REPRODUCTIVE FREEDOM

# International Studies in Human Rights

VOLUME 60

*The titles published in this series are listed at the end of this volume.*

# Reproductive Freedom

## In the Context of International Human Rights and Humanitarian Law

*by*

MAJA KIRILOVA ERIKSSON

*Professor of International Law, Faculty of Law, Uppsala University, Sweden*

MARTINUS NIJHOFF PUBLISHERS
THE HAGUE / BOSTON / LONDON

**Library of Congress Cataloging-in-Publication Data is available**

ISBN 90-411-1249-9

Published by Kluwer Law International,
P.O. Box 85889, 2508 CN The Hague, The Netherlands

Sold and distributed in North, Central and South America
by Kluwer Law International,
675 Massachusetts Avenue, Cambridge, MA 02139, USA

In all other countries, sold and distributed
by Kluwer Law International, Distribution Centre
P.O. Box 322, 3300 AH Dordrecht, The Netherlands



*Printed on acid-free paper*


Kluwer Law International incorporates the publishing programmes of
Graham & Trotman Ltd, Kluwer Law and Taxation Publishers,
and Martinus Nijhoff Publishers.



Printed and bound in Great Britain by Antony Rowe Limited.

To my daughter Maria

# Table of Contents

## Part III. Gender-based Violence – a Grave Violation of the Non-discrimination Principle and a Major Obstacle to Reproductive Freedom

### Chapter 7. Violence Against Women as an International Issue



### Chapter 8. The *Ad Hoc* International Tribunal for the Former Yugoslavia

# Acknowledgements

This book has been in process for several years and a great number of people have contributed to its completion. To all of them who have helped to bring it into being I wish to express my gratitude.

Most particularly I would like to thank the librarians at: the Faculty of Law in Uppsala, the Dag Hammarskjöld Library, the Library at Harvard Law School, the Library of Congress in Washington D.C. and the Library of the Max-Planck-Institut für öffentliches Recht und Völkerrecht in Heidelberg for patient responses to many queries and for invaluable help.

I also wish to thank Mark Boseley and Kjell Eriksson for suggesting a number of very useful linguistic alterations and making editorial comments.

I owe much to the financial support from the Swedish Council for Research in the Humanities and Social Sciences and the Emil Heijnes Stiftelse.

*Uppsala, January 1999* — *Maja Kirilova Eriksson*

*Part I*

# Gender Equality Under International Law

*"All human beings are born free and equal in dignity and rights"*
Article 1, Universal Declaration of Human Rights

*Chapter 1*

# The Significance of the Topic

## 1.1. The Centrality of Women's Human Rights for the Future Development of Humanity

Mankind has managed to send rockets to the moon and to outer space, yet there are deeply rooted problems on earth that continue to reduce the potential of half of the world's population and deprive the human race of untold resources. Tragically, women are most often the ones whose human rights are violated and they will never gain full dignity until their human rights are truly respected and protected. The abuses have continued because the history of women has been a history of silence.[1] Their perspectives have seldom been recognised and are still not accommodated enough in current international law. This is mainly because international law in concept and practice has remained a gendered system that marginalises women. Women's issues have simply been "at the periphery of international human rights",[2] and international treaty bodies have ignored and "continue to ignore" the fact that human rights violations often have a gender dimension, by and large because women have been and are still underrepresented at the governmental and intergovernmental level, in international human rights law-making and in supervisory mechanisms.[3]

---

[1] *J.W. Scott*, The Problem of Invisibility, in Retrieving Women's History, S.J. Kleinberg (ed.), UNESCO 1988, pp. 5–30; *A. Byrnes*, Women, Feminism and International Human Rights Law – Methodological Myopia, Fundamental Flaws or Meaningful Marginalization? Australian Yearbook of International Law 1992, Vol. 12, p. 7; *C. Bunch*, An equal voice, in Human Rights: the new consensus, R. Reoch (ed.), London 1994, p. 28.

[2] *A. Gallagher*, Ending the Marginalization: Strategies for Incorporating Women into the United Nations Human Rights System, HRQ 1997, Vol. 19, pp. 283 and 305. Also Professor Meron has observed that "under modern international law (t)he protection of women's rights does not appear to have been a priority item". *T. Meron*, Shakespeare's Henry the Fifth and the Law of War, AJIL 1992, Vol. 86, p. 30.

[3] *G. Van Bueren*, The Challenges for the International Protection of Family Members' Rights as the 21st Century Approaches, paper presented at the 8th World Conference of the International Society of Family Law, Cardiff 1994, p. 12 and *H. Charlesworth*, Human Rights as Men's Rights, in Women's rights, human rights, J. Peters & A. Wolper (eds.), New York 1995, p. 105; *K.D. Askin*, War Crimes Against Women, The Hague 1997, p. 253, note 840. A recent survey made by Gallagher shows that treaty bodies with a greater percentage of women members have displayed higher levels of gender sensitivity. *A. Gallagher*, p. 293. There has, *e.g.*, never been a woman judge at the European Court of Justice. On the extent to which violations of women's human rights have been addressed by the various human rights mechanisms see UN Doc. E/CN.6/1996/9.

Nevertheless, several human rights issues of significance for women's rights have recently received renewed interest and have obtained their long-deserved attention and moved to the top of the international human rights agenda. Women's human rights have become a fundamental concern of the United Nations and regional organisations, which have been established with the aim to promote and protect human rights. The slow historical process from disregard towards the recognition of women's rights as an integral part of international human rights law reached its culmination at the 1993[4] World Conference on Human Rights in Vienna.[5] The Vienna Declaration and Program of Action which was adopted by 180 Governments by consensus[6] contains a number of very extensive paragraphs on women's rights, *e.g.*, Part I, § 18, where it is stated:

> "The full and equal participation of women in political, civil, economic, social and cultural life, at the national, regional and international levels, and the eradication of all forms of discrimination on grounds of sex are priority objectives of the international community".[7]

It proclaims furthermore that: "The human rights of women and the girl child are an inalienable, integral and indivisible part of universal human rights".[8]

Unlike previous United Nations declarations such as the UDHR and the Teheran Declaration of 1968 which set forth human rights concepts in gender-neutral terms, the Vienna Declaration embodies the idea of substantive equality and it makes explicit reference to various kinds of women's rights. There is indeed a shift of thinking from viewing the discrimination against women as only a women's issue to studying it as an issue affecting the whole society. Moreover, the Fourth World Conference on Women, which took place in September 1995 in Beijing (hereinafter

---

4 The second (the first International Conference on Human Rights was held in Teheran in 1968) World Conference on Human Rights convened by the UN took place in Vienna from 14 to 25 June 1993. Among the aims of the conference were: a) to review and assess the progress made in the field of human rights since the adoption of the Universal Declaration of Human Rights and b) to identify obstacles and ways, in which they can be overcome to further progress in this area. More than 6,000 individuals participated from all over the world representing governments, intergovernmental and non-governmental organisations and national human rights institutions. Six Heads of States, more than 70 Ministers of Foreign Affairs and 23 Ministers of Justice delivered statements.

5 Women's groups submitted some 150,000 signatures from 115 countries in 1992 to the United Nations requesting women's rights to be included on the agenda of the Vienna Conference. *G. Binion*, Human Rights: a Feminist Perspective, HRQ 1995, Vol. 17, p. 524. See also *C. Bunch*, Strengthening Human Rights of Women, in World Conference on Human Rights, M. Nowak (ed.), Vienna 1994, pp. 32–42.

6 One of the advantages of UN conferences adopting human rights documents by consensus is undoubtedly that their texts can be viewed as generally accepted. Yet it has been stressed that it is also disadvantageous to apply this principle since it involves a substantial risk of a few recalcitrant governments preventing the adoption of progressive provisions. *T. Meron*, International Criminalization of Internal Atrocities, AJIL 1995, Vol. 88, p. 555.

7 UN Doc. A/Conf.157/22, reprinted in I.L.M. 1993, Vol. 32, p. 6.

8 For a review of the achievements of the Vienna Conference see generally *D.J. Sullivan*, Women's Human Rights and the 1993 World Conference on Human Rights, AJIL 1994, Vol. 88, pp. 152–167.

the Beijing Conference) emphasised the connection between the advancement of women and the progress of society as a whole.[9] It stressed like the 1995 UN Development Programme Report on Human Development that: "Investing in women's capabilities and empowering them to exercise their choices is not only valuable in itself but it is also the surest way to contribute to economic growth and overall development".[10] In addition, the significance of the realisation of women's rights has also been accentuated in connection with the emphasis put on the centrality of democracy as a prerequisite for future development.[11] The achievement of equality between women and men has been considered an important goal in strengthening democratic societies. It is asserted that the general welfare of everyone "can be increased by a decrease in the oppression of women".[12] It is also a widely accepted view today that sustainable development cannot be achieved without the full participation of both women and men in all aspects of productive and reproductive life.

The need for gender equality and the importance of the issues related to the improvement of the status of women were repeated throughout recent UN International Conferences, *e.g.*, on population and development, which were held in September 1994 in Cairo (hereinafter the Cairo Conference),[13] on social development

---

[9] Fourth World Conference on Women: Action for Equality, Development, and Peace, Beijing Declaration and Platform for Action (hereinafter Beijing Declaration), UN Doc. A/50/744, 10 November 1995, § 38.

[10] See also UNDP, Human Development Report 1996, p. 6. On the other hand there seems to exist a firm theoretical basis for the assertion that economic development influences the degree to which women's rights are realised. *S.C. Poe, D. Wendel-Blunt & K. Ho*, Global Patterns in the Achievement of Women's Rights to Equality, HRQ 1997, Vol. 19, pp. 827–835.

[11] A reference to discrimination against women and its detrimental effect on the development of nations is to be found in § 7 of the preamble of the UN Convention on Elimination of All Forms of Discrimination against Women and reads as follows: "discrimination against women violates the principles of equality of rights and respect for human dignity, is an obstacle to the participation of women, on equal terms with men, in the political, social, economic and cultural life of their countries, hampers the growth of the prosperity of society and the family and makes more difficult the full development of the potentialities of women in the service of their countries and of humanity". The Convention (Women's Convention hereinafter) was adopted on 18 December 1979 by GA Res. 34/180, 34 UN GAOR Supp. No. 46 at 194, UN Doc. A/34/46 and it entered into force 3 September 1981, reprinted in 19 I.L.M. 1980, Vol. 33. Similar ideas have been expressed in the literature as well. In the view of Karin Lundström, *e.g.*, the prohibition of gender-based discrimination is "an unconditional, minimum demand in states professing to be democratic, constitutional states". *K. Lundström*, Jämlikhet mellan kvinnor och män i EG-rätten, Uppsala 1999, p. 431.

[12] *F. Olsen*, Feminism Across Frontiers, paper presented at the 8th World Conference of the International Society of Family Law, Cardiff 1994, p. 4.

[13] The Cairo Conference was initiated by the UN in 1989. (ECOSOC Res. 1989/91) It was the third United Nations conference on population issues. The first one was the 1974 World Population Conference, which was convened in Bucharest and the second was the 1984 International Conference on Population, which took place in Mexico City. The Preparatory Committee (PrepCom) held its first substantive session in New York from 4 to 8 March 1991. At this session the objectives and themes of the Conference were defined. Six clusters of priority issues were identified: population, environment and development; population policies and programmes; population and women; family planning, health and family well-being, population growth and demographic structure; and population distribution and migration. These themes were addressed and discussed by a number of expert group meetings organised by the Population Division of the Department of Economic and Social Information and Policy Analysis of the UN Secretariat, in

in Copenhagen and on women in Beijing. The Fourth UN Conference on Women placed women's human rights at the heart of the international agenda.[14] Furthermore, the full and equal enjoyment by women of all human rights has been considered a *priority* for governments and for the United Nations.[15]

The empowerment[16] and autonomy of women were important ends in themselves and constitute central human rights objectives. As Marcuse has argued, "self-realisation" is the ultimate object of social life. It has been clearly stated by the UN treaty bodies that empowering women to take decisions about their sexuality and their fertility also empowers them in other domains, such as household decision-making and participation in educational and economic life.[17] Reproductive rights are in other words essential if women are to become full and equal partners with men in society and they play a crucial part in a larger struggle for equality. Of significance is also that women should have access to reproductive health services since that would facilitate their ability to realise their choices,[18] *i.e.*, to regulate the timing of their childbearing and to avoid unwanted and mistimed pregnancies and unsafe abortion. However, these aspects of reproductive freedom, which are crucial for women's status and health, still remain unsettled under international law. While men may be concerned about reproductive

---

consultation with UNFPA. Moreover, a series of regional population conferences was held in Africa, Asia, Europe, Latin America, the Caribbean and the Middle East. The PrepCom had accredited over 900 NGOs at its three sessions. (UN Doc. A/CONF.171/7 and Add.1) Despite three sessions of the PrepCom a number of key issues were left to be resolved in Cairo. An agreement among delegates had still to be reached on the definitions of, *inter alia,* family planning, reproductive and sexual health and rights and safe motherhood.

[14] The five regional preparatory meetings, which were held in 1994 in Argentina, in Austria, in Jordan, in Indonesia and in Senegal, each produced a final document. They are as follows: the Regional Programme of Action for the Women of Latin America and the Caribbean (UN Doc. E/CN.6/1995/5/Add.3); the Regional Platform for Action-Women in a Changing World-Call for Action from an ECE Perspective ( UN Doc. E/CN.6/1995/5/Add.4); the Arab Regional Preparatory Meeting (UN Doc. E/CN.6/5/Add.5); the Jakarta Declaration and Plan of Action for the Advancement of Women in Asia and the Pacific (UN Doc. E/CN.671995/5/Add.1) and the African Platform of Action (UN Doc. E/CN.6/1995/5/Add.2). All of them reflect, albeit to a varying degree, the idea of women's rights as an integral part of human rights law. The Beijing Conference itself stands for equality, development and peace.

[15] *Supra* note 7, Part II, 3, § 36.

[16] Women's empowerment is the process through which women gain better control over their lives. It can be viewed as a continuum of several interrelated and mutually reinforcing components, such as: 1. Awareness building about women's situation, discrimination, and rights and opportunities as a step towards gender equality. 2. Capacity building and skills development, especially the ability to plan, make decisions, organise and carry out activities. 3. Participation and greater control and decision-making power in the home community and society. 4. Action to bring about greater equality between men and women. *M. Karl*, Women and Empowerment: Participation and Decision-Making, London 1995, p. 14. See also *J. Rowlands*, Questioning Empowerment. Working with Women in Honduras, Oxford 1997; *S. Wieringa*, Women's Interests and Empowerment: Gender Planning Reconsidered, Development and Change 1994, Vol. 25, pp. 829–848.

[17] UN Doc. CEDAW/C/1996/3/Add. 1, § 13.

[18] *K. Tomaševski*, European Approaches to Enhancing Reproductive Freedom, The American University Law Review 1995, Vol. 44, p. 1048.

freedom, their lives are not actually threatened by its absence. But women's lives are very much affected by matters that involve reproduction, and for women "in areas of high maternal mortality full reproductive freedom may mean the difference between life and death".[19] This is one of the important reasons for my deciding to undertake the following study.

In addition, I found that there is still little research that directly addresses the particular questions of how and why women's reproductive freedom is violated from the point of view of public international law.[20]

## 1.2. The Scope and Outline of the Present Work

The following study is organised in four parts. It takes the definition of reproductive freedom[21] as its main subject of examination in the context of international human rights and humanitarian law. In addition, an evaluation of the prospects for its realisation will be made. Since this author seeks to ground the right to

---

[19] *J. Peters & A. Wolper,* Introduction, in Women's rights, human rights, J. Peters & A. Wolper (eds.), p. 2. That reproduction affects women in a special way has been recognised by Judge Dooling who has held in the *McCrae v. Califano* case that a woman's right to decide upon abortion when her health is at stake is "nearly allied to her right to be". Citation in *R.P. Petchesky*, Reproductive Freedom: Beyond "A Woman's Right to Choose", SIGNS, Journal of Women in Culture and Society 1980, Vol. 5, p. 666.

[20] I would like, however, to mention here the following valuable contributions to the human rights law literature: *R.J. Cook,* Human Rights in Relation to Women's Health, WHO 1993; *R. Dixon-Mueller*, Population Policy & Women's Rights, Transforming Reproductive Choice, London 1993; *K. Tomaševski*, Human Rights in Population Policies, Lund 1994 and *C.A.A. Packer*, The Right to Reproductive Choice, Åbo 1996. While the first excellent essay focuses mainly on the health dimension of reproductive freedom, the second and third studies consist mainly of an analysis of population policies measured by human rights criteria. The last mentioned monograph comprises a discussion of the components of the right to reproductive choice and the contemporary cultural, religious and demographic issues, which present challenges to its application. Despite its useful systematisation it lacks, however, the theoretical framework of modern legal theories. See also *J. Looks*, Book Reviews, EJIL 1998, Vol. 9, pp. 421–422.

[21] This author makes use of the word "freedom" instead of "choice" as a value framework for modern feminist approaches to the study of law. I have found Carol Gould's understanding of freedom as meaning self-development, reciprocity and democracy very useful. Reciprocity in this context presupposes and goes beyond formal (*de iure*) equality in that it involves the recognition by each agent of the differences of the other, in terms of the other's own projects and goals. In the mutual form of reciprocal relations "each agent consciously endeavors to act in such a way as to enhance the agency of the other". *C. Gould*, Private Rights and Public Virtues: Women, the Family, and Democracy, in Beyond Domination. New Perspectives on Women and Philosophy, New Jersey 1983, p. 6. I should mention, however, that several authors have introduced various terms relating to the topic of my research which mainly reflect differences in emphasis, *e.g.*, the right to reproductive choice, the right to reproductive self-determination, the right to reproductive decision-making etc. This author assumes that with regard to a theory of reproductive freedom, the critical issue for feminists along with the definition of the right to choose (reproductive choice) is the conditions under which such choices are made. For a short review of the definition of these terms see *C.A.A. Packer*, p. 15.

reproductive freedom on the principle of gender equality,[22] the first part of the book will be devoted to an analysis of this basic[23] and universally accepted principle[24] of civilisation, which has inspired human rights law and which constitutes the justification for all human rights. I will in other words approach several legal aspects of reproductive freedom in the context of the overall goal of the international community to advance the status of women and to achieve *de iure* as well as *de facto* gender equality.[25] I shall, however, try to make a coherent analysis of reproductive freedom, *i.e.*, integrating both ideas of equality and of woman's autonomy,[26] which I do not consider as mutually exclusive principles but rather complementary and supportive. I shall apply different feminist methods[27] in my enquiry since I believe that they have potentials to improve the application of international law to ensure better respect and realisation of women's rights. The feminist perspective, which I have

---

[22] Abortion is ,*e.g.*, sometimes seen to have liberating potential for women and consequently affecting their status. See *K. Engle*, After the Collapse of the Public/Private Distinction: Strategizing Women's Rights, in Reconceiving Reality: Women and International Law, Studies in Transnational Legal Policy No. 25, D.G. Dallmeyer (ed.), ASIL , Washington D.C. 1993, p. 148; *R.J. Cook*, Reservations to the Convention on the Elimination of All Forms of Discrimination against Women, Virginia Journal of International Law 1990, Vol. 30, p. 643. During the Council of Europe high-level meeting in preparation for the Beijing Conference it was made clear that the right to free choice in matters of reproduction and lifestyle was fundamental for women. The enjoyment of sexual and reproductive rights was considered as a prerequisite for women to have genuine self-determination and for gender equality. *Council of Europe*, Equality and Democracy: Utopia or Challenge?, Strasbourg, February 1995, p. 25.

[23] Sir Lauterpacht underlined the importance of the claim to equality as "the most fundamental of the rights of man. It occupies the first place in most written constitutions. It is the starting point of all other liberties". *H. Lauterpacht*, An International Bill of the Rights of Man, New York 1945, p. 115.

[24] For the purpose of my study I shall rely mainly on two definitions. Firstly, a principle is according to Dworkin "a standard that is to be observed not because it will advance or secure an economic, political or social situation deemed desirable, but because it is a requirement of justice or fairness or some other dimension of morality". *R.M. Dworkin*, The Philosophy of Law, Oxford 1977, p. 43. Secondly, Professor Fitzmaurice suggests that a principle is something "which underlines a rule, and explains or provides the reasons for it". *G. Fitzmaurice*, The General Principles of International Law Considered from the Standpoint of the Rule of Law, RdC 1957, Vol. II, p. 7.

[25] Professor Koskenniemi has rightly observed that "law is understood to exist for the pursuit of social goals". He continues, however, by stressing that "there is constant disagreement about correct goals". *M. Koskenniemi*, From Apology to Utopia. The Structure of International Legal Argument, Helsinki 1989, p. 2. It is my presumption that there is a common commitment to the goal of gender equality in the international society at present and which corresponds to the needs of more than the half of the population of our planet.

[26] The two ideas have developed from different philosophical traditions and have, therefore, been often seen as contradictory. The first one is based, according to Petchesky, on the "social position of women and the socially determined needs which that position generates". *R.P. Petchesky*, p. 662. The second idea derives from the biological connection between women's bodies, sexuality and reproduction. It has inspired arguments based on the principle of bodily integrity (bodily self-determination), *i.e.*, women ought to be able to control their own procreative capacities.

[27] There is a diversity of feminism, which makes it responsive to the different needs and concerns of different women. On the plurality of feminist legal theories and methods see sub-chapter 2.2.; *R.J. Cook*, Women, in The United Nations and International Law, C.C. Joyner (ed.), New York 1997, p. 182; *K. Lundström*, p. 34.

taken up, may place this study within the Newstream.[28] Scholars who associate themselves with this school of thought argue for a new international law, which is more contextual and more inclusive. One of the strategies of the Newstream is "the incorporation of multiple perspectives into the law-making process and the contextualisation of legal problems in their social, political and cultural background".[29] Thus, Newstream scholars seek to redefine the conceptual basis of international law by incorporating into legal analysis among other things gender perspectives.

My hypothesis is that the asymmetrical approach to gender equality[30] which is centred around the concept of difference, *i.e.*, the ability to give birth is the most obvious point of difference between the sexes, is the most appropriate to be applied in respect of reproductive freedom. I will, furthermore, argue for an expansive definition of the term "equality" as to include among others affirmative governmental action. However, this does not preclude or eliminate the need for women to struggle for their individual human rights in various settings. In this regard international jurisprudence of human rights developed by supervisory bodies for the protection of various human rights will be examined. I shall try to answer the question of whether the decision-making institutions are champions of gender equality.

Another central question to be explored in Chapter 2 of this survey will be the status of the principle of non-discrimination and equality[31] in contemporary international law. In this respect I will discuss the question of whether it qualifies as a principle of *ius cogens*. The traditional sources of international law have been identified as one of the obstacles for the effective remedy of women's issues.[32] Moreover, it has been maintained, not without reason, that the concept of *ius cogens* has "privileged the experiences of men over those of women, and it has provided a protection to men that is not accorded to women".[33] Many governments

---

28 For a review of the differences between the two schools of thought labelled as Mainstream and Newstream see *D.Z. Cass*, Navigating the Newstream: Recent Critical Scholarship in International Law, NJIL 1996, Vol. 65, p. 370.

29 *D.Z. Cass*, p. 370.

30 Asymmetrical equality is result-oriented, *de facto*, substantive equality.

31 According to some writers on international law doctrine, equality and non-discrimination are positive and negative statements of the same principle. In consequence I make use of the singular form of the noun "principle". See *W. McKean*, Equality and Discrimination under International Law, Oxford 1985, p. 285; *Y. Dinstein*, Discrimination and International Human Rights, Israel Yearbook of Human Rights 1985, Vol. 15, p. 11; *J.E.S. Fawcett*, The Application of the European Convention on Human Rights, Oxford 1987, p. 24; *A.F. Bayefsky*, The Principle of Equality or Non-Discrimination in International Law, HRLJ 1990, Vol. 11, p. 1. See furthermore the separate opinion of Judge R.E. Piza Escalante in the Advisory Opinion of 19 January 1984- *Amendments to the Naturalization Provisions of the Constitution of Costa Rica* – issued by the Inter-American Court of Human Rights, which reads as follows: "the concepts of equality and non-discrimination are reciprocal, like the two faces of one and the same institution. Equality is the positive face of non-discrimination. Discrimination is the negative face of equality". IACHR Advisory Opinion OC-4/84, Ser. B, No. 4, § 10.

32 *H. Charlesworth, C. Chinkin & S. Wright*, Feminist Approaches to International Law, AJIL 1991, Vol. 85, p. 613 and *H. Charlesworth & C. Chinkin*, The Gender of Jus Cogens, HRQ 1993, Vol. 15, pp. 64–76.

33 *H. Charlesworth & C. Chinkin*, ibid., p. 65.

have not understood women's rights as part of human rights law and few of them have been committed to women's equality as a basic human right.[34] In the search for grounds for the justification of certain norms, the place within the hierarchy of legal rules is still an important consideration with regard to how compulsory and obligatory they are. It is needless to say what a positive impact on the justification of women's human rights there would be if the principle of non-discrimination and gender equality were deemed as belonging to one of the most fundamental and highly valued interests of the whole international community.

The rationale of reproductive freedom can be explained on the basis of the international community's obligation "to assist the individual with the fulfilment of minimum needs",[35] *i.e.*, to live a life with dignity. Human rights are, in other words about what is necessary for living a desirable life. They are an affirmation of the notion of an authentic need. Human rights are, therefore, conceived in contemporary international law as "part and parcel of the integrity and dignity of the human being".[36] Women's ability to decide whether, when, if, and with whom to have sex and have children is a fundamental component of their human rights and of their human dignity.[37] Human dignity has implications as to how human beings ought to be treated and human rights constitute a possible articulation of that. Much of my argumentation for a dynamic treatment of women's human rights will be in consequence based on the concept of human dignity in the sense that it connotes "an ontologically given (independent of human evaluation) equal moral standing of every human individual".[38] In other words, the right to equal concern and respect is assumed to be a natural right[39] possessed by all human beings without distinctions as to birth and other characteristics. Especially gender-based[40] discrimination has

---

[34] *C. Bunch*, Transforming Human Rights from a Feminist Perspective, in Women's rights, human rights, J. Peters & A. Wolper (eds.), p. 12.

[35] *C.A.A. Packer*, p. 1.

[36] *R. Higgins*, Problems and Process – International Law and How to Use It, Oxford 1994, p. 96.

[37] *R. Dixon-Mueller*, p. XI.

[38] *P. Sundman*, Human Rights, Justifications, and Christian Ethics, Uppsala 1996, p. 94.

[39] In this regard, this author sustains much the same conception of basic moral rights as has been proposed by Stoics, Romans, medieval Christians and modern rationalists. It implies that every human being possesses basic rights simply by virtue of being human, and that human rights are derived from a common morality subscribed to by the vast majority of humankind. See on this topic *M. Granston*, Women's Rights Are Human Rights, in The Human Rights Reader, W. Laquer & B.M. Rubin (eds.), New York 1989; *J. Donelly*, Universal Human Rights in Theory and Practice, Oxford 1989; *R.E. Howard*, Human Rights and the Search for Community, 1995; *C. Bunch*, Women's Rights as Human Rights: Towards a Re-Vision of Human Rights, HRQ 1990, Vol. 12, at 486.

[40] Though the concept "sex-based discrimination" is overwhelmingly used in the domestic legislation of a number of states and also partly in the international law doctrine, I prefer the use of the expression "gender- based discrimination" instead for several reasons. First of all in some languages the use of the word sex may in itself constitute a form of indirect discrimination. In addition the word "sex" "has come to mean a sensual activity rather than biological distinction with legal implications". *G.H. Flanz*, Gender-based discrimination in spite of equal treatment laws? Legal and linguistic aspects, in Festschrift für Felix Ermacora, M. Nowak et al. (eds.), Strasbourg 1988, p. 439. I may establish here that the word "sex" has been used to mean a biological category (*i.e.*, biological identity) to which everyone belonged (*i.e.*, the male or female sex). These differences between men and women are fixed and unchangeable. They do not

been considered by the international community as an offence against human dignity and an infringement of human rights. I may mention in this regard that already in 1949 the UN Secretary General's definition of the principle of equality, was based on that ethical concept. It reads as follows: "Human dignity implies that human beings are to be treated as ends in themselves and not as mere means to an

---

change over time and between cultures. The term "gender" on the other hand, which not so long ago was permissible only as a technical term in grammar (*i.e.*, masculine or feminine nouns) refers to the socially constructed roles of women and men in public and private life (*i.e.*, social identity). It is thus, not simply a modern word for "sex". Today many feminists and social scientists have been using "gender" to refer specifically to roles that are assigned to men or to women by society, as opposed to the biological roles and functions of each sex. The critical point is that there are not just gender differences, but there are fundamental gender inequalities. During the preparations for the Beijing Conference the term "gender" was intensively discussed. Those who wanted to bracket the term suspected that there was a hidden agenda behind its use, *i.e.*, tolerance of non-heterosexual identities and orientation and inclusion of the right of lesbian couples to conceive children through artificial insemination and their right to legally adopt their partner's children. Others pointed out that there is no word for "gender" in many languages. Because of this controversy a special working group under Namibia's leadership was set up at the March 1995 PrepCom meeting in New York to arrive at an agreed understanding. Many of the delegates had assumed that the word "gender" was simply a polite way of saying "sex" to avoid the secondary meaning which sex has in English and that "gender" referred to male and female human beings. On the other hand, the supporters of the "gender perspective" believed that their understanding of the meaning of "gender" as referring to "socially constructed roles" was accepted today. The focus on gender would ensure that the emphasis remains on how society constructs opportunities and life chances. The gender constructs have operated to discriminate against and to subordinate women and thereby prevent them from enjoying fully their rights. At the end it was this second meaning of the word "gender" that gained most support and was promoted. It was said that wherever the term "gender" appears in the Beijing final document it is to be understood as its common meaning within the UN and its general use. The word "gender" has consequently evolved as differentiated from the word "sex" to express the reality that women's and men's roles and status are socially constructed and subject to change over time and between cultures. See on that topic the report of the informal contact group on gender, UN Doc. A/CONF.177/L.2, 7 July 1995, The report of the Expert Group Meeting on the development of guidelines for the integration of gender perspectives into human rights activities and programs, UN Doc. E/CN.4/1996/105, p. 13; UN Doc. E/CN.6/1999/4, p. 23; *D.L. Rhode*, Justice and Gender, Cambridge, Massachusetts 1989; *G. Binion*, p. 511; *C.A. MacKinnon*, Difference and Dominance: On Sex Discrimination, in Feminist Legal Theory, K.T. Bartlett & R. Kennedy (eds.), San Francisco 1991, p. 8 and the same author, Feminism, Marxism, Method and the State, *ibid.*, p. 195; *J.C. Williams*, Deconstructing Gender, *ibid.*, p. 111 and *K.T. Bartlett*, Feminist Legal Method, *ibid.*, p. 387; *D. Sullivan*, Integration of Women's Human Rights into the Work of the Special Rapporteurs, UNIFEM, New York 1996, p. 4. Catharine MacKinnon explains in her second essay on the page mentioned above that she uses the words "sex" and "gender" relatively interchangeably since "Sex is thought the more biological, gender the more social. The relation of each to sexuality varies. Since I believe sexuality is fundamental to gender and fundamentally social, and that biology is its social meaning in the system of sex inequality, which is a social and political system that does not rest independently on biological differences in any respect, the sex/gender distinction looks like a nature/culture distinction".

It may be noted here, in addition, that Article 7(3) of the Statute of the International Criminal Court (hereinafter ICC) provides: "For the purpose of this Statute, it is understood that the term 'gender' refers to the two sexes, male and female, within the context of society. The term 'gender' does not indicate any meaning different from the above".

end".[41] From the above I may draw the conclusion that the core concept of human dignity constitutes the very basis of human rights.[42] Therefore, the protection of equality in dignity and equality of rights is one of the very important aims of international law instruments. Equality in this sense is, furthermore, the common denominator in the interpretation and application of fundamental human rights and as such it is universal. All forms of deprivation of human dignity are consequently unacceptable.[43] Mr. Clapham suggests a twofold approach to the protection of dignity:

> "Everyone's humanity is to be respected and the conditions for everyone's self-fulfilment (or autonomy or self-realisation) must be created and protected".[44]

Following this line of thought, it becomes obvious that there is a strong connection between living a life in dignity and good health. The right approach to health issues must, therefore, be based according to Professor Leary "on fundamental human rights principles, particularly the dignity of persons and non-discrimination (equality)".[45] The physical and mental well-being of women is the very basis for enhancing equality between the sexes and it is vital for the empowerment of women. For that reason many of the documents presented in preparation of the Cairo Conference and thereafter focus on women's reproductive health. So, how does this term relate to reproductive freedom? It has been maintained that reproductive freedom in such a context is considered not only as having the legal option, but also the economic means and social conditions that make it possible effectuate one's choice. Part two of the present book will reveal possible answers to that question. Dr. Nafis Sadik, the Secretary General of the Cairo Conference and Executive Director of the United Nations Population Fund (UNFPA), has explained that the Cairo Programme of Action, covering the next 20 years, "starts from the reality of the world we live in, and shows us the path to a better reality". Moreover, she emphasised that this document "has the potential to change the world".[46] Thus, advancing gender equality and ensuring women's ability to control

---

41 The Main Types and Causes of Discrimination, Memorandum submitted by the Secretary General, UN Commission on Human Rights, UN New York 1949, p. 4 (hereinafter Memorandum). The concept of human dignity is, however, problematic. There are a few authors, who, with reference to traditional African societies, claim that human dignity and human rights are two distinct notions. It is claimed that safeguards to human dignity in these societies are based on duties and not on human rights. *J. Donnelly*, Human Rights and Human Dignity: an analytical critique of non-Western conceptions of human rights, American Political Science Review 1982, Vol. 76, p. 312 *et seq.*

42 Human rights derive, as stipulated in the preambles (§ 2) to the UN Covenant on Civil and Political Rights and (§ 2) to the Covenant on Economic, Social and Cultural Rights "from the inherent dignity of the human person".

43 UN Doc. E/CN.4/Sub.2/1989/19, p. 19.

44 *A. Clapham*, The "Drittwirkung" of the Convention, in The European System for the Protection of Human Rights, R.St.J. Macdonald, F. Matscher & H. Petzold (eds.), Dordrecht 1993, p. 206.

45 *V.A. Leary*, Justiciability and Beyond. Complaint Procedures and the Right to Health, The Review 1995, No. 55, p. 109.

46 UN Doc. POP/572, 14 September 1994, p. 1.

their own fertility are identified as the cornerstones of population and development-related programmes. Still criticism exists regarding the Western feminist preoccupation with a woman's right to abortion. It has been argued that the abortion issue is of less significance "to many Third World women because population control programs often deny them the chance to have children".[47] In my view statistics clearly indicate that unwanted pregnancies cause a great number of deaths, especially in the Third World countries. It is estimated that currently 500,000 women die each year, mostly in developing countries, of pregnancy-related sequelae.[48] There is an on-going debate as to whether abortion is comprised in the right to family planning as articulated in UN documents and which lends itself to differing interpretations. If it turns out that abortion is a component of that right, then it is protected by human rights law provisions, *e.g.*, Article 16(1)(e) of the Women's Convention. Does the increasing concern for maternal health and gender equality as expressed in recent international documents legitimate the demands for a *de lege ferenda* expansion of women's reproductive freedom to comprise legal abortion if necessary? This author argues that the recent endorsement of the new concept "reproductive health" requires among other things a holistic and comprehensive approach to existing law, *i.e.*, linking several human rights provisions with the right to family planning and the right to found a family. In other words, the notion "family planning" needs to be integrated into a wider framework, which addresses women's overall health, well-being and status. I shall in that respect employ a gender-based approach to treaty interpretation and the method that seeks to realise the objectives and purpose of a treaty, *i.e.*, a teleological method of interpretation of the relevant substantive articles on reproductive freedom. My point of departure for the present study is that international law is no exception to the law of nature that is change. The Greek philosopher, Heraclitus, expressed this historic truth 2500 years ago by saying: "*Panta rei*" (everything flows, changes). Neither is international law static. It is constantly developing by revision in content, expansion in scope and improvement of the means of securing compliance, so that it is kept in accord with the needs of the international community. One can even say that the problem of

---

[47] See *C. Bulbeck*, cited in H. Charlesworth & C. Chinkin & S. Wright, Feminist Approaches to International Law, AJIL 1991, Vol. 85, p. 619.

[48] UN Doc. A/CONF.157/PC/61/Add.9, p. 8; *R.J. Cook*, Women's International Human Rights Law: The Way Forward, HRQ 1993, Vol. 15, p. 241. About 25–50% of the maternal deaths are caused by unsafe abortions performed in order to interrupt unwanted pregnancy. Women living in developing countries have mortality rates 200 times higher than women living in Europe and in North America. *R.J. Cook*, International Protection of Women's Reproductive Rights, the New York University Journal of International Law and Politics, 1992, Vol. 24, pp. 646 and 648. The issue of unsafe abortions gathered over 100 participants from 20 African countries and a dozen international agencies at the IPPF Conference in Mauritius in March 1994. Unsafe abortions were recognised there as a major public health problem in Africa and an important social problem, since some 10,000 African women undergo every day unsafe abortions and many of them die. In the adopted "Mauritius Declaration", 18 of the African governmental delegations committed themselves among other things to tackle the vicious cycle of unwanted pregnancy and unsafe abortion and to liberalise restrictive laws and minimise barriers to safe abortion. See also UNICEF idag, Stockholm 1998, No. 4, p. 22.

change, flexibility and adaptability is acute and urgent in the field of international law.[49] A rigid approach to the interpretation of human rights treaties would be in conflict with their terms, the Vienna Convention on the Law of Treaties and the modern approach which international monitoring bodies take to human rights instruments. Human rights law has a dynamic character,[50] and a teleological interpretation of the provisions of the Women's Convention among other treaties, rather than a historical one, will lead to the result of their wide application covering more aspects of reproductive freedom and covering the protection of women from any danger of unequal treatment, either in vertical or in horizontal relations.[51] It is the ambition of this author to show that the content of established international human rights and humanitarian law norms and principles can be broadened through evolutive interpretation,[52] which also can stimulate the evolution of domestic laws in ways that enhance rights protection. Women can consequently use the existing international law framework to advance their legal

---

[49] On the inherently dynamic character of international law see *Lung-Chu Chen*, An Introduction to Contemporary International Law, New Haven 1989.

[50] Since this author puts emphasis on the dynamic nature of law, part of my reasoning has been influenced by arguments advanced by process-oriented lawyers like Rosalin Higgins. See, for example, her work *Problems and Process – International Law and How to Use It*, Oxford 1994, and *Policy Consideration and the International Judicial Process*, ICLQ 1968, Vol. 17, pp. 58–59. However, my thoughts reflect at times a conglomeration of different theories of international law.

[51] By adopting a teleological method of interpretation, the European Court of Justice has been able to focus on the spirit of the treaties and thus give effectiveness to the Community law even in areas where no specific legislation exists. The teleological method of interpretation has, *e.g.*, allowed the Court in the *Hellmut Marschall v. Land Nordrhein – Westfahlen* case to define the permissible scope of discrimination by assessing its functionality to a certain purpose, namely that of furthering gender equality. The ECJ ruled that: "It follows that a national rule in terms of which, subject to the application of the saving clause, female candidates for promotion who are equally as qualified as the male candidates are to be treated preferentially….(m)ay fall within the scope of Article 2(4) if such a rule may counteract the prejudicial effects on female candidates of the attitudes and behaviour described above and thus reduce actual instances of inequality which may exist in the real world". Case C-409/95, Judgment of 11 November 1997, sec. 3, ECR I-6363.

[52] Most of the contemporary human rights norms do not adequately take into account the reality of women's lives. There appears to be a number of major historical barriers to inclusive definitions of human rights, *i.e.*, which incorporate the specific needs and concerns of women. Among these mentioned has been the fact that international law-making institutions have been, and to a great extent continue to be, dominated by men. This is reflected in the content and emphasis in international human rights and humanitarian law. The mainstream human rights bodies have in consequence exempted themselves from responsibility in the area of women's rights by the creation of specialised bodies like the CSW and CEDAW solely to address women's issues. See *C. Bunch*, Women's Rights as Human Rights: Towards a Re-Vision of Human Rights, HRQ 1990, Vol. 12, p. 486; *H. Charlesworth*, What Are Women's International Human Rights, in Human Rights of Women, R.J. Cook (ed.), Philadelphia 1994, p. 58; *C. Bunch*, Transforming Human Rights from a Feminist Perspective, in Women's rights, human rights, J. Peters & A. Wolper (eds.), p. 13; *E. Friedman*, Women's Human Rights: The Emergence of a Movement, *ibid.*, p. 20 and *H. Charlesworth*, Human Rights as Men's Rights, *ibid.*, p. 104. The Report of the Secretary-General on the follow-up to the Beijing Conference emphasises how important it is to interpret existing human rights norms creatively "so that they can be applied to those experiences of women which are different from those of men". UN Doc. E/CN.6/1998/5, § 100.

rights[53] and that way to avoid the preservation of a parallel universe for women in the human rights area. Furthermore, it is my sincere conviction that the rules of law are not isolated enclaves in a legal system, but they have an internal coherence and make up a system of law. This analysis suggests that human rights are interconnected. Thus, systematic interpretation of international law norms could throw light on the content of provisions by the inclusion of related norms in the evaluation. A holistic approach to provisions of relevance to reproductive freedom based on their interpretation through establishing a link among several human rights and considering them in the light of recent developments, such as the final documents of international conferences,[54] might forward their extensive reading.

In Part II of this monograph I shall consider the different aspects (positive and negative) of individual articles on reproductive freedom under international law from a gender perspective with the Woman's Convention providing the normative framework for the examination. The negative aspect of reproductive freedom allows couples to decide on the number, timing and spacing of births without state intervention. In the Cairo Declaration the international community agreed, *e.g.*, that demographic goals should not be used to control individual behaviour in regard of human reproduction. Still in many countries where family planning schemes are launched, governments support them primarily for demographic reasons. Only a small number of countries support family planning explicitly for human rights reasons.

Several questions, which merit consideration, will be addressed. For example, will the fear of the possible consequences of over-population in certain parts of the world rule out commitment to human rights? Thus, high rates of population growth

---

[53] The Canadian political scientist and philosopher Christian Bay has in various works advocated the notion "needs" as an alternative to "rights". *C. Bay*, Peace and Critical Political Knowledge as Human Rights, Poltical Theory 1980, Vol. 8, pp. 331–334. Also Rosalind Petchesky rejects the concept of rights (women's right to choose in connection with the goal of women's movement – reproductive freedom) in favour of "social and individual need" as the key concept in the fundamental feminist analysis. According to her needs in contrast to rights, which are abstract and inherently static, always refer to concrete, individual concerns and historical circumstances. *P.R. Petchesky*, p. 670. In the view of this author rights and needs are not comparable and they are not mutually exclusive. Both terms do not compete with each other, on the contrary. Human rights should accommodate different human needs since the general function of human rights is to protect human needs, *i.e.*, to protect the interests of all human beings in the sense of their well-being (dignity). By that I do not mean a fixed conception of human needs, but rather a contextualistic, dynamic conception and understanding of different persons' authentic needs. See generally, *C. Nino*, The Ethics of Human Rights, Oxford 1991; *C. Nino* (ed.), Rights, Aldershot 1992 and *N. MacCormick*, Legal Rights and Social Democracy, Oxford 1982.

[54] CEDAW experts stressed, *e.g.*, on 17 January 1995 during the review of the country reports under the Women's Convention that Bolivia should implement the decisions of the Cairo Conference. Press Release WOM/787, CEDAW 263rd meeting, 1995. The Committee issued at that session (14th) a suggestion No. 8 on the follow – up to the Cairo Conference. In recalling the provisions of Articles 10(h), 12 and 16(1) of the Women's Convention, CEDAW requested coordination among the human rights monitoring bodies in order to facilitate the follow – up to the Cairo Programme of Action. Report of CEDAW, UN Doc. A/50/38,1995, pp. 11–12. It should also be mentioned that the HRC requested at its session in 1996 that two of its members prepare proposals for reviewing its reporting guidelines so that they take into account the recommendations made by the Cairo and the Beijing Conferences. UN Doc. HRI/MC/1996/2, § 106.

have been seen as a hindrance to future increase in per capita income, and population increase is associated with growing poverty and hunger and a general decline of the quality of life for millions of people.[55] May such considerations legitimise incentives to influence decisions on family size? Are coercive measures of population control such as compulsory sterilisation and forced abortion compatible with human rights standards?

The second positive aspect of reproductive freedom requires that governments provide reproductive health services and access to information and education in order to empower and enable individuals and couples to make responsible reproductive choices. At the Vienna Conference on Human Rights, partnership between men and women on the basis of equal rights and responsibilities was considered a major challenge for the modern family.[56] The United Nations GA proclaimed a year thereafter 1994 as the International Year of the Family with the motto "Building the smallest unit of democracy at the heart of society".[57] If the family is to aspire to be a democratic structure then gender equality within the family is a must. In the programme[58] for that year a major concern for women's situation was expressed in paragraph 24:

> "Affected as women are by continuing social, economic, cultural and political upheavals and pressures, they should be enabled to explore new opportunities for education and employment and to balance work and familial responsibilities".

As essential to a wider sharing of familial roles and responsibilities the full, informed and joint participation in family planning decisions by both spouses is stressed in paragraph 22 of the same document, in other words, the active involvement of men in all areas of family responsibility,[59] including family planning, should be encouraged. Moreover, familial well-being is conditioned by the ability of families to make informed and sensitive choices concerning fertility. Needless to say, health, the most important prerequisite for improving the status of women, is

---

[55] *United Nations*, Population, Newsletter No. 49, New York, June 1990, p.1. The interrelationship between "economic problems, especially with regard to countries, which are in the process of economic development" and population growth was articulated by the GA in its Resolution 1217(XII).

[56] See UN Doc. A/CONF.157/Add.6,12 June 1993, p. 3. The relationship between the status of women and family planning was stressed already at the first World Conference on Human Rights, which took place in 1968 in Teheran. See UN Doc. A/CONF.32/41.

[57] UN GA Res. 44/82, 8 December 1989.

[58] 1994 International Year of the Family, Building the smallest democracy at the heart of society, UN Centre for Social Development and Humanitarian Affairs, Vienna 1991, p. 17.

[59] The shared responsibility (for children and family) concept was introduced in the section dealing with equality in the World Plan for the Implementation of the Objectives of the International Women's Year adopted at the Mexico World Conference in 1975. There it is emphasised that women can not be equal if they accept all the traditional responsibilities of mother, worker and citizen. This view has been reinforced in the Programme of Action for the Second Half of the U.N. Decade for Women adopted at the Copenhagen Conference (UN Doc. A/CONF.94/35) and in the Forward-Looking Strategies for the Advancement of Women to the Year 2000 adopted at the Nairobi Conference (UN Doc. A/CONG.116/28/rev.1). See generally *A.S. Fraser*, The U.N. Decade for Women, Documents and Dialogue, Colorado 1987.

largely dependent on the realisation of the woman's right to control her fertility. The incidence of unwanted pregnancies is itself very high in several regions of the world, suggesting among other things women's lack of control over their reproductive roles in an unequal sexual partnership.

Since the individual has responsibilities towards other human beings in the exercise of his human rights, he/she is limited by the rights and freedoms of others.[60] At times the interests of the parents-to-be may also conflict. Whose interest, then, should be given priority in a situation when pregnancy is not welcomed by one of the parents-to-be? The father may claim that he has an interest in parenthood. Does international law give specific rulings in such situations? The case law of the international organs dealing with the protection of individuals' human rights is not extensive on this subject. However, some of the issues referred to have been dealt with within the Council of Europe and the Organization of American States. International concern within the UN about the necessity of finding a middle course between foetal protection and women's rights dates from the beginning of the 1980s when this issue was openly addressed and debated primarily by CEDAW[61] and the CSW.[62]

The rapid advances in medical science and biology have in recent years given rise to numerous other complicated questions concerning the legal protection of the foetus. Scientific progress, giving the human being a decisive influence over the biological process, hitherto under the unique power of nature, has offered the individual greater freedom to decide if, when and under what conditions to become a parent. Sub-chapter 5.3.3. of my survey will deal with new procreative techniques. Normative and conceptual issues raised by these resent innovations in human reproduction such as *in vitro* fertilisation, parenting through contract (surrogate motherhood) *etc.*, shall be examined. In order to be effective, international law must keep pace with the time. I agree very much with the words of Professor Edgar Bodenheimer that "law must intelligently link the past with the present without ignoring the pressing claims of the future".[63]

---

[60] Every individual has the duty to respect the life, liberty and security of person of others. See Article 3 in the Universal Declaration on Human Rights (hereinafter UDHR) and Article 6 in the International Covenant on Civil and Political Rights (hereinafter ICCPR).

[61] CEDAW – The Committee on the Elimination of Discrimination against Women is a treaty body established to monitor compliance with the Women's Convention (hereinafter CEDAW).

[62] The United Nations Commission on the Status of Women (hereinafter CSW) was established in 1946 with the mandate to submit proposals, recommendations and reports to ECOSOC on instruments relating to the status of women and the promotion and protection of the human rights of women. Many important documents were adopted under the sponsorship of the CSW as the Convention on the Political Rights of Women, the Convention on the Nationality of Married Women, the Convention on the Consent to Marriage, Minimum Age for Marriage, and Registration of Marriages, the Declaration on the Elimination of Discrimination against Women, the Convention on Elimination of All Forms of Discrimination against Women and the Draft Declaration on Violence against Women. In other words, the main activity of the CSW has been in standard settings. See generally on the historical background and the work of the CSW:UN Doc. A/CONF.157/PC/61/Add.5,1993, p. 5 ff.

[63] *E. Bodenheimer*, Jurisprudence – The Philosophy and Method of the Law, Cambridge, Massachusetts 1962, p. 218.

This study will also pay attention to the legal response in human rights law to, among other things, the situation of young woman confronted with an unwanted pregnancy.[64] It is not until recently that the magnitude of the problem connected with adolescence pregnancies has been recognised.

Part three of the study looks at gender-based violence as a grave violation of the non-discrimination principle and under certain circumstances of reproductive freedom. I attempt to show in Part III that gender-based crimes and violence against women constitute the ultimate expression of the lack of equality between women and men[65] and therefore it has increasingly become to be considered a question of human rights.[66] Men may be of course, also the victims of violence, however, such violence has not occurred as a part of a pattern of gender-based abuse. Violence deprives women of their ability to achieve full equality. It is a violation, which includes the right to life, liberty and personal, mental and physical integrity, the right not to be subject to torture or cruel, inhuman or degrading treatment, the right to equal protection before the law and equality within the family. The issue of violence is connected with reproductive freedom when rape, *e.g.*, results in forced pregnancy. In other words, rape is a crime of extreme violence and the denial of reproductive freedom. Women in the former Yugoslavia have been subjected, during the recent war, to systematic rape and other forms of sexual assault. These crimes raised profound and urgent concern in the international community. I will consequently address the issue of forced pregnancy through rape and the nature of the crime rape in the context of the armed conflicts in the former Yugoslavia and in Rwanda. I will subsequently elaborate on several legal issues involved, *e.g.*, whether rape and other sexual offences are included in the concepts "crimes against humanity" and "grave breaches" of the 1949 Geneva Conventions. I will also discuss the issue of rape as a weapon of genocide and as a method of torture. Prosecution of it might lead to the creation of a stable foundation for a "broader legal treatment of rape as a human rights violation in peacetime as well as in war".[67]

---

64 The term "unwanted pregnancy" refers within the official vocabulary of population analysis to "those pregnancies that do not fall within the range of motherhood schedules having the material, economic, or psychological conditions to carry the pregnancy to term and to welcome the birth of a child". *A.R. de Alonso*, Unwanted vs. Unplanned Pregnancies: Conceptual Differences and Emotional Implications on the Experience of Abortion, in Unwanted Pregnancies and Public Policy: An International Perspective, H. Correa (ed.), New York 1994, p. 17.

65 MacKinnon has identified rape, sexual harassment, incest, pornography and abortion as sources of women's inequality. *C. MacKinnon*, Toward a Feminist Theory of the State, Cambridge 1989. See also *S. Wright*, Human Rights and Women's Rights, in Human Rights in the Twenty-First Century: a Global Challenge, *K.E. Mahoney & P. Mahoney* (eds.), Dordrecht 1993, p. 80.

66 UN Doc. E/CN.6/1995/3, § 22. It is true that women, especially in sexual relations, often find that their saying is persistently and systematically invalidated and such invalidation would be incompatible if the two sexes actually shared the same status as individuals. *C. Pateman*, Feminist Critique of the Public/Private Dichotomy, in Public and Private in Social Life, S.I. Benn & G.F. Gans (eds.), p. 213.

67 *D. Aydelott*, Mass rape during war: prosecuting Bosnian rapist under international law, Emory International Law Review 1993, Vol. 7, p. 631. See also *K.D. Askin*, War Crimes Against Women-Prosecution in International War Crimes Tribunals, The Hague 1997.

In this regard the present author will examine the function and the prospects for success of the *ad hoc* Tribunal for the former Yugoslavia, the applicable laws, the crimes covered, the persons to be held accountable etc.

While rape occurs throughout the world in the context of marital and non-marital relations, forced pregnancy has been difficult to be regarded as a violation of international human rights norms. Much of this reality subsists because international law "reinforces still dichotomies between public and private spheres of action".[68] The result of this approach is an acceptance of the condemnation of human rights violations solely in the public sphere, *i.e.,* violations of the human rights of the individual by state authorities. In other words, international law is mainly focused on the first type of actions. This distinction has been detrimental to women, since discrimination against women most frequently occurs in the private sphere. Domestic violence is a human rights violation that is unique to women. It has, however, remained for too long a time unregulated and invisible. Yet in large parts of the world the family is the main milieu, where a woman's daily life is conducted, especially in certain parts of Africa and Asia.

Here the traditional rules related to state responsibility should be further developed in order to encompass state accountability for private acts of violation of basic human rights.[69] Recent international realities have resulted in the gradual expansion of international responsibility for massive violations of human rights to include also individuals and groups.[70] Chapter 9 elaborates on that issue. The present author seeks to clarify the character of the state's obligations under international law with regard to reproductive freedom and deals with the prospects of its realisation.

Finally, Part IV concludes this book. It contains views concerning the way forward in the form of a number *de lege ferenda* proposals. The aim of this study is, however, not to provide definite and easy answers to the questions above referred to. Rather, I wish to elucidate the complexity of these issues and hopefully provide ideas for some international strategies on the topic in the shaping of our common future. At the Beijing Conference the Chinese saying "Women hold up half of the sky" was often heard. If half of the sky falls, men are not safe either. So, both men and women should work together to keep the sky up.

It is my conviction that international law can be transformed in order better to take into account women's lives and to respond to women's needs and experiences. It is also my hope that this book will illustrate how the substance of several

---

[68] *H. Charlesworth & C. Chinkin*, The Gender of *Jus Cogens*, HRQ 1993, Vol. 15, p. 69; See also *H. Charlesworth, C. Chinkin & S. Wright,* Feminist Approaches to International Law, AJIL 1991, Vol. 85, p. 625; *R.J. Cook*, Women's International Human Rights Law: The Way Forward, HRQ 1993, Vol. 15, p. 230; *K. Lundström*, pp. 66–67.

[69] Discriminatory acts may be committed by: 1. An official authority or any of their agents. The main types are legal rules and their enforcement. 2. Private people. These are: a) Acts or omissions, the effect of which is to deny or limit the legal rights of individuals belonging to a particular group or b) Other acts, which result in discriminatory treatment in social relations. See UN Memorandum, p. 39.

[70] *T. Buergenthal*, The Normative and Institutional Evolution of International Human Rights, HRQ 1997, Vol. 19, p. 719.

international law norms can be elaborated from the point of view of women. The reinterpretation of already existing human rights norms is but the first step and there is a great challenge awaiting us. It is my belief that international law norms are powerful tools for the promotion of several, basic values like dignity,[71] justice and health.

[71] Such an approach may be associated with the policy-oriented school of international law which has been mainly represented by scholars like Myres, McDougal, Lasswell and Chen and who place human dignity as primary among all values which are relevant in the social processes that take place within the international community. *M. McDougal, H. Lasswell and L. Chen*, Human Rights and World Public Order-The Basic Policies of an International Law of Human Dignity, New Haven 1980.

*Chapter 2*

# Non-Discrimination and Gender Equality – Some Conceptual Deliberations

> "Equality!! The first desire of nature,
> the first need of man,
> chief bound of all legitimate society!"
>
> *The Manifesto of Equality*,
> Francois-Noel Babeuf
> and Sylvain Marechal

## 2.1. Introduction

For many centuries there was a prevailing view that a state had an absolute right to treat its citizens as it chose. Only in relatively recent times have states accepted, in their agreements with each other, various duties towards all individuals within their jurisdictions. The creation of international human rights law acquired international significance first after the tragic events that preceded and took place during the Second World War. The need to protect human rights in the future with appropriate international institutions was apparent to the international community. Provisions relating to equality and prohibition of specific forms of discrimination were considered essential and became a prominent feature of international human rights instruments adopted within global as well as regional organisations. They reflected the rising awareness both in governments and in peoples, in the legal, political and moral necessity of guaranteeing to all individuals equal dignity.

Much of the history of the United Nations is the history of human rights. One of the main purposes of the organisation called for the achievement of international co-operation in promoting and encouraging respect for human rights and fundamental freedoms for all human beings without distinction as to race, sex, language and religion.[1] The UN is firmly committed to gender equality and its Charter is the

---

[1] See Article 1(3) of the UN Charter. Earlier drafts of the Charter reveal that the text outlawing discrimination on the basis of sex was introduced later due to the pressure exercised by women delegates and the representatives of 42 NGOs accredited to the founding conference. The United Nations and The Advancement of Women 1945–1995, UN New York 1995, p. 10.

first[2] universal law-making treaty explicitly to mention the principle of equality between men and women. Paragraph 2 of the Preamble proclaims the determination of the peoples of the UN to "reaffirm faith in fundamental human rights, in the dignity and worth of the human person, in the equal rights of men and women". Thereby the goal of gender equality has become a contractual obligation of all states members of the organisation. The Charter is today nearly universally accepted since its acceptance is a condition for becoming a member of the UN.[3]

In addition, three other articles 13(1)(b), 55(c) and 76(c) of the UN's Charter assert equality and require the realisation of human rights and fundamental freedoms "for all without distinction as to race, sex, language or religion". In consequence international human rights law has greatly emphasised the treatment of women and men as human beings equal in value and dignity. The establishment of the Commission of the Status of Women as early as in 1946 demonstrates that great importance was ascribed within the UN to the principle of gender equality. The CSW aspires to promote respect for and the realisation of the right of women to be equal to men in their legal and social status.[4] States have to take measures by the year 2000 to achieve such equality.[5] Universal respect for gender equality is consequently the goal of the international community and non-discrimination is one of the means of achieving this goal. Therefore, the prohibition of discrimination is the core principle of international law in the human rights field.[6] The principle constitutes an integral part of the Universal Declaration of Human Rights (Articles 1 and

---

[2] General protection of human rights and non-discrimination were not matters of major concern to the League of Nations. Several proposals for equality or non-discrimination clauses were put forward during the drafting of the Covenant of the League of Nations. They were, however, unsuccessful. A few delegations raised issues of importance for the status of women, but the principle of equality between men and women was not specifically mentioned in the League's Covenant of 28 April 1919. The Covenant did on the other hand declare that member countries should discourage trafficking in women and children and by that it prepared the ground for the UN's treaty of 1949 outlawing the exploitation of prostitution. The significance of this provision can also be seen in that it denounced the treatment of women as commodities which was considered to perpetuate women's low status in society. For a historical review of the League of Nations work on women's issues see: The United Nations and The Advancement of Women 1945–1995, *ibid.*; *S. Skogly*, Article 2, in The Universal Declaration of Human Rights, A. Eide et al (eds.), p. 58; *A.E. Zimmern*, The League of Nations and the Rule of Law 1918–1935, New York 1939; *Y. Saito*, Judge Tanaka, natural law and the principle of equality, in The Living Law of Nations, G. Alfredsson & P. Macalister-Smith (eds.), Kehl 1996, pp. 400–401.

[3] The UN Charter came into force on 24 October 1945. It had been ratified by 186 states by the end of 1998.

[4] The effect of this well-intentioned initiative to assign the CSW the mandate to deal with all women's issues has proved instead to contribute to the marginalisation of women's rights, and to a treatment of women's rights as something different, and of lesser importance, than other human rights.

[5] See The Nairobi Forward Looking Strategies of Implementation for the Advancement of Women. Förenta Nationernas kvinnokonferens i Nairobi, Aktstycken utgivna av Utrikesdepartementet, Ny serie II: 42, Stockholm 1986.

[6] *M. Bossuyt*, L'interdiction de la discrimination dans le droit international des droits de l'homme, Brussels 1976.

2), and a number of multilateral human rights treaties[7] contain provisions of relevance for the right of women to be free from all forms of discrimination. The Universal Declaration of Human Rights was the first international human rights document, where the idea of equality as an ultimate human goal was reflected. The UDHR mirrors spiritual and moral tenets, which are central to all cultures. Article 1, in which the principle of equality has been expressed, was already during the drafting of the Declaration recognised as the "cornerstone" of the whole document.[8] The principle of equality and non-discrimination is here based on the dignity of the human person.[9] Representatives of states, furthermore, agreed that inequality did in fact exist, but the statement in Article 1 meant "that the right to freedom and equality was inherent from the moment of birth".[10]

General non-discrimination rules are likewise contained in regional[11] human rights conventions, *e.g.*, Article 14 in the European Convention[12] and Article 1 in the American Convention on Human Rights.

---

[7] ICCPR (Articles 2(1),3,4), ICESCR (Articles 2(2),3), the UN Convention on the Rights of the Child (Article 2(1)) and the Women's Convention (Articles 1,2,4).

Whereas the principle of equality and non-discrimination was established almost beyond discussion in the UN Charter, it was under attack during the drafting of the UDHR. The representative of South Africa maintained, *e.g.* , that "not now or ever would certain people enjoy equal rights" and that women could never have the same rights as men. Minutes of the US delegation to the third regular session of the GA, 14 October 1948, US(P)/A/M(Chr)/15, box 60, US mission to the UN, RG 84, NARA, cited in *Å. Samnoy*, Human Rights as International Consensus, R 1993:4, Bergen 1993, p. 81. The first article of an early draft of the UDHR stated that "All men are brothers". It was Mrs. Eleanor Roosevelt, a United Nations delegate representing the United States of America with considerable authority, who in cooperation with feminists from especially Latin America, advanced her opinion and argued persuasively for the inclusion of the principle of equality between men and women, so the drafts of the UN Charter and Article 2 of the Universal Declaration were revised. *B.W. Cook*, Eleanor Roosevelt and Human Rights: The Battle for Peace and Planetary Decency, in Women and American Foreign Policy: Lobbyists, Critics, and Insiders, E.P. Crapol (ed.), New York 1987, p. 99; *L. Reanda*, The Commission on the Status of Women, in The United Nations and Human Rights, P. Alston (ed.), Oxford 1992, p. 266; *K. Tomaševski*, Women and Human Rights, p. 98; The United Nations and The Advancement of Women, p. 11; *B. Andreassen*, Eleanor Roosevelt – verdenserklaringens mor?, Mennesker og rettigheter 1998, Vol. 16, pp. 349–376.

[8] *T. Lindholm*, Article 1, in The Universal Declaration on Human Rights, A. Eide *et al.* (eds.), p. 42. In my opinion the wording of Article 1 could also be understood as a statement of a fact, that all persons are equal in dignity.

[9] In 1949 the UN Secretary General defined the principle of equality as a principle based on the ethical concept of the dignity of the human person. Thus, "human dignity implies that human beings are to be treated as ends in themselves and not as mere means to en end". See Memorandum, p. 4.

[10] *A.Eide et al.*, p. 48.

[11] See Article 2 of the Arab Charter on Human Rights which was adopted on 15 September 1994 by the 22 states which form the League of Arab States. The treaty has not yet entered into force. For the text see International Commission of Jurists, The Review 1996, No. 56, pp. 57–64.

[12] Noteworthy is that the very first draft of the European Convention as presented by Mr. P.-H. Teitgen on 5 September 1949 did not contain a reference to sex as a prohibited ground of discrimination in its general clause on discrimination. It was only after a statement made in favour of an inclusion of this ground by the Danish delegate in the plenary session of the Consultative Assembly of the Council of Europe that sex was enumerated among the grounds for prohibited discrimination in the draft text of the convention. This proposal was approved later on at the Conference of Senior Officials in June 1950 in Strasbourg. See Doc. Council of Europe, INF/2/E,3; Doc. A.116.2 and docs. CM/WP 1(50) 15.

Article 18(3) of the African Charter on Human and Peoples' Rights[13] imposes a duty on states parties to eliminate "every discrimination against women and also to ensure the protection of the rights of the woman and the child as stipulated in international declarations and conventions". This provision displays consequently a linkage to the UN Convention on the Elimination of All Forms of Discrimination Against Women[14] as well as to other relevant international instruments, *i.e.*, the UN Declaration on the Elimination of Violence Against Women (1993), the Vienna Declaration (1993) and the Beijing Declaration (1995). On the other hand, the provisions of the African Charter containing individual duties encourage individuals to behave in accordance with the "conservation of values particular to traditional African civilisations". So, according to Article 29(7) each person has the duty "to preserve and strengthen positive African cultural values in his relations with other members of the society". Many African governments commonly use African culture and traditions as an excuse for not amending national laws to recognise women's rights.[15] Deep-rooted African values include "clear differentiations of roles and rights based on gender".[16] On this basis I may assume that African women to a great extend are hindered from the enjoyment of their human rights and

---

*P.-H. Teitgen*, Introduction to the European Convention, in The European System for the Protection of Human Rights, R. St. J. Macdonald, F. Matscher & H. Petzold (eds.), Dordrecht 1993, pp. 3–14; *M. Ragazzi*, The Concept of International Obligations *Erga Omnes*, Oxford 1997, p. 119. The Committee on Legal and Administrative Questions of the Consultative Assembly was assigned the task of preparing a draft of a European Convention. The Committee's proposal on the non-discrimination clause (Article 5) reads as follows: "The fundamental rights and freedoms enumerated above shall be guaranteed without any distinction based on race, colour, sex, language, religion, political or other opinion, national or social origin..". Collected Edition of the *Travaux Préparatoires* 1975, Vol. I, p. 178 *et seq.*

Moreover, the principle of equality before the law and of equal protection of the law does not appear in the European Convention. The text includes only a provision prohibiting discrimination. From that one might draw the conclusion that the European Convention does not give a prominent place to the idea of gender equality and non-discrimination. *A. Eide & T. Opsahl*, p. 13. See also *K.J. Partsch*, Discrimination, in The European System for the Protection of Human Rights, R. St. J. Macdonald, F. Matscher & H. Petzold (eds.), p. 574.

On the other hand, the Vienna Declaration of the Heads of State members of the Council of Europe, which was adopted in October 1993, contains a very strong commitment to the principle of equality, as the Heads of State ensure there the "respect of the principles, which are fundamental to our common European tradition: equality before the law, non-discrimination, equal opportunity, freedom of association and assembly as well as to participate actively in public life".

[13] In 1998, 51 out of 53 African States members of the OAU had ratified or acceded to the African Charter.

[14] Like the definition of discrimination contained in the Women's Convention this article places obligations upon African states to eliminate discrimination against women specifically and not merely on grounds of sex as such.

[15] *F. Butegwa*, The Challenge of Promoting Women's Rights in African Countries, in Ours By Rights, Women's Rights as Human Rights, J.Kerr (ed.), London 1993, p. 40.

[16] *C.E. Welch*, Human Rights and African Women: a Comparison of Protection Under Two Major Treaties, HRQ 1993, Vol. 15, p. 554; *N.K.A. Busia*, Kvinners rettigheter i Afrika, Mennesker og rettigheter 1995, Vol. 14, p. 288.

may easily become victims of violence in the name of retrograde traditional practice.[17] Traditional values should, however, not be used to legitimatise practices contrary to women's human rights. A number of aspects of customary law in Africa are discriminatory against women,[18] because custom traditionally has reflected male interests and dominance over women. Therefore, the African Commission[19] has been requested to interpret "African values and traditions in a positive way" with a view to universal standards.[20] There is implicit recognition in the African Charter of the fact that cultural values in Africa cannot remain static. International principles of human rights provide a solid basis for negating retrogressive traditions and customs, which are adverse to the position of women in Africa.[21] Thus, regional systems for the protection of human rights must be consistent with universal standards and cannot depart from such obligations, since there is strong support in modern international law for the view that the principle of non-discrimination and gender equality is of general application on the basis of customary international law.

The recognition of the equality in dignity and human rights of women and men as a priority issue for the UN and its member states is one of the most important messages that echoes from recent UN Conferences such as the Vienna World Conference on Human Rights Conference in 1993,[22] the International Conference on Population and Development in 1994,[23] the Fourth World Conference on Women in 1995[24] as well as the UN's fiftieth anniversary year in 1995.

Clearly, the prohibition of gender-based discrimination is fundamental and universal. Yet, in international law a consensus is lacking with respect to the exact

---

[17] UN Doc. A/CONF.157/PC/63/Add. 26, 27 April 1993, p. 2. In the preparational process for the Vienna World Conference on Human Rights in 1993, several African governments questioned the universal application of current international human rights law, claiming that it is not appropriate to certain social and cultural systems. In other words, there was a tendency to relativise human rights. In the Tunis Declaration, adopted by 41 states, at the African Regional Preparatory Meeting in November 1992, the issue of universality emerges in an apparently contradictory manner. Whereas the second operative paragraph states: "The universality of human rights is unquestionable; their protection and promotion constitute a duty for all States without regard to their political, economic or cultural system", the fifth operative paragraph declares that: "No preconceived model, however, can be prescribed on a universal scale". This statement is obviously contrary to the principle of the universality of human rights, which was thereafter endorsed in § 5, Part I of the Vienna Declaration and Programme of Action adopted at the 1993 Conference. The text of the Tunis Declaration is reprinted in Human Rights – The New Consensus, London 1994, *R. Reoch* (ed.), p. 288.

[18] *A. Armstrong et al.*, Uncovering Reality: Excavating Women's Rights in African Family Law, International Journal of Law and the Family, December 1993, p. 314 *et seq.*

[19] The African Commission on Human and People's Rights was established in 1987 after the coming into force of the African Charter on Human and People's Rights on 21 October 1986.

[20] *W. Benedek*, The Judiciary and Human Rights in Africa, HRLJ 1990, p. 251.

[21] *C. Beyani*, Toward a More Effective Guarantee of Women's Rights in the African Human Rights System, in Human Rights of Women, R.J. Cook (ed.), Philadelphia 1994, p. 297.

[22] See Part I, § 18 of the Vienna Declaration and Programme of Action.

[23] The Cairo Programme of Action, especially Chapters I and VII.

[24] The Beijing Declaration and Platform for Action sets the agenda for the UN and governments' work for achieving gender equality from the year 1995 to 2000.

scope of the terms "equality" and "discrimination",[25] the conceptual relationship between them and how they operate in a normative context. The point of departure of my analysis will be that equality in contemporary international law is increasingly being considered as having a twofold nature, thereby comprising "formal" equality as well as "substantive"/*de facto* equality.

Among various legal theories on gender equality two schools of thought can be identified as being prevailing: the symmetrical approach[26] and the asymmetrical approach.[27] This is, of course, a very simplistic systematisation of the great number of distinctive ideologies on gender equality represented in legal theory.[28]

---

[25] There is an assumption that equality and non-discrimination as general principle of law become meaningful in a legal context when supplemented by more specific rules. During the preparatory work on Article 1 of the UDHR, Mr. R. Cassin emphasised that this provision stated general principles "within the framework of which individual rights were defined". UN Doc. A/C. 3/SR 173, p. 4. A corresponding description of the notion "equality" has been presented by Mrs. R.Ben-Israel as follows: "It is an empty vessel, that acquires meaning by incorporating external values, without which it would remain a mere linguistic formula". *R. Ben-Israel*, Equality in Labour Law, Conference Papers Part II, 1st World Law Conference "Law in Motion", Brussels September 1996, p. 169. See also *A. Eide & T. Opsahl*, p. 2. In feminist literature "discrimination" is one of the key concepts most often used to define women's estate and the relations between the sexes in a patriarchal society. *A.G. Jónasdóttir*, Love Power and Political Interests, Örebro Studies No. 7, Kumla 1991, p. 89.

In legal theory there exist consequently numerous distinct ideas of equality. Some authors have advanced the view that the principle of equality has no substantive content of its own and that it derives its content from substantive rights. Others have argued that equality indeed is an independent legal norm. In addition, the standpoint has been taken that equality is but one of several components in the prohibition of discrimination. *T.R. Hervey*, Justification for Sex Discrimination in Employment, London 1993, p. 26. When Mr. L.Despouy presented in 1996 at the UN his final report on human rights and extreme poverty, he recalled that in human rights law an intrinsic link between dignity and equality has been established and that these two concepts together constitute the foundations of the principle of non-discrimination. For the various cited views see *P. Westen*, The Empty Idea of Equality, Harvard Law Review 1982, Vol. 95, pp. 537, 580 and 592.

[26] Christine Littleton distinguishes two models of the symmetrical vision, assimilation and androgyny. The first theory seems to be widely accepted by national courts. It indicates that the law should require that women be treated as men already are, because women, given the chance, are or could be just like men. The second model also emphasises that women and men are very much like each other, but equality requires that both sexes are treated as androgynous persons would be. The value placed on the principle of androgyny by some feminist writers is that it enables "men and women alike – and equally – to develop aspects of their nature repressed by the stereotypical exhortations and expectations of society, permitting them to eschew ways of being with which they find themselves ill at ease". *C.A. Littleton*, Reconstructing sexual equality, in Feminist Legal Theory, K.T. Bartlett & R. Kennedy (eds.), San Francisco 1991, p. 35.

[27] Asymmetrical approaches include "special rights", "accommodation", "acceptance" and "empowerment". The starting point for these approaches is the acknowledgement that the prohibition of discrimination on the basis of sex takes into account asymmetrical relations between men and women. It is to be interpreted as being aimed at the protection of groups, which have been confronted and/or are still confronted with structural disadvantage and subtle patterns of systematic discrimination. See *L. Code*, Simple equality is not enough, Australian Journal of Philosophy 1986, Vol. 48, p. 53 and *T. Loenen*, p. 269.

[28] For a thorough presentation of the major hypothesises on gender equality see: *K.T. Bartlett & R. Kennedy*, Feminist Legal Theory, San Franciso 1991 and *F.E. Olsen*, Feminist Legal Theory I:

Still, I find such a division of the various categories as useful and suitable for the purpose of this study. The variance between them reflects mainly their position in relation to the question of whether equality contains a formal as well as a substantive feature.

Formal/symmetrical equality is often associated in the context of , *e.g.*, EC law and in some national jurisdictions with the term "direct discrimination". This type of discrimination occurs where a person is treated less favourably on the grounds of his/her sex than someone of the opposite sex.[29] Direct discrimination relates to causality and comparison. Firstly, there must be a causal connection between the victim's sex and the treatment he/she has received. Secondly, the unfavourable status of this treatment is established by way of comparison with a person of the opposite sex. Professor Bernhardt has explained that: "Gehalt und Tragweite jedes der Diskriminierungsverbote bedürfe einer detaillierten Untersuchung, um feststellen zu können, wie weit Übereinstimmung und Unterschiede bestehen".[30]

A symmetrical approach to equality implies that the concept of discrimination applies equally to favoured and unfavoured groups. A purely formal concept of equality fails, in other words, to take proper account of the discrimination and discriminatory effect for an individual in consequence of her/his sex. This approach has been criticised from a feminist perspective for ignoring the nature of the social problem of gender-based discrimination. It is insufficient for redressing the inherited consequences of past discrimination and disadvantage women have suffered historically. The international community has, therefore, realised that gender equality cannot be achieved solely by the reliance on the strict formal approach to non-discrimination.[31] Unlike formal equality asymmetrical equality is result-oriented,

---

Foundations and Outlooks and II : Positioning Feminist Theory Within the Law, Dartmouth 1995. Robin Teske makes the point in her article "Power: An Interdisciplinary Approach" that it is difficult to characterise the "dozen schools of feminism". See Reconceiving Reality: Women and International Law, *D.G. Dallmeyer* (ed.), at 233. One should also bear in mind that there are many intersections and overlap between feminist theories and that feminist analysis has largely been missing in international law until the beginning of the 1990s. *H. Charlsworth*, Alienating Oscar? Feminist Analysis of International Law, in Reconceiving Reality: Women and International Law, D.G. Dallmeyer (ed.), pp. 2 and 14. See also *K. Engle*, International Human Rights and Feminism: When Discourses Meet, Michigan Journal of International Law 1992, Vol. 13, p. 517 ff. and *N. Lacey*, Unspeakable Subjects- Feminist Essays in Legal and Social Theory, Oxford 1998.

[29] Most writers seem to agree that the rationale for direct discrimination is corrective justice. Acts which discriminate directly are agent-relative and the victim may seek individual compensation from the defendant. The relationship is symmetrical in that compensation is granted according to the damage suffered. Corrective justice implies, in other words, a system of rights and duties that operates between people in individual cases.

[30] *R. Bernhardt*, Völkerrechtliche Verbote der Diskriminierung von Individuen, in J. Jekewitz *et al.* (eds.), Des Menschen Recht zwischen Freiheit and Verantwortung, Festschrift für K.J. Partsch, Berlin 1989, p. 99.

[31] The UN system has dedicated itself to ensure the universal recognition, in law, of the equality of rights between men and women as well as to explore ways to achieve substantial equality. Whereas the Women's Convention makes specific reference to *de facto* equality in connection with special measures, the Forward-Looking Strategies for the Advancement of Women explicitly distinguishes between *de iure*

*de facto* equality. The asymmetrical approach to equality allows positive discrimination to play an important role in advancing women's equality.[32]

The principle of non-discrimination is thus subordinated to equality and it is more limited in its scope. While the concept "equality" may refer to kinds of treatment, to aims and to results,[33] non-discrimination is generally linked to treatment. Nevertheless, the principle of non-discrimination fulfils useful functions in relations to all aspects of equality with the aim to prevent violations of each of them.[34] In the following section I shall examine the content and the relationship between the two concepts.

---

and *de facto* discrimination. Paragraph 48 says that: "The sharp contrasts between legislative changes and effective implementation of these changes are a major obstacle to the full participation of women in society. *De facto* and indirect discrimination, particularly by reference to marital or family status, often persists despite legislative action". Paragraph 33 recognises that "unless major measures are taken, numerous obstacles will continue to exist which retard the participation of women in political life, in the formulation of policies that affect them and in the formulation of national women's policies". Despite the fact that the final documents produced by four world conferences on women's rights clearly require that transitional special measures be used to achieve greater *de facto* equality between men and women, they also indicate their limited scope. Thus, states are sovereign in the implementation of the recommendations, and the realisation of their aims must be carried out in accordance with national conditions.

See the Report of the World Conference to "Review and Appraise the Achievements of the United Nations Decade for Women: Equality, Development and Peace". See UN Doc. A/CONF.116/28, July 1985 and § 42 of the Beijing Platform for Action. See also *N. Brunn & P.K. Koskinen*, Jämställdhetslagen, Helsingfors 1987, p. 41; The United Nations and Human Rights, UN New York 1984, p. 148 and *K. Tomaševski*, Women and Human Rights, p. 98.

[32] The notion "positive discrimination"/"positive action" denotes actions which aim at securing an equal share of social goods for different groups by departing from the principle of equal treatment and actively favouring people belonging to groups which have traditionally suffered from discrimination. Positive discrimination explicitly takes account of gender conscious criteria to further *de facto* equality. It comprises among other things preferential treatment and the introduction of quotas.

[33] As Forbes points out equality may denote generally "a moral belief, a rationalist precept, an *a priori* principle, a right, a means to an end, or an end in itself". *I. Forbes*, Equal Opportunity: Radical, Liberal and Conservative Critiques, in E. Meehan & S. Sevenhuijsen (eds.), Equality Politics and Gender, London 1991, p. 17. Nielson has argued that to have his or her needs equally met is an egalitarian goal that we should strive toward and that "quite independently of its attainment, there are certain rights that we shall have, the covering formula for which is the claim that we all are to be treated as moral equals". In other words, people have an equal right to respect and that none ought to be treated as a means only. *K. Nielson*, Radical Welfare Egalitarianism, in Equality, Selected Readings, L.P. Pojman & R. Westmoreland (eds.), New York 1997, p. 207.

[34] Professor Dinstein has, however, maintained that a phraseological distinction between non-discrimination and equality "has no real consequence" and it "produces no discernible practical results". Instead, he accentuates the procedural nature of the non-discrimination principle and its linkage to the enjoyment of substantive human rights. Nevertheless, Dinstein stresses that the line of division "between the procedural principle and some substantive human rights may be quite faint". *Y. Dinstein*, Discrimination and International Human Rights, Israel Yearbook of Human Rights 1985, Vol. 15, pp. 19 and 22. My proposition is that the achievement of gender equality is basic in its "own right". See the speech delivered by Mr. T.E. Worth cited in *N. Taub*, in International Conference on Population and Development, ASIL, Washington D.C. 1994, p. 13.

## 2.2. The Quest for a Dynamic Definition of Discrimination and Equality

### *2.2.1. Formal Equality*

#### *2.2.1.1. The Ideological Basis*

The philosophical and legal debate, which has surrounded both aspects of equality and the correlative categories of discrimination, have mainly concerned the question of whether they are founded on a corrective or a distributive notion of justice. The correlative relation between justice and equality is of vital importance to any anti-discrimination provision/law. Firstly, such legal norms/laws must necessarily possess an intelligible rationale for being. It is presumed that equality in the sense of uniformity, regularity, similarity and symmetry needs no reasons, whereas difference and unsystematic behaviour need as a rule justification.[35] Judge Tanaka has expressed this standpoint in his dissenting opinion in the *South West Africa* cases (Second Phase) as follows:

> "Equality being a principle and different treatment an exception, those who refer to the different treatment must prove its *raison d'Être* and its reasonableness".[36]

Secondly, the role of an anti-discrimination provision/legislation may alter substantially depending on the way justice is perceived.[37] If , for example, preferential treatment is to be justified from another standpoint than that of mere compensation for past discrimination, the relevant law must recognise distributive justice as one of its cornerstones. The issue of justification is significant in that it invites international supervisory human rights bodies and national courts to make very sensitive decisions about the social objectives of the treaties/legislation to be applied. The proponents for the symmetrical approach to equality usually justify their position on the basis of a) an *a priori* notion of justice, b) state neutrality and c) strong emphasis on the primacy of the individual.[38] The notion of *a priori* justice is regarded independently of any historical or political context. It is simply unaffected by the distribution of resources, benefits and disadvantages in society. The socio-economical background of particular group/s in society is thus of no relevance. Justice is, therefore, linked to particular events between particular subjects. The prohibition of discrimination applies equally to people from advantaged as well as disadvantaged groups. The symmetrical approach to equality is consequently based on the idea that the law must be the same for everyone and that the possession of

---

[35] *P. Westen*, p. 570. Most of the legal writers agree that a difference in treatment requires justification in terms of relevant and sufficient differences between the claimants. *M. Ginsberg*, On Justice in Society, Baltimore 1965, p. 79; *W. Frankena*, Some Beliefs About Justice, University of Kansas 1966, p. 8; *F.E. Oppenheim*, p. 63.

[36] ICJ, Reports and Judgments, Advisory Opinions and Orders, Judgment of 18 July 1966, p. 464; *I. Brownlie*, Basic Documents on Human Rights, Oxford 1981, p. 309.

[37] *A.E. Morris & S.M. Nott*, Working Women and the Law: Equality and Discrimination in Theory and Practice, London 1991, p. 12.

[38] *S. Fredman*, Reversing Discrimination, Law Quarterly Review 1997, Vol. 113, p. 577.

human rights should not be affected by specific grounds for discrimination. Thus, enjoyment of these rights should not be treated as depending on , *e.g.*, gender. The *a priori* notion of justice has been criticised, and rightly so, for assuming an ideal world, in which all human beings are on an equal footing. To deny the historical socio-economical status of a particular group any relevance when defining equality, is "to substitute the ideal for the reality".[39]

Justifications grounded on the idea of state neutrality presuppose that the state should be rather neutral as between its citizens. Preferential treatment of a particular group would be deemed undesirable, since it is viewed as an intervention with the purpose to further the interests of one group in society to the possible detriment of others. Writers who oppose the idea of a neutral state have emphasised that it is a delusion, since the policy of non-intervention usually favours the dominant group/s in society.[40] This is contrary to international human rights law, since "the state is bound to guarantee the realisation of fundamental rights for all, and not just for the most powerful".[41]

Finally, the primacy of the individual comprises the idea of merit and the idea of fault. The idea of merit implies treatment according to personal characteristics. Positive discrimination/positive action is, in consequence, suspect, since such policies are perceived to violate the right of the individual to be treated on the basis of his/her merits. This has been viewed as a violation of the very core concept of justice defined as the individual's claim to equality before the law. In the words of Abram:

> "Once we have abandoned the principles of fair procedures, equal opportunity, and individual rights in favour of the advancement of a particular group, we have opened the wide door to future abuses of all kinds".[42]

The above justification for a symmetrical approach to equality has been questioned, however, for the reason that what counts as merit may in itself be determined by gender or race-conscious criteria.

Legal norms embracing formal equality require equal treatment. The "equal treatment" doctrine appeared early in the feminist legal community. It is to a great extent based on a fragment of the well- known Aristotelian maxim on justice,[43] *i.e.*, that similarly situated individuals should be treated in the same way. The theory

---

39 Ibid.

40 *S. Fredman*, p. 579.

41 *T. Loenen*, Rethinking Sex Equality as a Human Right, NQHR 1994, Vol. 12, p. 268.

42 *M.B. Abram*, Affirmative Action: Fair Shakers and Social Engineers, Harvard Law Review 1986, Vol. 99, Nos 5–6, p. 1321.

43 Justice, according to Aristotle, comes in two different forms: corrective and distributive. Aristotle was the first to proclaim that things that are alike should be treated alike, while things that are unlike should be treated unlike in proportion to their unlikeness. Whereas the basis of the first part of his axiom lies in similarity, the second part has difference as its basis. The equal treatment of unlike things means, accordingly, inequality. The Aristotelian model of equality has, nevertheless, been strongly criticised in that it accepts "the validity of a male standard as human". In that way it marginalises a great part of women's experience. It has been maintained that the Aristotelian concept of equality does not relate to

comprises the impartial and consistent application of existing law rules and principles without taking account of motives and effects and regardless of the material outcome.[44] Since individuals are regarded as equal, only an equal application of the existing law with regard to every individual, whoever he/she is, is required (symmetry in law) including the demand that women have the right to be treated as men are. This actually constitutes the essence of the well-established formula requiring "equality before the law" and which has found expression in several human rights instruments.[45] The terms "equality before the law", "equal protection" and "non-discrimination" by way of law reflect, however, distinct ideas.[46] In

---

the reality of women's conditions. It rather perpetuates than eradicates inequality. Rape and battering are often given as examples of abuses based on sex differences. It is maintained that according to this theory they are "the permitted treating of unlikes unlike". In international law the concept of equality has traditionally been defined by the use of the androcentric model. Thus, if men are entitled to something, then women should be entitled to the same. The androcentric doctrine takes for granted and reinforces a status quo that is more favourable to male concerns than to female ones. *K.T. Bartlett & R. Kennedy*, Introduction, Feminist Legal Theory, p. 2. See also *S. Wright,* p. 79; *C.A. MacKinnon*, On Torture: a Feminist Perspective on Human Rights, in Human Rights in the Twenty-First Century: a Global Challenge, K.E. Mahoney & P. Mahoney (eds.), p. 30; *G. Rüpke*, Das Verbot Willkürlicher Gleichbehandlung in Seiner Bedeutung für Soziale Grundrechte, in Festschrift für F. Ermacora, pp. 484–485; *N.H. Kaufman & S.A. Lindquist*, p. 120; *C.A. MacKinnon*, Reflections on Sex Equality Under Law, p. 1286, especially note 28; *K.E. Mahoney*, in Human Rights of Women, R.J. Cook (ed.), p. 443 and *K. Lundström*, pp. 48–50. Others believe that Aristotle's writings can support feminist methods and epistemology. It has been stressed that he like many contemporary feminists assumes the natural sociability of the species. Moreover, his teleological virtues are directed to the end of society. *L.R. Hishman*, The Book of "A", Texas Law Review 1992, Vol. 70:971, pp. 972 and 986; *T. Loenen*, p. 257. The present author also suggests a more positive reading of Aristotle. I have found through non-dogmatic interpretation that the second part of his description of "equality" reflects a substantive, asymmetrical approach to equality.

44 *W. Williams*, Notes from a first generation, University of Chicago Legal Forum 1989, pp. 99–113. One might for good reasons question whether William's fears that if special benefits for pregnant women were permitted, then this approach would allow also "pregnancy to be treated worse than other disabilities" is well-grounded. *W. Williams*, The equality crisis: some reflections on culture, courts and feminism, in Women's Rights Law Reporter 1982, Vol. 7, p. 196.

45 See, *e.g.*, UDHR (Article 7), ICCPR (Article 26), CEDAW (Article 15), the American Convention (Article 24) and the African Charter (Article 3). See also the Preamble (§§ g (i) and g (v)) of the Universal Islamic Declaration of Human Rights adopted by the Islamic Council on 19 September 1981. However, a subsequent document, The Cairo Declaration on Human Rights in Islam of August 5, 1990, makes it clear that women do not have equal rights and responsibilities with men. Women and men have equal value ("equal in terms of basic human dignity") but different rights and different tasks in the Muslim society. Thus, the rights of Muslim men and women are considered equivalent rather than equal. See in addition *R.J. Cook*, Reservations to the Convention on the Elimination of All Forms of Discrimination against Women, p. 705.

46 The HRC in its GC No. 18 on non-discrimination has approached them en masse as not clearly distinguishable, and the singular form of the substantive "principle" has been used. Paragraph 1 of the GC reads as follows: "Non-discrimination, together with equality before the law and equal protection of the law without discrimination, constitutes a basic and general principle relating to the protection of human rights". The Committee based this statement on a systematic interpretation of the Covenant's provisions. It considered the relationship between Article 2 and Article 26 and not solely Article 2 as prohibiting discrimination. From that I may conclude that in the Committee's view non-discrimination in itself does not imply action in order to achieve *de facto* equality. It is only in combination with both rules that special measures designed to achieve material equality may be required. For the opposite view see *C. Bucchi*, pp. 71–87.

contrast to the principle "equality before the law", which is embedded in the theory of law and practice of continental Europe, the Anglo-Saxon clause granting everyone "the equal protection of the law",[47] which in international instruments often has been merged with the first one to appear in the same article,[48] has been regarded as to refer to material equality based on justifications related to justice, *e.g.*, comprising equal distribution of rights and equal opportunities.[49]

The principle of equality before the law is premised on a neo-liberal ideology, according to which the individual is perceived as the ultimate source of value and as an autonomous person, whose choices about his/her own life should enjoy the utmost respect. Outside interference, even when it is aimed at promoting equality, is rejected.[50] Equality in this sense relates to equal formal rights based on the philosophical supposition that men and women are born equal. In a few law dictionaries the notion "equality" is still defined as "the condition of possessing substantially the same rights, privileges, and immunities, and being liable to substantially the same duties".[51] Also within the legal doctrine a few authors[52] suggest that formal equality requires that the law must grant *identical* rights to women and men, whereas others mean that equality before law does not necessarily require that the extent and the content of the rights of all individuals are the same.[53] Nevertheless,

---

[47] Whereas the first maxim is to be found in many national constitutions since the French revolution, the second principle is historically related to the civil war in America and the adoption of the 14th Amendment to the US Constitution. The historical background might to a certain extent explain the process, in which the principle of equality gradually has been "transformed from a formal principle directed exclusively at law-applying organs into a substantive principle". *M.Nowak*, CCPR Commentary, p. 459.

[48] Article 7 (UDHR) as well as Article 26 (ICCPR) proclaim that all persons are "equal before the law and are entitled without any discrimination to the equal protection of the law". The *travaux préparatoires* of the UDHR do not shed much light on the intention behind Article 7. They do, however, reveal that there was a certain confusion on the part of the drafting Committee as to the meaning of the phrase "equal protection of the law". The precise meaning and the intended scope of it is nowhere explained. There was a lack of common understanding among the members of the third Committee concerning this concept. It was understood to mean either that "laws shall be applied equally" or that "all were equally entitled to the protection of whatever laws existed", *i.e.*, protection in general. The second alternative received considerable support from several delegations. For the discussions on this article see *N. Robinson*, The Universal Declaration of Human Rights, New York 1958, pp. 109–111 and *J.T. Möller*, Article 7, in The Universal Declaration of Human Rights, A. Eide *et al.* (eds.), pp. 118, 122 and 125. Also Article 26 of the ICCPR has been given the extensive meaning. See HRC GC No. 18, HRI/GEN/1/Rev.1, § 12. In its case law the HRC has observed that the principle of equal protection of the law, as contained in Article 7 of the UDHR "prohibits discrimination in law or practice" in any field regulated and protected by public authorities. HRC communications Nos. 172/1984 and 180/1984. On the legislative history of Article 26 of the ICCPR see *M. Nowak*, CCPR Commentary, pp. 465–469.

[49] Equal protection according to Vierdag can be realised through two methods: the negatively formulated-prohibition of discrimination- and the positively formulated-effective protection against discrimination. The latter may comprise special measures in order to obtain genuine equality. *E.W.Vierdag*, The Concept of Discrimination in International Law, The Hague, 1973, pp. 126–127. See also *A. Eide & T. Opsahl*, p. 19.

[50] *R. Ben-Israel*, p. 170.

[51] Black's Law Dictionary, St. Paul, Minnesota 1983, p. 279.

[52] For references see *T.K. Hervey*, p. 27.

[53] See *A. Byrnes*, p. 22.

the first proposition gained overwhelming support from governmental delegations during the drafting of Article 16 of the Women's Convention. The proposal presented by the CSW with regard to the wording of several sub-paragraphs of that provision referring to "equal rights" was replaced by the phrase "the same rights" instead.[54]

The formal acquisition of equality before the law has been assumed by some commentators to have solved the extensive imbalance of power. Other academic scholars have maintained that in practice the promise of the same rights is "thwarted by the inequalities of power (between men and women)".[55] The same legal rights do not necessarily lead to actual equality of opportunity within a given society. The main point in the argument of feminist theorists, who are in favour of the symmetrical approach to equality, is based on the presumption that since the same rules (identical rights should be granted to women and men) should apply to all concerned, this is the most appropriate way to counteract returning to separate spheres of ideology.[56] The similarities and even the "sameness" of men and women are stressed and the differences are minimised. Identification of women as unique is rejected on the basis that this has been used against them as, *e.g.*, in the mandatory leave laws in America. Thus, pregnancy has been invoked to rationalise discrimination against women.[57] Proponents of the equal treatment doctrine have complained that the law "draws irrational distinctions between men and women" instead of really being rational, objective and principled.[58] The symmetrical models of gender

---

[54] *L.A. Rehof*, Guide to the *Travaux Préparatoires*, pp. 168–186. In this respect I should mention that the HRC has in its GC No. 18 ( § 8) upheld the standpoint that the "enjoyment of rights and freedoms on an equal footing, however, does not mean identical treatment in every instance".

[55] *H. Charlesworth, C. Chinkin & S. Wright*, p. 635. See also *N. Hevener Kaufman & S.A. Lindquist*, Critiquing Gender-Neutral Treaty Language: The Convention on the Elimination of All Forms of Discrimination Against Women, in Women's rights, human rights, J. Peters & A. Wolper (eds.), p. 115; *C.A. MacKinnon*, Difference and Dominance: On Sex Discrimination, Feminist Legal Theory, in Feminist Legal Theory, K.T. Bartlett & R. Kennedy (eds.), p. 82.

[56] Under the theory of the separate spheres of men and women, the husband is considered the couple's representative in the public world and he is automatically seen as the breadwinner. The wife is merely the "centre of the private world of the family". In that way the dominance of male over female was preserved and promoted. *W. Williams*, The Equality Crisis, Some Reflections on Culture, Courts, and Feminism, in Women's Rights Law Reporter 1982, Vol. 7, p. 175. Similar ideas have been articulated throughout the centuries by a number of philosophers, among them Thomas Aquinas and Rousseau. Characteristic for their argument is the opinion that, since women and men are different as to natural or religious apprehension they should have different rights and opportunities and a different proportion of power. Women are seen first and foremost as private persons – wives and mothers – while men are also public persons, *i.e.*, breadwinners. *Eduards et al.* (eds.), Kön, Makt, Medborgarskap, Kvinnan i politiskt tänkande från Platon till Engels, Stockholm 1983, p. 148; *K. Lundström*, pp. 44–68.

The criticism of this ideology has been developed mainly on the basis of several controversial decisions delivered by the Supreme Court of the United States. *C. Bacchi*, Pregnancy, The Law and The Meaning of Equality, in Equality Politics and Gender, E. Meehan & S. Sevenhuijsen (eds.), London 1991, p. 72 ff.

[57] *C. Bacchi*, p. 77.

[58] See for references *F. Olsen*, Feminism and Critical Legal Theory: An American Perspective, International Journal of the Sociology of Law 1990, Vol. 18, p. 206. Natalie Kaufman and Stefanie Lindquist have supported this approach on the basis that there is no real objective application of the law.

equality fail, however, to take account of differences between groups of persons described as "equal" and of the prevailing hegemony since they advocate "gender-neutral" categories that do not rely on gender stereotypes to differentiate between men and women.[59] The potential risk in-built in gender-blind human rights has been described by Eva Brems in the following manner: "if neutrality comes down to blindness, human rights will further privilege the privileged and further disempower the disempowered".[60] Thus, the pervasive belief in the objectivity and gender neutrality of human rights norms has in the view of Anne Gallagher prevented the recognition of the fact that equal treatment of persons in unequal situations will "invariably operate to perpetuate rather than to eradicate injustices".[61] Therefore, many modern feminists have criticised the symmetrical approach to equality on the grounds that it only benefits women who meet male norms but not women who are occupied in traditional female activities. So, women face disadvantages as a result of their unique biological characteristics. It is apparent that the equal treatment doctrine is simply not capable of dealing with many aspects of reproductive freedom because of the "similarly situated" requirement. As Professor Cathrine MacKinnon has aptly put it: "Comparatively few men are raped and no men are denied abortions".[62] One may, therefore, conclude that the doctrine of formal/*de iure* equality requiring equal treatment in a way legitimises unequal and abusive conditions for women. Justification for equality claims with regard to reproductive freedom can, in my view, be made more successfully, on the whole, by using asymmetrical gender equality approaches. Quite clearly legislation sometimes has to take gender into consideration and provide differently for men and for women. One of the concrete consequences of the application of the "sameness" doctrine would be that the legal treatment of reproductive freedom and to a great extent gender-based violations cannot be handled as gender equality issues because, as Kathleen Mahoney rightly has pointed out, "the male comparators have no comparable disadvantage or need". This is also the reason, according to the same author, why the rape of women in war never has been prosecuted as a war

---

The law is merely interpreted in the view of both writers in a subjective and social realm, which colours the impact of the rights of women. What is taken as neutral is more likely to reflect a male perspective. Thus, legal rights do not stand alone but are embedded in the dominant social and cultural paradigm which may hinder women from enjoying equal human rights with men. Seen in this context the symmetrical theories of equality have proved to be of more symbolic than actual value to women. The structural inequalities continue to be seen as a question of legal reasoning rather than a matter of economics and politics. *N. Kaufman & S. Lindquist*, Critiquing Gender-Neutral Treaty Language: The Convention on the Elimination of All Forms of Discrimination Against Women, in Women's rights, human rights, J.S. Peters & A. Wolper (eds.), pp. 114–118; *M. McConnell*, Feminist Theory as the Embodiment of Marginalization, in Reconceiving Reality: Women and International Law, D.G. Dallmeyer (ed.), p. 70.

[59] *T.K. Hervey*, p. 28. See also *C.A. MacKinnon*, Toward a Feminist Theory of the State, Cambridge Mass. 1989, p. 217.

[60] *E. Brems*, Enemies or Allies? Feminism and Cultural Relativism as Dissident Voices in Human Rights Discourse, HRQ 1997, Vol. 19, p. 154.

[61] *A. Gallagher*, p. 290.

[62] *C.A. MacKinnon*, Difference and Dominance, p. 1297.

crime.[63] In other words, gender-neutral rules may constitute a barrier for the protection of women victimised by gender. They have not served women's interests well, since the specific experiences of women have been neglected and dealt with without proportionate emphasis in international human rights and humanitarian law. The asymmetrical models of gender equality represent in the light of what has been said above a significant challenge to contemporary international law and its institutions. The advantage of using these models, is, it has been argued, that they address "situations that do not victimise men as they do women"; they allow "for a women-centred solution without reference to male action" and they "can prescribe active public policy to achieve fairness rather than passive elimination of discriminatory laws and norms".[64]

*2.2.1.2. Governmental Commitment to* de iure *Equality*

Several country reports reviewed under human rights control-mechanisms and other documents suggest that most governments seem to have dealt with the international law requirement to guarantee formal (*de iure*) equality adequately.

A good indicator of the extent to which formal equality and *de iure* discrimination have been addressed in accordance with international human rights standards is the number of states that have accepted the Women's Convention as a treaty obligation. In 1985 there were (prior to the Nairobi Conference) only 39 states parties to the Convention. As of June 1990 (the first review of the Nairobi strategies) the number had increased to 105 and at the time of writing the Women's Convention has 161 parties.[65] The majority of them have enacted legal measures to ensure that women enjoy equality before the law. The first review of the implementation of the Nairobi Strategies, based on a great number of national reports, found that in the field of formal legislation there has been considerable progress in achieving *de iure* equality. Nevertheless, discriminatory legislative provisions continue to exist especially in the civil, penal and commercial codes and in certain administrative rules and regulations in many countries.[66] In several countries a woman may upon marriage be deprived of rights such as the independent ownership of property or the right to work or travel without her husband's consent. The UN Secretary-General emphasised in 1995 in his second review of the implementation of the Nairobi Strategies, which was based on 130 national reports, that many governments have

---

[63] *K.E. Mahoney*, Canadian Approaches to Equality Rights and Gender Equality in the Courts, in Human Rights of Women, R.J. Cook (ed.), p. 442. Violence against women is one of the major issues that women's human rights advocates have used to demonstrate how human rights law has excluded women. *E. Friedman*, Women's Human Rights: The Emergence of a Movement, in Women's rights, human rights, J. Peters & A. Wolper (eds.), p. 20 *et seq*. Other authors have pointed out the cultural construction of women's reproductive role and the continuance of this role within the family as a barrier contributing to the exclusion of women in human rights discourse. See *S. Wright*, Human Rights and Women's Rights: An Analysis of the United Nations Convention on the Elimination of All Forms of Discrimination against Women, in Human Rights in the Twenty-First Century, K.E. Mahoney & P. Mahoney (eds.), p. 77.

[64] *N. Haufman & S. Lindquist*, p. 114.

[65] Multilateral Treaties deposited with the Secretary-General, Status as of 26 March 1999.

[66] UN Doc. E/CN.6/1990/5, §§ 7, 100; *R. Dixon-Mueller*, p. 128.

taken steps to provide legal equality and the machinery necessary to implement it.[67] The enactment of equal opportunities laws is reported by a considerable number of countries. However, several countries, particularly in Africa, Asia and the Pacific,[68] have indicated that their domestic laws, policies and practices do not yet reflect all international norms and standards of relevance to gender equality. There is a broad concern regarding family and matrimonial laws, *e.g.*, sharing of family domestic chores and responsibilities within the family. Violence within the family continues to be another problematic area. Much points to the fact that changing discriminatory structures remains slowest in the area of family law.[69] The 1998 report of the UN High Commissioner for Human Rights on the follow-up to the Vienna Conference refers to many progressive changes that have taken place in recent years at the national level such as in constitutional and penal laws, prohibiting gender-based violence within the family, sexual assault etc. At the same time it is also pointed out there, that despite the large number of examples of progress with respect to *de iure* equality, women continue to be disproportionately subject to violations of human rights and that "the status quo remains intolerable".[70]

Also the Regional Platform for Action -*Women in a Changing World*- Call for Action from an ECE Perspective, reveals that there are still discriminatory laws and practices in many European countries which fail to conform to international standards and that there exist deliberate attempts to maintain women's subordination.[71] The Special Rapporteur on women's rights to the Inter-American Commission on Human Rights, pointed out in his final report to the Commission in 1998 that despite advances, problems still exist in the region with respect to, for example, *de iure* equality for women in the area of civil capacity. Discriminatory differentiation between men and women persists, *e.g.*, with respect to the authorisation to contract marriage, or to remarry; to parental authority etc.[72]

Clearly, the capacity of formal (*de iure*) equality to further gender equality is limited. Strict adherence to the formal equality doctrine may even develop into "an engine of oppression destructive of human dignity if the law entrenches inequalities in the political, economic, social, cultural or any other field of public life".[73] I shall

---

[67] A recent report presented at the 1st World Law Conference "Law in Motion", which took place in Brussels in September 1996, discloses that formal equality has been introduced into all the national legal systems under scrutiny (about 20 jurisdictions, representing different parts of the world). This is the current situation for the secular laws in contrast to religious law in the referred countries. *B. Verschraegen*, Equality in Family Law – The Influence of Constitutions and International Conventions, Conference Papers Part II, 1996, p. 11.

[68] A few provisions of the Latin American and the Caribbean Regional Programme of Action emphasise the need to make secondary legislation consistent with constitutional provisions that reflect international commitments and that there still persists gender-based discriminatory legislation, which reinforces women's unequal status in society and the family. UN Doc. E/CN.6/1995/Add.3, §§ 175, 183.

[69] UN Doc. E/CN.6/1995/3/Add.7, §§ 16, 21 and 26.

[70] UN Doc. A/53/372, § 42.

[71] ECOSOC, E/ECE/RW/HLM/L.3, §§ 11, 12 and 24.

[72] OEA/Ser.L/V/II.98, Doc. 7 rev., April 13, 1998, pp. 1017–1018.

[73] See the High Court of Australia in *Gerhardy v. Brown* (1985)57 ALR 472, 516, cited in *G. Triggs*, The Rights of "Peoples" and Individual Rights: Conflict or Harmony?, in The Rights of Peoples, J. Crawford (ed.), Oxford 1988, p. 148.

in the following, with this in mind, try to clarify the result-oriented treatment theories on gender equality and their relevance in the struggle to achieve *de facto* gender equality.

### *2.2.2. Substantive Equality*

#### *2.2.2.1. The Philosophical and Legal Basis*

With time the notion "equality" has been re-conceptualised in the legal context. Its dual dimension, which encompasses a formal equal treatment as well as equality in outcome, has become more noticeable. Gender equality has thus moved from comprising solely *de iure* equality towards equality on a higher level, *i.e.*, substantive/*de facto* equality, which is often understood in terms of "treatment as an equal" but is not necessarily the same.

Gender disadvantage, for example, is a starting point. Therefore, there is a clear connection between equality and justice. The concept "equality" may even be regarded as a prerequisite for social justice.[74] Aristotle's view that "Equality and justice are synonymous: to be just is to be equal, to be unjust is to be unequal", is indisputable today, just as it was more than 2,500 years ago.[75] Justice implies that social institutions be so arranged that everyone may achieve fulfilment. Article 1 of the UN Declaration on the Elimination of Discrimination against Women states:

> "Discrimination against women, denying or limiting as it does their equal rights with men, is fundamentally unjust and constitutes an offence against human dignity".[76]

In view of this it follows that justice requires in addition to equal treatment, treatment of women and men as equals in dignity, and that each person must be vouchsafed her/his due. The principle of equality has been recognised partly on this basis as one of the fundamental principles of democracy and government based on the rule of law. Equality between women and men is in such a context defined as a *sine qua non* of democracy and an imperative of social justice, *e.g.*, in the Declaration on Equality of Women and Men adopted by the Committee of Ministers of the Council of Europe on 16 November 1988.[77] According to this document, a just

---

[74] One should bear in mind, however, that neither justice nor fairness are static concepts. Rather, they are also context-specific and have evolved over time and place.

[75] *Aristotle*, Ethica Endemia VII.9.1241b; Ethica Nicomachea V.3 1131a–1131b, cited in *P. Westen*, p. 543, note 19. For the opposite view see *R. Nozick*, Justice does Not Imply Equality, in Equality, Selected Readings, L.P. Pojman & R. Westmoreland (eds.), p. 103.

[76] Similar statements may be found in the domestic jurisdictions in a great number of countries. I shall refer solely to one example, the Swedish Sex Discrimination Act of 1991. Its aim is considered to be to "guarantee justice to an individual". *R. Eklund*, The Swedish Case- the Promised Land of Sex Equality?, in Sex Equality Law in the European Union, Hervey & O'Keeffee (eds.), European Law Series 1996, p. 341.

[77] *P. Boucaud*, The Council of Europe's standard-setting activities relating to equality of the sexes, Strasbourg 1989, p. 42. See also European Committee for Equality between Women and Men, CEEG (88)1, Council of Europe, 1988. On equality as the rationale of democracy, see *C.S. Nino*, The Ethics of Human Rights, Oxford 1991, p. 242.

society secures the opportunity for women to participate on equal terms with men, in the social, economic, political and cultural lives of their countries. Societies which place women at a disadvantage because of their sex, are unjust.[78] This is why the achievement of equality between women and men is a matter of human rights and should not be seen in isolation as a women's issue. The principle of equality thus contributes to the coherent functioning of the international juridical order.

This dimension of the equality principle reflects what Aristotle termed "*justitia commutativa and justitia distributiva*".[79] In accordance with his theory four maxims of distributive justice have been developed: "1. To each according to his need. 2. To each according to his worth. 3. To each according to his merit. 4. To each according to his work".[80]

The distributive justice doctrine strives to achieve equality of outcome that will be reached by the redistribution of goods and power. Justice will be achieved it is believed by the adoption of positive action measures. The law-maker would have to promote equality in a more real sense through law.[81] This is the very basis for the reasoning of the second prevailing view in feminist theory, *i.e.,* the asymmetrical models of gender equality. A common presumption is that the legislator must provide for treatment of every person as equal in dignity, *i.e.*, any rules and policy that have a discriminatory purpose, effect and result are unjust and they should be adjusted so as to achieve substantial equality. The "equal protection of the law" provisions of international human rights conventions have been used, *e.g.*, on a domestic level, to secure the enforcement of criminal laws against private acts of violence against women. It has been argued that states parties must ensure that crimes against women are as thoroughly investigated and "as vigorously prosecuted as crimes that victimise men".[82]

In addition, there are some examples, albeit very few, in which criminal abortion laws were intended to deny women the equal protection of the law[83] and hinder the

---

[78] *E.W. Vierdag*, Non-discrimination and Justice, Archiv für Rechts- und Sozialphilosophie 1971, Vol. LVII, p. 187 ff. See also Mission Statement, § 1 of the Beijing Platform for Action, 1995.

[79] ICJ Rep. 1966, p. 305. Distributive justice concerns, as already mentioned before, distribution of social benefits and burdens proportionate to the worth or merit of the recipients. See selections from Aristotle's *Nicomachean Ethics* and *Politics Book III*, reproduced in Equality, Selected Readings, L.P. Pojman & R. Westmoreland (eds.), pp. 17–26.

[80] *G. Vlastos*, Justice and Equality, in Equality, Selected Readings, L.P. Pojman & R. Westmoreland (eds.), p. 122.

[81] *A. Eide & T. Opsahl*, p. 19. Paragraphs 5 and 12 of the HRC GC No. 18 express the Committee's standpoint that the ICCPR requires states parties to take measures to guarantee the equality of rights of the persons concerned, *e.g.*, to make certain that spouses have equal rights and that none of them is exposed to *de facto* discrimination. The members of the Committee consented that all persons should be guaranteed equal and effective protection.

[82] *R.J. Cook*, Accountability in International Law for Violations of Women's Rights by Non-State Actors, in Reconceiving Reality: Women and International Law, D.G. Dallmeyer (ed.), p. 104.

[83] See the cited Amicus Curiae Brief on Behalf of New Women Lawyers, Women's Health and Abortion Project, in *Roe v. Wade* at the Supreme Court level in *C.A. MacKinnon*, Reflections on Sex Equality Under Law, The Yale Law Journal 1991, Vol. 100, p. 1288, note 34. The main argument was

realisation of genuine equality between women and men. The present author holds the view that legalising abortion might have the effect of reducing the subordination of women and promoting substantial gender equality.

*2.2.2.2. Differential Treatment and Discrimination*

The second aspect of equality recognises in contrast to the first/*de iure* aspect, when it is appropriate to do so, that there are differences between men and women and it presupposes accommodation of life experiences within the applicable rules in order to redress past wrongs. Substantive equality may, therefore, require *unequal* treatment.[84]

Of great importance to this study is the question of whether the goal of equality between women and men requires that they should be considered alike, and in consequence treated in the same way, or unlike and thus be treated differently in relation to reproductive freedom. It is self-evident that men and women are not in the same position with respect to procreation. In which situations would then a differential treatment be deemed compatible with international human rights law norms? Does women's child-bearing function justify special treatment?

It appears that the requirement of equal treatment is supplemented by the understanding that differential/special treatment is acceptable, if the unequalness of the case in question is recognised. In support of this assertion I may refer to the well-known statement made by the Permanent Court of International Justice in the *Minority Schools in Albania case*, which reads as follows: "Equality in fact may involve the necessity of different treatment in order to obtain a result, which establishes an equilibrium between different situations".[85]

What makes this advisory opinion outstanding is the fact that the majority of the Court, as early as 1935, *i.e.*, a long time before the successful efforts in international law to establish the principle of equality as one of the most fundamental – "the starting point of all liberties"[86] – did not accept the formal approach to equality. It rather

---

based on the presumption that women bear "disproportionate share of the de jure and de facto burdens and penalties of pregnancy, child birth and child rearing". Statutes that deny a women the right to determine whether she will bear those burdens were consequently upheld to be in breach of the principle of equal protection of the laws. It was maintained, furthermore, that while sexual intercourse was equal, its consequences were not. Especially imposing upon woman the burdens of an unwanted pregnancy (pregnancy against her will) is objectionable. Seemingly in the litigations in *Webster v. Reproductive Health Services* one brief forwarded the argument that the denial of legal abortion constitutes sex discrimination and it is a violation of equality law. Unwanted (forced) pregnancy has been described as a source of oppression in the *Thornburgh* amicus brief filed by the NARAL. See *R. West*, Jurisprudence and Gender, in Feminist Legal Theory, K.T. Barlett & R. Kennedy (eds.), pp. 214–215.

[84] *I. Cameron & M.K. Eriksson*, An Introduction to the European Convention on Human Rights, Uppsala 1995, p. 107.

[85] The opinion is of considerable importance since the Court concluded that Albanian nationals who belong to racial, linguistic or religious minorities must enjoy the same treatment and security in law and in fact as other Albanian nationals. In the words of the PCIJ it "is indispensable to enable the minority to enjoy the same treatment as the majority, not only in law but also in fact". See the Advisory Opinion of the Permanent Court of International Justice on Minority Schools in Albania, PCIJ, Ser. A/B, No. 64, (1935), p. 19. See also Sir *H.Lauterpacht*, The Development of International Law by the International Court, London 1958, pp. 257–262.

[86] Sir *H. Lauterpacht*, An International Bill of the Rights of Man, New York 1945, p. 115.

required equality between members of the majority and minority to be genuine and effective. In other words, the result of the treatment is more important than the nature of treatment if it means favourable unequal treatment of the deprived and unprivileged in order to rectify their unequal status.[87] The PCIJ opinion has had a profound influence on contemporary juridical theories and judicial decisions arguing for special measures and/or affirmative action programmes. Such a non-formalistic, substantive approach to equality was demonstrated later by the Japanese member of the ICJ, Judge Kotaro Tanaka, in a dissenting opinion in the second phase of the *South West Africa Cases* in 1966. In his view individuals differ one from another and therefore their needs will be different. For that reason "to treat different matters equally in a mechanical way would be as unjust as to treat equal matters differently" and "to treat unequal matters differently according to their inequality is not only permitted but required".[88] From that follows that the mechanical application of the "equal treatment" principle without taking into account its effects and results may create injustice. At the same time it is also important to ensure that differential treatment does not engender injustice but that it instead conforms with the requirements of justice. It must be taken into account whether the differential treatment does or does not harm the sense of dignity of the individual in question. In my opinion several provisions dealing with freedom of procreation, which permit differential treatment between women and men (*i.e.*, treatment in accordance with different needs), may be invoked as required by reasonableness or be justified by the creation of justice.

The law may consequently establish unequal treatment based on biological differences, *e.g.*, sex and depending on its purpose be considered as non-discriminatory.[89]

---

[87] It is self-evident that the outcome of equal treatment might be rather different depending on the circumstances. As Vierdag has pointed out "if equal treatment is accorded to equals the result is equal social conditions; if equal treatment is accorded to unequals the result is unequal social conditions; likewise if unequal treatment is accorded to equals the result is unequal social conditions; if unequal treatment is accorded to unequals, then, depending on the factual unequalness and the character of the treatment: a) the inequality as to the social conditions has increased, has become wider, or b) the inequality as to the social conditions is compensated, a certain levelling has come about". See *E.W. Vierdag*, p. 13.

[88] Dissenting Opinion by Judge Tanaka in the South West Africa Cases (Second Phase) in ICJ Reports, Advisory Opinions and Orders, Judgment of 18 July 1966 p. 305. *I.Brownlie*, p. 461. Judge Tanaka makes on the applicants' submission the conclusive remark that the principle of equality "does not mean absolute equality, but recognises relative equality, namely different treatment proportionate to concrete individual circumstances". *Ibid.*, p. 468.

[89] The German Constitution enshrines in Article 3 II GG the principle of equality as follows: "Der Grundsatz der Gleichberechtigung steht einer rechtlichen Regelung, welche die objektiven biologischen und funktionalen Unterschiede von Mann und Frau entsprechend der Natur des jeweiligen Lebensverhältnissen berücksichtigt und dementsprechend differenziert, nicht entgegen. Creifelds Rechtswörterbuch, München 1970, p. 482. Section 31 of the Australian Sex Discrimination Act (1984) states that: "Nothing in the statute renders it unlawful for a person to discriminate against a man on the ground of his sex by reason only of the fact that the first mentioned person grants to a woman rights or privileges in connection with pregnancy or childbirth". Provisions of that kind are clearly consistent with Article 4(2) of the Women's Convention. On exceptions to equal treatment in the family law context in Australia see *D. Hodgson*, Equality: The Impact of Constitutions and International Agreements, in Gleichheit im Familienrecht, B. Verschraegen (ed.), Bielefeld 1997, p. 289.

Of course, if no consideration is taken of the result of a specific treatment, rules based on gender differences might give rise to distinctions, which are unfair, and they may perpetuate substantive inequalities. This would be the case if, *e.g.*, the law excludes pregnant women from unemployment benefits on purely biological grounds. Therefore, it is rational that deviation from the treatment requirement needs justification, *e.g.*, which outcome is acceptable in a democratic society based on the rule of law and where the principle "all are born equal in dignity" has been reinforced.

Thus, the difference between men and women should neither be ignored nor eradicated. The favourable unequal treatment of the weak and deprived would not be considered as discrimination. Discrimination is solely an illegitimate distinction or specific type of treatment, which can comprise wrongly equal and wrongly unequal treatment, *e.g.*, through equal treatment of individuals who are in an unequal position, or through unequal treatment of individuals who are in an equal position. Only the failure to treat all persons equally, where no reasonable distinction can be found between those favoured and those not favoured, constitutes consequently an element of the contemporary legal term "discrimination".[90] In the English language discrimination has two different connotations. One sense (the original one) of the word implies acknowledging differences, *i.e.*, distinguishing between people, things, or whatever. It is neutral in that it solely refers to making a distinction. On the other hand, *distinction*[91] is a term with a broader application than *discrimination* in the second pejorative sense of the word, meaning to "make unfair distinction",[92] since not all distinctions constitute discrimination. This approach has been accepted also by international human rights supervisory organs.

---

[90] Black's Law Dictionary, p. 244.

[91] Worth mentioning is the confusion in international law owing to the fact that both words (distinction and discrimination) were used to denote the same concept. Many of the French versions of human rights texts in which the English version employs "discrimination", use has been made of "distinction" instead. The French version has been seen as the result of a reluctance to adopt the Anglicism "discrimination". *A. Eide & T. Opsahl*, note 14. Article 14 of the European Convention on Human Rights speaks, *e.g.*, of distinction in the French version and of discrimination in the English version. The choice between distinction and discrimination has sometimes been left to translators as a matter of style. But also analogous texts in the same language show differences in this respect. Article 2(1) of the ICCPR prohibits distinctions on certain grounds, whereas the ICESCR prohibits discriminations on certain grounds. Even though the ICCPR kept the term "distinction" rather than changing it to "discrimination", Article 2 of the ICCPR is understood to mean discrimination. A study of the *travaux préparatoires* of the ICCPR shows that most of the delegations preferred the word "distinction" because the UN Charter and the UDHR made use of it. It was feared that the term "discrimination" would introduce a meaning implying action whereas "distinction" would not permit any differentiation whatsoever. Thus, the notion "discrimination" had at that time acquired a "separate shade of meaning". *S. Skogly*, in The Universal Declaration of Human Rights, A. Eide *et al.* (eds.), p. 63. The representative of Italy advanced arguments in support of making use of the word "discrimination" on the basis that there were instances in which the law "was justified in making distinctions between individuals or groups, but the purpose of the Article (2) was to prohibit discrimination in the sense of unfavourable and odious distinction which lacked any reasonable or objective basis". *P. Thornberry*, p. 281.

[92] *T.K. Hervey*, Justification for Sex Discrimination in Employment, London 1993, p. 24; *E.W. Vierdag*, p. 48. During the preparatory work on Article 7 of the UDHR, the French delegation was of the opinion that the term "discrimination" was equal to "invidious distinction". But the Chairman of the Commission was of another view. According to her "discrimination" had the same meaning as "distinction". *J.T. Möller*, p. 121.

The HRC has, *e.g.*, clarified that differentiation of treatment will not constitute discrimination if the criteria for it are "reasonable and objective and if the aim is to achieve a purpose which is legitimate under the Covenant".[93] From that follows that intentional differentiation in the sense that preferential treatment is given to a certain group and that others are excluded, such as distinction on the ground of sex, for the purpose of affirmative action in order to restore equality due to earlier discrimination is not comprised by the notion discrimination in its second sense.[94] Compensatory unequal treatment of unequals in order to reach equal social conditions was approved by the Permanent Court of International Justice in the Advisory Opinion on *German Settlers in Poland* of 1923. The Court claimed that: "There must be equality in fact as well as ostensible legal equality in the sense of the absence of discrimination in the words of the law".[95] Several decades later the HRC in its General Comment No. 18 on non-discrimination (§ 10) pointed out that "(i)n a State where the general conditions of a certain part of the population prevent or impair their enjoyment of human rights, the State should take specific action to correct those conditions". I may, therefore, conclude that differential treatment is compatible with the principle of equality in modern international law if actual equality, *i.e., de facto* equality can be achieved. And on the contrary, when a distinction is connected with a different *value* among and between people in terms of considering a group of persons being less worthy, resulting in unequal, unfair treatment or denial of rights to persons because of their belonging to this group, we can speak of violation of the principle of non-discrimination. So, discrimination conceived in this context means denial of the inherent equal worth of all human beings. The practical consequence of discriminatory actions would be that some people are disadvantaged, whereas others are endowed with privileges and benefits. It is in this sense the notion "discrimination" has been used in the legal terminology. A common feature of the definitions of discrimination as incorporated in international human rights treaties is also that they all refer to arbitrary and unjust distinctions made between individuals for the sole reason that they belong to a particular category. In other words, prohibited discrimination in international law comprises unequal and unfavourable treatment of human beings, who belong to a given natural or social group.[96]

The UN Secretary General delimited the term "discrimination" in the manner described above already in 1949 in his memorandum "The Main Types and Cases of Discrimination" as follows:

> "Discrimination includes any conduct based on a distinction made on grounds of natural or social categories, which have no relation either to individual capacities or merits, or to the concrete behaviour of the individual person".[97]

---

[93] HRC, GC No. 18, § 13.

[94] See *T. Opsahl & A. Eide*, p. 21.

[95] P.C.I.J., Advisory Opinion on *Settlers of German Origin in Territory Ceded by Germany to Poland*, 10th September 1923, Ser. B, No. 6, p. 24.

[96] *L. Hannikainen*, Peremptory Norms (jus cogens) in International Law, Helsinki 1988, p. 469.

[97] UN Memorandum, p. 9.

The fact that discrimination is not merely an attitude but comprises a conduct manifested outwardly has been confirmed thereafter in numerous international documents, among them the following four ensuing universal human rights conventions. The Convention against Discrimination in Education, adopted by UNESCO in 1960 accentuates that:

> "For the purpose of this Convention, the term 'discrimination' includes any distinction, exclusion, limitation or preference, which, being based on race, colour, sex... has the purpose or the effect of nullifying or impairing equality of treatment."

The 1958 ILO Convention concerning Discrimination in respect to Employment, declares in Article 1(a):

> "For the purpose of this Convention the term 'discrimination' includes: a) Any distinction, exclusion or preference made on the basis of race, colour, sex, ... (w)hich has the effect of nullifying or impairing equality of opportunity or treatment in employment or occupation".

The UN Convention on Elimination of Racial Discrimination of 1969 defines discrimination in Article 1 as:

> "(t)he term 'racial discrimination' shall mean any distinction, exclusion, restriction or preference based on race, colour, descent, or national or ethnic origin which has the purpose or effect of nullifying or impairing the recognition, enjoyment or exercise, on an equal footing, of human rights and fundamental freedoms in the political, economic, social, cultural or any other field of public life".

Article 1 of the Women's Convention gives the following definition of what constitutes discrimination:

> "For the purpose of the present Convention, the term "discrimination against women" shall mean any distinction, exclusion or restriction made on the basis of sex which has the effect or purpose of impairing or nullifying the recognition, enjoyment or exercise by women, irrespective of their marital status, on a basis of equality of men and women, of human rights and fundamental freedoms in the political, economic, social, cultural or any other field of public life".

This definition is of considerable breadth and encompasses a broad range of issues. A comparison between the above referred definitions discloses first of all that Article 1 of the Women's Convention establishes in contrast to the other corresponding provisions that the Convention deals with discrimination directed specifically against women and not generally with discrimination based on sex as other human rights treaties do. Simply, it does not deal with discriminatory practices affecting men. That problem is dealt with in other international human rights instruments. The definition contained in the Women's Convention develops instead the legal norm "from a sex neutrality norm that requires equal treatment of men and women, usually measured by how men are treated, to recognise that the distinctive characteristics of women and their vulnerabilities to discrimination merit a specific legal response".[98] The Convention can in that way respond to the particular nature of women's disadvantages.[99] The reason for that is spelled out in the preamble. It acknowledges that despite various United Nations efforts to promote equality between men and women, "extensive discrimination against women continues to exist". The adoption of the Woman's Convention was, therefore, necessary in order to address a number of areas of law and social institutions which perpetuate the continuation of discrimination against women and which prevent them from reaching *de facto* equality. Thus, the Convention is not limited to formal equality but it mandates equality of result. It expressly provides that affirmative action shall not be considered discriminatory.

The definition of "discrimination against women" employed in the Woman's Convention is very similar to the definition of "discrimination" contained in the other three above mentioned conventions. It describes which practices, *i.e.,* any gender distinction, exclusion or restriction with an adverse impact on women, constitute discrimination. A comparison between the definitions makes it also apparent that there is another important difference in material parts. Firstly, the legislators of the Women's Convention have excluded the word "preference" from its text. It does not mention that preference based on gender would mean discrimination against women.

Clearly, this makes the definition of "discrimination" in the Women's Convention more limited and it has been predicted on this ground that this circumstance can have "direct implications" for women's right to equality since it allows employers, *e.g.*, to choose a man in preference to a woman for employment. It has also been claimed that this weakness reflects but the long history of discounting the right of women to equality.[100] On the other hand, while the Convention on Racial Discrimination applies in "the political, economic, social, cultural or any other field of public life", the Women's Convention reaches also into private behaviour ("civil or any other field"), such as domestic violence and family planning.[101] Private rights are essential to

---

[98] *R.J. Cook*, Accountability in International Law for Violations of Women's Rights by Non-state Actors, in Reconceiving Reality: Women and International Law, D.G. Dallmeyer (ed.), p. 105. The same author argues that "the particular nature of discrimination against women and their distinctive characteristics is worthy of a legal response". International Protection of Women's Reproductive Rights, Journal of International Law and Politics 1992, Vol. 24, p. 679.

[99] *R.J. Cook*, Women, in The United Nations and International Law, C.C. Joyner (ed.), p. 188.

[100] *L.A. Donner*, Gender Bias in Drafting International Discrimination Conventions: The 1979 Women's Convention Compared with the 1965 Racial Convention, in California Western International Law Journal 1994, Vol. 24, p. 248.

[101] *S.C. Zearfoss*, The Convention for the Elimination of All Forms of Discrimination against Women: Radical, Reasonable, or Reactionary?, Michigan Yearbook of International Legal Studies 1991, Vol. 12, pp. 907–909; *R.J. Cook*, Reservations to the Convention on the Elimination of All Forms of Discrimination Against Women, p. 669 and *K. Engle*, After the Collapse of the Public/Private Distinction: Strategizing

women's equality. The fact that the Convention encompasses even interpersonal, private relations is one of the crucial elements of its potential strength with regard to gender equality. Otherwise, all the reviewed provisions prohibit unintentional as well as intentional discrimination, *i.e.,* they accentuate the purpose[102] or the effect of the action/s and therefore can be classified as result-oriented definitions of equality.

These developments within international organisations are to a certain extent reflected in the definitions presented in the legal doctrine. A general definition of discrimination has been elaborated by Professor Tomuschat[103] according to which discrimination is an invidious treatment that introduces unreasonable classifications within the specific context of the rights concerned. *Invidious* (harmful) treatment is consequently the key element. It is regularly based on attitudes of superiority or inferiority. This is very much in line with the understanding of the term "discrimination" as arbitrary or invidious distinction reflected in the case law of international organs for the protection of human rights, especially the European Commission and the European Court of Human Rights. Discrimination introduces in other words, an inequality of treatment of an arbitrary nature. The acts of inequality of treatment may take many forms such as: imposing disabilities and imposing odious obligations.[104]

Sexism is but a clear example of invidious treatment. It is a form of discrimination, which is directed towards an entire sex and is the most universal form of discrimination. Discrimination on the grounds of sex happens because of deeply rooted attitudes, values, beliefs, customs and practices based upon the belief that women are inferior to men, since they are born with different physiological, psychological and spiritual characteristics.[105] Sexism is consequently "not a legal aberration but a pervasive, structural problem".[106] The far reaching provision (Article 5), which has been considered as one of the "jewels in the crown"[107] of the

---

Women's Rights, in Reconceiving Reality: Women and International Law, D.G. Dallmeyer (ed.), p. 144. Mentioned should be also the fact that CEDAW's Recommendation No. 19 on Violence against Women recognises violence against a woman because she is of the female sex as a form of discrimination. This is but an expansion of the definition of discrimination in Article 1 of the Women's Convention. This understanding has been thereafter reaffirmed in numerous global and regional instruments, among them the 1993 UN Declaration on the Elimination of Violence against Women and the 1994 Inter-American Convention on Violence against Women. Regrettably Article 1 of the draft Protocol to the African Charter on Human and People's Rights concerning the Rights of Women which is currently under review and which generally is influenced by the Women's Convention, omits the important reference as to the application of the discrimination definition in fields of private life. On the other hand, Article 13 defines violence against women as all acts directed against women as such, including "the imposition of arbitrary restrictions on or deprivation of fundamental freedoms in private or public life". See 22nd Ordinary Session of the African Commission on Human and Peoples' Rights, November 1997, The Final Communiqué, § 13.

[102] The draft referred to above on additional protocol to the African Charter excludes in its definition of discrimination against women this essential subjective element.

[103] *C. Tomuschat*, Equality and Non-Discrimination under the International Covenant on Civil and Political Rights, in Festschrift für Hans-Jürgen Schlochauer, 1981, p. 715.

[104] UN Memorandum, p. 26.

[105] *B. Reardon*, Discrimination, World in Focus, Sydney 1977, Vol. 2, Nr. 2, p. 10.

[106] *H. Charlesworth et al.*, p. 266.

[107] *R. Dixon-Mueller*, p. 199.

Women's Convention, demands a state party "to modify the social and cultural patterns of conduct of men and women, with a view to achieving the elimination of prejudices and custom and all other practices which are based on the idea of inferiority or the superiority of either the sexes or on stereotyped roles for men and women". In other words, states parties to the Convention can not keep their traditions and attitudes reflecting the inferiority of women if they want to avoid breaching its prohibition of discrimination. Preservation of cultural practices, which are hostile to woman's equality, may consequently be suspect under the Women's Convention. One may, therefore, question on legitimate grounds the compatibility of the ingredients of several Islamic documents which try to reformulate human rights concepts in an Islamic framework with the contemporary understanding of international law. They continue to support the patriarchal pattern of male superiority established in Shari'a.[108] Professor Bunch has explained in this regard the failure in international law to see the oppression of women as a political matter on the basis that the subordination of women is viewed as natural and even inevitable in some parts of the world instead of as "a politically construed reality maintained by patriarchal interests, ideology and institutions".[109] According to the same author the struggle for continuing this reality consists of the control of women's reproductive rights and related areas.

In conclusion, I may establish that discrimination is a very complicated phenomenon that has many different forms, which are closely connected with each other and are consequences of each other. Betty Reardon[110] has described the whole process of injustice as a vicious circle. Discriminatory acts originate from prejudice and most forms of discrimination are actually based upon it. Prejudice and discrimination are reciprocally related. There occurs a mutual inter-action. Prejudice leads or causes a predisposition to respond favourably or unfavourably, *i.e.*, to discriminate. It contributes to a behaviour or action tending to differentiate a person or group of individuals from others to his/her or its detriment. Such behaviour often means devaluation of individuals belonging to a particular group. Discrimination in its turn leads to inequality and systematic oppression resulting very often in violence, which again gives rise to prejudice. The discriminating group usually possesses greater power (politically and socially) and/or has a superior economic position. Against this background proponents for one of the asymmetrical models of gender equality, the so called "empowerment" theory, argue that in order to respond directly to the concrete and lived-out experience of women, one should focus on subordination and domination. It has been maintained that the goal of

---

[108] *A.A. An-Na'im*, State Responsibility Under International Human Rights Law to Change Religious and Customary Laws, in Human Rights of Women, R.J. Cook (ed.), p. 183.

[109] *C. Bunch*, Transforming Human Rights from a Feminist Perspective, in Women's rights, human rights, J. Peters & A. Wolper (eds.), p. 14. Patriarchal institutions are built on power hierarchies of age and gender in which girls and women have limited control over their sexual lives, *i.e.*, the number and spacing of their children. Patriarchal control can also produce very early arranged marriages and polygyny. *R. Dixon-Mueller*, pp. 5 and 25.

[110] *B. Reardon*, p. 1.

gender equality can be easier achieved if we concentrate our efforts "on the conditions that have produced the problem, such as the separation of home and work and the consequent barriers for women and structures for men".[111] In essence this theory, which the present author has found most suitable for the purpose of this study, requires law, practice and/or policy to empower women and/or to breakdown male domination in order for *de facto* equality to be achieved. Empowerment means women's right to have power over their lives. So, laws, practices and policies should take account of the realities of women's lives and if they contribute to the subordination of women they are violative of the principle of equality and the prohibition of discrimination.[112] Different treatment of women and men is legitimate when necessary "to effectuate its overall goal of ending women's subordination".[113] In other words, substantial equality may require unequal (differential) treatment, which may include equality of opportunity or affirmative action.

*2.2.2.3. Equality of Opportunity*

In reality, women have not been given the chance to compete on equal basis with men in several areas of social life. Therefore, to equalise opportunity, recognition of the effects of history, background and social conditions is indispensable.[114] For

---

[111] *L.M. Finley*, Transcending equality theory: a way out of the maternity and the workplace debate, Columbia Law Review 1986, Vol. 86, p. 1169. Another well-established scholar, Sullivan, alleges that the public/private distinction reinforces power relations and structural inequalities within society. *D. Sullivan*, The Public/Private Distinction, in Women's rights, human rights, J. Peters & A. Wolper (eds.), p. 128. See also *D.L. Rhode*, Justice and Gender, Cambridge Mass. 1989, p. 320. In modern feminism the demand for change of power structures within governments and international organisations that permit and ensure continuation of male domination is a "constant theme". *H. Charlesworth et al.*, pp. 255 and 266; *H. Charlesworth*, Cries and Whispers, NJIL 1996, p. 564. See also *E.M. Svensson*, Vems tryckfrihet - hans, hennes eller hans och hennes, in 13 kvinnoperspektiv på rätten, G.Norborg (ed.), p. 247. Equality is viewed there as freedom from systematic subordination because of sex. Professor Olsen holds the view that it might be possible to protect women from discrimination by empowering them against male coercion. *F. Olsen*, Statutory Rape: A Feminist Critique of Rights Analysis, in Feminist Legal Theory, K.T. Bartlett & R. Kennedy (eds.), p. 308. On the dominance approach see *C.A. MacKinnon*, Difference and Dominance: On Sex Discrimination, in Feminist Legal Theory, K.T. Bartlett & R. Kennedy (eds.), pp. 81–94. According to MacKinnon "practices which express and reinforce the social inequality of women to men are clear cases of sex-based discrimination". *C.A. MacKinnon*, Sexual Harassment of Working Women: A Case of Sex Discrimination, 1979, p. 174. Other researchers have emphasised that these theories fail to accommodate the interests of all women since some women, *e.g.*, lesbians, do experience time in their lives free from male domination and non-subordination. *P.A. Cain*, Feminist Jurisprudence: Grounding the Theories, in Feminist Legal Theory, K.T. Bartlett & R. Kennedy (eds.), p. 273.

[112] Violence against women, *e.g.*, both violates and impairs or nullifies the enjoyment by women of human rights and fundamental freedoms. It is according to the Preamble of the UN Declaration on the Elimination of Violence against Women of 1993, "a manifestation of historically unequal power relations between men and women, which have led to domination over and discrimination against women by men and to prevention of their full advancement, and that violence against women is one of the crucial mechanisms by which women are forced into a subordinate position compared with men". UN Doc. A/48/629, p. 334.

[113] *C.A. Littleton*, p. 39. See in addition *DuBois et al.* (eds.), Feminist Discourse, Moral Values, and the Law-A Conversation, Buffalo Law Review 1985, Vol. 34, p. 11 ff.

[114] *K. O'Donovan & E. Szyszczak*, Equality and Sex Discrimination Law, Oxford 1988, p. 4.

these reasons the doctrine of equal opportunities has been adopted to legitimise the distribution of benefits in society. Since equal opportunity is about competing on an equal basis, those who suffer from historical, economical and social disadvantages must be supported until they reach a level where they can compete equally with others. In this way the equal opportunities model recognises the extent to which a person's opportunities may be distorted by structural discrimination.[115] However, once this starting-point is reached individuals are seen to enjoy equal opportunities, and fairness requires that they be treated according to merit.[116] Even though the notion of equal opportunities contains an element of asymmetry in that it recognises the extent to which a person's opportunities may be restricted by his or her belonging to a group, subject to past or present discrimination, the doctrine has been criticised for being too formal.[117] Its efficiency may be hampered by a strong belief in individualism. The doctrine on equality of opportunity recognises on the one hand the extent to which a person's opportunities may be reduced by structural discrimination. On the other hand, it seems to ignore the fact that merit-based competition in itself is not entirely unproblematic. The distinction between equality of opportunity and equality of result is, furthermore, unclear and ambiguous.[118] The complex interaction between opportunities and results makes equal opportunities difficult to assess. Only in retrospect can one determine whether two persons of different sex have enjoyed equal opportunities.

Many egalitarians[119] hold the view that equality of opportunity and freedom are compatible and mutually supportive concepts. By further elaborating the principle of freedom as a basis for the interpretation of the term "equality", *i.e.*, inequality is seen as a serious impediment to freedom, the late Norwegian Professor Opsahl and Mr. Eide[120] have proposed the following three features of the term "freedom" as central for the understanding of genuine (*de facto*) equality.

The individual must:

1. Have available an equally wide range of significant opportunities as others,
2. be equally independent of others in deciding on the use of the options and
3. be equally free to determine his/her own values and priorities.

The above model reflects ideas common for the distributive justice theories. One among them is Rawls' model of justice, which is constructed on fairness and equality. According to John Rawls all social primary goods such as liberty and opportu-

---

[115] *S. Fredman*, p. 579.

[116] *K. O'Donovan & E. Szyszczak*, p. 3.

[117] *N. Lacey*, p. 413.

[118] *D. Schiek*, Sex Equality Law After Kalanke and Marschall, ELJ 1998, Vol. 4, p. 162; *S. Fredman*, p. 586.

[119] Others mean that when equality requires equalisation of outcomes, the conflict between liberty and equality is "both dramatic and inescapable". *J.S. Fishkin*, Liberty Versus Equal Opportunity, in Equality, Selected Readings, L.P. Pojman & R. Westmoreland (eds.), p. 148.

[120] A. Eide & T. Opsahl, p. 3.

nity are to be distributed equally unless an unequal distribution is advantageous to the least favoured ("the least well off") and on the condition that they are open to everybody by a system of fair, equal chances. In other words, distributive justice should be implemented to ensure that each person enjoys full respect for her/his human dignity.[121] This approach has found some support in international law.[122] The advancement of women and the achievement of gender equality are considered to be a condition for social justice and they are according to § 41 of the Beijing Platform for Action "the only way to build a sustainable, just and developed society".

Equality of opportunity ensuring equal access to education,[123] to health services and to resources in general, is consequently first and foremost a matter of freedom and freedom implies freedom of choice, which is essential in matters of procreation.

The necessity to strive for greater gender equality with regard to available opportunities has been emphasised also by other legal writers in the doctrine.[124] Liberal thinkers like Professor Dworkin have also shown sympathy to such a conception of equality. He holds the view that equality comprises a right to "an equal distribution of some opportunity or resource or burden".[125] Based on the fact that human beings are differently situated, *i.e.*, differences exist in biology, and people have different needs, Ronald Dworkin introduces the concept of "treatment as an

---

[121] *J. Rawls*, A Theory of Justice, Oxford 1972. See *S. Davidson*, Human Rights, Philadelphia 1993, p. 35 ff.

[122] At the same time some legal theorists like Professor Thomas Franck have elaborated a critical approach to the theory and terminology used by John Rawls. Franck's book *The Power of Legitimacy among Nations* deals with the issue of justice in international law. After applying the methodology of Rawls' theory of justice the author asserts that the two aspects of fairness-legitimacy and distributive justice are frequently in tension. While the former favours status quo, the latter favours change. He reaches, however, the conclusion that legitimacy rather than justice should be the prime goal of an international law system. See *H.H. Koh,* Why Do Nations Obey International Law?, The Yale Law Journal 1997, p. 2643.

[123] It has also been recognised that education affects child survival, which makes it an important factor in fertility decline and it diminishes preference for large families. Statistics show that women in developing countries with secondary education marry later, *i.e.*, at an average age of 21 years versus 19 years for women with primary education and 17 years for women with no education. Well educated women have, furthermore, their first child later, *i.e.*, at an average of 23 years versus 20 for women with primary education and 19 for women with no education. *J.G. Speth*, Towards a new global strategy, People & The Planet 1994, Vol. 3, No. 3, p. 36. See, *e.g.*, § 26 of the Beijing Declaration in which Governments expressed their determination to promote "women's economic independence, including employment". Education is, according to § 42 of the Cairo Programme of Action, the most important means of empowering women.

[124] *G. Fürst-Mellström & M. Sterner,* Kvinnors värde i männens värld, Angered 1983, p. 81. Mentioned should be, however, that the concept of "equal opportunity" has been criticised for ensuring only that the rules of entry into competition are the same for all. It has been assumed that this notion means solely that "those who compete on merit have an equal starting point" and nothing more. It is obvious that solely relying on "equal opportunity" interpreted in such a restrictive manner, would not be enough for the realisation of *de facto* equality. *K. O'Donovan & E. Szyczczak*, p. 4.

[125] *R. Dworkin*, Taking Rights Seriously, London 1978, p. 227.

equal", which according to him is more suitable in taking consideration of and giving equal concern to individuals, than emphasising the "same treatment". This fundamental right to "treatment as an equal" derives from the central tenet of liberalism that everybody should be treated with equal respect and concern. Moreover, this right, argues Dworkin, is the source "both of the general authority of collective goals and of their authority that justify more particular rights".[126]

It may be noted here, in addition, that there are two different notions of equal opportunity. Weak equal opportunity (the so called "formal equal opportunity"), which leaves the matter of initial starting points untouched and strong equal opportunity (so called "substantive equal opportunity"), which holds that individuals ought to have equal life chances to fulfil themselves. This equal opportunity would be equivalent to equal outcomes.[127] The first notion of "equal opportunity" may be a necessary but it is not sufficient condition for genuine equality in society since it constitutes a procedural equality, dictating uniformity in procedures across all persons, and guaranteeing nothing about the outcomes "across individual or ascriptively differentiated groups".[128] For that reason I have found that the result-oriented theories (emphasising the correlation between aim and outcome) have greater potential as a model for gender equality. By applying these models of equality it would be easier to consider whether a specific treatment results in upholding disadvantages in social reality for one of the sexes.

With time the asymmetrical, result-oriented theories seem to have gained greater acceptance within the UN and other international organisations. They have been reflected in several international instruments on human rights. During the 1970s emphasis was put within the UN on the equality of opportunity. This approach was given a prominent place in the World Plan of Action agreed upon in Mexico City in 1975 at the First Women's World Conference, when Governmental delegations agreed that:

> "(t)he world community has proclaimed that the full and complete development of a country, the welfare of the world and the cause of peace require the maximum participation of women as well as men in all fields".[129]

For that purpose the achievement of equality between men and women must comprise that both sexes having equal rights, opportunity and responsibilities to enable them to develop their talents and capabilities for their own personal fulfilment and the benefit of society.[130] Shortly thereafter the United Nations

---

[126] *R. Dworkin, ibid.*, p. XV.

[127] *L.P. Pojman & R. Westmoreland* , Introduction: The Nature and Value of Equality, in Equality, Selected Readings, p. 7.

[128] *W. Darity*, Equal opportunity, equal result and social hierarchy, Praxis International 1987, Vol. 7, p. 178.

[129] *F.P. Hosken*, Toward a Definition of Women's Human Rights, HRQ 1981, Vol. 3, No. 2, p. 3.

[130] *UN Centre for Social and Humanitarian Affairs*, Law and the Status of Women, in Columbia Human Rights Law Review 1977, Vol. 8, p. 1.

Decade for Women[131] (1976–1985) was proclaimed by the UN General Assembly. Equality in terms of its objectives was understood not only as a legal equality, the elimination of *de iure* discrimination, but also as including equality of rights as to responsibilities and opportunities for the participation of women in development, both as beneficiaries and as active agents. The goal of *de facto* gender equality has since then gradually become a real priority within the UN.[132] The ECOSOC recalled, *e.g.*, in resolution 1990/15 that *de iure* equality constitutes only the first step towards *de facto* equality.

Dr. Sadik, Executive Director of the UNFPA, recognised in 1993 that "without equal opportunities for women and men, the prospects for achieving full human rights, democracy and development are seriously jeopardised".[133] The same year the Vienna Conference on Human Rights encouraged states in § 42 of the Vienna Declaration and Programme of Action to supply information on the situation of women *de iure* and *de facto* in their reports to treaty monitoring bodies. The international community intensified its efforts towards *de facto* equality during the years that followed and gender equality became a key issue at other major UN Conferences on various human rights issues as well.

The above cited and several other statements illustrate that there has been an evolution in UN standard-setting with regard to both aspects of gender equality, and it is apparent that today there is indeed universal consensus about genuine equality for all people as being an essential element in the construction of just and democratic societies for the 21st century. It has been firmly established that women should have equal rights, obligations and opportunities with men in all fields and at all levels of development in regional documents as well, *e.g.*, the Jakarta Declaration for the Advancement of Women in Asia and the Pacific[134] (Article 2) which was prepared for the Beijing Conference. Moreover, the Arab Plan of Action

---

[131] See resolution 3520 (XXX), reprinted in *Förenta Nationernas kvinnokonferens i Köpenhamn*, Stockholm 1981, p. 90. In 1980 the Copenhagen World Conference adopted a Programme of Action for the Second Half of the United Nations Decade for Women: Equality, Development and Peace, which was endorsed by the General Assembly the same year in its resolution 35/136. In connection with the activities of the Decade, three world conferences dealing with among others the issue of gender equality were held in Mexico City in 1975, in Copenhagen in 1980 and in Nairobi in 1985. All the adopted final documents stressed the need for intensified action to promote *de facto* equality between men and women.

[132] See § 10 of the Beijing Platform for Action. As to developments at the regional level the Declaration on Equality of Women and Men which was adopted within the Council of Europe in 1988, is worth mentioning. The legislators after making the observation that inequalities between women and men still persist *de iure* and *de facto*, welcomed past and present actions aimed at the achievement of equal rights and opportunities for women and men worldwide and at regional and national levels. The text of this document is reprinted in A Thematic Guide to Documents on the Human Rights of Women, *G. Alfredsson & K. Tomaševski* (eds.), The Hague 1995, pp. 44–45.

[133] Development and Cooperation for Human Rights and Democracy, Ministry for Foreign Affairs, Sweden, Stockholm, February 1993, p. 35.

[134] UN Doc. E/CN.6/1995/5/Add.1, 4 January 1995. See also the African Platform of Action adopted at Dakar in November 1994 which expresses similar concern. UN Doc. E/CN.6/1995/5/Add.2, 29 December 1994.

for the Advancement of Women to the Year 2000 declared as a general objective to guarantee equal opportunities in education for females (§ 29), job opportunities in both public and private institutions (§ 31b) and (§ 34).[135] Establishing mechanisms and procedures to guarantee women's equal opportunity for advancement in public, political and union careers is required in the Latin American and the Caribbean Programme of Action 1995–2000, (§ 160).[136] The ECE High-Level regional preparatory meeting for the Beijing Conference reaffirmed in its final document that the promotion of equality between women and men requires a more equitable sharing of authority and responsibilities in family life, in work and in society, as well as a better share of economic and political power. Equal opportunities for men and women are needed for the release of full human potential. Partnership between women and men is the most suitable concept on which to evolve a new social contract based on gender equality and parity.[137]

A move far beyond the formal recognition of equal rights between women and men to the identification of areas and specific problems that women face in the exercise of their rights is clearly distinguishable. It has necessitated the understanding that the lack of opportunity suffered by women under hundreds of years is the result of the assumed superiority of the male sex. In many societies, including Europe, women were, until the 19th century,[138] considered to be their husbands' and fathers' property, with the consequence of their being subject to male authority. Customs, which keep women in subordinated position, still exist today in the daily life of women in many countries. According to the report of the UN Working Group on Slavery from September 1992 obstacles to equality between the sexes are many and varied. Often the roots can be found in religious and cultural traditions.[139] Of greatest importance in this respect is cultural heritage, a result of thousands of years of development. However, the recognition of the diversity of cultures must not be used to justify the relativisation of the universal nature of the principle of gender equality[140] and thereby use culture and/or traditions as an excuse for the neglect and even breach of international law obligations.

---

[135] UN Doc. E/CN.6/1995/5/Add.5.

[136] UN Doc. E/CN.6/1995/5/Add.3.

[137] ECOSOC, E/ECE/RW/HLM/L.3, 15 September 1994, § 2 b and d.

[138] The Council of Europe's standard-setting activities relating to equality of the sexes, Strasbourg 1989, p. 30.

[139] Social and cultural barriers are named as an important hinder for the achievement of *de facto* equality between women and men in Rec. No. R(90)4 of the Committee of Ministers to Member States of the Council of Europe on the Elimination of Sexism from Language. See EG(90)3, p. 1. Many scholars, among them Anne Gallagher have identified justifications by governments for both *de iure* and *de facto* discrimination against women on the basis of culture, religion or ethnicity as a main problem within the field of women's rights. The relativist approach does not only deny the basis of the principle of universality and indivisibility of human rights, but "serves to obscure violations committed against women, to perpetuate an ideological resistance to the notion of women's human rights, and to inhibit a unified response from the international community". *A. Gallagher*, p. 291.

[140] See the Conclusions of the Seminar on the Democratic Principle of Equal Representation – Forty Years of Council of Europe Activity, EG/Sem (89),5 rev., Strasbourg 1989, p. 2.

According to the *Opsahl/Eide* model of freedom, the second dimension of the principle of equality – *equality in fact* – which aims at looking for ways to make men and women equally independent, in terms of reducing the dependence of the woman on the man (as regards decision-making in all areas of law as well as economically) is of central importance to the advancement of women.

Bearing this in mind, one should remember that the vast majority of women, who are victims of human rights violations, are disempowered. Therefore, the asymmetrical "empowerment" model for gender equality, which may include temporary special measures, affirmative action programmes *etc.* seems to be the most convenient theory with which to approach gender inequality. Documents from the time before[141] the Beijing Conference and afterwards witness that the "empowerment" doctrine has found great acceptance within the United Nations. The commitment to women's empowerment, autonomy and improved political, social, economic and health status is rooted in numerous international declarations and treaties. In 1994 the following definition of the notion "empowerment" was presented by the UNDP:

> "Empowering women means extending choices: choices about if and when to get married, choices about education, employment opportunities, controlling the social and physical environment: choices about if and when to get pregnant, and ultimately about family size. Empowering requires that husbands, partners, family members, and communities help to promote a healthy environment free from coercion, violence or abuse, in which women are free to use community services on a basis of equality".[142]

This very extensive description of "empowerment" underlines the importance of women's ability to take greater control over their own destinies, to have the right to be independent and to have choices in life.

---

[141] Chapter IV, Section 4.1 of the Cairo Programme of Action declares that the empowerment and autonomy of women and the improvement of their status is "a highly important end in itself". However, Chapter IV, § 4.3(a) refers to both gender equality and gender equity. One of the objectives was stated to be to achieve "equality and equity based on harmonious partnership between men and women". This compromise was a necessary solution in order to avoid "paralysing debates" on the issue whether equality comprises substantive equality along with formal equality and to facilitate the adoption of the final document by consensus. *N. Taub*, International Conference on Population and Development, ASIL, Washington D.C. 1994, p. 14. This circumstance shows in regard to the interpretation of the notion "equality" that the cultural relativists had a strong position in Cairo. It simply reflects the existing opposition to the inclusion of *de facto* equality in its substance. The Western delegations in Beijing were more successful. They managed to delete the term "equity" in the final text. It was instead underlined that a partnership between women and men based on equal rights, in both public and private spheres, was fundamental. See, in addition, the Preamble and Article 2 of the Jakarta Declaration (1994); § 25 and Commitment 5 of the Copenhagen Declaration (1995) and § 28 (b), 46, 73 (d) of the Copenhagen Programme of Action (1995). All these documents make use of the word "equity" in the sense that human rights do not need to be equal for men and women. However, both in the Habitat Agenda and in the Istanbul Declaration (1996) particular attention was paid to the promotion of gender perspectives in the sense of empowering women.

[142] *N. Sadik*, The State of World Population 1994, UNDP 1994, p. 7.

The Beijing Declaration considers empowerment of women fundamental for gender equality since 10 years after the Nairobi Conference (1985) *de facto* equality between women and men has not been achieved (§ 24). Therefore, one of the major objectives of the Platform for Action as laid out in § 9 is the empowerment of all women.[143] In this connection the full realisation of all human rights and fundamental freedoms of all women is considered essential for the empowerment of women. It was, furthermore, clearly stated at the Beijing Conference that empowering women to take decisions about their sexuality and their fertility also empowers them in other domains, such as household decision-making and participation in educational and economic life.[144]

The Conference emphasised, furthermore, the interrelation between the advancement of women and the progress of society as a whole.[145] The UN Secretary-General was in consequence to propose the establishment of an inter-agency task force on the empowerment and the advancement of women.[146] This confirms the assertion that both aspects of the principle of gender equality have attained their deserved prominence in the UN. It is almost beyond argument that they constitute part of the law of the United Nations. Still a controversy exists as to whether the desired societal goal of equality should be attained through preferential treatment.

#### *2.2.2.4. Affirmative Action*

President Lyndon Johnson, in a commencement address at Howard University in Washington, D.C., in June 1965, acknowledged that equality of opportunity is not enough for achieving *de facto* equality. He told the graduating class: "You do not take a person who for years has been hobbled by chains, liberate him and bring him to the starting line of a race and say, 'You are free to compete with others', and still justly believe that you have been completely fair".[147] It is apparent that it is not enough just to open the gates of opportunity. All must have the ability to walk through those gates. In other words, while equality remains unfulfilled, special measures or affirmative action programmes[148] for certain social groups such as

---

143 See also UN Doc. A/RES/50/203, 23 February 1996.

144 UN Doc. CEDAW/C/1996/3/Add.1, § 13.

145 Paragraph 41 of the Platform for Action reads: "Empowerment of women and equality between women and men are prerequisites for achieving political, social, economic, cultural and environmental security among all people".

146 UN Doc. A/50/744, 10 November 1995, § 38. In the beginning of 1996 the Secretary-General appointed Mrs. R. Green to act as his special advisor on gender issues to help ensure the system-wide implementation of the Beijing Platform of Action. UNGA 51st sess. Suppl. No. 38 (A/51/38).

147 Internet, http://www.essential.org/ussa/foundati/aamyths.html., 16 November 1996.

148 Affirmative action is a legal term with a long history in the labour law promulgated during the early years of this century in several Western democracies. It has been used by employers and educational institutions to overcome past and continuing discrimination in order to enable, *e.g.*, qualified women to compete equally for education and jobs. The domestic regulations in several of these countries provide today for affirmative action plans where: 1. There is a firm basis to believe that the employer to which the plan applies has discriminated against the group favoured by the plan in the past and 2. The plan is temporary and seeks only to eliminate discriminatory practices. See generally on affirmative action: *R. Kennedy*, Persuasion and Distrust: A Comment on the Affirmative Action Debate, Harvard

women are not considered discrimination. They constitute today an essential part of the equality principle.[149] Article 4 of the Women's Convention sets down, *e.g.*, that such measures are legitimate for the purpose of the acceleration of *de facto* equality. In consequence CEDAW recommended in its General Recommendation No. 5 that states parties should make more use of "temporary special measures such as positive action, preferential treatment or quota systems to advance women's integration into education, politics and employment".[150] Affirmative action[151] may consequently take many forms, depending on the context. The term has been interpreted by CEDAW as well as by the HRC[152] in a rather extensive manner, *i.e.,* so as to comprise temporary special measures, positive state action, preferential treatment and quota systems. Often some of these words were used interchangeably.[153] Whereas in contemporary

---

Law Review 1986, Vol. 99, p. 1327 ff.; *C.M. Koggel*, A Feminist View of Equality and its Implications for Affirmative Action, Can. J.L. Jur. 1994, Vol. 7, p. 43 ff.; *J.R.Lindgren & N.Taub*, The Law of Sex Discrimination, New York 1993, p. 248; *Affirmative Action Review*, Report to the President, The White House, Washington D.C. 1995, Chapter 2.

[149] *A.F. Bayefsky*, The Principle of Equality or Non-Discrimination in International Law, p. 26.

[150] UN Doc. A/43/38, 1988, p. 109.

[151] In response to the civil rights movement President John F. Kennedy issued Executive Order No. 10925/6.3.1961, which for the first time explicitly referred to "affirmative action" connotating a favourable and so unequal treatment with the aim to eliminate the effects of past discrimination. See *M. Stathopoulos*, Equality in the Law of Contract, Conference paper, Brussels, September 1996, Part I, p. 288.

In its contemporary use in the US the term "affirmative action" stems from Title VII of the Civil Rights Act and Executive Order No. 11246 from 1965. *R. Eklund*, Gender-based affirmative action, in Lex Ferenda, J. Rosén (ed.), Stockholm 1996, p. 43.

Today affirmative action programmes are not only hotly debated but are even under attack in some parts of the US. On July 20, 1995, the University of California Regents voted to remove consideration of race, ethnicity, religion, gender, colour or national origin in government hiring, contracting and education. Similar measures are proposed in the following seven states: Washington, Colorado, Texas, Arizona, Florida, Ohio and Michigan. While the Clinton Administration continues to support affirmative measures, opinion polls show as of October 31, 1996, growing opposition to the implementation of affirmative action in the sense of preferential treatment or quotas. The majority of California voters supported Proposition 209 on November 5, 1996, which would if adopted ban state and local affirmative action programmes in public education, hiring and contracting, designed to assist women and members of minority groups. Before the referendum Proposition 209 supporters circulated a letter, signed by 26 law professors from across the country, declaring that the initiative will not dilute sex discrimination protections. Opponents countered with a statement, signed by 75 Californian law professors, that the measure "constitutionally authorizes discrimination against women and girls in a manner that is much broader than any current law". *B. Stall*, Prop. 209's Fate May Hinge on 2 Words, L.A. Times, 31 October 1996. The Federal Appeals Court upheld Proposition 209 on 8 April 1997. However, the American Civil Liberties Union already is preparing an appeal and the case is expected to reach the US Supreme Court. *R. Price*, Preference ban upheld in California, USA Today, April 9, 1997, p. 1A. In addition, the United States Supreme Court has become increasingly conservative on affirmative action. Although recent decisions deal with racial issues, it is reasonable to believe that they may have impact on gender issues. For references to relevant case law see *L.D. Elrod*, Equality in Family Law, USA, in Gleichheit im Familienrecht, B.Verschraegen (ed.), p. 271.

[152] HRC GC No. 4/13, § 2. UN Doc. A/36/40.

[153] *R. Eklund*, p. 29. Affirmative action became one of the focal points in public policy on women in Western Europe mainly in the course of the 1980s. Moreover, affirmative action and positive discrimination may also be used interchangeably.

international law documents in the context of gender equality mostly reference to temporary special measures[154] and/or positive action has been made, there is some confusion in the general debate as to the content of the term "affirmative action". It seems that some agree upon the presumption that the notion covers temporary special measures and/or positive action.[155] Others, among them several governments in Western Europe, *e.g.*, tend to extend its content also to include "preferential treatment"[156] or a "quota system" for certain members of society. Opponents usually label such an interpretation of the phrase as "reverse discrimination".[157] The controversy about affirmative action has become more pronounced since the mid of the 1990s in the US and the Government has recently in response to public pressure developed clarifying policy principles on that issue. Any affirmative action programme must accordingly be eliminated or reformed if it: "(a) creates a quota, (b) creates preferences for unqualified individuals, (c) creates reverse discrimination, or (d) continues even after its equal opportunity purposes have been achieved".[158]

A similar shift towards a more strict and narrow interpretation of the notion "affirmative action", *i.e.*, in relation to a quota system expressly favouring women, has been discernible within the European Communities. The European Court of Justice handed down a judgment on 17 October 1995[159] implying a restrictive interpretation of Article 2(1) and 2(4) of the Council Directive 76/207/EEC of 9 February 1976 on the implementation of the principle of equal treatment for men and women

---

[154] Interestingly it was the representative of the United States who during the preparatory work on Article 4 of the Women's Convention stated that affirmative action might be unconstitutional and therefore suggested that this provision should be deleted. UN Doc. A/32/218, p. 8.

[155] Article 4 of the draft additional protocol to the African Charter requires states parties to take "specific positive action in those areas where *de jure* and *de facto* discrimination against women in law and in fact continues to exist".

[156] Professor Dinstein upholds a strict distinction between permanent preferential treatment and affirmative action. Affirmative action signifies according to him "that historically disadvantaged groups, (b)enefit from temporary preferences designed ultimately to bring about equality and to disappear". The temporal element of the affirmative action programme is considered by the same author as an "indispensable condition" for the application of such measures. *Y. Dinstein*, Discrimination and International Human Rights, pp. 16–17.

[157] The term "reverse discrimination" accentuates discrimination, *i.e.*, preferential (systematic) treatment given to a member of a specific group at the expense of others who are not members of the preferred group. During the drafting of the Women's Convention the delegations of France and the United Kingdom took the position that the convention should in no way require governments to impose "reverse discrimination", since save in certain carefully defined circumstances this would represent a permanent departure from the objective of equal status and opportunities and would not be in the long-term interest of women themselves. The UK observed, however, that positive action should be permitted in specific fields designed to equalise the opportunities open to women in situations where this is necessary to overcome an undesirable historical link. See UN Doc. E/CN.6/591, p. 7; *L.A. Rehof*, p. 68; *J. Bussemaker*, Equality, Autonomy and Feminist Politics, in Equality Politics and Gender, E. Meehan & S. Sevenhuijsen (eds.), p. 61; *J. Outshhorn*, Is This What We Wanted? Positive Action as Issue Perversion, in Equality Politics and Gender, E. Meehan & S. Sevenhuijsen (eds.), p. 115; *T. Gür*, Positiv särbehandling är också diskriminering, Stockholm 1998.

[158] Memorandum for Heads of Executive Departments and Agencies, Evaluation of Affirmative Action Programs, The White House, July 19, 1995.

[159] Case C-450/93 *Eckhard Kalanke v. Freie Hansestadt Bremen* , 35 I.L.M. 1996, pp. 268–273.

as regards access to employment, vocational training and promotion, and working conditions. The Court of Justice arrived at the conclusion that the legislation of the Bremen State (Federal Republic of Germany) under consideration, where candidates for a job who are of different sexes and are equally qualified, are not in conformity with the aforesaid principle because women are automatically and unconditionally, *i.e.*, in an absolute manner, to be given priority for appointment or promotion in sectors where they are under-represented. Under-representation of women was deemed to exist when they do not make up one half of the staff in the personnel category (defined by function and salary levels). The Court held, furthermore, that the domestic provisions in question involve discrimination on grounds of sex since it is not legitimate to favour by a quota a person simply because of sex and that they "go beyond promoting equal opportunities"[160] and overstep the limits of the exception in Article 2(4) of the relevant directive. This ruling constitutes a retreat from the idea of affirmative action in the broad sense, which the Court of Justice of the European Communities earlier has expressed in its case law.[161] In that case the Court supports the idea of achieving only formal (equal treatment, as between individuals belonging to different groups) and not substantive (in the sense of equal treatment as between groups)[162] gender equality. I agree very much with the pronouncement of the Swedish Professor Ronnie Eklund who rightly observed that "It is a mystery why the Court of Justice of the European Communities chose to take a narrow view when thinking of the fact that the same Court has paved the way to the enforcement of the sex equality principle in other landmark decisions in the past".[163] Whether the decision of the *Kalanke* case will have a negative effect upon the domestic law of states members of the EU and will substantiate future restrictive decisions in European countries which implement quotas, or not, is a subject for dispute in the legal literature. While some academic writers maintain that this judgment may have a negative impact on the domestic laws in several countries,[164] the Office of the Equal

[160] The Court found that although the Council Directive (Dir. 76/207) on the Implementation of the Principle of Equal Treatment for Men and Women as Regards Access to Employment, Vocational Training and Promotion, and Working Conditions, expressly permits measures to promote equal opportunity for men and women, it does not permit the type of *automatic* preferences for women prescribed by the German law. *Op. cit.* § 22.

[161] See, *e.g.*, Case 312/86 *Commission v. France*, 1988, ECR 6315 where the Court emphasised that Article 2(4) allows measures, even discriminatory in appearance, which are intended to eliminate or reduce actual instances of inequality existing in the reality of social life. *J. Outshoorn*, p. 113.

[162] See the Advocate General's opinion in the *Kalanke* case.

[163] *R. Eklund*, p. 51.

[164] Especially Austria, Denmark, Finland, Italy, The Netherlands and Sweden are mentioned in this regard. Professor Eklund predicts that the Swedish provisions of 1 July 1995 (SFS 1995:936, *The Ordinance on Certain Appointments as a Professor and Research Assistant to Promote the Principle of Equality*), which comprise preferential treatment for the underrepresented sex in regard of appointment of university professors and research assistants, will "apparently directly violate EC sex equality law". *R. Eklund*, The Swedish Case, p. 350. The mentioned regulation was adopted with the purpose to redress the numerical imbalance between men and women in the Swedish university sector. According to section 3(2) and (3) women have a right to be appointed before male candidates, even when a man possesses higher qualifications. The difference in qualifications must, however, not be so large as to make

Opportunities Ombudsman in Sweden (*Jämställdhetsombudsmannen*) holds the opinion that the ECJ ruling is limited to the facts of the case before the Court and that it should be read narrowly. The judgement may have relevance only in regard to such national rules as in the case in question and which unconditionally and without exception guarantee preferential treatment for women. It is maintained that this is not the case with relevant Swedish provisions, which appear to be sex-neutral and non-compulsory. No person is automatically excluded from consideration. Sweden may, therefore, in the view of the Ombudsman continue to implement its affirmative action policy comprising quotas on voluntary basis.[165] Despite the above judgment it seems to me that today in Europe there is not sufficient support for the replacement of the concept of equality of outcome by the concept of formal equality. In support of this assumption I would like to mention the recent decision of the European Court in the *Marshall* case[166] and that the European Commission proposed to the European

---

the positive action in conflict with the equality requirement in the Swedish constitution. The application of the Ordinance Act is supposed to be limited to a short time. The Appeal Board of the University recently asked the ECJ for an advisory opinion on this matter.

Noteworthy is that CEDAW during the consideration of the Ethiopian report in accordance with the Woman's Convention, welcomed the affirmative action efforts for women at university level. UN Doc. CEDAW/C/SR.292, 293 and 299, 24 January 1996. See IHRR 1997, Vol. 4, No. 1, p. 181.

165 Jämställdhetsombudsmannen, Dnr S95/6940/Jäm, Stockholm 31 January 1996. As regards active measures to promote gender equality in Sweden, section 9 of the 1991 Equal Opportunities Act provides that: " Where the balance between women and men at a workplace is, on the whole, uneven in a certain type of work or in a certain staff category, the employer shall make special efforts when recruiting new staff to obtain applications from the sex that is under-represented and endeavour to ensure that the proportion of employees of that sex is gradually increased". Hence, an employer may choose to recruit a woman or a man for a certain job with the motivation that either sex is under-represented. The legislative history of the provisions on affirmative action clarifies that "the breakeven line is often set at 40 per cent". For the opposite view see *R. Eklund*, pp. 37 and 49. The author argues that there are good grounds to assume that the *Kalanke* judgment will indeed have an impact upon the application of the Swedish law. For a thorough and objective analysis of the Swedish situation see *T. Sigeman*, Tjänstetillsättning vid universiteten i rättsligt perspektiv, in Festskrift till Stig Strömholm, Uppsala 1997, pp. 769–795. See also *N. Björklund*, Affirmative Action: The *Kalanke* Case and its Implications at EU Level and in Sweden, JT 1997–1998, No. 1, pp. 68–85.

166 On the 11 November 1997 the Court of Justice of the European Communities surprisingly reversed its earlier standpoint in the *Kalanke* judgment by relying on the notion of a "savings clause", which allows for consideration of the individual merits of the male candidate for a job and it accepted preferential treatment of women on the basis of Article 2(1) and (4) of the Council Directive 76/207/EEC of 9 February 1976 in the *Hellmut Marschall v. Land Nordrhein-Westfalen* case (No. C-409/95, http://europa.eu.int/ju). The clause mentioned does not guarantee absolute and unconditional priority for women. In other words, the decision implies that in official sectors (in that case within the school system) in which fewer women than men are employed in the relevant higher grade post in a career group, "women must, unless reasons specific to a male candidate predominate, be given priority where male and female candidates for promotion are equally qualified". Thus, the deep rooted prejudice and stereotyping of women's roles do not allow them to have equal life chances as men have. In the view of the Court "even where male and female candidates are equally qualified, male candidates tend to be promoted in preference to female candidates particularly because of prejudices and stereotypes concerning the role and capacities of women in working life and the fear, for example, that women will interrupt their careers more frequently". Ibid., § 29. For those reasons and to help restore balance to labour markets, the Court decided that a national rule such as that at issue in the *Marschall* case may be necessary to promote

Parliament in connection with the interpretation of the *Kalanke* judgment amendment of the relevant directive to mean that possible measures to promote equal opportunity for men and women "shall include the giving of preference".[167] In this regard I may also add that in a case of a norm conflict, universal rules on human rights take precedence over regional ones and that human rights should "be interpreted in favour of the individual who is the object of international protection".[168]

Since it has become clear that enforcement of equal opportunity is necessary but is insufficient as a means and end to break longstanding patterns of discrimination, the conviction is still strong that affirmative action is needed and that its aim should be to ensure that a legally required result is actually produced, *i.e.*, to remedy subjugation of women and to challenge gender hierarchies which continue to keep women at a disadvantage. Legal norms and/or policies affecting freedom of procreation require assessment in terms not only of formal principle but also of concrete consequences.

While the idea of affirmative action made a breakthrough in the US in the early 1960s and in the 1970s within Western Europe,[169] its acceptance is, however, of a relatively recent date in contemporary international law. In contrast to the progressive statements made by the PCIJ before the foundation of the UN, some of the UN's organs adopted during the early years of the organisation's existence, a moderate approach toward the dual nature of the equality principle. In 1954 the UN Sub-Commission on Prevention of Discrimination and Protection of Minorities discussed, *e.g.*, at its seventh session several aspects of the term "discrimination". It acknowledged that protective and compensatory measures intended to help backward groups achieve equality of opportunity do not constitute discrimination. However, it did not approve any form of *numerus clausus* or quota system, on the ground that that would ignore the principle of equal treatment of all.[170] Two decades later the objectives of the World Plan of Action, which were adopted at the

---

equality of opportunity. Positive action will, however, not be appropriate when the male candidate is more qualified than the female candidate. For a comment on the case see *J.A. Mertus*, A Commentary on case No. C-409/95, Marschall v. Land Nordrhein Westfalen, AJIL 1998, Vol. 92, pp. 296–300.

[167] The official position of the Commission was that "quota systems which fall short of the degree of rigidity and automaticity provided for by the Bremen law have not been touched by the Court's judgment". Communication on Kalanke Ruling, *J.A. Mertus*, p. 298.

The Swedish delegation together with the Austrian made a formal proposal on 6 of May 1997 during the ongoing negotiations for amendments of the EU treaty including a preferential treatment clause in it. Gender equality should, according to the Swedish Government , be brought into the European Union as a fundamental goal. The result of the negotiations is very similar to Sweden's proposition. The new adopted Article 13 (ex 6a) of the EC Treaty provides the Council with a legal basis for unanimously adopting, on a proposal from the Commission and after consulting the Parliament, measures to combat discrimination based on sex, racial or ethnic origins, religion or belief, disability, age or sexual orientation. Gender equality is included as one of the aims of the Community (Article 2 of the EC Treaty), whilst Article 3 sets of the objective of eliminating inequalities, and promoting gender equality in the accomplishment of the Union's aims. See Riksdagens Proposition 1997/98:58 om Amsterdamfördraget, Stockholm 1998, p. 81; *M. Droege*, Maastrichtfördraget, Fördragssamling, Europarätt, Uppsala 1997, p. 425 ff.

[168] IACourtHR, *In the Matter of Vivianna Gallardo et al.*, No. G./101/81, Decision of November 13, 1981, Ser. A: Judgments and Opinions, § 16.

[169] *N. Brunn & P.K. Koskinen*, Jämställdhetslagen, Helsingfors 1987, p. 38.

[170] *W. McKean*, pp. 130–131.

World Conference in Mexico and which form the basis for action during the UN Decade for Women to achieve equality, require affirmative action in the sense of "compensatory activities to correct accumulated injustices".[171] It is apparent that the compensation argument, *i.e.*, requiring rectification measures of the historical inequalities between men and women and seeking to compensate for past wrongs, has been given priority. Characteristic for later developments within international law is that emphasis instead has been put on the need for affirmative action on the basis of distributive justice arguments. Public awareness has arisen that significant progress toward social justice will require alternative frameworks. Thus, special measures should reflect the need to promote the compelling societal interest in the integration of disadvantaged groups into society and equal opportunity. Today affirmative action is still largely considered a measure designed to re-establish equality, which has been disturbed by the manifest imbalance of justice as well as to eliminate continuing discrimination. Affirmative action is considered to be a kind of social restitution and an attempt to create a more democratic society. It empowers the state to make special provisions for the advancement of any socially backward group. In other words, it seeks to ensure equality and fairness. Therefore, it is wrong to consider affirmative action as discrimination and as contrary to the principle of equality. Adopting special measures for the sole purpose of securing adequate advancement of certain groups and individuals demands such protection as may be necessary in order to secure for such groups and individuals equal enjoyment of their human rights. Affirmative action programmes in search of equality in law and in fact, for all persons, are called for to create systems and procedures to prevent future discrimination.

The HRC has, as has already been mentioned, endorsed affirmative action for certain limited purposes. One of the very first General Comments on the articles of the ICCPR produced by the HRC (GC No. 4) deals with the realisation of equal rights for men and women. It is emphasised there the importance of "affirmative action designed to ensure positive enjoyment of rights"[172] to be taken by states parties to the Covenant. In a subsequent General Comment on non-discrimination[173] the HRC evolved its position as follows: "(t)he principle of equality sometimes requires States Parties to take affirmative action in order to diminish or eliminate conditions, which cause or help to perpetuate discrimination prohibited by the Covenant". The states must furthermore report on the actual position of women in all areas of social life.[174] In 1995 the HRC, after it reiterated the basic character of

---

[171] *A.S. Fraser*, p. 83. See paragraphs 20, 62 and 63 of the Mexico Declaration (1975).

[172] HRC, GC 4, HRI/GEN/1/Rev.1, 1994, § 2, p. 4.

[173] HRC, GC 19, HRI/GEN/1/Rev.1, 1994, § 10, p. 28. On 14 October 1994 the presessional working group of the Committee recommended that a general comment be adopted on the status and human rights of women under the Covenant. In 1995 the HRC announced that the GC on Article 3 may be revised.

[174] *M. Nowak*, CCPR Commentary, p. 70. In regard to the ICESCR, it has been asserted that its mandate goes beyond affirmative action since it recognises that extraordinary efforts must be made to bring women up to the starting line. This would also require that the male norm at the starting point should be replaced with a female one, which takes into consideration child birth capacities. *B. Stark*, The "other" half of the international Bill of Rights as a postmodern feminist text, in Reconceiving Reality: Women and International Law, D.G. Dallmeyer (ed.), p. 26.

the principle of non-discrimination, pointed out again that states parties should, if necessary, take affirmative action to eliminate conditions that foster the perpetuation of discrimination prohibited by the Covenant.[175]

Similarly the Woman's Convention recognises that the formal prohibition of discrimination is insufficient to redress its inherited consequences. The combating of factual inequality calls for positive action rather than mere prohibitions. The Convention covers in other words the substantial concept of equality, which justifies affirmative action programmes.[176] Article 4(1) of the Women's Convention enables states parties to take affirmative action in the form of reversed differentiation in favour of women until the objectives of equality have been achieved. This provision provides states with the possibility to eliminate *de iure* as well as *de facto* discrimination.

> "Adoption by States Parties of temporary special measures aimed at accelerating *de facto* equality between men and women shall not be considered discrimination as defined in the present Convention, but shall in no way entail as a consequence the maintenance of unequal or separate standards".

Also the UN Special Rapporteur on Minorities, Mr. Eide, justifies affirmative action in his report on protection of minorities on the basis of the overall aim within the international community to ensure the equal enjoyment of human rights and freedoms and to secure the adequate advancement of certain disadvantaged groups.[177]

The special measures should be, however, as recognised in international law instruments, of temporary character. Such measures must not continue after the need for them has disappeared. It is prescribed in Article 4(1) of the Women's Convention that: "(t)hese measures shall be discontinued when the objectives

---

[175] UN Doc. A/CONF.177/9, § 9. The HRC noted during its consideration of the US report under the Covenant that the effects of past discrimination in society have not yet been fully eradicated, which makes it difficult to ensure the full enjoyment of the rights provided for under the ICCPR to everyone within the US jurisdiction. Therefore, the Committee emphasised the need for the Government to increase its efforts to "prevent and eliminate persisting discriminatory attitudes and prejudices" against women including "where appropriate through the adoption of affirmative action". The HRC expressed, furthermore, the hope that, when determining whether currently permitted affirmative action programmes for minorities and women should be withdrawn, "the obligation to provide Covenant's rights in fact as well as in law be born in mind". UN Doc. CCPR/C/SR.1401–1402 and SR.1405–1406, 29 and 31 March 1995.

[176] *H. Charlesworth et al.*, p. 265.

[177] Affirmative action is accordingly "preference, by way of special measures, for certain groups or members of such groups (typically defined by race, ethnic identity or sex) for the purpose of securing adequate advancement of such groups or their individual members in order to ensure equal enjoyment of human rights and fundamental freedoms". *A. Eide,* Protection of Minorities: Possible ways and means of facilitating the peaceful and constructive solution of problems involving minorities, UN Doc. E/CN.4/Sub.2/1993/34, § 172.

of equality of opportunity and treatment have been achieved".[178] Also within the doctrine most scholars reject the idea of a permanent differentiation in the rights or status of the members of certain groups.[179]

Several countries reported to CEDAW already in 1985 on the implementation of the Women's Convention that they have adopted temporary special measures aimed at accelerating *de facto* equality. Sweden mentioned, for example, that "preferential treatment"[180] is tolerated in connection with the promotion of gender equality at work throughout the employer's organisation. Canada cited affirmative action programmes designed to relieve economic disadvantage or to attempt to achieve equal opportunity in employment. They helped employers to remedy the effects of past discrimination.[181]

In addition to the Women's Convention, a number of other UN documents, mainly of policy character, like the Nairobi Strategies of 1985 refer to special measures and positive action in several provisions, *e.g.,* §§ 61, 72, 84 as well as § 56 (b) of the Copenhagen Programme of Action (1995), reaffirm special measures as a powerful means to achieve *de facto* equality.

It is obvious that over the years progress has been achieved within the international community at the norm-setting level with regard to substantial equality. But how effective has the implementation of the special measures been? Despite some of the gains made by domestic law prohibiting gender discrimination, discrimination still persists. To grant to women the same formal rights that men have has not been shown to be a sufficient condition to promote material equality. Governments have remedied only the most overtly discriminatory aspects of legislation. So, in 1990 the majority of states reports on the review of the implementation of the Nairobi strategies indicated that bridging the gap between the elimination of *de iure* and *de facto* discrimination against women is their "most difficult task in attaining the goal of equal rights for women".[182] The ratification of the Women's Convention and making all domestic legislation in conformity with it will not end the discrimination of women. Changing societal perception and attitudes is a slow process that will leave a gap between *de facto* and *de iure* equality between the sexes for a long time. Explanations for the lack of advancement have varied but

---

[178] It was the United States' delegation which introduced the idea of not maintaining unequal standards and discontinuing action when objectives had been reached. Also representatives from the UK observed during the drafting of Article 4 of the Women's Convention that positive actions should be seen, essentially, as a temporary measure which in the long term should become unnecessary. Finland supported this paragraph, which was according to it, justified in societies where women had traditionally been in subordinate positions. UN Doc. E/CN. 6/L. 688; UN Doc. E/CN.6/591, p. 7; *L.A. Rehof*, p. 69.

[179] *W. Kymlicka*, Multicultural Citizenship, Oxford 1995, p. 4.

[180] See Sweden's reports under the ICCPR regime, which confirm adherence to temporary measures of affirmative action: CCPR/C/58/Add.7, 1990, p. 5 and CCPR/C/95/Add.4, 1994, p. 8.

[181] UN Doc. A/CONF. 116/13, 5 June 1985, § 53. Some Governments do not , however, accept the legitimacy of affirmative action. The governmental delegation of Sri Lanka informed, for example, CEDAW that no affirmative action was put in place in the country because "it would cause antagonistic reactions against women when it caused women to be placed in unfairly advantageous positions". UN Doc. A/47/38, § 412.

[182] UN Doc. CN.6/1990/5, §§ 112, 239.

several countries stressed the obstacle provided by a system of traditional cultural values, beliefs[183] and patterns contributed to the reassertion of existing inequality, assigning women to demeaning roles and a status that prohibits them from enjoying full and equal participation in society. Gendered family structures and uneven power relations in the family are among the cited sources of women's oppression. Even Sweden's record is not perfect with regard to *de facto* gender equality, although the country has been ranked as number one in the gender development (GDI) and gender empowerment (GEM) indexes used by the UNDP in 1995 as well as in 1996.[184] This reality motivates the necessity to continue and to intensify the efforts, including affirmative action, to achieve genuine equality. Within the UN there is a noticeable increase of activities in this regard. The following few examples of devoted engagement on the part of the UN highest officials are illustrative. The UN Secretary-General encouraged governments on several occasions during the middle of the1990s to implement affirmative action programmes in those areas where there are the present-day consequences of past gender discrimination.[185] The UN High Commissioner for Human Rights has also stressed that in regard to human rights treaties it is important to identify areas of specific gender discrimination which require that state parties enact legal and administrative measures including affirmative action to achieve equality between women and men.[186]

Most recently during the Beijing Conference several governments, among them the representatives from Malawi expressly supported affirmative action to redress gender inequality in access to education *etc*. Uganda's delegation stated that the country's Constitution has provided for an Equal Opportunities Commission to monitor and supervise the implementation of laws made to affect affirmative action in favour of women. Women shall have accordingly the right to affirmative action for the purpose of redressing the imbalance created by history and traditional customs.[187] The Philippine's delegation reported that several types of affirmative

---

[183] Many of the reservations to the Women's Convention were motivated by the inconsistency of some interpretations of Islamic law and custom with the notion of sexual equality. *H. Charlesworth et al.*, p. 633.

[184] UNDP, Human Development Report of 1995, p. 75 and of 1996, p. 33. Whereas the GDI index is based upon factors relating to life expectancy, educational attainment and adjusted real income, the GEM index takes into consideration women's participation in decision-making as well as ability to participate actively in the economic and political life of a given country. Women's empowerment is a conscious national policy in Sweden and the legislation on gender equality forms "part of a relentless campaign seeking to change the social mores, the natural inertia and the old patterns exhibited by people in general". *R. Eklund*, The Swedish Case, p. 339. See also *M.K. Eriksson*, Gender Equality in Sweden, in Gleichheit im Familienrecht, B. Verschraegen (ed.), pp. 189–215. See also SOU 1998:6, Ty makten är din…Myten om det rationella arbetslivet och det jämställda Sverige, Stockholm 1998, p. 1 *et seq.*

[185] UN Doc. A/49/378, 12 September 1994, § 87(1). See also *B. Boutros-Ghali*, Translating the Momentum of Beijing into Action, in The Beijing Declaration and The Platform of Action, UN New York 1996, p. 2.

[186] UN Doc. E/CN.4/1995/98, § 68.

[187] We may find many examples in the literature in which African authors are very supportive of affirmative action programmes and who see them as necessary in order to redress the imbalance that women have been subjected to for decades. See, *e.g.*, *F. Khabo*, The Legal Status of Women in Lesotho-the Notion of Marital Power- A Case for Reform, in The Equal Status and Human Rights of Women, R. Wallenberg Institute, Report No. 20, Lund 1995, p. 22.

action are being promoted to raise the status of Philippine women. The Prime Minister of Norway in her closing statement on 15 September 1995 underlined that affirmative action worked in Scandinavia. The so called Scandinavian model of equality puts emphasis on the material element, *i.e.*, the equal material outcome of a certain treatment.[188] The Beijing Platform for Action, which upholds the Women's Convention and builds upon the Nairobi Strategies, pays significant attention to special/positive measures as a means to achieve gender equality. Paragraph 83(f), *e.g.*, urges governments to take "positive measures to increase the proportion of women gaining access to educational policy- and decision-making".[189]

Also at the regional level several documents of high-level political commitments reflect consensus as to the necessity to implement special measures/to take positive action to achieve gender equality. The adoption of specific measures to redress past and present imbalances between women and men were proposed by African Governments in the Dakar Declaration (§ 105(c)). Taking affirmative measures to ensure equality is also explicitly mentioned in the Latin American and the Caribbean Programme of Action (§§ 151, 164 and 166). Finally, Part B, C, D and H of the Jakarta Plan of Action (1994) affirm special/positive measures in the context of gender equality.[190]

Within the Council of Europe the Declaration on Equality of Women and Men, adopted in 1988, requires states to adopt strategies which should provide for suitable measures, including temporary special measures aimed at accelerating *de facto* equality between women and men, in particular in relation to the rights of couples and the eradication of violence in the family and in society (§ VI). One year later the second European Ministerial Conference on equality between women and men adopted policies to accelerate the achievements of "real gender equality". Among the adopted recommendations mentioned have been special temporary measures designed to accelerate the realisation of *de facto* gender equality such as positive action programmes in order to eliminate systematic discrimination (§ 3(v)).[191]

---

[188] Sweden, Norway, Finland and Denmark belong to the UNDP's top-ranking countries in this respect. *A. Dahlberg*, Jämställdhetslagen som paradox och dekonstruktion, in 13 kvinnoperspektiv på rätten, G. Nordborg (ed.), Uppsala 1995, p. 23. However, the representative of the Nordic Council to the Beijing Conference remarked that even though Nordic legislation on gender issues is in 1995 at an advanced state, reality, however, does not always meet the expectations engendered by the laws and that much remains to be done for women to be *de facto* equals to men. WOM/BEI/861, 12 September 1995.

[189] The report of the UN Secretary-General with the title "Peace: Women in international decision-making" reveals that one of the most significant and prevailing gaps between *de iure* and *de facto* equality is the low participation of women in politics and decision-making. CSW E/CN.6/1995/12, § 4.

[190] The Executive Secretary of the Economic and Social Commission for Asia and the Pacific (ESCAP) stated at the Beijing Conference that although many countries in the region have provided for de iure equality for women under the law, de facto equality is "usually elusive". UN Press Release WOM/BEI/21, 6 September 1995.

[191] The text of these documents has been reproduced in A Thematic Guide to Documents on the Human Rights of Women, *G. Alfredsson & K. Tomaševski* (eds.), p. 45 and p. 87.

### 2.2.3. Concluding Remarks

In summing up I may affirm that violation of the principle of non-discrimination on the basis of sex and equality as established in international law instruments is along with racial discrimination one of the most serious kinds of discrimination. Recently the UN Commission on Human Rights in its Resolution 1995/85 reaffirmed that discrimination on the basis of sex is contrary to the Charter of the UN. The fulfilment of equality for women with men on the other hand would, therefore, mean "the realisation of rights that they have been denied as a result of cultural, institutional, behavioural or attitudinal discrimination".[192] For that purpose both aspects of gender equality in contemporary international law: the formal ( *de iure)* equality, *i.e.*, equality in law, which precludes discrimination of any kind,[193] and substantial or *de facto* equality (equality in fact, which may accord different treatment in order to attain genuine equality), *e.g.*, appropriate special measures including in certain cases affirmative action, have important functions to perform with the aim to prevent violations of each of them. Moreover, it is now generally accepted that the definition of "discrimination" does not include temporary special measures for socially and economically deprived groups.

Several of the substantive provisions in central human rights documents are aimed at achieving not only *de iure* equality, but particularly *de facto* equality, which allows the various groups to enjoy the same social development. The goal of *de facto* equality is fundamental to those instruments. Thus, guaranteeing legal (*de iure*) equality of men and women is not sufficient in achieving gender equality. Clearly, international law accepts in many instances the normative rather than the purely formal view of what equality requires. It has become apparent that formal equality has masked material inequality. This hypothesis is of outmost importance to my analysis of reproductive freedom where the relevant differences between men and women with regard to human reproduction are taken into consideration. This view on equality goes together with a broad conception of "autonomy", which is also vital to human rights and freedoms. It reflects the idea of the self-fulfilling individual and accommodates the different situations of women and men. The notion may, furthermore, comprise special rights for a given group in specific circumstances, such as a right to legal abortion.

The symmetrical approach to gender equality is, consequently, not an adequate theory for the purpose of my study. The present author will instead apply the asymmetrical approach to gender equality, which includes among other things "empowerment" and "special rights" features. Under international law the principle of non-discrimination should be analysed and applied in terms of *de facto* equality. Every distinction must pursue a legitimate aim, be just, reasonable and proportionate to the aim sought.

---

192 United Nations Action in the Field of Human Rights, UN New York 1988, p. 118.

193 This aspect of equality may fulfil important functions on the level of law creation and/or on the level of law application

I will, furthermore, argue in line with Deborah Rhode's reasoning[194] that women's oppression and denial of reproductive freedom are indeed inter-connected. Despite the rights discourse and the feminist critique of rights-based strategies,[195] this author believes that the existing human rights framework can accommodate women's needs through, *e.g.*, systematic and teleological methods of interpretation of legal rights and that they can be successfully invoked in relation to gender inequality. In Ann Scales' words "the principle of equality requires that we look to see whose dignity is most at stake, whose point of view has historically been silenced and is in danger of being silenced again, and that in the ordinary case we choose that point of view as our interpretation".[196] Thus, there must be, as far as that is possible, an equal concern on the part of the international community to satisfy the genuine needs of all human beings. Some aspects of gender equality are comprised within humanitarian law and the third part of this study will examine ways to confront ignored types of gender oppression and discrimination, such as practices of sexual and reproductive abuses specifically directed against women.

In addition to rendering structural changes, rights can be used to urge changes in inadequate laws. By assisting in the transformation of laws, human rights might in that way be helpful in social reconstruction. Despite the failure of the human rights system to take into consideration to a great extent women's situation, this branch of international law can be expanded. Existing human rights norms have to be revised in the light of women's differences and needs and if necessary new human rights be created. Human rights are not necessarily inherently static and abstracted from social conditions. On the contrary, the problem with current rights-based strategies is merely "that they have operated within a limited institutional and imaginative universe".[197] In my view human rights open up the possibilities for change. They can be used to benefit women as well. They can empower women. Much depends, however, upon if and how women use them. So I shall in the next sub-chapter examine the relevant practice of international organs for the protection of human rights.

---

194 *D.L. Rhode*, Feminist Critical Theories, in Feminist Legal Theory, K.T. Bartlett & R. Kennedy (eds.), p. 343. I will make use both of "liberal" and "radical" feminist analysis since I agree very much with Charlesworths' standpoint that they are not rival theories and that such a classification is of no particular significance in the context of international law. *H. Charlesworth*, Cries and Whispers: Responses to Feminist Scholarship in International Law, NJIL 1996, Vol. 65, p. 559.

195 Several feminist scholars have argued that the concept of rights is "masculinist and patriarchal, a concept that came into its own with the rise of capitalism". Most critical feminist scholars have, therefore, viewed rights-based theories as an ineffective means of social change since rights analysis see the individual in social isolation. *H.B. Holmes & S.R. Petersen*, Rights Over One's Own Body: A Woman-Affirming Health Care Policy, HRQ 1981, Vol. 71, p. 79. See also *K. Engle*, Female Subjects of Public International Law: Human Rights and the Exotic Other Female, New England Law Review 1992, Vol. 26:1509, p. 1522; *E.M. Schneider*, The Dialectic of Rights and Politics: Perspectives from the Women's Movement, in Feminist Legal Theory, K.T. Bartlett & R. Kennedy (eds.), pp. 318–319; *F. Olsen*, Statutory Rape: A Feminist Critique of Rights Analysis, in Feminist Legal Theory, K.T. Bartlett & R. Kennedy (eds.), p. 305.

196 *A. Scales*, Feminist Legal Method: Not So Scary, UCLA Women's L.J. 1992, Vol. 2, p. 27.

197 *D.L. Rode*, ibid., p. 343.

## 2.3. Jurisprudence and Authoritative Statements of International Treaty Bodies

### *2.3.1. Introduction*

Six Committees of Experts, or treaty bodies, were established within the UN to monitor the implementation of the rights guaranteed in certain conventions.[198] The type of supervisory procedure most commonly applied and accepted is the reporting procedure. In addition, there is a special procedure, the so called international complaint procedure, which is contained in the major international instruments and which provides individuals and groups with an effective means of challenging the actual implementation of human rights treaties by states that ratified them and accepted these procedures. These supervisory mechanisms strengthen in other words the principle of the international accountability of governments in the area of human rights.[199]

Particular allegations of violations of human rights might also lead to a clarification of the content of the rights involved,[200] *e.g.*, the different aspects of the principle of equality and non-discrimination in relation to reproductive freedom. The following sub-chapter will, therefore, be devoted to a review of the case law and the authoritative statements delivered by international supervisory organs. It is important to emphasise in this respect that even though the following survey of existing human rights treaty regimes will be made on an individual basis and each treaty system will be reviewed on its own merits, *i.e.*, each treaty constitutes a

---

[198] These are as follows: The Human Rights Committee (HRC) established under the ICCPR, The Committee on Economic, Social and Cultural Rights (CESCR) which oversees the implementation of the ICESCR, The Committee on the Elimination of Racial Discrimination (CERD) established under the Convention on the Elimination of All Forms of Racial Discrimination, The Committee Against Torture (CAT) established under the Convention against Torture and Other Cruel, Inhuman or Degrading Treatment or Punishment, The Committee on the Elimination of Discrimination against Women (CEDAW) established under the Women's Convention and the Committee on the Rights of the Child (CRC) established under the Convention on the Rights of the Child. The Group of Three established under the Convention on the Suppression and Punishment of the Crime of Apartheid has suspended its meetings. See *M. O'Flaherty*, Human Rights and the UN, Practice before the Treaty Bodies, London 1996.

[199] *T. van Boven,* The International System of Human Rights an Overview, in UN Centre for Human Rights, Manual on Human Rights Reporting, New York 1991, p. 3. It should be mentioned that there are, in addition to treaty institutions, other types of supervisory mechanisms, which have their constitutional basis in the Charter of the UN, *e.g.*, the Commission on Human Rights and its special rapporteurs on countries, thematic rapporteurs etc, to which I shall refer in the other parts of the book. Their valuable contributions to human rights will be taken into account in the context of the subject matter for the present enquiry.

[200] The representative of the Swiss Government replying to a question concerning the views adopted by the HRC under the Optional Protocol to the ICCPR, said that although Switzerland has not yet acceded to the Protocol, the views adopted by the Committee under that instrument helped to determine the interpretation that should be given to the guarantees stemming from the Covenant and thus had to be taken into account by the Swiss courts. Several decisions of the Federal Tribunal referred explicitly to the Committees' case law. UN Doc. CCPR/C/SR. 1539, 9 January 1997.

separate legal regime with its own obligations and own monitoring body, we should bear in mind that they are not self-contained regimes but a part of a universal human rights system.[201] In addition, the UN Committees face similar problems in several areas ( *e.g.*, reservations) as well as share similar goals. It is for this reason that the existing global human rights bodies have increased their efforts to co-ordinate with each other. The UN General Assembly has authorised periodic meetings between the chairpersons of the Committees. Since 1984 meetings of the chairpersons have taken place annually.[202] In compliance with the provisions of the Vienna Declaration and Programme of Action, the chairpersons of the UN human rights supervisory mechanisms devoted, *e.g.*, their sixth meeting in 1995 to examine ways of more effectively monitoring the human rights of women.[203] I should also mention that the treaty-bodies are made up of experts which makes their role a much more legal and less political one than that of other UN bodies.

The United Nations General Assembly has, furthermore, on several occasions emphasised the importance that it attaches to regional human rights systems as a complement to the United Nations system. Thus, the impressive human rights jurisprudence as regards the interpretation of provisions contained in regional treaties, similar to those comprised in universal human rights treaties built up by the European Commission and Court of Human Rights and the Inter-American Commission and Court of Human Rights, are of great importance and relevance for the UN treaty bodies activities. The proposition that the interpretation accorded to a particular legal norm by the appropriate treaty body should not necessarily affect, in any way, the approach to an identical or very similar norm by another body has been "consistently contradicted by the policy and practice of virtually all of the relevant bodies".[204] Since there is a risk of divergent interpretation of human rights

---

[201] Evidential support for that perception can be found in several statements made by governmental representatives of states party to human rights treaty/ies as for example the representative of San Marino who stated with reference to questions raised under Article 3 of the ICCPR during the consideration of the periodic report that there is a desire within the Republic to accede to the Women's Convention but the smallness of the country's internal administrative structure influenced the international obligations which it was able to undertake. UN Doc. A/45/40,1990, p. 99, § 448. Another example may be found under the ICESCR reporting procedure. The CESCR asked Uruguay during the consideration of its report to consider the possibility of ratifying the Protocol of San Salvador additional to the American Convention on Human Rights. UN Doc. E/C.12/1994/20, § 118.

[202] During the 8th meeting in 1997 the focus of the discussion was the final report of Professor Philip Alston on the effective functioning of the treaty bodies, which was presented to the 53rd session of the Commission on Human Rights. Among the most controversial proposals in that report was the suggestion that ultimately there was need for consolidation of the committees into one committee charged with reviewing the implementation of all six treaties. One of the advantages would be harmonisation of the jurisprudence.

[203] The transfer of the Division for the Advancement of Women back to New York and its incorporation in the Department for Policy Coordination and Sustainable Development in 1993 has had the consequence of ending the perceived isolation of CEDAW in Vienna. The Committee held its 14th session in 1995 in New York.

[204] UN Doc. A/44/668, 1989, p. 17.

protected by the various treaties,[205] it is extremely important as regards human rights standards to maintain the highest possible degree of normative consistency.[206] It is not only necessary for the increase of legal certainty but also in order to prevent problems for the national courts seeking to apply the conventional provisions, which have been incorporated in the legislation of a great number of the states parties to the treaties. In this regard the need for greater co-ordination amongst the treaty bodies themselves with the view to facilitate the development of a common jurisprudence on women's human rights has been strongly advocated in the legal literature.[207]

### *2.3.2. The Human Rights Committee*

The International Covenant on Civil and Political Rights (ICCPR) was adopted by the General Assembly on 16 December 1966 and entered into force 23 March 1976. As of October 1998, there were 140 states parties to the Covenant.

Whereas discrimination on the basis of sex under the Covenant is prohibited specifically in Article 2(1), equality in the enjoyment of the enumerated rights is stipulated in Article 3. The latter provision can be considered as having an accessory character, *i.e.*, it refers only to the rights mentioned in the Covenant.[208] Even though the HRC has suggested a liberal interpretation of Article 3 in its GC 4/13 (§ 3), it is clear that the scope of application of Article 3 is more limited than that of Article 26 in which the general right to equality and prohibition of discrimination is guaranteed. It provides that:

> "all persons are equal before the law and are entitled without any discrimination to the equal protection of the law. In this respect, the law shall prohibit any discrimination and guarantee to all persons equal and effective protection against discrimination on any ground such as race, colour, sex, language, religion or other opinion, national or social origin, property, birth or other status".

---

[205] During the 6th session (Geneva 18–22 September 1995) of the Chairmen of the human rights treaty-monitoring bodies concern was expressed as to the danger of the increased number of monitoring bodies undermining the system unless new international instruments take account of the need for greater coherence. The same year the expert group meeting on the development of guidelines for the integration of gender perspectives into human rights activities and programmes concluded that it was impossible to elaborate a generic set of guidelines in respect of the application of a gender perspective and that are of relevance for all human rights bodies and investigatory mechanisms. It was suggested instead that "tailored" guidelines should be elaborated to fit the needs of each of them. See UN Doc. E/CN.4/1996/105. At the same time I should also mention that the issue of gender equality has been on the agenda of the annual meeting of the chairpersons of treaty bodies since 1994. A few recommendations have been adopted with the aim to develop a common strategy in this regard.

[206] See ECOSOC res. 1987/4, § 8.

[207] *A. Gallagher*, p. 308.

[208] A comprehensive article-by article analysis of the Covenant is contained in the impressive work by *M. Nowak*, U.N. Covenant on Civil and Political Rights, CCPR Commentary, Kehl 1993.

The aforesaid provision does not specify any limitations when it comes to the protection of rights against discrimination. It gives rise to an autonomous[209] and not a subordinate right to equality and non-discrimination unlike Article 14 in the European Convention, which can be invoked only in combination with one of the rights set forth there or in the additional protocols.[210] In other words, the principle of gender equality and non-discrimination is embodied in the ICCPR in relation to any of the rights enunciated. Moreover, Article 26 envisages obligations on states parties to ensure substantive equality.

Individuals from a state which is a party to the first Optional Protocol[211] may bring a complaint to the Human Rights Committee (HRC) alleging that their rights under the Covenant have been violated by the state party. As of October 1998, 93 state parties to the Covenant were parties to the first protocol. In addition, the Committee has a competence according to Article 41 to receive and act upon allegations of violations made by states parties against other states parties provided the relevant party has agreed to subject itself to such a procedure. As of October 1998, 34 States parties had made such declarations.

The HRC, which is composed of eighteen members, four of whom, as of October 1998 were women,[212] enjoys considerable authority from the very fact that it comprises distinguished experts from all parts of the world, and they have conducted their role as an expert body independent of political considerations (Article 28 of the ICCPR). The UN Special Rapporteur on torture and other cruel, inhumane or degrading treatment or punishment stated, *e.g.*, in one of his reports that: "The Human Rights Committee is a highly authoritative body... Its views should be taken with greatest possible seriousness".[213]

---

[209] The HRC has in the earlier referred GC on non-discrimination interpreted Article 26 as a free-standing equality norm. In its view the provision "(p)rovides in itself an autonomous right. It prohibits discrimination in law or in fact in any field regulated and protected by public authorities". UN Doc. HRI/GEN/1/Rev.1, p. 28, § 12.

[210] Several of the HRC members pointed out during the review of the Swiss report under the Covenant that the argument put forward by the Swiss Government (§ 484 of the national report CCPR/C/81/Add.8) to justify the reservation that it had entered concerning Article 26 of the Covenant, namely that it is important to avoid creating two different levels of protection under international instruments, *i.e.*, under the Covenant and under the European Convention, was hardly well-founded. In the view of Mr. Lallah, if the European Convention had been drafted, like the Covenant in 1966 and not in 1950, its safeguards would undoubtedly have been identical to those in Article 26 of the Covenant. Mr. Lallah together with Mrs. Evatt, Mr. Ando, Mr. Pocar and Mr. Bhagwati hoped, therefore, that the Swiss Government would give serious thoughts to and shortly be in a position to withdraw that specific reservation. The Swiss representative responded by saying that the legislation governing divorce was being revised and the new draft law on the subject made no distinction between men and women. However, the revision of the law would not yet have any immediate effect on the reservation entered in respect of Article 26 of the Covenant. UN Doc. CCPR/C/SR. 1539, 9 January 1997.

[211] The implementation mechanism of the ICCPR is regulated in Articles 28–45 of the Covenant and in the first Optional Protocol.

[212] Mrs. Chanet is at present the Chairperson of the HRC. One should remember, however, that for the first seven years of its existence the HRC did not have any women members. *G. Van Bueren*, The International Law on the Rights of the Child, Dordrecht 1995, p. 384.

[213] UN Doc. E/CN.4/1993/26, § 594.

*2.3.2.1. The Case Law of the HRC*

Even though the Human Rights Committee is not a judicial organ in the strict sense, the final views which it adopts after considering individual communications "follow a judicial pattern"[214] and constitute a primary means of interpretation of the ICCPR in accordance with the Vienna Convention on the Laws of Treaties of 1969. The Committee has been very active since its establishment and it has developed valuable jurisprudence. The number of cases regarding gender equality decided by the HRC is, however, very limited. It has mainly condemned discrimination on the basis of sex which has been "deliberately enacted in states parties' legislation".[215] In 1987 the Committee dealt with three communications against the Netherlands[216] which were based on Article 26 of the Covenant and made a substantive determination on the merits of the cases. The HRC arguments were almost identical in all the relevant cases. The first case (*Broeks v. the Netherlands*) was about the discriminatory nature of the benefits by virtue of Article 13(1) of the Dutch Unemployment Benefits Act 1979. According to this provision a married woman had to prove that she was in fact a breadwinner in order to benefit from the rules. There was no similar requirement foreseen for married men in the legislation. On that ground the author of the communication raised the question of whether the principle of equality and non-discrimination as guaranteed under the Covenant was respected by the Netherlands. The Committee pointed out that although Article 26 requires that legislation should prohibit discrimination, it does not of itself contain any obligation with respect to the matters that may be provided for by domestic legislation. However, the Committee underlined that when such legislation was adopted in the exercise of a state's sovereign power, then such legislation must comply with Article 26 of the Covenant. The HRC found in this regard that the domestic legislation in question did not guarantee to all persons equal and effective protection

---

[214] *D. McGoldrick*, The Human Rights Committee: its role in the development of the International Covenant on Civil and Political Rights, Oxford 1994, p. 53.

[215] *R.J. Cook*, Women, in The United Nations and International Law, C.C. Joyner (ed.), p. 197; *R.J. Cook*, International Human Rights Law Concerning Women: Case Notes and Comments, Vand. J. Transnat'l L. 1990, Vol. 23, p. 779 *et seq.*

[216] Communication No. 172/1984, *S.W.M. Broeks v. the Netherlands*. Report of the HRC, GAOR 39 session, Suppl. No. 40, UN Doc. A/42/40, pp. 139–150. See also Communication No. 182/1984, *F.H. Zwaan-de Vries v. The Netherlands*, Decision of 9 April 1987, in ICCPR, Selected Decisions of the Human Rights Committee under the Optional Protocol, UN New York 1990, Vol. 2, p. 209; *L.G. Danning v. the Netherlands*, Communication No. 180/1984, UN Doc. CCPR/C/29/D/180/1984, 16 April 1987. In the latter case the applicant was disabled after an accident. Mr. Danning received social insurance benefits but he claimed that he was a victim of discriminatory treatment, since the relevant provisions of the Dutch legislation ensured higher payment to married individuals than to single persons. Though the applicant lived in a common-law marriage, he was excluded from the higher social benefit. The HRC came, however, in this case to the conclusion that the differential treatment was based on objective and reasonable criteria. The facts consequently did not support a finding of a violation of Article 26 since in the view of the Committee: "the decision to enter into a legal status by a marriage, which provides, in Netherlands law, both for certain benefits and for certain duties and responsibilities, lies entirely with the cohabiting persons. By choosing not to enter into marriage, Mr. Danning and his cohabitant have not, in law, assumed the full extent of the duties and responsibilities incumbent on married couples". *Supra* §§ 14–15.

against discrimination. Subsequently the Committee came to the conclusion that the differentiation on the grounds of sex in this case was not reasonable. It placed married women at a disadvantage compared with married men. The circumstances in which the applicant found herself at the material time and the application of the then valid Netherlands law made her a victim of a violation, based on sex, of Article 26 of the ICCPR because she was denied a social security benefit on an equal footing with men. In the second case, related to the unequal rights of married women, the HRC pronounced:

> "Thus, a differentiation, which appears on one level to be one of status is in fact one of sex, placing married women at a disadvantage as compared with married men".[217]

The Netherlands removed this discriminatory provision in its national legislation in 1985, *i.e.*, before the HRC dealt with the above mentioned cases. The importance of these cases lies, however, in the Committee's reasoning that the principle of non-discrimination as enunciated in Article 26 of the ICCPR would apply even if a particular subject-matter is referred to or covered in other international instruments and not by the Covenant itself, *i.e.*, the protection against discrimination guaranteed by the ICESCR. In consequence and by analogy, women's rights covered by the Woman's Convention[218] would be permitted to be subjected to the supervisory jurisdiction of the HRC and especially its jurisdiction based on the Optional Protocol. While the governmental representative of the Netherlands argued in the *Broeks* case for a restrictive interpretation of Article 26 on the basis that the ICCPR and the ICESCR established two different monitoring systems and that a provision was made for an individual complaint procedure only with respect to the ICCPR, the Committee decided that it is not hindered from examining an allegation of discrimination with regard to economic and social rights.[219] The *Broeks* case opens

---

217 The *F.H. Zwaan de Vries* case, ibid. § 14.

218 *Supra*, p. 149, § 12.1. On the other hand, according to rule 90(b) of the HRC's Rules of Procedure, the Committee is empowered to declare an individual complaint inadmissible, if it is considered not sufficiently substantiated. The HRC has, however, not yet applied this provision in order to avoid consideration of a communication dealing with the principle of non-discrimination as regards a right not enumerated in the Covenant.

A similar reasoning was employed by the HRC in the *Pauger v. Austria* case, (Communication No. 415/1990, HRC Annual Report UN Doc. A/47/40, 1992) which also concerned widows. The HRC came to the conclusion that domestic provisions, which gave widowers fewer benefits than widows, were not based on objective and reasonable grounds. The Austrian Pension Act provided until 1995 for full pension benefits to widowers only if they have no other source of income. This does not apply to widows. The Committee found consequently the gender-specific distinction at issue not reasonable and concluded that the applicant has been discriminated on the basis of sex. This case indicates that the HRC preferred to apply a formal interpretation of equality and in that way avoided taking into consideration the fact that the great majority of widows at that time were in a more disadvantageous financial situation compared with widowers. For that reason some authors have rightly criticised that decision. See *T. Loenen*, p. 264.

219 The *Broeks* case, § 8.3.

the possibility for women to use the individual complaint procedure under the Covenant on Civil and Political Rights in a broad manner, provided that the state, against, which the communication is brought up, has ratified the Optional Protocol.

It should also be mentioned that by applying the principle of non-discrimination in a number of other cases, *e.g.*, dealing with immigration law or unemployment benefits, the HRC has established a new application area for the Covenant to apply to practically all areas regulated by public authorities.[220] This assertion may be supported by the ruling of the HRC itself in the Dutch cases as follows:

> "The Committee is of the view that the (ICCPR) would still apply even if a particular subject matter is referred to or covered in other international instruments, e.g., the International Convention on the Elimination of All Forms of Racial Discrimination, the Convention on the Elimination of All Forms of Discrimination Against Women, or, as in the present case, the (ICESCR)".[221]

The wide scope of application of Article 26 gives further strength to the idea of the principle of equality as being of fundamental importance in a theory of rights and among human rights in particular. The Committee through its case law was in a way trend-setter in regard to the current prevailing doctrine on the interdependence and indivisibility of human rights, which was established and generally accepted by consensus first in 1993 at the Vienna Conference on Human Rights.

The HRC develops its jurisprudence as regards interpretation of the provisions of the Covenant through individual cases as well as its general comments.[222]

---

[220] *C. Scott*, The Interdependence and Permeability of Human Rights Norms: Towards a Partial Fusion of the International Covenants on Human Rights, Osgoode Hall Law Journal 1989, Vol. 27, p. 770 *et seq.*; *K. Tomaševski*, Women and Human Rights, London 1993, p. 45.

[221] *Supra* note 216, § 12.1.

[222] See Article 40(3) of the Covenant. It is generally accepted today that the HRC's general comments have received increased importance in "legal, academic, governmental and non-governmental contexts". UN Doc. A/CONF.157/PC/62/Add.11/Rev.1,1993, § 250. They are, moreover, considered as a "strong body of jurisprudential insights into the various provisions of the Covenant". *P. Alston*, The Committee on Economic, Social and Cultural Rights, in The United Nations and Human Rights: A Critical Appraisal, P.Alston (ed.), Oxford 1992, p. 494. Also McGoldrick, who despite a moderate attitude towards the legal value and quality of the Committee's GC, does not hesitate to say that "the general comments serve rapidly to develop the jurisprudence of the HRC under the Covenant. They are potentially very important as an expression of the accumulated and unparalleled experience of an independent expert human rights body of a universal character". *D. McGoldrick*, p. 95. See also *A. Gallagher*, p. 307 and The United Nations and Human Rights 1945–1995, p. 51. Professor Bea Verschraegen advances the argument that not all the general comments have legal value as interpretations of the Covenant's provisions. Thus, in her view "Allgemeine Bemerkungen werden von einem Teil der Lehre als autoritative Interpretationen des IPBPR qualifiziert. In dieser generellen Form ist dies allerdings unrichtig. Denn die Allgemeinen Bemerkungen enthalten eine Reihe von sog. 'Soll-Vorschriften', die den Staaten blosse Obliegenheiten auferlegen, vor allem in bezug auf das Ausmass ihrer Berichtspflicht". *B. Verschraegen*, Die Kinderrechtekonvention, Wien 1996, p. 70.

As of January 1998, the HRC has adopted 26 general comments, two of which replaced earlier ones. During its 56th session in 1996, the Committee decided to begin work on the updating of GC No. 4(13) on Article 3 of the Covenant and to prepare new general comments on Articles 2 and 12 and, subsequently on Articles 21 and 22.

General comments provide states parties with an in depth consideration of the right discussed and of the responsibilities of the state parties in relation to the guarantees of that right. As regards the scope of Article 26, the HRC stated in 1989 in its General Comment,[223] which reflects the case law referred to earlier,[224] that the term discrimination should be understood to imply any "distinction, exclusion, restriction or preference, which is based on any ground such as... sex... which has the purpose or effect of nullifying or impairing the recognition, enjoyment or exercise by all persons, on an equal footing, of all rights and freedoms".

In other words, equality does not necessarily mean identical treatment in every instance. Moreover, according to the HRC not every differentiation in treatment will constitute discrimination provided that the aim is to achieve a purpose, which is legitimate under the ICCPR and provided that the differentiation made is based on *reasonable* and *objective* criteria.

The HRC has consistently applied this test, for instance, also in a case against the Netherlands[225] dealing with the domestic General Widows and Orphans Act. The applicant claimed that she was a victim of a violation of Article 26 of the ICCPR, since, according to the law, a disabled man, whose (former) wife dies retains the right to a disability allowance, but a disabled woman, whose (former) husband dies does not retain the right to a disability allowance, but qualifies instead as beneficiary under the General Widows Act. The state party argued in its defence that the purpose with the act had been to give widows an additional protection, which widowers do not enjoy. The Government of the Netherlands pointed out that: "At the time when the General Widows and Orphans Act was passed, it was customary for husbands to act as bread-winners for their families, and it was therefore desirable to make financial provisions for dependants in the event of the bread-winner's premature death".[226] The HRC found no violation of Article 26 of the Covenant, since:

> "(t)he unfavourable result complained of by Mrs. Vos follows from the application of a uniform rule to avoid overlapping in the allocation of social security benefits. This rule is based on objective and reasonable criteria, especially bearing in mind that both statutes under which Mrs. Vos qualified for benefits aim at ensuring to all persons falling thereunder subsistence level income".[227]

However, two members of the HRC, Mr. Wennergren and Mr. Urbina, delivered a dissenting opinion, in which they arrived at an opposite conclusion to the major-

---

223 UN Doc. CCPR/C/21/Rev.1/Add.1, § 7.

224 The HRC found a violation of Article 26 also in the *Ato del Avellanal v. Peru* case, Communication No. 202/1986, in which the applicant had been denied the right to sue in Peruvian courts because, according to the Peruvian Civil Code, when a woman is married only the husband is entitled to represent matrimonial property before the courts. HRC, Annual Report UN Doc. A/44/40, 1989.

225 *Vos v. the Netherlands* case, Communication No. 218/1986, HRC Annual Report, UN Doc. A/44/40, 1989, p. 232.

226 *Ibid.*, § 8.6.

227 *Supra* note 225, § 12.

ity. In their opinion the failure of the Dutch legislation to allow for a "modicum of flexibility in its implementation" should serve as a basis for classifying the differential treatment unjustifiable.[228]

Moreover, the HRC in its General Comment of 1989[229] on the content of Article 26 of the CCPR articulated the distinction between discrimination and differentiation as follows:

> "Not every differentiation of treatment will constitute discrimination, if the criteria for such differentiation are reasonable and objective and if the aim is to achieve a purpose, which is legitimate under the Covenant".

This is a crucial, and generally accepted in international law, criterion when determining the lawfulness of differentiation.[230] Thus, differential treatment is justified if it has an objective aim, derived from the public interest. Furthermore, Article 26 is intended to ensure equality of treatment and not identical treatment and does not preclude differentiation between individuals.

The "similarity and difference" test of treatment has been applied by the HRC in the *S. Aumeeruddy-Cziffra et al. v. Mauritius* case,[231] in which the Committee found that a violation of Article 26 of the Covenant had occurred. Thus, the immigration and deportation law of Mauritius subjected foreign husbands of native women to restrictions as regards their residency, whereas foreign wives of native men were not subjected to similar limitations. The Committee concluded that "an adverse distinction based on sex is made, affecting the alleged victims in their enjoyment of one of their rights. No sufficient justification for this difference has been given".[232] Several years later the Committee could note with satisfaction that

---

[228] *Ibid.*, § 4.

[229] UN Doc. CCPR/C/21/Rev.1/Add.1, § 12.

[230] *P. Sieghart,* The International Law of Human Rights, Oxford 1983, p. 75 *et seq.*; *I. Brownlie,* Principles of Public International Law, p. 597.

[231] Communication No. 35/1978, HRC, Selected decisions under the Optional Protocol, Vol. I, UN New York 1985, pp. 67–72. Regrettably, the HRC did not discuss the issue of gender discrimination in the *S.Lovelace v. Canada* case (Communication No. 24/1977, HRC views in UN Doc. A/36/40) which dealt with among other things the issue of loss of rights and legal status as an Indian after the applicant married a non-Indian man. Sandra Lovelace alleged that the provisions of the Indian Act (Section 12(1)b) were inconsistent with Article 3 of the ICCPR since there was no similar provision for a loss of Indian status for Indian men who married a non- Indian woman. The HRC recognised that the relevant provisions of the Indian Act, although not legally restricting the right to marry as laid down in Article 23 (2) of the Covenant, entails a serious disadvantage on the part of the Indian woman who wants to marry a non-Indian. However, the Committee did not discuss the issue of gender discrimination but it focused rather on the right to preserve the identity of the tribe under Article 27. Neither did the Committee examine the general provisions against discrimination in Articles 2 and 26. Only one member of the Committee, Mr. N. Bouziri took the view in an individual opinion that Articles 3 and 26 of the Covenant had been violated since the provisions of the Indian Act were discriminatory between men and women and he found that "Mrs. Lovelace is still suffering from the adverse discriminatory effects of the Act". UN Doc. A/36/40, p. 175.

[232] *Ibid.*, § 9.2.(b).

this case has urged necessary reforms of the legislation in questions on the domestic level so as to remove the element of gender discrimination.[233]

The HRC jurisprudence shows some similarities with the case law of the European organs for protection of human rights. Apart from the criteria of reasonableness and objectivity[234] reference to a proportionality reasoning has been made on several occasions by the late Professor Opsahl, a former member of the HRC and who also served at the European Commission on Human Rights.[235]

*2.3.2.2. The Reporting Procedure*

Treaty bodies work towards accomplishing their mandate also by reviewing and questioning reports submitted by states on a periodic basis. Article 40(1) of the ICCPR requires states parties to submit reports on measures taken, on progress made and difficulties encountered in the implementation of the rights defined in the Covenant.[236] This can include a discussion of matters such as legislative provisions, judicial findings, policy etc.[237] The HRC in its consideration of states reports is neither a judicial nor even a quasi-judicial body.[238] There is still uncertainty as to whether the Committee as such can make evaluations of the compliance or non-compliance of individual states and to formally express criticism of the contents of their reports.[239] However, the HRC issues annual reports to the GA containing the concluding observations of the HRC following the consideration of

---

[233] Under the existing UN procedures the views of the treaty body are not considered as formally binding on the state party as a matter of international law. Nevertheless, there is agreement that they are of high authority. When reviewing the third periodic report of Mauritius (UN Doc. CCPR/C/64/Add.12) in April 1996, the HRC welcomed an amendment to the Constitution which adds sex to the grounds on which discrimination is prohibited and the amendment to the Citizenship Act prohibiting gender discrimination. Mentioned should be that in 1990 the HRC created the post of the Special Rapporteur for the follow-up on views. His mandate comprises determination of whether views, *i.e.*, the Committees' decisions on the merits under the first Optional Protocol rendered by the HRC had been implemented on the domestic level. As examples of the influence of the HRC's decisions on domestic law I may refer to Canada, the Government of which amended its legislation following the decision in the *Lovelace* case. Finland changed its law in response to the *Hartikainen* case, even though the HRC did not find a violation of the Covenant. *A.H. Robertson & J.G. Merrills*, Human Rights in the World, Manchester 1993, p. 68.

[234] For a comprehensive review of the HRC jurisprudence see *D. McGoldrick*, The Human Rights Committee, Its Role in the Development of the International Covenant on Civil and Political Rights, Oxford 1994. A valuable compilation with comments on earlier case law has been prepared by *A. de Zayas, J.T. Möller & T. Opsahl*, Application of the International Convention on Civil and Political Rights under the Optional Protocol by the Human Rights Committee, GYIL 1987, Vol. 28, pp. 9–64.

[235] *M. Nowak*, CCPR-Kommentar, p. 506, note 72.

[236] In the years after 1983 the HRC has organised its work by examining one by one most of the core provisions of the Covenant.

[237] States parties are expected to submit their first report within one year of the entry into force of the Covenant and afterwards they should submit reports every five years.

[238] *F. Pocar*, The International Covenant on Civil and Political Rights, in Manual on Human Rights Reporting, UN New York 1991, p. 120.

[239] *T. Opsahl*, The Human Rights Committee, in The United Nations and Human Rights, P. Alston (ed.), p. 412; *J. Donnelly*, Universal Human Rights in Theory and Practice, Ithaca 1989, p. 209; *A.H. Robertson & J.G. Merrills*, pp. 48–49.

each country report and which are presented collectively.[240] They give us some ideas about the HRC's understanding of different substantial articles in the Covenant. In the view of Professor McGoldrick, the final observations as well as the principle subjects of concern expressed by the HRC reflect its common position on a specific matter.[241] Professor Alston has also emphasised the significance of the Committee's concluding observations in jurisprudential terms.[242] The importance of the periodic reporting procedure by states parties to relevant treaty bodies has been stressed in the GA Res. 43/115 as follows: "The effective implementation of instruments on human rights, (n)ot only enhances international accountability in relation to the protection and promotion of human rights, but also provides states parties with valuable opportunities to review policies and programmes affecting the protection and promotion of human rights and to make any appropriate adjustments".[243] The reporting procedure has indeed provoked changes in national law, for example, in Sweden and in Canada and it has turned to be a valuable promotional mechanism.

In the consideration of country reports the issue of gender equality (both its aspects *de iure*[244] and *de facto*) has been pursued by individual members of the HRC and all states parties to the Covenant have been asked "for facts regarding women's enjoyment of rights on an equal basis with men".[245] Even in the pattern of questioning emerging during the HRC consideration of periodic reports since the 1980s "non-discrimination and equality of sexes has become a standard heading"[246]

---

[240] This decision of the HRC to produce collective views rather than opinions of individual members was for the first time put into practice during its session in April 1992 in New York. UN Doc. A/47/40, § 45. On the controversy that may arise in connection with the question of what legal value to be given to a certain question or comment made by an individual member of the HRC during the consideration of a country report see *D. McGoldrick*, p. 83.

[241] *D. McGoldrick*, pp. 83–84. This author supports the view that the comments of the HRC on a state report can be regarded as a supplementary means of interpretation under Article 32 of the Vienna Convention on the Law of Treaties. See also *A. Spiliopoulou Åkermark*, Justification of Minority Protection in International Law, Uppsala 1996, pp. 134–135.

[242] UN Doc. A/CONF.157/PC/62/Add.11/Rev.1, § 33.

[243] UN Doc. A/CONF.157/PC/62/Add.11/Rev.1, § 92.

[244] Inequality according to law in respect of inheritance rules, family law (especially rules on divorce) and nationality has often been pointed out as inconsistent with the Covenant. See the comments of the HRC in regard to the Libyan report (IHRR 1995, Vol. 2, No. 2, pp. 436–438) and the report from Morocco (IHRR 1995, Vol. 2, No. 2, pp. 439–442).

[245] *T. Opsahl*, Equality in Human Rights Law, p. 57. In its GC No. 4/13 adopted on 28 July 1981, the HRC required information from the states parties about gender equality in practice with particular reference to the role of women. In accordance with rule 62 of the rules of procedure, the HRC establishes working groups which meet before each session to prepare lists of issues concerning the reports to be considered by the Committee. The HRC may, however, offer suggestions for amendments or improvements before adopting the list. See UN Doc. HRI/GEN/1/Rev.1, pp. 4–5.

[246] *T. Opsahl*, ibid., p. 58. See also *K. Tomaševski*, Women and Human Rights, p. 109. The updated guidelines for periodic reports provide that information "should concentrate especially on (f)actors affecting and difficulties experienced in the implementation of the Covenant including any factors affecting the equal enjoyment by women of covered rights". UN Doc. CCPR/C/5/Rev.2, 1995. States are currently requested to provide gender specific information in their periodic reports.

and an item in discussing every governmental report.[247] A few examples are provided below, which illustrate the pattern of dialogues between the HRC and representatives of governments.

At its 46th session (1992) the HRC, when reviewing the 3rd periodic report of Senegal, made remarks on a number of obstacles for the achievement of *de facto* gender equality. Among them the continued existence of polygamy, which is degrading to women, was especially named. Also the institutionalisation of the man as the head of the household prevents true equality between the spouses.[248] The same year the HRC stressed when considering the periodic report of Tanzania[249] that gender equality cannot be secured by legislation alone but through education, social and economic measures.[250] The Committee has regularly raised questions with regard to the *de facto* situation of women in several other countries[251] and in the case of Zambia and Guatemala[252] it noted that customs and traditions constitute an obstacle to the effective implementation of the Covenant, particularly in regard to equality between men and women.[253] The Committee recommended during the consideration of the Zambian report in 1996[254] that the Government review its laws to ensure full equality for women in all aspects of social and economic relationships, particularly with regard to laws governing the status of women, and it called for comprehensive anti-discrimination laws and, where appropriate, affirmative action measures. In its 1995 report to the GA, the HRC raised the issues of women's rights in Japan, Cameroon, Togo, Nepal and Jordan. The Committee deplored the fact that these countries had not yet embarked on all the necessary reforms to eliminate conditions still impeding gender equality. It also emphasised the need for efforts by governments to eliminate discriminatory attitudes and prejudices against women in order to ensure their equal rights, as set out in Article 3 of

---

[247] *M. Nowak*, CCPR Commentary, p. 447, notes 93 and 94. The annual reports of the HRC since 1995 are manifestation of the Committee's increasing gender sensitivity, since it addressed several aspects of women's human rights in the concluding observations, which follow the examination of the state party report.

[248] UN Doc. CCPR/C/64/Add.5.

[249] UN Doc. CCPR/C/42/Add.12.

[250] The HRC urged the representatives of Togo during the consideration of that country's report to undertake educational and administrative measures in order to fulfil the obligations arising from Article 3 of the Covenant. In the context of gender equality members of the Committee expressed concern about the on-going trade with women. See IHRR 1995, Vol. 2, No. 1, pp. 164–168. See also comments made upon the situation of women in Nepal. IHRR 1995, Vol. 2, No. 2, pp. 430–432.

[251] See, *e.g.* , UN Doc. CCPR/C/82/Add. 1, reflecting the HRC's discussion during its 53rd session in 1995 when its members pointed out to the representatives of Yemen that measures have to be undertaken in order to eradicate the present lack of equality of the sexes in many areas of law and *de facto*. On the other hand the Committee complimented Spain, for example, during its 56th session in 1996 on its progress in the promotion of equal opportunity for women.

[252] HRC, 56th session, March–April 1996, UN Doc. HRI/CORE/1/Add.47.

[253] The HRC underlined once again during its consideration of the third periodic report from Jordan the obligation for the Government to change traditions and customs that hinder the realisation of gender equality in the country. IHRR 1995, Vol. 2, No. 1, pp. 161–163.

[254] HRC, 56th session, March–April 1996, UN Doc. HRI/CORE/1/Add.22/Rev.1.

the Covenant.[255] At its 55th session the HRC reviewed Sweden's fourth periodic report.[256] The Committee noted that there remain areas where women are subject to *de facto* discrimination, in particular with regard to equality remuneration. The members of the Committee were also concerned that, despite guarantees of equality in the Constitution of the Russian Federation and in labour legislation, the *de facto* situation of women is one of continuing inequality.[257] The failure to ensure equal remuneration for work of comparable worth and the persistence of attitudes and practices which impose child-rearing and other domestic responsibilities entirely on women, contribute to this inequality and to discrimination in the work place. During its session in March 1995 the HRC expressed its satisfaction to the USA delegation in regard to the statement of understanding made by the Government at the time of ratification of the Covenant that the principle of non-discrimination is construed by the Government as not permitting distinctions among the sexes which would not be legitimate under that treaty.[258] On the other hand, the Committee emphasised in its recommendations the need for the Government to increase its effort to prevent and eliminate persisting discriminatory attitudes and prejudice against women including, where appropriate, through the adoption of affirmative action. It hoped also that, when determining whether at that time (1995) permitted affirmative action programmes for women should be withdrawn, the obligation to provide Covenant's rights in fact as well as in law should be borne in mind.[259]

In addition, the HRC has in recent years considered protection of women against violence in the context of gender equality. The Committee recommended the Italian Government,[260] the Government of Slovenia,[261] the Government of the UK and Northern Ireland[262] and Nepal[263] after concluding the review of their periodical reports to ensure that women are protected from all kind of violence. During its 57th and 58th sessions (1996), which took place in Geneva, the HRC recognised the uniqueness of the Nigeria's cultural and religious traditions and practices but

---

[255] UN Doc. A/50/40; A/CONF.177/9, 21 August 1995, § 8. The Committee has also observed that patriarchal attitudes and behaviour existed in Cyprus, which hindered the realisation of women's rights. IHRR 1995, Vol. 2, No. 1, pp. 172–174. Moreover, the Committee pointed to the representatives of the Government of Sri Lanka during its 54th session in 1995 that the minimum age of twelve years for girls to marry under Muslim law was a source of concern.

[256] UN Doc. CCPR/95/Add. 4.

[257] UN Doc. CCPR/C/79/Add. 54.

[258] UN, Multilateral Treaties Deposited with the Secretary-General, Status as at 31 December 1995, p. 130. The reservation implies that the Government "understands distinctions based upon (s)ex.., as those terms are used in Article 2, paragraph 1 and Article 26, to be permitted when such distinctions are, at minimum, rationally related to a legitimate governmental objective". It further "understands the prohibition in paragraph 1 of Article 4 upon discrimination in time of public emergency, based solely on the status of...(s)ex- not to bar distinctions that may have a disproportionate effect upon persons of a particular status".

[259] UN Doc. CCPR/C/SR. 1401–1402 and SR. 1405–1406, 29–31 March 1995.

[260] IHRR 1995, Vol. 2, No. 1, p. 169.

[261] IHRR 1995, Vol. 2, No. 1, pp. 175–177.

[262] HRC, 54th session, July 1995.

[263] IHRR 1995, Vol. 2, No. 2, p. 431.

stated that such factors must be subservient to the protection of fundamental human rights and could not be used as a justification for denying human rights to women. The Committee raised concern over gender inequalities arising out of practices such as polygamous marriages and the high death rates of women during childbirth and infant mortality.[264] At that session the HRC noted the progress made in Brazil with regard to gender equality, among other things the prohibition of sterilisation certificates which employers had required of women as a prerequisite for employment.[265] Among the Committee's main concerns during its sessions in 1997 was the lack of *de facto* gender equality in Colombia, Bolivia, Georgia and Lebanon. The Committee members expressed dissatisfaction with the persistence in India of practices harmful to females such as foeticide, sati (self-immolation of widows), infanticide and dowry-related violence. The Committee noted, furthermore, that religious norms treat women as second class citizens in the fields of marriage, divorce and inheritance rights.[266]

### *2.3.2.3. Concluding Observations*

In view of the above I may conclude that the HRC has in recent years shown a tendency to be more gender sensitive[267] in its work ( *i.e.*, consideration of periodic reports, formulation of general comments and adopting of views concerning communications),[268] in the sense that it has began to integrate women's issues according to the recommendations of the Vienna Declaration. First of all the Committee has approached both aspects of gender equality (*de iure* as well as *de facto*) especially in the context of examination of country reports. In its earlier work the HRC has emphasised formal/*de iure* rather than substantive/*de facto* discrimination. Until now the HRC has not devoted much effort to discussing reproductive freedom and gender-based violence in the review of country reports. These issues have still to be considered and then hopefully in the context of gender equality. The attention to specific women's issues is still in general uneven. The Committee is very subtle in its concluding observations on the various country reports of the states parties. Nevertheless, it has found in several countries that both aspects of discrimination of women persist and it has urged the states in question to redress these situations. The Committee has also stressed that traditional customs, prejudice and religion are not acceptable as reasonable justification for differential treatment among men and women. Therefore, the meagre case law on that issue is surprising. I may establish that the complaint procedure is a possibility not well used by women yet, espe-

---

[264] UN Doc. CCPR/C/SR. 1505, 13 August 1996.

[265] UN Doc. CCPR/C/SR. 1508, 16 July 1996.

[266] ISHR, Human Rights Monitor 1997, Nos. 39–40, pp. 43 and 45.

[267] It has been maintained, not without reason, that the increased sensitivity to gender issues by the Committee is the result of the increased number of female members. *A. Gallagher*, p. 298.

[268] The HRC itself has characterised its functions under the Covenant with the objective of giving effect to the rights recognised there as "advisory and monitoring" (in the consideration of state reports and in the formulation of general comments), as "inquiring and investigative" (with respect to complaints from individuals) and as "conciliatory" (with respect to communications from states). The United Nations and Human Rights 1945–1995, p. 49.

cially women living in Third World countries. The vast majority of the cases dealing with gender-based discrimination relate to European realities. Many factors obstruct access to the UN complaint procedure. It is obvious, however, that absence of knowledge necessary for the use of that system is a major one. Many countries with a poor record on human rights have, in addition, not yet accepted the individual right to petition.

The small number of communications on gender equality results in the limited value of the case law. The HRC has not yet provided an answer to controversial questions to be dealt with in this study, *e.g.*, procreative rights etc. Neither has the Committee applied the asymmetrical approach to gender equality in its case law. On the contrary a predominant feature of the case law reviewed here is the HRCs' preference for a formal interpretation of the principle of equality and non-discrimination. There is a tendency for the HRC to concentrate on the examination of circumstances for when a differential treatment of various persons or groups of persons is permissible or discriminatory (*i.e.*, differential treatment constitutes discrimination only when it is not based on reasonable and objective criteria) rather than to look at the discriminatory effects of the laws, which were perceived as gender neutral. The views of the Committee, as for example, in some of the Dutch cases, reflect often outmoded assumptions about women's role in society. In other words, the HRC has not taken gender disadvantage as a starting point in its analysis of equality for which it has been rightly criticised in the literature.[269] On the other hand, the decisions on individual cases dealing with violations of Article 26 imply an interpretation of the prohibition of discrimination to include an obligation for the states parties in their national laws to ban all forms of discrimination.[270] The Committee has shown also willingness to deal with gender equality issues in a creative way. It has taken the standpoint that equal and effective protection against discrimination is an autonomous right and it has extended it to economic, social and cultural rights, which indeed are of great importance to women, that might be of relevance, *e.g.*, the right to health and access to procreative services. Moreover, its General Comment on non-discrimination constitutes advancement in that it brings a modern understanding of equality, *i.e.*, as requiring substantive equality to be brought into focus. The Committee confirmed its dynamic approach towards the principle of equality in its understanding of Article 26 as prohibiting discrimination "in law and in fact in any field regulated and protected by public authorities".[271] The Committee has also been progressive in that it requires governments to redress *de facto* equality and reminds them of their obligation to undertake affirmative action, if needed, to ensure the positive enjoyment of the guaranteed rights. However, earlier formulated general comments relating to among others the right to life and the prohibition of torture should be up dated in order to better take account of women's needs. The General Comment

---

[269] *A.F. Bayefsky*, pp. 5 and 10, referring to the *P.P.C. v. The Netherlands* case, (Communication No. 212/1986, UN Doc. A/43/40, p. 244, § 6.2.) where the HRC explicitly stated that the scope of Article 26 did not extend to equality in result.

[270] *M. Nowak*, CCPR-Kommentar, p. 505.

[271] UN Doc. HRI/GEN/1/Rev.1, p. 28, § 12.

No. 19 on Article 23 is also disappointing because of its very weak language and its lack of analysis of the obstacles for achieving gender equality within family structures. It lacks, furthermore, comment as to how the HRC views the use of new reproductive techniques. Better integration of gender perspective in the work of the HRC is consequently needed as well as a greater consistency between its general comments, case law and comments on country reports.

### *2.3.3. The Committee on Economic, Social and Cultural Rights*

The Committee on Economic, Social and Cultural Rights (CESCR) was established by ECOSOC in 1985 to monitor the application of the ICESCR.[272] International supervision of states parties to the Covenant is accomplished primarily through periodic reports from the states on their compliance with duties under the treaty. The Committee studies them and makes general observations on them. The consideration of reports by the Committee is a process aiming at the creation of "a deeper awareness and understanding" of the provisions of the Covenant.[273]

In addition to examining reports from state parties, the Committee also makes general comments on the scope and meaning of the provisions of the Covenant.[274] The fundamental principle of indivisibility and interdependence of all the rights defined in the two Covenants has consistently been affirmed by the various international bodies. It constitutes a part of the current doctrine relating to human rights. The Vienna Declaration urges the world community to treat human rights globally in an equal manner on the same footing and with the same emphasis. Still there is a difference in structure of implementation between the two sets of rights contained in both Covenants. The existence of two different regimes for the two

---

[272] The GA adopted the ICESCR on 16th December 1966. As of 24 June 1998, 137 states were parties to the Covenant. The supervisory organ of the Covenant was composed initially of delegates to ECOSOC and subsequently of governmental experts. Due to dissatisfaction with its work, the Council decided to replace it with an Expert Committee on the implementation of the Covenant similar to the HRC. That Committee has been in existence since 1987. For a general background to the creation of the CESCR and its principle activities see *P. Alston*, The Committee on Economic, Social and Cultural Rights, pp. 473–509. For an overview and historical background of economic and social rights see *H.J. Steiner & P. Alston* (eds.), International Human Rights in Context, Oxford 1996, pp. 256–323. See also *M. Craven*, The International Covenant on Economic, Social and Cultural Rights: A Perspective on Its Development, Oxford 1995; *A. Eide, C. Krause & A. Rosas* (eds.), Economic, Social and Cultural Rights, Dordrecht 1995.

[273] *P. Alston*, The International Covenant on Economic, Social and Cultural Rights, in Manual on Human Rights Reporting under Six Major International Human Rights Instruments, New York 1991, p. 73.

[274] The Committee began as from its 3rd session the preparation of general comments with a view to assisting the states parties fulfil their reporting obligations. For the text of the six general comments adopted by the CESCR as of January 1996 see IHRR 1996, Vol. 3, pp. 79–103. The general comments make up not only "a strong body of jurisprudential insights" into the various provisions of the Covenant, but in the case of the CESCR also "a means of laying down some solid foundations for the future development of its jurisprudence". *P. Alston*, The Committee on Economic, Social and Cultural Rights, p. 494.

categories of rights "reflect the traditional perception that these rights are essentially different from each other".[275] However, recent developments in this regard are evidential of a change of attitudes towards greater emphasis on the indivisibility of rights.[276]

The CESCR functions very much like the HRC. It has, however, adopted a somewhat new approach to the reporting procedure, by conducting a "much more adversarial type of dialogue with representatives of governments".[277] The Committee receives, moreover, information from a wide range of sources. It encourages active participation from NGOs and IGOs in its sessions and it has agreed to the principle of considering at least one non-reporting state at each of its sessions etc.[278] This is of significance for the current focus that the Committee places upon assessing inadequacies in, or concern about, the performance of countries party to the treaty, "since most of the reports, which are submitted are very superficial and appear to be designed to camouflage rather than to reveal problems".[279]

The CESCR elaborates on rights, the content of which overlap with some rights contained in the ICCPR. According to Professor Alston, who is the current chair of the CESCR, discrimination may be understood "to cover any distinction, exclusion, restriction or preference, which is based on any ground such as... (s)ex, and which has the purpose or effect of nullifying or impairing the recognition, enjoyment or exercise by all persons, on an equal footing, or all of the rights set forth in the Covenant".[280]

The CESCR has interpreted Articles 2(2) and 3 as requiring both measures to prevent discrimination and positive measures, which may include affirmative action, in order to compensate for past discrimination and to correct *de facto* discrimination.[281]

---

[275] *M. Pellonpää*, Economic, Social and Cultural Rights, in The European System for the Protection of Human Rights, R.St.J. Macdonald, F. Matscher & H. Petzold (eds.), Dordrecht 1993, p. 858.

[276] An optional protocol has been, however, under consideration by the CESCR since its fifth session. By ratifying such an optional protocol, a state party would recognise the competence of the Committee to receive communications from individuals or groups alleging that their rights under the Covenant had been violated. The deliberations on this matter were concluded by the CESCR at its 15th session in 1996 and a final report was forwarded to the Commission on Human Rights. UN Doc. E/CN.4/1997/105. Several governments have commented upon this protocol. UN Doc. E/CN.4/1998/84.

[277] *M. Nowak*, The Need for an Optional Protocol to the International Convention on Economic, Social and Cultural Rights, The Review, December 1995, No. 55, p. 155; *D. Matas*, Economic, Social and Cultural Rights and the Role of Lawyers: North American Perspectives, The Review, December 1995, No. 55, p. 129.

[278] NGOs, irrespective of consultative status, are urged to address the Committee on the first afternoon of each session. At the 14th session, a one day informal session was held where representatives of NGOs presented their views. In addition, the Committee has invited a variety of experts who have a particular interest in, and knowledge of, some of the issues under review, to contribute to its discussion.

[279] *A.R. Chapman*, A New Approach to Monitoring the International Covenant on Economic, Social and Cultural Rights, The Review, December 1995, No. 55, p. 25.

[280] *P. Alston*, The Purposes of Reporting, in Manual on Human Rights Reporting, UN New York 1991, p. 47.

[281] *P. Alston*, ibid., pp. 47–48.

The Committee pays particular attention to the measures undertaken by states parties to ensure the equal rights of men and women to the enjoyment of all economic, social and cultural rights set forth in Articles 6 to 15 of the ICESCR. The Committee has since its establishment requested gender-specific data from governments and it requires them to provide information on both the *de iure*[282] and *de facto* situation of women with respect to, among others, rights to marriage and family (Article 10) and the right to health (Article 12). The Committee expressed concern at its 13th session in 1995[283] about the *de facto* situation of women in Portugal with regard to the right of equal treatment at work and the right to equal remuneration.[284] Similar concern was expressed one year later at its 14th session with regard to the periodic report presented by Spain. The Committee noted that there was an extremely high unemployment rate in Spain, particularly among women and the existence of discrimination against them regarding the right to equal pay. On the other hand, members of the Committee welcomed in 1996 the measures taken by the Finnish Government to outlaw gender-based discrimination in all sectors and especially the criminalisation of marital rape. The CESCR found it in its suggestions and recommendations extremely troubling that many forms of discrimination existed in Algeria, in particular as they are often contained in the legislation.[285] The CESCR discussed the treatment of men and women in matters of marriage and it noted that the right to choose freely a spouse is not fully guaranteed to Algerian women. The violence exercised against women within the family is a source of profound concern to the Committee since the problem is not sufficiently addressed by the authorities in terms of either prevention or punishment.

The Committee underlined in its suggestions that it considers it to be of "utmost importance"[286] that special attention be given to the problem of discrimination against women.

---

[282] In regard to the implementation of Article 10 of the Covenant, the Committee expects reports to indicate the existence of any constraints of a formal or informal nature, of the ability of intending spouses to exercise their free consent in regard to marriage. The Committee noted, for example, during the consideration of the report presented by Suriname that there is inconsistency in the fact that while young persons attain majority at the age of 21, men may marry from the age of 15 and women from the age of 13. In the Committee's view the difference in the marriageable ages for men and women did not appear to conform with the provisions of Article 2 and 10 of the Covenant. Moreover, the Committee expressed its deep concern about the possibility under Surinamese law that a marriage partner may be appointed without his or her consent, which in general appears to affect women more disadvantageously than men. The Committee urged the Government in its general suggestions and recommendations that laws permitting persons to marry without the acknowledgement or consent of the other partner be abolished and that the problem of violence against women be legally addressed. UN Doc. E/C.12/1995/18, §§ 159 and 164. The Committee recommended likewise the Byelorussian delegation during the consideration of its second periodic report in 1996 to review its legislation in order to bring it into conformity with the Covenant at all levels and to combat discrimination against women.

[283] CESCR report on the 12th and 13th session UN Doc. E/C.12/1995/18; E/1996/22.

[284] UN Doc. E/C.12/1995/18, § 94.

[285] UN Doc. E/C.12/1995/18, § 293.

[286] *Supra*, § 299.

Other examples of violations reflecting discriminatory policies and actions by states parties include among others lack of reproductive health services in primary care. It has become clear through the consideration of the periodic reports that women's health needs are rarely given equal resources. In many parts of the world women bear an undue proportion of health problems and discrimination is a frequent cause of the violation of the right to health.[287] As examples of the violation of Article 12 (the right to health) of the Covenant reference has been made to the coercive birth control practices, including abortions and large-scale sterilisation, being carried out in several Asian countries.[288]

As a further illustration of the Committee's concern with issues related to gender equality (aspects that are of relevance to our study), I shall refer to the consideration of a few country reports. Reviewing the initial report of the Philippines at its 12th session in 1994,[289] the Committee discussed issues of concern under the right to health as, for example, the lack of campaign on family planning. It recommended also the creation of stronger judicial and other remedies to redress the grievances of women who suffer from domestic violence.

One year later during its 13th session in 1995 the Committee expressed concern over reported domestic violence against women this time in Norway[290] and in Mauritius.[291] Especial attention was given to the rise in teenage pregnancy, the prohibition of abortion by law, and the high rate of suicide in Mauritius.

During its 16th session in 1997 the CESCR discussed abortion, female circumcision and prostitution in the context of gender equality when reviewing the report of Libya.

In summarising I may affirm that the CESCR has shown some sensitivity by incorporating gender perspectives into its work. The list of issues and questions that have been raised during the consideration of periodic reports and the concluding observations on states parties reports support this assertion.[292] However, the lack of clarity as to the definition and scope of these rights and obligations of states parties as enunciated in the ICESCR have hampered implementation and monitoring of the relevant, for this study, economic and social rights. The right to health has yet to be conceptualised in a gender perspective.[293] While the Committee has

---

[287] *V.A. Leary*, Justiacibility and Beyond: Complaint Procedures and the Right to Health, The Review, December 1995, No. 55, p. 120.

[288] *A.R. Chapman*, p. 34.

[289] UN Doc. E/C.12/1995/18, §§ 111, 129.

[290] UN Doc. E/C.12/1995/18, § 225.

[291] UN Doc. E/C,12/1994/20, §§ 172, 180 and UN Doc. E/C.12/1995/18, § 245.

[292] In addition, it should be mentioned that the Committee decided at its session in 1996 to appoint two of its members to study the desirability of reviewing the reporting guidelines in order to take into account the recommendations made during recent UN Conferences like the Cairo and the Beijing world conferences. *A. Gallagher*, p. 302.

[293] The link between the right to reproductive choice and the right to health has been explored by *C.A.A. Packer*, pp. 5–6. For a discussion on the content of the right to health in a gender perspective see *R.J. Cook*, Human Rights in relation to Women's Health, WHO 1993. *A.R. Chapman*, The Minimum Core Content of the Right to Health, AAAS, Washington D.C., December 1997, forthcoming

been very creative in suggesting that Article 12 encompasses the right to a safe and healthy environment, even though the Covenant does not explicitly recognise a right to environmental well-being as such,[294] the Committee has avoided discussing reproductive freedom in a broad manner in the context of the right to health. Neither has the Committee formulated a general comment setting the parameters for its interpretation of this, for women, so important provision. One explanation might be that the CESCR still consists of only two women out of eighteen members. This leads us to the conclusion that the CESCR has to face formidable challenges on the eve of the 21st century.

### *2.3.4. The Committee on the Rights of the Child*

The Committee on the Rights of the Child (CRC) is a special monitoring body that has been set up under the UN Convention on the Rights of the Child to oversee state compliance with the provisions of the Convention.[295] In 1998 eight out of ten members of the Committee were women. The Conference of the states parties to the Convention decided on 12 December 1995 to enlarge the membership of the Committee to 18 experts.[296] Governments that have ratified the treaty have pledged to report periodically on their performance of conventional obligations. The CRC may deliver proposals and general recommendations on the basis of the information it has received. Among the most frequently voiced criticisms of the CRC is that it has never issued a General Comment. Therefore, the Committee decided at its 16th session in 1997 to begin to draft General Comments.

---

[294] *P. Alston*, The Purposes of Reporting, p. 65.

[295] The Convention on the Rights of the Child was unanimously adopted by the UN General Assembly on 20 November 1989. As of December 1998, 191 states had ratified or acceded to the Convention. The Convention is, thus, unique in the response it has met. It has almost universally been ratified, and this suggests that it reflects emerging customary law. A disadvantageous fact is, however, that the Convention does not contain any provision for individual or inter-state complaints. The only implementation mechanism is the reporting procedure referred to in Article 44. States are obliged to submit an initial report on measures they have adopted to give effect to the rights guaranteed under the Convention within two years of its entry into force in the state concern. Thereafter, periodic reports must be submitted every five years.

Several authors, among them Geraldin Van Bueren, have suggested that further improvement of the system of protection of children's rights can be achieved by the adoption of an additional protocol to the Convention comprising a right of individual petition. In her view, extending the right to petition "would be both egalitarian and evolutionary". *G. Van Bueren*, p. 411. The CRC can though exceptionally raise a significant case, through its urgent procedure, and has in fact done so in a couple of instances. *T. Hammarberg*, Making Reality of the Rights of the Child, Jönköping 1996, p. 18. Generally on the rights of the child see: *P. Alston, S. Parker & J. Seymor*, Children's Rights and The Law, Oxford 1992; *M. Freeman & P. Veerman*, The Ideologies of Children's Rights, Dordrecht 1992; *M. Freeman* (ed.), Children's Rights: A Comparative Perspective, Dartmouth 1996; *UNICEF*, The Implementation Handbook for the Convention on the Rights of the Child, Geneva 1998.

[296] The GA endorsed the enlargement at its 1995 session. To enter into force, the amendment must be approved by two thirds of the state parties.

A number of the activities of the Committee concerning the implementation of the Convention have a direct bearing on issues of gender equality, because the human rights of the girl child are also under the protection of the Convention. Already at the beginning of its existence the CRC agreed during the discussion on its methods of work in respect of the consideration of reports, that "the gender issue was extremely important and the Committee should aim at understanding the causes of the marked differences between data for boys and girls".[297] Nowadays the Committee co-operates with other human rights bodies. One of its members follows the activities carried out by CEDAW and informs the CRC on main developments. The CRC has been holding since 1993 general, thematic discussions, *e.g.*, on the rights of the girl,[298] about once a year. The results of these meetings may serve as a basis for the work on interpreting the articles of the Convention and they may also lead to a request for a UN study on a specific topic.

One general principle, as identified by the Committee, is that all children should enjoy their rights, *i.e.*, that no child should suffer discrimination. Article 2 of the Convention states that non-discrimination applies to all of the rights set forth in it. The Committee has often emphasised in its suggestions and recommendations to the states parties that the principle of non-discrimination, as provided in Article 2, must be vigorously applied, and that an "active approach should be taken to eliminate discrimination against certain groups of children, most notably girl children".[300] In the view of the CRC the application of this principle should not depend upon budgetary resources.

In the process of the examination of state reports, the CRC has discussed various aspects of significance for the *de iure* and *de facto* situation of the girl-child. When considering reports submitted by states parties, the Committee has often stressed the need for concerted efforts on specific problems, such as discrimination against the girl child, among others discrimination in inheritance,[301] early marriage,[302]

---

297 UN Doc. CRC/C/1991/SR.12, 10 October 1991, § 10.

298 See UN Doc. CRC/C/38, 1995.

299 *T. Hammarberg*, p. 18.

300 UN Doc. A/49/41, 1994, § 43.

301 The CRC found the legislation in the United Republic of Tanzania as discriminatory against women and girls in matters of inheritance since boys are heirs in the first and second degree and girls are of the third degree only. They are not allowed to inherit clan land or their parent's estate. UN Doc. CRC/C/8/Add.14 ,1 June 1994, p. 8, § 31.

302 The Committee has on several occasions emphasised that there is a clear sexist reasoning behind the higher age limit for males in regard to marriageable age. Thus, it was assumed that the male would be the provider and the head of the household and therefore require greater physical and emotional maturity, whereas the basic role of the female was to carry out domestic chores and to reproduce. UN Doc. CRC/C/SR.54, 21 January 1993, p. 2, § 5. The Committee underlined during its 11th and 12th sessions in 1996 that the girl child is subjected to discrimination if she is subject to a lower marriageable age. The CRC recommended, *e.g.*, the Government of Yemen to ensure that its domestic laws are fully compatible with the Convention and are non-discriminatory. For that reason the marriageable age for boys and girls should be the same. UN Doc. CRC/C/15/Add.21, 25 April 1994. The same view was expressed in regard to the legal and *de facto* situation in Guatemala. The persistence of traditional practices and attitudes on matters, such as early marriage in Cyprus and in Lebanon, were also considered as

maternal health care, early pregnancies,[303] family planning education[304] and services, the sale and trafficking of children[305] etc. Such concerns, as well as suggestions for different measures are reflected in the concluding observations adopted by the Committee at the very end of the monitoring process. They constitute authoritative statements of the Committee's findings. Even though their legal value is not equal to a judgement of a human rights court, they have impact on states behaviour,

---

contrary to the Convention. The CRC found during the consideration of the initial report of Morocco in 1996 (UN Doc. CRC/C/15/Add. 60) that the early marriageable age and the fact that it is lower for girls than for boys constitutes a lack of conformity with the Convention. The Committee made similar remarks upon reviewing the report from Uruguay. In the view of the CRC a low age of marriage for girls tended to have a discriminatory effect on them since they could be under pressure to marry, to the detriment of their education and possible future careers. UN Doc. CRC/C/SR.140, 14 April 1994, p. 4, § 16. See in addition the CRC recommendations to the Government of Indonesia, UN Doc. CRC/C/15/Add.7, 18 October 1993, p. 2, § 10; UN Doc. A/49/41, 1994, p. 36, § 135. In other words, in the view of the Committee biological development should not be the only criterion for marriage. Marriage also requires the partners to have reached a degree of maturity and judgement to enable them to act responsibly within society.

[303] Another source of concern for the CRC is the increasing number of pregnant adolescents and single mothers especially in Latin America, for example, in Colombia. See UN Doc. CRC/C.SR.115, p. 4, § 15. The high rate of early pregnancy in Uruguay, the existence of which became apparent during the consideration of its initial report in 1996 by the CRC, was a source for real concern. The Committee has established in the case of Costa Rica that the main causes of abandonment of children included teenage pregnancy. The high number of teenage pregnancies as a result of early sexual activity was seen as "symptomatic of underlying social problems". UN Doc. A/49/41, 1994, p. 46, § 220; UN Doc. CRC/C/SR.92, 5 October 1993, p. 11, § 61. Teenage pregnancies and their negative impact on girls were underlined by the CRC in its recommendations to the Government of Namibia (UN Doc. CRC/C/15/Add. 14, 7 February 1994, p. 2, § 8) and at its 16th session in 1997 in regard to the situation in Trinidad & Tobago, Togo, Laos, Uganda and the Czech Republic.

[304] The CRC considered that greater efforts should be made by the Government of Romania to provide family education, to develop awareness of the equal responsibilities of parents, to disseminate widely knowledge about modern methods of family planning and thereby to reduce the practice of abortion. UN Doc. CRC/C/15/Add. 16, 7 February 1994, p. 3, § 15. Also in the case of Colombia the Committee underlined the importance of counselling services for young people as a preventive measure aimed at lowering the high incidence of teenage pregnancies. UN Doc. CRC/C/15/Add. 15, 7 February 1994, p. 3, § 15. See also the CRC Suggestions and Recommendations to the Government of Costa Rica: UN Doc. CRC/C/15/Add. 11, 18 October 1993, p. 3, § 16.

[305] In Article 35 of the Convention the state parties are compelled to take all measures to prevent the sale or trafficking in children for any purpose or in any form. See UN Doc. A/49/41, 1994, p. 22, § 39. In regard to the situation in China and in Nepal the Committee condemned the practice of selective infanticide, trafficking, sale and kidnapping of girls and son preference. See UN Doc. CRC/C/15/Add. 57, 1996. The Committee urged China to design its family planning policy in a manner so as to avoid any threat to the life of children, particularly girls. The CRC recommended, furthermore, that "clear guidance be given to the population and the personnel involved in the family planning policy" to ensure that the aims it promotes are in accordance with the principles of the Convention. The Committee acknowledged the information provided by the Chinese Government including that the non-registration of new-born girls constitutes a major factor contributing to the imbalance in the ratio of boys and girls. At the same time the Committee pointed out that deficiencies in the registration system lead to children being deprived of basic safeguards for the protection of their rights, including in the areas of child trafficking, sale and maltreatment, abuse or neglect. UN Doc. CRC/C/SR. 298–300, 28 May 1996, IHHR 1997, Vol. 4, pp. 207–210. See for further examples on that issue the records of the 13th session of the CRC regarding the review of the initial report of Nigeria. UN Doc. CRC/C/15/Add. 61, 1996.

*e.g.*, can lead to improved observance and better realisation of human rights norms. In addition, there is a clear linkage on violation of the Convention and development aid.[306] Many donor countries, thus, use implementation of the Convention as an instrument in its negotiations concerning aid. States parties are frequently requested with regard to Article 2 of the Convention to identify specific and concrete measures taken to combat discrimination against girls, including measures to eliminate and prevent discriminatory attitudes and prejudices.[307] The Committee recommended, for example, the government of El Salvador in its concluding observations to the consideration of its report to undertake strategies and educational programmes along with dissemination of information in order to counter certain prejudices which affect children negatively, such as "gender-based discrimination (known as 'machismo')".[308]

In its 1995 report[309] the CRC expressed concern about issues related to gender-based discrimination in a number of countries, such as Bolivia, Viet Nam, the Russian Federation, Egypt, El Salvador, Indonesia, Romania, Sudan and Pakistan. A major effort was recommended to widen educational campaigns so that they focus on substantive gender equality and the role of parents in the prevention of gender-based violence and abuse in the family. During its general discussion of the girl child on 22 January 1995, the CRC fully recognised that gender inequality was mainly caused by discrimination, the persistence of traditions and prejudices, neglect, exploitation and violence. The Committee emphasised the importance of the complementary and mutually reinforcing nature of the Convention and the Women's Convention at international and national levels.

The Convention on the Rights of the Child also establishes the basic right of the child, wherever possible, to know his/her parents (Article 7). The right to know one's origin is a specific aspect of the right to an identity. Without such a right the child would be deprived of the possibility of having "a true conception of himself".[310] On this ground there is a growing body of opinion, which recognises the need for children to seek and receive information about their origins. It has been argued that the only method to preserve their identity is to have complete knowledge of that identity (genetic and biological), including that of their genetic antecedents.[311] However,

---

[306] On the basis of Article 45(b) of the Convention, the CRC shall transmit requests for assistance to the specialised UN agencies, UNICEF and other competent bodies. See also *T. Hammarberg*, p. 19.

[307] UN Doc. CRC/C/SR.113, 21 January 1994, p. 11, § 35.

[308] UN Doc. CRC/C/15/Add. 9, 18 October 1993, p. 3, § 18.

[309] UN Doc. A/49/41.

[310] *L. Nielsen*, The Right to a Child versus the Rights of a Child, in Parenthood in Modern Society, J. Eekelaar & P. Sarcevic (eds.), Dordrecht 1993, p. 218. See Part II of this study.

[311] *G. Van Bueren*, p. 122. This argument has been advanced in the context of children's right to obtain access to their adoption records. In the view of the present author, despite some differences between adoption and artificial reproduction in the factual situation, the above mentioned reasoning can, by analogy, successfully be applied to AID (artificial insemination by donor), *i.e.*, also in the context of children conceived with the help of the new procreative techniques. G.Van Bueren has also taken the position that the right of children who are born by AID to the name of the genetic donors is similar and "equally compelling" to the rights of adopted children to have access to the identity of their biological parents. Ibid., p. 126.

there are a few situations where this is not possible, among others when a child is conceived by donation. State practice on this particular matter is not consistent. In several countries the identity of the donor is kept secret. The CRC has dealt with the possible contradiction between the provision of the Convention establishing the right of a child to know his or her origins with the policy of Norway in relation to artificial insemination, namely keeping the identity of sperm donors secret.[312] This is also of relevance for the legal situation in other countries, which upheld similar rules. The French report, for example, declares that their domestic legislation allows the child access to his/her origins, without making such access an absolute right. In the view of the French authorities this is not in contradiction to Article 7 of the Convention, which grants the child the right to know his parents, but "only as far as possible".[313] One of the cases referred to when the minor will encounter an obstacle is when there has been medically-assisted procreation with a third party donor. The standard practice, which is confirmed in the French bill of bioethics, guarantees the anonymity of the donor. It is argued that it is in the interest of everyone, the donor, so as to avoid any actions against him, the couples, who have recourse to these procedures, might find that the practice would become rarer if the identity of the donors could be revealed, and the child, "who should be a child like any other without having to face problems of a dual relationship".[314] Some of the members of the CRC seemed to be sceptical as to the validity of these arguments during the consideration of that report and the Swedish legal solution, *i.e.,* the law does not provide for anonymity of sperm donors, was given as an example of how this complex issue could be regulated. The representative of France agreed that there are indeed different opinions also in France and therefore the issue was at that time under debate in the Parliament.[315] It is disappointing that the CRC has not expressed itself in a more categorical manner with regard to the issue of balancing of the conflicting rights and how to weight the donor's right to privacy against the child's right to seek and receive information which is necessary for the preservation of its identity. On the other hand, my earlier cited examples show that the CRC has taken up a great number of issues which are suspect under the non-discrimination principle and which are not expressly regulated by the Convention. The Convention does not, for example, prohibit *verbatim* early marriages as Article 21 of the African Charter on the Rights and Welfare of the Child[316] does. However, the CRC has on several occasions pointed out how harmful child marriage can be for the child's growth and development. The Committee has frequently declared that the lower minimum age for marriage is discriminatory and as a result deprives girls of the benefit of other protections afforded by the Convention. This allows us to agree with the general perception of the CRC as being

---

[312] UN Doc. CRC/C/15/Add. 23, 23 April 1994, p. 2, § 10.

[313] UN Doc. CRC/C/3/Add. 15, 4 June 1993, p. 31, § 197.

[314] *Supra*, § 198.

[315] See UN Doc. CRC/C/SR.150, 14 April 1994 and UN Doc. CRC/C/SR. 141, 15 April 1994, § 18.

[316] For the legislative background of this treaty see *G. Van Bueren*, The African Charter on the Rights and Welfare of the Child: A New Children's Treaty, International Children's Rights Monitor 1991, Vol. 8, p. 20 ff.

one of the "more gender-sensitive" UN Committees.[317] Its understanding of gender equality includes a substantive element and in its activities the CRC has looked beyond *de iure* discrimination to *de facto* discrimination of girls.

### *2.3.5. The Committee on the Elimination of All Forms of Discrimination against Women (CEDAW)*

#### *2.3.5.1. General Background*

The fifth part (Articles 17–22) of the Women's Convention contains provisions on the supervisory system. A Committee on the Elimination of Discrimination against Women was established under Article 17 of the Convention. It consists of 23 experts of high moral standing and competence in the fields covered by the Convention.[318] The main mandate of CEDAW is consideration of the reports of states parties in accordance with Article 18 of the Convention. Countries which have ratified or acceded to the Convention (as of October 1998 their number is 161)[319] must submit a national report, initially within one year of signing, and then at least every four years, on measures to ensure women's equality with men in the political, social and cultural life and on progress made in its implementation. This treaty does not provide for the submission of complaints either by states or individuals. There is subsequently no body of jurisprudence elaborating upon the scope and content of the various treaty provisions and which can be used as guide-lines in its interpretation. It should be, however, mentioned that ECOSOC has now adopted CEDAW's suggestion No. 7 of 1995 on elements for an optional protocol. The CSW started the drafting of the protocol in March 1996[320] and in March 1997 it

---

[317] *A. Gallagher*, p. 302.

[318] The Committee has been, with one exception (the Swedish member Mr. J. Nordenfelt, during the years 1982–1984) an all-female committee. It has been argued on this background that the composition of CEDAW has caused some tensions between the Committee and the states representatives who, often, are male. Thus, the questions and questioners have become adverse in nature, as a result of which the representatives of states parties have felt victimised and have responded defensively. *R. Jacobson*, The Committee on the Elimination of Discrimination against Women, in The United Nations and Human Rights, P. Alston (ed.), p. 459. On the other hand, only about half of the experts who have served as CEDAW members are lawyers in contrast to other human rights supervisory organs. See International Human Rights in Context, Law, Politics, Morals, *H.J. Steiner & P. Alston* (eds.), p. 912; CEDAW/C/1995/7, § 172.

[319] The Beijing Platform for Action sets a goal of universal ratification of the Women's Convention by the year 2000. The United Nations and The Advancement of Women 1945–1996, p. 67.

[320] Report of CEDAW, 15th session 1996, GA 51st session, suppl. No. 38 (A/51/38). A formal proposal for the establishment of a petition procedure, through an optional protocol, was made at the Vienna Conference in 1993 and the Vienna Declaration and Programme of Action mandated CSW to draft an optional protocol for complaints under the Convention. Thereafter the Platform of Action that was adopted at the Beijing Conference requested Governments to support the process initiated by the CSW with the view of elaborating such a protocol and with the aim of its entering into force as soon as possible. See UN Doc. A/CONF.157/23, § 40 and UN Doc. A/CONF.177/20, Chapter I, Annex II, Sec. I, § 230(k). See also *T. Meron*, Enhancing the Effectiveness of the Prohibition of Discrimination against Women, AJIL 1990, Vol. 84, p. 216; *A. Byrnes*, CEDAW's 10th session, NQHR 1991, Vol. 3, p. 353 and the Report of the Secretary-General, Elaborating of a draft Optional Protocol to the Convention on the Elimination of All Forms of Discrimination against Women, UN Doc. E/CN.6/1996/10.

completed a first reading of a draft optional protocol. Several commentators, among them Andrew Byrnes, suggest that despite the fact that there are still many important issues to be resolved, there is a real prospect that the drafting of an optional protocol to the Women's Convention will be completed by 1998/99.[321] This would undoubtedly be a major step forward in bringing clarity to the normative content of the treaty through the development of detailed jurisprudence of the Convention in reply to complaints or petitions. CEDAW has consequently at present no formal power to interpret the Women's Convention authoritatively but in the course of its work implicitly.[322] The interpretation of some of the provisions contained therein is reflected in the questions of CEDAW members to the representatives of state parties during the consideration of their periodic reports.[323]

### *2.3.5.2. Monitoring the Women's Convention*

The Committee examines the national reports in public meetings at which government representatives are present. Thus, after a state party has presented its written report to CEDAW, members may ask questions, request additional information, or seek clarification on a range of subjects. The most frequently asked question concerns the lack of adequate statistical data in the reports since in most cases they reproduce the existing national legislation (constitutional and other provisions relating to non-discrimination) which provides only a partial view of the situation of women in that country.[324] The Convention requires the eradication also of *de facto* discrimination and without figures on the actual situation of women, *de facto* discrimination remains invisible. The Committee noted, for example, during the consideration of the Chilean report that in the discussion of the implementation of the articles contained in the Convention, more attention was given to responses having to do with legal and normative provisions, and not enough information was pro-

---

321 *A. Byrnes*, Slow and steady wins the race? The development of an optional protocol to the Women's Convention, paper presented at the 91st Annual Meeting of the ASIL, Washington D.C. April 1997, p. 1. For a general review on the background to the development of the protocol see *A. Byrnes & J. Connors*, Enforcing the Human Rights of Women: A Complaints Procedure for the Convention on the Elimination of All Forms of Discrimination against Women, Brooklyn Journal of International Law 1996, Vol. 23, p. 679 ff.; The United Nations and the Advancement of Women 1945–1996, p. 54. It may be noted here that the Chairperson of the Open-ended Working Group on the Elaboration of a Draft Optional Protocol to the Women's Convention, introduced the draft report of the group to the CSW in 1998. A revised draft optional protocol and an enabling resolution were adopted, however, at the 2nd and 3rd meetings of the WG on 11 March 1999. UN Doc. E/CN.6/1999/WG/L.1/Add.1.

322 *A. Byrnes*, The "Other" Human Treaty Body: The Work of the Committee on the Elimination of Discrimination against Women, Yale Journal of International Law 1989, Vol. 14, p. 46.

323 CEDAW has suggested that "by looking at the questions asked and raised over time by the Committee under the various articles during the constructive dialogue, its views about the nature of the State Parties' obligations under the Convention will emerge". UN Doc. CEDAW/C/1995/7, § 305.

324 *R. Jacobson*, p. 461; *K. Tomaševski*, Women and Human Rights, p. 122. States parties' non-compliance with reporting obligations has been a concern of the Committee for many years. As of 3 February 1999, about 165 reports were overdue. This is really a critical and intolerable situation since reviewing national reports is for the time being the only way for CEDAW to monitor states compliance with their treaty obligations.

vided on concrete actions. This made it impossible to determine the extent of the gap between *de facto* and *de iure* equality.[325] As has been outlined in the preceding section 2.2.2.2., the definition of discrimination according to the Women's Convention differs from the ones in other treaties in the sense that it deals with discrimination directed against women rather than discrimination on the basis of sex. In other words, the Women's Convention does not address discriminatory practices experienced by men.[326] Article 1 of the Women's Convention is the universally accepted definition on what constitutes discrimination against women. The definition is very extensive and comprises a broad range of issues as well as substantial equality.

At the end of the consideration of the national reports CEDAW presents concluding comments (suggestions and recommendations) on reports of individual states.[327] They are included in the Committee's annual report to the General Assembly. The comments are designed to highlight the most important points raised during the dialogue and identify particular areas of progress as well as issues of concern on which the Committee wishes the state party to report in its next periodic report. Below I have selected for illustrative purposes some comments made by CEDAW to selected countries, which indicate the variety of ways in which the principle of gender equality is to be implemented, especially in areas of relevance to my study.[328] A basic feature of the Convention is that women must be as free as men to make choices in such areas as marriage and family life, including reproduction. CEDAW monitors developments in states parties with regard to abortion for example. It habitually raises questions about the laws in place and whether illegal abortions are performed. Moreover, the Committee inquires about the health impact on women and about measures in place, or planned, to prevent unwanted pregnancies.[329]

---

[325] UN Doc. A/50/38, § 154.

[326] *Z. Ilic* (member of CEDAW), The Convention on the Elimination of All Forms of Discrimination against Women, in Manual on Human Rights Reporting, UN, New York 1991, p. 156. In its report on the preparatory work of Article 1 the CSW described the deliberations by governmental delegations on the content of this provision as being divided between those who felt that the convention should deal only with discrimination against women, and those who felt it should deal with discrimination on the grounds of sex as a whole. The proponents for the second view maintained that discrimination could either be defined specifically as discrimination against women or as discrimination against either sex. However, the first proposal was accepted by the majority of the delegates and subsequently incorporated in the conventional text. For a detailed background to the discussions see *L.A. Rehof*, Guide to the *Travaux Préparatoires* of the United Nations Convention on the Elimination of All Forms of Discrimination against Women, Dordrecht 1993, p. 46 (hereinafter cit. Guide to the *Travaux Préparatoires*). See also *K. Törnudd*, Finland and the International Norms of Human Rights, Dordrecht 1986, p. 258.

[327] The procedures for the formulation of concluding comments are to be found in the report of the Committee's 13th session, UN Doc. A/49/38, §§ 813–816. See also UN Doc. CEDAW/C/1997/5, §§ 12–16.

[328] CEDAW has since the early 1980s frequently raised questions dealing with abortion laws and practices. It is apparent that since the Cairo and Beijing Conferences the quality of reporting on the issues of reproductive freedom has increased dramatically, *i.e.*, nearly every state has reported and has been questioned on several elements of reproductive choice.

[329] UN Doc. CEDAW/C/1995/7, §§ 423–439.

Questions raised by CEDAW frequently venture into examining whether a specific law, policy or practice is consistent with the requirements of the Convention. At its 14th session in 1995 CEDAW expressed concern about laws in Chile, which contain discriminatory provisions and the maternal mortality resulting from clandestine abortions. Members of the Committee noted that though abortion was illegal, it was nevertheless practised widely.[330] The Committee recommended, therefore, that the Government revise the extremely restrictive legislation on abortion.[331] CEDAW made a recommendation for de-penalisation of abortion in St.Vincent and the Grenadines "in order to guarantee safe abortion".[332] On the other hand the Committee expressed its concern about the legislation which criminalises abortion in Venezuela but it did not recommend its repeal. However, at its 17th session in 1997, CEDAW called for steps to secure the enjoyment of women in Italy of their reproductive rights by, *e.g.*, guaranteeing them access to safe abortion services in public hospitals.

The alarming levels of teenage pregnancy were also discussed. CEDAW noted furthermore the lack of any explanation for the high rate of teenage pregnancy in the report of Mauritius.[333] It called, moreover, for a review of the statutory laws, which impose sanctions upon women in Namibia for illegal abortion. The Committee identified in addition teenage pregnancies, which were punished by expelling girls from school and increasing the high drop-out rates for girls, as an issue of concern.

The Committee was also critical to the high maternal mortality rates from clandestine abortions in Peru. It recommended the Government to review the law on abortion, taking into consideration the health needs of women and to consider the suspension of the penalty of imprisonment for women who have undergone illegal abortion procedures.[334] More importantly the Committee recommended the Government of the Philippines to carry out its suggestions to make reproductive and sexual health services available and accessible to all women in all regions.[335] CEDAW requested, moreover, a review of the requirement of spousal consent for abortion, which existed in Turkey, a requirement, which it found to be in contravention of Article 15 of the Convention.[336] It was suggested that the related provisions of the Penal Code be revised in order to ensure women the full protection of the law on equal terms with men.

In addition, CEDAW expressed concern about reports of rape (especially those affecting indigenous and peasant women), gang rape and custodial rape which had been documented by human rights organisations in Peru and other countries.

---

330 The representative from Chile remarked that although abortion was illegal, in 1990 one out of three pregnancies had ended in abortion. UN Doc. A/50/38, § 107.

331 UN Doc. A/50/38, §§ 152 and 158.

332 Report of the 16th session (1997), UN Doc. A/52/38, Part I, p. 28, § 148.

333 UN Doc. A/50/38, § 211.

334 UN Doc. A/50/38, § 446.

335 UN Doc. CEDAW/C/1997/L.1/Add.8, §§ , 19 and 27.

336 UN Doc. CEDAW/C/1997/L.1/Add.5, § 36.

Another specific form of particularly grave gender-based discrimination is domestic violence. It has been frequently debated by CEDAW during the monitoring procedure. As one of the most insidious forms of violence, domestic violence puts women's health at risk and impairs their ability to participate in family and public life on a basis of equality.[337] With this in mind the Committee welcomed the criminalisation of marital rape in Finland in 1995.[338] On other occasions the Committee expressed its deep concern about deficiencies in the legal system of the Philippines with regard to violence against women, in view of the fact that domestic violence was not specifically penalised by law and that it was surrounded by silence.

CEDAW emphasised during the consideration of Venezuela's report that it should respond effectively to problems such as domestic violence, early pregnancy and elimination of stereotypes. It was noted that Venezuela had not made the necessary changes to its legal system and this continued to reinforce patriarchal patterns of behaviour. CEDAW recommended that the Government fulfil the commitments, which it had made in adopting the Beijing Platform for Action.[339] Thus, in regard of states obligations in accordance with Article 5 of the Women's Convention, CEDAW has emphasised the need to identify what type of traditional and cultural practices hamper women's advancement. The Committee also tries to determine the extent to which such practices create an obstacle to women's equality and perpetuate their inequality. Subsequently, through its questioning CEDAW establishes what measures the state party has taken, or proposes to take to modify social and cultural patterns of conduct.

While many countries report that national laws comply with Article 16(1) of the Convention, others still have regulations that contravene it. In this regard in 1996 members of the Committee found the minimum legal age for marriage in Ukraine, which was not the same for girls as for boys, inconsistent with the Convention's provisions.[340]

The issue of trafficking in women from foreign countries for the purpose of prostitution and bride trade has been dealt with on several occasions, *e.g.*, during the consideration of the reports from Norway and Finland.[341]

CEDAW has made a contribution to understanding and expanding the definition of discrimination, which includes special measures of protection for women, such as, for example, maternity benefits by holding that such legal provisions do not constitute discrimination if they are designed to promote gender equality. The monitoring procedure indicates that the principle of gender equality has over time been recognised in national legislations. Domestic practices, however, are still not fully oriented towards *de facto* equality.[342] Even countries with very good records on

---

337 UN Doc. CEDAW/C/1995/7, § 466.

338 UN Doc. A/50/38, § 356.

339 UN Doc. CEDAW/C/1997/L.1/Add.6, §§ 27, 28 and 36.

340 UN Doc. A/51/38, § 293.

341 UN Doc. A/50/38, § 359.

342 *K. Ahooja-Patel*, Women's Rights, in International Law: Achievements and Prospects, M. Bedjaoui (ed.), Paris 1991, p. 1126.

gender equality have been criticised by CEDAW for recent developments. The Committee noted, for example, with concern the challenges currently facing efforts to implement temporary special measures in Denmark to hasten gender equality, such as the removal of quotas by political parties. In the view of the members of CEDAW although the participation of women in politics is at a higher level than other countries, Denmark has yet to reach a level of gender parity in the political sphere.[343] It suggested that temporary special measures should be maintained and even strengthened. Other states, which were also encouraged by CEDAW during its session in 1997 to put in place affirmative action programmes, include St.Vincent and the Grenadines as well as the Philippines. Temporary special measures with numerical goals and timetables should be initiated, according to CEDAW, in Turkey in accordance with article 4(1) of the Convention, in particular in the political sphere and the public sector.[344] In regard to Slovenia, the Committee recommended that the judiciary should be made aware of the meaning of indirect and structural discrimination, *de facto* equality and the concept of temporary special measures.[345]

*2.3.5.3. Request for Reports on an Exceptional Basis*

It should also be mentioned that CEDAW has, in accordance with the practice of other human rights bodies, requested exceptional basis reports from the states on the territory of the former Yugoslavia. The report from Croatia, for example, documented and identified the gender-specific impact of war. The representative of that country recalled during the dialogue that the Government had made a commendable effort to collect information relating to the violation of women's rights by encouraging women to provide testimonies of those violations. Testimonies by women constituted in her view "not only the source of information on violations, but also a form of psychological support and therapy that were badly needed by women who had experienced the physical and emotional scars of rape".[346] Five hundred testimonies of women, victims of various maltreatment, were collected. Among those cases rape accounts for 10 per cent. Sixty per cent of the raped women were, at the same time, victims of torture and maltreatment. It is believed, however, that the actual number of raped women is much higher that that reported. As a consequence of rape four children were born. The representative informed the Committee that women who became pregnant as a consequence of rape in the course of the military conflict had a right to abortion. Women could also decide whether to keep children conceived as a result of rape or offer them for adoption.[347] Nevertheless, CEDAW recommended above all that it is necessary to break the silence concerning sexual abuse and aggression of which women are victims, identify the guilty parties and bring them before national and international courts and

---

[343] UN Doc. CEDAW/C/1997/L.1/Add.7, §§ 14 and 20.

[344] UN Doc. CEDAW/C/1997/L.1./Add.5, § 52.

[345] UN Doc. CEDAW/C/1997/L.1/Add.3, § 28.

[346] UN Doc. A/51/38, § 560.

[347] *Supra*, § 563.

provide financial compensation to the victims. It noted, furthermore, with dismay that rape became during that armed conflict systematic in nature and was used as a "weapon of war" to submit women to humiliation and torture and so leave their homes.[348]

*2.3.5.4. Preparation of General Recommendations*

In conformity with Article 21 of the Convention, CEDAW has adopted a policy of making general recommendations to states parties on matters raised in the context of its examination of periodic reports. CEDAW only began to develop jurisprudence from the Convention, based on its consideration of country reports in 1989, and in 1991 it decided to start with a systematic adoption of general recommendations dealing with the interpretation of each of the substantive articles contained in the Convention.[349] As of its session in 1997, CEDAW had adopted a total of 22 general recommendations and 15 suggestions.[350] While some address technical and procedural matters, a number of them contribute in my view substantially to the understanding of the normative content of different articles comprised in the Women's Convention. Though the recommendations are not binding as such on states parties, they focus attention on the important substantial issues of the Convention and reflect the experience acquired by the Committee in reviewing the situation in many different countries. They contribute to the progressive implementation of that particular treaty and are considered as "scholarly work with regard to their analytical quality and comprehensiveness".[351] General Recommendation No. 19 on the elimination of violence against women is, for example, a very thorough, substantive and in-depth analysis of that subject matter within the framework of the Convention. It provides recommendations for action to be taken by states parties as to methods for its eradication and remedies which should be available to women who are victims of violence. I shall deal with this recommendation and recommendation No. 21 on equality in marriage and family relations more in detail in parts II and III of this study. It should also be mentioned that CEDAW decided at its 17th

---

[348] *Supra*, §§ 586, 591.

[349] *R. Jacobson*, p. 471. At its 14th session in 1995 CEDAW considered a draft recommendation on Articles 7 and 8 of the Convention, which will continue at the session in 1996. See UN Doc. CEDAW/C/1994/4. In addition, CEDAW decided in 1995 that priority would be given to the preparation of a general recommendation to Article 2. For an analysis of the content of that article based on country reports see UN Doc. CEDAW/C/1995/4.

[350] Suggestion No. 8 on the Follow-up of the International Conference on Population and Development is of particular interest for my study because it in "recalling the provisions of articles 10(h), 12 and 16(1)(e) of the Convention, with respect to..(t)he right of access to family health and family planning education, the right to equality in health services and the right to equality in deciding freely and responsibly the number and spacing of children", requested coordination among all the human rights bodies to promote the effective exchange of information to facilitate the follow-up to the Cairo Programme of Action. UN Doc. A/50/38, pp. 11–12. See in addition UN Doc. A/52/38, 1997.

[351] UN Doc. CEDAW/C/1995/7, § 260. Katarina Tomaševski views recommendations as the Committee's guidance for "best practice" in translating the Women's Convention into domestic law and practice. *K. Tomaševski*, A Primer on CEDAW for International Development Co-operation Personnel, SIDA, Stockholm 1998, p. 11.

session in 1997 that its next general recommendation would be on women and health (Article 12 of the Women's Convention).

The term "discrimination" in itself, however, has not been an issue on which a general recommendation has been prepared by CEDAW. On the other hand, an extensive definition of the concept has been elaborated in a report of 1995[352] in the following terms:

> "Discrimination is not limited to legal concerns, but encompasses any discrimination suffered by women on the basis of sex whether through law, from the operation of laws that are assumed to be gender-neutral or because of social, economic and cultural factors to which women are subject. Consequently, there are both obligations of conduct and obligations of result for States parties".

Moreover, from the analytical work on reports of states parties[353] which has been done by the Committee, clearly recognisable measures for the prevention[354] and ways for the elimination of gender-based discrimination of the kind that is comprised under the Women's Convention have materialised. They have been identified as follows:

1. Introduction of national legislation (Articles 2 and 3),[355]
2. Temporary special measures to establish *de facto* equality of women with men and to be discontinued when the objectives of equality have been achieved (Article 4) and
3. Measures to modify customary laws and practices based on stereotypes of the superiority or inferiority of either sex (Article 5).[356]

*2.3.5.5. Some Concluding Remarks*

What relevance has all of the above for our subject matter, *i.e.*, women's right to reproductive freedom? CEDAW has through its questions put to governmental

---

352 UN Doc. CEDAW/C/1995/4, § 11.

353 See, *e.g.*, UN Doc. CEDAW/C/CRP.15, UN Doc. CEDAW/C/CRP.15/Add.1; CEDAW/C/1995/4 and CEDAW/C/1995/7.

354 Prevention of discrimination has been generally considered within the UN as impeding any conduct which denies or restrains the right of a person to equality.

355 An important means to promote the elimination of gender discrimination is consequently law. Gender inequality is largely founded on differences between legal rights for women and men. Therefore, in the view of CEDAW the denial of equal rights should be fought by legal measures and social treatment by education and other social measures. Some states parties to the Women's Convention, *e.g.*, Cuba and Hungary, reported to CEDAW already in 1985 that discrimination against women was a separate offence punishable under law. Cuba provided for imprisonment for periods ranging from six months to three years or a fine or both for anyone who discriminated against another person. UN Doc. A/CONF.116/13, § 59, 5 June 1985. Mongolia has specified that any attempt to deny women equal rights in whatever way was punishable by law. UN Doc. CEDAW/C/1995/4, § 31.

356 CEDAW was alarmed, for example, by the religious and cultural practices perpetuating domestic violence, discrimination against women in inheritance and the continuing practice of female genital mutilation in Uganda. UN Doc. A/50/38, § 332.

representatives during the review of national reports, its comments and general recommendations identified its position on several elements of that right.

It has occasionally put forward the proposition that since it is the woman's body, which is involved in a pregnancy and not that of the man and she physically bears the child, her decision on whether to continue a pregnancy or not must prevail. The number and spacing of children have an impact on women's lives and also affect their physical and mental health. For these reasons, women are according to the Committee "entitled to decide on the number and spacing of their children".[357] It has also denoted that a free choice in procreation matters promotes gender equality. Thus, equality between women and men, in terms of the Women's Convention, means that both sexes be given the same formal and practical opportunities to develop their resources in all fields as in working life. Equal does not necessarily mean the "same" in the context of the Convention. In the debate during the preparatory process on its text, a representative of the delegation of the GDR stated that in his country's domestic jurisdiction "both spouses should decide on the number and spacing of their children by mutual agreement, failing such agreement, the decision was taken by the wife alone".[358] Thus, the woman is equal to the man in dignity and rights but she differs from him in her nature and mission and consequently in needs.[359] This interpretation of Article 16 was generally accepted during the drafting of the Women's Convention.

In other words, a distinction based on sex is justifiable, and even desirable, when the purpose of it is to diminish disadvantages.[360] Distinctions made because of physical characteristics are legitimate when they are based on physiological differences between men and women in the procreative process. The family is a partnership of equals, but the principle of equality can not be satisfied on the same basis as regards procreative rights. Gender-based discrimination occurs when men and women are treated differently, though they are in a similar situation. In reproductive capacity men and women are not similarly situated. Thus, the threats in nature, which endanger life and bodily integrity, justify the enjoyment of the rights on an *unequal* basis.[361] However, a basic factor causing inequality in many different societies and throughout history has been and is still the division of labour between the sexes justified on the basis of the childbearing function of women. This in its turn has led to the restriction of women's tasks and responsibilities mainly to the domestic sphere, making them unequal in activities outside the family and allowing them only limited access to decision-making processes in society.[362]

---

357 CEDAW, General Recommendation No. 21, § 21, CEDAW/C/1995/7.

358 UN Doc. A/32/218, § 128.

359 *W. McKean*, Equality and Discrimination under International Law, Oxford 1983, p. 184.

360 *B.G. Ramcharan*, Equality and Non-Discrimination, in The International Bill of Rights: The Covenant on Civil and Political Rights, L. Henkin (ed.), New York 1981, p. 258; *P. Sieghart*, The International Law of Human Rights, Oxford 1983, p. 17.

361 *L.A. Rehof*, Guide to the *Travaux Préparatoires*, p. 372.

362 Förenta Nationernas kvinnokonferens, p. 92.

On the other hand, arguments have been put forward in the scholarly literature based on the fact that since the gametes of both women and men[363] are needed for procreation, the two parents-to-be should be treated in like manner. I shall return to this issue in Part II of this study.

CEDAW has, as has already been mentioned, declared that a law would not be discriminatory if it made an exception to the principle of equality between men and women with reference to the unique situation of women regarding pregnancy and childbirth, *e.g.*, rules establishing a right for women to maternity leave. A law would be considered discriminatory if its application were not restricted to one gender, *i.e.*, if it contained rules other than those relating to reproductive differences and were of relevance to both men and women but it allocated benefits to men only or to women only. Pregnancy-related disadvantages, *e.g.*, exclusion from education or employment (when non-pregnancy is a requirement for employment) might be considered as unjust discrimination, since only women are exposed to it.[364]

CEDAW has, through the adoption of concluding comments and the preparations of detailed general recommendations, interpreted the definition of discrimination very broadly and it has also covered practices, which are discriminatory in their effect. On the other hand, CEDAW makes use of a rather weak language in its suggestions to states parties and it has not explicitly declared that a specific law, policy or practice is in breach of the Convention. Yet, a comprehensive understanding of the normative content of several of the rights guaranteed in the Convention has to emerge.

Needless to say, CEDAW is the only specialised body within the UN with competence to supervise states' compliance with their treaty obligations with respect to women's rights. This fact and its composition makes it undoubtedly the most women – sensitive supervisory body which has most extensively, compared to other human rights bodies, applied asymmetrical models of gender equality. The Committee has also shown willingness to look into grave violations of rights experienced by women during armed conflict.

The absence of a complaint procedure so far has diminished, however, the potential of the Women's Convention. The detailed examination of individual complaints provides an invaluable context in which to develop a body of jurisprudence elaborating upon the scope of, for example, the term "gender-based discrimination" and "reproductive freedom". As Geraldine Van Bueren has rightly emphasised, the principal advantages of a petitioning system consist in that "complaint mechanisms provide a more direct, effective and speedier remedy"[365] than the reporting system. Another obstacle for effective and integral implementation of the Convention, which I shall discuss in the following chapters of this book, is the great number of

---

363 A gamete is a reproductive cell, which can unite with another to form the cell that develops into a new individual. See *M. Coleman*, p. 627.

364 *R.J. Cook*, Human Rights in Relation to Women's Health, pp. XI and 27.

365 *G. Van Bueren*, p. 411.

reservations[366] that states parties have made under the regime of that treaty. Therefore, the recently taken clear standpoint by CEDAW when reviewing the report of Morocco that the reservations made by its Government, particularly the reservation to Article 2 (the commitment to eradicate discrimination), which is considered as one of the Convention's central provisions, "to be contrary to the object and purpose of the Convention and incompatible with international law"[367], is encouraging. The Committee was also concerned that the combination of reservation to Articles 2 and 16 leave no room for evolving concepts of Islamic law. CEDAW pointed out, in addition, that reservations of that kind seriously undermine the proper implementation of the Women's Convention and that it hoped that Morocco would envisage the withdrawal of the reservations. The formulation of a new comprehensive general recommendation on reservations based on the Committee's experience and practice developed under the expanded guidelines for reports and taking into account the HRC's GC No. 24 on reservations is but a necessary goal for the activities of CEDAW in the immediate future.[368]

### *2.3.6. The European Commission and the European Court on Human Rights*

#### *2.3.6.1. Institutional Background*

The system of international control established by Article 19 of the European Convention on Human Rights provides for a Commission and a Court of Human Rights.[369] The principal function of the European Commission (consisting of

---

[366] As of 1 January 1997, 49 states had accompanied their ratifications of the treaty with formal reservations involving 11 different articles. The largest number of substantive reservations concern the provisions on the elimination of discrimination in marriage and family. The text of the reservations and objections is contained in UN Doc. CEDAW/SP/1996/2. See also UN Doc. CEDAW/C/1997/4.

[367] UN Doc. CEDAW/C/1997/L.1/Add.2, § 15.Bangladesh, Egypt and Iraq, which also apply Shari'a Law, have submitted reservations concerning the very obligation to eliminate gender discrimination. Numerous objections were raised to these reservations. CEDAW has amended its guidelines for reports, so that it requires states parties which have entered general reservations that do not refer to a specific article of the Convention, or reservation to Articles 2 and 3, to make a particular effort to report on the effect and interpretation of them, since the Committee "considers these to be incompatible with the object and purpose of the present Convention". UN Doc. CEDAW/C/7/Rev. 2; UN Doc. CEDAW/C/1995/7, § 327, UN Doc. CEDAW/C/1997/4, § 19.

[368] The work of the International Law Commission on the definition of reservations and interpretative declarations is also of relevance. See the 1998 Report of the Special Rapporteur, UN Doc. A/CN.4/491.

[369] Under the amendments made by Protocol No. 11, the Commission will be merged with the Court and a new single, permanent Court will be created. It will perform the functions of the previous Commission and Court. Its jurisdiction will be exclusive, *i.e.*, the role of the Committee of Ministers (made up of the Foreign Ministers of each of the member States) under Article 32 will be abolished. But the Committee will continue to supervise the execution of judgments. The text of the Protocol and the explanatory report is published in HRLJ 1994, Vol. 15, pp. 86–96. For a commentary see *A. Drzemczewski & J. Meyer-Ladewig*, Principal Characteristics of the New ECHR Control Mechanism, HRLJ 1994, Vol. 15, pp. 81–86 and *J. Meyer-Ladewig*, Reform of the Control Machinery, in The European System for the Protection of Human Rights, R. St. J. Macdonald, F. Matscher & H. Petzold (eds.), Dordrecht 1993, pp. 909–927. See also *K. de Vey Mestdagh*, Reform of the European Convention on Human Rights in a Changing Europe, in The Dynamics of the Protection of Human Rights in Europe, Essays in Honour of Henry G. Schermers, Vol. III, R. Lawson & M. de Blois (eds.), Dordrecht 1994, pp. 350–360.

members equal to the number of parties to the Convention) is to review "applications", *i.e.*, complaints from persons, groups of individuals, NGOs, and states alleging violations of the rights guaranteed by the Convention and its Protocols. If a friendly settlement cannot be reached, the Commission may report its opinion on the state's compliance with the Convention. The reports are formally not legally binding. They are, however, generally accepted by states as authoritative statements. Within three months of the Commission's report, either the Commission or the state in question may refer the case to the European Court of Human Rights (composed of a number of judges equal to that of the member-states of the Council of Europe) for binding decision. Thus, its judgement is binding on the respondent state.[370]

The Court hears the cases referred to it by the Commission, the respondent state or another interested state, or by individuals from those states which have ratified Protocol No. 9 to the Convention. The competence of the Court extends among others to all cases "concerning the interpretation and the application of the Convention"[371] duly referred to it. It should be mentioned that the Court is in its interpretation of the Convention "very anxious to build up a coherent body of case law".[372] It is, thus, reluctant to diverge significantly from earlier judgements.

It has been suggested that the secret of the success which the European regime has enjoyed, *i.e.*, being "the most developed system of legal protection worldwide",[373] lies in the "unprecedented formal strength and completeness" of its procedures and that they are implemented "with scrupulous impartiality".[374]

*2.3.6.2. Non-discrimination*

Non-discrimination does not have the same, specific, foundational designation in the Statute of the Council of Europe or the Preamble to the European Convention as it does in the UN Charter. Nor is there an equivalent to Article 26 of the ICCPR, which provides comprehensive protection against discrimination in all those activities, which the state member chooses to regulate by law. Instead, the reach of Article 14 of the European Convention is restricted to protecting persons against discrimination only with respect to the rights and freedoms set out elsewhere in the Convention. It is impossible to summarise the voluminous and detailed jurisprudence of the European Commission and the European Court on Human Rights[375] dealing with different aspects of discrimination in the present sub-chapter. None the

---

[370] Although the judgments of the European Court do not as such bind other states, states seem to tend to review continuously the implications for their national law of cases concerning other states. *I. Cameron & M.K. Eriksson*, An Introduction to the European Convention on Human Rights, p. 42. See also *F. Sundberg*, The European Experience of Human Rights Proceedings: The Precedent Value of the European Court's Decisions, Akron Law Review 1987, Vol. 20, pp. 629–647; *H. Danelius*, Mänskliga rättigheter i europeisk praxis, Stockholm 1997, p. 379.

[371] Article 45 of the Convention.

[372] *I. Cameron & M.K. Eriksson*, p. 42.

[373] *F.G. Jacobs & R.C.A. White*, The European Convention on Human Rights, p. 404.

[374] *J. Donnelly*, Universal Human Rights in Theory and Practice, London 1989, p. 214.

[375] By the end of 1998, more than 600 judgments had been issued by the Court.

less, I can perhaps convey a picture of their approach by examining the subject matter of, and decisions in, some of its leading cases relating to the prohibition of discrimination, *e.g.*, on the basis of sex and reproductive freedom.

Article 14 of the European Convention, which provides that the rights and freedoms enumerated in the Convention are to be secured without discrimination on the ground of sex,[376] has given rise to several important cases. However, the principle of non-discrimination determines the field of application of equality without adding a further human right to the catalogue.[377] This article has not been given independent existence, *i.e.*, it is complementary and it has a dependent relationship to the substantive rights of the Convention. It can be applied only where the facts fall within the ambit of one or more of the other articles. This has remained so despite several strong arguments in the doctrine to extend the scope of Article 14 to imply a general prohibition of discrimination and despite the dynamic approach[378] adopted by the Court towards interpreting the rights contained in the Convention. Article 14 thus differs substantially from the protection offered by Article 26 of the ICCPR[379] and

---

[376] Article 14 of the European Convention on Human Rights reads as follows: "The enjoyment of the rights and freedoms set forth in this Convention shall be secured without discrimination on any ground such as sex, race, colour, language, religion, political or other opinion, national or social origin, association with a national minority, property, birth or other status".

[377] *K.J. Partsch*, Fundamental Principles of Human Rights: Self-Determination, Equality and Non-Discrimination, in The International Dimensions of Human Rights, K. Vasak (ed.), UNESCO 1982, Vol. 1, p. 62. The Swedish Judge Mrs. B. Sundberg-Weitman in her essay "Legal Test for Applying the European Convention on Human Rights and Freedoms in Adjudicating on Alleged Discrimination", NTIR 1980, Vol. 49, pp. 31–32 distinguishes between three different schools of thought in regard to the function of Article 14. The first school's view consists in the idea that the ban on discrimination as expressed in Article 14 cannot ever apply unless there is also violation of some specific right or freedom safeguarded by the Convention. The second school maintains that Article 14 is indeed an operative provision applicable independent of other provisions, *i.e.*, it is applicable in conjunction with some other article/s even where the minimum protection guaranteed by that article has not been violated. Furthermore, reference has been made to Sir Fitzmaurice who has argued that an application of Article 14 presupposes that the discriminatory act is "afforded" by the conventional guarantees. The non-discrimination rule applied when the relevant act did not violate the main article as such, but when its implementation was discriminatory. *B. Sundberg-Weitman*, Rättssäkerhet och godtycke- Strasbourg-domstolens tolkning av artikel 14 i konventionen till skydd för de mänskliga rättigheterna, in Skrifter till minnet av H.G.F. Sundberg, Institutet för offentlig och internationell rätt Nr. 40, Stockholm 1978, p. 37. See generally on Article 14, *P. van Dijk and G.J.H. van Hoof*, Theory and Practice of the European Convention on Human Rights, Deventer 1990, pp. 532–548; *K.J. Partsch*, Discrimination, in the European System for the Protection of Human Rights, R. St. J. Macdonald, F. Matscher & H. Petzold (eds.), pp. 571–593.

[378] On the interpretative methods applied by the European Court see *J.G. Merrills*, The Development of International Law by the European Court of Human Rights, Manchester 1993; *F. Matscher*, Methods of Interpretation of the Convention, in The European System for the Protection of Human Rights, R. St. J. Macdonald, F. Matscher & H. Petzold (eds.), pp. 63–83; *H. Golsong*, Interpreting the European Convention on Human Rights Beyond the Confines of the Vienna Convention on the Law of Treaties?, pp. 147–163.

[379] Judge Rolv Ryssdal, the former President of the European Court, brought this factual situation to the attention to the participants of the 7th International Colloquy held at Lund in 1990 and expressed the hope that these problems should be re-examined "under present-day conditions in order to prepare the necessary steps for their improvement". Doc. Court (90)152, p. 6. See *K.J. Partsch*, p. 571; *J. Bernhard & T. Lehmann*, Den Europeiske Menneskerettighedskonventionen, København 1985, p. 139; *L.A. Rehof & T. Trier*, Menneskeret, København 1990, p. 390 ff.

all initiatives to strengthen the principle of equality and non-discrimination within the European system through the adoption of new standards have failed in the past.[380] It has been maintained that the reason for that might be the fear within the Council of Europe about the unpredictable scope of such a provision and burdening the present system of the Convention.[381]

On the other hand, even if the substantive rights and freedoms at stake as such have not been infringed, there may have been discrimination, contrary to Article 14, involved. To that extent, the European Court has held that Article 14 is autonomous.[382]

In a relatively few cases before the Commission and the Court, the applicant has claimed to be a victim solely of discrimination. Most of the cases concern claims of substantive rights and in addition that discrimination contrary to Article 14 has occurred.

In the *Belgian Linguistic* case, which was brought by 324 French-speaking citizens and which related to certain aspects of the laws on the use of language in education in Belgium, the European Court dealt with the difficult problem of interpretation of what forms of differential treatment constitute discrimination. It did not argue that Article 14 prohibits all inequalities of treatment since they can be designed to benefit the less privileged group of individuals. The Court ruled instead that not every difference in treatment amounts to discrimination within the meaning of Article 14. By referring to "the principles, which may be extracted from the legal practice of a large number of democratic states", the Court declared that the principles of equality of treatment was violated if a distinction had no *objective* and *reasonable* justification. In other words, substantive equality may require unequal treatment. The Court, furthermore, established that:

> "In spite of the very general wording of the French version 'sans distinction aucune', Article 14 does not forbid every difference in treatment in the exercise of the rights and freedoms recognised. This version must be read in the light of the more restrictive text of the English version 'without discrimination'. The competent national authorities are frequently confronted with situations and problems, which, on account of differences inherent therein, call for different legal solutions. Moreover, certain legal inequalities tend only to correct factual inequalities".[383]

---

[380] A reference to equality before the law was, for example, deleted from the draft Convention without any discussions during the preparatory process. Later initiatives to include in an additional protocol a provision similar to that of Article 26 of the ICCPR have been unsuccessful as well. *A. Eide & T. Opsahl*, p. 25.

[381] *A. Eide & T. Opsahl*, p. 26 and *K.J. Partsch*, p. 592.

[382] *Abdulaziz, Cabales and Balkandali* case, ECHR Judgment of 28 June 1985, Ser. A, No. 94, § 71.

[383] *Belgian Linguistics* Case, (Case relating to certain aspects of the laws on the use of languages in education in Belgium – hereinafter cited as *Belgian Linguistics* Case), ECHR Judgment of 23 July 1968, Ser. A, No. 6, § 10.

The Court has repeated its interpretation of Article 14 in that case[384] in several subsequent judgements, which have added some modifications. Today one might say that the Strasbourg organs have developed a similar test to the one applied by the HRC when deciding about discrimination.[385] They must consequently, in relation to every case, establish whether there is:

1. a comparable situation, where treatment differs,[386]
2. an objective and reasonable justification for the difference in treatment concerned,
3. a legitimate aim for the distinction (the distinction must pursue a legitimate aim)
4. a reasonable relationship of proportionality between the means employed and the aim sought to be realised thereby.[387]

The principle of proportionality implies that any state intervention would be lawful if it is necessary in order to protect some legal interests and if the intervention is not disproportionate in relation to the expected advantages.

In addition, the European Court on Human Rights has articulated that the existence of the above mentioned relationship must be appreciated in the knowledge of the legal and factual features, which characterise the life of the society in the state, which is to answer for the measure in dispute.

*2.3.6.3. Non-Discrimination and some Aspects of Reproductive Freedom*

Several cases have been brought before the Strasbourg organs dealing with allegations of discriminatory measures on the ground of sex and which relate to many

---

[384] The Court's thesis on the meaning of discrimination as developed in the *Belgian Linguistic* case has been criticised in the doctrine as the weaker alternative of two possible. A stronger definition would imply that differential treatment is justified only if "without regard to the purpose of the measures in question, the facts themselves require or permit differential treatment". *F.G. Jacobs & R.C.A. White*, p. 287. See also *K.J. Partsch*, p. 586.

[385] The major difference between the European Court and the HRC is that the previous one uses a qualified test, *i.e.*, it includes the fourth requisite (proportionality) as cited above. *T. Loenen*, p. 262.

[386] *The Sunday Time* Case, ECHR Judgment of 26 April 1979, Ser. A, No. 30, § 70. In the *Lithgow and Others v. the UK* case the European Court established that Article 14 "safeguards persons (including legal persons) who are placed in analogous situations against discriminatory differences in treatment", § 177. See also *Van der Mussele v. Belgium*, ECHR Judgment of 23 November 1983, Ser. A, No. 70, §§ 22–23.

[387] The European Court held in the *Belgian Linguistic* Case that: "the principle of equality of treatment is violated if the distinction has no objective and reasonable justification. The existence of such a justification must be assessed in relation to the aim and effects of the measure under consideration, regard being had to the principles, which normally prevail in democratic societies. A difference of treatment in the exercise of a right laid down in the Convention must not only pursue a legitimate aim: Article 14 is likewise violated when it is clearly established that there is no reasonable relationship of proportionality between the means employed and the aim sought to be realised". *Op. cit.*, § 10. See also *Lithgow and Others v the UK*, ECHR Judgment 8 July 1986, Ser. A, No. 102, § 177; *Inze v. Austria*, ECHR Judgment 28 October 1987, Ser. A, No. 126, § 41; *Darby v. Sweden*, ECHR Judgment 23 October 1990, Ser. A, No. 187, § 31.

different areas.[388] The Convention organs have in a number of them reached the conclusion that discrimination against men has occurred almost entirely in family law, in particular in relation to children.[389]

Article 14 is of special importance in relation to Article 12, *i.e.*, in relation to marriage and the founding of a family. The Commission, as well as the Court, has up to the present shown unwillingness to include marriage between persons of the same sex among the guarantees of the Convention. They have instead upheld an interpretation of Article 12 as being limited to persons of the opposite biological sex.[390] Moreover, the Commission has ruled in the *C.Kerkhoven, A.Hinke & S.Hinke v. The Netherlands* case[391] that same-sex parents cannot be equated with a man and a woman living together and therefore the second applicant does not have a right to parental authority over the first applicant's child.[392] Thus, the claim raised by Mrs. Kerkhoven and Mrs. Hinke, who have a stable lesbian relationship and who considered themselves to be the social parents of the third applicant, who biologically is the second applicant's son and to be victims of discrimination in comparison to heterosexual couples (Article 8 was invoked in conjunction with Article 14 of the Convention), was not endorsed by the Commission. The Commission recalled that it has found in the past that despite the evolution of attitudes towards homosexuality, a stable homosexual relationship between two women does not fall within the scope of the right to respect for family life ensured by Article 8 of the Convention and therefore the application was found to be manifestly ill-founded within the meaning of Article 27(2) of the Convention.

Other sensitive issues of relevance which have arisen include the question of whether medical termination of pregnancy is permissible under the Convention[393]

---

388 Family life – see ECHR *Marckx v. Belgium*, Judgment of 13 June 1979, immigration policy – ECHR *Abdulaziz, Cabales and Balkandali v. the UK*, Judgment of 28 May 1985, custody, care and access – *W. Hendriks v. the Netherlands*, European Commission Report of 8 March 1982, *X.v. Switzerland*, case No. 10956/84, ECHR Judgment of 3 October 1987, etc. See also *M. Buquicchio-de Boer*, Sexual equality in the European Convention of Human Rights, a survey of case-law, Strasbourg 1989, EG(89)3 and *M. Buquicchio-de Boer*, Equality between the sexes and the European Convention on Human Rights, A Survey of Strasbourg Case-Law, Human rights files No. 14, Strasbourg 1995; *J.A. Frowein & W. Peukert*, Europäische MenschenRechtsKonvention, EMRK-Kommentar, Kehl 1996, pp. 455–459.

389 *M. Buquicchio- de Boer*, ibid., p. 22. See *Keegan v. Ireland*, ECHR Judgment of 26 March 1994, HRLJ 1994, Vol. 15, pp. 193–201.

390 Issues arising under this article are examined in detail in The Right to Marry and to Found a Family, *M.K. Eriksson*, Uppsala 1990. See also Application No. 14573/89 *Eriksson & Goldschmidt v. Sweden*, European Commission on Human Rights, D.R. 63, p. 213 and *Cossey v. UK*, ECHR, Judgment of 27 September 1990, Ser. A, No. 184.

391 Application No. 15666/89, 19 May 1992. See *M. Buquicchio-de Boer*, p. 19.

392 The applicants complaint that the Dutch authorities' refusal to vest the first applicant with parental authority over the third applicant constitutes an unjustified interference with their right to respect for their family life and that they are discriminated against as, unlike heterosexual couples, they cannot enjoy their rights under Article 8 of the European Convention with regard to parental authority.

393 I shall deal with several of the cases in depth below in Part II of this study. Generally I may assert that both conventional institutions have taken a hesitant approach in handling such cases. However, the European Commission has rejected an interpretation of the Convention as recognising an unqualified right to life for an unborn child, and a minority of the Commission placed legal abortion in the

and whether information on medical services (abortion) available in other countries which are unlawful in the country where the information is provided is included in the freedom of expression as protected by the Convention.[394] Furthermore, in the view of the Commission sterilisation may in certain circumstances involve a violation of Articles 2 and 3 of the Convention.[395]

Further, since the advancement of the equality between the sexes constitutes a *major* goal of the member states of the Council of Europe,[396] the European Court has ruled that "very weighty reasons would have to be advanced before a difference of treatment on the grounds of sex could be regarded as compatible with the Convention".[397] The European Court emphasised that since the advancement of the equality of the sexes is a major goal within the Council of Europe, the margin of appreciation will be narrowed in the context of gender discrimination.[398] The European Court confirmed once again this standpoint in the case of *Schuler-Zgraggen v. Switzerland*.[399] It found, by eight votes to one (the Turkish Judge

---

*Brüggemann and Scheuten v. the FRG* case in the context of gender equality. See *M.K. Eriksson*, The Legal Position of the Unborn Child in International Law, GYIL 1993, Vol. 36, pp. 86–130.

394 In the *Open Door and Dublin Well Woman and others v. Ireland* case (ECHR Judgment of 29 October 1992, Ser. A No. 246) the Court, *e.g.*, came to the conclusion that the right of women to obtain information concerning abortion facilities outside the jurisdiction of Ireland by the way of non-directive counselling is comprised within Article 10 of the Convention.

395 *F.G. Jacobs & R.C.A. White*, pp. 43 and 179.

396 Resolution 855 (1986) of the Parliamentary Assembly of the Council of Europe on equality between men and women notes "the obstacles to equality between men and women.. in stereotyped attitudes" and it recalls that "equality can only be achieved by changing the roles of both women and men, and that to this end a new and more even division of labour and responsibilities between women and men must be brought about" (§§ 3 and 5). As from 1 January 1992 the Committee of Ministers within the Council of Europe decided to promote the former Committee for Equality between Women and Men to the status of a steering committee (CDEG) in order to emphasise the importance it gives to the question of the realisation of equality between women and men. See Council of Europe, Information sheet, No. 30, Strasbourg 1993 (H/INF (92))2, p. 71. See also *K. Tomaševski*, Reproduction, Rights and Reality, pp. 1047–1048 and *J. Schokkenbroek*, The Prohibition of Discrimination in Article 14 of the European Convention and the Margin of Appreciation, HRLJ 1998, Vol. 19, p. 21.

397 See the *Abdulaziz, Cabales & Balkandali v. the UK*, ECHR Judgment of 28 May 1985, Ser. A, No. 94, § 78.

398 Ibid, § 80. The Court indicated also in the *Van Raalte v. Netherlands* case that the margin of appreciation is considerably reduced in the area of gender equality. ECHR, Judgment of 21 February 1997, § 42.

399 ECHR, Judgment of 24 June 1993, Ser. A, No. 263. In 1976 Mrs. Margit Schuler-Zgraggen was granted a half-pension by the appropriate Compensation Office in Canton Uri (Switzerland), as she had contracted tuberculosis. She was dismissed from her working place effectively from 1979 on account of her illness. She was subsequently granted a full pension, which was prolonged in 1981 and 1982. In May 1984 she gave birth to a son. The Invalidity Insurance Board of the Canton Uri cancelled her pension in 1986 on the grounds that her family circumstances had changed after the birth of her child and her health had improved. In other words, she was able to look after her home and her child. An appeal by Mrs. Schuler-Zgraggen to the Canton Uri Invalidity Insurance Appeals Board, in which she had claimed a full pension or, alternatively, a half-pension, was dismissed in 1987. In 1988 the Federal Insurance Court considered to what extent the applicant was restricted in her activities as a housewife but not her ability to work in her former job, as it proceeded on the assumption that, having a young child, she would have given up gainful employment even if she had not had health problems. It is interesting to note that the European Commission of Human Rights by nine votes to six expressed the opinion in its

Gölcüklü), that there had, indeed, been a violation of Article 14 taken together with Article 6(1) of the European Convention, since the assumption made by the Swiss Federal Insurance Court that, once the applicant had become a mother, she would have given up work even if she had not had health problems, amounted to discrimination on the ground of sex. Thus, the presumption of the Federal Insurance Court that women give up work when they give birth to a child was the sole basis for the reasoning and was decisive for the introduction of a difference of treatment based on the ground of sex only.[400] The Court discerned no adequate and very weighty reasons in the case before it for such a difference of treatment. Moreover, there was no reasonable and objective justification for it.

On the other hand, the European Court found in the *Rasmussen* case[401] that difference of treatment[402] between the applicant (Mr. Per Rasmussen) and his former wife with regard to paternity of a child born during the marriage was justified by the interests of the child since:

> "The difference of treatment established on this point between husbands and wives was based on the notion that such time-limits were less necessary for wives than for husbands, since the mother's interests usually coincided with those of the child".[403]

Despite the fact that the standards of "justification" and "reasonableness" are very vague and that the respondent state may apply the doctrine of a margin of appreciation[404] this particular case and the subsequent case law have established

---

report adopted on 7 April 1992 that there had been no violation of Article 14 taken together with Article 6(1). Four of the dissenting members expressed, however, the view that the applicant had been subject to discrimination on the ground of sex. Professor Frowein and Sir Basil Hall stated that "the Federal Insurance Court proceeded, in its appreciation of evidence, from a conception of the role of sexes which, in so far as expressed in such a general and sweeping manner, appears outdated and has no objective and reasonable justification, as would be required by Article 14 of the Convention". Also Professor Trechsel in dissenting opinion considered the approach of the Federal Insurance Court as a residue of gender discrimination. In his view one of the important tasks of the Commission is to contribute to the elimination of all forms of discrimination based on sex. *Op. cit.* § 128.

[400] The Court underlined that "As worded in the Federal Court's judgment, the assumption cannot be regarded-as asserted by the Government- as an incidental remark, clumsily drafted but of negligible effect. On the contrary, it constitutes the sole basis for the reasoning, thus being decisive, and introduces a difference of treatment based on the ground of sex only". *Schuler-Zgraggen* case, § 67.

[401] *Rasmussen v. Denmark*, ECHR Judgment of 28 November 1984, Ser. A, No. 87. The Danish Government changed the legislation as to the establishment of the same time-limits for men and women in paternity proceedings already at the time when the case was pending before the European Commission on Human Rights, *i.e.* , in 1982.

[402] Whereas men are subject to time-limits in paternity matters in Denmark, women are not.

[403] Ibid. § 41. Generally on the concept "margin of appreciation" see *R. St. J. Macdonald*, The Margin of Appreciation, in The European System for the Protection of Human Rights, R. St. J. Macdonald, F. Matscher & H. Petzold (eds.), pp. 83–125 and *H.C. Yourow*, The Margin of Appreciation Doctrine in the Dynamics of European Human Rights Jurisprudence, The Hague 1996.

[404] States parties to the European Convention enjoy a certain margin of appreciation in assessing whether and to what extent differences in otherwise similar situations justify a different treatment in law. However, it is for the European Court to give the final ruling in this respect. Thus, the scope of the

helpful guidelines for the understanding of the principle of non-discrimination under international law.

### *2.3.6.4. Conclusions*

The examples selected above illustrate the potential scope of Article 14.[405] They suggest that distinctions, which indirectly affect women negatively, may be challenged under Article 14.[406] The evolutive theory of interpretation, which both conventional organs frequently apply, places great emphasis on contemporary cultural and sociological notions such, *e.g.*, gender equality. Although the male-dominated European Commission (there are only two female members) and the Court (only one Judge is female)[407] have generally applied a formal approach to equality, both organs have on several occasions shown gender-sensitivity as to the different social and economic positions of men and women in society as, for example, in the *Rasmussen* case and when challenging sex stereotyping as in the *Schuler-Zgraggen* and *Burghartz*[408] cases.

Additionally, the recent findings of the Strasbourg organs in the *C.R. v the United Kingdom* and *S.W. v. the United Kingdom* cases,[409] especially the Court's strong

---

margin of appreciation will vary according to the circumstances, the subject-matter and its background. See *Abdulaziz, Cabales and Balkandali v. the UK* judgment, § 72; *Rasmussen* judgment, § 40. For a thorough analysis of the concept of "margin of appreciation" see *R. St. J. Macdonald*, The Margin of Appreciation, in The European System for the Protection of Human Rights, R. St. J. Macdonald, F. Matscher and H. Petzold (eds.), pp. 83–124.

405 Noteworthy in this regard is the separate opinion of Mr. Balta expressed in the *Grandrath v. Federal Republic of Germany* case, that the enjoyment of the rights and freedoms set forth in the European Convention "may not be made subject to any kinds of discrimination other than those which are either inherent in the nature of the right in question or are designed to remedy existing inequalities". Report of the European Commission of Human Rights, 12 December 1966, cited in *F.G. Jacobs & R.C.A. White*, p. 287, note 6.

406 *T. Loenen*, p. 263.

407 This is Mrs. Elisabeth Palm from Sweden. See *J.W.F. Sundberg*, Domare med mission, Institutet för offentlig och internationell rätt, nr. 111. I may mention in this respect that the new European Court of Human Rights will be effective in September 1998. Eight of the newly forty elected judges are women. DN, 1 September 1998, p. 3.

408 *Burghartz v. Switzerland*, Appl. No. 16213/90, Judgment of 22 February 1994, Ser. A, No. 280-B. A gender stereotype in Swiss legislation, which mandated married couples to adopt the husband's name as the family name and in that way prevented the free choice of the family name, was the issue discussed in this case. The Court argued that the choice of one of the surnames as the family name in preference to the other one did not represent a greater deliberateness on the part of the husband than on that of the wife, and it was, therefore, unjustified to provide different legal consequences in each case. Consequently the difference in treatment contravened Article 14 taken together with Article 8 of the Convention. Of interest to quote is also the Commission's standpoint in that case, that "tradition in itself no longer suffices to justify the difference of treatment on the ground of sex". Op. cit. § 66.

409 Case of *S.W. v. the UK*, Appl. No. 20166/92, Judgment 22 November 1995 and case of *C.R. v. the UK*, Appl. No. 20190/92, Judgment of 22 November 1995. Both applicants were charged with rape (respectively attempted rape and assault) under the British Sexual Offences Act of 1956 and complained that this constituted a breach of Article 7 of the Convention since they were convicted in respect of conduct committed against their wives, which at the time in question was not a criminal offence. The Court referring to the English Law Commission's argumentation that "recognition of women's equality of status with men in marriage and outside it and of their autonomy over their own bodies" is essential ruled that "the abandonment of the unacceptable idea of a husband being immune against prosecution

wording with regard to rape, emphasising its "essentially debasing character", are evidential as to their modern approach on gender issues. The European Court moreover established in a recent decision that the rape of a detainee (a 17 year old girl) by an official of the Turkish State constitutes "an especially grave and abhorrent form of ill-treatment"[410] and amounts to torture.

Significant to this study is also the newly adopted Convention for the Protection of Human Rights and Dignity of the Human Being with regard to the Application of Biology and Medicine within the Council of Europe, which is the first international treaty prohibiting the use of techniques of medically assisted procreation for the purpose of choosing a future child's sex, "except where serious hereditary sex-related disease is to be avoided" (Article 14).[411] The underlining reason for this provision is the protection of the dignity and identity of the human being without discrimination. The European Court of Human Rights has the competence on the basis of Article 29, to give under certain circumstances and without direct reference to any specific proceeding pending in a court, advisory opinion on legal questions concerning the interpretation of that Convention.

Finally, I may mention that several commentators consider the European Convention on Human Rights and its case law as supportive to the concept of substantial equality even though this notion has not yet been sufficiently developed and applied. Professor Partsch, for example, declares resolutely that from the text of Article 14 "it follows that not only an equal application of the existing law is required, but even more important, that the legislator must provide for equal treatment of every person. Formal equality is not sufficient; what is required is material and effective equality".[412]

Other scholars like Mahoney have criticised the predominant use of the "similarity and difference" model by international supervisory bodies when dealing with discrimination. In her view this test:

> "(u)ses a male standard of equality and renders women copies of their male counterparts. Thus, women are forced to argue either that they are the same as men and should be treated the same, that they are different but should be treated as if they were the same, or that they are different and should be accorded special treatment".[413]

---

for rape of his wife was in conformity not only with a civilised concept of marriage but also, and above all, with the fundamental objectives of the Convention, the very essence of which is respect for human dignity and human freedom" ( §§ 44–respectively 42). In consequence the Court reached unanimously the conclusion that there had been no violation of the Convention.

[410] Case of *Aydin v. Turkey*, (57/1996/676/866), Judgment of 25 September 1997, § 83.

[411] The Convention was open for signatures on 4th April 1997. Sverige, Regeringen, Social departementet, S97/2187/S. The text of the Convention has been reprinted in HRLJ 1997, Vol. 18, pp. 135–151. For a review of the Convention's history and its implication for Swedish law see *E. Rynning*, Mänskliga rättigheter och biomedicin- om Europarådets konvention och svensk rätt, in De lege, Uppsala 1997, pp. 311–351.

[412] *K.J. Partsch*, p. 584.

[413] *R.J. Cook*, Women's International Human Rights Law: The Way Forward, HRQ 1993, Vol. 15, p. 239.

Mahoney suggests instead the test of "disadvantage", which has been applied by the Supreme Court of Canada[414] and which has been discussed earlier in this chapter, to be used by the international organs for the protection of human rights in the future when determining whether gender discrimination has occurred. It is my conviction as well that this latter approach has both the potential, and is better positioned, to reflect and further develop the dynamics of contemporary international law in favour of equality between men and women. The evolutive method, whereby the European Convention is considered as a living instrument and is interpreted in the light of present-day conditions,[415] is appropriated and well suited for that purpose.

### *2.3.7. The Inter-American Commission on Human Rights and the Inter-American Court of Human Rights*

#### *2.3.7.1. The Inter-American System*

The inter-American system for the protection of human rights has evolved within the framework of a regional inter-governmental organisation-*the Organization of American States* (OAS).[416] The system has today two distinct sources, giving rise to a dual institutional structure of protection. One has its origins in the Charter of the OAS[417] and the other was created by the American Convention on Human Rights (hereinafter the American Convention), which entered into force on 18 July 1978.[418] Both parts of the system share a common institution, the "procedural heart of the regime",[419] the Inter-American Commission on Human Rights, which was created in 1959 and which has general competence in the field of human rights under the Charter-based regime as well as under the American Convention.

Most importantly, the normative standards developed under both parts of the system overlap and influence the development of each other.[420] The 1948 American Declaration of the Rights and Duties of Men (hereinafter the American Declaration) and the American Convention contain catalogues of fundamental

---

[414] *Andrews v. Law Society of British Columbia*, 1989,1 S.C. R.143, ibid., p. 240. According to this test it is sufficient for a person belonging to a disadvantaged group to show that the law and social behaviour "maintain or worsen the disadvantage". See *C.A. MacKinnon*, p. 31, note 31.

[415] *Tyrer v. the UK* case, Judgment of 25 February 1978, Ser. A, No. 26, § 31.

[416] On the inter-American human rights system in general see *T. Buergenthal*, The Inter-American System for the Protection of Human Rights, in Human Rights in International Law, T. Meron (ed.), Oxford 1984, pp. 451–454; *T. Buergenthal*, International Human Rights in a Nutschell, St. Paul Minn. 1995, pp. 123–166; *M.K. Eriksson*, Skydd av mänskliga rättigheter. Det interamerikanska systemet, Uppsala 1994; *T. Buergenthal & D. Shelton*, Protecting Human Rights in the Americas, Cases and Materials, Kehl 1995; *J.S. Davidson*, The Inter-American Human Rights System, Dartmouth 1997.

[417] This part of the system applies to all 37 Member States of the OAS. In Article 3 (l) of the Charter, the American States reaffirm and proclaim as a principle of the organisation "the fundamental rights of the individual without distinctions as to race, nationality, creed or sex".

[418] As of April 1998, 25 states are parties to it. OEA/Ser.L/V/II.98, Doc. 7 rev, April 13, 1998, p. 1059.

[419] *J. Donnelly*, p. 216.

[420] *T. Buergenthal*, International Human Rights, p. 124; *S. Davidson*, Human Rights, Philadelphia 1993, p. 128.

human rights and freedoms very similar to that of the UDHR[421] and the ICCPR. From these I may find relevant for my study: the right to equality before the law and equal protection of the law (Article 24 of the Convention)[422] and prohibition of gender discrimination, *i.e.*, "to have the rights and duties established ... without distinction as to race, sex..." (Article II of the Declaration) and the obligation of states to respect the rights and freedoms recognised in the Convention "without any discrimination for reasons of (s)ex." (Article 1of the Convention and Article II of the Declaration).

*2.3.7.2 The Inter-American Commission on Human Rights*

The Commission has been empowered to expose and rectify violations of the substantive norms contained in the American Declaration in relation to all members of the OAS and the American Convention in relation to States parties to it. In short the Commission performs the assigned functions by means of three main methods: by processing individual complaints of human rights violations, preparing and publishing reports on the general human rights situation in a given member state, and proposing measures to be taken by the OAS in order to increase the respect for human rights in the region. The first two procedural activities of the Commission constitute the most significant work. Any person, group of persons or legally recognised NGO may submit petitions to the Commission with regard to alleged violations of human rights protected by the Declaration or the Convention. Here follows a short review of the relevant part of the Commission's case law.

In interpreting the meaning of the right to equality before the law in a case concerning Haitian boat people seeking asylum in the United States,[423] the Commission based its reasoning mainly on earlier interpretations of Article 7 of the UDHR and Article 26 of the ICCPR. It argued that the prohibition of discrimination is intended to ensure *de facto* equality, not identity, of treatment. Therefore, the provisions in question would not preclude reasonable differentiations between individuals or groups of individuals. Subsequently the Commission pointed out that a breach of Article II of the American Declaration[424] arises "not only in the application of a substantive right but also in respect of any unreasonable differentiation in respect of the actual treatment of persons belonging to the same class or category"

---

[421] Mentioned should be that the American Declaration was adopted 7 months before the UDHR.

[422] Also Article 4(f) of the Inter-American Convention on the Prevention, Punishment and Eradication of Violence Against Women (see below) is worded in the same manner.

[423] Inter-American Commission on Human Rights, Report No. 51/96, Decision of the Commission as to the merits of Case 10.675, March 13, 1997, OAS, OEA/Ser.L/V/II.95, Doc. 7 rev, 1997, pp. 550–610.

[424] The Declaration was adopted as a non-binding resolution. Today it is, however, considered to be the normative instrument that embodies the interpretation of the OAS Charter (Article 3j). See Inter-American Court, Advisory Opinion OC-10/89 "Interpretation of the American Declaration of the Rights and Duties of Man within the Framework of Article 64 of the American Convention on Human Rights", 14 July 1989. See also the pronouncement of the Inter-American Commission on the juridical status of the Declaration in the *Baby Boy* case in 1981. *D. Shelton*, Abortion and the Right to Life in the Inter-American System: The Case of "Baby Boy", HRLJ 1981, Vol. 2, p. 309; *G.T. Mastaglia*, Human Rights Legal System in Member States of the OAS which have not ratified the American Convention on Human Rights, ASIL, Human Rights Interest Group, Newsletter 1997, Vol. 7, pp. 22–24.

and, therefore, this provision was violated by the United States in respect of the applicants who were interdicted on the High Seas in contradistinction to the position of Cubans and nationals of other countries who were favourably treated by being brought into the country by the United States Coast Guard.

In a case concerning Argentina,[425] the Commission analysed the right to equal protection by the law in connection with an alleged violation of the right to property. It referred in its argumentation to the grounds on which discrimination can be claimed in the case law of the Strasbourg organs as well as in the Inter-American Court of Human Rights advisory opinion OC-4/84 to which we shall return later on. With this background the Commission ruled that the petitioner in the case before it has not been able to supply information to prove that there has been no "objective and reasonable justification" for the different treatment. Regrettably, the Commission manifested here a rather restrictive approach to equality in that it pronounced the following: "In effect, the right to equal protection of the law cannot be assimilated to the right to equal outcome in judicial proceedings involving the same subject matter".[426] Subsequently, the petitioner's claim was declared ill-founded with respect to Article 24 of the Convention.

In recent years the Inter-American Commission has addressed human rights violations with gender-specific causes through its individual petition system and its monitoring functions.[427] I shall now mention a few cases of relevance to my discussion and which raised the issue of discrimination against women. In case No. 10.506 (Argentina)[428] the complaint alleged, for example, that the Argentine state, and particularly the prison authorities who routinely carried out vaginal inspections of the women visitors to a special unit, acted in violation of Article 24 relating to the general non-discrimination principle established by Article 1.1 of the American Convention. In the view of Mrs. X, such inspections served to stigmatise, denigrate, and oppress women as such, and because they are relatives of prisoners. Moreover, Mrs. X argued that the practice is discriminatory, since the women are neither the perpetrators nor suspected of any offence and it targets certain persons. The Commission noted that a vaginal search involves the invasion of a woman's body, and to be lawful it must meet a four-part test: "1. it must be absolutely necessary to achieve the security objective in the particular case; 2. there must not exist an alternative option; 3. it should be determined by judicial order; and 4. it must be carried out by an appropriate health professional".[429] After taking into consideration the facts in that particular case,[430] the Commission arrived at the

---

425 Inter-American Commission on Human Rights, Report No. 39/96, Case 11.673, October 15, 1996, OAS doc. 7 rev, 1997, ibid., pp. 76–92.

426 OAS doc. 7 rev., p. 84.

427 In addition, the Commission sponsored in 1996 a conference entitled "Women, Human Rights and the Inter-American System: An Agenda for Action". One of the themes which were addressed at that gathering concerned different approaches to the elimination of discrimination against women.

428 Inter-American Commission on Human Rights, Report No. 38/96, October 15, 1996, OAS doc. 7 rev, pp. 50–76.

429 OAS doc. 7 rev, p. 65.

430 Mrs. X and her daughter refused to be examined, and the inspections were not performed.

conclusion that by conditioning the visit with an intrusive measure and not providing appropriate guarantees, the prison officials unduly interfered with the applicant's and her daughter's rights. The Commission also found that such inspections violate the right to physical and moral integrity (Article 5 of the Convention) in relation to Article 1.1. It recommended, therefore, that the Government of Argentina adopt the necessary domestic legislation to adjust it to the obligations established by the American Convention. This is but a manifestation of a sympathetic attitude of the Commission towards women's situation.

Yet another case brought before the Inter-American Commission to invoke the right to equal protection in conjunction with the non-discrimination principle in the context of gender-based discrimination was that of the Costa Rican citizen Mrs. González.[431] The applicant based her claim on the fact that the rules for a 12 kilometre race excluded the categories of "juveniles" and "veterans" for female runners although these categories were established for male runners. Moreover, the petitioner complained that there was a difference in the prizes for male and female runners, *i.e.*, the amount for the first prize for male runners was higher than that for the first prize for the female runners, and that this was discriminatory action which prejudiced her. Finally, Mrs. González alleged that the Costa Rican law which provides that all competitive sports must provide equal prizes for men and women was not observed by the national authorities in practice, such as the municipality of Heredia, which organised discriminatory foot-races. This case was, however, declared inadmissible *ratione personae*, in accordance with Article 47 (b) of the American Convention, since a case cannot be presented before the Commission *in abstracto*. The applicant did not qualify to run in the "veterans" category because she was under the age of 40 at the time of the race and she chose not to run in the "adult" category. Thus, as in the European system for the protection of human rights, an individual cannot institute an *actio popularis* and present a complaint against a law without establishing some active legitimisation justifying her standing before the Commission. It is not sufficient for an applicant to claim that the mere existence of a law violates her rights under the American Convention. It is necessary that the law has been applied to her detriment.

For the time being two cases are pending before the Inter-American Commission one concerning alleged discrimination against women in domestic provisions of family law and the other relating to domestic violence.

Human rights violations, which have, gender specific causes and consequences are generally linked to the problem of discrimination primary of women. For example, the Inter-American Convention on the Prevention, Punishment, and Eradication of Violence Against Women "Conventíon of Belém do Pará",[432] stipu-

---

[431] Inter-American Commission on Human Rights, Report No. 48/96 on admissibility, Case 11.553, October 16, 1996. OAS doc. 7 rev, pp. 119–126.

[432] The Convention was adopted in Brazil on June 9, 1994 and entered into force on March 5, 1995. As of April 1998, 27 states are party to it. Many of the region's countries have published pamphlets and other types of documents to publicise the text of the Convention. OAS, Inter-American Commission of Women, OEA/Ser.L/II.2.28; CIM/doc. 5/96, 26 July 1996, p. 2; OEA/Ser.L/V/II.98, Doc. 7 rev, April 13, 1998, p. 1078.

lates in article 6 that the right of every woman to be free from violence must include the right to be free "from all forms of discrimination".

Of great practical significance is that Article 12 of the above mentioned convention empowers the Inter-American Commission to review petitions on violations of that treaty.

Also during its on- site visits to various countries and when considering the country reports, the Inter-American Commission has increasingly dedicated attention to women's rights and gender equality issues and it has on several occasions observed that the lack of respect for women's rights persists in many countries, which results in *de facto* and *de iure* instances of discrimination. When the Commission visited Haiti during 1995, it interviewed women who played an important role in the formation of democratic institutions in the country and who had been victims of politically motivated rape. In fact, a whole sub-section of its report[433] (Chapter IV) reviews instances of violence against women and sexual abuse. The Commission clearly recognised sexual violence as a serious human rights violation. In the great majority of cases it was demonstrated, according to the Commission's observations, that the acts of sexual abuse were committed by representatives of the army and the police and their armed civilian auxiliaries, with the authorisation or tolerance of the illegal regime. Therefore, the Commission was able to conclude that this circumstances constituted a violation of Article 5 (the right to humane treatment) and Article 11 (protection of honour and dignity) of the American Convention. Of significance for the development of human rights law is that the Commission has classified rape and the threat of rape against women as torture in that "it represents a brutal expression of discrimination against them as women".[434] The Commission considered also the use of rape as a weapon of terror as a crime against humanity under customary law. This view has been retained by the Commission in its extensive analysis of the crime rape in a case brought before it against Peru[435] and with which I shall deal in more detail in Part III of this study.

The Inter-American Commission has in its most recent activities shown great devotion to the *de iure* and *de facto* situation of women in the region. The 1996 Annual Report of the Inter-American Commission to the General Assembly of the OAS contains, for example, in the chapter on human rights development in Guatemala a special sub-section which is devoted to "Equality and the Rights of Women"[436] in which the Commission indicated that it continues to follow the

---

433 OAS, Inter-American Commission on Human Rights, Report on the Situation of Human Rights in Haiti, OEA/Ser.L/V/II.88, Doc. 10 rev, February 9, 1995.

434 *Supra*, p. 44.

435 OAS, Annual Report of the Inter-American Commission on Human Rights 1995, OEA/Ser.L/V/II.91, Doc. 7 rev, February 28, 1996, pp. 157-201.The case of *Mejía Egocheaga and another v. Peru* is also published in Butterworth's Human Rights cases 1996, pp. 229–267.

436 OAS doc. 7 rev, ibid., pp. 730–731. The same is true for the report on the situation of human rights in Brazil, which contains a chapter on the human rights of Brazilian women. OAS, OAE/Ser.L/V/II.97, Doc. 29 rev.1, September 29, 1997, pp. 129–137. See in addition the report on the Situation of Human Rights in Ecuador, OEA/Ser.L/V/II.96, Doc. 10 rev.1, April 24 1997 and the 1998 Report on the Situation of Human Rights in Mexico.

efforts made by the Government to reform the Civil Code, especially provisions concerning the role and representation of spouses within the marital unit so that women have the full capacity to exercise their rights and freedoms on the basis of equality. In addition, during its 85th session, the Commission appointed Mr. Claudio Grossman to serve as its Special Rapporteur on the theme of women's rights. His mandate includes both *de facto* and *de iure* discrimination, which may hinder women from exercising their rights and freedoms, protected by the American Declaration and Convention. The principal objective of the rapporteur's study has been defined as "to assist the member states of the OAS by identifying instances of discrimination which are inconsistent with inter-American human rights guarantees".[437] It is expected that such inconsistencies will be remedied. The Special Rapporteur presented his final report to the Commission in 1998, which approved it on March 6, 1998.

*2.3.7.3. The Inter-American Court of Human Rights*

The function of protecting human rights within North and South America is not exclusively reserved for the Inter-American Commission. As earlier mentioned there is also a court *-the Inter- American Court of Human Rights-* created by the American Convention and which is also competent in this field. The Court is an autonomous judicial institution of the inter-American human rights system whose purpose is to interpret and to apply the American Convention.[438] It has in other words, apart from its power to pronounce binding judgments on contentious issues, an important advisory jurisdiction on all international human rights instruments,[439] which has generally proved very effective.

Contentious proceedings are instituted in order to adjudicate allegations of human rights violations committed by states parties to the Convention, which have recognised the competence of the Court.[440] These proceedings differ from those of advisory opinions in that they are condemnatory in nature "leading to the classification of the defendant state as a delinquent".[441] The decisions of the Court are binding. However, the Inter-American System does not provide for means by which to ensure compliance. The case law produced by the Court to date is very limited and none of the decided cases is of direct relevance to my study. In contrast

---

[437] *Supra*, OAS doc. 7 rev., p. 751.

[438] On the origins, structure and work of the Court see *S. Davidson*, The Inter-American Court of Human Rights, Dartmouth 1992.

[439] According to Article 64(1) of the American Convention, the object of the request for an advisory opinion to the Court may be "the interpretation of this Convention or of other treaties concerning the protection of human rights in the American states". Mrs. Quiroga suggests that the Inter-American Commission of Women (CIM), which has a very broad competence in the field of human rights, might profit from the court's advisory jurisdiction. It could request, for example, an opinion on the interpretation of the term gender equality. This has not been the case yet. See *C.M. Quiroga*, The Battle of Human Rights, Gross, Systematic Violations and the Inter-American System, Dordrecht 1988, p. 176.

[440] By April 1998, 19 states had accepted its jurisdiction.

[441] Judge R.E. Piza Escalante in the Gallardo case (*In the Matter of Viviana Gallardo et al.*) No. 101/81, Judgment of November 13, 1981, § 24.

to its poor activity with regard to contentious jurisdiction, the Inter-American Court has used its advisory jurisdiction extensively. Thus, the main part of the Court's work has, until recently, has consisted of formulating advisory opinions. Advisory proceedings are designed to assist OAS organs and member states in an unformalistic manner to accomplish their international human rights obligations. While the former jurisdictional power is modelled on that of its European counterpart, the latter is unique and much wider than those conferred on the European Court by the Second Protocol to the European Convention. Advisory opinions often contain interesting legal analysis regarding in most cases provisions of the American Convention. They also carry considerable weight despite the fact that they are not binding in a strict judicial sense. The broadness of the Court's advisory competence has, however, not yet been used to specify the concept of gender discrimination. On the other hand, the Inter-American Court of Human Rights has given an advisory opinion (the fourth advisory opinion dealing with acquisition of the Costa Rican nationality) which reflects its understanding of the term "non-discrimination". The Court underlined that the prohibition of discrimination in the American Convention "springs directly from the oneness of the human family and is linked to the essential dignity of the individual".[442]

This case concerned the formula adopted in Costa Rica's Constitution, which gives women, but not men, who marry Costa Ricans, a special status for the purpose of naturalisation. In considering this legal position the Inter-American Court referring to the decision of the European Court in the *Belgian Linguistic* case found that:

> "No discrimination exists if the difference in treatment has a legitimate purpose and if it does not lead to situations, which are contrary to justice, to reason or to the nature of things. It follows that there would be no discrimination in differences in treatment of individuals by a state when the classifications selected are based on substantial factual differences and there exists a reasonable relationship of proportionality between these differences and the aims of the legal rule under review. These aims may not be *unjust* or *unreasonable*, that is, they may not be arbitrary, capricious, despotic or in conflict with the essential oneness and dignity of humankind" (italics added).[443]

In consequence, the Court pronounced that the proposed amendment to the naturalisation provision, which stipulates preferential treatment in cases of naturalisation

---

[442] IACHR, Advisory Opinion OC-4/84, January 19, 1984, *Proposed Amendments to the Naturalization Provisions of the Political Constitution of Costa Rica*, Ser. B, No. 4, San José 1984, § 55.

[443] Costa Rica was the first country to make use of its right established in Article 64(2) of the American Convention on Human Rights – the power to consult the Court regarding the compatibility or incompatibility of a domestic provision with the American Convention. IACHR, Advisory Opinion OC-4/84, January 19, 1984, § 57. See also Annual Report of the Inter-American Court of Human Rights, OAS, OEA/Ser. L/V/II.66, doc. 10 rev 1, 1985, p. 62.

applicable to marriage, and which favours only one of the spouses, constitutes discrimination incompatible with Articles 17(4) (equality of the rights of the spouses) and 24 of the American Convention since it was based on outdated notions of paternal authority and conjugal inequality. The Court also referred to Article 1 of the 1933 Montevideo Convention on the Nationality of Women which declares that "there shall be no distinction based on sex as regards nationality".[444] This was in the Court's view a "decisive impulse towards equality of treatment on the international plane".[445] This interpretation of the American Convention is clearly intended to bring the domestic legislation of Costa Rica into line with the international provisions in force in the inter-American system for the protection of human rights.

In a subsequent advisory opinion[446] the Court touched upon the issue of discrimination on the grounds of economic status in a cursory manner. It explained that "protection of the law" consists of "the remedies the law provides for the protection of the rights guaranteed by the American Convention". After referring to its own judgments in contentious cases, the Court recalled that there is a duty for states parties to the American Convention "to organize the governmental apparatus and, in general, all the structures through which public power is exercised, so that they are capable of juridically ensuring the free and full enjoyment of human rights".[447]

The latter indicates that the Inter-American Court has, as have the European Court and the HRC, adopted the test of differentiation and proportionality when determining what constitutes discrimination in the terms of the American Declaration and Convention on Human Rights.

### *2.3.7.4. Some Concluding Remarks*

In reviewing the inter-American system for the protection of human rights, we must remember that most countries in the Americas have experienced dictatorial governments. The Inter-American Commission and Court have operated consequently in quite different circumstances to those in Europe.[448] Their attention has, therefore, been mainly focused on human rights violations such as extra-judicial executions, detention without trial, interrogation accompanied by torture, arbitrary arrests on a massive scale, total absence of judicial remedies etc.. As a result, gender based violations have until recently been ignored or paid less concern. The political envir-

---

444 IACHR, *Proposed Amendments*, § 65.

445 *S. Davidson*, p. 347. The same author has interpreted the Court's position in the above cited case as implying that Article 24 "prohibits both formal and material discrimination, but that it also preserves the possibility of positive discrimination arising from affirmative action programmes". Ibid., p. 346.

446 Inter-American Court of Human Rights, Advisory Opinion OC-11/90, "*Exceptions to the Exhaustion of Domestic Remedies (Art. 46(1), 46(2) and 46(2)(b) American Convention on Human Rights*", of August 10, 1990. Ser. A, No. 11. See especially §§ 22 and 23.

447 *Supra*, § 23.

448 Professor Buergenthal who has served 12 years on the Inter-American Court suggested recently that the accession of the former East block countries to the European Convention is likely to produce similar difficulties for the European system. Several Latin American governments are confronting economic and social problems making it difficult for the Inter-American Court to fully enforce the American Convention. ASIL Newsletter 1997, p. 11.

onment in the region is, however, gradually changing as a consequence of the ongoing transition to democracy. This positive development has also had the effect of raising the awareness in Latin America that women's rights should be treated and analysed as human rights. The case law of the Inter-American Commission remains very limited as regards issues dealing with gender-based discrimination and it is not sufficient to draw any definite conclusion as to whether it is in favour or not of the use of the asymmetrical approach to equality. The all male Commission, which consists of seven members, each an authority in the field of human rights, has, however, through its current very extensive interpretation of the notions "torture" and "rape" and through its powers to review instances of violence against women on the basis of the Convention of Belém do Pará, shown a willingness and inclination to contribute to the progressive development of international law in favour of women's legal position. The Commission is very well positioned and it has considered gender equality in its overall activities (for example, in various reports) also in an extensive manner, *i.e.*, including *de facto* as well *de iure* elements in the definition of equality.

The Inter-American Court is, at the time of writing, composed of seven judges, all of them men. However, one woman, the judge Sonja Picado Sotela, was a member of the Court between 1989 and 1995 and served as its Vice-President.[449] Even though the new democratic governments in Latin America have shown they are prepared to support the Court and to accept its rulings, still very few states have actually done so. This is a factual situation, which restricts the scope of the contentious jurisdiction of the Court severely. Noticeable is also that none of the decided cases has dealt with gender-based discrimination. Thus, the quest for an effective judicial implementation of the American Convention that enhances the validity of the substantive rights of the human rights system of the Americas continues.

The reluctance of the Commission to submit cases for judicial solution and the existence of the advisory jurisdiction as a possible alternative might to certain extent explain the shortcomings of the Court's contentious procedure. Advisory opinions have a valuable utility since they enforce the norms of the Convention without specifying any government as a violator of human rights, *i.e.*, they are preventive rather than reparative. They may also contribute to the evolution of law of the American Convention and to international human rights law in general.[450] The Court has not used its full potential and it has not yet made a legal pronouncement on gender equality in this respect.

### *2.3.8. The African Commission for Human and Peoples' Rights*

#### *2.3.8.1. A Background of the African Charter*

On 17 June 1981, the Assembly of Heads of State and Government of the Organization of African Unity adopted the African Charter on Human and People's

---

[449] At the time of writing Mrs. Sotela is Costa Rica's ambassador to the USA.

[450] *T. Buergenthal*, International Human Rights, p. 166.

Rights (known as the "Banjul Charter"). Despite great scepticism expressed about its future acceptance, five years after the Charter's adoption it entered into force on 21 October 1986.[451]

The Charter differs considerably in many ways from existing universal human rights conventions, as well as from its other regional counterparts, both in the enumeration and articulation of the rights and freedoms protected and in the means of their implementation.[452] The Charter puts emphasis in its preamble on African culture and historical traditions as well as, it has been said, reflecting in its entire text the African conception of law.[453] Traditional values could, and are sometimes, used to legitimise practices which are incompatible with human rights. Customary rules, *e.g.*, often place women at a disadvantage. One can maintain that the status of women in Africa is generally dictated by deep-seated values and a tradition of patriarchy which include differential standards.[454] Traditional structures (among others the extended family)[455] of present-day Africa may actually be considered the greatest obstacle for the promotion of women's rights. The lack of emphasis on such rights is obvious in the generally inferior status of women in Africa. It is, therefore, in my view peculiar that it has been claimed that the African Charter has been designed to meet the specific needs of the African people. At the same time,

---

[451] For the history and content of the Charter see: *R. Gittleman*, The African Charter on Human and Peoples' Rights: A Legal Analysis, Virginia Journal of International Law 1982, Vol. 22, pp. 667–714; *E.G. Bello*, The African Charter on Human and Peoples' Rights, Recueil des Cours 1985–86, pp.13–268; *B.O. Okere*: The Protection of Human Rights in Africa and the African Charter on Human and Peoples' Rights: A Comparative Analysis with the European and American Systems, HRQ 1984, Vol. 6, pp. 141–179; *E. Kodjo,* The African Charter on Human and Peoples' Rights, HRLJ 1990, Vol. 11, pp. 272–283; *P. Amoah*, The African Charter on Human and Peoples' Rights – An Effective Weapon for Human Rights?, African Journal of International and Comparative Law 1992, Vol. 4, p. 231 ff.; *I. Österdahl*, Räddaren i nöden? Den afrikanska stadgan för människans och folkens rättigheter, SvJT 1993, s. 134 ff.

[452] As at the time of writing there is no African Court on Human Rights to settle disputes between states or to decide on individual cases. However, calls have been made for the establishment of such a court and the OAU decided on 14 December 1997 to establish an eight member African Court on Human Rights. For the different arguments in favour of the foundation of an African Court see *R. Sock*, The Case for an African Court on Human and Peoples' Rights: From a Concept to a Draft Protocol Over 33 Years, African Topics 1994, pp. 9–10; *E.A. Ankumanh*, The African Commission on Human and Peoples' Rights, The Hague 1996, pp. 194–195.

[453] *K.M. Baye & B. Ndiaye*, The Organization of African Unity (OAU), in The International Dimensions of Human Rights, K. Vasak (ed.), UNESCO 1982, Vol. 2, p. 588.

[454] *T.W. Bennett*, Human Rights and African Customary Law, Cape Town 1995, p. 80; *C.E. Welch*, Human Rights and African Women: A Comparison of Protection under two Major Treaties, HRQ 1993, Vol. 15, p. 554; *C. Beyani*, Toward a More Effective Guarantee of Women's Rights in the African Human Rights System, in Human Rights of Women, R.J. Cook (ed.), Philadelphia 1994, p. 299.

[455] Discrimination based on gender occurs within the family structures where women are in an inferior position to men. As a rule they cannot negotiate a marriage and terminate it. Women are, moreover, precluded from inheritance. As we all know control of property "is the key to social empowerment". *T.W. Bennett*, p. 86. An example of a discriminatory cultural practice which still exists (called Troskosi) entails, *e.g.*, that young girls are given to traditional priests as payment for alleged crimes committed by male members of their families to serve in slavelike conditions on their farms and to bear their children. *E.A. Ankumah*, p. 119.

the treaty recognises, as earlier pointed out in the preamble, its adherence to the principles of human rights and freedoms contained in other human rights instruments adopted by the UN, and refers in particular to the UDHR.

As to the scope and content of civil and political rights in the African Charter, it covers a wide array, including a general prohibition against discrimination (Article 2)[456] and a very comprehensive clause concerning the prohibition of discrimination against women (Article 18(3)), to which I have referred earlier, rights such as the right to equality before the law and to equal protection hereunder (Article 3). On the other hand, the Charter makes no mention of important rights to be found in other international instruments as, *e.g.*, the right to a free choice of a marriage partner. Gender equality is closely related to custom and marriage. Arranged/forced marriages, to a great extent child marriages, are still practised on a large scale in Africa. They are clearly in conflict with the fundamental right to marry and the prohibition of discrimination on the basis of sex, *i.e.*, women are not guaranteed the same freedom to marry as men.[457] It has been argued that the omission of a right to marry with full and free consent in the African Charter is "indicative of the drafters' intention not to deviate from customary practices relating to women in general and with marriage in particular".[458]

The vagueness of most of the rights enshrined in the African Charter and the inclusion of a much criticised feature, *i.e.*, "claw-back" clauses, allowing states to curtail rights by the adoption of national legislation, present obstacles to the effectiveness of the African Commission. The Charter gives, however, wide powers to the Commission to interpret its provisions (Article 55(3)). This particular function of the Commission, which obviously is very similar to the advisory jurisdiction of the Inter-American Court, could become very important in practice in that it may enable the Commission to ensure that the interpretation of the African Charter's provisions is compatible with the general human rights law. However, it seems that the Commission has been until today generally reluctant to interpret the substantive provisions of the Charter in a dynamic way.

### *2.3.8.2. The Mandate of the African Commission*

Like the previously discussed regional conventions, the African Charter provides for the establishment of an African Commission for Human Rights[459] with promotional and protective functions (Article 30). In other words, it exercises formal quasi-judicial functions. It is composed of 11 members and it has been, since its inception (June 1987), entirely male until November 1993. The appointment of two

---

[456] The reference to the rights and freedoms in the Charter suggests that the general non-discrimination clause has like the corresponding provision of the European Convention limited application and can be invoked solely with other substantive provisions of the African Charter.

[457] Arranged (forced) marriages are according to contemporary human rights norms considered to be slavery-like practices. *M.K. Eriksson*, The Rights to Marry and to Found a Family, p. 78.

[458] *E.A. Ankumah*, p. 156.

[459] See generally: *E.A. Ankumah*, op. cit.; *A.C. Odinkalu*, Proposals for Review of the Rules of Procedure of the African Commission of Human and Peoples' Rights, HRQ 1993, Vol. 15, pp. 533–548.

women commissioners (in 1993 respectively 1995) was the result of relentless efforts by several NGOs.

The protective function of the Commission comprises a communication procedure. This enables it to hear complaints against member states, investigate the alleged violation, and announce their findings, opinion, and suggestions as to sanctions and compensation. This procedure consists of two parts, one copes with communications from member states, and one deals with "other communications", which includes individual complaints (see Articles 47 and 55 of the Charter). At the same time, it must be stressed that the Commission does not deal with individual violations of human rights but only with "special cases, which reveal the existence of a series of serious or massive violations of human and people's rights". One of the specific features of the African Charter in this regard is consequently that it also recognises class action (*actio popularis*).

The Commission does not publicise many of its activities, and in addition to the limited material available we may only establish that it has not developed jurisprudence on the relevant issues of our study.[460] More exactly, the Commission has not yet received any communication alleging violations of women's rights. By the end of 1993 none of the 108 individual communications received by the African Commission under the African Charter on Human and Peoples' Rights contained any allegation of violation of women's human right/s. The discourse of traditional values and custom might have had implications on that factual situation. Most of the cases submitted to the African Commission, as of the time of writing, involve allegations of human rights violations such as extra-judicial executions, on-going torture etc.[461] The only complaint so far which is of some relevance to my research concerns the criminalisation in Zimbabwe of male and not female homosexual conduct. Even though the communication was withdrawn, the Rapporteur of the Commission made a general pronouncement at the Commission's 16th session in 1994 that: "Although homosexuality and lesbianism are gaining recognition in certain parts of the world, this is not the case in Africa. Homosexuality offends the African sense of dignity and morality and is inconsistent with positive African values".[462]

Thus, the African Commission, or at least some of its members, has adopted a very restrictive approach on the issue of homosexuality.

---

460 Until 1994 the Commission has only published the number of communications it had received and those which it had declared admissible. Since 1994 it has started to provide the public with general information on the status of communications. The Commission has not disclosed the names of the states against whom the complaints have been filed. Neither has it described the nature of the cases under review. *E.A. Ankumah,* pp. 2 and 38; *W. Benedek*, Human Rights News, NQHR 1994, p. 469; *S. Malmström* & *G. Oberleitner*, Human Rights News: Africa, 17th Session of the African Commission on Human and Peoples Rights, NQHR 1995, p. 295. The Commission prepares Annual Activity Reports which are published after approval by the Assembly of Heads of State and Governments of the OAU. The review of the Commission's activities appears since 1991 in its Review. The annual reports are also published in the IHRR.

461 *E.A. Ankumah*, pp. 113, 117 and 135.

462 *Supra*, p. 174.

Generally up till now the work of the Commission has dealt mostly with the examination of state reports. Thus, as a control and monitoring function, the Commission considers periodic reports prepared by state parties on legislative or other measures taken with a view to giving effect to the Charter's provisions (Article 62). It seems that in its examination of state reports the Commission has seldom raised questions of relevance to women's rights[463] although in its guidelines for the submission of state reports it refers to the Women's Convention, *i.e.*, states should provide information on, for example, institutions which can ensure the equal treatment of women and men. The guide-lines for national periodic reports point out that: "Discrimination against Women in Africa is of such widespread occurrence that the Commission would like to receive reports on measures to eliminate this anachronism".[464] Yet, the periodic reports[465] received by the Commission give only little attention to women's rights. Some of the reports do not even mention the issue of discrimination against women at all.[466]

It is important to note that the Commission has used its promotional competence more creatively. It has frequently organised seminars on issues of great interest and concern. During its activities between 1992–1996, one of the seminars dealt specifically with the status of women under the African Charter. Moreover, during March 1995, just prior to the 17th session of the African Commission, Women in Law and Development in Africa organised a workshop on "Women and the African Charter" at which members of the Commission participated. The drafting of an additional protocol to the African Charter to strengthen the protection of women's rights and the appointment of a special rapporteur on women's rights was recommended. This proposal and the creation of an African Court on Human and People's Rights are among the crucial matters that have been incorporated in an Action Plan for the term 1997–2002.[467] Of significance for making the African system for the protection of human rights more gender sensitive is undoubtedly the draft additional protocol on the Rights of African Women. It contains several very progressive provisions and if the text were to be adopted as it is formulated at the beginning of 1998, it would imply a clear improvement of *de lege lata*. I would like to mention specifically Article 6, which requires states not to accept marriages without the free and full consent of both parties and that a married woman shall have the right to keep her maiden name. Polygamy is, furthermore, prohibited and Article 15 urges states to take measures to grant women "the right to abortion and the means to exercise that right".

---

[463] The Commission has, however, expressed the view during the consideration of the Zimbabwean report that the domestic legislation which exempts women and not men from the death penalty is in contravention of Article 3 of the Charter (equality before the law).

[464] African Commission on Human and Peoples' Rights, Documentation OAU, No. 1,1991, p. 68.

[465] At the beginning of 1994 about 20 states parties have submitted biennial country reports.

[466] *C.E. Welch*, The African Commission on Human and Peoples' Rights: A Five Years Report and Assessment, HRQ 1992, Vol. 14, p. 565.

[467] *O.W. Thiis*, The International Human Rights Machinery, in Manual on Human Rights Monitoring, Norwegian Institute of Human Rights, Oslo 1997, p. 30.

*2.3.8.3. Concluding Remarks*

The African Charter undoubtedly constitutes an important step in the establishment of the rule of law on the African continent. Its full realisation, however, especially in relation to gender equality still meets strong resistance from many governments.[468] The African Commission exhibits, in addition, several procedural and structural defects.[469] It lacks the authority to bind states to its decisions. A real hinder for the Commission's effectiveness is the fact that its findings and recommendations are subject to the approval by the OAU's supreme body, the Assembly of Heads of State and Government (AHSG), which is a political body. Another obstacle is that all measures it ever takes in its review of communications remain confidential until the AHSG decides otherwise (Article 59(1)). On the other hand, of special importance for raising the awareness of and mobilising support for women's human rights issues is that the African Commission, unlike some other supervisory human rights bodies, has allowed maximum participation of NGOs (many of them having an impressive representation of women) in its work. By mid 1998, more than 170 NGOs held observer status with the Commission. NGOs have made a positive impact on the work of the Commission.[470] NGOs, especially those concerned with women's rights, have been continually urging the African Commission to consider with earnestness the serious violations of human rights (*e.g.*, the practice of servile marriage, which precludes reproductive freedom) experienced by women on the continent. Nevertheless, *de iure*[471] and *de facto* discrimination based on gender, continues to impede the realisation of women's rights.[472] Thus, the protection afforded by the African Charter has remained largely illusory for African women and the system has not yet come into full operation in this regard. Hopefully as a human rights supervisory body, the African Commission will in the near future use the African Charter in a more creative and dynamic manner so that it can provide an evolutionary interpretation of the Charter in favour of gender equality.

Issues and practices which need urgent and greater attention and which fall short of modern human rights norms to be considered by the Commission include among others the question of whether the practice of female genital mutilation and rape constitute torture, cruel, inhuman and degrading treatment in violation of Article 5 of the African Charter; does forced marriage which is allowed by a customary law constitute a contemporary form of slavery?; does the practice of polygyny[473] in the light of AIDS infringe upon the right to health? Another issue, which is of

---

[468] *T.W. Bennett*, p. 83.

[469] Severe criticism has been expressed in regard to the competence and integrity of some members of the Commission. It has been argued that certain governmental positions may be the source of a conflict of interests and may negatively influence Commissioners in their ability to function as independent experts. *E.A. Ankumah*, pp. 14 and 18; *C.E. Welch*, p. 570.

[470] *C.E. Welch*, p. 55.

[471] Great number of African countries have to adopt laws on marriage age and laws requiring women's consent to marriage.

[472] *C.E. Welch*, p. 551.

[473] Polygyny is also seen as a "direct cause of female subordination". *T.W. Bennett*, p. 120.

significance for the status of women in Africa, centres on the inter-connection between adolescent pregnancy and violation of the right to education. In spite of the large scale nature of the above mentioned practices, the African Commission has up to date not received any complaints in this regard. There is, therefore, not a sufficient basis for making a general proposition that the African Commission has been gender-sensitive in its work.

### *2.3.9. Summary and Concluding Comments*

Summing up our discussion in Chapter 2 I may draw some preliminary conclusions.

The principle of non-discrimination on the basis of sex and gender equality figures prominently in all the binding human rights instruments under review. In addition, the asymmetrical approach to equality has gained great acceptance in a number of high-level political commitments reflected in several declarations adopted at UN's conferences during the 1990s.

The prohibition of discrimination on the basis of sex is, in addition, expressed in several provisions of international humanitarian law treaties providing for treatment "without any diverse distinction founded on sex".[474] Furthermore, Article 14 of the Third Geneva Convention requires that women "shall in all cases benefit by treatment as favourable as that granted to men". The prohibition of discrimination in the context of the relevant rules has been understood rather as a prohibition of unfavourable distinction than as a general prohibition of differentiated treatment.[475]

Prohibited discrimination in international law is, furthermore, generally perceived as a conduct on the part of agents of the government in a given country. Only during the last years have inter-personal relations in this respect become increasingly relevant in international human rights and humanitarian law, as we shall see later on in the following parts of my enquiry.

I have observed that, despite some variations in the formulations, the normative content of the principle of non-discrimination is essentially the same in the reviewed treaties. It is, therefore, of great importance that the provisions in questions are interpreted and applied in a uniform way by the different supervisory bodies. Since judicial reasoning is to a substantial degree conditioned by the judge's/expert's own conceptions, which largely depends upon one's background, the membership of these bodies is rather crucial. It is apparent from the earlier review of the various human rights regimes that there are indeed important differences in the composition, function and powers of the supervisory human rights

---

474 These are Articles 12 of the First and Second Geneva Conventions, Article 16 of the Third Convention, Article 27 of the Fourth Convention and Article 75 of Additional Protocol I and Article 4 of Additional Protocol II. Article 3 in all four Geneva Conventions on the protection of war victims from 1949 includes as well prohibition against discrimination on the basis of sex. At the end of 1998 the Geneva Conventions had 188 parties. See http://www.un.org./Depts/Treaty, 1998–10-10.

475 *F. Krill*, The Protection of Women in International Humanitarian Law, in International Review of the Red Cross 1985, No. 249.

organs established under the three regional systems[476] on the one hand and the universal one on the other. Much of the effectiveness of a human rights body depends not only on its size but also on the competence as well as credibility of its members. The African Commission and the Inter-American Commission and Court are small in their composition, which may become a real hinder for their efficiency in the future.[477] Another important feature relating to legitimacy and effectiveness is not only the geographical but also equitable gender balance. Thus, the conditions for membership should include reference to equitable gender distribution. Despite being human rights bodies upholding the principle of gender equality, several of the Committees still have few women members. With equal gender representation on the Committees and Commissions/Courts, it is more likely that expanded understanding of equality will occur. More women increase, in other words, the prospects of the application of a gender-based approach to treaty interpretation by the supervisory body in question. Even though some positive changes have occurred, *i.e.*, in the case of the African Commission, the appointment of more female members on the existing bodies is urgently needed. With the exception of CEDAW and the CRC, the remaining human rights bodies are dominated by a single gender – the male.

The co-existence of several complaint systems in regard to human rights at the universal and regional levels may lead, if at the same time the same complaint is submitted to other international bodies, to "the adoption of conflicting decisions or to a denial of justice".[478] However, in practice, as Tardu has pointed out, conflicting decisions have so far been avoided, among other things because of "a great deal of

---

476 Mention should be made here that some evidence of progress in regard to regional regimes for the protection of human rights in the Arab world and in Asia and the Pacific is discernible. The 1994 Arab Charter of Human and People's Rights earlier referred to, contains arrangements for supervision and implementation, including both a commission on human rights and a court. The Asian Human Rights Commission has recently issued, after consultation with 100 Asian NGOs, a final draft of an Asian Charter on Human Rights. The document does, however, not mention any supervisory body. It is admitted in § 9.1 of the Charter that "In most Asian societies women suffer from discrimination and suppression. The causes of their oppression lie both in history and contemporary social and economic systems". The text of the 1997 NGO Asian Charter on Human Rights is reprinted in *F. de Varennes*, Asia-Pacific Human Rights Documents and Resources, The Hague 1998, pp. 133–147. See also Focus, Newsletter of the Asia-Pacific HRIC, Osaka, June 1997, p. 13. For more comprehensive information on the process of developing a sub-regional human rights body in ASEAN see 58th meeting of the UN Commission on Human Rights, 23 April 1996 UN Doc. /CN.4/1996/64.

477 Professor Buergenthal has recently made us aware that there are many economic, social and political obstacles which the African human rights system faces today and which make the task of the African Commission extremely difficult. He also reminds us of the fact that also the treaty bodies established within the UN framework may in the near future be unable for financial reasons to fulfil their supervisory functions in a satisfactory manner. Continuation of the present situation may lead to the system collapsing, as the process of ratification by more and more states parties leads to ever-greater burdens for the committees. *T. Buergenthal*, The Normative and Institutional Evolution of International Human Rights, HRQ 1997, Vol. 19, p. 717.

478 *M.E. Tardu*, The Right of Individual Complaint to the United Nations for Violations of Human Rights, in International Human Rights Law, Theory and Practice, I. Cotler & F.P. Eliadis (eds.), The Canadian Human Rights Foundation 1992, p. 415. Also Professor Alston has pointed to the growing risks of inconsistency as standards proliferate and new treaty bodies are created. UN Doc. A/CONF. 157/PC/62/Add. 11/Rev. 1, 1993, p. 10.

*de facto* cross-fertilisation between procedures (*i.e.*, several persons being members of two or three complaint bodies at the same time or successively)".[479]

In order to prevent a normative chaos the chairs of the UN committees began initially to meet biennially and since a few years ago annually.[480] The issue of gender has been, as earlier mentioned, since, 1994 on the agenda of these annual meetings. As a further step to avoid the adoption of conflicting definitions of human rights by the different UN bodies, a compilation of general comments and general recommendations has been produced by the human rights treaty bodies.[481] A related idea would be to encourage representatives from the six committees to draw up joint General Comments.[482]

I might also mention that the European and Inter-American Courts on Human Rights have been engaged in a dialogue with each other since 1969 and have established regular meetings for the judges serving on both bodies.[483] There is consequently no normative disparity in the case law of the above mentioned organs on our subject matter.

This is in line with the effort within the international community to maximise normative consistency in order "to improve the chances of a coherent overall international human rights regime evolving, and to reduce the likelihood of widely diverging and even directly incompatible approaches and interpretations"[484] of human rights norms. Neither is this situation contrary to the widely accepted principle that regional instruments shall complement the adopted universal standards on human rights. So, the regional human rights instruments have an important role to play in the international efforts to promote *universal* respect for and observance of human rights and fundamental freedoms.

The significance of the jurisprudence of international organs lies also in the fact that decisions of the various bodies have contributed to changing and harmonising the legislation and practice of several states with international law standards.[485] Yet, the number of decided cases regarding different aspects of gender equality is

---

479 *M.E. Tardu*, ibid., p. 417.

480 See *P. Alston*, Long-term approaches to enhancing the effective operation of bodies established under United Nations human rights instruments, UN Doc. A/CONF.157/PC/62/Add.11, 1993; *A. Gallagher*, p. 308. As already mentioned earlier, Professor Alston proposed in his report to the UN Human Rights Commission in 1997 a series of measures to rationalise the reporting system, which has turned out to be too burdensome for developing countries and to make the procedures of different UN's committees similar before approaching the subject of a possible merging of treaty monitoring bodies. A possible solution would be that one supervisory body reviews country reports and another (preferably as a human rights court) deals with petitions.

481 UN Doc. HRI/GEN/1/Rev.1, 29 July 1994.

482 ISHR, Human Rights Monitor 1997, Nos. 39–40, p. 51.

483 The former President of the European Court, Mr. R. Ryssdal, has underlined the importance of such a co-operation on the basis that: "In view of the universality of human rights on the one hand, and the differences of local social and legal traditions on the other, frequent dialogue is essential". Council of Europe, Colloquy "Democracy and democratisation: a dialogue between Europe and Latin America", Strasbourg 1986, p. 27.

484 UN Doc. A/CONF.157/PC/62/Add.11/Rev.1,1993, p. 10.

485 As regards the legal effects of the HRC's decisions see UN Doc. A/CONF.157/PC/60/Add.5, p. 37, for the European system see *I. Cameron & M.K. Eriksson*, pp. 124–134.

very small. The jurisprudence of international human rights supervisory bodies in accordance with the treaty norms under which they operate confirms the understanding of the norm of gender non-discrimination as a sex-neutral norm requiring equal treatment of men and women. But this pervasive belief "in the underlying objectivity and 'gender neutrality' of core rights has prevented recognition of the fact that equal treatment of persons in unequal situations will invariably operate to perpetuate rather than to eradicate injustice".[486] The international organs have, thus, generally applied in their case law a rather formal, symmetrical approach to equality, thereby leaving untouched the causes and conditions of inequality. My evaluation of the case law has, furthermore, shown that with very few exceptions the supervisory bodies continue to ignore that some human rights violations have gender dimension. Human rights of significance for women's status have to be analysed in a more creative manner. Thus, limited understanding of rights leads to limited compliance and understanding of obligations. On the other hand, the effectiveness of human rights law is more than simple compliance. Conceptualisation is as important as a realisation of human rights norms. Therefore, a dynamic approach to normativity is necessary. Women have their own specific problems and sometimes only special measures can meet their needs. Therefore, I would like to stress once more that the asymmetrical approach to the concept of discrimination is better situated to accommodate women's interests. Only the few dissenting members of the European Commission have placed reproductive freedom in the context of gender equality as we shall see in the next part of this study.

While the definition of discrimination has been very broadly interpreted by the HRC and the right to equality has been considered as an autonomous right, the Strasbourg organs still apply the non-discrimination principle as subordinate to other substantive provisions. At the same time the general comments and other statements, *i.e.*, in connection with the review of states reports made by the international organs, reflect a modern understanding of equality, *i.e.*, as requiring substantive equality and in certain instances even obligation to undertake affirmative action in order to uplift previously disadvantaged groups. It is apparent from the aforesaid that greater consistency in the approach to equality and non-discrimination in all activities of the UN committees is needed.

I have also noted that most of the international supervisory organs apply the limited doctrine of *stare decisis, i.e.,* they refer to their previous judgment/statement in which they consider they have made a particularly important ruling on some legal principles. This ensures a certain degree of continuity and predictability in the organ's decisions. Nevertheless, this does not preclude the supervisory bodies from deviating from their earlier case law.[487] Thus, human rights treaties best serve their purpose if they are considered as living instruments, *i.e.*, designed to meet the needs of society, including women at the time of their application and interpretation rather than the time of their adoption. Closely connected with the

---

[486] *A. Gallagher*, p. 290.

[487] *F.G.E. Sundberg*, The European Experience of Human Rights Proceedings, p. 631.

consideration of the aim and purpose of a given human rights convention is the principle which requires that "the interpretation of a treaty should be such as to make it most effective and useful".[488] The European Court of Human Rights has often chosen the method of interpretation, which leads to effective protection of the individual rights to be guaranteed. The Inter-American Court has, furthermore, stressed the importance of interpreting human rights norms in favour of the individual "who is the object of international protection" in the *Gallardo* case.[489]

Human rights are broadly conceived and are, therefore, adaptable. While some of the human rights bodies have adopted a progressive dynamic approach and liberal open minded attitude on women's issues, which can enhance the status of women, others appear to have adopted a conservative, strictly legalistic and dogmatic approach towards the interpretation of treaty provisions.

Moreover, I have discerned that gender sensitivity is uneven in the activities of the various international bodies. The latest developments suggest that there is a noticeable increase in gender sensitivity, but that the CEDAW, the CRC and the Inter-American Commission on Human Rights seem to have gone furthest in incorporating a gender perspective into their contemporary overall work.

Notwithstanding my criticism, we should not overlook the potential significance of existing implementation procedures under international human rights law to focus on women's experience and thereby to change current gender inequality and to reduce discrimination against women.

---

488 *S. Davidson*, p. 69; *F. Matcher*, Methods of Interpretation of the Convention, in The European System for the Protection of Human Rights, R. St. J. Macdonald, F. Matscher & H. Petzold (eds.), pp. 63–83.

489 IACourtHR, *In the Matter of Vivianna Gallardo et al.*, No. G/101/81, Decision of November 13, 1981, Ser. A, § 16

*Chapter 3*

# The Principle of Non-discrimination on the Basis of Sex and Gender Equality – A Candidate for *Ius Cogens* Status

## 3.1. The Function of *Ius Cogens* Norms in International Law

Progressive development of modern international law presupposes the existence of an international public order containing some few selected rules having the character of *ius cogens*.[1] Such rules stand on a higher level in the legal system with regard to their compulsiveness and obligatoriness. As Koh has put it states "may have greater incentives to comply with some treaties, but greater obligations to comply with others, for example, those enforcing *jus cogens* norms".[2]

My previous presentation has shown that there is no doubt that the principle[3] of non-discrimination on the basis of sex and equality occupies a significant position in the field of human rights. However, the question of whether it might pretend to be a rule of *ius cogens* rather than *ius dispositivum* has still to be answered. Which place the principle occupies in a hierarchy of legal norms has a symbolic and practical impact. It allows clarification of priorities. *Ius cogens* rules are elite norms and create obligations for all states. Those peremptory norms are of highest rank and

---

[1] *Ius cogens* as a technical term means compelling law. A definition of the concept *ius cogens* is contained in Article 53 of the Vienna Convention on the Law of Treaties of 1969: "A peremptory norm of general international law is a norm accepted and recognised by the international community of States as a whole as a norm from which no derogation is permitted and which can be modified only by a subsequent norm of general international law having the same character". The literature on *ius cogens* is extensive. See generally on *ius cogens* as a legal institution: *E. Suy and others*, The Concept of Jus Cogens in Public International Law, in Lagonissi Conference on International Law, Papers and Proceedings, Vol. II, Geneva 1967, p. 17 *et seq.*; *J. Sztucki,* Jus Cogens and the Vienna Convention on the Law of Treaties; A Critical Appraisal, Vienna 1974; *C.L. Rozakis*, The Concept of Jus Cogens in the Law of Treaties, Amsterdam 1976; *G.M. Danilenko*, International *Jus Cogens*: Issues of Law-Making, EJIL 1991, Vol. 2, pp. 42–66. See also for references on this subject matter in *Sir R. Jennings & Sir A. Watts*, Oppenheim's International Law, London 1992, pp. 7–8 and *M. Byers*, Conceptualising the relationship between *Jus Cogens* and *Erga Omnes* Rules, NJIL 1997, Vol. 66, pp. 214–215 and *M. Ragazzi*, The Concept of International Obligations *Erga Omnes*, Oxford 1997, p. 43, note 1.

[2] *H.H. Koh*, p. 2641.

[3] Even though one might distinguish between the terms "rule" and "principle", they are very often used in the international law literature interchangeably and so will I since there seems to be an agreement that *ius cogens* may include both. *M. Ragazzi*, pp. 136–137.

below them there are other binding norms of customary and conventional rules. In other words, *ius cogens* norms are universally applicable norms and are of normative superiority. The theory of *ius cogens* consequently introduces a distinction between peremptory and merely binding norms.

Much of the importance of the *ius cogens* doctrine consists, in other words, in "its symbolic significance in the international legal process",[4] since it introduces notions of superiority and universality into international law. It is, therefore, of relevance to my study to answer the question of whether non-discrimination on the basis of sex and gender equality are included among the "most fundamental and highly-valued interests"[5] of the international community. The normative status of the non-discrimination principle provides an important tool with which to strengthen arguments in international law against many forms of discrimination against girls and women. In our case, it would also be of value to determine the ambit of a number of broad reservations attached to the Women's Convention. Reservations will "only be effective as long as they do not trespass on areas which are part of the body of jus cogens".[6] Another practical function of *ius cogens* norm emanates from Article 53 of the Vienna Convention on the Law of Treaties which implies that a treaty would become void if "at the time of its conclusion, it conflicts with a peremptory norm of general international law". An additional impact of *ius cogens* norms signifies that the international community of states as a whole retains the right to impose a peremptory norm on a limited number of recalcitrant states.[7] In other words, states are bound by *ius cogens* norms irrespective of their free consent.[8] Since *ius cogens* rules seem to preclude persistent objection, states cannot contract out of such a rule.[9] These norms may not be altered or excluded by states in their international life. Rules of *ius cogens* indicate and illustrate the continuing development in international law away from considerations based on the principle of states' sovereignty towards the evolution of international law as an all-embracing universal legal order. This has been encapsulated by Professor Meron who asserts that the concept of *ius cogens* reflects "the quest of the international community for a normative order, in which higher rights are invoked as particularly compelling moral and legal barriers to derogations from and violations of human rights".[10]

While there is still no authoritative pronouncement by an international court on the normative status of the principle on non-discrimination on the basis of sex, the

---

[4] *H. Charlesworth & C. Chinkin*, The Gender of Jus Cogens, HRQ 1993, Vol. 15, p. 66.

[5] *G. Christenson*, Jus Cogens: Guarding Interests Fundamental to International Society, Virginia Journal of International Law 1988, p. 587.

[6] *G. Van Bueren*, p. 57.

[7] *L. Hannikainen*, pp. 5–6.

[8] *Ius cogens* norms are controversial particularly because they are non-consensual and yet binding. *K.D. Askin*, p. 240. At the same, time Professor Koskenniemi has emphasised that "what those norms are is determined by consent". *M. Koskenniemi*, From Apology to Utopia, p. 283.

[9] *M. Ragazzi*, p. 67; *L. Hannikainen*, p. 213; *C.L. Rozakis*, p. 78; *P. Weil*, p. 430.

[10] *T. Meron*, Human Rights and Humanitarian Norms as Customary Law, Oxford 1989, p. 8.

European Commission on Human Rights, though not explicitly referring to the *ius cogens* character of the prohibition of discrimination on the grounds of sex, expressed its view in the case of *Abdulaziz, Cabales and Balkandali v. the United Kingdom* that gender as a specific ground for the prohibition of discrimination is one of the most central ones as regards the principle of non-discrimination. Thus, "(h)eading the citation of prohibited forms of discrimination under Article 14 of the (European) Convention is that of discrimination on grounds of sex".[11]

While Judge Tanaka in a dissenting opinion in the South-West Africa Case (second phase) took a clear position that "surely the law concerning the protection of human rights may be considered to belong to the jus cogens",[12] the International Court of Justice has only occasionally expressed the view that the principle of equality and non-discrimination (on certain grounds) constitutes a part of *ius cogens* as for instance in the *Barcelona Traction* case[13] and in the *Namibia* advisory opinion.[14]

Within the international law doctrine a number of international law jurists support the idea of *ius cogens* as an indispensable foundation of the international legal order.[15] According to Professor Brownlie, the freedom from gender discrimination belongs to "the least controversial examples"[16] of *ius cogens*. The same author argued that, if protection against race discrimination is a part of *ius cogens*, so ought sex discrimination to be. This author adheres to Brownlie's view that if racial discrimination universally is rejected as an admissible derogation from the principle of equality, this should be true for gender. After all more than half of the world's population consists of women. In addition, I would like to submit that the UN Charter and other relevant international law instruments do not distinguish

---

[11] A great number of cases have been lodged with the European Commission on Human Rights by women living in the United Kingdom complaining of gender discrimination contrary to Article 14 of the Convention in the realisation of their right to respect for family life contained in Article 8 of the Convention. The Commission selected three of these applications, namely Application No. 9214/80, *Abdulaziz*, Application No. 9473/81, *Cabales*, Application No. 9474/81 and *Balkandali vs UK*, Application No. 9474/81. See the Report of the European Commission of 12 May 1983, § 103. After reviewing them, the Commission came to the conclusion that the applicants had been victims of discrimination on the grounds of sex, in violation of Article 14 taken together with Article 8 as a result of unjustified differences of treatment in securing the right to respect for their family life. According to domestic rules, it was easier for a man settled in the United Kingdom than for a woman so settled to obtain permission for his or her non-national spouse to enter or remain in the country for settlement. The European Court of Human Rights ruled that discrimination on the grounds of sex was the result of norms that were incompatible with the European Convention. See ECHR Judgment 28 May 1985, Ser. A, No. 94, p. iii.

[12] *I. Brownlie*, Basic documents, p. 454.

[13] *Barcelona Traction, Light and Power Co. Ltd.* case (Belgium v. Spain), Judgment of 5 February 1970, ICJ Rep. 1970 §§ 33–34.

[14] Namibia (Advisory Opinion), ICJ Rep.1971, §§ 72–75. ICJ has referred to *ius cogens* norms also in the *US Diplomatic and Consular Staff in Teheran,* ICJ Rep.1980, pp. 30–31, *Military and Paramilitary Activities in and Against Nicaragua*, ICJ Rep.1986, p. 14. For a thorough review of the jurisprudence of international tribunals which has some bearing upon the question of *ius cogens* see *J. Sztucki*, pp. 12–16.

[15] See references in *H. Charlesworth & C. Chinkin,* pp. 66–67.

[16] *I. Brownlie*, Principles of International Law, Oxford 1990, p. 513.

between race and sex in the provisions, which prohibit discrimination. Therefore, there is no reasonable ground to accord these classifications different priorities. We must at the same time admit that there is still no general agreement as to the precise content[17] of the concept *ius cogens* and that very few examples of *ius cogens* enjoy unanimous support. It has still to be elaborated in the jurisprudence of international organs and in the practice of states.

The International Law Commission itself stated in its commentary to Article 53 of the Vienna Convention on the Law of Treaties[18] that "since there is no simple criterion by which to identify a general rule of international law as having the character of Jus Cogens"[19] difficulties will be experienced in the application of the rule of *ius cogens*. The following sub-chapter will serve as an illustration to that proposition.

### 3.2. Rules, which have been Identified as Part of the Concept of *Ius Cogens*

Although the major difficulty related to *ius cogens* is the identification of such norms, there are a number of suggestions with regard to rules that qualify as principles of *ius cogens*. Since *ius cogens* is an evolving concept according to the principles accepted by the international community, its substance has been expanded during the years.

I shall give below some examples, in chronological order, of different views in scholarly writings as to the content and how the catalogue of *ius cogens* has increased.

Prior to the establishment of the League of Nations (LN) in 1919, there is some evidence that some norms, especially within maritime law (*e.g.*, prohibition of piracy), fulfilled the criteria of peremptory norms. The prohibition of the international slave trade was also considered as a peremptory norm.[20]

During the period after the establishment of the LN but before the founding of the UN, several norms of international law developed which had the characteristics

---

[17] Prior to the adoption of the Vienna Convention on the Law of Treaties, there have been views expressed in international law doctrine that *ius cogens* does not exist. Professor Schwarzenberger, for example, has maintained that international law on the level of unorganised international society does not know of any *ius cogens*. See: *G. Schwarzeberger*, A Manual of International Law, Vol. 2, London 1960. For scholarly scepticism see references in *M. Byers*, p. 215. Professor Verdross on the other hand is of the opinion that all rules of general international law created for a humanitarian purpose and certain principles embodied in Article 2 of the UN Charter had the character of *ius cogens*. See *A. Verdross*, Jus Dispositivum and Jus Cogens in International Law, AJIL 1966, Vol. 60, p. 217 *et seq*; Forbidden Treaties in International Law, AJIL 1937, Vol. 31, p. 571 *et seq*. See also *E. Schwelb*, Some Aspects of International Jus Cogens as Formulated by the International Law Commission, AJIL 1967, Vol. 61, p. 948 *et seq*.

[18] 1155 UNTS 331, reprinted in 8 I.L.M. 1969 p. 679.

[19] ILC, Report UN GA, XXI session, OR, Supp. 9, p. 76.

[20] *L. Hannikainen*, pp. 67, 78; *F. Capotorti*, L'Extinction et la Suspension des Traités, Recueil des Cours (RdC) 1971, Vol. III, at 522.

of peremptory norms. Among them the prohibition of wars of aggression was most widely agreed upon. The PCIJ played a significant role in clarifying the content of *ius cogens*.[21]

In the early 1930s von der Heydte classified *ius cogens* norms in three categories. The first one included norms that are indispensable to the existence of every legal order. The second category referred to norms closely bound up with the character of inter-state relations and finally the third category comprised norms in the existence of which the international community has an interest.[22]

The most noteworthy development as regards *ius cogens* is, however, the work of the International Law Commission (ILC)[23] on the text of the Vienna Convention on the Law of Treaties. The Commission did not give in its draft any examples of rules that could be categorised as *ius cogens* since it recognised that contemporary international law is in a process of rapid development, and it would be unwise to do so.[24] Several of the delegations at the Vienna Conference during the discussions on Article 53 gave, however, examples of norms, which in their view , were peremptory ones of general international law. According to a compilation of the records of the meetings produced by Professor em. Sztucki, some of the selected *ius cogens* rules were as follows: 13 delegations proposed prohibition of genocide, 12 delegations suggested prohibition of slavery, 7 delegations were in favour of human rights and 2 named the prohibition of racial discrimination.[25] After the adoption of the Vienna Convention, several writers have commented upon *ius cogens*, especially its content.

According to Roberto Ago *ius cogens* includes: "the fundamental rules concerning the safeguarding of peace, fundamental rules of a humanitarian nature (prohibi-

---

[21] The *Lotos* case, PCIJ Reports, Ser. A, No. 10, p. 5.

[22] *F.A. von der Heydte*, Die Erscheinungsformen des zwischenstaatlichen Rechts: jus cogens und jus dispositivum im Völkerrecht, Zeitschrift für Völkerrecht 1932, p. 471. Professor em. Sztucki has rendered a comprehensive compilation of propositions made in the international law doctrine, prior to the Vienna Convention coming into force in 1980, regarding norms considered to possess the nature of *ius cogens*. Accordingly most authors supported the prohibition of slavery and genocide. Thereafter followed fundamental norms of humanitarian nature and the prohibition of traffic in women and/or children. *J. Sztucki*, pp. 81–83.

[23] I should in this respect also mention Article 19 (3) of the ILC draft of a convention on state responsibility (UNGA OR, 51st session Suppl. 10, A/51/10) in which the definition of international crimes refers in my opinion to *ius cogens* rules, even though not *expressis verbis*, that are considered evident: "a serious breach of an international obligation of essential importance for the maintenance of international peace and security, such as that prohibiting aggression; a serious breach of an international obligation of essential importance for safeguarding the right of self-determination of peoples, such as that prohibiting the establishment or maintenance by force of colonial denomination; a serious breach on a widespread scale of an international obligation of essential importance of safeguarding the human being, such as those prohibiting slavery, genocide and apartheid; a serious breach of an international obligation of essential importance for the safeguarding and preservation of the human environment, such as those prohibiting massive pollution of the atmosphere or of the seas". *J.A. Frowein*, Jus Cogens, in Encyclopedia of Public International Law, R. Bernhardt (ed.), Instalment 7, Amsterdam 1984, p. 328. For more recent work of the ILC on that draft see *G. Lysen*, State Responsibility and International Liability of States for Lawful Acts, Uppsala 1997.

[24] YBILC 1966, ii, pp. 247–249. See also *O. Schachter*, p. 343.

[25] *J. Sztucki*, pp. 119–120.

tion of genocide, slavery and racial discrimination, protection of essential rights of the human person in time of peace and war), the rules prohibiting infringement of the independence and sovereign equality of States, etc."[26]

A well-known international lawyer and former President of the International Court of Justice, Jiménez de Aréchaga, enumerated the following rules as being *ius cogens*: "they include the prohibition of use or threat of force and of aggression, the prevention and repression of genocide, piracy, slave-trade, racial discrimination, terrorism or taking of hostages".[27] Professor Henkin, who also has been a former president of the ICJ, has found that *ius cogens* norms in contemporary international law include the prohibition of the use or threat of force and of aggression, the prevention and repression of genocide, piracy, slave-trade, racial discrimination, terrorism or the taking of hostages.[28] Even though this exemplification of the *ius cogens* has gained many advocates during the years, it has been rightly criticised as reflecting "a male perspective of what is fundamental to international society that may not be shared by women or supported by women's experience of life".[29]

Other legal writers have made suggestions that are more inclusive. Professor em. Detter De Lupis introduces in her monograph "The Concept of International Law" a theory according to which rules of basic importance to the survival of the international society are "prophylactic rules" in international law. The author describes this new concept, which in my view corresponds to the concept of *ius cogens,* as follows: "rules prohibiting force in general, as well as the substratum of human and humanitarian rights".[30]

In the modern doctrine the Finnish international lawyer, Hannikainen, has put together a comprehensive list of norms which in his view are considered as peremptory in contemporary international law. They are as follows:[31]

"1. the prohibition of aggressive armed force between States;
2. respect for the self-determination of peoples;

---

[26] *R. Ago*, Introduction au droit des traités à la lumière de la Convention de Vienne, RdC 1971, Vol. III, p. 324.

[27] *E. Jiménez de Aréchaga*, International Law in the Past Third of a Century, RdC 1978, Vol. I, p. 64.

[28] *L. Henkin*, International Law Cases and Materials, New York 1987, p. 470.

[29] *H. Charlesworth & C. Chinkin*, p. 67.

[30] *I. Detter De Lupis*, The Concept of International Law, Stockholm 1987, p. 32. In the second edition of this monograph Ingrid Detter identifies the core of human rights belonging to the "bare substratum" as follows: "Now there are fairly clear rules that individuals enjoy certain basic rights: they must thus not be subjected to genocide, slavery, apartheid, or to other forms of racial discrimination or to torture. To these rights must be added the freedom of expression." *I. Detter,* The Concept of International Law, Stockholm 1993, p. 48. In a textbook of international law the same writer defines the prophylactic rules as "those, which are designed to prohibit harm to international society. To this group we can count rules, which forbid the use of force, between states, or, between groups, such as insurgents, freedom fighters or terrorists, between such groups and states, or between states and individuals by violating Human Rights. Some prophylactic rules concern the protection of international society from environmental damage or excessive waste of natural resources". *I. Detter,* International Law, Stockholm 1991, p. 206.

[31] *L. Hannikainen*, p. 317.

3. respect for basic human rights;[32]
4. respect for basic rules, which guarantee the international status, order and viability of sea, air and space areas outside national jurisdiction;
5. respect for the basic norms of the international law of armed conflicts., *i.e.,* the law of war."

Decisions of municipal courts and international arbitral tribunals, as well as the opinions given by the *ad hoc* Arbitration Commission on the former Yugoslavia, contain references to *ius cogens*.[33]

In the light of what has been said above, I may conclude that despite the wide range of existing views there is today pervasive support for the presumption that basic human rights ought to be considered as part of *ius cogens*. Nevertheless, there is still some controversy as to which human rights are to be considered basic and whether all basic human rights fulfil the criteria of peremptory norms. The purpose of this study and its limited space does not allow us to undertake a lengthy discussion on that matter. I shall return, however, to this issue below in section 3.4. The present author adheres to the view of writers in international law doctrine who agree that at least the common non-derogable rights listed in universal human rights conventions ought to be defined as basic.[34] Of interest for my survey is then whether the principle of non-discrimination and equality belongs to the list of these basic human rights. There are, in addition, authors who have taken a slightly more reluctant position but who have questioned whether the exclusion of the prohibition of discrimination on the basis of sex from the list of basic human rights belonging to *ius cogens* is justifiable.[35] According to others the prohibition of discrimination against women obviously belongs to the notion of basic human rights.[36] Equality of human beings before the law and the prohibition of discrimination on the basis of sex is given the most central place in international instruments. The fact that the principles are included throughout the UN Charter accords them "a preeminent position in the field of human rights".[37] According to McKean, it is generally

---

[32] Also Professor Frowein has listed rules concerning the basic rights of the human person, *i.e.*, fundamental human rights as part of *ius cogens*. *J.A. Frowein*, Jus Cogens, p. 328.

[33] Opinion No. 2 of the Arbitration Commission mentions respect for fundamental human rights among the "normes imperatives du droit international général". See *M. Ragazzi*, pp. 47, 69.

[34] Professor Theodoor van Boven has presented some weighty arguments in favour of distinguishing fundamental (called by the same author elementary or supra-positive rights) from other human rights. Accordingly the former category of rights lies "at the foundation of the international community". These rights are valid under all circumstances and they are non-derogable. *T.C. van Boven,* Distinguishing Criteria of Human Rights, in The International Dimensions of Human Rights, K. Vasak (ed.), Vol. 1, p. 48. Henkin and Dinstein have, on the other hand, criticised the assumption that fundamental rights would coincide with non-derogable rights in a public emergency. See *M. Ragazzi*, p. 143.

[35] *B. Sima & P. Alston*, The Sources of Human Rights Law: Custom, Ius cogens & General Principles, Australian YIL 1992, Vol. 12, p. 82.

[36] *I. Brownlie,* Universality of Human Rights in a Pluralistic World, Council of Europe, Strasbourg 1990, p. 93.

[37] *D. Shelton*, Improving the Status of Women Through International Law, Whittier Law Review 1987, Vol. 9 , p. 414.

agreed that Articles 1 and 2 of the UN Charter are peremptory norms of general international law binding on members and non-members alike.[38] As of June 1998, 185 states were members of the organisation.[39] The importance of the prohibition of discrimination on the basis of sex and gender equality may be measured also by the frequency with which it is included in practically all instruments dealing with human rights issues. Judge van Dijk classifies prohibition of discrimination into the category of the "very core of human rights", not only because it is proclaimed as a non-derogable right, *i.e.*, it can never be suspended, but because it is a right, without which "human existence is impossible, both physically and mentally".[40] In the domestic sphere the principle of gender non-discrimination and equality is included in virtually every state and it has become an integral part of the constitutions of most countries in the world.[41] Botswana, which has not ratified yet the conventions containing the relevant provisions, has prohibited discrimination on the basis of sex in its constitution. With this background it might be possible to argue that the principle of non-discrimination on the basis of sex and gender equality possess the character of *ius cogens* rule.

I shall now return to Article 53 of the Vienna Convention on the Law of Treaties as a starting point in order to set out criteria for that purpose and for identification of *ius cogens* rules. The above provision establishes the general definition of *ius cogens* in international law and it contains according to Hannikainen[42] four of the criteria for the identification of a peremptory norm. Thus:

"1. They are norms of general international law.
2. They have to be accepted by the international community of States as a whole.
3. They permit no derogation.
4. They can be modified only by new peremptory norms."

Lauri Hannikainen suggests, furthermore, that a fifth criterion be added to the four above mentioned, namely: "A fifth criterion is derivable from the purpose of jus cogens: peremptory norms protect overriding interests of the international community of States; therefore obligations under peremptory norms are owed by States to the international community of States".[43]

---

[38] *W. McKean*, p. 280.

[39] Web site: http:/www.un.org/Overview/unmember.htm.

[40] *P. van Dijk*, A Common Standard of Achievement, NQHR 1995, p. 115. In line with this reasoning it would be possible to argue that some aspects of reproductive freedom can be considered as having attained the status of *ius cogens*. Prohibition of violations of sexual integrity can be included within several of the non-derogable rights, *e.g.*, prohibition of torture and other inhuman or degrading treatment. In addition, Kelly Askin, suggests that since rape committed during the course of armed conflict is a war crime, it has received *ius cogens* status. *K. Askin*, p. 141. See also *J. Fitzpatrick*, Human Rights in Crisis, Philadelphia 1994, pp. 35, 63.

[41] The Albert Sloman Library Law and Human Rights Page at Essex University contains world constitutions (http://libwww.essex.ac.uk/plus/humr/html). See also *L. Hannikainen*, p. 468.

[42] *L. Hannikainen*, p. 3.

[43] Ibid., p. 207.

Consequently for a norm to be considered peremptory, all five criteria must be satisfied.

## 3.3. Norms of General International Law

### *3.3.1. General Discussion*

I shall start my enquiry on the question of the status of the principle of non-discrimination on the basis of sex and gender equality by exploring the first of the above mentioned criteria, namely the requirement to be a "norm of general international law".

According to the late Professor Akehurst, a rule of *ius cogens* can be derived from customary law and possibly from treaties.[44] This view is supported by reports of the ILC and several international scholars.[45]

In the American Restatement of Foreign Relations Law the view has been taken that freedom of gender discrimination "may already be a principle of customary international law".[46]

There is a widespread view in the doctrine[47] that the prohibition of discrimination, at least with respect to the grounds of race and sex,[48] has already become a principle of customary international law and that it, therefore, is even binding on states, which have never expressly agreed to it. The late Professor Lillich[49] suggested that the principle of non-discrimination (equal protection) is part of customary law. Scholars like Lung-Chu Chen, McKean and Hannikainen[50] may be mentioned among those who support the idea that non-discrimination on any ground is a fundamental component of human rights and is as such part of customary law

---

[44] *M. Akehurst*, The hierarchy of the sources of international law, BYIL 1974–1975, Vol. 47, p. 273.

[45] For references see *P. Thornberry*, International Law and the Rights of Minorities, Oxford 1992, p. 98. The ILC has, however, refused to make a distinction between, or give priority to, specific sources of international law for the purpose of ascertaining the peremptory character of a norm. *J. Sztucki*, p. 73.

[46] *A.F. Bayefsky*, The Principle of Equality or Non-Discrimination in International Law, p. 21.

[47] *L. Henkin, R.C. Pugh, O. Schachter & H. Smith*, International Law, Cases and Materials, St. Paul, Minnesota 1987, p. 998; *J.E. Guertin*, Customary international law and women's rights, Detroit College of Law Review, p. 138; *A. Bayefsky*, The Principle of Equality or Non-Discrimination in International Law: Implications for Equally Rights in the Charter, in Righting the Balance: Canada's New Equality Rights, L. Smith (ed.), 1986, pp. 123–25; *B.G. Ramcharan*, Equality and Nondiscrimination, in The International Bill of Rights: The Covenant on Civil and Political Rights, L. Henkin (ed.), New York 1981, p. 246; *Y. Dinstein*, Discrimination and International Human Rights, Israel Yearbook of Human Rights 1985, Vol. 15, p. 11.

[48] See references in *L.M. Hitch*, Non-discrimination and the rights of the child, Article 2, Journal of Human Rights 1989, Vol. VII, p. 50 and *J. Oraa*, Human Rights in States of Emergency in International Law, Oxford 1992, p. 263.

[49] *R. Lillich*, Civil Rights, in Human Rights in International Law: Legal and Policy Issues, T. Meron (ed.), Oxford 1984, p. 115.

[50] *Lung-Chu Chen*, An Introduction to Contemporary International Law, Yale University Press 1989, p. 179; *W. McKean*, p. 44 and *L. Hannikainen,* p. 718. See also *T. Einarsen,* Discrimination and Consequences for the Position of Aliens, NJIL 1995, Vol. 64, p. 430.

and consequently of *ius cogens*. McKean argues for good reasons "for accepting that the principles of equality and non-discrimination, in view of their nature as fundamental constituents of the international law of human rights, are part of the jus cogens".[51] Kelly Askin maintains, in addition, that especially after 1993 there is a clearly identifiable "trend toward treating gender discrimination as a violation of customary international law".[52] There are, nevertheless, few commentators on international law, who are not prepared to recognise discrimination on the basis of sex either as a customary law rule or as a *ius cogens* norm. As generally accepted impermissible discrimination only systematic racial discrimination is referred to.[53]

Professor Meron assumes that: "(t)he repetition of certain norms in many human rights instruments is in itself an important articulation of state practice and may serve as evidence of customary international law".[54]

Professor Alston has elaborated the following test, a so – called *quality control*, for human rights to be considered part of international customary law:

> "1. the proposed right must be fundamental; 2. it must be universal in the senses both that it is universally or very widely recognised and that it is guaranteed to everyone, and 3. it must be capable of sufficiently precise formulation to give rise to legal obligations on the part of a state, rather than merely setting a standard of conduct".[55]

The claim of a norm to be fundamental and the demand that it enjoys very wide recognition is consequently of primary importance. This author has taken the view in the previous discussion that gender non-discrimination and equality should be considered a basic[56] human right.

Professor Dinstein has taken the position that the prohibition of discrimination "in the exercise of human rights"[57] constitutes part of customary law. He argues, however, against separating basic from ordinary human rights since such a distinction "would be without foundation in the theory and practice of human rights. All human rights are interchangeably depicted as fundamental freedoms. Any attempt to rate some of them as more basic than others would be confusing and ill-advised".[58]

---

[51] *W. McKean*, p. 283.

[52] *K. Askin*, p. 231.

[53] *V. Dimitrijevich*, 7th International Colloquy on the European Convention on Human Rights, Council of Europe, H/Coll(90)7, 1990, p. 3. See also *C.E. Welch*, p. 574.

[54] *T. Meron*, pp. 92–94. As evidence of sources Professor Meron refers to the UN Charter, the UDHR, global agreements, regional agreements, general support for UN resolutions, incorporation of human rights provisions into national constitutions, etc.

[55] *P. Alston*, Conjuring Up New Human Rights: a Proposal for Quality Control, AJIL 1984, Vol. 78, p. 607.

[56] I prefer the phrase "basic" right to the phrase "fundamental" partly because the ICJ has used the former term. Both expressions are, however, used interchangeably in official documents and in the literature. See *M. Ragazzi*, p. 139.

[57] *Y. Dinstein*, Discrimination and International Human Rights, p. 11.

[58] *Y. Dinstein*, The *erga omnes* Applicability of Human Rights, in Archiv des Völkerrechts 1992, Vol. 30, p. 17.

Norms of general international law are of general applicability, *i.e.*, they create obligations and/or rights for at least a large majority of states or other subjects of international law.[59]

A visible indication that a great majority of states have accepted a candidate for *ius cogens* status would be broad state participation in, and acceptance of, relevant international instruments (treaties, declarations, resolutions and others) establishing or embodying the norm. In other words, the proportion of the states that have ratified the international document in question is important. Therefore, I have to explore whether the majority of states have accepted obligations under the principle of non-discrimination on the grounds of sex.

As already pointed out, prohibition of discrimination on the basis of sex is included in all general conventions on human rights. These conventions are further developments of the Universal Declaration. The Declaration has evolved into a very important instrument and it is the primary source of global human rights standards. It is an accepted view in contemporary international law that the UDHR "has acquired a legal aura",[60] *i.e.*, it creates binding obligations on states, partly because it was passed without a negative vote and because many of its provisions have been incorporated in national constitutions and international agreements.[61] From the

---

[59] *L. Hannikainen*, p. 208.

[60] *T.J. Farer & F. Gaer*, The UN and Human Rights, in A. Roberts & B. Kingsbury (eds.), United Nations, Divided World, Oxford 1993, p. 249.There are several statesmen and scholars who have concluded that the UDHR has become binding as international custom in accordance with Article 38 of the Status of the International Court of Justice. See, *e.g., A. Eide & G. Alfredson*, Introduction, in The Universal Declaration on Human Rights, A. Eide *et al.* (eds.), p. 7. It is, furthermore, stated in The Human Development Report (UNDP) 1996 on page 25 that "The Universal Declaration of Human Rights is universally accepted as binding customary international law". Moreover, there are scholars who argue that the UDHR as a whole has become binding as customary law (see , *e.g.,* the Special Representative of the UN Commission on Human Rights, R. Gallindo Pohl's Report on the Human Rights Situation in the Islamic Republic of Iran, UN Doc. E/CN.4/1987/23, at 4–5) and *J.C. Salvedo*, Human Rights, Universal Declaration (1948), Encyclopedia of International Law, Vol. 8, p. 307. Most scholars seem, however, at least to agree that many of the principles embodied in the UDHR can be regarded as a part of customary international law. For the latter position see *A.H. Robertson & J.G. Merrills*, p. 27; *G. Melander*, FN-systemet, in FN och de mänskliga rättigheterna, B. Dunér (ed.), Falun 1995, p. 15. See for references *K. Askin*, p. 230, note 726. Other scholars have found the Declaration's norms to constitute *ius cogens*. Yet, the ILA Committee on the Enforcement of Human Rights reached the conclusion in a report which refers to those authors that many, if not all of the rights elaborated in the UDHR, are nowadays recognised as constituting rules of customary law that even with respect to protected rights, state practice does not support a conclusion that there is full compliance with the principle of equality. That makes it difficult to prove the necessary requirement of state practice. The International Law Association, Report of the 66th Conference held at Buenos Aires, Argentina, 14 to 20 August 1994, Buenos Aires 1994, pp. 526, 539 and 545.

[61] McKean considers the UDHR to have acquired the status of customary law since it is referred to in numerous resolutions, statements and declarations. *W. McKean*, p. 274. These arguments and the statement made by 171 representatives for Governments who participated in the 1993 Vienna Conference on Human Rights, whereby they reaffirmed their commitment to the purposes and principles of the UN Charter and the UDHR as well as their belief in the importance of the Universal Declaration in setting standards for human rights, leads us to the conclusion that the UDHR is at least, to a certain extent, part of international customary law, mainly because of its general and inspirational character.

UDHR derive, for instance, the two UN covenants (ICCPR and ICESCR) as well as regional conventions[62] on human rights. All of them contain a prohibition of gender discrimination and require equality between the sexes. Universal acceptance and adherence is presupposed.[63] The ICCPR has been ratified as of October 1998 by 140 states and the ICESCR by 137 states. Some 29 small countries (populations under one million) have not ratified either of the covenants. Only two states are not yet party to any human rights treaty. Moreover, the Women's Convention treats specifically the prohibition of discrimination against women in all its forms. In other words, sexual discrimination along with racial discrimination are the only two grounds of discrimination "(w)hich have had sufficient degree of international agreement so as to permit the promulgation of specialised treaties devoted solely to non-discrimination on these bases".[64] This Convention was adopted in the United Nations GA by a vote of 130-0-10 and has been ratified as of September 1998 by 161 states, *i.e.*, 87,5% of the whole international community , in the sense of members of the UN. The Women's Convention belongs to the conventions that enjoy, alongside with the Convention on the Rights of the Child and the 1949 Geneva Conventions, the highest number of ratifications and accessions and it is consequently universal in reach.[65] Here I might compare the prohibition of discrimination on the basis of sex with the prohibition of racial discrimination, which is universally rejected as an inadmissible derogation from the principle of equality. There is today almost unanimous support for the idea that the prohibition of racial discrimination is the subject of an international custom and that it belongs to *ius cogens*. Yet the UN Convention on the Elimination of All Forms of Racial Discrimination has, in fact, much fewer ratifications[66] than the Women's Convention.

This high level of international commitment to the non-discrimination principle on the grounds of sex clearly indicates its universal acceptance.[67] There is, furthermore, a close link between human rights as part of, and protected by, customary international law and *ius cogens* and reservations to multilateral treaties. The HRC expressed the position in its General Comment No. 24/52 that: "Reservations that offend peremptory norms would not be compatible with the object and purpose of the Covenant" and "Accordingly, provisions in the Covenant that represent

[62] The European Convention for the Protection of Human Rights and Fundamental Freedoms, the American Convention on Human Rights, and the African Charter on Human and Peoples' Rights.

[63] The Sub-Commission on Prevention of Discrimination and Protection of Minorities has established on the basis of res. 1 B(XXXII) a sessional Working Group on the Encouragement of Universal Acceptance of Human Rights Instruments. See UN Doc. E/CN.4/1350; UN Doc. A/CONF.157/PC/60/Add.4, p. 9 and Sub-Commission res. 1992/1.

[64] *A.F. Bayefsky*, p. 20.

[65] The four Geneva Conventions of 1949 have more or less achieved universal ratification.

[66] As of October 1998 the Convention had 150 parties. Web site <http:/www.un.org./Depts/Treaty>.

[67] Despite the difficulties for Islamic nations to bring internationally recognised human rights standards into conformity with Shari'a, the right to equality between men and women is vigorously asserted in the Islamic Declaration of Human Rights of December 19, 1981, approved by the League of Arab States and the Cairo Declaration on Human Rights in Islam of August 5, 1990 adopted at the 19th Islamic Conference. UN Doc. A/45/421/5/21797, p. 199; *F. Ermacora, M. Nowak & H. Tretter*, International Human Rights, Vienna 1993, p. 324.

customary international law (and *a fortiori* when they have the character of peremptory norms) may not be subject of reservations". In the view of the Committee in the case of non-derogable provisions[68] not constituting customary international law, states have "a heavy onus to justify such a reservation".[69] Clearly, most of the non-derogable provisions constitute the very foundation of each human rights treaty and therefore cannot be reserved. This would be contrary to the object and purpose of the treaty.[70] This author adheres to the opinion that reservations to provisions reflecting *ius cogens* should not be permitted. Thus, I agree to some extend with the criticism put forward with regard to the Human Rights Committee's proposition that *any* provision that represents customary international law may not be the subject of a reservation on the basis of the argument that customary law may be subject to modification by treaty law.[71] In the doctrine Professor Meron has taken the view that reservations to conventional provisions, which are only declaratory of customary law, would "not necessarily be excluded as incompatible with the object and purpose of the treaty".[72] Obviously, for those, who are of the opinion that the Women's Convention embodies customary principles, it would be more difficult to rule on the incompatibility of a reservation than

---

[68] The Women's Convention does not comprise a derogation clause, which provides that suspensions will not be allowed in emergencies in respect of certain articles. On the other hand, as Packer has observed, it would be easy to argue that Article 2 of the Convention is a non-derogable right because should this right be suspended "the entire foundation on which the Women's Convention is built collapses, rendering it impotent". *C.A.A. Packer*, p. 130.

[69] HRC, General Comment No. 24/52 adopted on 2 November 1994, UN Doc. CCPR/C/22/Rev1/Add. 6, p. 1, §§ 8-10, reprinted in HRLJ 1995, Vol. 16, p. 1ff.

[70] The Dutch and Belgian Governments have on several occasions objected to reservations to non-derogable articles in the general human rights treaties. *I. Cameron & F. Horn*, Reservations to the European Convention on Human Rights: The Belilos Case, GYIL 1990, Vol. 33, p. 108. The Inter-American Court applied this approach in the *Restriction to the Death Penalty* case, IACHR Advisory Opinion OC-3/83 of 8 September 1983, Ser. A, No. 3, § 61.

[71] See *M.Nowak*, The Activities of the UN Human Rights Committee: Developments from 1 August 1992 to 31 July 1995, HRLJ 1995, Vol. 16, p. 380. The Government of the US goes even further in its standpoint on that subject matter. It declared that the Human Rights Committee's proposition that any reservation which contravenes a norm of customary international law is *per se* incompatible with the object and purpose of the treaty as "wholly unsupported by and is in fact contrary to international law". Observation by the United States of America on General Comment No. 24(52) transmitted by letter dated 28 March 1995. UN Doc. A/50/40, reprinted in HRLJ 1995, Vol. 16, pp. 422–424. Moreover, the Government of the UK expressed some doubts about the HRC's argumentation that because human rights treaties "are for the benefit of individuals, provisions in the Covenant that represent customary international law may not be the subject to reservations". The UK stressed that this is a view not shared by most commentators, and states have not expressly objected to reservations on this ground. Observations by the United Kingdom on GC No. 24 transmitted by letter dated 21 July 1995, UN Doc. A/50/40, reprinted in HRLJ 1995, Vol. 16, pp. 424–426. The French Government also made an observation on that issue. It found that the customary rule concept "can in no way be equated with a peremptory norm of international law". Observation by France on GC No. 24 on Reservations to the ICCPR. The text has been reprinted in IHRR 1997, Vol. 4, pp. 6–8.

[72] *T. Meron*, Human Rights and Humanitarian Norms as Customary Law, Oxford 1991, p. 15. For the opposite view see *T. Giegerich*, Vorbehalte zu Menschenrechtsabkommen: Zulässigkeit, Gültigkeit und Prüfungstendenzen von Vertragsgremien, ZaöRV 1995, 55/3, p. 780.

for those advocating that the principles of non-discrimination on the basis of sex and gender equality are part of *ius cogens*. Other scholars have supported the idea that reservations to peremptory norms or norms of customary international law should be impermissible.[73]

To put it in another way, a state cannot, by reserving its position, avoid its obligations under *ius cogens*, or under customary international law, "unless the reservation is part of a policy of persistent and effective dissent from the norm in question".[74] Reservations to human rights treaties have, however, developed into a serious problem in international law.

### *3.3.2. The Problem of Reservations*

#### *3.3.2.1. Generally*

Reservations, sometimes of considerable weight, are attached to a great number of treaty provisions. The fact that multilateral treaties relatively often exclude reservations, wholly or partly, shows the possibility that reservations can adversely affect the regulatory régime established by the treaty in question, as a whole.[75] The objectivity and coherence of the convention régime may be impaired.[76] Moreover, reservations tend to diminish the validity of the legal norm concerned and even legitimating its violation.[77] The universal nature of human rights standards may be, in addition, severely undermined by adherence to a convention accompanied by a reservation. The legal machinery which conventions institute may, in addition, be weakened and fall short of the goal of harmonising relevant domestic laws. Thus, reservations often reveal a tendency of states not to want to change a particular law and/or practice and sometimes that tendency is elevated to a general policy.[78] As reserving states are no longer bound by the same international undertakings, reservations make it difficult to determine the obligations of each state.

---

[73] *I.M. Sinclair*, The Vienna Convention on the Law of Treaties, Manchester 1973, p. 212; *D.B. Bowett*, Reservations to Non-restricted Multilateral Treaties, BYIL 1976–1977, p. 89; *R.J. Cook*, Reservations to the Convention on the Elimination of All Forms of Discrimination Against Women, p. 684.

[74] *D.W. Greig*, Reservations: Equity as a Balancing Factor, Australian Year Book of International Law 1995, p. 75.

[75] This is emphasised in Article 19(c) of the 1969 Vienna Convention on the Law of Treaties by the recognition that, even when a treaty is silent on the question of reservations, they can be incompatible with the very object and purpose of the treaty, and consequently inadmissible.

[76] The General Assembly of the Council of Europe recommended on this ground among others that it "considers it advisable and even necessary that the number of reservations made in respect of Council of Europe conventions be considerably reduced". Recommendation 1223(1993), GA debate on 1 October 1993 (51st Sitting), Council of Europe Doc. 6856, Report of the Committee on Legal Affairs and Human Rights.

[77] *A. Zoller*, Analytical Report on the 44th Session of the Sub-Commission, Human Rights Monitor, Nos. 7–8, September 1992, p. 10. See generally *R.J. Cook*, Reservations to the Convention on the Elimination of All Forms of Discrimination against Women, p. 643; *H. Charlesworth, C. Chinkin & S. Wright*, p. 633.

[78] HRC, GC No. 24/52, § 13.

The Women's Convention has been the subject of more reservations than any other major human rights treaty.[79] Comparatively large number of governments have made substantive reservations[80] to basic articles of the treaty such as Article 2 of the Convention, which is a central provision, since the object and purpose of the treaty is set out here. Therefore, they are to be considered inadmissible as contrary to international law. The intentions of the Women's Convention have been severely undermined by extensive reservations and they might for good reasons be deemed as contrary[81] to the aim of the Convention, which is banning all forms of discrimination against women. They would appear to undermine the basic philosophy of the Convention. Some of the existing reservations go even "to the heart of both values of universality and integrity".[82] It is, therefore, deplorable that the international community has tolerated this type of reservation[83] for such a long time.

*3.3.2.2. The Permissibility and Pattern of Reservations*

Theoretically all reservations should be subjected to the test of validity. Article 19 of the VCTL enumerates three categories of reservations that are deemed inadmissible: reservations that are expressly prohibited by treaty, reservations that do not

---

[79] Some states have entered reservations to the Women's Convention but not to corresponding provisions of other treaties to which they are party. Such behaviour is undoubtedly inconsistent with the requirements of a coherent approach to human rights protection. Thus, reservations under one treaty must be consistent with obligations under another treaty incumbent on the reserving state. *L. Lijnzaad*, Reservations to UN-Human Rights Treaties, Ratify and Ruin?, Dordrecht 1995, p. 97.

[80] A number of states have withdrawn their reservations after accomplishing necessary adjustments in national law or after deciding that the reservations do not affect existing domestic jurisdiction in the way it was expected. See *A. Byrnes*, CEDAW's 10th Session, p. 356.

[81] The criteria which a reservation must meet in order to be permissible are contained in Articles 19–23 of the Vienna Convention on the Law of Treaties. According to Article 19 "a State may, when signing, ratifying, accepting, approving or acceding to a treaty, formulate a reservation unless: a) the reservation is prohibited by the treaty; b) the treaty provides that only specified reservations, which do not include the reservation in question, may be made; or c) in cases not falling under subparagraphs (a) and (b), the reservation is incompatible with the object and purpose of the treaty". Still there is a great difference of approach regarding compatibility and acceptability of a reservation in international law. The various conventions dealing with human rights contain rules that may differ considerably from each other. Some explicitly allow reservations or certain kinds of reservations, others do not authorise reservations at all. Moreover, there are treaties that do not mention the question of reservations as such. See on that subject *B. Clark*, The Vienna Convention Reservations Regime and the Convention on Discrimination against Women, AJIL 1991, Vol. 85, p. 281 *et seq*; *C.A.A. Packer*, p. 127. It should also be mentioned that the ILC appointed at its 46th session in 1994 a special rapporteur (Mr. A. Pellet) for "the law and practice relating to reservations to treaties". The ILC had in 1995 before it the Special Rapporteur's first report. UN Doc. A/CN.4/470 and Corr.1. The most recent (third) report was discussed at the Commission's fiftieth session in 1998. UN Doc. A/CN.4/491.

[82] *R.J. Cook*, Reservations to the Convention on the Elimination of All Forms of Discrimination Against Women, p. 644.

[83] I may mention here that the reservation made by Belgium to Article 2 of the ICCPR, which contains prohibition of discrimination on the basis of sex, on the grounds that the exercise of royal powers is limited to men, has not been objected to by other states. UN Doc. CCPR/C/2/Rev.3. The text is reproduced in *M. Nowak*, CCPR Commentary, p. 751.

belong to those reservations that are preclusively permitted by the treaty, or reservations that are incompatible with the object and purpose of the treaty. The VCTL is, however, silent on the question of how to determine compatibility of a reservation with a treaty. Today it seems that there is agreement that the object and purpose of a treaty are of great significance when deciding on the permissibility of a reservation. An obligation implied in the object and purpose rule is that it leads to distinguishing between the core and non-core obligations in the treaty.

Article 28(2) of the Women's Convention restates a fundamental rule of international law of treaties, *i.e.*, that a reservation "incompatible with the object and purpose of the present Convention shall not be permitted".[84] The Convention does not, however, establish any specific criteria of incompatibility that would facilitate states in their determination as to when its object and purpose have been contravened.[85] Nevertheless, several commentators have emphasised in this regard the significance of the first five articles of the Convention in the fulfilment of its objectives.[86] Of relevance to mention is that by applying the object and purpose test to the ICCPR, the HRC commented that a reservation to the "obligation to respect and ensure the rights, and to do so on a non-discriminatory basis (Article 2(1)) would not be acceptable".[87]

As of June 1994, over forty of the then 133 states parties had entered more than 91 substantive reservations[88] with respect to their obligations to implement the Women's Convention. The reservations are of different types. Some of the reservations were designed to avoid any obligation to rise above existing domestic law and

---

[84] The ICJ used in its advisory opinion on reservations to the Genocide Convention the object and purpose of the treaty as "the yardstick for both reservations and for objections". *L. Lijnzaad*, p. 81.

[85] CEDAW has frequently put questions to reserving states parties during consideration of their reports about their reservations in order to determine whether the object and purpose of the treaty have been impeded. *R.J. Cook*, Reservations to the Convention on the Elimination of All Forms of Discrimination Against Women, p. 708.

[86] *R.J. Cook*, ibid., p. 648; UN Doc. CEDAW/C/1997/4, § 6.

[87] HRC, GC No. 24/52, § 9. Reservations to the obligation in Article 2(2) to implement the Covenant rights domestically and to the derogation clause in Article 4 were also considered by the Committee as incompatible with the object and purpose of the Covenant. The Government of the US has entered a reservation to Article 6(5) of the ICCPR which is a non-derogable right according to Article 4. After considering the initial report under the ICCPR of the US, the HRC issued a comment on 7 April 1995 stating that the US reservation to Article 6(5) is incompatible with the object and purpose of the ICCPR. It recommended that the Government of the US withdraw the reservation. The HRC based this comment on its GC No. 24/52. The HRC did not, however, consider the legal effects of the US reservation. Neither did the objecting states to the American reservation make a statement that the reservation would constitute an obstacle to entry between themselves and the US. See UN Doc. CCPR/C/79, Add. 50.

[88] *E. Stamatopoulou*, Women's Rights and the United Nations, in Women's rights, human rights, J. Peters & A. Wolper (eds.), p. 38. As at 8 January 1996, 49 States Parties had made, and not subsequently withdrawn, reservations to the Women's Convention. See generally, UN Fact Sheet No. 22, Discrimination against Women: The Convention and the Committee, Geneva 1994, Annex II; UN Doc. A/CONF.177/7, 21 June 1995, § 48; UN Doc. CEDAW/C/1997/4, §§ 7–12. For a list containing the remaining substantive reservations to the Women's Convention in 1998 see *K. Tomaševski*, A Primer on CEDAW, p. 16.

practice.[89] A number of governments have invoked religion and/or culture[90] as reasons for not considering themselves bound by the provisions of the Convention.[91]

States which have attached such reservations and which refer to the commitment to eradicate discrimination in all its forms (Article 2) include Bangladesh, Egypt, Iraq, Libya, Malawi,[92] Tunisia and the United Kingdom. The greatest number of reservations is submitted in relation to non-discrimination in family law (Article 16).[93] Four states explicitly invoke in their reservations the Convention's incompat-

---

[89] Professor Henkin deems such reservations to be of "dubious propriety" since the Convention in question would be futile. *L. Henkin*, U.S. Policy on Human Rights Conventions, AJIL 1995, Vol. 89, p. 343. Lijnzaad has argued, furthermore, that reservations indicating the prevalence of national legislation are very undesirable because they are contrary to the "progressive development of the international protection of human rights". *L. Lijnzaad*, p. 323. Human rights treaties are, in other words, intended to improve the protection in a country rather than maintain a standstill. Reliance on domestic law may also lead to insecurity for the other states parties. Therefore, the reservation which the UK has made to Article 2(f) and (g) on the basis of constantly reviewing its legislation related to the elimination of discrimination against women can be questioned. Such a reservation, as in the case of reservations for religious reasons, does not provide the required certainty about the state's obligations.

[90] Culture has a variety of meanings and many philosophical and ideological doctrines have been developed. Today it is assumed that culture refers to a "whole of basic views and fundamental values related to human existence, to the major questions about life and death, to the relations among and between human beings, groups of people and their structures, to the creative attitude of man with regard to his environment, nature , technology and to his experience of time and space". *M. Eyskens*, Culture and Progress, Conference paper, Law in Motion, Brussels September 1996, p. 1. See also UN Doc. CN.6/1995/Add.2. Culture is not a static conception since culture and law shape each other in many and varied ways. Law suppresses, however, some values and reinforces others. Thus, there is evidence today that a universal human rights law has triumphed over the diverse influence of culture and that the right to gender equality is a core value for the international community.

[91] Generally on the various reasons for making reservations see *F. Horn*, Reservations and Interpretative Declarations to Multilateral Treaties, The Hague 1988, pp. 14–22; *L. Lijnzaad*, pp. 77–80.

[92] The Government of Malawi withdrew its reservation dealing with traditional customs in 1991.

[93] The countries that have made reservations are as follows: Bangladesh, Brazil, Egypt, France, India, Iraq, Ireland, Jordan, Libya, Luxembourg, Malta, Mauritius, Korea, Thailand, Tunisia, Turkey and the United Kingdom. Only Malta's reservation to which I shall return in Part II of the study has impact on the right to reproductive freedom.

Article 16 is of special importance to my enquiry on reproductive freedom. One could argue that reservations to this provision would be incompatible with the object and purpose of the Women's Convention since each and every provision in treaties which ban discrimination "contribute to the goal of the treaty". CEDAW itself has indicated Article 16 to be a provision essential to the object and purpose of the Convention. The Committee has even suggested that there is *communis opinio* on the core value of among others Articles 2 and 16. *L. Lijnzaad*, pp. 82; 303–304. One could also use the weaker argument based on the HRC's GC No. 24/52 that at least part of Article 23(2) of the ICCPR which corresponds to Article 16 of the Women's Convention constitutes customary international law and, therefore, may not be subject to reservations. Professor Nowak has, however, reminded the readers that there is neither a common practice or *opinio iuris* for such an assumption. *M. Nowak*, The Activities of the UN Human Rights Committee: Developments from 1 August 1992 through 31 July 1995, HRLJ 1995, Vol. 16, p. 381. Nevertheless, reservations of that kind might reasonably be viewed as imprecise and indeterminate and thereby contrary to the certainty required for the acceptance of a clear legal obligation. *C. Chinkin*, Reservations and Objections to the Convention on the Elimination of All Forms of Discrimination against Women, in Human Rights as General Norms and A State's Right to Opt Out, J.P. Gardner (ed.), British Institute of International and Comparative Law 1996, p. 65.

ibility with Shari'a(t), the central core of Islam.[94] Bangladesh, for example, did not consider as binding upon itself the provisions of Article 2 as they conflicted with Shari'a law.[95] Similarly, Egypt acceded to the Convention subject to a broad-based reservation. The Government of Egypt expressed willingness to comply with Article 2, provided that such compliance did not run counter to the Islamic Shari'a.[96] A reservation by Iraq stated that approval of, and accession to, the Convention should not mean that the Republic was bound by the provisions of Article 2(f) and (g). Preservation of religious or customary laws appears basic to the reserving states parties in question under the Convention.[97] This suggests that Muslim countries regard Islamic law as superior to international human rights law[98] and that there are fundamental inconsistencies between Shari'a and international human rights standards. Reservations of that kind manifest bad faith on the part of the reserving state

---

[94] Shari'a(t) as a technical term means the Canon law of Islam. It is based on two sources: 1. the Holy Qur'an – the very word of God, (the collected sayings of the Prophet Muhammad) and 2. Sunna – the practice of the Prophet. See *Asaf A.A. Fyzee*, Outlines of Muhammadan Law, Oxford 1993, p. 14 *et seq.* One should, however, bear in mind that there is a tremendous diversity in the Muslim world. Different schools of jurisprudence co-exist alongside civil codes derived from European legal systems and customary laws from the pre-islamic past. With respect to women's status, it has been argued that "the ambiguity of the religious texts makes the process of interpretation crucial". On the other hand, there is no central, authoritative interpretation of religious doctrine, which means that the same texts can be used to legitimatise divergent views in regard to the position of women. Thus, local customs, attitudes and institutions have influenced the interpretation and application of Shari'a in the different Muslim countries. *C.M. Obermeyer*, in Power and Decision, The Social Control of Reproduction, G. Sen & R.C. Snow (eds.), p. 60; *A.A. An-Na'im*, The Rights of Women and International Law in the Muslim Context, Whittier Law Review 1987, Vol. 9, p. 494. See also *S.H. Amin*, Islamic Law and its Implications for Modern World, Royston 1989. CEDAW made an attempt, which was unsuccessful, in 1987/88 to initiate a study into the rights of women under Islamic Law. Many Muslim countries were offended as they thought it was a neo-colonialist attempt to impose Western values on Islamic societies. The purpose and effect of the requested study were seriously questioned and it was felt that CEDAW entertained arbitrary and inappropriate assumptions about Islamic law. *M.K. Eriksson*, The Right to Marry, p. 204; UN Doc. E/1987/SR. 11; *C.A.A. Packer*, p. 121.

The Holy See has also formulated reservations to human rights treaties with reference to religious norms. *W.A. Schabas*, Reservations to the Convention on the Rights of the Child, HRQ 1996, Vol. 18, p. 478.

[95] The text of the reservation is as follows: "The Government of the People's Republic of Bangladesh does not consider as binding upon itself the provisions of Article 2, ..(a)s they conflict with Sharia Law based on the Holy Quran and Sunna". Multilateral Treaties Deposited with the Secretary-General: Status as at 31 December 1995, p. 169.

[96] Multilateral Treaties, ibid., p. 169. Reservations to Article 2 that exclude the establishment of means to amend national laws and culture to eliminate discrimination against women are according to CEDAW "highly questionable since one of the primary objectives of the Convention is an obligation of means". UN Doc. CEDAW/C/1995/4, § 100; UN Doc. A/CONF.177/7, 1995, § 48. Reservations of that type have also been viewed as "imprecise and indeterminate and thereby contrary to the certainty required for the acceptance of a clear legal obligation". UN Doc. CEDAW/C/1997/4, § 6.

[97] In the general observations regarding the report of Iraq under the Convention, CEDAW experts pointed to the fact that there seems to be a contradiction between the above mentioned reservations and the view that Shari'a guaranteed women equality with men. UN Doc. A/48/38, 28 May 1993, p. 18, § 37.

[98] *A.A. An-Na'im*, Human Rights in the Muslim World: Socio-political Conditions and Scriptural Imperatives, Harvard Human Rights Journal 1990, Vol. 3, p. 21; *S.H. Amin*, p. 10.

because they place domestic law above international law.[99] Many Shari'a norms still mandate religious and gender discrimination, giving non-Muslims and women subordinate status. Allowing treaty parties to the Women's Convention to invoke Islam and their culture as the defence for their non-compliance with the terms of the Convention can be questioned on the ground of the requirement in article 5 for parties to "modify the social and cultural patterns of conduct of men and women with a view to achieving the elimination of prejudices and customary and all other practices which are based on the idea of the inferiority or the superiority of either of the sexes". In other words, culture and religion cannot be used to legitimise the discriminatory treatment of women. It has been observed that "no social group has suffered greater violation of its human rights in the name of culture than women".[100] Thus, discriminatory practices like rape, dowry deaths are either avoided or defended by members of the international community.[101]

Reservations invoking Shari'a law entail problems related to the question of cultural relativism in respect of human rights. The cultural relativistic approach expresses in general terms the conviction that there are no universal standards by which all cultures may be judged. The legitimacy of using values taken from Western culture to judge institutions of non-western cultures is denied. Cultural relativists contend that critique against, for example, the treatment of women in the Middle East, reflects an insensitive, ethnocentric approach to human rights issues linked to cultural imperialism.[102] Very strong opposition against the idea that human rights norms are universal was observable during the preparatory work for, and during, the 1993 World Conference on Human Rights.[103] However, the universal

---

[99] It has been suggested that the best way of tackling reservations on the grounds of religion would be to focus on the specificity and thereby classify them as insufficient and contrary to the idea of *lex scripta*. On the specificity requirement see *R.J. Cook*, p. 655; *B. Clark*, pp. 310–311; *L. Lijnzaad*, pp. 320–321; *C.A.A. Packer*, pp. 133–134. Sweden, together with a few other countries, has argued that the wide and vague reservations of particularly those states, which make reservations on the basis of religion, are incompatible with the object and purpose of the Women's Convention. UN Doc. CEDAW/C/1997/4, § 15.

[100] *A. Rao*, The Politics of Gender and Culture in International Human Rights Discourse, in Women's rights, human rights, J. Peters & A. Wolper (eds.), p. 169. For similar views see *A.E. Mayer*, Cultural Particularism as a Bar to Women's Rights: Reflections on the Middle Eastern Experience, in Women's rights, human rights, J. Peters & A. Wolper (eds.), p. 177; *A.D. Reuteln*, International Human Rights: Universalism Versus Relativism, Sage 1990; *D. Donoho*, Relativism Versus Universalism in Human Rights: The Search for Meaningful Standards, Stanford Journal of International Law 1991, Vol. 27, pp. 354–391; *R. Howard*, Cultural Absolutism and the Nostalgia for Community, HRQ 1993, Vol. 15, pp. 315–338; *A.A. An-Na'im*, State Responsibility Under International Human Rights Law to Change Religious and Customary Laws, in Human Rights of Women, R.J. Cook (ed.), pp. 167–189; *H. Bielefeldt*, Muslim Voices in the Human Rights Debate, HRQ 1995, Vol. 17, pp. 587–617.

[101] *L. Southard*, Women's Rights and the Culture of International Law, ASIL, Human Rights Interest Group Newsletter 1996, Vol. 6, pp. 14–18. Generally on some cultural traditions and their compatibility with international law see *W. Schmale*, Human Rights and Cultural Diversity, Goldbach 1993.

[102] *A.E. Mayer*, ibid., p. 178.

[103] A small but very vocal group of governments representing countries as culturally dissimilar as Syria, Libya, Sudan, Yemen, Iran, Iraq, Pakistan, India, Burma, China, Indonesia, Malaysia, Cuba, Mexico and Columbia, challenged the universality of the application of the human rights standards by

nature of human rights has been reaffirmed in many paragraphs of the final document – *the Vienna Declaration and Programme of Action*,[104] which was adopted on 25 June 1993 at the Conference. As human rights belong to human beings, they are of a universal nature, and the standards should be equally applied world-wide without any discrimination. Thereafter *the Beijing Declaration and Platform for Action* stressed that "while the significance of national and religious particularities and various historical, cultural and religious backgrounds must be born in mind, it is the duty of States, regardless of their political, economic and cultural systems, to promote and protect all human rights and fundamental freedoms".[105] The Conference agreed that governments should limit the extent of any reservation to the Convention, formulate any such reservation as precisely and narrowly as possible, ensure that no reservation were incompatible with the object and purpose of the Women's Convention and review reservations regularly with a view to their withdrawal.[106]

*3.3.2.3. Acceptance and Objections to Reservations*

Article 20 of the VCTL regulates the acceptance of an admissible reservation which is necessary for it to become binding. Every state party to a treaty has the discretion to choose between accepting or objecting to an admissible reservation. The HRC has, however, expressed the view that the VCTL is not suitable to determine the problems of reservations to human rights treaties. This is because human rights concern rights of individuals and not inter-state exchanges of mutual obligations, and states often do not see any legal interest or need to object to reservations.[107] Therefore, the absence of protest from states does not imply the compatibility or incompatibility of a reservation with the object and purpose of, *e.g.*, the ICCPR.

The determination of the compatibility of reservations with treaty law may have to take place within the compulsory dispute-settlement procedure of Article 29 of the Women's Convention. The issue can be referred, in other words, to the International Court of Justice. Regrettably this provision is rendered largely ineffective by the many reservations to it. So far no state has challenged another state party and no one has sought an advisory opinion from the Court on the compatibility of reservations. It seems that it is unlikely that this situation will arise.[108]

---

using arguments of cultural integrity. This author had the possibility to follow closely the preparatory process for the UN Vienna World Conference on Human Rights. See on cultural relativity and human rights, *A.A. An-Na'im,* Toward a Cross-Cultural Approach to Defining International Standards of Human Rights, in Human Rights in Cross-Cultural Perspectives, A Quest for Consensus, A. Ahmed-An-Na'im (ed.), Philadelphia 1991, p. 22 ff.

[104] UN Doc. A/Conf.157/22. See, *e.g.*, Part I, Chapter III, § 1, § 5, § 6, § 32.

[105] UN Doc. A/CONF.177/20, Chapter II, § 9.

[106] UN Doc. CEDAW/C/1997/4, § 20.

[107] The Chairpersons of the UN's treaty bodies recalled during their meeting in Geneva in February 1998 that human rights treaties, by virtue of their subject matter and the role they recognise to individuals, cannot be placed on precisely the same footing as other treaties with different characteristics.

[108] The Sub-Commission on Prevention of Discrimination and Protection of Minorities requested in 1993 the Secretary-General to seek the views of CEDAW and the Commission on the Status of Women as to the desirability of obtaining an advisory opinion on the validity and legal effect of far-reaching reservations made by states when ratifying the Women's Convention, which contradict the very principle

Since there is no definition of the terms under which a reservation may be deemed incompatible with the Women's Convention, then the only feasible option open to a state party and the primary responsibility for evaluating the compatibility of a reservation lies, according to international law, with the other states parties. Thus, they can lodge an objection to a reservation they consider incompatible with the object and purpose of the treaty and raise the matter at meetings of the states parties. There is today a continuing dispute among certain states parties on the compatibility issue.

Nevertheless, in my view in the case of the Women's Convention, reservations should be measured according to whether or not they would hamper the elimination of discrimination against women, which is the *raison d'être* of the Convention.

Few states have elaborated on the content of the "object and purpose" of the Convention and have included four factors as decisive in the determination of the compatibility of a reservation. Accordingly it is of importance whether the reservation is made to a general provision (*i.e.*, Article 2), whether the reservation deals with a particular crucial aspect of equality, whether the reservation involves the entire provision or specific elements of it and finally whether the reservation affects women in "a significant facet of national life".[109]

Objections have been occasional, made only by some states and the grounds and legal consequences have not always been specified. The pattern is so unclear that it is not safe to assume that a non-objecting state has found a particular reservation to be valid.

A number of states parties to the Women's Convention have challenged the legality of some of the reservations on the grounds of Article 28 of the Convention, which does not permit reservations "incompatible with the object and purpose of the present Convention".[110] States have adopted a variety of approaches to counter

---

of the Convention. I agree with the view that currently, building up pressure against recalcitrant governments by repetitive findings of all human rights treaty bodies that reservations that undermine the thrust of international human rights law should be outlawed, seems to be appropriate measure to urge governments to withdraw reservations.

Nevertheless, during several work-shops at the Beijing NGO-Forum '95 it was argued, as academic commentators have done on other occasions, that there is a danger today in seeking an advisory opinion on that subject matter because of the dangers of the male dominated ICJ delivering a restrictive interpretation of Article 28 of the Women's Convention which will be more detrimental to the achievement of the Convention's goal than having the matter left undecided. On the different work-shops that took place in Huairou see Forum '95, *N. Hijab & B. Wiig* (eds), The Independent Daily of the NGO Forum on Women, Beijing 1995. For the doctrine's standpoint on that issue see *L.Lijnzaad*, p. 335.

[109] UN Doc. A/41/608 at 6, cited in *L. Lijnzaad*, p. 330.

[110] This provision is based on principles deriving from the Vienna Convention on the Law of Treaties and the advisory opinion of the International Court of Justice (ICJ) concerning reservations to the Convention on the Prevention and Punishment of the Crime of Genocide. See UN Doc. E/CN.6/SR.673, p. 10.

According to Professor Theo van Boven, when states parties to a treaty do object to certain reservations, this appears to be motivated, in most cases, by the desire to serve the common interest of defending the integrity of the standards enunciated in the treaty rather than by the wish to pursue their own individual interest *vis-à-vis* other states parties. Book Review in HRQ 1992, Vol. 14, p. 567.

reservations, which they believe are incompatible with the object and purpose of a treaty. Germany,[111] Mexico, the Netherlands and Sweden[112] are the states that have objected most frequently to reservations to Article 2 and 16 of the Women's Convention. These countries have shown consistency in their objections which gives them undoubtedly greater weight.

There are some variations with regard to the motivation of the obligations. Whereas Sweden and Germany, for example, underline the incompatibility of the objected reservation with the object and purpose of the Convention, Mexico refers to inconsistency with other human rights obligations accepted by the reserving state.

Sweden stressed in its objection to the reservations made by Egypt and Mauritius that incompatible reservations "contribute to undermine the basis of international contractual law".[113] Thus, incompatible reservations undermine the credibility of treaty law and are doubtful in regard to the intentions of the reserving state. Sweden has, moreover, observed as regards the reservations of Thailand, Tunisia, Bangladesh and Brazil that:

> "Indeed the reservations in question, if put into practice would inevitably result in discrimination against women on the basis of sex, which is contrary to everything the Convention stands for. It should also be born in mind that the principles of the equal rights of men and women and of non-discrimination on the basis of sex are set forth in the Charter of the United Nations as one of its purposes, in the Universal Declaration of Human Rights of 1948 and in various multilateral instruments, to which Thailand, Tunisia and Bangladesh are parties".[114]

Some reservations are so broad and vague that it is difficult to determine exactly what states are reserving because they do not indicate the provision/s at which they are aimed. About 12 general reservations have been entered against the Women's Convention. The Maldives made, for example, a general and very provocative

[111] The governments of Denmark, the Federal Republic of Germany, Finland, Norway and Sweden objected to the reservation made by the Libyan Arab Jamahiriya that the country's accession to this treaty "cannot conflict with the laws of personal status derived from the Islamic Shariah". UN Doc. CEDAW/SP/13/Rev.1, p. 16 and UN Doc. A/45/426, Annex III.

[112] Sweden's strong engagement in these issues has been ascribed the country's genuine commitment to the principle of full equality for women, as "evidenced in its feminist domestic policies". *A.E. Mayer*, p. 185. On recent objections to reservations to human rights treaties made by Sweden see *L. Magnuson*, pp. 359–360.

[113] *L.A. Rehof*, p. 281; UN Doc. CEDAW/C/1997/4, § 13. Similarly Finland stated in its objection to Kuwait's reservation to Article 16 that it had an unlimited and unspecified nature that may contribute to undermining the basis of international human rights treaties.

[114] Multilateral Treaties, ibid., pp. 179–180. The Government of Sweden noted, furthermore, that, as a matter of principle, the same objection could be made to the reservations made by Egypt, Mauritius, the Republic of Korea and New Zealand.

reservation to the whole Women's Convention on 1 July 1993. It implies that the Government:

> "will comply with the provisions of the Convention except those which the government may consider contrary to the principles of the Islamic Shari'a upon which the laws and traditions of the Maldives is founded. Furthermore, the Republic of Maldives does not see itself bound by any provisions of the Convention which obliges it to change its Constitution and laws in any matter".[115]

All states parties to a treaty have the opportunity to consider reservations and to react. Nevertheless, the number of objecting states is very small. For the most part states do not object to reservations. Some believe that it is preferable to accept a reservation than to keep a state outside the régime of the Convention.[116] Inaction should, however, not be considered automatically as an intention to consent to a reservation.[117] On the other hand, although I do not have any empirical evidence, it cannot be totally wrong to assume that objections have influenced states to withdraw their reservations.

CEDAW regards the question of reservations to the Convention as a very serious matter. The Treaty Section of the Office of Legal Affairs of the UN Secretariat expressed an opinion, after the inquiry made by CEDAW on the implications of Article 28(2) of the Convention, that neither the Secretary-General, as depository, nor CEDAW,[118] has the mandate to determine the compatibility of

---

[115] Multilateral Treaties, ibid., p. 172. See also UD Promemoria, UD Rättsavdelningen, R4, 1994-10-20, p. 2. On the Swedish reaction to that reservation see *O. Mårsäter & S. Spiliopoulou Åkermark*, Otillåtna reservationer, Maldivernas reservation mot kvinnodiskrimineringskonventionen, Mennesker og rettigheter 1995, Vol. 13, pp. 382–399. Sweden claimed in its objection that the above mentioned reservation is incompatible with the object and purpose of the Convention. It is too general and it is of a serious nature. The effect of the reservation would be total freedom for the country not the take any of the required measures to adapt national legislation to international standards.

[116] *G. Van Bueren*, p. 397.

[117] On the reasons for such inertia on the part of most governments see *D.W. Greig*, p. 132. Like the HRC, CEDAW has argued that the absence of protests by states parties to reservations does not imply compatibility with respect to the treaty and it considers that it may be up to the Committee itself to make this determination. HRC GC No. 24/52, § 13.

[118] Here I should mention that CEDAW at its third session in 1984 sought an opinion from the Office of Legal Affairs of the United Nations Secretariat on the scope of admissible reservations. In the legal note received from the Treaty Section of the Office it was stated that although reservations undoubtedly affect the application of the Women's Convention and the Committee might have to comment thereon in its reports to the GA in this context, the functions of the CEDAW "do not appear to include a determination of the incompatibility of reservations". See UN Doc. CEDAW/C/L.1/Add.20. Furthermore, CEDAW expressed at its sixth session in 1987 concern in relation to the significant number of reservations that appeared to be incompatible with the object and purpose of the Convention. Therefore, it welcomed in its General Recommendation No. 4 adopted at that session the decision of states parties to consider reservations at its meeting in 1988; UN Doc. A/42/38.

reservations with the Convention as well as to make a final judgement on the validity of reservations.[119]

Nevertheless, CEDAW adopted at its eleventh session in 1992 a General Recommendation No. 20 concerning reservations. It proposed the introduction of a procedure in the Convention to examine the validity and legal effects of reservations. The Committee recommended that, in connection with preparations for the World Conference on Human Rights in 1993, states parties should:

> "a) Raise the question of the validity and the legal effect of reservations to the Convention in the context of reservations to other human rights treaties; b) Reconsider such reservations with a view to strengthening the implementation of all human rights treaties; c) Consider introducing a procedure on reservations to the Convention comparable with that of other human rights treaties".[120]

States are, furthermore, urged in this document to withdraw reservations that are contrary to the object and purpose of the Convention or such that are otherwise incompatible with international treaty law.

Following the Conference CEDAW addressed again the issue of reservations at its 13th session in 1994 and amended the guidelines in which it requested states parties which have entered general reservations, or reservations to Articles 2 and 3 of the Convention, to make a particular effort to report on the effect and interpretation of them, since the Committee "considers these to be incompatible with the object and purpose of the treaty".[121]

The deliberations in this sub-chapter allow us to draw some conclusions. Firstly, objections to reservations are not a conclusive test as to the existence of customary law.[122] Secondly, reservations to norms of *ius cogens* nature and to most of the non-derogable rights, would be deemed today inadmissible by the great majority of

---

[119] Report of CEDAW, 3rd session 1984, GA OR 39th Sess. Suppl. No. 45 UN Doc. A/39/45, Annex III, p. 55; *L. Lijnzaad*, p. 331; UN Doc. CEDAW/C/1997/4, § 17. Several academic writers have, however, argued persuasively that "inherent competence exists in any human rights treaty which establishes supervisory organs with the competence to interpret and apply the treaty in a dispute between contracting parties or between a party and an individual", *i.e.*, to determine the validity of a reservation. *I. Cameron & F. Horn*, p. 96. See in addition HRC GC No. 24/52, § 11 and *T. Giegerich*, p. 779. The ILA recommended recently that the UN GA should pass a resolution that supports direct treaty body involvement in reservations. ILA, Report of the sixty-seven Conference-Helsinki 1996, London 1996, p. 354. The ILC suggests also that although human rights treaties do not explicitly provide for the competence of treaty bodies to determine the validity of reservations, such bodies necessarily have this competence. Preliminary Report of the ILC on the work of its 48th session, GA OR, 55 session UN Doc. A/51/10, Chapter VI, § 137; UN Doc. CEDAW/C/1997/4, § 27.

[120] General Recommendation No. 20, Eleventh session 1992, UN Doc. A/47/38.

[121] UN Doc. CEDAW/C/1995/7, § 327. The Beijing Platform for Action urges Governments in § 230(c) to limit the extent of any reservation to the Convention and regularly review them with a view to withdrawing them, and "withdraw reservations that are contrary to the object and purpose of the Convention or which are otherwise incompatible with international treaty law". UN Doc. CEDAW/C/1997/4, § 19.

[122] A norm may fall within the notion *ius cogens* without qualifying at all as international custom as defined in the ICJ status. *See B. Simma & P. Alston*, p. 104.

the members of the international community. It is, therefore, not surprising that reservations to the non-discrimination principle have been objected to by other states. Even though they merely preclude the legal effects of the provision as between the reserving and objecting state they "inevitably shed some degree of light on State's interpretation of core obligations"[123] and, in my view, they are indicative of *ius cogens* obligations. As demonstrated above, there is an increasing opinion expressed by the objecting states as to the incompatibility of reservations to core obligations, which contravene the object and purpose of human rights treaties, and which, among other things, is the elimination of discrimination based on sex, as well as the inadmissibility of reservations contrary to *ius cogens*.

In addition, the latest development in international refugee law, which has moved towards greater acceptance of gender discrimination as a relevant ground for obtaining refugee status according to the 1951 Geneva Convention on the Status of Refugees and the 1967 Protocol Relating to the Status of Refugees,[124] *i.e.*, discrimination can constitute persecution under certain circumstances,[125] supports the assertion that the principle of non-discrimination on the grounds of sex should be considered a principle of general international law. Persecution for Convention reasons has included the threat of deprivation of life and other basic human rights. Thus, the idea of persecution is linked to the idea of core human rights as understood in international human rights instruments.

## 3.4. *Ius Cogens* Norms Permit No Derogation

An imperative norm of international law is a norm from which no derogations are permissible. The principle of non-derogability of basic human rights is of vital importance for their protection in emergencies. It has, therefore, been considered as a general principle of law according to Article 38 of the ICJ Statute.[126]

---

[123] *C.A.A. Packer*, p. 128.

[124] 189 UNTS 137; 19 UNTS 6223; 606 UNTS 267.

[125] See generally *G.S. Goodwin-Gill*, The Refugee in International Law, Oxford 1996, p. 43 *et seq.* The UNHCR has on several occasions recommended and some countries have indeed recognised women asylum-seekers to be conventional refugees because they have been persecuted because they have transgressed discriminatory rules of conduct. These persons have been considered as persecuted as a social group in order to obtain that status.

See Guidelines on the Protection of Refugee Women, UNHCR 1991, § 54; Conclusion No. 39 of the Executive Committee of the UNHCR Programme on Refugee Women and International Protection, October 1993; UNHCR, Refugee, Asylum Seekers and Displaced Women in the ECE Region, Vienna 1994, p. 7.

In other words, the "social group" category has been expanded to encompass "gender claims". On the other hand, very few refugee receiving countries in the Western hemisphere accept women victims of gender-specific abuses, such as domestic violence, as refugees. *P. Goldberg*, Any Place but Home: Asylum in the United States for Women Fleeing Intimate Violence, Cornell International Law Journal 1993, Vol. 26, p. 565; *N. Kelly*, Gender-Based Persecution: Assessing Asylum Claims of Women, Cornell International Law Journal 1993, Vol. 26, p. 658 and SOU 1995:75, Svensk flyktingpolitik i globalt perspektiv, Stockholm 1995, p. 57. See, in addition, Part III below.

[126] For references see *J. Oraá*, Human Rights in States of Emergency in International Law, Oxford 1992, p. 264, note 14.

As already debated in section 3.2., the prohibition against derogation from peremptory norms encompasses all grounds for violating peremptory norms and all acts contradicting these norms.[127] According to many legal scholars, the fact that a certain right is non-derogable, provides strong evidence regarding the status of *ius cogens*.[128] I shall below explore which the current non-derogable obligations are regarding the principle of equality and non-discrimination deriving from multilateral conventions. Most human rights treaties include a restriction on measures taken by the state party in derogation of treaty obligations. Yet, those treaties produce different lists of non-derogable rights. Article 4(1) of the ICCPR stipulates, for example, that in time of public emergency the equal treatment of men and women should remain intact. The provision provides as follows:

> "1. In time of public emergency, which threatens the life of the nation and the existence of which is officially proclaimed, the States Parties to the present Covenant may take measures derogating from their obligations under the present Covenant to the extent strictly required by the exigencies of the situation, provided that such measures are not inconsistent with their obligations under international law and do not involve *discrimination* solely on the ground of race, colour, *sex*, language, religion or social origin" (italics added).

Whereas the above text can be interpreted as permitting states parties to derogate from the principle of non-discrimination provided that the other conditions for derogation are met, there is strong support for the view that provisions related to the prohibition of discrimination cannot, in fact, be derogated from.[129] The HRC stated boldly in its General Comment No. 24/52 that reservations to the obligation to respect and ensure the rights and to do so on a non-discriminatory basis, would not be acceptable.[130]

Article 4 of the ICCPR specifies, moreover, the provisions from which no derogation can be made. The principle of non-discrimination when then applied to those rights is in itself entrenched from derogation.

---

[127] *L. Hannikainen*, p. 248. See also *A. Gómez Robledo*, El Ius Cogens Internacional, UNAM, Mexico City 1982.

[128] *R.B. Lillich*, US Ratification of the Human Rights Treaties – With or Without Reservations?, Charlottesville 1981, p. 120; *L. Hannikainen*, p. 263. It is worth mentioning, however, that two different criteria have been used in the adoption of lists of non-derogable rights. The first one refers to rights that are absolutely fundamental and indispensable for the protection of the human being. It could be, therefore, safe to argue that these rights are a part of *ius cogens*. The second criterion relates to those human rights where the derogation of which would not have any direct bearing on the emergency situation. In other words, not all rights of profound importance have in fact been made non-derogable, because their suspension is irrelevant to the legitimate control of the state of national emergency. *J. Oraá*, p. 94. See also *A.-L. Svensson-McCarthy*, Minimum Humanitarian Standards-from Cape Town Towards The Future, The Review 1996, pp. 9–13.

[129] *J. Oraá*, p. 102.

[130] HRC, GC No. 24/52, CCPR/C/21/Rev.1/Add.6, § 9.

According to Article 27 (1) of the American Convention on Human Rights, the main conditions for derogations are that those measures do not involve discrimination on certain grounds (among them sex):

> "In time of war, public danger, or other emergency that threatens the independence or security of a State Party, it may take measures derogating from its obligations under the present Convention... (p)rovided that such measures are not inconsistent with its other obligations under international law and do not involve *discrimination* on the ground of race, color, *sex*, language, religion, or social origin" (italics added).

Of further interest to this study is paragraph 2 of Article 27, which contains reference to the specific non-derogable rights under the American Convention. Among them we may find Article 17 dealing with the rights of the family. In paragraph 4 of that article it is stipulated that the states parties "shall take appropriate steps to ensure the equality of rights and the adequate balancing of responsibilities of the spouses as to marriage and during marriage".

Article 15 of the European Convention confers on states parties a wide scope for action in the case of emergency but it omits an explicit reference to the principle of non-discrimination as a condition for derogation. Neither has the non-discrimination provision been given independent existence, *i.e.*, autonomous standing in the European Convention as already pointed out earlier. Nevertheless, since this principle qualifies all of the substantive provisions as if it were a part of each one in the convention, it constitutes part of the non-derogable rights of the European Convention.

## 3.5. Is the Principle of Non-Discrimination on the Basis of Sex and Equality Recognised and Accepted by the International Community?

Whereas the evidence of a customary rule of international law requires evidence of wide-spread state practice, another criterion for determining whether a legal norm has a *ius cogens* status is that it "is accepted and recognised by the international community of States as a whole".[131] Thus, an overwhelming majority of states is required, "cutting across cultural and ideological differences".[132] The majority of writers who have commented upon the subject seem to agree that the lack of acceptance of a few states is no obstacle for a norm to achieve the status of *ius cogens*. Support for the presumption that it is not necessary that a peremptory norm be accepted and recognised as such by every single state can also to be found in the preparatory works of the Vienna Convention on the Law of Treaties. That subject matter was considered by the Chairman of the Drafting Committee of the Vienna

---

[131] See Article 53 of the Vienna Convention on the Law of Treaties. International community means in this context the totality of territorial sovereign states, with the possible exception of such state or states, which have been excluded from the membership of the community. *L. Hannikainen*, p. 4.

[132] *P. Malanczuk*, Akehurst's Modern Introduction to International Law, London 1997, p. 58.

Conference on the Law of Treaties, Mr. Yaseen, who explained the meaning of the phrase "as a whole" in the following manner:

> "By inserting the words "as a whole" in Article 50 the Drafting Committee had wished to stress that there was no question of requiring a rule to be accepted and recognised as peremptory by all States. It would be enough if a very large majority did so; that would mean that, if one State in isolation refused to accept the peremptory character of a rule, or if that State was supported by a very small number of States, the acceptance and recognition of the peremptory character of the rule by the international community as a whole would not be affected".[133]

In other words, a small minority group of states behaving in a manner contrary to the content of a norm would not disqualify it from its peremptory character. The International Law Commission has been on the other hand stricter in its interpretation of the phrase "the international community of States as a whole". As early as 1976 the ILC indicated that the phrase certainly did not mean the requirement of a unanimous recognition by all members "but recognition by all essential components of the international community" of states, since a requirement of unanimous recognition by all the members of that community would give each state an inconceivable right of veto.[134] In practice, that would mean that a norm must find acceptance and recognition by nearly all states since it cannot be imposed on a significant minority of states.[135] But, since this question has remained without any authoritative legal answer, it seems, therefore, that the prevailing view in contemporary international law is the liberal interpretation of the requirement of universal acceptance, *i.e.*, not to use strictly a numerical test.[136] On this basis we may suggest that there is today considerable agreement in the international community at large on the prohibition of discrimination on the basis of sex.

### 3.6. Peremptory Obligations are Owed by All States to the International Community

Since the main purpose of *ius cogens* is to protect certain overriding interests and values of humanity, states owe peremptory obligations to the international community. In this regard the concepts of *ius cogens* norms and *erga omnes* obligations (*i.e.*, obligations towards the international community as a whole)[137] are closely linked to each other. Obligations *erga omnes* are primarily concerned with the legislative and enforcement procedures of the international law system. Yet the

---

[133] *L. Hannikainen*, p. 210.

[134] ILC 1976 Report on the work of its 28th session, UN Doc. A/CN.4/Ser. A/1976/Add.1, at 119.

[135] *L. Hannikainen*, p. 211.

[136] *J. Sztucki*, pp. 99–100.

[137] *Erga omnes* means literally "as against all". As Arangio-Ruiz has asserted *erga omnes* rules provide for obligations which "bind simultaneously each and every addressee State with respect to all the others". *M. Ragazzi*, p. 201.

second topic is also related to *ius cogens* since the violation of the asserted norms would be deemed "to be an offence not only against the state directly affected by the breach, but also against all members of the international community".[138]

The well-known *obiter dictum*, which was incorporated in the judgement delivered by the ICJ in the *Barcelona Traction* case, was the first to address this issue. The Court recognised here that states have an obligation to respect fundamental rights of the "human person" towards the international community (*erga omnes* obligations) and that obligations are applicable *erga omnes* "in view of the importance of the rights involved".[139] From that I may conclude that major international human rights issues can no longer be classified as falling exclusively within the domestic jurisdiction of a country. They are vital to the international community and all states can, therefore, be held to have a legal interest in the protection of human rights. Professor Schachter has remarked in this respect that *erga omnes* obligations express "a collective interest of the community in the rights of all persons irrespective of nationality and it suggests the need for a 'guardian' of that interest who would act solely on the basis of law and objective facts".[140] This means that each state has legal standing to call for *erga omnes* obligations to be fulfilled and to assert the responsibility of any other state that fails to observe them. In the words of Professor Meron "when a state breaches an obligation *erga omnes*, it injures every state, including those not specially affected".[141]

Even though the principle of *erga omnes* obligations has found wide recognition in international law,[142] still the question remains open as to which the *erga*

---

[138] *P. Malanczuk*, p. 59.

[139] See *Barcelona Traction, Light & Power Co. (Belgium v. Spain)* case, 3 ICJ Reports 1970, § 32, where the Court held that: "an essential distinction should be drawn between the obligations of a State towards the international community as a whole, and those arising *vis-à-vis* another State in the field of diplomatic protection. By their very nature the former are the concern of all States. In view of the importance of the rights involved, all States can be held to have a legal interest in their protection; they are obligations *erga omnes*". See, however, the more restrictive and much disputed ruling of the ICJ in the *East Timor* case where the Court declared that its Statute precludes it from deciding "a dispute between States without the consent of those States to its jurisdiction". *East Timor (Portugal v. Australia)* case, Judgment of 30 June 1995, 90 ICJ Reports 1995, p. 101. See also *S.M. Schwebel*, The Treatment of Human Rights and of Aliens in the International Court of Justice, in Fifty Years of the International Court of Justice, V. Lowe & M. Fitzmaurice (eds.), 1996, pp. 327–350.

[140] *O. Schachter*, International Law in Theory and Practice, p. 345.

[141] *T. Meron*, Human Rights and Humanitarian Norms as Customary Law, Oxford 1991, p. 191.

[142] *J.A. Frowein*, Die Verpflichtungen *erga omnes* im Völkerrecht und ihre Durchsetzung, in Völkerrecht als Rechtsordnung, Internationale Gerichtsbarkeit, Menschenrechte, Festschrift für Hermann Mosler, R. Bernhardt *et al.* (eds.), 1983, p. 250; *K. Wolfram*, Besonderheiten der internationalen Kontrollverfahren zum Schutz der Menschenrechte, in Aktuelle Probleme des Menschenrechtsschutzes, W. Kälin *et al.* (eds.), Heidelberg 1994, pp. 88-89; *C. Annacker*, The Legal Régime of *Erga Omnes* Obligations in International Law, Austrian JPIL 1994, Vol. 46, p. 131 *et seq.*; *J.A. Frowein*, Reactions by Not Directly Affected States to Breaches of Public International Law, RdC 248 (1994-IV), pp. 345–437; *D. Shelton*, Letter from the Chair Human Rights Interest Group, ASIL 1997, Vol. 7, No. 3, p. 1.

The fourth World Conference on Women recognised that human rights constitute "a legitimate concern of the international community". UN Doc. E/CN.4/1995/98, § 88, p. 29. I may also mention that a great number of subjects on the UN Commission on Human Rights agenda is but a proof of collective responsibility and solidarity duty. UN Doc. E/CN.4/1995/98, § 133, p. 40.

*omnes* obligations are and as to their distinction from *ius cogens*. Some scholars have taken a cautious view. The argument has been advanced that the two concepts refer to different aspects of the same rules.[143] It has also been suggested that the ICJ in the *Barcelona Traction* case, when referring to *erga omnes* obligations, had in mind only the human rights which qualified as *ius cogens* norms. As the ICJ indicated there, *erga omnes* obligations "derive, for example, in contemporary international law, from the outlawing of acts of aggression, and of genocide, as also from the principles and rules concerning the basic rights of the human person, including protection from slavery and racial discrimination".[144] Three out of the four examples of obligations *erga omnes* given by the International Court relate to human rights. This enumeration of what the content of *erga omnes* is seems, however, not to be exhaustive. It can be considered as an exemplification of that notion. In 1989 the Institute of International Law commented on the principle of non-intervention and the *erga omnes* obligations by states concerning fundamental human rights. Accordingly a "(s)tate shall not be entitled to invoke the principle of non-intervention in matters essentially pertaining to its national competence in order to escape the consequences of activities attributable to it stemming from dereliction of its duty to ensure, pursuant to international law, the enjoyment of human rights within the area of its jurisdiction".[145] In other words, the question of universal supervision of states' compliance with international law obligations regarding basic human rights has been asserted. Of some relevance is also the statement made by President Jimmy Carter on 12 November 1980 when ratifying the Convention on the Political Rights of Women that: "Human rights in general and women's rights in particular are matters of legitimate concern to the international community and are not subjects with exclusively domestic ramifications".[146]

The standpoint that even though not all human rights amount to *ius cogens*, every such right (primarily the ones contained in the UDHR) gives rise to *erga omnes* obligations[147] is in my view more appealing than the preposition that only *ius cogens* norms may have *erga omnes* character. Thus, not all human rights belong to the *ius cogens* category, but due to their "very nature"[148], *i.e.*, they relate to the inherent dignity of every person, all of them are natural obligations towards the international community. In my view the notion *ius cogens* is narrower than

---

[143] On the various standpoints see *M. Byers*, Conceptualising the Relationship between *Jus Cogens* and *Erga Omnes* Rules, NJIL 1997, Vol. 66, Nos. 2–3, p. 21.

[144] ICJ, Reports 1970, ibid., § 32.

[145] Human Rights Monitor, No. 21 May 1993, ISHR Geneva, p. 6.

[146] *M. Halberstam & E.F. Defeis*, Women's Legal Rights. International Covenants an Alternative to ERA?, New York 1989, p. 63.

[147] See for references on the resolution on that subject matter adopted by the Institute of International Law in 1989 in *Y. Dinstein*, The *erga omnes* Applicability of Human Rights, Archiv des Völkerrechts 1992, Vol. 30, p. 17. A similar view is shared by Professor Meron. *T. Meron*, Human Rights and Humanitarian Norms as Customary Law, p. 194.

[148] *B.-O. Bryde*, Thesen zum Referat, in Aktuelle Probleme des Menschenrechtsschutzes, W. Kälin *et al.* (eds.), p. 187.

*erga omnes* in that *ius cogens* rules generally[149] constitute *erga omnes* obligations, whereas *erga omnes* obligations may exist on the basis of rules which do not necessarily have *ius cogens* status.[150]

The principle of non-discrimination on the basis of sex protects a key common interest of the international society and even though there is still some uncertainty as to its *ius cogens* status today on the basis of the above, I suggest that this principle has *erga omnes* character as to standing and obligation. This would imply that states have standing to complain according to the existing complaint procedures about violations of this obligation by another state.[151]

## 3.7. Concluding Remarks

Taking all that has been said above into consideration, I may conclude that the principle of non-discrimination on the basis of sex and equality constitutes a principle of general international law[152] and that there are some indications of a growing support for the emergence of a peremptory prohibition of discrimination on the grounds of sex in contemporary international law. Despite the controversy on the precise scope of *ius cogens* in the doctrine, prohibition of discrimination on the basis of sex has in recent time been more frequently incorporated in the catalogue of *ius cogens* norms by some well-established scholars, and it seems that the traditional view on that subject matter is in a process of changing. Kelly Askin has argued that the increased activity in international law in the 1990s "towards affording greater protection status, and equality to women", is evidential for a trend toward *ius cogens* status for gender based abuses.[153]

This author has used, in addition, other arguments to support the contention that the principle of non-discrimination on the basis of sex and gender equality is a strong candidate to a *ius cogens* status. I have referred among other things to the judicial incorporation and impressive legislative embodiment of the prohibition of discrimination on the grounds of sex on the international as well as on the national[154] level, which clearly signals its overwhelming acceptance as a basic

---

[149] There are some, albeit very few, examples of situations in which certain legal relations resulting from *ius cogens* rules do not operate *erga omnes*. Mr. Ragazzi mentions in this regard the invocation of the invalidity of a treaty. *M. Ragazzi*, p. 194.

[150] *M. Byers*, p. 212. See also *T. Meron*, Human Rights Law-Making in the UN, Oxford 1986, p. 187; *R. Macdonald*, Fundamental Norms in Contemporary International Law, CYIL 1987, Vol. 25, p. 138. For an extensive discussion on the identification of fundamental rights see *M. Ragazzi*, p. 143.

[151] *L. Hannikainen*, pp. 725–726; *O. Schachter*, General Course in International Law, RdC 1982, Vol. 178, p. 182.

[152] *J. Oraá*, p. 269.

[153] *K. Askin*, p. 242.

[154] A few examples may illustrate the state of affairs. A part of the domestic legislation in Botswana was held *ultra vires* the constitution because it discriminated against women. The High Court in Tanzania found customary law contrary to the constitution which expressly prohibits gender discrimination. *M.A. Freeman*, Women's Human Rights in Domestic Legal Systems, HRQ 1994, Vol. 16, p. 569 ff.

human rights norm. Sex, is furthermore, one of the few prohibited grounds for discrimination in the UN Charter and in the UDHR. Members of the international community are thus bound by this principle on the basis of the UN Charter, even if they do not ratify the various conventions aimed at the elimination of discrimination against women. At the same time I admit that the status of the principle is a question open to discussion and that there are grounds for opposite opinions. Some states have not yet ratified the central human rights conventions and those who have done so have made extensive reservations to provisions indispensable for gender equality. Thus, these states seem to have considered it possible to contract out of the rule on non-discrimination on the basis of sex and gender equality. As was demonstrated in Chapter 2, especially sub-section 2.2.1.2., the fact remains at present that gender discrimination in some form or other exists in almost all countries in the world. State practice is not consistent and that makes it difficult to support the position that there is full compliance with the principle of non-discrimination and equality. It is obvious that there is still a gap between rhetoric and reality. Nevertheless, the fact that international law doctrine, especially the one concerning the validity of *ius cogens,* does not always reflect international practice has been acknowledged by Professor em. Sztucki.[155] Of relevance to the present issue is also the conclusion drawn by Professor Meron that the ICJ's more recent approach as to the existence of customary international law in the human rights field "accords limited significance to state practice, especially to inconsistent or contrary practice, and attributes central normative significance to resolutions both of the United Nations and of other international organisations".[156] The burden of proving custom established in the field of human rights and humanitarian law is thus less onerous in these than in other fields of international law.

International law is a dynamic legal order and interpretation of the notion *ius cogens* serving the fundamental values of humankind cannot lag behind the realities of the international society. There is, in other words, a need for evolution of the normative structure in the direction of the overall objectives (gender equality being such an example) of the international community.

Finally, this author fully agrees with the view taken by Professor Charlesworth and Professor Chinkin that *ius cogens* doctrine is still predominantly male-oriented in the sense that *ius cogens* "has privileged the experiences of men over women, and it has provided a protection to men that is not accorded to women".[157] The time has thus come to modify and to adjust the concept of *ius cogens* to the needs and values of modern societies. A rigid and static approach to international law conflicts with the attitude which international bodies take to human rights norms. Therefore, the content of *ius cogens* should not be viewed as defined once and for all. It is the constant reinterpretation, reinvention and modification of law that allows it to be viable over time. As Professor van Boven has observed, in such a

---

155 *J. Sztucki*, pp. 93–94.

156 *T. Meron*, Human Rights and Humanitarian Norms as Customary Law, p. 108.

157 *H. Charlesworth & C. Chinkin*, p. 65.

process new peremptory norms may emerge.[158] Upgrading of the principle of non-discrimination on the basis of sex and equality on the hierarchical scale of international law norms would, besides important practical implications, be of great symbolic significance since it would serve as a powerful warning signal that international society will not tolerate its violation. International institutions for the promotion and protection of human rights have key functions with respect to this process of revitalisation and transformation of international law.

---

[158] *T.C. van Boven*, Survey of the Positive International Law of Human Rights, in The International Dimensions of Human Rights, K. Vasak (ed.), Vol. 1, p. 107.

*Part II*

# Reproductive Freedom – Its Core Component Elements

*Chapter 4*

# The Current Discourse

## 4.1. General Overview

Mrs. Eleanor Roosevelt, the Chairman of the Committee appointed within the Commission of Human Rights, which was entrusted with the drafting of the Universal Declaration on Human Rights, observed in 1958 that universal human rights begin "in small places, close to home – so close and so small that they cannot be seen on any maps of the world. Unless these rights have meaning there, they have little meaning elsewhere…".[1] This important statement is still very much valid for our time and for our subject matter. Unless woman's reproductive freedom is secured within the personal sphere of relationships, several human rights of significance for women will remain wishful thinking. Most of the relevant international instruments[2] contain provisions, which promote an equitable balance between the protection and preservation of the family *per se*, and the protection of its individual family members. Safeguarding the unity and harmony of the family should not be done, in other words, at the expense of the individual human rights of its members, especially not women's and children's rights. Yet the preservation of family and culture has very often been used as a rationale for the denial of human rights to women.[3] In the majority of Muslim societies and in many Third World countries, there is still a tension between the interests of the community and the family unit on the one hand, and the interests of the individual woman and/or child on the other.

How can we than achieve a balance in which the interests of both the individuals and the community/family are maximised? Which interests should prevail when

---

[1] Mrs. Roosevelt's speech "The Great Question" is reproduced in *E. Partnow*, The New Quotable Woman, New York 1993, p. 279. For a review of Mrs. Roosevelt's contributions in regard to gender issues during the early work of the UN, see The United Nations and The Advancement of Women 1945–1996, UN New York 1996, p. 11.

[2] Article 16 of the UDHR, Article 10(1) of the ICESCR, Article 23 of the ICCPR and Article 17 of the American Convention.

[3] *M.A. Freeman*, The Human Rights of Women in the Family: Issues and Recommendations for Implementation of the Women's Convention, in Women's rights, human rights, J. Peters & A. Wolper (eds.), p. 149.

they conflict with each other? In a utopian ideal society, the "general will" of the society coincides with that of the individual. That is, the general will does not supersede but it meets and provides for the interests of the individuals. Conflicts of interest have been solved differently in different cultures and at different times. The balance of rights and interests shift from country to country and depends, among other factors, on the political ideas of liberalism and communitarianism. Liberal ideas favour the individual's rights and freedoms to a greater extent than communitarian ones, which imply that the interests of the community should prevail. To put it very sweepingly, liberal ideas are found and expressed in the individualistic Western cultures, and communitarian ideas in the Third World. International law has tried to balance the need to protect human rights against other needs with which they may occasionally come in conflict. However, the degree to which it is permissible to curb human rights and exactly what grounds justify restrictions of the rights of others remain contested questions.[4]

Procreation is fundamental to the very existence and survival of mankind. Therefore, questions related to human reproduction are of vital importance and involve both the family unit and society as a whole. Since time immemorial the human being has striven to protect his most elementary instinct to procreate. In primitive societies and subsequent successive civilisations, these aspirations have been gradually transformed into rights and obligations, embodied and protected by customary, religious and later on in legal rules.

The right to make decisions about procreation is a basic human right, because it is essential to a contemporary concept of the free individual, and if a right is arguably necessary to the freedom of an individual, *i.e.*, to have power to direct his own life, it is to be considered fundamental.[5] In other words, it is essential to secure women's reproductive rights, since the ability to decide freely and in an informed manner the number and spacing of one's children is "the first step in enabling women to exercise other choices".[6] Reproductive freedom is *sine qua non* for the attainment of any real equality between women and men. It confers, moreover, important benefits not only on women, but equally on the child/ren to be born and on society as a whole. Thus, if parents are entitled to plan for parenthood, the result will be better conditions for the children to be born. To let chance be decisive in matters of pregnancy will not always result in the most favourable conditions for future parenthood.

---

[4] Professor van Dijk has remarked on this dilemma by pointing out that what is established in Article 29(2) of the UDHR, *i.e.*, "In the exercise of his rights and freedoms, everyone shall be subject only to such limitations as are determined by law solely for the purpose of securing due recognition and respect for the rights and freedoms of others and of meeting the just requirements of morality, public order and the general welfare in a democratic society", holds "good for the exercise of the rights and freedoms by the other persons". In consequence the problem of achieving the right balance is not resolved, but rather made more complicated. *P. Van Dijk*, A Common Standard of Achievement, NQHR 1995, Vol. 2, p. 119.

[5] *T.H. Lackland*, Towards Creating a Philosophy of Fundamental Human Rights, in Columbia Human Rights Law Review 1975, Vol. 6, p. 489.

[6] A/CONF.157/PC/61/Add.9, p. 8. See also the *Study on the Interrelationship of the Status on Women and Family Planning*, UN Doc. E/CN.6/575/Rev.1, § 31.

The contemporary understanding of reproductive freedom in international law considers it as a composite right which comprises the right to marry and to found/establish a family,[7] the right to family planning, the right to reproductive health, the right to equality and non-discrimination, the right to information and education, to physical integrity[8] and to private and family life.[9] These core elements are separate human rights on their own and they are to be found in different international instruments. Nevertheless, all of them interact with each other in a dynamic way,[10] thereby strengthening women's reproductive freedom within the realm of international human rights law. Provisions of relevance should, therefore, be viewed in a holistic way. I shall *inter alia* make use of textual-analytical as well as systematic methods of interpretation[11] of the human rights norms in question, *i.e.*, establishing a link among them and, in addition, considering them in the light of recent developments including the final documents adopted at recent UN conferences.[12]

---

[7] Since marriage is no longer a legal precondition for the foundation of a family, the right to found/establish a family has a separate existence within the meaning of the provisions in several human rights instruments.

One might observe that there is a slight variation of language in the wording of Article 10(1) of the ICESCR as compared to the comparatively well-established usage in universal, *e.g.*, the UDHR and the ICCPR as well as regional (the European Convention) documents of the phrase "to found a family". It would have to be assumed, however, that the drafters of the ICESCR had intended a similar meaning to that established in the UDHR from which the right is understood to derive from. To establish a family is virtually synonymous with founding a family. On the other hand Article 17(2) of the American Convention provides that men and women of marriageable age have the right to marry and to "raise a family". This provision has not yet been subject to close scrutiny or analysis by the inter-American human rights institutions. It has been, however, maintained that the American Declaration and the Protocol of San Salvador use the words "establish" and "form" in respect of creating a family, and that indicates a right to procreate, whereas it may not be arguable that the expression "to raise" a family comprises such a right. *S. Davidson*, p. 328.

[8] Part III of this study will be devoted to discussion of some aspects of this right in the context of reproductive freedom.

[9] *R. Dixon-Mueller*, pp. 12–15; *R.J. Cook*, International Human Rights and Women's Reproductive Health, in Women's rights, human rights, J. Peters & A. Wolper (eds.), p. 259. For a definition of the right to reproductive choice, which seems to be more limited than the one of reproductive freedom, see *C.A.A. Packer*, p. 18. Rebecca Cook has in her definition of the right to reproductive self-determination included the right to the benefits of scientific progress. *R.J. Cook*, Putting the "Universal" into Human Rights, Populi 1993, Vol. 20, p. 13.

[10] C.*A.A. Packer*, p. 16.

[11] On the systematic method of interpretation see *K. Larenz*, Methodenlehre der Rechtswissenschaft, Berlin 1975, pp. 313–315; *S. Strömholm*, Rätt, rättskälla, rättstillämpning, Stockholm 1991, pp. 491–403; *O. de Schutter*, L'intreprétation de la Convention Européenne des Droits de l'Homme, Revue de droit international de science diplomatiques et politiques 1992, pp. 90–91.

[12] Audrey Chapman has recently argued, on the basis of the Covenants' lack of sensitivity to women's needs, that it is important to interpret the rights contained therein in the light of subsequent international human rights instruments. *A.R. Chapman*, The Minimum Core Content of the Right to Health, p. 7. Judge Alvarez has argued convincingly in a dissenting opinion as early as in the beginning of the 1950s for the employment of the evolutive method of interpretation of treaties. In his view "it is necessary to avoid slavish adherence to the literal meaning of legal or conventional texts; those who drafted them did not do so with a grammar and a dictionary in front of them; very often, they used vague or inadequate expressions. The important point is, therefore, to have regard above all to the spirit of such documents...(a)nd indeed the *new* requirements of international law". (Italics added) The *Anglo-Iranian Oil co.* Case (Preliminary Objections), ICJ, Judgment of 22 July 1952, p. 126.

While bearing this in mind, I shall for several reasons[13] focus mainly on the right to found a family and to family planning and I shall place it in a broader reproductive health framework and in conjunction with gender equality.[14] Thus, while reproduction as a female experience involves insemination, gestation and childbirth, men's involvement is limited to only the first stage of this process. Considering reproduction from the perspective of feminist theory,[15] it seems obvious to me that men's limited involvement with reproduction makes the use of asymmetrical models of gender equality most suitable. At the same time, our ability medically to intervene in biological processes has raised new ethical and legal questions like: "Is an abortion as the right to freely interrupt pregnancy without the consent of the partner equal to the right of a man to be the master of his sperm? Does this right end with ejaculation or after fertilisation but before pregnancy?"[16] The separation of procreation from sexual relations has considerable implications for the rights of all parties concerned, *e.g.*, genetic parents, commissioning parents, children born by means of new technologies, single women, post-menopausal women, homosexual people etc. Three women can claim to be the mother of a child born by assisted procreation, *i.e.*, "where donor oocytes, surrogate womb and commissioning women are involved".[17]

With this background in mind it is of outmost importance to explore the question of whether access to legal abortion and/or safe abortion services as well as access to new reproductive techniques[18] should be considered essential elements of human rights already in force, such as the right to family planning and to found a family. Can these rights be used as forceful pressure for creating conditions conducive to greater gender equality and better health for women?

---

[13] The most important one is limited space. Moreover, the first element of reproductive freedom, *i.e.*, the right to marry with free and full consent, which indeed has an impact on reproductive freedom, has already been the subject of an enquiry in a book which this author published in 1990 and to which I have already made references.

[14] Inattention and neglect of women's reproductive health in the legislative and regulating frameworks of countries, have been recognised as part of a systematic discrimination against women. See Strategy for Development Cooperation, *Sexual and Reproductive Health and Rights*, SIDA, Stockholm 1997, p. 12 and UN Doc. E/CN.6/1999/4, § 9.

[15] *G. Binion*, Feminist Theory Confronts US Supreme Court Rhetoric: the Case of Abortion Rights, International Journal of Law, Policy and Family 1997, Vol. 11, p. 67.

[16] *B. Verschraegen*, Equality in Family Law, *Law in Motion*, General Report, Part II, Brussels 1996, p. 47.

[17] *D. Evans*, Creating the Child, in Creating the Child, D. Evans (ed.), The Hague 1996, p. 6. The result of the newly (in 1996/97 in Huntington Reproductive Centre, California) used reproductive technique of partial egg donation is that the child born out of this procedure has three parents, two mothers and one father. *A.-L. Haverdahl*, Ägg från två kvinnor ger äldre större chans att bli gravida, SvD 15 June 1998, p. 8.

[18] As we shall see in the following sub-chapter, the new term "reproductive health" as defined in most recent consensual international documents comprises *inter alia* prevention and appropriate treatment of infertility.

These corollaries of reproductive freedom are highly controversial and are likely to remain so unless the essence of the concept is clearly grasped. My starting point for the discussion would be to use teleological and sociological[19] methods of interpretation of the relevant treaty provisions as well as the principle of "maximum effect"[20] when determining whether the scope of the above rights might lead to an expansive reading of them, thereby allowing the coverage of a wide range of various aspects of reproductive freedom. It is clear that this approach to interpretation extends the obligations of the treaty parties, sometimes beyond their intended undertakings.[21] At the same time the intention of contracting states to human rights treaties has been and still is to protect the individual against the threats of the past as well as against the threats of the future.[22] Moreover, as Professor Nowak has observed "generally recognised rules of interpretation for human rights texts call for a liberal interpretation of rights ("*in dubio pro libertate*") and a narrow interpretation of restrictions".[23] The European Court of Human Rights has often relied on the maxim that individual liberties need a broad interpretation (interpretation which leads to effective protection of the individual rights), whereas restrictions on them require a restrictive interpretation.[24] Especially basic human rights ought to be interpreted rather towards freedom of action than imposing restrictions upon them.[25]

---

[19] Whereas the 1969 Vienna Convention on the Law of Treaties omits any reference to this method of interpretation, the European Court of Human Rights has applied it frequently. The sociological method of interpretation "points at developments in society as a means of interpretation. It takes into account attitudes in society, for example, *vis-à-vis* moral questions, in order to establish the meaning of a legal provision". *M. de Blois*, The Fundamental Freedom of the European Court, in The Dynamics of the Protection of Human Rights in Europe, R. Lawson & M. De Blois (eds.), Dordrecht 1994, p. 55.

[20] See the *South West African* case (second phase), ICJ Judgment of 18 July 1966, p. 48. With regard to the interpretation of legal texts, the Court observed that "in the application of the teleological principle of interpretation, treaties must be given their maximum effect in order to ensure the achievement of their underlying purpose".

[21] It was, for example, clear during the preparation of the Convention on the Rights of the Child that the contracting parties could not reach any agreement as far as abortion and modern medical reproduction technologies were concerned. *B. Verschraegen*, Die Kinderrechtekonvention, Wien 1996, p. 20.

[22] *F.G. Jacobs & R.C.A. White*, The European Convention on Human Rights, Oxford 1996, p. 32.

[23] *M. Nowak*, CCPR Commentary, p. 412.

[24] There is a wealth of literature on this issue. I would like, however, to refer to the works of the following authors: *J.G. Merrills & R. Bernhard*, Thoughts on the interpretation of human rights treaties, Mél Wiarda, 1988, p. 70; *M. Delmas-Marty*, The European Convention for the Protection of Human Rights. International Protection versus National Restrictions, Dordrecht 1992, Part III; *F. Matscher*, Methods of Interpretation of the Convention, in The European System for the Protection of Human Rights, R. St. J. Macdonald, F. Matscher & H. Petzold (eds.), p. 67.

[25] *P.I. Schick*, Law and Moral Dilemmas affecting Life and Death, Council of Europe, Strasbourg 1990, p. 60.

## 4.2. Exploring Contemporary Concepts

### *4.2.1. The Concept of "Reproductive Health"*[26]

#### *4.2.1.1. Its Emergence*

Reproductive health is a new subject of regulation in the area of international human rights law. The process of articulating it more clearly is continuing. In recent years governments have been slowly but steadily giving increased priority to reproductive health, motivating a shift from demographic concerns to concerns about meeting the needs of individuals for reproductive health information and services. In this environment a new approach towards family planning has evolved. It is now considered in relation to other methods of regulation of fertility and in the context of health, and so it has been materialised in the concept of women's "reproductive health". This explains to a certain extent why "reproductive health" has been confused with the provisions of family planning and maternal and child health services only, or rather the provisions of family planning and child health services exclusively. The concept is, however, much more complex than that. While acknowledging the importance of family planning, the broad approach to reproductive health is "not limited to child-bearing ages alone and that reproductive health concerns men as well as women".[27] Nevertheless, the right to obtain the means of family planning is closely connected with the right to health as guaranteed in international law.[28] Reproductive freedom in such a context is then considered not only to mean having the legal option, but also the economic means and social conditions that make it possible to effectuate one's choice in reproduction.

---

[26] Groups involved in international family planning introduced the term "reproductive health" as early as the 1970s. Their aim was to broaden the notion of "human reproduction" to include more than fertility regulation and to stress the health aspect of family planning programmes. One can safely assert that it is indeed the international women's health movement through close co-operation with the women's human rights movement that has managed during the last years to achieve this conceptual shift from two separate concepts, *i.e.*, to merge the right to family planning and the right to health into one.

The Vienna Programme of Action includes specific references to women's right to health and to safe maternity. But even though the document recognises the importance of women's enjoyment of the "highest standard of physical and mental health throughout their life span", the term "reproductive health" as such was not even mentioned during the negotiation process. Though the Vienna Declaration and Programme of Action has been a success when it comes to defining women's human rights in armed conflicts and condemning of gender based-violence against women, it does not touch upon the issue of reproductive freedom in an expansive manner. The World Conference affirmed solely in § 41 in the context of the Women's Convention and the Teheran Declaration "a woman's right to accessible and adequate health care and the widest range of family planning services".

[27] UN Doc. E/CN.9/1996/2, § 4.

[28] *N. Taub*, International Conference on Population and Development, ASIL Washington D.C. 1994, Issue Papers on World Conferences, No. 1, pp. 7–8. See also UN Doc. E/CN.6/1999/4.

*4.2.1.2. The Cairo Programme of Action*

The term "reproductive health" as such was set out for the first time in a universal governmental document[29] in Chapter VII (§ 7.2.) of the ICPD Programme of Action.[30] There reproductive health is described as a state of complete physical, mental and social well-being, and not merely the absence of diseases or infirmity, in all matters relating to the reproductive system and to its functions and processes. The attainment of reproductive health also enables women to go safely through pregnancy and childbirth and provides couples with the best chance of having a healthy infant. Implicit in that definition, therefore, is the need for people to have the capability of reproducing (prevention and appropriate treatment of infertility) and the freedom to decide if, when and how often to do so. That would, moreover, include prevention of, or cure from, an unwanted and mistimed pregnancy. In other words, comprehensive health care must also comprise access to safe abortion services.[31] Nevertheless, such services are still generally regarded as a kind of back up when contraceptives fail as well as a way of avoiding complications from unsafe abortions.[32] By considering abortion in the context of health[33] the controversy on

---

[29] In preparation for the Cairo Conference, women's health advocates representing women's networks in Asia, Africa, Latin America, the Caribbean, the U.S. and Western Europe adopted a "*Women's Declaration on Population Policies*", focusing on women's reproductive health. As important aspects of sexual and reproductive health not only pregnancy, delivery and postpartum care were included but also "safe and legal abortion services; safe choices among contraceptive methods including barrier methods, information, prevention and treatment of STDs, AIDS, infertility, and other gynaecological problems, child care services; and policies to support men's parenting and household responsibilities". The text of the declaration has been reprinted by the International Women's Health Coalition, New York, March 4, 1993.

On the regional level, when adopting the guiding principles for women in development by the OECD/DAC in 1988, a connection between primary health care and family planning was made in § 363, in such way that the later has been considered an important component of the first. See DAC Principles for Effective Aid. Development Assistance Manual, OECD, Paris 1992, p. 97.

[30] UN Doc. A/CONF.171/13, 18 October 1994. See also UN Doc. E/CN.6/1995/3/Add.3, § 43.

[31] Paragraph 7.6 of the Programme of Action states that "All countries should strive to make accessible..., (a)bortion as specified in paragraph 8.25, including prevention of abortion and the management of the consequences of abortion". Several commentators support the idea of the notion "reproductive health" as implying that fertility regulation can be achieved without health hazards and terminating unwanted pregnancies. *I. Aitken & L. Reichenbach*, Reproductive and Sexual Health Services: Expanding Access and Enhancing Quality, in Population Policies Reconsidered, G. Sen, A. Germain & L.C. Chen (eds.), p. 178; *M. Fathalla*, Reproductive health: a global overview, Annals of the New York Academy of Sciences 1991, cited in *R.J. Cook & M.I. Plata*, Women's Reproductive Self-determination: evolutionary models, Development 1994:3, p. 30; *R.P. Petchesky*, Introduction, in Negotiating Reproductive Rights, R.P. Petchesky & K. Judd (eds.), London 1998, p. 9.

[32] Unsafe abortion is defined as a procedure for terminating an unwanted pregnancy either by persons lacking the necessary skills, or in an environment lacking the minimal standards, or both. WHO, The Prevention and Management of Unsafe Abortion, Report of a Technical Working Group, Geneva, WHO/MSM/92.5. This definition was used in the ICPD's Programme of Action. The Cairo Conference is the first UN conference to address unsafe abortion as a major public health concern. However, the first review of the implementation of the Nairobi strategies revealed in 1990 that induced abortions, which were numerous and for the most part carried out clandestinely, and adolescent pregnancies, which were on the rise, constitute a threat to the lives of women and girls. UN Doc. E/CN.6/1990/5, § 152.

[33] Chapter VIII (Health, Morbidity and Mortality), paragraph 8.20 of the Programme of Action includes the objective to reduce greatly the number of deaths and morbidity from unsafe abortion.

the legal status of abortion was somewhat side-stepped at the Cairo Conference. In that way focus turned to the serious health effects[34] of unsafe abortions with the aim to promote the development of safe abortion services to all who need them. I may draw the conclusion that the intention of the drafters of this document was to remove existing legal restrictions and making abortion legal,[35] so that all abortions that take place are safe. In support of my assertion, I may refer to the statement of the Honourable Timothy Worth on behalf of the US delegation, who said that: "(o)ur position...is that abortion should be safe, legal and rare".[36] Still the issue of access to abortion services was not resolved at that conference.

An extensive formulation of the concept "reproductive health" was highly contested by conservative forces that considered an expansion of the term "a euphemism for contraception, sterilisation and abortion".[37] The Holy See stated in its reservation to the final document of the ICPD that on the basis of the preamble it assumed that the document does not contain the affirmation of a new internationally recognised right to abortion.[38] The preambular § 1.15 does, indeed, declare that the Cairo Conference "does not create any new international human rights". On the other hand, in § 1.8 it is written that because of major shifts in attitudes among the world's people and leaders in regard to reproductive health and family planning "a new comprehensive concept of reproductive health,[39] including family planning

---

[34] In addition, "pregnancies that come too early, too late, too often and too closely spaced intervals in women's reproductive lives" may also affect women's health adversely. *R.J. Cook*, Human Rights in Relation to Women's Health, WHO, Geneva 1994, p. 13.

[35] The fact that several Latin American governments felt it necessary to clarify their position on that issue supports the proposition that de-criminalisation of abortion was one of the priority issues for the conference. Argentina, *e.g.*, underlined that "reproductive health" may not be interpreted as restricting the right to life or abrogating the condemnation of abortion as a method of birth control or an instrument of population policy. UN Doc. A/CONF.177/20, p. 157. The representative of the Dominican Republic said that the term in question does not include abortion or interruption of pregnancy as a component and that the reservation applies to all regional and international agreements referring to these concepts. *Ibid.*, p.159. Peru interpreted "reproductive health" as not including abortion "as a method of birth control or family planning". *Ibid.*, p. 171. Venezuela accepts the term solely if it does not include abortion or voluntary interruption of pregnancy. *Ibid.*, p. 176.

The Holy See reaffirmed its reservations expressed at the conclusion of the Cairo Conference concerning the interpretation of "reproductive health" and "reproductive rights" in the sense that it does not consider abortion or abortion services to be a dimension of them. *Ibid.*, p. 163. Kuwait expressed the view that § 94 contravenes the Islamic Law (Shari'a). *Ibid.*, p. 167.

[36] *S.P. Johnson*, World Population-Turning the Tide, Three Decades of Progress, London 1994, p. 361.

[37] *R.J. Cook*, The Elimination of Sexual Apartheid: Prospects for the Fourth World Conference on Women, ASIL, Issue Papers on World Conferences, Washington D.C. 1995, No. 5, p. 19.

[38] UN Doc. A/CONF.171/13, p. 147.

[39] The Holy See did, on the other hand, accept the concept of "reproductive health", but solely as a "holistic concept for the promotion of the health of men and women". However, its representatives have frequently maintained that it is necessary to continue to work on a more precise definition of that notion. UN Doc. A/CONF. 171/13, p. 147. Others, among them the Nordic countries, considered the ICPD's final document as "breakthrough language concerning reproductive health and reproductive rights- a concept based on the recognition of the basic right of all couples and individuals to decide freely and responsibly the number, spacing and timing of their children and to have means and information to do so". U.N., Information Centre for the Nordic Countries, POP/572, 1, 14 September 1994.

and sexual health, as defined in the present Programme of Action" has emerged. Implementation of this reproductive health approach requires family planners and health administrators to plan jointly the realisation of the programmes. It also urges them to integrate services shaped to the specific needs of diverse clients in different settings and available to all who need them.[40] Finally, the notion "reproductive health" includes protection against sexual violence. Gender-based discrimination and violence are the causes of many reproductive health problems.

*4.2.1.3. The Beijing Declaration and Platform of Action*

After the Cairo Conference the concept "reproductive health" has been increasingly used in the international debate. It has been repeated and re-utilised in several regional[41] and global documents, *e.g.,* in the Beijing Declaration and Platform for Action, § 94, where family planning and regulation of fertility are discussed in the context of reproductive health.[42] It should be mentioned that the adopted version of § 94 was one of the main subjects of controversy. It was, therefore, put in brackets[43]

---

[40] *I. Aitken & L. Reichenbach*, p. 178; *A. Hardon*, Introduction, in Reproductive Rights in Practice, A. Hardon & E. Hayes (eds.), London 1997, p. 6.

[41] See, for example, § 30 of the Arab Plan of Action for the Advancement of Women to the Year 2000, which was adopted in November 1994 in Amman. UN Doc. E/CN.6/1995/5/Add.5 and § 9.5 in the 1997 Asian Charter on Human Rights (NGO), in *F. de Varennes*, Asia-Pacific Human Rights Documents and Resources, The Hague 1998, p. 142.

[42] The provision reads as follows: " Reproductive health therefore implies that people are able to have a satisfying and safe sex life and that they have the capability to reproduce and the freedom to decide if, when and how often to do so. Implicit in this last condition are the right of men and women to be informed and to have access to safe, effective, affordable and acceptable methods of family planning of their choice, as well as other methods of their choice for regulation of fertility which are not against the law, and the right of access to appropriate health-care services that will enable women to go safely through pregnancy and childbirth and provide couples with the best chance of having a healthy infant". UN Doc. A/CONF.177/20. See in addition Principle 4 of the Jakarta Declaration for the Advancement of Women in Asia and the Pacific (ESCAP 1994) which was adopted in preparation for the Beijing Conference. See A Thematic Guide to Documents on the Human Rights of Women, *G. Alfredsson & K. Tomaševski* (eds.), p. 50. Comprehensive reproductive health including fertility regulation has been identified as a major area for UN policy, programme and project intervention in the recently proposed "System-wide Medium-term Plan for the Advancement of Women 1996–2001", Report of the Secretary General, Follow up to the Fourth World Conference on Women, UN Doc. E/CN.6/1996/CRP.2, § 69. See also the Report of the Secretary-General, Synthesized report on national action plans and strategies for implementation of the Beijing Platform for Action, 22 December 1997, §§ 64–75 (hereinafter cited as the Synthesized report 1997).

[43] Despite the consensus reached in 1994, 35 % (468 sets of brackets-each delineating an area of disagreement that needed further negotiations) of the bracketed language of the draft Platform for Action for Beijing remained in square brackets, compared to 15% of the language, which was in brackets before the Cairo Conference. Much of the bracketed language in the Beijing draft document was the same language, which was agreed upon at Cairo and almost all of it was related to women's reproductive rights and reproductive health. One of the presented theories in this connection maintains that the opposition to the abortion issue was not well organised at Cairo and it realised afterwards the impact that the Cairo document will have on the international community, especially on the lives of women. *K. McDonald*, Reproductive rights under attack, 2 IPPF, Challenges, Women's health, Women's rights, 1995, p. 15. On the other hand, some key actors appeared to shift from earlier positions and signalled early their desire to reach agreement. The Holy See, *e.g.,* assured the Beijing Conference that it did not wish to unravel any existing agreements and was not seeking to re-open debates from Cairo.

before the conference, flagging the failure to reach consensus. On the other hand, only a few states submitted written statements as to their interpretation of the term "reproductive health". Despite a minor opposition, there is today ample support for the concept of "reproductive health" as described above and as strongly asserted in the final documents of the two major UN's conferences (Cairo and Beijing).

In light of the above, it is apparent that the phrase "reproductive health" is broader than the rather narrow concepts of "fertility regulation" and "family planning". It includes elements of both[44] but it expands beyond a focus on controlling births, since it incorporates an awareness of the social and cultural context in which reproduction and child bearing is carried out, and puts it in the context of gender equality and the empowerment of women. As some authors have put it, the notion of reproductive health "is shaped not only by medical conditions, but also by social forces and power relationships that range from the level of the family to that of international institutions".[45] In other words, this term recognises that to address reproductive health issues successfully, we must address the reproductive rights of women *and* men and the social behaviour and cultural practices that affect reproductive health outcomes. Reproductive freedom provides the framework in which to achieve reproductive health. Again, access to family-planning information and services is an important instrument for its realisation.[46] Reproductive health incorporates all the previous approaches dealing with reproduction and health, focusing only on specific aspects of them in a comprehensive manner.

This expansive and broad understanding of the notion "reproductive health" makes it difficult to accept a proposed interpretation of Article 12 of the Women's Convention[47] which protects the right to health as incorporating reproductive health.

---

[44] *H.H. Pyne*, Reproductive Experiences and Needs of Thai Women: Where Has Development Taken Us, in Power and Decision, The Social Control of Reproduction, G. Sen & R.C. Snow (eds.), p. 36. See also UN Doc. CEDAW/C/1996/3/Add.1, § 13; UN Doc. E/CN.6/1996/CRP.2, §§ 69, 84; UN Doc. E/CN.9/1996/2, § 38; UN CN.9/1996/5, § 14. Access to safe and legal abortion was encouraged by members of CEDAW in their discussions on several aspects of women's health issues on 3 February 1995. Press Release WOM/809, 284th Meeting (1995). A couple of years earlier members of CEDAW asked representatives of the Nicaragua's Government about the prospects of adopting a general policy for reproductive health in the country and whether the Government was carrying out any programme to deal with the problem of clandestine abortion, which was referred to as the third most common cause of death among mothers. UN Doc. GA, A/48/38, 1993, § 391. Unwanted pregnancy and unsafe abortion were discussed in the context of reproductive health during a recent meeting of experts which took place in Addis Ababa. See the Report of the Expert Group Meeting on Adolescent Girls and Their Rights, Addis Ababa, Ethiopia, 13–17 October 1997, EGM/AGR/1997, Rep.1, 6 November 1997, § 41. Abortion was also mentioned with regard to women's reproductive health in some national plans for implementation of the Beijing Platform for Action. See the Synthesized report 1997, § 67.

[45] *C.M. Obermeyer*, Religious Doctrine, State Ideology and Reproductive Options in Islam, in Power and Decision, The Social Control of Reproduction, G. Sen & R.C. Snow (eds.), p. 59.

[46] UN Doc. A/CONF.171/4, 1994, § 110.

[47] *K.H. Martinez & B. Romney*, International Family Planning Cuts Undermine Human Rights, ASIL, Human Rights Interest Group, Newsletter 1998, Vol. 8, p. 20.

## 4.3. The Concept "Regulation of Fertility"

### *4.3.1. The Cairo Programme of Action*

Several other definitions of vague terms were discussed and developed at the Cairo Conference. "Regulation of fertility" was one of those newly introduced concepts. Here it was included for the first time in a universal document, the ICPD Programme of Action.[48] The WHO, as well as the majority of participants at the ICPD, took the standpoint that "fertility regulation" should be considered as a wider concept than "family planning", since it emphasises the prevention or the termination of unwanted pregnancy,[49] *i.e.,* abortion, *per se.* Thus, the term was understood to connote a means of achieving a decline in fertility. At the same time, it was also contended that abortion should be used for fertility control when no other means are available. The initial § 7.1, *i.e.,* the adopted § 7.2 in the ICPD's final document, proclaimed that men and women have the right to obtain access to methods of fertility regulation. More than 70 delegates commented on this paragraph and debated at length the replacement of the phrase "fertility regulation" with "family planning". Thus, many delegations assumed that the previous term clearly included abortion. The World Health Organisation proposed that the working definition of "fertility regulation" to be used during the course of the Cairo Conference should comprise: "family planning, delayed childbearing, the use of contraception, treatment of infertility, interruption of unwanted pregnancies and breastfeeding".[50] This definition was presented by WHO in response to a comment on Nigeria's interpretation of "family planning" as a broader term than "fertility regulation". In consequence, I may establish that "family planning" today is regarded by the international community as a less comprehensive phrase than "fertility regulation" and as separate from abortion. This view was subsequently reflected in paragraph 8.25 of the ICPD final document, which underlines that: "In no case should abortion be promoted as a method of family planning". This provision has been embodied thereafter in § 106 (k) in the Beijing Declaration and Platform for Action. Much support for such an interpretation may be found in the reactions, *i.e.*, arguments put forward for the replacement of "fertility regulation" with "family planning", of several states" representatives to the Cairo Conference, generally known for their strong opposition to abortion. The countries were the Philippines, the Dominican Republic, Libya, Honduras, Argentina, Peru, the Holy

---

[48] Within the NGO community, the Guidelines for the Distribution and Use of Fertility Regulation Methods (WEMOS), which were adopted in 1989, frequently refer to this phrase as including "hormonal methods, barrier methods such as condoms and diaphragms, natural methods, sterilisation and safe abortion services". A Thematic Guide to Documents on the Human Rights of Women, *G. Alfredsson & K. Tomaševski* (eds.), p. 249.

[49] Abortion is the common and at times it has been the primary means for dealing with the problem of unwanted pregnancies.

[50] Earth Negotiations Bulletin, 7 September 1994, Vol. 6, p. 2. The term "fertility regulation" has been used in similar wording, *i.e.*, comprising among other things family planning in the Report of the Secretary General presented at the CSW's 14th session, UN Doc. E/CN.6/1996/CRP.2, § 85.

See, Malta and Malaysia. When it became obvious that the phrase "regulation of fertility" would be retained in the final text, reservations were orally expressed by the representative of El Salvador, Nicaragua[51] as well as of Honduras, marking a minority view.[52] The representative of the latter state based his argument on the Declaration of the Fifteenth Summit of Central American Presidents, adopted in Costa Rica on 20 August 1994.[53] Also the delegates of Paraguay made it clear at the conference that the inclusion of the term "interruption of pregnancy", as part of the concept of regulation of fertility, made the concept unacceptable to his country.[54] The Dominican Republic entered a reservation on the same subject, *i.e.*, accepting a content of the terms "reproductive health", "reproductive rights" and "regulation of fertility" and "other terms" as excluding the concept abortion. It is of interest to note that according to their statement, this reservation should also apply to all regional and international agreements referring to these concepts. Malta and the Holy See thought the same.[55] The delegations of these states were, however, not persuasive enough, inasmuch as "fertility regulation" was not cut out in the text. In

---

[51] The representative of Nicaragua explained that: "We accept the concepts of "family planning", "sexual health", "reproductive health", "reproductive rights" and "sexual rights" expressing an explicit reservation on these terms and any others when they include "abortion" or "termination of pregnancy" as a component. Abortion and termination of pregnancy can under no circumstances be regarded as a method of regulating fertility or a means of population control". UN Doc. A/CONF.171/13, p. 139.

[52] It reads as follows: "As far as reproductive rights, reproductive health and family planning are concerned, we wish to express reservations, as the other Latin American countries have done: we should never include abortion within these concepts, either as service or as a method of regulating fertility". UN Doc. A/CONF.171/13, p.137. Malta's reservation is very much in the same line.

[53] The statement reads as follows: "As a consequence of this, one accepts the concepts of "family planning", "sexual health", "reproductive health", "regulation of fertility", "reproductive rights" and "sexual rights" so long as these terms do not include "abortion" or "termination of pregnancy", because Honduras does not accept these as arbitrary actions; nor do we accept them as a way of controlling fertility or regulating the population". UN Doc. A/CONF.171/13, p. 138.

[54] UN Doc. A/CONF.171/13, p. 140. Argentina submitted a written statement to the Programme of Action, pointing out that: "The Argentine Republic cannot accept the inclusion of abortion in the concept of "reproductive health" either as a service or as a method of regulating fertility". UN Doc. A/CONF.171/13, p. 142.

[55] UN Doc. A/CONF.171/13, at 143 and 148. Regarding the terms "sexual health", "reproductive rights" and "reproductive health", the Holy See did not consider abortion or access to abortion as a dimension of these terms. Moreover, a concern has been expressed that the final document, as opposed to the earlier documents of the Bucharest and Mexico City Conferences, recognises abortion as a dimension of population policy and, indeed of primary health care, *i.e.*, abortion services belong within primary health care as a method of choice.

With reference to the terms "contraception", "family planning" and "regulation of fertility", the Holy See did not change its well-known position concerning those family planning methods which the Catholic Church considers morally unacceptable.

The delegation of Ecuador entered a similar reservation on the meaning of the above concepts pointing out that as they are used within the context of the ICPD's Programme of Action, "could involve abortion". The Government of Guatemala made a reservation on the whole of Chapter VII and relevant parts of Chapter VIII with the motivation that the GA's mandate to the Cairo Conference did not extend to the creation and formulation of rights such as, *e.g.*, "reproductive rights", "reproductive health" and "fertility regulation". *Ibid.*, at 144–145.

the final version of the ICPD Programme of Action "fertility regulation" was only altered into "regulation of fertility" (§ 7.2), which does not signify any change in its content. Therefore, the inclusion of this provision, implying that safe and legal abortion has been recognised as a means of fertility control and that individuals shall have access to it, is but one of the hard-won gains of the Cairo Conference. Several of the above mentioned states maintained the same reservations on the Beijing Declaration and Platform for Action.[56] Argentina, for example, declared that it continues to condemn abortion as a method of birth control. In the statement of the Holy See, it was underlined that the language used in the Beijing Declaration in regard to fertility regulation "could be interpreted as including societal endorsement of abortion".[57] As a matter of fact, the International Bank for Reconstruction and Development (IBRD) has included abortion methods under the category of "Other Fertility Regulation Methods".[58] Also a recent UN report reflects the understanding that abortion is indeed one of "the most widely used" methods of fertility regulation.[59]

### *4.3.2. The Impact of the Final Documents Adopted at the Cairo and Beijing UN Conferences*

While the Cairo Programme of Action and the Beijing Declaration and Platform of Action lack legally binding quality in terms of contemporary international law, they do bear great authority since they have been endorsed by the vast majority of governments.[60] Both conferences adopted without a vote the final documents on 13 September 1994, respectively on 15 September 1995.[61] The documents were subsequently endorsed by resolutions of the United Nations General Assembly.[62] In

---

[56] See UN Doc. A/CONF.177/20, pp. 157–176. Paragraph 17 of the Beijing Declaration stipulates that states are convinced that "the explicit recognition and reaffirmation of the right of all women to control all aspects of their health, in particular their own fertility, is basic to their empowerment".

[57] *Supra*, at 162.

[58] IBRD, Effective Family Planning Programs 1993, pp. 94–95; *C.A.A. Packer*, p. 74.

[59] UN Doc. E/CN.9/1996/2, § 54. See also Strategy for Development Cooperation, SIDA, p. 22.

[60] Approximately 180 governments agreed upon the Cairo Programme of Action. The Beijing Declaration and the Platform of Action was adopted unanimously by 189 countries. It should also be mentioned that the Main Committee of the ICPD succeeded in adopting *ad referendum* the entire Programme of Action on 12 September 1994.

[61] The fact that the documents were approved by so many states does not change the nature of obligations they generate. Noteworthy is that only the US delegation declared explicitly that it would not interpret the Beijing Platform of Action as legally binding.

[62] UN GA Res. 49/128 of 19 December 1994; GA Res. 50/124 of 20 December 1995 and GA Res. 50/203 of 23 February 1996.

For a discussion on the legal value and implications of the UN GA resolutions see *O. Schachter*, International Law in Theory and Practice, Dordrecht 1991, pp. 84–105; *I. Detter*, International Law, Stockholm 1991, pp. 285–319. The on-going debate on the status of certain declarations and resolutions of the UN is closely related to the concept of "soft law". Professor Weil has defined the term "soft law" as follows: "The term 'soft law' is not used solely to express the vague and therefore, in practice, uncompelling character of a legal norm but is also used at times to convey the sublegal value of some non-normative acts, such as certain resolutions of international organizations..." *P. Weil*, Towards

consequence, it has been maintained that they "embody globally accepted policy norms and recommendations".[63]

Moreover, the Beijing Platform of Action has emerged from a preparatory process more participatory and inclusive than any other in history. Nevertheless, the impact of both world conferences will be measured by the concrete actions undertaken by states and international organisations to fulfil the goals of the final documents. The existing differing viewpoints among governments on fertility regulation are thus of practical importance, since it is up to the individual state to implement the ICPD Programme of Action and the Beijing Platform for Action.[64] The large number of reservations on health and sexuality reflects abiding political and cultural differences that the Cairo and Beijing conferences exposed and reflected but could not realistically be expected to resolve. At the same time the reservations show, in my opinion, that opposing governments calculated that provisions on these issues might be custom-making. Therefore, they excluded themselves through the "persistent objector" rule from the application of the rules when they become general law. Persistent objection influences the applicability of customary international law but not its creation and its very existence. In other words, if one government refuses to recognise a rule as one of law, there is nothing to prevent the other states from accepting it *inter se*. By that I am not asserting that the broad

---

Relative Normativity in International Law, AJIL 1983, Vol. 77, p. 414. For a critical and thorough analysis of the concept in the doctrine see *J. Sztucki*, Reflections on International "Soft Law", Festskrift till Lars Hjerner, Studies in International Law, Stockholm 1990, pp. 499–575. Professor Sztucki considers the term "soft law" as "counterproductive, inadequate, misleading and even dangerous", since it leads to relativisation of normative values in international law in the sense that certain rules are being regarded as more binding than others. See also *T. Gruchalla-Wesierski*, A framework for understanding "soft law", McGill Law Journal 1984, Vol. 30, pp. 37–88; *C.Ingelse*, "Soft Law"?, Polish Yearbook of International Law 1993, Vol. 20, pp. 75–90; *F. Francioni*, International "soft law": a contemporary assessment, in Fifty years of the International Court of Justice-Essays in honour of Sir Robert Jennings, Lowe & Fitzmaurice (eds.), Cambridge 1996, pp. 167–178; *J. Klabbers*, The redundancy of soft law, NJIL 1996, Vol. 65, pp. 167–182.

[63] *L. Katzive & K.H. Martinez*, Roe v. Wade in the Global Context: International Recognition of Abortion Rights, ASIL, Human Rights Interest Group Newsletter 1998, Vol. 8, No. 1, p. 4.

[64] Issues relating to implementation and follow-up did not receive sufficient attention in Cairo. However, Chapter XVI calls on the GA to organise a regular review of the implementation of the Programme of Action. The UN General Assembly has, furthermore, decided to review the progress in implementing the Beijing Platform for Action on a regular basis, starting in 1996 and culminating in the year 2000 with a review of both the Nairobi Forward-looking Strategies and the Platform. Paragraphs 4 and 6 of GA resolution 50/203 (1996) establish that governments have the primary responsibility for implementing the Platform for Action and that commitment at the highest level is essential for its implementation. The GA, ECOSOC and the CSW will play the primary role in the overall policy-making and follow-up of both documents. The Commission on the Status of Women will review at its 43rd session in March 1999 analytical reports on two critical areas of concern of the Beijing Platform for Action: "Women and health" and "Institutional mechanisms for the advancement of women".

As noted in § 297 of the Platform for Action, states should, as soon as possible and preferably by the end of 1995, begin to develop strategies to implement it. They should be developed together with plans of actions, preferably by the end of 1996. With regard to the reference to commitments in § 293 (commitments on national level), states have the primary responsibility for implementing the Platform of Action. See UN, The UN and The Advancement of Women 1945–1996, p. 69.

content of the right to reproductive health has already acquired the status of a customary law rule. I solely maintain that the small group objecting states is not sufficient to prevent its emergence as a rule of law.

It seems that there is agreement in contemporary understanding of international law that GA resolutions may generate new law norms with regard to the process of the formation of customary law or treaty law. Thus, the declarations resulting from the mentioned conferences are considered as "signposts of the direction in which international human rights law is developing".[65] In other words, it is important to retain in my study a line between the law *de lege lata* and the law *de lege ferenda*.

The significance of the mentioned instruments consists also in that they will influence states, participants in the mentioned conferences, but which are not parties to the Women's Convention, and other human rights treaties of relevance, in their international conduct and hopefully domestic law.[66] They can acquire considerable weight in "structuring international conduct"[67] even though not on the basis of legally binding obligations. Also Professor Chinkin has strongly suggested that the role of soft law instruments should not be underestimated since in her view they also "play a major role in the development of international law and both are needed for the regulation of States' activities and for the creation of expectations".[68] The final documents of the Cairo and Beijing Conferences may also "raise the public awareness and consciousness" as well as stimulate positive changes within states.[69]

Thus, both conferences should not be viewed in isolation. Their results will have a far-reaching impact on future meetings within the UN like subsequent conferences that are linked to similar issues. Thereby new, weaker language cannot be permitted.

While the norms contained in the final documents of the UN Conferences in question cannot be invoked *per se* to secure legal protection, they may have a certain effect in the judicial/quasi judicial decision-making as "supporting arguments in interpreting the law as it stands".[70] Thus, what is important for our subject matter is that these documents ought to be taken into consideration by the

---

[65] *R.J. Cook*, Human Rights in Relation to Women's Health, p. 29.

[66] At the CSW's session in March 1996, which was intended as a general discussion on the follow-up of the Beijing Conference, the representative of Brazil stated, *e.g.*, that the Platform for Action had inspired innovative policies within the country. For that purpose special measures were included in the Programme for the Integral Assistance to Women's Health.

[67] *P. Malanczuk*, p. 54.

[68] *C.M. Chinkin*, The Challenge of Soft Law: Development and Change in International Law, ICLQ 1989, Vol. 38, p. 850. Judge Higgings has also expressed the view that resolutions of international organisations play "a significant role in creating norms". *R. Higgins*, Problems and Process, p. 28. See also Brownlie who holds that "the normative impact of an instrument does not necessarily depend upon its formal legal status". *I. Brownlie*, International law at the fiftieth anniversary of the United Nations, 255 Recueil de Cours 1995, p. 80.

[69] *C.A.A. Packer*, p. 22.

[70] *P. Malanczuk*, p. 55.

international supervisory bodies in their interpretation of the relevant rules in existing human rights treaties.[71]

There is nothing that indicates that there is any customary law basis for the right to reproductive health in its comprehensive version earlier referred to, and that is the reason why I shall focus on conventional law as the source for the elements forming reproductive freedom.

[71] Paragraph 36 of GA Res. 50/202 (1996) requests CEDAW within its mandate, to take into account the Platform for Action, when considering reports submitted by states parties. CEDAW recommended, *e.g.*, after the consideration of Ukraine's report under the Women's Convention, that the Government should in subsequent reports provide information on the status of implementation of commitments made at the Beijing Conference. UN Doc. CEDAW/C/SR.302, 1996, § 25.

*Chapter 5*

# Family Planning in a Wide Perspective

With regard to reproductive freedom we may notice that the unqualified use of several terms of importance to our study is rather confusing. There is, *e.g.*, an ongoing debate on whether abortion is comprised in the term "family planning", which lends itself to different interpretations, or in "regulation of fertility" or in both. If it turns out that abortion is included in the first right, then human rights law provisions protect it. This will not be the case if abortion is only an element of the term "regulation of fertility", since it has not yet been incorporated as a human right in any judicially binding international instrument.

## 5.1. Fertility Regulation in Relation to Family Planning

My proposition is that family planning and abortion are connected. Nevertheless, abortion has to be distinguished generally from family planning, since it cannot be considered as a desirable method of family planning, but rather as a means to reduce the number of abortions.[1] In other words, this author subscribes to the view

---

[1] *M.K. Eriksson*, The Right to Marry and to Found a Family, p. 141. Some of the recommendations (*e.g.*, Recommendation No. 18, subparagraph (e)) adopted by the International Conference on Population, which was held in Mexico City in 1984, include a passage that refers to the need to help women to avoid abortion and that abortion should in no case be promoted as a method of family planning. The recommendation referred to was the subject of a heated debate and was one of the few instances where a governmental delegation (from Sweden) requested a separate statement, which indicated that while joining the consensus reached on that issue, it wanted to express the understanding of the Swedish Government that one step towards the elimination of illegal abortion, was the provision of access to abortions that were legal and safe. UN Doc. A/CONF. 171/4, § 124. The US delegation denounced abortion and declared that it would not give aid to family-planning programmes that offered it. In consequence the final document spurned abortion. The years after the Mexico City conference, the WHO took the official standpoint that abortion must not be considered as a method for family planning. In 1990 at an international conference in Tbilisi representatives of WHO declared that the organisation does not hold any position with regard to abortion, but is of course concerned with its health implications. At the same conference the UNFPA stated that it does not regard abortion as a means of family planning. *K. Sundström*, Abortion- A Reproductive Health Issue, Stockholm 1993, p. 65. Another example is Sweden, a country with a liberal approach to the abortion issue. In the *travaux préparatoires*

that the term "family planning" is narrower in scope than "fertility regulation" or "regulation of fertility". At the same time, it must be acknowledged that there are scholars, such as Ms. Sundström, who have shown a preference to give the term "family planning" a broader meaning, *i.e.*, understood to cover methods, services and programmes for "fertility regulations". According to the same writer, the main methods for fertility regulation include: 1. Social control of sexuality and reproduction 2. Contraception and 3. Abortion safe or unsafe.[2] Ms. Sundström, consequently, considers abortion to be a method for fertility regulation, and since she regards "family planning" to contain "fertility regulation", both concepts comprise abortion.

Some support for such a position may be found in statements made in the international fora. At the third UN Conference on Women in 1985, representatives for the organisation Third World Women demanded their right to: "all methods of family planning, including abortion as a back-up method, and to choose ourselves what is best for us in our situation". CEDAW in its report to the same conference comprised under the title "Family planning and counselling" information on abortion laws in states parties to the Women's Convention. Many governments had indicated that abortion was legal and free of charge. Only two states, the Philippines and Rwanda, reported that abortion was forbidden.[3]

There are other, albeit very few, examples of documents in which the term "family planning" has been given an extended interpretation. Among them I may mention a relatively recent report of the UN Secretary-General on Human Rights and Scientific and Technological Developments which comprises a heading "Family planning: artificial insemination and abortion".[4]

WHO applies, in addition, a very broad working definition of family planning, according to which the term is but one of the methods of fertility regulation, which includes delaying childbearing, the use of contraception, treatment of infertility, interruption of unwanted pregnancies and breastfeeding.[5]

Also CEDAW seemed on one occasion to have subsumed regulation of fertility under family planning. In its General Recommendation No. 21 (§ 23), dealing with

---

to the Swedish Abortion Act (SOU 1983:31,15) it is emphasised that abortion was to be regarded as an emergency measure and only a part of the wider issue of fertility regulation. It was not to be made a deliberate alternative to family planning by preventive methods. In addition, I may also mention the Regional Programme of Action for the Women of Latin America and the Caribbean, 1995–2001, presented at Beijing, which underlined that while governments of that region recognised the importance of abortion as a public health problem, abortion should in no case be considered a method of family planning. UN Doc. E/CN.6/1995/5/Add.3,1995, § 88.

[2] *K. Sundström*, p. 17.

[3] UN Doc. A/CONF. 116/13, § 249. Also in the legal doctrine there are references to abortion as a family planning method. See, *e.g.*, *E. Mercado,* Consequences of unwanted pregnancies in Bolivia: an overview, in Unwanted Pregnancies and Public Policy: An International Perspective, *H. Correa* (ed.), New York 1994, p. 179 and *A.B. Marcelino*, Combating Opposition in the Philippines, IPPF 1996, No. 1, p. 30.

[4] UN Doc. E/CN.4/1995/74, §§ 102–110.

[5] Statement made by representatives of WHO at the Cairo Conference. See Earth Negotiations Bulletin, 7 September 1994, Vol. 6, p. 2.

Article 16(1)(e), *i.e.*, family planning issues, we may find the following illustrative clarification: "where there are freely available appropriate measures for the voluntary regulation of fertility" the health of the members of the family improves.

Still this author considers the examples above as a too insufficient basis for a conclusion that CEDAW views Article 16(1)(e) of the Women's Convention, the most significant conventional provision protecting reproductive freedom, as comprising a right to fertility regulation including abortion. There is, in other words, considerable doubt as to whether family planning as guaranteed in treaty law includes the right to abort unwanted foetuses. In my view, such a right is not yet part of the Women's Convention and therefore not the law *de lege lata*, *i.e.*, part of the international human rights law. This is, however, not to establish that a right to access to abortion services might not be derived from other human rights provisions.

## 5.2. The Emergence of the Concept "Family Planning"

The acceptance of the concept "family planning" as a basic human right is relatively recent in public international law. The term was introduced after World War II, and it was first used in a UN resolution adopted in 1965 by the UN Commission on the Status of Women. It is stated there that: "married couples should have access to all relevant educational information concerning family planning".[6] It was, however, not until the first UN Conference on Human Rights held in Teheran 1968 that matters of procreation and family planning were specifically related to human rights. In Article 16 of the Proclamation adopted at this conference, it is said that: "Parents have a basic right to determine freely and responsibly the number and spacing of their children".[7] The right to family planning has repeatedly been restated and further elaborated in international documents since 1968, if not always by name. So, family planning was defined as a human right in Article 14(f) of the concluding document adopted at the World Population Conference in Bucharest in 1974 as follows: "All couples and individuals have the basic right to decide freely and responsibly the number and spacing of their children and to have the information, education and means to do so". The right of couples and individuals to decide the number, spacing and timing of their children was endorsed in §§ 7.2 and 7.3 of the IPCD final document and in § 95 of the Beijing Declaration. In addition, § 223 of the Beijing Platform for Action establishes that reproductive rights "rest on the recognition of the basic right of all couples and individuals to decide freely and responsibly the number, spacing and timing of their children".

---

[6] *N. Petrić*, The Status of the Human Right to Planned Parenthood in International Resolutions, in *Planned Parenthood in Europe: A Human Rights Perspective*, P. Meredith & L. Thomas (eds.), London 1986, p. 49.

[7] Final Act of the International Conference on Human Rights, Teheran 22 April to 13 May 1968, UN Doc. A/CONF.32/41. The term "family planning" was, however, used first in the United Nations context in a resolution adopted by the Commission on the Status of Women in 1965. It was, however, not related to human rights *per se*.

Even though the importance of these documents should not be underestimated, since resolutions of the GA may have a crucial role in the norm-creating process of international law, of greater significance for my discussion is whether and, if so, how the principles reflected in them are specified in treaty law. Family planning as a human right was first proclaimed in a universal treaty in Article 16(1)(e) of the Convention on Elimination of All Forms of Discrimination against Women. This treaty creates legal obligations today for the majority of states in the world and requires them to take all appropriate measures to ensure that women have the same right as men to decide "freely and responsibly on the number and spacing of their children and to have means to enable them to exercise this right".

## 5.3. The Substantive Content of the Right to Family Planning

### *5.3.1. The Committee's on Elimination of Discrimination against Women (CEDAW) Interpretation*

The ultimate challenge of the XXI st century is that of giving greater substance to existing norms on human rights. The lack of specific content of the term "family planning" in international law documents, as well as other factors, seems to have given rise to some scepticism, and doubts have been expressed in the doctrine as to whether there *is* after all such a universally accepted right to family planning.[8] In the view of the present author, though doubt may be justified in regard to the vague character of the norm, this fact should not be exaggerated. I admit that there exist considerable difficulties in reaching consensus world wide on the exact meaning of the notion, but rules that are expressed in abstract or ambiguous wording do not necessarily deprive them of their legal character. What rules with indeterminate language, *i.e.*, the usage of flexible wording, permit is a scale of possible degrees of implementation. Therefore, it might be wise to explore whether there are any statements by international (quasi) judicial organs, which might cast some light as to the content of the right mentioned above. Thus, so far it is only CEDAW, which has adopted – in 1993 – recommendation No. 21[9] to states parties on equality in marriage and in family relations. In relation to the issue under consideration, it should be noted that this fact is of relevance. To start with, the Committee reached the conclusion that the responsibilities in bearing and raising children affect women's personal development and they impose inequitable workloads on them. The impact on their physical and mental health that comes with the right to decide the number and spacing of their children is similar, and therefore women have the right to decide the number and spacing of their children.[10] This is a rather new approach to

[8] *K. Tomaševski*, Human Rights in Population Policies, A Study for SIDA, Lund 1994, pp. 19 and 95.

[9] CEDAW, General Recommendation on equality in marriage and in family relations, UN Doc. E/CN.6/1993/CRP.2. See also CSW, Res. 38/6, Gender equality in population programmes, Commission on the Status of Women, UN Doc. E/CN.6/1994/14, pp. 18–21.

[10] CEDAW, General Recommendation, *ibid.*, § 21.

the explication of the Convention's requirements. Moreover, the recommendations create criteria by which the Committee may measure the state party's compliance with the provisions of that treaty.

The main components of the right to "family planning", though the term is not explicitly mentioned, have been identified therein as follows: guaranteed sex education and availability of family planning services, *i.e.*, availability of safe and reliable methods of contraception. Then the Committee continues its deliberations by emphasising the importance of freely available and appropriate measures for the voluntary regulation of fertility for the health and well-being of all members of the family. In other words, family planning and regulation of fertility are considered as inter-related issues in the broader context of health.[11] And yet, the avoidance of the term "family planning" *verbatim* is indicative that it might have become outmoded, or that it is too restrictive, and that it ought to be replaced by the more comprehensive umbrella term "reproductive health".

Since CEDAW's recommendation is the only authoritative interpretation in existence of the right to family planning, it will serve as the basis for my further deliberations.

### *5.3.2. Religious Resistance to an Extensive Interpretation of the Notion "Family Planning"*

Religious norms are often invoked against an extensive interpretation of the right to family planning. Whereas in religions like Judaism the foetus is not seen as a person before birth and "abortion is not only permissible, but indeed required if the life of the mother is threatened by continuing the pregnancy",[12] Catholicism and Islam,[13] *e.g.*, limit the application of human rights in this area. Although there are

---

[11] See *A.R. Chapman*, pp. 14–15 and *K.H. Martinez & B. Ronney*, International Family Planning Cuts Undermine Human Rights, ASIL 1998, Human Rights Interest Group Newsletter, p. 20. The last mentioned scholars maintain that the established right to health includes the right to family planning.

[12] *S. Jenkins*, Abortion Rights, Poor Women, and Religious Diversity, in From Abortion to Reproductive Freedom, Transforming a Movement, M.G. Fried (ed.), Boston 1990, p. 152. Nevertheless, the Jewish tradition in pre-Christian and early Christian times considered abortion as wrong, although it was allowed when necessary to save the life of the mother. *J. Connery*, Abortion in Roman Catholic Perspective, Loyola University Press 1977, p. 18.

[13] Human rights documents emanating from Islamic organisations follow an approach in many respects different from human rights standards. In the preamble of The Cairo Declaration on Human Rights in Islam, adopted by the 19th Islamic Conference of Foreign Ministers in 1990, it is explained that for reasons that lie in the nature of the Shari'a "the highest Islamic state and religious law", Islamic nations in parts of the African, Asian and Arab land masses, have difficulties in bringing internationally recognised human rights standards into conformity with Shari'a. In Article 7 it is stipulated that "both the foetus and the mother must be protected and accorded special care". Access to family planning is obviously not envisaged as a right. UN Doc. A/45/421/5/21797, p. 199. See also *F. Ermacora, M. Nowak & H. Tretter*, International Human Rights, Documents and Introductory Notes, Vienna 1993, pp. 324–327. The above cited text is much more restrictive compared with Article XIX (a) of the Universal Islamic Declaration of Human Rights adopted earlier by the Islamic Council on 19 September 1981, which envisages every person's right to marry and to found a family. A Thematic Guide to

no official statements within Buddhism and Shintoism on the subject of abortion, there are some indications of negative attitudes towards its performance. Devotion to the unborn child, for example, is a common occurrence in Buddhist temples.[14]

Ensuring compatibility of religious norms with human rights law has become one of the main controversies today. The attitude of the Catholic Church towards the right to family planning has found expression in the 1983 Charter of the Rights of the Family. There it is said that:

> "The spouses have an inalienable right to found a family and to decide on the spacing of births and the number of children to be born, taking into full consideration their duties towards themselves, their children already born, the family and society, in a just hierarchy of values and in accordance with the objective moral order which excludes recourse to contraception, sterilisation and abortion".

The Church has since not moderated its view on this subject. On the contrary, at a meeting between Mrs. N. Sadik (the Secretary-General of the Cairo Conference) and Pope John Paul II on 18 March 1994, the latter repeated his previous opposition to modern contraception, sterilisation and abortion. As indicated by the Pope anything other than periodic abstinence in marriage is considered contrary to the moral law inscribed in the human heart, and is an assault on the sacredness of life.

---

Documents on the Human Rights of Women, *G. Alfredsson & K. Tomaševski* (eds.), p. 54. Also the preamble of the Arab Charter on Human Rights, which was adopted on 15 September 1994, (not yet in force) mentions that certain internationally recognised human rights are omitted in the text, because there is a common assumption that they are not acknowledged in Islam. The text of the Charter is reprinted in International Commission of Jurists, The Review 1996, No. 56, pp. 57–64 and in HRLJ 1997, Vol. 18, pp. 151–154.

The Arab Plan of Action for the Advancement of Women to the Year 2000, which was presented at Beijing, states on the other hand that governments in the region should review all legislation related to women in order to bring it into line with the rapidly changing conditions in Arab societies in such a way that it does not contradict original religious values. UN Doc. E/CN.6/1995/5/Add.5, § 25.

At the same time, we cannot ignore the fact that Muslim countries have very different policies regarding reproductive rights even though political leaders pretend to act in conformity with Islam. The Qur'an is not explicit on the issue of family planning. Interpretations vary depending on whether the community is Shia or Sunni. Thus, Islam like other religions is relatively open, containing the seeds of both liberal and conservative approaches to reproduction. There are, *e.g.*, four main schools of thought within the Sunni sect. The following examples may be illustrative of the diversity in the Muslim world. Tunisia offers both contraception and free abortion services to women, whereas women in Bangladesh may be subjected to forcible contraception and abortion. Turkey has enforced a law that permits abortion for a variety of reasons during the first 120 days of pregnancy. Most Islamic schools of law agree that abortion is acceptable before ensoulment and unacceptable afterwards. The Malikis school of jurisprudence considers that ensoulment happens near the end of the first trimester. In consequence abortions are allowed until that point. However, in Oman, Yemen and the United Arab Emirates abortion is prohibited unless it is necessary to save the women's life. See World Abortion Policies 1994, UN Department for Economic and Social Information and Policy Analysis, Population Division.

[14] *K. Nakatani*, Japan, in Abortion and Protection of the Human Foetus, J. Frankowski & G.F. Cole (eds.), Dordrecht 1987, p. 228.

The Vatican became one of the most active participants at the Cairo Conference objecting to all references to abortion and contraceptives in the final document and declaring specifically abortion evil. Also in the Pope's "Letter to Women"[15] the Church's teaching[16] on this matter was reaffirmed. On 14 November 1995 the representative of the Holy See, by presenting a report before the CRC, reaffirmed that the Charter of the Rights of the Family, makes "explicit the sense of the right to life in all dimensions, being the protection and absolute respect of the life of a child from its conception, excluding abortion ...".[17] In other words, it reflects the Catholic ethical position.

Several states (mainly Catholic) have taken the opportunity on several occasions to express their disapproval in relation to an extended understanding of the term "family planning". The delegation from Peru made, for example, at the Cairo Conference an oral interpretative statement in regard to the concept of "family planning", which was thereafter attached to the final document as an interpretative reservation of § 8.25.[18] The Constitution's recognition of the fundamental role of the family and the role of parents in responsible parenthood and maternity was emphasised implying everyone's right to use methods of family planning they wish "provided that it does not place life at risk". In this context the Peruvian Government refers to Article 2 of its Constitution, "which accords to everyone the right to life from the moment of conception; abortion is rightly classified as a crime in the Criminal Code of Peru, with the sole exception of therapeutic abortion". In addition, the reservation implies a restrictive interpretation of the terms "reproductive health", "reproductive rights" and "fertility regulation", *i.e.*, a total exclusion of abortion on the previous grounds. These terms were considered as "gateways for legal abortions".[19] We may on the other hand take note that the majority of Catholic countries did not make any reservations at all to the notions mentioned above. On

---

[15] The papal letter was released on 10 July 1995 at the Vatican. The prolific Pope John Paul II has published 10 papal letters. Also in the 11th Encyclical *"Evangelium Vitae" – "Gospel of Life"*, signed on 30 March 1995, he addresses, *e.g.*, the issue of abortion, which according to him is but an encroaching "culture of death" that threatens human dignity. He pleads for the creation of an alternative "culture of life" that respects human dignity from conception to the moment of death. Of relevance on this issue is also his latest book *"Crossing the Threshold of Hope"* (1994), especially pp. 12, 65, 204–211. Much of his message is concerned with human rights. In this regard the Pope underlines that "the legalisation of the termination of pregnancy is none other than the authorisation given to an adult, with the approval of an established law, to take the lives of children yet unborn and thus incapable of defending themselves" (*ibid.* p. 205). For the Pope, abortion is a form of "murder", a violation of the Biblical commandment against killing. But to my knowledge abortion is not mentioned as such in the Bible.

[16] The Church's teaching authority is binding on all Roman Catholics and it is irreversible. At the same time many Catholic theologians and Church members believe that when there is a doubt (*e.g.*, there is no definitive doctrine on person-hood), there should be a freedom to make an individual choice. *S. Jenkins*, p. 152.

[17] UN Doc. CRC/C/3/Add.27. Article 4(a) of the Charter says that "Abortion is a direct violation of the fundamental right to life of the human being".

[18] UN Doc. A/CONF.171/13, p. 150.

[19] *C.A.A. Packer*, p. 74.

the contrary, countries like Bolivia, Columbia and El Salvador expressly supported the Beijing Declaration and Spain even expressed satisfaction, especially with the Chapter on reproductive health.

Finally, I may conclude that international treaty law is rather unhelpful on the issue of family planning since none of the existing treaties defines the concept. Despite considerable confusion on that topic, there seems to be a general agreement that the right to family planning, as defined in the spirit of contemporary human rights law, consists of two main elements: the right to procreate and the right not to reproduce,[20] *i.e.*, reflecting the diversity of fertility-related situations, which women must cope with. Some women are unable to conceive, others are unable to avoid pregnancy and/or have too many pregnancies to be able to restrict the size of their family.

### *5.3.3. The Right to Procreate*

#### *5.3.3.1. Some Justifications for the use of Modern Technologies of Human Reproduction*

The beginning of family formation may be either marriage or parenthood, or both. The positive element of the right to family planning[21] and the right to found/establish a family is related to individuals' and couples' right to decide to *have* a child, *i.e.*, it implicitly guarantees a right to procreate.[22] As pointed out in the liter-

---

[20] In the doctrine a proposal has been made to expand the concept of reproductive freedom to include adoption rights in the sense that the mother who has given birth to a child should have a right to give up her child and an infertile woman should have a right to parent a child who has no parent. *E. Bartholet*, Adoption Rights and Reproductive Wrongs, in Power and Decisions, The Social Control of Reproduction, G. Sen & R.C. Snow (eds.), p. 177.

[21] As earlier mentioned, none of the international instruments defines the term "family planning". However, Professor Evans has presented a definition, which I have found suitable to be applied for the purpose of my study. It reads as follows: "(f)amily planning is a phenomenon whereby humans moderate and intervene in what would otherwise be essentially a biologically-regulated process in order to achieve a chosen outcome-a family of a given size, or no family at all". *M. Evans*, A Right to Procreate?, Assisted Conception, Ordinary Procreation and Adoption, in Creating the Child, D. Evans (ed.), p. 137. A similar view has been expressed by Professor Cook who has emphasised the duty of states to create the possibility for individuals to act themselves in matters of procreation. According to her "the act of foundation of a family goes beyond a passive submission to biology". *R.J. Cook*, Women's Health and Human Rights, Geneva 1994, p. 30. According to the same author a governmental inaction to prevent or remedy the source/s of infertility would violate the right to found a family. *R.J. Cook*, International Human Rights and Women's Reproductive Health, Studies in Family Planning 1993, Vol. 24, No. 2, p. 80. See also *R.J. Cook & B. Dickens*, Ethics and Values in Family Planning: Legal and Legislative Aspects, in Ethics and Human Values in Family Planning: XXII CIMS Conference Highlights, J. Barzelatto, A.M. Capron & Z. Bankowski *et al.* (eds.), Geneva 1989, p. 123; *R.J. Cook*, International Human Rights and Women's Reproductive Health, p. 265. For the opposite standpoint see the arguments advanced by the Vatican in UN Doc. E/CN.4/1995/74, § 114 and in *C.A.A. Packer*, p. 49.

[22] Thus, it can be maintained that this right requires states to facilitate assisted reproduction by removing any rules, which prevent individuals from treatment that will overcome their inability to have children. *M. Tardu*, Relationships between human rights and population issues, in Population and

ature on this subject the new assisted reproductive technologies constitute a significant challenge to the traditional view of procreation[23] and they are, therefore, legally a troublesome aspect of reproductive freedom. Their use raises several questions with legal and ethical implications. Some of these are: does the right not to be prevented from having a child entail the right to be provided with a child? Is there any entitlement to assisted conception services? Because assisted procreation often implies that third parties are involved and that society might be obliged to satisfy individuals' claims the question of justification arises.

Even though medical intervention in procreation (*e.g.*, use of assisted reproductive technology)[24] increases the range of personal choices and decisions, certain relevant aspects of the right to found a family/to family planning has had less priority in the context of human rights. Technological reproduction has been considered much later as an equally valid claim as the right not to be prevented from procreating. Nonetheless, it is to be recalled that still multiple interpretations of the right to

---

Human Rights, UN New York 1990, p. 55; *M.K. Eriksson*, The Right to Marry, p. 153. See also Statens Medicinsk-etiska Råd, Assisterad befruktning, Stockholm 19 april 1995, p. 15; *J.A. Frowein & W. Peukert*, Europäische MenschenRechtsKonvention, Kehl 1996, p. 424; Strategy for Development Cooperation, SIDA, p. 9; *R.P. Petchesky*, p. 9; *J. Looks*, Book Reviews, EJIL 1998, Vol. 9, p. 421. While some writers are of the opinion that international human rights law does encompass a general right to reproduce, others upheld the view that the right to procreate is not established as such in international law. For the first opinion see *H. Little*, Non-Consensual Sterilisation of the Intellectually Disabled in the Australian Context: Potential for Human Rights Abuse and the Need for Reform, Australian Yearbook of International Law 1993, Vol. 14, p. 205 and for the second see, *e.g., C.A.A. Packer*, p. 54. On the national level it appears that especially within common law jurisdictions there is a significant body of judicial opinion recognising the right to reproduce. *H. Little*, ibid., p. 210.

[23] *L. Nielsen*, The Right to a Child versus the Rights of a Child, in Parenthood in Modern Society, J. Eekelaar & P. Sarcević (eds.), Dordrecht 1993, p. 213. New technologies for assisted reproduction comprise: artificial insemination (thereafter AI), *in vitro* fertilisation (thereafter IVF) and embryo transfer (thereafter ET). There are three types of artificial insemination, homologous, heterologous and mixed. The last mentioned method implies that the infertile husband's semen is mixed with a donor's semen and used to inseminate the wife of the husband. *B.K. Padgett*, Illegitimate children conceived by artificial insemination: does some state legislation deny them equal protection under the fourteenth amendment?, in Annual Survey of Family Law, University of Louisville Journal of Family Law 1994, Vol. 32, p. 517.

*In vitro* fertilisation is a treatment, which involves obtaining mature eggs through surgical procedures, fertilising them outside of the body in a petri dish, and then reinserting the embryo into the woman's uterus. IVF is generally applied when utilising the couple's own gametes, but IVF may include one or more donated gametes. IVF is widespread in GrBr and in Australia. Its use is so far expressly prohibited by law only in the Canton of St. Gallen in Switzerland. See *E.R. Bernat*, Rechtsfragen medizinisch assistierter Zeugung, Frankfurt am Main 1989, p. 21.

Embryo transfer is a form of AI. It is done for genetic reasons or because a woman is sterile and cannot produce any ova. ET is non-surgical transfer of a fertilised ovum from a donor, who has been artificially inseminated with the sperm of the infertile patient's husband. The fertilised ovum is flushed out and immediately transferred to the infertile woman's uterus. Embryo donation may also be combined with surrogacy.

[24] The term "assisted reproduction" is used to describe techniques involving the manipulation of sperm, eggs or embryos. *J. Parsons*, Assisted Conception: The State of The Art, in Creating the Child, D. Evans (ed.), p. 13.

procreate ranging from the strictest[25] to the most liberal[26] remain. Generally speaking two perspectives on the use of medical technology to ensure the right to found a family/to family planning can be discerned: a child-oriented[27] and a parent-oriented. International human rights law has not yet delivered any clear answer as to how to resolve tensions between these two approaches. Proponents for the first approach warn of the potential dangers of objectification of the child and they justify access to reproductive technologies solely on the grounds of possible benefits for the child to be born. Thus, the legislator must, according to this view, guarantee protection of certain interests of the new-borns, *e.g.*, the right to know one's genetic origin, to have two parents of different sex, etc.[28] In consequence, few national legislatures have placed the interest (welfare) of the child to be born to the fore when decisions concerning access to assisted procreation services are to be taken. Justification for

---

[25] Opposition to assisted procreation, in terms of the denial of the existence of such a right, is often based on arguments related to the necessity of avoiding interference with natural processes which new technologies entail. Natural human procreation is explained in terms of God's will, *i.e.*, the right form of human procreation is that given or willed by God. The Vatican Congregation for the Doctrine of the Faith has, for example, condemned *in vitro* fertilisation along with all other artificial forms of procreation (even AIH) as threats to the sanctity of the conjugal act, to the family and human dignity. In addition, it has been argued that any interference whatsoever with what it regards as natural forms of procreation would lead humanity to "a condition of moral numbness". UN Doc. CN.4/1995/74, § 114. It seems, however, that this view no longer enjoys general support among Catholic countries as will be demonstrated in the following discussion. For a review of the arguments put forward by the proponents of the natural procreation position in the legal doctrine see *D.L. Steinberg*, The depersonalisation of women through the administration of "*in vitro* fertilisation", in The New Reproductive Technologies, M. McNeil, I. Varcoe & S. Yearley (eds.), London 1990, pp. 74–122; *N. Pickering*, *Ad hominem*, in Creating the Child, D. Evans (ed.), pp. 114–116; *R.A. McCormick*, Reproductive technologies: ethical issues, in Encyclopedia of Bioethics, W.T. Reich (ed.), Vol. II, New York 1982, pp. 1454–1464. For a German viewpoint see *T. Ramm*, Die Fortpflanzung-ein Freiheitsrecht?, JZ 1989, p. 861 ff. Some of the restrictive views as to the use of reproductive techniques have been expressed within the realm of regional organisations. A delegate to the Council of Europe, for example, condemned officially the practice of artificial insemination as "a world campaign to undermine marriage and the family". *M. Stanworth*, The Deconstruction of Motherhood, in Reproductive Technologies, Gender, Motherhood and Medicine, M. Stanworth (ed.), Oxford 1987, p. 23.

The Greek Orthodox Church, on the other hand, has not taken a definite position on the matter of assisted reproduction. The importance of the exercise of the free will of the individual in matters of marriage and child bearing for his salvation has instead been emphasised. *P. Dalla-Vorgia*, Assisted reproduction in Greece, in Creating the Child, D. Evans (ed.), pp. 279–280.

[26] Those who favour a broad interpretation of the relevant terms assume that the desire to procreate is an essential characteristic of the human condition and therefore there is a natural, basic right to procreate which requires absolute protection including positive action from governments. Also the human value of the fulfilment of the parenting need has been emphasised. In consequence, obligations on the part of society are asserted to ensure that "in those individuals who are disadvantaged in the relevant biological respects, certain normal levels of functioning be restored and maintained". *M. Evans*, p. 129. See also *D. Neri*, Child or Parent Oriented Controls of Reproductive Technologies?, in Creating the Child, D. Evans (ed.), p. 149. See also *S. Bok*, Population and Ethics: Expanding the Moral Space, in Population Policies Reconsidered, G. Sen, A. Germain & L.C. Chen (eds.), p. 16; *B.K. Padgett*, p. 520.

[27] *A. Haverdahl*, BO kritisk till allas rätt att ha barn, SvD 5 October 1997, p. 4.

[28] *L. Nielsen*, The Right to a Child versus the Rights of a Child, pp. 217–218.

this kind of regulation is often based on the Kantian understanding of human dignity and the intrinsic value of human beings, *i.e.*, that humanity ought to be considered as an end and never as a mere means.

Scholars adhering to the second approach, who prioritise the rights of the prospective parents, maintain on the other hand that: "Ein solcher Aufruf, Fortpflanzung nicht mehr als unabdingbares Fatum (der Frau) anzusehen, wäre nicht kinder- und familienfeindlich, sondern hätte eine Stärkung der Selbstbestimmung und-verwirklichung des Menschen und damit letztlich seiner Würde zum Ziel"[29] and therefore the prospective parents are free to decide whether or not to resort to the new reproductive techniques.[30] In order that all persons have equal opportunity to become parents, they must have the means to do so.

Treatment of infertility can be also considered from a gender equality perspective, because of its differential impact on the lives of women.[31] As a consequence, the view that women's reproductive health includes services for treatment of infertility has gained greater acceptance today.[32] Thus, some of the new technologies widen the choice for women and they have the potential to empower women.[33] Much of this is because parallel to technical development the number and combinations of mother roles is on the increase and it allows several alternative choices, *i.e.*, when and under what conditions to mother. Instead of being subject to biological destiny, reproductive capacity is under such circumstances considered as a unique source of power. Others, among them representatives of a group of radical feminists, have articulated arguments supportive for the standpoint that the medicalisation of procreation manifests a gender bias. Assisted procreation is then considered as a "strategy for increasing the power of the male dominated medical profession at the cost of the disempowerment of women".[34] Proponents of this idea do not see the development of reproductive technologies as an expansion of reproductive freedom but rather as a form of patriarchal exploitation of women. It is submitted that the modern techniques are about fulfilling the traditional feminine role, *i.e.*, being a mother.[35] For these reasons some of the women's movements in the Scandinavian countries have to a large extent been hostile towards the use of the

---

[29] *M. Palm-Risse*, Der völkerrechtliche Schutz von Ehe und Familie, Berlin 1990, p. 147.

[30] *D. Neri*, p. 145.

[31] *International Women's Health Coalition*, Reproductive Tract Infections in Women in the Third World, New York 1991, p. 5. The report referred to above of the Secretary-General on national action plans reveals that several countries raise the issue of mainstreaming a gender perspective into health coordination mechanisms, especially in reproductive health as a priority. UN, Synthesized report on national action plans, Secretary-General, 22 December 1997, § 73.

[32] *R.J. Cook*, International Human Rights and Women's Reproductive Health, p. 258.

[33] See for support of this presumption references in *J. Wajcman*, Delivered Into Men's Hands? The Social Construction of Reproductive Technology, in Power and Decision, G. Sen & R.C. Snow (eds.), p. 158 and *E.R. Bernat*, Rechtsfragen medizinisch assistierter Zeugung, Frankfurt am Main 1989, p. 3.

[34] *D. Evans*, p. 4.

[35] See *S. Bok,* Population and Ethics: Expanding the Moral Space, in Population Policies Reconsidered- Health, Empowerment, and Rights, G. Sen, A. Germain & L.C. Chen (eds), p. 16.

new technologies for procreation.[36] Generally it would not be wrong to conclude that there is no unified feminist stance towards the new reproductive technologies.[37]

One of the main arguments of the protagonists for the second approach (parent-oriented) towards family planning has been, however, that infertility constitutes a disease and therefore it is justified that medicine intervenes to put it right. Supportive of such an idea is the fact that in the context of the new concept "reproductive health", reproductive health services cover fertility and infertility management. Some of the plans and strategies for the implementation of the Beijing Platform for Action prepared as a follow-up to the Fourth World Conference on Women refer specifically to the treatment of infertility in the context of reproductive health.[38]

The causes of infertility are complex. There might be environmental, heritable, pathological as well as socio-behavioral factors. Infertility may also be closely linked to the incidence of unsafe abortions.

Statistics from the beginning of the 1990s show that the number of infertile couples[39] is considerable, and there are indications that the number is even increasing, especially in the industrialised world. World-wide between 8 per cent and 12 per cent of couples, *i.e.*, 50 to 80 million people, experience some form of infertility during their reproductive lives.[40] Approximately 10% of the couples in Sweden fail to have the child/children they would like. Nevertheless, not everyone who approaches a doctor on the grounds of involuntary childlessness can be helped to become pregnant. Swedish experience reveals for example that only 50% or so of all cases after investigation and treatment lead to a pregnancy.[41] Clearly, infertility

---

36 *L. Nielsen*, Legal consensus and divergence in Europe in the area of assisted conception-room for harmonisation? in Creating the Child, D. Evans (ed.), p. 318. Several references to feminist arguments, which have been put forward in the Scandinavian countries, can be found in the earlier cited publication of the Medicinsk-etiska Rådet, Stockholm 1995, p. 16. According to those arguments the new techniques for procreation strengthen men's (doctors) power over women's bodies, and in that way reproductive freedom becomes restricted.

37 *J. Gallagher*, pp. 145–146.

38 Synthesized report on national action plans, Secretary-General, 22 December 1997, § 67.

39 In the USA 14% of wives between the ages of 30 and 34 are infertile; 25% of wives aged 35 to 39 are infertile. See *K. Schaefer*, In-vitro Fertilisation, Frozen Embryos, and The Right to Privacy – Are Mandatory Donation Laws Constitutional, Pacific Law Journal 1990, Vol. 22, No. 1, p. 87. Other figures show that 15% of about 65 million couples of reproductive age in the USA have an infertility problem. *P. Soupart,* Present and Possible Future Research in the USA of Human Embryos, in Abortion and the Status of the Fetus, B. Bondeson *et al.* (eds.), p. 68. In Sweden in 1993 about 250,000 couples out of a population of 8 million were infertile. See Aftonbladet, Stockholm 20 October 1993, p. 5. Statistics from 1995 refer to 100,000 couples. Statens Medicinsk-etiska Råd, p. 16. See also *R.H. Blank*, Reproductive technologies and public policy: the gap widens, in Unwanted Pregnancies and Public Policy, H. Correa (ed.), p. 27; *E. Bartholet*, p. 188.

40 *N. Sadik*, The State of World Population 1994, UNFPA, p. 15. According to a more recent study infertility affects about 8 % of people in the developed countries and about 30% of people in the developing countries, representing between 500 and 900 million individuals in the world. *G.C. Di Renzo, E.V. Cosmi & G. Caserta*, Control of Human Reproduction, in Creating the Child, D. Evans (ed.), p. 29.

41 SOU 1994:37, Stockholm 1994, p. 41. Experience in Russia shows that AID is effective in 28% to 85% of cases, depending of course on the nature of the infertility treatment. *A.J. Ivanyushkin*, New Reproductive Technologies in Russia, in Creating the Child, D. Evans (ed.), p. 270.

constitutes a health need in certain situations, but not all people perceive it in that way.[42] One of the reasons for disagreement in this regard is the existence of different definitions of the notion "health". Jean Martin has made a very useful distinction between the individual, professional and community approach. In his view, health is the ability to function normally in society. Whereas health is considered from the individual perspective merely as "the balance between what the individual wants to do and can do", the concept is from the professional and community perspective regarded as the absence of disease and the ability to function normally in society is strongly emphasised.[43] However, both approaches may be used for the justification of the use of assisted conception services.

Viewing infertility as a health need can, of course, be challenged on the basis that the new reproductive technologies leave the infertile medical status of the persons making use of them unchanged, *i.e.*, they do not restore normal reproductive functioning. IVF, *e.g.*, does not alter the ability of the woman to conceive naturally. The health authorities in a great number of countries refuse to purchase such services because they do not consider infertility an illness. It is pointed out that assisted procreation does not cure the condition of infertility.

Others consider infertility to be a serious disability,[44] which may cause marital difficulties, *e.g.*, psychological stress. Therefore, it is believed that a stronger case can be made by labelling infertility as a social need.[45] What would then be in focus would be the social and psychological suffering that can be caused by childlessness and its negative effect on marriage. International human rights norms, which attach significance to the protection of the family and family life, would constitute then the basis for the justification of the use of procreative techniques. On the other hand, it must be admitted that such grounds for justification are not enough strong for the upholding of a general right to a child.

Involuntary childlessness may also generate costs related to treating physical disorder and emotional trauma. With this background it could be possible to claim that AI services are necessary for the full development of the individual's personality in a democratic community. Most men and women in the world regard living in a family with children as an essential element of their personal life. Children are symbols of continuity and renewal.[46] But also in this respect there are divergent

---

[42] For persuasive argumentation as to whether infertility is or is not a health need see *D. Evans*, The Clinical Classification of Infertility, in Creating the Child, D. Evans (ed.), p. 57; *S. Holm*, Infertility, Childlessness and the Need for Treatment, in Creating the Child, D. Evans (ed.), pp. 65–75.

[43] *J. Martin*, Prioritising Conception Services: A Public Health Perspective, in Creating the Child, D. Evans (ed.), p. 249.

[44] On the domestic level of legislation, for example, in New Zealand, issues of accessibility to assisted procreation are treated in the light of human rights legislation, which outlaws discrimination on the grounds of disability. *B. Atkin*, New Zealand, The International Survey of Family Law 1994, A. Bainham (ed.), The Hague 1996, p. 384.

[45] In the current academic debate, social reasons for the use of assisted conception techniques comprise single women and lesbian couples, who wish to have a child but without the involvement of a man. *J. Parsons*, p. 15.

[46] *J. Gallagher*, Eggs, Embryos and Foetuses: Anxiety and the Law, in Reproductive Technologies, Gender, Motherhood and Medicine, M. Stanworth (ed.), Oxford 1987, p. 148.

views on the extent to which begetting children is valuable. Besides, it has been argued that the problem of childlessness can be alleviated through adoption.[47] While this author finds that argument reasonable and strong – adoption takes care of children who are abandoned or unwanted – one should bear in mind that adoption as a matter of law is not universally accepted, *i.e.*, in Muslim countries.

It is the view of this author that human rights norms in matters such as procreation can foster coexistence among different ethical perspectives, *i.e.*, they may reflect the moral pluralism that exists on this issue. Supervisory bodies can adopt an interpretation of the notions "the right to found a family" and of "family planning" consistent with principles of a rational ethic as well as being coherent and compatible with a general frame of values expressed by a given society.[48]

Within international law none of the provisions in human rights treaties clearly supports a claim right to access to infertility treatment, (*i.e.*, all existing methods).[49] Certainly, an interpretation based on a reliance upon the primacy of the text of the treaty and on an examination of the *travaux préparatoires* of the ICCPR and the Women's Convention suggests that the right to found a family/to family planning was solely related to individuals, who have a pre-existing physiological capacity to procreate.[50] In other words, one does not have a right to the ability to have children in the sense that it is a state's duty to assist in creating it. This position has been strengthened by the HRC on the basis of its definition of the right to found a family, which refers to "the possibility to procreate and live together".[51] Also subsequent authoritative interpretations by the HRC reinforce rather a restrictive understanding of Article 23 of the ICCPR. Moreover, none of the international bodies with competence to deal with human rights issues has in its jurisprudence yet considered the question of whether an individual or a couple has a right to claim access to use of techniques for artificial insemination.

Nevertheless, in the opinion of this author it may be argued that the right to beget a child relates to the human rights sphere irrespective of the means of procreation. From the states' positive obligation under human rights treaties, *e.g.*, to ensure that individuals actually enjoy the rights guaranteed to them, it follows that states have a duty to facilitate human reproduction, even by artificial insemination which has been practised for over 100 years.[52] Artificial insemination is today the most widely used form of reproduction-aiding technologies. In other words, there ought to be remedies for all causes of infertility. One can arrive at this conclusion

---

[47] *S. Holm*, p. 75; *K.W. Ruyter*, The example of adoption for medically assisted conception, in Creating the Child, D. Evans (ed.), p. 180.

[48] *L. Nielsen*, Legal consensus and divergence in Europe in the area of assisted conception-room for harmonisation? in Creating the Child, D. Evans (ed.), p. 306.

[49] *M. Palm-Risse*, pp. 152–153; *C.A.A. Packer*, p. 54.

[50] *C.A.A. Packer*, p. 47.

[51] GC No. 19/38 on Article 23 of the ICCPR, UN Doc. CCPR/C/21/Rev.1/ Add.2, § 5.

[52] *M. Eichler*, Human Rights and the New Reproductive Technologies – Individual or Collective Choices?, in Human Rights in the Twenty-First Century, K.E. Mahoney & P. Mahoney (eds.), p. 875, note 2.

by applying the principle of dynamic and contextual[53] interpretation of human rights treaties,[54] *i.e.*, to interpret conventional texts as "living instruments"[55] in accordance with contemporary circumstances. We live, in other words, in an age in which assisted conception is a reality, at least in the technically developed world. Treatment of infertility has also increasingly been included in the concept of family planning during the recent past years.[56] Promotion of research on all methods of fertility regulation in order to expand reproductive choice is one of the topics included in the final document adopted at the Cairo Conference in September 1994. Paragraph 7.6 of the Platform for Action states that reproductive health care includes among others "prevention and appropriate treatment of infertility". The same year the CSW reaffirmed the recommendations of the Cairo Conference by res. 38/6 that an important goal remains to be striven for, namely universal access to assistance in preventing and overcoming infertility.[57] The UN Secretary-General acknowledged in his 1994 report, dealing with among other things artificial insemination, that legally binding rules of international human rights law are indeed of relevance to issues arising from advances in biomedicine.[58] Some scholars have also suggested that Article 15(1)(b) of the ICESCR, which establishes the right for everyone to "enjoy the benefits of scientific progress and its applications" in combination with Article 12 (right to health), could be invoked as comprising states obligations to promote assisted procreation.[59] Others feel that such a conclusion "would be misleading and erroneous" since the previous provision does not confer obligations on the state "to furnish an individual with the means to enjoy according to the individual's desire".[60] Of relevance is, in addition, the on-going dispute on whether infertility should be classified as ill-health and/or as a disability.

If the right to procreate can be considered as part of existing human rights, then they would seem to entail "*prima facie* equitable opportunities, for everyone who so wishes, to gain access to the system of providing assisted conception services".[61]

---

[53] The World Conference on Human Rights, held in Vienna 1993, emphasised that everyone had the right to enjoy the benefits of scientific progress and its applications. Also the final documents adopted at the Cairo and the Beijing conferences are of relevance when considering the context.

[54] *J.G. Merrills*, The Development of International Law by the European Court of Human Rights, Oxford 1988, p. 74; *M. Palm-Risse*, pp. 141–144. While the European Court of Human Rights has had considerable recourse to the teleological approach to interpretation, the elements of teleology are not that frequently used in the jurisprudence of other international organs for the supervision of human rights.

[55] The European Court of Human Rights applied for the first time the technique of evolutive interpretation in 1978 when considering the *Tyrer v. the UK* case. ECHR, Judgment of 18 January 1978, Ser. A, No. 25, § 31.

[56] *A.B. Marcelino*, p. 30.

[57] UN Doc. E/1994/27, Chapter I, Section C.

[58] UN Doc. E/CN.4/1995/74, §§ 101–118.

[59] For a discussion of the medical aspects of artificial reproductive technologies see *J.K. Mason*, Medico-Legal Aspects of Reproduction and Parenthood, Aldershot 1990.

[60] *C.A.A. Packer*, p. 49.

[61] *M. Evans*, p. 127.

But even in the event that a right to being assisted to conceive is emerging, this is not say that the right would imply having and bringing up a child "free from social scrutiny". Neither does it mean that this should happen with the active assistance of society's resources.[62]

Today a large part of the discussion on the scope of the right to procreate is centred on the issue of access, on which most disagreements remain, *i.e.*, who should qualify to receive assisted conception services and who should not. My proposition is, therefore, that even if I can establish that a right to procreate can be derived from existing human rights norms through their extended interpretation, the right should not be viewed as absolute. Each society should be able, on legitimate grounds, to restrict the liberty of some to protect other individuals. Thus, international law does not guarantee unrestricted access to assisted procreation techniques and unrestricted practice of them.

Assisted procreation involves many different techniques and we shall in the following undertake enquiry of the legal implications of their use.

### *5.3.3.2. Alternatives to the Conventional Method of Conception*

#### 5.3.3.2.1. Homologous and Heterologous Artificial Insemination

Homologous insemination implies that a woman is artificially inseminated with the sperm of the husband or companion. For this reason, this specific procreative technique has generally not created any legal problems. Homologous insemination is consequently widely accepted,[63] although it is practised on a large scale only in the modern industrial societies, where comprehensive policies are now being introduced to encourage childbearing and to raise the birth-rate.

By applying the principle of dynamic interpretation of human rights norms, *e.g.*, the right to found a family/to family planning, it would mean that if homologous insemination, by which a family is founded on legal bounds corresponding to natural descent, is forbidden by law[64] or states authorities deny persons access to the required techniques, *e.g.*, to clinical facilities, it would constitute an infringement of Article 12 of the European Convention on Human Rights, Article 23 of the ICCPR and Article 16(1) of the Women's Convention. Two arguments may be advanced for such a proposition. First of all the procedure involving AIH is not complicated. It is so simple that a woman can perform the process herself. Secondly, the procedure is generally inexpensive and therefore inadequate legal regulation, or non-regulation at all, would not be effective and it would not prevent people from using it.

At the same time I admit that governments in Asian, African and some Latin American countries are struggling with the phenomenon of over-population, and

---

[62] *M. Evans*, pp. 130 and 132.

[63] *M. Palm-Risse*, pp. 148–153. See furthermore *Rädda Barnen*, Barnets rättigheter, Stockholm 1991, p. 280.

[64] Libya is the only country in the world so far which has introduced rules banning all forms of AI. Reference is made hereby to the Quaran, Sura XLII, 50. See *E.R. Bernat*, p. 27.

doubts have been expressed as to whether Article 23 of the ICCPR may be interpreted so extensively.[65] This holds good also for the Women's Convention.

While AIH has not provoked any legal debate, *heterologous* insemination, *i.e.*, AI with the use of donated gametes[66] has remained a subject of controversy, even though it is an old phenomenon. AID was used, *e.g.*, for the first time in clinical practice as a treatment of infertility, for example, in Sweden in the 1920s[67] and in England in the late 1930s. Since then the practice of AID has grown considerably. The conceptive technologies were generally extended to include IVF in the late 1970s.[68] In the UK alone there are about 50 clinics today offering such treatment.[69]

The domestic jurisdictions of a number of countries have, however, still a restrictive approach as regards the use of AID, though in some of them official attitudes have changed over time from rejection through indifference to qualified acceptance, such as in the case of Great Britain.[70] So far there is no consensus on the issue, neither on the universal level nor on the regional level, as for instance in the countries members of the Council of Europe. There are only a few very vague principles elaborated by CAHBI reflecting the position of the majority of experts.[71] In short, one of the principles (Principle 1a-b)[72] expresses the acceptance of the use of donors' gametes in circumstances which justify such use. Only a minority of experts was of the view that techniques involving gametes or embryo donation should not be permitted at all. The support for AID is, in my view, still too weak to

---

[65] *M. Nowak*, CCPR-Kommentar, p. 433. Recent statistics show that population growth is much more massive than earlier presumed; the figures substantially exceed those earlier arrived at. The population growth is at present highest in the poor African countries located between the Sahara and the equator and parts of south Asia (Pakistan, India, Bangladesh). In 1994 5.3 billion people populated the globe. According to a UN estimation the global population will be six billion by 1998 and about 8.5 billion people in 2025. *N. Sadik*, UNFPA, The State of World Population, New York 1994, p. 1.

[66] AID is insemination of a woman by the use of donated gametes or a mixture of donor and husband's sperm. *D. Morgan*, p. IX. AID can be carried out in three ways. The first is through professional services such as a sperm bank. The second is through the utilisation of a third parties as intermediaries. And the final, third method of AID is insemination with a donor known by the woman through a direct arrangement between the woman and the donor. *R.H. Blank*, p. 29.

[67] *Å. Saldeen*, Barn och Föräldrar, Uppsala 1997, p. 109.

[68] *M. Stanworth*, pp. 10–11; *Å. Saldeen*, supra, p. 113.

[69] *J. Dewar*, p. 119; *N. Pfeffer*, Artificial Insemination and Infertility, in Reproductive Technologies, Gender, Motherhood and Medicine, M. Stanworth (ed.), p. 92.

[70] *J. Dewar*, Fathers in Law? The Case of AID, in Birthrights, Law and Ethics at the Beginning of Life, R. Lee & D. Morgan (eds.), London 1989, p. 120.

[71] *I. Fahrenhorst*, Fortpflanzungstechnologien und Europäische Menschenrechtskonvention, EuGRZ 1988, p. 129. On the other hand, AID is regulated and practised widely in almost all Eastern European countries. In the former Soviet Union, *e.g.*, a great number of women have been inseminated with the sperm from a donor. SvD 21 October 1991. *D. Morgan*, pp. 20–22. In addition, the 1997 European Convention on Human Rights and Biomedicine contains some principles of importance to our topic, such as the prohibition of sex-selection during application of techniques of medically assisted procreation (Article 14).

[72] CAHBI is a committee of experts on progress in the biomedical sciences relating to human artificial procreation within the Council of Europe. See Human Artificial Procreation, Legal Affairs, Council of Europe, Strasbourg 1989.

enable it to be categorically established in the provisions relating to family planning and the right to found a family as defined in international human rights law. Within the doctrine Professor Hegnauer, for example, has argued that "(t)he basic right to have children embraces exclusively the right to beget children with one's *own* gametes".[73]

A conservative approach to AID is mostly to be found in countries with Roman Catholics making up a majority of their population. As already mentioned, the Catholic Church has constantly been negative to the application of AID. It has referred to AID as a grave assault on the Holy sacrament of marriage and family[74] and as a violation of natural law, since it introduces a third party into the procreative process. The child's interest is defined as knowing it is a product of love. For that reason it is submitted that the ties between marriage, sexuality, love and reproduction should not be loosened.

The issue of confidentiality and the child's right to personal identity and to know the identity of its genetic forbears have stimulated legal controversy in the case of AID. Experts who do not accept techniques involving donation of gametes or embryos have argued that the secrecy coupled with AID will, with a great degree of probability, have a harmful effect on the child. The dilemma concerning the child's knowledge of its biological identity cannot be avoided. Nevertheless, the anonymity of the donor is carefully maintained in most jurisdictions representing different parts of the world, where AID is practised. Such countries include among others Australia, Israel, Norway, Russia, Spain and the Republic of South Africa.[75] In Norway the argument has been put forward that knowledge of the identity of the donor might create conflicts between the social parent and the child. Therefore, the identity of the donor is to be kept secret.[76] Similar arguments have been articulated in New Zealand. A survey was carried out in 1985, there with the aim to explore the extent of AID practice in the country. Only 45% of the practitioners felt it was desirable for a child conceived as a result of AID to be told of its origins.[77]

---

[73] *C. Hegnauer*, Human Rights and Artificial Procreation by Donor, in Parenthood in Modern Society, J. Eekelaar & P. Sarcević (eds.), p. 208.

[74] *Vatikanische Glaubenskongregation*, Instruktion über die Achtung vor dem beginnenden menschlichen Leben und die Würde der Fortpflanzung. Antworten auf einige aktuelle Fragen, Vatikanstadt 1987. Here I may mention the Holy See's reservation to Article 24 of the Convention on the Rights of the Child, which provides that "Family planning education and services to include only natural methods of family planning". Poland, a country with a great number of Catholics, stated in its declaration to the same article that: "Family planning and education services should be in keeping with the principles of morality".

[75] *J. Thévoz*, The Right of Children to Information Following Assisted Conception, in Creating the Child, D. Evans (ed.), p. 198; *A.J. Ivanyushkin*, p. 271. On the legal situation in Australia see *D. Hodgson*, Equality: The Impact of Constitutions and International Agreements, in Gleichheit im Familienrecht, B. Verschraegen (ed.), p. 295; *E. Blyth*, Donor assisted conception and donor offspring rights to genetic origins information, The International Journal of Children's Rights 1998, Vol. 6, p. 237.

[76] Act No. 68 of 12 June 1987.

[77] *M. Henaghan*, Law Reform and Human Reproduction in New Zealand – Implications for Parent and Child, Conference paper presented at the VIIth World Conference of the International Society on Family Law, Opatija 1991, p. 19.

Others, like Sweden, Germany and Austria, have abandoned the doctrine of anonymity of the donor.[78] In Sweden, for example, the "Sverne report"[79] stressed the importance of the child's need to know its origins in order to establish his own identity. Article 4 of the Law on Insemination in force in Sweden since 1 March 1985 reads:

> "A child conceived as a result of insemination is entitled to be advised of the content of the record kept by the hospital concerning the donor of the sperm, provided the child has reached sufficient maturity. The local Social Welfare Committee shall assist the child in obtaining this information when he so desires".[80]

This provision entitles the child on reaching maturity to be informed of the identity of the donor. In other words, the need for the child to know its roots is considered essential in Swedish society.[81]

On the national level of jurisdiction[82] arguments in favour for the child's right to know its origins in the context of parentage are most frequently based on references to Article 7(1) of the UN Convention on the Rights of the Child of 20 November 1989, which reads as follows: "The child shall be registered immediately after birth and shall have the right from birth to a name, the right to acquire a

---

[78] *J.V. Martínez*, p. 221. Sweden was the first country in the world to adopt a law allowing the child conceived with the help of AID to obtain information about the biological father (*i.e.*, the sperm donor). *Å. Saldeen*, Barnets rätt till sitt ursprung, in De lege, Rättsvetenskapliga studier tillägnade Carl Hemström, Uppsala 1996, p. 272. For legal developments in the same direction in Switzerland see *O. Guillod*, Switzerland: Everyone has the right to know his or her origins, University of Louisville Journal of Family Law 1994, pp. 465–466. For remarks on the regulations in Austria see *E. Bernat*, Austria: Legislating for assisted reproduction and interpreting the ban on corporal punishment, University of Louisville Journal of Family Law 1994, p. 251.

[79] The title of the report is: "Den gravida kvinnan och fostret – två individer, Om fosterdiagnostik, Om sena aborter", SOU 1989: 51, Stockholm 1989, p. 125. See, furthermore, *N. Bruce,* The Child's Right to Know, in International Children's Rights Monitor 1986, Vol. 3, p. 14; Socialdepartementet, andra rapport av Sverige, konventionen om barnens rättigheter, Stockholm 1997, p. 46.

[80] Law on Insemination, No. 1140 of 20 December 1984. See, furthermore, *Å. Saldeen,* Barn och föräldrar, Uppsala 1997, pp. 108–113.

[81] However, the effect of this law has been that a great number of Swedish couples seek treatment with donor insemination in countries where the donor anonymity is guaranteed, *e.g.*, in Denmark. *L. Nielsen*, Procreative Tourism, Genetic Testing and the Law, Paper presented at the 8th World Conference of the ISFL, Cardiff 1994, p. 4.

[82] The Swedish Ombudsman on Children's Rights (BO) has requested, for example, a change in the existing national legislation as to who is to be registered as the child's parent(s) in the registry books (Lag om folkbokföringsregister, SFS 1990:1536) so that the law may in the future contain information about the donor who is considered as the genetic father. The public is, however, not expected to have unrestricted access to this kind of information. Barnombudsmannens årsrapport 1996, Stockholm 1996, pp. 53–56. Similar ideas are expressed in Motion till riksdagen av M. Israelson, Folkbokföringsregister 1996/97:s13030

nationality and, as far as possible, the right to know[83] and be cared for by his or her parents". Shortly after the adoption of the Convention the German Federal Constitutional Court established in a decision of 31 January 1989 that "the right to know one's parentage is recognised as part of the general right of personality protected by the Constitution".[84]

An interpretation of the above mentioned provision in the UN Convention on the Rights of the Child as implying prohibition of anonymity of the donor has been questioned in the doctrine on the basis of the legislative work on the Convention.[85] Generally it has been opposed on the ground of the realities of daily life. It is submitted that there is often some uncertainty as regards the biological identity of a person's parents, and therefore one should be prepared to uphold a claim to a right to know one's biological origins not only for children born through artificial insemination, "but for any child, including those born within valid marriage as a consequence of an adulterous relationship and adopted children".[86] According to Swedish statistics one out of ten children has another father than the one officially registered.[87] In Norway, on the other hand, the reason given for preserving the anonymity of a

---

[83] The inclusion of the phrase "the right to know" one's parents in this article is due to a common proposal presented by the delegations of Algeria, Egypt, Iraq, Jordan, Kuwait, Libyan Arab Jamahiriya, Morocco, Oman, Pakistan and Tunisia, whereby the declared purpose of it was to ensure the psychological stability of the child, *e.g.*, the right to know one's parents was considered quite essential for the child (of importance to his physical and mental growth and helped to form his personality) and equal to his or her right to a name and nationality. UN Doc. E/CN.4/1989/48, § 94; UN Doc. E/CN.4/1989/WG.1/WP.4. On the other hand, the expression "as far as possible" contained in the same article implies a risk for arbitrary interpretation. Declarations and reservations concerning Article 7 have been made by the Czech and Slovak Federal Republic, Kuwait, Poland, Thailand and Tunisia with the effect that the provision is being made subject to national laws and prevailing practices affecting the confidentiality of the child's origin in certain cases (adoption). Only the declaration of the Czech and Slovak Federal Republic establishes explicitly that "in cases of irrevocable adoption and artificial fertilisation, which are based on anonymity, non-communication of a natural parent's name is not in contradiction with this provision". See UN Doc. CRC/C/2/rev.2 (1993). A number of alternative formulations aiming to replace the words "as far as possible" put forward by the representatives of the USA, Sweden and New Zealand were, however, rejected. *S. Detrick*, The United Nations Convention on the Rights of the Child, A Guide to the "*Travaux Préparatoires*", Dordrecht 1992, p. 129.

[84] BVerfGE 79, 256, NJW 1989, p. 881 ff. The case has been discussed in *R. Frank*, Germany: Blood versus "more" social ties, University of Louisville Journal of Family Law 1994, p. 335. See also *E. Deutsch*, Assisted Procreation in German Law, in Creating the Child, D. Evans (ed.), p. 337. Similarly, Austria has on this basis incorporated the relevant provision in its national legislation with the result that semen donors will not enjoy a right to anonymity. According to the Act on Procreative Medicine of 14 May 1992 a child born as a result of AID may request information regarding the identity of the donor on reaching the age of 14. See *E. Blyth*, p. 237.

[85] *B. Verschraegen*, Die Kinderrechtskonvention, p. 20. The author emphasises that " Ebenso wie über die Problematik des Schwangerschaftsabbruchs konnten sich die Verhandlungsstaaten über die Frage der Fortpflanzungsmedizin nicht einigen". It is submitted that Article 7(1) was introduced to cover "secret adoptions". *G. Van Bueren*, p. 125. My previous discussion in sub-chapter 2.3.4. has revealed that the CRC has not yet taken a categorical standpoint on the impact of this provision in regard to new procreative techniques and specifically on the question of anonymity of a sperm donor.

[86] *G. Ferrando*, Artificial Insemination in Italy, in Creating the Child, D. Evans (ed.), p. 263.

[87] SvD 17 October 1991, p. 2.

sperm donor is among others considerations for the child and its family.[88] Others have argued that there might be a need for pertinent factual medical information,[89] which must be seen to be in the interest of the child, *i.e.*, it protects its right to health. The interests of the child to know, who its biological parents are, should consequently override the interests of parents in maintaining secrecy and of donors to remain anonymous. The UN Convention on the Rights of the Child promotes, in the view of the proponents for this idea, respect for the child's autonomy and that knowledge of one's origins is indispensable for healthy psychological development.[90] Human dignity and the right to develop one's personality are frequently mentioned as justifications for the demands for the child to know what determines his/her individuality.[91] It has also been pointed out that the secrecy surrounding donor insemination may undermine family relationships[92] in the sense that confidence and trust may be difficult to be upheld in the relationship between the child and parents.

Assisted conception creates a variety of situations, which, depending on the means employed, results in different repercussions on family life and relations within the family. For that reason, I may note that positions concerning the appropriateness of access to AID services vary very much among scholars and practitioners in different countries. In some countries sperm donation is allowed but not egg donation.[93] Several countries, among them Sweden, prohibit embryo

---

[88] *M. Halvorsen*, The act relating to the application of bio-technology in medicine with particular regard to questions in family law, in The International Survey of Family Law 1996, A. Bainham (ed.), The Hague 1998, p. 326.

[89] For medical reasons the right to know one's biological parents has a clear connection with accessible information such as the donor's blood group or hereditary diseases which occur in the family. The Warnock Committee, for example, observed that individuals' desire to know about their medical history is indeed of value in diagnosing an individual's medical problems. *M. Warnock*, Report of the Committee of Inquiry into Human Fertilization and Embryology, London 1984, § 6.85.

[90] *J.H. Hubben*, Donor Anonymity in the Dutch Draft of an Artificial Insemination Act, in Creating the Child, D. Evans (ed.), p. 211. See also *A. Eriksson & Å. Saldeen*, Parenthood and Science-Establishing and Contesting Parentage, in Parenthood in Modern Society, J. Eekelaar & P. Sarcević (eds.), pp. 77–78; *K.W. Ruyter*, The Example of Adoption, in Creating the Child, D. Evans (ed.), p. 186.

[91] *J.V. Martínez*, Anonymity of the Donor in the Spanish Act, in D. Evans (ed.), p. 221.

[92] See for references: *S. Colombok, R. Cook, A. Bish & C. Murray*, Families Created by the New Reproductive Technologies: Quality of Parenting and Social and Environmental Development of the Children, Society for Research to Child Development, London 1995, p. 286.

[93] On the variety of legal solutions in the Scandinavian countries see *L. Nielsen*, The Right to a Child versus the Rights of a Child, pp. 214–215; *K. O'Donovan*, What shall we tell the children?, Reflections on children's perspectives and the reproduction revolution, in Birthrights, Law and Ethics at the Beginning of Life, R. Lee & D. Morgan (eds.), p. 96.

Even though opinions are divided, egg donation for the purpose of *in vitro* fertilisation is prohibited by law, *e.g.*, in Sweden, in 1995, however, a proposal was made by a Commission according to which egg donation should, under certain preconditions, be permissible in the future. *Å. Saldeen*, Sweden, Rights of the unborn child and questions of custody, access and residence, in The International Survey of Family Law 1995, The Hague 1997, A. Bainham (ed.), pp. 477, 481; *Å. Saldeen*, Barnets rätt till sitt ursprung, p. 257. See also the memorandum presented in April 1995 by the Swedish Council on Medicine and Ethics (Statens Medicinsk-etiska Rådet). The majority of the Council's members were of the view that egg donation, with the exception of *in vitro* fertilisation with both eggs and sperm donor, should be permitted. Others like the Swedish Ombudsman on Children's Rights finds egg donation

donation.[94] In Germany and in Austria egg as well as embryo donation is forbidden.[95] In Denmark egg donation is lawful.[96] Because of deep disagreements it seems to be a very difficult task to elaborate uniform standards on that subject matter across national boundaries. On the other hand, prohibitive rules might be difficult to uphold in the interdependent world we are living in today. In addition, there is also a risk that enterprises of that kind go underground. The European freedom of movement has produced such problems. Thus, people may exercise their reproductive choices in less restrictive countries than the home country. This new phenomenon has been called "procreative tourism".[97] Swedish women travel, for example, to Finland and Great Britain in order to undergo egg donation.[98] Regulation within the realm of human rights would be in such a context desirable and justifiable on the basis of effectiveness of human rights norms. Otherwise, individuals rights will show too great a variation from place to place.

Therefore, only internationally shared values can forward ethical considerations in assisted procreation and accord them a central place. Such a framework, which assures human dignity, welfare of the conceived child and the informed consent of the parents to be, is currently absent within international human rights law but is badly needed. There is a general agreement amongst contemporary scholars that the adoption of general principles like non-commercialisation (commercialisation leads to dehumanisation of procreation) of the use of procreative methods and access to information about the effects or side effects of treatment with the view to artificial procreation reflect more commonly shared values.

---

incompatible with Article 3 (which reflects the doctrine of the best interest of the child) of the UN Convention on the Rights of the Child, since it is a procedure contrary to nature; it breaks the natural link between uterus and egg, *i.e.*, in egg donation the female genitor is neither carrier, nor caring mother. There is in other words a possibility for the manipulation of the identity of the mother. *L. Sylwander*, Äggdonation svek mot barnen, DN 29 November 1995, p. 4; Barnets rätt till sitt ursprung, barnombudsmannens årsrapport 1996, p. 53. See also *T. Sverne*, Äggöverflyttning inte till barnets bästa, Läkartidningen 1995, p. 3473 ff.

[94] In *in vitro* fertilisation there are five stages of producing a child and they may involve five separate persons: female genitor, male genitor, female carrier, social mother and social father. In embryo donation the genitors are separated from the other three functions. See *K. O'Donovan*, p. 96.

[95] See the German Embryo Protection Act of 13 December 1990 and the Austrian Act No. 275 of May 1992 on Procreative Medicine. For comments on the Austrian law see *D. Neri*, p. 155, note 16; *E. Bermat*, The Interaction of Rationality and Freedom of Conscience in Legislation on Controversial Bioethical Issues, in Creating the Child, D. Evans (ed.), pp. 169–170.

[96] Act No. 503 of 24 June 1992. On the recent more comprehensive legislation on this topic, *i.e.*, Act No. 460 on assisted reproduction of June 10, 1997 see *L. Nielsen & A. Kronborg*, Legislation on assisted reproduction, reports on adoptions, the family principle and the individual principle and blessing registered partnership, in The International Survey of Family Law 1996, A. Bainham (ed.), The Hague 1998, p. 137. Egg donation may take place under certain preconditions. AI with the egg donated by another woman may not take place, *e.g.*, if the identity of the donating woman is known in advance by the recipient woman or the recipient couple.

[97] *L. Nielsen*, Procreative Tourism, Genetic Testing and the Law, p. 1; *D. Evans*, Creating the Child, p. 9; *L. Nielsen*, Legal consensus and divergence in Europe in the area of assisted conception-room for harmonisation?, p. 305.

[98] *A.-L. Haverdahl*, Ofruktsamma får ägg i Finland, SvD 6 March 1996, p. 8.

In assisted procreation women bear a greater amount of inconvenience and risk than men do. Therefore, feminists have drawn attention to the negative impact upon women which new technologies may have, *i.e.*, subjecting them to "invasive and risky procedures more suitably labelled experimentation than therapy".[99] Women's bodies become then, it is said, vehicles for the new technologies. Therefore, the relevance of women's informed consent has been repeatedly stressed. For such reasons, many national legislations contain, for instance, prohibitive provisions in regard to, for example, commercial surrogacy.

Biomedicine has undergone dramatic developments in recent years and fertilisation, for example, may very soon become unnecessary since there is a possibility of the cloning of human embryos.[100] Technical methods, ensuring the right to procreate, have already been challenged on ethical grounds because it is said, they may have "damaging repercussions for human values"[101] and they might be "socially disruptive".[102]

Informed consent, as well as access to information, does have a bearing on equality issues in several ways. First of all the principle of equality "compels the giving of a guarantee to the new-born of a right of a knowledge both of the modality of his/her birth, and of his/her genetic origins, as is common in adoption".[103] In my view though, widespread and accepted anonymity of the donor in AID (the anonymity of the donor is considered essential for the success of donation) contravenes several provisions of the UN Convention on the Rights of the Child as well as the general principle of non-discrimination and equality. For example, the child conceived by AID is discriminated against compared to the child conceived by intercourse or AIH since it is deprived of the possibility of identifying himself with his parents.[104]

---

[99] G. Correa cited in *J. Gallagher*, Eggs, Embryos and Foetuses: Anxiety and the Law, in Reproductive Technologies, Gender, Motherhood and Medicine, M. Stanworth (ed.), p. 145.

[100] Cloning means that early cleaving embryos are disaggregated and each cell used as a separate embryo. Then all the embryos from each cleaving embryo would be identical. *J. Parsons*, Assisted conception: the state of the art, in Creating the Child, D. Evans (ed.), p. 23. Several proposals for the enactment of legislation prohibiting, with criminal sanctions, several aspects of the new reproductive techniques, such as using embryos in research related to cloning etc.. have been discussed within the UN. UN Doc. E/CN.4/1995/74, p. 27. The 1997 European Convention on Biomedicine contains prohibition of the creation of human embryos for research purposes and it requires states where the law allows research on embryos *in vitro*, to ensure adequate protection of the embryo (Article 18). In addition, 17 out of 40 of the member states of the Council of Europe signed on 12 January 1998 a protocol to the above mentioned convention, which prohibits cloning of human embryos. See Additional Protocol to the Convention for the Protection of Human Rights and Dignity of the Human Being with regard to the Application of Biology and Medicine, on the Prohibition of Cloning Human Beings, ETS No. 168. The text of the treaty is reproduced in IHRR 1998, Vol. 5, No. 2, pp. 523–526.

[101] *L. Nielsen*, The Right to a Child versus the Rights of a Child, p. 215.

[102] The well-known Warnock Committee, which was established by the British Government in 1982 and reported in 1984, rejected the technique of egg donation by uterine lavage on the basis of physical risks of among others unwanted pregnancy in the donor woman. It was also stressed that both women would be pregnant from the same genetic parents and the existence of the donor mother-to-be would challenge the common categories of motherhood. That was considered to be socially disruptive. *J. Wajcman*, p. 160.

[103] *D. Neri*, p. 151.

[104] *C. Hegnauer*, p. 211.

From the prospective of gender equality, several writers have maintained that the most frequent gamete donation occurs in case of male infertility and, therefore, donors' anonymity is a "male (patriarchal) concern to protect male pride (property) in hiding male infertility and non-biological paternity in a pluralistic society".[105] In case the proposition is true that women prefer openness,[106] in the sense that they reject anonymity in oocyte donation, then it is obvious that rules protecting the anonymity of a donor represent patriarchal thinking. Once again I may establish that there is a legal area where gender sensitivity is negligible. In order to overcome this, society should promote greater acceptance of male sterility and more openness on that issue.

At the same time, it must be admitted that we have practically no empirical data as to whether the laws in Sweden, Germany, Austria and Switzerland, which do not protect the anonymity of the sperm donor, do so because of considerations of gender equality. In my view, they rather reflect a consideration of children's interests in that prominence is given to the significant consequences which follow from the preservation of all the rights and interests of the children born as a consequence of AID. A Committee of Inquiry in Sweden, for example, accentuated that "The child's interests must take precedence over those of prospective parents, donors or physicians".[107]

In addition, I believe that the above mentioned national laws may also indicate that social parenthood[108] (*i.e.*, social and emotional bounds) is as equally valuable as biological ties.

A common feature of the new reproductive technologies is also the alienation of the father from the process of conception, which in itself "may put a strain on marriage"[109] and it may be counterproductive of gender equality.

Gender equality issues have also arisen, for example, in the Swedish debate in connection with the question of the appropriateness of egg donation. It has been argued that since sperm donation is allowed so should egg donation be.[110] It is contended that acceptance of both methods would ensure that there will be no unreasonable differentiation in approach to male and female infertility. In consequence, children should have a right to access to the identity of the sperm donor as well as to the genetic mother in case of egg donation. Another argument has been that infertile men are given the possibility, through artificial procreation, to

---

[105] *J.M. Thévoz*, p. 198. Ruyter agrees that secrecy and anonymity ensures the father's "possible sense of shame" is concealed. *K.W. Ruyter*, p. 186.

[106] Some scholars maintain that there is enough evidence in support of this proposition. See *P. Pierre & M. Christine*, Pour les Suissesses la route des ovules passe par Paris, Journal de Genève 1993, p. 6.

[107] Justitiedepartementet, Barn genom insemination. Huvudbetänkande av inseminationsutredningen SOU 1983:42, Stockholm 1983, p. 57. Also the 1994 Governmental Bill, which contains a proposal for amendments to the Secrecy Act, emphasised that a child's interest in obtaining knowledge concerning its biological origins is significant and therefore "the protection of the integrity of the mother and any men must be secondary to the child's interest". *Å. Saldeen*, Sweden, p. 444.

[108] For a general discussion on the legal implications stemming from the various terms according to Swedish law see *A. Agell*, Äktenskap, samboende, partnerskap, Uppsala 1998; *A. Agell* (red.), Familjestöd, familjebegrepp, underhållsskyldighet mot barn, Uppsala 1996.

[109] *S. Colombok et al.*, p. 286.

[110] Statens Medicinsk-etiska Råd and *Å. Saldeen*, Barnets rätt till sitt ursprung, p. 257.

become a social parent and therefore also infertile women should have such an opportunity.[111]

Finally, the existence of a fertilised egg outside the woman's body has given rise to questions related to equality issues. The well-known case *Davis v. Davis* from the USA[112] may serve as a good illustration. The Court of Appeal in Tennessee ruled unanimously in favour of the ex-husband, *i.e.*, that the potential father could prevent his ex-wife's control of the fertilised eggs, in the sense of preventing their donation to a childless couple. No priority was made in this case between the woman's right to procreate and the man's right not to beget a child (in situation where no pregnancy has taken place). Justice Martha Daughtrey argued that the right to privacy as recognised by the Constitution of the USA includes the right to procreate. However, this right consists in her view of two rights of *equal* significance: the right to procreate, and the right to avoid procreation. Against this background the above ruling has been considered as "the first indication of an emergent men's right to control fertility and conception".[113] In effect, this ruling gives the man a power of veto over continuing the process. The decision has, therefore, not surprisingly been used in argumentation in favour of strengthening the position of men in the procreative process, *i.e.*, the one accomplished with the help of alternative methods,[114] as opposed to the case in the natural course of procreation. From

---

[111] References are to be found in *T. Sverne*, p. 1393.

[112] For a comment on the case see *R. Deech*, The Rights of Fathers: Social and Biological Concepts of Parenthood, in Parenthood in Modern Society, J. Eekelaar & P. Sarcević (eds.), p. 25; *N. Lewin*, Jerusalem Post, 17 September 1996 and *R. Schutz*, The Right to Parenthood: Surrogacy and Frozen Embryos, in The International Survey of Family Law 1996, A. Bainham (ed.), The Hague 1998, p. 237. The background of the case (*Davis v. Davis* (1992) 842 South Western Reporter 2d 588) is in short the following. A married couple (Mary Sue Davis and Junior Lewis Davis) stored seven embryos with a clinic in preparation for transfer to the wife's womb. But before the process of implantation started, the couple divorced. By the time the case reached the Court of Appeal, Mary Sue no longer wanted to use the eggs herself. She preferred instead to give them to an childless couple for implantation. Her ex-husband objected to that. In contrast to the reasoning of the Court of Appeal, the dilemma of how to balance the competing rights of the woman to procreate and of the ex-husband not to become a father against his own will was solved by the trial judge in the lower Tennessee courts in favour of the mother. The reason for that being that embryos were in his view unborn children and therefore it is in their interest to be given the chance to live. Thus, it was not out of consideration for gender equality that was decisive for the outcome of the case but rather consideration for the unborn child. Similarly one of the judges in the Israeli Supreme Court (Justice Tirkel) based his reasoning on the *Nachmani* case ( *Daniel Nachmani v. Ruti Nachmani,* F.H.(C)2401/95, C.A. 15587/93) to which I shall return in the section below, on the proposition that embryos represent the very existence of potential life. Therefore, in his view the prospect of creating life is a weighty ground for giving priority to the woman's right to become a mother over the man's right to refuse parentage. In addition, Justice Kedmi took the position that the right to complete the creation of the embryos, which has been started, with the consent of both donors of gametes must prevail over the right to destroy them. This is, of course, a bothersome approach, especially in relation to an emerging right to abortion. At the same time one, should bear in mind the circumstances of this specific case, whereby the woman had practically no other alternatives of achieving biological motherhood since she had lost her uterus to cancer.

[113] *R. Deech*, p. 25.

[114] In the Israeli Supreme Court's first verdict in the *Nachmani* case, the majority of justices were of the opinion that a husband's consent should be required at every stage of *in vitro* fertilisation, as it is in most of the Western world, because forcing a man to become a parent against his will would violate his fundamental human right to personal autonomy.

the perspective of equality before the law, such an expansion of men's reproductive freedom may be difficult to be challenged. It is, at the same time, a fact that there is a difference in regard to the efforts involved in the donation of eggs and sperm, which may justify the use of asymmetrical models of law. It is apparent that the reasoning in the above case supports the idea of equality of rights rather than equality of outcome. The legal situation in the USA, as well as elsewhere, is however not uniform on that topic. A more recent case *Kass v. Kass*[115] which was handled by a New York Court in 1995 is explanatory. The trial judge ruled in favour of a woman who wanted, as part of a divorce proceeding she had filed, to have control over five frozen pre-embryos for possible implantation in her own uterus, on the basis that a husband's *in-vivo* rights and his control over the procreative process end with ejaculation.[116] A husband has, according to Judge Roncallo, no greater right when the egg is in a hospital freezer than when it is in its mother's womb. Thus, under the circumstances of the case, which differ from the ones in the previous case, *i.e.*, there is an existing family, the court did not find any reasons why the husband should have more rights in an *in vitro* situation. The judge's decision can be characterised as gender sensitive since it was based exclusively on the distinction between male and female roles in procreation. Thereby, the foundation for the reasoning in the *Davis v. Davis* decision was rejected. Also the dissenting opinion of Justice Tal in the *Nachmani* case rests on the view that since a man may not demand the termination of a pregnancy, even if it is based on fraud and deceit, so is he precluded from demanding the cessation of the fertilisation and implantation process. Both processes involve, according to him, "intervention in a woman's body, desecrating her dignity and modesty, which the law will not recognize".[117] Others have opposed this standpoint since they disagree as to the existence of any analogy (when a surrogate mother may be involved) with the right to terminate pregnancy, which involves the woman's rights over her own body.

Despite the normative vacuum in international law and the scarce case law on national level, I may draw a preliminary conclusion that even in assisted procreation the asymmetrical models of gender equality seem to be the most suitable for application. Where there is, for example, a continuing process of *in vitro* fertilisation, the positive right of motherhood should prevail over the negative right of refusal to parenthood. Thus, these two rights are not symmetrical.

#### 5.3.3.2.2. Surrogate Motherhood

One issue, which is closely related to that of alternative methods of procreation and which at the same time is an especially controversial social innovation, is surrogate motherhood. Surrogacy is a reproductive alternative, which aims at overcoming involuntary infertility.[118] This is a method not exclusively dependent on

---

115 *L.D. Elrod*, USA, in Gleichheit im Familienrecht, B. Verschraegen (ed.), p. 283.

116 *B. Verschraegen*, Equality in Family Law, General Reports Part II, Brussels 1996, p. 46.

117 *A.F. Landau*, Jerusalem Post, 7 October 1996, p. 1.

118 *D. Morgan*, Surrogacy: An Introductory Essay, in Birthrights, Law and Ethics at the Beginning of Life, R. Lee & D. Morgan (eds.), p. 78.

advanced technology. It has been practised for centuries and there are plenty of examples throughout our history as to different forms of surrogate motherhood. Reference to the story of Sara, Abraham and Hagar in the Old Testament of the Holy Bible has frequently been made.[119] In international law there are no explicit provisions of relevance to the subject, neither in the case law nor in the authoritative statements of the international organs dealing with the supervision of human rights norms. The term surrogacy has been defined, on the other hand, in principle I (e) of the Document on Human Artificial Procreation prepared by CAHBI within the Council of Europe.[120] According to it "Surrogate mother means a woman, who carries a child for another person and has agreed before pregnancy that the child should be handed over after birth to that person" who will become the social and legal mother of the child and thereby entitled to custody. Three different types of surrogate mothers are covered, that is "those who carry embryos obtained by using the gametes of the couple who are to receive the child, those whose own gametes have been used in conjunction with those of the male member of the couple or a donor and those who carry an embryo obtained with the gametes of male and female donors".[121] The notion consequently relates to a situation, where a heterosexual married or cohabiting couple wishes to have a child but that they lack the capacity to procreate – either one or both of them. By contributing their gametes and/or the gametes of donor/s, an embryo will be generated, which then is implanted in another woman. This woman, the so – called surrogate mother will then carry to term the child for the commissioning persons. An important requirement for surrogacy arrangement is in practice that the surrogate mother before the pregnancy has agreed to hand over the child after the birth to the intended parents.

Even though the majority of the countries in the world have not yet ruled on the question of the legal status of surrogate motherhood, the absence of specific laws does not mean that the phenomenon is non-existent. It has been estimated that about 400 children have been born as a result of surrogacy arrangements between 1980 and 1996.[122] The general picture as far as the legal response to this occurrence on the domestic level is concerned reflects a great variety of solutions. Whereas surrogacy as such, *i.e.*, in all its forms, is strictly prohibited, for example, in France,[123] in

---

[119] *J. Zipper & S. Sevenhuijsen*, Surrogacy: Feminist Notions of Motherhood, Reconsidered, in Reproductive Technologies, M. Stanworth (ed.), Oxford 1987, p. 119; *D. Morgan*, ibid, p. 63; *I. Fahrenhorst*, Fortpflanzungstechnologien und Europäische Menschenrechtskonvention, EuGRZ 1988, p. 126.

[120] The purpose of the report mentioned is according to the Committee to "contribute in the first place to pre-legislative harmonisation in this field". It is expected that states members of the Council of Europe by taking the principles contained therein into consideration will be able to avoid a legal vacuum or conflict between their legal systems. *Council of Europe*, Human Artificial Procreation, p. 7.

[121] *Council of Europe, Legal Affairs*, supra, p. 16.

[122] *A.-L. Haverdahl*, Få klara bli surrogatmor, SvD 17 March 1996, p. 11.

[123] *L. Nielsen*, Legal consensus and divergence in Europe in the area of assisted conception-room for harmonisation? in Creating the Child, D. Evans (ed.), p. 315.

Spain,[124] in the Czech Republic[125] and in Japan,[126] British law does not forbid it explicitly.[127] In New Zealand applications for IVF surrogacy have been frequently rejected.[128] In Sweden and in Norway surrogacy, when egg-donation is involved, is explicitly prohibited by law. In Denmark announcement and procurement for surrogacy are liable to punishment.[129] Surrogacy has, thus, in the Scandinavian countries been considered as not being in accord with the existing basic ethical and legal principles of those societies. Especially the use of a surrogate mother for non-medical reasons, *i.e.*, merely convenience and where there is payment for the service involved, has proved difficult to justify. For that reason commercial surrogacy is almost universally condemned. Exception to this restrictive approach is, however, to be found in the USA, where the most developed commercial market for surrogacy nowadays exists. Nevertheless, some consider surrogacy contracts void.

Even though surrogacy has gender implications – women are after all the surrogate mothers – there is no unified feminist stance towards it. Some consider surrogacy as a forced pregnancy, since "a woman's body incubates a child she does not want to raise" and thereby incompatible with reproductive freedom.[130] I can object to statements of that kind on the basis that there is indeed an element of voluntariness in surrogacy arrangements. The evidence of it is the surrogate mother's consent when signing a surrogacy contract. Surrogacy has, furthermore, been considered as a degradation of motherhood, *i.e.*, an "exploitative debasement of motherhood",[131] since it is unreasonably arduous for the surrogate mother. The surrogate mother is merely seen then as a victim of exploitation, because she submits herself to a man's reproductive plans.[132] Focus has also been put on the fact that a surrogate mother may be subject to psychological problems after handing over the baby, or even that she may refuse to give the new-born to the commissioning couple as the *Monza* case demonstrates.[133] It has been supposed, therefore, that it would not be wrong to

---

124 *G.G. Cantero*, Gleichheit vor dem Recht, in Gleichheit im Familienrecht, B. Verschraegen (ed.), p. 139.

125 *J.F. Haderka*, Über einige Fragen der Gleichheit im heutigen tschechischen Familienrecht (mit Berücksichtigung der Einflüsse des Verfassungs- und Völkerrechts), in Gleichheit im Familienrecht, B. Verschraegen (ed.), p. 238.

126 *K. Yamauchi*, Gleichberechtigung im japanischen Familienrecht, in Gleichheit im Familienrecht, B. Verschraegen (ed.), p. 339.

127 *J. Sándor*, Legal Approaches to Motherhood, in Creating the Child, D. Evans (ed.), p. 164.

128 *B. Atkin*, New Zealand, in The International Survey of Family Law 1994, A. Bainham (ed.), The Hague 1996, p. 382.

129 Act No. 326 of 4 June 1986. See *L. Nielsen*, The Right to a Child versus the Rights of a Child, p. 7.

130 *R.H. Axelrod,* Whose womb is it anyway, are paternal rights alive and well despite Danforth?, Cardozo Law Review 1990, Vol. 11, No. 3, p. 705.

131 *Commonwealth Secretariat*, Issues in Reproductive Health Law in the Commonwealth, London 1986, p. 97.

132 For references on this position see *J. Zipper & S. Sevenhuijsen*, p. 120 and in addition *L.R. Hirshman*, The Book "A", in Feminist Legal Theory II, F.E. Olsen (ed.), p. 329.

133 The Italian judge ruled in this case that surrogacy agreements are null and void and he declared such contracts, like the British courts have done in a few cases, as contrary to public policy and morals. For a discussion of this case see *G. Ferrando*, Artificial insemination in Italy, in Creating the Child, D. Evans (ed.), pp. 259–260.

assume that as a rule an attachment to the foetus arises during pregnancy. Several states have for such reasons introduced rules that only women who already have own children may enter into a surrogacy contract.

At the same time there is almost world-wide consensus that surrogacy contracts are not enforceable. Unforeseeability does, however, not effect the parties when they comply with their contractual obligations. The gestating mother is given a right to renounce the contract and receive custody of the child. An argument in favour of accepting surrogacy internationally, which has often been put forward, is that since women may decide on whether to have an abortion or not, they should also be allowed to offer their body for surrogacy if they want to do so. This argument is prevalent among a great number of feminists. They, furthermore, claim that surrogacy as a reproductive alternative should be included in the right to found a family and to family planning. It has been maintained that the greatest gift a woman can give to another woman is a child. Thus, surrogacy is seen as an appreciation of pregnancy. Reference can be made here to a study concerning surrogacy practice in the USA. According to the results of the survey, 66% of the women questioned have given the answer that they would like to be surrogate mothers again. As regards attitudes towards surrogacy, about 86% of the questioned persons approved of surrogacy.[134] On the other hand, about 22% of the surrogate mothers included in the study have experienced that the most difficult aspect of the surrogacy process, and which might be used as a reason for not approving such practices, is giving up the baby. In other words, they emphasised the potential risk of custody battles, which may harm the child because of the social implications it causes. References to the principle of the best interests of the child,[135] as expressed in the UN Convention on the Rights of the Child, have been made in this regard. British courts have, for example, found surrogacy involving artificial insemination as "against public policy", since such a contract involved "the sale and purchase of a child".[136] Thus, the argument that has been advanced against legalisation of surrogacy in that regard underlines the high risk that the ability of a woman to give birth to a child will lead to pregnancy being treated as a commodity and that a clear parallel can be drawn with baby selling. The obvious risk of the commercialisation of motherhood has been stressed, especially when the reward for the services goes beyond compensation for the expenses and losses of the surrogate mother. The high risk for exploitation of underprivileged women living in the Third World countries

---

[134] *D. Macphee & K. Forest*, Surrogacy: Programme Comparison and Policy Implications, International Journal of Law and the Family 1990, pp. 309 and 312.

[135] The existing legal ban on surrogacy in Switzerland has been motivated on the basis of the relationship between the child and the surrogate mother. In other words, "Aus der rechtlichen Konstruktion des Kindesverhältnisses zur Mutter ergibt sich auch ohne weiteres, daß Leihmutterschaften in der Schweiz nicht zulässig sind". *T. Geiser*, Gleichheit im Familienrecht-Schweiz, in Gleichheit im Familienrecht, B. Verschraegen (ed.), p. 97. Another issue which is closely related with the best interests of the child is the child's own identity. It has happened that the commissioning parents have changed the birth certificate so as to appear to be the natural parents in the register.

[136] *J. Sándor*, p. 163.

should not be ignored. Surrogacy as an aspect of reproductive freedom has, in my view, rightly been criticised on these grounds. While most of the new reproductive technologies have been designed in the rich Western countries, they are used throughout the world. Practices have already occurred when frozen gametes have been implanted in a great number of women living in the developing countries and who have not been duly informed about the consequences of such arrangements.[137] On the other hand, to "protect" women from their own decisions is a way of denying them the ability to take responsible decisions and rationally grounded choices. An unjustified breach of a woman's freedom of choice might in this respect be said to facilitate the enforcement of paternalistic views.[138] Surrogate motherhood, in my view, is itself morally neutral. Hence, if, by way of illustration, two sisters decide to carry out a surrogacy and no money is involved the surrogate motherhood can be seen as an act of charity.

Opponents of surrogacy have, furthermore, pointed to the risk that a situation occurs when the infertile couple has built up expectations of the child to be born and which are not met in reality, *e.g.*, the child is not born healthy but with an HIV-infection. It might also happen that the couple renounces responsibility for a child born with a handicap. Situations such as these would in my opinion contribute to the dehumanisation of our society. A Swedish example[139] illustrates well the difficult problems that might arise out of surrogacy arrangements. It took a paternity suit, in which it turned out that the husband of the surrogate mother was in fact the biological father of the child, to solve a dispute about responsibility for the handicapped child. This shows us how important it is to rule in surrogacy contracts as to who will take the responsibility in cases when the surrogate mother delivers a child with a handicap.

Legal questions with gender implications arose in Israel in connection with the earlier referred-to *Nachmani* case. The main issue at stake was the woman's (Ruti) quest to have one of her 11 frozen eggs, which have been fertilised *in vitro* by her ex-husband (Danny), implanted in a surrogate mother, since this was the only hope for her of ever becoming a genetic mother. Both parties had signed a contract with a surrogate institute. But circumstances since then had changed. Danny separated from Ruti and he was living with another woman who had borne him a child. He wanted to stop the process of surrogacy and claimed that he had the right not to be compelled to be a parent against his will. For reasons of equality, justice and public policy, the Supreme Court decided in 1991 on the basis of arguments that since the wife is entitled to decide on abortion on her own, the husband should have the right to discontinue the process of implantation of ova fertilised with his sperm at any

---

[137] The UN Special Rapporteur on Violence against Women warns the international community about the negative consequences of such practices for women. Thus, in her view the practice of surrogate motherhood "has also resulted in the exploitation of the bodies of women from the third world". UN Doc. E/CN.4/1995/42, § 56.

[138] *D. Machee & K. Forest*, p. 100.

[139] *Rädda Barnen*, Barnets rättigheter, Stockholm 1991, p. 288.

time before pregnancy.[140] The dissenting judge, on the other hand, argued that the wife should be able to have a child as a part of her self-fulfilment. The majority opinion was heavily criticised, and following an additional hearing the Court (seven to four votes) reversed on 12 September 1996 its earlier decision in favour of the wife. So, Ruti was given custody over the frozen embryos and she was allowed to go ahead with their implantation. Nevertheless, on one point the majority of justices were united, namely that since the baby will be carried by a surrogate, the issue of a woman's right over her own body is not relevant. The relevant issue instead is the supremacy of the right to have children over the right not to be a parent. Owing to the precedent-setting nature of this case, the ruling is a very good illustration not only of how to resolve disputes about frozen embryos, but also of the application of the principle of equality of outcome rather than achieving equality of rights, *i.e.*, the asymmetrical model of gender equality.[141]

Yet another case, the *Monza* case in Italy, demonstrates that in a surrogacy arrangement the surrogate mother (the biological mother) may be accorded a weaker position than that of the biological father. Thus, the court decided here on the basis of the best interests of the child in favour of the father in a dispute in which the surrogate mother refused to fulfil the contract and to hand over the new-born child. The consequences of such a situation have helped the articulation of the most powerful arguments against surrogacy from the feminist point of view, *i.e.*, the eradication of the *mater semper certa est* principle with instead "the power of men as sole begetters being reaffirmed".[142] From the gender perspective, it is therefore more advantageous to make non-commercial surrogacy[143] legal and thereby secure respect for the above mentioned rule, *i.e.*, the right for the surrogate mother to keep the child after its birth against the claim of the biological father, when she does not have a relationship with him.

---

[140] *T. Einhorn*, Equality in Israeli Family Law, in Gleichheit im Familienrecht, B. Verschraegen (ed.), p. 319. The minority of the judges relied in their reasoning on the concept of equality between the sexes (it attempted to equalise the legal position of men and women in relation to procreation) in the 1996 decision and it held the view that each of the two parties should have equal rights to stop the IFV-surrogacy arrangement. It has been rightly pointed out in the doctrine that even though in case of IVF conception does not occur inside the body of the woman, there is still a difference in the nature of the donation of the gametes of the two sexes, which may justify different legal treatment. See *R. Schutz*, p. 248, note 54.

[141] Following the 1996 decision of the Supreme Court Ruti began looking for a surrogate mother in Israel. Danny Nachmani, the ex-husband of Ruti Nachmani, appealed then to the Haifa District Court to prevent her from using an Israeli surrogate. He asked the district court to forbid her from having the frozen embryos at Assuta Hospital implanted unless she did so under the terms of the Surrogacy Law (The Surrogacy Agreements Law was passed in 1996), which requires the agreement of both parents. The Haifa District Court rejected Danny's suit on the basis that both parties had agreed to implant the fertilised eggs in a surrogate mother abroad before the Surrogacy Law was passed and therefore it does not apply in this case. However, the Supreme Court issued on 25 November 1996 a temporary injunction to prevent Ruti from implanting her eggs in a surrogate mother until the court hears her ex-husband's appeal.

[142] *J. Zipper & S. Sevenhuijsen*, p. 129. Support for the biological father's right to final and ultimate control over his sperm has been expressed on other occasions by women active within the legal profession. See for references, *E. Hertzog*, Byline, Jerusalem Post, 16 September 1996, p. 1.

[143] Arguments against commercial surrogacy may be based on the principle of distributive justice, since not many families can afford such an arrangement.

The two above cases, and in the absence of a decision by an international supervisory organ of human rights, have shown that disputes arising out of surrogacy contracts can be solved in a gender sensitive manner as well as in a manner contrary to achieving substantive equality, *i.e.*, equality of result. To avoid extreme differences in national regulations, international human rights law should, therefore, reflect divergent moral views about procreation, in the sense of a flexible conception of reproductive freedom, but at the same time it is of value that there is a normative framework as, for example, one in line with the principles proposed by CAHBI on regional level, which clearly cover the present issue. The law has, in other words, to be adjusted to the scientific and social changes that have taken place. Therefore, the expert members of CAHBI seem to have accepted non-commercial surrogacy. Some of the reasons behind this are based on the understanding that it is better to regulate surrogacy in order to protect the surrogate mother rather than the infertile couple. Principle 15 § 4 Part VI of CAHBI's report deals, for example, with the requirements for the use of AI for the conception of a child to be carried by a surrogate mother. Thus, states may: "in exceptional cases fixed by their national law, provide, while duly respecting paragraph 2 of this principle, that a physician or an establishment may proceed to the fertilisation of a surrogate mother by artificial procreation techniques, provided that:

a) the surrogate mother obtains no material benefit from the operation;
b) the surrogate mother has the choice at birth of keeping the child".[144]

While CAHBI's recommendations are not to be considered as any expression of existing law, the Committee's views are, however, of great significance in the clarification of that law and of contemporary understanding of how law must respond to social realities.[145] In fact, the Parliamentary Assembly of the Council of Europe has adopted several of its recommendations and thereby giving them considerable political weight.[146]

To conclude, legal regulation of surrogacy may be justified in order to protect the weakest party in the arrangement, *e.g.*, the prospective new-born and the surrogate mother.

---

144 *Council of Europe*, Human Artificial Procreation, p. 39.

145 Within the literature Martina Palm-Risse has convincingly argued that on the basis of the jurisprudence of the Strasbourg organs it may be assumed that a surrogate mother under certain conditions already enjoys the protection of Article 8 of the European Convention. In her view "Daraus läßt sich jedenfalls für die Beziehung auch genetisch beteiligter Leihmütter zu dem Kind der Schluß ziehen, daß in diesem Verhältnis weitaus eher der Ansatz eines Familienlebens besteht als mit den bislang unbeteiligten Auftraggebern. Verweigerte also die Leihmutter nach der Geburt die Herausgabe des Kindes, könnte sie sich auf ihr Recht auf Achtung des Familienlebens berufen". *M. Palm-Risse*, p. 208.

146 CAHBI's principles could be used, for example, by the European Court of Human Rights, if a relevant issue is brought before it for consideration in the future, to forward an expansive reading of Article 12 of the European Convention.

### *5.3.3.3. Access to Assisted Procreation*

#### 5.3.3.3.1. Married and Cohabiting Couples

One of the major questions that arises in the context of access to the new procreative techniques is: Who should qualify to receive those services and who should not? I shall try to answer the question by looking at contemporary understanding of the notion "family" in international law.

Even though the concept of family occurs in most of the central human rights instruments,[147] there is not a single universally accepted definition of it.[148] Neither is there any universal consensus with regard to its functions, probably because they are different and changing.

Human rights treaties that contain the notion of family have so far been interpreted restrictively, *i.e.*, excluding same-sex partners and in the recent past at the regional level (within the Council of Europe), even excluding unmarried heterosexual partners.[149]

Even though the language of Article 12 of the European Convention on Human Rights signifies that the right to found a family is closely connected with the right

---

[147] References to the family in international legal instruments are contained in *United Nations Department of Public Information*, Human Rights and The Family, DPI/1203, May 1992, p. 4. For an analysis of the contents of the relevant provisions in global as well as regional human rights treaties see *M. Palm-Risse*, Der völkerrechtliche Schutz von Ehe und Familie, note 100.

[148] While some authors simply conclude that "the conventional approach which seeks to identify essential and irreducible characteristics of the phenomenon has failed to locate it within specific definitional boundaries", others discuss the notion of family on the basis of the following elements: household, blood relationship and marriage (or cohabitation). This citation is to be found in *I.S. Malila*, Shifting Definitional Boundaries of the Family: Notes from the Field, a paper presented at the ISFL, 9th World Conference, which took place in Durban in July 1997. The second approach has been applied by among others *J. Trost*, Familjen i Sverige, p. 14. See in addition *A. Agell*, Familjebegrepp och lagstiftningsideologi i svensk rätt, in Festskrift udgivet i anledning af Àrmanns Snaevars 70 års foedelsdag, Reykjavik 1989. Some feminists consider the family as a "reactionary institution and a primary locus for the oppression of women". *F.G. Olsen*, p. 1497. On that basis they have criticised the traditional approach in international law of viewing the privacy of family as sacrosanct and of abstaining from regulating the relations within a family as well as lacking a clear standpoint on the protected functions of a family, thereby leaving the vulnerable members (children and women) unprotected. Especially the patriarchal, nuclear family has been seen as the most important source of woman's oppression. As Stella Omniyi has put it: "in the culturally sacrosanct family men retain a material, sexual and moral dominance which they are not willing to surrender". *S. Omiyi*, African Women, The Family and Human Rights Abuses, in African Women & Human Rights, Issue 8, December 1993–May 1994, p. 12. For the opposing view see *D. O'Leary*, Gender: the Deconstruction of Woman, a paper distributed during the NGO Forum '95 in Beijing. The author predicts that "without strong families based on stable marriages between men and women, the society will deteriorate into anarchy". *Supra*, p. 22.

[149] *K. O'Donovan*, Family Definitions and Human Rights: Rights to Respect for Private and Family Life under the European Convention on Human Rights, in Family Law and Family Policy in the New Europe, J. Kurczewski & M. Maclean (eds.), Aldershot 1997, p. 38; *M. Palm-Risse*, p. 211; *I. Cameron & M.K. Eriksson*, p. 93; *B. Verschraegen*, Gleichgeschlechtliche "Ehen", p. 42. According to the jurisprudence of the Strasbourg organs, it has been necessary for the applicant/s to show that some legal or blood relationship exists and that the element of dependency is clear in order to enjoy the guaranteed rights under the Convention.

to marry (*i.e.*, the use of the singular form "this right"),[150] it can be, in my view, also invoked separately. Also according to Article 17(2) of the American Convention, Article 10(1) of the ICESCR and Article 23(1) of the ICCPR the right to marry and to found/establish a family are linked with each other.[151] Also here the singular form of the noun "right" has been used. A textual interpretation of these provisions makes it, therefore, uncertain whether unmarried couples can claim a right to found a family.[152] But as I have earlier argued this method of interpretation is not satisfactory in regard to human rights norms. Their meaning should be elucidated with the context among other things in mind so that the treaty can be read as a whole. At the same time, I should also mention that the crucial role of national laws under the relevant provisions is apparent. Some of the above mentioned provisions (*e.g.*, Article 17(2) of the ACHR) refer explicitly to the fact that the right to found a family shall be exercised in accordance with conditions required by domestic law. This means, for instance, that all familial forms consistent with the legal peculiarities the contracting parties are protected by the respective convention[153] and which can make the field of application of the notion wider. In addition, a systematic interpretation, *i.e.*, when the provisions which guarantee the right to found a family are being read in conjunction with the provisions which ensure respect for family life[154] (*i.e.*, the protection of the integrity of the family) and the prohibition of discrimination, may forward a more flexible understanding of the notion family. Thus, taking into consideration the importance of coherence in the conventional regime and of uniform interpretation, it seems to me inappropriate to interpret the concept of family more narrowly in the first kind of rules than in provisions dealing with family life.

---

[150] The European Court based its conclusions in the *Rees v. UK* case among other things on reference to Article 12 and that there the right to marry and to found a family is used in the conjunctive form as a single right. ECHR, Judgment of 17 October 1986, Ser. A, No. 106, p. 19.

[151] Only the Women's Convention omits such a clear link between the right to marry and to found a family (Article 16(1)(e)). On the basis of the formulation of Article 16(1)(d), which guarantees the same rights and responsibilities as parents, "irrespective of their marital status", and on the basis of the discussions during the drafting process of the Convention, I assume that this treaty equalises in some respects *de facto* family unions with *de iure* unions. See *L.A. Rehof*, p. 176 and the reference to CEDAW's General Recommendation No. 21 which follows below.

[152] In the view of Professor Fawcett they cannot. *J. Fawcett*, The Application of the European Convention, Oxford 1987, p. 226.

[153] Professor Nowak has put forward arguments, which speak in favour of an extensive interpretation of the right to found a family as guaranteed in the ICCPR. In his view the explicit omission of a reference to "this right" in the Covenant, as is the case in the European Convention as well as the rejected motion submitted by France during the drafting of the provision in question and which sought to restrict the definition of family to the marital family, supports the proposition that Article 23(1) should be understood in the "overall context of a provision guaranteeing comprehensive, institutional protection to the family in all its various cultural forms", *i.e.*, including *de facto* family unions. *M. Nowak*, CCPR Commentary, p. 413.

[154] The cohabitation relationship between homosexual persons does not in itself constitute family life but it falls within private life according to Article 8 of the European Convention. *F.G. Jacobs & R.C.A. White* (eds.), The European Convention on Human Rights, p. 176.

Over the years there has been a profound change in attitudes towards marriage in Europe.[155] In response to these developments in social and political attitudes, the Strasbourg organs have taken a broad view of family by extending the notion "family life" to include a man and a woman who are not married but who have children together, as long as there is effective cohabitation. As I have observed at the beginning of Part II of this study, formalised marriage has been steadily losing its status, especially in Western countries, where cohabitation without marriage has increased. We may notice, in other words, a de-linking of marriage from family foundation, as originally envisaged in international human rights standards[156] and an increasing acceptance of *de facto* family unions as well.[157] On the other hand, the case law of the European Commission and Court suggests that the doctrine of full equality between married and unmarried fathers in respect of protection of their right to family life is not yet accepted. Thus, their differential (in the sense of discriminatory) treatment has been justified on the grounds that states parties are in a position to adopt policies with the aim to promote marriage-based family life.[158]

Due to social changes and economic developments, the family (its forms and functions) is also undergoing constant world-wide transformation. It has, therefore, been rightly characterised as a concept in "transitional development".[159] Most of the UN mechanisms for the protection of human rights have been receptive to these changes. At its 39th session in 1990 the HRC adopted, for example, a rather flexible General Comment on Article 23. This is a provision on which very few

---

[155] *M.K. Eriksson*, The Right to Marry, p. 154; *K. Tomaševski*, Reproduction, Rights, and Reality: How Facts and Law can Work for Women, The American University Law Review 1995, Vol. 44, p. 1040.

[156] *M.K. Eriksson*, supra, p. 131.

[157] I may mention here the *Keegan v. Ireland* case, which was decided by the European Court of Human Rights in 1994. The Irish Supreme Court's argument concerning protection of the family was based on the statement that Article 41 of the Irish Constitution relates only to the family based on marriage. The European Court came, however, to another conclusion, namely that the notion "family" as referred to in Article 8 of the European Convention is not confined solely to marriage-based relationships but may encompass other *de facto* "family" ties where the parties are living together outside of marriage. ECHR, Judgment of 26 March 1994, § 44. The text is reprinted in HRLJ 1994, Vol. 15, pp. 193–201. In the *Kroon v the Netherlands* case the European Court recalled its earlier view that the notion "family life" in Article 8 is not confined solely to marriage-based relationships and that it may encompass other *de facto* family ties. ECHR, Judgment of 27 October 1994, Ser. A, No. 297–C.

[158] The previous British Prime Minister John Major announced at the Conservative Party Conference in 1993 the policy of getting "back to basics", *i.e.*, reasserting traditional family values. The reasoning behind this was determined to a large extent by the perception of the supposed detrimental effect of fatherless families on crime and the notion that the welfare state encourages lone parenthood and in that way encourages teenage mothers' dependence on benefits. For comments on this issue in greater depth see *M.D.A. Freeman*, England: Back to Basics, University of Louisville Journal of Family Law 1995, Vol. 33, p. 329–353. Within the literature Martina Palm-Risse has taken the standpoint that it seems to be compatible with the European Convention on Human Rights that states parties may give marital unions preferential treatment "um Anreize für künftige Eheschließungen zu schaffen". *M. Palm-Risse*, p. 241.

[159] *G. Van Bueren*, p. 68.

states deliver any information in their periodic reports. The Committee, therefore, urged state parties to indicate in their periodic reports whether various forms of family "such as unmarried couples and their children or single parents and their children" are recognised and protected by domestic law and practice.[160] The Human Rights Committee emphasised in its comment that it is impossible to give a universal definition of the family, since it is universally acknowledged that the family has many forms,[161] and the concept of family "may differ in some respects from State to State, and even from region to region within a State".[162] Also in its understanding of Article 17 of the Covenant, the HRC accommodates a range of different family structures within the notion of family. While the word family remains undefined, it must in its view include "all of those comprising the family as understood in the society of the State Party concerned".[163] In accordance with this broad, non-traditional view, several writers in the doctrine consider the scope of Article 23(1) of the ICCPR to include protection of the marital families as well as of extra-marital ones.[164] CEDAW has to a great extent joined this standpoint, which is reflected in § 13 of the 1994 Committee's General Recommendation No. 21 on Equality in Marriage and Family Relations.[165]

Since the beginning of the 1990s it has been acknowledged on several occasions and in several consensual documents adopted within the UN how important it is to

---

[160] Paragraph 2 of the GC, No. 19, 39th Session of the HRC, 1990, HRI/GEN/1/Rev.1, 29 July 1994, p. 29.

[161] In the African context, for example, the family is defined to include a wider field of relatives than are usually considered in the Western context. It has not without reason been maintained that African women's position within marriage and family can only be understood in the context of the extended family. *P. Letuka & A. Armstrong*, Which Law?, Which Family?, Which Women?, Problems of Enforcing CEDAW in Southern Africa, Paper presented at the 8th World Conference of the International Society of Family Law, Cardiff 1994, p. 11.

[162] Ibid., § 2. It has been assumed that Article 23 of the Covenant protects "not only monogamous marriages and the nuclear family prevalent in industrialised States, but also, for instance, polygamous marriages set down in Islamic law or the extended family common in African cultures". *M. Nowak*, CCPR Commentary, p. 403. It is also noteworthy that the Strasbourg organs have ruled that Article 8 of the European Convention may cover protection of polygamous families. See *T. Opsahl*, The Convention and the right to respect for family life, in Privacy and Human Rights, A.H. Robertson (ed.), Manchester 1970, p. 213. In my view it is unreasonable to accept polygamy as a protected value by the Covenant on the basis that there is an obligation for the states parties to implement the equality of spouses progressively (Article 23(4)). Also CEDAW has clearly stated in § 14 of its General Recommendation No. 21 that "Polygamous marriages contravene a woman's right to equality with men, and can have such serious emotional and financial consequences for her and her dependants that such marriages ought to be discouraged and prohibited". Also in an earlier study carried out by CEDAW polygamy and bigamy have been viewed as impediments to women's equal status in the family and in society. See UN Doc. CEDAW/C/1993/4, p. 5. See also *M.K. Eriksson*, The Right to Marry, p. 192.

[163] UN Doc. A/36/40, p. 134.

[164] For references see *M. Nowak*, CCPR Commentary, p. 405, note 20.

[165] The text of this paragraph reads as follows: "The form and concept of the family can vary from State to State, and even between regions within a State. Whatever form it takes, and whatever the legal system, religion, custom or tradition within the country, the treatment of women in the family both at law and in private must accord with the principles of equality and justice for all people, as article 2 of the Convention requires".

respect the variety in which families are organised throughout the world. Here follow some examples. The difficult task of establishing a universal definition of a family was stressed at the Vienna World Conference on Human Rights in June 1993. The delegates agreed that there is no simple view and no easy definition of the family, since types of families differ in different countries.[166] In 1994 the UN Secretary-General stressed in § 67 of the fourth review and reappraisal of the World Population Plan of Action that "the family in all its forms is the cornerstone of the world community" and that in this respect the plan does not endorse any particular form of family more than any other.

The Copenhagen Declaration and Programme of Action, which was adopted at the World Summit for Social Development in March 1995, states in its principle 23(h) that: "In different cultural, political and social systems various forms of family exist" and that each form should be entitled to receive comprehensive protection and support.[167] Several of the provisions contained in the Beijing Declaration of 1995 endorse this acceptance of plurality. Paragraph 29 establishes, for example, that "in different cultural, political and social systems various forms of the family exist".[168]

Despite the above-described developments, we should bear in mind that there are still states which take a limited view of the meaning of family. A few governments "qualified" their conception of the term "family" during recent UN's conferences along religious or cultural lines.[169]

---

[166] UN Doc. A/CONF.157/6, p. 2.

[167] See also Section G, § 80 of the document.

[168] The Secretary-General of the World Muslim Congress said at Beijing that "All unsanctioned forms of cohabitation are a violation of the sanctity of life". UN Press Release, WOM/857, 8 September 1995. Several governments from Latin America underlined that they recognise the "traditional family as the basic unit of society". WOM/861, 12 September 1995. This despite the fact that the governments from Latin America and the Caribbean agreed in the Regional Programme of Action that while there is a legal recognition of the variety of family structures in the region, there is still a predominance of the patriarchal concept of the family. UN Doc. E/CN.6/1995/5/Add.3, § 212.

[169] The representative of the Holy See, Mr. R. Martino declared, for example, in Cairo during the ICPD that "The Holy See strongly rejects any attempts to weaken the family or to propose a radical redefining of its structure, such as assigning the status of family to other life-style forms". With reference to the term "couples and individuals", the Holy See reserved its position with the understanding that this term is to mean "married couples and the individual man and woman who constitute the couple". UN Doc. A/CONF. 171/13, p. 148. See also the reservations made by Egypt and the Islamic Republic of Iran, ibid., pp. 144 and 149. Essentially the same states clarified in written statements at Beijing that they understand the term "couple" in relation to matters of procreation to mean "married couple". The representative of the Holy See submitted, for example, a reservation to the Beijing Declaration and Platform of Action in which it was stressed once again that the family "is the basic unit of society and is based on marriage". UN Doc. A/CONF.177/20, p. 163. The Government of Guatemala made a reservation to the same document stating that "the protection of the family is guaranteed on the legal basis of marriage". The representative of Peru submitted a similar statement. UN Doc. A/CONF.177/20, p. 161 and p. 171. At the same time there are also examples of Catholic countries as, for example, Honduras, which could join the consensus in the adoption of the Beijing Declaration and which pointed out in a written statement that "marriage and de facto unions are under the protection of the State". UN Doc. A/CONF.177/29, p. 165.

The aforesaid leads us to the conclusion that in regard to the availability of artificial reproductive techniques, it would not be wrong to assume that one precondition can legitimately be upheld by international law, namely the existence of a stable family relationship, such as married or cohabiting heterosexual couples. This was also the opinion expressed by the vast majority of the expert members of CAHBI[170] in the recommendations referred to earlier. A small minority considered that the new techniques for assisted procreation should be limited to married couples only. The correct view, therefore, would seem to be that the contextual and systematic reading of the right to found a family (Article 12) may allow the European Court in future considerations of relevant applications not to restrict it beyond a reasonable limit and to forward its dynamic understanding, *i.e.*, to include also cohabiting persons.

In addition, both the Commission and the Court have often relied, when determining the scope of the rights protected by the European Convention, on comparative surveys of the laws of states parties. In most European countries artificial insemination is today available not only to *de iure* family unions but also to couples living in stable, heterosexual family unions.[171]

The gradual re-evaluation of the notion of family towards greater flexibility and tolerance, a development, which is consistent with dominant social realities, is also clearly conceivable in other parts of the world, as for example in Latin America. Even though until the middle of the present century the disapproval of unmarried cohabitation was very extensive in Latin America, several countries have enacted laws and/or national courts have begun to bestow legal status on *de facto* family unions under certain conditions. In Argentina, for example, a Senate State Commission recommended recently among other things that the new techniques for assisted procreation may be used by married and cohabiting couples.[172]

Cohabitation without marriage is widespread all over the world[173] with one major exception: most of the Muslim world does not accept it.[174] Since heterosexual *de facto* family unions fulfil the same functions as married couples there is no reasonable ground to treat them differentially (discriminatorily) in matters of

---

[170] See *Council of Europe*, Human Artificial Procreation, p. 17.

[171] This is, for example, the case in Austria, Denmark, France, Germany, Greece, Italy, the Netherlands, Norway, Spain and Sweden. In Hungary, on the other hand, assisted conception is only available for married women who have a permanent address in the country. *L. Nielsen*, Room for Harmonisation?, p. 310.

[172] *D.B. Inigo*, Argentina: Cohabitation and Assisted Human Fertilization, University of Louisville Journal of Family Law 1995, Vol. 33, p. 273.

[173] For references to countries where this form of family life has become an established form see UN Doc. CEDAW/C/1993/4, pp. 7 and 14.

[174] *M. Palm-Risse*, p. 230. See the reservations of the Islamic Republic of Iran, of the Libyan Arab Jamhiriya and Malaysia to the Beijing Declaration and Platform for Action. The Government of the last mentioned country expressed, for example, its conviction that "reproductive rights should be applicable only to married couples formed of the union between a man and a woman". UN Doc. A/CONF.177/20, p. 169.

procreation.[175] Such an approach is consistent with today's rapidly shifting social conditions and attitudes and the intention of international organs to uphold diversity of family arrangements, in which the nuclear family based on marriage is only one among many.

I agree, therefore, with Professor Nowak that there are good reasons to argue that there is not only one standard way of life and that unmarried couples should enjoy the same right to found/establish a family as that which follows from marriage. However, in the absence of authoritative statements on that particular right in the light of the new developments in bio-medicine it is the future that will show us whether the new forms of family life arising out of the use of new techniques for assisted procreation may lead to an expansion of the concepts of family/family life as protected by human rights norms.

### 5.3.3.3.2. Single Women and Lesbians

*A. Single Women*

Infertility affects not only married and cohabiting heterosexual couples but also single women. It has been, therefore, maintained that even single persons should be given the possibility to resort to the new reproductive techniques. Such claims are often based on the assumption that refusal to guarantee access to AI techniques for individuals on the ground of their civil status or sexual orientation constitutes discrimination and violation of their human right to family planning and to found a family. Different rationales, which I shall comment below, are given for and against propositions of that kind.

Firstly, the argument has been put forward that it is already too late to oppose the practice of the use of AID on single women since it is practically impossible to control its application. Thus, single women can undertake AI on their own.[176]

---

[175] Martina Palm-Risse argues in this respect as follows: "Die vergleichbare tatsächliche Situation und Funktion rechtfertigen es also, stabile nichtehliche Lebensgemeinschaften dem Schutz des Rechts auf Achtung des Familienlebens zu unterstellen". Ibid., p. 199. As an example I may refer to the situation in Norway. Before 1994 unmarried/cohabiting women were barred from assisted reproductive treatment, but since cohabitation became a normal phenomenon in the country, the new Act Relating to Application of Biotechnology in Medicine no longer discriminates against unmarried couples. *M. Halvorsen*, The act relating to the application of biotechnology in medicine with particular regard to questions in family law, The International Survey of Family Law 1996, A. Bainham (ed.), The Hague 1998, p. 325.

[176] Two of the experts within CAHBI were, for example, in favour of permitting access to artificial insemination for single women since in their view AI can be performed by single persons directly anyway. This is in line with an resolution earlier adopted by the European Parliament according to which "family (p)olicy cannot in any way stand in the way of progress towards ensuring that women have their own derivative rights". For the first pronouncement see Council of Europe, Human Artificial Insemination, Ibid., p. 17. See also *B. Kritchevsky*, The Unmarried Woman's Right to Artificial Insemination: a Call for an Expanded Definition of Family, Harvard Women's Law Journal 1981, Vol. 4, p. 4. For the cited text of the European Parliament's resolution of June 9, 1983 see Council of Europe, Directorate of Human Rights, Doc. H/INF(83), April-October 1983, p. 120.

In support of the validity of the CAHBI members' assertion I shall refer to the following. In response to the legal situation of their children several lesbian women have started a debate in the Swedish press in which they make use of the above-mentioned argument. They have also admitted that self-insemination

Secondly, the de-linking of marriage and parenthood as discussed in the previous sub-chapter has, in addition, given rise to arguments for making the new techniques for assisted procreation available to single women and to same-sex couples. For these reasons the assertion in several articles in central human rights documents that the family is "the natural and fundamental group unit of society", and as such it is entitled to protection by the state, has become a subject to extensive controversy. Raine Eisler has captured the essence of the matter in the following:

> "with whom to have intimate relations, whether or not to conceive, whether or not to carry a pregnancy are *not* family rights. They are individual rights even though they may involve personal choices or actions that characteristically take place within the family".[177]

The fact remains, however, that the provisions of the relevant human rights documents, with the exception of the Woman's Convention, recognise a couple's right to found a family/family planning and that there is no explicit reference to individuals in this respect. This circumstance can be criticised from the gender perspective, since the wording of the texts endorses gender inequality.[178] The decision-making of a couple in many cultures still cannot be characterised as equal. Greater awareness about gender equality issues and pressure from various women groups have among other things resulted in formulations of the right to family planning/to found a family in hortatory international documents adopted since the mid of 1970s, which comprise entitlement for both the couple and the individual. We may give as an example § 14 (f) of the Plan of Action, which was adopted at the World Population Conference in Bucharest in 1974. It reads as follows: "All couples and individuals have the basic right to decide freely and responsibly the number and spacing of their children".[179] It would be correct to assume that a teleological, systematical and contextual interpretation of treaty provisions in the light of this and similar provisions would require that women have a right to control their fertility in their capacity as individuals in order to realise the goal of gender equality. At the same time I ought also to mention that in some of the documents adopted at recent UN conferences[180] the emphasis, as we shall see later on in my discussion on

---

with the sperm either from friends or anonymous donors is a very common phenomenon among lesbians and that such practices are nearly impossible to prevent in practice. *C. Gustavsson*, Han har 2 mammor, Aftonbladet, 28 April 1997, p. 23. For comments on this issue see *B. Verschraegen*, Gleichgeschlechtliche "Ehen", pp. 75–76.

177 *R. Eisler*, Integrating the Private and Public Spherese: Toward a New Partnership in Human Rights, (unpublished paper ), London 1990, p. 4.

178 *K. Tomaševski*, Human Rights in Population Policies, p. 66; *C.A.A. Packer*, p. 81.

179 Report of the UN World Population Conference, UN Doc. A/CONF.60/19,1974. In addition § 12 of the Declaration on the Equality of Women and their Contribution to Development and Peace of 1975 (adopted in Mexico City) stipulates that: "Every couple and every individual has the right to decide freely and responsibly whether or not to have children". See the Report of the World Conference of the International Women's Year, UN Doc. E/CONF.66/34,1976.

180 See, for example, § 7.3 of the Cairo Programme of Action and the reservations submitted by certain states in relation to the use of the word individual, as well as § 95 of the Beijing Platform for Action.

responsible parenthood, has been clearly put on the importance of involving both men and women on an equal footing in decision-making on procreation.

Single women's right to procreate has not been so far explicitly acknowledged by international human rights bodies. Only CEDAW has produced an authoritative pronouncement of some relevance to our issue. In its General Recommendation No. 21 (§ 22) the Committee established that: "decisions to have children or not, while preferably made in consultation with spouse or partner, must not nevertheless be limited by (these)". But this means only that it is the individual woman forming part of the couple, and not the person living as single, who should enjoy a right to reproductive freedom according to the Woman's Convention. This contemporary understanding holds true for the other human rights instruments.[181]

Opponents to the view that the right of single women to procreate by means of AID should be recognised attach the greatest importance to the wellbeing of the child. They suggest that in assisted procreation, as in adoption, individuals who want to become parents should undergo scrutiny tests with regard to their suitability as parents.[182] The predominant norm in this regard throughout the world is the married/cohabiting heterosexual couple. In consequence those who do not fit in this traditional pattern are as a rule deemed "unsuitable for treatment".[183] It has been maintained in addition that since the right to found a family/to family planning is not absolute, certain limitations[184] in its exercise can be justified in order to protect the rights and interests of others, especially the child to be born. In consequence, the leading principle – *the best interest of the child* – as expressed in Article 3 of the UN Convention on the Rights of the Child, ought to take precedence over other values. On this basis, it is submitted that the desire to have a child should, therefore, not be satisfied at the expense of the interests of the child to be born.

On the regional level references are frequently made in this regard to the *Jonston v. Ireland* judgment,[185] delivered by the European Court on Human Rights, and in which the fundamental right of the child to have a normal family life was emphasised. The upshot of this case is, in short, that states have an obligation under the European Convention to ensure that children born out of wedlock acquire dual affiliation. Thus, the fundamental rule in international law that every child shall have the right to a normal family life was once more[186] given principal importance

---

[181] In regard to the content of Article 23(2) of the ICCPR Professor Nowak promptly declares that: "At the core of the right to found a family is *the right of two parents to have children*". CCPR Commentary, p. 26.

[182] *M. Evans*, p. 134.

[183] *L. Doyal*, Infertility-a Life Sentence? Women and the National Health Service, in Reproductive Technologies, Gender, Motherhood and Medicine, M. Stanworth (ed.), p. 182.

[184] On the other hand I cannot deny that there is a certain risk in giving states broad margins of discretion when deciding upon limitations on who should and who should not have access to AI that these decisions can be taken on arbitrary grounds. It is extremely difficult to create tenable tests for the suitability of a person as a parent. There is simply no accepted definition of good parenting.

[185] *Johnston and Others v. Republic of Ireland*, ECHR Judgment of 18 December 1986, Ser. A, No. 112.

[186] A somewhat similar reasoning may be found in the ruling of the European Court in the *P. Marckx v Belgium* case, ECHR Judgment of 13 June 1979, Ser. A., No. 31.

in this judgment. Much of the above argumentation reflects an attitude that for the healthy and harmonious development of a child's personality both a mother and a father are necessary. The proponents of a restrictive interpretation of the right to found a family/to family planning refer in addition to empirical studies of the consequences of divorce for children and which show that children obviously are best benefited by a stable two-parent nuclear family.[187] On that basis it is claimed that both women and men provide important psychological and material support for the child's normal growth, important from the very beginning for the child's socialisation. The mother's and father's roles are thus seen as complementary. Such a family is considered by the great majority of states to be the natural environment[188] for children and as such it still has a role to play in modern society. Growth is not only about material prosperity but also about establishing one's own identity. Article 18(1) of the Convention on the Rights of the Child stipulates that both parents have common responsibilities for the upbringing and development of their child. Furthermore, Article 5(b) of the Women's Convention recognises: "The common responsibility of men and women in the upbringing and development of their children".

The strong conviction of the value of the family that has found expression in the central conventions on human rights has also been used in the argumentation against the recognition of single women's right to procreate. References were made to among others Article 23 of the ICCPR where the family is described as "the natural and fundamental group unit of society". Also Article 10(1) of the ICESCR stipulates that "the widest possible protection and assistance should be accorded to the family, which is the natural and fundamental group unit of society". This international concern for the well-being of the family was furthermore demonstrated within the UN by proclaiming the year 1994 as the International Year of the Family. In Part III, A, paragraph 6 of the Programme for that year it was stated:

> "In spite of the many changes in society that have altered its role and functions, it continues to provide the natural framework for the emotional, financial and material support essential to the growth and development of its members, particularly infants and children".[189]

---

[187] *E.S. Scott*, Rational Decisionmaking About Marriage and Divorce, Virginia Law Review 1990, Vol. 76, p. 72 *et seq.*

[188] On the other hand, the concept "family environment" as incorporated in the Convention on the Rights of the Child has been interpreted in the literature in an extensive manner in the sense that it "is broader than the family and overcomes the historic and some would argue unjustifiable biological restraints on the protection of family life". *G. Van Bueren*, The Challenges for the International Protection of Family Members' Rights as the 21st Century Approaches, Paper presented at the 8th World Conference of the International Society of Family Law, Cardiff 1994, p. 6. There is, however, no evidence that the drafters intended to interpret the expression in that way. Neither has the CRC yet discussed it in the light of new procreative techniques.

[189] *Centre for Social Development and Humanitarian Affairs*, 1994, International Year of the Family, Building the smallest democracy at the heart of society, UN, Vienna 1991, p. 12.

Furthermore, § 5 of the preamble to the UN Convention on the Rights of the Child establishes:

> "(t)he family, as the fundamental group of society and the natural environment of the growth and well-being of all its members and particularly children, should be afforded the necessary protection and assistance so that it can fully assume its responsibilities within the community".

The considerable weight in international law given to the concept of parental responsibility towards the child to be born forms consequently[190] a significant part of the above argumentation.

Even though arguments have been presented in favour of the use of AI on single women by referring to the fact that the traditional family unit, comprised of a mother, a father and a child, is not always established in practice, or it might have a very short existence, since death or separation leave a great number of parents single (*i.e.*, a guarantee cannot be required for the child to be brought up by a father *and* a mother), this author agrees that there is indeed a value in starting a child's life within a traditional family structure rather than in an incomplete family.

In conclusion, as international law stands today there is in my opinion not enough support in conventional law and/or in the case law of international human rights supervisory bodies for the view that AID may also be applied in cases of single women. This is also the case in reality, since the majority of states refrain from using AID on unmarried (not cohabiting in stable heterosexual relations) women, totally or with far-reaching restrictions as regards access to such treatment services. A recent survey of national laws in Europe discloses that the main rule seems to be that single women and lesbians may not benefit from medically assisted conception.[191] I shall in what follows give some examples. According to the Austrian Act on Procreative Medicine, which entered into force on 1 July 1992, AI is allowed only in the case of a married or a stable heterosexual union. Single women are consequently not given lawful access to any form of assisted conception. In the United Kingdom as well as in France legislation was recently introduced that would restrict official insemination to heterosexual, married women.[192]

---

[190] Parental responsibilities are defined in a recommendation prepared by the Committee of Ministers of the Council of Europe in 1984 (Recommendation No R (84) 4) "as a collection of duties and powers, which aim at insuring the moral and material welfare of the child, in particular by taking care of the person of the child, by maintaining the personal relationships with him and by providing for his education, his maintenance, his legal representation and the administration of his property". Moreover, § 6 of the explanatory memorandum says: "...it was agreed that the term 'parental responsibilities' better described the modern concept, according to which parents are, on a basis of equality between the parents and in consultation with their children, given the task to educate, legally represent, maintain, etc. their children. In order to do so they exercise powers to carry out duties *in the interests of the child* and not because of an authority, which is conferred on them in their own interests." (this author's italics).

[191] *L. Nielsen*, Room for Harmonisation?, p. 310.

[192] *J. Dorf & G.C. Pérez*, Discrimination and the Tolerance of Difference: International Lesbian Human Rights, in Women's rights, human rights, J. Peters & A. Wolper (eds.), p. 328.

A liberal approach, *i.e.*, making access to the new procreative techniques available to single women, exists today only in a small number of European countries such as the Netherlands, Spain and Russia.[193]

*B. Single Lesbian Women and Same-Sex Couples*

While sexuality (distinctions based on sexual identity) is not mentioned in any of the human rights treaties, several countries in different parts of the world[194] have during recent years introduced "sexual orientation"[195] as a ground upon which discrimination should be avoided. On this basis among other arguments have been advanced within the literature and in cases brought before national courts that reproductive freedom is a primary issue for women of any sexual orientation.[196]

Within international law the issue of banning discrimination on the grounds of sexual orientation was substantially discussed for the first time in a UN forum during the Beijing Conference in 1995. The attempts to adopt the draft Platform for Action containing four references to "sexual orientation" were however unsuccessful.[197] Only a few countries, among them Israel, submitted a written statement to the Beijing Declaration and Platform for Action, which suggests that in the light of the interpretation given to the words "other status" by, *e.g.*, the HRC[198], "we interpret the words 'other status' to include sexual orientation".[199]

---

[193] Artificial fertilisation and embryo implantation is performed on single women in the Russian Federation as a matter of right since 1993. *A.Y. Ivanyushkin*, p. 272.

[194] In New Zealand the Human Rights Act of 1993 bans discrimination on the grounds of sexual orientation. *B. Atkin*, p. 384. Some Bundesländer in Germany (Brandenburg and Thuringia) have, furthermore, in their constitutions provisions that prohibit discrimination on the grounds of sexual orientation. *B. Verschraegen*, Gleichheit im Familienrecht, in Gleichheit im Familienrecht, B. Verschraegen (ed.), p. 34. In addition, most of the jurisdictions in Canada have adopted legislations which guarantee protection against discrimination based on sexual orientation in matters of, for example, employment. *M. Bailey & N. Bala*, p. 91.

It ought to be mentioned also that since 1 April 1998 there is in Sweden a special ombudsman against discrimination on the basis of sexual orientation in working life. *E. Bäckstrand*, HomO börjar jobba i april, SvD 15 May 1998, p. 12.

[195] For arguments in favour of the assertion that sexual orientation amounts to a separate and recognisable status see *W. Morgan*, Sexuality and Human Rights, The First Communication by an Australian to the Human Rights Committee under the Optional Protocol to the International Covenant on Civil and Political Rights, The Australian Year Book of International Law 1993, Vol. 14, p. 282.

[196] *J. Dorf & G.C. Pérez*, p. 330.

[197] While the delegations of 33 states supported the references to "sexual orientation", 22 delegations opposed their inclusion in the final document. *D. Sanders*, Getting Lesbian And Gay Issues On The International Human Rights Agenda, HRQ 1996, Vol. 18, p. 90.

[198] Equality rights were invoked on the basis of Article 26 of the ICCPR by Nicholas Toonen, a homosexual activist and citizen in Australia but who was residing in Tasmania in regard to the Tasmanian criminal law which in his opinion discriminated on the basis of sex by applying only to male homosexual activities. It is noticeable that the HRC chose to avoid the interpretation of the expression "other status". It simply ruled that the concept of "sex" within the meaning of Article 26 of the Covenant included "sexual orientation" and that the Tasmanian law violated Mr. Toonen's right to privacy. See *Toonen vs. Australia*, Communication No. 488/1992, UN Doc. CCPR/C/50/D/488/1992. The HRC expressed its views on 31 March 1994.

[199] UN Doc. A/CONF.177/20, p. 167. In addition the USA in its interpretative statement to the Beijing document took the following position: "The United States Government has a firm policy of non-

So far the only reference to women's rights in procreative matters, irrespective of sexual orientation, is explicitly contained in § 9.5 of the 1997 Asian (NGO) Charter on Human Rights. It reads as follows: "The recognition of sexual preference or orientation must be genuine and real, and all other overt and covert ways of denying such preference based on social habits or cultural inhibitions and other forms of social oppressions is a violation of human rights".[200]

On the European level, within the Council of Europe, in 1990 the International Lesbian and Gay Association (ILGA) decided to press for an additional protocol to the European Convention. This protocol should prohibit discrimination on the nature of sexual orientation. The proposal has as at the time of writing not advanced. In 1993, however, the Parliamentary Assembly adopted a declaration stressing the need to end the practice of discrimination against homosexuals in former Eastern-block countries and in consequence Lithuania reformed its laws.[201]

Despite some significant, progressive decisions delivered by the European Commission and the European Court regarding the human rights of homosexuals, both organs have been reluctant to discuss homosexual relations within the provisions for family life. In the case of *Kerkhoven, Hinke & Hinke v. The Netherlands*, which I discussed in Part I of his study, the Commission demonstrated clearly its negative standpoint to childrearing by a homosexual couple. The Commission, as well as the Court, has moreover as a rule[202] abstained from making use of the non-discrimination provision of the Convention. The European Commission of Human Rights recently preferred, for example, to avoid determining whether a difference based on sexual orientation in the law of the UK in regard to the minimum age for consensual male homosexual relations compared to the age of consent for consensual heterosexual and lesbian relations, is a matter which should be considered as a difference on grounds of "sex" or "of other status".[203]

In light of the non-discrimination principle, which is of great value in the EU, steps have been taken in recent years to obtain equal treatment between homosexuals

---

discrimination on the basis of sexual orientation and considers that the omission of this reference in paragraph 46 and elsewhere in the Platform for Action in no way justifies such discrimination in any country". Ibid., p. 174.

200 *F. de Varennes*, p. 142.

201 *D. Sanders*, pp. 81–82. Romania on the other hand has refused to take any action to repeal its anti-homosexual criminal law. The Penal Code Modification of Article 200, of February 3, 1994 calls for prison terms of up to five years for homosexual activities.

202 The European Commission in the case of *E. Sutherland v. the UK*, reached, however, the conclusion that there had been a violation of Article 8 taken in conjunction with Article 14 of the Convention.

203 Appl. No. 25186/94, *E. Sutherland v. the UK*, Report of the Commission adopted on 1 July 1997. The Commission was of the opinion that regardless of whether the difference in treatment of heterosexuals and homosexuals is based on "sex" or "other status", "given that it impinges on a most intimate aspect of affected individuals' private lives, the margin of appreciation must be relatively narrow". It concluded, therefore, that there was no objective and reasonable justification for the maintenance of a higher minimum age of consent for male homosexual than for heterosexual acts and that the application discloses discriminatory treatment in the exercise of the applicant's right to respect for private life under Article 8 of the Convention. Ibid., §§ 57 and 66. See <http://www.dhcommhr.coe.fr/eng/25186R31.E.html>. The case is still pending before the European Court.

and heterosexuals within the member states of the Union. The European Parliament affirmed its conviction, for example, in a resolution "On equal rights of homosexuals and lesbians in the EC", which it adopted on 8 February 1994,[204] that: "all citizens must be treated equally, irrespective of their sexual orientation" and therefore it considered that the European Community is under obligation to apply the principle of equal treatment, "irrespective of each individual's sexual orientation", in all legal provisions already adopted or which may be adopted in the future. Moreover, the EC Staff Regulations were amended in 1998 to prohibit discrimination against Community employees on the basis of their sexual orientation. However, the European Court of Justice emphasised in its in the literature already much criticised[205] judgment in the case of *Lisa Grant v South-West Trains*[206] that discrimination on the grounds of sexual orientation cannot be regarded as discrimination on the basis of "sex" which is prohibited under European law.[207] It rejected the reasoning of the Advocate General Elmer that the South-West Trains, Ltd. could not justify its discriminatory policy on the basis of its private conceptions of morality, which disfavoured same-sex partnerships. Finally, the Court took the position that, although the national legislations in some of the member states of the Community regulate same-sex partnerships in a manner "equivalent to marriage", they treat such relationships as comparable to unmarried heterosexual partnership only for limited purposes. The fact remains , thus, that the majority does not recognise same-sex relationships at all.[208] On the other hand, the ECJ observed that this situation might change after the 1997 Treaty of Amsterdam comes into force. On a proposal from the Commission and after consulting the European Parliament, a legislation prohibiting discrimination on the grounds of sexual orientation can be adopted, provided that there is unanimous support for it within the Union. Other regional and global (with the exception of the HRC) organs and intergovernmental institutions have remained silent on the issue discussed above.

---

[204] Res. No. A3–0028/94, 8 February 1994, Official Journal of the European Communities, No. C 61/40, 28 February 1994.

[205] *P. Noorlander*, The Right to Sexual Orientation; Recent Developments in Europe, ASIL, Human Rights Interest Group, Newsletter 1998, Vol. 8, pp. 6–9; *L.R. Helfer*, *Grant v. South-West Trains, LTD.* Case C-249/96, AJIL 1999, Vol. 93, p. 202.

[206] Case C-249/96, ECJ, Judgment of 17 February 1998. See <http://curia.eu.int/sv/act/9806sv.htm>.

[207] In its judgment of 30 April 1996, in the case *P v S and Cornwall County Council*, C-13/94 the ECJ produced a ruling that dealt in depth with the scope of the Community's rules prohibiting discrimination based on sex. The Court held that the Equal Treatment Directive which is in force within the Community and which prohibits employment discrimination "on grounds of sex", precluded the dismissal of a male-to-female transsexual because of her gender reassignment. In the Court's opinion the scope of the directive "cannot be confined simply to discrimination based on the fact that a person is of one or other sex". ECJ, 1996, ECR 2143, 2 CMLR 247.

[208] *Grant v. South-West Trains, LTD.*, Judgment, §§ 29–36. It may be noted here, in addition, that on 28 January 1999, the First Instance of the EC Court rejected the argumentation in the *D. v. Council* case (Case T-264/97) that the Community should treat its employees' same-sex partnership contracts as equivalent to marriage for the purposes of awarding a household allowance.

On the national level the courts, for example, in Canada have applied legislation that prohibits discrimination on the basis of sexual orientation to ensure lesbian women full access to artificial insemination.[209] Belgium has, in addition, reviewed national law[210] in such a way that lesbian woman are now entitled to obtain insemination.

The question under discussion arises often in respect of marriage. While the relevant provisions in universal and regional human rights instruments do not expressly prohibit marriage by persons of the same sex, several of them are formulated in terms of "men" and "women" (*e.g.*, Article 16 of the UDHR). Only Article 10(1) of the ICESCR makes use of the expression "intending spouses", *i.e.*, a term not related to sex. On the other hand, a subject to state protection in the same provision is the traditional family.[211] The human rights organs, which have had opportunity to review cases dealing with this issue, have not treated a stable relationship between two persons of the same sex as equivalent to marriage or to *de facto* family union. Despite greater frankness and openness for homosexuality and homosexual relations[212] which is apparent in recent years in Europe,[213] the Strasbourg organs have not departed from their earlier case law according to which the state parties to the European Convention must be permitted to exclude

---

[209] The case *Korn v. Potter* (1996) B.C.J. 692 (B.C.S.C) is a good illustration of this issue. See *M. Bailey & N. Bala*, Child support guidelines, parental mobility, and redefining familial relationships, in The International Survey of Family Law 1996, A. Bainham (ed.), The Hague 1998, p. 91.

[210] Reference to the new rules can be found in SOU 1993:98, Partnerskap, Del B, Betänkande av Partnerskapskommittén, Stockholm 1993, p. 89; *A. Brewaeys, H. Olbrechts, P. Devroey & A.C. Van Steirteghem,* Counselling and selection of homosexual couples in fertility treatment, Human Reproduction 1989, Vol. 4, p. 7.

[211] The *travaux préparatoires* to the ICESCR indicate, in addition, that the drafters meant the term "marriage" to imply a heterosexual character to the relationship.

[212] Studies suggest that the percentage of individuals within a given population likely to prefer sexual relations with individuals of their own sex are between 4% and 12%. See *E. Heinze*, Sexual Orientation: A Human Right, Dordrecht 1995, p. 18, note 85. Within the EU there are approximately 35 million citizens of the Community, depending on the method of calculation used, who are homosexual. See reference in § 42, Opinion of Advocate General M.B. Elmer in the case C-249/96. See <http://www.egale.ca/legal/grant.txt>.

[213] None of the human rights conventions contains a provision that defines homosexuality as a human right. However, the ECHR's decision in *Dudgeon vs. United Kingdom*, is seen as a landmark in international human rights law for homosexuals. The Court noted that "marked changes" in the domestic laws of the European states, made the law in Northern Ireland, which criminalised adult homosexual activity out of date in the U.K. and in Europe as a whole. ECHR, Judgment of 22 October 1981, Ser. A, No. 22. Other cases that show that the ECHR has played a role in decriminalising homosexual activity is *Norris vs. Ireland* (ECHR Judgment of 26 October 1988, Ser. A, No. 142) and the *Modinos v Cyprus* case (ECHR Judgment of 22 April 1993, Ser. A, No. 259). The European Court demonstrated in the last mentioned case a more flexible attitude towards homosexuality compared with its earlier case law. Thus, the Court held that the Attorney General's policy not to prosecute male homosexual conduct in private between adults is not in itself a sufficient guarantee for the right to private life. At the same time, it is obvious that the fact that the Commission and the Court rule that homosexual relationships do not lie within the provision on respect for family life but rather private life narrows the possibility of using the Convention.

from marriage persons "whose sexual category itself implies a physical incapacity to procreate either absolutely, (o)r in relation to the sexual category of the other spouse".[214]

On the other hand, the European Parliament decided on 8 February 1994 with a bare majority to appoint a working group to deal with the question of how to avoid discrimination of homosexual individuals. It became obvious that there is support for the idea of homosexual marriage and the adoption of children by homosexuals. The Parliament adopted a resolution, to which I referred earlier, and which can be considered as a radical reform. It calls, *e.g.*, for an end of the unequal treatment of homosexuals under the laws on adoption. The legislative and administrative powers of the EU have an integrating effect in that they lead to some degree of legal unity among member states. Moreover, all the members of the EU have ratified the European Convention on Human Rights and have recognised the jurisdiction of the European Court.

In other parts of the world, homosexual relationships are still forbidden by law in several countries, and those who choose to live out their sexual nature risk persecution. They can be subjected to severe penalties, sometimes even the death penalty.[215]

The conclusion I can derive from the above is that, despite certain developments in the attitudes and in domestic laws dealing with homosexuality, according to rules of contemporary international law homosexuals may not claim a right to marry and to found a family.[216]

---

[214] *M. Rees v. UK*, Report of the European Commission, adopted on 12 December 1984, p. 18. Also the European Court has underlined the heterosexual character of the marriage in the *Rees* and the *Cossey* cases. In the words of Professor Verschraegen "Zu Recht entschied das Gericht, daß punktuelle Abweichungen vom traditionellen Ehebild noch keine generelle Rechtsentwicklung darstellen, die eine Abkehr vom tradierten Ehebild rechtfertigen". *B. Verschraegen*, Gleichgeschlechtliche "Ehen", p. 42.

[215] See, for example, *C.L. Taylor*, Legends, Syncretism, and Continuing Echoes of Homosexuality from Pre-Columbian and Colonial México, in Latin American Male Homosexuality, S.O. Murrey (ed.), 1995, p. 93; *D. Sanders*, p. 71.

[216] See generally *M.K. Eriksson*, The Right to Marry and to Found a Family, Uppsala 1990. The European Commission of Human Rights has in its case law, as earlier mentioned, classified a stable homosexual relationship as private rather than family life. The Commission has held that the family "merits special protection and therefore the difference in treatment is objectively and reasonably justified". *S v. the UK*, 47 D&R 1986, p. 279. *M. Palm-Risse*, pp. 199–200. This aspect of the jurisprudence of the European organs has given rise to heavy criticism from lesbian and gay groups. For references see *W. Morgan*, p. 287.

Similarly the HRC expressed concern during the review of the periodic report presented by the US at its session in March 1995 that the "serious infringement of private life in some states which classify as a criminal offence sexual relations between adult consenting partners of the same sex carried out in private and the consequences thereof for their enjoyment of other human rights without discrimination". CCPR/C/SR. 1401–1402 and SR. 1405–1406, 29–31 March 1995. See in addition *C. Folder*, The Netherlands, Re-thinking Marriage, Parenthood and Adoption, in The International Survey of Family Law 1995, A. Bainham (ed.), The Hague 1997, p. 362.

While some national courts, among them the Hungarian Constitutional Court,[217] the Supreme Court of Canada,[218] several courts within the USA[219] and the German Constitutional Court,[220] found that same-sex couples are not discriminated against as far as the right to marry[221] is concerned, others like the Dutch Supreme Court reached the opposite conclusion in 1990.[222] The latter proposed that any change in this matter should be made by the legislator. In consequence thereof, a majority of the Parliament in the Netherlands required recently the Government to prepare a legislation according to which homosexuals can marry and adopt a child.[223] To the knowledge of this author, such a regulation entered into force on 1 January 1998.[224] In addition, the Supreme Court of Hawaii found in its decision in the case *Basher v. Lewis/ Bear v. Mike*[225] that "sex" was a suspect category. It ruled that the denial of

---

[217] The Court delivered a decision in 1995 according to which the refusal to register a marriage of same-sex couple was not a denial of the right to marry. Neither does it constitute discriminatory treatment in this regard. The Court emphasised that: "das Institut der Ehe in unseren Kultur, unserem Recht und auch unserer Tradition eine Lebensgemeinschaft von einem Mann und eine Frau sei". *E. Weiss*, Ungern, in Gleichheit im Familienrecht, B. Verschraegen, p. 267.

[218] The *Layland v. Ontario*, 1993, 14. O.R. (3d) 658 (Gen.Div.) case illustrates this position. Yet in another case of 1995, the *Egan v. Canada* (12 R.F.L. 84th) 201, 124, D.L.R. (4th) 609 (S.C.C.), which was decided by five to four votes by the Canadian Supreme Court, the majority of the judges based their arguments on the presumption that "homosexual relationships are not 'spousal' in nature". One Justice referred to the heterosexual couples' "unique ability to procreate" as a legitimate ground for differential treatment. This decision was, however, overruled in 1996 when the Ontario Court of Appeal affirmed in another case *M. v. H.* that "spouse" includes also unmarried homosexual couples. See *M. Bailey & N. Bala*, pp. 92–93. At the time of writing this decision, which was appealed, is pending before the Supreme Court of Canada.

[219] For references to cases up to 1995 in which various courts have abstained from recognising same-sex marriages see *S.N. Katz*, The United States, State Regulation and Personal Autonomy in Marriage: how can I marry and whom can I marry?, in The International Survey of Family Law 1996, A. Bainham (ed.), The Hague 1998, p. 495, note 16. It should be mentioned that the United States Supreme Court has not yet ruled that homosexuals are a suspect class. Ibid., p. 496, note 18. See also *L.D. Elrod*, pp. 272–274.

[220] For a review of the German debate up to 1994 see *B. Verschraegen*, Gleichgeschlechtliche "Ehen", pp. 155–167.

[221] The most frequently used argument against same-sex marriage in decisions of international organs as well as in several jurisdictions is that marriage traditionally has been defined as the voluntary union "of one man and one woman, to the exclusion of all others". The citation resembles the words of Lord Penzance in the *Hyde v. Hyde* case. See *K. Mck. Norrie*, Reproductive Technology, Transsexualism and Homosexuality: New Problems for International Private Law, ICLQ 1994, Vol. 43, p. 767.

[222] *P. Vlaardingebroek*, (I)nequality in Netherlands Family Law, in Gleichheit im Familienrecht, B. Verschraegen (ed.), p. 34. The Dutch Supreme Court argued in a decision from 1989 that the non-discrimination provision of the European Convention does not impose any obligation on the Dutch Government to introduce any "legislative provision for social parenthood for lesbian and homosexual couples". *C. Forder*, p. 363.

[223] *P. Vlaardingerbroek*, p. 155. For an overview of the situation in the Netherlands up to 1994 see *B. Verschraegen*, Gleichgeschlechtliche "Ehen", pp. 139–153.

[224] See *S. Schultz*, Gaykampen är långt ifrån vunnen, SvD, 4 January 1999, p. 4.

[225] 852 P.2d44 (Haw. 1994); Hawaii Cir Ct 1st Cir, No. 91–1394. Following this controversial decision, the United States Congress passed (the US senate rejected by 85 to 14 same-sex marriage in federal law on 10 September 1996) the Defence of Marriage Act, which establishes that each state could choose whether or not to recognise same-sex marriages. President Clinton signed the Act on September 21, 1996. To date 25 states have banned them outright. *E. Rudulph*, A Different Father's Day, in Time, December 29, 1997– January 5, 1998, p. 69. See also International Herald Tribune, 12 September 1996, p. 3.

the legal status of being married to a same-sex couple, *i.e.*, the sex-based classification in HRS 572-1, *prima facie* and as applied, "is unconstitutional and in violation of the equal protection clause of article I, section 5 of the Hawaii Constitution".[226] In addition, there seems to exist overwhelming support in the American literature in favour of the legalisation of same-sex marriage.[227]

Several European countries have, meanwhile, enacted laws on registered/domestic partnership. None of them makes use of the word "marriage" for this kind of relationship[228] and in no country are homosexual couples afforded the same benefits as married heterosexual couples.[229] Such a legal solution is in my view not in conflict with the principle of non-discrimination and equality. Thus, the main purpose of the legislation in the Nordic countries was to equalise the social status of homosexual and other forms of cohabitation.[230] The ideological foundation, for example, for a draft legislation on registered partnership which was submitted to the Government of Sweden in June 1990 by the National Board of Health and Welfare was the belief in human equality "both individually and under the law, together with the acknowledgement that homosexual love is of equal value to heterosexual love".[231]

Nevertheless, some differences in treatment by law still remain. For example, not even the liberal legislation in Denmark, which is of relevance for couples of the same sex ensuring them the right to register their partnership,[232] entitles them jointly to adopt a child from a third party. Stepchild adoption is according to these provisions prohibited. As mentioned before, according to the Act on Assisted Reproduction of 1997, access to assisted reproduction is only available to a woman who is married or is cohabiting with a man.[233] Thus, the proposal made by the Ethical Advisory Committee in Denmark that single women and lesbians should, on the basis of legal rules, be allowed to obtain artificial insemination, *in vitro* fer-

---

226 Judge Kevin S.C. Chang, Honolulu, December 3, 1996. See <http://www.hawaii.gov/lrb/cpt6.html>.

227 For references on writings in favour and against recognition of same-sex marriage see *S.N. Katz*, p. 502.

228 Opponents of same-sex marriage have argued that marriage should not be seen as a privilege. It is a patriarchal and sexist institution that lesbians and gays should not enter into. For references see *R. Colker*, Marriage, in Feminist Legal Theory II, F.E. Olsen (ed.), p. 239.

229 *J. Dorf & G.C. Pérez*, Discrimination and the Tolerance of Difference: International Lesbian Human Rights, in Women's rights, human rights, J. Peters & A. Wolper (eds.), p. 327; *R. Colker*, p. 239.

230 *L. Nielsen*, Family Rights and "Registered Partnership" in Denmark, International Journal of Law and the Family 1990, Vol. 4, p. 305.

231 *Å. Saldeen*, Sweden: Family Counselling, the Tortious Liability of Parents and Homosexual Partnership, University of Louisville Journal of Family Law 1995, Vol. 33, pp. 519–520.

232 This innovative legal regime is modelled on marriage and most of its legal consequences. Act of Registration of Partnership, No. 372 of June 1989 is in force since 1 October 1990. See further *L. Nielsen*, Family Rights and the "Registered Partnership" in Denmark, p. 297 *et seq*; *L. Nielsen*, Equality before the Law-Family Law, in Gleichheit im Familienrecht, B. Verschraegen (ed.), p. 181; *B. Verschraegen*, Gleichgeschlechtliche "Ehen", pp. 107–118. In Norway the Act of Registration of Partnership has been in force since 1 August 1993 and in Iceland since 1996. See *B. Verschraegen*, Gleichgeschlechtliche "Ehen", pp. 118–126 and *D.T. Björgvinsson*, Iceland, General Principles and Recent Developments in Icelandic Family Law, in The International Survey of Family Law 1995, A. Bainham (ed.), The Hague 1987, p. 226.

233 *L. Nielsen & A. Kronborg*, p. 136.

tilisation and egg-donation was not included in the Act.[234] Similarly, the Norwegian Act Relating to the Application of Biotechnology in Medicine of 1994 excludes women living in registered lesbian partnership from assisted reproduction treatment.[235] The same is valid for the situation in Iceland.[236]

In Sweden the Partnership Committee recommended in November 1993 the passing of a law[237] under which two persons of the same sex will be able to enter into partnership through a registration procedure, which, in principle, corresponds to the procedure in a civil marriage ceremony. The law (*The Registered Partnership Act*) was adopted in 1994 and it entered into force on 1 January 1995.[238] The legal consequences of a partnership correspond essentially to the legal consequences of a marriage with some exceptions. Partners will, for example, not be able to adopt children, neither jointly nor individually, not even through what is known as stepchild or next-of-kin adoption.[239] Furthermore, lesbians will not have access to artificial insemination or other forms of artificial conception. Thus, the only consideration to be made in this respect is the child's best interests. The Partnership Committee emphasised in this respect that: "(f)ailing a reasonable degree of consensus among researchers on the possible consequences to a child of growing up in a homosexual family, it is not appropriate for homosexual couples to be enabled to adopt or to be given access to various forms of artificial fertilisation. For the same reason I feel that it should not be possible for homosexual couples to be made joint custodians of children".[240] It is maintained that adoption must be to the child's advantage and that insemination should only be permissible if the future child will "presumably have good conditions to grow up in".[241]

In summarising the debate on the sensitive matter under discussion here, different arguments can be generally grouped in the following way.

The basis for arguments against the marriage of same-sex partners centres round the discussion of the appropriateness of, for instance, lesbian women as parents.[242]

---

234 *L. Nielsen*, The Right to a Child versus the Rights of a Child, p. 215.

235 *M. Halvorsen*, p. 325.

236 *D.T. Björgvinsson*, p. 226.

237 The Partnership Act, SOU 1993:98, Del A, p. 69.

238 Lag 1994:1117 om registrerat partnerskap. *M.K. Eriksson*, Gender Equality in Sweden, in Gleichheit im Familienrecht, B. Verschraegen (ed.), p. 199. For a review of the content of the law see *A. Agell*, Äktenskap, Samboende, Partnerskap, Uppsala 1998, pp. 263–275. See also *M. Bogdan*, Registrerat partnerskap och svensk internationell privaträtt, SvJT 1994, pp. 773–784. *B. Verschraegen*, Gleichgeschlechtliche "Ehen", pp. 126–137.

239 I should also mention here that the Supreme Administrative Court (Regeringsrätten) in Sweden decided in June 1993 to consider a case (mål 6305–92) of relevance for homosexuals' right to adopt a child. See SOU 1993:98, Del A, p. 60. Such a right has not been granted yet. Nevertheless, there is an on-going debate in the Swedish parliament on this issue. *H. Andersson*, Homosexuella par måste få möjlighet att adoptera barn, SvD 26 April 1997, p. 7.

240 SOU 1993:98, Del A, p. 34.

241 Ibid., p. 33.

242 A significant part of the first circuit court opinion in the *Bear v. Miike* case is devoted to a discussion of that kind. Dr. Pruett testified, for example, that biological parents have a predisposition which helps them in parenting children and that the same-sex relationship does not provide the same type of learning

It is thus assumed that children will not be given appropriate gender role models. The implication of this argument is that the official recognition of homosexual marriage may result in the deconstruction of gender itself.[243] Others oppose this view on the basis of modern developments, *i.e.*, that the distinct gender roles that "husband" and "wife" play, involving the authority of the male and the dependence of the female, are no longer so typical, at least not in Western societies.[244]

It has also been claimed that it is not yet scientifically proven that children can be hampered in their development if they are the product of AID applied on lesbian women living single or in a couple relationship. It is said that it is the quality of the family relationship and not the sexual orientation of the mother, which is decisive for the child's development. Statistical data reveal that in 1997 there were about 40,000 children in Sweden living with homosexual parents[245] and that there has not been any evidence that their development has been inauspicious. Also an American Psychological Association study has concluded that children of homosexual parents turn out "no better or worse than children of heterosexuals".[246]

It has been, however, admitted that there are no long-term studies on the subject. This research has, therefore, been widely criticised as unreliable and as not being representative enough.[247]

Yet another argument that has been used with a certain frequency by the Strasbourg organs,[248] in their case law as well as in domestic jurisdictions focuses on biology, is that same-sex couples cannot bring children into being.[249] This

---

model or experience for children as does male-female parenting, "because there is an overabundance of information about one gender and little information about the other gender". However, Dr. Pruett concludes that parents' sexual orientation does not disqualify them from being good, fit and loving parents. (Ibid., § 25, § 27, § 33) Also Dr. Brodzinsky testified that research shows that the sexual orientation of parents is not an indicator of parental fitness. Ibid., § 104. According to a third expert, Dr. Bidwell, lesbian and gay parents raise children that "are just as healthy and well-adjusted as those raised by different-sex couples". Ibid., § 113.

Of relevance to mention further is that only the minority of the Commission on Sexual Orientation in Hawaii expressed serious concern about the adverse effect that the legalisation of homosexual marriage will have on the social, sexual and psychological development of children. State of Hawaii, Report of the Commission on Sexual Orientation and the Law, 1996, <http://www.hawaii.gov/lrb/cpt6.html>.

243 *D. Herman*, Rights of Passage-Struggles for Lesbian & Gay Legal Equality, p. 147.

244 *W.M. Hohengarten*, Same -sex marriage and the right to privacy, The Yale Law Journal 1994, Vol. 103, p. 1513.

245 *H. Andersson*, p. 7; Aftonbladet, 28 April 1997, p. 23. In the Netherlands approximately 20,000 lesbian and gay couples are living on a durable basis and also caring for children. *P. Vlaardingerbroek*, Changing Family Forms and the Law of Succession, paper prepared for the ISFL Conference in Durban 1997.

246 *E. Rudulph*, p. 69.

247 SOU 1993:98, Del A, p. 26.

248 See, for example, the comments made in the essay of *G. Cohen-Jonathan*, p. 432, note 111.

249 The slogan of Women's International Task Force (Terra Femina) at Beijing was "Humankind is made up of two sexes and this difference is the mainspring of life". Another somewhat to the above mentioned connected argument is based on the idea that same-sex partnership cannot contribute to society in comparable manner as heterosexual families do. In other words: "Eine homosexuelle Lebensgemeinschaft kann einer Ehe mit all ihren rechtlichen, sozialen und gesellschaftlichen Folgen nicht gleichgestellt werden, da sie keinen vergleichbaren Beitrag für die Gesellschaft leisten kann". *H. Neisser*, Editorial, in B. Verschraegen, Gleichgeschlechtliche "Ehen", p. 7.

proposition has been opposed by, for example, Dr. Eggebeen in the *Baehr v. Miike* case, on the grounds that people marry and want to get married for reasons other than having children and that those reasons are "valuable and important".[250] As an additional counter-argument it has been asked "Since heterosexual couples can be adoptive parents and become parents through AID, why not homosexuals?". It has also been mentioned in this regard that stepparents who, even though not the biological parents, love, care for and stimulate children.

Despite dramatic social changes in the Western world signifying greater tolerance towards gay people and lesbians, it is still my conviction that in decision-making about availability of new procreative technologies, the overriding principle should be that the interests of the child are of paramount importance. I very much agree with the reasoning behind the proposed governmental bill on artificial procreation and on paternity by the Ministry of Justice in Finland in regard to the requirements expected of a heterosexual couple, that a balanced life for the expected child ought to be ensured.[251] It is a great advantage for a child to be brought up by a couple with the different roles of different sexes, and society should not contribute to situations, which from the very beginning are divergent. They are essential for the full development of the child's character and personality, apart from material welfare.

5.3.3.3.3. *Post Mortem* Insemination

Even though the use of the partner's cryo-preserved semen after his death or of sperm retrieval from the dead partner are rare, such practices have been in recent years intensively debated as, for example, in the United Kingdom, in the USA and in Israel.[252] Some of the reasons behind the controversy are the circumstances[253] under which such procedures have taken place. It has been pointed out that where the consent of the deceased man is absent, such a procedure resembles "an embezzlement".[254]

Several of the arguments presented in the sub-chapter above could also be used to suggest that *post mortem* insemination should be banned in international law. It can be claimed, for example, that there is so far no recognised right in human rights

---

250 *Baehr v. Miike*, ibid., § 46.

251 CEDAW Convention, Second periodic report by Finland, Helsinki 1993, p. 71.

252 Sperma tas från döda män, SvD, 29 December 1996, p. 8; Fick barn med döde maken. Aftonbladet, 21 Maj 1998, p. 12; Nyfödd–men pappan dog för fyra år sedan, Expressen, 8 April 1999, p. 13.

253 In the well-known case of Diane Blood the sperm was taken through invasive procedure and frozen while the husband was lying on a life support machine, *i.e.*, he was unconscious and there was no written consent. Despite the court's finding that the procedure is illegal and that it should not have taken place, Mrs. Blood won the litigation and the IVF procedure was completed not in the UK but in a Belgian clinic. As at the time of writing Mrs. Blood has announced that she is pregnant and awaiting to give birth to the child conceived with the sperm of her dead husband at the beginning of 1999. TT-Reuter, 28 June 1998. The case was reported also in the Swedish press: Döde makens sperma insemineras, SvD, 7 February 1998, p. 5. The recent birth (March 1999) of the baby Brandolyne Vernoff in Los Angeles, who was conceived posthumously, has been criticised on ethical grounds. See, *e.g.*, Scottish Daily Mail, 17 July 1998, p. 2.

254 *Di Renzo, Cosmi & Caserta*, p. 33.

law for widows to demand access to stored gametes or embryos. This would be valid for ET to widows even though the right to family planning as guaranteed in international law implies a right for the individuals who form part of a couple to decide *when* to have a child, *e.g.*, to control the timing of childbearing. It can be also argued from a gender perspective that since a pregnancy achieved through *post-mortem* insemination would affect the woman's body, she should not be hindered in her decision to give birth to the couple's child, by imposing a husband's veto in the shape of requiring his consent.

In my view a sound family life requires the natural continuity of the generations. A child conceived posthumously will in most jurisdictions not only be disregarded for the purpose of succession to and inheritance from the father, but it will also deliberately be denied an upbringing with a father.

For some of these reasons CAHBI rejected the idea of the legalisation of *post mortem* insemination. Among the explanations for such a prohibition[255] the Committee mentioned:

> "(t)he first and most important one is that, in the case of post-mortem procreation, the future child is condemned at the outset to be born without a father. This fact is certainly not in harmony with the condition laid down in Principle I, paragraph 1, as to the existence of conditions ensuring the welfare of the child. In addition to this…(s)uch practice would also create serious legal problems of paternity and inheritance rights to which the present state of civil law of most member states would provide no satisfactory answer".[256]

Apart from the profound psychological problems arising, posthumous insemination leads to different children being accorded different status. This would in my view be incompatible with the extensive interpretation of Article 8 of the European Convention articulated by the European Court on Human Rights in the *Johnston v. Ireland* case,[257] as well as with the principle of the best interests of the child as guaranteed by the UN Convention on the Rights of the Child.[258] It demands that children should receive equal treatment without distinctions of any kind, such as, *e.g.*, birth status, which includes children being born in or out of wedlock as well as a result of artificial insemination.

On the national level legal regulation of the issue at hand varies among countries. According to the 1997 Danish Act on Assisted Reproduction the man's semen

---

[255] In principle 7§ 4 it is stated that "Artificial procreation with the semen of the deceased husband or companion shall not be allowed". Council of Europe, Human Artificial Procreation, p. 37.

[256] Council of Europe, op. cit., p. 24.

[257] *Johnston et al. v Republic of Ireland*, ECHR Judgment of 18 December 1986, Ser. A. No. 112.

[258] For a discussion on the principle "best interests of the child" see *S.A. Wolfson*, The Theoretical Underpinning of the "Best Interests of the Child", in The Ideologies of Children's Rights, M. Freeman & P. Veerman (eds.), Dordrecht 1992, pp. 7–29; *J. Wolf*, The Concept of the "Best Interest" in Terms of the UN Convention on the Rights of the Child, ibid., pp. 125–135; *G. Van Bueren*, The International Law on the Rights of the Child, pp. 45–51.

should be destroyed during a process of assisted procreation in the event of the man's death.[259] The same applies to the use of eggs of deceased women. In Germany *post-mortem* insemination is, in addition, unlawful.[260] On the other hand *post-mortem* insemination is allowed ten months after the death of the husband in Spain.[261]

It ought also to be mentioned here that cases dealing with the question of the lawfulness of *post mortem* insemination have been tried in domestic courts, *e.g.*, *Parpalaix v CECOS et Federation Francaise des Centres d'Etudes et de Conservation du Sperme* case in France. The court reached the conclusion that, since one of the aims of marriage is procreation, nothing in natural law prohibits the use of *post mortem* insemination.[262] A few years later (in 1994) new legislation was enacted in France banning posthumous insemination and according to which both members of the couple must be alive and consent in order to have access to a procedure of medically assisted procreation.

To conclude, the national attitudes towards *post-mortem* insemination differ but it seems that there is a growing consensus today within Europe for its proscription. This is an additional legal area in which norm-setting activity within international human rights law is needed.

5.3.3.3.4. Conclusions

The sub-chapter above has clearly illustrated that medical advances have challenged our traditional views of family, parentage and sexuality.[263] The twentieth century has been an era of rapid change; there has been a gradual expansion in family law in several jurisdictions to accommodate cohabiting heterosexual unions as well as lesbians and gay men couples.

Given the controversial nature of the issue and despite a growing consensus that discrimination against homosexuals should not be tolerated, legislations and courts (national as well as international) have been as a rule reluctant to accord homosexuals the same rights as heterosexual persons in several fields of law. While the European Commission and the European Court of Human Rights have dealt, for example, with issues of legal recognition of gender change, parental rights of transsexuals etc,[264] both organs have upheld the traditional understanding of marriage as a heterosexual union.

The non-discrimination principle has, moreover, not yet been expanded as to respond to changes in societies. The European Court has so far preferred to abstain from determining an issue, which falls within the ambit of Article 14 once the

---

[259] *L. Nielsen & A. Kronborg*, p. 137.

[260] *L. Nielsen*, Room for Harmonisation?, p. 310.

[261] *G.G. Cantero*, Gleichheit vor dem Recht, Spanien, in Gleichheit im Familienrecht, B. Verschraegen (ed.), p. 139.

[262] *D. Morgan & R.G. Lee*, Human Fertilization and Embryology Act 1990, London 1991, p. 29.

[263] *K. Mck. Norrie*, p. 767.

[264] *G. Van Bueren*, Annual Review of International Family Law, in The International Survey of Family Law 1996, A. Bainham (ed.), The Hague 1998, p. 6.

matter has been resolved under another provision of the Convention. Only the HRC has included sexual orientation within the prohibition of discrimination on the grounds of "sex" contained in the ICCPR. On the whole, however, the *Dudgeon*, the *Modinos*, the *Sutherland* and the *Toonen* cases to name but a few, bear witness that homosexual rights issues are on the current international human rights agenda.

While several countries have guaranteed cohabiting couples of the same-sex virtually identical treatment to legally married persons in many areas that are not linked to marriage,[265] *e.g.*, matrimonial property,[266] in inheritance, social security, taxation regimes, labour law, pension provisions, immigration and adoption,[267] procreative matters are as a rule excluded. I have in this regard addressed several of the ethical and legal problems linked to assisted reproduction. This author has been able to demonstrate that contrasting views exist on issues about the acceptability of AID, of surrogacy, of insemination of single (including lesbian) women, of the anonymity of donors, etc. Alongside with that there is a high level of agreement that artificial insemination should not be performed on persons who are not living as a stable heterosexual couple, or on a woman over the age of 45–50[268] or after a partner's death. I may give some examples here. In Sweden there is a general consensus in favour of prohibiting egg donation as a form of treatment for women who have passed the menopause out of consideration for the child, as well as on the grounds that it "involves a method beyond that permitted by nature".[269] Also in Denmark the 1997 Act on Assisted Procreation stipulates that artificial reproduction may not take place when the applicant is older than 45 years.[270]

This leads us to the conclusion that reproductive freedom in the context of modern procreative techniques does not imply that there is in international law a recognised right to have children whatever the circumstances are. In other words, the new techniques of assisted procreation are not available to everyone who desires their use.

---

[265] I agree with Judge Levinson in the *Baehr v. Lewin* case that it is difficult to produce well-founded arguments based on the consideration of the gender-equality principle that same-sex marriages are suspect on the grounds of discrimination on the basis of sex, since in my view marriage law treats men and women equally. For the opposite standpoint, see the majority ruling in the *Baehr v. Miike* case. There are, in addition, writers who presuppose that "the best strategy for attaining equality from a feminist as well as lesbian perspective was to get straight people to stop marrying rather than to change the law to permit lesbian and gay people to be able to marry". *R. Colker*, p. 323.

[266] *J.F. Haderka*, p. 225.

[267] New Jersey became the first state within the USA to explicitly allow lesbian and gay couples to adopt children jointly. Previously, homosexuals in the state could adopt only as individuals. The new court-affirmed agreement implies that homosexual couples must be treated as full equals with heterosexual couples also in the area of child rearing. Nevertheless, adoption policy is made case by case. *E. Rudulph*, p. 69.

[268] On the other hand in Italy there is no age condition for access to assisted conception. *G. Ferrando*, Artificial Insemination in Italy, in Creating the Child, D. Evans (ed.), p. 264; *L. Nielsen*, Legal consensus and divergence in Europe in the area of assisted conception- room for harmonisation?, pp. 309 and 311.

[269] SOU 1994:37, p. 43; The Council for Medical Ethics, citation in *Å. Saldeen*, Rights of the unborn child, p. 481.

[270] *L. Nielsen & A. Kronborg*, p. 136.

In spite of that refusal to offer access to procreative services to lesbian couples who wish to have them, donor insemination has been considered as a discrimination on the grounds of sexual orientation and that "to deny equality of treatment to relationships which will not procreate appears perverse".[271] Consideration of the issue from the feminist perspective has urged scholars to claim that: "if we are to construct a feminist international law that adequately addresses the human rights of all women-that allows for the construction of identities different from the norm-it must respond far more fully to the abuse of lesbians".[272] This argument can apply also to women who have passed the natural menopause age (*i.e.*, all human rights instruments refer to "everyone" regardless of age), women infected with HIV[273] and people suffering from physical and intellectual handicaps. It has been argued that a blanket rule excluding a whole category of people would be difficult to justify on the basis of existing human rights norms. In the words of Professor Nowak "Because the right to found a family,..(i)s guaranteed without express proviso, the *permissibility of State restrictions* on…(a)rtificial procreation is *to be interpreted narrowly*".[274] Also other scholars have taken the view that it would be unjust to uphold that unmarried and single women are less capable of raising a child than married couples who raise unwanted and unexpected children.[275]

The availability of AI techniques is, furthermore, selective in that the state makes priorities if it provides the resources. Access to the benefits of some techniques such as IVF are often related to the ability to pay since such treatment is generally excluded from health insurance coverage.[276] Application of the equality test may, however, require that, in order to ensure equal opportunity to become a parent, economic barriers or alternative forms of reproduction, such as the cost of donor insemination, *in vitro* fertilisation, or embryo transfer, must be lessened.

Even so it seems that there is agreement within the scholarly writings that in the context of modern forms of artificial procreation, limitations and restrictions with regard to access to techniques for medically assisted procreation, can be viewed as permissible if they are necessary to protect the rights of others, *i.e.*, the child to be born. This would mean that marital status, age and the sexual orientation of women can be considered as acceptable grounds for the limitation of their reproductive freedom.

It is also important at the same time that in jurisdictions where there are no limitations on reproductive freedom, children born as a result of the new birth technologies are not discriminated against, in spite of the fact that a single/lesbian

---

[271] See for reference *G. Van Bueren*, The Challenges for the International Protection of Family Members' Rights as the 21st Century Approaches, p. 5.

[272] *J. Dorf & G.C. Pérez*, p. 332.

[273] As earlier mentioned some countries, among them France and the United Kingdom do not allow AID treatment of unfertile couples with HIV. *J. Dorf & G.C. Pérez*, p. 328.

[274] *M. Nowak*, CCPR Commentary, p. 414.

[275] *J. Sándor*, p. 162.

[276] In Sweden IVF is considered as a borderline category, for which the public funds may cover the costs. *I. Martin*, p. 250.

mother is the only legal parent.[277] In procreation matters, when AID is used, the donor's identity is kept secret in most domestic jurisdictions. It has been asserted[278] that infertile couples, among others, are reluctant to be treated if the donor is identifiable. This situation can in my view hardly be judged as compatible with international human rights law. Thus, the conclusions of the European Court of Human Rights in the *Gaskin v. UK* case[279] are of significance in this respect. In accordance with the European Commission's interpretation of Article 8, saying that "everyone should be able to establish details of their identity as individual human beings and that in principle they should not be obstructed by the authorities from obtaining such very basic information without specific justification",[280] the European Court has ruled that the interests of the individual seeking access to records relating to his private and family life must be secured when a contributor to the records is either not available or improperly refuses consent. By analogy we may argue that every child shall have access to information identifying its biological father.[281] In the case of children conceived with the use of AID, the biological father is excluded from legal paternity. He is relieved of any obligations towards the child[282] and the child will be in theory and practice fatherless. In the case of normal couples the social parent is to be the legal parent and this is not the case when a single (lesbian) woman becomes a mother with the help of AID. Therefore, the rationale for not making AID permissible for single/lesbian woman, *i.e.*, the paramount importance of a father, seems reasonable.

Developments in science have produced dilemmas that are awaiting legal solutions on the national as well as on the international level. Profound changes demand matching changes in law and practice. There is a need, therefore, of clear

---

[277] Professor Cook has also referred to some of the implications of the denial of equal rights for same-sex relationships for children, *i.e.*, that a parent's same sex partner cannot legally be recognised as a step-parent to adopt or take care of the child in, *e.g.*, a situation of the parent's death. *R.J. Cook*, Human Rights and Reproductive Self-Determination, The American University Law Review 1995, Vol. 44, p. 1010.

[278] *J. Masson & C. Harrison*, Identity: Mapping the Frontiers, paper presented at the VIIIth World Conference of the International Society of Family Law, Cardiff 1994, p. 8. In Great Britain HUEFA (The Human Fertilization and Embryology Act of 1990) provides that where a child is born as a result of donated gametes, the legal father is the mother's husband or partner unless he did not consent to the procedure or it did not take place at a licensed clinic. According to this act, individuals have a right after the age of 18 to know whether they were or (might have been) born as a result of treatment and may be provided with non-identifying information. In other words, the person will not be able to find out the donor's identity. See *D. Morgan & R. Lee*, pp. 162–167.

[279] *Gaskin case*, ECHR Judgment of 7 July 1989, Ser. A, No. 160.

[280] *Supra,* § 39. As regards recovery of identity, Article 8(2) of the Convention on the Rights of the Child provides: "Where a child is illegally deprived of some or all of the elements of his or her identity, States Parties shall provide appropriate assistance and protection with a view to speedily reestablishing his or her identity".

[281] Ibid., § 49.

[282] In the case *G v. The Netherlands*, Application No. 16944/90 the European Commission on Human Rights concluded that the biological link between a semen donor and the conceived child is not in itself sufficient ground to guarantee the donor a right to respect for family life with the child on the basis of the European Convention. Of some interest in this regard is the European Court's decision in the *Kroon v The Netherlands* case. See ECHR Judgment of 27 October 1994, Ser. A, Vol. 197–C.

articulation of the non-discrimination principle on the norm-setting level as well as on the norm using level in the context of procreation.

The increased internationalisation of life has made it possible that, *e.g.*, within the European Union, European citizens may seek medical treatment within its member states. As Professor Deech[283] has rightly observed, in the question of fertility this may allow "forum shopping" for the least regulated clinics. Reality has thus pushed us into a state of a *fait accompli*. There is, therefore, a strong need to seek harmonisation of legislation to regulate practices across national borders. The preamble of the 1997 European Convention on Human Rights and Biomedicine underlines "the need for international co-operation so that all humanity may enjoy the benefits of biology and medicine". A general recognition of the need for international co-operation in "order to ensure that mankind as a whole benefits from the life sciences and to prevent them from being used for any purpose other than the good of mankind" has in addition found expression in the conclusions contained in the 1995 UN Report on Human Rights and Bioethics.[284]

Our discussion has shown that international law has not addressed most of the issues raised by the new reproductive technologies and some of them are even unregulated on the domestic level.[285] Since they challenge basic values, which underlie human rights, the regulatory gaps are in the view of this author unfortunate. With a great degree of probability they may contribute to the upcoming of a highly lucrative, discriminatory commercial fertility industry.

Some of the reasons behind this reality are that the legislative process and the process of realisation of already existing human rights norms in international law are very slow. This is a fact that has been acknowledged on several occasions, *e.g.*, as in the following statement: "the rapid development of science and its technological applications which have taken place in recent decades have not been accompanied by an appropriately *urgent, profound and continuous consideration* of their implications for human rights".[286] (italics added) Thus international law fails often to respond quickly to new developments in society and medicine and sometimes international human rights bodies even try to avoid difficult moral aspects in their decision-making and/or in their supervisory activities.

All this speaks in favour of my assertion that a dynamic, contextual interpretation of existing human rights norms should be encouraged. It would help revitalise existing standards and at the same time it may also lead to strengthening the value of the newly adopted consensual documents which are more reflective of current realities.

---

283 *R. Deech*, Oral presentation made at the ISFL Conference in Durban 1997.

284 UN Doc. E/CN.4/1995/74, § 154.

285 Professor Nielsen has on the basis of the existing extensive national differences in regard to legal solutions of the issues under discussion concluded that the possibility of "a comprehensive policy, or of legislation encompassing all of the problems related to fertility, infertility and the human embryo" even within the EU "may never be forthcoming". *L. Nielsen*, Legal consensus and divergence in Europe in the area of assisted conception- room for harmonisation?, p. 316.

286 *Supra*, note 284, § 152.

### *5.3.4. Women's Right not to Procreate*

#### *5.3.4.1. Contraception*

While the emphasis of human reproduction has in human rights law traditionally been put on non-interference, non-intervention and freedom from governmental control,[287] the increased concern for women's health and gender equality as expressed in contemporary international law documents has moved the focus towards the demand to provide couples and individuals with the means[288] which are necessary for the exercise of reproductive freedom. In other words, the right to obtain family planning information and services will enable them to limit, space the number of children as well as to remain childless if so desired.

One of the first international documents[289] acknowledging family planning as a basic human right declared: "We believe that the majority of parents desire to have the knowledge and *the means* to plan their families; that the opportunity to decide the number and spacing of children is a basic human right" (italics added). Paragraph 41 of the Vienna Declaration and Programme of Action reaffirms, furthermore, women's' right "to accessible and adequate health care and the widest range of family planning services".[290] A distinctive feature for pronouncements of this kind is that they do not determine the term "means". Neither do they specify any particular form of family planning services as required.[291] While the consensus documents resulting from the recent UN Conferences confirm that access to contraceptives and a free and informed choice of methods for family planning have been accepted world-wide as fundamental human rights,[292] one issue remains unresolved

---

[287] In other words, national laws tolerating coercive practices such as forced sterilisation and forced abortions would constitute, as I shall demonstrate below, a violation of the right to found a family/to family planning as well as of the right to health.

[288] The content of the term "means" includes material products as well as services. This does not, however, imply as Packer has observed that governments are obliged to "provide *all* kinds of family planning services nor any *particular* kind of service". (Italics added) *C.A.A. Packer*, p. 70. Another writer draws the conclusion on the basis of the relevant international documents that governments are expected not to intervene to prevent people from "obtaining or using a contraceptive method". *R. Dixon-Mueller*, p. 13.

[289] Declaration on Population adopted on 10 December 1966 by World Leaders. See Human Rights Aspects of Population Programmes, UNESCO 1977, p. 110.

[290] UN Doc. A/CONF.157/23,1993, p. 19. Paragraph 7.2 of the Cairo Programme of Action stipulates that in order to ensure reproductive health, women and men must have "access to safe, effective, affordable and acceptable methods of family planning of their choice". Similarly § 94 of the Beijing Platform for Action explains that reproductive health comprises a right for men and women "to be informed and to have access to safe, effective, affordable and acceptable methods of family planning of their choice".

[291] Among the mentioned methods of fertility regulation which states ought to guarantee in accordance with § 4 of the 1989 NGO-Guidelines for Distribution and Use of Fertility Regulation Methods (WEMOS), we may find the following: "hormonal methods, barrier methods such as condoms and diaphragms, natural methods, sterilization and safe abortion services". The text of the document is reprinted in A Thematic Guide to Documents on the Human Rights of Women, *G. Alfredsson & K. Tomaševski* (eds.), pp. 249–251.

[292] A right to have access to contraception can be claimed on the basis of, *e.g.*, Article 12 of the Women's Convention, which provides for: "access to health care services, including those related to family planning". CEDAW recommended at its session in 1993 states parties to the Convention to: "(a)dvise on whether safe and reliable methods of contraception are available to women" in the respective countries. UN Doc. E/CN.6/1993/CRP.2, § 47.

and it continues to be a subject for controversy internationally as well as nationally, namely access to abortion services. For these reasons and because of the wealth of literature[293] on the topic of the use of contraceptives, I shall in the following very briefly touch on some gender equality aspects of access to contraceptives. I shall explore instead more comprehensively the question of whether there is enough support for the preposition[294] that access to abortion services is an essential ingredient of the right to family planning as articulated in recent UN's consensual documents, thereby constituting an important element of reproductive freedom.

In treaty law the negative element of the right to family planning, as stipulated in Article 16(1)(e) of the Women's Convention,[295] infers first and foremost a freedom for the individual to decide *not*[296] to have a child at a certain point of time as well as to choose to remain childless.[297] The right to choose not to have children at all is consequently an integral part of women's reproductive freedom.[298] Such an interpretation of the relevant provision was given by CEDAW at its session in 1993 in a comment on the content of Article 16 (1)(e) as follows:

> "Women's right to full and free exercise of their reproductive functions, including the right to decide whether to have children or *not,* must not be limited by spouse or government, and women must also be guaranteed access to information about safe contraceptive methods, sex education and family planning services" (italics added).[299]

A self-evident interpretation of the right to family planning has been that it demands equal access to family planning services for men and women, *i.e.,* women

---

[293] The World Health Organisation's Publications catalogue "Women and Health" gives a good idea of the great number of published books on that topic. A more recent publication ought, however, to be mentioned here: *A. Hardon & E. Hayes* (ed.), Reproductive Rights in Practice, A Feminist Report on the Quality of Care, London 1997. For general and more specific information see <http://www.law-lib.utoronto.ca/diana>.

[294] *R. Dixon-Mueller*, p. 4.

[295] The text of the article reads as follows: "States parties shall take all appropriate measures to eliminate discrimination against women in all matters relating to marriage and family relations and in particular shall ensure, on a basis of equality of men and women: the same rights to decide freely and responsibly on the number and spacing of their children and to have access to the information, education and means to enable them to exercise these rights".

[296] As regards the right not to procreate, distinction is often upheld between non-abortifacient procedures, such as contraception and contragestion on the one hand, and abortion on the other.

[297] A number of studies carried out by family planning administrators in various countries disclose, however, that most of the people who use contraceptives intend to postpone rather than to avoid future conception.

[298] Several feminist writers have, however, expressed deep disappointment with the feminist movement for not making the choice not to have children as a *fundamental* part of a feminist agenda. Instead, they say, "maternal revivalism" has occurred which has even been extended to the lesbian community. See Childless by Choice: A Feminist Anthology, *I. Reti* (ed.), Santa Cruz 1992.

[299] UN Doc. E/CN.6/1993/CRP.2, 25 February 1993, § 46. See, in addition, the earlier mentioned General Recommendation No. 21, (§ 22) adopted by CEDAW, UN Doc. A/49/38 as well as UN Doc. CEDAW/C/1995/7, § 465.

shall have the right to obtain contraceptives without spousal authorisation.[300] Thus, domestic legislations providing for a veto right for the husband, as regards his wife's use of contraceptives, constitute gender bias and are clearly contrary to the right of non-discrimination on the grounds of the sex and the gender-equality principle.[301] Professor Cook has, in addition, argued that denial of access to means of fertility control for women constitutes a violation of the liberty of persons as defined in a number of human rights treaties.[302]

It is quite obvious that whether women will be able or not to assert their right to make a free choice of a fertility regulation method has very much to do with gender relations as well as with their ability to exercise other human rights.[303] In strong patriarchal regimes marked by male dominance, there is very little or no room at all for woman's decision making with regard to contraceptives' use. A study performed in Egypt illustrates this assertion well. After a law reform was carried out in 1982, which repealed spousal veto for women who wished to attend family planning clinics, the number of female clients had increased by 26% immediately.[304]

Nevertheless, husband disapproval is only one among several reasons why women do not use or stop using contraceptives. Social pressures, religious beliefs as well as concern about health complications are mentioned as further reasons.[305] The last mentioned reason could be one explanation why the most widespread applied contraceptive method throughout the world still is sterilisation, with an estimated use of about 70%[306] in some countries. What causes most concern in this regard is that there is little sufficient and reliable information, as well as statistical, evidence available as to the extent of coercion and discriminatory treatment that occurs in the performance of sterilisations. The incidence of sterilisation of women

---

300 *R.J. Cook & J.M. Haws*, The United Nations Convention on the Rights of Women: Opportunities for Family Planning Providers, International Family Planning Perspectives 1986, Vol. 12, p. 50.

301 For examples of currently existing restrictions in terms of spousal consent upheld by law and/or governmental policies see *A. Hardon*, p. 17. See also *K. Tomaševski*, Human Rights in Population Policies, p. 43. Such a requirement exists in the domestic jurisdictions of, *e.g.*, Gambia, Papua and New Guinea. See *Commonwealth Secretariat*, The Convention on the Elimination of All Forms of Discrimination Against Women, The Reporting Process–A Manual for Commonwealth Jurisdiction, London 1988, p. 26. Generally in countries, where Sharia'(t) is the rule of law, spousal consultation for women's access to family planning services is required. See *R.J. Cook & D. Maine*, p. 340.

302 *R.J. Cook*, International Protection of Women's Reproductive Rights, p. 697.

303 At the beginning of 1970s a consensus was reached within the UN that the ability to regulate "the timing and number of births is one central means of freeing women to exercise the full range of human rights to which they are entitled". Study on the Interrelationship of the Status of Women and Family Planning, UN Doc. E/CN.6/575/Rev.1, 1973. See in addition *R.J. Cook*, *supra*, note 302, p. 684 and *M.K. Eriksson*, The Right to Marry and to Found a Family, p. 142 *et seq.*; *R. Dixon-Mueller*, p. 13.

304 *K. Tomaševski*, Women and Human Rights, p. 19.

305 UN, The World's Women 1995, Trends and Statistics, New York 1995, p. 19. For extensive and well-researched information (including further references) on contraceptive use and their availability see *S. Coliver & S. Gruskin*, Global Overview, in The Right to Know, S. Coliver (ed.), p. 89 ff. and *A. Hardon*, Setting the Stage: Health, Fertility and Unmet Need in Eight Countries, in Reproductive Rights in Practice, A. Hardon & E. Hayes (eds.), pp. 22–31.

306 *K. Tomaševski*, Human rights in family planning, unpublished paper, SIDA, Stockholm, April 1993, p. 3.

without their informed consent seems to be a major issue in, *e.g.*, India, Brazil and Mexico.[307]

From the gender perspective it is apparent that existing international human rights norms *per se* (*i.e.*, their ordinary meaning)[308] and states' practices do not reflect an asymmetrical approach to gender equality in regard to the availability and choice alternatives for the use of various contraceptives. The burden of contraception continues to fall disproportionately upon women. There are many more means of contraceptive intervention for women than for men,[309] which in practice inhibits equal access for men and women to contraception. A related issue, which has been raised by feminists, concerns women's health. It has been rightly claimed that women are more exposed to health risks than men are,[310] *e.g.*, in connection with the use of certain fertility regulation methods such as hormonal pills, hormonal injections, IUDs etc. Feminists have also charged that "most of the research has been done on female methods because male scientists are reluctant to pursue technologies that put men at any risk from side effects or that might be perceived as interfering with male sexuality".[311] There is a clear need for expanding the range of contraceptive methods to be offered to men. This might, of course, result in the limitation of what some authors have called woman's "actual power" to make a man father or not.[312]

To succeed in family planning, services must, in addition to being available, include balanced, objective information about method options. Free and informed choice is, therefore, one of the other very important elements of reproductive freedom to be discussed next.

### *5.3.4.2. Freedom of Information*

#### 5.3.4.2.1. Achieving Universal Consensus

Information and education[313] are crucial components of reproductive health, making informed consent and responsible, voluntary, deliberate choices about childbearing and parenting possible. Knowledge of human rights is indispensable

---

[307] IWRAW, Human Rights in the Family, January 1993, p. 19. Nevertheless, a new law was enacted in 1995 in Brazil outlawing such practices. The authorities are obliged according to its provisions to investigate claims of coercion, fraud or misinformation in the procurement of consent to sterilisation. *R. Reichmann*, Brazil, in The Right to Know, S. Coliver (ed.), p. 125; *A.O. Ortega, A. Amuchástegui & M. Rivas*, "Because They Were Born From Me", in Negotiating Reproductive Rights, R.P. Petchesky & K. Judd (eds.), p. 163.

[308] On the other hand, CEDAW has taken into consideration the inequitable burdens of work on women in connection with the raising of children as well as the effect that childrearing can have on their education and personal development by the elaboration of its General Recommendation No. 21. In § 21 it is stipulated that "Women are entitled to decide on the number and spacing of their children".

[309] This is also valid for the situation in Western countries. See, *e.g.*, Facts in Brief, Women and Reproductive Health in the United States, The Alan Guttmacher Institute, New York and Washington 1994.

[310] WHO, Women's Health, Improve our Health, Improve the World, Geneva 1995, p. 21.

[311] *R. Dixon-Mueller*, p. 48.

[312] *M.T. Meudelrs-Klein*, p. 133.

[313] Lack of access to education leads to ignorance about information regarding health care and family planning. Illiteracy affects maternal health and decision making. A number of studies show that illiterate

for their exercise, since its absence is the best environment for their violations. In other words, possessing information on the rights that women should enjoy enables women to demand them. It gives them power and provides them with the ability to master their own destiny. The need to provide women with information on their rights was recognised long ago within the international community. Access to family planning information and quality family planning services was specifically referred to as a "long recognised basic right for all individuals"[314] at the 1993 World Conference on Human Rights in Vienna.[315] Mentioned among the main objectives of the ICPD Programme of Action is the improvement of the "quality of family planning advice, information, education, communication, counselling and services" (§ 7.14(d)). Also the Beijing Platform for Action places reliable counselling, accessible information, especially on sexuality and reproduction, among the actions to be taken by governments (§ 107(e)). In addition, one of the UN's critical areas of concern in the Medium-term Plan for the Advancement of Women (1996–2001) constitutes reproductive health. This part of the document is based on a pragmatic and participatory approach with the goal of providing individuals and couples with access to information and services to prevent unwanted pregnancies "that are too early, too closely spaced or too late".[316]

In international treaty law, women's right to information and counselling on family planning is explicitly expressed in among others Articles 10(h),[317] 14(2)(b) and 16(e) of the Women's Convention.[318] Several other universal[319] as well as

---

women tend to have more children at shorter intervals between them and that educated women give birth to fewer children as their level of education increases. *S. Bergström & A. Molin,* International maternal health care 1993. Advanced international training programme. Poverty and reproductive health, Uppsala 1994, p. 26. See also *R. Dixon-Mueller*, p. 122. On education as a powerful means for the empowerment of women see *K. Tomaševski*, Women and Human Rights, pp. 24–30. For an ample analysis of the rights regarding information and education in the context of reproductive rights see *R.J. Cook*, International Protection of Women's Reproductive Rights, pp. 710–719; *R.J. Cook*, Human Rights and Reproductive Self-Determination, The American University Law Review 1995, pp. 1011–1013; *L.P. Freedman*, Censorship and Manipulation of Reproductive Health Information, in The Right to Know, S. Coliver (ed.), pp. 1–31.

[314] The right to information on family planning was stipulated in Article 14(f) of the World Population Plan of Action, 1974 and in recommendation No. 25 of the World Population Plan of Action, 1984.

[315] UN Doc. A/CONF.157/6, p. 3.

[316] UN Doc. E/CN.6/1996/CRP.2, § 71.

[317] This provision ensures women access to "specific educational information to help to ensure the health and well-being of families, including information and advice on family planning". Packer suggests that in a systematic reading of Article 10(h) the word "access" used in the sense of seeking and receiving the desired information on family planning would, *e.g.*, lead to a broader interpretation of the text than otherwise would be possible if one only relies on its general meaning. As a consequence the same author believes that state parties should be obliged not to "hinder free approach to, or obstruct admission of, information" as well as to perform some activity/ies. *C.A.A. Packer*, p. 66. For a systematic interpretation of Article 16(1)(e) in conjunction with Article 10(h) see UN Doc. CEDAW/C/1995/7, § 465.

[318] CEDAW is explicit in its General Recommendation No. 21, § 22 that "In order to make an informed decision about safe and reliable contraceptive measures, women must have information about contraceptive measures and their use, and guaranteed access to sex education and family planning services, as provided in article 10(h) of the Convention".

[319] See Article 19(1) of the ICCPR, Article 12 of the ICESCR and Article 24(2)(f) of the UN Convention on the Rights of the Child.

regional treaties[320] on human rights contain, in addition, specific provisions as regards freedom of information as a right on its own merits (the right to seek, receive and impart information) regardless of frontiers.

From the feminist viewpoint it is apparent that only when women have full knowledge about the ramifications of accepting or rejecting a particular method of family planning, including explanations of medical procedures and their risks and benefits, can decision-making on reproduction be voluntary. Bearing this in mind, many of the delegations at recent UN Conferences insisted that the final documents should strongly recommend that access to family planning information/education never be restricted. In consequence states must not prohibit the dissemination of information on methods of fertility regulation, including information about abortion facilities.[321] Such a prohibition would infringe the freedom of expression as set out in the human rights conventions, which includes among other things the freedom to receive information. Denying women this right will seriously limit their ability to retain control over their health and their educational and social status.

The recent inclusion of reproductive health as a central component in women's human rights would, furthermore, infer an emerging right to non-directive counselling to enable women to make free, fully informed choices among various methods of fertility regulation as well as other health services. The international texts of a declarative nature also mean that women should require information and services not just in the reproductive ages but before[322] as well as after.

State practice is, of course, at variance in regard to accessibility to family planning information/education, and there is no fully reliable criterion to measure compliance with international law requirements in that respect. However, several studies support the proposition that the proportion of women who claim in various surveys to have knowledge of at least some contraceptive methods and where to obtain them has "grown remarkably" in most parts of the world with some few exceptions, such as sub-Saharan Africa.[323] I shall illustrate this situation by mentioning only one example of extensive information campaigns on family planning services, including abortion, which occur, *e.g.*, in Asia. In the province of Quang-Ninh (Vietnam), for example, there is a one-minute television programme every day, a television play every month and a page in the newspapers every week about these issues. In the mountainous, coastal and minority areas, where it is not common for most people to have access to TV, information is spread by loudspeakers in the rice fields.

---

320 The following provisions may be invoked to obtain family planning information: Article 10(1) of the European Convention, Article 13(1) of the American Convention on Human Rights and Article 9 of the African Charter.

321 Professor Cook has taken the position that "The attempt by public authorities, social agencies, and religious institutions to limit information regarding reproductive health services, including not only contraceptive and abortifacient methods, but also controversial means to increase the chance of having a child of a particular sex, discloses authoritarian instincts that are inimical to health protection and safety and, more corrosively, to individual liberty and social freedom". *R.J. Cook*, Human Rights and Reproductive Self-determination, p. 1011.

322 I shall return to the issue of adolescents' rights below.

323 *R. Dixon-Mueller*, p. 114.

Moreover, a magazine, "Happy Family", about family planning services is distributed to every family in Vietnam by the NCPFP (the National Committee on Population and Family Planning).

Since there is no case law pursuant to Article 19(2) of the ICCPR, neither have the inter-American human rights bodies rendered decisions of relevance and which could help us to clarify the framework of the right to family planning information, I shall below review the jurisprudence of the European judicial bodies on that matter.

5.3.4.2.2. The European Experience

The case law of the European judicial organs[324] indicates that the right to receive information should be paramount. At the same time the right can be limited (as the case is in other conventions) on the grounds of public health and morals. The European Court of Human Rights has often allowed a wide margin of appreciation,[325] *i.e.*, national authorities are given the power to decide that certain information should not be imparted because of its immoral nature, in matters of morality on the basis that a common European position is lacking. This has, however, not prevented the Court from scrutinising and materially reconsidering decisions made by domestic authorities in a particular case, *i.e.*, despite the country's (Ireland) justification of the prohibition of giving information on abortion on moral grounds.[326]

Despite the absence of any uniform policy in the member states of the European Union and the Council of Europe today, in the view of the cases I will refer to, there is a clear tendency towards a greater uniformity[327] of domestic legislation even on controversial issues. The existing case law of the European Court of Justice (ECJ) and the European Court of Human Rights concerns companies engaged in non-directive counselling of pregnant women in Ireland, including advice on obtaining abortions in clinics in the United Kingdom. The Supreme Court of Ireland has found such activities unconstitutional. The international judicial organs are of the view, however, that a ban on information about lawful services related to pregnancy and its termination constitutes a violation of the freedom of expression. Ireland has been the only member country in the European Community and the Council of Europe opposing legalised abortion. The question may be raised whether the EC law and the standards of the European Convention on Human Rights might not be able to decree the introduction of legal abortion services in

---

324 For an analysis of the case law of the European treaty bodies on matters of information see *S. Coliver*, The Right to Information Necessary for Reproductive Health and Choice under International Law, The American University Law Review 1995, Vol. 44, pp. 1279–1303.

325 On the different tests of determining whether a state has acted within its margin of appreciation see *P. van Dijk & G. van Hoof*, Theory and Practice of the European Convention on Human Rights, Deventer 1990, p. 588. See also the *Bowman v. The UK* case, ECHR Judgment of 19 February 1998.

326 *Open Door Counselling Ltd and Dublin Well Women vs Ireland*, ECHR Judgment of 24 March 1992, Ser. A, No. 246, § 61.

327 To achieve a harmonisation of the legal regimes of all the members of the EC as far as the abortion issue is concerned is not an easy task. On one side there are countries with a very conservative approach to abortion, *e.g.*, Belgium and Germany, and there are societies with more liberal views such as the Netherlands and the United Kingdom.

Ireland, since the binding decisions of the European organs do promote a uniform interpretation and application of the human rights guaranteed. The answer would today be that unfortunately this has not been the case yet.

Two cases against Ireland highlight some of the relevant aspects of the freedom of information question in relation to family planning. Both decisions uphold the right of women to receive information on abortion services without interference by the public authorities.

The first of these was the *Grogan case*.[328] It was decided by the Court of Justice of the European Communities. During the 1980s many pregnant women with unwanted pregnancies went to England for abortions. Information concerning abortion was available from a number of organisations. The Society for the Protection of Unborn Children (SPUC), a company, the purpose of which is to prevent the decriminalisation of abortion, sought to restrain the activities of two such organisations. Therefore, it submitted a case against a number of persons, who in their capacity as representatives of one of three students' associations published an annual guidebook with names, addresses, *etc.*, of a number of clinics in the United Kingdom, where services for the medical termination of pregnancy were available. The SPUC claimed that any publication of the aforementioned information is contrary to Article 40.3.3 of the Irish Constitution, where the right to life of the unborn child as from the moment of conception has been guaranteed. In addition to that argument, reference was made to the fact that Irish common and criminal law make it an offence to procure or attempt to procure an abortion, to administer an abortion or to assist in an abortion by supplying any noxious thing or instrument.[329] The European Court of Justice, after considering the merits of the case, delivered its judgment on 4 October 1991, in which it came to the conclusion that termination of pregnancy in the member states of the EC constitutes a medical activity, which is covered by the term (cross-border) "service" within the meaning of Article 60 of the Treaty of the European Economic Community. The Court rejected SPUC's argument that abortion is immoral and that it cannot come within the definition of service. In its view, since the information initiative was not connected with the promotion of the economic interests of abortion clinics,[330] the factual situation had to be seen merely as a manifestation of the freedom of expression. Implicitly, the ECJ acknowledged that there is a corollary right to receive information about a service, including abortion clinics. At the same time we may also notice that the emphasis was put by the Court on the drafter's intention to guarantee the fundamental freedom of consumers to receive services found in a member state. So, persons receiving medical treatment are recipients of services and are entitled to the benefit of the free movement provisions of the EEC treaty. Nevertheless, a right for women residing in

---

[328] Case C-159/90, *The Society for the Protection of Unborn Children Ireland Ltd v S. Grogan and Others*. The text of the decision has been reproduced in HRLJ 1991, Vol. 12, pp. 455–471.

[329] Sections 58 and 59 of the Offences against Person Act 1861.

[330] For this reason the Court could rule that a prohibition of the distribution of information did not constitute a restriction on the promotion of economic services within the meaning of Article 59 of the Treaty of Rome.

Ireland can be derived from European Community law – the provisions of the Treaty of Rome dealing with the freedom to provide services – to obtain information about abortion clinics in member states of the European Community and even to use the medical facilities in those countries in order to terminate their pregnancies. This interpretation of the Community law is very much consistent with the meaning of Article 10 of the European Convention on Human Rights,[331] according to which everyone has the right "to receive and to impart information and ideas without interference by public authority and regardless of frontiers". The European Convention is an important source also for the European Community legal order, though the ECJ does not consider itself bound by the European Convention. Of particular note as regards the case referred above is the Advocate-General Van Gerven's inclination against restricting a pregnant woman from travelling abroad to have abortion. In his view "Measures which would be disproportionate – in as much as they would excessively impede the freedom to supply services – would include for example a ban on pregnant women going abroad".[332] It has been asserted that his warning on restricting the movement of pregnant women influenced the adoption of the secret Protocol No. 17 to the Maastricht Treaty.[333] However, later developments compelled the Irish Government to launch the following Solemn Declaration: "This Protocol shall not limit the freedom to travel between member states or to obtain or make available in Ireland, in accordance with conditions which may be laid by Irish legislation, information relating to services lawfully available in Member States".

In consequence of the injunction,[334] which the Supreme Court of Ireland granted to the plaintiffs mentioned above, the defendants brought the case to the European Commission on Human Rights, on 19 August and 22 September 1988,[335] asking for determination as to whether the injunction amounts to an infringement of Article 10 of the European Convention. Both the European Commission and the Court reached the conclusion that the injunction constituted a breach of the freedom of expression. The European Court of Human Rights ruled in a decision of 29 October 1992 (by fifteen to eight votes)[336] that the existing ban in Ireland on counselling

---

[331] Human rights treaties of which member states are part, supply guidelines within the framework of the European Community law. See, *e.g.*, ECJ Judgment of 14 May 1974 in Case 4/73, *Nold v Commission* 1974, ECR 491, § 13.

[332] *Ibid.*, 3 CMLR, 1991, pp. 849 and 875, § 29.

[333] The protocol reads as follows: "Nothing in the Treaty of the European Union or in the Treaties establishing the European Communities or in the Treaties or Acts modifying or supplementing those Treaties shall affect the application in Ireland of Article 40.3.3. of the Constitution of Ireland". See *P. Ward*, Ireland: Abortion: "X" + "Y" = ?!, University of Louisville Journal of Family Law 1994–95, Vol. 33, p. 401; *J. Hadley*, Abortion, Between Freedom and Necessity, London 1996, p. 20.

[334] The Supreme Court of Ireland ruled as follows: "It is ordered that the defendants and each of them, their servants or agents be perpetually restrained from assisting pregnant women within the jurisdiction to travel abroad to obtain abortions by referral to a clinic, by the making for them of travel arrangements, or by informing them of the identity and location of the method of communication with a specified clinic or clinics or otherwise". I. R. 1988, pp. 593 and 627.

[335] Applications Nos. 14234/88 and 14235/88.

[336] *Open Door and Dublin Well Women v. Ireland* case, §§ 387–388. This case dealt with the issue of women's right to travel outside the Irish jurisdiction to obtain an abortion not lawfully available in Ireland and provisions in Ireland of information and assistance in respect to abortion abroad.

women on the availability of abortion services abroad violates Article 10(1) of the European Convention. Thus, the applications concerned the restrictions placed on the applicant clinics (Dublin Well Women Centre Ltd. and Open Door Counselling) by Irish authorities in order to prevent them from providing non-directive pregnancy counselling to pregnant women as to the location or identity of, or method of communication with, abortion clinics in Great Britain. In the view of the European Court recognition of the right to life of the unborn as established in the Irish Constitution does not exclude a right to receive information on how to procure an abortion abroad. The European Court did not, however, rule on whether the European Convention guarantees a right to abortion. It said that "it is not called upon to examine whether a right to abortion is guaranteed under the Convention"[337] in this particular case, since the applicants had not claimed that the Convention contains such a right. By applying the test of "proportionality",[338] the majority of the Court arrived at the conclusion that the gain of Ireland's policy to protect the life of the unborn was not a compelling justification to abridge the freedom of speech as protected by the Convention. However, several dissenting judges, a few of them stemming from countries with cultures influenced by the Catholic church, took the standpoint that the imposed restriction was not disproportionate and that there was a reasonable margin of states' discretion in the field of the protection of morals. Of further interest to my study is the evidence presented by the applicants as to the adverse implications for the health of Irish women arising from the injunction in the present case, namely: "1. An increase in the birth of unwanted and rejected children; 2. An increase in illegal and unsafe abortion; 3. A lack of adequate preparation of Irish women obtaining abortion; 4. Increase in delay in obtaining abortions with ensuing increased complication rates; 5. Poor aftercare with a failure to deal adequately with medical complications and a failure to provide adequate contraceptive advice".

The above reviewed case law achieved favourable results even though limited. The concrete impact of the decisions of international organs on the domestic application of Article 40.3.3 of the Irish Constitution can be demonstrated by reference to the Supreme Court of Ireland decision on The *Attorney General v. X and Others case* on 5 March 1992.[339] The Supreme Court held unanimously that abortion within the state could be lawful in certain circumstances and that the right to life of the unborn as expressed in the Irish Constitution is not absolute. The Court clarified the circumstances in which it will regard the mother's life as being in danger. In the light of the circumstances of the case it ruled consequently that balancing the right to life of the fourteen and a half year old girl against the right to life of the unborn was necessary. The Court found that the substantial risk to the life of the mother in

---

[337] *Ibid.*, § 66.

[338] For a lengthy exploration of this test see *M.-A. Eissen*, The Principle of Proportionality in the Case-Law of the European Court of Human Rights, in The European System for the Protection of Human Rights, R. St. J. Macdonald, F. Matscher & H. Petzold (eds.), pp. 125–147.

[339] Supreme Court of Ireland, Dublin, Judgment of 5 March 1992, *The Attorney General v. X and Others*. The text of the decision has been reprinted in HRLJ 1992, Vol. 13, pp. 210 *et seq.*

this case could only be avoided by the termination of her pregnancy and that termination of that kind is permissible with regard to a true interpretation of Article 40.3.3. of the Irish Constitution. The effect of the Supreme Court decision was that legislative and/or constitutional changes were found to be necessary. Therefore, a referendum took place in Ireland on 25 November 1992, in which people were asked to vote on an amendment of Article 40.3.3 of the Constitution as to the right to life, travel and information. The right to life amendment was turned down by the majority of the population, obviously since it would have left undisturbed the existing affirmation in Article 40.3.3 of the Constitution of the right to life of the unborn. The current constitutional position, therefore, is as set out in the decision of the Supreme Court in the "*X*" case, *i.e.*, making the rules concerning abortion more permissive. The Irish Government has committed itself to introducing legislation to regulate this position. The other two proposals received the majority's support in the referendum with the consequence that the Government in 1995 introduced a new piece of legislation, *The Regulation of Information* (Services Outside the State for the Termination of Pregnancies), in order to regulate the availability of information on abortion services, which are obtainable outside the state, to all pregnant women and not only those who are in a situation described in the "*X*" case.[340] This development of the national law of Ireland is fully in conformity with the judgments of the European Court of Human Rights in the *Open Door* case and in the Court of the European Communities in the *Grogan* case. In this way Europe shows itself to be a modernising influence. Thus, Ireland cannot uphold restrictions on the dissemination of information concerning the identity and location of abortion facilities in other states. Neither can women's right to travel abroad for an abortion be restricted. There is no pressing, social need for restrictions of that kind. Neither would such measures be proportionate. In other words, the EC law and the European Convention have a tremendous role to play in reconciling domestic abortion law with international human rights standards. The case law of the international organs consequently provides for greater uniformity in Europe, having a concrete impact on the national law of the member states of the Council of Europe and the European Union. In order to ensure enforcement of international law, national law should be coordinated with international law. Countries with restrictive laws can be forced to introduce more liberal rules on the subject matters of concern. Thus, in a suitable case in the future the European Court of Human Rights

---

[340] The law permits among others doctors, counsellors and social workers engaged in pregnancy advice to give names, addresses and telephone numbers of agencies abroad, where Irish women may lawfully undergo abortion provided that this information is objective and non-directive (*i.e.*, it does not advocate and promote, *e.g.*, termination of pregnancy). *S. Coliver*, Ireland, in The Right to Know, S. Coliver (ed.), p. 169. At the same time Paul Ward remains us that the above mentioned Bill precludes any commercial links between information providers and abortion clinics. It was precisely on the basis of such a failing link that the ECJ could rule in the *Grogan* case that the imposed restrictions in Ireland on the students' right to receive information were justifiable and not contrary to European Community Law. *P. Ward*, Republic of Ireland, Life, Death and Divorce, in The International Survey of Family Law 1995, A. Bainham (ed.), The Hague 1997, p. 296.

might, *e.g.*, by using the comparative method of interpretation rule that abortion be legalised. The effect of international case law and/or the "*X*" case on the domestic jurisdiction of Ireland has not been the introduction of a right to abortion *per se*. However, under the "*X*" case test (based on the existence of a real and substantive threat to the life of the mother) there is now a limited class of persons who are entitled to a legal right to abortion.[341] Moreover, impeding legislation ought not restrict the right to obtain and provide information (the international organs did not apply interpretative methods that would have extended the right to expression to comprise *counselling*, which involves a higher degree of societal performance) on abortion services available within the member states of the EU and the Council of Europe.

A feminist perspective on reproductive freedom values "intensive counselling on the risks and benefits"[342] of each method of fertility regulation, because it takes account of each woman's particular circumstances and then every individual woman would be placed in the best position to know what suits her best. Feminists have also pointed out that the knowledge and information about how "to delay birth, space additional births, stop childbearing, or avoid pregnancy"[343] will not only improve women's health but it will significantly contribute to their self-determination, thereby facilitating the achievement of substantial gender equality. It seems reasonable to assume that those who oppose information/knowledge of pregnancy prevention do so because they see it as a threat, *i.e.*, it can weaken patriarchal control over women's reproductive capacity and life.

The right to information is, therefore, essential for ensuring that reproductive choices are made by women voluntarily and free from outside pressures/coercion. Without full and impartial information on various family planning methods and services, the parameters of reproductive freedom can be manipulated not only by husbands but also by governments in, *e.g.*, pursuit of their population policies[344] as we shall see in the following sub-chapter.

#### *5.3.4.3. Freedom from Governmental Interference with Decision-Making*

##### 5.3.4.3.1. Generally

The right of the individual to choose on matters related to procreation is an inherent right in itself. It is an activity that falls within the private domain and thereby comes within the concept of "privacy".[345] While the right to found a family/family planning and the right to privacy are separate rights, there is a considerable amount

---

[341] In his address to the Cairo Conference on 6 September 1994, the Irish representative Mr. B. Howlin acknowledged that "policy and legislation in relation to the circumstances in which the termination of pregnancy may be permitted is a matter for each country to determine for itself".

[342] *R. Dixon-Mueller*, p. 208.

[343] Op. cit., p. 116.

[344] *S. Coliver*, The Right to Information, p. 41.

[345] The right to privacy is guaranteed by all major global as well as regional human rights treaties, *e.g.*, Article 17(1) of the ICCPR, Article 8(1) of the European Convention and Article 11(2) of the American Convention.

of overlap between them. As it has been noted in the literature, for some purposes the right to found a family/to family planning may be considered to be part of the right to private life.[346] The common denominator for these rights is that they are regarded primarily as "negative rights", *i.e.*, they are to be viewed as "safeguards against intrusions into private lives by the public authorities".[347] Despite their significance for the realisation of reproductive freedom, the relevant conventions permit states to place some restrictions upon them.[348] Treaty law allows, in other words, for interference by public authorities in the privacy of people (in the sense of influencing their reproductive behaviour) under certain conditions, *i.e.*, that the interference is not unlawful and arbitrary. Such arbitrary interference contains in the words of Professor Nowak "elements of injustice, unpredictability and unreasonableness".[349] While the conditions, under which the right to privacy may be limited, have been specified in the case law of several of the international human rights bodies, it seems that there is still disagreement about and uncertainty in regard to the interpretation of the content of the term "interference" since it is qualified by "arbitrary". It is generally agreed that there must be some kind of balance between the interests of the state to ensure the well-being of the country on the one hand[350] and the individual's right to free and voluntarily decision-making on procreative matters in privacy on the other hand. The Woman's Convention (Article 16(1)(e)) modifies, for example, decision making on the number of children by the adverb "responsible", to which I shall return below. The question remains therefore: how to identify the borderline between arbitrary and non-arbitrary interference? I shall in the following make an attempt to define the boundaries of the private zone, which the state should not transgress according to international human rights law.

#### 5.3.4.3.2. Forced Abortions and Forced/Compulsory Sterilisations

While the scope of the protection of private live in the context of procreation remains unexplored in the case law of international human rights bodies, CEDAW has delivered some important, and for the purpose of this study, useful statements, which I shall employ as guidelines in my search for an answer to the above raised question. First of all the Committee commented in its General Recommendation No. 21 that some country reports on the domestic implementation of the Women's

---

[346] *R.J. Cook,* Protection of Women's Reproductive Rights, p. 703. The same author argues, in addition, that the right to private life includes the right of private resort to abortion. *R.J. Cook*, Human Rights and Reproductive Self-determination, p. 1000.

[347] *K. Tomaševski*, Human Rights in Population Policies, p. 59.

[348] The HRC has, for example, acknowledged that the right to privacy is a "relative rather than absolute right". HRC General Comment No. 16/32 on Article 17, UN Doc. CCPR/C/21/Rev.1, p. 20. The European Commission on Human Rights has on the other hand in the case *X v UK*, (Application No. 6564/74, D&R, Vol. 2, p. 106) considered the right to found a family, as defined in Article 12 of the European Convention, as an "absolute right", *i.e.*, not allowing any state interference whatsoever.

[349] *M. Nowak*, CCPR Commentary, p. 291.

[350] Family planning programmes in most countries were seen as part of an over-all socio-economic planning. *M.K. Eriksson*, The Rights to Marry and to Found a Family, pp. 148–153.

Convention disclosed coercive practices such as forced pregnancies,[351] abortions or sterilisation which it considers to affect women's physical and mental health adversily and to infringe the rights under Article 16(1)(e) of the Convention. The Committee provided such an interpretation of Article 16, *i.e.*, that "compulsory sterilisation or abortion, (i)nfringes the right of women to decide on the number and spacing of their children" in § 22 of its earlier General Recommendation No. 19. With this in mind CEDAW has taken the standpoint that: "Decisions to have children or not, while preferably made in consultation with spouse or partner, must not nevertheless be limited by spouse, parent, partner or Government".[352] It was ascertained that there is a general agreement that where there are freely available appropriate measures for the voluntary regulation of fertility, the health and well-being of all members of the family improve. For the reasons given above CEDAW, therefore, called upon states parties to ensure that measures are taken by them to prevent coercion in regard to fertility regulation and reproduction.[353] Among scholars Professor Peukert supports the idea that direct state interference aimed at the destruction of the foetus (*i.e.*, forced abortion) would violate the right to found a family as protected by the European Convention.[354] This understanding holds good for forced sterilisations. Coercive birth control practices, including forced abortions and large-scale sterilisation, have been considered in the literature as a violation of the right to health as guaranteed in treaty law, *e.g.*, Article 12 of the ICESCR.[355]

Declaratory documents since the mid-1980s reinforce the above notion of decision-making in matters of reproduction, *i.e.*, free from governmental interference. On the regional level I may mention the resolution on a Charter on the Rights of Women in Childbirth which was adopted by the European Parliament/EEC in 1988. It emphasised that at the heart of reproductive choice is the principle that "maternity should be entered into on the basis of free will".[356]

---

[351] I shall deal with this form of coercion more in depth in Part III of my study. However, I ought to mention here that the 1993 Vienna Declaration condemns forced pregnancy in Part II, § 38. On this basis it has been suggested that that expression might be interpreted so as to include *legally* forced continuation of pregnancy. If victims of rape, *e.g.*, are denied abortion by public authorities on the basis of law and/or practice, and thereby force them to bear children resulting from rape, such a conduct would constitute coercion. It can be, therefore, argued that governmental toleration of forced pregnancy falls within the concept of "arbitrary interference". It constitutes, furthermore, violation of the physical integrity of the person and it is a serious violation of reproductive freedom. See *R.J. Cook*, Human Rights and Reproductive Self-determination, p. 997 and *R. Boland, S. Rao & G. Zeidenstein*, Honoring Human Rights in Population Policies: From Declaration to Action, in Population Policies Reconsidered: Health, Empowerment and Rights, G. Sen, A. Germain & L.C. Chen (eds.), p. 100.

[352] UN Doc. HRI/GEN/1/Rev.1, § 22.

[353] UN Doc. CEDAW/C/1995/7, § 465 at 28.

[354] *W. Peukert*, Human rights in international law and the protection of unborn human beings, in Protecting Human Rights: The European Dimension, F. Matscher & H. Petzold (eds.), Köln 1988, p. 513.

[355] *A.R. Chapman*, p. 14.

[356] Official Journal of the European Communities, 18 July 1988, p. C 187.

Coercion in reproductive matters was, furthermore, banned at the Cairo Conference in 1994.[357] Article 7(12) in the ICPD Programme of Action states that: "The principle of informed free choice is essential to the long term success of family planning programs. Any form of coercion has no part to play". It was also acknowledged that while demographic goals legitimately are the subject of government development strategies, they "should not be imposed on family planning providers in the form of targets or quotas for the recruitment of clients". Also the Beijing Declaration stresses in § 97 that the human rights of women "include their right to have control over and decide freely and responsibly on matters related to their sexuality", including reproductive health and freedom from coercion. Furthermore, Article 115 of the Platform for Action defines forced sterilisation and forced abortion, coercive/forced use of contraceptives, female infanticide and prenatal sex selection as acts of violence against women.[358]

In the light of the above, it may be concluded that in regard to the number as well as the frequency with which international declaratory and authoritative statements have been made in recent years on the issue under discussion, there is support for the presumption that the following examples of compulsory non-procreation measures can be indicated as unjustified, arbitrary governmental interference with the exercise of reproductive freedom and which are contrary to international law: forced abortion[359]

---

[357] Attention to the significance of guarantees for the free and informed choice of methods for fertility regulation was given prior to the documents adopted at recent UN conferences in § 8 of the NGO Guidelines for the Distribution and Use of Fertility Regulation Methods (WEMOS) 1989. It is said there that "No woman or man is sterilized without their fully informed consent. This means that they are aware that sterilization is irreversible".

[358] Several delegates, representatives of governments, to the Beijing Conference condemned such practices in their speeches. The USA' s First Lady, Hillary Clinton expressed the view on 5 September 1995 that it is a violation of human rights when women are denied the right to plan their own families, and that "includes being forced to have abortions or being sterilised against their will". The representative of the USA, Mrs. M. Albright, to the Conference said categorically on 6 September 1995 that: "No women, whether in Birmingham, Bombay, Beirut or Beijing, should be forcibly sterilised or forced to have an abortion". In addition the Chief of the Federal Department of the Interior of Switzerland declared on 8 September 1995 that forced abortion, forced sterilisation, prenatal sex selection are particularly grave violations of women's human rights. Press Release, WOM/857, 8 September 1995.

[359] Women who become pregnant without receiving official authorisation, after already having had one child, have been required, *e.g.*, in China to abort the foetus. There are credible reports, which contain data on a large number of abortions conducted in the last trimester of pregnancy. Some are as late as the ninth month. There have been, in addition, eyewitness reports of abortion forces, rounding up women in rice fields, handcuffing them, and trussing them to operating tables. Such practices have occurred in China in accordance with, for example, the implementation of Article 14 of the Sichuan Family Planning Regulation of 1987. Authorities are permitted to search homes or suspected hide-outs of women "illegally" pregnant, and who fear being forced to undergo abortion. Women who already have one child have been threatened in the province of Guangdong with sterilisation. *B. Lintner*, Protester i Kina, Upplopp mot barnbegränsning, SvD 8 September 1997, p. 7. Also Amnesty International has reported in early 1996 that public authorities have coerced doctors to kill new-born children outside the quota. Amnesty Press, Stockholm 2/1996.

According to the 1994 Maternal and Child Health Care Law, pregnant women diagnosed as having certain infectious diseases will be "advised" to have an abortion. The law requires, furthermore, that couples who have serious hereditary diseases remain childless and those who are already pregnant terminate the pregnancy. This plan for avoidance of undesirable births has been considered as a "campaign

and forced sterilisations.[360] Irrespective of these current developments in human rights law, upon examining state practice today it is evident that coercion in matters of procreation still occurs. Laws and thereupon following practices which allow for non-consensual sterilisation can be found even in some democratic Western societies, *e.g.*, Austria, Australia, Belgium, Finland, France, Germany, etc.[361]

The consequences of sterilisation are far-reaching since it leaves no room for future decisions on procreation. It is an irreversible procedure, which not only infers with the right to bodily integrity but it deprives the individual in question of the ability to reproduce. In the context of the principle of equality, coercive/compulsory sterilisation practices are an especially grave violation of the very basis of human rights, human dignity, since certain individuals are defined as biologically and socially worthless.

Eugenic movements in various countries[362] have periodically argued for the necessity of compulsory control of family planning and upholding restrictions in the exercise of reproductive freedom. This is in order to protect society from the offspring of certain groups. So, the coercive sterilisation law targeting Gypsies, as well as persons considered unfit to beget children, such as mentally backward persons or criminals, in the former Czech and Slovak Republic[363] was based on such motives.

---

for forced sterilization and abortion". *Z. Hong*, The Testimony of Women Writers: The Situation of Women in China Today, in Women's rights, human rights, J. Peters & A. Wolper (eds.), p. 97. See generally on the issue: *J. Hardley*, p. 94; Human Rights in China: Caught Between Tradition and The State, New York 1995, p. 39; *R. Boland, S. Rao & G. Zeidenstein*, p. 98; *Hsia Chang et al.*, Human Rights in the People's Republic of China, 1988, p. 259; *E. Munoz* (ed.), 1995 Directory of Persecuted Scientists, Eugineers and Health Professionals, Washington D.C. AAAS 1995, pp. 164–165; *Amnesty International*, Women in China: Imprisoned and Abused for Dissent, October 1995, pp. 6–8.

[360] Compulsory sterilisation has been practised on a large-scale in India and China, especially during the 1960s and 1970s. *L.J. Macfarlane*, The Theory and Practice of Human Rights, London 1985, p. 59. In response to that, people fearing persecution because of governmental policy of forced abortion and/or coercive sterilisation were granted political asylum in, *e.g.*, the USA during early 1990s. Practice seems, however, to have changed in recent years. On 6 September 1996 a San Francisco Court handed down a decision, for example, in the case of *De You Chen* implying that a risk for forceful sterilisation and opposition to China's one child policy cannot be considered as a political act, and therefore, cannot be a ground for political asylum. The petitioner and his wife fled from China in 1993 after refusing to interrupt a third pregnancy. Their house was torn down and the authorities decided to sterilise the husband. The Court did not argue in relation to any abuse of a human right. It referred instead to the fact that President Bush's proposal for a law granting asylum to persons under threat of abortion and sterilisation had not entered into force.

[361] *T. Lundin & E. Andersson*, Tyska lagar om sterilisering ännu kvar, SvD 29 August 1997, p. 4; TT-Reuter, Sydney, as cited in SvD 16 December 1997, Australien, olaglig sterilisering pågår ännu; *B.E. Rosin*; Tvångssterilisering fortsätter i Frankrike, SvD 11 September 1997, p. E1.

[362] The most frequent mentioned example in this regard is the 250,000 sterilisations that were carried out under the Nazi Hereditary Health Law. Several other countries adopted as, for example, Sweden in 1935 similar laws during the 1930s and 1940s. In 1932 the Eugenic Society in the United States reported that at least 26 states had passed compulsory sterilisation laws and that thousands of "unfit" persons had already been surgically prevented from reproducing. Native American, Chicana, Puerto Rican and Black women have been sterilised in disproportionate numbers. *A. Davis*, Racism, Birth Control, and Reproductive Rights, in From Abortion to Reproductive Freedom, Transforming the Movement, M.G. Fried (ed.), pp. 20–23.

[363] *K. Tomaševski*, Human Rights in Population Policies, p. 26.

Discriminatory, compulsory and coercive measures against various minorities[364] and indigenous peoples[365] in their right to found a family/family planning, constitute a violation of Article 2(d) of the Genocide Convention which condemns measures (such as involuntary sterilisation) imposed with the intention of preventing births with the objective of limiting the number of racial, ethnic or religious groups. Such practices are, furthermore, a breach of the prohibition of discrimination on racial grounds as guaranteed by international law.

Eugenic arguments have, as already indicated above, been advanced in favour of forced abortions and sterilisations in order to avoid the birth of disabled children.[366] The target groups of such policies have often included intellectually disabled girls and women. There has been an assumption that these groups of people are "incapable of controlling their reproductive behaviour by virtue of their reduced capacities of judgment".[367] Despite assumptions of that kind having been discredited by research, international human rights norms in regard of the rights of mentally disabled persons remain inadequate, as has rightly been pointed out in the literature.[368]

What is even more surprising is that despite there being a very long history of sterilisation abuses, the issue has not been given high priority by the feminist movement. Nor have human rights activists paid it the attention it deserves. State practices reveal that apart from discrimination on racial grounds and on the grounds of disability, also discrimination on the basis of sex has occurred to a great extent. Thus, far more women than men have been sterilised, *e.g.*, Swedish studies have shown that more than 90 per cent of the individuals that have been sterilised well into the 1970s were women,[369] despite the fact that the operation is more dangerous than a

---

[364] With regard to allegations of forced sterilisation of members of the Tibetan minority in China see *Whitfield* (ed.), Briefing Paper on China 1993, pp. 46–47.

[365] A great number of women have been forcefully sterilised by the Indonesian authorities in East-Timor with the obvious intent to minimise the ethnic group's chances of survival. *I. Agda*, Tvångssteriliseringar i Östtimor, UNICEF idag, Stockholm 1998, No. 1, p. 21.

[366] As an example of legislation incompatible with human rights law, I may mention the Chinese (People's Republic of China) Eugenics law of 1 June 1995, which has been designed among other things to "avoid new births of inferior quality and heighten the standards of the whole population". See the cited source in *C.A.A. Packer*, p. 51.

[367] For references see *C.A.A. Packer*, p. 88.

[368] *H. Little*, Non-Consensual Sterilisation of the Intellectually Disabled in the Australian Context: Potential for Human Rights Abuse and the Need for Reform, Australian Yearbook of International Law 1993, Vol. 14, p. 213; *C.A.A. Packer*, p. 89.

[369] Whereas the Swedish law in question did not proscribe compulsory sterilisations, it was applied in a woman-hostile manner. Sterilisations were carried out on three indications: medical, social and racial. In regard to the social indication, 100 per cent of the sterilised persons were women. A great number of them were seeking an abortion. A prerequisite for that was they would then be sterilised. The results of several empirical studies have initiated very intensive debate in Sweden in recent years, in the literature (See, *e.g.*, *G. Broberg & N. Roll-Hansen*, Eugenics and the Welfare State, Michigan 1996; *M. Runcis*, Steriliseringar i folkhemmet, Stockholm 1998; *A. Nelson*, Kring födelse och död–några juridiska reflexioner, Annales Societatis Litterarum Humaniorum Regiae Upsaliensis 1997, pp. 110–138) as well as in the press. See, *e.g.*, *S. Leijonhufvud*, Hisnande överdrifter om steriliseringarna, SvD 26 September 1997, p. E3; *L. Truedson*, Tvångssteriliseringar utreds, SvD 27 August 1997, p. 2; *J. Larsson*, Bär vi skuld för dåtidens fel?, SvD 22 February 1998; *I. Sanner*, Indignation gör syn på sterilisering ohistorisk, SvD, 25 June 1998, p. 14;

vasectomy for men. This is in my view clearly an expression of gender inequality and of a "paternalistic attitude towards woman's sexuality and fertility".[370]

Coercive sterilisations and forced abortions are often the result of governmental policies aimed at reducing the number of children in the respective country, such as for example the single-child family planning policy in China,[371] and the maximum of two children policy in the Socialist Republic of Vietnam.[372] In my view several of the earlier referred to human rights provisions in various treaties may be invoked to secure the right for individuals to decide the number and spacing of their children. According to the UN Special Rapporteur on Violence against Women, Mrs. Coomaraswamy, the one-child policy violates "a woman's right to physical integrity and security of person, and the right of both parents freely to determine the timing and spacing of their children".[373]

Besides, limitations regarding the maximum number of children may lead, as seen in Asia, to the widespread son-preference and female infanticide, which quite obviously reinforce gender inequality. The World Bank has made the following observation with regard to this: "In China the one-child policy has been challenged by an apparent preference for sons. The same bias in favour of sons exists in Korea".[374]

Compulsory abortions for single women as well as migrant women, as this has been the case in China, is a measure, which demonstrates an additional gender bias.[375]

Another phenomenon connected with the "one birth per couple" policy, and which has adverse effects on gender equality, is that when a family has a baby girl, the girl is often not registered as the hope for a son lives on with the parents. It has been suggested that there are over a million unregistered women in China today. The negative effects of non-registration on those persons' legal status are obvious.[376]

---

*E. Sidenbladh*, Tvångssteriliserade bör få ersättning föreslår utredning, SvD 27 January 1999, p. 8; *E. Wikström*, Steriliserad för sin fattigdom, SvD 6 April 1999, p. 7. The Swedish Government decided in March 1999 to grant compensation to the victims of forceful sterilisations during 1935–1945.

[370] *H. Little*, p. 211.

[371] *China Intercontinental Press*, How China Implements its Family Planning Programs, Beijing September 1995, p. 1. In 1991, The Communist Party of China's Central Committee summarised China's family planning policy as follows: "Encourage late marriage and late pregnancy, and fewer but healthier births; and encourage one child for every couple except in special circumstances where permission is granted for birth of a second child". Information Office of the State Council of the People's Republic of China, Human Rights in China 1991, p. 67; "White Paper", The Situation on Chinese Women 1994.

[372] Vietnam, Population and Family Planning Policies 1988, Council of Ministers Decision No. 162 Concerning a Number of Population and Family Planning Policies, Article 2, § 1.

[373] UN Doc. E/CN.4/1996/53, § 95.

[374] *The World Bank*, World Development Report 1984, Washington D.C. 1985, p. 178.

[375] UN Doc. E/CN.4/1996/53, § 96.

[376] The CRC's concluding observations in connection with the consideration of China's report under the Convention on the Rights of the Child, in May 1996, are illustrative. The Committee expressed first of all its concern in regard to the deficiencies in the registration system in China, which had led to children being deprived of basic safeguards for the promotion and protection of their rights, for example, "in the areas of child trafficking, abduction, sale and maltreatment, abuse or neglect". In the Committee's view family planning policy must be designed to avoid any "threat to the life of children, particularly girls". China's Government was urged to take further action for the maintenance of strong and comprehensive measures to combat the abandonment and infanticide of girls. UN Doc. CRC/C/SR.298–300, §§ 16, 36.

The great attention given internationally in mass media to the coercive measures and the sanctions for non-compliance with the one-child policy in China resulted in not only condemnation by the international community but also withdrawals of financial support to the country.[377] China has generally responded by arguing that these measures are interference in matters which are essentially within the domestic jurisdiction of a state.[378] The Government strongly opposed the extensive critique of its family planning programme and population control measures as contrary to respect of human freedom by stating that: "Any such practice of interfering in China's internal affairs has not only deviated from the basic principle set up in the field of population by the international community, but it has also violated the established principles of international law".[379] The term "interference" as used in this context has a vague character. It can include such measures as international criticism or negative media coverage, which, however, is not comprised in any prohibitive rule of international law. Besides, the practical significance of the doctrine of national sovereignty *versus* human rights has been minimised through the latest developments in international human rights law. Nevertheless, some changes in attitude have been perceived recently, primarily because of the structure of an ageing population. For this reason the public authorities have announced that some easing of the one-child policy might be expected in the near future.[380]

While the spacing of pregnancies is important for the health of mother and child, its effects on society are very few, if any at all. Therefore, I agree with Corinne Packer that to interfere with individuals' decisions in regard to pregnancies, in quick succession or spaced over many years would seem "always arbitrary". Thus, the right to decide the spacing of one's children should be viewed "to be an absolute freedom".[381] Yet, such practices still occur today, as for example in Vietnam. According to regulations from 1988, specific intervals of time between the births of children in each family are being prescribed. Each couple is allowed to have two children with a space of 3–5 years between them. The recommended childbearing age is 22 years of age or older for women, and 24 years of age or older for men. People are also advised not to have children after the age of 35.

In addition, I should mention that some societies emphasise the *moral/religious* obligation of the spouses to procreate and to restrict their reproductive freedom, for instance, to abstain from contraception. Although it cannot be denied that societal interest in reproduction to a certain extent is legitimate, aggressive pro-natalist policies which can be equated with coercive methods to make individuals beget chil-

---

377 *K. Tomaševski*, Human Rights in Population Policies, p. 27.

378 Naturally, coercion or the use of force in implementing family planning regulations, including forced abortions and sterilisations, is officially opposed by the Chinese Government. It has, however, admitted that incidents of coercion occasionally take place, usually in remote areas. Country reports on China and the one child policy, in Refugee Survey Quarterly 1995, Special Issue, p. 91. See also *J.S. Aired*, Slaughter of Innocents: Coercive Birth Control in China, London 1990, p. 12.

379 *Information Office of the State Council of the People's Republic of China*, Family Planning in China, Beijing 1995, p. 34.

380 *K. Nielson*, Kineser kan tillåtas ha fler barn, SvD 14 October 1997, p. 5.

381 *C.A.A. Packer*, p. 56.

dren cannot be justified within the realm of international human rights law. With the 1979 Revolution, the Islamic Republic of Iran rejected family planning programmes as an imperialist mechanism. Increasing the population was a goal to strengthen the Muslim nation. Abortion and sterilisation were outlawed and the minimum legal age for marriage was reduced to nine for girls.[382]

Manipulation and withholding of information about side-effects and alternative contraceptive measures may also be regarded as an element of "coercion", if it prevents the free choice of the individuals.

5.3.4.3.3. Coercion in Relation to HIV/AIDS

Another important question of current interest is whether states may introduce restrictions in their domestic law and/or administrative practice on the right to family planning/to found a family by explicitly referring to the risks and consequences of HIV infection, as compatible with human rights. Some biological, social and physiological features predispose women to greater vulnerability to most sexually transmitted diseases, including AIDS.[383] It may, of course, be argued that the protection of the health of the mother and the unborn child constitutes a legitimate aim for governmental intervention. At the same time there seems to be an international consensus, manifested during the International Consultation on AIDS and Human Rights held at Geneva in July 1989, that it is not of "sufficient weight"[384] to justify measures against the mother's wishes. Even though the rapid spread of HIV is a cause for great concern, non-discrimination in regard to free decision-making is also vital in cases of pregnant women with HIV/AIDS. Thus, mandatory abortions or sterilisations for HIV-infected women would be a violation of the human right to found a family and the right to family planning as well as of her right to dignity and integrity,[385] as protected by international law, and cannot in my view be justified on any legal grounds. Despite that it is now known that out of ten children born to mothers who are HIV-positive, between 6 and 8 will be unaffected; many pregnant

---

[382] The population growth reached subsequently 4 per cent per year, *i.e.*, one of the highest rates ever seen anywhere. *N. Mac Farquhar*, Iran's New Ideal: Small Families, International Herald Tribune, 9 September 1996, p. 2. *C.M. Obermeyer*, Religious Doctrine, State Ideology, and Reproductive Options in Islam, in Power and Decision, The Social Control of Reproduction, G. Sen & R.C. Snow (eds.), pp. 67–71; *A. Mirhosseini*, After the Revolution: Violation of Women's Human Rights in Iran, in Women's rights, human rights, J. Peters & A. Wolper (eds.), p. 73. However, since the early 1990s Iran has one of the world's more aggressive programmes to encourage smaller families.

[383] The Secretary- General of the International Federation of the Red Cross referred in his speech at the Beijing Conference to estimates according to which by the year 2000 over 13 million women will have been infected by HIV. Press Release, WOM/BEI/861, 12 September 1995.

[384] Report of an International Consultation on AIDS and Human Rights, New York 1991, p. 49. See also *P. Sieghart*, AIDS and Human Rights, A UK Perspective, London 1989. Generally on family law restrictions in connection with AIDS see Die Probleme von AIDS, *B. Schünemann & G. Pfeiffer* (red.), Baden-Baden 1988.

[385] *S. Gruskin*, Negotiating the Relationship of HIV/AIDS to Reproductive Health and Reproductive Rights, The American University Law Review 1995, pp. 1191–1206. See also UN Doc. E/CN.6/1999/4, §§ 21 27.

women with HIV have experienced pressure in several countries, most often from doctors, to terminate their pregnancies.[386]

5.3.4.3.4. Public Authorities' Use of Incentives and Disincentives

In the view of this author governments must not intervene in the sphere of family planning, whether by the use of reward or punishment, in order to influence people who have "too many" children or "too few", because this is an insidious form of coercion. Applying policies of that kind is not only a breach of the right to decide freely on the number of one's children (Article 16(1)(e) of the Women's Convention) but it will result in social inequality – the financial situation of the family is in most societies dependent on the number of children. Sanctions against large families, for example, loss of tax benefit, may infringe upon the rights not only of the parents but also of the child/ren. Besides, such measures have not been very effective in modifying fertility levels. The use of substantial material incentives, which has been practised frequently in some countries, especially in Asia,[387] may indirectly prevent the free choice of the spouses. For people living under the incessant threat of starvation, the scope for making a free choice on family size is very narrow. If, as in China in recent years, it is legally established that a family allowance will not be paid if the number of children in a family exceeds the limit set by the state,[388] this, too, will constitute a violation of the right concerned.[389] Mme Yu told recently the UN Commission on Population and Development that families who prefer fewer children are better-off, with the state offering them preferential treatment, for example, access to low-interest loans and to the means and techniques of production. Besides, single-child insurance and an old-age security system have been set up, thus reducing rural people's need for more children.[390]

---

[386] Proposals concerning involuntary sterilisation of infected women has been discussed in the legal literature by *H. Amaro*, Women's Reproductive Rights in the Age of AIDS, New Threats to Informed Choice, in From Abortion to Reproductive Freedom, Transforming the Movement, M.G. Fried (ed.), pp. 253 ff.

[387] The countries that can be mentioned in this regard are first and foremost India, Korea, Pakistan, Taiwan, Sri Lanka, Turkey, China. *L. Gordon*, Birth Control in America, p. 339. Rewards for compliance with the one-child policy in China, *e.g.*, has been in urban areas more substantial than in rural areas. Many include privileges regarding housing, food subsidies, medical care, education, a monthly health allowance, job promotions. In rural areas the main incentives for adhering to family planning regulations usually involve more land and grain rations. *X. Peng*, Demographic Transition in China: Fertility Trends since the 1950s, Beijing 1991, pp. 50–51.

[388] In 1993 legal regulations authorised birth control lifting subsidised health insurance and food coupons for any child after the third. In addition, before getting a marriage license, couples must submit a stamped form indicating that they attended a special lecture on birth control methods at their area clinic. *N. Mac Farquhar*, p. 2.

[389] Official penalties generally include fines, as well as the loss of paid medical care, of paid education and of food rations for the unauthorised child. It can also include dismissal or demotion for the parents as well as other punishments. *Population Crisis Committee*, China's Family Planning Programme, Beijing 1991, p. 23.

[390] Peng Yu, Representative of China at the 29th Session of the UN Commission on Population and Development, General Debate on National Experience in Population Matters, New York, 26 February 1996. See also *L. Yang & J. Hamand*, Backers of the People, in China, IPPF 1996, No. 1, p. 28.

Another human rights issue is the fact that quite severe disincentives, some of which can be regarded as penalties, are imposed on the citizens in the Republic of Vietnam, not by a court but by a political institution, the People's Committee. Families with more than two children must, *e.g.*, contribute to a social support fund, which includes funds for education and health care, and do make socially beneficial labour. Families with more than the permitted number of children must pay a housing or land rent calculated at a high price for the extra space they request.[391] According to decision No. 1664 (§ 4b), in force since 1992 in the Quang Ninh province, couples in agricultural areas with more than two children have to pay fines equalling 80–200 kg of raw rice every year for five years. Government or military employees will receive a reduced salary or can even be discharged. In addition, families with three children or more will not be permitted to move into the urban centres of municipalities, cities and industrial zones.

So, here is a society with different disincentives for different groups. As a consequence there is an obvious risk of discrimination and of difficulty in upholding the principle of equality before the law – the chief consideration in a state governed by the rule of law.

Finally, I may establish that there seems to be sufficient grounds for the assertion that financial burdens influence reproductive decision-making. Therefore, the right to family planning would also be violated if care facilities, health subsidies, maternity leave and access to land in rural areas are conditional on compliance with state-imposed restrictions on the number of children. This would be arbitrary interference despite governments' justification for policies of that kind that they want to limit population growth in accordance with foreseeable estimates of available resources and that failure to achieve such limits "will doom many individuals to a manner of life incompatible with human dignity".[392] Even though a pregnancy has social consequences, the chief function of a state is to protect individual rights.

### *5.3.4.4. Coercion of Women in Custody*

A great number of Amnesty International reports reveal widespread custodial violence against women. Women who are detained have been abused, most often sexually, by prison officers,[393] the police and the military in several countries. The UN Special Rapporteur on Violence against Women has explained in the following terms why custodial violence is even on the increase: "Abuse of power by government agents, usually police or military personnel, under non-transparent and highly

---

[391] Council's of Ministers Decision No. 162, § 6.

[392] *J.P. Hanigan*, Unwanted pregnancies and the common good, in Unwanted Pregnancies and Public Policy, H. Correa (ed.), p. 3.

[393] Custodial rape is an issue, which falls within the ambit of violence against women, and I shall discuss it therefore in Part III of the study. Nevertheless, I shall give here one example of such practices, which demonstrate a particular severe gender bias. In Iran after the 1979 Islamic Revolution, a way to improve one's qualifications is to rape detained women, especially virgin girls, irrespective of the reason for their imprisonment. Rapes of that kind have been regular and have often taken place as a punishment in public. *A. Mirhosseini*, After the Revolution: Violations of Women's Human Rights in Iran, in Women's rights, human rights, J. Peters & A. Wolper (eds.), p. 75.

unequal conditions, together with the impunity accorded to such agents, constitute the basis on which custodial violence ferments and grows".[394]

A pregnant woman is particularly vulnerable to torture and/or to detention in cruel and degrading conditions. She risks miscarriage and severe injury from any untreated medical complications of her pregnancy. The UN Special Rapporteur on Violence against Women has also stressed that the psychological and gynaecological sequelae of extreme forms of custodial violence, "are further compounded by inadequate or unavailable medical treatment".[395] There is a body of principles in international law directed towards safeguarding the physical safety of detainees and prisoners.[396] These standards are, however, formulated in gender-neutral language, thereby excluding the need for special protection of women in detention. Thus, there is no specific set of rights elaborated in regard to detained women's reproductive freedom. The issue is, for example, not explicitly included in the Women's Convention. Among the reasons for the neglect of women in vulnerable position it has been mentioned that: "The world of prison has been created by men for men and although it would be quite simple to introduce a sound penal policy for women's prisons, it has not been done in practice".[397] Against this background ECOSOC has adopted several resolutions that relate to violence against detained women, which is specific to their sex.[398] But irrespective of these documents very few countries have expressed concern for the situation of women in prison in their reports on the implementation of the Nairobi strategies in 1990. CEDAW called, therefore, on several occasions attention to the need for special law and/or administrative measures on a domestic level to protect pregnant women prisoners.[399] The necessity to protect women from ill-treatment and violence was one of the major areas of concern during the Cairo and Beijing Conferences as well.[400] Notwithstanding these efforts made by the international community to come with grips with the problem, several governments still ignore the special needs for protection of pregnant women in custody.

---

[394] UN Doc. E/CN.4/1995/42, § 248.

[395] Ibid., § 249.

[396] See, *e.g.*, The UN Standard Minimum Rules for the Treatment of Persons in Detention and Imprisonment, the ICCPR, the European and American Convention on Human Rights, the UN and the European Conventions against Torture, the UN Declaration on Violence against Women. For further general and more specific provisions of relevance for the issue under discussion see *K. Tomaševski*, Women and Human Rights, p. 74.

[397] *E. Gimenez-Salinas i Colomer*, Spain, in Imprisonment Today and Tomorrow, D. Van Zyl Smit & F. Dunkel (eds.), Deventer 1991, p. 359, cited in *K. Tomaševski*, Women and Human Rights, p. 71.

[398] See,*e.g.*, ECOSOC Res. 1986/29 of 23 May 1986 and Res. 1990/5 of 24 May 1990. Member states of the UN were urged by these documents "to take appropriate measures urgently, as necessary, to eradicate acts of physical violence against detained women".

[399] UN Doc. A//48/38, § 399. See also Amnesty International, Rape and Sexual Abuse: Torture and Ill-treatment of Women in Detention, New York 1991.

[400] Also during the World Summit for Social Development which was held in March 1995, states committed themselves to taking effective measures to combat and eliminate all forms of violence against women in accordance with international instruments and declarations (commitment 5 h). Violence against women was considered as a growing threat to the security of individuals, families and communities everywhere.

The number of pregnant women detained in South America, *e.g.*, is still very high. Many of them are held under intolerable conditions and are subject to treatment that contravenes contemporary human rights law. Not seldom have they been frequently kicked and beaten, and they have with malicious aforethought been assigned to heavy labour in order to provoke a miscarriage. Such acts fall in my opinion within the prohibition of forced abortion.

It is apparent from the above that in order to ensure relevant protection to women in custody, the asymmetrical approach to gender equality requires a kind of protection different from the one designed for men in custody. This can be achieved among other ways by the dynamic interpretation of existing human rights provisions, which provide a valuable but for the time being limited net of protection, so that they might include the unique problems for imprisoned women as pointed out above. States should pursue, in addition, by all appropriate measures and in accordance with Article 4 of the UN Declaration on Violence against Women and without delay, a policy of eliminating this kind of violence against women.

### *5.3.4.5. Coercion in the Private Sphere*

#### 5.3.4.5.1. Relations between Non-State Actors

Human rights are, in the context of classical international law, primarily designed to protect individuals against the abuse of power by a state, *i.e.*, its own agents. Through the application of the "*Drittwirkung*" doctrine, human rights law may, however, place obligations upon states to prevent and respond to acts committed by individuals, *e.g.*, agents of the family, in order to protect the exercise by the individual of her/his fundamental rights and freedoms. The UN Commission on Human Rights adopted a resolution on the elimination of violence against women[401] at its session in April 1996, in which the duty of governments to refrain from engaging in violence against women and to take appropriate and effective action concerning acts of violence against women, "whether those acts were perpetrated by the State or by private persons", is emphasised. One commentator has summarised this development in international law as follows: "The emergence of gender discrimination on the human rights agenda broadened the reach of human rights from 'vertical' relations between individuals and governments, to 'horizontal' relations, namely between private individuals, within families and communities, and ultimately within couples".[402] The implications of the recent developments in the case law of the Inter-American and the European Court on Human Rights indicate that these international organs have taken a step towards the recognition of the applicability of the

---

[401] UN Doc. E/CN.4/1996/L.83. See also Article 2 of the 1994 Inter-American Convention on the Prevention, Punishment and Eradication of Violence Against Women, "Convention of Belém do Pará", which has been in force since 3 March 1995. Violence against women is defined as acts that occur within the family or domestic unit and that occur in the community. See *T. Buergenthal & D. Shelton*, Protecting Human Rights in the Americas, Kehl 1995, p. 645.

[402] *K. Tomaševski*, Human Rights in Population Policies, p. 40. See also *A. Clapham*, The Drittwirkung of the Convention, in The European System for the Protection of Human Rights, R. St. J. Macdonald, F. Matscher & H. Petzold (eds), p. 163. See, in addition, Part IV of this study.

regional conventions on behaviour in the private sphere, a fact which is of great significance.[403] In consequence, freedom of choice as the core element of the right to found a family, as well as of the right to family planning, means that a person does not have a right to beget a child with a particular person, so that even for persons living in marriage there is no obligation for the wife to become pregnant, nor for the husband to impregnate her. Since parentage is a basic freedom and not an obligation, neither of the spouses may compel the other spouse to have children. The consent of both prospective parents throughout the process of procreation creates the basis of equality required by the legal system. Marital rape and forced impregnation as expressions of gender inequality[404] are, therefore, included in the UN definition of violence.[405] Rape by the husband is, moreover, considered a violation of Article 16(1)(e) of the Women's Convention.[406] Still, in many parts of the world coercion amounting to violence against women, including rape, is a frequent occurrence within the family.[407] In societies where there is no real partnership between the spouses, and the man is considered to have absolute authority within the family unit, including matters of procreation, gender is here the sole basis of discrimination. Thus, there is a presumption in patriarchal societies that a "wife gives herself up to the husband by entering into the contract of marriage".[408] Practices of this kind are in obvious contradiction to human rights rules, according to which decisions on procreation should rest *equally* on both spouses (Article 16(1)(e) of the Women's Convention). Violence against women in the form of rape affects women's ability to protect themselves from unwanted pregnancies as well as sexually transmitted diseases, HIV included. In other words, rape can have serious consequences for women's reproductive health.

Another phenomenon, though not falling within the term "violence" but still contradictory to the above mentioned Convention's demand that human rights be enjoyed on an equal footing among the family members, is the legal empowerment of the husband to veto his wife's access to family planning services, including abortion.[409]

---

[403] The regional developments have influenced also the work on human rights standards within the UN. The Vienna Declaration and Programme of Action of 1993 calls, for example, governments and the UN to eliminate violence against women in public and private life as a human rights obligation.

[404] Rape has often been characterised as the "primary instrument of control in a patriarchal society". UN Doc. E/CN.4/1995/42, § 172.

[405] A clear and very comprehensive definition of the notion "violence against women" is contained in § 1 the UN Declaration on the Elimination of Violence against Women adopted by a GA resolution on 20 December 1993. See The United Nations and the Advancement of Women, 1945–1995, New York 1995, p. 459. See also CEDAW, General Recommendation No. 19, Violence against Women, adopted in 1992, UN Doc. CEDAW/C/1992/L.1/Add.15.

[406] UN Doc. CEDAW/C/1993/4, § 60.

[407] On the various types of violence within the family including practices that affect women's reproductive freedom see UN Doc. E/CN.4/1995/42, §§ 117–171; UN Doc. E/CN.4/1996/53, §§ 64–65.

[408] UN Doc. E/CN.4/1995/42, § 181.

[409] Indonesian authorities introduced in 1996 rules allowing spousal veto in regard to family planning services on the island of Lombok with the disparaging motivation that wives at home on their own should not be tempted to wrongful acts while their husbands are away. Jakarta Post, 8 October 1996.

5.3.4.5.2. Resolving Conflicting Interests – A Test for Gender Equality

Sometimes there might be a difference of opinions and interests between a pregnant woman and the father-to-be as regards the continuation or interruption of pregnancy. A pregnancy may be unwanted by the woman, who is pregnant, by the man who has impregnated her, or by both.[410] Voluntary abortion clearly has an impact on the interests of the male partner, but does he have a right to prevent or to insist on the birth of his child? What about a man's decision taken without the consent of his female partner to undergo a castration operation? Are the rights involved in both situations symmetrical?

It has been argued that since the foetus is as much genetically part of the man as of the woman, putative fathers have a moral stake in the decision concerning woman's access to abortion. The UDHR, as well as other human rights documents, recognise that one person's human rights may conflict with those of another person. Still, there are no principles for determining the priority between conflicting rights.[411] CEDAW has, however, in its analysis of the content of Article 16 of the Women's Convention concluded that: "The rights allocated to both spouses as individuals should not depend on the one receiving permission from the other, thereby placing one spouse in an inferior position".[412]

In early Roman society a right to decide upon abortion belonged to the *pater-familias* (the head of the household) rather than the mother.[413] Men enjoyed a very powerful position in the family and children were treated as if they were the possession of the father. He had, for example, the right to leave unwanted children in the wilderness to die if he wished to reject them. This power over life and death was gradually curtailed. Eventually, exposure of children to death was totally prohibited in the late Empire, but such practices continued and were not outlawed in other societies, as for example until the 13th century in Sweden.[414] With time women were ensured stronger guarantees for their right to private life, and nowadays a father has no possibility of taking action on behalf of the unborn child against the mother's will to undergo abortion.

The European Commission on Human Rights in the *Paton v. United Kingdom* case[415] dealt with the question whether a national regulation protecting pregnant

---

[410] A recent country study shows, *e.g.*, that in Bolivia in the majority of the cases (about 64%) the decision for abortion was taken jointly by the couple. In 25% of the cases, it was only the woman's decision and in 4% it was solely the husband's decision. *E. Mercado*, Consequences of Unwanted Pregnancies in Bolivia: An Overview, in Unwanted Pregnancies and Public Policy, H. Correa (ed.), p. 184.

[411] *L. Henkin*, International Law: Politics and Values, Dordrecht 1995, p. 188.

[412] UN Doc. CEDAW/C/1993/4, § 161. The representative of Tunisia referred during the review of the country report by CEDAW at its meeting on 23 January 1995 to the fact that in regard to abortion the husband's agreement is not required and that the decision to continue or interrupt a pregnancy "is the wife's prerogative".

[413] *M. Andreev*, Rimsko častno pravo, Sofia 1971, p. 170; *M. Bartošek*, Rimskoje pravo, Moscow 1989, p. 239; *A. Borkowski*, Textbook on Roman Law, London 1994, pp. 102–142.

[414] *Rädda barnen*, Barnets rättigheter och samhällets skyldigheter, lagar och regler, Stockholm 1991, p. 35.

[415] Application No. 1416/78, The Report of the European Commissions adopted on 13 March 1980.

women from being compelled to continue an unwanted pregnancy by her husband's veto of her abortion is to be considered compatible with the European Convention. One of the considered questions was whether a prohibition of the termination of pregnancy after the 12th week under the 1967 Abortion Act could constitute interference with the husband's right to private life. The European Commission expressed the opinion in this regard that the European Convention was not breached in the particular case. So, the right of the husband to respect for private life (having an interest in the birth of his child) had to give way to the woman's right to privacy. Consequently, abortion is primarily a matter for the pregnant woman to decide upon. The Commission held, moreover, that the applicant's right to privacy could not be interpreted as to cover a legal right to require to be consulted on his wife's decision.

The question of a man's legal interests in abortion in general and the compatibility of national law (Norwegian) concerning abortion issues and the standards of the European Convention was raised before the European Commission in another case, the *Knudsen v Norway* case.[416] The Commission ruled that the applicant was not affected differently by the domestic legislation than other citizens and declared the application incompatible *ratione personae* with the provisions of the European Convention on March 8, 1985. The applicant insisted that an amendment to the Norwegian Abortion Act, which authorised the woman herself to make the final decision whether or not to terminate the pregnancy before the end of the 12th week of pregnancy, implied "abandonment of every legal protection of the budding human life and involved in principle a denial of the foetus' s human worth".[417] The applicant claimed, moreover, that the said Act was in conflict with basic Christian values and Article 2 of the European Convention and that it therefore should be declared void. Mr. Knudsen was, furthermore, of the opinion that he had a direct legal interest in the examination of the acceptability of the Norwegian Abortion Act in relation to the European Convention, because he had risked and lost his office as vicar of Balsfjord within the Norwegian State Church on account of his views on the abortion issue. The European Commission stressed, however, that a priest who could not be deemed as a potential father could not be considered to be the victim[418] of the violation he alleged. Therefore, he had no right to petition.

The consequences of the case law referred above may briefly be established as follows: Abortion cannot be subject to the consent of the husband, and he cannot oppose it on the grounds of existing provisions in the European Convention on Human Rights.[419]

---

[416] Application No. 11045/84, 42 D&R, p. 247 *et seq.*

[417] *Ibid.*, at 250.

[418] The ECHR interpreted the requirement to be a "victim of a violation" in the sense of the European Convention to mean that the person has to be *actually* affected by the violation of a human right. See the *Klass and Others v. Germany* case, ECHR Judgment of September 6, 1978, Ser. A, No. 28.

[419] I may also refer, with regard to the legal stance at national level, to the 1976 *Planned Parenthood of Central Missouri v. Damforth* case, in which the Supreme Court of the United States overturned a law requiring a married woman to obtain her husband's consent for an abortion, stating that a woman's right to choose abortion is not subject to the veto of her spouse. See also *R.J. Cook*, International Human Rights and Women's Reproductive Health, in Women's rights, human rights, J. Peters & A. Wolper (eds.), p. 264.

In my view this position is justifiable for several reasons. Forced sexual intercourse, also in the form of marital rape, sometimes occurs for the purpose of securing the conception of a child in the family, a situation in which the woman's right to choose to become a parent or not is clearly violated. Women with poor or no education at all and no financial independence are clearly in an inferior position to negotiate issues like the planning and spacing of their children. They are often at risk of violence from uncooperative spouses. Within a great number of domestic jurisdictions, rape or physical force within marriage does not constitute a crime.[420] Under such circumstances the innocent part with the weaker position has to be protected, and a requirement of the husband's permission for abortion cannot be justifiable.

There are also examples in the case law of national jurisdictions where the right of the pregnant woman to decide on abortion without regard to her partner's preferences has been recognised.[421] The Supreme Court of the USA has, for example, based its decisions in two significant cases on arguments related to the following two interests of the pregnant woman, namely: rearing burdens and gestational burdens.[422] Even though no aspects of gender equality were explicitly considered, in practice the mentioned grounds have justified the different (asymmetrical) legal position of a man and a woman with respect to reproductive freedom, which on the whole might have a positive effect in regard to the realisation of substantial equality for women.

I may, consequently, conclude that women have, in accordance with international human rights law as well as domestic jurisdictions, been guaranteed a freedom of choice with respect to the continuation of a pregnancy. A man can neither compel nor prevent abortion. As the right to family planning is formulated in international law, the male partner has a right to participate in the decision-making process and nothing else. This position has, however, been questioned in the scholarly writings on the basis of whether it is compatible with the principle of equality before the law. Professor Meron has, for example, advanced the argument that: "Because men have equal rights with women in matters of family planning, abortion... (w)ould be not a woman's individual right, which she might exercise independently of consent of the father".[423]

---

420 *L.J. Macfarline*, p. 58; *R.J. Cook*, Human Rights in Relation to Women's Health, p. 12. On the other hand, there is also a tendency within the domestic legal systems of several states to recognise rape between spouses as an offence. The German Parliament, for example, passed through a draft law making rape within marriage a criminal offence by the votes 318 in favour and 306 against, on 9 May 1996. See in addition UN Doc. A/44/38, Suppl. No. 38, § 309; UN Doc. E/CN.4/1996/53, §§ 64–65 and the more recent cases dealing with marital rape decided by the ECHR and which I have discussed in Part I of this study.

421 See *M.N. Coleman*, Embryo Transplant, Parental Conflict, and Reproductive Freedom: a Prospective Analysis of Issues and Arguments Created by Forthcoming Technology, Hofstra Law Review 1987, Vol. 15, p. 611.

422 *Ibid.*, at 613.

423 *T. Meron*, Human Rights Law-Making in the United Nations. A Critique of Instruments and Processes, Oxford 1986, p. 72.

With regard to state practice, there are albeit very few examples in the national legislation of countries in Asia and in Africa that require a husband's authorisation for a woman's abortion.[424]

Even though the HRC's General Comment No. 16 dealing with privacy did not explicitly mention this issue, provisions providing for veto power for the husband in procreation matters are unquestionably incompatible with contemporary human rights law. CEDAW underlined in its comment on Article 16 (1)(e) that: "Women's right to full and free exercise of their reproductive functions, including the right to decide whether to have children or not, must not be limited by spouse or government".[425]

Finally, I may establish that a man cannot find justification on the basis of existing human rights law for the use of coercion in order to compel a woman to have an abortion, if she does not want to. In such a case one may argue that he has had the chance of making a choice, when deciding to use contraceptives or not in order to prevent an unwanted pregnancy, before he had sexual intercourse.

5.3.4.5.3. Son Preference and Sex-Selective Abortions

Another issue regarding reproductive freedom, which has only recently been addressed by international human rights law, is the use of sex-determination technology by parents for the purpose of sex-selective abortion. The UN Special Rapporteur on Violence against Women among others has condemned such practices, since in her view the use of "reproductive technology which allows for preselection of the sex of the child has resulted in the killing of female foetuses and selective abortion".[426] The term violation has been, furthermore, broadened to include "female infanticide and prenatal sex selection" in the Beijing Declaration and Platform for Action, strategic objective L. 7, § 283 (d).

In the view of this author it is apparent that the freedom of choice compatible with international norms on human rights cannot comprise a freedom of the spouses to decide on their child's sex if that would result in total devaluation of one of the sexes. The great number of selective abortions of female foetuses in India and China is but a manifestation of such a devaluation of women. Nevertheless, it has been argued that since there is a demand for sex selection, freedom of choice includes freedom to have a child of one's own choice. Proponents of this view try to justify the preference for sons over daughters, a world-wide occurrence though it is most marked in South Asia and the Middle East, by saying that choosing the sex of a child is a logical extension of the right to family planning. Such practices do not only curtail the access to food, health and education to girl children, but may prevent them from being born. The majority of families living in India, Pakistan,

---

[424] *R.J. Cook & J.M. Haws*, p. 51. In Islamic law spousal consultation for access to family planning services, including abortion, is required in general. *R.J. Cook & D. Maine*, Spousal Veto over Family Planning Services, The American Journal of Public Health 1987, Vol. 77, pp. 340– 343.

[425] UN Doc. E/CN.6/1993/CRP.2, § 46.

[426] UN Doc. E/CN.4/1995/42, § 56.

Nepal, Bangladesh, South Korea, Syria, Jordan and China are known for their strong preference for male children. This is very much because in those societies the family lineage is carried through the male line.[427] It is obvious that the prevalence of son preference in Asian societies is "historically rooted in the patriarchal system".[428] Sons are seen as potential earners as well as sources of future support. Another reason for this practice is the social and cultural stigma attached to having a girl child, *i.e.*, it means the considerable costs (dowry)[429] of marrying off a daughter. It is presupposed that if the daughter does not marry she will remain dependent upon her family. It has been said at the same time that the high level of the sex-selective abortions in India arises from the societal attitude "that regards girl children as a social and economic burden".[430] Therefore, prenatal tests designed to discover abnormalities of the foetus are being widely used in China,[431] India[432] and the Republic of Korea, to determine the gender of the child, resulting in abortion or female infanticide if it is a girl. This conduct is clearly contrary to the prohibition of discrimination on the ground of sex as endorsed in central

---

[427] *G. Van Bueren*, The International Law on the Rights of the Child, p. 309. Various practices resulting from preference of sons are considered to be comprised by the first universal treaty to prohibit harmful traditional practices, *i.e.*, the Convention of the Rights of the Child (Article 24(3)). Similarly, discriminatory practices of preference for male children were previously outlined in the 1986 Report of the Working Group on Traditional Practices affecting the Health of Women and Children. UN Doc. E/CN.4/1986/42. At the same time one of the most well-known maxims of Hindu religion concerns the significance of *kanya dan* (the gift of a daughter), which implies that a father must give a daughter away in marriage in order to guarantee his salvation. *B.D. Miller*, Unwanted Daughters in Northwest India, in Unwanted Pregnancies and Public Policy, H. Correa (ed.), p. 194.

[428] UN Doc. E/CN.4/1995/42, § 155.

[429] The practice of dowry and bride-price not only leads to young women becoming objects of speculation for their parents, but it certainly contributes to the low status of women. A woman may even lose her life if she has brought an insufficient dowry, as in the many reported cases from India. See *E. Bumiller*, May You Be the Mother of a Hundred Sons, New York 1990, pp. 46–49, 111–112 and *I. Jaising*, Violence against Women: The Indian Perspective, in Women's rights, human rights, J. Peters & A. Wolper (eds.), p. 53.

[430] UN Doc. E/CN.4/1996/53, § 94. See also *K. Askin*, p. 251.

[431] The Government has, however, recently initiated legal reforms strictly forbidding foetus sex appraisal with modern medical means for non-medical purposes. Authorities were, in addition, urged to "seriously investigate and deal accordingly with such criminal acts as killing, trading and cruelly injuring new-born baby girls". The Programme for the Development of Chinese Women, 1995–2000, Beijing 1995, p. 22.

[432] The Government of India has adopted an Pre-natal Diagnostic Techniques Act in September 1994, which is expected to prevent the results of pre-natal procedures from being used as a reason for the abortion of female foetuses. UN Doc. E/CN.4/1996/53, § 94. At the same time some studies show that criminalising access to information on foetal sex has only made the information more expensive and decreased the possibilities for regulation or quality control. Therefore, it has been proposed that equal inheritance to family property (payment of dowry for girls and boys is closely linked to the inheritance system) should be required in law and practice and it may help to resolve the problem. The exclusion from family property is considered to create the impetus for large dowry payments at the time of marriage. *R. Balakrishnan*, The Social Context of Sex Selection and the Politics of Abortion in India, in Power and Decision, The Social Control of Reproduction, G. Sen & R.C. Snow (eds.), p. 279.

documents of international law,[433] as I pointed out at the beginning of this subsection, and it has been determined as a form of violence within the family.[434] First and foremost discrimination based on sex is wrong when it is based on false and invidious beliefs about persons of one sex or the other, *i.e.*, when the worth of a human being is conditioned by its sex. Secondly, the desire to preselect sex, except for certain medical reasons, *i.e.*, to avoid the birth of a child with a sex-linked disease such as Duchenne's muscular dystrophy, may unjustly harm those discriminated against. Nevertheless, even the use of sex preselection on medical grounds has been morally questioned. Academic commentators have argued that such circumstances would result in the abortion of perfectly normal foetuses of the one sex, *e.g.*, male foetuses suffering from haemophilia, while they lead to the birth of some female children who might be carriers of the genetic disease.[435] One may also wonder whether the argument that sex-selective abortions must be regarded as an injustice against an individual person is very strong at all, bearing in mind that the case law of the European organs for the protection of human rights shows that the foetus, according to the European Convention, does not have an absolute right to continued existence. Thus, abortion on whatever grounds under the first trimester of pregnancy has not been held contrary to this human rights treaty. Yet, Corinne Packer has suggested that while it "remains unlikely that any universal human rights provisions apply to foetuses", Article 2 of the European Convention read "alone or in conjunction with Article 14 on non-discrimination may be invoked to protect a foetus from abortion".[436]

Another proposal which has been made in the scientific debate suggests that sex-selective abortions should be rejected because they might lead to other forms of positive eugenics, which are morally objectionable, *i.e.*, preselection of traits that are desired, such as a certain intelligence quotient. In my opinion a distinction must be upheld between a possible legal toleration of selecting for *desirable* traits as opposed to screening out *undesirable* traits. Each of the procedures must be discussed separately. It is obvious that some of the preselective abortions belonging to the first group would have lesser social significance than sex-selective ones. The long-term social consequences of sex-preselection would probably be detrimental to women and society as a whole. It would lead to the institutionalisation of perceptions that males should continue to be more highly valued, *i.e.*, they would remain in possession of the structural power, comprising among other things the control of economic, legal and other key social institutions. It would lead to the confinement

---

433 The HRC included abortion of female foetuses during the examination of the governmental report of India under the ICCPR, for example, in its questions on non-discrimination and equality between sexes. *K. Tomaševski*, Women and Human Rights, p. 87. The Nepalese delegation expressed on 5 September 1995 at the Beijing Conference serious concern about these practices in developing countries in the context of gender-equality.

434 UN Doc. E/CN.6/1995/3, § 6.

435 *M.A. Warren*, The Ethics of Sex Preselection, in The Ethics of Reproductive Technology, K.D. Alpern (ed.), Oxford 1992, p. 234.

436 *C.A.A. Packer*, pp. 64–65.

of women to subordinated "female" roles. In consequence, I may establish that individuals' freedom of choice in terms of international law implies only a choice of the number of children that one wishes to have and when to have them but not to have a child of one's own choice.

Nevertheless, the view has often been taken that it is better for the spouses to choose the sex of the baby by technical means rather than forcing them to have several daughters before producing a son. This is said to increase the probability of the couple having a child of their own choice. The usage of such techniques would also help reduce population growth in the Third World. However, such reasoning must be strongly disapproved of as being contrary to human rights law. The cultural and social perceptions that such practices perpetuate and generate as regards women are clearly contrary to the prohibition of discrimination on the ground of sex. An approach of this kind is, moreover, counterproductive to the international community's aspiration to enhance the social and legal status of women and it is contrary to the principle of gender equality. Several provisions embodied in recent[437] universal human rights documents rest upon this strong consequentialist argument for banning sex preselection. One of the objectives of the ICPD Programme of Action as mentioned in § 4(16) is, for example, to eliminate the root causes of son preference, "which result in harmful and unethical practices regarding female infanticide and prenatal sex selection". Governments are urged on the basis of § 4(23) to take the necessary measures to prevent such practices. Alongside the encouragement to national leaders to "speak out and act forcefully against patterns of gender discrimination within the family, based on preference for sons", the need of equitable inheritance rights is emphasised. Other long-term measures of importance in this context are the enactment of legislation which: 1. Enables women to maintain their maiden name and to pass it on to their children so that the desire, where it exists, to continue the family name is fulfilled;[438] and 2. Guarantees social security for elderly people in order to free them from dependence upon economic support.

In addition to that the practice of dowries must be eradicated.

Also the Fourth World Conference on Women singled out for special attention the problem of son preference.[439] Governments as well as international organisations were urged in § 107(a) of the Beijing Declaration and Platform for Action to give priority to the elimination of harmful practices such as son preference and early marriage. It was also underlined that one of the important actions to be taken

---

[437] At the regional level, however, member states of the Council of Europe were encouraged already in 1986, on the basis of recommendation No. 1046 to prohibit the preselection of sex through genetic manipulation.

[438] Mrs. Bhutto said in her address to the Beijing Conference on 4 September 1995 that boys are wanted in her part of the world to satisfy the ego: "they carry on the father's name". Members of the Japanese delegation reported at the same occasion that their Government is considering reviewing the legal system pertaining to marriage, *e.g.*, by introducing a legal measure that permits a couple to retain their respective surnames after their marriage.

[439] See §§ 39 and 259 of the Beijing Declaration and Platform for Action.

by states in this regard is to enact and enforce legislation against prenatal sex selection (§ 124(i)).

Finally, sex selection may have unpredictable results, including a sharp imbalance in the sex ratio. Disturbing this balance can have grave consequences. One of the results could be increased violence and civil unrest. Recent data presented by the CSW show that for every 100 females delivered into the world there are 105 males born.[440] Since female human beings are generally biologically more resistant, the surplus of male infants is nature's way of balancing the sex ratio in the population. There are, however, parts of the world where this male-to-female imbalance is never overcome, probably because of sex-selective abortions as well as because of the practice of infanticide. In India, where the scientific selection technology has frequently been used[441] and the birth of a daughter is considered a serious calamity, only one out of 1,000 aborted foetuses is male. In addition, female children still have a higher death rate, caused mainly by neglect, than males.[442] The striking discrepancy in the sex-ratio was observed once again at the Women's Conference in Beijing and it was underlined that it is a cause for concern.[443] India, *e.g.*, is short of 50 million women. In China the average sex ration is 125 boys for every 100 girls (in some provinces the sex ratio is 164 new-born boys for every 100 girls).[444] Still there is no indication that scarcity will raise women's value to their benefit. Therefore, one of the strategic objectives as defined in the Beijing Platform for Action (part L. 2) is the encouragement of governmental actions as well as actions by international and non-governmental organisations to eliminate the root causes of son preference. Social acculturation processes over generations are not easy to breakdown, but the task is not impossible. The growing awareness globally about the phenomenon of sex-selective abortion as a gender bias, which must be eradicated gives us, however, some hope.

### *5.3.4.6. Responsible Choice*

Most of the international documents containing provisions on the right to family planning mention individuals' or couples' right to make decisions on procreation

---

440 UN Doc. E/CN.6/1995/3/Add.3, § 26. In India there are 957 females aged four years or under for every 1,000 males in the population. UN Doc. E/CN.6/1995/3/Add.3, § 27. According to UNICEF estimates there are 100 million fewer women than would be expected from general demographic trends. See UN Doc. E/CN.4/1996/53, § 98. There is unfortunately some confusion in the literature with regard to what is to be considered as the normal (natural) sex ratio. According to Packer in Europe and North America the normal sex ratio at birth is 106 females to 100 males. *C.A.A. Packer*, p. 64, note 163. On the other hand, Balakrishnan says that the biological sex ratio is commonly accepted as 105 males per 100 females at birth since male infants have a lower chance of survival than females. The biological sex ratio compensates in other words for the greater vulnerability of male infants. It evens out as children grow older. *R. Balakrishnan*, p. 267.

441 *W. Harcourt*, Bio-Medical Interventions: Young Women's Future Choice or Control?, Development 1990, No. 1, p. 63.

442 UN Doc. E/CN.4/1995/42, § 158.

443 The Beijing Declaration, § 259. See also UN Doc. E/CN.6/1995/Add.1, § 52.

444 *B.D. Miller*, p. 202 and *J. Hadley*, p. 97.

freely in conjunction with the adverb "responsibly". Yet none of them defines it. The concept of responsibility in the context of reproductive freedom has been elaborated in a number of documents since the late 1960's. Article 4 of the Declaration on Social Progress and Development adopted by the GA in 1969 states that: "Parents have the exclusive right to determine freely and responsibly the number and spacing of their children".[445] There was consensus among states delegations that this right should take priority over all other considerations, but at the same time the right to have children was tied to the responsibility of the couple not to have more children than they can support. Parents were expected to guarantee their children a life in dignity, that is, to ensure them food and clothing, to take care of them and to give them a good upbringing. The concept of responsible parenthood was further particularised in paragraph 14(f) of the World Population Plan of Action of 1974, which stresses the importance for couples and individuals, as regards family planning, to take consideration of their own situation as well as the implications of their decisions for the balanced development of their children and of the community[446] and the society in which they live. In other words, a limitation on the freedom of reproductive choice was introduced, since the right- bearers were expected to take decisions on procreation after considerations as to: 1. Their own situation, 2. The impact of the decision on their (living and future)[447] children and 3. Considerations of the community and society in which they live.

To become a parent is indeed one of the most complex lifetime decisions that individuals and couples are called upon to make. Becoming a *responsible* parent involves a sustained commitment to the economic, social and psychological support of the child for several years. In the words of Ruth Dixon-Mueller, individual reproductive behaviour "is to be governed by a sense of social responsibility".[448] Thus, the choice to enter parenthood involves the assessment of current and likely future circumstances in several matters. The private life and the wishes of the individual/couples will necessarily encroach upon the life of the community as a whole. A government can, therefore, determine how far it has responsibility to interfere with a certain right in the interest of societal control as well as in order to protect the rights and freedoms of others. Thus, it seems to me that justification can be found in human rights law to assert that the government after all may decide

---

[445] UN Doc. GA, Res. 2542(XXIV), 11 December 1969.

[446] On the other hand, Sandra Coliver has expressed the view that Article 16(1)(e) of the Women's Convention, *i.e.*, the only treaty provision of relevance, "does not include the notion of responsibility to the community". She continues by stating that the inclusion of the word "responsible" as a qualifier to the right to decide on the number and spacing of one's children can make it, however, possible for governments to argue "that they are entitled to limit the right on the grounds of achieving national interests". *S. Coliver*, The Right to Information, p. 546.

[447] Ten years later after the adoption of the above mentioned document this phrase was added to the above definition in recommendation No. 30 of the UN Conference on Population held at Mexico City in 1984.

[448] *R. Dixon-Mueller*, pp. 15–19. See in addition *H.M. Sass*, Responsibilities in Human Reproduction and Population Policy, in The Contraceptive Ethos, S.S. Spicker, W.B. Bonderson & H.T. Engelhardt (eds.), Dordrecht 1987, pp. 137–138.

whether a decision on family planning matters is responsible or not. Both the World Population Plans of Action (1974 and 1984) state that population policies should, among other things, be consistent with "national goals and values". In the IPCD Plan of Action (§ 7(3)) it is recognised that "the formulation and implementation of population-related policies is the responsibility of each country". A request is added to that inference that the promotion of responsible exercise of reproductive rights should be the fundamental basis for governmental and community-supported policies and programmes in the area of reproductive health.

An interesting feature in consensual documents from the 1990s, *e.g.*, § 7(3) in the IPCD Programme of Action and § 95 of the Beijing Declaration, is that they do not any longer uphold a request for the consideration of one's own needs in decision-making on procreation. The emphasis in family planning, consequently, embraces today not only individual, personal choices but mainly choices about relationships with others. Thus, I might say that the current interpretation of the term family planning involves a higher degree of individual responsibilities towards coming generations and towards our planet as a whole. China has embraced these changes and has sought justification for its family planning program for the years 1995–2000 on this basis. Public officials have remarked that if an unlimited population growth is allowed "the interests of the majority of the people, including those of new-born infants, will be seriously harmed".[449] Moreover, an effective solution to China's population problems (the country is the home of more than one-fifth of the world's population) is seen not just as a responsibility towards the well-being of the Chinese people and future generations, but "it is a duty owed to maintaining the stability of the world's population", *i.e.*, it is in the common interests of all humanity.[450] Such a policy could be considered as compatible with the latest developments in determining the term "responsible parenthood", provided that it is based on voluntariness. One should, however, bear in mind that not only is coercion contrary to human rights but "people cannot be held responsible when denied choice".[451] Similarly, Corinne Packer has stated that responsible reproductive behaviour "in no way releases a State from its obligations to ensure access to family planning information and services since an individual must have these in order to behave 'responsibly'".[452]

Finally, I ought to mention that during the Cairo, the Beijing Conferences and the Copenhagen World Summit for Social Development[453] governments from all over the world agreed that changes in both men's and women's attitudes are necessary in order to achieve a harmonious partnership between men and women and that promotion of equal responsibility, among other things responsible reproductive behaviour, is essential. Male responsibility in family life, the Cairo Conference declared, must be included in the education of children from the earliest ages. I

---

[449] Family Planning in China, p. 37.

[450] Op. cit.., at 39.

[451] *K. Tomaševski*, Human Rights in Population Policies, p. 22.

[452] *C.A.A. Packer*, p. 60.

[453] See § 4(24), § 4(27) of the ICPD' s Plan of Action and § 96 in The Beijing Declaration; Commitment 5 (g) of the 1995 Copenhagen Declaration on Social Development.

agree very much with this newly introduced approach in regard to responsible procreation behaviour. Family planning is not just a "woman's issue": it affects women as well as men. However, as Mr. Martino – the representative of the Holy See[454] to the Cairo Conference- observed, it is women who are most often "the principle victims of such irresponsible behavior". Encouragement of joint decision-making in the family and male support for his partner's choices related to reproduction are vital for a participatory orientation to reproductive health.[455] At the same time it is important to underline that the above approach presupposes that social institutions are structured in ways that do not perpetuate gender-based discrimination. The Cairo and Beijing Declarations are real challenges to cultures where men dominate reproductive decision-making. Therefore, we have to be aware of the risk that the formulations in these declaratory documents can be used in such a manner as to curtail women's abilities to exercise their reproductive freedom. Where parents disagree on the number of children for example, the men's views will usually prevail today in patriarchal societies.[456]

Parenthood is a consequence of a joint action, even though in the process of reproduction there exists inherent inequality, since pregnancy cannot be divided between parents and the dangers arising from unwanted pregnancy are different for men and women. However, still in some parts of the world, such as in African societies, the procreative capacities of women are under the control of men. In patriarchal-masculinist cultures fertility is considered a manifestation of power and virility. Consequently, men are negative to their wives' participation in fertility control.[457] Procreation is, moreover, seen as the primary function of wifehood.[458] On the other hand, if a father cannot compel a woman to accept the burdens of motherhood, it is arguable that a mother cannot force a man to accept the burdens of fatherhood. A woman's reproductive function should, consequently, not abrogate the man's right to participate in the decision to become a parent, because her decision affects the man's rights. Thus, he becomes legally liable for the child. There are not only financial but also emotional considerations in regard to forced fatherhood. It is important to protect both potential parents from imposed parenthood. If the woman declares falsely that she is using contraceptives in order to mislead her partner and the man relies on that assurance, her behaviour is a breach of trust. The man, then, has no standing whatsoever in the decision to terminate a pregnancy.

---

[454] Professor Mary Ann Glendon, the Head of the delegation of the Holy See to the Beijing Conference, also underlined that: "responsible procreation requires especially the equal participation and sharing of responsibility by husbands". Beijing, 5 September 1995.

[455] *N. Sadik*, The State of World Population, UNFPA, New York 1995, p. 36.

[456] Ibid., p. 37.

[457] *B.W. Harrison*, Our Right to Choose, Boston 1983, p. 162. To counteract this fact a resolution (Res. (78) 37) was adopted by the Committee of Ministers of the Council of Europe as early as 1978, which called on governments to amend their laws to ensure equality between the spouses especially in cases where the legal position of a wife is inferior to that of a husband, *e.g.*, where he has the sole right to take decisions.

[458] *R.T. Nhlapo*, Biological and Social Parenthood in African Perspective, Conference paper, Opatija 1991, p. 24.

The woman has the possibility to interrupt the pregnancy, if she has been forced into intercourse, but the man does not have that choice. In my opinion, the principle of equality and non-discrimination implies that each party to an intercourse shall bear equal responsibility for preventing unwanted pregnancy. If it is not prevented, neither of the two can later complain.[459]

### *5.3.4.7. Denial of Legal and/or Safe Abortion – A Governmental Coercion?*

#### 5.3.4.7.1. Universal Trends

In the previous sub-chapters I have explored some of the more or less uncontroversial elements of reproductive freedom. In the following I shall deal with the "thorniest problem of all",[460] *i.e.*, the question of whether abortion (the right to abort unwanted foetuses and/or access to safe[461] services) can be considered as an element of this freedom.

The growing concern internationally and nationally for maternal health[462] and the legal and social position of women in society,[463] as expressed in contemporary

---

[459] *P. Shifman*, Involuntary Parenthood: Misrepresentation as to the Use of Contraceptives, International Journal of Law and the Family 1990, Vol. 4, No. 3, p. 284.

[460] *C.A.A. Packer*, p. 71. Participants in the abortion debate represent in their extreme what has been described as clash of absolutes, *i.e.*, a conflict between two fundamental values, fetal life and procreative autonomy. No possibility of compromise exists in this controversy as long as it revolves around the "polarising question whether the foetus is a person having rights and interests of its own". See *M.A. Graber*, Rethinking Abortion, Equal Choice, the Constitution, and Reproductive Politics, Princeton 1996, p. 16 and *C.P. Schlegel,* Landmark in German Abortion Law: The German 1995 Compromise Compared with English Law, International Journal of Law, Policy and the Family 1997, Vol. 11, p. 56.

[461] A definition of "coercion" in respect of family planning should, according to some writers, include "not only forced abortion, sterilization, and contraceptive use, but also the denial of safe reproductive health services, including denial of safe abortion". *K.H. Martinez & B. Romney*, p. 24, note 29.

[462] In its analysis of Article 16 and other provisions of the Women's Convention, CEDAW stated in 1993, *e.g.*, that Article 16 is "closely related to Articles 2 and 12 of the Convention". UN Doc. A/48/38, § 636. Several authors have discussed the linkage between the regulation of fertility and the right to health. See, *e.g., R.J. Cook*, Human Rights in Relation to Women's Health; *C.A.A. Packer*, p. 70, *R. Dixon-Mueller*, p. 110 ff. See in addition §§ 92 and 97 of the Beijing Declaration and Platform for Action. Even countries that oppose abortion, such as Chile, stated at the Beijing Conference that while the Government reiterates its rejection of abortion it considers abortion a subject that must be addressed as a serious public health problem.

[463] Already in 1974 the World Population Conference recognised that the right to family planning had immediate benefits for the health, well-being and economic independence of women. Thereafter, both CEDAW and the CSW have produced comments of relevance. At its eighth session (1989) members of CEDAW, *e.g.*, asked Government representatives from Ireland during the consideration of its report under the Women's Convention, whether "the fact that abortion was illegal was not considered by the Government to be contrary to the objectives of equality of opportunity and self-determination enshrined in the Convention". The Committee requested, furthermore, data on deaths resulting from illegal abortions and it also wished to know if anything was being done to change the law. UN Doc. A/44/38, Suppl. No. 38, § 89. In 1993 CEDAW requested representatives from among others, Iraq and Kenya, to present more information on legislation and statistics on abortion under Article 12 of the Women's Convention. UN Doc. A/48/38, §§ 70, 128, 352 (France), § 438 (Republic of Korea), § 582 (England). In 1995 the CSW stressed the fact that the ability of women to control their own fertility was one important basis for the enjoyment of other human rights and it enables them to achieve their personal objectives. In consequence, all women should be in a position to plan and to organise their lives. UN Doc. E/CN.6/1995/3/Add.3, §§ 5 and 16.

international law documents, have legitimated the demands for an expansion of women's reproductive freedom to comprise legal abortion[464] if necessary. Even though it is hardly arguable that a legal ban of abortion in itself constitutes discrimination against women,[465] forcing a woman to bear the burden of an unwanted pregnancy by upholding prohibitive rules on abortion, will, however, have a discriminating effect in its practical results.[466] Thus, forced pregnancy imposes a heavy burden on women, severely restricting their lives. Men are not similarly affected.[467] In the words of Professor Dworkin an unwanted pregnancy "frustrates a woman's creative role in framing her own life".[468] Secondly, legal denial of abortion can also be considered as a violation of women's freedom of reproductive choice (including the ability to control the involuntary use of their bodies). It is against this background that I shall make an attempt to find possible justifications for a right to abortion as a component of the right to family planning.

In the absence of explicit textual (treaty) provisions, which might support such an assumption I shall look among others at authoritative statements, made by international supervisory bodies. CEDAW has, for example, encouraged states in the recommendations adopted at its session in 1993 to "provide information on the incidence of interruption of pregnancy and what legislative measures are in place to

---

[464] The term is sometimes used by the public to refer to induced abortions. Within the scholarly literature on that issue Professor Ronald Dworkin's starting sentence in his book "Life's Dominion" on page 3 that: "Abortion... (m)eans deliberately killing a developing human embryo" is somewhat provocative. Within international law, abortion was defined by WHO in 1950 in a more neutral manner as follows: "all foetal deaths in the early period up to nineteen weeks and intermediate period up to twenty eight weeks of gestation, whereas the term stillbirth should apply to the latest period". *B.W. Harrison,* Our Right to Choose, Towards a New Ethic of Abortion, Boston 1983, pp. 193–194.

[465] Mark Graber has argued on the other hand that abortion should be legal, because statutory bans have a history (in the USA) of being enforced in ways that intentionally discriminate against poor persons and persons of colour who have frequently been forced to choose between a dangerous abortion and an unwanted child. *M.A. Graber*, pp. 52 and 63.

[466] I shall return to the relationship between abortion rights and gender equality below but I shall already here refer to some of the authors who have examined the issue from that perspective. *R. Dixon-Mueller*, p. 135 and *G. Binion*, Feminist Theory Confronts US Supreme Court Rhetoric, p. 79 with further references in note 1. Significantly, several members of CEDAW expressed the view during the consideration of Colombia's fourth periodic report in 1999 that the legal prohibition of abortion was discriminatory and that overturning it was something the Government could do automatically and without delay. UN, Press Release WOM/1096, 3 February 1999.

[467] Apart from the argument based on lack of total control of the circumstances, in which women become pregnant, *i.e.*, in the case when men forcibly impregnate women, there is a need for a right to abortion as long as mothers live in a social situation of relative disadvantage. A freedom of choice about abortion will remain consequently necessary. Legal abortion is required in a context of women's cumulative inequality. In other words, the argument for freedom of choice as regards abortion is strengthened when it is based on the demand in international law to improve gender equality. *S. Martin,* A Women Centered Approach to Laws on Human Reproduction, in Human Rights in the Twenty-first Century, K.E. Mahoney & P. Mahoney (eds.), Dordrecht 1993, p. 913; *J. Sándor*, p. 157. Similar arguments have been put forward in discussions on national jurisdictions as, *e.g., J. Sinclair*, South Africa, From the Interim to the Final Constitution, in The International Survey of Family Law 1996, A. Bainham (ed.), The Hague 1998, p. 446 and *M.A. Graber*, p. 33 with the references contained in note 17.

[468] *R. Dworkin*, Life's Dominion, An Argument about Abortion and Euthanasia, London 1993, p. 97.

regulate it".[469] But is this a sufficient foundation for the hypothesis that CEDAW actually, by applying the dynamic method of treaty interpretation, can forward an evolution of the perception of the concept of family planning so that it includes a right to legal abortion and access to abortion services, and that the right as such can be interpreted into the Women's Convention?[470] The reservation made by the Government of Malta,[471] in regard to the content of Article 16(1)(e), when ratifying that treaty, is indicative and supportive of my presumption to some extent. It implies that Malta considered itself not bound by Article16 (1)(e) because of the fear of a probable interpretation of the right to family planning as imposing an obligation on states parties to legalise abortion. Packer believes on the other hand that the absence of reservations similar to that of Malta "does not necessarily imply that the remaining States Parties to the Convention interpret abortion as a method of family planning, only that they have not felt it necessary to make an explicit statement in this regard".[472] While it could be admitted on the factual basis that some signatory states to the Women's Convention still uphold restrictive laws on abortion, I find Packer's statement somewhat speculative because it is also true that there is a clear tendency towards liberalisation of abortion laws in most jurisdictions world-wide, as I shall demonstrate later on in this part of the study.

If my assumption is correct, then CEDAW's expansive understanding of family planning might also influence the interpretation and the implementation of other international documents containing provisions of relevance. As earlier mentioned, the contemporary approach towards international human rights law is to regard it as a coherent set of rules. Moreover, there seems to be growing recognition of the idea that priority should be given to such an interpretation of provisions contained in human rights treaties that they can afford the best protection or status to the individual. In other words, human rights norms should be interpreted in favour of the individual, which after all is the object of international protection.[473] Finally, the contemporaneous/dynamic interpretation of a treaty provision might require that the most recent documents be consulted. Therefore, I shall in what follows examine the final documents arising out of recent UN Conferences and which reflect the evolving consensus of the international community on the issue under discussion.

---

469 UN Doc. E/CN.6/1993/CRP.2, § 47.

470 Members of CEDAW interpreted the Women's Convention as requiring access to all methods of fertility control, including abortion already in 1983 when reviewing the country report from Ecuador. See *R.J. Cook & J.M. Haws*, p. 52. See also UN Doc. A/39/45, Suppl. No. 45, Vol. I, §§ 72, 169 and Vol. II, §§ 84, 257; UN Doc. A/42/38, Suppl. No. 38, §§ 97, 416 and UN Doc. A/43/38, Suppl. No. 38, §§ 154, 321. In addition, I may also mention that CEDAW in its analysis of Article 16 referred to the UN Expert Group Meeting on Family Planning which took place in 1992 and which rejected any attempt on the part of governments or international organisations "to prohibit abortion entirely". UN Doc. CEDAW/C/1993/4, § 115. See in addition the examples cited in *C.A.A. Packer*, p. 74, note 195 and CEDAW's comments on country reports during its 1999 session <http:www.wom.1096.html.>.

471 *L.A. Rehof*, p. 265. See also UN Doc. CEDAW/C/1995/6, § 30 and Annex 3.

472 *C.A.A. Packer*, p. 75.

473 See IACourtHR, *In the Matter of Viviana Gallardo et al. v. Costa Rica*, No. G/101/81, Decision of November 1981, Ser. A, Judgments and Opinions, § 16.

To start with, I may note that these declaratory documents are only to a certain extent supportive of the idea of an extensive interpretation of the right to family planning as indicated above. At the Cairo Conference the reference to "legal abortion" in the draft § 8.25 (dealing with family planning) was the one that gave rise to the most heated debate during the whole conference. Decriminalisation of abortion and eradication of existing repressive practices related to that issue was a proposal put forward by the Norwegian delegation.[474] It brought about criticism that this international gathering had become a conference on the abortion issue instead of on population matters. Malta's delegation took the standpoint in this regard that a state cannot be expected to legalise something it considers illegal. In addition, Afghanistan, Guam and Honduras required that the reference to legal abortion in the final document be deleted. The Holy See asserted that it attaches great importance to the question of maternal death and endorses those aims of the relevant paragraph that address women's health, but for moral reasons it does not approve of legal abortion.[475] In other words, these delegations perceived the proposed provision as favouring legal abortion, and in the view of the Holy See, its approval might elevate it to "the level of a right".[476] Reservations similar to the ones cited

---

[474] Mrs. Gro Harlem Brundtland, who at that time was the Norwegian Prime Minister, emphasised in her speech on 5 September 1994 that: "Morality becomes hypocrisy if it means accepting mothers suffering or dying in connection with unwanted pregnancies and illegal abortions, and unwanted children living in misery".

[475] Speaking before the adoption of the Programme of Action, the observer for the Holy See said that: "The Holy See affirms that human rights begin at the moment of conception. Thus, it could never accept population programmes that condone abortion". UN Doc. Press Release POP/572, 2, 14 September 1994.

The Vatican's Permanent Observer Mission enjoys UN status identical to Switzerland's (*i.e.*, as a non-member state permanent observer). This status places restrictions upon an entity's role at the UN. But because the UN treats the Holy See as a state, the Roman Catholic Church is able to participate fully and to vote in most UN's conferences. In some of the latest conferences on various human rights issues, the Holy See has taken such a high profile position that has sparked world-wide attention and raised questions regarding its status at the UN. Arguments have been advanced that the Holy See does not meet the criteria for statehood and that it is in reality the governing arm of a religious and not a civil institution. In fact, the Vatican has never made a formal membership (UN) application. The credibility of its report to the Beijing Conference was, moreover, challenged on several grounds. It was argued among other things that taking into account the structure of the Holy See there are no women taking part in its policy making, neither is there any indication that in the development of the Vatican's documents of relevance consultations with women have been made voluntarily. In other words, the position reflected in this document was said to be one sided–that of men. Women-Church Convergence, Equal is as equal does: Challenging Vatican views on women, IPPF 1995, No. 2, pp. 10–13. While the Holy See is a party to a few human rights treaties, it is not a party to the Women's Convention.

It might be of some interest to mention that several NGOs presented a Petition to withdraw UN observer status from the Holy See during the NGO Forum at the Beijing Conference. See, *e.g.*, a publication of the Centre for Research on Population and Security, North Carolina. See also the mailed petitions to CFFC, Washington. The petition of the Holy See was considered by many delegates as overreaching its observer status and obstructing with increasing frequency the action and development of consensus among member states. The Holy See had publicly opposed the credentials of certain women's NGOs seeking accreditation to the Beijing Conference at the 1995 CSW meeting. *R.J. Cook*, Human Rights in relation to Women's Health, p. 10.

[476] Statement delivered by H.E. R.R. Martino on 7 September 1994.

above were indicated by the delegations from Argentina, Peru and the Dominican Republic. The representative of Jordan, supported by Libya, said that his country would interpret the discussed paragraph in accordance with Islamic law. On the other hand, Zambia's delegation affirmed that keeping the reference to legal abortion in the Cairo Programme of Action was their rock bottom position. It seems that the latter position was also the majority's. However, consensus on that provision was not reached until the very last day of the conference and its formulation became weaker than proposed. Thus, it just refers to "circumstances in which abortion is not against the law", *i.e.*, it does not require the legalisation of abortion *per se*. UN conferences are processes of inter-state negotiations between different parties and are to some extent based on documents adopted at regional level by governments and international organisations. Several decisions made nationally and internationally in preparation for the Cairo Conference reflect the existing tensions between demographic goals, democratic values, interventionist anti-natalist or pro-natalist policies, reproductive and sexual health programs, and they all contributed to the very complicated negotiations in Cairo. The major obstacle in the adoption of a progressive provision was a handful of countries, the so-called "hard-liners", among them the Holy See, Honduras, Nicaragua, Malta, Benin, Morocco, Guatemala and Argentina with obstructive anti-contraception/abortion tactics. Still, women's advocates succeeded in weakening the position of this group; and as a consequence increasing women's opportunities for decision-making on their fertility, sexuality and child bearing options was recognised as a fundamental premise for women's empowerment. On that basis it was maintained that women should have access to safe contraception and legal abortion under broader health care. Thus, a major achievement of the Cairo Conference is that unsafe abortions[477] were considered a threat to the health of women (Article 12.17). It was pointed out that unsafe abortions are threatening the health of women in reproductive age more than anything else world-wide.[478] Reality shows indeed that unsafe, illegal abortions are a major contributing factor to maternal mortality in many countries. According to estimates 70,000 (it may be as many as 200,000)[479] women die each year as a result of undergoing avoidable, unsafe abortions. These deaths are needless. Most of them could be prevented if women had access to decent health care. Recent figures show that approximately 30 to 60 million abortions occur each year. They take place both in societies where abor-

---

[477] The term "unsafe abortion" is defined in a footnote to §§ 7.44 and 8.25 of the ICPD's Programme of Action as follows: "Unsafe abortion is defined as a procedure for terminating an unwanted pregnancy either by persons lacking necessary skills or in an environment lacking the minimal medical standards or both".

[478] *J.L. Jacobson*, Women's reproductive health, the silent emergency, World Watch Institute 1991, p. 5. See also UN Doc. A/171/4, § 167.

[479] UNICEF & UNIFEM, Convention on the Elimination of All Forms of Discrimination, New York 1995; WHO, Complications of Abortion, Geneva 1995. See also *R.P. Petchesky & J.A. Weiner*, Global Feminist Perspective on Reproductive Rights and Reproductive Health, Congress Report, New York 1990, p. 2; *R. Dixon-Mueller*, p. 141.

tion is absolutely prohibited[480] and in those where it is not. At least half of them are illegal and performed under unsafe conditions.[481] The incidence of unsafe abortion is highest in South America in spite of the Catholic Church's influence in the countries of this region. The estimated rate of unsafe abortion is the lowest in Asia among developing regions.[482]

In addition, unsafe abortions cause long-term bad health for at least one million others. Between 125,000 and 200,000 women die every year from complications resulting from an abortion, of which the majority occurs in developing countries such as Ethiopia, Colombia and Bangladesh.

We may notice that the term "unsafe abortion" has been given a broad meaning. It comprises not only illegal abortions. It also covers situations where there is a doubt that the legislated right to abortion actually provides women with access to safe abortions. Lack of legal restrictions on abortion has, for example, not ensured access to safe abortions as evidenced by the relatively high incidence of unsafe abortions (estimated by WHO at 30 unsafe abortions per 1,000 women aged 15–49 years) in the former USSR, despite the availability of abortion on request since 1956.[483]

It is apparent that the basic UN Programme of Action has broadened considerably from the one adopted at the end of the Mexico City Population Conference in 1984. Family planning has expanded to include, among other important issues, women's reproductive health and the promotion of women's equality. The importance of the Cairo Conference is that its blueprint (the final document) will serve as a guide for international population activities as well as national actions over the next 20 years.

This legal development was reaffirmed and further elaborated at the Conference in Beijing, where the abortion issue became only one of the major advances over previous conferences. Paragraph 106(k) of the Beijing Declaration and Platform for Action contains a commitment for states to consider reviewing laws containing punitive measures against women who have undergone illegal abortions. As during the Cairo Conference so in Beijing, about twenty states out of 181, a small but determined group of states from Latin America, the South-East Asian regions and

---

480 The Brazilian Penal Code, *e.g.*, classifies induced abortion among crimes against life. Irrespective of that induced abortions are widely carried out. Estimates vary from 1 million up to 6 million abortions per year. Moreover abortion was at the beginning of the 1990s the fifth leading cause of hospitalisation in the country. *E. Hardy et al.,* Illegal Induced Abortion Among Female Employees of A Brazilian University, in Unwanted Pregnancies and Public Policy, H. Correa (ed.), p. 110; *J. Pitanguy*, Feminist Politics and Reproductive Rights: The Case of Brazil, in Power and Decisions, The Social Control of Reproduction, G. Sen & R.C. Snow (eds.), p. 117. See also *S.G. Diniz, C. De Mello de Souza & A.P. Portella*, Not Like Our Mothers, in Negotiating Reproductive Rights, R.P. Petchesky & K. Judd (eds.), p. 61.

481 *K. Sundström*, p. 12; Swedish Government Official Reports, SOU 1994:37, *M. Bygdeman & K. Lindahl*, Sex education and reproductive health in Sweden in the 20th century. Report for the International Conference on Population and Development in Cairo 1994, Stockholm 1994, p. 35.

482 The United Nations, The World's Women 1995, Trends and Statistics, New York 1995, p. 43.

483 UN Doc. E/CN.9/1996/2, § 55.

several Arab states, indicated that they did not condone abortion and expressed a reservation to that specific provision.[484] Some of them referred to traditional values and cultural principles as a justification for the reservation (the Maldives, the Dominican Republic, Iraq, Nigeria), others to domestic legislation[485] and religious practices[486] (*e.g.*, Benin, the Philippines, Ecuador, Kuwait, Libya, and Morocco). At the same time it is noteworthy that a great number of countries from various geographical regions of the world and with populations linked up with one or several of the major religions of the world (*e.g.*, India, Bolivia, Colombia, El Salvador, South Africa, Tanzania, Spain on behalf of the EU) declared that they had no reservations whatsoever on the final document. On the contrary, they were very satisfied with its wording and expressly supported it.

---

[484] UN Doc. A/CONF.177/20, 157–177. It is noteworthy, however, that only the delegations of the Dominican Republic, Ecuador, Nicaragua and Peru entered reservations to § 220 of the Regional Programme of Action 1995–2001, which was adopted in preparation for the Beijing Conference in 1994. This document endorsed § 8.25 of the ICPD. UN Doc. E/CN.6/1995/5/Add.3.

[485] The Argentine delegation took a position based, as it said, on the legal tradition of the country and the practice of its courts, that Article 106(k) does not constitute "a proposal to decriminalise abortion or exempt from criminal responsibility those who may be accomplices or participants in this offence". UN Doc. A/CONF.177/20, § 158. Argentina submitted the same reservations concerning the Regional Programme of Action for the Women of Latin America and the Caribbean, adopted in Santiago, Chile in June 1995.

[486] The Peruvian President Mr. Fujimori criticised in his speech at the closing plenary of the Beijing Conference on 15 September 1995, the Catholic hierarchy in Peru for opposing the country's comprehensive family planning policy.

A striking feature from the Beijing Conference is that representatives from about twenty Islamic states who took the floor to comment on the Declaration and Platform for Action noted reservations to the final text in regard to the demand to review punitive domestic laws for illegal abortion since; they maintained, it was not in conformity with Islamic law. On the other hand, the Prime Minister of Pakistan, Mrs. Bhutto, representing a Moslem country, stressed in her speech at the opening Plenary on 4 September 1995 that it is not the religion itself but social prejudices that deny women's rights. This is in contrast to the assertion made by three male professors representing the Al-Azhar University at the Cairo Conference who said that Islam was not against family planning generally but it allowed abortion only to save the mother's life or health. Although the *fatwas*, or religious proclamations by this university, carry much weight amongst Muslims, these statements were heavily challenged as not being the authentic message of Islam by several Muslim NGOs and Muslim feminists participating in the Cairo Conference. *R. Hassan*, Women in Islam: Qur'anic ideals versus Muslim realities, IPPF 1995, No. 2, p. 8. This is a clear hardening of the prior to that conference general Islamic position according to which abortion is allowed until ensoulement, which is believed to take place after the first trimester. Some Muslim scholars consider that ensoulement occurs after 120 days, others that it occurs after 80 or even 40 days. Until these days had passed, the foetus did not count as a human life. Algeria (this article is based upon the statements of several contributors who wish to remain anonymous), in The Right to Know, S. Coliver (gen. ed.) p. 114; *C.M. Obermeyer*, A Cross -Cultural Perspective on Reproductive Rights, HRQ 1995, Vol. 17, p. 378.

Within the scholarly literature Aristotle wrote in one of his biological treatises (History of Animals, Book VII, Ch. 3, 583 b) that the male embryo develops a human soul about 40 days after conception, whereas a female foetus acquires its soul at about 90 days. For much of its history, the Christian Church believed in the delayed-ensoulement principle and allowed first trimester abortions. It was first in 1869 that Pope Pius IX forbade all abortions and declared that the soul was present from the instant of conception. See *R. Dworkin*, Life's Dominion, pp. 40–44; *J. Hadley*, p. 31.

The medical profession nowadays appears to follow the viability criteria.

From the above I may draw the conclusion that there is a clear tendency in the international community to recognise the adverse effects of unsafe abortions on women's health,[487] and the need to decriminalise inducive abortion has been stressed. Several arguments were presented at the Beijing Conference against the opponents of legal abortion, among other things that legalisation would not, as feared, increase abortion rates. Empirical data has been presented on several occasions, which shows that this fear lacks factual grounds (*see* next sub-chapter). On the contrary, statistics from countries with liberal legislation on abortion show that the rate of abortions stabilises a short time after the progressive reforms and even declines. Principally, the legislation prescribes where and under which medical circumstances women can undergo surgery. Several indications likewise support the assertion that illegal abortions are commonly resorted to in countries with a restrictive legislation.[488] Illegal abortions are generally unsafe, inasmuch as they are often performed by an unskilled provider. The risk of death from such an abortion is 100 to 1,000 times greater than from one performed by a qualified provider.[489] Therefore, the requirement contained in the recent UN documents mentioned above implying that "abortion shall be safe" and that women shall "have access to quality services for the management of complications arising from abortion" is a small but nonetheless a step forward in establishing an obligation for states to provide women with *safe* abortion services. Both UN Conferences stressed that states must make attempts to eliminate the need for abortion. Safe and effective means of contraception and sterilisation as well as the elimination of certain types of violence against women (*e.g.*, rape) would guarantee the freedom of choice without resort to abortion for women. Women resort to abortion predominantly under duress. Therefore, restrictive and punitive laws on abortion are not very effective in preventing abortion as such. They only affect the procedure in such a way that often women who must have a clandestine abortion expose their health and lives to risk. So, the controversy emphasises nowadays[490] not so much the question of whether or not to accept abortion, but merely *what* kind of abortion we will have and how to legitimise it.

5.3.4.7.2. European Consensus

At the regional level the Committee of Ministers within the Council of Europe recommended already in the mid 1970s in a resolution No. (75)29 with the title

---

[487] The Minister for Foreign Affairs of Finland argued on 6 September 1995 at the Beijing Conference that the right to health includes sexual and reproductive rights and that safe abortion is essential to those rights. UN Press Release, WOM/BEI/21, Beijing 1995.

[488] SOU 1983:31, p. 30; UN Doc. E/CN.9/1996/2, § 55. The incidence of unsafe abortions varies from a high of 30 or more unsafe abortions per 1,000 women aged 15–49 years in Eastern and Western Africa, Latin America and the Caribbean to fewer than 2 unsafe abortions per 1,000 women aged 15–49 years in Northern Europe and Northern America. See also Strategy for Development Cooperation, SIDA, p. 23.

[489] UNFPA, The State of World Population 1995, p. 48.

[490] *E. Hardy et al.*, p. 109.

"On legislation relating to fertility and family planning", governments members of the organization to "take all necessary steps to eliminate the practice of illegal abortion with its attendant dangers".[491] This document sets out guide-lines for among other things the attainment of a greater unity between the member states of the Council of Europe on the matter of fertility regulation. Principle D (3) of the resolution requires that abortion, when permitted by domestic law, should be available as a medical service to all women regardless of their social or economic position. States are, furthermore, requested to eliminate the practice of illegal abortion with its accompanying dangers (Principle D (4)).[492] The resolution is perfectly clear as to the standpoint that abortions should not be made *illegal* in the member states of the Council of Europe. On the other hand, a resolution of the Committee of Ministers is still considered by the majority as a category of "soft law" instruments. It has been maintained that such a document prescribes important international principles but not yet as binding law. On the other hand, non-legal instruments may have regulatory effects, as Professor em. Sztucki has observed: "by influencing national legislation and judicial decisions, or by constituting directly *ratio decidendi* in disputes on the international level".[493]

In the opinion of this author, the term "soft law" presupposes different phases in the law-making process in international law. Neither does such a view necessarily exclude the possibly compelling role which non-legal norms can play in international law. In that way even provisions of a non-legal character, on the pre-normative stage (embryonic norm), may have significant juridical relevance for our subject matter. Moreover, the above mentioned resolution reflects the prevailing opinion concerning the quest for the legalisation of abortion and making it safe, within a regional international organization.

Several years later, in 1990, the European Parliament adopted a resolution, dealing with the abortion issue, in which it expressed its conviction that "judicial prosecution is not an acceptable way of reducing its incidence".[494] The emphasis here was put on the right to the self-determination of women with regard to their fertility and their own lives.

The current developments within international organizations, mapped out in the review above, are very much in line with recently presented theories in the human rights law doctrine. Coercion has, for example, been defined in a very extensive

---

491 See (§ D) of the Res. (75)29 on Legislation relating to Fertility and Family Planning of 14 November 1975 adopted by the Committee of Ministers. Collection of the Council of Europe's work relating to equality between women and men (1950–1988), European Committee for Equality between Women and Men, Council of Europe, Strasbourg 1989, p. 129.

492 The delegations from Belgium and the Federal Republic of Germany reserved, however, their governments' right not to comply with the text of principle D, paragraph 4. The representative of Ireland expressed his Government's view that it did not consider itself obliged to comply with the text of the resolution as a whole. However, all three countries have since liberalised their very restrictive abortion laws, as we shall see in the next sub-section.

493 *J. Sztucki*, Reflections on International "Soft Law", p. 568.

494 *S. Detrick*, The Irish case, International Children's Rights Monitor 1992, Vol. 9, p. 6.

manner so that it includes also the denial of safe and legal abortion.[495] Considering it the other way around, abortion is an important means of ensuring women's right not to be forced into unwanted motherhood. It is, instead, a means to ensure a voluntary and responsible motherhood.

In addition to the sources discussed above of relevance for a right to legal abortion and/or access to abortion services, I shall also explore whether there is any support for the current approaches to abortion in international law on the domestic level.

5.3.4.7.3. Societal Attitudes Towards Abortion as Reflected in National Laws

Interruption of unwanted pregnancies is a phenomenon with an ancient history. Early-term abortion has been practised at all times and places. Ideas about and attitudes towards abortion have, however, to a great extent depended on what legal status has been attached to the foetus. They have also depended on the influence of religious norms in a certain society. Views about abortions are as diverse among nations as among individuals. Consequently, opinions on the abortion issue have varied from serious condemnation[496] to acceptance and to regulating it by law or even prescribing it.[497]

This diversity of, at times, contradictory views about the legal status of abortion may to a certain extent explain the hesitancy of the international organs dealing with human rights issues to take a clear standpoint on this important legal issue.

---

[495] *R. Boland, S. Rao & G. Zeidenstein*, Honoring Human Rights in Population Policies: From Declaration to Action, in Population Policies Reconsidered, G. Sen, A. Germain & L.C. Chen (eds.), p. 100; *K. Tomaševski*, Human Rights in Population Policies, p. 73; *R.J. Cook*, Human Rights and Reproductive Self-determination, p. 997.

[496] In the laws of Assyria *lex talonis* from the 10th century BC abortion was punishable with the death penalty. *C. Blomquist*, Medicinsk etik, Stockholm 1971, p. 164. According to Roman Law (Digest 47.4.1.), abortion was considered dishonourable, since it deprived the husband of his children with impunity. Therefore, a woman performing abortion could be sentenced to temporary exile. *R.H. Fee*, Abortion and Exposure in Ancient Greece: Assessing the Status of the Fetus and "New-born" from Classical Sources, in Abortion and the Status of the Foetus, W.B. Bondeson, H.T. Engelhardt, S.F. Spicker & D.H. Winship (eds.), Dordrecht 1983, p. 291. Abortion has very commonly been considered a serious criminal offence and is prosecuted in states with dictatorial regimes. So, during the Ceausescu dictatorship in Romania, for example, abortion became punishable by law in the mid 1960s. Abortion was regarded by the regime as a matter of state population policy with the consequence that the state was considered to have a right by various means to ensure population growth. Women were subjected to random pregnancy tests to confirm that they did not abort their foetus. Since 1966 until 1989 governmental statistics show that about 300 women per year died because of illegal abortions. *C.A.A. Packer*, p. 71; *E. Nilsson*, Fortsatt starkt stöd för abort, SvD 8, 24 April 1993. In our days we may identify numerous active militant anti-abortion societies also in countries with liberal abortion laws. See, for example, Abortion debate focuses on Florida, Acid attacks precede visit by hundreds of opponents, June 2, 1998, USA Today, p. 2A.

On different ideas about legal settlement of the controversy about abortion see generally *R. Dworkin*, Life's Dominion, p. 11 *et seq.*

[497] A common rationale for desirable abortion in some traditional societies is the so called "improper" paternity. In East Africa the Masai mandate abortion if the father is an "old, weak, or infirm man". See *L.H. Tribe*, Abortion, The Clash of Absolutes, New York 1990, p. 54. Abortion was widely approved and was a common practice in ancient Greece. Philosophers such as Plato and Aristotle saw the use of abortion as a means of family planning. *R.H. Fleen*, p. 290.

*A. Categorisation of Domestic Laws*

Current world-wide approaches[498] to abortion, as reflected in national laws, can roughly be described with the help of the following distinguishing features, which to some extent are typical of the great variety of legal solutions to the issue. Within the ***first*** category fall jurisdictions (about 50), in which abortion is completely banned or allowed only when the woman's life would be endangered, if the pregnancy is carried to term, for example, in countries such as Afghanistan, Chile,[499] Ecuador, Nigeria,[500] the Philippines, Saudi Arabia, Zaire.[501] In some of these countries abortion is regulated within the realm of criminal law and it is punishable. In Nepal, for example, women risk lengthy terms of imprisonment for self-induced abortion.[502] Regulations of that kind are often justified on the grounds of the right to life of the foetus.[503] Still,

---

[498] Most examples of prohibitive and restrictive laws on abortion are to be found in Latin America, parts of the francophone Africa and partly North Africa. See *R.J. Cook*, International Protection of Women's Reproductive Rights, p. 667; *R. Lahti,* Law and Moral Dilemmas Affecting Life and Death; Council of Europe, CJ-DE/XX (90)5, Strasbourg 1990, p. 18.

[499] *L. Katzive & K.H. Martinez*, Roe v. Wade in the Global Context: International Recognition of Abortion Rights, ASIL, Human Rights Interest Group Newsletter 1998, Vol. 8, p. 5; OAS,CIM, National Report: Chile, OEA/Ser.L/II.2.28, 1996, p. 10.

[500] *A. Hardon & E. Hayes*, p. 18.

[501] See World Abortion Policies 1994, UN Department for Economic and Social Information and Policy Analysis, New York 1994. Totally in 173 of the world's 191 countries abortion is permitted to save the life of a woman, *N. Sadik*, The State of World Population 1995, p. 43.

[502] *K. Tomaševski*, Human Rights in Population Policies, p. 74. An estimated 75% of all women incarcerated in Nepal are there for having had an abortion. *L. Katzive & K.H. Martinez*, p. 5.

[503] The national laws in several countries use *implantation* (implantation begins 6–7 days after fertilisation and can be described as the process whereby the embryo becomes burrowed in the lining of uterus) or *conception* (conception occurs at the time of implantation in the uterine mucosa, *i.e.*, about 14 days after fertilisation) as the beginning of protection of the unborn child. Fertilisation is generally defined as the fusing together of the maternal and paternal genetic material from the sperm and the egg. I may mention in this regard that embryo experiments are banned from 14 days after fertilisation onwards according to national as well as international principles. The 14th day is considered important because it is said that until then cells are pluripotential. Thus, it is not known whether they will develop into any hydatiform mole, into twins, into one embryo, or degenerate into nothing. See generally *A. Redelbach*, Protection of the Right to Life by Law and by Other Means, in The Right to Life in International Law, B.G. Ramcharan (ed.), Dordrecht 1985, p. 198 *et seq.*; *A. Wolkinger*, Lebensbeginn durch Menschenhand?, in E. Bernat (ed.), Graz 1985, p. 89 ff.; *A. Leist* (ed.), Um Leben und Tod, Frankfurt am Main 1990; the dissent opinion of Dr. Cabra in the *Baby Boy* case, case No. 2141 (United States), Inter-American Commission on Human Rights, resolution 23/81, OEA/Ser.L/V/II.54, doc. 9, rev.1, p. 16.

Aristotle seemed to consider the foetus a "human being" in the full sense of the term from the time it was formed. He maintained that formation took place 40 days after conception in the male foetus and 90 days in the female foetus. At that time the human soul was infused. Only abortion of the formed foetus was considered a murder. The morality of abortion was consequently related to the issue of whether a human soul was present or absent. In other words abortion prior to that stage, especially if the foetus was female, was not considered as the deliberate killing of another human being. *Aristotle*, Politics, book VII, sec. XIV, London 1944, p. 623. Thomas Aquinas, the Christian philosopher, believed likewise that the formation of the male embryo took 40 days and 80 days for girls. Aborting a foetus before that did not involve depriving a soul of the opportunity of baptism and was not considered a crime. Interestingly, distinctions on the ground of the sex of the foetus in the context of abortion were reflected in the national laws in a number of European countries and disappeared as late as the 19th century.

prohibitive law and religion have been powerless to stem the tide of up to four million illegal abortions every year in Latin America.[504]

Within the ***second*** category fall some 81 countries having statutes authorising abortion on broad medical grounds and for juridical reasons (incest or rape) but not for social reasons alone or on request. It seems, however, that these restrictions on a woman's freedom of procreative choice are rarely strictly upheld in reality,[505] because every day approximately as many as 150,000 unwanted pregnancies are terminated through induced abortions.[506] Still, interpreting abortion data is difficult, since surveys in many countries indicate that abortion is grossly under-reported and the availability of reliable statistics is very limited. Abortion is often a secret business.

Most jurisdictions, which have liberalised their abortion laws, have also extended abortion eligibility so as to include traditional reasons such as family circumstances and new reasons such as AIDS or HIV infection. 56 countries belonging to this category allow abortion on social and medical grounds.[507]

The ***third*** category comprises the national laws of 41 countries, which allow abortion on a woman's demand. Thus, an unconditional right to abortion on a woman's request is guaranteed. Even in these jurisdictions, however, women do not have a right to abortion during the whole of the pregnancy. A distinction is made between the early and late stages of gestation by the vast majority of legislators. Thus, the right to abortion implies that women are in a position to decide whether or not to perform an abortion only during the early stages of pregnancy.[508] In other words, they are not obliged to give any reasons and need not specify any grounds for having an abortion during the first three months of pregnancy. During the second trimester up to viability,[509] states usually have regulations on the grounds for abortion. After viability only the life and health of the woman serves as grounds for abortion. This approach is to a great extent based on the American model developed in the *Roe v. Wade* case,[510] implying a test of balancing the competing interest

---

[504] Allan Gutmacher Institute, Clandestine Abortion: A Latin American Reality, New York 1994.

[505] *R.J. Cook,* International Protection of Women's Reproductive Rights, p. 669. According to statistics about 30–40 million legal abortions are performed in the world a year. On the other hand, given the clandestine nature of unsafe abortion, its incidence is very difficult to gauge. WHO has estimated that some 20 million unsafe abortions are performed each year. UN Doc. E/CN.9/1996/2, § 51.

[506] WHO, Reproductive health: a key to a brighter future, Biennial Report 1990–1991, Special 20th anniversary issue, New York 1992. See also UN Doc. A/CONF.171/4, § 125.

[507] *M.F. Fathalla,* Fertility Control Technology: a Women-Centered Approach to Research, in Population Policies Reconsidered, G. Sen *et al.* (eds.), p. 227. See also UN Doc. A/CONF.171/4, § 126.

[508] Some of the countries with liberal abortion laws have, however, made it subject to being restricted to licensed practitioners or facilities. *R. Dixon-Mueller*, p. 171.

[509] It has been argued that the viable foetus and the newly born child show no greater difference than the fact that the foetus receives its nourishment through the navel string and the born child through its mouth. It is also underlined that even when the foetus is still *in uterus* it would be capable of independent life, and its chance of surviving outside the mother's womb is considerable.

[510] 410 US113 (1973). Justice Blackmun held in his opinion in this case: "The right of privacy, whether it be founded in the Fourteenth Amendment's concept of personal liberty and restrictions upon state action, as we feel it is, or... in the Ninth Amendment's reservation of rights to the people, is broad

of the mother and the state's interest in the foetus. The United States Supreme Court declared in this case that any state law that makes abortion illegal in order to protect the foetus within the first two trimesters of pregnancy is unconstitutional. However, states are permitted to regulate abortion in the second trimester of pregnancy in order to protect the mother's health. In this respect the Court applied a dynamic concept of viability by stating that viability usually occurs at about 28 weeks but it may occur earlier, even at 24 weeks.

An interesting feature of countries with a permissive abortion system is that the rate of abortions is kept relatively low, for instance in the Netherlands and Japan,[511] while Romania, when a strict abortion law was in force, had one of the highest abortion rates.[512] Statistics show that the number of abortions has even decreased after the liberalisation of the abortion regulations in Hungary,[513] Denmark[514] and Finland.[515] In the district of Stockholm (Sweden) abortions declined with 13.5% during 1993.[516] Consequently, several countries with a liberal approach to abortion have not shown that the legislation itself is counterproductive to the legal protection afforded to the foetus,[517] since abortion occurs less frequently than in many

---

enough to encompass a woman's decision whether or not to terminate her pregnancy". *Supra*, at 153. After this judgment the Supreme Court had to decide in a number of cases involving different issues of state regulation of abortions. The essential position of *Roe v. Wade* in establishing a core right for a woman to terminate her pregnancy before viability was reaffirmed in the *Planned Parenthood v. Casey and Casey* case (112 S. Ct.2791 (1992)) on June 29, 1992. However, the majority (five out of nine members of the Court) applied a new test for state regulations of abortions, *i.e.*, the undue burden test (the test implies that regulations imposing substantial obstacles to woman's choice about abortion create undue burden on the woman). Since Pennsylvanian law prohibited doctors from performing an abortion on a married woman without a written proof that her spouse had been notified of the abortion, this provision imposes an undue burden on a woman's right to have an abortion and was considered therefore unconstitutional. Ibid. at 2829. On the other hand, there were partially concurring and partially dissenting opinions by four Justices of the Court. A fact, which has motivated Justice Blackmun's concern about future developments, expressed in the following way: "All that remained between the promise of Roe (vs. Wade) and the darkness of the plurality was a single flickering flame.. now, just when so many expected the darkness to fall, the flame has grown bright... I fear for the darkness as four justices anxiously await the single vote necessary to extinguish the light". Ibid. at 2844.

511 *H.P. Kee*, Abortion in Singapore: a Legal Perspective, ICLQ 1993, Vol. 42, p. 392. See also *K. Shiota*, Induced abortion and unwanted pregnancies in Japan, in Unwanted Pregnancies and Public Policy, H. Correa (ed.), p. 145 and *J. Hadley*, p. 137. See also Strategy for Development Cooperation, SIDA, p. 23.

512 *M.A. Glendon*, Abortion and Divorce in Western Law, Boston 1987, p. 60. See also UNFPA, The State of World Population 1995, p. 156.

513 UN Doc. CEDAW/C/13/Add.1, Amendment 1, p. 6.

514 UN Doc. CEDAW/C/13/Add.14, § 20.

515 UN Doc. CEDAW/C/5/Add.56, § 24.

516 *F. Mellgren*, Aborterna minskar i länet, SvD, 11 February 1993, p. 8. See also SOU 1994:37, Stockholm 1994, pp. 33–35. The legal right to abortion in Sweden has resulted in an improved health situation, fewer unwanted pregnancies and a decreasing number of abortions in the whole country. Statistical Yearbook, Stockholm 1995, p. 320. See also *Women and Men in Sweden*, Facts and Figures 1998, Statistics Sweden, Stockholm 1998, p. 20.

517 *P. Westman*, Protection of the Unborn Child and the Rights of Parents, SvJT 1993, Vol. 78, p. 479 *et seq.*

countries where it is considered a crime. Thus, law has an impact on the safety of abortion but not on the numbers. There is no sufficient factual basis for the fear that legal abortion promotes promiscuity. Moreover, these countries have a very high total fertility level. Also in countries belonging to the former communist block, for example Russia, Albania and Romania, the number of abortions has fallen by as much as 23% in 1993 in comparison to the number of abortions performed in 1989. It is believed, however, that here not the legality *per se* but the increased poverty in society is the reason for this development.

*B. Current Developments*

The international picture of abortion laws shows at present many contrasts. Along with the attitudinal changes, which have led to the increased legalisation of induced abortion,[518] we may also observe a tendency towards a more restrictive approach to abortion in a few European countries with a previously liberal attitude. In Germany, *e.g.*, the Federal Constitutional Court (*Bundesverfassungsgericht*) in Karlsruhe declared on 28 May 1993,[519] by a six-two ruling in a 183-page-decision, substantial parts of the liberal law regulating abortion adopted in 1992 with a clear majority as a compromise for the reunified Germany,[520] incompatible with the Basic Law of Germany, which in Article I, § 1 and Article 2, § 2 establishes unlimited duty upon the state to protect unborn life. According to this decision abortion is unlawful, but it is not penalised.[521] The judgment has mainly practical implications, since, if abortion is considered unlawful, no state-supported compulsory public health

---

[518] South Africa, for example, a country with highly restrictive law of abortion, adopted in 1996 a new and very liberal legislation (Choice on Termination of Pregnancy Act), which took effect on February 14, 1997. Abortion becomes in consequence available at the woman's request during the first 12 weeks of pregnancy. *L. Katzive & K.H. Martinez*, p. 4; *J. Sinclair*, South Africa, From the Interim to the Final Constitution, in The International Survey of Family Law 1996, A. Bainham (ed.), The Hague 1998, p. 446.

[519] Bundesverfassungsgericht, Zweiter Senat, Urteil vom 28 Mai 1993, 2 BVFG 2/90; 2 BVFG 4/92; 2 BVFG 5/92; NJW, Heft 26, 1751,1993.

[520] Before the reunification of West and East Germany in 1989 the national laws regulating abortion in both countries differed greatly. Whereas in the German Democratic Republic abortion was permitted on demand, *i.e.*, the law spoke of a woman's right to an abortion, in West Germany a doctor's certificate was required justifying the necessity of the abortion (on medical, genetic, ethical grounds or because of social hardship) in each single case. Counselling was mandatory. The so-called *Indikationslösung* has been in force since 18 May 1976, (BGBl 1976, I, 1213) making the termination of pregnancy within the first twelve weeks of pregnancy punishable under the criminal code. Therefore, it was believed that the Pregnancy and Family Assistance Law from 27 July 1992 (BGBl 1992, I, 1398) had adequately balanced these varying concerns. A termination of pregnancy within the first twelve weeks remained non-punishable if the pregnant woman consulted a recognised office. However, this law did not take effect.

[521] "Schwangerschaftsabbrüche, die ohne Feststellung einer Indikation nach der Beratungsregelung vorgenommen werden, dürfen nicht für gerechtfertigt (nicht rechtswidrig) erklärt werden. Es entspricht unverzichtbaren rechtsstaatlichen Grundsätzen, daß einem Ausnahmetatbestand rechtfertigende Wirkung nur dann zukommen kann, wenn das Vorliegen seiner Voraussetzungen unter staatlicher Verantwortung festgestellt werden muß". Die Entscheidung des Bundesverfassungsgerichts zum Schwangerschaftsabbruch vom 28 Mai 1993, Juristen Zeitung, 2 Sonderausgabe 7 Juni 1993.

insurance programme can cover the costs of an abortion.[522] Of significance is, however, that the Court approved the last decision competence of the woman concerning the termination of pregnancy. The decision of the Federal Court from 1993 comprising the provisional regulation of "*Fristenlösung*",[523] *i.e.*, implying that women may perform abortion during the first 12 weeks of pregnancy under special conditions, *e.g.*, must pay for the abortion themselves, remained the law in force until October 1995.[524]

At the same time, I cannot ignore the fact that action towards a greater liberalisation of laws on abortion, *i.e.*, in favour of a more permissive stance, has been growing steadily in many countries, notably in Belgium, in Romania,[525] in Albania,[526] in Spain,[527] in Bulgaria[528] and in Italy,[529] where access to legal abortions has been made easier by recent legislation, although abortion is far from being available on request. In other European countries, *e.g.*, Ireland, such efforts have been less successful. Thus, to procure an abortion in Ireland still remains a criminal offence. On the other hand, impeding legislation ought not to any longer, *i.e.*, on the basis of decisions of international organs, restrict the right to obtain and provide information on abortion.

---

[522] In other words, abortion shall not as a rule be performed in state-funded clinics. The creation of such a medical system, where performance of abortion is dependent upon the financial power of a woman, is in the view of this author difficult to defend. Several other writers have pointed to the fact that the costs of terminating a pregnancy will be a "heavy burden for many German women". *R. Frank*, Federal Republic of Germany: Three Decisions of the Federal Constitutional Court, University of Louisville Journal of Family Law 1995, Vol. 33, p. 357.

Nevertheless, a special statute, the *Women's Aid Act* concerning abortions in special cases, was passed in 1995 which applies to women who have restricted financial means or assets. *C.P. Schlegel*, p. 48.

[523] *Fristenlösung* (straffreie Abtreibung in den ersten drei Monaten der Schwangerschaft) was based on women's right to self-determination, *i.e.*, women may decide themselves whether or not to perform abortion during the first three months of pregnancy. The availability of abortion on request was a part of a package of equal opportunity measures for women. In other words, the previous law on discontinuation of pregnancy dated 9 March 1972 (GBl 1972, I, 89) which was in effect in the GDR, expressly referred to a woman's right to an abortion. See *M.K. Eriksson,* The Legal Position of the Unborn Child in International Law, GYIL 1993, Vol. 36, p. 261; *F.K. Fromme*, Rechtswidrig, aber nicht strafbar – der Weg zur Abtreibung wird im Westen kürzer, Frankfurter Allgemeine Zeitung, 16 June 1993, p. 3.

[524] The *Schwangeren und Familienhilfeänderungsgesetz* came into force partly in October 1995 and partly on 1 January 1996. BGBl 1995, I, 1050–57. The recent German law constitutes a kind of mixture of the time-limit model (*Fristenlösung*), the pro-child counselling model (*Beratungslösung)* and the indication model (*Indikationslösung*). It corresponds to a large extent to the decision of the Constitutional Court referred to above. For a more in depth comment on recent developments in Germany see *C.P. Schlegel*, pp. 36–63.

[525] Abortion is now permitted at the woman's request during the first 14 weeks of pregnancy. *J. Hadley*, p. 177; *L. Katzive & K.H. Martinez*, p. 5.

[526] Whereas abortion was completely suppressed by the former Albanian regime, in June 1991 the Albanian Ministry of Health authorised abortion on request. *E. Sahatci*, Albania: Discovering the human right to family planning, IPPF 1995, p. 25; *J. Hadley*, p. 177.

[527] *M.A. Glendon*, p. 11.

[528] *K. Tomaševski*, Human Rights in Population Policies, p. 75.

[529] *R. Dworkin*, p. 5. Between 1967 and 1987 abortion laws were liberalised in about 65 countries. *S. Coliver*, The Right to Information necessary for Reproductive Health and Choice under International Law, p. 64.

So, I may conclude that this very brief account of domestic legal solutions of the abortion issue indicates that according to statistics about 48% of the world's population lives in countries (22% of the states members of the UN) with a very liberal attitude towards abortion, *e.g.,* abortion is there an unconditional right upon a woman's request.[530]

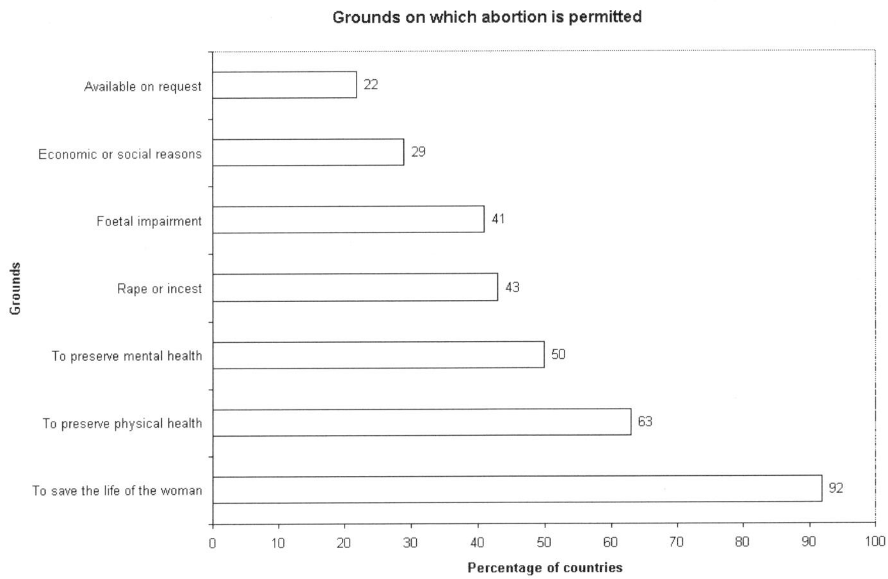


All these countries have acceded to relevant conventions on human rights. This is a fact which cannot be immaterial when considering the demand for the decriminalisation of abortion in recent international law documents. There is, in addition, a clearly recognisable global trend toward a liberalisation of rules on the interruption of pregnancy. I may at the same time point out that a very substantial minority of states allow abortion on request, even though, on the other hand, a great number of countries continue to maintain laws that criminals abortion.[531] This gives us a little support for the presumption that a right to abortion is increasingly being legally enforced and is gaining world-wide acceptance today. I may only suggest that on the basis of what has been said above, the majority of states favour at

[530] At the same time one should remember that many of the reforms leading to liberal abortion laws in the countries of Central- and Eastern Europe were primarily motivated by the goal to protect women from the negative impact of unsafe and illegal abortion on their health rather than a conviction that a woman had a legal right to terminate her pregnancy. *S. Coliver & W. Nowicka, Poland,* in The Right to Know, S. Coliver (ed.), p. 270.

[531] For 39% of the world's population, abortion is still illegal. *L. Katzive & K.H. Martinez,* p. 5.

present legal regulation of abortion on certain conditions. The indications for legal abortion vary. While medical reasons are broadly accepted, social and economic indications are more rare. It has been, however, pointed out that laws regulating abortion have limited a capacity to influence the phenomenon *per se*. Other living conditions for women, such as economic and educational, seem to influence its performance more than legislation.[532] In other words, permissive abortion law and practice does not necessarily imply a higher incidence of abortion. And restrictive abortion laws or /and practice can not automatically be connected with lower abortion rates.[533]

### *5.3.4.8. Access to Abortion Services*

Of crucial importance for women's ability to exercise the right to their own choice in procreation matters is the second element of the right to family planning, *i.e.*, the right to implement such decisions. It is decisive, because "it acknowledges that the abstract right to make a decision is meaningless if the conditions needed to carry it out do not exist".[534] The relevant provision of the Women's Convention reflects this line of reasoning, since it entitles women to demand means necessary for the exercise of their right to family planning, such as access to contraception methods and not merely information on fertility. Furthermore, Articles 12(1) and 14(2)(b) of the same Convention place states parties under a duty to take appropriate measures to ensure access to "family planning" services. Such an obligation has been restated in Article 24(2)(f) in the Convention on the Rights of the Child, where states parties undertake to develop, in addition to preventive health care, guidance for parents' family planning education and services.

The self-evident interpretation of this right comprises equal access to family planning services, in the sense that women shall have the right to obtain contraceptives without spousal authorisation.[535] CEDAW considered recently that the requirement of spousal authorisation for abortion (in the case of Turkey) contravened Article 15 of the Woman's Convention.[536]

However, the *travaux préparatoires* of the relevant provisions are silent on the question of whether access to (safe) abortion services are also included therein. Neither did CEDAW mention it *verbatim* in the text of its General Recommendation No. 21. At the same time § 21 of the same document establishes that women are entitled to be "guaranteed access to sex education and family planning services". CEDAW has in consequence urged several governments, among them Italy's,

---

532 *H. Correa*, The Impact of Abortion Legislation, in Unwanted Pregnancies and Public Policy, H. Correa (ed.), p. 156.

533 CEDAW experts noted during their discussion on women's health issues at the 286th meeting, 3 February 1995, that where contraception and abortion services are widely available, the incidence of abortion was often quite low.

534 *L.P. Freedman*, Censorship and Manipulation of Reproductive Health Information, in The Right to Know, S. Coliver (ed.), p. 6.

535 *R.J. Cook & J.M. Haws*, p. 50.

536 UN Doc. CEDAW/C/1997/L.1/Add.5, § 36.

during the consideration of their periodic reports, to guarantee women access to safe abortion services in public hospitals.[537]

The understanding of the right to family planning as including access to safe abortion services has, however, been confirmed earlier, at the World Conference with the aim to review and appraise the achievements of the UN Decade for Women, which took place in Nairobi in 1985. In the recommendations adopted at the Conference it was stated among other things that: "(l)egal, good-quality abortion services should be made easily accessible to all women".[538]

The 1993 Vienna World Conference on Human Rights recognised the importance of the enjoyment by women of the highest standard of physical and mental health and reaffirmed women's right to "accessible and adequate health care and the widest range of family planning services".[539] Access to abortion services was not verbally mentioned in the final document. But only one year thereafter, in 1994, some 181 states agreed that one of the important goals of the ICPD Programme of Action, as defined in paragraph 7.16, is to provide "universal access to a full range of safe and reliable family planning methods and to related health services which are not against the law" by the year 2015. Governments are especially urged to remove unnecessary legal, medical, clinical and regulatory barriers to information and to access to family planning services and methods in order to make it easier for couples and individuals to take responsibility for their own reproductive health (§ 7. 20). Abortion services are mentioned in § 7.6, according to which all countries shall strive to make them available through the primary health-care system with reference to § 8.25. Thus, state action is required as to minimising the negative health impact of unsafe abortions. This is one of the areas where substantial progress was later on achieved at the Beijing Conference, since the Beijing Platform for Action expanded beyond the earlier texts in adding that abortions where they are not against the law "should be safe" (§ 106 (k)).

Unfortunately, I am unable here to draw any far reaching conclusions in regard to whether safe abortion services are existing and affordable in reality to all who need them on the national level, since no large-scale studies have been undertaken on this issue.[540] The UNFPA referred in a report from the year 1995 only to the fact

---

[537] See Part I of this study and UN Doc. CEDAW/C/1997/L.1/Add.8, § 19. In the Nordic countries, *e.g.*, all abortions are performed in public hospitals. Abortion is in these societies integrated into the general health care. The situation is similar in several other European countries. See Ministry of Health and Social Affairs, Shared Power Responsibility, Stockholm 1994, p. 74; *C. Forder*, The Netherlands, in The International Survey of Family Law 1995, A. Bainham (ed.), The Hague 1997, p. 380. In the USA abortion facilities are, on the other hand, left to private initiatives and most women have to pay for the abortions themselves. *J. Rademakers*, Abortion Laws and Practice: An International Comparison, in Unwanted Pregnancies and Public Policy, H. Correa (ed.), pp. 165–167.

[538] UN Doc. A/CONF.116/5/ Add. 6.

[539] UN Doc. A/CONF.157/6, Part II,12 June 1993, § 41.

[540] *J. Zeitlin, R. Govindaraj & L.C. Chen*, Financing Reproductive and Sexual Health Services, in Population Policies Reconsidered, G. Sen, A. Germain & L.C. Chen (eds.), p. 246. For a case study on the availability of abortion services in a number of countries in different parts of the worlds see *A. Hardon & E. Hayes* (eds.), Reproductive Rights in Practice, London 1997.

that "120 million women would be using family planning if (a)ffordable services were easily available" and that most women in developing countries do not have access to safe abortion services.[541] An inquiry carried out in late 1995, based on the response of 78 developing countries, identifies that 38% of them did not have any abortion services available as required in § 8.25 of the ICPD Programme of Action.[542] One explanation for this undesirable state of affairs can be found in the poor allocation of governmental resources to such activities. Family planning services account for less than 0.5 per cent of governmental budgets of developing countries and "less than 1.5 per cent of all foreign aid" to these countries.[543] It is apparent that in order to be able to implement the Cairo and the Beijing documents the donor governments, the international donors, as well as the developing countries themselves, have to increase expenditures in order to meet the requirements for increasing the safety of abortion services to all. Safe abortion should not be an option only for high-income and rich women. Governments should provide some funding at least for those who are in need but who cannot afford such services. The denial of state funding would make it difficult, if not impossible, for poor women to exercise their reproductive freedom.[544] Yet another problem for women living in rural areas in developing countries is that even if abortion services are for free, it can be expensive to get to them because of transportation costs. Loss of income can also be an additional burden. Health centres and clinics are often located too far away. In Kenya about 23 per cent of the women in fertile age live farther than 8 km to a health facility.[545]

The above mentioned circumstances lead us to the conclusion that a legal right to abortion might in reality be of lesser importance for women if abortion services are not accessible. Abortion may be legal and yet unsafe. And on the contrary safe abortion services may be available despite legal constraints. Abortion services are available, for example, in Bangladesh, as well as in some areas in Malaysia and in Indonesia, despite restrictive legal rules on abortion.[546] Another example is Belgium, where abortion was illegal until 1990, but it was available, safe and inexpensive. The ideal solution would be if abortion were legal, safe, affordable[547] and

---

541 UNFPA, The State of World Population 1995, pp. 31 and 47.

542 UN Doc. E/CN.9/1996/3, § 27.

543 *S. Coliver & S. Gruskin,* Global Overview, p. 85.

544 Within the literature Audrey Chapman has considered laws and practices that obstruct women's access to full reproductive health services as violations of commission under Article 12 of the ICESCR. *A.R. Chapman*, p. 14. In addition, there are several researchers who support the idea of reconceptualising abortion as a health care need for all women and viewing it as integral to women's reproductive health needs. *J. Brodie*, p. 141. On the other hand, defining legal abortions as a technical-medical solution (as in the case of Canada) has also led to arbitrary and inconsistent treatment of women by hospitals and abortion has been in practice "illusory for many Canadian women". *J. Brodie*, p. 130. The Canadian case is a good illustration of the preposition that even a medical definition of abortion does not necessarily ensure access to safe abortion services.

545 *J.W. Kabeberi-Macharia*, Kenya, in The Right to Know, S. Coliver (ed.), p. 190.

546 UNFPA, The State of World Population 1995, p. 43. *R. Dixon-Mueller*, pp. 172–173.

547 A primary focus of attention of the UN system's strategy for the years 1996–2001 in regard to support for reproductive health is defined in terms of "availability, accessibility and affordability of health services and related information for all women and girls, and their ability to use them". UN Doc. E/CN.6/1996/CRP.2, § 71.

rare, since neither the law nor the religious norms will stop a woman who desperately needs an abortion. Still the scope of states obligations in regard to the right to access to family planning services has to be articulated by international supervisory organs.

The lack of family planning counselling and services for adolescents, which causes damage of different types[548] to this group in most of the world, merits special attention and I shall, therefore, devote the next sub-chapter to their specific needs.

### *5.3.4.9. Adolescent Pregnancy and Abortion*

#### 5.3.4.9.1. Definition of Adolescence

Adolescence has come to be known as the stage of life during which individuals reach sexual maturity. It is a period of transition from childhood to adulthood,[549] which makes it "a period of time of development that is increasingly recognised both as an important determinant of future health and as a specially vulnerable period of life".[550] Adolescent reproductive behaviour has become an emerging international concern,[551] especially in regard to the sexual risk-behaviour of young people leading to among other things teenage pregnancy and unsafe abortion. When pregnancy occurs, the most disadvantaged adolescents, *i.e.,* those who live in poor urban areas, single unemployed young women who have no means of support, are likely to resort to unsafe abortion.[552]

Despite the fact that the majority of the international documents dealing with the right to family planning, as well as in the domestic laws of many countries, the concept "individuals" has in that regard not been considered generally to apply to adolescents.[553] Thus, the right might be limited to persons of a certain minimum age.[554] On the basis of the argument that definitions of childhood and adulthood vary across cultures, adolescents and their rights are often mentioned in separate paragraphs in most international documents, thereby leaving a considerable space for states' "margin of appreciation" in regulating their legal status. Recommendation No. 29 of the World Population Plan of Action from 1984 is illustrative in referring

---

548 *C.A.A. Packer*, p. 83.

549 In 1974 the WHO defined adolescence as a period of life which: 1. The individual progresses from the point of the initial appearance of sex characteristics to that of sexual maturity, 2. The individual's psychological process and patterns of identification develops from those of a child to those of an adult and 3. A transition is made from the state of total socio-economic dependence to one of relative independence. *S. Bergström, A. Molin & G.W. Povey*, International maternal health care 1993, Uppsala 1994, p. 46.

550 UN Doc. E/CN.9/1996/2, § 9.

551 See the recommendations adopted at the UN Expert Meeting on "Adolescent Girls and their Rights" which was held in Addis Abeba in October 1997. UN Doc. EGM/AGR/1997/Rep.1. See in addition UN Doc. CN.6/1998/2, §§ 149–156.

552 *J.W. Kabeberi-Macharia*, p. 192.

553 *G. Van Bueren*, The International Protection of Family Members' Rights as the 21st Century Approaches, HRQ 1995, Vol. 17, p. 741; *G. Van Bueren*, The International Law of the Rights of the Child, p. 32.

554 *C.A.A. Packer*, p. 84.

to: "suitable family planning information and services should be made available to adolescents within the changing socio-cultural framework of each country".

5.3.4.9.2. Universal Recognition of the Special Needs of Adolescents

Adolescent sexuality has gained increasing acceptance during the past years as an important element in the right to family planning.[555] Adolescents are a growing segment of society. There will be over one billion of them in the near future.[556] Human rights- and women's organisations have gradually realised that the fact remains that gender discrimination often begins at the early stages of life and it will be difficult to remedy its effects without starting with the creation of conditions to eradicate practices affecting adversely the girl adolescent. Social pressures, for example, influence early marriage and pregnancy, establishing at an early age a pattern of high fertility and poor sexual and reproductive health that severely limits their ability to pursue educational and employment opportunities and which would narrow and reduce the range of options later in their life.[557] As a result of the rise of the awareness on that issue within the international community, the ICPD Programme of Action dedicated the entire section E of Chapter VII to adolescents.[558] After admitting that the reproductive health needs of adolescents as a group "have been largely ignored to date by existing reproductive health services", the emphasis is here placed on their need of information. Thus, education in sexual behaviour for the future generation of women is highlighted as the key issue to change. It is agreed that it should mainly contribute to making adolescents understand their sexuality and to help them prevent unwanted pregnancies, STDs and the risk of infertility.[559] Poor educational opportunities is one reason among others, which is recognised in § 7.42 as a factor in the high levels of adolescent childbearing. Therefore, states recognised the importance of adolescent participation in designing programmes that respond to their needs. Also one of the objectives contained in the ICPD Programme of Action is to "substantially reduce all adolescent pregnancies through the promotion of responsible and healthy reproductive and sexual behaviour, including voluntary abstinence, and the provision of appropriate

---

[555] *A.B. Marcelino*, p. 30.

[556] Today more than half of the world's people are below the age of 25. About a third are between the ages of 10 and 24; some 80 per cent of these live in developing countries. UNFPA, The State of World Population 1998, p. 39.

[557] In Africa, 25–40 per cent of pregnancies among married girls are unintended and abortions among girls aged 15–19 account for perhaps a tenth of the 50 million abortions performed each year. UNFPA, The State of World Population 1994, p. 16. See also UN Doc. E/CN.6/1995/Add.2, §§ 16 and 42.

[558] Members of CEDAW have regularly during the consideration of periodic country reports, *e.g.* Kenya's, asked questions as to whether pregnant teenagers had difficulties in being accepted by their families and/or society. UN Doc. A/48/38, 28 May 1993, § 129. Also the CRC recommended at its 16th session in October 1997 to 5 (these are Trinidad & Tobago, Togo, Laos, Uganda and the Czech Republic) out of 6 states, whose periodic reports were under consideration, to work more on solving the problem of teenage pregnancies. See in addition *C.P. Cohen & A. Wolthius*, Practice and Implementation, Committee on the Rights of the Child: Eighth Session Reports of State Parties, The International Journal of Children's Rights 1995, Vol. 3, p. 263.

[559] Paragraph 7.41.

services and counselling".[560] Legal barriers preventing adolescents from receiving reproductive health information and services should be removed. On the other hand, according to § 7.45 states are exhorted to "safeguard the rights of adolescents to: privacy, confidentiality, respect and informed consent" with respect to cultural values and cultural backgrounds. In other words, the access to information and services for adolescents may still be limited to what is found appropriate within the context of national laws. This was a necessary compromise during the negotiation process on the final document since Islamic leaders contested parts of it relating to adolescents in its whole. They said they were concerned about promiscuity and the spread of Western immorality.

However, it is confusing that the document makes use of the expression "young people" in several of its provisions. In section D (§ 7.37), for example, which is concerned with human sexuality and gender relations, the importance of sexual education and information of young people and especially male responsibility in such matters is emphasised. According to WHO's statement made in 1989, the term "young people" applies to those from 10 up to 24 years, while "adolescents" refers to persons between 10 and 19 years of age and finally "youth" is defined as between 15 and 24. In other words, "young people" comprises both "adolescents" and "youth".[561]

5.3.4.9.3. Risks and Consequences of Adolescent Pregnancy

Concern about the sexual behaviour of adolescents continued to increase after the Cairo Conference as the recognition of the health and the socio-economic consequences of precocious pregnancy becomes widespread. It is known now that one quarter of the 500,000 women who die every year from pregnancy- and childbirth-related causes are teenagers.[562] Many of adolescent pregnancies are unintended and unwanted. Because adolescents are sometimes unwilling or unable to seek appropriate health care or wait longer in the gestation period to obtain help, induced abortion presents a greater risk to their health than to an adult woman. Children of very young mothers face higher risks of infant morbidity and mortality. The fourth review and appraisal of the World Population Plan of Action presented at the Cairo Conference[563] indicated that abortions are increasingly becoming the main response to unwanted pregnancies,[564] while at the same time a belief in the social desirability

---

560 Paragraph 7.44.

561 See WHO, The reproductive health of adolescents: a strategy for action, Geneva 1989; Ford Foundation, Reproductive health: a strategy for the 1990s, p. 7. See also UN Doc. E/CN.9/1996/2, § 8.

562 UN Doc. E/CN.6/1995/3/Add.3, § 34. In the developing countries between 10,000 and 100,000 teenage girls die following illegal abortions. See *M. Benson*,Our sisters abroad, in Rädda barnen och vi, special issue, Stockholm 1996, p. 30.

563 UN Doc. A/CONF.171/4, § 139.

564 Abortion among adolescents has accounted for 15–25 per cent of the total of reported legal abortions in a number of countries, according to recent UN estimates. UN Doc. E/CN.9/1996/2, § 56. Nevertheless, the rates of unwanted pregnancies among young, single women are rising. In Latin America as many as 60 per cent of the pregnancies befalling women between 15 and 19 years old are unwanted. *J. Hadley*, p. 44. In some countries, *e.g.*, in the USA, there are laws requiring parental consent/notification for minors seeking abortion. *M.G. Fried*, Transforming the Reproductive Rights Movement: The Post-Webster Agenda, Boston 1990, p. 4.

of early marriage and early child-bearing continues to prevail in many countries,[565] despite the fact that recommendation 18 subparagraphs b-g, adopted at the Mexico City Conference, stressed the importance of education in order to change attitudes about early child-bearing. There is still a need for legislation at the domestic level to curb early marriage. In some parts of the world the ages of puberty and marriage have been traditionally linked. In the 1993 Vienna Declaration[566] states are urged to repeal existing laws and regulations and to remove customs and practices that discriminate against and cause harm to the girl child.[567] CEDAW has, moreover, interpreted Article 16(2)[568] of the Women's Convention to preclude states parties from permitting or giving validity to a marriage between persons who have not attained their majority. Notwithstanding the definition of a child contained in Article 1 of the Convention on the Rights of the Child, implying that "a child means every human being below the age of eighteen years unless, under the law applicable to the child, majority is attained earlier", CEDAW has expressed the standpoint in its General Recommendation No. 21,[569] that the minimum age for marriage should be 18 for both men and women.[570] One of the arguments put forward in support of this text was that when minors marry and have children, particularly girls, their health can be adversely affected and their education would be most probably impeded. Girls who marry early do not only become pregnant early but they also tend to have more children and at shorter intervals than the ones who marry later. There are more than 15 million girls aged 15 to 19 who give birth each year. They run a significantly higher risk of complications during pregnancy and premature birth.[571] The Committee on the Rights of the Child emphasised in January 1995 the compatibility of the two Conventions. It said that both instruments "have a complementary and mutually reinforcing nature". As I have shown in Part I of my study, the CRC

---

[565] About 18 per cent of the girls in Asia, 16 per cent in Africa and 8 per cent in Latin America are married by the age of 15. UNFPA, The State of World Population 1995, p. 39. This reality of widespread toleration of child marriages might explain the very few ratifications, which the 1962 UN Convention on Consent to Marriage, Minimum Age for Marriage and Registration of Marriages has received. See also *M.K. Eriksson,* The Right to Marry and to Found a Family, pp. 54–55. While teenage pregnancy is a universal problem, the reasons behind vary with different cultures. In the Middle East, Southeast Asia and Africa teenage pregnancies are the result of early marriage. In the USA it is believed that the increasing number of single-parent families is a major factor in teenage pregnancies. In Latin America, *e.g.*, in Peru, studies show that 90 per cent of the young mothers aged 12 to 16 in a hospital were rape victims. UN DPI, New York 1995, WOM 95–01657.

[566] UN Doc. A/CONF.157/24, Part I, Chapter III.

[567] States' obligation to discourage early marriage constituted an important strategic objective in the report of the Asia and Pacific region as well as the report by the African countries presented at the Beijing Conference. See UN Doc. E/CN.6/1995/5/Add.1, p. 5; UN Doc. E/CN.6/1995/5/Add.2, § 96(h).

[568] This provision declares that the betrothal and the marriage of a child shall have no legal effect.

[569] UN Doc. HRI/GEN/1/Rev.1, § 36, pp. 97–98.

[570] UN Doc. CEDAW/C/1995/7, § 465. This is a considerable improvement compared with the requirement contained in Article 6 (3) of the UN Declaration on the Elimination of Discrimination against Women where child marriage and the betrothal of young girls only before puberty shall be prohibited.

[571] WHO, The reproductive health of adolescents, pp. 7–9; The Beijing Declaration, § 268; *A. Rwomire*, Adolescent fertility in African countries: causes, consequences, and policies, in Unwanted Pregnancies and Public Policy, H. Correa (ed.). p. 102.

has often focused in its discussions of the periodic country reports on problems such as discrimination against girl children, early marriage or denial of educational opportunities for girls.[572]

Also Article 11(6) of the Charter of the Rights and Welfare of the African Child adopted by the OAU in 1990, stipulates categorically that: "Child marriage and the betrothal of young girls shall be prohibited". Still, recent studies show that there is a lack of commitment to raise the minimum legal age for marriage as well as to effectively enforce the prohibition of child marriages in large parts of Africa.[573] On the other hand, statistics included in a report recently presented to the CSW by the Secretary General[574] bear evidence of other disturbing circumstances. They not only show a rise in teenage pregnancies in Africa,[575] but they also indicate that young men are refusing to marry. It is suggested that this unwillingness to marry and to assume family responsibility might be the result of their inability to sustain a family. In consequence teenage pregnancy outside marriage has become mostly problematic and critical, pre-empting the educational, vocational and social experience of persons at an early stage in their life cycle.[576] Teenage pregnancy may also imply, especially in the industrial countries, a longstanding dependency upon public financial assistance.

Within the Asia region where there is a recognisable shift towards later marriages, child marriages are still practised. Therefore, the issue of child marriages was currently reflected in the Jakarta Plan of Action in Principle 5(iii) where states are urged to create a socio-economic environment conducive to the elimination of all child marriages as "a matter of urgency".[577]

These contemporary developments have undoubtedly contributed to the fact that adolescents as a particularly vulnerable group receiving immense attention at the Women's Conference in Beijing. In § 268 of the Platform for Action it is stipulated that early child-bearing continues to be an impediment to improvements in the educational, economic and social status of women in all parts of the world. The Beijing Platform for Action urges governments in § 274(e) to raise the minimum age for marriage, where necessary, in order to eliminate discrimination against the girl child. Thus, early marriages and early motherhood "can severely curtail educational and employment opportunities and are likely to have a long-term adverse impact on their and their children's quality of life". Adolescents often become pregnant because they lack essential knowledge about sex, contraception, pregnancy etc.

---

[572] See UN Doc. E/CN.6/1995/3/Add.10, § 32. See also CEDAW's analysis of the content Article 16 of the Women's Convention, UN Doc. CEDAW/C/1993/4, § 151.

[573] *K. Tomaševski*, Human Rights in Population Policies, p. 64. Another reason is that young women marry older men who compel them to become pregnant during adolescence. *A. Rwomire*, p. 100.

[574] UN Doc. E/CN.6/1996/5.

[575] Some authors even speak in terms of "epidemic proportions". *A. Rwomire*, p. 99.

[576] After birth the infants of teenage mothers often face greater health and developmental risks. *P.A.M van den Akker*, Unmarried young girls and motherhood, an international comparison, in Unwanted Pregnancies and Public Policy, H. Correa (ed.), p. 82; *A. Rwomire*, p. 104.

[577] A Thematic Guide to the Documents on the Human Rights of Women, *G. Alfredsson & K. Tomaševski* (eds.), p. 209.

Among the required actions to be taken by governmental, international and non-governmental organisations, mention has been made of education and dissemination of information to girls, especially adolescent girls, regarding "the physiology of reproduction, reproductive and sexual health" § 281(e).[578] Wide-ranging sex education has been shown to delay the onset of sexual activity. Sex education promotes responsible sexual behaviour and even abstinence. Several governmental delegations at the Beijing Conference considered this provision controversial and preferred its alteration on the basis of the argument that giving adolescents such information promotes early sexual activity and constitutes a violation of parental rights. The member countries of the European Union were the ones that succeeded in setting the tone in the discussions and achieved a compromised text, which implies that the best interest and the rights of the child have to be given primary consideration in all actions, including measures to meet the educational and service needs of adolescents to enable them to deal in a positive and responsible way with their sexuality. However, a reference to the rights and duties of parents and legal guardians to provide "in a manner consistent with the evolving capacities of the child, appropriate direction and guidance" was included. On the other hand, parental rights are not contravened by the right to sexual education as ruled by the European Court of Human Rights in the *Kjeldsen, Madsen and Pedersen v. Denmark* case.[579] The applicants, all parents, were opposed to "integrated" and hence compulsory sex education. On ethical grounds they preferred to conduct their children's sex education themselves, but their request for exemption from sex instruction for their children was rejected by the competent authorities. The Danish state was attempting to warn children against matters, which it considered to be of concern, for instance, the excessive frequency of births out of wedlock and abortions. The European Court held that those considerations were indeed of a moral order, but they were general in character and did not entail overstepping the bounds of what a democratic state might regard as public interest. Moreover, it did not affect parent's right to advise their children. In other words, a child who wishes to attend sex education classes offered in school may do so even if the parents were opposed.

The most significant measure to reduce adolescent pregnancy and unsafe abortion would be to make contraceptive services and information, as well as sex education[580] in general, accessible to adolescents world-wide.

---

[578] In many African countries, a girl cannot receive reproductive health education until she marries. Only then can she be accepted as a woman. Therefore, the right of adolescents to access to family planning information that may have a bearing on their health was considered as a topical issue at Beijing. However, the regional Programme of Action for the Women in Latin America and the Caribbean, 1995–2001, which was adopted in September 1994 in preparation for the Beijing Conference, sets up a more extensive strategic action in this area, since it urges states to design "compulsory sex education programmes, at the level of school boards, from the first year of school". UN Doc. E/CN.6/1995/5/Add.3, § 91, § 233.

[579] ECHR, Judgment of 7 December 1976, Ser. A, No. 23.

[580] The availability of sex education has been considered as the most important factor in the Netherlands, a country having the lowest number of unwanted pregnancies and abortions among teenagers in the world. *Y. Rademakers*, p. 59.

*Chapter 6*

# Legal Abortion – An Emerging Human Right in International Law?

## 6.1. Developments on the Universal Level

### *6.1.1. The Women's Convention*

Since the nineteenth century women have fought to ensure their right to abortion in order to facilitate their choice *not* to reproduce.[1] Within the UN the issue of women's access to legal abortion and counselling as well as to services has been of major concern to expert members of CEDAW. Nevertheless, the Committee has, as already mentioned in Part I of this study, at present no formal power to interpret the Woman's Convention authoritatively but in the course of its work implicitly.[2] The interpretation of some of the provisions contained therein is reflected in the questions of CEDAW members to the representatives of states parties during consideration of their periodic reports. These questions identify in my opinion CEDAW's collective perception[3] of among other things the meaning of Article 16 (the right to family planning) as guaranteed by the Convention. When a great number of similar questions are frequently raised by experts during CEDAW's sessions dealing with a specific substantial issue under the Convention and there is no dissent among the experts, the questions are to be considered as a shared view and as an expression of a high degree of consensus among CEDAW experts. There is, furthermore, a new practice evolving in the work of CEDAW, entailing that individual members act as co-ordinators of questions in relation to specific articles. Moreover, a pre-session Working Group has been established, since the 9th session, which meets before each subsequent session to prepare a list of issues and questions relating to the country reports to be considered at the CEDAW's session to come. Many questions relating to abortion have frequently been asked in relation to a number of periodic

---

1 *L. Doyal*, p. 186.

2 *A. Byrnes*, The "Other" Human Rights Treaty Body: The Work of the Committee on the Elimination of Discrimination Against Women, Yale Journal of International Law 1989, Vol. 14, p. 46.

3 CEDAW has suggested that "by looking at the questions asked and issues raised over time by the Committee under the various articles during the constructive dialogue, its views about the nature of the States Parties' obligations under the Convention will emerge". UN Doc. CEDAW/C/1995/7, § 305.

country reports.[4] Members of CEDAW have on different occasions interpreted the Women's Convention as requiring access to all methods of fertility control including abortion. In other words, an abortion choice must be legally available and, furthermore, it could be seen to place an obligation on the state to provide such services.[5] CEDAW has consequently indicated that it does not consider the issue of legal abortion as being outside the state parties' treaty obligations. The issue of women's access to abortion counselling and to safe abortion services has also been of major concern to expert members of CEDAW. Several members of CEDAW required, for example, in their discussion of women's health issues during the 284th meeting (3 February 1995) access to safe and legal abortions. It was noted that in countries with widely available contraception – and abortion – options the incidence of abortion was often quite low. In its consideration of states parties' reports in regard to Article 12 (2), which is considered as imposing a limited duty on states to provide free health care,[6] the Committee has required information about any family planning policy in place in the state party in question. CEDAW also habitually determines whether abortion is legal and if so, whether, and what kind of, legal restrictions there are, and whether illegal abortions are performed. The interplay of several provisions, for example, Articles 12 and 16 of the Convention, constitutes a part of the context which might prove significant in the process of interpretation.

On the other hand, CEDAW has not yet mentioned what specific requirements the Women's Convention may impose on the substance of domestic abortion laws. It is obvious that the existence of tremendous differences in the national legislation as regards the grounds for the lawful performance of abortion and which reflect different degrees of permissiveness in the judicial systems world-wide, makes such a standpoint a very sensitive issue.

Of further importance for the clarification of the content of the established rights in the Women's Convention is the recently developed practice by CEDAW of preparing and adopting general recommendations of a detailed nature dealing with

---

[4] Some illustrative examples can be found in the following documents: UN Doc. CEDAW/C/5/Add.23 (1983); UN Doc. CEDAW/C/CRP.15/Add.1 (1990); UN Doc. CEDAW/C/CRP.15 (1990); UN Doc. CEDAW/C/1995/4, § 87 (1995). See furthermore my references in sub-chapter 2.3.5.2. of Part I of this study.

[5] Article 12 of the Women's Convention has been interpreted by CEDAW in the sense that family planning services including abortion should be assured to women in the states parties to the Convention. See *B.G. Elder,* Human Rights and the United Nations, Crime and Social Justice 1986, Vol. 25, p. 21. See also UN Doc. CEDAW/C/1995/7, §§ 422, 428 and 430. The drafting history of this provision reveals that some countries were opposed to the mention of "family planning services" in § 1, since these did not exist everywhere and it was feared that it could lead to a refusal to ratify the Convention. Several other delegations felt, however, that the Convention should reflect the desired state of affairs and it should serve as a guide-line for the future. UN Doc. A/C.3/33/L.47, §§ 114 and 116. See also *L.A. Rehof,* pp. 144–146.

[6] Article 12(2) reads as follows: "Notwithstanding the provisions of paragraph 1 of this article, States Parties shall ensure to women appropriate services in connection with pregnancy, confinement and the post-natal period, granting free services where necessary, as well as adequate nutrition during pregnancy and lactation". See for a commentary *H.J. Steiner & P. Alston,* International Human Rights in Context, Law, Politics, Morals, Oxford 1996, at 909.

various substantive issues. These recommendations are to be considered as collective pronouncements of an international human rights monitoring body and ought in my opinion to have judicial authority, despite the fact that several writers in the legal doctrine do not consider them binding on states parties to the Convention.[7] CEDAW itself regards the general recommendations as an "important source of jurisprudence of the Convention", since they contribute to the understanding of the normative content of the rights contained therein.[8] In regard to this activity the timing of certain international events seems to have been decisive for the selection of specific issues for the preparation of general comments. The pronouncement of the International Year of the Family (1994) within the UN contributed, for example, to the choice of "The Family" as the theme to be examined by CEDAW and it resulted in its recommendation No. 21, in which the meaning of Articles 9, 15 and 16 of the Women's Convention were explored,[9] and which has served as a starting point for my study. It appears to this author that when issuing this recommendation CEDAW has relied on the teleological approach, *i.e.*, the provisions in question were interpreted in the light of the Convention's object and purpose. This theory is especially suitable in the field of general multilateral conventions, particularly those of the social, humanitarian and law-making type.[10] I have earlier taken the standpoint that human rights conventions have law-making character. They permit, therefore, interpretation of the enumerated rights in accordance with developments in different spheres of life with time.

### *6.1.1.1. Legal Abortion – A Prerequisite for Gender Equality*

> "If men could become pregnant,
> abortion would be a sacrament"[11]

The general nature of the relevant human rights provisions on reproductive freedom opens the opportunity to approach the abortion issue by means of interpretation.[12]

---

[7] *A. Byrnes*, The "Other" Treaty Body, at 345. Andrew Byrnes finds, however, the general recommendations of CEDAW as "particularly persuasive interpretations" of the Women's Convention and he points to the fact that they have been invoked on several occasions before domestic courts and tribunals. *A. Byrnes*, Human Rights Instruments Relating Specifically to Women, With Particular Emphasis on the Convention on the Elimination of All Forms of Discrimination Against Women, in Advancing the Human Rights of Women: Using International Human Rights Standards in Domestic Litigation, A. Byrnes, J. Connors & L. Bik (eds.), London 1997, pp. 46–47.

[8] UN Doc. CEDAW/C/1995/7, § 490.

[9] General Recommendation 21(thirteenth session): Equality in marriage and family relations, UN Doc. HRI/GEN/1/Rev.1, pp. 90–100.

[10] *D.J. Harris*, Cases and Materials on International Law, London 1991, p. 767. CEDAW has recently emphasised that it has assumed an important role in the international arena, not only in monitoring the implementation of the Women's Convention but beyond, through its contribution to the "progressive development of international human rights law". UN Doc. CEDAW/C/1995/7, § 165.

[11] Outrageous Acts and Everyday Rebellions, New York 1983, p. 9, cited by *Gayle Binion*, Feminist Theory Confronts US Supreme Court Rhetoric, p. 80, note 24.

[12] *C.A.A. Packer*, p. 74.

The Vienna Convention on the Law of the Treaties, which depicts generally accepted principles of law on the interpretation of treaties, gives a prominent position to the teleological method. According to Article 31, paragraph 1 of the Convention:

> "A treaty shall be interpreted in good faith in accordance with the ordinary meaning to be given to the terms of the treaty in their context and in the light of its object and purpose".

In general terms the promotion of equality between men and women and the elimination of all forms of discrimination against women, which "violates the respect for human dignity",[13] can be identified as the object and purpose of the Women's Convention. This principle has found expression in its Preamble. In other words, among the aims of that treaty we may find the protection of the basic value, which entails respect for woman's dignity and well-being, and the attainment of substantial equality between women and men. Each and every one of the provisions in the Women's Convention is aimed at achieving this goal. Moreover, basic values like human dignity lend legitimacy to the legal system.

Closely linked with human dignity is control over reproduction and sexuality, which has been considered as an essential element of it.[14] Such an approach would also imply that one of the most important grounds for the justification of the adoption of permissible legal rules on abortion, would be respect for human dignity of women.[15] Justification of legal rules relates primarily to explanations why they ought to be respected. Human dignity has implications as to how human beings ought to be treated. The essence of human rights comprises according to Marsha

---

[13] Most of the human rights instruments stress the worth of the individual. The Preambles of the UN Charter likewise and of the Women's Convention refer to the "dignity and worth of the human person". The Preambles of the UDHR and the ICCPR speak of the "inherent dignity" of the human person. In addition I may mention here that the Committee of Ministers of the Council of Europe wished to stress in October 1987 that "human rights and fundamental liberties flow from the recognition of the inherent dignity of human kind". *P.-H. Imbert*, Rights of the Poor, Poor Rights?, The Review, December 1995, No. 55, p. 86.

Principle I of the Cairo Declaration establishes, furthermore, that all human beings are born "equal in dignity". Mr. A. Gore emphasised in his statement at the Cairo Conference that the "inherent dignity of every individual woman, man and child on this planet, is a basic value enshrined in all of our major religions, traditions and principles increasingly shared by men and women all around the world". Also § 8 of the Beijing Declaration reaffirms the commitments by states to "the equal rights and inherent dignity of women and men".

[14] *L.P. Freedman*, p. 5. See also the keynote address by Dr. N. Sadik at the 3 September 1994 to the delegates to the Cairo Conference.

[15] I should, however, mention here that criticism has been put forward in regard to argumentation which connects woman's freedom to decide in procreative matters and the concept of human dignity as follows: "such actions are clearly not celebrations or vindications of human dignity and freedom, but a confession of our failure to push back the walls of necessity to find more human solutions to our problems". *J.P. Hanigan*, Unwanted Pregnancies and the Common Good, in Unwanted Pregnancies and Public Policy, H. Correa (ed.), p. 13.

Freeman respect for human dignity and for the capacity "to make responsible choices, regardless of gender or geography".[16] The principle of the dignity of a person, as understood in contemporary human rights law, enables individuals to realise a chosen life plan[17] (*i.e.*, to be free to make decisions about one's reproductive destiny without coercion from the government or outside factors) and relinquish access to certain goods or acquire access to others.[18] Against this background access to legal abortion has been considered to be of particular importance to women because "how reproduction is managed and controlled is inseparable from how women are managed and controlled".[19] Abortion is an issue that fundamentally affects the life and the well-being of a woman and conditions her social status. Thus, the welfare of women can be used as justification for their legal right to abortion.[20] This has been emphasised also in national court decisions.[21] If women are unable to decide on procreation matters, they will be deprived of benefits regarding "their health, education or employment and their roles in family and public life"[22]

---

[16] *M.A. Freeman*, The Human Rights of Women in the Family: Issues and Recommendations for Implementation of the Women's Convention, in Women's rights, human rights, *J. Peters & A. Wolper* (eds.), p. 149.

[17] In the light of the above, the premise of the right to family planning as guaranteed in Article 16 of the Women's Convention would be that marriage must be a partnership of equals in which each spouse has the opportunity to develop her or his capacities. See *M.A. Freeman*, p. 157. Legal abortion considered in this context would provide opportunities in which women can realise their potentialities and talents.

[18] *C.S. Nino*, The Ethics of Human Rights, p. 129. Justice Blackmun in the *Thurnburgh v. American College of Obstetricians and Gynecologists* case (1986) made a very forceful assertion of the right to abortion as follows: "Few decisions are more personal and intimate, more properly private, or more basic to individual dignity and autonomy, than woman's decision (w)hether to end her pregnancy". *Ibid.*, at 2185. See also *A.H. Henkin* (ed.), Human Dignity, The Internalization of Human Rights, New York 1979; *O. Schachter*, Human Dignity as a Normative Concept, AJIL 1983, Vol. 77, p. 849 ff.

[19] *S. Atkins and B. Hogget*, Women and the Law, Oxford 1984, p. 83. Also Davis underlines that birth control, including abortions when necessary, is a fundamental prerequisite for the emancipation of women. According to the same author it was not a coincidence that women's consciousness of their reproductive rights was born within the organised movement for women's political equality. *A. Davis*, Racism, Birth Control, and Reproductive Rights, in From Abortion to Reproductive Freedom, J. Fried (ed.), pp. 15–18; *L.L. Heise,* Freedom Close to Home, in Women's rights, human rights, J. Peters & A. Wolper (eds.), p. 250.

[20] *S.E. Romans-Clarkson*, What Role for Induced Abortion in the Management of Unwanted Pregnancies? in Unwanted Pregnancies and Public Policy, H.Correa (ed.), p. 136. Criminalisation of abortion at any stage of pregnancy would constitute discrimination against women on the grounds of sex. *J. Sándor*, p. 157.

[21] See, *e.g.*, the US Supreme Court decision in the *Roe v. Wade* case. Of special interest here is Justice Harry Blackmun's opinion.

I may also mention that the right to gender equality was seen as crucial to the question of abortion in the argumentation for liberalisation of the South African abortion law. The newly adopted law's preamble refers to the achievement of equality as well as non-sexism. *J. Sinclair*, p. 446.

[22] *McDougal, Lasswell & Chen,* Human Rights for Women and World Public Order: the Outlawing of Sex-Based Discrimination, AJIL 1975, Vol. 69, pp. 497–504. The 1994 African Platform for Action stresses in § 15 that women's ability to exercise "control over their fertility is a major step in enabling them to make the necessary choices in other areas". UN Doc. E/CN.6/1995/Add.2.

and there will be very few and limited social options for them. Limitation of fertility has been a definite factor in the increasing levels of female participation in public spheres. As was clearly stated at the Beijing Conference in 1995, empowering women to take decisions about their sexuality and their fertility also empowers them in other domains.[23] In other words, the status of women is inextricably linked with fertility. Consequently women's educational level, employment status and their position in the family influence the size of family.[24] To formulate an abortion right in the context of gender equality would necessitate focusing on the assurance of woman's autonomy, *i.e.*, requiring affirmative needs-oriented initiatives on the part of the state, which can guarantee the preconditions for self-realisation. This means an expansion of the doctrine based on privacy right,[25] which merely invokes the notion of non-interference by the state. Protection of dignity against this background would mean not only respect for everyone's humanity but also the creation of the necessary conditions for everyone's self-fulfilment. The UN Secretary General emphasised as early as in 1949 that "human dignity implies that human beings are to be treated as ends in themselves and not as mere means to an end".[26] Professor Leary, too, underlines the notion that "the concept of rights grows out of a perception of the inherent dignity of every human being",[27] and therefore the use of the rights language in connection with reproductive freedom underscores that the dignity of women must be central in all its aspects.

Within the doctrine Andrew Clapham[28] advocates, in addition, that dignity and democracy, which are the two basic values to be protected by the European Convention on Human Rights, ought to be used as "the tools with which to analyse human rights in the private sphere". This approach could without difficulty be applied in regard to universal treaties dealing with women's rights too, since, in the

---

[23] UN Doc. CEDAW/C/1996/3/Add.1, § 13. The African Platform for Action, which was adopted at a regional governmental conference in 1994, stresses in § 15 that women's ability to exercise "control over their fertility is a major step in enabling them to make the necessary choices in other areas". UN Doc. E/CN.6/1995/Add.2, § 15.

[24] *A.S. Fraser*, The U.N. Decade for Women, Documents and Dialogue, London 1987, p. 46.

[25] In the USA abortion has been, for example, legally justified as part of a constitutional right to privacy. Rhonda Copelon has argued that the privacy doctrine is inadequate as a theory for reproduction and sexual self-determination "because it perpetuates the myth that the right to choose is inherent in the individual" instead of acknowledging that choices are shaped, facilitated, or denied by social conditions. *R. Copelon*, From Privacy to Autonomy: The Conditions for Sexual and Reproductive Freedom, in From Abortion to Reproductive Freedom, M.G. Fried (ed.), p. 38. Privacy must be, in other words, transformed into the affirmative right to self-determination and grounded on the broader principle of equality. Within the jurisdiction of the USA in the litigation in *Webster v. Reproductive Health Services*, one amicus curiae brief forwarded the argument that the denial of legal abortion constitutes sex discrimination. See *C.A. MacKinnon*, Reflections on Sex Equality Under Law, The Yale Law Journal 1991, Vol. 100, p. 1288; *R. West*, Jurisprudence and Gender, in Feminist Legal Theory, K.B. Bartlett & R. Kennedy (eds.), pp. 214–215.

[26] UN Commission on Human Rights, The Main Types and Causes of Discrimination, Memorandum submitted by the Secretary General, p. 4.

[27] *V.A. Leary*, Justiciability and Beyond, p. 110.

[28] *A. Clapham*, The "Drittwirkung" of the Convention, in The European System for the Protection of Human Rights, R. St. J. Macdonald, F. Matscher & H. Petzold (eds.), p. 203.

words of Judge Rosalin Higgins, human rights are understood as "part and parcel of the integrity and dignity of the human being".[29]

Consideration of the context of a treaty may include, furthermore, review of related agreements among the states parties as well as other documents adopted by the international community.

Seen in a historical perspective it was not until the announcement of the UN Decade for Women (1975–1985) that planned parenthood in international law in the sense of a right to procreative freedom[30] was coupled with the advancement of women's status in society. The link between women's position and their ability to take decisions as regards their fertility was further reaffirmed during the 1984 International Conference on Population in Mexico as follows:

> "The ability of women to control their own fertility forms an important basis for the enjoyment of other rights: likewise the assurance of socio-economic opportunities on an equal basis with men and the provision of the necessary services and facilities enable women to take greater responsibility for their reproductive lives".[31]

Women's right to determine whether to have or not to have children in this context was confirmed at the World Conference in Nairobi in 1985[32] and thereafter it was endorsed in principle 4 and Chapter 7 of the ICPD Programme of Action. Several of the provisions on reproductive health in the Beijing Declaration and Platform for Action are interrelated with gender equality and empowerment of women. I may, therefore, conclude that the standpoint that women's right to reproductive freedom "through invoking the prohibition of all forms of discrimination against women may be considered a fundamental key that opens up women's capacity to enjoy other human rights" has gained prominence.[33]

---

[29] *R. Higgins,* Problems and Processes-International Law and How to Use It, Oxford 1994, p. 96. The concept of human dignity is, however, problematic. Some academic commentators claim that with reference to traditional African societies human dignity and human rights are two distinct notions. Thus, safeguards to human dignity in these societies are based on duties and not on human rights. *J. Donnelly*, Human Rights and Human Dignity: an analytical critique of non-western conceptions of human rights, American Political Science Review 1982, Vol. 76, at 312. Others tend to consider human rights and human dignity as synonyms. Mr. Khushalani emphatically argues, *e.g.*, that the right of women to their dignity "is a fundamental, substantive, legal and inalienable right". *Y. Khushalani*, Dignity and Honour of Women as Basic and Fundamental Human Right, The Hague 1982, p. 153. As to the practical effects of acknowledging the linkage of human rights to human dignity and using it as a means of justifying the later, Professor Henkin thinks that it has "encouraged a tone and mood" as well as it has "discouraged definitions". *L. Henkin*, International Law: Politics and Values, p. 185.

[30] Increased concern as regards the abortion issue was given during the Copenhagen World Conference in 1980 thanks to the activities and pressure of the Copenhagen NGO Forum (Forum 80). See also *R.J. Cook*, International Human Rights and Women's Reproductive Health, in Women's rights, human rights, J. Peters & A. Wolper (eds.), p. 261.

[31] *P. Senanayake*, Family Planning, UN Doc.EGM/SSMAW/1988/WP. 2.

[32] UN Doc. A/CONF.116/5/Add.6, 2.

[33] *R.J. Cook*, International Human Rights and Women's Reproductive Health, p. 261.

Fear of the economic and social burdens of unwanted parenthood and social inequality may be eliminated by advancing the freedom to choose safe abortion when needed and so facilitate a woman's ability to combine motherhood and family life with equal opportunities to personal fulfilment and a professional career. This would have a positive impact on the children to be born too. Thus, studies dealing with situations in Third World countries have shown that the health and survival of infants rise in direct relation to the education of the mother. Yet, only about 40% of the women in Africa and in parts of Asia are literate. In some countries illiteracy rates among women are as high as 97%.[34] A right to legal and safe abortion is on this basis motivated, if women are to be able to plan their lives rationally, without unwanted random interruption. Unwanted pregnancies create future risks, psychological as well as physical and are obstacles in achieving *de facto* equality among men and women. Family planning consequently, as stated in Article 16(1)(e) of the Women's Convention, is crucial to women and their status. CEDAW has indicated during discussions with governmental representatives, when reviewing reports on the implementation of the Convention, that it considers Article 16 as a provision essential to the object and purpose of the Women's Convention and that it constitutes its *raison d'être*.[35] Article 16 is consequently a core obligation. This view seems to be furthermore widely accepted by representatives of the international law doctrine.[36]

Having the aforesaid in mind and taking into consideration several international studies,[37] official pronouncements of international organs and state practice, the objectives of family planning may be summarised as follows:

1. The enhancement of both the status of women and the exercise of human rights;
2. The improvement of opportunity for attaining self-determination;
3. Enabling the voluntary efforts of an individual to postpone, prevent or encourage conception as well as to continue or interrupt pregnancy;
4. The protection of the rights of the child to be wanted and the importance of substitute families for those children without their natural parents;

---

[34] Convention on the Rights of the Child, United Nations Centre for Human Rights, Note No. 6, Geneva 1991.

[35] On the other hand, the HRC in its controversial general comment, (GC No. 24/52 of 2 November 1994, UN Doc. CCPR/C/21/Rev.1/Add.6, § 8), on issues relating to reservations to multilateral treaties, referred in its very comprehensive list, solely to reservations on the right of a person of marriageable age to marry, excluding the right to found a family, as incompatible with the object and purpose of the Covenant. The enumeration of provisions that may not be the subject of reservations is based on the Committee's understanding of Covenant provisions "that represent customary international law (and *a fortiori* when they have the character of peremptory norms)". Thus, the HRC rejected the opinion that all the rights of the UDHR (which includes also the right to found a family) have achieved the status of customary international law.

[36] *L. Lijnzaad*, Reservations to UN-Human Rights Treaties, Ratify and Ruin*?*, pp. 303–304.

[37] See, *e.g.*, UN, Social Welfare and Family Planning, Department of Economic and Social Affairs, New York 1976.

5. The promotion of the concept of responsible parenthood, within which parents have the right and the duty to secure the best conditions for the physical and emotional development of their children.

Focusing on and applying the object and purpose test to the Women's Convention, it would seem that an extensive interpretation of the notion "family planning" as including legal and safe abortion is needed, especially with reference to the results from the Cairo and Beijing Conferences. One of the strengths of the final documents adopted at these conferences is that they link family planning and reproductive health with the empowerment of women and the enhancement of their status. Professor Cook has, in addition, convincingly argued that Article 12 of the Women's Convention is offended by restrictive abortion laws since such rules do "have a significant impact in perpetuating women's oppression". Thus, gender inequality results from the fact that women's health is affected by contraceptive failure.[38] The present author agrees with Ruth Dixon-Mueller that the ability to terminate an unwanted pregnancy legally and safely can be considered as an element both of the right to family planning and to health.[39]

From the emphasis placed upon the teleological method of interpretation it follows that human rights instruments must be given a dynamic interpretation, *i.e.*, taking into account present day conditions and developments.

Another argument supporting an expansive interpretation of the Woman's Convention would be the attempt in international human rights law to choose an interpretation which leads to an effective[40] and progressive protection of the individual rights to be safeguarded. Thus, human rights treaties are for the benefit of persons within its jurisdiction.[41]

On the other hand, even a human rights treaty cannot be interpreted too widely, in the sense of reflecting changes so as to introduce into it a new right that was not intended to be included when the document was drafted.[42] After all CEDAW did not by the adoption of its Recommendation No. 21, as it did in the case with the General Recommendation No.19, express the view that the prohibition of abortion and/or unsafe abortion *per se* should be regarded as a breach of the Women's Convention. In Recommendation No. 19 CEDAW firmly placed gender-based violence within the conventional obligations even though it is not explicitly mentioned in the treaty text. The Committee stressed furthermore that states parties should take measures to eliminate violence against women.

---

[38] *R.J. Cook*, International Human Rights and Women's Reproductive Health, p. 261.

[39] *R. Dixon-Mueller*, p. 110. According to the same writer, abortion falls "clearly and logically under the rubric of the right to family planning". Ibid., p. 164. See also *L. Katzive & K.H. Martinez*, p. 5.

[40] *F. Matscher*, Methods of Interpretation of the Convention, in The European System for the Protection of Human Rights, R. St. J. Macdonald, F. Matscher & H. Petzold (eds.), p. 67.

[41] HRC, GC No. 24, UN Doc. CCPR/C/21/Rev.1/Add.6, § 8.

[42] *D.J. Harris, M. O'Boyle & C. Warbrick*, Law of the European Convention on Human Rights, London 1995, p. 8.

Within the doctrine Professor Meron has shown for similar reasons some caution as to the possible inclusion of a right to abortion within the family planning activities addressed in Article 16(1)(e) of the Women's Convention.[43]

### *6.1.2. Other Universal Instruments*

#### *6.1.2.1. The Covenant on Civil and Political Rights*

My starting point of view in Part I of this study was that international human rights law should be seen as a coherent system implying that the obligations under one human rights treaty will have to be consistent with the obligations under another treaty. Therefore, I shall in the following present a short overview of other international treaty provisions which might be of relevance in the argumentation for a right to abortion.

To begin with, no case dealing with the issue of abortion has been considered by the HRC under the First Optional Protocol to the ICCPR. On the other hand, under Article 40 of the Covenant, which directs a very important implementation mechanism, the HRC has elaborated a large number of general comments comprising authoritative interpretations of the rights embodied in the ICCPR. Few states have officially declared that they do not consider the GC adopted by the HRC as legally binding, though they consider them as commanding "great respect given the eminence of the Committee" and the status of the Covenant.[44] They are also intended to assist states parties in their implementation of the Covenant. As regards clarification of the content of the right to found a family in accordance with Article 23, the Committee in its GC No. 19 of 1990 expressly avoided mentioning abortion. It only referred to the state's obligation when deciding family planning policies and that they should be compatible with the provisions of the Covenant. Neither did the Committee in its GC No. 6 (on the right to life) and in GC No. 16 (on the right to privacy)[45] address the possible implications of the relevant provisions on the reproductive rights of women and their access to abortion services. Article 6 of the Covenant, which guarantees the right to life, is of special importance to the abortion issue. An examination of the *travaux préparatoires* reveals that a prospective life was not intended to be protected from the moment of conception. The proposal made by Belgium, Brazil, Mexico and Morocco to amend this

---

[43] *T. Meron*, Human Rights Law-Making in the United Nations, at 72. See also *C.A.A. Packer*, pp. 74-75.

[44] See Observation by the United Kingdom on General Comment No. 24, HRLJ 1995, Vol. 16, p. 424. See also the Observation by the United States of America on General Comment No. 24(52), ibid., at 422 where it is declared that the Covenant "does not impose on States Parties an obligation to give effect to the Committee's interpretations or confer on the Committee the power to render definitive or binding interpretations of the Covenant". This part of the argumentation might be formally correct but one should emphasise the importance of leaving the interpretation of international legal instruments to international institutions and not to each state party in order to ensure the coherence of the human rights law system.

[45] The texts of the mentioned general comments have been reprinted in UN Doc. HRI/GEN/1/Rev.1.

provision and which was designed to make it clear that the article would apply "from the moment of conception" was rejected by a vote of 31 to 20 with 17 abstentions[46] on the grounds among other things that the domestic laws differ on this matter.

In addition to its general comments, the HRC has expressed its perception of the meaning in regard to several provisions during its consideration of periodic reports, which I have commented upon in sub-chapter 2.3.2.2. of Part I in my study. A great number of questions have been put forward by individual expert members of the HRC to representatives of governments during the review of their country reports indicating strong support for the interpretation of Article 6 in the sense that it provides for a developmental protection for the foetus and the existence of a woman's right freely to decide on an interruption of her pregnancy during its first stages.[47] During the consideration of a number of periodic reports,[48] members of the HRC have also asked under what circumstances abortions were authorised in the respective jurisdictions. Thus, there is a clearly recognisable presumption that abortion is lawful in the domestic jurisdictions subject to consideration. It is, however, unclear whether all members of the HRC agree with a question or a comment on a particular issue under the Covenant put forward by an individual expert. Therefore, there is still some uncertainty as to whether the interpretation of each provision of the Covenant is based on consensus within the entire HRC. On the other hand, the HRC presents as a rule in its annual reports to the GA the issues, in a summarised form, which all members have found to be of great importance. This can be taken as evidence for an existing consensus on the substantial issues at hand. Moreover, an academic commentator, McGoldrick, has argued that the common position of all members of the HRC becomes apparent in the final observations presented at the end of the consideration of each state's report.[49]

In conclusion, I may note that there are some indications, albeit not always unequivocal, that a limited right to abortion might be comprised within the provisions of the ICCPR, since the HRC has not opposed the view that abortion does not constitute any violation of human rights obligations. On the contrary, the Committee has abstained to declare that the unborn child's right to life is included

---

[46] UN Doc. A/C.3/SR.820. A similar debate on Article 3 of the Universal Declaration of Human Rights resulted in the adoption of a general formula, which does not *verbatim* articulate any prohibition of abortion. However, several delegations have expressed doubts as to whether Article 3 should be considered as comprising the legality of (all) provoked abortions. *L.A. Rehof*, Article 3, in The Universal Declaration of Human Rights, A Commentary, A. Eide *et al.* (eds.), p. 76; UN Doc. A/C.3/L.654.

[47] *D. Shelton*, International Law on Protection of the Fetus, in Abortion and Protection of the Human Foetus, S. Frankowski *et al.* (eds), p. 12.

[48] *W.A. Schabas*, Substantive and Procedural Hurdles to Canada's Ratification of the American Convention on Human Rights, HRLJ 1991, Vol. 12, p. 408. When considering the country report of Italy, one of the members of the HRC stated that he "thought the abortion laws so strict that they infringed perhaps on religious grounds the woman's freedom in that respect". See *D. McGoldrick*, The Human Rights Committee, p. 330.

[49] *D. McGoldrick*, op. cit., p. 83.

within the realm of Article 6. At the same time Professor Cook and others[50] have rightly criticised the contemporary interpretation of this provision as "essentially male oriented" since it ignores the deaths of women from pregnancy-related causes. She suggests, moreover, that a woman's right to life under Article 6 should "entitle her to have access to basic reproductive health services".[51]

*6.1.2.2. The Convention on the Rights of the Child*

A few of the reservations entered by states parties with respect to Articles 1 and 6 of the Convention on the Rights of the Child are of some relevance to the abortion issue. First of all we may notice that out of 191 states parties to the Convention only two, Argentina and Guatemala, have stated in their declarations to Article 1 that they shall interpret the term "child" as a human being from conception to 18 years of age.[52] In consequence, the unborn child's right to life is protected in these jurisdictions and abortion is illegal.[53] Other countries like China, France and Tunisia have at the same time referred in their reservations or declarations to the Convention to their national legislation, which allows voluntary interruption of pregnancy. In their view the Convention should not be interpreted to impede the application of the rules already in force.[54] No government has yet objected to that. Moreover, the previous Swedish member of the CRC, Mr. Hammarberg, stated at the Committee's first session in October 1991 that:

> "The Committee should not take up the issue of the rights of the child before birth, since States parties had not assumed any such obligations under the Convention. If the Committee had doubts on the subject, it should begin by requesting a special study on that important and sensitive issue, which would retrace the history of the negotiations that had led to the Convention and bring out the divergent views expressed at the time."[55]

This has not been the case yet. It seems, therefore, that it would not be wrong to assume that the prevailing opinion is still that the child's "inherent right to life" contained in Article 6(1) of the Convention, as well as in other international treaties, does not apply as from the moment of conception. In practice this means that voluntary, early interruption of an unwanted pregnancy would be judged as

---

[50] See *J. Connors*, General Human Rights Instruments and Their Relevance to Women, in Advancing the Human Rights of Women, A. Byrnes, J. Connors & L. Bik (eds.), p. 33.

[51] *R.J. Cook*, International Human Rights and Women's Reproductive Health, p. 262.

[52] *B. Verschraegen*, Die Kinderrechtekonvention, pp. 112–113.

[53] Abortion is defined in the domestic law of these countries as an offence against life, *i.e.*, it is considered as criminal conduct in which the death of the foetus is caused deliberately, "within the mother's womb or by its premature expulsion". UN Doc. CEDAW/C/Gua/1–2, § 210.

[54] Also the Swedish legislator argued in the preparatory work for the ratification of the Convention that the Swedish Abortion Act is not incompatible with Article 1 and 6 of the Convention. Governmental Bill, prop. 1989/90:107, Godkännande av FN-konventionen om barnens rättigheter, Stockholm 1990, p. 29.

[55] UN Doc. CRC/C/1991/SR.11/, 6, § 27.

compatible with these provisions of international treaties. It has been discussed, moreover, within the HRC what was best for the child and the argument has been advanced that every child should have the right to be born as a desired child.

### 6.2. Developments on the Regional Level

#### *6.2.1. Within Europe*

Within the Council of Europe the Strasbourg organs for the protection of human rights have so far left open the question whether, if at all, and if so, to what extent, access to legal and safe abortion is guaranteed by the European Convention on Human Rights. The first case considered by the European Commission, which directly confronts access to abortion as a privacy right (Article 8), was the *Brüggemann and Scheuten v. the FRG* case.[56] The majority of the European Commission arrived at the conclusion that not every termination of pregnancy was a matter solely about the mother's right to private life, since pregnancy creates a close connection between her life and the developing foetus.[57] Professor Opsahl stated, however, in a dissenting separate opinion, that "punishment of unlawful abortion, or the threat of it, cannot be justified on any of the grounds set out in Article 8(2)" of the European Convention. The European Commission pointed out, furthermore, in the same case that when the European Convention entered into force there was no "evidence (therefore) that it was the intention of the Parties to the Convention to bind themselves in favour of any particular solution under discussion", *i.e.*, a time limitation as regards an interruption of pregnancy.[58] At the same time, in a separate opinion Mr. Opsahl, Mr. Nørgaard and Mr. Kellberg persuasively argued that "laws regulating abortion ought to leave the decision to have it performed in the early stage of pregnancy to the women concerned". The Nordic members of the European Commission continued their reasoning by saying that the "Fristenlösung, based on self-determination, is the most consistent with what we think a right to respect for private life in this context ought to mean in our time".[59] This view was upheld by the European Commission in a later case involving abor-

---

[56] Application No. 6959/75, YB 19, 382, D&R 10, at 100. See also the Report of the European Commission adopted on 12 July 1977. The application concerns the criminal law on the termination of pregnancy in the Federal Republic of Germany. The applicants, two women, alleged that the judgment of the Federal Constitutional Court, which established that the criminal law is void insofar as it allows the interruption of pregnancy during the first twelve weeks without requiring any particular reason of necessity (indication), interfered with their right to respect for their private life under Article 8 (1) of the European Convention. Interestingly, despite the fact that the applicants had not been denied abortion under the new law and they were not pregnant, the Commission recognised that they could be considered as "victims" of it. But the European Commission concluded unanimously that the present case did not disclose a breach of Article 8 of the Convention.

[57] The Report of the European Commission, ibid., at 116.

[58] Application No. 6959/75, The Report of the European Commission, ibid., § 64, at 117.

[59] The Report of the European Commission, ibid., at 120.

tion, *H v Norway,*[60] in which the lawful abortion of a fourteen-week-old foetus on social grounds was held not to be contrary to the Convention. Such a pregnancy could place a woman in a "difficult situation of life" according to the Commission's majority.

I may conclude from the examples of the case law under the European Convention referred to above that abortion for health and social reasons in the first weeks (12–14 weeks) of the pregnancy has been regarded as compatible with the Convention. In consequence, Article 2 (the right to life) does not impose any far-reaching restrictions on the domestic legislator's right to set conditions for abortion. The abortion cases have consisted of complaints that restriction on abortion has limited the private rights (Article 8) of the applicants to self-determination in regard to procreation matters.

### *6.2.2. The Inter-American Human Rights System*

The Inter-American Commission on Human Rights has used argumentation similar to that of the European Commission in the *White and Poter v. USA* (Baby Boy) case.[61] According to the claimants, the intentional interruption of pregnancy constitutes an offence against the right to life and it is a violation of the American Declaration of the Rights and Duties of Man. The Commission came in this case to the conclusion that none of the rights in the American Declaration had been violated. It found that the right to life of the foetus as outlined in that document is not absolute. The Commission referred to a number of states that permitted abortion. Thus, a ban of abortion from the moment of conception was rejected because it would have invalidated the laws in force at that time in eleven member states of the Organization for the American States. The Commission based several of its arguments on an examination of the legislative history of the relevant articles in the American Declaration as well as in the American Convention on Human Rights.[62]

The above referred cases, general comments and general recommendations permit reciprocal influence and impact, which is in my view one of the goals in human rights law, namely to achieve normative uniformity.[63]

From the legal situation in the majority of countries and the concern by the international community to accord, albeit limited, protection to the unborn child[64] I may

---

[60] Application No. 17004/90 (1992), unreported.

[61] Resolution 23/81, Case 2141/United States 6 March 1981, Annual Report of the Inter-American Commission on Human Rights 1980–1981, OAS/Ser. L/V/II.54 doc.9 rev., 16 October 1988, pp. 25–33.

[62] *T. Buergenthal & D. Shelton*, pp. 77–84.

[63] Professor Kiss has emphasised in this regard how important it is that no system for the protection of human rights be "considered in isolation". All systems (universal, regional and national) must be studied and applied simultaneously. See *T. Buergenthal & D. Shelton*, p. VII.

[64] *M.K. Eriksson*, The Legal Position of the Unborn Child, p. 95; *L. Katzive & K.H. Martinez*, p. 4. The European Commission came to the conclusion in the *Paton v. UK* case that under certain circumstances, such as the late stage of pregnancy, the unborn child is protected under the European Convention. A similar argument has been advanced in regard to Article 6 of the ICCPR by Professor Henkin in his book *The International Bill of Rights*, p. 122.

conclude that women's right to abortion is generally accepted only at the early stage of pregnancy. Therefore, national legislation may impose limits upon post-viability abortion[65] without contravening the human rights of the mother.

### 6.3. Some Concluding Remarks

In the sub-chapter above I have addressed the abortion issue in the context of existing and evolving human rights law. I have demonstrated that international law during the previous years has become more responsive to women's needs. However, women's perspectives have still not been sufficiently included in the legal considerations by the international supervisory organs in regard to several human rights treaty provisions. Recent statistics show, furthermore, that women's reproductive aspirations are seldom fulfilled and that they still have inadequate control over their reproduction.[66] This author has argued that the recent endorsement of the new concept "reproductive health" requires among other things a holistic and comprehensive approach to existing law, *i.e.*, the linking of several human rights provisions with the right to family planning and the right to found a family. In other words, the notion "family planning" needs to be integrated into a wider framework, which addresses women's overall health, well-being and status.

In my view equality claims in regard to procreative freedom can be successfully brought with the help of asymmetric (result-oriented) models of equality, which may include justifications for special rights, *i.e.*, a right to abortion and access to services. Thus, criminal abortion laws can be considered as a hinder to the realisation of genuine equality between women and men.[67] An additional argument could be inferred from the *sui generis* nature of human rights treaties.

Though my survey has shown that the discussed terms, such as family planning, do not *de lege lata* include access to legal abortion,[68] the scope and the content of human rights evolve continuously. International law has generally seldom had a proactive role; it is merely receptive and responsive to social and other developments.

---

[65] *B.M. Knoppers*, Modern Birth Technology and Human Rights, AJIL 1985, Vol. 33, p. 22.

[66] The percentage of births reportedly unwanted ranges from 2 to 26 in Africa, 6 to 21 in Asia and 5 to 35 in Latin America and the Caribbean. The percentage of births reportedly mistimed ranges from 6 to 52 in Africa, 8 to 28 in Asia and 13 to 25 in Latin America and the Caribbean. UN Doc. E/CN.9/1996/2, § 32.

[67] Carla Obermeyer has similarly stressed that an "examination of reproductive rights entails a consideration of the status of women in society". *C.M. Obermeyer*, A Cross-Cultural Perspective on Reproductive Rights, HRQ 1995, Vol. 17, p. 369.

[68] There are, however, writers who have argued that this is already the case. See, *e.g.*, *R. Dixon-Mueller*, p. 164; *S. Isaacs*, Reproductive Rights 1983: An International Survey, Columbia Human Rights Law Review 1983, p. 311. For a further discussion and references on that issue see *S. Correa & R. Petchesky*, Reproductive and Sexual Rights: A Feminist Perspective, in Population Policies Reconsidered, G. Sen *et al.* (eds.), pp. 116–117; *S.A. Rumage*, Resisting the West: The Clinton Administration's Promotion of Abortion at the 1994 Cairo Conference and the Strength of the Islamic Response, California Western International Law Journal 1996, Vol. 27, p. 7, note 19.

This means that the increasing concern for maternal health and the legal and social position of women in society, as expressed in contemporary international law documents, can legitimate the demands for an *de lege ferenda* expansion of the relevant provisions in human rights treaties so as to comprise legal abortion and access to safe abortion services if needed. This survey has also been illustrative of the global trend toward the liberalisation of national laws and practices on abortion. Thus, through the legalisation of abortion the detrimental effects of wide-spread illegal abortion on the health of women and adolescents girls can be diminished.

Professor Cook[69] has, as earlier mentioned, argued that a positive right to abortion could be based on a claim to preserve the woman's health. Thus, an unwanted pregnancy may endanger a woman's health. Safe abortion is an important element of the right to health.[70] Unsafe abortion has been referred to as the most neglected underlying cause of reproductive ill-health, constituting a major public health issue in the final documents adopted at the Cairo and at the Beijing Conferences. The most recent developments in international law are consequently supportive of this theory.

Denying abortion often implies also a long-lasting disadvantage for the unwanted children subsequently born. They may be abandoned or raised in circumstances, which their parents wanted to avoid. Besides, many governments have tried to abolish abortion, but none has succeeded. Instead they have driven such practices underground and/or created a lucrative travelling industry, *i.e.*, women who can afford it travel abroad in order to have an abortion. It is apparent that a heavy burden falls on the poor and disadvantaged. Therefore, working for the decriminalisation of abortion all over the world should be the minimal response of the international community to existing reality. Most women, given the choice, would not seek the experience of abortion, but if they do, it should be available to them in a legal, safe, accessible and affordable service. A clear advantage of linking abortion to health issues is that it may be easier for women to argue for abortion services to be considered as a part of a public health service and that way it should be paid for out of public health funds. Anti-abortion strategy often denies abortion to be a health issue. It is accordingly about "killing babies".[71] One possible disadvantage of defining abortion solely as a health issue, and disconnecting it from its human rights context, would be that doctors will be the ones to be arbiters of its necessity. This may curtail women's entitlement to decide themselves.

---

[69] *R.J. Cook*, International Protection of Women's Reproductive Rights, p. 720. The same author has also claimed that the right to found a family includes "the right to maximise the survival prospects of a conceived or existing child" through among others abortion. *R.J. Cook*, International Human Rights and Women's Reproductive Health, p. 265. I may also mention here that abortion in Canada is justified as part of an entitlement to health.

[70] *R. Dixon-Mueller*, p. 165. See also UN Doc. CN.6/1998/2, §§ 64-75.

[71] The statement delivered by Mr. Galea, the representative of Malta to the Cairo Conference on 8 September 1994, is illustrative of that. He stressed among other things that: "The national legislation of our country, reflects our culture and our respect for human life in that it forbids the taking of human life, including abortion".

It remains to be seen whether the international supervisory bodies for human rights protection will show willingness to take the challenge by the application of the dynamic method of interpretation of treaties to forward an evolution of existing human rights law in the sense of also comprising access to legal abortion and services. At present, the very few reviewed international cases suggest that international human rights law does not oppose abortion at the early stage of pregnancy, *i.e.*, up until the end of the first trimester.[72] However, there is still no strong support for the proposition that there is a formally recognised enforceable right to abortion under international law. Such a right is in my view only at an embryonic stage since only 22 per cent of the states members of the UN guarantee an unconditional right to abortion upon woman's request. But such a right is in a process of evolving.[73] It should be considered as an important element of reproductive freedom. The full potential of international human rights framework in this respect has not yet been used up. Some recent developments are supportive of the presumption that international human rights organs have become more aware of their "role as a stimulator"[74] for the progressive development of law.

---

[72] Medical, ethical and social concerns serve as the foundation, upon which laws are based. The European Court of Human Rights endorsed the view in the *Rees v. The UK* case that: "The need for appropriate legal measures should therefore be kept under review having regard particularly to scientific and social development". ECHR, Judgment of 7 October 1986, Ser. A, No. 106, § 47. In the legal context the *different* stages of foetal development have influenced decisions on when societal concerns for the protection of the foetus may override the request for abortion by the woman. Philosophical and theological reflections on the issue of abortion have, on the other hand, shown that they can only illuminate this complex issue but cannot deliver indisputable answers to it. Christian Munthe, a Swedish philosopher, has identified five different positions on the abortion issue among philosophers and theologians. He arrives at the conclusion that "none of the arguments put forward in the debate are both valid and sound". *C.Munthe*, Livets slut i livets början, En studie i abortetik, Stockholm 1992, p. 406.

[73] See the reference to the US State Department's message to US embassies in preparation for the Cairo Conference with instructions to inform their host governments that "the United States believes that access to safe, legal and voluntary abortion is a fundamental right of all women". *S.A. Rumage*, p. 77.

[74] *J. Boerefijn*, Towards a Strong System of Supervision: The Human Rights Committee's Role in Reforming the Reporting Procedure under Article 40 of the Covenant on Civil and Political Rights, HRQ 1995, Vol. 17, p. 785.

*Part III*

# Gender-based Violence – a Grave Violation of the Non-discrimination Principle and a Major Obstacle to Reproductive Freedom

*Chapter 7*

# Violence Against Women as an International Issue

## 7.1. Introduction

> "Discrimination against women is a deadly disease. More women and girls die every day from various forms of gender-based discrimination and violence than from any other type of human rights abuse".[1]

Violence against women has recently emerged as a serious human rights issue[2] on the global human rights agenda and its implications for gender equality have subsequently become more obvious.[3] I shall in this part of my study explore the

---

[1] Amnesty International, Report 1995, p. 5. WHO considers violence against women as a major public health issue, since it leads to psychological trauma, depression, substance abuse, injuries, sexually transmitted diseases, suicide and death. UN Doc. E/CN.6/1995/14, Chapter IV, § 24. See in addition UN Doc. E/CN.4/1995/42, § 75 and *L.L. Heise*, Freedom Close to Home: The Impact of Violence against Women on Reproductive Rights, in Women's rights, human rights, J. Peters & A. Wolper (eds.), p. 238.

[2] *C. Bunch*, Transforming Human Rights from a Feminist Perspective, in Women's rights, human rights, J. Peters & A. Wolper (eds.), p. 15. See for further references *K.D. Askin*, War Crimes Against Women, p. 253.

[3] Violence is increasingly being recognised as linked to the social, economic, and political inequality that women experience and at the same time, reinforcing that inequality. UN Doc. E/CN.6/1990/5, § 362; UN Doc. E/CN.6/1995/3, § 11. The European Committee for Equality between Women and Men (CEEG) has referred to sexual violence by men against women as "a consequence of unequal power relationship between women and men". It stated furthermore that sexual violence against women "seriously violates fundamental human rights, such as individual freedom, dignity and physical integrity" and therefore its eradication should be given a high priority.

See Proposal for a Council of Europe Programme for the achievement of real equality between women and men, to be implemented under the 3rd Medium-Term Plan (1987–1991), Strasbourg 1988, CEEG (88)4, p. 7

The Beijing Declaration and Platform for Action contains, furthermore, a whole chapter on violence against women (D), where it is stated in § 112 that violence against women is an obstacle to the achievement of gender equality. The same provision continues as follows: "It violates and impairs or nullifies the enjoyment by women of their human rights". CEDAW has also, as we shall see in the following, dealt with the problem of violence within the equality paradigm. *J. Fitzpatrick*, The Use of International Human Rights Norms to Combat Violence Against Women, in Human Rights of Women, R.J. Cook (ed.), Philadelphia 1994, pp. 535 and 556. The UN Special Rapporteur on violence against women noted in her first report to the Commission on Human Rights that "Violence against women is a manifestation

link between gender-related violence, primarily in the context of armed conflict,[4] and reproductive freedom. My proposition is that sexual violence[5] against women is a severe obstacle for the realisation of their reproductive freedom[6] and thereby the achievement of substantial gender equality. Forced pregnancy and forced motherhood through rape, which is a crime of extreme violence, may constitute, depending on the context, a breach of human rights law as well as of international humanitarian law. Moreover, when gender-specific violence involves non-derogable rights, such as freedom from gender discrimination, torture and genocide, the right to be free from sexual violence is itself non-derogable.[7]

Another challenge for my examination will be to try the thesis that the application of asymmetrical models of equality as well as gender-sensitive interpretation of humanitarian law treaties could forward a broad reading of existing key notions in regard to violence against women, such as for example torture and genocide.

---

of historically unequal power relations between men and women, which have led to domination over and discrimination against women by men and to the prevention of their full advancement. (I)t is one of the crucial mechanisms by which women are forced into a subordinate position compared with men". UN Doc. E/CN.4/1995/42, § 49.

See in addition *C.N. Niarchos*, Women, War, and Rape: Challenges Facing The International Tribunal for the Former Yugoslavia, HRQ 1995, Vol. 17, p. 678; *J. Gardam*, Women and The Law of Armed Conflict: Why the Silence?, ICLQ 1997, Vol. 46, p. 65; UN Doc. E/CN.4/1997/47, § 9.

[4] Targeting women for gender-specific violence during armed conflicts has been widespread and pervasive throughout our history. Yet international humanitarian law has not adequately taken account of the reality of women's experience of warfare. Much of the insight, *i.e.*, the reasons behind and proposals for how to move forward, of feminist scholars in regard to the inadequacy of the human rights law is valid for our analysis of the rules of armed conflict. I shall study the shortcomings of humanitarian law through gender-sensitive eyes. On the historical invisibility of gender-specific violations see *K.M. Pratt & L.E. Fletcher*, Time for Justice: The Case for International Prosecutions of Rape and Gender-Based Violence in the Former Yugoslavia, Berkeley Women's Law Journal 1994, Vol. 9, p. 80; *J. Gardam*, p. 55; *E.A. Kohn*, Rape as a Weapon of War: Women's Human Rights during the Dissolution of Yugoslavia, Golden Gate University Law Review 1994, Vol. 24, pp. 201–202; UN Doc. E/CN.4/1995/42, § 79; UN Doc. E/CN.4/Sub.2/1998/13, § 13.

[5] The term "sexual violence" refers to "any kind of violence carried out through sexual means or by targeting sexuality". *M.C. Bassiouni & M. McCormick*, Sexual Violence, an Invisible Weapon of War in the Former Yugoslavia, Occasional Paper No. 1, DePaul University College of Law 1996, Chicago, p. 3.

The *ad hoc* Tribunals Statute's do not comprise a definition of the notion "sexual violence". Nevertheless, the Akayesu indictment issued by the *ad hoc* Tribunal for Rwanda clarifies it in a broad and progressive manner. Accordingly, "acts of sexual violence" include "forcible sexual penetration of the vagina, anus or oral cavity by a penis and/or of the vagina or anus by some other object, and sexual abuse, such as forced nudity". It appears that the Trial Chamber inferred this definition from proscriptions against "inhuman acts", acts causing "serious bodily or mental harm", and "outrages against personal dignity". *Prosecutor v. Akayesu*, case No. ICTR-96-4, 13 February 1996, amended, No. ICTR-96-4-I, 17 June 1997, § 10A. See *D.M. Amann*, Prosecutor v. Akayesu, AJIL 1999, Vol. 93, p. 199.

[6] The UN Special Rapporteur on violence against women has emphasised that violence against women has been one of the major factors which has prevented the realisation of human rights goals in the twentieth century. UN Doc. E/CN.4/1995/42, § 47.

[7] *A. Aafjes*, Gender Violence: The Hidden War Crime, WLD International, Washington D.C. 1998, p. 59.

Despite the fact that violence against women is widespread and long-standing[8] many forms of it have inadequately been recognised as human rights violations largely because this kind of violence has for centuries remained invisible. This issue has been considered as extremely sensitive, since it relates to sexual and cultural attitudes.[9] In other words, systematic and sporadic forms of violence have to a great extent been justified on religious and cultural grounds.[10] Women have been afraid to raise this issue and claim their rights because of the high probability of their not being believed.[11] Rape, for instance, is generally more difficult to prove than physical injuries.[12]

It was only a few years ago that violence against women was identified as one of the critical areas of concern by the United Nations, and drew the attention of the international human rights community during the 1993 Vienna Conference on

---

[8] A regional Conference on intra-familial violence which was held in Phnom Penh in December 1994 concluded that violence within the family is endemic and prevalent in the countries of the Asian region, but it is only in the last 20 years that it has been discussed as a problem pertaining to the public arena with serious consequences for gender equality. It was also stressed that women continue to be specific targets of violence in situations of armed and non-armed conflicts. The Arab Plan of Action for the Advancement of Women to the Year 2000, refers also to the fact that women in that region of the world suffer from all forms of violence, such as violence in the family, "forcing them into marriage", rape during wars etc.. UN Doc. E/CN.6/1995/5/Add.5, § 38. In addition the ECE regional Platform for Action of 1995 establishes that violence against women still affects women in all countries of the ECE region and that sexual violence constitutes a major issue of concern. E/ECE/RW/HLM/L.3, § 25. See also the African Platform for Action of 1994, UN Doc. E/CN.6/1995/Add.2, § 10.

[9] *A.S. Fraser*, p. 87.

[10] Attention to this occurrence has been paid in § 4 of the UN Declaration on the Elimination of Violence against Women in the sense that states are urged not to "invoke any custom, tradition or religious consideration to avoid their obligations with respect" to the elimination of violence against women.

[11] In a number of Moslem countries reporting rape, *e.g.*, without presenting sufficient proof, is considered a crime with the consequence of imprisonment. In Pakistan Zina (adultery) is in the domestic legislation coupled with rape (Zina-bil-Jabr). A rape victim not in a position to provide proof of rape by the alleged rapist will be charged with adultery. In Karachi Jail alone the statistics for 1989 show that 62 women had been arrested under the Zina Ordinance. Punishment for adultery is rigorous in Pakistan. It results in imprisonment for not less than four years or more than ten years, including a fine, or, as a maximum, life imprisonment. See Asian Seminar on Trafficking of Women and Children, Pakistan 1990, pp. 5 and 22; *K. Tomaševski*, Women and Human Rights, p. 75; ACFOD, Tackling New Challenges, Women in Action, Bangkok 1991, p. 81; *K. Mumtaz*, The Woman not the Womb: Population Policy in Pakistan, Development 1994:1, p. 27.

[12] *H. Charlesworth, C. Chinkin & S. Wright*, p. 629. According to Article 177, Chapter 23 of the Japanese Penal Code severity of force or threat is required in order for an act to be considered a crime of rape. Consequently, the police do not treat an incident as a crime unless a woman has suffered serious injury. If there are no visible physical wounds, the police will dismiss the case because of "no available evidence". Thus, no consideration is taken to the fact that the act committed by the man is against the woman's will. *Y. Tsunoda*, Patriarchy and Violence against Women, Workshop paper, Japan 1992. Still, many other governments do not consider rape, sexual assault and sexual abuse as serious crimes comparable with other kinds of physical assault. *C.A. MacKinnon*, On Torture: a Feminist Perspective on Human Rights, in Human Rights in the 21st Century, A Global Challenge, K.E. Mahoney & P. Mahoney (eds.), p. 29.

Human Rights. The Vienna Declaration and Programme of Action called governments and the UN to eliminate violence against women in public and private life[13] as a human rights obligation.[14] Violence against women was thereafter considered a global problem and its elimination an essential objective for the international community at the World Summit for Social Development in Copenhagen as well as at the Beijing Conference.[15]

## 7.2. Some Definitional Deliberations

Within international treaty law, paragraph 15 of the preamble of the Women's Convention stipulates that states parties to the Convention shall adopt the measures required for the elimination of discrimination against women "in *all* its forms and manifestations" (italics added). Even though the term "violence" is not verbally mentioned in the definition of discrimination in Article 1, a "proper",[16] contemporary interpretation of it would include it by implication. The idea that gender-based violence constitutes a form of discrimination, which seriously inhibits women's

---

[13] Violence against women focuses on aspects of different forms of control and coercion exercised through a hierarchical and patriarchal gender relationship in the family and society. The idea of the family being sacred and above sanction has contributed to keeping violence in the home a highly underreported crime.

In macho cultures, especially in Latin American countries, rape generally has been considered a private rather than a public crime. *M. Morgan*, Founding Mothers: Women's Voices and Stories, Boston University Law Review 1990, Vol. 70, No. 1, p. 45.

A very extensive definition of the expression "domestic violence" has been presented by the Women's and Children's Treatment Committee, Colorado in 1990 as follows: "domestic violence is the infliction of any bodily injury or harmful physical contact or the destruction of property or threat thereof as a method of coercion, control, revenge or punishment upon a person with whom the actor is involved in an ongoing intimate relationship". *D.Q. Thomas & M.E. Beasley*, Domestic Violence as a Human Rights Issue, HRQ 1993, Vol. 15, p. 37.

[14] See Section I, § 18 and Section II (B.(3), 38).

[15] The progressive development resulting in the recognition that women's rights are human rights and that abuse of women is no less important than other human rights violations, began, however, during the UN Decade for Women, from 1975 to 1985. In 1989 the UN study "*Violence Against Women in the Family*" strongly emphasised the necessity of giving priority to international and national action combating violence against women. Violence against women was, furthermore, recognised as a *universal* problem. The same year CEDAW required states parties to the Women's Convention in its General Recommendation No. 12 to protect women against violence of any kind, including its occurrence within the family. General Recommendation No.12, Violence against women, CEDAW 8th session. The text of the document is reprinted in *L.A. Rehof*, p. 312. See *R. Carrillo*, Violence Against Women: An Obstacle to Development, in Gender Violence, A Development and Human Rights Issue, C. Bunch & R. Carrillo (eds.), Center for Women's Global Leadership, New Jersey 1991, pp. 24–26; *J.F. Connors*, Violence Against Women in the Family, New York 1989, p. 14.

I should also mention that several human rights treaties include provisions of relevance for the protection of women from violence to some of which I shall return below.

[16] See UN Doc. E/CN.4/1995/42, § 85; *J. Fitzpatrick*, p. 557. Further support for this assumption is also the fact that CEDAW on several occasions has recommended that the issue of violence against women be included in the periodic reports submitted to it by the states parties to the Convention.

ability to enjoy their human rights and basic freedoms on a basis of equality with men,[17] was expressed by CEDAW in its General Recommendation No.19 formulated in 1992. I can, therefore, safely argue that gender-based violence, which includes "physical, mental, or sexual harm or suffering, threats of such acts, coercion and other deprivations of liberty", may constitute a breach of specific provisions of the Women's Convention (*e.g.*, those of relevance for reproductive freedom) irrespective of whether the term "violence" is being expressly mentioned there or not. Thus, enforced sterilisation and forced abortion are mentioned, *e.g.*, in § 22 of the Recommendation. Rape in the family context is in addition described as a form of violence, which impairs gender equality (§ 23). In my view also forced pregnancy ought to be considered as comprised within the term "violence against women". I maintain this on the basis of § 114 of the Beijing Declaration which includes in acts of violence against women in situations of armed conflict the following: "murder, systematic rape, sexual slavery and forced pregnancy".

Such an extensive and creative interpretation of the term "discrimination", which will provide guidance to the states parties to the Women's Convention, is very much in line with the ruling of the European Court on Human Rights in the *Wemhoff* case, in which it expressed its view concerning the interpretation of human rights treaties that it is necessary to "seek the interpretation that is most appropriate in order to realise the aim and achieve the object of the treaty, not that, which would restrict to the greatest possible degree the obligations undertaken by the Parties".[18]

A clear and very comprehensive definition of the notion "violence against women" is furthermore contained in the UN Declaration on Violence against Women of 1993, which places violence against women within the framework of violation of human rights obligations and gender equality. The notion refers, for instance, to physical, sexual and psychological harm. The strong emphasis on the equality aspect of violence against women can be the result of the fact that the delegations of the 48 member states participating in the meeting for the preparation of the draft text were composed of 41 men and 58 women.[19] According to Article 1 of the Declaration, violence against women "means any act of gender-based violence that results in, or is likely to result in, physical or psychological harm or suffering to women, including threats of such acts, coercion or arbitrary deprivations of liberty, whether occurring in public or private life". Furthermore, a number of

---

[17] See paragraph 1, General Recommendation No. 19: Violence against Women, adopted by CEDAW at its 11th session in January 1992. UN Doc. CEDAW/C/1992/L.1/Add.15. This recommendation undoubtedly stimulated and influenced the outcome of the UN Declaration on the Elimination of Violence against Women in 1993.

[18] *Wemhof v. Germany*, ECHR Judgment of 27 June 1968, Ser. A, No. 7, p. 23.

[19] Women 2000, Violence against Women, New York 1992, No. 4, p. 2. In regard to the legislative history of this document I may mention among others that ECOSOC adopted resolution 1991/18 on the basis of a recommendation by the CSW, which called for the development of a framework for an international instrument dealing with the issue of violence against women. As a result an expert group meeting was convened in November 1991 to prepare a draft Declaration on the Elimination of Violence against Women. The final text of the draft declaration was adopted by the General Assembly in 1993.

examples of situations comprised within the definition are given in Article 2 as follows:

> "Violence against women shall be understood to encompass, but not be limited to, the following:
>
> a) Physical, sexual and psychological violence occurring in the family, including battering, sexual abuse of female children in the household, dowry-related violence, marital rape, female genital mutilation[20] and other traditional practices harmful to women, non-spousal violence, and violence related to exploitation;
>
> b) Physical, sexual and psychological violence occurring within the general community, including rape, sexual abuse, sexual harassment and intimidation at work, in educational institutions and elsewhere, trafficking in women and forced prostitution;
>
> c) Physical, sexual and psychological violence perpetrated or condoned by the State, wherever it occurs."

In the light of the above definition I may conclude that gender specific violence against women in both the *private* and *public* spheres of social life constitutes the gravest form of sexual discrimination. Domestic (inter-personal) violence against women has been viewed as a "mechanism of the patriarchal control of women"[21] based on the presumption of female inferiority. Violence against women is thus not only a manifestation of the unequal distribution of power between women and men,[22] but it is also an instrument in maintaining this situation. Therefore, Article 4(c) of the Declaration urges states to take all appropriate measures to eliminate violence against women, whether perpetrated by the state or by private persons. Though very comprehensive the definition of "discrimination" in the 1993 Declaration may be applied only to acts perpetrated by an individual and/or agent/s of the state. It excludes laws, policies or structural inequalities that could be considered violent. Nevertheless, the advantage of the Declaration consists of its being the only document, even though of hortatory nature, universal in its coverage, *i.e.*, it is

---

[20] Female genital mutilation (FGM) is a term comprising traditional practices, which involve the removal of the external genital organs on female children and young women around the world. This phenomenon is a grave breach of several of the elements of reproductive freedom. Empirical studies have confirmed that the operation involves significant risks of damage to the mental and physical health of girls and women. FGM is carried out in at least 25 countries and it is estimated that, on a global scale, 85 to 114 million girls and women have been genitally mutilated. *K. Kruse*, Genital Mutilation – a Cultural Right?, in Terra Viva, Vienna 16 June 1993, p. 9. See also *K. Lee*, Female Genital Mutilation-Medical Aspects and the Rights of Children, The International Journal of Children's Rights 1994, p. 36; CEDAW's General Recommendation No. 14 on Female Circumcision, 9th session 1990; UN Plan of Action for the Elimination of Harmful Traditional Practices Affecting the Health on Women and Children, UN Doc. E/CN.4/Sub.2/1994/10/Add.1; UN Doc. E/CN.4/1996/53, §§ 104–116.

[21] *R.J. Cook,* Women's International Human Rights Law, p. 249.

[22] ECOSOC's res. 1990/15 expresses the view that violence against women derives from their unequal status in society. See also UN Doc. E/CN.6/1994/4, § 10.

of relevance for non-parties to the Women's Convention. At the same time I have already in the previous parts of my study argued for the inclusion of current international documents of relevance when interpreting human rights in a evaluative and contextual manner.

The deficiencies of the 1993 Declaration can be diminished at the regional level through the application of the Inter-American Convention to Prevent, Sanction and Eradicate Violence Against Women from 1995,[23] which is the only treaty on women and violence and which provides for supervisory procedure (Chapter IV).[24] The Convention has adopted a comprehensive definition approach (Articles 1 and 2). It also places violence against women in the context of gender equality (Article 6). One of the Convention's key provisions involves furthermore the seriousness of physical, sexual and psychological violence against women in both public and private life. It condemns violence inflicted within the family, the home or any other personal relationship, including rape, sexual abuse, and violence perpetuated or tolerated by the state (Article 2).

Article 4(c) of the Convention protects in addition women's rights to security of the person. In my view the following types of violence against women such as acts

---

[23] For sources and comments on the text, see the references contained in Part I, sub-chapter 2.3.7.4. of this study. The text of the treaty has been reproduced in Protecting Human Rights in the Americas, Cases and Materials, *T. Buergenthal & D. Shelton* (eds.), Kehl 1995, pp. 645–648.

[24] As of the end of 1997, the Convention has only been invoked in one petition, which is still pending before the Commission. Annual Report of the Inter-American Commission on Human Rights 1997, OEA/Ser.L/V/II.98, Doc. 7 rev, April 13, 1998, p. 999.

It is worth mentioning here that there is a special procedure available within the UN system, under which a person can lodge an individual complaint of discrimination on the ground of sex to the Commission on the Status of Women.

The mandate of the CSW is according to ECOSOC's resolution 5(I) and 11(II) of 1946 to prepare recommendations and reports to ECOSOC on promoting women's rights in political, economic, civil, social, and educational fields; to make recommendations on urgent problems requiring immediate attention in the field of women's rights with the object of implementing the principle that men and women shall have equal rights, and to develop proposals to give effect to such recommendations. The mandate of the CSW was broadened in 1987 on the basis of ECOSOC's resolution 1987/22. The Commission shall promote the objectives of equality, development and peace, monitor the implementation of measures for the advancement of women and review and appraise progress made at the national, subregional, regional, sectoral, and global levels.

However, there has been a negligible number of communications in the confidential list considered under that procedure, in which allegations of discrimination against women have been dealt with. They have covered allegations of failure to accord women equality in the provisions of the civil and criminal law in a number of countries, widespread patterns of official and private violence against women and allegations of forced abortion or sterilisation.

On the other hand, this procedure provides neither redress for individual grievances nor permits a detailed study of particular situations. Nor does it provide for any follow up. In other words, the CSW procedure is only one of examining communications as a source of information and only for the purpose of identifying general trends and patterns of violations against women. The only major issue that has been identified is violence against women in detention, on which CSW has expressed its concern on a number of occasions. See UN, Report of the Secretary-General, Monitoring the Implementation of the Nairobi Forward-Looking Strategies for the Advancement of Women, Examining Existing Mechanisms for Communications on the Status of Women, UN Doc. E/CN.6/1991/10, p. 9.

of murder,[25] rape,[26] forced prostitution and trafficking[27] in women, female genital mutilation and forced pregnancy, would also constitutes abuse of the right to security of the person.

Sexual and other aspects of gender-based violence place women at high risk when it comes to physical and mental traumas, diseases as well as unwanted pregnancies. Wars and armed conflicts often lead to increased[28] sexual assault and other

---

[25] Dowry death, a crime constituting violence against women, has increased tremendously during the last years. Solely in India dowry deaths have increased in five years (1987–1991) by 170 per cent. See Planned Parenthood Challenges 1993, Vol. 2, p. 45. *I. Jaising*, Violence Against Women: The Indian Perspective, in Women's rights, human rights, J. Peters & A. Wolper (eds.), p. 53.

[26] Rape is an extreme act of violence. However, the term "rape" has not been defined under international law. Recently, the Trial Chamber of the Rwandan Tribunal pronounced in the Akayesu judgment that: "while rape has been defined in certain national jurisdictions as non-consensual intercourse, variations on the act of rape may include acts which involve the insertion of objects and/or the use of bodily orifices not considered to be intrinsically sexual". *Prosecutor v. Akayesu*, case No. ICTR-96-4-T, Judgment of 2 September 1998, § 597.

A number of studies show, in addition, that rape is not an aggressive expression of sexuality, "but it is a manifestation of anger, violence and domination of a woman. The purpose is to degrade, humiliate and subjugate her". *R. Seifert*, War and Rape, Analytical Approaches, Women's International League for Peace and Freedom, New York 1993, p. 2.

[27] Trafficking in women implies the transportation, sale and purchase of women for the purpose of sexual use. The UN Convention for Suppression of Traffic in Persons and of the Exploitation of Others, in force since 1950, condemns in unequivocal terms compelled prostitution and trafficking in women. Despite the fact that these practices have been characterised as slavery-like practices, and in being so are prohibited in a *peremptory* manner, very few states have ratified the convention. See *B. Whitaker*, Updating the Report of the Working Group on Slavery, UN Doc. E/CN.4/Sub.2/1982/20 and Add.1.

The General Secretariat of the International Police Organisation INTERPOL already in 1974 in a report submitted to the UN on the "Traffic in Women" exposed these practices of serious violations of women's human rights and required action for the elimination of these practices. The findings in the report were, however, suppressed. See *K. Barry*, Female Sexual Slavery: Understanding the International Dimensions of Women's Oppression, HRQ 1981, Vol. 3, p. 49.

The trafficking in women has been the concern of the WG on Contemporary Forms of Slavery, which in 1991 elaborated the Programme of Action for the Prevention of Traffic in Persons and the Exploitation of Women and which has been endorsed by the Sub-Commission and the Commission on Human Rights. UN Doc. E/CN.4/Sub.2/1991/41. Subsequently, the Special Rapporteur Ms. Linda Chavez on Contemporary Forms of Slavery devoted a whole Chapter (Chapter 4) in her report to that issue. UN Doc. E/CN.4/1997/47.

Article 6 of the Women's Convention requires from states parties to undertake all appropriate measures to suppress all forms of traffic in women and exploitation of women in the form of prostitution. Surprisingly, CEDAW has not yet paid much attention to the implementation of this specific article. The Committee has observed, however, in its report to the Cairo Conference in 1994 (A/CONF.116/13) that most of the state parties to the Women's Convention have reported that they have provided legal measures to combat prostitution and other forms of traffic in women. See in addition UN Doc. E/CN.6/1995/3; UN Doc. CN.6/1995/5/Add. 3, § 195; E/ECE/RW/HLM/L.3, §§ 62 and 90; UN Doc. CN.4/1996/53, §§ 73–76; UN Doc. CN.4/Sub.2/1996/ §§ 29–30. The Beijing Declaration has also addressed this issue and stated in § 122 that the use of women in international prostitution and trafficking networks has become a major focus of international organised crime. Finally, § 9.2. of the 1997 Asian Charter on Human Rights (NGO) considers trafficking in women as one of the most evident forms of oppression and gender inequality. See *F. de Varennes*, p. 141.

[28] On the existence of a military rape differential in war and in peace see *M. Morris*, By Force of Arms: Rape, War, And Military Culture, Duke Law Journal 1996, Vol. 45, No. 4, p. 653.

forms of gender-based violence (*e.g.*, rape and forced pregnancy) against women, a fact, which requires special attention and specific protective and punitive measures. If victims of rape are denied abortion and are forced to bear children resulting from rape, it is a clear violation of their reproductive freedom as protected under international law. I shall, therefore, in the following explore several issues of gender-based violence against women in armed conflicts.

## 7.3. Violence Against Women in Armed Conflicts

Women in large numbers have been subjected to gender-based violence such as systematic rape, sexual slavery, forced abortion,[29] forced impregnation,[30] and forced pregnancy[31] in times of war as well as armed and social conflict.[32]

The armed conflicts on the territory of the former Yugoslavia have given rise to human rights violations and violation of the rules of international humanitarian law involving acts of rape, forced prostitution and other sexual abuses on an unprecedented scale on European soil after the Second World War. These events have provoked a strong world opinion condemning the atrocities and have resulted in the

---

[29] Forced abortion and forced miscarriage as forms of sexual violence were discussed during the Akayesu trial. See *Prosecutor v. Akayesu*, Judgment §§ 416–460.

[30] Forced impregnation has been defined by Kelly Askin as follows: "(A) Elements of the offence. (1) That the accused committed or ordered to be committed an unlawful act upon a certain named or described person with an intent to forcibly impregnate that person; and (2) That the certain named or described person became pregnant as a result of the act". Not only intercourse but also forced insemination medically would be covered by this definition. *K.D. Askin*, pp. 398–399. A similar definition of forced impregnation has been presented by Astrid Aafjes as follows: "forced impregnation is an impregnation that results from an assault or series of assaults on a woman perpetrated with the intent that she become pregnant". *A. Aafjes*, p. 6.

[31] A generally accepted meaning of the term "forced pregnancy" in the mentioned above context is that it relates to the confinement or restriction of liberty of a woman impregnated as a result of rape with the intent that the pregnancy proceeds to term. This term was, however, the most controversial aspect of the definitional provisions related to violence against women during the Diplomatic Conference of Plenipotentiaries held in 1998 in Rome for the elaboration of the Statute of the ICC. Some governments felt that the term "forced pregnancy" could be interpreted as a means of challenging domestic anti-abortion laws. Others, among them many Muslim states, opposed the inclusion of the notion on the ground that "forced pregnancy" was not a new crime but rather the consequence of the crime rape, which was already incorporated in the text. Therefore, "forced pregnancy" was defined in a restrictive manner as "the unlawful confinement, of a woman forcibly made pregnant, with the intent of affecting the ethnic composition of any population or carrying out other grave violations of international law. The definition shall not in any way be interpreted as affecting national laws relating to pregnancy". (Article 7(2)(f) of the ICC Statute) The text of the Statute is available in IHRR 1999, Vol. 6, pp. 232–285. On the issue of forced pregnancy see *K.H. Martinez*, The International Criminal Court: Ending Impunity for Reproductive Rights, Violations Involving Sexual Violence, ASIL, Human Rights Interest Group Newsletter 1998, Vol. 8, p. 22; *Human Rights Watch*, Justice in The Balance, New York 1998, p. 18; *M.H. Arsanjani*, The Rome Statute of the International Criminal Court, AJIL 1999, Vol. 93, p. 31 and *D. Robinson*, Defining "Crimes against Humanity" at the Rome Conference, AJIL 1999, Vol. 93, p. 53, note 63.

[32] Women have been raped in recent years in civil strifes, for example, in Cambodia, in Liberia, in Peru, in Somalia and in Uganda.

creation of the *ad hoc* international criminal Tribunal for their persecution. The following sub-chapter will focus mainly on a legal analysis of the nature of the above mentioned crimes affecting a great number of women and girls.[33] In this connection the question of responsibility for the perpetrators of the abuses will be explored, since averting impunity is of vital importance for the prevention of continued violations of women's rights. In addition, other features, for example, the structure and the procedural rules of the *ad hoc* Tribunal will be briefly outlined and discussed in a gender sensitive manner. It is not possible, however, in the space available to review the vast body of these rules. Similar proposals for punishing the perpetrators of international crimes in Rwanda and the establishment of a permanent international criminal court will constitute a comparative element in my deliberation below albeit in a limited manner.

### *7.3.1. General Remarks*

After the tragic experience of, and the atrocities committed before and during, the Second World War, a system for the maintenance of international peace and security was established within the United Nations that was intended to be comprehensive and universal in its application. The effort of states to regulate their inter-state relations on the basis of the rule of law rather than recourse to the use of force,[34] *i.e.*, their desire to settle disputes by peaceful means, consequently found expression in the prohibition of the threat or use of force in international relations under the terms of Article 2(4) of the UN Charter.[35] The prohibition of use of force is a

---

[33] I shall consult the work of those who interpret and elaborate upon the relevant norms such as domestic, regional, and universal courts, as well as *ad hoc* tribunals, domestic legislatures, international publicists and NGOs.

[34] For a review of treaties containing prohibitions on the use of force by states see *K. Skubiszewski*, Use of Force by States. Collective Security. Law of War and Neutrality, in Manual of Public International Law, M. Sorensen (ed.), London 1968, pp. 739–855. See also *I. Brownlie*, International Law and the Use of Force by States, Oxford 1963; *B. Asrat*, Prohibition of Force Under the UN Charter–A Study of Art. 2(4), Uppsala 1991, p. 13 and *R. St. J. Macdonald*, The Use of Force by States in International Law, in International Law: Achievements and Prospects, M. Bedjaoui (ed.), Dordrecht 1991, pp. 717–740. Questions related to the use of force are discussed in historical perspective by A. Roberts and B. Kingsbury, The UN's Roles in International Society since 1945, in United Nations, Divided World, The UN's Roles in International Relations, *A. Roberts & B. Kingsbury* (eds.), Oxford 1993, pp. 1–63; *M. Howard*, The Historical Development of the UN's Role in International Security, ibid., pp. 63–81; *B. Urquhart*, The UN and International Security after the Cold War, ibid., pp. 81–104. Mentioned should also be made of Boutros-Ghali's An Agenda for Peace of 1992, which presents new visions of the UN's role in international security matters. *B. Boutros-Ghali*, An Agenda for Peace: Peacemaking and Peacekeeping, New York 1992 and Supplement to an Agenda for Peace: Position Paper of the Secretary-General on the Occasion of the Fiftieth Anniversary of the United Nations, New York 1995. See also *P. Wallensteen* (ed.), Preventing Violent Conflicts, Past Record and Future Challenges, Uppsala 1998.

[35] This provision reads as follows: "All Members shall refrain in their relations from the threat or the use of force against the territorial integrity or political independence of any State, or in any other manner inconsistent with the purposes of the United Nations".

fundamental obligation of states[36] and is one of the most basic principles of modern international law. It largely restricts the right of states to use force. Despite the ban on the use or threat of armed force against another state, except when exercised in individual self-defence or collective security, and despite the fact that international society is changing as well as political patterns, the causes for armed conflicts have not vanished over the years. The international community has not yet achieved its primary goal of abolishing the use of force in international relations. On the contrary, armed conflicts still occur and human suffering has not diminished. This reality conditions the necessity for applicable rules in armed conflicts, which contribute to the regulation of the conduct between the parties involved and which may promote the maximum of humaneness in the conflicts, for example, to ensure decent treatment for protected persons. It is needless to point to the fact that every person caught up in armed conflicts is affected. However, there is also an awareness that women, though they only rarely are involved in the decisions leading to armed conflicts and, more important, seldom perpetrate them, are affected in a particular way by the conflicts. Women are exposed to various dangers and threats in armed conflicts as civilians as well as because of their "physical nature and dual role in society",[37] which makes them vulnerable in wartime. They are wounded or killed,[38] driven from their homes, detained for arbitrary reasons and separated from their families. Women have been, and still are, victims of torture, disappearance and systematic rape; practices that have been and continue to be used as weapons of war. Systematic and organised violation of women's bodies by the male of the rival parties at times of conflict has been seen as "if to put the seal of victory over the rival".[39] Women were subjected to violence in conflict situations because they happen to be the wives, mothers, daughters or sisters of the men the authorities cannot capture. They are victimised in order to shame their male relatives or to coerce them into surrendering. Moreover, many of the abused women are from the most marginalised and vulnerable sectors of society, such as indigenous or peasant women, refugees or displaced women.[40] The unique suffering of women justifies their entitlement to a gender-specific protection under international humanitarian law. It has been argued that of the approximately 560 articles in the Geneva

---

[36] *B. Asrat*, p. 38. This rule is of universal validity, *i.e.*, even the few states which are not members of the United Nations are bound by it because it is a rule of customary international law. Moreover, the provision applies to all kinds of use of force, regardless of whether or not it constitutes a technical state of war. See generally *O. Bring*, FN-stadgans Folkrätt, Stockholm 1992, p. 78 ff; *P. Malanczuk*, Akehurst's Modern Introduction to International Law, London 1997, p. 369.

[37] *Y. Khushalani*, Dignity and Honour of Women as Basic and Fundamental Human Right, The Hague 1982, p. 548. See in addition ICRC, Women and War, Special Brochure, Geneva 1995, p. 7.

[38] Of the 50 million persons killed during World War II, it was estimated that 26 million were in the armed forces while 24 million were civilians, including many women. The proportion of civilians among the dead was in some instances as high as 90%. *F. Krill*, The Protection of Women in International Humanitarian Law, International Review of the Red Cross, No. 249, Geneva 1985. On the effect of warfare on women see *J. Gardam*, pp. 58–61; *K. Askin*, p. 93 and *R. Carrillo*, pp. 32–33.

[39] UN Doc. E/CN.6/1995/5/Add.1, § 44.

[40] UN Doc. E/CN.6/1995/3, § 8.

Conventions and the Additional Protocols about 40 are of specific concern to women.[41] Article 27(2) of the fourth Geneva Convention,[42] *e.g.*, prescribes explicitly that women must not be subjected to attacks on their honour, rape, enforced prostitution, or any form of indecent assault. Yet, for a better understanding of this specific sphere of public international law as a starting point a short overview of the characteristic features of international humanitarian law will be made.

### *7.3.2. Definition and Historical Development of Modern International Humanitarian Law*

> "This law is not static, but by continued adaptation follows the needs of the changing world".[43]

The term "international humanitarian law" was originally used to govern the rules related to the humanitarian treatment of victims of war,[44] especially non-combatants. In contemporary international law the term "international humanitarian law" is used interchangeably with the terms "law of war" and "law of armed conflicts".[45] The United Nations has shown preference for the latter term. A well-established definition of international humanitarian law is contained in the Commentary on the Additional Protocols to the Geneva Conventions of 8 June 1977.[46] It reads as follows:

---

[41] *F. Krill*, Protection of Women, note 35.

[42] The convention previous to that, the Geneva Convention of 27 July 1929 relative to the prisoners of war, provided for special treatment and consideration for women. See *M. Tabory*, The Status of Women in Humanitarian Law, in International Law at a Time of Perplexity, Y. Dinstein & M. Tabory (eds.), Dordrecht 1989, p. 942; *J. Fitzpatrick*, International Norms and Violence against Women, in Human Rights of Women, R.J. Cook (ed.), p. 546.

[43] International Military Tribunal (Nuremberg), Judgment and Sentences (October 1, 1946), reprinted in AJIL 1947, Vol. 41, p. 219.

[44] In the beginning, rules of international humanitarian law were simply said to be applicable during a state of war. *L. Doswald-Beck*, International humanitarian law, in International Institute of Human Rights, 23rd study session, Strasbourg 1992, p. 5. However, the notion of "war" has over the years been replaced by the expression "armed conflict". *R.R. Baxter*, The Duties of Combatants and the Conduct of Hostilities, in International Dimensions of Humanitarian Law, UNESCO, Paris 1988, p. 93. For an excellent review of the historical development of international humanitarian law see *G.I.A.D. Draper*, The Development of International Humanitarian Law, in International Dimensions of Humanitarian Law, ibid., pp. 67–93; *L.C. Green*, The Contemporary Law of Armed Conflict, Manchester 1993, pp. 1–31; *D. Fleck* (ed.), The Handbook of Humanitarian Law in Armed Conflicts, Oxford 1995 and *K.D. Askin*, pp. 18–46.

[45] This author prefers, like the ICRC, the use of the term "international humanitarian law" instead of the phrase "law of armed conflict", which other writers apply because in their view the previous expression is "misleading to the extent that it conveys an impression that these rules are based on purely humanitarian considerations". *J. Gardam*, p. 62. See also ICRC, International Humanitarian Law, Geneva 1998, p. 5.

[46] Commentary on the Additional Protocols of 8 June 1977 to the Geneva Conventions, *J. Sandoz, C. Swinarski & B. Zimmermann* (eds.), The International Committee of the Red Cross (ICRC), Geneva 1987, p. XXVII. See also the following definition proposed by Mr. Pictet: "Humanitarian law constitutes that important part of international public law which finds its inspiration in humane ideals, and which

"The expression international humanitarian law applicable in armed conflicts means international rules, established by treaties or custom, which are specifically intended to solve humanitarian problems directly arising from international or non-international armed conflicts and which, for humanitarian reasons, limit the right of Parties to a conflict to use the methods and means of warfare of their choice or protect persons and property that are, or may be, affected by conflict. The expression is often abbreviated to international humanitarian law or humanitarian law".

From the content of the text follows that the definition comprises two major elements: the first element refers to rules on the conduct of hostilities, which limit the methods that may be used to achieve the objectives of the conflict; the second involves rules for the protection of victims, which provide for the care of persons who are not participating or are no longer directly involved in hostilities. These individuals may be wounded, shipwrecked, prisoners of war and civilians.

In this respect the strict division should be mentioned which traditionalists uphold between the "Law of Geneva", which is based on the Geneva Conventions of 1864 and 1929 and the four Geneva Conventions of 1949, and the two Additional Protocols of 1977 on the one hand and the "Law of The Hague" on the other hand, which was codified as far back as 1868 (St. Petersburg Declaration Renouncing the Use, in Time of War, of Explosive Projectiles under 400 Grammes Weight), then modified in 1899 (The Hague Convention II) and in 1907 (the Fourth Hague Convention Respecting the Laws and Customs of War on Land and its Annexe). The view has been challenged on the obvious interrelationship between these two sets of rules. In the words of Professor Dinstein "the Geneva Conventions are derived from The Hague Conventions".[47] Of interest here are also the preambles of the 1899 and the 1907 Hague Conventions, which contain the so-called Martens Clause named after the Russian lawyer and delegate at the first Hague Conference in 1989, Fyodor Fyodorovich de Martens.[48] This clause affirms the pre-existing principles of international law in the following manner: "Until a more complete code of the laws of war has been issued, the High Contracting Parties deem it expedient to declare that, in cases not included in the Regulations adopted by them, the inhabitants and the belligerents remain under the protection and the rule of the principles of the law of nations, as they result from the usages established among civilised peoples, from the laws of humanity, and the dictates of the

---

focuses on the protection of the individual in time of war". *J. Pictet*, International Humanitarian Law: Definition, in International Dimensions of Humanitarian Law, UNESCO, Paris 1988, p. xx.

[47] *Y. Dinstein*, Human Rights in Armed Conflict: International Humanitarian Law, in Human Rights in International Law, Legal and Policy Issues, T. Meron (ed.), Oxford 1988, p. 345.

[48] Many scholars consider the Martens clause one of the greatest importance in modern international law "especially in rebutting any suggestions that States are free to behave as they wish within their own territory". *J. Detter De Lupis*, The Law of War, Cambridge 1987, p. 157. See in addition *F. Kalshoven*, Constraints on the Waging of War, Geneva 1991, p. 14. Others are of the opinion that the exact significance of the clause is difficult to assess. *C. Greenwood*, Historical Development and Legal Basis, in The Handbook of Humanitarian Law in Armed Conflict, D. Fleck (ed.), Oxford 1995, p. 29.

public conscience". Both conventions remained for decades the most central documents containing rules on the humanitarian aspects of the law of armed conflict.[49] A great number of the rules emanating from the Law of Hague have been incorporated in the 1977 Protocols.[50] Modern international humanitarian law was consequently mainly codified as a branch of law after the Second World War, more precisely in 1949 and 1977. In other words, the contemporary development is very much reflected in the Geneva Convention (I) for the Amelioration of the Condition of the Wounded and Sick in Armed Forces in the Field of 12 August 1949; Geneva Convention (II) for the Amelioration of the Condition of the Wounded, Sick and Shipwrecked Members of Armed Forces at Sea of 12 August 1949; Geneva Convention (III) relative to the Treatment of Prisoners of War of 12 August 1949; Geneva Convention (IV) relative to the Protection of Civilian Persons in Time of War of 12 August 1949;[51] Protocol Additional to the Geneva Conventions of 12 August 1949, and Relating to the Protection of Victims of International Armed Conflicts (Protocol I), of 8 June 1977;[52] Protocol Additional to the Geneva Conventions of 12 August 1949, and relating to the protection of victims of non-international armed conflicts (Protocol II), of 8 June 1977.[53]

Finally, I may assert that this impressive body of international instruments constitutes the foundation of contemporary international humanitarian law and it is the principal treaty-based source of that law, although by no means the only one. Like the other parts of international law, humanitarian law also consists of various rules of customary law.[54]

---

[49] The Law of Hague has been enlarged through later agreements such as the Geneva Protocol for the Prohibition of the Use in War of Asphyxiating, Poisonous or other Gases and of Bacteriological Methods of Warfare of 1925, the 1954 Convention for the Protection of Cultural Property in the Event of Armed Conflicts, the Convention on the Prohibition of the Development, Production and Stockpiling of Bacteriological (Biological) and Toxin Weapons and on Their Destruction of 1972, the Convention on Prohibitions or Restrictions on the Use of Certain Conventional Weapons, which May be Deemed to be Excessively Injurious or to Have Indiscriminate Effects of 1980, the 1993 Convention on the prohibition of the development, production, stockpiling and use of chemical weapons and on their destruction; the 1995 Protocol relating to blinding laser weapons, the 1996 Revised Protocol on prohibitions or restrictions on the use of mines, booby traps and other devices and the 1997 Convention on the prohibition of the use, stockpiling, production and transfer of anti-personnel mines and on their destruction.

[50] The text of the mentioned conventions can be found in various collections and is reprinted in The Laws of Armed Conflicts: a Collection of Conventions, Resolutions and Other Documents, *D. Schindler & J. Toman* (eds.), Dordrecht 1988. For a comprehensive review of the history of the codification process as regards the international law of armed conflict see *F. Kalshoven*, Constraints on the Waging of War, Geneva 1991, pp. 7–21; *E.K. Kwakwa*, The International Law of Armed Conflict: Personal and Material Fields of Application, Dordrecht 1992, pp. 9–42.

[51] 75 UNTS, pp. 31, 85, 135, 287.

[52] Additional Protocol I to the Geneva Conventions of 12 August 1949, and relating to the Protection of Victims of International Armed Conflicts,12 December 1977,1125 UNTS 3.

[53] Additional Protocol II to the Geneva Conventions of 12 August 1949, and relating to the Protection of Victims of Non-International Armed Conflicts,12 December 1977, 1125 UNTS 609.

[54] *Y. Dinstein*, Human Rights in Armed Conflict, p. 345; *T. Meron*, Human Rights and Humanitarian Norms as Customary Law, Oxford 1991.

Even though there are some fifty provisions of international humanitarian law which relate to the principle of non-discrimination on the basis of sex,[55] or provide special protection for women, the existing law is as, I shall demonstrate below, deficient in taking fully into account women's needs, particularly in prohibiting and/or punishing reproductive crimes.

### *7.3.3. The Interrelationship of International Humanitarian Law and International Human Rights Law*

> "Peace is the underlying condition for the full observance of human rights and war is their negation".[56]

International humanitarian law on the one hand, which for instance deals with the protection of victims of armed conflict, *i.e.*, protection of non-combatants or persons placed *hors de combat*, as well as protection of civil property, and international human rights law on the other hand, have historically evolved as distinct bodies of public international law. The central aim of both branches of law is, however, to protect the individual though they do so in different circumstances and in different ways. It can be, therefore, maintained that both regimes "share the same concerns and underlying goals".[57] Thus, the rules of humanitarian law are applicable in times of armed conflict and human rights provisions are generally, that is with the exception of rules on non-derogable rights, applicable in peace. International human rights law lacks rules on the methods and means of combat. Both systems have, furthermore, a different institutional background, *i.e.*, the system for the protection of human rights operates within the United Nations and within regional organisations, whereas the ICRC and the Red Cross movement are primarily the ones concerned with the implementation of international humanitarian law. A further difference between the two regimes is that humanitarian law to a great extent reflects the classical international law conception, *i.e.*, as an inter-state law system. In other words, the individual has no *locus standi* before international organs. The most recent development, *i.e.*, the greater willingness of the international community to prosecute war criminals, shows, however, that this assumption is not entirely correct. Equally valid is the argument that one of the most important aims of humanitarian law is to protect individuals and not states in the first place.

---

[55] The existing set of rules of humanitarian law aiming at limiting violence and protecting the fundamental rights of civilians in time of armed conflict have been criticised by feminist scholars as insufficient for the safeguard of the non-discrimination principle since they "take the experience that men have of warfare as their starting point" and not of women. *J. Gardam*, p. 64. The same writer argues, furthermore, that humanitarian law seen from the gender perspective, reinforces gender differences in the sense that it privileges the protection of men. This not only by upholding a distinction between men and women, but also because it differentiates between combatants and non-combatants. See *J. Gardam*, Gender and Non-Combatant Immunity, Transnational Law & Contemporary Problems 1993, p. 345.

[56] Resolution adopted at the 1968 World Conference on Human Rights at Teheran.

[57] *J. Gardam*, p. 56.

International human rights law regulates the relationship between states and individuals and with the nowadays increasing acceptance of the application of the *Drittwirkung*-doctrine also the relationship between individuals.

Because of the above mentioned differences there is still disagreement in the doctrine[58] about the question of 1) whether international humanitarian law is to be considered as an integral part of the international law of human rights, which is a wider concept and is the basis for humanitarian law, 2) or whether both branches are distinct, that is they are branches in their own right, or 3) whether humanitarian law is the wider concept, which includes both the law of war and human rights law.[59]

To begin with I may ascertain that there seems to be a well-established perception and wide acceptance in contemporary international law that "human rights is the genus of which humanitarian law is a species".[60] This standpoint has also been formulated in the way that the rules of the laws of armed conflict are but a "specific subset of human rights norms applicable in extreme circumstances".[61] Also the Winner of the 1991 Paul Reuter prize awarded by the ICRC, Mr. Edward Kwakwa, has argued in similar terms: "Although it antedates human rights law in terms of codification, the ensemble of the law of war is, in the truest sense, a part of human rights law".[62]

Other scholars, among them Ingrid Detter De Lupis have shown preference for the second view, *i.e.*, instead of establishing a hierarchical order between humanitarian law and human rights law to consider the two areas of law on a horizontal level. This means that emphasis is put on the idea of the two branches of law as co-existing and having different distinctive features and different circumstances of application.[63] The honorary Vice President of the ICRC, Mr. Jean Pictet, has in support of this stand-

---

[58] *L. Doswald-Beck*, The Civilian in the Crossfire, Journal of Peace Research 1987, Vol. 24, No. 3, p. 251 *et seq.*; *A. Eide*, The laws of war and human rights-differences and convergences, Studies and essays on international humanitarian law and Red Cross principles, in honour of Jean Pictet, *C. Swinarski* (ed.), ICRC, Geneva 1984, p. 675 *et seq.*

[59] The prominent writer Jean Pictet has suggested that also refugee law and certain other aspects of international law concerning social relations might be included in a concept of humanitarian law defined in a broad manner. See *A. Eide*, p. 675.

[60] *A.H. Robertson,* Human rights as the basis of international humanitarian law, Acte du congrès international de droit humanitaire, San Remo 1970, p. 174, cit. in *I. Detter De Lupis*, The Law of War, p. 131; *A.H. Robertson & J.G. Merrills*, Human Rights in the World, Manchester 1993, p. 277.

[61] I.P. Blishchenko quoted in *H. McCoubrey*, International Humanitarian Law, Dartmouth 1990, p. 5.

[62] *E. Kwakwa*, p. 180. See also *T. Buergenthal*, International Human Rights, Minnesota 1988, p. 190.

[63] *I. Detter De Lupis*, The Law of War, p. 131. See also *F.J. Hamson*, Human rights law and international humanitarian law: two coins or two sides of the same coin?, Bulletin of Human Rights 1991/1, New York 1992, p. 46. As Mr. David Petrasek has explained "Human rights advocates fear that the realism built into humanitarian law (for example, through such notions as military necessity) will compromise the idealism of human rights law. On the other hand, those used to basing their advocacy on international humanitarian law fear that the politicisation associated with human rights work will compromise the neutral and purely humanitarian nature of their work". *D. Petrasek*, Moving Forward on the Development of Minimum Humanitarian Standards, AJIL 1998, Vol. 92, p. 560.

Professor Dinstein has, for example, declared by analysing the interplay of human rights in peacetime and wartime that: "In any event, international humanitarian law must not be confused with international human rights". *Y. Dinstein*, Human Rights in Armed Conflict, p. 346.

point argued in a similar manner: "In conclusion, the two systems are related but distinct, and must remain so. They are complementary, and indeed complement each other admirably".[64] At the same time, by illustrating the interdependence imposed by the intrinsic logic of the two bodies of law and the interests of their beneficiaries, he does not exclude the feasibility of bringing both branches under one all-embracing term with the title "humane law", which shall comprise "all international legal provisions ensuring respect for and full development of the human being".[65]

As to the third alternative approach of defining the concept of humanitarian law, there are but a few scholars today that hold the view in favour of humanitarian law being the wider concept and of considering a part of the human rights law as its subset.[66]

Within the framework of the United Nations, the first UN Conference on Human Rights, which took place in Teheran in 1968, emphasised in its final document the Proclamation of Teheran, the need to protect human rights in all situations, be there a state of peace or war. For that purpose the Proclamation used the term "human rights in *armed conflicts*" (emphasis added). This concept was meant to relate to victims of armed conflicts and rules regarding the prohibition and limitation of the use of certain methods and means of warfare without making distinction between rules that are humanitarian in their content or other rules. In this respect we should also remember that various organs of the UN have in a consequent manner viewed international humanitarian law from the angle of human rights law. A number of resolutions with the title "Respect for human rights in armed conflicts" explicitly confirming this approach have been adopted by the General Assembly, especially during the period between the 1960s and the 1970s.[67] The convergence of human rights and humanitarian law has been emphasised in later resolutions as well. An important example is resolution 1989/24 of the Sub-Commission on Prevention of Discrimination and Protection of Minorities on "Human rights in times of armed conflict".[68] The same title was given to several reports received by the GA from the Secretary-General. This factual situation has been referred to as evidence for the

---

[64] *J. Pictet*, International Humanitarian Law: Definition, p. xxi. On the recent introduction of a new terminology, *i.e.*, "fundamental standards of humanity" within the UN see *D. Petrasek*, p. 557.

[65] *J. Pictet*, op. cit.

[66] *O. Bring*, Folkrätt för totalförsvaret, Stockholm 1994, p. 30.

[67] See Res. 1776(XVII) of 7th December 1962, Res. 2027(XX) of 18th November 1975, Res. 2444(XXIII) of 19th December 1968, Res. 2597(XXIV) of 16th December 1969, Res. 2674(XXV) of 9th December 1970, Res. 2677(XXV) of 9th December 1979, Res. 2852(XXVI) of 20th December 1971, Res. 3032(XXVII) of 18th December 1972, Res. 3102(XXVIII) of 12th December 1973, Res. 3319 (XXIX) of 14th December 1974, Res. 3500(XXX) of 15th December 1975, Res. 31/19 of 24th November 1976.

[68] See also the Report of the Secretary-General on Education dealing among others with the question of respect for human rights in armed conflicts, UN Doc. E/CN.4/Sub.2/1991/5, *A. de Zayas*, Human Rights and Humanitarian Law, NJIL 1994, Vols. 61/62, p. 260. Mention should also be made of the UN's publication "United Nations Actions in the Field of Human Rights" of 1988 and its previous editions, containing a chapter entitled "Protection of human rights in armed conflicts". New York 1988, pp. 283–296.

perception that humanitarian law is a recognised branch of human rights law which relates to human rights in times of armed conflict.[69]

The desire to contribute to a more solid respect for, and observance of, human rights in all situations during peace-time as well as wartime has also found expression in the earlier referred to Declaration of Minimum Humanitarian Standards prepared by an expert meeting and adopted at Turku (Finland) in December 1990. This document has received significant international attention.[70] Its legal foundation is the non-derogable standards of human rights law as well as the humanitarian law standards.

In summing up the above it may be concluded that considerable attention has been paid to the important relationship between international humanitarian law and human rights, not in the least because of practical considerations.[71] It is my conviction that despite the fact that these two legal systems to a great extent have different substantial content (*ratione materiae*), different *ratione personae* applicability,[72] different history and apply different implementation procedures,[73] they overlap at certain points, since concern for the protection of the dignity and the integrity of the

---

[69] *A.H. Robertson & J.G. Merrills*, p. 281.

[70] The declaration was submitted in 1991 to the UN Sub-Commission on Prevention of Discrimination and Protection of Minorities for discussion. The text was subsequently considered in 1995 by the UN Commission on Human Rights, which in its turn asked the Secretary-General in 1997 to prepare a report on the question of fundamental standards of humanity. The analytical report (UN Doc. E/CN.4/1998/87) was submitted to the Human Rights Commission at its session in 1998 and it was decided by resolution 1998/29 that the study of the issue shall continue also during 1999. See *T. Meron & A. Rosas*, A Declaration of Minimum Humanitarian Standards, AJIL 1991, Vol. 85, pp. 375–381; UN Doc. CN.4/Sub.2/1991/55; *D. Petrasek*, p. 557.

[71] In the doctrine of public international law a number of prominent scholars have analysed the interrelationship between international humanitarian law and human rights, among them: *Y. Dinstein*, The Law of Armed Conflict and Human Rights: Convergence and Integration, Strasbourg 1974, The International Law of Inter-State War and Human Rights, Israel Yearbook of Human Rights 1977, Vol. 7; *G.H. Aldrich*, Human Rights in Armed Conflicts: Developments of the Law, The Department of State Bulletin, Washington 1973, Vol. 68; *H.G. Espiell*, Human Rights and international humanitarian law, Bulletin of Human Rights 1991/1, New York 1992, pp. 13–25; *C. Sepúlveda*, Interrelationship in the Implementation and Enforcement of International Humanitarian Law and Human Rights Law, American University Law Review 1983, Vol. 33, p. 117 *et seq.*; *C. Sommaruga*, Human Rights and International Humanitarian Law, Bulletin of Human Rights 1991/1, New York 1992, pp. 55–63; *T. Meron*, The protection of the human person under human rights law and humanitarian law, Bulletin of Human Rights 1991/1, New York 1992, pp. 33–46; *H.S. Levie*, Violations of Human Rights in Time of War as War Crimes, in War Crimes in International Law, Y. Dinstein & M. Tabory (eds.), The Hague 1996, 123–141.

[72] In human rights law the rights of the *individual* human being, independent of which group he or she belongs are decisive, whereas international humanitarian law prescribes a differential status, *i.e.*, a different degree of protection is foreseen on the basis of to which category the individual belongs.

[73] I shall briefly give a few examples of international monitoring mechanisms in situations of armed conflicts. Provisions dealing with the implementation and monitoring of international humanitarian law are to be found in Articles 8–11 of the four Geneva Conventions of 1949. Article 8 common to the first, second and third Geneva Conventions and Article 9 of the fourth Convention require that these conventions "shall be applied with the co-operation and under the scrutiny of the Protecting Powers whose duty is to safeguard the interests of the Parties to the conflict". In other words, the institution of Protecting Powers is compulsory. The Protecting Powers may perform a number of different functions under each of the four Geneva Conventions. But this system has been applied very seldom and in very few cases, *i.e.*, in 1956 (the Suez crisis), in 1961 (the Goa conflict), in 1971–1972 (the Indo-Pakistan conflict) and in 1982 (the Falklands-Malvinas conflict). See *E. Kwakwa*, p. 164. Furthermore, there are provisions,

individual constitutes the basis of international humanitarian law as well as of human rights law. Therefore, the drawing of distinct borderlines between both bodies of law is artificial and even counter-productive.[74] I have, therefore, adopted a more flexible approach, whereby the focus is put on the interrelationship and gradual convergence of human rights and humanitarian law. In this respect, of relevance to my discussion here is also the principle of the non-derogability, according to which even in situations of public emergency (war is the most serious one) threatening the life of the nation (*i.e.*, internal or international armed conflicts), there are a number of human rights, which can never be suspended by the states parties to the respective treaties.[75]

---

which provide for a procedure of good offices through the ICRC or other impartial humanitarian organisation recognised by the parties to the conflict. I should also mention that Article 90 of the first Additional Protocol to the Geneva Conventions provides for the establishment of an independent International Humanitarian Fact-Finding Commission for investigation of alleged violations of the conventions. The Commission was set up recently and it held its first meeting in 1992. See *A. Rosas*, International monitoring mechanisms in situations of armed conflict, in Monitoring Human Rights in Europe, A. Bloed *et al.* (eds.), Dordrecht 1993, p. 229; *A. Reinish*, The International Fact-Finding Committee According to Article 90 Additional Protocol to the Geneva Conventions and its Potential Enquiry Competence in the Yugoslav Conflict, NJIL 1996, Vol. 65, pp. 241–255.

It should be mentioned that the Commission's mandate is very narrow and depends on the express recognition of its jurisdiction of the parties involved in the conflict. Moreover, the Commission can carry out its inquiries only on the request of one of the High Contracting Party, which has recognised its competence. Also the publicity of the Commission's findings is subject to all parties' consent.

There is, moreover, no reporting obligation for the states parties to the relevant conventions on humanitarian law as the case is in human rights law. Much of the implementation of humanitarian law relies consequently on the national legislation of the states. See generally on the issue of monitoring the implementation of international humanitarian law: *F. Kalshoven*, pp. 61–70; *L. Boisson de Chazournes*, The collective responsibility of states to ensure respect for humanitarian principles, in Monitoring Human Rights in Europe, A. Bloed *et al.* (eds.), pp. 247–261; *R.H.F. Austin*, The Law of International Armed Conflicts, in M. Bedjaoui (ed.), pp. 786–787; *Y. Sandoz*, Implementing International Humanitarian Law, in International Dimensions of Humanitarian Law, pp. 259–283. As to the existing different implementations procedures on human rights, see the comparative study carried out by Mr. *Tardu*, The Right of Individual Complaint to the United Nations for Violations of Human Rights, in International Human Rights Law, Theory and Practice, in The Canadian Human Rights Foundation 1992, I. Cotler & F.P. Eliadis (eds.), pp. 405–434; *P. Alston & M.E. Tardu*, Human Rights: The International Petition System, New York 1985, Vol. III, Part II.

74 It has been emphasised that especially in situations of internal violence-where there is considerable overlap and complementarity of both branches of relevant law-upholding "distinctness can be counter-productive". UN Doc. E/CN.4/1998/87, § 99.

75 While the concept of non-derogable rights has been discussed in Part I of this study, I ought to mention here that in regard to states' obligation to respect the non-derogable clauses there are significant differences between the various human rights treaties. The American Convention contains, for example, very flexible criteria as to the required intensity of the threat to the security and the independence of a treaty state before it may impose an emergency regime. The ICCPR permits derogations in time of "public emergency, which threatens the life of the nation" (Article 4). The European Convention refers to "war or other public emergency threatening the life of the nation" (Article 15). The American Convention makes the exercise of the right to derogation dependent on "war, public danger, or other emergency that threatens the independence or security of a State Party" (Article 27). In other words, states parties to the later conventional regime may more easily derogate from their human rights obligations and proclaim a state of emergency in less grave emergencies than are required according to the other relevant conventions. Clearly, the Inter-American regime of derogation is more favourable to states than the others. *M.K. Eriksson*, Skydd av mänskliga rättigheter, det interamerikanska systemet, Uppsala 1994, pp. 85–90.

Thus, applying the rules of international humanitarian law in armed conflicts does not prevent or exclude the application and observance of human rights law at the same time.[76] Thus, both sets of rules are most frequently applied concurrently. Therefore, it is not surprising that the most recent developments in international law indicate an attitude of striving for a compromise between the major different views among states on the above-discussed subject. This approach has facilitated the bridge building between the two branches of law. Thus, representatives of the International Committee of the Red Cross articulated this current position in the Report on the Protection of War Victims of 1993 in the following way: "it should be stressed that human rights law and international humanitarian law are complementary".[77] Another indication of the increasing convergence of both regimes is the UN Convention on the Rights of the Child, which is expressly concerned with both the principles of international human rights treaty law and the application of international humanitarian law. Thus, in relation to children both branches of law are no longer considered as distinct.[78] Such a holistic starting-point of considering human rights and humanitarian law as interdependent is in my view of overwhelming importance for the efforts of the international community to achieve full realisation of human rights (including those of women) universally and in all situations and should be encouraged. It must be born in mind that the most basic link between international humanitarian law and human rights law is international obligations of states to guarantee an effective protection of the life and the dignity of the individual human being.

### *7.3.4. Basic Principles of International Humanitarian Law*

The basic sources of humanitarian law are as already mentioned the four Geneva Conventions of 1949 for the protection of war victims, which as of March 1998 were ratified by 188 states, and the two additional Protocols of 1977 dealing with the protection of victims of international conflicts and internal armed conflicts.[79] The four conventions are consequently among the most widely ratified international treaties. This is, however, not the case with the additional protocols, despite the fact that many of the provisions contained there are considered to reflect rules of customary international law.[80]

---

[76] *A.-L. Svensson-McCarthy*, Minimum Humanitarian Standards-From Cape Town Towards the Future, The Review 1997, Nos. 58–59, p. 13 ff.

[77] International Conference for the Protection of War Victims, ICRC Report on the Protection of War Victims, Geneva, June 1993, p. 31. See also *ICRC*, International humanitarian law, Answers to your questions, ICRC Geneva 1998, p. 40.

[78] *G. Van Bueren*, The International Law on the Rights of the Child, p. 349. See also the draft additional Protocol to the Convention which deals with the protection of children in times of armed conflicts. UN Doc. E/CN.4/1995/6.

[79] At the time of writing there are 137 states parties to Protocol I and 127 states parties to Protocol II.

[80] See the case *Military and Paramilitary Activities in and against Nicaragua* (Nicaragua v. United States of America), Merits, 1986 ICJ Rep. 14, Judgment of 27 June 1986. In this case the International Court of Justice ruled that the common articles 1 and 3 of the Geneva Conventions are embodying customary international law. Article 3 prohibits at any time and in any place whatsoever: "a) Violence to

Since protecting the humanitarian principles of the international community in situations of armed conflict is the main purpose and aim of these documents, one of the most central principles of that law is upholding *humanity*,[81] meaning that all kinds and degrees of violence that are not necessary for the overpowering of the opponent are prohibited. In other words, the requirement of military necessity and restraint on the conduct of belligerents is the very basis of international humanitarian law. Yet another important principle of international humanitarian law is the safeguard of the equal right of all war victims independent of whether they belong to the party of the aggressor or to the party of the victim, to protection and assistance. Also, the Geneva Conventions and the additional protocols affirm the international responsibility of all the parties to armed conflicts in order to ensure that they respect international humanitarian law. On the other hand, the recent active involvement of the United Nations, especially the Security Council and other intergovernmental organisations in matters that are traditionally governed by international humanitarian law, has given rise, not without sufficient grounds for serious concern, as to the consequences of this "politicisation" of international humanitarian law. Thus, it is believed that this tendency constitutes a real danger to, and is inconsistent with, the very basis of humanitarian law – the impartiality, the humanity and the neutral approach.[82] Since it is beyond the framework of this study to explore in depth the notions that influence the development of international humanitarian law in general, I shall therefore concentrate only on the specific issues of relevance for the protection of women's reproductive freedom and for the achievement of gender equality.

Major international instruments prohibit discrimination on the ground of sex in the states' exercise of the right to derogation. The non-discrimination principle includes the prohibition of gender-based violence and it is consequently incorporated both in international humanitarian law and in human rights law. International

---

life and person, in particular murder of all kinds, mutilation, cruel treatment and torture; b) Taking of hostages; c) Outrages upon personal dignity, in particular humiliating and degrading treatment; d) The passing of sentences and the carrying out of executions without previous judgement pronounced by a regularly constituted court, affording all the judicial guarantees, which are recognised as indispensable by civilised peoples". A detailed analysis of the customary character of various rules of humanitarian law has been presented by the eminent jurist *T. Meron*, Human Rights and Humanitarian Norms as Customary Law, pp. 3–79. See also another publication of the same writer, The protection of the human person under human rights law and humanitarian law, Bulletin of Human Rights 1991/1, New York 1992, pp. 34–35.

[81] This principle implies according to Mr. Sommaruga that: "war must not serve as an outlet for anger nor as a justification for any form of inhumane treatment". *C. Sommaruga*, Human rights and international humanitarian law, Bulletin of Human Rights 1991/1, New York 1992, p. 57. Other notions that influence modern international humanitarian law are *military necessity*, *i.e.*, the belligerent may use the force necessary to overpower the opponent, and *chivalry*, *i.e.*, a certain degree of fairness is to be observed, including a certain mutual respect. This, in effect, guarantees the minimum of civilisation in the armed conflict by the imposition of order and the ability to trust the adversary in essential matters.

[82] *J. Patrnogic*, Introductory Comments on the Current Problems of International Humanitarian Law, in Current Problems of International Humanitarian Law, San Remo 1993, p. 54.

humanitarian law contains a number of provisions prohibiting gender discrimination. Articles 12 of the First and Second Geneva Conventions, Article 16 of the Third Convention, Article 27 of the Fourth Convention and Article 75 of Additional Protocol I and Article 4 of Additional Protocol II require a treatment "without any adverse distinction founded on sex". Furthermore, Article 14 of the Third Convention stipulates that women "shall in all cases benefit by treatment as favourable as that granted to men".

The serious violations of humanitarian law committed during the armed conflicts in former Yugoslavia (1991–1995), which have especially affected women's reproductive freedom, brought the atrocities into focus for the whole international community. They provoked a strong response to the effect that this conduct of behaviour was widely condemned, and prosecution of the criminal acts was called for. The massive, world-wide public opinion found expression in a number of important international documents, and gender-based violence against women in armed conflicts[83] was brought to the fore and became one of the very central issues for consideration during the UN second World Conference on Human Rights in 1993 and subsequent international gatherings. The overwhelming majority of the delegates to the Vienna Conference stressed the importance for the whole international community to strive towards and to act decisively for the elimination of violence against women in armed conflicts, both in public and private life. The consensus on that particular subject matter was reflected in § 38 of the Vienna Declaration where it is stated that:

---

[83] A distinction is being upheld in international law between international and internal armed conflicts. Since the international community for many decades has focused on international armed conflicts, there are more comprehensive rules elaborated to regulate that area of law. In an international armed conflict, women as members of the civilian population benefit from rules in international humanitarian law, which impose various kinds of limitations on the conduct of hostilities. The relevant rules may be traced back to the Hague Conventions of 1899 and 1907 which to a great extent have become part of customary law and which are further developed in Additional Protocol I. Article 48 provides that the parties to a conflict "shall at all times distinguish between the civilian population and combatants and between civilian objects and military objectives and accordingly shall direct their operations only against military objectives". Furthermore, women shall be especially protected against any attack on their honour, in particular against rape, enforced prostitution, or any form of indecent assault. (Article 27(2) of the Fourth Convention and Articles 75, 76 of Additional Protocol I).

However, international humanitarian law is today increasingly applied in situations of non-international armed conflicts as well. In relation to non-international armed conflicts, Article 13 of Additional Protocol II establishes that: "the civilian population as such, as well as individual civilians, shall not be the object of attack". Besides, a great number of the on-going armed conflicts are of a mixed character. In addition, it should be mentioned that in the case of armed conflict of a non-international character, besides the guarantees of Article 3 of all four Geneva Conventions, women and children are explicitly protected against rape, enforced prostitution or any form of indecent assault and shall be treated without any adverse distinction. Article 4 of Additional Protocol II forbids "outrages upon personal dignity, in particular humiliating and degrading treatment, rape, enforced prostitution and any form of indecent assault". See *J. de Preux*, Special protection of women and children, International Review of the Red Cross, 1985, No. 248, p. 300; *F. Krill*, The Protection of Women in International Humanitarian Law, International Review of the Red Cross 1985, No. 249; *A.-L. Svensson-McCarthy*, pp. 1–30; *M. Bothe*, War Crimes in Non-International Conflicts, in War Crimes in International Law, Y. Dinstein & M. Tabory (eds.), pp. 293–305.

> "Violations of the human rights of women in situations of armed conflict are violations of the fundamental principles of international human rights and humanitarian law. All violations of this kind, including particularly murder, systematic rape, sexual slavery, and forced pregnancy, require a particularly effective response".[84]

The 1995 Beijing Declaration contains, moreover, a whole chapter (E) devoted to women in armed conflicts. In § 132 it is stated that "All violations, including in particular murder, rape, including systematic rape, sexual slavery and forced pregnancy require a particularly effective response". These formulations in recent consensual documents reaffirm first of all the principles already embodied in various General Assembly resolutions, *e.g.*, Res. 2675 (XXV), that fundamental human rights, *i.e.*, norms of peremptory character, continue to apply fully in armed conflicts. Protection of physical and mental integrity is a very basic necessity for the survival of a human being. Therefore, the right to life, which is a fundamental value of civilised societies, is placed on top of the hierarchy of human rights. On the other hand, it is important also to stress that the right to life and the right to health are inseparable. If health cannot be guaranteed and maintained for reasons of the crimes against women (including reproductive crimes), which are enumerated in § 38 of the Vienna Declaration, the life of the individual concerned is in danger. Secondly, the recent international commitments to co-operate in order to prevent and to punish[85] the perpetrators of the crimes referred to adds a new dimension to international humanitarian law, since by listing the different forms of violations of women's human rights in equal terms, the prohibition of *all* of them in peremptory terms is authorised. Thus, the aforementioned prohibited practices qualify to be defined and prosecuted as war crimes. This is a very encouraging development, which a couple of months before the adoption of the Vienna Declaration was confirmed by resolution 827 of the UN Security Council.[86] The Security Council expressed therein its grave alarm at continuing reports of mass killings, massive, organised and systematic detention and rape of women and its determination to put an end to such crimes. It declares that serious crimes against women are punishable

---

[84] UN Doc. A/Conf.157/22, Part II, § 38.

[85] The use of the expression "effective response" in the cited paragraph of the Vienna Declaration has been, however, subject to some criticism. Mrs. Donna Sullivan holds the view that this provision "stops short of calling for prosecution of those gender-specific abuses that constitute war crimes, grave breaches or crimes against humanity", since it simply urges effective response. *D.J. Sullivan*, Women's Human Rights and the 1993 World Conference on Human Rights, AJIL 1994, Vol. 88, p. 156.

[86] Resolution 827 (1993) of 25 May 1993, reprinted in HRLJ 1993, Vol. 14, Nos. 5–6, p. 197. The Security Council has been preoccupied by information regarding widespread and flagrant violations of international humanitarian law involving rape also in the following resolutions: Res. 780 (1992) of 6 October 1992, Res. 787 (1992) of 16 November 1992, Res. 809 (1993) of 2 March 1993, Res. 820 (1993) of 17 April 1993, Res. 836 (1993) of 4 June 1993 and Res. 844 (1993) of 18 June 1993. The text of these resolutions is reprinted in: Role of the Competent United Nations Bodies in the Implementation of International Humanitarian Law, *International Institute of Humanitarian Law*, San Remo, September 1993.

offences under international humanitarian law. The awareness and the significance of an urgent response in prosecuting such war crimes against a large number of women and girls committed in connection with the armed conflicts in the former Yugoslavia, furthermore, resulted in the Security Council adopting, on 25 May 1993, the Statute of the *ad hoc* international Tribunal for the former Yugoslavia.[87] Similar action was taken by the Security Council in regard to the situation in Rwanda. By adopting resolution 955 on 8 November 1994,[88] the *ad hoc* international criminal tribunal for Rwanda was established. The expectations for the prosecution of gender crimes by these tribunals in that they may "change drastically the way wartime abuses against women have been perennially ignored, and to establish firmly that wartime abuses against women will henceforth be rigorously prohibited, prosecuted, and punished" are very high.[89] The progressive development of international humanitarian law has been, since the establishment of both *ad hoc* tribunals, rapid.[90] Time will tell us how seriously the international community is prepared to deal with women's issues in the context of international humanitarian law.

---

[87] The Statute of the *ad hoc* Tribunal was presented by the UN Secretary–General after extensive consultations with member and non-member states of the UN, inter-governmental organisations, etc. See Report of the Secretary-General pursuant to paragraph 2 of Security Council Resolution 808 (1993), UN Doc. S/2504, especially §§ 18–25. Prior to the adoption of the Statute, several member states put forward suggestions and made proposals on the creation of an international tribunal, *e.g.*, France (S/25266), Italy (S/25300) and Sweden (S/25307). Moreover, the Secretary- General received comments from the ICRC and a great number of international NGOs. Many of the formulations of the provisions of the Statute also reflect already existing international instruments and texts previously prepared by the UN Committee on International Criminal Jurisdiction, the ILC and the ILA. See *M. Bergsmo*, p. 372.

[88] SC Res. 955(1994) with annexed Statute, reprinted in 33 ILM, 1994, p. 1602 *et seq.*

[89] *K.D. Askin*, p. 259.

[90] According to Professor Meron international humanitarian law has "developed faster since the beginning of the atrocities in the former Yugoslavia than in the four-and-a-half decades since the Nuremberg Tribunals and the adoption of the Geneva Conventions for the Protection of Victims of War". *T. Meron*, War Crimes Law Comes of Age, AJIL 1998, Vol. 92, p. 463.

I may also mention that the Beijing Declaration as well as some of the regional plans of Action (for Asia and the Pacific) require governments to strongly condemn, among other things, the systematic rape of women in situations of armed conflict and to support calls for the perpetrators of such crimes to be punished. UN Doc. E/CN.6/1995/5/Add.1. Of great significance for the progressive development of international humanitarian law is also the Rome Statute of the International Criminal Court (UN Doc. A/CONF.183/9), which was adopted on 17 July 1998 and which I shall comment below. The Statute is in the words of Philippe Kirsch and John Holmes "a historic achievement" and "the culmination of many decades of hope and hard work". *P. Kirsch & J.T. Holmes*, The Rome Conference on an International Criminal Court: The Negotiating Process, AJIL 1999, Vol. 93, p. 12.

*Chapter 8*

# The *Ad Hoc* International Tribunal for the Former Yugoslavia

## 8.1. General Developments Prior to its Creation

The idea of bringing into existence an international criminal court is not a new one. Several attempts have been made earlier in history to create international tribunals for the prosecution of persons accused of committing war crimes. There are a few examples of military trials prior to the First World War.[1] After the end of the war the establishment of a High Tribunal was discussed by a Commission appointed by the Allied Powers at the Preliminary Peace Conference of Paris in January 1919.[2] The main purpose of that tribunal was meant to be the prosecution of war crimes committed by the forces of the enemy powers (Germany and its allies). The proposal was, however, opposed and rejected by the representatives of the USA[3] and Japan, partly because of the Commission's recommendation to expose high officials to individual responsibility, and it therefore did not become a part of the

[1] The very first documented precedent of international criminal trial dealing with among other things rape of innocent civilians by the troops of Peter von Hagenbach dates from 1474. *V. Morris & M.P. Scharf*, An Insider's Guide to The International Tribunal for The Former Yugoslavia, New York 1995, p. 1; *K.D. Askin*, p. 5, note 11. Generally on historical precedents of the *ad hoc* tribunals see *M.C. Bassiouni*, Introduction to the History of Establishing an International Criminal Court, in International Criminal Law, Vol. III Enforcement, M.C. Bassiouni (ed.), New York 1987, pp. 181–185; *M.C. Bassiouni*, Crimes Against Humanity in International Criminal Law, Dordrecht 1992, pp. 192–199; *L.S. Sunga*, pp. 18–20; *G. Schwarzenberger*, International Law as Applied by International Courts and Tribunals, Vol. II, The Law of Armed Conflict, London 1968; *H. von Hebel*, An International Tribunal for the Former Yugoslavia, NQHR 1993, pp. 438–439; *H. Roggemann*, Der Internationale Strafgerichtshof der Vereinten Nationen von 1993 und der Krieg auf dem Balkan, Berlin 1994, pp. 42–43; *M.C. Bassiouni & P. Manikas*, The Law of the International Criminal Tribunal for the Former Yugoslavia, New York 1996, pp. 199–202.

[2] The Commission was given a broad mandate. It was requested to examine and report on, *e.g.*, the responsibility of the authors of the war, the degree of responsibility for the members of enemy forces and any other individuals and the constitution of a criminal court for the prosecution of those responsible for the breaches of the laws of war. Of special interest to my study is the findings of the Commission submitted to the Preliminary Peace Conference in which it enumerated 32 war crimes. Among them we can find torture of civilians, rape and abduction of girls and women for the purpose of enforced prostitution. The United Nations War Crimes Commission, History of the United Nations War Crimes Commission and the Development of the Laws of War, London 1948, pp. 34–35.

[3] *M. Lippman*, Nuremberg: Forty Five Years Later, Connecticut JIL 1991, Vol. 7, p. 7.

Treaty of Versailles, which was signed on 28 June 1919.[4] In consequence Articles 228 to 230 of that treaty declare that the German Government is obliged to surrender war criminals guilty of acts in violation of the laws and customs of war to the Allies.[5] The victorious powers, furthermore, attempted on the basis of Article 227 of the same treaty to prosecute the German Emperor, Kaiser Wilhelm II of Hohenzollern, who was accused of crimes against *inter alia* international morality. The matter was, however, not proceeded with for the simple reason that the Kaiser fled to the Netherlands where he was granted asylum and the Dutch refused to extradite him to stand trial because of the political nature of the case.

Many ideas about an international criminal court were presented and debated within the Advisory Committee of distinguished jurists during its work on the draft statute of the Permanent Court of International Justice (cited also as the World Court). The Committee's Chairman, the Belgian Lord Descamps, put forward a formal proposal on that subject. It was, however, not adopted, since there were serious disagreements among his colleagues as to the questions relating among other things to the imposition of criminal responsibility under international law on individuals acting for, and on behalf of, their respective states as well as the question of whether individuals were to be prosecuted for their individual conduct.[6] The movement for the creation of an international criminal court gained support in 1934 after the assassination of King Alexander of Yugoslavia.[7] However, it was not until the end of the Second World War that perpetrators of war crimes were convicted by international tribunals (Nuremberg and Tokyo[8]). After these trials had discharged their functions, the UN requested the ILC to explore the feasibility of the creation of an international criminal court. The conclusions of the Commission were in favour of this idea and the GA accordingly appointed in 1951 and 1953 a special Committee to prepare a draft statute of an international criminal court. The draft was presented in 1953 but unfortunately no action followed.[9] This was very much

---

[4] Treaty of Peace with Germany, entered into force on 10 January 1920. 11 Martens Nouveau Recueil, 323. See also *I.P. Blishchenko,* Responsibility in Breaches of International Humanitarian Law, in International Dimensions of Humanitarian Law, UNESCO 1988, p. 283.

[5] Later on the Allied Powers decided not to carry out these provisions, for several reasons, and they agreed instead to permit the German Government to prosecute the war criminals itself. The result of the trials was, however, disappointing. *L.S. Sunga*, p. 24; *M. Lippman*, pp. 10 –11.

[6] *S. Glueck*, War Criminals – Their Prosecution and Punishment, New York 1944, pp. 91–92. For a discussion of the Committee's deliberations and decisions see also *M. Lippman*, pp. 13–14.

[7] This incident prompted the adoption of the Convention for the Prevention and Punishment of Terrorism and a Convention for the Creation of an International Criminal Court by the League of Nations in 1937. But the practical problems associated with the creation of an international criminal court seem to have been considered serious obstacles, since no state ratified the second above-mentioned treaty. *M. Lippman*, p. 14.

[8] For an insightful background of the Tokyo trial see *B.V.A. Röling & A. Cassese*, The Tokyo Trial, Oxford 1993 and *K.D. Askin*, pp. 117–126.

[9] Two draft statutes were presented in 1951 and 1953. Neither of them were acted upon pending the adoption of the Draft Code of Offences Against the Peace and Security of Mankind. *M.C. Bassiouni*, Introduction to the History of Establishing an International Criminal Court, p. 184. See also The Work of the International Law Commission, UN New York 1966.

because of the reluctance on the part of the majority of states to support the work on that draft, partly because of lack of consensus on important matters of a *ratione materiae* as well as of a *ratione personae* character. The legitimacy of disobeying superior orders was resisted by some states. At the same time, in 1950, the GA called upon the ILC to prepare a draft code of offences against the peace and security of mankind. The Commission decided to limit the scope of the draft to offences containing a political element and endangering the maintenance of international peace and security. Therefore, international crimes such as slavery and trafficking in women and children were omitted. In 1953 the ILC revised its elaborated draft in the light of the observations received from governments, but in 1954 the GA postponed further consideration of it until a definition of the term "aggression" was submitted. A special Committee was appointed for that purpose and the definition of "aggression" was finally approved in 1974. A couple of years later, in 1981, the GA invited the ILC to resume its work on the draft Code of offences. This was also done but regrettably without any success due to the international climate. During the Cold War there were neither favourable conditions nor the political will[10] to achieve an agreement on the creation of a permanent international criminal court. A concrete result could consequently not be achieved until the end of the Cold War.[11] The tensions between the Great Powers disappeared and the political climate was then favourable towards achieving widespread recognition of the need for an international enforcement of criminal responsibility for violations of humanitarian law. The GA was in 1989 accordingly able to request the ILC to address the issue of the creation of an international criminal court or other international criminal trial mechanism "with jurisdiction over persons alleged to have committed crimes, which may be covered under the (Draft Code of Offences against the Peace and Security

---

In the meantime, two UN conventions (on genocide and apartheid), containing provisions which foresaw the establishment of an international criminal tribunal in the future, came into force. Thus, the Convention on the Prevention and Punishment of the Crime of Genocide was the first universal instrument to codify the jurisdiction of an international criminal court. Article VI of that convention provides that: "persons charged with genocide or any of the other acts enumerated in article III shall be tried by a competent tribunal of the State in the territory of which the act was committed, or by such international penal tribunal as may have jurisdiction with respect to those Contracting Parties, which shall have accepted its jurisdiction". Article V of the Convention on the Suppression and Punishment of the Crime of *Apartheid* stipulates that: "Persons charged with the acts enumerated in article II of the present Convention may be tried by a competent tribunal of any State Party to the Convention, which may acquire jurisdiction over the person of the accused or by an international penal tribunal having jurisdiction with respect to those States Parties, which shall have accepted its jurisdiction". Regrettably this has not become a reality yet. I should, however, mention that the Statute for the Creation of an International Criminal Jurisdiction to Implement the International Convention on the Suppression and Punishment of the Crime of *Apartheid* was opened for signature as early as 1981.

[10] The idea of an international criminal court has been seen by many governments as an infringement of national sovereignty. National courts should, according to these opponents, have exclusive jurisdiction over crimes committed in the territory of the state concerned. *J. Borgen*, En internasjonal straffedomstol, Mennesker og rettigheter 1994, No. 3, p. 260.

[11] See *B. Broms*, The Definition of Aggression, Recueil des Cours 1977, Vol. I, pp. 319 *et seq.*

of Mankind)".[12] Undoubtedly the ILC gained from this situation and was at last[13] able to review its draft statute of a permanent criminal court at its 45th session, 3 May to 24 July 1993. A second reading of the draft took place at its 46th session.[14] Finally the ILC adopted the complete draft Statute for the proposed court in July 1994 and it presented it to the 49th session of the UN General Assembly. The General Assembly could agree only on setting up an *ad hoc* Committee to review the draft Statute and report back in 1995.[15] The draft was then revised by a UN Preparatory Committee during two years of meetings (1996–1998)[16] and finally the statute was adopted on 17 July 1998 at the Diplomatic Conference for an International Criminal Court in Rome. The creation of a standing criminal court may thereby become "a reality before the end of the twentieth century",[17] provided that sixty instruments of ratification, acceptance, approval or accession are deposited with the Secretary-General of the UN (Article 126 of the Statute).

---

[12] UNGA Res. 44/39 adopted on 4th December 1989, UN Doc. A/44/49. For a review of the work of the ILC at the beginning of the 1990s see ICJ, The Establishment of a Permanent International Penal Court, UN Doc. A/CONF.157/PC/62/Add. 17, 3 June 1993, pp. 5–6.

Professor Bassiouni, who earlier has prepared and presented a Draft International Criminal Code, has given a thorough historical background on the efforts to establish a permanent international criminal court in A Draft International Criminal Court and Draft Statute for an International Criminal Tribunal, 1987. See also Draft Statute International Criminal Tribunal, 9 Nouvelles Etudes Pénales, 1992 and Amnesty International, The quest for international justice: Time for a permanent international criminal court, Report July 1995, IOR 40/04/95.

[13] The ILC was in 1993 able to transmit the Working Group's preliminary Draft for an International Criminal Tribunal to the GA. Report of the ILC on the Work of its 45th session, GAOR, 48th Session, Suppl. No. 10, UN Doc. A/48/10. On general questions of an international criminal trial mechanism see *G. Eiriksson*, The Work of the International Law Commission at its 44th session, NJIL 1994, Vols. 61/62, pp. 374–375.

[14] Report of the ILC on the Work of its 46th session, GAOR, 49th Session, Suppl. No. 10, UN Doc. A/49/10. See, in addition, the report of the Special Rapporteur Mr. Thiam, UN Doc. A/CN.4/460, 15 April 1994.

[15] *J. Crawford*, The ILC Adopts a Statute For An International Criminal Court, AJIL 1995, Vol. 89, p. 415. The same year Amnesty International called for the adoption of the necessary treaty no later than 24 October 1996, which marks the end of the 50th anniversary of the United Nations. Amnesty International, Report 1995, p. 40.

[16] For a more detailed background on the work around the draft statute for an international criminal court see *B. Broms*, The Establishment of an International Criminal Court, in War Crimes in International Law, Y. Dinstein & M. Tabory (eds.), pp. 183–197; General Assembly, Preparatory Committee on International Criminal Court, in Human Rights Monitor 1997, Geneva, Nos. 39–40, pp. 5–10; *M. Palatsi*, Proposed International Criminal Court. Aspects on Jurisdiction, in Essays on International Law, Finnish Branch of ILA, Helsinki 1998, No. 7, pp. 99–150. See also UN Doc. A/Ac.249/1998/L.13; *I. Tallgren*, Completing the "International Criminal Order", NJIL 1998, Vol. 67, pp. 107–137. *A. Zimmermann*, Die Schaffung eines ständigen Internationalen Strafgerichtshofes. Perspektiven und Probleme von der Staatenkonferenz in Rom, Zeitschrift für ausländisches öffentliches Recht und Völkerrecht 1998, Vol. 58/1.

[17] *T. Meron*, War Crimes Law Comes of Age, AJIL 1998, Vol. 92, p. 463. See also *C. Cissé*, An Effective and Independent International Criminal Court before the End of the Century?, International Law Forum Du Droit International, Zero Issue 1998, p. 6.

This progressive general development in the post Cold War period towards a broad agreement on the establishment of an international criminal court and narrowing of the doctrine of state sovereignty undoubtedly strengthens the system of international law and also rendered it possible more than 45 years after the Nuremberg and the Tokyo trials the S. C. to create for the first time *ad hoc* international tribunals, albeit with limited jurisdiction,[18] entrusted with the power to try war criminals. The crisis in former Yugoslavia and in Rwanda made it clear to the world that the only urgent and effective response to the need to prosecute those responsible for mass and flagrant human rights violations and breaches of international humanitarian law, in order to deter future violations, is to create *ad hoc* tribunals[19] instead of waiting for the completion of the ILC tasks on that matter. In addition to that, Professor Crawford has considered the intensive and detailed media coverage of the atrocities perpetrated during the armed conflicts in the former Yugoslavia and in Rwanda in contrast to the rather similar situations in Burundi and Sudan, but which were "internationally less visible", as "crucial" for the creation of the *ad hoc* criminal trials.[20]

---

[18] The two established *ad hoc* tribunals fulfil short-time needs in only two areas of the world.

[19] Like the Yugoslav Tribunal, the creation of the Rwanda Tribunal was preceded by an impartial Commission of Experts, which was established on the basis of S.C. Res. 935 (1994), (UN Doc. S/1994/1125 of 4 October 1994) for the purpose of examining and analysing information with a view to providing the Secretary-General with its conclusions on the evidence of grave violations of international humanitarian law committed on the territory of Rwanda, including the evidence of possible acts of genocide. The Commission strongly recommended in its preliminary report (the Commission submitted its final report S/1994/1405 to the Secretary-General on 29 November 1994) that the S.C. take all necessary and effective measures so that individuals responsible for serious international crimes committed in Rwanda during the armed conflict, triggered on 6 April 1994 (On that date President Habyarimana was killed together with President Cyprien Ntaryamira of Burundi when their plane was hit by a rocket), could be brought to justice before an independent and impartial international criminal tribunal. The following three persons were appointed to serve on the Commission, each in a personal capacity: Chairman – Mr. Atsu-Koffi Amega (Togo), Ms. Haby Dieng (Guinea) and Mr. Salifou Fomba (Mali).

On the basis of Res. 955 the Security Council subsequently, on the 8 November 1994, decided to establish an *ad hoc* Rwanda Tribunal. Thus, the one-step process (*i.e.*, through a resolution) of the creation of the Rwanda Tribunal was different from the two-stage process (the request for a report was followed by its approval by the S.C.) for the Yugoslav Tribunal. The 1994 resolution on Rwanda is the culmination of a series of resolutions in which the S.C. has condemned the systematic and widespread violations of international humanitarian law in Rwanda and, in particular, the mass killing of civilians with impunity. According to preliminary estimations between 500,000 and 1 million persons belonging to the Tutsi minority were the victims of the massacres. The Tutsi minority made up about 15% of the approximately 7.2 million people living there in early 1994. However, we should bear in mind that Hutu who opposed the killings were also targeted. It is also expected that the Rwanda Tribunal will investigate allegations of, and prosecute gender-specific, war crimes. *L.S. Sunga*, The Commission of Experts on Rwanda and the Creation of the International Criminal Tribunal for Rwanda/A note, HRLJ 1995, Vol. 16, p. 121; Proposition 1995/96:48 Lagstiftning med anledning av den av Förenta Nationerna inrättade tribunalen för Rwanda mm., Stockholm 1996. See also *P. Akhavan*, The International Criminal Tribunal for Rwanda: The Politics and Pragmatics of Punishment, AJIL 1996, Vol. 90, p. 502. Generally on the UN's role in Rwanda see The United Nations and Rwanda 1993–1996, New York 1997.

[20] *J. Crawford*, The ILC Adopts A Statute For An International Criminal Court, p. 407.

## 8.2. The Legal Foundations and Objectives of the *Ad Hoc* Tribunal

The *ad hoc* Tribunal for the former Yugoslavia (the official name is "International Tribunal for the Prosecution of Persons Responsible for Serious Violations of International Humanitarian Law Committed in the Territory of the Former Yugoslavia Since 1991")[21] came into existence on the basis of the two UN Security Council resolutions No. 808 of 22 February 1993[22] and No. 827 of 25 May 1993.[23] Both are related to Chapter VII of the UN Charter, which is entitled "Action with respect to threats to the peace, breaches of the peace, and acts of aggression".[24] Since the key terms in that provision are not closely defined, it is up to the Security Council to decide what constitutes a threat to the peace. The late Professor Akehurst has argued that this regulation shows a "political realism"[25] and consequently gives free hands to the Security Council to interpret the expression "threats to the peace" extensively, *i.e.*, whenever it deems it necessary and more or less as it wants. Various situations have been considered by the S.C. as constituting such a threat.[26] The Security Council determined for the first time of its existence that crimes against international humanitarian law[27] and

[21] At its first session at The Hague in November 1993, the *ad hoc* Tribunal decided that its name should be abbreviated as "The International Tribunal For Crimes in Former Yugoslavia", *P.S. Szasz*, The Proposed War Crimes Tribunal for Ex-Yugoslavia, New York University Journal of International Law and Politics 1993, Vol. 25, p. 405.

[22] S.C. Res. 808, UN Doc. S/RES/808, 1993.

[23] S.C. Res. 827, UN Doc. S/RES/827, 1993.

[24] Article 39 under Chapter VII provides that: "The Security Council shall determine the existence of any threat to the peace, breach of the peace, or act of aggression and shall make recommendations, or decide what measures shall be taken in accordance with Articles 41 and 42, to maintain or restore international peace and security". For a comment on the interpretation of the relevant provision and for further references see *O. Bring*, FN-stadgan och världspolitiken, Stockholm 1994, pp. 80–82; *B. Simma* (ed.), The Charter of the United Nations: A Commentary, Oxford 1994; *P. Malanczuk*, pp. 364–367.

[25] *M. Akehurst*, A Modern Introduction to International Law, London 1984, p. 181. Between 1945 and 1991 the Security Council has authorised the use of force in two cases (South Korea and Congo) for purposes other than self-defence. Between 1991 and 1994 the Council authorised the use of force under Chapter VII of the Charter in five cases (in the Gulf, Somalia, the former Yugoslavia, Rwanda and Haiti). See The Report of the Commission on Global Governance, Our Global Neighbourhood, (hereinafter referred to as Our Global Neighbourhood), Oxford 1995, p. 237.

[26] Most of them have been civil wars with serious human suffering in different forms. *R.B. Lillich*, Humanitarian Intervention through the United Nations: Towards the Development of Criteria, ZaöRV 1993, Vol. 53/3, pp. 557–575; *P.S. Czasz*, Centralized and Decentralized Law Enforcement: The Security Council and the General Assembly Acting under Chapters VII and VIII, in Allocation of Law Enforcement Authority in the International System, J. Delbrück (ed.), Berlin 1994, pp. 17–38; *F. Danelius*, FN:s Säkerhetsråds befogenheter. Något om utvecklingen i teori och praktik, i Tandlös eller Tiger, P. Ahlin (red.), Stockholm 1995, p. 89; *M. Falk*, The Legacy of Humanitarian Intervention, A Review in Light of Recent UN Practice, Stockholm 1996; *O. Ramsbotham*, Humanitarian Intervention in Contemporary Conflicts, Oxford 1996; *S.D. Murphy*, Humanitarian Intervention, The United Nations in an Evolving World, University of Pennsylvania Press 1996; *I. Österdahl*, Threat to The Peace, Uppsala 1998, p. 85.

[27] The frequent reference to violations of humanitarian law as the major factor in the determination of a threat to peace made by the Security Council has been viewed as an important precedent in international law. *T. Meron*, War Crimes in Yugoslavia and the Development of International Law, AJIL 1994, Vol. 88, p. 79.

genocide, including gender-based violence, represent in the case of former Yugoslavia a threat to international peace as required by Chapter VII of the Charter. This is in my opinion a groundbreaking decision in that issues related to women's reproductive freedom[28] were placed on the agenda of the highest organ within the hierarchy of the United Nations. This author agrees, therefore, with those who see the creation of the *ad hoc* tribunals as a departure from the traditional *Realpolitik* paradigm. Despite several good arguments against the widening of the powers of the S.C., *i.e.*, involving a political organ in situations related to serious violations of human rights, the unusual enforcement measures mentioned above were in my view indispensable at the time in question. I may consequently establish that the Security Council's decision and action in regard to the particular circumstances of the former Yugoslavia as well as of Rwanda were unique and necessary responses to a practical need.[29] Since the S.C., acting through various resolutions in accordance with Article 40 (Chapter VII) of the UN Charter, had exhausted provisional measures, the establishment of *ad hoc* tribunals was considered an effective means to contribute to restoring and maintaining international peace and security. Yet this conduct was very much due to the new approach towards the Security Council's role of its permanent members[30] after the end of the Cold War when a new world order emerged. The world is no longer divided between East and West. The stalemate that paralysed

---

[28] This is also a clear signal that the international community will not repeat the grave injustice done to numerous women subjected to gender-based violence during the WW II by failing during the Nuremberg Tribunal to prosecute the perpetrators of well documented crimes including torturous rape, forced sterilisation and forced abortion. *K.D. Askin*, p. 102.

[29] The Special Rapporteur on the Situation of Human Rights in the Territory of the Former Yugoslavia, Mr. Mazowiecki, urged on several occasions in his reports the international community to establish an international tribunal in order to bring to justice the perpetrators of all war crimes and crimes against humanity, including rape, since there was no recourse to justice for victims of human rights violations inside the territory of the former Yugoslavia. See UN Doc. E/CN.4/1993/50, p. 74, § 72. As regards the situation in Rwanda see the recommendations of the Special Rapporteur Mr. R. Degni-Séqui, UN Doc. E/CN.4/1995/70, p. 19; UN Doc. E/CN.4/1995/71, p. 12. The decisions to establish the tribunals demonstrate at the same time the reactive nature of international law. Several writers have observed that in the case of Rwanda there was an opportunity to take preventive action against the acts of genocide, but there was as some have remarked "little willingness". *P. Akhavan*, The International Criminal Tribunal for Rwanda: The Politics and Pragmatics of Punishment, AJIL 1996, Vol. 90, p. 501.

[30] The five permanent members, the so called Great Powers: the Republic of China, France, Russia, the United Kingdom of Great Britain and Northern Ireland and the United States of America enjoy an exceptional status within the UN since it is within their responsibility to decide upon measures for maintaining international peace and security. In addition, there are six rotating non-permanent members who serve each for two years on the Council. Since 1963 the number of the non-permanent members has been increased from six to ten.

The Security Council's primary function of maintaining international peace and security is exercised by a) specific settlement of such international disputes as are likely to endanger international peace and security and b) the taking of enforcement action. For a discussion on the power of the S.C. under Chapter VII of the UN Charter see *M.W. Reisman*, The Constitutional Crisis in the United Nations, AJIL 1993, Vol. 87, pp. 83–100; *T.D. Gill*, Legal and some political limitations on the power of the UN Security Council to exercise its enforcement powers under Chapter VII of the Chapter, NYIL 1995, pp. 30–138.

the Security Council for decades and the threat of the use of the veto that benumbed it[31] no longer exist. The permanent members have started to co-operate rather than to compete for the solution of urgent major problems. The Security Council can, therefore, today more easily make decisions that bind all member-states of the organization. This is also true in regard to the authorisation of enforcement action under the collective security provisions of Chapter VII of the Charter.[32] Therefore, it is generally thought that all the members of the Security Council can agree upon the fact that the situation in former Yugoslavia, which reveals massive and grave breaches of international humanitarian law,[33] constitutes a threat to international peace and

---

[31] Each of the permanent members of the Security Council has a veto over Council decisions on non-procedural questions. As a consequence, the Security Council was during the years of the Cold War often rendered powerless to deal with many conflicts because of the vetoes, in all 279 of them. It has been maintained that neither the Soviet Union nor the United States of America would have ratified the UN Charter without the veto provision. Since 1990 the veto has hardly been used. International observers emphasise that with the end of the Cold War the system of collective security "as conceived by the founding fathers of the United Nations at San Francisco has become fully operational". On the changing pattern of the use of veto by the five permanent members of the S.C. see *A. Roberts & B. Kingsbury*, p. 10; *P. Malanczuk*, p. 375; *E. Kussbach*, Role of the Competent United Nations Bodies in the Implementation of International Humanitarian Law, in Current Problems of International Humanitarian Law, International Institute of Humanitarian Law, San Remo 1993, p. 31;*B. Urquhart*, p. 81.

For a review of various proposals for further expansion of the S.C. see *A. Roberts & B. Kingsbury*, pp. 39–44; *M. Bertrand*, The Historical Development of Efforts to Reform the UN, in United Nations, Divided World, A. Roberts & B. Kingsbury (eds.), pp. 431–432; *P. Wilenski*, The Structure of the UN in the Post-Cold War Period, in United Nations, Divided World, A. Roberts & B. Kingsbury (eds.), pp. 441–445; *E. Konrula & T. Kanninen*, Reforming the Security Council: The International Negotiation Process Within the Context of Calls to Amend the UN Charter to the New Realities of the Post-Cold War Era, LJIL 1995, Vol. 8, p. 337 ff.; *D. Bills*, International Human Rights and Humanitarian Intervention: The Ramifications of Reform of the UN's Security Council, Texas International Law Journal 1996, Vol. 31, pp. 107–130; *L.B. Sohn*, Important Improvements in the Functioning of the Principal Organs of the United Nations That Can Be Made without Charter Revision, AJIL 1997, Vol. 91, pp. 652–663.

[32] The Security Council's primary responsibility for the maintenance of international peace and security confers it, according to Article 13 of the Statute of the ICC, the power to refer a case, involving serious crimes of significance to the international community and connected with situations that threaten international peace and security, to the Prosecutor. These are situations in which Chapter VII of the UN Charter applies. During the preparatory work on the Statute some states, among them the United States, expressed the view that it would have been preferable if this provision vested even wider powers in the Council (*i.e.*, that the S.C. authorisation be required for any case to reach the Court), whereas others found such a regulation unsustainable, with reference to their view that the Council is a political body. Thus, the majority of the countries were not in favour of an expansive role for the S.C. in the operation of the second track of the system (*i.e.*, cases referred to the ICC by States Parties or the Prosecutor). This predominant view influenced the outcome of the final document adopted in Rome (See Articles 14 and 15 of the Statute). *S. Suikkari*, Debate in the United Nations on the International Law Commission's Draft Statute for an International Criminal Court, NJIL 1995, pp. 213–214; *M.P. Scharf*, Rome Diplomatic Conference for an International Criminal Court, ASIL, Flash Insight, June 1998, p. 2.

[33] See for instance UN Doc. S/RES/713 of 25 September 1991, which is the first resolution on the conflicts in former Yugoslavia establishing that the situation there constitutes a threat to, and a breach of, the peace. The S.C., therefore, decided to impose a complete embargo on all deliveries of weapons and military equipment. I should also mention in this context that Resolution 752 of 15 May 1992 comprised a reference to the violations of human rights and humanitarian norms. Thus, the S.C. required the parties to the conflict to cease immediately "any attempts to change the ethnic composition of the population". Of

security and requires effective measures in order to secure the maintenance of peace. This background shows that the *ad hoc* Tribunal for the former Yugoslavia has not been established as the previous military tribunals by the victorious states parties to an armed conflict, *e.g.*, the agreement by the Government of the United States of America, the Provisional Government of the French Republic, the Government of the United Kingdom of Great Britain and Northern Ireland and the Government of the Union of Soviet Socialist Republics for the prosecution and punishment of the major war criminals of the European axis,[34] but by third states members of a global

---

further interest to my study is resolution 798 of 18 December 1992 in which the S.C., taking note of the reports on systematic detention and rape of women in Bosnia and Herzegovina, demands that "all the detention camps and, in particular, camps for women should be immediately closed".

For a review of various historical and other factors leading to the conflict on the Balkan Peninsula see: *J. Grotzky*, Balkankrieg. Der Zerfall Jugoslawiens und die Folgen für Europa, München 1993; *H. Roggemann*, Krieg und Frieden auf dem Balkan. Historische Kriegsursachen, wirtschaftliche und soziale Kriegsfolgen, politische und rechtliche Friedensvoraussetzungen, Berlin 1993 and Der Internationale Strafgerichtshof der Vereinten Nationen von 1993 und der Krieg auf dem Balkan, Berlin 1994, pp. 10–20. On the history and political background of the *ad hoc* Tribunal for the former Yugoslavia see *M.P. Scharf,* Balkan Justice: The Story behind the First International War Crimes Trial since Nuremberg, Durham 1997.

Also the situation in Rwanda was considered by the S.C. as an international threat to peace and security under Chapter VII of the Charter despite the fact that the basic character of the armed conflict in Rwanda during the period from 6 April to July 1994 can be viewed as predominantly non-international in character. Responding to strong world reaction, the S.C. decided to establish an international *ad hoc* Tribunal for Rwanda.

[34] The judges who served at the Nuremberg trial were consequently appointed by the four Allied powers, *i.e.*, F. Biddle (USA), H.D. de Vabres (France), Sir G. Lawrence of Great Britain and I.T. Nikitchenko (Soviet). In this regard, historical documents have revealed that the Allied powers did not consider it "practical" to permit other states to participate in the tribunal as a matter of right. *M. Lippman*, p. 22. This is maybe one of the reasons why Göring in his defence speech at Nuremberg repeatedly emphasised that the victors always will be the judges whereas the vanquished will always be the accused. Also academic commentators have observed that the "Allies' selective prosecution contributed to the perception of victors' justice". For objections to the Trial see: *A.G. Finch*, The Nuremberg Trial and International Law, AJIL 1947, Vol. 41, pp. 20–37; *F.J. Berber*, Some Thoughts on the Laws of War and the Punishment of War Crimes, in Essays on International Law, M.K. Nawaz (ed.), Leyden 1976, pp. 260–265.

On the other hand, it seems that most commentators recognise that the Nuremberg trial satisfied the standards of procedural justice. As a response to the charge of "victors' justice" Justice R.H. Jackson stressed, *e.g.*, that in the future, the principles which are embodied in the Charter would be applied against any nation "which disregarded their requirements". *M. Lippman*, pp. 38–39. See furthermore *H. Lauterpacht*, The Law of Nations and the Punishment of War Crimes, BYIL 1944, Vol. 21, p. 83; *Q. Wright*, The Laws of the Nuremberg Trial, AJIL 1947, Vol. 41, pp. 38–72; *T. Taylor*, The Concept of Justice and the Laws of War, Columbia Journal of International Law 1974, Vol. 13, p. 202; *V. Morris & M.P. Scharf*, pp. 2–11.

By contrast the judges at the Tokyo Trial represented a greater number of countries. They were nationals of eleven countries, among them Australia, Canada, China, France, India, The Netherlands, The Philippines and the USA. At the same time the view has been put forward that although the history of the Tokyo Trials is quite similar to that of Nuremberg, the former have not become as important a precedent since some of the judges dissented from several aspects of the judgment. American Bar Association, Report, p. 5. There is yet another difference between the two tribunals, which I would like to mention. Whereas the Nuremberg Tribunal was created by a multilateral agreement, the Tokyo Tribunal was established by Special Proclamation of the Supreme Commander for the Allied Powers.

In regard to the situation in former Yugoslavia, the party to the armed conflict who has been accused of committing the bulk of the international crimes has most often been the strongest party in the conflict. *H. von Hebel*, p. 443.

organisation and acting on the legal basis of their treaty obligations to maintain international peace and security. It is, like the International Tribunal for Rwanda, a subsidiary organ to the S.C. within the meaning of Article 29 of the Charter.[35] Thus, it is dependent in administrative and financial matters on various United Nations organs. However, it is important to stress that the *ad hoc* Tribunal has to perform its functions independently of political considerations, *i.e.*, that it will not be subject to the authority of the Security Council as regards the performance of its judicial tasks.[36] Mr. Richard Goldstone, the very first Chief Persecutor of the *ad hoc*

---

[35] Article 29 of the Charter provides: "The Security Council may establish such subsidiary organs as it deems necessary for the performance of its functions".

[36] In the normal course of events, the establishment of an international tribunal would be, after detailed elaboration of the legal issues, based on a treaty. Such a treaty could have been drafted and adopted by the UN General Assembly or by a specially convened intergovernmental conference. Several governments seem to have a clear preference for this approach. The Chinese delegation, for example, declared that despite their vote in favour of the S.C. Res. 827 (1993), this was not to be viewed as an approval of the legal approach involved, since its consistent position was "that an international tribunal should be established by concluding a treaty so as to provide a solid legal foundation for it and ensure its effective functioning". UN Doc. S/PV.3217, p. 33. In consequence, the Chinese delegation abstained from voting on the S.C. Res. 955 (1994) on the creation of an international Tribunal for Rwanda. Also the ILC has maintained the view that an international criminal court should be created by treaty with an annexed Statute, as in the case of the Nuremberg Tribunal. Also eminent scholars, among them Professor Crawford, have taken the view that "the secure and, in the long run, the only appropriate way to create an international criminal court" is by legislation, *i.e.*, treaty. *J. Crawford*, supra, note 20, p. 416. See also *T. Meron*, International Criminalization of Internal Atrocities, p. 554.

According to the newly adopted Statute of the ICC, the Court shall be created by a multilateral treaty under the control of states parties to the statute.

Yet, in the light of the particular case of former Yugoslavia there was agreement among the majority delegations that the treaty approach, *i.e.,* that an international criminal court could be established through a separate convention, had serious disadvantages in regard to the necessity of an *expeditious* and *effective* implementation of the decision of the Security Council. (italics added) See UN Doc. S/2504, § 22. In addition to the time factor (it might take years to reach the required number of ratifications for such a treaty), yet another important reason for the creation of the *ad hoc* Tribunal on a legal basis other than by means of a special treaty was the probable non-participation of states crucial to the successful prosecution of war criminals, *e.g.*, Serbia and Montenegro. *P.C. Szasz*, p. 411; *V. Morris & M.P. Scharf*, pp. 41–42; *K. Lescure & F. Trintignac*, International Justice for Former Yugoslavia, The Working of the International Criminal Tribunal of the Hague, The Hague 1996, p. 8; *M.C. Bassiouni*, The Law of the International Criminal Tribunal for the Former Yugoslavia, p. 220.

Also the establishment of the *ad hoc* Tribunal for Rwanda was based on a Chapter VII resolution in order to ensure a *speedy* and *expeditious* method of establishing the Tribunal. Nevertheless, there are some differences as to the circumstances under which the resolutions leading to the establishment of both *ad hoc* tribunals were adopted. While the Government of Rwanda first requested the S.C. to establish an international tribunal, the states of the former SFRY did not participate in the debates about the creation of a criminal tribunal. Rwanda was, moreover, a sitting non-permanent member of the S.C., and voted against the resolution 955(1994). For the reasons behind Rwanda's objection see *A. Obote-Odora*, The Judging of War Criminals: Individual Criminal Responsibility Under International Law, Stockholm 1997, p. 295.

It has been assumed that the Bosnian and the Croatian governments have expressed themselves in favour of a tribunal, whereas the Federal Republic of Yugoslavia (Serbia and Montenegro) and the Bosnian Serbs have explicitly opposed the idea. *H. von Hebel*, p. 443. See also *R. Akhavan*, The International Criminal Tribunal for Rwanda, p. 504.

Tribunal, through his announcement on 24 April 1995 that the leaders for the Bosnian Serbs, Mr. Radovan Karadžić and Mr. Ratko Mladić, were suspected of serious violations of the rules of international humanitarian law, confirmed the Tribunal's firm determination to prosecute the persons really responsible for giving the orders and the inspiration for the crimes committed on the territory of the former Yugoslavia.[37] The fact that such an official notification could render the on-going peace negotiations more difficult, and even make them impossible in the future, influenced by no means the work of the *ad hoc* Tribunal. On the contrary, this fact illustrates clearly the Tribunal's determination to accomplish successfully one of its objectives, namely "to bring to justice the persons who are responsible for crimes perpetrated in former Yugoslavia" (S.C. Res. 827(1993)). Paragraph 1 of the S.C. Resolution 808(1993) supports the above mentioned aim of the *ad hoc* Tribunal by declaring that the international tribunal "shall be established for the prosecution of persons responsible for serious violations of international humanitarian law committed in the territory of the former Yugoslavia since 1991".[38] This provision reaffirms in its turn the content of the Security Council resolution 764 of 13 July 1992 and resolution 771 of 13 August 1992. The first of those requires states to fulfil their obligations under international humanitarian law and the second underlines individuals' liability for committing or ordering the perpetration of grave breaches of the Geneva Conventions of 1949. In fact, the 1995 "*General Framework Agreement for Peace in Bosnia and Herzegovina*"[39] declares that those who have committed crimes which threaten international peace and security – genocide, crimes against humanity and war crimes – will be brought to justice. The Dayton agreement gives IFOR, the peace implementation force, the authority to arrest any indicted war criminal it encounters. The peace agreement also provides for a Bosnia – Herzegovian constitution to prohibit anyone indicted by the *ad hoc* Tribunal from holding public office if they try to evade its authority. In other words, they have to appear in The Hague.[40]

The special circumstances surrounding the creation of the Yugoslavia Tribunal may partly give an explanation to some of the features, which make it unique. Firstly, the international *ad hoc* Tribunal for former Yugoslavia is the first tribunal

---

[37] See below sub-chapter 8.3.

[38] Since 1997 the Prosecutor of the Tribunal has started to implement a strategy that calls for indicting only the high-level offenders. *S.D. Murphy*, Progress and Jurisprudence of the International Criminal Tribunal for the former Yugoslavia, AJIL 1999, Vol. 93, p. 59.

[39] The agreement was drafted during negotiations at the Wright Patterson Air Force Base in Dayton, Ohio in November 1995 and it was signed in Paris on 14 December 1995, UN Doc. S/1995/999. The text has been reprinted in 35 ILM 75, 1996.

[40] The Human Rights Annex (Annex VI) to the Dayton agreement obliges each party in Bosnia-Herzegovina to give the Tribunal unrestricted access to all sites and persons. For an interesting discussion on human rights as an integral part of conflict prevention, peacemaking and peacekeeping see *Anonymous*, Human Rights in Peace Negotiations, HRQ 1996, Vol. 18, pp. 249–258; *P. Akhavan*, The Yugoslav Tribunal at the Crossroads: The Dayton Peace Agreement and Beyond, HRQ 1996, Vol. 18, pp. 259–285; *F.D. Gaer*, UN-Anonymous: Reflections on Human Rights in Peace Negotiations, HRQ 1997, Vol. 19, pp. 1–8; *Z. Pajić*, A Critical Appraisal of Human Rights Provisions of the Dayton Constitution of Bosnia and Herzegovina, HRQ 1998, Vol. 20, pp. 125–138.

established after the Nuremberg and Tokyo trials to try war crimes. Secondly, the elected eleven judges represent different parts of the world (three judges are from the Americas, three are from Asia, two are from Africa, two are from Europe and one is from Australia). It is quite obvious that the *ad hoc* Tribunal is truly *international*[41] as are its rules of procedure. Thirdly, the Yugoslavia Tribunal is also the first trial established during on-going armed conflicts.[42] All this makes the *ad hoc* Tribunal in the words of Professor Antonio Cassese (the then Tribunal's President[43]) "a novel and experimental institution", which is to be considered as "a momentous advance in the world community, for this institution is called upon impartially to vindicate and enforce the abiding demands of humanity".[44]

Nevertheless, the defence of the Bosnian Serb Duško Tadić,[45] the first suspect[46] to stand trial at the *ad hoc* Tribunal in The Hague, made an initial objection to the

---

[41] The Nuremberg and Tokyo tribunals have been described as "multinational tribunals, but not international tribunals in the strict sense". Röling cited in UN Doc. A/49/342, ibid., p. 11. On the other hand, Professor Meron has observed that the question of whether the *ad hoc* Tribunal for former Yugoslavia is the first or the second truly international criminal tribunal is not indisputable, since "The post-World War II Nuremberg and Tokyo tribunals are regarded by some commentators as victor's courts". *T. Meron*, War Crimes in Yugoslavia and the Development of International Law, AJIL 1994, Vol. 88, p. 78.

The judges, elected on the basis of the GA decision of September 1993 (UN Doc. A/DEC/47/328), are the following: Mr. Antonio Cassese, Italy; Ms. Elizabeth Odio Benito, Costa Rica; Mr. Georges M. Abi-Saab, Egypt; Mr. Jules Deschenes, Canada; Mr. Claude Jorda, France; Mr. Adolphus G. Karibi-Whyte, Nigeria; Mr. Haopei Li, China; Ms. Gabrielle Kirk McDonald, USA; Mr. Rustam S. Sidhwa, Pakistan; Sir Ninian Stephen, Australia and Mr. Lal Chand Vohrah, Malaysia. The eleven judges took office on 17 November 1993.

[42] In the case of Rwanda, the civil war had ended by the time the *ad hoc* Tribunal for Rwanda was established.

[43] Judge Gabrielle Kirk McDonald was elected on 19 November 1997 to act as President of the Tribunal.

[44] UN Doc. A/49/342, S/1994/1007, p. 49.

[45] *Tadić's* trial began on May 7, 1996. The defence counsel for *Tadić* referred before the trial in an interview by V. Vasić-Janeković (Institute for War & Peace Reporting, London) to the opinion of Yugoslav lawyers and scholars that a court, permanent or *ad hoc*, can only be formed by a convention or treaty binding on all signatories. In their view it is contrary to law to impose a court on other countries, if they don't accept it. Subsequently the defence for *Tadić* argued during the trial at The Hague that the *ad hoc* Tribunal for the former Yugoslavia was not lawfully established, since an international tribunal must be created by an international treaty and not by an resolution of the S.C., unless the UN's Charter were amended in that respect. *Prosecutor v. Tadić*, Case No. IT-94-1-T, Trial Chamber, decision on defence motion on jurisdiction, HRLJ 1995, Vol. 16, p. 426 § 2. Professor V.A. Vasilijević at the Institute of Criminology and Sociological Research (Yugoslavia) has advanced the argument in a paper presented at the International Conference "Justice in Cataclysm" in Brussels 1996 that "its (the S.C.) decision in 1993 to set up an international *ad hoc* tribunal to reinforce the already implemented measures in Chapter VII of the UN Charter seems also unconvincing and leaves scope for unnecessary andfor international legal order and ethic-very harmful disputes". *V.A. Vasiljevic*, International Criminal Tribunal for the Former Yugoslavia and Temptations of International Legal Order, p. 12.

[46] Some of the allegations against *Tadić* included sexual violence against males and females, *e.g.*, castration and rape. Survivors of the Omarska camp have reported that Tadić "personally raped one woman detainee, murdered thirteen men, and tortured scores of others". *Prosecutor v. Tadić*, case No. IT-94-1-I, Decision on Jurisdiction, 14 December 1995, §§ 2.6, 2.7, 4.3 and 5. The text is available at the following address: <http://www.courttv.com/download/serb/docs/dtjurisd.txt.>. See generally the Tribunal's web site on Internet: <http://www.ictr.org.>. See also *M.P. Scharf*, Balkan Justice, p. xi.

indictment, challenging the Tribunal's jurisdiction and legitimacy.[47] The defence argued that the Tribunal had not been legally established because the Security Council lacked the power to do so, and, furthermore, that it had no competence to decide upon this question.[48] The initial objection was first tried by the Trial Chamber II and subsequently, upon an interlocutory appeal by the defence, by the Appeals Chamber. The Trial Chamber arrived at the conclusion in its decision of 10 August 1995 that it "will have no authority to investigate the legality of its creation by the Security Council".[49] In other words, it lacks competence to deal with this argument of the defence. The Trial Chamber underlined at the same time that due to the nature of the conflict, an adjudicatory body is a "particularly appropriate measure to achieve lasting peace in the former Yugoslavia"[50] and it dismissed the challenge to the Tribunal's jurisdiction by the defence. The Appeals Chamber rendered its decision in the *Tadić* case on October 2, 1995,[51] in which it ruled among others that the Tribunal had been lawfully established, that the S.C. had the power in the circumstances in question to invoke Chapter VII of the UN Charter[52] and in contrast to the Trial Chamber that the Tribunal had competence to rule on a plea against its jurisdiction based on the invalidity of its creation by the S.C.[53] The Trial Chamber could subsequently try the merits of the case. In doing so, the Tribunal

[47] For a commentary on this case see generally *G.H. Aldrich*, Jurisdiction of the International Criminal Court for the Former Yugoslavia, AJIL 1996, Vol. 90, pp. 64–69; *W.H. von Heinegg*, Zur Zulässigkeit der Errichtung des Jugoslavien-Strafgerichtshofes durch Resolution 827(1993), Humanitäres Völkerrecht 1996, Vol. 9, pp. 71–84; *K. Koschorreck & M. Müller*, Report on the International Criminal Tribunal for the Former Yugoslavia, GYIL 1996, Vol. 39, pp. 407–433; *K.D. Askin*, Sexual Violence in Decisions and Indictments of the Yugoslav and Rwandan Tribunals: Current Status, (thereafter cit. Sexual Violence), AJIL 1999, Vol. 93, pp. 100–105.

[48] International Tribunal for the Former Yugoslavia, Case No. IT–94–1-AR72, reprinted in HRLJ 1995, Vol. 16, p. 437; 35 ILM 32, 1996.

[49] *Prosecutor v. Tadić*, Case No. IT-94-1-T, Decision on Jurisdiction, § 5.

[50] Ibid., § 31.

[51] *Prosecutor v. Tadić*, Case No. IT-94-1-AR72, Appeal on Jurisdiction, pp. 437–492.

[52] Another question which was raised by the defence was whether the S.C. can delegate its own executive powers to a subsidiary, judicial body. The Tribunal found that the establishment of a judicial body does not imply a delegation of the executive powers of the Council, nor is there any judicial power within the Security Council that could possibly be delegated to a judicial body-the Council is a solely executive body. *Prosecutor v. Tadić*, Case No. IT-94-1-AR72, Appeals Chamber, Decision of 2 October 1995, §§ 37–38.

[53] The Appeals Chamber concluded that the Tribunal had constitutional jurisdiction to review the *Tadić* case, based upon the competence laid upon it by the S.C. through the adoption of the Statute of the Tribunal; a principle known in international law as "Kompetenz-Kompetenz" (jurisdiction to determine its own jurisdiction). *The Prosecutor v. Tadić*, Case No. IT-94-1-AR72, Decision by the Appeals Chamber, 2 October 1995, § 18. Judge Li was, however, of dissenting opinion on this matter. Like the Trial Chamber he held that it was outside the competence of the Tribunal to review the question of the legality of the resolutions of the S.C. For the full text of the separate opinion of Judge Li see HRLJ 1995, Vol. 16, pp. 466–469. See in addition *L. Verruci*, The First Steps of the International Criminal Tribunal for Former Yugoslavia, European Journal of International Law 1995, Vol. 6, p. 134 ff.; *C. Warbrick & P. Rowe*, The International Criminal Tribunal for Yugoslavia: The Decision of the Appeals Chamber on the Interlocutory Appeal on Jurisdiction in the Tadić Case, ICLQ 1996, Vol. 45, pp. 691–696; *J.E. Alvarez*, Nuremberg Revisited: The Tadić Case, European Journal of International Law 1996, Vol. 7, p. 247 ff.

found the defendant guilty on 11 of the 34 counts, and sentenced him on 14 July 1997 to 20 years' imprisonment.[54] The *Tadić* case is not only of utmost importance for the development of international humanitarian law but it constitutes also an important precedent for the future cases to be considered by the *ad hoc* Tribunal for the Former Yugoslavia[55] as well as by the *ad hoc* Tribunal for Rwanda,[56] domestic courts and the ICC. The *Tadić* case has contributed, furthermore, to the strengthening of the status of the individual as a subject of international law.

## 8.3. The Jurisdiction of the *Ad Hoc* Tribunal

The special nature of both *ad hoc* Tribunals required limited jurisdiction in regard to territory, time and the applicable substantive law. Professor Bassiouni, Professor Meron,[57] and several other scholars have extensively commented upon and analysed several aspects of the temporal, territorial, personal jurisdiction of the *ad hoc* Tribunal for the former Yugoslavia as well as the substantive law of the Tribunal. These issues are for the most part beyond the scope of my study, so I shall treat them in the following very briefly and I shall extract only aspects that are of relevance for reproductive freedom in the context of humanitarian law.

### *8.3.1. The Tribunal's Jurisdiction Ratione Loci and Ratione Temporis*

The Statute of the *ad hoc* Tribunal provides for the territorial jurisdiction to extend to the territory of the former Socialist Federal Republic of Yugoslavia, called former Yugoslavia. Land surface, airspace and territorial waters are included in that jurisdiction. (Article 8 of the Statute)[58]

---

[54] *Prosecutor v. Tadić*, Case IT–94–1-T, The Trial Chamber's Decision, May 7, 1997, appears at 36 ILM 908, 1997; IHRR 1997, Vol. 4, No. 3. pp. 645–848. See also UN Doc. A/52/375, p. 10. The judgment in the *Tadić* case is the very first of its kind since the decisions at Nuremberg and Tokyo and I shall return to it on several occasions in this part of my study.

[55] Third Annual Report of the International Tribunal for the former Yugoslavia, UN Doc. A/51/292, 1996, p. 17. See also *M.P. Scharf's* commentary on the case in AJIL 1997, Vol. 91, p. 719.

[56] The Trial Chamber 2 of the Rwanda Tribunal rejected, *e.g.*, the defence challenges to the jurisdiction of the Tribunal in the *Kanyabashi* case by stating that it "respects the persuasive authority of the decision of the Appeals Chamber of the International Criminal Court for the Former Yugoslavia and has taken careful note of the decision rendered by the Appeals Chamber in the Tadić case". *Prosecutor v. Kanyabashi*, Decision on Jurisdiction, Case No. ICTR-96-15-T, International Criminal Tribunal for Rwanda, June 18, 1997, § 4. For a comment on that case see *V. Morris*, Prosecutor v. Kanyabashi, AJIL 1998, Vol. 92, pp. 66–70.

[57] See especially *M.C. Bassiouni*, The Law of the International Criminal Tribunal for the Former Yugoslavia, pp. 293–334. In regard to Meron's production I have referred to several of his articles published in the American Journal of International Law.

[58] The territorial jurisdiction of the *ad hoc* Tribunal for Rwanda covers international crimes committed by Rwandanese citizens not only on the territory of Rwanda but also in neighbouring states. The S.C. has in this respect encompassed the refugee camps in Zaire and other neighbouring countries in which violations of international humanitarian law are alleged to have been committed in connection with the conflict in Rwanda. See UN Doc. S/1995/134, p. 4; *P. Sob*, The Dynamics of International Criminal Tribunals, NJIL 1998, Vol. 67, pp. 147–148.

Regarding the temporal jurisdiction of the *ad hoc* Tribunal for the former Yugoslavia, it is empowered only to review international crimes committed on or after the 1 January 1991 (Article 8 of the Statute).[59] The UN Secretary-General stressed in his report on the subject of establishing the *ad hoc* Tribunal, which provides explanations and analyses of the various legal issues of concern, together with a draft statute for the International Tribunal, that "this is a neutral date, which is not tied to any specific event".[60] The advantage of such a solution consists in that it makes it possible to avoid requiring a definite standpoint as to the character (international or internal) of the armed conflict in former Yugoslavia. The choice of this particular date may seem remarkable since the *ad hoc* Tribunal was established as late as in 1993.[61] However, according to the rapporteurs under the CSCE Moscow Human Dimension Mechanism to Bosnia-Herzegovina, the Ambassadors Hans Corell, Helmut Türk and Gro Hillestad Thune the principle of legality had not been contravened by that.[62]

The jurisdiction of the *ad hoc* Tribunal does not preclude or hinder jurisdiction by national courts with respect to serious violations of humanitarian law. In other words, the national law of former Yugoslavia can provide the legal basis for trials in domestic courts at least in the successor republics, in which the law has not been changed.[63] Nevertheless, at the domestic level there might exist certain limitations in regard to *ratione temporis* requirements for the prosecution and punishment for criminal offences.[64]

---

[59] The temporal jurisdiction of the *ad hoc* Rwanda Tribunal is, on the other hand, limited to only one year. Thus, it shall try people responsible for the specified crimes committed between 1 January and 31 December 1994. It has been maintained that the date of 1 January 1994 captures the planning stage of the crimes in question. UN Doc. S/1995/134, p. 4.

[60] UN Doc. S/2504, § 62. Secretary-General's Report on Aspects of Establishing an International Tribunal for the Prosecution of Persons Responsible for Serious Violations of International Humanitarian Law Committed in the Territory of the Former Yugoslavia, 3 May 1993 (hereinafter Secretary-General's Report). The text of the report is reprinted in HRLJ 1993, Vol. 14, pp. 198–210. See also *V. Morris & M.P. Scharf*, pp. 118–119. Some writers hold the view that the date of "1 January 1991" marks the outbreak of hostilities in the territory of former Yugoslavia. *K. Lescure & F. Trintignac*, p. 17.

[61] Most of the evidential material presented to the Tribunal suggests that the majority of the crimes that have been committed during the time between April and August 1992 on the territory of Bosnia and Herzegovina. *M. Bergsmo*, Den internationale domstol for forbrytelser i det tidligere Jugoslavia, Mennesker og rettigheter 1996, Vol. 14, p. 32.

[62] *H. Corell, H. Türk & G.H. Thune*, Proposal for an International War Crimes Tribunal for the Former Yugoslavia, CSCE 9 February 1993, p. 54. The principle of legality implies among other things a prohibition against an act that, at the time of commission, was not criminalised as an offence. *P.O. Träskman*, Should we take the condition of double criminality seriously?, in Double Criminality, Studies in International Criminal Law, N. Jareborg (ed.), Uppsala 1989, p. 148.

[63] The former Yugoslavia was a treaty party to the major conventions relating to human rights and humanitarian law, *i.e.*, the four 1949 Geneva Conventions and the two 1977 Protocols thereto and has subsequently given effect to the assumed obligations in the national legal system. None of the successor states has renounced any of these treaties. See *H. Corell, D. Türk & G.H. Thune*, pp. 53–54 and *M. Bothe*, pp. 293–304.

[64] One should bear in mind that also Article 1 of the Convention on the Non-Applicability of Statutory Limitations to War Crimes and Crimes Against Humanity of 26 November 1968, which entered into force on November 11, 1970 (8 I.L.M. 68, 1969), is still relevant in questions dealing with temporal jurisdiction. According to this provision, no statutory limitation shall apply to war crimes "as

For natural reasons there is no fixed date announced for when the *ad hoc* Tribunal's jurisdiction must cease. Since the *ad hoc* Tribunal was created on the basis of a S.C. decision, which was linked to the restoration and the maintenance of international peace on the territory of the former Yugoslavia, "the life span"[65] of that Tribunal depends upon the normalisation of the situation, which was considered a threat to or breach of peace. In other words, once peace has been achieved in the territory of the former Yugoslavia, the Security Council can, on the basis of Article 39 of the UN Charter, decide that the *ad hoc* Tribunal shall discontinue its functions. It is important to note at the same time that this provision relates not only to the restoration of peace but also to the *maintenance* of international peace and security.[66] Undoubtedly this is to some degree a paradoxical situation, since in my view an effective implementation of criminal responsibility as a means of securing peace can be truly realised after peace has been achieved and when the functioning of the judicial system/s is normalised. In this regard Roggemann has convincingly argued that:

> "(d)ie Funktionen eines internationalen Strafgerichts sich nicht in Prävention erschöpfen, sondern auch Rechtsbewährung und damit Rechtsfrieden im Täter-Opfer-Verhältnis bewirken, zur zeitgeschichtlichen Aufklärung und zur Stabilisierung nationalen Rechtsbewußtseins beitragen soll, so ist davon auszugehen, daß dies erst unter Friedensbedingungen und vielfach Jahre oder Jahrzehnte nach Tatbegehung erst möglich sein wird. Das Beispiel der Strafverfahren gegen NS-Täter in Deutschland und anderswo in Europa zeigt dies".[67]

---

they are defined in the Charter of the International Military Tribunal, Nürnberg, of 8 August 1945 and confirmed by resolutions 38(I) of 13 February 1946 and 95(I) of 11 December 1946 of the General Assembly of the United Nations, particularly the 'grave breaches' enumerated in the Geneva Conventions of 12 August 1949 for the protection of war crimes" and crimes against humanity "whether committed in time of war or in time of peace as they are defined in the Charter of the International Military Tribunal, Nürnberg, of 8 August 1945 and confirmed by resolutions 3(I) of 13 February 1946 and 95(I) of 11 December 1946 of the General Assembly of the United Nations, eviction by armed attack or occupation and inhumane acts resulting from the policy of apartheid, and the crime of genocide as defined in the 1948 Convention on the Prevention and Punishment of the Crime of Genocide, even if such acts do not constitute a violation of the domestic law of the country, in which they were committed", irrespective of the date of their commission.

Unfortunately very few states have ratified this treaty. It has been argued that the Convention "offends certain basic principles of justice since it would extend jurisdiction over crimes irrespective of when they were committed". *L.S. Sunga*, p. 64.

[65] UN Doc. S/2504, § 28. See also *H. von Hebel*, p. 446. The fact that the *ad hoc* Tribunal can be abolished by a S.C. resolution at any time has been considered by some international law scholars as a rather disturbing fact, adding a great amount of insecurity. *J. Crawford*, The ILC Adopts a Statute for an International Criminal Court, p. 416.

[66] *M.C. Bassiouni*, The Law of the International Criminal Tribunal, pp. 249–251.

[67] *H. Roggemann*, p. 50. For a somewhat different opinion in regard to the *ad hoc* Tribunal's temporal jurisdiction, see *C. Hollweg*, Das neue Internationale Tribunal der UNO und der Jugoslawienkonflikt, JZ 1993, p. 980.

At the time of writing the continued existence of the Tribunal has not been challenged and it seems that there is a wide support for its important role in the process of reconciliation and the maintenance of peace in this region of Europe.

### *8.3.2. The Tribunal's Jurisdiction Ratione Materiae*

The most fundamental question in regard to the *ad hoc* Tribunal's subject matter jurisdiction is connected with the determination of the international crimes that it is empowered to prosecute and to try. A number of studies submitted to the Security Council during the preparatory work on its Statute indicate that the Tribunal's "mandate should be reasonably limited to grave breaches of criminal law committed in the mass, and systematically, and that have given rise to international indignation".[68] There was a presumption that otherwise the *ad hoc* Tribunal might be overloaded. This approach influenced undoubtedly the outcome of the legislative process of the Tribunal's Statute. Thus, a number of internationally recognised principles of criminal law formed the basis for several provisions of the Statute. Among them we may find the earlier mentioned principle of legality, *i.e.*, there can be no crime or punishment without a pre-existing law (*Nullum crimen, nulla poena, sine lege).*[69] In order to comply with this principle the Security Council decided that only international humanitarian law norms should be of relevance for the Tribunal's jurisdiction *ratione materiae*, for which there is no doubt regarding their legal validity, *i.e.*, the applicable rules are those of international humanitarian law, which are part of international customary law. With this background I may affirm that the *ad hoc* Tribunal will deal with **two** groups of legal norms: war crimes and crimes against humanity,

---

[68] *B. Broms*, Security Council Resolution 808 (1993), in Current International Law Issues, Nordic Perspectives, Essays in Honour of Jerzy Sztucki, O. Bring & S. Mahmoudi (eds.), Stockholm 1994, p. 59.

[69] The principle of legality is also reflected in Articles 22, 23 and 24 of the Statute of the ICC. With regard to crimes under general international law, this provision decrees that the accused must not be held guilty unless the act or omission in question has constituted a crime under international law at the time of its commission, whereas with regard to treaty crimes, it says that the treaty of relevance must be applicable to the conduct of the accused under the appropriate national law of the state party to the treaty. The prohibition of retroactive penal measures is undoubtedly a fundamental principle of justice and it is *per se* a fundamental (non-derogable) human right. It is considered as a customary and even peremptory norm of international law. *T. Meron*, International Criminalization of Internal Atrocities, p. 565, The Normative Impact on International Law of the International Tribunal for Former Yugoslavia, in War Crimes in International Law, Y. Dinstein & M. Tabory (eds.), pp. 213–215, War Crimes Law Comes of Age, p. 464. The argumentation used by the *ad hoc* Tribunal regarding the substantive criminal provisions to be applied reveals a delicate balancing. On the one hand, discernible is the intention to fulfil the purpose of its creation, *i.e.*, to convict war criminals, a task that in many aspects requires a legal approach acquainted with the progressive doctrine that has developed in human rights law. On the other hand, there is an essential requirement that the above mentioned principle is properly attended. On the basis of the existing case law I may suggest that the principle has been duly implemented both by the Trial Chamber and the Appeals Chamber in, *e.g.*, the *Tadić* case. The Trial Chamber ruled in that case that the principle of *nullum crimen sine lege* was respected by the Tribunal since Article 3 of the Geneva Convention is recognised as part of customary international law and the criminal code of Yugoslavia criminalised the offences in question. *Prosecutor v. Tadić*, Case No. IT-94-1-T, at 74.

in particular genocide. In concrete terms the Tribunal's Statute refers in its Article 2 to "grave breaches" of the Geneva Conventions of 1949. Article 3 deals with "violations of the customs of war".[70] The interpretation and application thereof by the Nuremberg Trials is explicitly recommended by the UN Secretary-General as the legal basis for the competence of the Tribunal in this area.[71] Article 4 expresses the definition of the crime genocide in accordance with the Convention on the Prevention and Punishment of the Crime of Genocide of 9 December 1948.[72] Finally, Article 5 of the Statute embodies crimes against humanity as formulated in the Charter of the International Military Tribunal of 8 August 1945 with specific reference to rape.[73] The rules are applicable irrespectively of the internal or international character of the conflict.[74] The above allows us to conclude that crimes against peace are not included in the mandate of the *ad hoc* Tribunal for the former Yugoslavia.

Furthermore, it must be noted here that despite the fact that the Geneva Conventions of 1949 do not use the term war crimes in relation to grave breaches, according to prominent publicists "there can be no doubt that the latter constitute war crimes and are concerned with individual responsibility for breaches of the laws of war".[75] This view is also supported by Article 86(5) of Protocol I of 1977, according to which all grave breaches either of the Conventions or of the Protocol "shall be regarded as war crimes", whereas "other breaches" require merely preventive measures. According to Article 146(3) of the fourth Geneva Convention, all states parties are under the obligation to "take measures necessary for the suppression of all acts contrary to the provisions of the present Convention other than grave breaches defined in the following Article". In other words, the expression

---

[70] This provision reflects Articles 23, 25, 27 and 28 of The Hague Convention (IV) Respecting the Laws and Customs of War on Land and the Regulations annexed thereto of 18 October 1907.

In the view of the *ad hoc* Tribunal's Appeals Chamber the common Article 3 of the Geneva Conventions is included in Article 3 of its Statute on the basis of "the intent of the Security Council and the logical and systematic interpretation of Article 3 (of the Statute) as well as customary international law". *Prosecutor v. Tadić,* Case No. IT-94-1-AR72, at 71. See *P. Akhavan*, The International Criminal Tribunal for Rwanda, p. 503.

[71] UN Doc. S/25704, §§ 41 and 44. See also *V. Morris & M.P. Scharf*, pp. 69–72 and *M.C. Bassiouni*, The Law of the International Tribunal, pp. 505–509.

[72] 78 UNTS, p. 277 *et seq*. The Convention was adopted by the GA Res. 260 (II) with 55 votes in favour and none against. It entered into force on January 12, 1961.

[73] UN Doc. S/2504, § 35.

[74] The decisive question, when it comes to applicable law, is whether the alleged crimes were committed in a state of international or internal armed conflict, since the rules of international humanitarian law still differ in this respect. The topic has been, however, vividly and thoroughly discussed and explored by the parties to the *Tadić* case, *e.g.*, by legal scholars etc. and I shall return to it below. I may mention here that Tadić denied that there had been an armed conflict at all, where the alleged crimes were committed. Despite differences in argumentation on this matter, the S.C., the Trial Chamber and the Appeals Chamber came to the same conclusion, namely that the conflict on the territory of former Yugoslavia has had internal as well as international elements.

[75] *I. Brownlie*, p. 563. See also Article 8(2) of the ICC Statute which says that: "For the purpose of the Statute, 'war crimes' means: (a) Grave breaches of the Geneva Conventions of 12 August 1949, namely any of the following acts against persons or property protected under the provisions of the relevant Geneva Convention…".

"suppression" has been interpreted as not necessarily "effected through the application of criminal law".[76]

In evaluating the subject matter jurisdiction of the *ad hoc* Tribunal for former Yugoslavia, I may establish that it has been given a competence to punish a wide range of crimes under public international law. Four categories of internationally recognised crimes are identified in the Statute of the *ad hoc* Tribunal. Pursuant to Articles 1–5 of its Statute the Tribunal will have jurisdiction over the following:

a) grave breaches of the 1949 Geneva Conventions (Article 2 of the Statute)
b) violations of the laws or customs of war (Article 3 of the Statute)
c) genocide (Article 4)
d) crimes against humanity (Article 5).

It has been suggested that Articles 2 and 3 of the Statute will constitute the basis for the most of the activity of the Tribunal, since "any act that might constitute a crime against humanity or genocide would also be a war crime".[77] Until today the majority of the cases of indictment the prosecutor has indeed based his/her argumentation on these rules. It should also be mentioned here that the Tribunal has through its jurisprudence and the use of the teleological method of interpretation contributed to the "expansive reading of customary humanitarian law".[78] This is also of some relevance for the *ad hoc* Tribunal for Rwanda, since certain organisational and institutional links have been established between the two Tribunals in order to ensure a unity of legal approach.[79]

---

[76] *J.J.E. Schutte*, The System of Repression of Breaches of Additional Protocol I, in A.J.M. Delissen & G.J. Tanja (eds.), p. 178. Professor Meron has pointed to the greatest disadvantage in the creation of the category of "other" breaches being "less categorically penal". *T. Meron*, International Criminalization of Internal Atrocities, p. 564.

[77] *J.C. O'Brien*, The International Tribunal for Violations of International Humanitarian Law in former Yugoslavia, AJIL 1993, Vol. 87, p. 645. The list of public indictments as of March 1999 supports this presumption.

[78] *T. Meron*, War Crimes Law Comes of Age, p. 465.

[79] The subject matter jurisdiction of the Rwanda Tribunal comprises violations of international humanitarian law which may either be committed in both international and internal armed conflicts, such as the crime of genocide and crimes against humanity, or may be committed only in internal armed conflict, such as violations of Article 3 common to the four Geneva Conventions and as further elaborated in Article 4 of Additional Protocol II. This provision prohibits the following acts against "all persons who do not take a direct part or who have ceased to take part in hostilities: a) Violence to the life, health and physical or mental well-being of persons, in particular murder as well as cruel treatment such as torture, mutilation or any form of corporal punishment; b) collective punishments; c) taking of hostages; d) acts of terrorism; e) outrages upon personal dignity, in particular humiliating and degrading treatment, rape, enforced prostitution and any form of indecent assault;... ".

A comparison with the Statute of the Yugoslavia Tribunal shows that the S.C. has preferred a more expansive approach as regards the applicable law in the case of the Rwanda Tribunal's jurisdiction. Thus, Article 4 of the later Statute includes as above mentioned violations of Additional Protocol II, which as a whole has not yet been considered as a part of customary international law. This development is expected to have "enormous normative importance" for the international humanitarian law. *T. Meron*, International Criminalization of Internal Atrocities, p. 559; *P. Akhavan*, p. 503 and *T. Meron*, War Crimes Law Comes of Age, p. 464.

Despite the significant shortcoming of the Statute for the *ad hoc* Tribunal for the former Yugoslavia in that it identifies "rape" explicitly as a crime only in one (Article 5) of the categories of violations of international humanitarian law, it is my assumption that some aspects of gender-based violence (including reproductive crimes) may be prosecuted as a grave breach, as customary war crime, as genocide, or as a crime against humanity. Bearing in mind the poorly written crime-catalogue in the Tribunal's Statute, I shall in the following sub-chapters explore the question of 1) whether rape and forced pregnancy are covered by several of the notions in the different provisions of the Tribunal's Statute and if so, according to which of the above mentioned categories and 2) whether the crimes rape and forced pregnancy[80] should be considered as independent international crimes and therefore separately indictable.

*8.3.2.1. Grave Breaches*

The subject matter jurisdiction of the *ad hoc* Tribunal as defined in Article 2 of the Statute is the following: "The International Tribunal shall have the power to prosecute persons committing or ordering to be committed grave breaches of the Geneva Conventions of 12 August 1949". The provision continues by enumerating the following acts against persons or property that are protected under the provisions of the relevant Geneva Conventions[81] as grave breaches:

"a) wilful killing;
b) torture or inhumane treatment, including biological experiments;
c) wilfully causing great suffering or serious injury to body or health;
d) extensive destruction and appropriation of property, not justified by military necessity and carried out unlawfully and wantonly;
e) compelling a prisoner of war or a civilian to serve in the forces of a hostile power;
f) wilfully depriving a prisoner of war or a civilian of the rights of fair and regular trial;
g) unlawful deportation or transfer or unlawful confinement of a civilian;
h) taking civilians as hostages".[82]

---

[80] The American Bar Association recommended in its Report on the International Tribunal to Adjudicate War Crimes Committed in former Yugoslavia, (Washington D. C. 1993, pp. vi, 14–15), certain modifications of the *ad hoc* Tribunal's Statute. It suggested, *e.g.*, expansion of sub-paragraph (g) (rape) of Article 5 to include specific reference to enforced prostitution, forced pregnancy, and other widespread sexual offences reportedly committed in former Yugoslavia and as described in the Secretary General's Report (§ 48). *K.E. Puls*, A Commentary on the preparatory work published in Boston University International Law Journal 1994, Vol. 12, p. 14.

[81] An important provision, which defines the term "grave breaches" though in a non-exhaustive manner and which has inspired Article 2 of the *ad hoc* Tribunal's Statute to a great extent, is Article 147 of the Fourth Geneva Convention (civilians). See also the wording of Article 50 of the First Geneva Convention (wounded and sick); Article 51 of the Second Geneva Convention (maritime) and Article 130 of the Third Geneva Convention (prisoners of war).

[82] A similar but much more detailed provision has been incorporated in the Statute of the ICC. Article 8(2)(§ xxii) includes among others the crimes of "(r)ape, sexual slavery, enforced prostitution, forced pregnancy, enforced sterilization, or any other form of sexual violence also constituting a grave breach of the Geneva Conventions".

The first observation, which can be made after reading the text above is that the list of grave breaches of international humanitarian law within the jurisdiction *ratione materiae* of the *ad hoc* Tribunal covers the definitions of grave breaches according to the four Geneva Conventions of 1949, which are by no means identical and which refer to the same acts as those enumerated in Article 6 (b) of the London Charter. The Conventions reflect customary international law applicable in international armed conflict. Thus, the character of the conflict is significant for the application of the rules related to "grave breaches". Article 2 of the Tribunal's Statute does not explicitly state that the crimes in question have to be committed in an international conflict. The Trial Chamber II interpreted this provision in the *Tadić* case as being self-contained and independent of the Geneva Conventions, save in relation to the definition of protected persons and property, and thus applicable to internal as well as international conflicts.[83] The Appeals Chamber did not agree with the Trial Chamber's interpretation and it applied a more restrictive and formal approach in this regard compared to the unorthodox view of the Trial Chamber. It ruled, on the opposite, that Article 2 of the Statute only allowed prosecution of acts "perpetrated against persons or property regarded as 'protected' by the Geneva Conventions under the strict conditions set out by the Conventions themselves".[84] It continued by stating that the Geneva Conventions only protect people or persons that are caught up in an international armed conflict. Nevertheless, the Appeals Chamber left it up to the Trial Chamber to determine, *in casu*, the status of the conflict and thus the applicability of the article.[85] The Trial Chamber had no difficulty in concluding that prior to the withdrawal of the Yugoslav People's Army (the JNA) there existed an

---

[83] The events leading to the indictment of Tadić occurred in the opstina Prijedor, Bosnia-Herzegovina. According to the Prosecutor, Serb forces, beginning on or about 23 May 1992, attacked Bosnian Muslims and the Croat population centres in Prijedor. Most of the Muslims and Croats were forced from their homes and seized by the Serb forces, and thousands were unlawfully confined in the Omarska, Keraterm and Trnopolje camps. The crucial question in the *Tadić* case was if the victims of the crimes that Tadić was accused of were in the hands of a party of which they were not nationals. In other words, the question was raised of whether the conflict in opstina Prijedor was international or not. The Prosecutor asserted that the accused participated in the attack on, seizure, murder and maltreatment of Bosnian Muslims and Croats in opstina Prijedor both within the camps and outside the camps. Before the Appeals Chamber the defence made the assertion that there did not exist an armed conflict in Prijedor at the relevant time and therefore the Tribunal lacked jurisdiction. *Prosecutor v. Tadić*, Case No. IT-94-1-AR72, § 79. It is interesting to note that the USA *amicus curiae* brief to the Tribunal regarded the conflict as being international and that Article 2 of the Statute applied to both international and internal conflicts. *Amicus Curiae Brief* presented by the Government of the United States of America filed on June 23, 1995, § 25–35.

[84] Ibid., § 81. See also *Prosecutor v. Rajić*, Case No. IT-95-12-R61, ICTY 13 September 1996, § 34. For a comment on the case see *O. Swaak-Goldman* in AJIL 1997, Vol. 91, pp. 523–532.

[85] Critics of the Appeals Chamber's decision argue that it has complicated unnecessarily the future work of the Tribunal, since it has to make judgment in each case as to the character of the conflict in which the alleged offences occurred. *G.H. Aldrich*, Jurisdiction of the International Criminal Court for the Former Yugoslavia, AJIL 1996, Vol. 90, pp. 64–69. Others claim that although the Appeals Chamber might have chosen a more difficult approach than that of the Commission of Experts, it is justified. Whether the actual armed conflict is international or internal is a mixed question of fact and law, and the answer to the question will decide by which substantive provisions the defendant's acts will be judged. Such an important question can not be determined without full consideration of all evidence. *C. Greenwood*, International Humanitarian Law and the *Tadić* case, European Journal of International Law 1996, Vol. 7, p. 257.

international conflict in Bosnia-Herzegovina. It had more trouble determining the nature of the conflict after May 19, 1992. The crimes that the defendant was accused of were committed after that date. The majority of the Trial Chamber found that the conflict was internal, and thus the people living in Prijedor were not protected persons within the meaning of Article 4 of the Fourth Geneva Convention, *i.e.*, Article 2 of the Statute was not applicable.[86] Consequently, the charges made pursuant to the Geneva Conventions were considered inapplicable and Tadić was found not guilty on all the counts that were based on that provision. The Tribunal thus did not take any standpoint as to whether rape may be prosecuted or not as a grave breach of the Geneva Conventions.[87] Having determined that Article 2 was not applicable, the Trial Chamber turned to Article 3 of the Statute which had been held applicable both to international and internal conflicts by the Appeals Chamber.

I may, however, note that although the Geneva Conventions and the Protocol[88] explicitly contain prohibition of rape as, *e.g.*, Article 27 of the Fourth Geneva Convention,[89] the term "rape" is not mentioned among the enumerated examples of

---

[86] The President of the Trial Chamber, Judge McDonald disagreed with the majority's conclusion that the civilians in Prijedor were not protected persons. In her view the evidence presented by the Prosecutor showed among other things that Serbia and Montenegro had effective control over the VRS (the armed forces of Republic Serbska). The evidence proved, moreover, that the creation of the VRS was a legal fiction and that practically everything remained the same after the formal withdrawal by the JNA. Separate and Dissenting Opinion of Judge McDonald Regarding the Applicability of Article 2 of the Statute, § 7.

[87] Yet the *Tadić* case is in my view of symbolic importance with regard to prosecution of gender-based violence since it is the very first indictment dealing specifically with rape, sexual abuse and sexual slavery of women and girls. It is the first time that rape and sexual assault have been investigated for the purpose of prosecution under grave breaches of the Geneva Conventions and as a war crime and a crime against humanity. The part of the indictment which concerned rape of a female prisoner in the Omarska camp charged Tadić with committing: **count 2**: a grave breach recognised by Article 2(b) of the Statute (inhuman treatment); and **count 3**: a violation of the laws or customs of war recognised by Article 3 of the Statute (cruel treatment); and **count 4**: a crime against humanity recognised in Article 5(g) of the Statute (rape). This pattern of charging the accused under Articles 2, 3 and 5 of the Statute in respect of each incident has been repeated in the indictments in other cases as well. Eight Bosnian Serbs have been, for example, charged thereafter for grave breaches of the Geneva Conventions (torture), Article 5 (f) of the Tribunal's Statute for committing rape. See *The Prosecutor v. D. Gagović and others*, Case No. IT-96-23, <http://www.un.org/icty/indictment/english/98-13-07.htm.>.

[88] Grave breaches are listed in Articles 11, § 4 and 85 of Additional Protocol I of 1977. Article 76 of the same instrument contains an explicit prohibition of rape.

[89] The first part of Article 27(2) reads as follows: "Protected persons are entitled, in all circumstances, to respect for their persons, their honour, their family rights, their religious convictions and practices, and their manners and customs. They shall at all times be humanely treated, and shall be protected especially against all acts of violence or threats thereof and against insults and public curiosity.

Women shall be especially protected against any attack on their honour, in particular against *rape*, enforced prostitution, or any form of indecent assault". (italics added) Forced pregnancy may be considered as implicitly covered by the prohibition of any "form of indecent assault" contained in Article 27 of the fourth Geneva Convention. This provision has, however, limited significance since it ensures protection only for those women who are in the hands of a state party to the conflict of which they are not nationals. In other words, as it has been pointed out in the literature, women of the same nationality as their captors, or from a neutral or co-belligerent state, or states not parties to the Convention, lack the protection it guarantees. *C.N. Narchos*, p. 676, note 164; *K.M. Pratt & L.E. Fletcher*, Time for Justice:

"grave breaches"[90] which are subject to international jurisdiction. This is the reason behind why Article 2 of the Statute lacks reference specifically to "rape".[91] Rape and sexual assault are instead "subsumed in offences that are explicitly identified as grave breaches",[92] *i.e.*, torture, inhuman treatment, wilfully causing great suffering, or serious injury, to body and health. Others mean that by reading Article 27 (IV Geneva Convention) and Article 147 of the same Convention together, it should become obvious that rape constitutes a grave breach of the Convention.[93] The above discussion illustrates the assessment that treaty law, as it stands today, does not reflect the special needs of women and their different experience of warfare as compared to men.[94] Several scholars have, therefore, rightly criticised Articles 2 and 3 of the Tribunal's Statute as too restrictive in regard to sexual offences.[95] The *ad hoc* Tribunal for the former Yugoslavia continues so far to uphold the failure of international humanitarian law to deal equally with women's and men's experience of armed conflicts.[96] A few writers have, therefore, suggested that the Geneva Conventions be amended by an additional protocol or annex so that rape and sexual assault are specifically mentioned within the definition of grave breaches.[97]

Recognising the weakness of existing rules of relevance to the topic which this author explores, it is my assumption that this does not prevent the Tribunal from considering rape and forced pregnancy as violations of the normative provisions of international humanitarian law, which prohibit such violence since it is indisputably a brutal attack on women's physical integrity. Moreover, when rape has been committed under humiliating and aggravating circumstances indicating use of extreme coercion or threat of force[98] (including sexual mutilation) such acts should be deemed as covered by the definition of torture and inhuman and degrading treatment in international law.

---

The Case for International Prosecutions of Rape and Gender-Based Violence in the Former Yugoslavia, Berkeley Women's Law Journal 1994, Vol. 9, p. 90.

Additionally, I may assert that gender-specific abuses are covered by Article 14 of the third Geneva Convention, since it requires that women "be treated with all the regard due to their sex".

90 During the preparatory work on Article 2 of the Statute NAWO has suggested that forced prostitution and forced pregnancy constitute grave breaches of the Fourth Geneva Convention. *V. Morris & M.P. Scharf*, p. 373.

91 *V. Morris & M.P. Scharf*, p. 67.

92 *M.C. Bassiouni*, The Law of the International Tribunal, p. 564; *K.D. Askin*, p. 309.

93 *T. Meron*, Rape as a Crime Under International Humanitarian Law, pp. 424–427. See also *V. Morris & M.P. Scharf*, p. 67, note 221.

94 *E.A. Kohn*, pp. 201 and 209; *C.N. Niarchos*, p. 672; *K.M. Pratt & L.E. Fletcher*, p. 88.

95 *C. Chinkin*, Rape and Sexual Abuse of Women in International Law, European Journal of International Law 1994, Vol. 5, p. 332; *D. Shraga & R. Zacklin*, The International Tribunal for the Former Yugoslavia, EJIL 1994, Vol. 5, pp. 360–380; *K.D. Askin*, p. 983.

96 *J. Gardam*, p. 73.

97 *J. Gardam*, p. 77; *K.D. Askin*, p. 322.

98 Judge Fitzmaurice stated in his separate opinion in the *Ireland v. The United Kingdom* case that: "Torture is torture whatever its object may be,..., provided it is inflicted by force". ECHR, Judgment of 18 January 1978, Ser. A, No. 25, p. 129. See *M.E. Tardu*, The United Nation's Convention against Torture and Other Cruel, Inhumane or Degrading Treatment or Punishment, NJIL 1987, Vol. 56, p. 320, note 6.

Considering rape in such a context, I can safely argue that the crime is comprised within the term "grave breaches"[99] of international humanitarian law and as such it is included in Article 2 § b and § c of the *ad hoc* Tribunal's Statute.

8.3.2.1.1. Rape as a Grave Breach of Humanitarian Law

Paragraph b of Article 2 of the *ad hoc* Tribunal's Statute contains the notions "torture" and "inhumane treatment". Both terms may embody protection against rape and forced pregnancy. The common elements in the notions are based on the obligation under international law to protect the integrity and dignity of the human being. However, the scope of neither of the expressions has yet been precisely and unambiguously defined in the context of international humanitarian law. Therefore, existing definitions and case law to human rights treaties might be of some help in exploring their substance. The ICTY has, *e.g.*, frequently referred to human rights instruments, in its jurisprudence. This is, in my view, a reasonable method of ascertaining the content of both terms, since the prohibition in international law against torture and inhumane treatment is applicable in all situations, *i.e.*, it is not susceptible to derogations under international human rights law. This means that no state, in circumstances such as state of war and national emergency, is allowed to resort to the use of torture. Therefore, one may argue that the prohibition of the use of torture is an integral part of customary international law and belongs to the *ius cogens* norms.[100] As an illustration I shall, for instance, refer to Article 2(2) of the UN Convention against Torture, which indicates that no exception from the prohibition against torture may be made under any circumstances, including war or other public emergency. Nor is the prohibition of torture in Article 7 of the ICCPR derogative.[101] On the contrary, it is expressed in unconditional terms.

---

[99] Ms. Mary Robinson has also taken the position that rape of women and girls in situations of armed conflict, "whether civil or international, constitutes by definition a grave breach of international human rights and humanitarian law". *M. Robinson*, Message from the United Nations High Commissioner for Human Rights, in Common Grounds, Violence Against Women in War and Armed Conflict, Asian Center for Women's Human Rights (ASCENT) 1998, I.L. Sajor (ed.), p. 20. See also *A. Brunet & S. Rousseau*, Acknowledging Violations, Struggling Against Impunity: Women's Rights, Human Rights, in Common Grounds, *op. cit.*, p. 43.

[100] UN Doc. E/CN.4/1986/15, p. 1, § 3; *Y. Dinstein*, The Right to Life, p. 122; *M. Nowak & W. Suntinger*, International mechanisms for the prevention of torture, in Monitoring Human Rights in Europe, A. Bloed *et al.* (eds.), p. 145. For an extensive reference to the predominant view in the international law doctrine on that subject see *L. Hannikainen*, p. 502; *M.C. Bassiouni*, International Crimes: Jus Cogens and Obligations Erga Omnes, in Accountability for International Crimes and Serious Violations of Fundamental Human Rights, M.C. Bassiouni & M.H. Morris (eds.), p. 68; UN Doc. E/CN.4/Sub.2/1998/13, § 52. The Trial Chamber of the ICTY established, *e.g.*, in the *Prosecutor v. Furundžija* case that the prohibition of torture imposes obligations *erga omnes* upon states and has acquired the status of *ius cogens*. *Prosecutor v. Furundžija*, Judgment of 10 December 1998, §§ 151 and 153.

[101] This implies in my view that future interpretation of human rights instruments should take account of the *ad hoc* Tribunal's rulings. It has been submitted in the literature that the HRC intends to revise its comment of Article 7 to include all forms of sexual abuse, rape and violence against women occurring as acts of war or in a theatre of armed conflict. *A. Brunet & S. Rousseau*, p. 48.

8.3.2.1.2. Rape as Torture

Rape can, and it has often been used, as a method of torture in armed conflicts. The gravity of the offence of torture qualifies it as a grave breach under all four Geneva Conventions. An interesting indication is, however, that all these Conventions put torture on "an equal footing with inhumane treatment" as grave breaches, *i.e.*, with the consequence of establishing universal criminal jurisdiction[102] for both kinds of behaviour.

This legal approach is somewhat modified in the case of the other international law instruments containing the prohibition against torture and inhumane treatment. The UN Convention Against Torture (Article 1), the ICCPR (Article 7), the European Convention (Article 3) and the American Convention on Human Rights (Article 5) differentiate between these two types of conduct.[103] At the same time, it is evident from the existing case law on that subject matter that the margin of appreciation in establishing whether or not the circumstances in each specific case amount to torture or instead constitute inhumane treatment is rather great. The outcome in most cases is, therefore, uncertain and I may also establish that the borderline between acts constituting torture and inhumane treatment is for the most part not self-evident. On the other hand, more significant is the fact that the judicial consequences of classifying actions as the one or the other have been deemed as relatively unimportant.[104] Others have contrary to that maintained that, in the case of the UN Convention against Torture, the distinction between these two types of conduct does indeed "have important legal consequences, affecting both the extent of the obligations undertaken by the states parties and the availability of the various procedures".[105] The universal jurisdiction clause does not, *e.g.*, apply to acts considered as inhumane or degrading treatment. In addition to this comment,

---

[102] *J.J.E. Schutte*, p. 184. See Article 50 of the First Geneva Convention, Article 51 of the Second Geneva Convention, Article 130 of the Third Geneva Convention and Article 147 of the Fourth Geneva Convention. Prohibitions of torture, of cruel, inhumane or degrading treatment or punishment and of brutality are comprised in several other provisions of these documents and of the Additional Protocols. Among these I may mention Article 3, common to the four Conventions, Article 12 of the First Convention, Article 12 of the Second Convention, Articles 13 and 87 of the Third Convention, Article 32 of the Fourth Convention, Articles 11 and 75 of Additional Protocol I and Article 4 of the Additional Protocol II. See furthermore on the issue of universal jurisdiction *T. Meron*, International Criminalization of Internal Atrocities, pp. 572–574.

[103] This perspective was actually introduced in the text of the 1975 UN Declaration against Torture and other Cruel, Inhumane and Degrading Treatment and Punishment. However, the European Commission on Human Rights distinguished in its case law (*the Greek case*) as early as 1969 torture from inhumane or degrading treatment. Report of the Commission, 5 November 1969, YB Vol. 12, at 186. See also the *Aydin* case in which the European Court emphasised that this distinction "would appear to have been embodied in the Convention to allow the special stigma of "torture" to attach only to deliberate inhuman treatment causing very serious and cruel suffering". ECHR, *Aydin v. Turkey*, Judgment of 25 September 1997, § 82.

[104] *M.E. Tardu*, The United Nations Convention against Torture and Other Cruel, Inhumane or Degrading Treatment or Punishment, p. 309; *H. Danelius*, Protection Against Torture in Europe and the World, in The European System for the Protection of Human Rights, R. St. J. Macdonald, F. Matscher & H. Petzold (eds.), p. 266.

[105] *A. Byrnes*, The Committee against Torture, in The United Nations and Human Rights, P. Alston (ed.), Oxford 1992, p. 514.

Mr. Hans Danelius has expressed the view that upholding the differentiation approach may have considerable political as well as psychological implications for states.[106] Therefore, I shall in the following search for supportive and representative statements in the international community as to the recognition of rape as torture on the one hand and rape as inhuman treatment on the other hand, as well as the joint prohibition of torture and inhuman treatment, in a chronological order.

The International Committee of the Red Cross (ICRC) recognised as early as 1958 in the Commentary on the Fourth Geneva Convention that its Article 147, which prohibits acts of wilfully causing great suffering or serious injury to body and health, shall be regarded as covering rape and, under certain circumstances, violation of the prohibition of torture and inhuman treatment.[107]

Within the UN the prohibition of torture and inhuman treatment has been a priority theme for several human rights organs. In his 1991 report presented at the annual session of the UN Commission on Human Rights,[108] the Commission's previous Special Rapporteur on Torture, Professor Kooijmans, has analysed the phenomenon of torture and has also elucidated circumstances when rape has been used as a means to force the adversary to surrender and with the purpose of forcing members of a particular ethnic group to leave their habitual place of residence and to seek refuge in other countries. The significance of that document consists among other things in its broad and flexible interpretation of the term "torture". Thus, it is one of the few official statements at that time which considers the practice of rape as a violation of the prohibition of torture and inhuman treatment according to international human rights law.

The Special Rapporteur of the same UN body, Mr. Tadeusz Mazowiecki, has in his report on the situation of human rights in the territory of the former Yugoslavia, which he submitted at the 49th session of the Commission on Human Rights in 1993, also argued in favour of an interpretation of the crime rape whereby it is covered by the international definition of torture. Mr. Mazowiecki, in developing his reasoning on the subject matter, stated that: "Rape in this context is a grave breach of the Fourth Geneva Convention (Article 147) and as such, a war crime (Additional Protocol I)".[109]

---

[106] *H. Danelius*, Protection Against Torture in Europe and the World, p. 266.

[107] The ICRC has interpreted the expression "grave breaches" under Article 147 of the Fourth Geneva Convention as inclusive of rape in that it constitutes "torture or inhuman treatment wilfully causing great suffering or serious injuries to body and health". International Committee of the Red Cross, Aide-Mémoire, 3 December 1992, cited in *E.A. Kohn*, p. 210.

[108] UN Doc. E/CN.4/1991/17. See also UN Doc. E/CN.4/1992/17 and Add.1; UN Doc. E/CN.4/1993/26; UN Doc. E/CN.4/1994/31 and UN Doc. E/CN.4/1995/34. Professor Kooijmans served as a Special Rapporteur on Torture to the UN Commission on Human Rights from 1985 to 1993. After his appointment as the Netherlands' Minister of Foreign Affairs in 1993, Mr. Rodley has been acting as the thematic Rapporteur on Torture. Nigel Rodley has taken the position that rape is an especially traumatic form of torture. UN Doc. E/CN.4/1995/34 and UN Doc. E/CN.4/1997/7. See also *M. Nowak & W. Suntinger*, p. 158; *D. Blatt*, Recognizing Rape as a Method of Torture, NY University Review of Law & Social Change 1992, Vol. 19, p. 833.

[109] UN Doc. E/CN.4/1993/50, p. 20, § 89. For similar pronouncements supporting this particular standpoint see *T. Meron*, Rape as a Crime under International Humanitarian Law, p. 426 and the first report of the UN Special Rapporteur on Violence against Women Mrs. R. Coomaraswamy, UN Doc. E/CN.4/1995/42, p. 63.

In the same year, the participants of the high level International Conference for the Protection of War Victims, which was held in Geneva from August 30 to September 1, 1993, declared solemnly in § 3 of the unanimously adopted Declaration at the Conference that: "We are alarmed by the marked increase in acts of sexual violence directed notably against women and children and we reiterate that such acts constitute grave breaches of international humanitarian law".[110]

Following this encouraging development, CEDAW also took the view that rape and other violent acts constitute grave breaches of the Fourth Geneva Convention and of customary humanitarian law.[111] Shortly, thereafter, this standpoint gained strong support from an Expert Group consisting of 10 experts of all regions of the world including governments and NGOs, scholars and practitioners. The group presented in 1994 to the CSW, and subsequently to ECOSOC, its conclusions and recommendations for the eradication of violence against women in the family and in society. The experts declared that: "Rape in internal and international armed conflict, including individual acts of rape as well as systematic rape, should be prosecuted as a war crime and as a grave breach of the 1949 Geneva Convention".[112] One year afterwards, the Secretary-General took the position in his report on "Peace-women in international decision-making" that "Rape is the conduct of war and it should be defined as a serious war crime comparable to terrorism or torture".[113]

Also at the regional level various official statements confirm the consensus as to the necessity to apply an extensive interpretation of the term "torture" which also comprises rape so as to be able to prosecute the perpetrators. Given the manner in which, and the scale on which, rape has been perpetrated in the Bosnia-Herzegovina conflict, the EC investigative mission declared in its final report that rape is "a particularly humiliating and degrading treatment and a clear form of torture".[114] Also, according to the Declaration of the Committee of Ministers of the Council of Europe of 1993, rape is considered as a serious violation of human rights, since it "constitutes an attack on the physical and mental integrity and on the dignity of the victims". Though there is no explicit reference as to which particular human rights are meant, the prohibition against torture and inhuman treatment as such is, in my view, not excluded but on the contrary, as one of the most fundamental freedoms aimed at the protection of a person's integrity and dignity, it is highly relevant in regard to the statement above. In favour of this assumption speaks also the fact that the European Commission on Human Rights, which operates within the Council of Europe, has considered rape of women committed by Turkish troops during the invasion of Cyprus as a violation of the prohibition against torture and inhuman treatment in Article 3 of the European

[110] ST/DPI/1291; ST/DPI/1364. The text of the Declaration is reprinted in The Review 1993, No. 51, pp. 56–58. The very same year the Government of the United States declared that it also interpreted rape as a grave breach under the Geneva Conventions. *E.A. Kohn*, p. 210.

[111] UN Doc. E/CN.4/1994/5, § 22, p. 7.

[112] UN Doc. E/CN.6/1994/4, p. 21.

[113] UN Doc. E/CN.6/1995/12, § 45(a).

[114] UN Doc. S/25240, p. 3.

Convention.[115] In recent years rape has acquired greater attention within the context of human rights law. The European Court, as well as the Inter-American Commission on Human Rights, have found in their case law rape to be a violation of the prohibition of torture.[116] The Commission declared categorically that "rape represents not only inhumane treatment that infringes upon physical and moral integrity under Article 5 of the Convention, but also a form of torture in the sense of Article 5(2) of that instrument".[117] Of relevance to this study is also the argument advanced by the Commission that rape and the threat of it against women also qualifies as torture in that it represents "a brutal expression of discrimination against them as women".[118] Most interestingly, the Commission says that the Statute of the *ad hoc* Tribunal for the former Yugoslavia incorporates rape as a "grave breach" of the Geneva Conventions.[119]

At the high-level ECE regional preparatory meeting for the Fourth World Conference on Women, the delegations representing the European governments agreed in § 13 of the preambular declaration of the "Regional Platform for Action" that murder, torture, systematic rape, forced pregnancy and forced abortion, and especially policies of so-called "ethnic cleansing" constitute grave violations of the human rights of women, particularly in times of armed conflict, and are to be deemed unacceptable.[120] Governments are urged to uphold the standards set out in international humanitarian and human rights law. According to Article 63 of the above mentioned document, perpetrators of such crimes should be punished and "such practices and violations immediately stopped". On the other hand, the confusing fact ought to be mentioned that the proposed amendment to Article 63 "perpetrators of such war crimes" presented by the NGO caucus, which took place

---

[115] *Cyprus v. Turkey*, Application Nos. 6780/74, 6950/75, Report of the European Commission on Human Rights adopted on 10 July 1976, §§ 373–414.

Turkey invaded Cyprus in July 1974 and the Turkish soldiers committed various types of human rights abuses. The Turkish troops were accused of, among other things repeated rapes of Cypriot women of all ages and mental conditions. Nevertheless, the decision by the Commission to consider the rapes definitely as "inhuman treatment" and possibly, but not expressly, as torture under Article 3 of the European Convention has been rightly criticised in the doctrine. See *D. Blatt*, p. 856. See generally on the issue *J. Fitzpatrick*, The Use of International Human Rights Norms to Combat Violence Against Women, p. 566; *A. Byrnes*, The Committee against Torture, p. 519; *T. Meron*, Rape as a Crime Under International Humanitarian Law, p. 425; *M.C. Bassiouni*, The Law of the International Criminal Court for the Former Yugoslavia, p. 586.

[116] See ECHR, Judgment in the *Aydin v. Turkey* case and the decision of the Inter-American Commission in the *Mejía Egocheaga and other v. Peru*. Both cases have been discussed in part I of this study. See also the *Dianna Ortiz v. Guatemala* Case No. 10.526, IACHR, Annual Report of the Inter-American Commission on Human Rights 1996, OEA/Ser.L/V/II.95, March 14, 1997, pp. 360–361. The Inter-American Commission considered, in addition, other forms of sexual torture such as "blows to the breasts and stomach, often inflicted on pregnant women with the intention of causing them to abort or damage their ability to have children" as a serious human rights violation. IACHR, Report on the Situation of Human Rights in Haiti, OEA/Ser.L/V/II.88, February 9, 1995, §§ 123–124.

[117] *Supra*, The Report on Haiti, § 133.

[118] Ibid., § 134.

[119] Ibid., § 136.

[120] E/ECE/RW/HLM/L.3/Rev.2, 20 October 1994, p. 7.

before the intergovernmental meeting, was not adopted by the diplomatic conference because of disagreement among delegations on the wording to be used. Neither was there any consensus as to the proposed amendment of Article 63 (bis)(4), which said that: "The international community must explicitly define systematic rape as a war crime subject to prosecution". This is but an isolated example of a more moderate, and I hope only occasional, attitude on a regional level to the inclusion of rape within the term "grave breach" of international humanitarian law and "war crime".

Of greater importance is anyway the expressed universal consensus on that matter, since regional interpretations of norms of international law shall be complementary and not contrary to universal ones. The international impartial Commission of Experts established in 1992 with the purpose of providing the Secretary-General with conclusions based on investigations of grave breaches of the 1949 Geneva Conventions in the territory of the former Yugoslavia, deemed in its final report of 27 May 1994 that Article 147 of the Fourth Geneva Convention "includes rape and other sexual assaults as constituting torture or inhumane treatment".[121] In addition, the members of the Commission argued that these acts are prohibited because they are "wilfully causing great suffering or serious injury to body or health". In other words, the Commission draws a connecting and very significant link between paragraph (b) and paragraph (c) of Article 2 of the *ad hoc* Tribunal's Statute based on Article 147 of the Fourth Geneva Convention.

In the international law doctrine Professor Meron, a great authority in international humanitarian and human rights law, has described the progress in combating rape internationally in the following way: "Indeed, under the weight of the events in former Yugoslavia, the hesitation to recognise that rape can be a war crime or a grave breach has already begun to dissipate".[122] Kathleen Pratt and Laurel Fletcher believe that rape and other forms of gender-based violence, when committed against protected persons (Article 4 of the Fourth Geneva Convention), "clearly constitute violations of the 'grave breach' provision of the Geneva Conventions" and may therefore properly be prosecuted under Article 2 of the *ad hoc* Tribunal's Statute.[123] Kelly Askin has used the aim and purpose of the provisions that are sought to provide as much protection as possible to persons protected by the Geneva Conventions as a basis for her argument that "since grave breach language is internationally expansive, a 'grave breach' of the 1949 Geneva

---

[121] UN Doc. S/1994/674, p. 28. Generally on the work of the Commission of Experts see *M.C. Bassiouni*, Investigating Violations of International Humanitarian Law in the Former Yugoslavia, Occasional Paper No. 2, International Human Rights Law Institute, DePaul University College of Law 1996. See also *M.P. Scharf*, Balkan Justice, pp. 42–49.

[122] *T. Meron*, Rape as a Crime under International Humanitarian Law, p. 426. Also other international commentators have asserted that rape violates the prohibition of torture and other, cruel, inhuman, or degrading treatment or punishment. International Human Rights Law Group, No Justice, No Peace, 1993, p. 52; *D. Blatt*, p. 821; *R. Copelon*, Gendered War Crimes: Reconceptualising Rape in Time of War, in Women's rights, human rights, J. Peters & A. Wolper (eds.), p. 201.

[123] *K.M. Pratt & L.E. Fletcher*, p. 96.

Conventions necessarily would be intended to protect civilians from sexual assault".[124] These are but a few examples of statements within the international law doctrine reflecting an ever growing consensus about the contemporary reading of the "grave breach" provisions in the Geneva Conventions as inclusive of rape and sexual assault.[125]

This tendency to understand humanitarian law provisions in an expansive way has been confirmed, moreover, by the unanimous adoption of the excellent report on violence against women submitted by the UN Special Rapporteur on Violence Against Women Ms. Radhika Coomaraswamy at the 51st session of the Commission on Human Rights in 1995. Among the issues which have attracted the rapporteur's particular attention is the urgency of adopting measures to eliminate gender-based violence against women in public and private life. Rape is explicitly defined in the report as a grave breach of international humanitarian law. In the view of Ms. Coomaraswamy "rape of women and girls in situations of armed conflict, whether civil or international, constitutes by definition a grave breach of international human rights and humanitarian law".[126] In her next reports Ms. Coomaraswamy considered rape in the context of torture.[127] The UN Special Rapporteur on Contemporary Forms of Slavery, Ms. Linda Chavez, has furthermore characterised rape and sexual abuse as torture and inhuman treatment in that it "causes suffering and serious bodily injury".[128] In her view systematic rape can be used as an instrument of torture, or an abhorrent instrument of warfare, and it is therefore to be seen as a grave breach under international humanitarian law.[129]

The above review of official statements within the UN bears clear evidence in support of my position that rape under certain circumstances should be covered by the notion "torture".[130] It, therefore, constitutes a grave breach of humanitarian law when committed in armed conflicts. A closer look at the content of "torture" as defined in international law treaties and the existing case law on that subject matter follows below.

---

124 *K.D. Askin*, p. 311.

125 See in addition *E.-J.F. Daes*, New Types of War Crimes and Crimes Against Humanity: Violations of International Humanitarian and Human Rights Law, International Geneva Yearbook, Dordrecht 1993, p. 63; *R. Seifert*, War and Rape, Analytical Approaches, WILPF 1993, p. 2; *A. Heiberg*, Torture og vold mot kvinner i krig, Mennesker og rettigheter 1994, Vol. 12, p. 146; *R. Copelon*, Surfacing Gender: Reconceptualizing Crimes against Women in Time of War, in Mass Rapes, A. Stiglmayer (ed.), London 1994, p. 199; *D. Aydelott*, p. 612; *C.N. Niarchos*, p. 683; *M.C. Bassiouni & M. McCormick*, Sexual Violence, p. 31; *M.C. Bassiouni*, The Law of the International Criminal Tribunal for the Former Yugoslavia, p. 564; *A. Obote-Odora*, p. 260; *J. Gardam*, p. 77; *A.Aafjes*, pp. 27–28.

126 UN Doc. E/CN.4/1995/42, § 261.

127 UN Doc. E/CN.4/1996/53, § 46 and UN Doc. E/CN.4/1998/54, p. 14.

128 UN Doc. E/CN.4/Sub.2/1996/26, § 15. See also UN Doc. E/CN.4/Sub.2/1998/13, §§ 53–55.

129 UN Doc. E/CN.4/Sub.2/1996/26, § 14. See also UN Doc. E/CN.4/Sub.2/1993/44 §§ 1–2.

130 This perspective has been reflected in a recent document UN Doc. E/CN.6/1998/5, § 68. In fact, the prosecutor at both the ICTY and the ICTR has indicted individuals for rape as a grave breach of international humanitarian law, *i.e.*, torture and wilfully causing great suffering or serious injury to body and health.

8.3.2.1.3. The Definition of Torture

Many provisions in the major human rights conventions, as well as in humanitarian law, contain the prohibition in absolute terms of torture. However, there have been considerable problems when attempts have been made to define precisely the content of the notion "torture" in international law. This is partly due to the want of an authoritative treaty definition and general pronouncement about the kind of actions falling within the term. Article 1(2) of the 1975 UN Declaration on the Protection of All Persons from Torture and Inhumane or Degrading Treatment or Punishment[131] was the first provision in an international document that delivered a definition, which became a source of inspiration for the treaty provisions adopted later on that subject matter. It reads as follows: "torture constitutes an aggravated and deliberate form of cruel, inhumane or degrading treatment or punishment". The earlier mentioned 1977 Additional Protocols to the Geneva Conventions, which were adopted two years later, contain categorical prohibition against torture being used against civilians and prisoners of war. These provisions do not, however, define the term "torture". Neither are the concepts of torture and inhuman treatment defined within the human rights conventional law, *i.e.*, the ICCPR, the European and the American Conventions on Human Rights.[132] This omission has been remedied first by the UN Convention against Torture and other Cruel, Inhuman or Degrading Treatment of 1984 (Article 1(1)).[133] Moreover, the importance of that convention consists in its supervisory mechanism, *i.e.*, the Committee Against Torture (CAT), which has been guided in its activities by the desire to provide an universal substantive interpretation of the term torture and inhumane treatment consistent with other universal and regional human rights treaties' provisions. On the other hand, some scholars have challenged CAT's aspiration. It has been pointed out that:

> "What "torture" means for the work of one body will depend on the text, purpose, and history of its enabling instrument, as well as on its own practice and the relevant practice of States".[134]

However, since the late 1980s a commonly accepted understanding in the contemporary international law doctrine is that the term "torture", as defined in international human rights instruments, consists of the following four elements:

1) severe physical and/or mental pain and suffering;
2) the infliction of pain and suffering is intentional;

---

[131] GA Res. 3452 (XXX) of 8 December 1975. The text is reprinted in Human Rights, A Compilation of International Instruments, UN New York 1983, pp. 82–83. See generally *R. Kühner*, Torture, in Encyclopaedia of Public International Law, R. Bernhardt (ed.), Instalment 8, Amsterdam 1985, pp. 510–513.

[132] In can be noted here that this is also valid for the European Convention Against Torture of 1987. Nevertheless, this convention has established a committee which has the mandate to visit any place of detention within the territory of the states parties at short notice, in order to investigate among other things if torture is occurring there.

[133] GA Res.39/46, Annex, UN Doc. A/39/51, p. 197, hereinafter UN Convention on Torture.

[134] *A. Byrnes*, The Committee against Torture, p. 513.

3) the act is committed for specified purposes;
4) there is some form of involvement of a public official, whether active or passive, *i.e.*, commission or authorisation of an act of torture.[135]

The crucial element of the universally accepted term "torture" is the infliction of severe pain or suffering upon a victim. But what is severe pain and what is suffering? There is no answer to this question in the *travaux préparatoires* to the UN Convention on Torture. It seems to me that the prohibition of torture relates to acts that cause physical pain, as well as to acts that cause mental suffering to the victim.[136] In the first case, pain is connected merely with bodily integrity, whereas in the second case suffering is more oriented towards emotional disturbances. Such an interpretation partly finds support in the statement made by the European Commission of Human Rights in the *Greek* case in connection with the process of defining the notion of "non-physical torture". The Commission unanimously concluded that the latter term covered "the infliction of mental suffering by creating a state of anguish and stress by means other than bodily assault".[137] Also the explanation given by the delegation of the United Kingdom during the preparatory work on Article 3 of the European Convention is supportive in regard to my interpretation of

---

[135] *R. Copelon*, Intimate Terror: Understanding Domestic Violence as Torture, in Human Rights of Women, R.J. Cook, (ed.) p. 122. The fourth element of the definition of torture which requires that torture takes place in the public realm has been rightly criticised and considered as an obstacle in its application to instances of violence against women which occur in the private, non-governmental sphere. Professor Charlesworth assumes that "if violence against women is understood not just as aberrant 'private' behaviour but as part of the structure of the universal subordination of women, it can never be considered a purely 'private' issue": the distinction between "public" and "private" action in the context of violence against women is not a useful or meaningful one". *H. Charlesworth*, Human Rights as Men's Rights, in Women's rights, human rights, J. Peters & A. Wolper (eds.), p. 107.

In assessing whether a violation of the prohibition of torture according to the European Convention on Human Rights has occurred, the following three elements are to be considered: 1. the intent to ill-treat, 2. a severe suffering (physical or psychological) and 3. lack of any justification for that suffering. In addition, Professor Cassese introduces a fourth element, namely "the *imputability* of the misbehaviour to one of the Contracting States". *A. Cassese*, Prohibition of Torture and Inhuman or Degrading Treatment or Punishment, in The European System for The Protection of Human Rights, R. St. J. Macdonald, F. Matscher & H. Petzold (eds.), p. 229.

[136] It is beyond question that rape in general causes severe physical pain and suffering as well as it causes psychological and emotional trauma. Amnesty International stated in the report *Women in the Front Line* that rape was "both a physical violation and injury, and an assault on a woman's mental and emotional well-being". AI, London 1990, p. 18. The Inter-American Commission on Human Rights noted in the *Majia v.Peru* case that rape causes physical and mental pain. See also UN Doc. E/CN.4/1997/47, § 20. My assumption may be supported by the ICTY's ruling in the *Furundžija* case. The Trial Chamber determined that torture as a war crime consists of "(i) the infliction, by act or omission, of severe pain or suffering, whether physical or mental; in addition (ii) this act or omission must be intentional; (iii) it must aim at obtaining information or a confession, or at punishing, humiliating, coercing the victim or a third person, or at discriminating, on any ground, against the victim or a third person; (iv) it must be linked to an armed conflict; (v) at least one of the persons involved in the torture process must be a public official or must at any rate act in a non-private capacity, *e.g.*, as a *de facto* organ of a State or any other authority-wielding entity". *Prosecutor v. Furundžija*, Judgment of 10 December 1998, § 162.

[137] *The Greek case*, p. 461.

the term "torture". Thus, it was underlined that no person shall be "subjected to imprisonment with such an excess of light, darkness, noise or silence, as to cause mental suffering".[138] In many aspects the scope of psychological torture can be considered wider than physical torture. Therefore, I may safely assume that physical and psychological torture have different characteristics. Thus, the use of the latter does not necessary comprise the use of physical torture.[139] Also Article 17 of the Geneva Convention Relative to the Treatment of Prisoners of War of 1949 emphasises that torture may be physical or mental. So, "No physical *or* mental torture, nor any other forms of coercion, may be inflicted on prisoners of war".[140] (italics added) On the other hand, the reasoning of the European Court of Human Rights in the case of *Ireland v. the United Kingdom* may lead to considerable confusion in this respect. The Court ruled, contrary to the Commission's view, that the five techniques used by the United Kingdom in the interrogation procedures in Northern Ireland did not constitute torture but fell into the category of inhuman treatment, since although they caused intense physical *and* mental suffering, they did not inflict suffering of the required "intensity and cruelty implied by the word torture".[141] This judgment is really challenging in that it reflects the very conservative approach of a majority of the Court to the definition of torture as comprising mainly physical pain and not necessarily mental suffering. Such an interpretation is in my view contradictory to the universal definition on torture and ought, therefore, to be considered as overruled in current international law. I also hope that the future decisions by the international supervisory bodies can throw some light and bring clarity as to the exact content and the differences between the two expressions: "pain" and "suffering". However, the upholding of a strict distinction between the two expressions is really not necessary, since both are comprised in the modern definition of torture.

Basically, the act of rape must attain a minimum level of severity if it is to fall within the scope of the universal definition of torture. The assessment of this minimum will, however, depend on all the specific circumstances of the concrete case. The European Court of Human Rights ruled in the *Ireland v. the United Kingdom* case, earlier referred to, that:

> "The assessment of this minimum is, in the nature of things, relative; it depends on all the circumstances of the case, such as the duration of the treatment, its physical or mental effects, and in some cases, the sex, age and state of health of the victim".[142]

---

[138] Cited in *J.E.S. Fawcett*, The Application of the European Convention on Human Rights, Oxford 1969, p. 35.

[139] *F. Malekian*, International Criminal Law, The Legal and Critical Analysis of International Crimes, Vol. I, Uppsala 1991, p. 380. See on that issue *C.M. Bassiouni*, The Law of the International Criminal Tribunal for the Former Yugoslavia, p. 567, note 182; *D. Blatt*, p. 853; *K.D. Askin*, pp. 315–316.

[140] In the UN commentary as regards the applicability of Article 5 of the Code of Conduct for Law Enforcement Officials of 1979, distinction has been made between "physical" and "mental" abuses in the context of the term torture.

[141] ECHR Judgment of 18 January 1978, Ser. A, No. 25, pp. 65–67.

[142] Ibid., p. 65, § 162.

This particular case and the remaining case law of the European Commission and the European Court of Human Rights on that subject matter indicate clearly that the difference made by both treaty bodies between torture and inhuman treatment is based on the assumption that torture causes greater suffering, *i.e.*, it is "*more serious or grave*" than acts, which are judged as inhuman treatment.[143] The European Commission held in the *Greek case* the view that torture is "generally an aggravated form of inhumane treatment".[144] The reference to "generally" indicates that the Commission might have deemed it necessary to have some kind of safety valve for doubtful cases.

On the universal level the UN Human Rights Committee has demonstrated in its case law the approach of not drawing a "sharp distinction" between the different prohibited forms of treatment. The members of the Committee agreed, however, in the General Comment on Article 7 of the ICCPR that a distinction between torture and inhuman treatment would depend on "the nature, purpose and severity of the treatment applied".[145] At the same time the Human Rights Committee did not consider it necessary to draw up a list of prohibited acts.

Interestingly, the Inter-American Convention to Prevent and Punish Torture of 9 December 1985[146] does not comprise in its definition of torture a requirement for the severity of the act, *i.e.*, a prerequisite for the inflicted pain and suffering to be of a certain degree. Torture is defined in Article 2 of the Convention merely as "the use of methods upon a person intended to obliterate the personality of the victim or to diminish his physical or mental capacities, even if they do not cause physical pain or mental anguish". No doubt this definition, compared with the conservative text of the UN Convention on Torture, to a great extent reflects contemporary developments in international law. As Maxime Tardu aptly puts it: "torturers do not appear to be fixated on pain as an end, but on the achievement of domination through personality distortion and surrender".[147] I may with this background assume that a modern international definition of torture would encompass not only the infliction of physical pain but also various methods of *humiliation*. In the words of Rhonda Copelon, in the contemporary understanding of torture, degradation is "both vehicle and goal".[148] For these reasons the Rwandan Tribunal opted in the *Akayesu* case for a broader and "more useful" definition of torture in international law. It emphasised that many rapes amount to torture and that both rape and torture

---

[143] *A. Cassese*, Prohibition of Torture and Inhumane or Degrading Treatment or Punishment, p. 241.

[144] *The Greek* case, p. 186.

[145] HRC, General Comment No. 20 on Article 7, adopted at the 44th session in 1992, UN Doc. HRI/GEN/1/Rev.1, 29 July 1994, p. 31, § 7. This GC replaced GC No. 7 on Article 7 of 1982. I may observe that no substantive changes were made as to the issue discussed here.

[146] O.A.S.T.S. No. 67. The Convention entered into force on 28 February 1987. As of April 1998 there were 13 ratifications deposited with the OAS General Secretariat. OEA/Ser. L/V/II.98, Doc. 7 rev, April 13, 1998, p. 1074.

[147] *M.E. Tardu*, The United Nations Convention against Torture and other Cruel, Inhumane or Degrading Treatment or Punishment, p. 305.

[148] *R. Copelon*, Recognizing the Egregious in the Everyday: Domestic Violence as Torture, Columbia Human Rights Law Review 1994, Vol. 25, p. 291.

are crimes that violate personal dignity since such acts are used for purposes such as "intimidation, degradation, humiliation, discrimination, punishment, control or destruction of a person".[149]

The UN definition of torture, furthermore, comprises another distinctive feature, *i.e.*, there is a presumption that torture in contrast to inhuman treatment is always performed for a certain purpose.

As to this element the purposes, for which the suffering has been inflicted and which are mentioned in Article 1[150] of the UN Convention on Torture, are to be seen merely as examples and not as an exhaustive enumeration.[151] Thus, as Maxime Tardu has observed, since the number of "conscious purposes" is "almost unlimited, any attempted list is bound to be incomplete".[152] Also in this respect the definition of "torture" in the American Convention to Prevent and Punish Torture is broader than the one in the UN Convention on Torture, since it provides that torture is the infliction of pain or suffering not only for a few specified purposes but for "any other purpose". Mr. Burger and Mr. Danelius have pointed to this important difference between the universal and the regional rules of relevance, and they have in their analysis of the term "torture", on the basis of a comparison of various texts, identified the common element of the enumerated purposes in the UN Convention on Torture, which can serve as an appropriate starting point in future deliberations. So, they declare that "In principle, the common element of the purposes referred to

---

[149] *Prosecutor v. Akayesu*, case No. ICTR-96-4-T, Judgment of 2 September 1998, §§ 6.4 and 7.7. See, in addition, § 596 where it is stated that "like torture, rape is a violation of personal dignity, and rape in fact constitutes torture when inflicted by or at the instigation of or with the consent or acquiescence of a public official or other person acting in an official capacity".

[150] Article 1 reads as follows: "1. For the purpose of this Convention, the term 'torture' means any act by, which severe pain or suffering, whether physical or mental, is intentionally inflicted on a person for such purposes as obtaining from him or a third person information or a confession, punishing him for an act that he or a third person has committed or is suspected of having committed, or intimidating or coercing him or a third person for any reason based on discrimination of any kind, when such pain or suffering is inflicted by, or at the instigation of, or with the consent or acquiescence of, a public official or other person acting in an official capacity. It does not include pain or suffering arising only from, inherent in, or incidental to lawful sanctions".

[151] For a historical review of the drafting process see *H. Danelius*, The International Protection against Torture and Inhumane or Degrading Treatment or Punishment, in Collected Courses of the Academy of European Law, 1993, Vol. II, p. 171. I should mention here that the Convention requires states parties only to provide "as full rehabilitation as possible" to the victims (Article 14(1)) for acts which amount to torture or cruel treatment as defined under the Convention. The Convention created, as already mentioned before, a treaty body (the Committee Against Torture) which is responsible for interpreting Articles 1 and 16 and applying them to complaints forwarded to it for review. Of relevance here is the Committee's consideration of a case dealing with the refusal by the Swedish authorities to grant asylum to a woman fleeing from persecution in Zaire and who had based her application among others on grounds of gender-based violence, *i.e.*, rape. See Communication No. 41/1996, *Pauline Muzongo Paku Kisoki v. Sweden*, IHRR 1997, Vol. 1, p. 78 ff.

[152] *M.E. Tardu*, ibid., note 147, p. 305. In support of this standpoint I refer to the view expressed by the European Commission on Human Rights in the *Greek case*: "the word 'torture' is often used to describe inhuman treatment which has a purpose *such as* the obtaining of information or confessions, or the infliction of punishment..". (italics added) YB 1969, Vol. 12, p. 186.

in the definition should /... / be understood to be the existence of some – even remote – connection with the interests of policies of the State and its organs".[153]

In the context of the armed conflicts in the former Yugoslavia, the final report of the independent Commission of Experts,[154] which has undertaken a pilot study of the rape issue, has indicated the existence of an overriding policy advocating the use of rape as a method of "ethnic cleansing", rather than a policy of omission, tolerating the widespread committing of rape. The report, moreover, identified several patterns of rape in regard to the reported cases. The first pattern involved individuals or small groups committing sexual assault in conjunction with *intimidation* of the target ethnic group.[155] The second pattern often included rape of women in public. The third pattern of rape is related to sexual assaults in detention.[156] According to evidential sources many of the surviving victims believe that they were detained for the purpose of rape. Yet another pattern of rape involves the detention of women in hotels or private homes for the purpose of sexually entertaining soldiers.[157] Even though a clear connection to the policy of ethnic cleansing is difficult to draw in these latter cases, it is of importance to pay attention to the statistics, which show that the sexually assaulted women in this group were more often killed after the rape than exchanged.[158]

It is obvious from the above that the second and the third required elements of the universal definition of "torture" are fulfilled in most of the reported cases related to the situation in the former Yugoslavia, since those who have committed sexual assaults, including rape, against women have done that for the purpose of terrorising and humiliating them as part of the policy of ethnic cleansing. The aim

---

[153] *Burger & Danelius*, The United Nations Convention against Torture, A Handbook on the Convention against Torture and Other Cruel, Inhumane and Degrading Treatment or Punishment, Dordrecht 1988, pp. 118–119.

[154] On the 26 October 1992 the Secretary-General appointed the following commissioners: Chairman – Prof. F. Kalshoven, Prof. M.C. Bassiouni, Commander W.J. Fenrick, Judge K. M'baye and Prof. T. Opsahl. On 19 October 1993 the Commission of Experts was reorganised because of the resignation of Prof. Kalshoven for medical reasons and the death of Prof. Opsahl. As new members of the Commission were appointed Ms. Chr. Cleiren and Ms. H.S. Greve. Prof. Bassiouni subsequently became the Chairman. The investigation methods employed by the Commission were the following: a) collection and analysis of information sent to or requested by the Commission; b) undertaking of investigative missions in the territory of the former Yugoslavia or in other countries; c) information gathering on behalf of the Commission by Governments, particularly in Austria, Germany, the Netherlands, Norway and the USA. See UN Doc. S/1994/674, pp. 9–10. See also *M.P. Scharf*, Balkan Justice, pp. 42–49.

[155] See also *D. Blatt*, p. 859 and *M.C. Bassiouni & M. McCormick*, p. 16.

[156] For reference to provisions designed to safeguard the honour of women and generally on the treatment of female prisoners of war see *M. Tabory*, pp. 942–945. See also *M.C. Bassiouni & M. McCormick*, p. 17. The Geneva Conventions focus on rape as a crime against the honour of women and do not consider it as a crime of gender-based violence. It has been pointed out that this is but a patriarchal dimension of rape. Such an attitude fails to recognise the fact that women too are raped as an enemy. As a crime of violence, rape violates the right to bodily autonomy and integrity and self-esteem "as well as standing in the community". *R. Copelon*, Gendered War Crimes, p. 201.

[157] See the *Gagović and Others v. the Prosecutor*, Case No. IT-96-23, counts 56–59, count 60 and counts 61–62 of the indictment.

[158] UN Doc. S/1994/674, pp. 58–59.

of the sexual assaults has very often been to "ensure that the victims and their families would never want to return to the area".[159] It is also apparent that these acts of rape have been committed for the purpose of intimidating and wilfully discriminating individuals belonging to a certain population group. Nevertheless, rape has occurred among and between all sides involved in the conflicts.

Consequently, as rape generally results both in pain and suffering of the exposed person and since the crucial element of the term "torture" is the infliction of severe pain or suffering,[160] I can on good grounds contend that rape ought to be comprised in the definition of torture, due to the serious health consequences generally connected with it (physical and mental). Rape can result in permanent disablement and/or have chronic traumatic consequences.[161] Very often this trauma is combined with a social stigma for the attacked person. In these circumstances women suffer "the double cruelty of victimisation by ethnic hatred".[162] Therefore, in regard to the intensity of the pain and the suffering following rape, the actuality of applying the provision prohibiting torture even when the result is less serious should not be excluded.

Considering the fourth element of the concept "torture", the UN Convention's approach is unfortunately very restrictive, since it only prohibits torture committed "by, or at the instigation or with the consent or acquiescence of a public official or other person... in an official capacity".[163] In other words, an act of torture committed by a private person against another individual will fall outside the scope of the

---

[159] UN Doc. S/1994/674, p. 59. See also UN Doc. E/CN.4/1995/42, §§ 277–281. See also *C.A. McKinnon*, Crimes of War, Crimes of Peace, UCLA Women's Law Journal 1993, Vol. 4:59, p. 66.

[160] Rape involves the infliction of pain to the most delicate and tender parts of the human body.

[161] The European Court of Human Rights concluded in the *Aydin v.Turkey* case that "rape leaves deep psychological scars on the victims which do not respond to the passage of time as quickly as other forms of physical and mental violence". ECHR, *Aydin v. Turkey*, Judgment of 25 September 1997, § 83.

The Prosecutor for the ICTY emphasised in her indictment in the *Gagović and Others* case (§ 6.5) that the physical and psychological health of many female detainees seriously deteriorated as a result of the sexual assaults. Some of the women became even suicidal. In § 7.1 reference is also made to one victim who can no longer have children as a result of the permanent gynaecological harm due to sexual assaults. Paragraph 1.8 of the *Kunarac* indictment (it is amendment of the original *Gagović and Others* indictment) of 13 July 1998 refers also to the fact that women who had been subjected to sexual assault "suffered psychological injury and emotional harm; some remain traumatised".

Health problems may include also sexually transmitted diseases, including HIV/AIDS, the consequences of mutilation and complications resulting from unsafe abortions etc... UN Doc. CN.6/1998/5, § 52. A study which was presented at the NGO-forum at Beijing 1995 reveals that about 35% of Rwandese soldiers were HIV-positive before the genocide of 1994. The author draws the conclusion that "(i)t is very likely that the extremely high degree of venereal diseases presently observed in women and the rape of girls and women during the genocide are directly linked". *E. Richter-Lyonette*, Mission on gender-based war crimes against women and girls during the genocide in Rwanda, Geneva 1996, p. 7. The UN Special Rapporteur on Violence against Women has, in addition, reported on the increase in HIV infections in Rwanda after 1994. UN Doc. E/CN.4/1998/54/Add.1, p. 21.

[162] *R.J. Cook*, Human Rights and Reproductive Self-determination, The American University Law Review 1995, Vol. 44, p. 997.

[163] The feasibility of applying the doctrine of *Drittwirkung* in relation to Article 3 of the European Convention on Human Rights (prohibition of torture and inhumane or degrading treatment or punishment) has already been raised by the Strasbourg organs. See *A. Cassese*, Prohibition of Torture and Inhumane or Degrading Treatment or Punishment, p. 260. For a critical view see *C.A. McKinnon*, Crimes of War, Crimes of Peace, p. 69.

UN Convention on Torture. In the course of the armed conflicts in the former Yugoslavia, most of the different patterns of committing rape mentioned above presuppose the existence of an overall policy, *i.e.*, the involvement of public officials. Also this requirement is consequently fulfilled in the majority of the reported cases.

Nevertheless, I should mention that private torture, *e.g.*, severe and systematic wife beating, has been considered as a subject of regulation in the context of torture and inhuman treatment in a number of the central global and regional human rights instruments.[164] Consequently, the term "torture" may be employed in many connections involving the suffering of a victim, *i.e.*, forced pregnancy.

Finally, another important aspect of the provisions related to the prohibition of torture is whether they ensure any effective protection from the threat of torture. A well-known statement made by the European Court of Human Rights in the *Campbell and Cosans* case illustrates that issue as follows: "(p)rovided it is sufficiently real and immediate, a mere threat of conduct prohibited by Article 3 may in itself conflict with that provision. Thus, to threaten an individual with torture might in some circumstances constitute at least inhumane treatment".[165]

In the light of the above, this author concludes that a clear international standard still does not exist by which to ascertain when rape is to be considered as torture and when it falls short of it. I have therefore found Kelly Askin's proposed definition of torture in the context of "grave breaches" very useful. According to her, the elements of the offence are the following:

> "(1) That the accused committed an act or omission resulting in the infliction of severe physical or mental pain or suffering upon a certain named or described person;
>
> (2) That such person was protected under one or more of the 1949 Geneva Conventions;
>
> (3) That the accused, at the time of such act, had the specific intent to inflict, or cause to be inflicted, severe physical or mental pain or suffering; and
>
> (4) That the act or omission was inflicted for such purposes as obtaining information or a confession, punishment, intimidation or coercion, or for any reason based on discrimination of any kind".[166]

Any act of sexual abuse, which meets the above requirements, would constitute torture and should be prosecuted as a grave breach of the Geneva Conventions.

8.3.2.1.4. Rape as Inhuman Treatment

According to the definitions contained in the various universal and regional treaties and the existing case law of relevance to that subject matter, the category of mis-

---

164 *M.E. Tardu*, The United Nations Convention against Torture and other Cruel, Inhumane or Degrading Treatment or Punishment, p. 306.

165 ECHR, Judgment of 25 February 1982, Ser. A, No. 48, p. 12, § 25.

166 *K.D. Askin*, p. 387.

behaviour called "inhuman treatment" has been described as "more general than that of torture".[167] As to the wording of the expression "inhuman treatment" in the treaties of concern as well as in Article 2 § b of the *ad hoc* Tribunal's Statute, I may establish that, since it is characterised by its vagueness and lack of clarity, there is a considerable freedom for the international supervisory bodies to interpret it widely. There are, therefore, no formal legal obstacles in my view to defining "inhuman treatment" as always covering rape of women.[168] Basically, the difference between torture and inhuman treatment is one of degree.[169] Torture is consequently more severe than inhuman treatment. This is why torture has been described as an aggravated form of inhuman treatment. Rape is, moreover, an act that not only injures women's bodily integrity and health but also their *dignity*. Or the other way around, injuring a woman's dignity constitutes inhuman treatment. In support of that assertion I may refer to a case decided by the European Court of Human Rights, in which it was argued that inhuman treatment should constitute "an assault on precisely that, which is one of the main purposes of Article 3 to protect, namely a person's dignity and physical integrity".[170] Also the HRC in its GC on Article 7 of the ICCPR established that the aim of this particular provision is "to protect both the dignity and the physical and mental integrity of the individual".[171] At the same time, inhuman treatment may be said to be degrading if it humiliates the victim in her/his own or others' eyes.[172] There is nowadays a well-established understanding in the international community that rape and other sexual assaults are not related to sexuality, but to dominance. Needless to say, such acts express an apparent need to humiliate and to degrade the attacked person. It has been argued that forced pregnancy has been used in some situations (in the context of the armed conflicts in the former Yugoslavia) as a weapon to further humiliate the rape victim by forcing her to bear the child/ren of the perpetrator.[173] Consequently, such behaviour constitutes inhuman and degrading treatment. Also the European Commission on Human Rights emphasised in the *Greek* case, when explaining what constitutes degrading treatment, that it is an act which "grossly humiliates the victim before others or drives him to act against his will or conscience". The Commission went on in its reasoning and stated that: "(a)ll torture must be inhuman and degrading treatment and inhuman treatment also degrading. The notion of inhuman treatment covers at least such treatment as deliberately causes severe suffering, mental or physical, which, in the particular situation, is unjustifiable".[174]

---

[167] *A. Cassese*, Prohibition of Torture and Inhumane or Degrading Treatment or Punishment, p. 229.

[168] *M.C. Bassiouni*, The Law of the International Criminal Court for The Former Yugoslavia, p. 564.

[169] *I. Cameron & M.K. Eriksson*, p. 52.

[170] *Tyrer v. UK*, Judgment of 25 April 1978, Ser. A, No. 26, p. 16, § 33.

[171] HRC, GC No. 20 on Article 7, HRI/GEN/1/Rev.1, 29 July 1994, p. 30.

[172] *Campbell and Cosans v. UK*, supra, note 165, pp. 13–14, §§ 30–31.

[173] UN Doc. E/CN.4/1998/54, § 7.

[174] *Cyprus v. Turkey*, Report of the European Commission on Human Rights adopted on 5 November YB, 1969, Vol. 12, p. 186, § 2. The Commission has confirmed this standpoint in several of the cases considered by it thereafter. See *A. Cassese*, ibid., p. 229.

Along with the above it should also be remembered that one of the important purposes of humanitarian law is to protect the civilian population on the basis of humanity. Also this speaks in favour of an extensive interpretation of the wording "inhuman treatment", *i.e.*, as comprising rape and forced pregnancy. Thus, these crimes constitute clear violations of the ban on practices against human dignity. As emphasised by Mr. Kushalani rape "is a grave injury to a woman's dignity and would definitely be considered as inhuman treatment, expressly denounced under the Convention" (the Fourth Geneva Convention).[175] Furthermore, the 1977 ICRC Commentary clarifies that "inhuman treatment" does not mean only physical injury or injury to health, but relates also to measures which "caused grave injury to (a person's) human dignity" and, therefore may, conceivably be considered as inhuman treatment. As to the interpretation of the phrase "wilfully causing great suffering" in Article 147 of the Fourth Geneva Convention, it is spelled out as encompassing "punishment, in revenge or for some other motive, perhaps out of pure sadism... (that) can quite legitimately be held to cover moral suffering also".[176] Hence, "inhuman treatment" may embrace "moral suffering" as well. In the context of the armed conflict in Bosnia-Herzegovina, arguments have been put forward on the basis of its ethnic character that also Article 85(4(c)) of Additional Protocol I, which prohibits "inhuman and degrading practices involving outrages upon personal dignity, based on racial discrimination", may be applicable in many instances.[177]

In certain cases, for the same reasons that were mentioned earlier, acts of rape could also be covered by Article 2 § c of the *ad hoc* Tribunal's Statute.[178] Opponents to this view have presented arguments that are mainly based on the principle of legality, requiring that punishable criminal acts shall be explicitly mentioned in the legal text to be applied. Still, the list of what is included under the term "grave breaches" is drafted in broad, general terms and it is, therefore, as I have shown earlier, suitable for extensive interpretations, which can hardly be said to be contrary to the principle of legality.

There are yet other examples of authoritative statements, which have been made by international organs and which support my position that rape indeed constitutes inhuman treatment. As early as 1958 the ICRC was of the opinion that the expression "inhuman treatment", as referred to in the definition of grave breaches of international humanitarian law, should be interpreted in the light of Article 27 of the Fourth Geneva Convention, *i.e.*, to cover rape.[179] Moreover, the Strasbourg supervisory bodies for the protection of human rights have through the application of a dynamic approach to treaty interpretation in their case law ruled that rape commit-

---

[175] *Y. Kushalani*, p. 44.

[176] 1977 ICRC Commentary, pp. 598–599.

[177] Helsinki Watch, War Crimes in Bosnia-Herzegovina, Vol. II, New York 1993, p. 20.

[178] Prohibition against rape and other sexual assaults, when deemed as wilful injury to the person, is also contained in the common Article 3 to the four 1949 Geneva Conventions and Article 4 § 2 of Additional Protocol II. These provisions are, however, applicable in armed conflicts of a non-international character. For a more extensive discussion on this matter see *K.D. Askin*, pp. 313–314.

[179] *T. Meron*, Rape as Crime under International Humanitarian Law, p. 426; *D.Q. Thomas & R.E. Ralph*, Rape in war, challenging the tradition of impunity, SAIS Review 1994, p. 41; *K.D. Askin*, p. 314.

ted during interrogation procedures at detention centres constitutes "inhuman treatment", a clear infringement of Article 3 of the European Convention on Human Rights. The arguments have been based on one of the main purposes of Article 3, namely to protect a person's dignity and physical integrity.[180]

So, bearing in mind that Article 27 of the Fourth Geneva Convention represents a customary rule of international law and the fact that in the view of some representatives of the contemporary international law doctrine, among them the Finnish scholar Lauri Hannikainen, "in international law rape and enforced prostitution are prohibited in peremptory terms",[181] *i.e.*, they belong to the *ius cogens* norms of contemporary international law, it is only reasonable to maintain that the prohibition of rape and forced prostitution has to be observed by all members of the international community and in all circumstances. Moreover, this type of violation as a grave breach of international humanitarian law falls under universal jurisdiction. In support of his statement, Mr. Hannikainen refers to the fact that ill treatment of civilian populations "was included in the definitions of 'war crimes' and 'crimes against humanity' in the Charter of the Nuremberg Tribunal and in other relevant documents of the Second World War settlement".[182] Professor Tomuschat has reasoned that the Statute of the *ad hoc* Tribunal for the former Yugoslavia "proceeds from the assumption that all the categories of criminal acts it lists, which are taken from the relevant international treaties on humanitarian law, have passed into the corpus of general international law and are thus binding on every State, including anyone of its nationals".[183] Despite this apparent obligation for the members of the international community, I should again point to the fact that all parties to the conflict in the former Yugoslavia are subject to the obligations under the 1949 Geneva Conventions and their Additional Protocols implying among other things the prosecution of persons, against whom a *prima facie* accusation of grave breaches has been made.

Furthermore, the eminent publicist Professor Meron has in two essays[184] on international humanitarian law demonstrated the emerging universal consensus in both the international law doctrine and in the view of the majority of states to consider rape a grave breach of international humanitarian law. This very strong international support for an extensive interpretation of the notion "grave breaches" as stipulated in Article 2 of the *ad hoc* Tribunal's Statute to cover the crime rape cannot and should not be ignored.

However, it remains to be seen how the *ad hoc* Tribunal itself will interpret the term "grave breaches" of humanitarian law. This is no doubt dependent upon the cases referred to it. There are many reasons to be optimistic about the future activities of the *ad hoc* Tribunal. It is encouraging to note that the Tribunal seems to be

---

[180] *M. Nowak*, CCPR Commentary, p. 131.

[181] *L. Hannikainen*, pp. 452, 510 and 671.

[182] *L. Hannikainen*, p. 668.

[183] *C. Tomuschat*, A System of International Criminal Prosecution is Taking Shape, The Review 1993, No. 50, p. 63.

[184] *T. Meron*, Rape as Crime under International Humanitarian Law, pp. 424, 428 and War Crimes in Yugoslavia and the Development of International Law, AJIL 1994, Vol. 88, p. 84.

prepared to apply a liberal approach to treaty interpretation – one of the many grounds for the indictment of all 21 individuals, based on the Geneva Conventions of 1949 in accordance with Article 2 of the Statute by the *ad hoc* Tribunal on 13 February 1995, is "forcible sexual intercourse" causing great suffering.[185] By employing the word "forcible" emphasis has again been put on the important element of the definition of violence against women, namely the use of a coercive form of power in order to compel the victim to do something that he or she would not otherwise do. Another positive feature is that the Tribunal in its rules of procedure makes use of the very broad wording "crimes of sexual assault". Rape is only one category of it. Moreover, the *Gagović and others* case, which is pending before the Tribunal deals with prosecution for rape as covered by the definition of "grave breaches" set out in Article 2 of the Statute. Recently, Hazim Delić was convicted by the ICTY of a grave breach of the Geneva Conventions for having raped two women on several occasions. He was sentenced to 20 years' imprisonment. In this case rape was specifically recognised as torture.[186] The Trial Chamber of the ICTY ruled, in addition, in the *Furundžija* case that rape could qualify under either its Article 2 jurisdiction or its Article 3 jurisdiction. Anto Furundžija was in consequence convicted of torture and outrages upon personal dignity, including rape. He was sentenced to 10 years' imprisonment.[187]

It is apparent from the discussion above that the assertion that rape when committed under certain circumstances, *e.g.*, multiple and repetitive rapes or gang rapes,[188]

---

[185] CC/PIO/004-E, p. 3. See Indictment No.2, §§ 22.8–22.10 of 13 February 1995; Indictment No. 3, §§ 4.2–4.4 of 13 February 1995. The indictment affirms that forcible sexual intercourse can be, among other things, torture under Article 5(f) and a grave breach of the Geneva Conventions (torture under Article 2(b)).

[186] *Prosecutor v. Delalić and Others*, case No. IT-96-21-T, Judgment of 16 November 1998.

[187] The Tribunal defined rape in this case in the following terms:"(i) the sexual penetration, however slight: (a) of the vagina or anus of the victim by the penis of the perpetrator or any other object used by the perpetrator, or (b) of the mouth of the victim by the penis of the perpetrator; (ii) by coercion or force or threat of force against the victim or third person. *Prosecutor v. Furundžija*, Judgment § 185. In the Nicolić Rule 61 decision (*Prosecutor v. Nicolić*, case No. IT-94-2-R61, 20 October 1995) the Trial Chamber of the ICTY invited the Prosecutor to amend the indictment to add charges of rape and other forms of sexual assault "either as a crime against humanity or as a grave breaches or war crimes" (§ 33). The Chamber took the position, in other words, that rape and other forms of sexual assault may fall within the definition of torture.

[188] See the investigations conducted by Helsinki Watch in War Crimes in Bosnia-Herzegovina, Vol. II, pp. 184, 214, 242, 345. The same organization has, furthermore, identified several members of a Bosnian Croat paramilitary group known as the "Fire Horses", who are accused of having engaged in a gang-rape of five Serbian women at Posavska Mahala. After the report of the crime, the Bosnian Croat police arrested the alleged rapists but then released them without prosecuting them. A well documented case of gang-rape is also presented as regards hundreds of women during early May 1992 in Doboj. Helsinki Watch, Prosecute Now!, pp. 13–14; 20–21. See also *M. Brandt*, citing international observers' report: "In southeastern Bosnia, Serbian forces use rape as one of many methods of torturing and humiliating women. The women are sexually mistreated during their detention, and many are gang-raped on one or more occasions", note 41, p. 1421. *C.N. Niarchos*, p. 657.

Several counts in the indictment concerning the *Gagović and others v. the Prosecutor* case relate to gang rape, *e.g.*, counts 1–12 (§§ 5.3, 6.4, 7.7), counts 36–55 (§§ 9.10, 9.20). Gang rape has apparently very frequent taken place in Rwanda during the genocide. *E. Richter-Lyonette*, p. 6. See also *Prosecutor v. Akayesu*, Judgment §§ 416–460; UN Doc. E/CN.4/1998/54, pp. 15–16 and UN Doc. E/CN.4/1998/54/Add.1, p. 10.

public rapes in front of a whole village and rapes committed in particularly sadistic[189] and brutal ways with the conscious intention to inflict a maximum of humiliation on the victims, their family and on the community they belong to,[190] constitutes torture as well as always inhuman and degrading treatment, is well-founded. Consideration should also be taken to the victim's age. Thus, according to evidential material in regard to cases of rape in the territory of the former Yugoslavia as well as in Rwanda, rape has encompassed the entire age spectrum including children. The Commission of Experts came, *e.g.*, to the conclusion, based on its investigative mission in the former Yugoslavia, that during the armed conflict "young women and virgins are targets for rape, along with prominent members of the community".[191] Moreover, the information received by the Commission indicates that girls as young as 7 years old and women as old as 65 have been raped while in captivity.[192]

I would like to point, furthermore, to the fact that also men have been sexually abused in the course of the armed conflict in the former Yugoslavia. Forceful castration[193] under humiliating circumstances, beating on the genitals as well as rape of men by men have left both physical and psychological scars on many. Paragraph 206 of the *Tadić* judgment illustrates this form of sexual violence well.[194]

---

[189] In Rwanda some women and girls were, *e.g.*, macheted and then raped immediately afterwards. UN Doc. E/CN.4/Sub.2/1996/26, § 10; *E. Richter-Lyonette*, p. 8.

Furthermore, in Rwanda during the genocide, as well as in the course of the conflicts in the former Yugoslavia, women and girls have been sexually abused with objects such as guns, broken bottles, with stones, with branches from trees and bushes etc. This kind of extremely brutal rape, when various objects have been used to cause pain, is in my view undoubtedly torture.

[190] Women, who have been interviewed by Helsinki Watch and the Women's Rights Project have referred to cases when rapists have openly stated their intention forcibly to impregnate women as "a haunting reminder of the rape and an intensification of the trauma it inflicts". Helsinki Watch, War Crimes in Bosnia-Herzegovina, Vol. II, p. 21. See also Helsinki Watch, War Crimes in Bosnia-Herzegovina: U.N. Cease-Fire Won't Help Banja Luka, 1994, pp.13–14. Here belong also the traumatic experiences of women interviewed by the Special Rapporteur on violence against women who have been forced to have intercourse with their own sons. UN Doc. E/CN.4/1998/54/Add.1, p. 20.

[191] See also *M.P. Scharf*, Balkan Justice, p. 168.

[192] UN Doc. S/1994/674, pp. 55, 59. The Croatian representative stated during CEDAW's 279th meeting on 31 January 1995, when reviewing a report on exceptional basis from Croatia on the situation of women there, that, according to documentation gathered from victims, rapes are committed against females as young as six and as old as 80. However, the most frequent rape victims are teenage minors "treated like slaves" in brothel camps. *J. Kuzmanović*, Legacies of Invisibility. Past Silence, Present Violence Against Women in the Former Yugoslavia, in Women's rights, human rights, J. Peters & A. Wolper (eds.), p. 58. Also in Rwanda girls as young as five years old have been raped. UN Doc. E/CN.4/Sub.2/1996/26, § 10. *C.N. Narchos*, p. 658; *K.D. Askin*, p. 319. The Trial Chamber of the ICTY reviewed in the *Tadić* case acts of sexual violence that have taken place in the Omarska camp. It quoted the testimony of a medical worker, who mentioned among other things the rape of girls being 12 years of age. *Prosecutor v. Tadić*, case No. IT-94-1-T, Judgment of 7 May 1997, § 175.

[193] For references to cases see in Helsinki Watch, War Crimes in Bosnia-Herzegovina, Vol. II, pp. 99, 186–187.

[194] *Prosecutor v. Tadić*, Judgment of 7 May 1997. See also the indictment of *Jelisić and Cesić, Brčko*, case No. IT-95-10, of 21 July 1995, amended on 3 March 1998 (§ 32). This part of the indictment refers to the fact that Cesić forced two Muslim brothers "to beat each other and perform sexual acts on each other in the presence of others, causing them great humiliation and degradation". See, in addition, the

Mistreatment of that kind constitutes clearly torture. Like other victims of war, men who have been sexually abused suffer from post-traumatic stress and their sexuality is often disturbed and by that it is reasonable to argue that their reproductive freedom is blurred. Even though the prohibition of rape of a homosexual character is not specifically referred to in the relevant provisions, violence of that type should equally be condemned and prosecuted on the basis of the non-discrimination principle.[195] There are consequently no legal obstacles for adopting such an expansive definition of rape in international law.

Finally, I have arrived at the conclusion that there are undoubtedly difficulties in drawing a meaningful distinction between torture and inhuman treatment[196] in the context of rape. An act of rape may constitute torture as well as inhuman and degrading treatment. It has been argued, therefore, that the strict upholding of such a distinction is unnecessary.[197] Similar arguments have been put forward as regards the delineation of a precise borderline between torture and the other forms of ill-treatment in the context of human rights law. The fact that these misbehaviours are simultaneously prohibited in absolute terms in the relevant provisions of the human

---

*Miljković and Others* indictment, case No. IT-95-9, of 21 July 1995 (count 36). One of the accused persons, Todorović was charged with instigating, ordering, and committing a grave breach of the Geneva Conventions, since he forced two men to perform sexual acts upon each other in the presence of several other prisoners and guards.

[195] In the view of Rhonda Copelon rape of men by men should be considered as crime of gender since it is "designed to humiliate through feminization". *R. Copelon*, Gendered War Crimes, p. 212. See on that particular aspect of the issue of sexual assaults the results of the investigations of the Commission of Experts, UN Doc. S/1994/674, p. 56; *K.D. Askin*, pp. 315 and 318; *M.C. Bassiouni*, The Law of the International Criminal Court for The Former Yugoslavia, p. 566, note 182, *M.C. Bassiouni & M. McCormick*, pp. 17–18 and p. 20.

It has been estimated that during the war approximately 4,000 men from Croatia were sexually abused. *G. Rebić*, Silent victims of a pathological aggressor, Večernji List, March 7, 1996, p. 6. Such incidents have, however, probably occurred also in relation to men belonging to the other groups involved in the conflict. It seems that this type of sexual violence has not been recorded in history.

[196] Judge Antonio Cassese, the former President of the ICTY, has in the context of Article 3 of the European Convention on Human Rights and by taking present-day conditions into account submitted the following interpretation of the provision: "a) neither in the case of "inhumane treatment or punishment" nor in that of "degrading treatment or punishment" would any intent to cause suffering be required; b) in the former case, however, a certain level of mental or physical suffering would be necessary and, in addition, would need to be out of proportion to the security and other considerations behind the "inhumane" measure or behaviour; c) in the case of "degrading treatment or punishment", a high level of debasement or humiliation would be needed; d) as for torture proper, it would be markedly distinct from the other two categories, as it would hinge on a specific purpose (that of extracting information or a confession, of punishing, intimidating or coercing, or of wilfully discriminating) and would in addition require a degree of mental or physical suffering higher than that needed for "inhumane treatment or punishment". *A. Cassese*, p. 247.

[197] One alternative way of establishing the different features of the two conducts of behaviour would be to achieve a wide consensus on a list of acts that would be considered to fall within the term "torture". This suggestion has been opposed by the UN's Special Rapporteur on Torture, Mr. Rodley, who argued that: "...a juridical definition cannot depend upon a catalogue of horrific practices; for it to do so would simply provide a challenge to the ingenuity of the torturers, not a viable legal prohibition". *N. Rodley*, The Treatment of Prisoners under International Law, Oxford 1987, p. 73.

rights conventions has been accentuated.[198] Still, concern has been expressed in the literature about the tendency to categorise rape under the heading of cruel, inhuman and degrading treatment rather than torture. In the view of Ariane Brunet and Stephanie Rousseau since "rape gives rise to and is accompanied by all sorts of physical and mental injuries", this crime should not be considered to be anything other than torture.[199]

Since Article 2 of the *ad hoc* Tribunal's Statute prohibits both kinds of mistreatment under the term "grave breach" of international humanitarian law, this should be sufficient for the successful prosecution of acts of rape, forced pregnancy and other sexual assaults that are considered grave breaches of international humanitarian law. Such a perspective is of importance not only from the practical point of view, but it has a moral dimension as well since it legitimises claims that all rape in war, not only mass or genocidal rape, be understood as torture and/or inhuman treatment. This author agrees at the same time with Kelly Askin that there might be some disadvantages to classify *all* rape as torture. In her view rape is "a recognised crime in and of itself, so classifying it *solely* as torture would obscure the gender specific nature of the crime. Also, the elements of torture are often more difficult to establish than rape".[200]

Defendants who have committed sexual violence in the context of the armed conflicts in the former Yugoslavia have been charged by the ICTY with "torture" in cases of multiple and repetitive instances of rape causing serious bodily harm or suffering and in situations where there is no serious physical injury, they have been charged with "inhuman treatment".

Of special relevance to this study with focus on reproductive freedom are crimes which affect the reproductive capacity of a person either by becoming pregnant against one's will or losing the capacity to reproduce as a result of sexual assault.[201] In other words, forced pregnancy, as well as forcible miscarriage/abortion (*i.e.*, rape which results in the termination of current pregnancy),[202] should also be considered as the equivalent of torture and given the status of "grave breaches" within the meaning of the Geneva Conventions.[203] The expressed intent to make women pregnant is a severe form of "psychological torture".[204] The unwanted pregnancy is, in

---

198 *L. Hannikainen*, p. 508, n. 202. On the other hand, Mr. Hannikainen himself has convincingly argued that not all inhumane or degrading treatment or punishment is actually prohibited in a peremptory manner. What is important to this study is that the same scholar considers rape of women as a brutal and cruel form of treatment and as such prohibited in peremptory terms. Ibid., p. 509.

199 *A. Brunet & S. Rousseau*, p. 45.

200 *K.D. Askin*, p. 321. For the opposite view see *R. Copelon*, Gendered War Crimes, p. 203.

201 Various unlawful medical procedures would be covered by the later offence, as well as repeated gang rapes with the result in forced sterilisation etc. See *K.D. Askin*, p. 401. Gagović was, *e.g.*, charged by the ICTY with a grave breach of the Geneva Conventions (*i.e.*, wilfully causing great suffering) on the basis that one of the victims of sexual violence can no longer have children. *Prosecutor v. Gagović and Others*, case No. IT-96-23, count 30.

202 *K.D. Askin*, pp. 320, 384 and 399.

203 For a similar opinion see *K.D. Askin*, p. 384.

204 *R. Copelon*, p. 202.

addition, a constant reminder of the terrifying violence that the woman in question has been exposed to. It is maybe not surprising that children born as a product of violence were "despised"[205] and often abandoned.

The reproductive elements of a crime can alternatively, according to Professor Bassiouni and other scholars, as in the case of forced pregnancy, be considered as a separate crime, *i.e.*, a crime in itself, because "the harm it causes is qualitatively and quantitatively different from that cased by sexual violence alone".[206] I shall discuss this aspect of violation of reproductive freedom below in connection with deliberations on the terms "ethnic cleansing" and "genocide". Nevertheless, it can be noted already here that such practices have occurred during the conflicts both in the former Yugoslavia and in Rwanda.[207]

Forced pregnancy and enforced sterilisation have been as mentioned earlier endorsed as separate war crimes[208] in Article 8 of the ICC Statute, and I shall in the following explore the notion of "war crimes".

### *8.3.2.2. Violations of the Laws or Customs of War*

#### 8.3.2.2.1. General Remarks

War crimes have historically been defined as violations of the laws and customs of war.[209] Among the earliest international documents[210] which contain a list of acts

---

[205] *E.A. Kohn*, p. 216. A UN team has presented a report in which 119 pregnancies from rape were identified in Bosnia-Herzegovina. The majority of those pregnancies, *i.e.*, 88 ended, however, in abortion. Many of the women who have left Bosnia too late to have an abortion have, however, abandoned their unwanted children. *D. Aydelott*, p. 625; *E.A. Kohn*, p. 216.

[206] *M.C. Bassiouni*, The Law of the International Criminal Tribunal for the Former Yugoslavia, p. 565, note 175. See in addition *D. Blatt*, p. 855; *K.D. Askin*, p. 384.

Some of the indicted persons according to the *Gagović and others v. the Prosecutor* case, have expressly emphasised that they want to impregnate the victims with children of the perpetrator's ethnicity. Drago Kunarac and Zoran Vuković, *e.g.*, told FWS-48 that she would now give birth to "Serb babies". Indictment, counts 36–55, § 9.3. The same is valid for the accused Dragan Zelenović. Indictment, ibid., § 9.13.

[207] *E. Richter-Lyonette*, p. 8; Prosecuting Human Rights Violations Against Women: The International Criminal Tribunals on The Former Yugoslavia and Rwanda, paper presented by representatives of the Jacob Blaustein Institute for the Advancement of Human Rights and The American Jewish Committee at the NGO Forum in Beijing 1995, p. 3.

[208] The Women's Caucus was in particular successful in its lobbying efforts to make delegations more supportive of the inclusion of gender-specific provisions in the treaty. Unanimous agreement was in consequence achieved during the preparatory work on the Statute in favour of specifying a provision concerning gender and sexual violence, *e.g.*, in the context of war crimes.

[209] It has been maintained that in "the widest sense" the notion of "war crimes" may include crimes against humanity as well as crimes against peace. *C. Meindersma*, Violations of Common Article 3 of the Geneva Conventions as Violations of the Laws or Customs of War under Article 3 of the Statute of the International Criminal Tribunal for the Former Yugoslavia, NILR 1995, p. 379, note 11.

[210] One of the first serious attempts on the national level to codify the law of war by providing comprehensive rules (including rape by a belligerent as a war crime) for the entire range of land warfare was the United States Lieber Code of 1863, *i.e.*, the Instructions for the Government of Armies of the United States in the Fields promulgated as General Orders No. 100 by President Lincoln in April 24, 1863, Washington D.C. See *A. de Zayas*, An International Criminal Court, NJIL 1994, Vols. 61/62, p. 272;

recognised as war crimes, mention should be made of The Hague Conventions of July 29, 1899 (No. II)[211] and of October 18, 1907 (No. IV).[212] In addition to these treaties, the Geneva Conventions of 1929 and 1949 comprise regulations of significance to the subject matter of this study. The first two conventions provide the foundation of what is internationally known as "the law of Hague". The main aim of these agreements, as expressed in their preambles is to: "revise the laws and general customs of war/... /for the purpose of modifying their severity as far as possible" in order to "diminish the evils of war so far as military necessities permit". In concrete terms, "the law of Hague" regulates the behaviour of belligerents in war, for example, the limitations on means and methods in the conduct of warfare. However, the protection of the civilian population as a basic principle was not specifically included. The protection of the victims of armed conflicts became the concern of the latter law, *i.e.*, "the law of Geneva". These factual circumstances have contributed to the division between the two sets of rules. However, with time these "two initial tracks"[213] have more or less merged into one. Moreover, a number of important steps have since that time been taken towards the punishment of war criminals. The legal concept of "war crimes" was further developed at the end of the Second World War in a more flexible manner in that a broad definition was introduced.[214] War crimes were perpetrated in all the countries occupied by Germany as well as on the High Seas. They were committed not only in every conceivable form of cruelty and horror, but also on a scale which never before had been experienced in the history of mankind. It is, therefore, not surprising that the International Military Tribunal, established for the trial of the Second World War offenders, decided to deal quite generally with the question of war crimes. Against this background the most serious war crimes were enumerated in article 6(b) of the Charter (hereinafter referred to as the London Charter) annexed to the Agreement and signed on 8 August 1945 by the Governments of France, the Soviet Union, the United Kingdom of Great Britain and Northern Ireland and the USA concerning the

---

*F. Kalshoven*, p. 13; *L. Doswald-Beck*, p. 252; *Y. Khushalani*, pp. 5–7; *G. Abi-Saab*, Non-International Armed Conflicts, in International Dimensions of Humanitarian Law, p. 217; *C. Meindersma*, p. 382, note 29. For a historical review on rules prohibiting the use of certain means of warfare see *R. Bierzanek*, War Crimes: History and Definition, in International Criminal Law, Vol. III, M.C. Bassiouni (ed.), New York 1987, pp. 21–41; *M.C. Bassiouni*, The Law of The International Criminal Tribunal for The Former Yugoslavia, pp. 576–579; *K.D. Askin*, p. 323.

211 T.S. No. 403.

212 T.S. No. 539.

213 *A. Eide*, The laws of war and human rights, p. 678. See also *I. Detter De Lupis*, The Law of War, p. 129.

214 The definition of war crimes previous to the Nuremberg Charter has been considered as narrower in the sense that it reflected the understanding of war crimes as constituting violations of the laws of war, *i.e.*, the laws of war are limited in application to specific technical methods in the use of weaponry, etc., or to specific situations. *L.S. Sunga*, Individual Responsibility in International Law for Serious Human Rights Violations, p. 26. It has, however, been maintained that the traditional perception of war crime from the very beginning implied illegitimate violence and the rights of prisoners of war as well. *I. Detter De Lupis*, op. cit. , p. 355.

creation of the International Military Tribunal in order to prosecute and punish the major war criminals of the European Axis Powers,[215] as follows:

> "**war crimes**: namely, violations of the laws or customs of war. Such violations shall include, but not be limited to, murder, ill-treatment or deportation to slave labour or for any other purpose of civilian population of or in occupied territory, murder or ill-treatment of prisoners of war or persons on the sea, killing of hostages, plunder of public or private property, wanton destruction of cities, towns or villages or devastation not justified by military necessity".

Provisions similar to the London Charter are found in the Charter of the International Military Tribunal for the Far East.[216] According to Article 5 (b) of the Charter, the Tokyo Tribunal shall have the power to try and punish war criminals that are charged with offences of conventional war crimes "namely, violations of the laws or customs of war". Of importance to this study is to note that while rape was ignored by the International Tribunal at Nuremberg, it was actually prosecuted in Tokyo as a war crime. Admiral Toyoda was accused of committing war crimes by tolerating, for instance, acts of rape.[217] Rape was in other words not treated as a crime for which the accused would be separately charged. During the Sino-Japanese War and the Second World War, about 200,000 Korean women and women from other nations were recruited or coerced and transported by the Japanese military to the so-called "comfort stations", where they were used as sex slaves.[218] The

---

[215] UNTS, Vol. 82, p. 279. The London Charter defines three categories of crimes falling within the jurisdiction of the Nuremberg Tribunal: crimes against peace, war crimes and crimes against humanity. For a comprehensive historical background of the drafting of the charter see *M. Lippman*, pp. 20–27.

[216] Tokyo Charter for the International Military Tribunal for the Far-East of January 1946, Department of State Bulletin US, Vol. XIV, No. 349, p. 362 et seq., TIAS No. 1589. On the legal contribution of the Nuremberg and Tokyo Tribunals see *B.V.A. Röling & A. Cassese*, The Tokyo Trial and Beyond, Oxford 1993, pp. 89–93.

[217] See *T. Meron*, Rape as a Crime Under International Humanitarian Law, p. 426. The Netherlands conducted, furthermore, trials which dealt with the crimes committed by the Japanese military during the World War II. A court in Batavia (which is now Jakarta) found a number of Japanese military defendants guilty of war crimes for acts including rape. UN Doc. E/CN.4/Sub.2/1998/13, § 62 ; *A. Utsumi*, How the Violence Against Women Were Dealt With in War Crimes Trials, in Common Grounds, I.L. Sajor (ed.), p. 193.

[218] From 1932 to 1945, hundreds of thousands of young women and girls served as "comfort women" or sex slaves to the Japanese military. Lured initially by the promise of work as nursing aid or cooks, these young women came mostly from Korea but also from China, the Philippines, Indonesia, Malaysia and the Netherlands. Instead of nursing and cooking, they found themselves to be prisoners and forced to "serve" 30–50 solders per day. When the war ended, most of the women were abandoned in caves where they were bombed, forced to commit suicide, murdered or killed aboard ships on their way home. First in 1980 a 56 year old professor from the Women's University in Seoul (Yoon Jung Ok) raised the issue, but publicity was given to it first in 1988 at an international conference on sex tourism. Today about 168 victims have come forth. The Korean Council for Women has demanded that the Japanese Government punish the criminals and pay legal reparation as well as revise Japanese textbooks. *S. Friedman*, Reparation, Forum '95, September 3, 1995, p. 1. See also Asia News, Empire of the Sun, Asian Student Association, Issue 3, September 1992, p. 8; *E.A. Kohn*, p. 205; *D. Aydelott*, pp. 594–597; *U. Dolgopol*, Women's Voices, Women's Pain, HRQ 1995, Vol. 17, pp. 127–154; *K.D. Askin*, pp. 62–85; UN Doc. E/CN.4/Sub.2/1998/13, § 6.

Japanese Government has not yet fully compensated the victims and not fully admitted its culpability.[219] Its position on the compensation issue has been to argue that all such claims were settled when Japan paid reparation to countries like China and the Philippines, which it occupied during the war. A number of international and national NGOs claimed at the World Conference on Human Rights in Vienna 1993 that it was this continued reluctance to face up to its war crimes that disqualified the country from obtaining a permanent seat in the UN Security Council. Among the most generally mooted countries for permanent membership of a reformed composition of the Security Council after the end of the Cold War and better reflecting geopolitical and geo-economic realities are Japan along with Germany, India, Indonesia, Brazil, Nigeria, Egypt and Mexico. Japan as an economic power, and the second largest contributor to the UN budget, is most widely recognised as a strong possible candidate.[220] However, Prime Minister T. Murayama extended on 18th July 1995 his country's apologies to all women forced into prostitution to serve Japan's armed forces before and during World War II. Supporters inaugurated at the same time a private fund for the victims.[221]

---

[219] Professor Yuji Iwasawa submitted in an oral presentation on 28 May 1998 at the ILA conference in Taipei that recently a Japanese court had awarded compensation to Korean women and that the decision was among others based on breach of international law. Nevertheless, in October 1998, Swedish newspapers reported that a court in Tokyo has rejected the requests for compensation from 46 Phillipino women who were subjected to sexual slavery during WW II. SvD, 10 October 1998, p. 7. See also UN Doc. E/CN.4/1998/54, pp. 8–9.

[220] *A. Roberts & B. Kingsbury*, p. 41; *M. Bertrand*, p. 431 and *P. Wilenski*, p. 442.

[221] The Government appointed nine prominent Japanese as executors of a special fund and 20 others as "petitioners" to collect donations to compensate victimised women from Korea, the Philippines, Indonesia, China and the Netherlands. Of an estimated 200,000 "comfort women", as the victims have come to be known, about 1,000 are believed to be still alive.

The Japanese delegation to the Beijing Conference in 1995 declared on 5 September that an "Asian Peace and Friendship Fund for Women" has been established, which is meant among others to express the Japanese people's atonement to former wartime "comfort women", reflecting Japan's "sincere remorse for its past history". For other official statements on the part of the Government, see also Report of the Special Rapporteur on Violence against Women on the mission to the Democratic People's Republic of Korea, the Republic of Korea and Japan on the issue of military sexual slavery in wartime, UN Doc. E/CN.4/1996/53/Add.1, § 131.

During the UN's Sub-Commission's 49th session (in 1997) the question of crimes committed during the Second World War by the Japanese army was brought up again and the speakers noted that the Japanese Government's position has changed, note of the "deep regret" expressed by the Government was taken, but it was at the same time emphasised that the Japanese Government had still not assumed its responsibility in this matter. Ms Gay McDougal was entrusted with the task of completing the study of systematic rape etc. for submission to the Sub-Commission at its 50th session in 1998. The appendix of her report (UN Doc. E/CN.4/Sub.2/1998/13) comprises an in depth analysis of the legal liability of the Government of Japan for "comfort women stations" established during the second World War. See also *M.J. Dennis*, The Fifty-Second Session of The UN Commission on Human Rights, AJIL 1997, Vol. 91, p. 168; *Y. Matsui*, History Cannot Be Erased, Women Can No Longer Be Silenced, in Common Grounds, I.L. Sajor (ed.), pp. 26–33; *Y. Tanaka*, Rape and War: The Japanese Experience, in Common Grounds, *op. cit.*, pp. 148–186; *A. Utsumi*, pp. 187–197; *R. Nishino*, The Comfort Women Issue and Responses of the Japanese Government, in Common Grounds, *op. cit.*, pp. 214–225.

Shortly after the Nuremberg and Tokyo trials a more extensive definition of the term war crimes was incorporated in Article II, § 1 (b) of the Law No. 10 promulgated by the Control Council for Germany:

> "*war crimes*: Atrocities or offences against persons or property constituting violations of the laws or customs of war, including, but not limited to, murder, ill treatment or deportation to slave labour or for any other purpose, of civilian population from occupied territory, murder or ill treatment of prisoners of war or persons on the seas, killing of hostages, plunder of public or private property, wanton destruction of cities, towns or villages, or devastation not justified by military necessity".

Here it is important to stress that the London Charter, the Tokyo Charter and the Control Council Law No. 10 were adopted at very short time intervals between them for the major purpose of punishing war criminals, who had committed offences before, during and after the Second World War.[222]

A modern conception of war crimes comprises according to the prominent scholars Professor McDougal and Professor Reisman the following:

> "War crimes are violations, by civilians or military personnel, of the international law of war. They include crimes against the peace, crimes against humanity and violations of the rules of conduct of hostilities, treatment of civilians and prisoners of war and belligerent occupation of enemy territory".[223]

Both writers observe, however, that although every violation would constitute a war crime, according to the recent developments in treaty law, a distinction has been made between "grave breaches" and other breaches of international humanitarian law. As already mentioned, much of the contemporary law on war crimes is to be found in the provisions of The Hague Conventions, in the Geneva Conventions of 1949 and to some extent in the provisions of the First Additional Protocol of 1977. It must be born in mind that even though Article 2 of the Statute of the *ad hoc* Tribunal for the former Yugoslavia does not explicitly mention the grave breaches stipulated in the latter document, several of them are to be considered as violations of the laws and customs of war.

War crimes can also be comprised in customary rules of war, which have been developed over centuries and are not contained in the above mentioned interna-

---

[222] I may observe that there is indeed an important difference in the language used in the three documents. Law No. 10, which was issued on 20 December 1945, omits the phrase "before and during the war" contained in the London Charter, *i.e.*, the previous law is applicable to crimes committed after the war as well. Furthermore, one important purpose of Law No. 10 was to create a uniform legal basis in Germany for the prosecution of war criminals and other offenders, except those who were dealt with by the International Military Tribunal. For the text of the law see Official Gazette of the Control Council for Germany, No. 3, Berlin 31 January 1946.

[223] *M.S. McDougal & W.M. Reisman*, International Law in Contemporary Perspective, The Public Order of the World Community, Cases and Materials, Mineola 1981, p. 1042.

tional documents. Nevertheless, there are still some problems in regard to the law applicable in non-international armed conflicts, since doubts as to the existence of any body of customary international law,[224] which includes the concept of war crimes, applicable in such conflicts have been expressed.

8.3.2.2.2. War Crimes in the Context of the *Ad Hoc* Tribunal's Statute

Article 3 of the Statute of the *ad hoc* Tribunal refers to violations of the laws and custom of international humanitarian law and gives examples of such violations as follows:

> "The International Tribunal shall have the power to prosecute persons violating the laws or customs of war. Such violations shall include, but not be limited to:
>
> a) employment of poisonous weapons or other weapons calculated to cause unnecessary suffering;
>
> b) wanton destruction of cities, towns or villages, or devastation not justified by military necessity;
>
> c) attack, or bombardment, by whatever means, of undefended towns, villages, dwellings, or buildings;
>
> d) seizure of, destruction or wilful damage done to institutions dedicated to religion, charity and education, the arts and sciences, historic monuments and works of art and science;
>
> e) plunder of public or private property".

With the exception of paragraph (a), Article 3 of the Statute exclusively enumerates different types of damage to property as violations of the laws or customs of war. On the other hand, the explicit reference to the applicability of customs of war opens the opportunity of widening the scope of this provision. This means that the list of violations of the laws or customs of war is not exhaustive and would not preclude an extensive interpretation of the provision for the purpose of the prohibition of rape and forced pregnancy.

---

[224] The treaty-based law applicable to internal armed conflicts consists of Article 19 of the 1954 Hague Convention on Cultural Property, the common Article 3 of the Geneva Conventions of 1949 and their Second Additional Protocol of 1977. There is a strong opinion, however, based on the ICJ judgment in the *Nicaragua v. United States of America* case, in favour of considering the common Article 3 as an expression of customary international law. The other treaty provisions are unlikely to be viewed as statements of customary law. UN Doc. S/1994/674, p. 15. See also *C. Meindersma*, Applicability of Humanitarian Law in International and Internal Armed Conflict, Hague Yearbook of International Law 1994, pp. 122–126. For a discussion of the norms applicable in non-international armed conflicts and internal strife, see *T. Meron*, On the Inadequate Reach of Humanitarian and Human Rights Law and the Need for a New Instrument, AJIL 1983, Vol. 77, p. 589 *et seq.*; *A. Eide, A. Rosas & T. Meron*, Combating Lawlessness in Gray Zone Conflicts through Minimum Humanitarian Standards, AJIL 1995, Vol. 89, p. 215 *et seq.*; *T. Meron*, International Criminalization of Internal Atrocities, pp. 574–576.

The UN Secretary-General referred in his explanatory report[225] to the Statute of the *ad hoc* Tribunal in regard to the scope of Article 3 that it is based primarily on the provisions contained in the 1907 Hague Convention (IV) Respecting the Law and Customs of War on Land and the Regulations annexed thereto which are declaratory of international customary law. Since the principle *nullum crimen sine lege* must be observed, only rules of international humanitarian law may be applied "which has beyond doubt become part of international customary law".[226] The Hague Regulations have found expression in the 1949 Geneva Conventions but there is still a difference between both sets of norms in that the previous ones also recognise "the right of belligerents to conduct warfare is not unlimited and that resort to certain methods of waging war is prohibited under the rules of land warfare".[227] In short, the conclusion may be drawn that since the 1907 Hague Convention views sexual violence as a war crime[228] and since many of the provisions of the Geneva Conventions, which are recognised as part of customary law condemn among others the crime rape, Article 3 of the Statute could be applied by the *ad hoc* Tribunal so as to cover the prohibition of rape and other forms of sexual violence (including reproductive crimes).

Moreover, the use of the expression "but not limited to" in Article 3 of the Tribunal's Statute has been interpreted as comprising "all relevant, well-established international law"[229] within the jurisdiction of the *ad hoc* Tribunal. Theoretically there should be no obstacles for the *ad hoc* Tribunal to apply in its interpretation of that article the provisions containing non-grave breaches under the Geneva Conventions as well as the common Article 3 and the Additional Protocols to these Conventions. Mr. O'Brien has convincingly put several arguments forward in favour of widening the scope of Article 3 of the *ad hoc* Tribunal's Statute in that way.[230]

There is increasing support for the standpoint that common Article 3 of the Geneva Conventions has become part of customary law[231] and that it is applicable

225 UN Doc. S/2504, §§ 41–44.

226 UN Doc. S/2504, § 34.

227 UN Doc. S/2504, § 43.

228 *M.C. Bassiouni & M. McCormick*, p. 32.

229 *J.C. O'Brien*, p. 646.

230 *J.C. O'Brien*, pp. 646–647. Moreover, Professor Menno Kamminga has taken the position that war crimes are offences that can be divided into two categories. The first category consists accordingly of grave breaches of the four Geneva Conventions of 1949 and Protocol I, *i.e.*, offences committed during international armed conflict and the second category consist of violations of common Article 3 of the Geneva Conventions and Protocol II, *i.e.*, serious violations committed during non-international armed conflict. *M.T. Kamminga*, The Exercise of Universal Jurisdiction in Respect of Gross Human Rights Offences, ILA, Taipei Conference 1998, Committee on Human Rights Law and Practice, p. 5.

231 *C. Meindersma*, p. 396; *A. Obote-Odora*, pp. 247–248; *S.D. Murphy*, p. 69; *K.D. Askin*, Sexual Violence, p. 97, note 3. See also the *Tadić* case, decision of 2 October 1995, §§ 102 and 134 and the *Furundžija* judgment, § 132. It could be mentioned here that Article 4 of the Rwanda Statute includes common Article 3 of the Geneva Conventions as well as violations of additional Protocol II of 1977, which has not yet gained universal recognition as part of international customary law. The indictment by the Rwandan Tribunal of Pauline Nyiramasuhuko and Arsene Ntahobali is of special significance in this regard. It charges both of them with serious violations of common Article 3 and Protocol II to the

to the entire conflict in the former Yugoslavia. Thus, violations of that article undoubtedly can and have been prosecuted by the *ad hoc* Tribunal. On the basis of a systematic interpretation of common Article 3 it is reasonable to conclude that its prohibitions include rape and other forms of sexual assault.[232]

After very long and thorough examination, the Appeals Chamber concluded in the *Tadić* case that the examples in Article 3 of the Tribunal's Statute were only an enumeration of violations and that this provision also included other infringements of international humanitarian law.[233] In short, the Appeals Chamber found that Article 3 was a general clause covering all violations of humanitarian law not falling under Articles 2, 4 or 5 of the Statute. It held that another interpretation would make the latter articles superfluous. In contrast to Article 2, Article 3 was considered applicable to both international and internal conflicts.[234] The Appeals Chamber held further that to be subject to prosecution under Article 3, the act must have violated either a customary rule of international law or a treaty rule which was binding on the parties at the time of the alleged offence, that the violation must be serious and that it must entail individual criminal responsibility.[235] Thus, according to the Tribunal:

> "if correctly interpreted, Article 3 fully realizes the primary purpose of the establishment of the International Tribunal, that is, not to leave unpunished any person guilty of any such serious violation, whatever the context within which it may have been committed".[236]

It has also been stressed in the literature that in the light of changing circumstances there is a perceived need for "international criminalization of the offences under common Article 3", *i.e.*, raising individual criminal responsibility for

---

Geneva Conventions. Count 7 alleges that, by committing rape, Mr. Ntahobali caused "outrages to the personal dignity, in particular humiliating and degrading treatment" of the concerned people. *Prosecutor v. Nyiramasuhuko & Ntahobali*, case No. ICTR-97-21-I, 26 May 1997.

232 *C.N. Niarchos*, p. 683; *C. Meindersma*, p. 381; *K.M. Pratt & L.E. Fletcher*, pp. 90 and 98; *P. Akhavan*, The International Criminal Tribunal for Rwanda, p. 503; *M.C. Bassiouni*, The Law of the International Criminal Tribunal for The Former Yugoslavia, p. 574; *J. Gardam*, p. 76; *K.D. Askin*, p. 330.

233 To support this conclusion, the Appeals Chamber cited statements from three of the permanent members of the S.C. (France, the United States and the United Kingdom). *Prosecutor v. Tadić*, Case IT-94-1-AR72, Appeal on Jurisdiction, §§ 87–89. Judge Li dissented from the majority's expansive interpretation of Article 3 since this in his view was "an unwarranted assumption of legislative power". Separate Opinion of Judge Li, ibid., § 13. The fact that the Appeals Chamber did not include grave breaches of the Geneva Conventions as a part of Article 3 has been questioned, since these offences have become part of customary law. *G.H. Aldrich*, p. 68; *T. Meron*, The Continuing Role of Custom in the Formation of International Humanitarian Law, AJIL 1996, Vol. 90, p. 234.

234 Interestingly, the Commission of Experts held in its report on the contrary that "violations of the laws or customs of war referred to in Article 3 of the Statute of the International Tribunal are offences when committed in international, but not in internal armed conflict". Final Report of the Commission of Experts, UN Doc. S/1994/674, § 54.

235 Ibid., § 94.

236 Ibid., § 92.

offences committed in non-international armed conflicts as well.[237] In other words, Article 3 of the Statute allows for the prosecution of persons who have committed rape and/or other forms of sexual assault in the course of a non-international armed conflict, independently of whether the act was widespread or systematic in character. In other words, under the provision referred to above a single act of rape and other forms of sexual assault constitute war crimes.

Finally, it should be mentioned that also other international treaties which are evidential of customary law, such as the 1956 Supplementary Convention on the Abolition of Slavery, the Slave Trade, and Institutions and Practices Similar to Slavery as well as the 1949 Convention for the Suppression of the Traffic in Persons and of the Exploitation of the Prostitution of Others[238] can serve as the basis for the prosecution of certain forms of sexual assault, *e.g.*, rape during unlawful detention and abduction. Evidence of the sexual victimisation of women in the conflicts in the former Yugoslavia coincide with the revelation of systematic abduction of women, described as "comfort women", who were subsequently forced into prostitution by the Japanese army during the World War II.[239] The indictments of several Bosnian Serbs in the *Tadić* and *Gagović and others* cases bear witness of the assumption that many girls and women have been forcibly detained in rape camps and that forced prostitution and sexual bondage in organised brothels have occurred.

Ms. Gay McDougal insists, in addition, in her final report on systematic rape, sexual slavery and slavery-like practices during armed conflict, on a link between rape and slavery. The report shows that rape during armed conflict is synonymous with sexual slavery. It demonstrates, furthermore, that sexual slavery and sexual violence when committed during armed conflict may be characterised under certain conditions as violations of *ius cogens* norms.[240]

Last but not the least, I agree with the view of Professor Bassiouni that forced impregnation and gestation must be treated as slave related practices as well since

---

[237] This group of offences has traditionally not been considered as criminal offences which are subject to universal jurisdiction. *D. Plattner,* The Penal Repression of Violations of International Humanitarian Law Applicable in Non-international Armed Conflict, International Review of the Red Cross 1990, Vol. 30, pp. 409–414. For arguments in favour of an extensive interpretation of Article 3 of the *ad hoc* Tribunal's Statute, see *T. Meron*, War Crimes in Yugoslavia and the Development of International Law, pp. 82–83 and *T. Meron*, International Criminalization of Internal Atrocities, p. 554. On recent developments on the national level which are also witness to an expansive interpretation of the concept "war crimes" see *M.T. Kamminga*, p. 6.

[238] See also the Report of the UN Secretary-General on Traffic in Women and Girls, UN Doc. A/51/309. For a more in depth deliberation of various relevant texts see *M.C. Bassiouni*, The International Criminal Tribunal for The Former Yugoslavia, p. 579–587; *D. Aydelott*, pp. 615–621, *K.D. Askin*, p. 331.

As of 28 April 1998, 119 states had ratified the 1956 Convention and only 72 had ratified the 1949 Convention.

[239] *D.E. Sanger*, Japan admits it ran army brothels during war, New York Times, 8 July 1992, p. 5.

[240] UN Doc. E/CN.4/Sub.2/1998/13, §§ 27–33. The Sub-Commission endorsed the rapporteur's recommendations by res. 1998/18 and requested that Ms.McDougal's mandate be extended for another year.

"Not only does the victim have no control over her body, the pregnancy amounts to forced labour".[241]

8.3.2.2.3. Rape as a Violation of the Laws and Customs of War

The brief review above shows that prohibitions of violations of the laws and customs of war are contained in a number of international instruments. Every violation of that law consequently constitutes a war crime. So does, for example, Article 46 of the Fourth Hague Convention of 1907,[242] which requires respect for the "family honour and rights". The expression "family honour" is in my opinion sufficiently broad to include protection of women against rape and other forms of gender-based violence. Since by such acts women's honour is wronged, it should not be regarded separately from the notion "family honour". There are plenty of examples of women who have been rejected by their families because of considerations of "family dishonour", made in the context of religion and culture during the armed conflicts in former Yugoslavia. One cannot exclude the probability of the enemy's motivation to perpetrate sexual abuses on the basis of the "knowledge of women's liability to consequent ill-treatment by their own families and communities"[243] following sexual assaults. At the same time this author fully agrees with the contemporary view that rape should be considered first and foremost a crime of violence (*i.e.*, it is an assault on the human dignity and bodily integrity of the woman), and not be dealt with in the context of protection of woman's honour. Thus, in the words of Ms. McDougal "the only party without honour in any rape or in any situation of sexual violence is the perpetrator".[244] The honour paradigm is, furthermore, linked to stereotypical concepts of chastity and virginity and thereby interconnected with the morality of the victim. Therefore, many women have abstained from reporting the sexual violence that has been perpetrated against them. Several writers and organisations have pointed out that there is no rational basis for making the prohibition of sexual violence depend on the honour and reputation of the victim.[245]

It is also of importance to note that cases that are not covered by the prohibition of crimes against humanity still may be considered under the prohibition of war crimes.[246] The following brief overview of the extensive investigation of the situation

---

[241] *M.C. Bassiouni*, The Law of the International Criminal Tribunal for The Former Yugoslavia, p. 583. Several NGOs have also urged that forced pregnancy as a result of rape must be prosecuted as a war crime. *C.A.A. Packer*, p. 151.

[242] The International Military Tribunal for the Far East (Tokyo Tribunal) took the view in its judgment in regard to The Hague Convention respecting the Laws and Customs of War and Land of 1907 that it was "good evidence of the customary law of nations". Judgment of the International Military Tribunal for the Far East of 1948, UN War Crimes Commission, Law Reports of Trial of War Criminals, Vol. 15, 1949, p. 13. The judgment is reprinted in The Law of War – A Documentary History, *L. Friedman* (ed.), Vol. II, New York 1972, pp. 1036–37.

[243] *R.J. Cook*, Human Rights and Reproductive Self-determination, p. 997.

[244] UN Doc. E/CN.4/Sub.2/1998/13, § 16.

[245] UN Doc. E/CN.4/1998/54, § 4; *M. Robinson*, pp. 20–21; *A. Brunet & S. Rousseau*, p. 37; *A. Aafjes*, pp. 1–4; *R. Copelon*, Gendered War Crimes, p. 201; *Human Rights Watch*, Justice in The Balance, p. 17.

[246] *J.C. O'Brien*, p. 645.

with regard to acts of rape committed during the armed conflicts in former Yugoslavia carried out by the impartial Commission of Experts, established pursuant to Security Council resolution 780 of 6 October 1992, can help to illustrate that issue.

A great part of the documentation and information received by the Commission throughout the various phases of the armed conflicts in former Yugoslavia refer to allegations of widespread and systematic rape and other forms of sexual assault.[247] Therefore, the commissioners decided at an early stage to examine the question of whether the systematic perpetration of such acts should be regarded as crimes in themselves, and if so, as war crimes or crimes against humanity.

The Commission of Experts conducted in depth investigations of the allegations and came to the important conclusion that all sides in the conflict had committed rape.[248] However, out of the 330 reported cases reviewed in its interim-report of February 1993 and, in addition to that, its later investigations reproduced in the final report of 1994, the largest number of victims have been Bosnian Muslims and the largest number of alleged perpetrators have been Bosnian Serbs.[249] Very few reports indicate the occurrence of acts of rape and sexual assaults between members of the same ethnic group. The perpetrators are military personnel, special forces, local police and civilians. Since the Commission established that a considerable number of the cases studied can be considered as part of an overall pattern, the conclusion could be drawn that a systematic rape policy existed. In support of this argument, the Commission has referred to two important factors: the coincidence in time between military action designed to displace civilian populations and widespread rape of the same population. Furthermore, group involvement of the members of the same military units in rape points to a command responsibility by commission or omission. The Commission also takes into consideration the manner in which this type of rape has been conducted, *i.e.*, in multiple locations and within a fairly close period of time (between May and December 1992). Yet another important factor referred to by the Commission is the contemporaneous existence of other violations of international humanitarian law in a given region and occurring simultaneously on the battlefield, in prison camps and in the civilian regions of occupied areas. In spite of all these factual circumstances, the Commission of Experts is very cautious in making a definite judgement on the issue of rape. It rather emphasises the circumstance that the question of a systematic rape policy

---

247 Report of the Commission of Experts, UN Doc. S/25240, Annex I. See also *H.-P. Gasser*, Der Internationale Strafgerichtshof für das frühere Jugoslawien und das "Kriegsrecht und die Kriegsgebräuche", in Humanitäres Völkerrecht, Deutsches Rotes Kreuz, Nr. 2, 1993, pp. 60–63; UN International Criminal Tribunal for the Former Yugoslavia, Press Release, The International Criminal Tribunal for the Former Yugoslavia Indicts a Former Camp Commander and Issues Warrants for his Arrest, The Hague, 7 November 1994, p. 2.

248 See UN Doc. E/CN.4/1994/5 and UN Doc. S/1994/674, p. 60.

249 UN Doc. A/48/858, 29 January 1994, p. 3 and UN Doc. S/1994/674, p. 60. The Commission's database identifies close to 800 victims by name and number, while 1,673 victims are referred to without a name. There are also 500 reported cases which refer to an unspecified number of victims. The reported cases identify some 600 alleged perpetrators by name. UN Doc. S/1994/674, p. 56.

still remains to be proven. Thus, it suggests that if further investigations prove that a nexus exists between these activities and the policy of "ethnic cleansing",[250] then

---

[250] It can be of interest to mention here that the term "ethnic cleansing" was first coined by the Croats and Bosnians during World War II. It has been estimated that over 500,000 Serbs were killed during that war and a million were driven from the territory to seek refuge in other countries. *M.P. Scharf*, p. 23.

The Commission of Experts defined the term "ethnic cleansing" in its Final Report as follows: "'Ethnic cleansing' means rendering an area ethnically homogenous by using force or intimidation to remove persons of given groups from the area". Final Report, UN Doc. S/1994/674, Annex p. 33.

The main objective of ethnic cleansing is according to Human Rights Watch observations "the removal of an ethnic group from a given area through murder, population exchanges, forced displacement, and terrorization". Human Rights Watch World Report 1995, p. 192. In this regard reference to Article 147 of the Fourth Geneva Convention, which provides that deportations and population transfers are "grave breaches" or war crimes, can be made.

In the context of the Bosnia-Herzegovina conflict, a policy and practice of ethnic cleansing has often followed after an area has been occupied by Serbian forces. The ethnic cleansing that has been practised by Serbian forces has been directed particularly against Muslims and Croats on the basis of their religion and ethnicity. The overall aim has been to create an ethnically homogeneous region to be administered by the Serbian authorities. I may mention here that the Serbs, Croats and Slovenes, Montenegrins and Macedonians were recognised as constituent nations of post-war Yugoslavia in 1946, whereas a Muslim national identity was recognised officially only in 1970. Although Slavic Muslims, a great number of Albanians and Turks living in the former Yugoslavia practise Islam, they are considered as three separate national groups. Helsinki Watch, War Crimes in Bosnia-Herzegovina, Vol. I, New York 1992, p. 22.

Helsinki Watch has summarised the following violations under the policy of ethnic cleansing: "summary executions of non-Serbian civilians, including children and elderly persons; arbitrary detention, torture and general mistreatment of non-Serbs, in prisons, detention camps or ghettos; forcible deportation of non-Serbs from Bosnia-Herzegovina and from Serbia; forcible displacement of non-Serbs, which is achieved either through terror bombardment and shelling; burning of non-Serbian villages and the destruction of Muslim and Croatian homes in ethnically mixed villages; summarily execute, torture, beat and otherwise mistreat prisoners of war, civilians and combatants *hors de combat* in their custody; make "disappear" non-Serbian combatants and civilian males; take hostages to exchange for captured combatants or to extract military concessions; deny medical care to wounded prisoners of war and civilians, including journalists; use prisoners as human shields; use hospitals and other medical establishments as military headquarters or as depots for weapons; indiscriminately shell and bomb Bosnian cities, towns and villages; use disproportionate and indiscriminate force, as well as attacks on civilian targets, to terrorise the civilian population; use disproportionate force against Bosnian military targets, thereby inflicting unnecessary and excessive damage on the civilian population; target for attack civilians, hospitals, heavily populated city centres and cultural and religious objects, continue to attack, hijack and obstruct international relief convoys, including U.N. vehicles and personnel, intended for civilians in besieged cities and towns; loot, burn and otherwise pillage Muslim and Croatian villages". Nevertheless, Helsinki Watch emphasises that all of the parties to the conflict have committed crimes and it refers to the fact that Muslim and Croatian forces: "take hostages for exchange for captured combatants; harass and intimidate Serbs in areas under their control; forcibly displace Serbian civilians from areas under their control; place artillery and other weapons close to hospitals and other civilian objects; loot and destroy property belonging to Serbs; shoot at UN vehicles; deliberately attack journalists; may be executing Serbian civilians and disarmed combatants". See Helsinki Watch, War Crimes in Bosnia-Herzegovina, Vol. I, pp. 195–198.

In conclusion, I may observe that as to the methods for ethnic cleansing used in Bosnia-Herzegovina, it is clear that they have varied considerably. However, in the context of this study the term covers grave discrimination, torture, maltreatment, mass executions, rape, etc. See UN Doc. E/CN.4/1993/50, p. 7. Ethnic cleansing has repeatedly been mentioned as one of the crimes to be repressed and punished internationally in the Security Council's resolutions Nos.: 752 § 6, 757 § 5, 771 § 2, 779 § 4, 787 § 7, 780 § 4, 819 § 2, 820 § 5, 824 § 4, 836 § 6.

it could be argued that rape has been used as an instrument of war. For that purpose the Commission of Experts at its ninth session adopted a "Plan of Action for an in-depth investigation of allegations of sexual assault, extra-judicial executions, torture and alleged violations of international humanitarian law in detention camps in connection with the hostilities in former Yugoslavia". After concluding its mandate the Commission kept its prudent attitude, which is demonstrated in its final report. There it is underlined that there are patterns of rape which strongly suggest "that a systematic rape policy existed in certain areas, but it remains to be proven whether such an overall policy existed, which was to apply to all non-Serbs".[251] From that statement it is apparent that there is a grounded presumption that many of the alleged rapes in former Yugoslavia constitute crimes against humanity. In addition, there will be cases falling outside this concept but which still can and should be considered as war crimes by the *ad hoc* Tribunal. A distinctive feature between a war crime and a crime against humanity is that the latter can be committed independently of an armed conflict and "even when committed during a conflict, /is/ not necessarily related to it".[252] As already pointed out before, to prove a crime of sexual violence in the context of war crime it will be enough to prove that the accused had sexual contact with a victim and that this victim did not consent to the act.[253]

This renewed attention to and emphasis on the observance and implementation of international humanitarian law since the beginning of the 1990s has on several occasions found expression within the international community. I shall in the following give some recent examples of the increasing international awareness as to the urgent need to eradicate war crimes.

The strong opinion condemning rape as a war crime was reflected in a resolution unanimously adopted at the world-wide World Veterans Federation's 51st meeting in 1993 as follows:

> "The World Veterans Federation condemns rape being used as a weapon of war and terror and demands that such rape should be considered as a war crime and appeals to the international community and to the persons bearing responsibility in the countries concerned, particularly in former Yugoslavia, to guarantee to these misused women and children the appropriate medical care and social services".[254]

The UN Human Rights Commission at its session of 1994 supported in a resolution the view that the abhorrent practice of rape and abuse of women and children in the areas of armed conflict in former Yugoslavia constitutes a war crime.[255] In

---

[251] UN Doc. S/1994/674, p. 60, § 253.

[252] *M.C. Bassiouni*, Regulation of Armed Conflicts, in International Criminal Law, Vol. I Crimes, M.C. Bassiouni (ed.), New York 1986, p. 225.

[253] *M.C. Bassiouni & M. McCormick*, p. 34; *K.D. Askin*, p. 388 ff.

[254] Doc. 51/C–8, April 1993 cited in *A.N. Heiberg*, Tortur og vold mot kvinner i krig, Mennesker og rettigheter 1994, No. 2, p. 145.

[255] Res. 1994/77 of 9 March 1994.

1995 the Commission again strongly condemned violations of women's human rights in armed conflicts, including rape and sexual abuse against women. In its resolution 1995/89, the Commission stated that the systematic practice of rape as a weapon of war against women and children constitutes a war crime that cannot be justified under any circumstances.

Also the Commission on the Status of Women adopted at its 1994 session a resolution,[256] in which its members strongly condemned the practice of rape and other sexual abuses of women in the areas of armed conflict in former Yugoslavia and declared that rape should be considered a war crime. The same year the report containing the conclusions and recommendations of the earlier mentioned expert group meeting was adopted by the CSW. Its § 82[257] expresses the contemporary predominant understanding in the international community of rape committed in international armed conflict, including individual acts of rape as well as systematic rape, as a war crime.[258]

The Report of the Secretary-General which was presented at the Fourth World Conference on Women says, furthermore, that action by governments is needed with regard to war-related violence against women, "such as mass rapes, forced pregnancies and other gender-specific abuses applied as a means of warfare, as war crimes and crimes against humanity",[259] so that they will be prosecuted by proper national and international institutions. The Beijing Platform for Action reaffirms in § 145(d) that "rape in the conduct of armed conflict constitutes a war crime".[260] The 26th International Conference of the Red Cross and Red Crescent in December 1995 condemned in resolution 2 A(g) sexual violence directed against any person and stressed that rape and forced prostitution in the course of an armed conflict, or instigated by any party to a conflict, constitute a war crime. Ms. Chavez concludes also that the definition of rape under international humanitarian law is evolving so as to classify it as a war crime.[261] The UN General Assembly expressed its conviction during its 51st session in 1996 that "the heinous practice of rape, in fulfilling the policy of ethnic cleansing, constitutes a deliberate weapon of war". It is affirmed that "rape in the conduct of armed conflict constitutes a war crime and that under certain circumstances it constitutes a crime against humanity and an act of genocide". (Resolution 51/115)

---

[256] Res. 38/9, UN Doc. E/CN.6/1994/14, pp. 25–29.

[257] UN Doc. E/CN.6/1994/4, p. 21.

[258] At this session (38th) of the CSW, the representative of the United States said that her country would press for the International Tribunal for the prosecution of war crimes in the former Yugoslavia and, in particular, prosecute rape as a war crime. CSW, 38th session, 7th meeting, 10 March 1994.

[259] UN Doc. E/CN.6/1994/10, p.19. It can be also mentioned that regional documents presented at the Beijing Conference in 1995, among them the Arab Plan of Action, stressed that gender-based violence during times of war "should be considered a war crime with no statute of limitations". UN Doc. E/CN.6/1995/5/Add. 5, § 39(h).

[260] Paragraph 9.2. of the 1997 Asian Charter on Human Rights (NGO) emphasises also that "rape is a war crime and crime against humanity". *F. de Varennes,* p. 141.

[261] UN Doc. E/CN.4/Sub.2/1996/26, § 6(b). See also UN Doc. E/CN.4/Sub.2/1998/13, §§ 56–73.

All these authoritative statements are a strong indication of *opinio iuris* on a less restrictive understanding of existing rules of international humanitarian law. Support for my assumption that rape and other forms of gender-based violence are to be viewed as war crimes and thereby as implicitly prohibited by Article 3 of the *ad hoc* Tribunal's Statute can be increasingly found also in the literature.[262] This approach has in fact been followed by both *ad hoc* tribunals, which have charged and prosecuted rape and other sexual violence as violations of the laws and customs of war.[263]

This author has, in addition, demonstrated above that rape has been prosecuted as a violation of a customary humanitarian law for long time, *i.e.*, before the creation of the *ad hoc* Tribunals and by the Tribunals as well. Although no principle of *stare decisis* is put into the Yugoslavia Tribunal's procedure, the conclusions of the Appeals Chamber in the *Tadić* case in regard to the definition of war crimes must be of major legal precedental importance.[264] In the words of Professor Meron "(t)he *Tadić* appeals decision of the Hague Tribunal, which confirmed the applicability of some principles of the Hague law to non-international armed conflicts and the criminalisation of violations of common Article 3 of the Geneva Conventions in such conflicts"[265] has assisted the creation of a favourable environment for the development of a modern and progressive understanding of international humanitarian law when drafting the Statute of the ICC. Taking into consideration the recent achievements may also result in reproductive crimes other than rape, *e.g.*, forced pregnancy and enforced sterilisation, which were criminalised as war crimes under the ICC Statute, being prosecuted under Article 3 of the *ad hoc* Tribunal's Statute.[266]

---

262 *T. Meron*, Rape as a Crime Under International Humanitarian Law, p. 426; *E. Stamatopoulou*, Women's rights and the United Nations, in Women's rights, human rights, J. Peters & A. Wolper (eds.), p. 42; *E.-J.A. Daes*, New Types of War Crimes and Crimes against Humanity, p. 62; *C.A. MacKinnon*, Crimes of War, Crimes of Peace, p. 84; *D. Aydelott*, p. 627 ff.; *K.D. Askin*, p. 329; *Human Rights Watch*, Justice in The Balance, pp. 15–16.

263 Furundžija was, *e.g.*, charged in counts 13 and 14 with a violation of the laws or customs of war (torture and outrages upon personal dignity, including rape). He was subsequently found guilty of these charges. *Prosecutor v. Furundžija*, Judgment of 10 December 1998. Also other accused, among them Delić (counts 20–23), Cecez (count 39), Delalić and Mucić (count 45) were charged by the ICTY with violations of the laws or customs of war. *Prosecutor v. Delalić and Others*, Judgment 16 November 1998. See also *Prosecutor v. Nicolić* Rule 61 decision, 20 October 1995, § 33; *Miljković and Others*, indictment of 21 July 1995, counts 37 and 52 and *Gagović* and *Others* indictment of 26 June 1996, § 4.8. The *Gagović and Others* indictment has been considered as a landmark indictment "because it focuses exclusively only on sexual charges. There is no precedent for this. It is of major legal significance because it illustrates the court's strategy to focus on gender-related crimes and give them their proper place in the prosecution of war crimes". Citation in *K.D. Askin*, Sexual Violence, p. 118.

264 *C. Warbrick*, p. 696.

265 *T. Meron*, War Crimes Law Comes of Age, p. 464.

266 The Women's Rights Project of Human Rights Watch, which was established in 1990 to monitor violence against women, has already urged the Prosecutor's office of the *ad hoc* Tribunal for the former Yugoslavia to prosecute forced pregnancy as a war crime. According to the same organisation US officials have during the summer of 1994 indicated that forced impregnation was "highly likely" to be prosecuted as inhumane treatment. Human Rights Watch World Report 1995, pp. 337 and 342.

### *8.3.2.3. Genocide*

#### 8.3.2.3.1. General Remarks

Genocide,[267] the gravest and the most severe form of violation of the non-discrimination principle, is a crime under international law irrespective of whether it is committed in time of peace or in time of war and regardless of the nature of the armed conflict, *i.e.*, regardless of whether it is an international or an internal armed conflict. Moreover, the outlawing of genocide today belongs to the peremptory norms (*ius cogens*) in international law and it is an *erga omnes* legal obligation, since it safeguards values of vital importance for humanity and corresponds to fundamental moral principles.[268] Thus, genocide presents a fundamental threat to

---

[267] The term "genocide" is a hybrid comprising the Greek "genos", which means race or tribe, and the Latin suffix "cide" meaning killing. It was introduced by the Polish-American jurist Raphael Lemkin in 1944 in his book "Axis Rule in Occupied Europe", p. 79. According to him the "realities of European life in the years 1933–45 called for the creation of such a term and for the formulation of a legal concept of destruction of human groups. The Nazis had embarked upon a gigantic plan to change permanently the population balance in occupied Europe in their favour. They intended to wipe out entirely the national-biological power of the neighbours of Germany so that Germany might win a permanent victory, whether directly through military subjugation or indirectly through such a biological destruction that even in the case of Germany's defeat the neighbours would be so weakened that Germany would be able to recover her strength in later years". *R. Lemkin*, Genocide as A Crime under International Law, AJIL 1947, Vol. 41, p. 147. Professor Lemkin has also actively encouraged and supported the UN's efforts to promote the adoption of treaty provisions prohibiting this crime. He was actually one of the experts consulted by the UN Division of Human Rights in the drafting process of the Genocide Convention. *S.K. Kapoor*, International Law, Bahadurganj, Allahabad 1990, p. 735; *W. McKean*, p. 106 and *P. Thornberry*, International Law and the Rights of Minorities, Oxford 1992, p. 66. See generally on the issue of genocide: *R. Lemkin*, Axis Rule in Occupied Europe, Washington 1944; *A.K. Kuhn*, The Genocide Convention and State Rights, AJIL 1949, Vol. 43, pp. 498–501; *A.G. Finch*, The Genocide Convention, AJIL 1949, Vol. 43, pp. 732–738; *J.L. Kunz*; The United Nations Convention on Genocide, AJIL 1949, Vol. 43, pp. 738–746; *E.I. Daes*, Protection of Minorities under the International Bill of Human Rights and the Genocide Convention, Xenion, Festschrift für P.J. Zepos, Athens 1973, Vol. II, p. 43 et seq.; *N. Ruhashyankiko*, Study of the Question of the Prevention and Punishment of the Crime of Genocide, UN Doc. E/CN.4/Sub.2/416, 1987; *B. Whitaker*, Revised and Updated Report on the Question of the Prevention and Punishment of the Crime of Genocide, UN Doc. E/CN.4/Sub.2/1985/6; *P.N. Drost*, The Crime of State, Vol. II, Genocide, Leyden 1959; *N. Robinson*, The Genocide Convention: A Commentary, New York 1960; Porter (ed.), Genocide and Human Rights, Washington 1982; *H.-H. Jescheck*, Genocide, in Encyclopaedia of Public International Law, Instalment 8, pp. 255–258; *M.N. Show*, Genocide and International Law, in Y. Dinstein & M. Tabory (eds.), International Law at a Time of Perplexity, Dordrecht 1989, pp. 797–820; *E. Staub*, The Roots of the Evil. The Origins of Genocide and Other Group Violence, New York 1989; *T. Zülch*, "Ethnische Säuberungen"-Völkermord für Grosserbien, Hamburg 1992; *I.W. Charny* (ed.), The Widening Circle of Genocide, Genocide Vol. 3, New Brunswick 1994; *H. Fein*, Genocide, Terror, Life, Integrity, and War Crimes: The Case of Discrimination, in The Conceptual and Historical Dimensions of Genocide, G. Andreopoulos (ed.), Philadelphia 1994, pp. 95–108.

[268] *R. Lemkin*, Genocide as A Crime Under International Law, p. 150; *L.R. Beres*, Genocide and Genocide-Like Crimes, in International Criminal Law, Vol. I, M.C. Bassiouni (ed.), p. 272; *M.N. Show*, p. 800. A well-known statement on the rules of *ius cogens* of relevance to our discussion has been delivered by the former President of the International Court of Justice, Professor Jiménez de Aréchaga as follows: "The substantive contents of *jus cogens* are likely to be constantly changing in accordance with the progress and development of international law and international morality. *Jus cogens* is not an immutable natural law but an evolving concept: the last phrase in the definition envisages the modification of *jus cogens* by the same process which led to its establishment". This text can be found in International

societies and the global social order. The prohibition of genocide applies consequently to all members of the international community rather than merely to parties to the convention on that specific matter. The UN Convention on the Prevention and Punishment of the Crime of Genocide (hereinafter referred to as the Genocide Convention) of 9 December 1948[269] states in its preamble that "genocide is a crime under international law, contrary to the spirit and aims of the United Nations and condemned by the civilised world".[270] The contracting states, furthermore, declare that, in case of failure to prevent genocide, those who are guilty of the crime must be punished whether they are constitutionally responsible rulers, public officials or private individuals.

The adoption of the Genocide Convention was motivated by the tragic experiences of the Second World War when millions of people, particularly Jews, Poles, Gypsies and various nationalities of the Soviet Union were exterminated simply because they belonged to a certain human group. Therefore, one of the main objectives of the Genocide Convention is to prevent the annihilation of a national, ethnic, racial or religious group of human beings as such. In other words, its aim is to ensure the protection of the right of human groups to their physical existence as groups. From that follows that the term "genocide" focuses on the collective element, *i.e.*, it is a group-oriented notion. The very first definition of genocide[271] in an international instrument is stipulated in the GA Res. 96 (I) of 1946 as follows:

> "a denial of the right of existence of entire human groups, as homicide is the denial of the right to live of individual human beings".

Genocide was subsequently defined in Article II of the Genocide Convention as acts committed with the intent to destroy a national, ethnical, racial or religious

---

Law, Cases and Materials, *L. Henkin et al.* (eds.), Minnesota 1987, p. 470. See *P. Thornberry*, pp. 95–100 and *L. Hannikainen*, pp. 456–464.

[269] The Convention on the Prevention and Punishment of the Crime of Genocide was adopted by the GA on December 9, 1948, (78 U.N.T.S. 277). It came into force on January 12, 1951. The Genocide Convention is widely accepted as part of the customary international law. See ICJ, *Reservations to the Convention on the Prevention and Punishment of the Crime of Genocide*: Advisory Opinion of 28 May 1951, ICJ Rep. 1951, p. 23. See also the case *Application of the Convention on the Prevention and Punishment of the Crime of Genocide (Bosnia-Herzegovina v. Yugoslavia (Serbia and Montenegro)),* Preliminary Objections, Judgment ICJ, July 11, 1996, § 31, the separate opinion of Judge Weeramantry, p. 5 and the separate opinion of Judge M. Kre, § 101. The text of the Court's Judgment is available through the ICJ web site at: <http://www.icj.org.>. See furthermore *E. Klein*, Genocide Convention (Advisory Opinion), EPIL II 1995, pp. 544–546; *K.D. Askin*, p. 338; *M. Palatsi*, p. 112.

[270] The GA considered the acts of genocide committed by the German Nazis during the Second World War at its very first session. One of the items on its agenda was named "Resolution on the Crime of Genocide". A document containing a condemnation of the crime was unanimously adopted on December 11, 1946 Res. 96 (I). The resolution contains the quoted sentence word for word. UN Yearbook 1946–1947, p. 255.

[271] The first international instrument to use this term was the indictment of 8 October 1945, which was brought against the war criminals at Nuremberg. *M.N. Shaw*, pp. 799 and 804.

group, by killing members of the group, causing serious bodily or mental harm to members of the group, deliberately inflicting on the group conditions of life calculated to bring about its physical destruction, imposing measures intended to prevent births within the group, or forcibly transferring children of the group to another group. The general language of the first definition was consequently replaced by an exhaustive enumeration of the categories comprised within the notion of genocide. The latter definition, furthermore, makes reference to the expression "killing members of the group", which indicates that killing some and not all members of a human group would constitute genocide provided the act was committed with the intent of destroying the group or a substantial part thereof.[272] The insertion in the definition of the words "in whole or in part" has been interpreted in a similar way by the UN Commission of Experts, *i.e.*, certain actions can be considered genocidal even if the designated group is not exterminated in its entirety.[273] Thus, genocide is an attack on the group as an entity, but the actions involved are carried out on an individual basis, *i.e.*, the individual is victimised only because he/she belongs to that specific group. The consideration of a proportionate scale as well as of total numbers should be according to some writers[274] an applicable factor for genocide to be relevant. As Bryant has put it:

> "Unless the intent were express,..the intent to destroy the group would be difficult to prove, except in those instances where the number of people of the group affected was significant. Practically speaking, then, the number of victims may be of evidentiary value with respect to proving the necessary intent".[275]

In making a comparison between the wording of the text in Article II of the Genocide Convention and Article 4 of the *ad hoc* Tribunal's Statute, it is apparent that the Genocide Convention has served as a model for the relevant provision in the Tribunal's Statute. Furthermore, Article 2 of the Statute of the International

---

[272] *T. Buergenthal*, International Human Rights, Minnesota 1988, p. 49.

[273] UN Doc. S/1994/674, p. 26.

[274] See, for example, *L.J. LeBlanc*, The United States and the Genocide Convention, 1991, pp. 44–51; *P.N. Drost*, p. 85; *M.C. Bassiouni*, The Definition of Aggression, p. 532; *L. Hannikainen*, p. 461. At the same time several scholars claim that nothing in the Genocide Convention prohibits an interpretation which will allow for its application in individual cases. It has been suggested that it would be "enough if only a handful of individuals or indeed only one person were killed provided the intent criterion" is present for it to be genocide. *M.N. Shaw*, p. 806. A similar view has been expressed by Professor Robinson who has argued that: "the murder of a single individual may be categorised as genocide if it constitutes one of a series of acts designed to attain the destruction of the people to which the victim belonged". *N. Robinson*, p. 58; *Y. Dinstein*, Collective Human Rights of Peoples and Minorities, ICLQ 1976, p. 106; *H. McCoubrey*, International Humanitarian Law: Regulation of Armed Conflicts, Vermont 1990, p. 140. See also the references in *K.D. Askin*, p. 342, note 1070 and the UN reports on the Study of the Question of the Prevention and Punishment of the Crime of Genocide, ECOSOC, Commission on Human Rights, UN Doc. E/CN.4/Sub.2/1978/416, § 50.

[275] Final Report of the Commission of Experts established pursuant to Security Council resolution 935 (1994), UN Doc. S/1994/1405, p. 32.

Tribunal for Rwanda is a verbatim version of that provision. The conventional definition has also been incorporated in Article 6 of the ICC Statute.[276]

It is obvious from the text below that Article 4 of the *ad hoc* Tribunal's Statute for former Yugoslavia is based entirely on the definition of the concept genocide embodied in Article II of the Genocide Convention. It reads as follows:

> "2. Genocide means any of the following acts committed with intent to destroy, in whole or in part, a national, ethnical, racial or religious group, as such:
> a) killing members of the group;
> b) causing serious bodily or mental harm to members of the group;
> c) deliberately inflicting on the group conditions of life calculated to bring about its physical destruction in whole or in part;
> d) imposing measures intended to prevent births within the group;
> e) forcibly transferring children of the group to another group;".

The definition identifies two elements of the crime: 1) the commission of one or more of the acts listed and 2) intent to destroy, in whole or in part, one of the groups protected. Each of the above indicated five kinds of acts constitutes the crime of genocide. Any combination of them is held as the same.[277] The Genocide Convention prohibits not only acts of genocide but also conspiracy or incitement and attempts to commit genocide as well as complicity in genocide (Article III). The fact that an attempt will be sufficient for criminal responsibility is persuasive evidence for how seriously and decisively genocide is regarded by the international community.

Even though genocide has been described as "a special case of crimes against humanity",[278] acts of genocide are nowadays covered by separate norms explicitly

---

[276] The ILC commented the inclusion of this crime in its draft Code as follows: "The enormous gravity of the crime of genocide and the fact that the General Assembly had drafted an international convention on its prevention and punishment as early as 1948 made it essential to include this crime in the draft Code and also facilitated the Commission's task". UN Doc. A/CN.4/L.464/Add.4, 1991. The ILC in clarifying its standpoint as regards crimes under general international law has, in addition, stated that: "(t)he prohibition of genocide is of such fundamental significance, and the occasions for legitimate doubt or dispute over whether a given situation amounts to genocide are so limited, that the Court ought, exceptionally, to have inherent jurisdiction over it.... (t)he case for conferring such "inherent jurisdiction" is powerfully reinforced by the Genocide Convention itself, which does not confer jurisdiction over genocide on other states on an *aut dedere aut iudicare* basis, but expressly contemplates its conferral on an international criminal court to be created (art. VI)". GAOR 49th session, Supp. No. 10, UN Doc. A/49/10, 1994, at 67.

[277] UN Doc. S/1994/674, p. 26.

[278] *J.C. O'Brien*, p. 648. The category of crimes against humanity has also been described as "the parent of genocide". Thus, the definition of the first term contained in the London Charter is broad enough to include genocide. *P. Thornberry*, pp. 58 and 63. But, as Professor Bassiouni emphasises, crimes against humanity as defined at Nuremberg "were considered either part of 'war crimes' or separate crimes connected to the conduct of war". *M.C. Bassiouni*, Introduction To The Genocide Convention, in International Criminal Law, Vol. I, p. 281.

prohibiting it. This means that the crime of genocide is a distinctive crime, independent of any connection with war crimes as was earlier the case.[279] One and the same act might consequently be considered either as constituting crime against humanity or genocide. The decisive element for that classification would depend on the second element of the definition, *i.e.*, *intent* to destroy a designate human group "because of its existence and character as a coherent community".[280] In other words, the definition of genocide excludes situations where the required specific intent does not exist.[281] Actual physical destruction is not required.[282] Intent is the deliberate will to commit a crime, whereas the word "motive" has been defined by the ILC as "impulse, which led the perpetrator to act or the feeling which animated him (racism, religious feelings, political opinion, etc.)".[283] Intent may be linked with a specific motive/s, but neither the Genocide Convention nor the *ad hoc* Tribunal's Statute make explicit reference to such a requirement. Thus, if the aim of the perpetrator:

> "... is to eliminate the victim because of the latter's race, religion or political beliefs, with no other interest, his act constitutes a crime against humanity, whereas if committed with intent to destroy, in whole or in part, a national,[284] ethnic, racial or religious group, it will be qualified as genocide".[285]

The motive is irrelevant for the definition of genocide. In other words, whatever the reasons or the motive/s might be for an attack on a human group, in absence of intent there will be no genocide. The requirement of a subjective element such as "intent" has been strongly opposed during the drafting of the Genocide Convention on the grounds that "it would enable those accused of genocide to escape punishment by claiming that there was no *mens rea*".[286] Thus, ascertaining the subjective intent to destroy is not an easy task. It is feared that if the prosecution would have

---

[279] *P. Thornberry*, pp. 90–91.

[280] *M.N. Shaw*, p. 805.

[281] *M.C. Bassiouni*, Crimes Against Humanity, The Need for a Specialized Convention, Columbia Journal of Transnational Law 1994, Vol. 31, p. 477; *L. Mansfield*, Crimes against Humanity: Reflections on the Fiftieth Anniversary of Nuremberg and a Forgotten Legacy, NJIL 1995, p. 315.

[282] *N. Robinson*, p. 58; *M.N. Shaw*, p. 805.

[283] ILC's commentary on Article 4 of the draft Code, UN Doc. A/CN.4/L.464/Add.4, 1991.

[284] Possible difficulties, which might arise when defining the criteria for the determination of the notion "national" group, have been described by *M.N. Shaw*, p. 807.

[285] *S. Glaser*, Droit International Pénal Conventionnel, Vol. I, Brussels 1970, p. 109, cited in *P. Thornberry*, p. 58. Professor Shaw has taken a partly different position on that subject matter. According to him: "The intention to destroy a group, wholly or partly, in order to constitute genocide must be coupled with the motive force of 'national, ethical, racial or religious' reasons for such behaviour. Thus, the destruction of a group for reasons of profit or during the course of a war and in the absence of such reasons or motives would not comply with the basic requirements of the genocide definition, although it may very well violate other rules of international law". *M.N. Shaw*, p. 806. In the context of the armed conflicts in the former Yugoslavia, Serbian soldiers have, *e.g.*, made use of the argument that they have not committed genocide, since, in their view, they have not deliberately sought to destroy Bosnian Muslims. They maintain that this population should be seen merely as victims of war. *L. Mansfield*, p. 315.

[286] *W. McKean*, p. 110.

to prove a specific intent to destroy the group as such in respect of the accused in each and every case in order to rebut the defence that ordinary murder rather than genocide had been committed, it would require an unreasonably high burden of proof.[287] Similarly, it is therefore feared that charges against low-level officials on the basis of the relevant article in the *ad hoc* Tribunal's Statute might meet considerable difficulties, since there must be a reliable proof of intention to destroy the designated group. This might require a strong linkage to involvement in a policy with this aim. But the replacement of the subjective element by an objective expression has attracted criticism as well, in that it would render it impossible to distinguish between genocide and ordinary murder and between genocide and other war crimes and crimes against humanity.[288] Besides, a subjective element can be measured by objective means. In the case of Rwanda it has been emphasised that "a clear and unambiguous intention", in view of the massacres perpetrated against the Tutsi ethnic group, is contained in the constant incitements to murder broadcast by the media (particularly Radio Télévision Libre des Milles Collines (RTLM)) and reproduced in leaflets. On the basis of that, it has been maintained that the genocide of the Tutsi population is not difficult to establish.[289] In addition, it has been pointed out that the intention can be deduced from several other facts: the preparations for the massacres, *e.g.*, distribution of firearms to the civilian population and training of members of the militias; the exceptional speed of events at the outset (roadblocks were set up all over Kigali just 30–45 minutes after the assassinations, even before they had been reported on the radio; the "screening" carried out at the roadblocks by militiamen and soldiers aimed essentially at the Tutsi, and finally the lists drawn up by the public authorities with the aim of identifying Tutsi, after which they were immediately executed.[290] In conclusion, the impartial UN

---

[287] UN Doc. S/1994/1405, p. 33.

[288] *P. Drost*, The Crime of State, Vol. II, Genocide, p. 82; *W. McKean*, p. 110; *M.N. Shaw*, p. 805.

[289] According to the very first indictment of the *ad hoc* Tribunal delivered on 12 December 1995, eight persons were accused, *inter alia*, of genocide and conspiracy to commit genocide in the mass killings of thousands of Tutsis in the Kibuye Prefecture of Western Rwanda. As of December 1998, some 20 individuals were charged for genocide.

While genocide charges have been included in a number of the indictments issued by the ICTY, the only trial as at the time of writing containing a genocide charge was that of *Kovačević*. It began in July 1998 but was terminated in August 1998 because of his death.

[290] UN Doc. E/CN.4/1995/71, pp. 4–5. The UN Special Rapporteur on the situation of human rights in Rwanda has reviewed cases of assassination of the Hutu population as well. According to Mr. R. Degni-Séqui, the massacres have indeed not spared the members of the Hutu ethnic group, but the Hutu moderate has been merely targeted as a traitor to his ethnic group, *i.e.*, for political reasons. Thus, the ethnic group *per se* has not been targeted, and therefore the acts constitute political assassinations. The major part of the victims have been human rights activists and political opponents. See also UN Doc. E/CN.4/1995/70, p. 5; *G. Prunier*, The Rwanda Crisis, History of a Genocide, New York 1995, p. 239; *A.J. Klinghoffer*, Folkemordet i Rwanda, Mennesker og rettigheter 1996, Vol. 14, pp. 1–9; The United Nations and Rwanda 1993–1996, The United Nations Blue Books Series, Vol. X, New York 1996, p. 7; *J.F. Metzl*, Rwandan Genocide and the International Law of Radio Jamming, AJIL 1997, Vol. 91, pp. 630–632; *H.N. Krug*, Genocide in Rwanda: Lessons Learned and Future Challenges to the UN Human Rights System, NJIL 1998, Vol. 67, pp. 176–178.

Commission of Experts expresses the opinion in its final report[291] that there is overwhelming evidence to prove that acts of genocide against the Tutsi were committed by Hutu elements in a concerted, planned, systematic and methodical way, in violation of Article II of the Genocide Convention.

Furthermore, the Commission of Experts held the view in its final report of 1994 on the situation in the former Yugoslavia that intent may be inferred from sufficient facts. In establishing the intent in certain cases "there will be evidence of actions or omissions of such a degree that the defendant may reasonably be assumed to have been aware of the consequences of his or her conduct".[292] Again it is underlined that the requirement of the presence of an intention to destroy the group as such and not necessarily the motive/s for that behaviour differentiates genocide from other types of war crimes. The *ad hoc* Tribunal's action so far favours this attitude. Željko Meakić (alternately referred to as Mejakić, Mejaković and Mehajić), Chief commander,[293] has been charged with the crime genocide by the *ad hoc* Tribunal for former Yugoslavia. He is accused, on the basis of Article 4 (a), (b) and (c) of the Statute, of intending to destroy, in whole or in part, the Bosnian Muslim and Bosnian Croat people as national, ethnic, or religious groups. With respect to the allegations it is emphasised that the subordinates of Meakić regularly and openly killed, raped and tortured prisoners.

In conclusion, I may ascertain that when acts of rape have been committed with the intent to destroy a specific national, ethnic or religious group in the territory of the former Yugoslavia, they will qualify as genocide. Internationally, there seems to be overwhelming agreement that all the groups that are objects for protection against genocide in the armed conflict of the former Yugoslavia, among them the Serbs, the Croats, the Muslims and the Gypsies, have status as ethnic groups. It has been assumed that they may also, at least to some extent,[294] be characterised by religion, ethnicity and nationality.

Of significance for the interpretation of the term "genocide" is, in the context of this study, among other things the question of whether it covers the policy of "ethnic cleansing". The notion has not been used in a consequent manner. It has

---

[291] The Commission conducted a field mission in Rwanda and its three neighbouring countries, Burundi, the United Republic of Tanzania and Zaire, from 29 August to 17 September 1994 in order to collect substantial information relating to grave violations of international humanitarian law and acts of genocide committed in Rwanda during the conflict. The Commission has also received documents from the Governments of Spain, the USA, France and Ireland, which in turn have received them mainly from NGOs and individuals.

Also the UN Special Rapporteur on Rwanda confirmed in his third report (UN Doc. S/1994/1157/Add.1) the constituent element of genocide, namely the discovery of mass graves and the existence of proof or indications of the planned genocide of Tutsis motivated out of ethnic hatred.

[292] UN Doc. S/1994/674, p. 26. On the requirement of intent see *Y. Dinstein*, Collective Human Rights of Peoples and Minorities, pp. 105–106.

[293] See in addition the investigations of Helsinki Watch, War Crimes in Bosnia-Herzegovina, Vol. II, pp. 115–117 and pp. 163–165.

[294] UN Doc. S/1994/674, p. 25. Even though Bosnian Muslims and Serbs have a common South Slavic ancestry, it has been submitted that they have developed separate religious, national and cultural identities. *V. Morris & M.P. Scharf*, p. 88; *M.P. Scharf*, Balkan Justice, p. 21.

been given several meanings and it has been considered as equivalent to several crimes, among them genocide.[295] It has been suggested that in the context of genocide "ethnic cleansing would be the intention, the motivation or the objective to induce the commitment of some offences".[296] In this regard it should be mentioned that the commitment of the crime genocide was invoked in a suit initiated on 20 March 1993 by the Government of Bosnia-Herzegovina against the Federal Republic of Yugoslavia, which was brought before the International Court of Justice.[297] The Republic of Bosnia and Herzegovina referred in its application to several provisions of the Genocide Convention as well as of the UN Charter.[298] It complained of acts of genocide committed by the Yugoslav forces against citizens of Bosnia and Herzegovina, *e.g.*, charges of rape as a form of genocide.[299] Yugoslavia responded by contending that the Government of Bosnia-Herzegovina was responsible for acts of genocide.[300] Both parties to the armed conflict requested

---

[295] Mr. Burkhalter, Director of Human Rights Watch has, for example, categorically stated that "Ethnic cleansing is genocide. The Serb practice includes the deliberate slaughter of civilians for no other reasons than they are Croat or Muslim", cited by *J. Webb*, Genocide Treaty, Ethnic Cleansing-Substantive and Procedural Hurdles in the Application of the Genocide Convention to Alleged Crimes in the Former Yugoslavia, The Georgia Journal of International and Comparative Law 1993, Vol. 23:377, p. 379, note 14. Professor Cathrine MacKinnon calls furthermore "ethnic cleansing" a "euphemism for genocide". In her view "here is first a genocide in which ethnicity is a tool for political hegemony: the war is an instrument of the genocide: the rapes are an instrument of war". *C. MacKinnon*, Rape, Genocide, and Women's Human Rights, in Mass Rape, A. Stiglmayer (ed.), p. 187. See also *A. Stiglmayer*, The Rapes in Bosnia, in Mass Rape, ibid., pp. 86–93; *E.-I.A. Daes*, New Types of War Crimes, pp. 58–59; *K. Lescure & F. Trintignac*, p. 26.

[296] *N. Lerner*, Ethnic Cleansing, in War Crimes in International Law, Y. Dinstein & M. Tabory (eds.), p. 116.

[297] Case concerning *Application of the Convention on the Prevention and Punishment of the Crime of Genocide (Bosnia-Herzegovina v. Yugoslavia (Serbia and Montenegro)),* Request for the Indication of Provisional Measures. 1993, ICJ Rep. 3, reprinted in ILM 1993, Vol. XXXII, pp. 888–902.

[298] ICJ, Communiqué No. 93/4, 22 March 1993, pp. 1–5. Professor D.Sokolović at the University of Sarajevo has argued that the tragedy of Bosnia should neither be considered as a civil or ethnic war, nor as a religious war, but merely as a planned and implemented crime – genocide. Thus, R. Karadžić announced six months before the tragedy started that genocide was an immediate aim. *D. Sokolović*, Organiseret forbrydelse, Mennesker og rettigheter 1995, No. 3, pp. 280–281. In addition, I may recall the fact that during the drafting process of the Genocide Convention it was argued that the promulgation of all forms of public propaganda promoting genocide should be an equally punishable act within the provisions of the Convention. OR GA, Third Session, Part I, Sixth Committee, 86th and 87th meetings. *F. Malekian*, p. 299. See also UN Doc. E/CN.4/Sub.2/1978/416, pp. 29–30.

[299] The Government of Bosnia-Herzegovina requested the International Court of Justice in its application to adjudge and declare that Yugoslavia (Serbia and Montenegro) and its agents and surrogates are under the obligation to cease and immediately desist from its breaches of for example: murder, summary execution, torture, rape, kidnapping, mayhem, wounding, physical and mental abuse, and the detention of the citizens of the Republic of Bosnia-Herzegovina. See ICJ, Judgment of July 11, 1996, ibid., note 350, § 13(d). It has been argued in the literature that mass rapes in Bosnia fit in the definition of genocide within the Genocide Convention and that this was "implicitly recognised" by the ICJ when issuing a provisional ruling regarding Serbian acts against Bosnia in the above mentioned case. *E.A. Kohn*, p. 207.

[300] The Government of Yugoslavia recommended that the International Court of Justice order the application of provisional measures *inter alia* to direct the authorities under the control of Mr. A. Izebegović to respect the Geneva Conventions of 1949 and the Additional Protocols, "since the genocide of Serbs living

consequently provisional measures under Article 41 of the Statute of the Court. To begin with the International Court of Justice stressed that it cannot and will not make a definitive finding of fact and that provisional measures will be made only to protect the established rights under the Genocide Convention. This is in my view a strong indication that the Court's understanding of, for instance, the policy of "ethnic cleansing" is covered by the term genocide. On this basis, the Court ruled that it had *prima facie* jurisdiction to issue its order under the Genocide Convention, to which Yugoslavia and Bosnia-Herzegovina are parties. The 15-member Court indicated by 13 votes to 1 in its Order of 8 April 1993 that pending its final decision:

> "the Government of the Federal Republic of Yugoslavia (Serbia and Montenegro) should in particular ensure that any military, paramilitary or irregular armed units, which may be directed or supported by it, as well as any organizations and persons, which may be subject to its control, direction or influence, do not commit any acts of genocide, of conspiracy to commit genocide, of direct and public incitement to commit genocide, or of complicity in genocide, whether directed against the Muslim population of Bosnia-Herzegovina or against any other national, ethnical, racial or religious group".[301]

This statement is, in my opinion, clear as to the perception therein reflected that the persons in power in Yugoslavia are being conducting or condoning acts of genocide. Partly on these grounds the relevant passage of the Order of the ICJ was objected by Judge Tarasov,[302] who argued that the provisional measures as formulated by the Court are very close to a pre-judgment of the merits of the case. The power of the International Court of Justice to indicate provisional measures under Article 41 of its Statute has the important object of preserving the respective rights of the parties against an irreparable prejudice, pending the decision on the merits of a dispute by the Court. This is motivated by the need to ensure "the possibility of the execution of whatever judgment the Court may subsequently render".[303] The International Court of Justice has only to consider *what* provisional measures may be called for in accordance with the mentioned provision. As a consequence the Court shall not make any definitive findings of fact, *i.e.*, investigating possible breaches of the Genocide Convention by either party, or of imputability. On the

---

in the 'Republic of Bosnia-Herzegovina' is being carried out by the commission of very serious war crimes". Moreover, the application refers to the fact that "Serbs are being detained because of their ethnic origin and subjected to acts of torture" and "may suffer the same fate as the Serbs in eastern Bosnia, which was the site of the killing and massacres of a few thousands Serb civilians". Ibid., p. 894.

[301] Ibid., p. 901; ICJ Communiqué No. 93/9, 8 April 1993, p. 1.

[302] Judge Tarasov appended a declaration to the Order. The judges voting in favour were: President Sir R. Jennings, Vice-President Oda, Judges Ago, Schwebel, Bedjaoui, Ni, Evensen, Guillaume, Schahabuddeen, Aguilar, Mawdsley, Weeramantry, Ranjeva and Ajibola.

[303] *J. Sztucki,* Interim Measures in The Hague Court, An Attempt at a Scrutiny, Deventer 1983, p. 70. See on interim protection generally *J.B. Elkind,* Interim Protection, A Functional Approach, The Hague 1981.

other hand, allegations of serious international crimes are likely to be controversies about the facts.[304] In this respect, Professor emeritus Sztucki has observed that the ICJ has as a matter of fact mostly dealt with cases in which interim protection has been granted "on the basis of events, which were certain since they already had taken place" or on the basis of events "the occurrence of which in the near future could be regarded as certain".[305] It is needless to say how important it is that the Court handles the case in question with the required impartiality and objectivity. Despite the fact that the Court's Order in the Yugoslavian case underlined that the facts and law of the dispute meanwhile remained unsettled, urging that both parties "should not take any action and should ensure that no action is taken, which may aggravate or extend the existing dispute over the prevention or punishment of the crime genocide, or render it more difficult of solution", the Respondent expressed the view that Bosnia-Herzegovina was seeking an interim judgment on the merits of a case, which is not covered by Article 41 of the ICJ Statute. It remains to be seen on the subject matter in the eventual judgment of the International Court of Justice how the elements of the international crime genocide will be interpreted and whether the question of criminal responsibility under the Genocide Convention will be resolved.[306] The ICJ has, according to Article IX of the Genocide Convention, jurisdiction over disputes concerning the interpretation and application of the Convention.[307] The application of the Republic of Bosnia-

---

[304] ILC's Working Group on the question of an international criminal jurisdiction, UN Doc. A/47/10, § 424.

[305] *J. Sztucki*, Interim Measures in The Hague Court, p. 105.

[306] The ICJ rejected all of the preliminary objections raised by Yugoslavia, among others that the Court lacked jurisdiction and that an international dispute was absent in the earlier referred Judgment of 11 July 1996. The ICJ found that it had jurisdiction to deal with the merits of the case on the basis of the existence of an international dispute between the two states that falls within the scope of Article IX of the Genocide Convention. By an order of January 22, 1998, the Court fixed the time-limit for Bosnia to submit a reply by April 23, 1998 and ordered Yugoslavia to submit a rejoinder by January 22, 1999.

A judgment on the merits of the *Genocide* case will be handed down only after the parties fully brief and argue it. On the basis of the above, it seems that hearings are not likely to start until 1999, *i.e.*, six years after Bosnia filed its application. *P.H.F. Bekker*, Application of the Convention on the Prevention and Punishment of the Crime Genocide, AJIL 1998, Vol. 92, p. 517. See also *P.H.F. Bekker & P.C. Szacz*, Application of the Convention on the Prevention and Punishment of the Crime Genocide, AJIL 1997, Vol. 91, pp. 121–126; *P.H.F. Bekker*, Recent Developments at the World Court, ASIL, Newsletter, March–April 1998, pp. 1 and 8.

[307] In this respect I should mention that the Government of Rwanda, when acceding to the Genocide Convention on 16 April 1975, entered a reservation with the following text: "The Rwandese Republic does not consider itself as bound by Article IX of the Convention". Article IX provides that: "(d)isputes between the Contracting Parties relating to the interpretation, application or fulfilment of the present Convention, including those relating to the responsibility of a State for genocide or for any of the other acts enumerated in Article III, shall be submitted to the International Court of Justice at the request of any of the parties to the dispute". On the other hand, the UN Commission of Experts has determined that there are "more than ample grounds to conclude that every provision laid out in article III of the Genocide Convention has been violated in Rwanda in the period from 6 April to 15 July 1994 in respect of a specific ethnic group as such". UN Doc. S/1994/1405, p. 31. See also UN Doc. E/CN.4/1995/70, pp. 46; UN Doc. E/CN.4/1995/71, pp. 5–8.

Herzegovina refers specifically to this provision as the basis of the jurisdiction of the Court.[308]

The abhorrent policy of "ethnic cleansing" carried out by Serbian forces in Bosnia-Herzegovina has earlier been considered as a form of genocide by the General Assembly in Res. 47/121 of 18 December 1992. This document was recalled by the UN Commission on Human Rights in its Res. 1994/77 of 9 March 1994 and adopted without a vote. On 23 December 1994 the GA again expressed its deep concern about the continuing and substantiated reports of widespread rape and abuse of women in the areas of armed conflict in former Yugoslavia and reaffirmed its understanding of the policy of ethnic cleansing as a form of genocide.[309] Also the Commission on the Status of Women expressed in a resolution adopted at its session in 1994 its outrage at the systematic practice of rape being used as a weapon of war and an instrument of "ethnic cleansing" against women and children in former Yugoslavia.[310] One year later the CSW adopted a resolution without a vote condemning the continuing abhorrent practice of rape and abuse of women and children in the areas of armed conflict in the former Yugoslavia. It expressed its conviction that the heinous practice of rape and abuse of women constitutes "a deliberate weapon of war in fulfilling the policy of 'ethnic cleansing' carried out by Serb forces in the Republic of Bosnia and Herzegovina".[311]

In conclusion, I would like to express my view that "ethnic cleansing" can fall within the meaning of the term genocide, since deliberate destruction of a human group may well take the form of "deportation or mass displacement, of internment

---

308 It should also be mentioned that on July 1993 a further request for provisional measures was made by Bosnia and Herzegovina, reiterating the complaints of the first one and in addition comprising other alleged sources of jurisdiction and offences, *i.e.*, the four 1949 Geneva Conventions on humanitarian law, the Hague Regulations of 1907 and the Nuremberg Charter, Judgment and Principles. However, the ICJ was content to reaffirm its earlier Order, since it took the position of not being able to accept any of the above referred instruments as *prima facie* sources of its jurisdiction. See *Application of the Convention on the Prevention and Punishment of the Crime of Genocide, Bosnia and Herzegovina v. Yugoslavia (Serbia and Montenegro), Provisional Measures*, 1993 ICJ Rep. 325, Order of September 13 1993. *R.Y. Jennings*, The United Nations at Fifty, The International Court of Justice after Fifty Years, AJIL 1995, p. 502.

309 GA Res. 49/205, 23 December 1994. See also the report reprinted in UN Doc. A/49/610/Add.3.

310 CSW Res. 38/9, UN Doc. E/CN.6/1994/14, p. 26.

311 It might be of some interest to note that following the adoption of the text, the representative of the Russian Federation said that his country had condemned, and would continue to condemn, human rights violations no matter which side was responsible. Nonetheless, in such a large-scale and bloody conflict as that taking place in the territory of the former Yugoslavia, there "cannot be angels in white and devils in black". Thus, each individual, regardless of ethnic origin, that was responsible for rape or violating the rights of women in the territory of the former Yugoslavia would be judged by the International Criminal Tribunal for the Former Yugoslavia. Furthermore, the representative emphasised the fact that the practice referred to – ethnic cleansing as a form of genocide – no longer existed. It had in the past and at that time Russia had opposed it. He explained the Russian position as follows: "(t)he United Nations, in its documents, must reflect today's realities, rather than the historic past in a distorted context". This standpoint partly explains the Russian Federation's voting against the retention of preambular § 8 of the draft resolution. Thus, 35 states voted in favour to 1 against and 5 abstained (Angola, Belarus, India, Madagascar and Namibia). UN Doc. E/CN.6/1995/L.10; CSW, 39th session, 12th meeting, 29 March 1995.

and enslavement with forced labour, of denationalisation by systematic terrorism, torture, inhuman treatment and physical intimidation measures".[312]

8.3.2.3.2. Rape – A Vehicle of Genocide

My point of departure in this section of the study is the assertion that intentional acts of rape committed for the purpose of destroying a specific human group[313] are included in the Genocide Convention's and the *ad hoc* Tribunal's definition of genocide both in the physical and in the biological sense. Acts of "physical genocide" are listed in Article II, §§ a, b, c of the Genocide Convention and in Article 4 §§ a, b, c of the *ad hoc* Tribunal's Statute. They imply the intentional destruction for genocidal purposes of the physical life – killing, bodily or mental harm – of a large number of persons who are members of a target group.[314] This is also the case with compelling abortions.[315] The second category, "biological genocide" is stipulated in Article II, § d of the Genocide Convention and in Article 4 § d of the

---

[312] *P.N. Drost*, The Crime of State, Vol. II, Genocide, p. 124.

[313] Of interest is to note here that the National Alliance of Women's Organizations submitted a proposal during the process of the drafting of the Genocide Convention that the definition of genocide should be extended to cover acts such as rape, forced prostitution and forced pregnancy on the basis of the argument that they "qualify as persecution-based offences because they constitute discrimination on the basis of gender" and that they are committed against a stable and identifiable group, namely women. *V. Morris & M.P. Scharf*, p. 88, note 279. Similar proposals to include gender as one of the targets groups protected by the Genocide Convention's definition have been made in the contemporary international law literature as well. Kelly Askin has argued persuasively in this respect that "controlling, manipulating or eliminating reproductive capabilities can obviously exterminate a group". *K.D. Askin*, p. 343. See also the discussions on Article 20(a) of the ILC draft statute for an international criminal court. UN Doc. A/50/22, Suppl. No. 22, §§ 60–61. A few writers have in this regard drawn parallels to the international standards for political asylum, which increasingly recognise gender as a source of persecution. *R. Copelon,* Surfacing Gender, p. 207; *C.N. Niarchos*, p. 679, note 184; *I.L. Sajor*, Our Common Grounds, in Common Grounds, I.L. Sajor (ed.), p. 5.

Among the motives for the rapes of an estimated 200,000 Bengali women during the war of independence from Pakistan the genocidal one, *i.e.*, the intention to destroy the racial distinctiveness of the Bengali people, has been mentioned on several occasions. See for example *R. Copelon*, Gendered War Crimes: Reconceptualizing Rape in Time of War, p. 197.

[314] There could be no doubt about the bodily as well as mental harm that victims of rape and forced pregnancy experience. Sexual violence causes often the death of the women exposed to it. There are reports suggesting that women in Bosnia-Herzegovina and Croatia who were raped by Serb soldiers and who did not became pregnant were often murdered. *A. Aafjes*, p. 20. See also *R. Seifert*, War and Rape, in Mass Rape, Stiglmayer (ed.), pp. 55–59; *C.A. MacKinnon*, Rape, Genocide, and Women's Human Rights, p. 187; *K.D. Askin*, p. 341; UN Doc. E/CN.6/1998/5, § 52.

In Rwanda, for example, the militiamen bearing the HIV-virus (Rwanda is one of the countries with the highest rate of HIV-positive persons) used it as a "weapon" during the genocide. Thus, they raped girls and women with the intent to transmit it to women of a particular ethnicity and to cause delayed death. Death has also resulted from gang rape, from complicated pregnancies etc. See UN Doc. E/CN.4/1996/68, § 20 and *R. Muzigo-Morrison*, Gender Issues Emerging From The Genocide in Rwanda and the Trials Taking Place in Arusha, paper of November 5, 1997, p. 3.

[315] Professor Lemkin called the techniques for abortions used by the Nazi doctors for "ktonotechnics", from the Greek *ktonos* meaning killing. *R. Lemkin*, Genocide as A Crime Under International Law, p. 148.

*ad hoc* Tribunal's Statute. It aims at the forcible prevention of births within the target group. Its objective is consequently to prevent the group's preservation and development. This is the case when marriages are prevented and reproduction is hampered by various means within the group, for example, compelling abortion, sterilisations and castrations.[316] Thus, by the imposition of enforced birth control, the group will undoubtedly be reduced in its size. Professor Lemkin has illustrated in his study *Axis Rule in Occupied Europe* the biological aspect of genocide by taking the following examples from the German Nazi practice during the Second World War:

> "measures to favour a lower birth rate in non-German populations and a higher rate in German groups/... / such as forcibly separating male from female, deliberate undernourishment of parents in order, *inter alia*, to lower the survival capacity of children born to weakened adults, and conversely, the payment of benefits to children fathered by German troops".[317]

Recently, the Trial Chamber of the Rwandan Tribunal stated in the *Akayesu* judgment that imposing measures intended to prevent births within a group should be constructed "as sexual mutilation, the practice of sterilisation, forced birth control, separation of the sexes and prohibition of marriages".[318]

Against that background I shall try to examine the question of whether raped and forcibly impregnated women in the course of the armed conflict in the former Yugoslavia have been the victims of genocidal measures. The view has been put forward by the prominent scholar Professor Catherine MacKinnon and the Pulitzer Prize winner Mr. Roy Gutman that the systematic raping of Bosnian women constitutes a central element of the term genocide.[319] According to both writers, forced impregnation has to be considered as an attempt to block procreation of the Bosnian Muslim group.[320] Also in the view of Rhonda Copelon forced impregnation is central to genocidal rape. It is "condoned as such, when it reflects an intent to harm the victimised race".[321] I agree very much with this view partly because

---

[316] Professor Lemkin called these techniques for "sterotechnics", from the Greek *steiros* meaning infertile or steirosis meaning infertility, ibid., p. 148.

[317] *P. Thornberry*, p. 61.

[318] *Prosecutor v. Akayesu*, Judgment § 508.

[319] On the other hand, in the view of Helsinki Watch rape can be used as a means of carrying out genocide, but the crime itself does not constitute genocide, "even when committed on a mass basis". Helsinki Watch, War Crimes in Bosnia-Herzegovina, Vol. II, p. 21.

[320] *A.K. Wing*, Book Reviews and Notes; Mass Rape. The War Against Women in Bosnia-Herzegovina, A.Stigmayer (ed.), University of Nebraska Press 1994, AJIL 1994, Vol. 88, pp. 849 and 850.

The Commission of Experts recommended in its final report to the S.C. that the Prosecutor "explore fully the relation between the policy of systematic rape under a responsible command as a crime against humanity on the one hand, and as such a policy as a crime of genocide, on the other". UN Doc. S/1994/1405, § 145. See furthermore *M.C. Bassiouni & M. McCormick*, pp. 32–33.

[321] *R. Copelon*, Gendered War Crimes: Reconceptualizing Rape in Time of War, p. 206.

proof has already been given to the assertion that a great number of impregnated women actually have been held captive beyond the legal period for the termination of a pregnancy in Croatia and Bosnia-Herzegovina. There can be little doubt about the intention of the perpetrators, namely that the captivity is carried out deliberately to make termination of the pregnancies impossible. Moreover, reproductive crimes inflict serious physical and/or mental injury contributing to the destruction of the targeted group. One can also, not without reason, assume that a woman may meet considerable psychological difficulties to procreate again after being raped (often repetitively for a long period of time). It has been submitted that very few if any of the "comfort women" during World War II were able subsequently to bear children.[322] In other words, inability to give birth again has "a direct link with the physical destruction of the group".[323]

The *Akayesu* judgment is precedent-setting in this respect. The Rwandan Tribunal emphasised that:

> "measures intended to prevent births within the group may be physical, but can also be mental. For instance, rape can be a measure intended to prevent births when the person raped refuses subsequently to procreate, in the same way that members of a group can be led, through threats or trauma, not to procreate".[324]

Acts of rape may consequently *indirectly* lead to the prevention of births within the target group and eventually lead to the group's destruction. The plaintiffs' allegations, presented in the *Doe v. Karadžić* and *Kadić v. Karadžić* cases,[325] of acts of

---

322 *R. Copelon,* op.cit., pp. 204–205; *K.D. Askin*, p. 401.

323 *A. Brunet & S. Rousseau*, p. 47.

324 *Prosecutor v. Akayesu*, Judgment § 509.

325 No. 93 Civ. 0878 (S.D.N.Y. Feb. 11, 1993). *Doe v. Karadžić* and *Kadić v. Karadžić* (No. 93 Civ. 1163 (S.D.N.Y., Mar. 1, 1993)) were the first lawsuits brought under the American Torture Victim Protection Act, which grants federal courts in the United States subject matter jurisdiction in a civil action for violations of international law. Both actions were class actions. Thus, many of the plaintiffs were sexually assaulted by military forces under the command and control of Karadžić. Some were thereby forcibly impregnated. *Doe I and II*, Second Circuit Brief (Docket No. 94–9035), at 4. Here follows a brief background of the cases. On 13 October 1995 the US Court of Appeals for the Second Circuit reinstated a class action lawsuit against R. Karadžić, charging him with responsibility for genocide, war crimes and crimes against humanity, including rape. On May 31, 1992, eight Bosnian-Serb soldiers raped a teenage prisoner (Jane Doe I), while she was imprisoned in a Bosnian-Serb concentration camp. This camp functioned as a "rape/death camp for women and a camp for reproducing 'Serbian' babies through forced impregnation". *M. Brandt*, Doe v. Karadžić: Redressing Non-State Acts of Gender-Specific Abuse Under the Alien Tort Statute, Minnesota Law Review 1995, Vol. 79, p. 1413.

On June 28, 1992, soldiers beat an eighteen-year-old women (Jane Doe II) while she watched Bosnian-Serb soldiers rape her mother. On September 7, 1994, these women and children, on behalf of themselves and all other victims of gross human rights abuses perpetrated by Bosnian-Serb forces, brought two related class action lawsuits (*Doe v. Karadžić* and *K. v. Karadžić*) in the United States against R. Karadžić. Plaintiffs personally served R. Karadžić with the suits while he was in New York in February 1993. The Center for Constitutional Rights, the International League for Human Rights and the International Women's Human Rights Clinic of the City University of New York Law School submitted the action on behalf of plaintiffs Doe I and Doe II (the plaintiffs filed their complaint anonymously

Bosnian-Serb forced impregnation of Muslims and Croats to increase the birth of Serbian children are based on a similar reasoning. Thus, they are considered to "impose measures intended to prevent births within the (Muslim and Croat) groups".[326] Therefore forced impregnation and forced pregnancy are regarded as fitting the definition of the crime genocide.

Another relevant circumstance, when discussing rape in the context of the definition of genocide, is the fact that in most Muslim societies a man's honour is dependent upon that of his wife. This means among others that in cases of rape a social stigma is attached to the entire family. Forced pregnancy often results, moreover, in the abandoning of the children thus born since the group most likely will not accept them. In Islamic communities the ethnicity of the father is as a rule determinative for the ethnicity of the offspring.[327] Consequently, there might be strong psychological barriers to overcome for men belonging to the Muslim party in an armed conflict to accept the continuation of family life with a raped woman. The husband and the other members of the family will blame the wife for not being able to protect her sexual purity and accordingly be considered as "unclean", leading most probably to her rejection. Many Muslim women will in like manner be socially marginalised and rejected by their former community. This type of gender-based violence brings consequently about the dissolution of the existing family structure,[328] which forms the basis of the ethnic group and of the nation. The long-term consequence may be a threat to the physical existence of the group. A certain support for my standpoint might be derived from the definition of the concept "destruction" as introduced by Professor Lemkin. According to him, genocide implies "a co-ordinated plan of different actions aimed at the destruction of essential foundations of life of national groups. The objectives of such a plan would

---

because of fear for their safety). The United States District Court for the Southern District of New York dismissed the lawsuit for lack of subject matter jurisdiction. Thus, the court refused to acknowledge, pursuant to the Alien Tort Statute, that certain international treaties and customary international law reach non-state conduct. However, the Court of Appeals disagreed with the District Court dismissal by holding that fundamental rules of international law apply to Karadžić and his force. Therefore, they can be held accountable in US courts for their actions. Worth mentioning is also that the US Government in September 1995 filed a brief with the Second Circuit, in which it urged the Court to reverse the lower court decision and allow the case to proceed. Academic commentators have also brought strong arguments in favour of the assertion that the Alien Tort Statute encompasses the acts of ethnic cleansing, including gender-specific abuses, that should be imputed to Karadžić as head of the Bosnian-Serb Republic and armed forces. *M. Brandt*, id., p. 1416 et seq. See furthermore Center for Constitutional Rights, An Activist Guide: Bringing International Human Rights Claims in United States Courts; Lawsuits Against Individuals, Corporations And Governments: a Remedy For Human Rights Abuses Against Women, New York 1995 and *T.R. Posner*, AJIL 1996, Vol. 90, pp. 658–663. See also *E. Johnson*, Kadić v. Karadžić and Doe I and II v. Karadžić: The Latest Stage in Alien Tort Act Jurisprudence, GYIL 1996, Vol. 39, pp. 434–467.

326 *M. Brandt*, p. 1445.

327 *K.D. Askin*, p. 339.

328 Professor Bassiouni has, in addition, pointed to the circumstance that in Islamic society a woman who has had sexual relations outside of marriage, despite the fact that she has not consented, will not be marriageable. *M.C. Bassiouni & P. Manikas*, The Law of the International Criminal Tribunal, p. 587; *K.D. Askin*, p. 339; *F.A. Kohn*, p. 204

be the disintegration of the political and social institutions of culture, language, national feelings, religion, and the economical existence of national groups, and the destruction of personal security, liberty, health, dignity, and even lives of the individuals belonging to such groups".[329]

In my opinion also the conscious policy of prolonged starvation of the designated group can lead to the prevention of births within that group. Numerous spontaneous abortions will be caused by the lack of food in combination with psychological traumas, again affecting the physical existence of the group. In other words, the characteristics of genocide in the biological and in the physical meaning of the term are in the above mentioned circumstances in evidence here.

However, as earlier pointed out the requirement of proof of the intent to destroy a designated human group can make it difficult to establish guilt as regards a majority of the perpetrators in the former Yugoslavia, with one major exception in my view, namely when rape has been committed in the special detention camps. There, women have repeatedly been raped until they have become impregnated. Then they have been held in detention for extended periods of time in order to past the period for obtaining legal abortions.[330] These women have consequently been subjected to forced maternity, *i.e.*, forced to give birth to children, whom the enemy considers belong to its own ethnic group.[331] Even though there is uncertainty as to the number of births that may result from acts of rape and the fact that a precise figure probably never can be ascertained, the investigative mission (called also the Warburton mission) into the treatment of Muslim women in former Yugoslavia, which was carried out in 1992 and in 1993 by a special team appointed by the EC, suggests in its final report a probable figure of 1,000 pregnancies based on an indicative figure of 20,000 women being raped. The Warburton mission observes in this respect, however, that estimates vary widely, ranging from 10,000 to as many as 60,000 victims involved. Moreover, the mission underlines that the Bosnia-Herzegovinian Muslim women indeed form the vast majority of the victims, but that there are

---

[329] *R. Lemkin*, Axis Rule in Occupied Europe, p. 79.

[330] Such practices have occurred also in the context of the genocide in Rwanda. *R. Muzigo-Morrison*, p. 3; *E. Richter-Lyonette*, p. 10; Prosecuting Human Rights Violations Against Women, J. Blaustein Institute, ibid., p. 3.

[331] *P. Granjon & P. Deloche*, Ex-Yugoslavie: Le viol devient une arme de guerre, Réfugiés 1993, No. 93, p. 43. In the context of the former Yugoslavia it has been argued that the strong "ethno-genetic narcissism, nationalism, and forced impregnation", whereby the children born as a result of rape were considered to be the ethnic products of their fathers only, "would indicate a desire to destroy the gene pool of the target ethnic group". *M.C. Bassiouni & P. Manikas*, p. 588. Several reports indicate that perpetrators taunted their victims with the words: "Now you'll have a Serb baby". International Human Rights Law Group, No Justice, No Peace, 1993, p. 3. See furthermore *D. Aydelott*, Mass Rape During War: Prosecuting Bosnian Rapists Under International Law, Emory International Law Review 1993, Vol. 7, p. 585; *Y.S. Wu*, Genocidal Rape in Bosnia: Redress in United States Courts Under the Alien Tort Claims Act, UCLA Women's Law Journal 1993, Vol. 4, p. 103; *M. Brandt*, p. 1421; *J. Kuzmanović*, p. 57; *C. Chinkin*, Rape and Sexual Abuse of Women, p. 333; *C.A. MacKinnon*, Crimes of War, Crimes of Peace, p. 67 and my earlier references to the *Gagović and others v. The Prosecutor* case.

Similarly in Rwanda, children of parents belonging to different ethnic groups, take on the ethnic identity of the father. *H.N. Krug*, p. 177. See also *Prosecutor v. Akayesu*, Judgment § 508.

many reports of the rape of Croat and Serbian women and children as well.[332] In this respect also the UN Special Rapporteur on Violence against Women, Mrs. Coomaraswamy, has paid much attention to the uncertainty of figures related to acts of rape. According to her the numbers of acts of rape committed by enemy troops have very often been used as war propaganda. In other words, the number of rapes committed by a belligerent's own troops is being underrated when reported, whereas the number of incidents with enemy involvement is exaggerated.[333] This author agrees with the reasoning of Rhonda Copelon that, *vis-à-vis* rape, it is not the massive numbers, but rather the patterns of abuse that are particularly important for its classification as a war crime, including genocide.[334] In addition, the UN Special Rapporteur on systematic rape has taken the position that with the necessary intent element "even a single act of rape may theoretically be ground for a persecution for the crime genocide".[335]

The existing uncertainty in regard to the required proof of intent to destroy a designated group in the context of the conflict in the former Yugoslavia has been challenged by Professor Paust,[336] who has argued that rape as part of proscribed methods or tactics covered by the paragraphs (b), (c) and (d) of the definition of the crime of genocide according to the Genocide Convention and the *ad hoc* Tribunal's Statute "need not involve systematic governmental planning or be committed against any civilian population".[337] Mr. Paust emphasises that the use of rape as part of the general strategy of "ethnic cleansing"[338] has been so widespread and frequent in Bosnia-Herzegovina that its "wilful or deliberate and systematic nature

---

[332] Report to the European Community Foreign Ministers, UN Doc. S/25 240, 3 February 1993, pp. 3 and 5. Helsinki Watch has been monitoring abuses committed during the armed conflicts in the former Yugoslavia since they began as well as in Slovenia and Croatia in the summer of 1991. On the issue of the number of women who have been forced to bear children consequent to rape, see Helsinki Watch, War Crimes in Bosnia-Herzegovina, Vol. II, pp. 21–22; pp. 228–229 and 233. Reference has been made to cases in which raped women from Bosnia have sought abortions at a hospital in Zagreb, but since it was more than ten weeks after conception, they were required by Croatian law to carry their pregnancies to term. Mentioned has also been made of the visit of a team of experts on the behalf of the U.N. Human Rights Commission in the former Yugoslavia in 1993, which has identified 119 pregnancies as a result of rape in 1992 in six major medical centres. A few Bosnian Muslims, among them Zejnil Delalić, Hazim Delić and Esad Landžo have been indicted by the ICTY for among other things rape of Serbian inmates at a prison camp in central Bosnia in 1992. *Z. Delalić & Others (Celebići)*, ICTY indictment of 21 March 1996. The *Celebići* case is the first case before the ICTY in which rape and sexual assault were prosecuted. Nevertheless, rape was not considered in the context of genocide.

[333] UN Doc. E/CN.4/1995/42, p. 67.

[334] *R. Copelon*, Gendered War Crimes: Reconceptualizing Rape in Time of War, p. 203.

[335] UN Doc. E/CN.4/Sub.2/1998/13, § 52.

[336] During the Vietnam war, Professor Paust was a Captain, JAGG, and on the faculty of the US Army Judge Advocate General's School. See *J.J. Paust*, Superior Orders and Command Responsibility, in International Criminal Law, Vol. III, Enforcement, M.C. Bassiouni (ed.), New York 1987, p. 73.

[337] See *J.J. Paust*, Correspondence, AJIL 1994, Vol. 88, p. 88.

[338] Several other commentators have supported the view that mass rape and other gender-specific sexual abuses, when carried out to further the Bosnian-Serb "ethnic cleansing" campaign, and when purposed to destroy Bosnian-Muslims, constitute acts of genocide. *E.A. Kohn*, p. 202; *L.E. Fletcher & K.M. Pratt*, p. 99; *M. Brandt*, p. 1432.

is self-evident", *i.e.*, the low-level military personnel did not need direct orders to understand that the use of this strategy was approved. Therefore, such circumstances are expected to lead to criminal dereliction and/or complicity. Here I should mention that Article 4 (3) of the *ad hoc* Tribunal's Statute, which reflects the relevant provision of the Genocide Convention, provides punishment for:

"a) genocide;
b) conspiracy to commit genocide;
c) direct and public incitement to commit genocide;
d) attempt to commit genocide;
e) complicity in genocide".

Genocide is consequently a crime, for which the responsible individuals shall be punished.[339] The rape of women in an organised fashion points to the fact that local commanders must know that their soldiers are committing this crime but doing nothing to stop the abuses. Unfortunately, as Helsinki Watch has observed, "the failure to punish rapists appears to be as consistent and widespread as the act of rape itself", despite the fact that soldiers on many occasions have identified themselves to their victims.[340] On the other hand, it is also known that rapists often have threatened their victims with future injury to themselves and their family members in order to ensure women's silence.

The Beijing Platform of Action establishes in § 145(d) that rape in the conduct of armed conflict constitutes under certain circumstances an act of genocide as defined in the Genocide Convention and governments must take all measures required for the protection of women and children from such acts and strengthen mechanisms to investigate and punish all those responsible and bring the perpetrators to justice.[341]

The provision on genocide might be applicable in cases of mass and systematic rape in connection with Article 7 of the *ad hoc* Tribunal's Statute dealing with personal responsibility for political and military leaders.[342] The first paragraph of the mentioned provision stipulates individual criminal responsibility for any person who "planned, instigated, ordered, committed or otherwise aided and abetted in the plan-

---

339 For an overview of the five acts punishable under the Genocide Convention see *P.N. Drost*, Vol. II, pp. 87–92.

Article 6 of the Genocide Convention provides: "Persons charged with genocide or any of the other acts enumerated in Article III shall be tried by a competent tribunal of the State in the territory of which the act was committed, or by such international penal tribunal as may have jurisdiction with respect to those Contracting Parties, which shall have accepted its jurisdiction." Though an international criminal tribunal has not been created for that purpose, universal jurisdiction to punish acts of genocide has been established as a matter of customary law. *Y. Dinstein*, The Defence of "Obedience to Superior Orders" in International Law, pp. 217–223; *M.N. Shaw*, pp. 815–818; *M.T. Kamminga*, p. 6. The case law on prosecutions based on the principle of universal jurisdiction has increased significantly since 1997. For a review of the most recent cases decided on domestic level see *M.T. Kaminga*, pp. 9–14.

340 Helsinki Watch, War Crimes in Bosnia-Herzegovina, Vol. II, p. 22.

341 UN Doc. A/CONF.177/20, 17 October 1995.

342 The charge of genocide has been used, as we shall see below, against superior authorities in the chain of command. See UN Doc. E/CN.4/Sub.2/1998/13. § 51; UN Doc. E/CN.4/1998/54, p. 16.

ning, preparation or execution" of, *e.g.*, the crime genocide. But since genocide is the ultimate crime, *i.e.*, the crime of crimes, I agree very much with the words of Mr. Ben Whitaker: "Punishment after the event, however desirable, does not supersede the priority challenge of preventing genocide".[343] The importance of Article VIII of the Genocide Convention should be underlined in this regard. It authorises any of the treaty parties to call upon "the competent organs of the United Nations to take such actions under the Charter of the United Nations as they consider appropriate for the prevention and suppression of acts of genocide or any of the other acts enumerated in Article III". In fact, I may establish that this provision has given support to the United Nations' reaction to the situations in the former Yugoslavia and Rwanda.

In summary, several forms of sexual violence whereby women's reproductive capacity[344] has been used as a means to prevent births within a specific group and causes its destruction may be considered as a form of genocide. Depending on the factual circumstances, the *ad hoc* Tribunals can prosecute rape (*e.g.*, in consequence of which the reproductive system of the individual in question has been permanently damaged), forced impregnation and forced pregnancy under the provisions dealing with genocide of their Statutes. In fact, the Office of the Prosecutor for both *ad hoc* Tribunals has issued indictments charging sexual violence as genocide and thereby establishing a clear link between sexual violence, forced impregnation and genocide.[345] In its significant contribution to the jurisprudence on gender-based crimes, the *Akayesu* judgment, the Rwandan Tribunal ruled that: "In patriarchal societies, where membership of a group is determined by the identity of the father, an example of a measure intended to prevent births within a group is the case where, during rape, a woman of the said group is deliberately impregnated by a man of another group, with the intent to have her give birth to a child who will consequently not belong to its mother's group".[346] The *ad hoc* Tribunal for the former Yugoslavia has also inferred that forced pregnancy may constitute evidence of genocidal intent. It concluded, *e.g.*, in the *Karadžić* and *Mladić* Rule 61 decision that "It would seem that the aim of many rapes was enforced impregnation".[347]At the same time several of the indictments issued by the ICTY are disappointing in this regard. Thus, I agree very much with the criticism expressed by Kelly Askin that Dragoljub Kunarac could have been charged of genocide for raping a woman and telling her that she "would now give birth to Serb babies".[348] Neither does the

[343] *B. Whitaker*, Genocide: the ultimate crime, in Human Rights, P. Davies (ed.), London 1991, p. 54.

[344] One of the distinctive feature of genocidal rape is according to Rhonda Copelon "the focus on women as reproductive vessels". *R. Copelon*, Surfacing Gender, p. 206. Professor Bassiouni has, in addition, noted that the majority of the raped women during the conflicts in the former Yugoslavia were of reproductive age. *M.C. Bassiouni & P. Manikas*, p. 588.

[345] UN Doc. E/CN.6/1998/5, § 53.

[346] *Prosecutor v. Akayesu*, Judgment § 508.

[347] *Prosecutor v. Karadžić and Mladić, Review of the Indictment Pursuant to Rule 61*, cases Nos. IT–95–5- R61 and IT–95–18-R61, 11 July 1996.

[348] *Prosecutor v. Gagović and Others*, amendment of the indictment, 13 July 1998, § 6.1. This criticism is also valid for the indictments of Janjić, Vuković, Janković and Zelenović. *Prosecutor v. Gagović and Others*, counts 36 55. *K.D. Askin*, Sexual Violence, pp. 119 and 121.

*Sikirica* indictment of 21 July 1995 contain rape charges in the context of genocide. Sikirica was the commander of the Keraterm camp where it is known that such forms of sexual violence have taken place.

### *8.3.2.4. Crimes against Humanity*

#### 8.3.2.4.1. General Observations

The traditional definition of the legal category "crimes against humanity"[349] covers grossly inhumane and atrocious offences, which are part of a large, widespread and systematic action against any civilian population[350] based on race, religion, nationality or political opinion. The International Law Commission has in its commentary to Article 4 of its draft Code observed that motives generally characterising a crime against humanity derive from "racial or national hatred, religion or political opinion".[351] An important limitation of the notion "crimes against humanity" envisages a presumption that the offences shall not be directed against individual civilians. The acts must, furthermore, be part of a policy of persecution or discrimination.[352] In other words, the perpetrators of crimes against humanity are mostly connected with an official authority. The crimes must consequently be of a systematic and organised nature.[353] This precondition makes a significant difference between the crime "grave

[349] For an in depth analysis of the notion "crimes against humanity" see *M.C. Bassiouni*, Crimes Against Humanity in International Criminal Law, Dordrecht 1992.

Even though the preambles of The Hague Conventions No. II of 1899 and No. IV of 1907 refer to the "laws of humanity", the term "crimes against humanity" was used as such and given substantive meaning for the first time by the Governments of Great Britain, France and Russia in a declaration of May 28, 1915, in which they considered the Turkish genocidal massacre of its Armenian minority in 1915 as "crimes against humanity and civilisation, for which all members of the Turkish Government will be held responsible together with its agents implicated in the massacres". *Y. Khushalani*, p. 14; *B.B. Ferencz*, p. 107; *L.S. Sunga*, p. 42. See also *E. Schwelb*, Crimes against Humanity, BYIL 1946, Vol. 23, pp.178–226; *M.C. Bassiouni*, Crimes Against Humanity, in International Criminal Law, Vol. III, pp. 52–53 and *M.C. Bassiouni & P. Manikas*, p. 589.

[350] This is a significant difference between the notion "war crimes" and the notion "crimes against humanity". The first comprises offences against soldiers as well. In the context of the *ad hoc* Tribunal's jurisdiction the Commission of Experts has underlined that the wording "any civilian population" should not lead to "any quick conclusions concerning people who at one particular point in time did bear arms". UN Doc. S/1994/674, p. 21.

[351] UN Doc. A/CN.4/L.464/Add.4.

[352] UN Doc. S/1994/674, p. 23; *P.N. Drost*, Vol. II, pp. 185–186. Professor Meron has criticised the Tribunal's holding in the *Tadić* case that "all crimes against humanity, not only persecution, require discriminatory intent" since this is in his view a departure from customary law, which does not require such intent. *T. Meron*, War Crimes Law Comes of Age, p. 465.

Professor Chinkin has, furthermore, observed that the requirement of a discriminatory behaviour as an element of the definition of crimes against humanity, is equally well provided by the gender discrimination in regard of crimes against women. *C. Chinkin*, Rape and Sexual Abuse of Women in International Law, p. 333. See also UN Doc. E/CN.4/Sub.2/1998/13, § 40. It is significant that the definition of crimes against humanity, which is contained in Article 7 of the ICC's Statute, does not require proof of a discriminatory motive.

[353] The Legal Committee of the United Nations War Crimes Commission referred to these prerequisites in its definition of crimes against humanity, as follows: "As a rule systematic mass action, particularly if it was authoritative, was necessary to transform a common crime punishable only under

breach" of international humanitarian law and the "crime against humanity", since occasional and isolated acts constituting offences under international law do not qualify as crimes against humanity by themselves. It is not the type of behaviour in itself (wilful killing, torture, rape, inhumane treatment, etc.) that constitutes the decisive element of the term's definition, but above all the scale, on which the crimes have been carried out against the civilian population. The Nuremberg Tribunal expressed during the proceedings its general opinion on the notion of crimes against humanity as follows:

> "The policy of terror was certainly carried out on a vast scale, and in many cases it was organised and systematic. The policy of persecution, repression and murder of civilians in Germany before the war of 1939, who were likely to be hostile to the Government, was most ruthlessly carried out".[354]

In sum, significant elements of the classical notion "crimes against humanity" are thus the character of the overall policy, the means employed to implement it and the number of victims affected.

Another major distinguishing feature of that notion is that it prohibits the relevant offences in all armed conflicts, be they of an international, a national or a mixed character. The term includes crimes committed in the circumstances of peace as well.[355]

---

municipal law, into a crime against humanity, which thus became also the concern of international law. Only crimes which either by their magnitude and savagery or by their large number or by the fact that a similar pattern was applied at different times and places, endangered the international community or shocked the conscience of mankind, warranted intervention by States other than that on whose territory the crimes had been committed, or whose subjects had become their victims". History of the United Nations War Crimes Commission, p. 178.

[354] *Nazi Conspiracy and Aggression*, Opinion and Judgment. United States Government Printing Office, Washington 1947, p. 84.

[355] The conclusion of the Inter-American Commission on Human Rights in its 1995 report on human rights in Haiti is a welcome contribution in this regard. The Commission stated that rape as a weapon of terror against women is a crime against humanity in peacetime. OEA/Ser.L/V/II.88, Doc.10 rev., February 9, 1995, § 135.

The defence in the *Tadić* case claimed that "the Tribunal only has jurisdiction under Article 5 of the Statute if it involves crimes that have been committed in the execution of or in connection with an international armed conflict" and broadening the scope of Article 5 to crimes when committed in armed conflicts of an internal character offends the *nullum crimen* principle. The Trial Chamber and the Appeals Chamber did not agree with this argumentation. In the view of the Trial Chamber, the nexus in the Nuremberg Charter between crimes against humanity and crimes against peace and war crimes was "peculiar" to the context of the Nuremberg Tribunal. Thus, no nexus is required in customary international law between crimes against humanity and the other two categories. It seems to me that the Trial Chamber expressed its disappointment in its conclusion that Article 5 of the Statute is more restrictive than the general definition of crimes against humanity recognised by customary international law, in that it requires a nexus with an armed conflict, be it international or internal. *The Prosecutor v. Tadić,* Defence motion on jurisdiction, Decision of 10 August 1995 (Trial Chamber II), §§ 77 and 83. With this in mind I would like to refer to a recent proposal made by Kelly Askin on a definition of crimes against humanity which would circumvent the limitations in the *ad hoc* Tribunals' Statutes as follows: "Crimes against humanity are serious violations of international humanitarian law, committed with the intent to destroy, physically or mentally, in whole or in part, any particular group or class of persons. Such crimes

In this respect the notion "crimes against humanity" is wider than "war crimes". Crimes against humanity are, furthermore, inhumane acts directed against a specific group or against any civilian population, *i.e.*, people who are not belligerents, be they enemy citizens, other non-citizens or the citizens of the own warring party.[356]

The legal category of international crimes discussed above is relatively new.[357] It was for the first time explicitly defined as a punishable offence under international law in an international document in Article VI of the Charter of the Nuremberg Tribunal (annexed to the London Agreement of 1945),[358] which has since come to represent general principles of international law and as such to be considered as one of the sources of international law as stated in article 38 of the Statute of the International Court of Justice.[359] The relevant provision reads as follows:

> "The following acts, or any of them, are crimes coming within the jurisdiction of the Tribunal, for which there shall be individual responsibility:... c) **Crimes against humanity**: Namely, murder, extermination, enslavement, deportation, and other inhumane acts committed against any civilian population, before or during the war, or persecutions on political, racial or religious grounds in execution of or in connection with any crime within the jurisdiction of the Tribunal, whether or not in violation of the domestic law of the country where perpetrated".[360]

---

include, but are not limited to, wilful killing, torture, and sexual assault". *K.D. Askin*, p. 348, note 1098. It can be also noted here that Article 7 of the ICC Statute does not require nexus between armed conflict and crimes against humanity. This opens in my view a new and unexpected possibility for the world community to start legal proceedings against violations of human rights. Of course, it would only be possible to apply this provision to situations where systematic or widespread violations occur, but there are many examples of these in modern history perpetrated by totalitarian regimes and dictators all over the world. For comments on Article 7 of the ICC see *D. Robinson*, pp. 43–57 and *M.H. Arsanjani*, pp. 31–34.

[356] *L. Hannikainen*, p. 435.

[357] Judge Röling has explained that: "The crime against humanity is new, not in the sense that those acts were formerly not criminal… (t)he newness is not the newness of the crime, but rather the newness of the competence to try it". Cited in *T. Meron*, International Criminalization of Internal Atrocities, p. 567, note 74.

[358] Nuremberg was chosen for symbolic reasons. The anti-Semitic "Nuremberg Laws" had been among other things decreed in 1935 there. They made marriage or sexual intimacy between Jews and Germans a criminal offence. *M.P. Scharf*, pp. 4 and 6. For a review of the Nuremberg Trials see *H.-H. Jescheck*, Nuremberg Trials, in Encyclopaedia of Public International Law, Amsterdam 1982, Instalment 4, pp. 50–57; *A. de Zayas*, Der Nürnberger Prozeß, in Macht und Recht, A.Demandt (ed.), München 1990, pp. 249–270.

[359] *I. Brownlie*, Principles of Public International Law, Oxford 1982, p. 562; *M.C. Bassiouni*, International Law and the Holocaust, Cal. W. ILJ 1979, Vol. 9, p. 235.

[360] The Tokyo Charter contains a similar wording in its definition of crimes against humanity stipulated in Article 5 (c): "Crimes against humanity: namely, murder, extermination, enslavement, deportation, and other inhumane acts committed against any civilian population, before or during the war, or persecutions on political or racial grounds in execution of or in connection with any crime within the jurisdiction of the Tribunal, whether or not in violation of the domestic law of the country where perpetrated. Leaders, organisers, instigators and accomplices participating in the formulation of the foregoing crimes are responsible for all acts performed by any person in execution of such plan".

Seen in the historical perspective it is apparent that this provision was a response to the need to redress and prosecute serious crimes committed on a vast scale and in an organised and systematic fashion during the Second World War and which were not regulated in international law as war crimes *strictu sensu*. War crimes in the latter sense do not comprise offences committed in peacetime, nor offences against individuals who are nationals of the offending State.

In analysing the wording of Article VI (c) of the London Charter, it seems to be quite clear that it refers to two types of crimes against humanity. The first kind comprises murder, extermination, enslavement, deportation, and other inhumane acts committed against any civilian population. The second category covers "other inhumane acts", *i.e.*, activities of a nature similar to the enumerated crimes and which are directed against any civilian population, not necessarily the entire population, whether or not such offences are in violation of domestic law. The expression "and other inhumane acts" indicates that the list of the mentioned activities is not exhaustive and exclusive. It may cover a wide range of inhumane acts. In this regard it can be noted that rape, sexual slavery and forced pregnancy are not mentioned in the London Charter. In my opinion, its wording, though not mentioning examples of sexual assaults explicitly, does not exclude rape as a crime against humanity. On the contrary, the flexibility of the language used facilitates such an extensive interpretation of the term. Mr. Khushalani declared categorically in this respect that: "there is no doubt whatsoever that the civilised nations of the world would have any difficulty in recognising rape of women as a crime against humanity as defined by the Charter under the provisions of "other inhumane acts".[361]

Neither is there any requirement in the definition of "crimes against humanity" that the entire population must be affected. Yet, there seems to be a kind of implied presumption that there must be a large number of victims. The use of the word "any" in Article VI (c) signifies that the crimes might be directed towards the perpetrator's own compatriots as well as towards populations in countries under belligerent occupation. The prohibition of crimes against humanity is in this respect revolutionary, since it challenges the predominant rule in traditional international law that a state was entitled to treat its own nationals as it pleased. Furthermore, the definition of crimes against humanity, according to the London Charter, presupposes that the inhumane acts and persecutions, in order to constitute such crimes, must be committed "in execution of or in connection with any crime within the jurisdiction of the Tribunal", *i.e.*, crimes against peace or war crimes. It appears from the reasoning of the Nuremberg Tribunal in its judgment that it applied this requirement in the above-mentioned way. Crimes against humanity were considered as accessory to crimes against peace and war crimes committed during World War II by Germany and Japan against alien populations. Persecution of crimes committed before the war was not covered by the Tribunal's jurisdiction. The restriction in the definition implying that crimes against humanity were punishable only if connected with crimes against peace or war crimes was later on removed

---

361 *Y. Khushalani*, p. 20. See also *C.N. Niarchos*, p. 677.

through the adoption of the Control Council Law No. 10 in December 1945. As a result, the subsequent trials ruled that crimes against humanity could be punishable even if unrelated to war, *i.e.*, crimes against humanity can be committed in times of war or in times of peace, and regardless of the nationality of the victim.[362] Gradually the concept of crime against humanity has been internationally accepted as an autonomous offence, *i.e.*, independent from that of war crimes.[363] As a practical matter, these two categories are in reality still often considered together "since they attract equivalent degrees of condemnation and call for the application of similar measures to secure their prohibition and punishment".[364]

So, as regards the jurisdiction of the *ad hoc* Tribunal for the former Yugoslavia, no connection with a crime against peace or with a war crime is required for an inhumane act to constitute a crime against humanity.[365] The Commission of Experts on the Former Yugoslavia has asserted that it considers crimes against humanity to be: "gross violations of fundamental rules of humanitarian and human rights law committed by persons demonstrably linked to a party to the conflict, as part of an official policy based on discrimination against an identifiable group of persons, irrespective of war and the nationality of the victim".[366] This development in contemporary international humanitarian law has for good reasons been considered as "a modest advance over the Nuremberg Charter".[367] Prosecution of crimes against peace was intentionally left out of the mandate of the *ad hoc* Tribunal, since the Security Council felt that a legal institution should not deal with political matters, *i.e.*, reviewing the question of who started the war, the causes of the conflict, etc. Thus, the Security Council has demonstrated a clear preference to "reserve to itself competence in the field of aggression and similar crimes against peace".[368]

More efforts were undertaken in the time after the Second World War to guarantee a minimum measure of fundamental rights to all human beings and to uphold

---

[362] *B.B. Ferencz*, Crimes Against Humanity, in Encyclopaedia of Public International Law, Instalment 8, p. 108.

[363] *T. Meron*, War Crimes in Yugoslavia and the Development of International Law, p. 86. Mr. Thiam has reflected this development in international law in his Fourth Report on the Draft Code of Offences Against the Peace and Security of Mankind as follows: "(t)he separation of crimes against humanity from war crimes has now become absolute. Today, crimes against humanity can be committed not only within the context of an armed conflict, but also independently of any such conflict". UN Doc. A/CN.4/1986/398, p. 54.

[364] Sir *R. Jennings* & Sir *A. Watts*, Oppenheim's International Law, Vol. I PEACE, 9th edition, p. 996.

[365] See the Interim Report of the Commission of Experts Established Pursuant to the Security Council Resolution 780(1992), UN Doc. S/25274, § 49.

[366] UN Doc. S/25274, Annex I, § 49. The Commission of Experts on Rwanda has likewise considered crimes against humanity as "gross violations of fundamental rules of humanitarian and human rights law committed by persons demonstrably linked to a party to the armed conflict, as part of an official policy based on discrimination against an identifiable group of persons, irrespective of war and the nationality of the victim, and includes acts such as the following: murder; extermination; enslavement; deportation and population transfer; imprisonment; torture; rape; persecutions on political, racial and religious grounds; other inhumane acts; apartheid". UN Doc. S/1994/1405, pp. 27–28.

[367] *C. O'Brien*, p. 650.

[368] UN Doc. A/49/342, S/1994/1007, p. 13. See also *M. Palatsi*, pp. 114–116.

human dignity. As an important step in that direction, the UN has through different actions confirmed and expanded the scope of crimes against humanity. The principles elaborated by the Nuremberg and Tokyo trials were unanimously confirmed by United Nations General Assembly resolution 95 (I) of 11 December 1946, with the title "Affirmation of the Principles of International Law of the Nuremberg Tribunal".[369] In consequence, resolution 177 (II), adopted on 21 November 1947 by the GA, entrusted the International Law Commission (ILC) to further formulate the principles of international law of relevance and to proceed with the drafting of the Statute of an International Criminal Court. The ILC Draft Code of Crimes against the Peace and Security of Mankind approved the principles laid down in the Charter and Judgment of the Nuremberg Tribunal and developed them further. In consequence, the Statute of the ICC contains a similar definition of crimes against humanity (Article 7) albeit wider in scope compared to the one in the Statute of the *ad hoc* Tribunal for the former Yugoslavia.[370] With this in mind I may safely conclude that the category of crimes against humanity is well recognised in contemporary international law. The importance of the documents referred to above for the firm establishment of crimes against humanity has been stressed by the UN Secretary-General as well. In the explanatory report presented in compliance with Security Council Res. 808 (1993), he describes the background of the crimes against humanity and refers to the Charter and Judgment of the Nuremberg Trial and Law No. 10 of the Control Council of Germany as the legal basis for the definition of the notion "crimes against humanity". In the latter document rape has been explicitly covered by that term, and it is from this law that the additional categories of conduct qualifying as crimes against humanity derive and that are stipulated in the *ad hoc* Tribunal's Statute. Therefore, the Secretary-General draws the conclusion in the mentioned report that in the context of the conflict in former Yugoslavia crimes against humanity have taken "the form of so-called "ethnic cleansing" and widespread and systematic rape and other forms of sexual assault, including enforced prostitution".[371] This standpoint was confirmed by the Secretary-General once again in a report delivered on 2 March 1994[372] during the preparatory process for the World Conference on Women in 1995. The Beijing Platform for Action reaffirmed thereafter in § 145(d) that rape in the conduct of armed conflicts constitutes under certain circumstances "a crime against humanity". Governments, international organizations were urged to investigate acts of

[369] UN Doc. A/RES/95(I), 1946.

[370] With regard to the specification of the crimes to be covered by the notion crimes against humanity, it was pointed out during the preparatory process on Statute of the ICC that there is a need to further elaborate the specific content of the existing definition and to revise and expand it in the light of subsequent developments in international humanitarian law. UN Doc. A/50/22, §§ 77–80. See also *C.K. Hall*, The First Two Sessions of the Preparatory Committee on the Establishment of an International Criminal Court, AJIL 1997, Vol. 91, p. 180. It may be noted here that the Rome Conference decided to establish a Preparatory Commission with the task to prepare, among other things, a text for the Elements of Crimes. This work must be completed by 30 July, 2000.

[371] UN Doc. S/2504, § 48.

[372] UN Doc. E/CN.6/1994/10, p. 19. See in addition UN Doc. E/CN.6/1995/14.

violence against women, in particular systematic rape and to prosecute all criminals responsible for these crimes. This issue has continuously been in focus since then. The Special Rapporteur on contemporary forms of slavery referred, for example, in her 1996 report to the growing recognition of acts of rape committed in wartime as crimes against humanity.[373]

In addition, several well established international NGOs, among them the Human Rights Watch, has, too, expressed the view that the systematic and widespread crimes, *e.g.*, rape, committed in the territory of the former Yugoslavia and as described and reported in the two-volume publication "War Crimes in Bosnia-Herzegovina" earlier referred to, constitute a sufficient "mass scale" to be considered as crimes against humanity and deserve "judicial prosecution against the appropriate parties as such".[374]

Mentioned could also be the resolution adopted by the Red Cross and Red Crescent at its 26th International Conference in 1996, in which it strongly condemned sexual violence, in particular rape, in the conduct of armed conflict as a war crime and under certain circumstances as a crime against humanity. The Conference encouraged the strengthening of the existing and creation of new mechanisms to investigate, bring to justice and punish all those responsible for the crimes in question.[375] The most recent NGO document of relevance to be noted here is the 1997 Asian Charter on Human Rights, which emphasises that systematic rape is a war crime and a crime against humanity.[376]

8.3.2.4.2. Rape as a Crime against Humanity

Acts of rape committed on a mass scale are considered today as crimes against humanity. Rape as an independent crime against humanity was for the first time mentioned specifically in Article II § 1 (c) of the Control Council Law No. 10 enacted by the four Powers in 1945. The article reads as follows:

> "*crimes against humanity*: Atrocities and offences, including but not limited to murder, extermination, enslavement, deportation, imprisonment, torture, rape, or other inhumane acts committed against any civilian population, or persecution on political, racial or religious grounds whether or not in violation of the domestic laws of the country where perpetrated".[377]

Despite Professor Meron's[378] call for caution not to overstate the moral and legal importance of this provision the view, with which I very much agree, has been put

---

373 UN Doc. E/CN.4/Sub.2/1996/26, § 25. See also UN Doc. E/CN.4/Sub.2/1998/13, §§ 38–45.

374 Human Rights Watch, Memorandum of Law, Elements of the International Crime of "Crimes Against Humanity" Applied in the Former Yugoslavia, p. 4.

375 Resolution 2, B(c), Geneva 1 January 1996. Moreover, recent legal developments serve to support the presumption that individuals are criminally responsible for serious violations of international humanitarian law committed in internal conflicts. *Human Rights Watch*, Justice in The Balance, pp. 7–8.

376 *F. de Varennes*, p. 141.

377 Control Council for Germany, Official Gazette, 31 January 1946, p. 50 et seq.

378 *T. Meron*, War Crimes in Yugoslavia and the Development of International Law, p. 84.

forward that Council Law No. 10 does not only succeed but it also interprets and spells out in specific terms the provisions of the London Charter including the definition of crimes against humanity.[379]

Rape has subsequently been recognised as a punishable crime against humanity under international law in Article 5 of the Statute of the *ad hoc* Tribunal for former Yugoslavia.[380] There it is expressed in the following way:

> "The International Tribunal shall have the power to prosecute persons responsible for the following crimes when committed in armed conflicts, whether international or internal in character, and directed against any civilian population:
>
> a) murder;
>
> b) extermination;
>
> c) enslavement[381];
>
> d) deportation;
>
> e) imprisonment;
>
> f) torture;
>
> g) rape;
>
> h) persecutions on political, racial and religious grounds;
>
> i) other inhumane acts".

Members of the Commission of Experts wished to ascertain their understanding of the term under discussion that the acts referred to above "correspond to what is already considered part of international customary law".[382] A strong support for the view that rape committed on a mass scale shall be prosecuted as crimes against humanity under customary international law was expressed in 1994 at the expert

---

[379] *Y. Khushalani*, p. 27.

[380] The corresponding Article 3 of the Statute of the International Tribunal for Rwanda is slightly different in the first part of the article. It says: " The International tribunal for Rwanda shall have the power to prosecute those responsible for the following crimes when committed as part of a widespread or systematic attack against any civilian population on national, political, ethnic, racial or religious grounds: a) murder; b) extermination; c)enslavement; d)deportation; e) imprisonment; f) torture; g) rape; h) persecution on political, racial and religious grounds; i) other inhumane acts". Of relevance to this study is to be mentioned that Article 7(1)(g) of the ICC's Statute adds to rape, enforced prostitution, forced pregnancy and enforced sterilisation as crimes against humanity.

[381] In the context of the mandate of the Rwanda Tribunal the relevant question has been raised as to whether women who have been given as a reward to "hardworking" killers will amount to slavery and be covered by Article 3 of the Statute which defines crimes against humanity. *R. Muzigo-Morrison*, p. 3.

[382] UN Doc. S/1994/674, pp. 22 and 28. See also *L. Henkin et al.* (eds.) International Law, p. 997. In this respect, it is worth mentioning that the listed acts of crimes against humanity in Article 5 of the *ad hoc* Tribunal's Statute are comprised within the common Article 3 of the Geneva Conventions of 1949 as well as in Article 4 § 2 of the Second Protocol of 1977. They were regarded as "codification of elementary dictates of humanity". UN Doc. S/1994/674, p. 23.

group meeting at Rutgers University organised by the UN Division for the Advancement of Women.[383]

The Commission of Experts stressed in its final report that Article 5 of the *ad hoc* Tribunal's Statute contains "minimum provisions, which must be respected, *a fortiori*, whether or not articles 2 or 3 are applicable to a specific conflict".[384]

The sad truth is that rape is a crime that has regularly occurred in wars. It serves, according to Professor Cook, in armed conflicts to "cast light on women's low status in their communities in peacetime".[385] Looking back in history we may find a great number of examples where rape of civilians has formed part of military tactics. Some of them are unparalleled in human history. Soldiers of Nazi Germany committed rape on a massive scale in occupied territories during the Second World War. Moreover, in areas where troops were stationed or through which they passed, innumerable women were made to enter brothels against their will.[386] The conquering Russian army on the other hand raped German women. During the Vietnam War rape was carried out in a systematic way also by American military personnel. A further example is the incidents of mass rape during the Iraqi occupation of Kuwait.[387] In 1971 mass rapes were committed in Bangladesh as a deliberate military scheme to intimidate the population,[388] and the most recent examples are related to the armed conflicts in Rwanda and in Bosnia-Herzegovina. As earlier established war crimes as well as crimes against humanity have been perpetuated on women in the course of the armed conflict in former Yugoslavia in the name of "ethnic cleansing".[389] As a part of the policy of "ethnic cleansing" the overall context of the large-scale victimisation of women has been considered by the Commission of Experts in its final report of 1994 as the element of "systematicy".[390] According to the ILC the

[383] UN Doc. E/CN.6/1994/4, § 82 p. 21. Of further importance for that issue is the recommendation produced by the same meeting dealing with the question of compensation for the victims of rape. In § 75 of the adopted document it is proposed that international mechanisms monitoring human rights violations should give attention to the question of reparations and compensation for acts of rape committed on a mass scale and considered as crimes against humanity.

[384] UN Doc. S/1994/674, p. 21.

[385] *R.J. Cook*, Human Rights and Reproductive Self-Determination, p. 997. See also *D.M. Koenig*, Women and Rape in Ethnic Conflict and War, Hastings Women's Law Journal 1994, Vol. 5, p. 129.

[386] *R. Copelon*, Gender War Crimes: Reconceptualizing Rape in Time of War, p. 197.

[387] *W. Kälin*, Report on the Situation of Human Rights in Kuwait under Iraqi Occupation, UN Doc. E/CN.4/1992/26, p. 47; *D. Aydelotte*, pp. 588–597; *A. Obote-Odora*, p. 254.

[388] The total disrespect and disregard of the protection against rape contained in Article 27 of the Fourth Geneva Convention in the conflict in Bangladesh was one of the reasons behind the repetition of that provision in Article 76(1) of Additional Protocol I.

[389] *A. Obote-Odora*, p. 257, note 1013. The *Tadić* case is of significance in this regard as well since as it has been pointed out that it documents the existence of the Serb policy of ethnic cleansing. *M.P. Scharf*, Comment on the Decision of 7 May, 1997, AJIL 1997, Vol. 91, p. 719.

[390] UN Doc. S/1994/674, p. 23; *D. Aydelott*, pp. 598–599. On the necessity to demonstrate the systematic or massive nature of certain acts in order to show that a crime against humanity has been committed see *K.D. Askin*, pp. 351–353. According to the same author, a strict textual interpretation of Article 5 of the Statute implies that crimes do not need to be massive, systematic or part of an official policy in order to fall within the jurisdiction of the Tribunal. This means that all instances of sexual assault (including random and isolated opportunistic rape) committed against protected persons can

systematic element relates to a constant practice or to a methodical plan to carry out the offence.[391] Against this background the argument put forward by Kelly Askin that "sexual assault could be classified as a systematic attack *vis-à-vis* as constituting a policy of persecution or discrimination against the female gender in general" is to be agreed with.[392]

The perpetrators of rape and other sexual assaults have had a common plan and therefore rape has, at least during the first years, followed an established and deliberate pattern in the conflict of the former Yugoslavia.[393] Once Serb military and paramilitaries entered a village, they used public rape to flush out the rest of the villagers. After establishing control, they then separated men from women. Men were detained, while women were systematically raped. The Special Rapporteur of the UN Commission on Human Rights in former Yugoslavia, Mr. Mazowiecki, has based his findings regarding cases of rape in ex-Yugoslavia on *on-site* investigations and information received by a large number of refugees in different European countries. In his report of 1993[394] he demonstrated that rape had been used as an attack on the individual victim as well as a method of "ethnic cleansing".[395] Also Amnesty International's research is evidential of rape, as well as other sexual abuses of women in Bosnia-Herzegovina, being carried out in an

---

"technically" be treated as crimes against humanity. *K.D. Askin*, p. 358. This position is partly in line with the statement made by the Tribunal in the *Tadić* case that: "a single act by a perpetrator taken within the context of a widespread or systematic attack against a civilian population entails individual criminal responsibility and an individual perpetrator need not commit numerous offences to be held liable". *Prosecutor v. Tadić*, Judgment of May 7, 1997, § 649. See also § 648. In the *Prosecutor v. Mrksić, Radić & Sljivančanin* case the Tribunal similarly ruled that "as long as there is a link with the widespread or systematic attack against a civilian population, a single act could qualify as a crime against humanity". In other words, a person who rapes a single women or a small number of women can be found guilty of a crime against humanity. See Review of the Indictment Pursuant to Rule 61, § 30, April 3, 1996, No-IT-95-13-R61. For a similar view see also UN Doc. E/CN.4/Sub.2/1998/13, § 43.

Article 3 of the Rwanda Tribunal's Statute is an expression of the above mentioned idea as well. The Special Rapporteur on the situation of human rights in Rwanda arrived, *e.g.*, at the conclusion that "the forms of rape similarly testify to their systematic nature". UN Doc. E/CN.4/1996/68, § 18. The qualifying concepts of "widespread" and "systematic" were discussed and defined by the ICTR in the Akayesu judgment as follows: "The concept 'widespread' may be defined as massive, frequent, large-scale action, carried out collectively with considerable seriousness and directed against a multiplicity of victims. The concept of 'systematic' may be defined as thoroughly organised and following a regular pattern on the basis of a common policy involving substantial public or private resources". *Prosecutor v. Akayesu*, Judgment § 6.4.

More importantly, Article 7 (1) of the ICC Statute uses both adjectives (widespread and systematic) disjunctively, *i.e.*, they are connected with or.

[391] Commentary to Article 21 of the ILC' draft Code. See Draft Report of the International Law Commission on the Work of its Forty-third Session, UN Doc. A/CN.4/L.464/Add.4, 1991.

[392] *K.D. Askin*, p. 352.

[393] Various patterns of rape and other forms of sexual assault have been identified in the literature. *M.C. Bassiouni & P. Manikas*, pp. 54–55.

[394] Report on the Situation of Human Rights in the Territory of Former Yugoslavia, UN Doc. E/CN.4/1993/50.

[395] See UN Doc. E/CN.4/1994/110, p. 44.

organised, widespread and systematic way.[396] Gender-based violence has been committed by all parties to the armed conflict in the territory of the former Yugoslavia. As earlier mentioned about 20,000 women have been raped up until August 1993.[397] In addition, one must calculate with the fact that the number of undocumented and unreported cases is presumably also very high. As the UN Special Rapporteur Mr. Mazowiecki has observed, many women are unwilling to speak about their experiences because of "severe traumatisation, feelings of shame, lack of trust, fear of awakening bad memories".[398] Further, another important reason for women's reluctance to testify sexual abuses is the fear of future reprisals.[399] Consideration should also be taken to the circumstance that women, who do not much wish to be identified as rape victims, may refer to their experiences in the third person. Thus, there is no reliable method of calculation of the figures in regard to rape. Still the results of the investigative mission carried out by the Commission of Experts points to the fact that systematic rape has occurred on a large scale, requiring "some level of organisation and group activity"[400] in the conflict of the former Yugoslavia. Seriously concerned about the alarming number of allegations concerning the practice of rape, the Committee of Ministers of Foreign Affairs of the Council of Europe in a Declaration on the Rape of Women and Children in the Territory of Former Yugoslavia unanimously adopted on 18 February 1993 concluded in Article 4 that:

> "the use of rape as an instrument of warfare and within the context of a strategy of ethnic cleansing – as is the case in the territory of former Yugoslavia – is a war crime and should be considered a crime against humanity".

The Committee of Ministers, recalling an earlier Declaration of 9 December 1992 on the systematic practice of rape in Bosnia-Herzegovina, in which it stated that "such a degree of barbarity, rarely seen, is intolerable" and that "those who perpetrate such crimes must realise that they shall not go unpunished", appealed to member states of the Council of Europe and the international community at large to

---

[396] Amnesty International, Report "Bosnia-Herzegovina – Rape and Sexual Abuse by Armed Forces", London, January 1993; *D. Petrasek*, Amnesty International, Monitoring human rights around the world, Refugees 1993, No. 92, p. 14 *et seq*.

[397] *P. Granjon & P. Deloche*, p. 42.

[398] UN Doc. E/CN.4/1993/50, pp. 71–72, §§ 51 and 58. The Special Rapporteur emphasised that cultural and religious traditions are another important factor decreasing women's readiness to tell about their experiences of rape since often the victim is blamed.

An interview with a victim of rape is very illustrative as to the above assertion. She simply explains that: "What happened to me, happened to many, but the women keep in secret. It is shameful. Thus, the mother conceals it if it happened to her daughter so she can marry and if it happened to an older woman, she wants to protect her marriage. It is a huge embarrassment, you know". Helsinki Watch, War Crimes in Bosnia-Herzegovina, Vol. II, p. 178.

[399] Evidence exists that perpetrators have threatened to kill the families of rape survivors if the women report their rape. The feelings of fear seem to increase in situations where the victim's husband or other family members are held in a detention centre administered by the perpetrator's forces. Human Rights Law Group, No Justice, p. 27.

[400] UN Doc. S/1994/674, p. 60.

ensure "that these atrocities cease and that their instigators and perpetrators are prosecuted by an appropriate national or international tribunal".[401]

Similar statements have been delivered by the EC investigative mission earlier referred to in its final report. In the view of the mission rape and enforced prostitution, practised on a wide scale, and for the purposes mentioned, against Muslim women in Bosnia-Herzegovina is "now a strong case for clearly identifying these abuses as war crimes" and crimes against humanity.[402]

Within the UN, the Commission on Human Rights at its 49th session, which took place from 1 February to 12 March 1993, dealt with rape and other sexual abuses of women in the territory of the former Yugoslavia in the context of crimes against humanity and war crimes, and it strongly condemned these abhorrent practices.[403] As a concrete measure the Commission urged UN's member states to exert every effort to bring to justice all those directly and indirectly involved in these outrageous international crimes and requested the Special Rapporteur on the situation of human rights in the territory of the former Yugoslavia to pursue an investigation into the rape and other sexual abuses of women and children in former Yugoslavia, including the dispatch of a team of experts.

Finally, I may establish that there is a difference as regards the jurisdiction *ratione materiae* of the *ad hoc* Tribunal, when analysing rape as a grave breach of international humanitarian law, and rape as a crime against humanity. The definition of crime against humanity requires that the crime is directed towards a civil population and must be carried out in an organised or systematic way. Because of the nature and scale of the crime, its commission requires "the use of the state's institutions, personnel and resources".[404] At the same time the Tribunal ruled in the *Tadić* case that a policy to commit crimes against humanity need not be formalised. It assumed, furthermore, that the existence of a policy can reasonably be deduced from the manner in which the acts take place.[405] It is also clear that acts committed by private individuals in their own capacity and without the state's complicity in the crime, would not fall within the category of crimes against humanity.

Under specific circumstances crimes against humanity can constitute war crimes at the same time.[406] However, crimes against humanity are more difficult to establish

---

401 Council of Europe, Information sheet No. 32, Strasbourg 1994, p. 157.

402 UN Doc. S/25240, p. 10.

403 The Commission adopted without dissent resolution 1993/8 which for the first time in history stated that rape in an armed conflict is an international crime. On the dramatic history of this resolution see *M.P. Scharf*, Balkan Justice, pp. 52–53.

404 *M.C. Bassiouni*, Crimes Against Humanity in International Criminal Law, p. 248; *S. Goldenberg*, Crimes Against Humanity- 1945–1970: A Study in Making and Unmaking of International Criminal Law, Western Ontario Law Review 1971, Vol. 10, p. 48.

405 *Prosecutor v. Tadić*, Judgment of May 7, 1997, § 653.

406 The Nuremberg International Military Tribunal indicates this possible situation in its judgment delivered on 30 September 1946 as follows: "The Tribunal therefore cannot make a general declaration that the acts before 1939 were crimes against humanity within the meaning of the Charter, but from the beginning of the war in 1939 war crimes were committed on a vast scale, which were also crimes against humanity; and in so far as the inhumane acts charged in the indictment, and committed after the beginning of the war, did not constitute war crimes, they were all committed in execution of, or in connection with, the aggressive war, and therefore constituted crimes against humanity". Ibid., p. 84.

and to prosecute in comparison with "war crimes" from the point of view of evidential requirements, since there must be elements of "acquisition of facts supporting policy planning, mass character and command responsibility".[407] It is, therefore, encouraging to note that the *ad hoc* Tribunal has already indicted several Serbs[408] for individual responsibility (Article 7(1) of the Statute) as well as command responsibility (Article 7(3) of the Statute) for crimes such as murder, rape, torture, committed by their subordinates.[409] Nevertheless, it is unclear what must be proven.[410] Taking into consideration the realities of the former Yugoslavia, it has been argued that it is difficult to form an opinion of whether rape is to be classified as a war crime or as a link in a military strategy. In my view the act of rape can be either or both, depending on the concrete circumstances at hand. The EC investigative mission arrived, on the basis of its on-site investigations in the territory of the former Yugoslavia, without any difficulties at the view that acts of rape of Muslim women have been "and perhaps still are" perpetrated in a systematic manner and on a wide scale in such a way as to be "sufficient to form an important element of war strategy".[411] Thus, rape has been considered by the EC mission not as incidental to the main purpose of the aggression, nor as a by-product of war but as serving a strategic purpose in itself. This argument was put forward by the Croatian representative during the consideration by CEDAW in January 1995 of the report on an exceptional basis from Croatia on the situation of women there. Mrs. Matek, said that mass rape had occurred in several places in the same way and led to the same terrible consequences. Hence, there were clear signs of "synchronised action". In her view, "such rape was directed and served the practical aims of aggression and conquest of new territory".[412]

Several academic commentators have argued that the practice of mass rape by Serb soldiers is not merely a private act, but it has been accomplished in order to

---

[407] *T. Meron*, Rape as a Crime under International Humanitarian Law, p. 428; *T. Meron*, War Crimes Law Comes of Age, p. 466.

[408] This expression has been used by the *ad hoc* Tribunal to comprise Bosnian citizens of Serbian descent or individuals for whom it is unknown whether they are Bosnian Serbs or citizens of Serbia proper.

[409] Some of the accused have been held criminally responsible for the acts of their subordinates in the rape of Omarska prisoners. The following persons may be mentioned: Z. Meakić, M. Kvočka, D. Prcac, M. Radić, M. Kos and M. Gruban, case No. IT-95-4-I. See also the *Tadić* case (count 4.4) and the *Gagović and others* case (*e.g.*, counts 19, 36 and 37).

In the Far East, a number of commanders were indicted, tried and convicted for failing to prevent subordinates from using sexual violence. *M.C. Bassiouni & M. McCormick*, p. 33.

[410] The charges of rape in the *Tadić* case (count 4.4) were unfortunately withdrawn before the trial began. The dropping of the rape charge is a great disappointment for all those who hoped that the *Tadić* case would set an important precedent conforming that rape is an international crime. See *Order on the Prosecution Motion to Withdraw Counts 2 through 4 of the Indictment without Prejudice*, case No. IT-94-1-T, 15 May 1996. See also *M. Leigh*, p. 82; *M.P. Scharf*, Balkan Justice, p. 113.

The *Tadić* case contains, nevertheless, a few "gender-significant paragraphs" in which the Trial Chamber reported, *e.g.*, on sexual violence in the Omarska camp. *K.D. Askin*, Sexual Violence, p. 102.

[411] UN Doc. S/25240, p. 4.

[412] CEDAW, 14th session, 279 Meeting, 31 January 1995.

facilitate ethnic cleansing[413] and therefore this systematic practice would meet the requirements of any definition of crimes against humanity.

Still, the establishment of the legal status and the definition of crimes under international law is a very difficult task to be faced in the near future following the needs of the contemporary world community.

From the above examination of the material jurisdiction of the *ad hoc* Tribunal for the former Yugoslavia I may, however, draw the conclusion that acts of rape and other forms of sexual assaults are included in the concept of "crimes against humanity". Indictments have been issued by both *ad hoc* Tribunals[414] and national courts[415] charging sexual violence as a crime against humanity (rape, enslavement, torture and other inhuman acts).

When the sexual offences do not qualify as crimes against humanity, there is still the possibility for the crimes "rape", "forced pregnancy" as well as other forms of sexual assault to be considered by the *ad hoc* Tribunal on the legal basis of Articles 2, 3 and 4 of its Statute as the circumstances in each case require.[416] Reproductive crimes can consequently fall within any of the following two categories, grave breaches of the Geneva Conventions or violations of the laws or customs of war or genocide. As to the jurisdiction of the Rwanda Tribunal, the Commission of Experts has taken the position that it considers rape to be both a grave breach of international humanitarian law and a crime against humanity. It argued that:

> "There are clear cases where rape, which undoubtedly constitutes 'serious bodily or mental harm', is perpetrated under a responsible command as a systematic policy alongside or as part of a larger policy that is "committed with intent to destroy, in whole or in part, a national, ethnic, racial or religious group, as such".

In consequence the Commission recommends that the Prosecutor "explore fully the relation between the policy of systematic rape under a responsible command as a crime against humanity on the one hand, and such a policy as a crime of genocide, on the other".[417]

---

413 *J. Gardam*, Gender and Non-Combatant Immunity, Transnational Law & Contemporary Problems 1993, Vol. 3, p. 345; *T. Meron*, Rape as a Crime under International Humanitarian Law, pp. 424–427; *E.A. Kohn*, p. 199; *M. Brandt*, p. 1420; *K.D. Askin*, p. 351.

414 *Human Rights Watch*, Justice in The Balance, p. 16; UN Doc. E/CN.6/1998/5, § 53. Among the relevant ICTY cases I may mention the following: the *Nicolić Rule 61* decision, § 33, *Meakić and Others*, § 19.9; *Miljković and Others*, counts 38 and 53; *Jelisić and Cesić*, count 35; *Gagović and Others*, counts 29, 56, 57, 60, 61 and 62. The Rwandan Tribunal, in addition, stated in the earlier referred to *Nyiramasuhuko and Ntahobali* indictment (count 6) that the rapes Ntahobali committed were "part of a widespread or systematic attack on a civilian population on political, ethnic or racial grounds" and they therefore constitute crimes against humanity. Moreover, the ICTR recognised in the *Akayesu* case (counts 13 and 14) rape and other forms of sexual violence as independent crimes constituting crimes against humanity.

415 *M.T. Kamminga*, p. 11.

416 Similar view has been expressed by *K.D. Askin*, p. 350.

417 UN Doc. S/1994/1405, p. 29.

Finally, the present author believes, that even a single case of forced impregnation and forced pregnancy where there is a link to a larger series of violations of fundamental human rights or humanitarian law that evidence a widespread or systematic attack against a civilian population, should also be prosecuted as crimes against humanity.[418]

### *8.3.3. The Ratione Personae Jurisdiction of the Ad Hoc Tribunal*

An important reason for the lack of controversies on the issue of *ratione personae* jurisdiction of the *ad hoc* Tribunal is probably the fact that the jurisdiction of that Tribunal concerns very specific proceedings. The legal basis of the *ad hoc* Tribunal, *i.e.*, the resolution adopted by the Security Council, makes its Statute binding upon all states affected by a trial without requiring a formal recognition of its jurisdiction.[419]

#### *8.3.3.1. The Defendants*

Criminal responsibility for individuals *in propria personam* can be traced back to the laws of war in the Middle Ages when a few international trials were held to try persons for acts that in modern international law are considered crimes against humanity.[420] Today international legal norms stipulating individual responsibility are universally recognised by the international community and regarded as part of customary international law, despite the fact that it took a long time for governments to decide upon the establishment of a permanent judicial organ to enforce them. Criminal jurisdiction is generally exercised by a state on the opposite side in the war in question, or by international tribunal. It would be no exaggeration to say that most parties to an armed conflict have shown unwillingness to prosecute and punish a perpetrator belonging to its own army.[421]

The *ad hoc* Tribunal for the former Yugoslavia has jurisdiction exclusively over natural persons, *i.e.*, states and organisations are excluded (Article 6 of the Statute).[422]

---

[418] UN Doc. S/2504, §§ 47–48. For a supportive standpoint see also *K.M. Pratt & L.F. Fletcher*, pp. 99–100. The UN Sub-Commission endorsed at its 50th session in 1998 the following view: "regardless of whether sexual violence in armed conflict occurs on an apparently sporadic basis or as a part of a comprehensive plan to attack and terrorise a targeted population, all acts of sexual violence, in particular during armed conflicts and including all acts of rape and sexual slavery, must be condemned and prosecuted". (Resolution 1998/8). See also *Prosecutor v. Msksić, Radić and Sljivančanin*, Review of the Indictment Pursuant to Rule 61 of the Rules of Procedure and Evidence, Case No. IT-95-13-R61, Trial Chamber, 3 April 1996.

[419] *C. Tomuschat*, p. 65.

[420] UN Doc. S/1994/1405, p. 33.

[421] The decision by the British judiciary not to prosecute several combatants who probably can be held responsible for grave breaches of humanitarian law during the Falklands war has been frequently cited as an example of the above statement. See for example *G. Melander*, Monitoring Humanitarian Law and Human Rights, Raoul Wallenberg Institute, Report No. 21, Lund 1995, p. 22 and *P. Malanczuk*, p. 353.

[422] Articles 5 and 6 of the Statute of the International Tribunal for Rwanda envisages individual criminal responsibility as well, using the same wording as the above mentioned provision of the *ad hoc* Tribunal's Statute.

War crimes and crimes against humanity can be committed both by persons acting as organs of the state,[423] *i.e.*, the leaders of the state, and the servants of the state. The individuals may act in their official capacity as officers and soldiers or personnel of POW camps, and as a third category, as individuals in their private capacity. All these three categories of criminals are equally punishable[424] under the *ad hoc* Tribunal's Statute for acts defined as criminal, therein including rape and other sexual assaults.[425]

On the question of individual responsibility it was submitted at Nuremberg that since international law is concerned with the actions of sovereign states no punishment for individuals is provided for. On that basis it was asserted that where the criminal acts are acts of a state, those who carry it out are not personally responsible but are protected on the ground of the state sovereignty-doctrine. The Tribunal rejected these submissions based on the traditional system of international responsibility, which mainly relates to states, and held that it has long been recognised that public international law imposes duties and liabilities upon individuals as well as upon states. In other words, the Nuremberg Tribunal refuted the classic view that international law applies to states only, and it ruled that individuals have indeed international duties, which transcend the national obligations of obedience imposed by the individual state. By that assertion the Tribunal established in its judgment the concept of individual responsibility, *i.e.*, the individual is liable for criminal action under international law and can be punished for it in a personal capacity. Its famous statement reads as follows:

> "Crimes against international law are committed by men, not by abstract entities, and only by punishing individuals who commit such crimes can the provisions of international law be enforced".[426]

---

423 It should be stressed, however, that states are responsible for the criminal acts of their own organs only when "they have failed to exercise due diligence in the prevention or the repression of the crime committed by the individual". *E.J. de Aréchaga & A. Tanzi*, International State Responsibility, M. Bedjaoui (ed.), p. 360. See also *M. Lippman*, p. 5 ff.

424 The Judgment in the Flick Trial reaffirmed in the following words the view that the general principle of individual responsibility refers equally to public and private perpetrators: "Acts judged criminal when done by an officer of the Government are criminal also when done by a private individual. The guilt differs only in magnitude, not in quality. The offender in either case is charged with personal wrong and punishment falls on the offender in *propria persona*. The application of international law to individuals is no novelty. There is no justification for a limitation of responsibility to public officials". Law Reports of Trials of War Criminals, London 1949, Vol. XV, p. 60. See also *O. Triffterer*, Dogmatische Untersuchungen zur Entwicklung des materiellen Völkerstrafrechts seit Nürnberg, Freiburg 1966; *L. Friedman*, The Law of War: A Documentary History, New York 1972, p. 1284.

425 On individual responsibility for sexual violence see UN Doc. E/CN.4/Sub.2/1996/26, §§ 49–53 and *K.D. Askin*, Sexual Violence, pp. 97–123.

426 Judgment of the International Military Tribunal, Transcript of Proceedings, p. 16878. In his final speech at the Nuremberg Trial Sir Hartley Shawcross made the following comment: "In no other sphere is it more necessary to affirm that the rights and duties of States are the rights and duties of men and that unless they bind individuals, they bind no one". This well-known passage is cited in *P.N. Drost*, The Crime of State, Vol. II Genocide, Leyden 1959, p. 127. For a review of arguments as to the legality of the punishment of the war crimes committed during World War II see *H. Lauterpacht*, The Law of Nations and the Punishment of War Crimes, BYIL 1944, Vol. 21, pp. 58–95.

The principle of individual responsibility for serious crimes was further developed after the establishment of the UN. Several multilateral treaties,[427] among them the Geneva Conventions of 1949, require states parties to provide for penal sanctions and the prosecution of persons committing or ordering any of the grave breaches of the Conventions[428] in their national legislations. The states parties must bring such persons before the national courts or extradite the offenders for trial to another state party. The relevant provisions make, however, a distinction between "grave breaches" and other infractions as earlier pointed out.[429] Thus, not all violations of the provisions of the Geneva Conventions may amount to grave breaches, *i.e.*, become an object of the above-mentioned prosecution. Moreover, each of the four Geneva Conventions defines the acts constituting grave breaches in accordance with the respective treaty.[430] I should also mention that very few states have so far in their municipal law adopted specific provisions for effective penal sanctions for the perpetrators of grave breaches as defined in the Geneva Conventions.

The principle of individual responsibility is, furthermore, re-emphasised in the *ad hoc* Tribunal's Statute. One of the principle objectives of the *ad hoc* Tribunal is set out in the preamble of resolution 827 (1993). It states that the Tribunal is: "to bring to justice the persons who are responsible for crimes perpetrated in former Yugoslavia".[431] As a result the Statute of the *ad hoc* Tribunal (Article 7) estab-

[427] See, *e.g.*, the relevant provisions of the Genocide Convention and the UN Convention on Torture.

[428] Several resolutions of the Security Council reaffirm that all parties to the armed conflicts on the territory of the former Yugoslavia are bound to comply with the obligations under international humanitarian law and in particular the 1949 Geneva Conventions, and that persons who commit or order the commission of grave breaches of the Conventions are individually responsible in respect to such breaches. See, for example, S.C. resolutions 764, § 10 and 808.

[429] See Articles 49, 50, 129 and 146 in the respective Geneva Conventions.

[430] See Articles 50, 51, 130 and 147 from the first through to the fourth Geneva Conventions. These provisions refer to acts such as wilful killing, torture or inhumane treatment of protected persons, wilfully causing them great suffering or serious injury to body or health, their unlawful deportation, and the taking of hostages.

[431] It is my personal conviction that securing individual accountability for war crimes is a prerequisite for a lasting peace in Bosnia-Herzegovina. Otherwise, the state of collective guilt might lead to new outbreaks of violence. Generally it is known that a majority of victims of crimes may experience difficulties forgiving the offenders for their conduct. Thus, the probability of an ever-widening cycle of retribution in the Balkans is high. To build the rule of law in that region is a necessary foundation for any lasting peace. Therefore, if nobody is held accountable and branded as criminal, the victims' feelings of hatred will occasion further violence. History has taught us, according to Roggemann: "Die historische Erfahrung – in Deutschland und anderswo – zeigt, daß nach blutigen Kriegen, Revolutionen und politischen Systemunrecht ('Regierungskriminalität') der innere Friede und damit letztlich auch die äußere Friedensfähigkeit von Gesellschaften nur (wieder)gewonnen werden können, wenn begangene Unrechtstaten möglichst vollständig aufgeklärt und in rechtsstaatlichen Verfahren – oder anderen Formen öffentlichen und kritischen Diskurses – verurteilt werden und auf diese Weise auch den Opfern und deren Angehörigen Genugtuung gegeben wird". *H. Roggemann*, p. 64. So, meting out justice is of outmost importance in preventing a continuation of the conflict. At the same time, it is a means of alleviating the victims or their relatives of their suffering. This is also true for the

lishes individual liability for persons guilty of committing crimes falling under the description of the acts declared punishable in this document.[432] The relevant provision in the *ad hoc* Tribunal's Statute reads as follows:

> "1) A person who planned, instigated, ordered, committed or otherwise aided and abetted in the planning, preparation or execution of a crime referred to in articles 2 to 5 of the present Statute, shall be individually responsible for the crime.

---

deeply shocked surviving victims of the massacres in Rwanda, whose greatest concern according to the Special Rapporteur, is "whether the perpetrators of genocide will be tried and punished". It is also the Governments' concern, since it does not wish to countenance impunity, which is regarded as a recurrent cause of the successive waves of massacres in Rwanda. Thus, pending the establishment of the international tribunal, people, who increasingly become impatient, have not hesitated to take the law into their own hands. (UN Doc. E/CN.4/1995/71, p. 8; UN Doc. E/CN.4/1995/70, pp. 10–11) Therefore, in this regard the view expressed by Judge Cassese that the only civilised alternative to the desire for revenge "is to render justice: to conduct a fair trial by a truly independent and impartial tribunal and to punish those found guilty" seems to be very much to the point. UN Doc. A/49/342, S/1994/1007, p. 12.

I should mention that perpetrators committing international crimes might theoretically gain amnesty, decided upon by international organs. In this respect reference has also been made to Article 6 (5) of Additional Protocol II, which seems to favour amnesty regulations after a conflict. On this basis it has been argued that amnesty can contribute to the "process of building and preserving peace". *H. von Hebel*, p. 455. This has, however, not been the case with the violators of international humanitarian law, whom the conflicts of former Yugoslavia have produced, even though the question of using requirements based on amnesty regulations as an important part of the peace negotiations seems not to have been totally excluded. The Dayton peace agreement did not provide amnesty for those accused of serious violations of international humanitarian law. But the UN did not declare clearly before that that amnesty for those who have planned, ordered or carried out war crimes in the former Yugoslavia would not be put "on the bargaining table". Human Rights Watch, Prosecute Now!, New York 1993, p. 2. On the other hand, Mrs. M. Albright, stated on 7 January 1994 on her departure from Pleso Airport, Zagreb, that the USA will not recognise an amnesty for war criminals. Also Cyrus Vance, the then U.N. mediator in the armed conflict, assured in a meeting with representatives of the Helsinki Watch that he would oppose any effort, as part of a peace settlement, to provide for an amnesty for individuals responsible for international war crimes. See Helsinki Watch, War Crimes in Bosnia-Herzegovina, Vol. II, New York 1993, p. 2.

History reminds us of the fact that amnesty laws have frequently been used as an effective means in negotiations. Recently, a number of Latin-American countries have adopted such rules on the domestic level. See *M.K. Eriksson*, Skydd av mänskliga rättigheter, pp. 57 and 82. There are also other examples that can be mentioned in this respect, such as the amnesty given to the Turkish officials responsible for the killing of about 600,000 Armenians in Turkey on the basis of the 1923 Treaty of Lausanne. My standpoint is that impunity of the perpetrators of war crimes, crimes against humanity and grave violations of basic human rights is a phenomenon that has to be strongly disapproved. It represents not only a denial of justice for the victims of human rights violations and breaches of humanitarian law but it also hampers the development of democracy. In this regard the *ad hoc* Tribunal for former Yugoslavia and the Tribunal for Rwanda have an essential function to fulfil.

[432] The following relevant cases from the jurisprudence of the ICTY and ICTR on charges of commitment of various forms of gender-based violence may be quoted here: the *Delalić and Others* case, the *Furundžija* case, the *Miljković and Others* case, the *Jelisić and Cesić* case, the *Gagović and Others* case and the *Ntahobali* case.

2) The official position of any accused person, whether as Head of State or Government or as a responsible Government official, shall not relieve such person of criminal responsibility nor mitigate punishment.[433]

3) The fact that any of the acts referred to in articles 2 to 5 of the present Status was committed by a subordinate does not relieve his superior of criminal responsibility if he knew or had reasons to know that the subordinate was about to commit such acts or had done so and the superior failed to take the necessary and reasonable measures to prevent such acts or to punish the perpetrators thereof.

4) The fact that an accused person acted pursuant to an order of a Government or of a superior shall not relieve him of criminal responsibility, but may be considered in mitigation of punishment if the International Tribunal determines that justice so requires".[434]

---

[433] A similar provision excluding the excuse of official position for punishability of criminal action, is contained in Article 27(1) of the ICC Statute. It reads as follows: "This Statute shall apply equally to all persons without any distinction based on official capacity. In particular, official capacity as a Head of State or Government, a member of a Government or parliament, an elected representative or a government official shall in no case exempt a person from criminal responsibility under this Statute, nor shall it, in and of itself, constitute a ground for reduction of sentence".

During the preparatory work on the above mentioned Statute several governments have in their observations in respect to this provision expressed criticism. It was felt that the question of immunity from jurisdiction to which officials may be entitled under international law was not sufficiently considered. UN Doc. A/CN.4/460, p. 26.

Reference has been made to the fact that under many constitutions the head of state cannot be tried by the regular courts of the country. Yet, Article 27(2) of the adopted text is quite clear on the point that "Immunities or special procedural rules which may attach to the official capacity of a person, whether under national or international law, shall not bar the Court from exercising its jurisdiction over such a person".

[434] See the almost identical Article 6 of the Statute of the International Tribunal for Rwanda. It reads as follows:

"1. A person who planned, instigated, ordered, committed or otherwise aided and abetted in the planning, preparation or execution of a crime referred to in articles 2 to 4 of the present Statute, shall be individually responsible for the crime.

2. The official position of any accused person, whether as Head of State or Government or as a responsible Government official, shall not relieve such person of criminal responsibility nor mitigate punishment.

3. The fact that any acts referred to in articles 2 to 4 of the present Statute was committed by a subordinate does not relieve his or her superior of criminal responsibility if he or she knew or had reason to know that the subordinate was about to commit such acts or had done so and the superior failed to take the necessary and reasonable measures to prevent such acts or to punish the perpetrators thereof.

4. The fact that an accused person acted pursuant to an order of a Government or of a superior shall not relieve him or her of criminal responsibility, but may be considered in mitigation of punishment if the International Tribunal for Rwanda determines that justice so requires".

It appears from the wording of Article 7(1) of the Tribunal's Statute that it shall deal with three levels of responsibility, that of political leaders, that of the commanders and that of subordinates or those merely carrying out orders.[435]

Two main aspects of individual responsibility for the commission of criminal acts under international law, the issue of command responsibility and the issue of defence of obedience to superior orders, which are of outmost importance in the context of the *ad hoc* Tribunal's jurisdiction, will be briefly reviewed in the following.

*8.3.3.2. The Issue of Command Responsibility*

The doctrine of command responsibility connotes two different conceptions of criminal responsibility: 1) The so-called *direct* responsibility for unlawful commander's orders, and 2) *Imputed* responsibility for a subordinate's unlawful conduct, which is not based on the commander's order.[436]

The first aspect of command responsibility, which indicates direct responsibility for the person who issued an offending order or related the order seems to be relatively easy to implement from the evidential point of view. The second aspect of command responsibility is to a great extent based on the commander's failure to act in order to:

> "1. prevent a specific unlawful conduct; 2. provide for general measures likely to prevent or deter unlawful conduct; 3. investigate allegations of unlawful conduct; and 4. prosecute, and upon conviction, punish the author of the unlawful conduct".[437]

---

[435] *K. Lescure & F. Trintignac*, p. 29; *M.C. Bassiouni & P. Manikas*, pp. 344–345; UN Doc. S/2504, § 54. This proposition is equally relevant for the perpetrators responsible for the atrocities in Rwanda. In this regard, it has been emphasised by the Special Rapporteur of the UN Commission on Human Rights that as far as the authorities or organs involved are concerned responsibility can immediately be apportioned to among others "The Rwandese State authority, such as a number of ministers, various elements of the government security forces such as the Presidential Guard, the Rwandese Armed Forces and the gendarmerie.. ". UN Doc. E/CN.4/1995/71, p. 7.

[436] *M.C. Bassiouni*, Crimes Against Humanity in International Criminal Law, Dordrecht 1992, p. 368; *M.C. Bassiouni & P. Manikas*, p. 345.

[437] *M.C. Bassiouni*, Crimes against Humanity, pp. 368 and 370.

Article 87 of the First Protocol to the Geneva Conventions provides a duty for the person in command to prevent any breaches of the Conventions as follows:

> "1. The High Contracting Parties and the Parties to the conflict shall require military commanders, with respect to members of the armed forces under their command and other persons under their control, to prevent and, where necessary, to suppress and to report to competent authorities breaches of the Conventions and this Protocol.
>
> 2. In order to prevent and suppress breaches, High Contracting Parties and Parties to the conflict shall require that, commensurate with their level of responsibility, commanders ensure that members of the armed forces under their command are aware of their obligations under the Conventions and this Protocol.
>
> 3. The High Contracting Parties and Parties to the conflict shall require any commander who is aware that subordinates or other persons under his control are going to commit or have committed a breach of the Conventions or of this Protocol, to initiate such steps as are necessary to prevent such violations of the Conventions or their Protocol, and where appropriate, to initiate disciplinary or penal actions against violators thereof".

For self-evident reasons it is obvious that difficulties can arise when determining the guilt, depending on the choice of standard to be applied as regards the commander's knowledge of the wrongdoing. A further source for potential uncertainties can constitute the essential element in the concept of command responsibility, especially "with respect to those in the higher echelons in the chain of command",[438] namely causation.

Both aspects of command responsibility are comprised within the *ad hoc* Tribunal's Statute. During the *Furundžija* trial the Trial Chamber of the ICTY discussed and analysed extensively both the *actus reus* and the *mens rea* necessary to sustain a charge of aiding and abetting in international law.[439]

In the course of the Nuremberg and Tokyo trials the doctrine of command responsibility, *i.e.*, the notion that a person who gives the order to commit a war crime or crimes against humanity is as equally guilty of the offence as the person actually committing it, gained wide approval. The Nuremberg Principles affirmed that even a head of state is not free from responsibility under international law for the commission of a crime under international law. It is, therefore, not surprising that all the written comments made by governments and submitted to the UN Secretary-General during the preparatory process on the Statute of the *ad hoc* Tribunal suggested the incorporation and implementation of that doctrine.[440] In this respect the Commission of Experts observed in its final report of 1994 that the doctrine of command responsibility is primarily directed at military commanders, because "such persons have a personal obligation to ensure the maintenance of discipline among troops under their command".[441] Truly, most cases in which the doctrine of command responsibility has been applied have been related to military and paramilitary personnel. In a few instances political leaders and public officials[442] have also been held liable for crimes under international law. In this regard the great importance of having the highest officials prosecuted has frequently been underlined, due to the difficulties otherwise of proving "intention", *i.e.*, when criminal acts are deliberately committed systematically and follow a policy, in order for the offences to be considered as genocide and/or crimes against humanity.

---

[438] *M.C. Bassiouni*, Ibid., p. 372.

[439] The Tribunal found that while "the *actus reus* consists of practical assistance, encouragement, or moral support which has a substantial effect on the perpetration of the crime, the *mens rea* requires the knowledge that these acts assist in the commission of the offence". *The Prosecutor v. Furundžija*, Judgment § 249. See also *The Prosecutor v. Tadić*, Judgment §§ 674 and 692 where the Judges of the Trial Chamber emphasised that "aiding and abetting includes all acts of assistance by words or acts that lend encouragement or support, as long as the requisite intent is present".

[440] UN Doc. S/2504, §§ 55–56.

[441] UN Doc. S/1994/674, p. 16.

[442] The criminal responsibility of public officials was discussed at the Nuremberg Trial. It was argued that: "The principle of international law, which under certain circumstances protects the representatives of a State, cannot be applied to acts, which are condemned as criminal by international law. The authors of these acts cannot shelter themselves behind their official position in order to be freed from punishment in appropriate proceedings". *P.N. Drost*, Genocide, p. 127. See also *H. von Hebel*, p. 451.

The principle of the punishability of any person without distinction whatsoever, *i.e.*, including persons in positions of authority, *e.g.*, heads of state or government, who bear actual and factual responsibility for the commission of acts of crimes as set out in the Tribunal's Statute, has obviously been considered important by the *ad hoc* Tribunal. The Tribunal's Prosecutor has, on the basis of Article 7 of its Statute, initiated an investigation into the criminal responsibility of Radovan Karadžić,[443] Ratko Mladić[444] and Mico Stanisić[445] arising out of indictments already issued by the *ad hoc* Tribunal[446] against various individuals in respect to war crimes and crimes against humanity as specified in Articles 2 to 5 of the *ad hoc* Tribunal's Statute.[447] The

---

443 He became the first President of the Bosnian Serb administration in Pale and is as such also the commander of the armed forces.

444 Ratko Mladić is a professional military officer and was the commander of the forces of the Second Military District of the JNA, which in effect became the Bosnian Serb army.

445 Milo Stanisić was the first minister of internal affairs of the Bosnian Serb administration in Pale. In that capacity he was responsible for the regular and special police forces at the regional and local level in the territory under Bosnian Serb control.

446 The indictments may be amended to include more recent crimes. The indictment declares that Karadžić and Mladić, "by their acts and omissions, and in concert with others, committed a crime against humanity by persecuting Bosnian Muslim and Bosnian Croat civilians on national, political and religious grounds. They are criminally responsible for the unlawful confinement, murder, rape, sexual assault, torture, etc., of civilians" (§ 19). Paragraph 22 of the indictment states, in addition, that "In many instances, women and girls who were detained were raped at the camps or taken from the detention centres and raped or otherwise sexually abused at other locations". (§§ 32 and 33). Both accused were indicted for superior criminal responsibility.

447 On July 25, 1995, the Tribunal issued 5 indictments charging a total of 24 Bosnian and Croatian Serbs, among others Radovan Karadžić and Ratko Mladić, with crimes ranging from genocide to breaches of the Geneva Convention. Among other high-ranking leaders who were indicted mention should be made of Milan Martić, the President of the former Croatian Serb Administration of Knin. Arrest warrants were issued for all the accused. They have been transmitted to all states, Interpol and the Implementation Force (IFOR). See *International Arrest Warrants and Orders for Surrender for Radovan Karadžić and Ratko Mladić*, July 11, 1996, 36 I.L.M. 92, 1997, pp. 92–95. See also *R. Dixon*, New Developments in the International Tribunal for the Former Yugoslavia. Prominent Leaders Indicted and Jurisdiction Established, LJIL 1995, Vol. 8, pp. 449–461.

Nevertheless, contrary to the terms of the Dayton Peace Agreement, some of the suspect persons held official positions a long time after the indictments. Moreover, since the first IFOR troops arrived in Bosnia and Herzegovina, spokespersons for IFOR and troop-contributing states have on several occasions stated that they would not search for persons indicted by the *ad hoc* Tribunal, but would detain suspect persons if they encounter them. See Amnesty International, International Criminal Tribunals, Handbook for government co-operation, AI Index: IOR 40/07/96, August 1996, p. 12; Fransk officer stoppade gripande av Karadžić, SvD, 28 April 1998, p. 4.

At the same time, it is to be noted that SFOR carried out its first arrest on 10 July 1997 (the person arrested was Milan Kovačević). UN Doc. A/52/375; S/1997/729, § 133. As at the time of writing (December 1998) nine indictees had been detained by SFOR and arrested by the Prosecutor of the ICTY. According to Professor Meron, several of the indicted persons have been captured *manu militari* under the umbrella of SFOR and NATO and brought to the Tribunal. *T. Meron*, War Crimes Law Comes of Age, p. 463.

The delay in bringing proceedings against the presumed perpetrators of the atrocities in the former Yugoslavia is a matter of concern. Thus, the principle leaders responsible for the crimes committed against international humanitarian law have yet to be arrested. There are, however, a few exceptions to which I shall refer here. To begin with Slavko Dokmanović, the Serb mayor of Vukovar, and principal suspect in the 1991 massacre of more than 200 people in the Croatian city of Vukovar, was, for example, arrested in

Prosecutor has expressed the view[448] that the matter of the individual criminal responsibility of these three persons in political, military or police leadership posi-

---

1997 by UN authorities and he was transferred immediately to the Tribunal's headquarters in The Hague. He hung himself unfortunately on 30 June 1998, just a couple of weeks before the Tribunal's decision was expected. A Croatian general charged with authorising hundreds of civilian killings in Bosnia in 1993, Tihomir Blaškić, went on trial on 25 June 1997. This is the first proceeding against a commanding officer since the end of World War II. Blaškić surrendered in April 1996 after the then US defence secretary Mr. Perry put pressure on the Croatian Government. Another trial which I may mention here is the Celebići trial which *inter alia* concerns command responsibility. UN Doc. A/52/375, p. 12.

Unlike the situation in the former Yugoslavia, persons in leading positions during the genocide in Rwanda in 1994, have been removed rather quickly from state institutions and their previous positions. A great number of them left the country and hid in refugee camps in neighbouring countries or went into exile elsewhere. It can be concluded there have been more favourable circumstances for arresting and prosecuting suspects for the atrocities in Rwanda than in the case of the former Yugoslavia. The former Prime Minister of Rwanda Jean Kambanda who bears first and foremost the responsibility for the genocide taking place in his country, was convicted of that crime by the *ad hoc* Tribunal on 4 September 1998 and he was sentenced to life imprisonment for six counts of genocide and crimes against humanity on 4 September 1998. *The Prosecutor v. Kambanda*, case No. ICTR 97-23-S, Judgment 4 September 1998. This is the first-ever sentence for genocide. Kambanda became the first person to accept culpability for genocide before an international court. In addition to Kambanda, three former ministers have been indicted by the ICTR. Pauline Nyiramasuhuko is one of them. She was a government minister and is the first woman ever to be indicted for genocide.

Jean-Paul Akayesu, the former mayor of the Taba commune, was also found guilty of genocide and crimes against humanity. On 2 October 1998, he was given three life sentences, plus 80 years' imprisonment for other violations of humanitarian law, including rape. Akayesu has appealed against the judgment. *The Prosecutor v. Akayesu,* Case No. ICTR-96-4-I.

Moreover, Colonel Bagasora, a leading member (Directeur de Cabinet) of the former Interim Government in Rwanda during the mass-killings of 1994, was arrested on 9 March 1996 in Cameroon and he was transferred to the Tribunal in Arusha in January 1997. (*Bagosora*, ICTR-96-8-T) See UN Doc. A/52/582; S/1997/868, pp. 26–28.

Joseph Kanyabashi, the former mayor of Ngoma commune was, furthermore, transferred by Belgium to Arusha on 7 November 1997. *Kanyabashi v. Prosecutor*, Scheduling Order No. ICTR-96-15-AR72, July 29, 1997. See generally on criminal responsibility in the context of the genocide in Rwanda *P. Akhavan*, The International Criminal Tribunal for Rwanda, p. 509. As at the time of writing there were twenty-two indictments against thirty-five former Rwandan officials. *K.D. Askin*, Sexual Violence, p. 100.

The view that an international tribunal should first and foremost try the leadership-level defendants can be criticised on the basis that this attitude can render significant injustice. Thus, a trial before an international tribunal tends to be more favourable for defendants than would be a trial before national courts. In other words, persons in leading position can escape capital punishment, whereas subordinates have already been subjected to the death sentence. There is a disparity in sentence in regard to the crimes committed in Rwanda since the Tribunal' s Statute rules out capital punishment, which is provided for in the Rwandese penal code. Two Catholic priests, Kayiranga and Nkuriye, were among the 22 individuals sentenced to death in April 1998 for participating in the commission of genocide during 1994 by the national courts.

Even though the Government of Rwanda has announced that it has opted for the categorisation of defendants, or accused, thereby ensuring that different categories of defendants receive penalties of varying severity depending on the nature of the offences or the status of the defendants, it has been submitted, not without reason, that " the most responsible defendants get the least harsh treatment". *M.H. Morris*, The Trials of Concurrent Jurisdiction: National and International Tribunals in the Wake of Mass Violence, conference paper, Brussels 1996, p. 6; *G. Gahima,* Rwanda: The Challenge of Justice in the Aftermath of Genocide, conference paper, Brussels 1996, pp. 3–4.

448 International Tribunal for the Prosecution of Persons Responsible for Serious Violations of International Humanitarian Law Committed in the Territory of Former Yugoslavia since 1991, Case

tions must be examined. Moreover, the Prosecutor argued that "it is that position of authority, which would have enabled the suspects to plan, instigate, or order the crimes in respect to which the above-mentioned investigations have been conducted, or given them the means to prevent the said crimes, or at least to punish their perpetrators".[449] The Prosecutor has, furthermore, conducted investigations into alleged serious violations of international humanitarian law committed by Bosnian Croat military and political leaders in the Republic of Bosnia-Herzegovina.[450]

As to the second aspect of command responsibility, *i.e.*, imputed responsibility, the central provision in a multilateral treaty should be mentioned, namely Article 86(2) of the First Protocol to the Geneva Conventions of 1949. It addresses the question of the superiors' criminal responsibility in connection with "failure to act" as follows:

> "The fact that a breach of the Conventions or of this protocol was committed by a subordinate does not absolve his superiors from penal or disciplinary responsibility, as the case may be, if they knew, or had information, which should have enabled them to conclude in the circumstances at the time, that he was committing or was going to commit such a breach and if they did not take all feasible measures within their power to prevent or repress the breach".

The present article is of the greatest importance in laying down the criminal responsibility of persons in command position, but before its adoption that issue was discussed at the Nuremberg and Tokyo Tribunals. One particular case, the case of General Yamashita[451] constitutes a good illustration in regard to the question of whether international humanitarian law imposes on an army commander a duty to

---

No. IT-95-5-D, *In the Matter of a Proposal for a Formal Request for Deferral to the Competence of the Tribunal Addressed to the Republic of Bosnia-Herzegovina in respect to Radovan Karadžić, Ratko Mladić and Milo Stanisić*, 16 May 1995, p. 4.

[449] Ibid., p. 13.

[450] *In the Matter of a Proposal for a Formal Request for Deferral to the Competence of the Tribunal Addressed to the Republic of Bosnia-Herzegovina in respect to Crimes Against the Population of the Lašva River Valley*, Case No. IT-95-6-D, 11 May 1995.

[451] *United States v. Yamashita*, 327 U.S. 1, (66 S. Ct.340, 90 L. Ed. 499, 1946). Of some relevance is also the *Hirota* case, according to which the Japanese Prime Minister was convicted of war crimes committed in the "rape of Nanking" incident since he did not stop the atrocities. 3 Judgment of the International Military Tribunal for the Far East 1, 1948, p. 160.

The question of individual criminal responsibility has, thereafter, been considered on several occasions. The well-known case from the days of the Vietnam war, the *My Lai (Song My)* case can be mentioned, where the "knowledge test" was of relevance. During the proceedings of this case a demand for the punishment of the higher officials in military as well as in civil positions was put forward. The company commander at My Lai was, however, not found guilty. Great emphasis was put on the actual knowledge of the "knew or should have known test" of the commission of the criminal acts in question. See International Law, *L. Henkin et al.* (eds.), p. 368 ; *J.J. Paust*, Superior Orders and Command Responsibility, pp. 81- 86; *J.F. Adicott & W.A. Hudson*, The Twenty-Fifth Anniversary of My Lai: A Time to Inculcate the Lesson, Military Law Review 1990, Vol. 139, pp. 153–185 ; *J.F. Addicott*, The Lesson of My Lai, The Military Law and Law of War Review 1992, Vol. XXXI, pp. 74–107.

take such appropriate measures as are within his power to control the troops under his command for the prevention of the specified acts which are violations of the law of war. General Tomoyuki Yamashita served as commanding general of the Japanese Army at Manila during the period between 9 October 1944 and 2 September 1945. Shortly after his surrender he was prosecuted by a Military Commission for war crimes committed by the Japanese armed forces in the Philippines. General Yamashita was convicted of dereliction of duty, *i.e.*, he should have taken such measures "as were within his power and appropriate in the circumstances to protect prisoners of war and the civilian population".[452] There was not enough evidence to connect the accused with ordering atrocities, such as the rape of hundreds of Filipino women, neither of having direct knowledge of them.[453] General Yamashita was, nevertheless, found guilty on the grounds that he condoned a general atmosphere of lawlessness that pervaded the troops under his command.[454]

The trial put considerable weight on the similarity of pattern aspect of the atrocities throughout the commission as a basis for command responsibility. General Yamashita was subsequently sentenced to death, despite his denial of knowledge of his subordinates' criminal conduct.

The argument used at the Yamashita trial is of interest to my discussion because it can be used by analogy in the context of crimes perpetrated during the armed conflicts on the territory of the former Yugoslavia.

In the context of the *ad hoc* Tribunal's jurisdiction it has been asserted[455] that the leaders of all the parties to the conflict in the former Yugoslavia are in the position and factually have exercised effective control over their civilian and military structures. Therefore, they cannot dissociate themselves from atrocities committed by their forces. Persons in command have a responsibility to see to it that their subordinates obey the law. The UN Special Rapporteur Mr. Mazowiecki has pointed to the fact that it is obvious that there have been no attempts "by any of those in position of power" to stop the rapes in the areas of armed conflict in former Yugoslavia.[456] Therefore, it seems to me that many cases may fit into the rule of command responsibility. There is ample evidence that persons in military and political command have failed to take reasonable corrective action[457] as regards sexual abuses of

---

452 *J.J. Paust*, Superior Orders and Command Responsibility, in International Criminal Law, Vol. III, Enforcement, M.C. Bassiouni (ed.), New York 1987, p. 83.

453 *M.C. Bassiouni*, Crimes Against Humanity, p. 378; *M.C. Bassiouni & P. Manikas*, pp. 355–357.

454 *M.P. Scharf*, Balkan Justice, p. 59.

455 UN Doc. E/CN.4/1993/50, p. 55.

456 Ibid., p. 55 and annex II.

457 Evidence concerning commanders' failure to condemn even if they have not ordered, gender-specific violence has been presented at the first Bosnian war crimes trial. At least one Serbian soldier has testified that local orders to rape Muslim girls and women were given by the head of Bosnian Serb armed forces, R. Karadžić. In this regard I may observe that the plaintiffs in the earlier referred *Doe v. Karadžić* case have not alleged that Karadžić has directly perpetrated any torts, but referred instead that under the well-established doctrine of command responsibility, they need not show that the defendant expressly ordered or was directly involved in the tortuous conduct. Thus, it should be enough to hold Karadžić liable for the acts imputed to him by simply asserting that he at least permitted his forces to commit the criminal acts. *M. Brandt*, pp. 1421 and 1442.

women. As a rule these acts have neither been sporadic nor isolated. It is difficult to believe that the widespread pattern of sexual violence has not been known to persons in command position.[458] With regard to corrective action Professor Paust has observed the following:

> "... prosecutions have been based partially on the failure to control troops, disregard of troop conduct, acquiescence in troop activity, dereliction of duty, general complicity (incitement, approval, aiding and abetting, accessory responsibility, conspiracy), failure to educate troops or to suppress crime, failure to prosecute troops who violate the law, failure to enforce the law generally, failure to maintain troop discipline, failure to investigate incidents, failure to report incidents to higher authorities, and at least in one case failure to resign from office".[459]

On the other hand, a superior political or military authority of forces committing atrocities cannot be made liable for any criminal action committed by his subordinates. The Commission of Experts has adopted a similar approach to that subject matter. Its members argued in the final report of 1994 that "isolated offences may be committed of which he has no knowledge or control whatsoever".[460] In other words, the superior must have had prior knowledge and necessary information[461]

---

In the context of this study the following cases illustrate the issue of command responsibility. Furundžija, the local commander of the Jokers (Bosnian Croat paramilitary forces) was, *e.g.*, alleged of sexual violence on the basis of his presence or authority when witness A was raped. He did nothing to prevent or stop the crime. Therefore, his acts or omission amounted in the view of the Trial Chamber of the ICTY to aiding and abetting of international law. Furundžija was in consequence found guilty and was sentenced to ten years' imprisonment. According to the *Delalić and Others* case, three of the accused persons held positions of authority at the Celebići camp. Their acts and omissions were the basis for charges of criminal responsibility for sexual violence. This is an important precedent in that the principle of command responsibility for gender-based crimes was extensively developed. See also the *Meakić and Others* case according to which six persons in position of authority were indicted for command responsibility for acts of sexual violence committed by their subordinates. The principle of leadership responsibility for crimes committed by subordinates has been, furthermore, applied in the *Sikirica and Others* case.

458 The notion of command responsibility is not limited to military or paramilitary structures. It comprises political leaders, government officials and civilian authorities. The Office of the Prosecutor of the ICTY indicted the highest ranking civilian officer in a municipality in Bosnia-Herzegovina who "knew or had reasons to know" that the chief of the Police in the area was about to force others to commit acts of rape and other forms of sexual assault. See *Prosecutor v. Miljković and Others*. The Trial Chamber of the ICTY ruled in the *Delalić and Others* case that the doctrine of command responsibility encompasses not only military commanders, but also civilians holding positions of authority and can have a *de facto* as well as a *de iure* character. *Delalić and Others*, Judgment §§ 363 and 378. See, in addition, UN Doc. E/CN.4/Sub.2/1998/13, § 78.

459 *J.J. Paust*, Superior Order and Command Responsibility, p. 79.

460 UN Doc. S/1994/674, p. 17.

461 The Secretary-General has clarified this requirement as follows: "This imputed responsibility or criminal negligence is engaged if the person in superior authority knew or had the reason to know that his subordinates were about to commit or had committed crimes and yet failed to take the necessary and reasonable steps to prevent or repress the commission of such crimes or to punish those who had committed them". UN Doc. S/25704, § 56. It is expected that the *mens rea* standard contained in Article 7(3) of the Statute will be clarified in the ongoing Blaškić trial.

enabling him to realise that the subordinate was actually committing, or that he was going to commit, criminal acts under international humanitarian law, and he must have failed to prevent or repress this conduct (Article 7(3) of the Statute).[462]

Finally, there is an obligation laid down in Article 7(3) of the *ad hoc* Tribunal's Statute for a person in command to prosecute and, if found guilty, to punish the perpetrator of the prohibited criminal act/s.[463]

### *8.3.3.3. The Plea of Respondeat Superior as a Defence*

Obedience to superior orders[464] is an issue relating for instance to the question of applicability of legal rules, which may preclude the imposition of personal responsibility under international law for those carrying out unlawful orders. It may be contended that in general there are two opposite views on that subject matter: the doctrine of *respondeat superior*, implying that a soldier committing an offence in obedience to superior orders is automatically and unconditionally excluded from liability, and the doctrine of absolute liability, according to which defence based on obedience to superior orders "does not create a defence *per se*, nor can it be taken into account within the compass of any other defence".[465] The rationale for the defence/justification of "obedience to superior orders" is according to Professor Bassiouni: "1. the hierarchical nature of the command military structure; 2. the need

---

Mr. O'Brien has argued on this issue that because of the extensive media, UN and governmental reporting of atrocities in former Yugoslavia, it will be "difficult for any person to plead ignorance". That includes persons in a command position as well. *J.C. O'Brien*, p. 652.

[462] The text of the relevant provision in the ICC Statute, Article 28 (1)(a) and (b), read as follows: "A military commander or person effectively acting as a military commander shall be criminally responsible for crimes within the jurisdiction of the Court committed by forces under his or her effective command and control, or effective authority and control as the case may be, as a result of his or her failure to exercise control properly over such forces, where: (a) That military commander or person either knew or, owing to the circumstances at the time, should have known that the forces were committing or about to commit such crimes; and (b) That military commander or person failed to take all necessary and reasonable measures within his or her power to prevent or repress their commission or to submit the matter to the competent authorities for investigation and prosecution".

[463] The Trial Chamber of the ICTY rejected, *e.g.*, the defence's argument in the *Blaškić* case that criminalising the failure to punish perpetrators was en *ex post facto* development in international criminal law. See also *Prosecutor v. Miljković and Others.*

[464] For a more detailed discussion on this subject matter see the book which is still considered as one of the most authoritative works on the subject *Y. Dinstein,* "The Defence of "Obedience to Superior Orders" in International Law, Leyden 1965. See also *L.C. Green*, Superior Orders in National and International Law, Leyden 1976; *J.L. Bakker*, The Defence of Obedience to Superior Orders: The Mens Rea Requirement, AJCL 1989, Vol. 17, pp. 55–70; *L.C. Green*, The Defence of Superior Orders in the Modern Law of Armed Conflict, Alberta Law Review 1993, Vol. 31, p. 320 *et seq.*; *J.W. Grayson*, The Defence of Superior Orders in the International Criminal Court, NJIL 1995, pp. 243–260.

Professor Dinstein defines the term "respondeat superior" in the way that it: "meant to point out not so much the responsibility of the superior as the lack of responsibility on the part of the subordinate committing an offence in pursuance of superior orders". Ibid., p. 8. See in addition *V. Morris & M.P. Scharf*, pp. 101–103.

[465] *Y. Dinstein*, The Defence of "Obedience to Superior Orders" in International Law, p. 68. See also in the same work pp. 21–87.

to maintain discipline in the military structure; and 3. the fact that a commanding officer is responsible for the acts of his subordinate".[466] However, in modern times the defence of "obedience to superior orders" has been made dependent upon "the legality of the order and the lawfulness of its foreseeable outcome".[467] Thus, if it is obvious that the order is illegal, the subordinate must disobey it. Otherwise he will be penalised for his criminal act. The "personal knowledge principle"[468] is based on the presumption that the defendant is aware of the illegality of the order. In this respect the Special Task Force of the American Bar Association Section of International Law and Practice pointed out in its Report on the International Tribunal to Adjudicate War Crimes Committed in the former Yugoslavia that the unqualified denial of defence of superior orders in the draft of the *ad hoc* Tribunal's Statute should be "revised or interpreted to recognise the defence of superior orders where a military defendant subject to superior orders in armed conflict did not know the orders to be unlawful and a person of ordinary sense and understanding would not have known the orders to be unlawful".[469] The text of the draft Statute was, however, not amended in its final form in accordance with this recommendation. As to its future interpretation, it remains to be seen what position the *ad hoc* Tribunal will take on that issue.

Here I ought to recall that there is a well established view in international law that ignorance of the law, or mistake of law, cannot serve as basis for a defence against criminal prosecution under international law and consequently does not relieve a person from criminal responsibility. It is not within the scope of this study to analyse in depth the validity of various theories on the issue of defence of obedience to superior orders. Therefore, it will suffice to observe here that the predominant view in international law seems to be that the doctrine of absolute liability reflects contemporary positive international law, whereas the doctrine of *respondeat superior* has very few adherents. It can be argued that it is a thing of the past. On the issue of defence, the Statute of the *ad hoc* Tribunal stresses the principle of individual liability and rejects totally the defence of superior orders. The liability to punishment of a subordinate who has either acted pursuant to an order of his government or of a superior and has thereby committed war crimes or crimes against humanity is regulated in Article 7(4) of the *ad hoc* Tribunal's Statute. The practical implication of this provision is that the subordinate cannot in the mentioned situations be relieved of criminal responsibility "provided a moral

---

466 *M.C. Bassiouni*, Crimes Against Humanity, pp. 399–400.

467 Ibid., p. 404. *Y. Dinstein*, op. cit., p. 9.

468 *Y. Dinstein*, ibid., p. 30; *A. Obote-Odora*, pp. 81–83.

469 Report, p. 38. See also *M. Leigh et al.*, Report on the International Tribunal to Adjudicate War Crimes Committed in former Yugoslavia, American Bar Association 1993, p. 40 and *K.E. Puls*, Report on the International Tribunal to Adjudicate War Crimes Committed in the Former Yugoslavia, Boston University International Law Journal 1994, Vol. 12, p. 148. The American Bar Association argued that the rejection of the plea of superior orders, as adopted by the Nuremberg Charter, may have been appropriate in prosecuting high-ranking Nazi officials. However, it should be considered in certain limited circumstances by the *ad hoc* Tribunal for the former Yugoslavia, *e.g.*, in the case of individual soldiers of lower ranks accused of criminal acts ordered by their superior, or in cases of intermediate commanders who "transmitted unlawful orders from higher authority to their subordinates".

choice was in fact available to him".[470] In other words, a crucial criterion for criminal liability under international law is the presence of a freedom of choice for the defendant "amounting to the moral and factual possibility of making choice of disobedience to superior orders and of insubordination to national authority",[471] *i.e.*, refusal to perform the incriminated act/s. It may be of interest to recall that also the first draft of the ILC Draft Code of Crimes Against the Peace and Security of Mankind contained an explicit reference to the moral choice test in Article 4, *i.e.*, superior orders are recognised as exculpatory.[472] Because of disagreement between governments on the use of the expression "moral choice" it was, however, replaced by the wording: "if, in the circumstances at the time, it was possible for him not to comply with that order". Also this text has been criticised by a few governments, and there are several proposals for improving the formulation of this provision.[473] On the other hand, in the Commentary to the draft Article 11 of the 1991 version of the ILC Draft Code the following explanation was given in the matter of moral choice: "Such circumstances would not exist in cases of irresistible moral or physical coercion, state of necessity and obvious and acceptable error".[474] An act of refusal presupposes that the subordinate would not expose himself by that conduct to "a greater harm than the one he is required to inflict".[475] However, it has been maintained that while the Nuremberg principles and the *ad hoc* Tribunal severely limit the defence of superior orders,[476] the

---

[470] UN Doc. S/1994/674, p. 18. This moral choice test has earlier been applied by the Nuremberg Trial when determining the punishability of a person. In this regard it was stressed that it is not the existence of the order in itself but merely whether a moral choice was in fact possible for the person in question that is decisive. The frequently quoted pronouncement of the Tribunal reads as follows: "The true test, which is found in varying degrees in the criminal law of most nations, is not the existence of the order, but whether moral choice was in fact possible". Judgment, p. 42. Relying on the French version of the judgment Professor Dinstein argues that: "the Tribunal did not establish a mere test but rather a criterion of penal responsibility/.... /. Consequently, if the conditions of the test are fulfilled, if there is no possibility of moral choice ('faculté de choisir') according to the French version – the defendant ought to be relieved of criminal responsibility and not just be subjected to a lenient punishment". After presentation of different possible substantive interpretations of the judgment in relation to Article VIII of the Nuremberg Charter, Professor Dinstein arrives at the conclusion that: "the moral choice test was meant to complement the provision of Article 8 and not to undermine its foundations, and that it does not permit the fact of obedience to orders to be considered for defence purposes". *Y. Dinstein*, pp. 149–152. It can be thus maintained that Article 7(4) of the *ad hoc* Tribunal's Statute is but an expression of the more restrictive view of the superior orders defence based on the Nuremberg Principles.

[471] *P.N. Drost*, p. 154.

[472] The text reads as follows: "The fact that an individual charged with a crime against the peace and security of mankind acted pursuant to an order of a Government or a superior does not relieve him of criminal responsibility if, in the circumstances at the time, it was possible for him not to comply with that order". Report of the ILC, Yearbook of the ILC 1951, pp. 123–124.

[473] UN Doc. A/CN.4/460, pp. 23–24.

[474] UN Doc. A/CN.4/L.464/Add.4.

[475] *M.C. Bassiouni*, Crimes Against Humanity, p. 410.

[476] UN GAOR, 49th Session, Supp. No. 10 (A/49/10), 1994. Under Article 33 the Court is obliged to consider applicable treaties, principles and rules of general international law, and rules of national law in evaluating the efficacy of the defence of superior orders. In this regard it has been suggested that the International Criminal Court may evaluate national law as evidence of custom in the law of war. But this is certainly a difficult task, since there is no universal agreement on that specific subject matter. Some

case law interpreting the international customary law[477] expresses a more liberal and expansive understanding of that defence. In the view of the present author the more restrictive approach to the principle of non-admissibility of the defence of non-punishability of the defendant by reason of having acted under authoritative command, today constitutes a customary rule of international law, which stems from the Charter[478] and the Judgment of the Nuremberg trial.[479] This presumption is mainly based on the argument that in the reverse situation all but the commander-in chief would be exculpated.[480] On the other hand, I must admit that though the mentioned provision in the *ad hoc* Tribunal's Statute expressly rejects any defence of superior orders, it does not exclude the application of the doctrine to a certain extent in mitigation of a sentence "if the International Tribunal determines that justice so requires". Circumstances that may have bearing on the sentence are, *e.g.*, a situation when coercion has been used or when there is a "lack of moral choice".[481]

Subordinates may be excluded from liability on the basis of internationally accepted defences, *i.e.*, a state of necessity, coercion and self-defence according to Article 31 of the ICC Statute.

As to the *ad hoc* Tribunal's jurisdiction, the Special Task Force of the American Bar Association recommended that the use of defence of superior orders should be limited to include only situations of duress, *i.e.*, if the defendant has committed the crime "to avoid death or serious harm to himself, as long as this threat is imminent, real, and inevitable".[482] According to Professor Bassiouni most legal systems recognise such a defence, but at the same time it varies with respect to the nature of the crimes. It is not accepted for the most serious crimes. [483] The Statute does not

---

countries, such as Great Britain, Sweden and Italy, do not recognise the defence of superior orders for violations of the laws and customs of war; others do. Under American military law, superior orders comprises the possibility of referring to "mistake of law" and is consequently recognised as a complete defence. *J.W. Grayson*, pp. 244, 248–249.

[477] *J.W. Grayson*, p. 248.

[478] Article VIII of the Nuremberg Charter establishes that: "The fact that the defendant acted pursuant to orders of his Government or of a superior shall not free him from responsibility, but may be considered in mitigation of punishment, if the Tribunal determines that justice so requires". I might mention that as early as in 1474 during the Breisach Trial when Peter von Hagenbach was tried for among other things murder and rape in an international context, the plea of the defence of superior orders was rejected. *L.C. Green*, p. 323; *J.W. Grayson*, p. 245.

[479] The following relevant passage from the Judgment may be quoted: "The rule that superior order is not a defence to a criminal act is a rule of fundamental criminal justice that has been adopted by civilised nations extensively. It is not disputed that the municipal law of civilised nations generally sustained the principle at the time that the alleged criminal acts were committed. This being true, it properly may be declared as an applicable rule of international law". Law Reports of Trials of War Criminals, Vol. XV, London 1949, p. 7.

[480] On justificatory grounds for superior orders as absolute defence against violations of international humanitarian law see *A. Obote-Odora*, p. 89.

[481] UN Doc. S/2504, § 57. See also *M.C. Bassiouni*, Crimes Against Humanity, pp. 438–446.

[482] *M. Leigh et al.*, p. 41.

[483] *M.C. Bassiouni*, Crimes Against Humanity, p. 441. Of relevance here is also the *Dražen Erdemović* case (*Prosecutor v. Erdemović*, Case No. IT-96-22-T, Appeals Chamber, October 7, 1997, final decision March 5, 1998), in which the accused was found guilty of shooting ten to one hundred

explicitly mention the availability of such a defence. However, it is assumed that the principle of individual responsibility might be excluded in exceptional circumstances for reasons such as "minimum age or mental incapacity, drawing upon general principles of law recognised by all nations".[484] In regard to the operation of the Rwanda Tribunal, the Commission of Experts has considered the defence of duress and mistake of fact as possible defence to individual allegations of serious human rights violations.[485]

For obvious reasons the category of subordinate perpetrators of criminal acts constituting violations of humanitarian law is the largest. Therefore, it can be argued that the great number of potential cases and "the fact that many defendants may find themselves in countries whose authorities are willing"[486] to bring them to justice does not make this category the most suitable for international proceedings. After all, as Professor Meron has observed, the fact that some trials would be subject of international, rather than national jurisdiction "concerns procedure rather than a fundamental principle of justice".[487] Furthermore, given the limited resources, which are at the *ad hoc* Tribunal's disposal, it is only reasonable to think that the other category of perpetrators, *i.e.*, persons in command, officers or officials, who were in charge and gave orders resulting in international crimes or the encouragement thereto, and the governmental and the military leaders, who

---

persons (according to his own statement he had killed about 70 persons) through participation near Pilica in the execution of men that had been transported from Srebrenica. *Erdemović* submitted that he had been threatened with death if he refused to participate in the summary executions. This argument was rejected by the Trial Chamber. Interestingly the Trial Chamber came to the conclusion that, in contrast to superior orders, duress could, in principle be invoked as a defence. It dismissed, however, the claim of duress in the particular case under review because of lack of proof. The Appeals Chamber was of another opinion on that subject matter. In the view of its members in international law, duress may not be regarded as a defence in cases of murder. It may, however, be taken into account by mitigating the punishment. The accused has appealed against the decision. The *Erdemović* case is also interesting in that the Prosecutor agreed, in return for his testimony against Karadžić and Mladić, to ask the Tribunal to give him a reduced sentence. He was actually sentenced to ten years' imprisonment. Since August 1998, *Erdemović* has been serving his sentence in Norway. UN Doc. A/52/375, p. 8; *J.C. Nemitz*, Aggravating and Mitigating Circumstances in International Humanitarian Law – The *Erdemović* Case, Humanitäres Völkerrecht 1997, p. 22 ff.; *S. Yee*, The *Erdemović* Sentencing Judgment: A Questionable Milestone for the International Criminal Tribunal for the former Yugoslavia, Georgia Journal of International Law 1997, Vol. 26, p. 263 ff.; *M.P. Scharf*, Balkan Justice, pp. 67 and 134; *O. Swaak-Goldman*, Comment on the case, AJIL 1998, Vol. 92, pp. 282–287; *K. Oellers-Frahm & B. Specht*, Die *Erdemović* Rechtsprechung des Jugoslawientribunals: Probleme bei der Entwicklung eines internationalen Strafrechts, dargestellt am Beispiel des Notstands, ZaöRV 1998, Vol. 58/2, pp. 389–414; *S.D. Murphy*, pp. 91–93.

[484] UN Doc. S/2504, § 58. Professor Bassiouni refers to the following defences, recognised in the major criminal justice systems on the universal level, which can be considered as general principles: "insanity; self-defence; mistake of law or fact; compulsion (coercion and duress); necessity; and, obedience to superior orders". *M.C. Bassiouni*, Crimes Against Humanity, p. 398. See also *N. Jareborg*, Essays in Criminal Law, Uppsala 1988, pp. 75–102 and Articles 26 and 31 (1) (a) and (b) of the ICC Statute.

[485] UN Doc. S/1994/1405, p. 34.

[486] UN Doc. A/49/342, S/1994/1007, p. 28.

[487] *T. Meron*, International Criminalization of Internal Atrocities, p. 566.

planned or tolerated the atrocities, should be a matter of priority for the international prosecution.[488]

To that end the concurrent jurisdiction of the *ad hoc* Tribunal with the jurisdiction of national courts over the same crimes can be efficiently used in order for the *ad hoc* Tribunal to be relieved of the bulk of cases dealing with the first category of perpetrators. Some explanation on this particular subject matter is, however, needed and follows below.

### 8.4. Exclusive or Concurrent Character of the *Ad Hoc* Tribunal's Jurisdiction?

By establishing the *ad hoc* Tribunal, the Security Council did not intend to deprive national courts of their jurisdiction over war crimes and crimes against humanity,[489] since such violations constitute both international and national crimes and "therefore (are) justiciable both in a national and international court".[490] As a consequence the *ad hoc* Tribunal was not vested with exclusive jurisdiction. Instead, from Article 9(1) of its Statute follows that the *ad hoc* Tribunal and national courts have concurrent jurisdiction[491] to prosecute persons for serious violations of inter-

---

488 This opinion can be objected to with regard to the suitability of making priorities on the subject matter in question. The first President of the *ad hoc* Tribunal Professor Cassese has thus stressed that: "the Tribunal will proceed against any person, regardless of status and rank, against whom the Prosecutor has issued an indictment confirmed by a judge of the Tribunal".

489 Worth mentioning is that the relationship of the jurisdiction of an *ad hoc* Tribunal and that of national courts might be approached from several perspectives: 1) *exclusive jurisdiction, i.e.*, the jurisdiction of the international body would replace that of national courts for certain crimes, 2) *concurrent jurisdiction*, which creates a situation of equality between the position of the international body and the domestic courts, 3) *preferential jurisdiction, i.e.*, the international tribunal would have its own priority jurisdiction and 4) *appellate jurisdiction, i.e.*, the international body would be the appeal instance in respect of national courts for certain crimes. All these aspects of a possible jurisdiction of an international tribunal versus that of national courts were discussed in depth during an international meeting of experts on the establishment of an international criminal tribunal, which was held by the International Centre for Criminal Law Reform and Criminal Justice Policy in Vancouver, March 22–26, 1993. It was pointed out that all the above mentioned options have their advantages and disadvantages. However, there appeared to be some consensus that in the case of the *ad hoc* Tribunal concurrent jurisdiction would be the more suitable and acceptable, particularly given the likely volume of cases. On this subject matter see generally *V. Morris & M.P. Scharf*, pp. 121–135.

490 United Nations War Crimes Commission, cited in *T. Meron*, International Criminalization of Internal Atrocities, p. 566.

491 Article 8 of the Statute of the International Tribunal for Rwanda contains a similar provision.

Countries which have accepted the principle of universal jurisdiction can prosecute without formal obstacles those suspected of committing serious violations of international law according to their domestic rules of criminal law. German courts have relied on this principle when prosecuting war criminals coming from the Balkans. *C.J. Safferling*, Comment on the case *Public Prosecutor v. Djajic*, No. 20/96, AJIL 1998, Vol. 92, pp. 528–532. Professor Kamminga has observed that since 1997 there has been a "significant and encouraging" prosecutoral activity on the domestic level based on the exercise of universal jurisdiction in respect of gross human rights and humanitarian law offences. *M.T. Kamminga*, p. 11.

national humanitarian law committed on the territory of the former Yugoslavia since January 1991. Nevertheless, of significance is the fact that the concurrent jurisdiction is subject to the primacy[492] of the *ad hoc* Tribunal. In accordance with Article 9(2) of the Statute, the *ad hoc* Tribunal may intervene at any stage of national proceedings and formally request the national courts to defer to the competence of the Tribunal "whenever this proves to be in the interests of justice".[493] Interestingly, the defence in the *Tadić* case challenged this jurisdictional provision by arguing that the primacy given over national courts by the UN was a violation of the sovereignty of States as expressed in Article 2 of the UN Charter and that the defendant had, moreover, a right to be tried by his national courts (*ius de non evocando*[494]). While the Trial Chamber took a very orthodox approach to the first challenge, and rejected the plea, on the grounds that the question of violation of sovereignty could only be raised by a state, and not by an individual,[495] the Appeals Chamber was of the opposite view in this matter. The principle upheld by the Trial Chamber was dismissed as anachronistic on the basis that: "Dating back to the

---

However, since there are still countries, *e.g.*, the United States of America and France, rejecting this principle, national prosecutoral structures cannot be considered as an "adequate substitute" for an international criminal court. *H. Roggemann*, p. 69. Besides, history has shown us the limitations of exclusive reliance on trials by national jurisdictions. At the same time Professor Meron has convincingly argued that the possible fear of states that the activities of international tribunals "might pre-empt national prosecutions" can stimulate "spurring prosecutions before national courts for serious violations of humanitarian law". *T. Meron*, International Criminalization of Internal Atrocities, p. 555.

[492] It could be noted here in regard to the jurisdictional relationship between the proposed ICC and national courts that the ICC Statute reflects the principle of complementarity. Nevertheless, unlike the *ad hoc* Tribunal's jurisdiction, the Statute of the ICC gives primacy to national jurisdictions. See UN Doc. A/50/22, §§ 29–51; *I. Tallgren*, Completing the "International Criminal Order", The Rhetoric of International Repression and the Notion of Complementarity in the Draft Statute for an International Criminal Court, NJIL 1998, Vol. 67, pp. 119–132; *M. Palatsi*, p. 133; *A. Cassese*, On the Current Trends towards Criminal Prosecution and Punishment of Breaches of International Humanitarian Law, p. 16.

[493] UN Doc. A/49/342; S/1994/1007, p. 13; *K. Lescure & F. Trintignac*, pp. 66–67.

[494] This principle may be found in the constitutional law of several civil law jurisdictions. Its purpose is to ensure that persons accused of certain types of crimes should retain their rights to be tried before the regular domestic criminal courts rather than by politically founded special tribunals established for that particular reason. After reviewing the human rights instruments relevant to this point, the *ad hoc* Tribunal came to the conclusion that the on-going trial is of advantage for the defendant, and *at least* as equally fair as a trial before a national court would be. The invocation of this right was considered ill-founded by the Tribunal and it was subsequently dismissed. *Prosecutor v. Tadić*, IT-94-1-AR72, Appeals on Jurisdiction, at 63. The same issue was raised in the *Kanyabashi* case, in which the Trial Chamber of the Rwanda Tribunal emphasised that "the Tribunal is far from being an institution designed for the purpose of removing, for political reasons, certain offenders from fair and impartial justice and have them prosecuted for political crimes before prejudiced arbitrators". The Tribunal could not find any violation of the principle in question. *Prosecutor v. Kanyabashi*, No. ICTR-96-15-T, Decision on Jurisdiction, June 18, 1997, at 8, IHRR 1999, Vol. 6, p. 85.

[495] The Trial Chamber relied on a series of national judgments, *e.g.*, the *Israel v. Eichmann* case as well as the more recent *Noriega* case, in which the relevant principle was laid down. The Appeals Chamber reaffirmed the principle of the cases above *per se*, but then pointed out the fundamental element that made it inapplicable: they were cases from national courts, relating to situations quite different from the present one. Instead the Appeals Chamber emphasised the non-national character of the alleged crimes, and quoted statements from among others the Italian *General Wagener* case. *Prosecutor v. Tadić,* at 57.

period when sovereignty stood as a sacrosanct and unassailable attribute of statehood, recently this concept has suffered progressive erosion at the hands of more liberal forces' work in the democratic societies, particularly in the field of human rights".[496] Since the Tribunal is dealing with a measure under Chapter VII of the UN Charter, the primacy of the Tribunal was found perfectly legal by the Appeals Chamber, and the plea regarding state sovereignty dismissed. Besides this argument, one can find two reasons of a more practical nature for the chamber to reassert the primacy for the international forum. Firstly, the Tribunal "must be endowed with primacy over national courts", otherwise "there would be a perennial danger of international crimes being characterised as 'ordinary crimes'".[497] Secondly, by holding this view, the Tribunal prevents the risk for the so-called "forum shopping" in this and other similar cases.[498]

Representatives of the International Commission of Jurists have on several occasions pointed out a number of possible negative consequences of the concurrent character of a court's jurisdiction.[499] It has been stressed that there is a potential jurisdictional conflict between two or more states and that of the *ad hoc* Tribunal. Against this background it has been argued that in order to avoid problems relating to the principle of *non bis in idem* (protection against double jeopardy),[500] it would have been better if the *ad hoc* Tribunal had been granted exclusive jurisdiction. Some of the advantages would have been upholding a better guarantee of uniform justice[501] for

---

[496] *Prosecutor v. Tadić*, ibid., at 55.

[497] In the words of the Trial and Appeals Chambers "Before leaving this question relating to the violation of the sovereignty of States, it should be noted that the crimes which the International Tribunal has been called upon to try are not crimes of a purely domestic nature. They are really crimes which are universal in nature, well recognised in international law and transcending the interest of any one State". *Prosecutor v. Tadić*, at 58 and 59.

[498] Ibid, at 65. See on the issue of forum shopping *M. Bogdan*, Svensk internationell privat-och processrätt, Stockholm 1995, p. 34 and *G.H. Aldrich*, p. 64.

[499] See, *e.g.*, UN Doc. A/CONF.157/PC/62/Add.17, 3 June 1993. See also *S.Oeter*, Kriegsverbrechen in den Konflikten um das Erbe Jugoslawiens, ZaöRV 1993, p. 26.

[500] This is a fundamental principle of the criminal law of a great number of the UN member states and it is consequently expressed in Article 20 of the Statute of the ICC. See also the European Convention on the International Validity of Criminal Judgments of 1970; *A. Nelson*, Swedish and Foreign Crimes in the Swedish Criminal Justice System, in N. Jareborg (ed.), Double Criminality, Studies in International Criminal Law, Uppsala 1989, p. 20; *M.N. Morosin*, Double Jeopardy and International Law: Obstacles to Formulating a General Principle, NJIL 1995, pp. 261–274; *M.C. Bassiouni & P. Manikas*, pp. 306–334.

[501] This can hardly be upheld, especially in view of cases which have already occurred, where alleged war criminals were not charged with war crimes but rather with violations of domestic criminal law. A Sarajevo court has, *e.g.*, tried and sentenced to death at least two Serbs for war crimes, including summary executions and the rape of civilians. As earlier pointed out the *ad hoc* Tribunal shall not apply the death penalty. In other words, if these cases were adjudicated by the Tribunal the persons who have committed the above mentioned criminal acts would at the most have been sentenced to life imprisonment. The Bosnian Government has, however, since then abolished the death penalty. As to war crimes trials in the FRY, seven members of the Croatian National Guard were sentenced to death or received long prison terms on June 26, 1992. Nevertheless, later the defendants were exchanged and handed over to Croatian authorities. As a consequence of amending and revising the Yugoslavia's Criminal Code, capital punishment was abolished in 1993. Helsinki Watch, Former Yugoslavia, War Crimes Trials in the Former Yugoslavia, 1995, pp. 35 and 38–39. See also *V.A. Vasiljević*, Zločini, Odgovornost, Beograd 1995 and Medunarodni Krivični Tribunal, Beograd 1996.

all accused and an avoidance of having governments that have sponsored atrocities prosecute those responsible. To encourage or sanction war crimes trials in any of the states that are parties to the armed conflict has been described as "functional equivalent to granting widespread amnesty", *i.e.*, acceptance of impunity for alleged criminals.[502] On the other hand, reality made such a regulation difficult to achieve mainly for political reasons but also for other reasons. We should, however, bear in mind the fact that the primacy of the *ad hoc* Tribunal over national courts and the requirement to observe the principle of *non bis in idem*, which is set forth in Article 10 of the Statute,[503] precludes a subsequent trial before a national court. The *ad hoc* Tribunal may, however, try the accused once again despite the fact that he has been tried in national courts under the condition that the offences are other than those revealed by the national court. Furthermore, in the following two circumstances the above mentioned principle does not preclude a subsequent trial before the *ad hoc* Tribunal:

> "a) The characterisation of the act by the national court did not correspond to its characterisation under the Statute or b) Conditions of impartiality, independence of effective means of adjudication were not guaranteed in the proceedings before the national courts".[504]

---

[502] Human Rights Watch, Former Yugoslavia, The War Crimes Tribunal: One Year Later, 1994, p. 2. The trials that have already taken place in the former Yugoslavia, *e.g.*, the one in Serbia against D.Vucković, a Serbian paramilitary responsible for gross human rights violations in Bosnia-Herzegovina, have been characterised by politicisation and disrespect of due process rights. It is even maintained that the prosecution's line of questioning in the above case, did more to assist the defence than to fulfil its own task. This is equally valid for the decisions to prosecute in Croatia where it has been apparent that ethnicity has been given weight in the determination to prosecute. Judges and prosecutors have been dismissed summarily or reprimanded because they have refused to obey the political authorities when adjudicating a case. See Helsinki Watch, Former Yugoslavia, 1995, pp. 2 and 14 ff.

[503] According to Rule 13 of the Rules of Procedure and Evidence, a Trial Chamber shall, on the basis of reliable information as regards initiated criminal proceedings against a person before a national court, request the national court permanently to discontinue its proceedings. If the state fails to do so, the President of the *ad hoc* Tribunal may report the matter to the Security Council.

In fact the prohibition against subjecting a defendant to more than one prosecution for the same offence, has been considered as one of "the oldest ideas found in western civilization". American Bar Association, Report, quoting *Bartkus v. Illinois* on p. 42, note 138.

On the other hand, the existence of provisions relating to a defendant's right to be free from double jeopardy on the national level, *e.g.*, Article 31 of the Croatian Constitution, has in practice not proved to be a strong guarantee for its observance by the domestic courts. International NGOs have reported cases involving violations of that particular right. See, *e.g.*, Helsinki Watch, Former Yugoslavia, p. 14.

[504] UN Doc. S/2504, § 66. When deciding upon the penalty to be imposed on the person convicted of a crime under the Statute of the *ad hoc* Tribunal, consideration has to be taken as to the extent to which the penalty imposed by a national court on the same person for the same acts already has been served (Article 10(3) of the Statute).

The American Bar Association has paid much attention to possible difficulties that might arise out of the rule allowing for retrial by the *ad hoc* Tribunal of a case previously heard by a national court in the enumerated situations. It has been feared that there might be obstacles in obtaining the list of the crimes charged by the national court if the country in question refuses to co-operate with the *ad hoc* Tribunal. The Tribunal might also be exposed to difficulties in connection with ascertaining necessary evidence in order to prove that the national proceedings were a "sham". *K.E. Puls*, p. 149.

Rule 9 of the Rules of Procedure and Evidence contains further clarification as to the cases in which the Prosecutor may make a formal request[505] to the Trial Chamber for a national court to defer a case to the *ad hoc* Tribunal. The following specific situations has been referred to:

> "(i) the act being investigated or, which is the subject of those proceedings is characterised as an ordinary crime;... (iii) what is in issue is closely related to, or otherwise involves, significant factual[506] or legal questions,[507] which may have implications for investigations or prosecutions before the Tribunal".

The question of request for deferral was raised in the very first case[508] before the *ad hoc* Tribunal. The then Prosecutor of the *ad hoc* Tribunal, Mr. Richard J. Goldstone, made an application pursuant to Rule (9 (iii))[509] of the Tribunal's Rules of

---

[505] The Prosecutor must first require national authorities to provide information on cases that are the subject of investigations or criminal proceedings in that State (Rule 8) and then, if he deems it appropriate, to request the Trial Chamber to issue an order for deferral to the competence of the Tribunal.

[506] The Prosecutor referred to the following factual questions, which he deemed may have implications for his investigations or any subsequent prosecutions in the case No. IT-95-5-D: "i) witnesses may be exposed to greater risks as their identities and evidence will already have been made public; ii) witnesses may be unwilling or unable to testify for a second time; iii) critical evidence stored in war zones in the Republic of Bosnia-Herzegovina could be damaged or lost before use by the International Tribunal; iv) witnesses may become confused as to the scope and authority of the two investigations; v) the International Tribunal is not a party to the conflict in the Republic of Bosnia-Herzegovina and has a better ability to obtain evidence world-wide; vi) deferral of these investigations may encourage Governments and other sources to furnish additional information to the International Tribunal that has thus far not been provided". Ibid., p. 7. See also case No. IT-95-6-D, pp. 4–5.

[507] In case No. IT-95-5-D the Prosecutor referred to the following legal issues as being of significance for the proceedings: "vii) issues relating to the principle of *non-bis-in-idem*; viii) there is the potential inadvertently to create inconsistent sworn evidence; ix) issues relating to possible trials *in absentia*, which may be held in the Republic of Bosnia-Herzegovina; x) it would be undesirable and not in the interest of justice if the decisions of a national court and of the International Tribunal were to conflict". Ibid., p. 8.

[508] The first case dealing with the prosecution of a Bosnian Serb war criminal, (Refik Sarić) who is residing in Denmark and which was brought before a national court, was decided on 25 November 1994 in Copenhagen by a district court. The perpetrator was sentenced to eight years imprisonment for committing atrocities such as murder and torture in the Dretelj camp. The conviction, which was based on grave breaches of the Third and Fourth Geneva Conventions in conjunction with the Danish Penal Code, was confirmed on appeal. *Prosecution v. Refik Sarić*, Supreme Court of Denmark, 15 August 1995. See furthermore *V. Morris & M.P. Scharf*, p. 125, note 376; *A. Cassese*, On the Current Trends towards Criminal Prosecution and Punishment of Breaches of International Humanitarian Law, EJIL 1998, Vol. 9, No. 1, p. 7. For recent cases reviewed under the jurisdiction of various European countries see *M.T. Kamminga*, pp. 10–11.

The first trial in the Serbian controlled part of Krajina in Croatia sentenced on 19 January 1995 Dušan Boljević to 20 years imprisonment for having committed war crimes.

On legal proceedings against persons suspected of being instigators of the genocide in Rwanda in, *e.g.*, Belgium, Canada and Switzerland see UN Doc. E/CN.4/1996/68, § 57.

[509] This rule has been applied in other cases as well, *e.g.*, in the earlier referred to *Erdemović* case. See *D. Beane*, The Yugoslav Tribunal and Deferral of National Prosecutions of War Criminals, ASIL, Newsletter, September–October 1996, pp. 1–4.

Procedure and Evidence entailing a formal request from the Tribunal to the Government of the Federal Republic of Germany for the deferral to the competence of the *ad hoc* Tribunal of the investigation of the activities of Duško Tadić by that government, in respect to events having occurred on the territory of the former Yugoslavia since 1 January 1991.[510] The Prosecutor declared in his application that Tadić had been arrested and taken into custody by the Government of the Federal Republic of Germany on 13 February 1994 on suspicion of having: 1) Aided and abetted the commission of genocide at Omarska in former Yugoslavia in 1992; 2) Compelled another person to murder three individuals at Omarska on 15 or 18 June 1992; 3) Assaulted and tortured Muslim detainees at Omarska in June 1992, contrary to the law of the Federal Republic of Germany. There was, moreover, an allegation that Tadić was involved in incidents of rape at Omarska, an allegation which was under investigation. In this respect the Trial Chamber observed the following:

> "At the Trnopolje camp Tadić was witnessed, on more than one occasion, to have been involved in the raping of Muslim women. On one occasion in the summer of 1992, Tadić was witnessed to have arrived at the Trnopolje area riding on a tank with a group of Serbian soldiers. Tadić and the soldiers were then involved in the rape of some Muslim women at a house outside the camp".[511]

The Prosecutor, furthermore, stressed that the case of Duško Tadić was significant for the investigations being undertaken against persons in higher positions than Tadić, responsible for serious violations of international humanitarian law committed in the territory of the former Yugoslavia since 1 January 1991. Thus, the Office of the Prosecutor investigated allegations of serious violations of international humanitarian law in the Prijedor region according to several sources including the report of the United Nations Commission of Experts established pursuant to Security Council Resolution 780 (1992). Tadić was considered a key witness in this respect. Moreover, in the view of the Prosecutor the *ad hoc* Tribunal was the appropriate forum to deal with the *Tadić* case, taking into account the seriousness

---

[510] United Nations, Case No. IT-94-1-D, *In the Matter of a Proposal for a Formal Request for Deferral by the Federal Republic of Germany in the Matter of Dušan Tadić also Known by the Names Dusǎn "Dule" Tadić*, International Criminal Tribunal for the Former Yugoslavia, 8 November 1994.

[511] Ibid., p. 9. I should also mention that the Registry of the *ad hoc* Tribunal on 13 February 1995 announced the indictments of twenty other individuals, most of them persons in an official position (camp commanders and camp guards) in the Omarska camp during the relevant time (the summer of 1992) and who have been involved in among other things incidents of rape. Warrants of arrest have also been issued against the defendants. The indictments against the 21 defendants are the result of a five-month investigation by a team of twenty investigators, attorneys and analysts from the Office of the Prosecutor. The evidence has been collected by travelling to twelve countries and interviews with some of the victims and witnesses. CC/PIO/004/-E, The Hague, 13 February 1995. See case No. IT-94-1-I, *Indictment against D. Tadić and G. Borovnića/ Responsibility for the killings within and outside* the *Omarska camp between May and August 1992*; case No. IT-95-4-I, Indictment against 19 members of the Serb forces (*Z. Meakić et al.*) who were commanders, guards or others responsible for the conditions and mistreatment of prisoners in the Omarska camp between May and August 1992.

and the nature of the crimes committed,[512] and the legal points, which were to be raised in connection with, for instance, the interpretation of the concept of armed conflict and the nature and manner of their proof. With reference to the investigations being carried out by the Prosecutor, the Trial Chamber established that the case of Duško Tadić involved:

> "i) genocide, through the policy of ethnic cleansing, and crimes against humanity, such as assault, murder, rape and persecution based on religious grounds; ii) the case of Duško Tadić cannot be separated from the cases of other alleged co-offenders; iii) the role of Duško Tadić and his status in the local militia are indispensable elements to show the role of other alleged co-offenders; and iv) this International Tribunal would not be acting in the proper interests of justice if some of these serious violations of international humanitarian law committed in the same territory and during the same period of time by alleged co-offenders, who are party to the same criminal plan, were judged in national courts and others before this International Tribunal".[513]

After receiving the above mentioned formal request from the *ad hoc* Tribunal, the Government of the Federal Republic of Germany raised the question as to the potential legal conflict between its national law in force and the formal request for deferral issued by the Trial Chamber. It declared that the domestic rules had to be changed until an extradition could be carried out.[514] This factual situation could not be side-stepped and caused a delay in the *ad hoc* Tribunal's proceedings until mid April 1995 when the accused was delivered to The Hague after the German parliament enacted necessary implementing legislation on March 31, 1995. On 29th October 1995 the Tribunal accepted the demand of the defence[515] of the suspect

---

[512] This was also the motivation for the Prosecutor's request to the Trial Chamber to issue an order for the deferral of all investigations and criminal proceedings in respect to *R. Karadžić, R. Mladić and M. Stanisić* (case No. IT-95-5-D) and an order of deferral of all investigations and criminal proceedings in respect to the crimes alleged to have been committed in the *Lašva* River Valley area (case No. IT-95-6-D).

[513] Ibid., p. 12.

[514] Given the current status of national regulations, it seems that many countries can experience similar difficulties in meeting their obligations under the *ad hoc* Tribunal's Statute. The American Bar Association has, *e.g.*, addressed the issue of judicial assistance and the potential problems which may arise in this context within the United States, and recommended that implementing legislation is needed in order to address the deficiencies in the laws in force and to comply with the requirements of the Statute. *K.E. Puls*, p. 150. This question was given significant attention at the Tribunal's first session. At its closing meeting the President of the *ad hoc* Tribunal underlined the necessity for states "not only to designate, in their domestic legal systems, a body responsible for dealing with any request from the Tribunal, but also to adopt the legislative or regulatory provisions required to give effect to the Tribunal's statute". UN Doc. A/49/342, S/1994/1007, p. 45. In 1998 some 20 states have enacted legislations to implement the *ad hoc* Tribunal's Statute and the Rules of Procedure and Evidence. In addition, a number of states have indicated their intention to promulgate such legislation in the near future.

[515] According to Mr. Scharf, Tadić's defence in Germany had no objections against the transfer of the proceedings to the ICTY. It has been assumed that Tadić's lawyers thought that, if convicted by Germany on the charge of genocide, Tadić faced automatically life imprisonment, whereas the ICTY could hand down a lesser sentence. *M.P. Scharf*, Balkan Justice, p. 100.

Bosnian Serb war criminal Tadić to postpone the trial till March 1996 in order to collect evidence to prove the innocence of their client. The defence challenged the authority to defer his prosecution pursuant to Rule 9(iii) of the Tribunal's Statute on the basis of the argument that the Tribunal lacked jurisdiction under the principle of *non bis in idem* and therefore his case should have remained in Germany for a final decision. The Prosecutor maintained rightly that while the indictment had been issued against Tadić, neither a judgment nor a sentence was pronounced by the national court in question. Thus, there did not exist any hinder to apply the relevant rules of the Tribunal's Statute.

It must be stressed that since the *ad hoc* Tribunal lacks direct enforcement powers, it must rely upon the domestic legal system and enforcement machinery of each state in order to perform the important tasks entrusted to it. In concrete terms, this means that all requests from the *ad hoc* Tribunal for the arrest, search, surrender or transfer of persons must be processed through the domestic system of the states concerned.[516] For that reason it is of outmost importance that all states fulfil their obligation to co-operate with the Tribunal. In order to ensure the co-operation of the German Government with the *ad hoc* Tribunal, the Trial Chamber referred at an early stage to Article 29[517] of the Statute and to a Note from the Secretary-General of the United Nations from 2 June 1993, in which he drew the attention of the international community to the obligations of states under § 4 of the Security Council Resolution 827 (1993) to co-operate with the *ad hoc* Tribunal and its organs.[518] In other words, in the concrete case it was underlined that a state cannot

---

516 UN Doc. A/49/342, S/1994/1007, p. 27.

517 This provision requires among other things judicial assistance related to the identification or location of persons, taking of testimony, arrest or detention, service of documents and surrender or transfer of persons to the *ad hoc* Tribunal. In a statement issued on 24 November 1995 the *ad hoc* Tribunal welcomed the Dayton peace agreement, noting that all parties agreed to "strictly fulfil their obligations to arrest and surrender persons indicted by the Tribunal. Nevertheless, the FRY, Republic Serbska and the Bosnian Croat authorities continue so far to refuse to arrest indictees". The President of the ICTY therefore appellated in strong wording to the international community to "put unceasing pressure on those non-cooperative parties to meet their international obligations to co-operate with the Tribunal". UN Doc. A/52/375, p. 3. See also the statement by the President of the S.C. made on August 8, 1996, on the situation in Bosnia and Herzegovina, UN Doc. No. S/PRST/1996/34 and the following article "Jugoslavien kräver att FN släpper krigsförbrytare", <http://www.dn.se/DNet/articles/23200–23299/index.html.>.

Articles 86 and 87 of the ICC Statute contain obligation for states parties to cooperate fully with the Court in its investigations and prosecution of crimes within the jurisdiction of the Court.

In contrast to the *ad hoc* Tribunal's jurisdiction not all member states of the UN are under obligation to accept the International Criminal Court's jurisdiction. Yet, states not parties to its Statute may assist the Court on the basis of an *ad hoc* arrangement, an agreement with such a state or any other appropriate basis (Article 87(5)).

518 Paragraph 4 lays down that all states "shall take any measures necessary under their domestic law to implement the provisions" of the Statute and comply with "request for assistance or orders issued by a trial chamber". Also the Rwanda Tribunal relies on the full and unreserved co-operation of states. The arrest of Colonel Bagosora, a leading member of the former interim Government in Rwanda, has been cited as the most significant example in this regard. Despite extradition requests from Rwanda and Belgium, he had been prosecuted because of his position, by the *ad hoc* Tribunal at Arusha. See *P. Akhavan*, The International Criminal Tribunal for Rwanda: The Politics and Pragmatics of Punishment, p. 509. On the

avoid compliance with its international obligations by invoking its municipal law,[519] which nowadays is a universally accepted principle of public international law. Furthermore, according to Rule 11 of the Tribunal's Rules of Procedure and Evidence, a failure to comply within sixty days with a request for deferral, the "Trial Chamber may request the President to report the matter to the Security Council". If despite the above said a warrant of arrest is not executed, it will not be possible for the *ad hoc* Tribunal to fulfil its judicial function. Such a situation may occur when the authorities of the territory concerned have not been able to locate the person or when they refuse to co-operate with the *ad hoc* Tribunal. The ICTY remains then in the words of Judge Cassese "like a giant without arms and legs".[520]

The defendant might also deliberately have eluded justice.[521] In such cases Rule 61 of the Rules of Procedure and Evidence of the Tribunal will apply, which allows the Tribunal to fulfil at least an important accusatory function. The President of the Tribunal may inform the Security Council thereof. Moreover, the application of Rule 61 implies that the accused person will publicly be branded an "international fugitive", *i.e.*, he will become a prisoner in his country of residence, and secondly he will become a hostage to political changes that may arise in his country of refuge. The person's position, be it of public, civil or military character, will unquestionably be seriously affected internationally as well as domestically.[522]

## 8.5. The Organisation of the *Ad Hoc* Tribunal

### *8.5.1. The Structure and the Seat of the Ad Hoc Tribunal*

Articles 11–15 of the Statute contain the relevant provisions for the organisation and structure of the *ad hoc* Tribunal for former Yugoslavia. Since the *ad hoc* Tribunal has been established for the purpose of prosecuting persons responsible for serious violations of international humanitarian law in the territory of the former

---

arrest of Elizaphan Ntakirutimana on February 26, 1998 in the US, on the basis of charges of genocide and crimes against humanity and his probable extradition to Arusha, see *P.J. Magnarella*, Can the US extradite fugitives to UN Criminal Tribunal for Rwanda?, ASIL, Human Rights Interest Group Newsletter, Vol. 8, No. 1, 1998, pp. 16–19. See also, Swiss ready to hand over Rwandan war crimes suspect, USA Today, August 3, 1996, p. 1; Amnesty International, International Criminal Tribunals, Handbook for government co-operation, AI Index: IOR 40/07/96, August 1996; UN Doc. E/CN.4/1996/68, §§ 56–57.

519 In two other earlier referred to cases (No. IT-95-5-D and No. IT-95–6-D) the Trial Chamber formally requested the Government of the Republic of Bosnia-Herzegovina that its national courts defer to the Tribunal all investigations and criminal proceedings respecting serious violations of international humanitarian law and invited the Government to take all necessary steps, both legislative and administrative, to comply with the request. The Government appearing as *amicus curiae* has indicated in both its written and oral statements on the cases above that it does not oppose the issue of a formal request.

520 *A. Cassese*, On the Current Trends towards Criminal Prosecution and Punishment of Breaches of International Humanitarian Law, p. 13.

521 Information Memorandum issued by the Information Office of the *ad hoc* Tribunal, p. 1.

522 *P. Malanczuk*, p. 359.

Yugoslavia, its structure reflects the functions it is expected to perform, *i.e.*, ensuring the fair and efficient administration of justice.[523] The *ad hoc* Tribunal is consequently composed of three organs: its judiciary, the Office of the Prosecutor and the Registry.[524] The judicial organ in its turn is composed of two levels of jurisdiction, *i.e.*, it is organised as a two instance court. This means that the cases will first be dealt with by the Trial Chambers (there are two Trial Chambers consisting of three judges each). In cases of appeal they will be considered by the single standing Appeals Chamber, which consists of five judges. The availability of an appeal institution is an important requirement in contemporary international criminal law.[525] The Chambers consist of in all eleven judges (Article 12).

Of crucial importance in regard to the composition and organisation of the *ad hoc* Tribunal is the question of the qualifications of the judges and their election. Thus, when the matter was under consideration, the predominant standpoint was that the judges should meet the highest standards of competence, experience, integrity, impartiality and independence (Article 13 of the Statute). On 17 September 1993 the UN General Assembly elected the eleven judges from a list submitted by the Security Council to serve to the *ad hoc* Tribunal.[526] They took office on 17 November 1993. Subsequently Professor Antonio Cassese was elected by the judges to act as President of the *ad hoc* Tribunal. He has upheld this position until 17 November 1997, when Ms. McDonald was elected to act as President of the Tribunal. In view of the nature of the crimes committed – numerous cases of rape and other kinds of sexual assault – it is vital that as many as possible of the judges are women.[527] Regrettably I may note that of the elected eleven judges only two are women: the Vice President of the Tribunal, Ms. Elizabeth Odio Benito, and the

---

[523] *V. Morris & M.P. Scharf*, p. 137.

[524] See Article 11 of the Statute.

The Tribunal for Rwanda consists, according to Article 10 of its Statute, likewise of three organs. It has separate Trial Chambers from the *ad hoc* Tribunal for the former Yugoslavia but the two Tribunals share the same Appeals Chamber (Article 12). The Prosecutor of the *ad hoc* Tribunal for the former Yugoslavia serves also as the Prosecutor of the Tribunal for Rwanda (Article 15(3)). After extensive and difficult negotiations, this solution was agreed upon as a compromise between on the one hand the recommendations of the Commission of Experts for Rwanda to expand the jurisdiction of the already established *ad hoc* Tribunal to comprise also competence over international crimes committed in Rwanda and on the other hand the proposal to create a completely separate tribunal for Rwanda. See *L.S. Sunga*, The Commission of Experts on Rwanda, p. 123. See also *M.C. Bassiouni & P. Manikas*, pp. 795–859.

On the composition and administration of the future International Criminal Court, see Part 4 (§§ 34–52) of the ICC Statute.

[525] *P.C. Szasz*, p. 428. I need also mention Article 14(5) of the ICCPR, according to which "Everyone convicted of a crime shall have the right to his conviction and sentence being reviewed by a higher tribunal according to law".

[526] The judges are elected for a term of four years. Yet, they shall be eligible for re-election. Casual vacancies are to be filled by the Secretary General in consultation with the Presidents of the General Assembly and the Security Council.

[527] Thanks to the intensive lobbying by the Women's Caucus among others, during the preparatory process of the ICC Statute, the adopted version of Article 36 (8)(a)(iii) requires "A fair representation of female and male judges" and subsection (b) adds that states parties should in the electoral process take into account the need to include judges with legal expertise on, *e.g.*, violence against women and children.

current President Ms. Gabrielle Kirk McDonald. In the case of the Trial Chamber of the Rwanda Tribunal, only one out of the six judges is a woman (Ms. Pillay). Professor Cook has illustrated the significance of having expertise on gender issues among the Tribunal's members by referring to the fact that only after the female judge had raised certain questions during the Akayesu trial, which started on 9 January 1997, could evidence of mass rapes be brought up, and the indictment was amended so as to include a count of rape.[528] None of the accused was charged with rape and/or other forms of sexual violence before that.

The *ad hoc* Tribunal's Statute, furthermore, entails a provision for a public prosecutor's office headed by a Prosecutor. This organ will initiate and conduct the investigations of the cases, prepare the indictments and prosecute the war criminals. The need of an independent office of prosecutor was determined by the necessity to ensure guarantees of impartiality and objectivity in the preparation of charges.[529] The Prosecutor must consequently be independent from other parts of the *ad hoc* Tribunal and must not receive instructions from any government. As the functions of the Prosecutor are of major importance, the Statute provides in Article 16 that he/she should be appointed by the Security Council upon nomination by the Secretary General. Also, qualifications similar to those of the judges are required. The Prosecutor should possess the highest level of professional competence as well as be experienced in the conduct of investigations and prosecutions of criminal cases. After difficulties in reaching an agreement in regard to the nominated persons, finally Mr. Richard J. Goldstone from South Africa was appointed by the Security Council[530] on 8 July 1994 as Prosecutor of the Tribunal.[531] By a resolution

---

[528] *R.J. Cook*, Women's Human Rights Resources (WHRR), ASIL Human Rights Interest Group, Newsletter 1998, Vol. 8, No. 2, p. 6. See also UN Doc. A/52/582, § 12; UN Doc. E/CN.4/1998/54, p. 11 and *K.D. Askin*, Sexual Violence, p. 98.

[529] ICJ, Towards Universal Justice, p. 35. See also *M. Bergsmo & M.J. Keegan*, Case Preparation for the International Criminal Tribunal for the Former Yugoslavia, Manual on Human Rights, Oslo 1997, Chapter 10, pp. 9–11; *V. Morris & M.P. Scharf*, pp. 157–168. On the role of the Prosecutor of the future ICC see UN Doc. A/50/22, § 25 and *K. Ambos*, The Role of the Prosecutor of an International Criminal Court from a Comparative Perspective, The Review 1998, No. 53, pp. 45–56.

[530] S.C., Res. 936 of 8 July 1994. See also *M. Bergsmo*, International Criminal Tribunal for the Former Yugoslavia, Recent Developments, HRLJ 1994, Vol. 15, p. 405.

[531] The Security Council approved by Res. 877 (1993) on 21 October 1993 Mr. Ramon Escovar-Salom of Venezuela as the *ad hoc* Tribunal's Prosecutor. However, before he took up his duties as the Prosecutor, he withdrew from his appointment in early February 1994, since he had decided to accept the appointment as Minister of the Interior in his home country. One of the undoubtedly most qualified candidates, Professor Bassiouni, did not receive the support of seven states members of the S.C. The reasons put forward have been criticised as hardly convincing: "Die Gründe, die für diese ablehnende Haltung u.a. Frankreichs, Großbritannien, Rußlands, auch der USA, genannt wurden,....., wirken nicht überzeugend: dieselbe (ägyptische) Herkunft wie der Generalsekretär, Herkunft aus moslemischen Glaubensbereich, die Ankündigung, ohne politische Rücksichten ermitteln und anklagen zu wollen. Wieviel effektive Aktionsfähigkeit die einzelnen Staaten diesem Strafgericht wirklich zugestehen wollen, muß sich angesichts derartige Vorbehalte erst erweisen". *H. Roggemann*, p. 49.

As Deputy Prosecutor for the Rwanda Tribunal Mr. Honoré Rakotomanana (Madagascar), was appointed. He assumed his functions on 1 March 1995 and initiated the operation of the Investigative/Prosecutorial Unit in Kigali. On 26 February 1997 Mr. Rakotomanana resigned from his post.

of 29 February 1996 the S.C. appointed Ms. Louise Arbour (Canada) the new Prosecutor for the Yugoslav and Rwanda Tribunals. At the initiative of the new Prosecutor a workshop on sexual violence was held from 23 to 27 March 1997. I should also mention the positive fact that when appointing the staff to the Office of the Prosecutor much consideration was actually taken to the sensitivity of the victims of rape and sexual assault. In the appointment of the staff, great importance was attached to the employment of qualified women. Moreover, in December 1994 the GA urged the Chief Prosecutor[532] to pay particular attention to the appointment to his office of experts specialised in the prosecution of crimes involving sexual violence.

The *ad hoc* Tribunal is served by the Registry consisting of the Registrar and other staff. The conditions of the service of the Registrar are those of an assistant Secretary-General to the UN (Article 17 of the Statute). The Dutch Professor Theo van Boven was first appointed by the Secretary-General after consultations with the President of the Tribunal to function as the Registrar. On 29 December 1994 Mrs. Dorothee Garrido-Nijgh replaced him. The Registry shall provide administrative and support services to the Chambers and the Prosecutor. Under the authority of the Registrar a special victims and witness unit has been set up with the responsibility, among other things, to "provide counselling and support for them, in particular in cases of rape and sexual assault" (Article 34 (A)(ii) of the Rules of Procedure and Evidence).[533] Also here there is a requirement with regard to the appointment of the staff members that consideration should be given to employing qualified women. The importance of paying attention to various psychological factors and the need to make social support available for the well-being of the victims of rape has earlier been emphasised by the UN Special Rapporteur, Mr. Mazowiecki. In his reports presented at the Human Rights Commission's annual sessions, he has pointed out the apparent risk for women of being revictimised through repeated interviews if account is not taken of the effects of chronic violence and trauma.[534] Needless to say, rape as a complete disregard for the rights

---

532 Res. 49/205. See also Res. 48/153 of 20 December 1993.

533 This and several other relevant documents have been reprinted in *V. Morris & M.P. Scharf*, An Insider's Guide to The International Criminal Tribunal for The Former Yugoslavia, Vol. 2. As of September 1998 some 150 witnesses from 20 countries have appeared before the Tribunal in a number of hearings.

Some authors have forwarded criticism as to the actual functioning of this unit. See, *e.g., F.J. Hampson*, The International Criminal Tribunal for the Former Yugoslavia and the Reluctant Witness, ICLQ 1998, Vol. 47, p. 51, note 4. Nevertheless, certain progressive developments were discernible. In June 1997, for example, the Victims and Witness Units of both Tribunals participated in a workshop with the purpose of developing procedures for harmonising their conduct. Gender sensitivity was but one of the issues of concern. UN Doc. A/52/375, § 98.

534 See, *e.g.*, UN Doc. E/CN.4/1993/50, pp. 19, 73, §§ 86 and 64.

The American Bar Association has also emphasised the importance of protecting the victims of rape from retraumatisation as well as ensuring protection from public humiliation. Report, pp. 32–33. Similar view has been taken by the Special Rapporteur on Violence against Women, UN Doc. E/CN.4/1995/42, § 281. See also *D. Beane*, p. 3.

An illustrative example which supports this preposition is the refusal to testify of one of the witnesses in the Tadić trial.

and dignity of the human being requires that those providing assistance to victims of rape and other forms of sexual abuses, be they women or men, have received special training. Therefore, the NGOs concerned may be better placed to provide practical assistance and psychological support to victims and witnesses before as well as after trials.[535]

Article 31 of the Statute provides that the seat of the *ad hoc* Tribunal will be The Hague in the Netherlands. A number of considerations have been taken when deciding that issue. Among those that should be mentioned are administrative efficiency and economy[536] as well as reasons of justice and fairness. For these reasons it has been underlined that it is not appropriate to have the *ad hoc* Tribunal situated in the territory of the former Yugoslavia or in any neighbouring state. On the other hand, the *ad hoc* Tribunal is free to conduct its proceedings wherever it decides to do so (Rule 4 of the Rules of Procedure and Evidence).

### *8.5.2. Due Process of Law*

An important requirement for a proper administration of justice is the existence of detailed rules governing the proceedings before a trial. The legitimacy of the *ad hoc* Tribunal for the former Yugoslavia will, therefore, to a great extent depend on the fairness of its proceedings and its impartiality. Since most of the central conventions on human rights contain extensive rules as to the procedural standards, which are reflected in the *ad hoc* Tribunal's rules of procedure and evidence, it appears that the defendants involved in the procedures of the *ad hoc* Tribunal have been secured much better legal guarantees compared to the standards of relevance applied during the post-World War II trials.

Here it will suffice to comment briefly on the main stages of the *ad hoc* Tribunal's proceedings. The Prosecutor must, according to Article 18 of the Statute, initiate investigations *ex officio* or on the basis of information received or obtained

---

[535] UN Doc. A/49/342, S/1994/1007, p. 29. See also Meeting the Health Care Needs of Women Survivors of the Balkan Conflict, The Center for Reproductive Law & Policy, New York, April 1993.

[536] The Secretary-General argued in favour of a European location since the UN already had an important presence in The Hague and Geneva. See UN Doc. S/2504, p. 210, § 131. As to the venue of the Tribunal for Rwanda, the Rwandan Government expressed preference to have the trials held on its territory in order to ensure that justice was not only done but also seen to be done, *i.e.*, "for the moral and educational value that its presence there would have for the local population". The UN Secretary-General came, however, on the basis of consideration of several political as well as practical factors to the conclusion in his report of 13 February 1995 (UN Doc. S/1995/134, p.10) that establishing the Rwanda Tribunal on that country's territory "would not be feasible or appropriate". Thus, ensuring complete impartiality and objectivity in the prosecution of persons responsible for crimes committed by both sides to the conflict is of outmost importance, and therefore it was argued that trial proceedings be held on neutral territory. In consequence, Arusha (the United Republic of Tanzania) was recommended as the seat of the Tribunal. By resolution 977 (1995) of 22 February 1995, the S.C. decided that, subject to conclusion of appropriate arrangements between the United Nations and the Government of the United Republic of Tanzania, the International Tribunal for Rwanda shall have its seat at Arusha. The Chambers and the Registry are located there as well. UN Doc. A/C.5/49/68, 29 June 1995; UN Doc. A/C.5/49/SR.65, 12 July 1995; UN Doc. A/49/945, 18 July 1995.

from any source.[537] After assessing the material the Prosecutor shall decide whether there is sufficient grounds to proceed further. In other words, the above provision prevents governments, which might be politically motivated, to initiate proceedings. Proceedings before the *ad hoc* Tribunal can neither be initiated by the alleged victim nor by his representative or an NGO.[538] After collecting evidence on his own initiative or based on complaints, information or reports received from individuals, governments, NGOs, IGOs or other sources,[539] the Prosecutor may commence the proceedings. A very important precondition for the successful functioning of the *ad hoc* Tribunal is consequently the availability of the necessary evidential material. Therefore, the first session of the *ad hoc* Tribunal, which was held from 17 November through 1 December 1993, was aimed at the preparation of the rules of procedures and evidence governing the pre-trial phase of the proceedings, the conduct of trials and appeals, the admission of evidence, the protection of victims and witnesses and other appropriate matters. The "Rules of Procedure and Evidence" were unanimously adopted on 11 February 1994 and came into force on the 14 March 1994.[540]

---

[537] It is feared that unlike the Nuremberg trials, where the majority of the atrocities were recorded in extensive documentation, in the case of the former Yugoslavia decisions "are rarely fully articulated or recorded". Therefore, persons hierarchically below those from whom they received the commands are expected to deliver important testimonies. Thus, it is assumed that the cases will to a great extent be witness-driven. *P.C. Szasz*, p. 422. The corresponding provision of the Statute of the Tribunal for Rwanda is Article 17. On production and presentation of evidence, as well as potential problems that may arise as a result of differing procedures regarding the collection and preservation of evidence and the taking of statements of suspects, see *M. Bergsmo & M.J. Keegan*, pp. 4–9; *D. Beane*, p. 3; *V. Morris & M.P. Scharf*, pp. 175–183; *M.C. Bassiouni & P. Manikas*, pp. 934–950.

A well known and respected NGO, Helsinki Watch, has in a document of 1993, "Prosecute Now!" identified 29 possible defendants by name. The selection of the cases has been done on the basis of the strength of the case, availability of evidence for immediate prosecution, diversity of defendants and alleged crimes. Thus, five of the cases charge Serbs with offences, two charge Croats and one charges Muslims. The allegations encompass a broad spectrum of war crimes, from gang rape to genocide. Some of the defendants, *e.g.*, persons connected with the Omarska prison camp, have later on been indicted by the *ad hoc* Tribunal.

[538] Individuals and international organisations are, as I have mentioned before, excluded from the right to complaint before the future International Criminal Court. The right of international organisations to complain was a subject of dispute in the ILC but it failed since the proposal did not gain general approval. UN Doc. A/CN.4/449, p. 24. During the fourth session of the Preparatory Committee on International Criminal Court, which was held in August 1997, New Zealand referring to the work done by the Women's NGO Caucus, argued in strong wording that the international community once again fails to response to women's needs since the text of the ICC Statute leaves the trigger mechanisms to states and the S.C. It was assumed that this would again contribute to the failure to address adequately the rights of women. Israel argued on the other hand that the *ad hoc* Tribunals do not have a complaint procedure. Other countries made several proposals on this important contentious issue. Granting *ex officio* powers to the Prosecutor was, for example, supported by a great number countries. Counter arguments were based among others on the fear that the ICC could otherwise be overwhelmed.

[539] UN Doc. A/49/342, S/1994/1007, p. 22.

[540] See UN Doc. IT/32 of 14 March 1994. The text has been reproduced in HRLJ 1994, Vol. 15, pp. 38–49. Non-compliance with the rules of procedure and evidence might lead to the act being declared null. Inconsistency with the fundamental principles of fairness will occasion a miscarriage of justice (Rule 5). The rules of procedure and evidence were modified in the beginning of 1995. See "Rules of Procedure and Evidence", IT/32/Rev 3, 30 January 1995. See also Rules of Procedure, IT/32/Rev.8, 23 April 1996, <http://www.un.org/ictr/index.htm.>.

Regarding the rules of procedure for crimes against women, the *ad hoc* Tribunal has emphasised the importance of the standards of evidence and the matter of credibility of the witnesses (Rule 96).[541] A large number of the witnesses called before both Tribunals are also victims. However, in exceptional cases victims of sexual abuses do not need to appear before the *ad hoc* Tribunal. Also, in order to protect the identity of the persons involved and to keep it confidential special measures are allowed.[542]

---

[541] It is apparent that credibility problems with witnesses may and actually have occurred as, *e.g.*, in the *Tadić* case, in which the credibility of witness L. was challenged by the defence council. Witness L. told the Tribunal that he falsely testified about Tadić's involvement in crimes at the Trnopolje camp. Problems can arise because witnesses are being interviewed on multiple occasions, under different circumstances and sometimes in different languages. *D. Beane*, p. 3; *M.P. Scharf*, Balkan Justice, p. 212.

On important aspects of the issue of judging the credibility of witnesses of various forms of sexual violence, see *M.C. Bassiouni & M. McCormick*, pp. 26–27.

[542] Witnesses' interests are first and foremost related to personal safety. Many of the witnesses who will be called on to testify at the *ad hoc* Tribunal fear reprisals against themselves and their families. Helsinki Watch has in this respect stressed that the possibility of retaliation will only be magnified if the trial take place before the war has ended. Public testimony will, therefore, not only endanger the physical safety of witnesses and their family members, but also their job security, pension, housing and ability to travel. Helsinki Watch, Procedural and Evidentiary Issues, pp. 8–9.

The *Tadić* case (*Decision on the Prosecutor's Motion Requesting Protective Measures for Victims and Witnesses*, case No. IT-94-1-T, 10 August 1995) is of relevance to this issue. The prosecution did not pursue rape charges contained in the indictment against Tadić because the alleged victim was too frightened to testify for fear of reprisals on her family in Bosnia. This despite the fact that she was one of the six witnesses who were placed under a witness protection program in which the Tribunal guaranteed them anonymity. The Prosecutor requested thus that certain victims and witnesses were heard *in camera*, that they be assigned pseudonyms and that their identity is not disclosed to the public and the media. Nine of the 40 witnesses testified under various sorts of protective measures. Few arguments brought forward in support of anonymity related to charges of sexual violence. The majority of the Trial Chamber could agree upon the necessity of granting such protective measures. Justice Stephen dissented in this regard. In his view withholding the identity of some of the victims and witnesses from the accused and his counsel indefinitely was contrary to the requirement of a fair trial. For support of the minority position see *M. Leigh*, Unnamed Witnesses Against Accused, AJIL 1996, Vol. 90, pp. 235–238. For very persuasive arguments and support of the majority view see *C.M. Chinkin*, Due Process and Witness Anonymity, AJIL 1997, Vol. 91, pp. 75–79; *M.P. Scharf*, Balkan Justice, p. 113. The procedure of non-disclosure of the identity of the victim to the public was also used in the case against Akayesu before the ICTR. The *Delalić and Others*, the *Blaškić* and the *Furundžija* cases are, in addition, of relevance to the present issue.

The Special Rapporteur on Violence against Women proposes, in addition, that an absolute prohibition on the identification of the witness to the accused could serve as an "incentive for victims to come forward". UN Doc. E/CN.4/1998/54, p. 17. The rapporteur has, in addition, expressed concern about the fact that there are no cases of sexual violence before the national courts in Rwanda. This is in her view a serious setback for the prosecution of gender-based crimes. Women were, thus, for several reasons hesitant to come forward with their testimonies. Many witnesses had been threatened and one-or two even killed. UN Doc. E/CN.4/1998/54/Add.1, pp. 10 and 14.

Of further relevance in this regard is also Article 21 (4)(e) of the Statute, which provides for the right to cross-examination, rather a broader right of confrontation as generally recognised in common law jurisdictions.

The progressive rules of procedure adopted by the *ad hoc* Tribunal, unfortunately do not exist for most of the war crime trials on domestic level. International NGOs have reported cases where victims of rape apparently were brought before the trial and did not testify of their own will. See, *e.g.*, Helsinki Watch, Former Yugoslavia, 1995, p. 44.

The positive trend of increased consciousness about gender issues has found expression in article 69 of the ICC Statute. The future Court is expected to take appropriate measures to protect "the safety,

According to Rule 96 no corroboration of the victim's testimony is required in cases of sexual assault and consent is not allowed as a defence where violence, duress, detention or psychological oppression are shown. The wording of Rule 96 (ii) was amended on 5 May 1994 as follows:

> "consent shall not be allowed as a defence if the victim a) has been subjected to or threatened with or has reason to fear violence, duress, detention or psychological oppression, or b) reasonably believed that if she did not submit, another might be so subjected, threatened or put in fear".

These rules clearly reflect, according to Copelon, the influence of a feminist approach to the crime rape.[543] Consent under the brutal conditions under which sexual assaults, rising to the level of international crimes, are committed, "would be ludicrous".[544] Neither shall prior sexual conduct of the victim of a sexual assault be admitted in evidence. The Tribunal issued an important decision of principle in this regard on 5 June 1997. The Trial Chamber determined in the *Tadić* case that the introduction of evidence concerning prior sexual conduct is totally forbidden by Rule 96(iv).[545] In other words, the information about a witness's abortion may constitute prior sexual conduct, but it was in the view of the Chamber not admissible as evidence.

During the earlier mentioned meeting of experts on the establishment of an international criminal court, which took place in March 1993 in Vancouver, it was recognised that investigations and prosecutions for mass rape practised as genocide may require extreme sensitivity, even including the development of some original procedures. This was all the more so because of the cultural and religious background of the victims.[546] In this respect I may mention that the Prosecutor can have the advantage of using important, already gathered, evidential material, *e.g.*, information collected by the Special Rapporteur of the UN Commission on Human Rights, the UN Commission of Experts established on the basis of the Security Council's resolution 780 of 1992,[547] the EC-observers in the territory of the former

---

physical and psychological well-being, dignity and privacy of victims and witnesses" (article 68(1)). As a special measure proceedings may take place *in camera* in the case of a victim of sexual violence or a child who is a victim or a witness (Article 68(2)).

543 *R. Copelon*, Gendered War Crimes, p. 210, note 16.

544 *M.A. Rasmussen*, Rules of Evidence for the International Criminal Court, NJIL 1995, p. 280.

545 UN Doc. A/52/375, § 37.

546 The Organization of the Islamic Conference has expressed strong concern for the protection of victims and witnesses (especially of rape and torture) and has suggested that the *ad hoc* Tribunal develops rules that will protect the victims from unnecessary invasions of privacy and from violent reprisals against themselves or their families. Views of the Islamic Conference, SCOR, UN Doc. A/47/920, 1993. Similar views on the necessity of culture and gender sensitivity when dealing with cases of sexual violence have been expressed in regard to the procedures before the Rwanda Tribunal. *R. Muzigo-Morrison*, p. 4.

547 S.C. Res. 780, UN Doc. S/RES/780, 1992. Professor Bassiouni was elected as a Chairman of the Commission after Kalshoven's resignation. He created an impressive documentation centre and database at DePaul University's Human Rights Law Institute. By April 1994, the centre had systematically catalogued and analysed over 64,000 documents and had created a computerised archive of over 300 hours

Yugoslavia and major international NGOs, *e.g.*, Amnesty International and Helsinki Watch.[548] Moreover, several states have provided the UN with useful reports containing information on violations of international humanitarian law in former Yugoslavia.

Collection of important material, *i.e.*, testimonies of war crimes, have been delivered in refugee camps and have been carried out through national authorities, *e.g.*, the Foreign Ministries of Germany, Sweden, Denmark and Norway. For the collection of evidence close co-operation between the *ad hoc* Tribunal and national authorities is essential, since they may have access to physical evidence and witnesses as well as practical measures for the arrest of the alleged persons.[549] In addition, the Ministry of the Interior of Bosnia and Herzegovina has claimed that it has collected and documented 13,000 cases of rape.[550]

If the Prosecutor reaches the conclusion that there is a *prima facie* case for prosecution, he/she will then prepare an indictment, which will be transmitted to a judge of one of the Trial Chambers. In the case of the indictment being confirmed, the judge may at the request of the Prosecutor issue orders and warrants for the arrest, detention, surrender or transfer of persons (Article 19(2) of the Statute). All orders or warrants are sent to the authorities of the state concerned to be executed. On arrest the accused will be transferred to The Hague. A special Detention Unit has been established within a governmental prison and close to the seat of the *ad hoc* Tribunal in The Hague. As of December 1998 the *ad hoc* Tribunal has taken custody of 26 of the 56 indicted persons (the vast majority of them being Serbs and some few Croats).[551]

---

of videotapes containing testimonies of individuals. Of relevance for this study is the investigation into rape and sexual assault which has been carried out by Commissioner Cleiren. 223 women who had been victims of or witnesses to rape were interviewed in seven cities in Bosnia and Croatia. Needless to say how useful this material and information will be for the prosecution of persons responsible for serious violations of international humanitarian law. *M.P. Scharf*, Balkan Justice, pp. 46–49.

[548] Helsinki Watch and other NGOs have been able to carry out impressive investigatory work, thereby identifying a number of cases where the evidence against particular individuals has appeared to be clear cut and easily documented. See Prosecute Now!, Helsinki Watch Releases Eight Cases for War Crimes Tribunal on Former Yugoslavia, News from Helsinki Watch, Vol. 5, No. 12, August 1, 1993; Helsinki Watch, Procedural and Evidential Issues for the Yugoslav War Crimes Tribunal: Resource Allocation, Evidentiary Questions and Protection of Witnesses, Vol. 5, No. 15, August 1993, p. 3.

Helsinki Watch has, furthermore, released in August 1992 and in April 1993 over 800 pages of extensive testimony on war crimes in the former Yugoslavia. See War Crimes in Bosnia-Herzegovina, Volumes I and II. The NGO investigations include, over and above the collection of testimony which can be presented at a trial, the identification of witnesses and the identification of alleged perpetrators for indictment. Both volumes are being updated with periodic additional protocols. As regards possible additional sources see *H. Roggemann*, pp. 28–29.

[549] Ms. Hampson has highlighted some of the practical problems that have occurred in regard to gathering evidence and the inability of states authorities to compel certain witnesses to testify. *F.J. Hampson*, pp. 55–73.

[550] Human Rights Watch, Prosecute Now!, p. 21.

[551] The ICTY has, in addition, issued an unknown number of sealed indictments hoping to catch some suspects off guard. At the end of 1998, the Rwandan Tribunal has issued 28 indictments against 45 people and has 32 of them in custody at Arusha. *D. Manasian*, The conscience of mankind, The Economist, December 5th, 1998, p. 12.

On the basis of Articles 18 and 20 of the Statute the suspect is during investigation entitled to legal assistance from a counsel of his own choice or in case of insufficient means to free legal assistance from the Tribunal. This is a unique feature of the *ad hoc* Tribunal. As Judge Cassese correctly has noted, it is for the first time in history that the accused will be held in a special detention unit governed not by national rules of detention, but under specific international standards. The *ad hoc* Tribunal adopted these standards on 5 May 1994.[552]

Another important precondition for the *ad hoc* Tribunal to carry out its important tasks in an effective manner is the existence and observance of extradition regulations.[553] According to the Statute's Article 29(2)(e) states shall comply without undue delay with any request of a Trial Chamber for "the surrender or the transfer of the accused to the International Tribunal". Much of the realisation of these provisions will depend upon the will of the national authorities to cooperate with the Tribunal. As of December 1998 eight indictees had been arrested by national law enforcement authorities and transferred to the ICTY.[554]

It must be born in mind in this regard that the 1949 Geneva Conventions require that either a state extradites a war criminal or ensures that he is punished in accordance with the domestic criminal system. This principle is based on the Roman maxim *aut dedere aut punire*.[555] As earlier mentioned, each state party to the Geneva Conventions is under the obligation to ensure that its national legislation contains "effective penal sanctions for persons committing, or ordering to be committed, any of the grave breaches" as defined in the conventions. The state is, furthermore, expected to "bring such persons, regardless of their nationality, before its own courts" unless it decides to "hand (them) over for trial" to another state party. Moreover, Article 49 of the first Geneva Convention, Article 50 of the second

---

552 UN Doc. A/49/342, S/1994/1007, p. 30. The text of the "Rules Governing the Detention of Persons Awaiting Trial or Appeal before the Tribunal or Otherwise Detained on the Authority of the Tribunal", Doc. IT/38/Rev.3 has been reprinted in HRLJ 1995, Vol. 16, pp. 116–121.

553 The GA adopted by resolution 3074 (XXVIII) of 3 December 1973 the "Principles of international co-operation in the detention, arrest, extradition and punishment of persons guilty of war crimes and crimes against humanity", which still constitute an important part of the international standard on that subject matter. States are urged to co-operate for the detention, arrest and extradition of persons against whom there is evidence that they have committed war crimes and crimes against humanity, in conformity with the Charter of the UN and the Declaration on Principles of International Law Concerning Friendly Relations and Co-operation among States. Generally on this issue see *M.C. Bassiouni & E.M. Wise*, Aut Dedere Aut Iudicare: The Duty to Extradite or Prosecute in International Law, Dordrecht 1995.

554 These persons are as follows: Aleksovski, Delalić, Delić, Erdemović, Landžo, Mucić, Tadić and Zigić. Six of them had been sentenced. *S.D. Murphy*, pp. 75 and 91.

555 *I. Detter de Lupis*, The Law of War, p. 357. See also *S.E. Nahlik*, From Reprisals to Individual Penal Responsibility, in Humanitarian Law of Armed Conflict Challenges Ahead, A.J.M. Delissen & G.J. Tanja (eds.), Dordrecht 1991, p. 175; *P.N. Drost*, p. 151; *T. Meron*, Human Rights and Humanitarian Norms as Customary Law, Oxford 1989, p. 209; *M.C. Bassiouni*, Crimes Against Humanity, pp. 499–527; *H. Wassgren*, p. 310; *N. Roth-Arriaza*, Sources in International Treaties of an Obligation to Investigate, Prosecute, and Provide Redress, in Impunity and Human Rights in International Law and Practice, N. Roth-Arriaza (ed.), New York 1995, p. 25; *J. Dugard & Van den Wyngaert*, Reconciling Extradition with Human Rights, AJIL 1998, Vol. 92, p. 209.

Geneva Convention, Article 129 of the third Geneva Convention and Article 146 of the fourth Geneva Convention prescribe obligations for the states parties to "take measures necessary for the suppression of" all other infractions of the conventions.

Once in custody the accused are entitled to internationally recognised standards,[556] among them the right to a fair and public hearing, to be presumed innocent until proven guilty, to be informed promptly and in detail in a language, which the accused understands of the nature and cause of the charges against him, adequate time to prepare for trial, trial without undue delay, the right not to be compelled to testify against himself (Articles 20 and 21 of the Statute and Rule 42 of the Rules of Procedure and Evidence). Article 21 provides that the right to a public hearing is "subject to Article 22 of the Statute". The latter provision contains, however, guarantees for the protection of witnesses to which I have referred earlier.

Though there is no explicit reference in the Statute of the *ad hoc* Tribunal, consideration has been taken to the important progressive development of law in regard to non-acceptance of trials *in absentia.*[557] In other words, a trial must not be conducted in the absence of the accused. Trials *in absentia* have been considered to "fundamentally undermine the authority" of international criminal courts, since

---

[556] These standards are embodied in several UN documents, such as the 1977 UN Standard Minimum Rules for the Treatment of Prisoners (res. 2076 (LXII) of 13 May 1977), the 1988 Body of Principles for the Protection of All Persons under Any Form of Detention or Imprisonment and the 1990 Basic Principles for the Treatment of Prisoners. Despite the fact that all sentences of imprisonment shall be supervised by the *ad hoc* Tribunal, or a body designated by it, different countries still have a great variety of standards with regard to the existing conditions in their prisons. The Tribunal's Statute does not explicitly prevent the unequal treatment of prisoners.

It is of course an irony that some of the main criminals who will be tried by the *ad hoc* Tribunals will enjoy better conditions in prisons than their subordinates who are subjected to national jurisdiction. It is a well known fact, for example, that in Kigali about 9,000 prisoners are awaiting trial in a prison built to hold only 2,000 persons. Statement made by the Rwanda representative to the Beijing Conference, Press Release WOM/857, 8 September 1995.

[557] The right of the accused to physical presence at the trial has earlier been stipulated in Article 14 (3) (d) of the ICCPR and it has been interpreted as to preclude trials *in absentia*. There is now sufficient evidence that this right has gained universal acceptance in public international law. Even the criminal trial system in China does not permit trials *in absentia*. Therefore, the proposal made by the French delegation during the drafting process on the Statute of the *ad hoc* Tribunal implying a possibility of trials *in absentia* was rejected. See UN Doc. S/25226, § 108. At the same time we cannot ignore the fact that a number of delegates in the GA's Sixth Committee during the drafting of the Statute for a permanent International Criminal Court have shown willingness to accept the possibility of trials *in absentia* in exceptional cases, exhaustively listed in the draft Article 44, since their domestic laws allow for such trials in certain circumstances. Nevertheless, Article 63 of the ICC Statute upholds the restrictive approach towards trials *in absentia*. *T.L.H. McCormack & G.J. Simpson*, p. 201; *S. Suikkari*, p. 216.

Of some relevance is also the report on war crimes trials in Croatia, which was presented in 1995, and which shows that thousands of persons, primarily Serbs, have been tried, most *in absentia*, for war crimes and crimes against humanity, including rape and forced pregnancy. Governments' estimations show that over 80% of the cases have proceeded without the presence of the accused. As reasons for that reference has been made to the fact that most of the accused have always been in Serbian-controlled areas of Croatia or other parts of the former Yugoslavia, or because several of the accused persons have been exchanged for Croatian prisoners held by Serbian forces during prisoners' exchanges. Helsinki Watch, Former Yugoslavia, 1995, pp. 3, 12, 28.

there is a risk for its factual basis to become highly unreliable.[558] On this basis it has been argued that the accused ought to have the opportunity to participate in the proceeding, in order to be able to confront the evidence presented against him, to present his own evidence and to be properly and effectively represented by counsel. Furthermore, individuals and organisations (IGOs and NGOs) may present written or oral submissions as *amicus curiae*. Judge Cassese has observed that the relevant provision (Rule 74) enables the *ad hoc* Tribunal to have access to independent expert advice on any legal issue as well as to permit other interested parties to present their views.[559]

If the accused is sentenced to imprisonment, the sentence will be served in a specific country, designated by the President among the ones that have indicated their willingness to accept convicted persons.[560] Thus, according to the *ad hoc* Tribunal's Statute (Article 24(1)), penalties to be imposed on a convicted person are limited to imprisonment. A convicted person may be sentenced to imprisonment for a term up to and including the remainder of his life (Rule 101 (A) of the Rules of Procedure and Evidence). From that follows that the *ad hoc* Tribunal does not possess the right to impose the death penalty.[561] As to the decision on the con-

---

[558] *C. Tomuschat*, p. 66. The Appeals Chamber of the ICTY argued in the *Blaškić* case that: "generally speaking, it would not be appropriate to hold *in absentia* proceedings against persons falling under the primary jurisdiction of the International Tribunal.....(i)t would prove extremely difficult or even impossible for an international criminal court to determine the innocence or guilt of that accused". *Prosecutor v. Blaškić*, 29 October 1997, § 59. Nevertheless, the Appeals Chamber took the position that proceedings *in absentia* may be warranted in cases involving contempt of court by witness. *S.D. Murphy*, p. 75.

[559] UN Doc. A/49/342, S/1994/1007, p. 29. Pursuant to Rule 74 a few NGOs together with a group of human rights scholars submitted a brief *amicus curiae* to the ICTR in 1997 urging the Prosecutor to conduct the necessary investigations and amend the *Akayesu* indictment to charge rape and other sexual violence within the framework of genocide, war crimes and crimes against humanity. See Amicus Brief, Respecting Amendment of the Indictment and Supplement of the Evidence to Ensure the Prosecution of Rape and Other Sexual Violence Within the Competence of the Tribunal, 27 May 1997.

[560] As of 24 February 1999 only four countries have accepted such obligations. These are Finland, Italy, Norway and Sweden.

According to Article 26 of the Statute of the Rwanda Tribunal, imprisonment shall be served in Rwanda or in any of the states on a list of states that have indicated to the S.C. their willingness to accept convicted persons. There is consequently an important difference as to the placement of convicted persons, since Rwanda is not like the former Yugoslavia, excluded from the list of states where prison sentences pronounced by the International Tribunal may be served.

[561] During the Nuremberg Trial, 12 of the 19 defendants convicted were sentenced to death by hanging. *M. Lippman*, p. 27; American Bar Association, Report, p. 7; *M.P. Scharf*, Balkan Justice, p. 10.

The main arguments in support of the non-application of the death penalty, which were put forward during the Vancouver meeting of experts in 1993, were based on the ongoing international efforts to abolish capital punishment, as well as the fact that the penalty was not included in conventions, even those dealing with such serious conduct as genocide. The death penalty has been abolished by for example the Sixth Additional Protocol to the European Convention on Human Rights (adopted in 1983 and in force since March 1, 1985), the Second Optional Protocol to the ICCPR (adopted by the GA Res. 44/128, UN Doc. A/44/49, 1989 and in force since July 11, 1991) and the Protocol of 1990 to the American Convention on Human Rights to Abolish the Death Penalty (in force since 28 August 1991). The death penalty is also ruled out in the ICC Statute. According to Article 77 it is possible to impose a term of imprisonment, including life imprisonment and/or a fine.

crete length of the imprisonment, the Tribunal is allowed to take into consideration the national law of the offender. It has been feared that penalties in accordance with national rules might not in all cases correspond to the gravity of the crimes, which have been perpetrated. Furthermore, many doubts have been expressed as to the enforcement of sentences. A person might be punished, *e.g.*, on the basis to the 1982 Criminal Code of the Socialist Federal Republic Yugoslavia to between 1 and 10 years' imprisonment for rape. If the act of rape has caused serious harm or even the death of the victim, the sentence shall be a minimum of three years' of imprisonment. This illustrates well the apprehensions expressed above, inasmuch as the punishment in my opinion does not correspond with the crime.

Finally, it may be contended that the *ad hoc* Tribunal has greater judicial legitimacy in comparison to its predecessors in Nuremberg and Tokyo. The extensive and carefully defined rules of procedure and evidence have the potential of securing the *ad hoc* Tribunal's impartiality, independence, and political neutrality as well as reflecting certain gender sensitivity.[562] This is a reliable basis and an important pre-

---

On the other hand, I may recall that for a number of the – for the *ad hoc* Tribunal's jurisdiction relevant – crimes, many states retain the death penalty. On this basis, Professor Crawford concludes that "it may be a mercy to be tried internationally". *J. Crawford*, The ILC Adopts a Statute for an International Criminal Court, p. 407.

As to the jurisdiction of the Rwanda Tribunal, the Rwanda Government strongly favoured the death penalty by referring to the in Rwanda existing demands for justice, "commensurate with the gravity of genocide". This proposal was rejected since it met strong opposition during the negotiations from most of the states. *L.S. Sunga*, p. 123.

[562] In the course of 1994 all sides to the conflict in the former Yugoslavia held trials or initiated investigations into crimes connected with the war. The first trial in the former Republic of Yugoslavia of a defendant accused of war crimes in Bosnia and Herzegovina began in November 1994. D. Vučković was charged with, *inter alia,* rape. However, Amnesty International has questioned the conditions under which the trials and investigations have been carried out, *i.e.*, they cannot be considered as a sufficient basis for a fair trial. Furthermore, the defendants are almost exclusively accused of crimes against individuals of the national group holding the trial. Almost all of the war crimes proceedings in Croatia have, *e.g.*, involved ethnic Serbs. By mid-1994, over 2,200 individuals had been charged in Croatia. But as observers have pointed out, these cases for the most part fall short of internationally accepted standards of fairness and due process. Authorities in the respective countries are clearly unwilling to prosecute abusive members of their own armed forces. At the same time the use of military courts to adjudicate members of their nation's own troops for war crimes has resulted in the introduction of a kind of impunity. Officially, the FRY has taken the standpoint that it would not extradite alleged war criminals, if these persons can be tried before the Yugoslav courts, since it questions the *ad hoc* Tribunal's impartiality on the grounds that its indicted defendants have been for the greater part Serbs. See Amnesty International, Report 1995, pp. 77 and 316; Helsinki Watch, Former Yugoslavia, pp. 5–9.

As regards the crimes committed in Rwanda, the Government brought the first people accused of genocide to court on April 6,1995, *i.e.*, one year to the day after the start of the killings. However, the cases were adjourned the same day in order to permit further investigation. This is sheer reluctance to confront the political ramifications of the trials. It has been claimed that the prosecutors in Kigali and Butare have long had more than a hundred cases each ready for presentation to the court and in which the vast majority of the accused have confessed to the crime. Another obstacle for bringing the guilty to justice is the fact that it can hardly be said that the judiciary has been independent in that country before. It has been claimed that there is continuing interference from the military demonstrating that the judiciary is not yet free to decide fully questions that belong solely to its domain. On the other hand, some national court systems have achieved better results with Rwandan fugitives, *e.g.*, the Belgian and Swiss,

requisite for the Tribunal's future success. The above mentioned rules, furthermore, provide a stable ground for the confidence and the co-operation of states. Moreover, the adoption of specific provisions for victims and witnesses of rape and other sexual assaults is a positive as well as a necessary development in contemporary international law. At the same time it is also important to stress that *ad hoc* tribunals "will never be a substitute for national courts".[563] Domestic courts still remain the main tool for the enforcement of international humanitarian law.

## 8.6. Some Concluding Remarks

Violence against women is a phenomenon occurring world-wide in public as well as in private life. It takes many shapes right across culture and class.

Numerous reports prepared by intergovernmental organisations and NGOs bear witness of reproductive abuses such as rape, forced impregnation and forced pregnancy, forced abortions, forced sterilisations, abortions of girl foetuses, occurring daily in all societies and in some places on a massive scale.

Violence against women is in other words a term, which covers a wide range of gender specific acts committed against girls and women by men. Since this is an issue related to gender inequality, it is today universally condemned and recognised as a violation of basic human rights and the rules of international humanitarian law. Many of the violations affect, furthermore, directly women's reproductive freedom in that they obscure its realisation. But while human rights aspects of gender violence has been given increasingly attention in international law since 1980s, it has remained until recently an issue of lesser priority in the context of humanitarian law. The mass rapes which have taken place in the armed conflicts in the former Yugoslavia[564] have received unprecedented publicity and could therefore contribute to the changed perception by the international community of rape in wartime. It is thus not any longer considered as a random or isolated wartime event but as one of the indispensable instruments of war.[565]

---

whereas the French have refused for a long time to deal with complaints of genocide. First on January 6, 1998, the French Court of Cassation decided that the *Wenceslas Munyeshyaka* case can be reviewed under French jurisdiction. *M.T. Kamminga*, p. 11. For other examples, see Human Rights Watch, Africa, Rwanda-the crisis continues, April 1995, Vol. 7, pp. 2–11. See generally on national trials in Rwanda UN Doc. E/CN.4/1998/54/Add.1, pp. 17–18.

[563] *T. Meron*, International Criminalization of Internal Atrocities, p. 555.

[564] Mass rape of women and girls (sometimes as young as five years old) often in public places, abduction of women and other types of sexual violence against women during the genocide in Rwanda are thoroughly and extensively documented by various human rights groups and NGOs. See UN Doc. E/CN.4/1995/42, p. 65, § 270. See also the 1996 study on the impact of armed conflicts on children, prepared and presented by Ms. Machel. UN Doc. A/51/306.

[565] Rape has been used as part of a deliberate policy of ethnic cleansing and a military strategy (Bosnia-Herzegovina); a political terror tactic (Haiti); an instrument of armed struggle (Kashmir, Bangladesh, Kuwait); an act of genocide (Rwanda and Bosnia-Herzegovina). *A. Brunet & S. Rousseau*, pp. 37–38; *A. Aafjes*, p. 5.

A large number of recent studies point to the evidential link between violence against women and the lack of equality and the imbalance of power between men and women in the family and in society.[566] Violence is used to keep the woman in a subordinate position against her will. In the words of Indai Sajor "rape is one of the most extreme expressions of the patriarchal drive towards masculine domination over the woman".[567] Thus, women when exposed to sexual violence are denied the ability to enter into sexual relations as equal partners. Therefore, if violence against women is to be eliminated, it is important to build settings, in which the balance of power between women and men is evened out, where women are full-scale actors and not acted upon. International humanitarian law, like human rights law, addresses gender equality in its requirements of non-discrimination on the basis of sex in the application of its protective provisions. Article 3 common to the Geneva Conventions of 1949 is but one example of a provision which prescribes humane treatment without discrimination on the basis of sex of all those who take no active part in the hostilities. This is very much in line with my standpoint that there is a growing convergence and applicability of both branches of law, *i.e.*, human rights and humanitarian law.[568] One of their common goals is to protect all civilians, including women and their fundamental rights under all circumstances. It, furthermore, coincides with the view expressed by CEDAW that rape and other forms of sexual violence (including reproductive crimes) constitute a form of discrimination prohibited by the Women's Convention and which inhibits women's ability to enjoy their legally guaranteed rights and freedoms on a basis of equality with men. Gender-based violence is consequently contrary to the duty to ensure the equal protection of humanitarian norms in time of international and internal armed conflicts or civil strife.[569] Nevertheless, relevant norms of humanitarian law disclose the equality paradigm in the sense of *de iure* equality instead of focusing on substantial equality. It can, therefore, be established that current humanitarian law

---

[566] As earlier mentioned the UN Declaration on the Elimination of Violence against Women states, *e.g.*, that violence against women is a manifestation of the historically unequal power relations which have lead to the domination over, and discrimination against, women and the prevention of their full advancement. The Inter-American Convention on the Prevention, Punishment and Eradication of Violence against Women emphasises the equality aspect of violence against women as well. Any form of violence against women is, in other words, an expression of oppression and harassment. *D. Wilsnak*, Den Besitz des Feindes beschädigen, Vergewaltigung im Krieg, Der Überblick 1993, No. 2, pp. 43–46 and UN Doc. E/CN.6/1994/4, p. 4. See also "Shared Power and Responsibility", National Report by the Government of Sweden for the Fourth World Conference on Women in Beijing 1995, Ministry of Health and Social Affairs, Stockholm 1994, p. 79 and *J.G. Gardam*, The Law of Armed Conflict: A Gendered Regime?, p. 176. Ms. Indai Sajor has rightly pointed out that the manifestations and causes of gender-based violence, such as of mass rape, sexual slavery, custodial violence, enforced prostitution and forced impregnation "Cannot be understood without attention being given to the patriarchal mode of society in general and the domination of men over women in all spheres of public and private life". *I.L. Sajor*, p. 2. See also *Y. Tanaka*, Rape and War: The Japanese Experience, in Common Grounds, I.L. Sajor (ed.), p. 179; *A. Aafjes*, p. 47; UN Doc. E/CN.6/1998/5, § 48.

[567] *I.L. Sajor*, op.cit., p. 3.

[568] For further references see *K.D. Askin*, p. 243, note 805.

[569] UN Doc. E/CN.4/1994/5, § 21, p. 7

is an incomplete, underdeveloped branch of law and much of it has to be adapted to modern realities. International humanitarian law does not fully accommodate the interests of women. It still neglects certain aspects of reproductive freedom. Therefore, the asymmetrical model of equality seems to be most useful in addressing sexual violence, which apparently prevents its realisation. Clearly, there is a greater likelihood for women to face rape and other forms of sexual assaults as civilians than there is for men. Needless to say, forced impregnation and forced pregnancy are forms of violence that are used specifically against women. Women's reproductive capacity makes them, in addition, particularly vulnerable to shortages of food and medical treatment.[570]

Substantive gender equality must, therefore, be recognised as an important factor in the determination of the validity of definitions of crimes under humanitarian law.

Part III of this study has demonstrated, however, that currently there is an ever growing international consensus that the crime rape and other sexual assaults committed in the conduct of armed conflicts be regarded as "an extremely grave violation of international humanitarian law".[571] Moreover, the present author's examination and analysis of the prohibition of sexual violence in international humanitarian law has illustrated that some forms of it, *e.g.*, under certain circumstances acts of rape, forced impregnation, forced pregnancy, enforced sterilisation, which are war crimes with *ius cogens* status, constitute an important component of *ius cogens* obligations under contemporary international law and are thereby subject to universal jurisdiction.

This is undeniably an encouraging development, since rape and other grave violations of women's reproductive rights under international humanitarian law committed all over the world have for centuries remained "the least condemned crimes",[572] and I would also like to add the least prosecuted crimes. Part III has shown, furthermore, that, albeit slowly progressing, there is indeed today an attitude change in the international community towards greater consciousness about the existence of gender-based violence and the obligation to encounter it.

The establishment of the *ad hoc* Tribunal for the prosecution of persons responsible for serious violations of international humanitarian law committed in the territory of the former Yugoslavia and the International Tribunal for Rwanda supports the preposition that we have reached a turning-point in the international community, a manifestation of a new and strong willingness to start to cope with serious international crimes and to prosecute the perpetrators of gender-specific crimes against women on the international as well as on the national level. In response the CSW in resolutions 38/9 of 1994 and 39/4 of 1995 as well as the UN General Assembly have encouraged the *ad hoc* Tribunal in a resolution of 23 December

---

570 *A. Aafjes*, p. 14.

571 UN Doc. E/CN.4/1994/5, § 16, p. 6.

572 UN Doc. E/CN.4/1995/42. As Ms. Mary Robinson has observed, it was only in 1992, "when reports were received about the rape and deliberate impregnation of thousands of women in the territories of the former Yugoslavia, that rape in wartime was first publicly discussed". *M. Robinson*, p. 19.

1994[573] to "give due priority to the cases of the victims of rape" in the areas of armed conflict, in particular in Bosnia-Herzegovina. In other words, it is the international community's expectation that the *ad hoc* Tribunal for the former Yugoslavia shall make important substantial contributions to the enforcement of the rules of international humanitarian law. On the other hand, one has also to be conscious of the difficulties that the *ad hoc* Tribunal might meet, and as a matter of fact has already encountered,[574] both on the practical level (*e.g.*, the extradition of war criminals from the territory of the former Yugoslavia;[575] in many cases of rape there are seldom witnesses and the ones who are still alive are difficult to be found and persuaded to participate in the process)[576] and on the judicial, technical level (mainly in connection with the compilation of evidential material,[577] but also personal difficulties occur for the victims of rape to relate the details of the circumstances when the crime was committed). The viability and the successful

---

[573] Res. 49/205. The CSW upheld this standpoint again during its session in 1995 when it declared that it would encourage the International Criminal Tribunal for the Former Yugoslavia to give due priority to victims of rape, particularly in Bosnia. CSW, 12th meeting, 29 March 1995. See also UN Doc. E/CN.6/1995/14.

[574] UN Doc. A/49/342, S/1994/1007, pp. 15–19. The allocation of sufficient funds to the international prosecutors as well as to the judicial system in Rwanda is one example of the true test of the international community's will to administer justice.

[575] Belgrade has persistently failed to cooperate with international human rights investigators, taking into account, for example, the circumstances around the admission of the UN Special Rapporteur for the former Yugoslavia and the monitors from the Conference on Security and Co-operation in Europe. Recently, the President of the ICTY, Judge McDonald, underlined in a letter to the S.C. of 22 October 1998 that the Government of the F.R.Y. continues to refuse co-operation with the Tribunal, by failing to arrest and transfer to its custody three of the in 1995 indicted persons. See ICTY, Press Release, JI/PIU/356-E, The Hague 22 October 1998. See also *H. Fox*, The Objections to the Transfer of Criminal Jurisdiction to the UN Tribunal, ICLQ 1997, Vol. 46, p. 434 ff. and *S.D. Murphy*, p. 65.

[576] From the gender perspective the rules for the protection of witnesses at trial adopted and applied by the ICTY is, therefore, a welcome innovation in international law. They have arisen from the prevalence of rape and gender-related violence among the violations at issue.

[577] A team of 21 investigators has already been faced with the arduous task of collecting first-hand evidence in order to bring to justice the perpetrators of the gross human rights violations and breaches of international humanitarian law norms on the territory of the former Yugoslavia.

As to the efficiency of the *ad hoc* Tribunal for Rwanda, I may with disappointment establish that it took too long a time until adequate staff was recruited. So, for example, only five professionals assisted the prosecutor in mid–1995 in examining the systematic slaughter that caused the death of between one half and one million people. As regards the national judicial system in Rwanda, only thirty-six judges, fourteen prosecutors, of whom only three had formal legal training, and assistant prosecutors were available to prosecute and try the accused. To show the shortage of staff, the above figures can be compared with the estimation made that in order to make the system fully functional at all levels, *i.e.*, from the communal courts up to the Supreme Court, nearly 700 magistrates would be required to serve as judges and prosecutors. One of the consequences of the above mentioned deficiency is that the vast majority of the persons in jail have been detained without due process. Moreover, the Minister of Justice and the prosecutor for Kigali have even expressed suspicion that as for as many as 20% of the prisoners jailed, there is no basis for charges. Human Rights Watch, Africa, pp. 5–6. Nevertheless, recent developments to which I have referred earlier in Part III, show that the prosecution of violations of international humanitarian law (including sexual violence), albeit slowly, has started to function. See in addition *T. Meron*, War Crimes Law Comes of Age, p. 463 and *A. Aafjes*, p. 103.

functioning of the *ad hoc* Tribunals are consequently dependent upon a number of factors. It is, however, expected that both Tribunals, like the Nuremberg Trials, will have a profound impact on the interpretation of international law. Consequently of great importance in determining what will be achieved will be the flexibility and readiness of the judges to interpret in a dynamic, creative and gender-sensitive way the vague articles of the Statutes so that perpetrators of reproductive crimes actually will be prosecuted for their atrocities. Much will depend on the activism of the judges as regards the interpretation of, for example, the crime rape and sexual assault, *i.e.*, whether it will be covered by one, two, three or four of the articles of the Statute for the former Yugoslavia. Thus, rape occurs in many contexts and it may, depending on the circumstances, be considered as a war crime, as a grave breach of international humanitarian law, as a crime against humanity or as genocide.

There might be indeed good reasons (of, for example, a psychological and symbolic nature) to strive for the prohibition of rape as well as explicitly naming other forms of reproductive abuses such as forced impregnation, forced pregnancy and forced sterilisation as a separate legal category of crime under international law in order to underline that they are conceived by the international community as offences of the gravest character against the life and the physical and mental integrity of the individual.[578] In the words of Ustinia Dolgopol "the naming of harms is an important exercise".[579] Forced impregnation and forced pregnancy should be dealt with as violations of women's reproductive freedom rather than as the natural consequence of rape, *i.e.*, as crimes itself and not mere consequences.[580]

On that basis it becomes obvious that the wording of the provisions of the *ad hoc* Tribunals' Statutes does not adequately reflect the applicable law to reproductive crimes. The application of one or other of the above mentioned provisions has been instead left as a question of interpretation and it will depend upon the gravity of the criminal act as well as the interests of the international community. The analysis of the possible content of relevant legal provisions of international humanitarian law in Part III of this study allows this author to submit that as a matter of interpretation rape and other reproductive abuses can easily be included in the provisions on crimes of genocide, war crimes and crimes against humanity. In addition, the scope of existing terms such as "torture" in various international instruments also can be interpreted more extensively so as to include rape and other forms of sexual assault.[581] Recent case law of the otherwise conservative European Court of Human Rights as well as of the inter-American organs for the protection

---

578 Arguments in this direction have been introduced by Professor D. Sokolović. See *D. Sokolović*, Organiseret forbrydelse, Mennesker og rettigheter 1995, No. 3, pp. 281–282.

579 *U. Dolgopol*, Rape as A War Crime- Mythology and History, in Common Grounds, I.L. Sajor (ed.), p. 136.

580 *A. Brunet & S. Rousseau*, p. 39; *K.H. Martinez*, p. 21. It is encouraging event that the UN Commission on Human Rights took a particular stand against violations of fundamental rights of women in situations of armed conflict, notably forced pregnancy, at its 54th session in 1998 (resolution 1998/52).

581 The Inter-American Commission on Human Rights addressed, for example, the issue of rape as torture under the American Convention on Human Rights as well as under the UN Convention to Prevent and punish Torture in the *Requel Martín de Mejía v. Peru* case.

of human rights[582] suggests that they have become increasingly more sensitive to gender issues and especially to gender-based violence.

In addition to the possibility of prosecuting reproductive crimes through creative interpretation of existing norms (*i.e.*, transforming the content of key concepts from a feminist perspective), the elaboration of a binding universal document, *e.g.*, additional substantive protocol to the Women's Convention or a separate Convention on Violence against Women, which will give visibility to the issue of reproductive crimes and which should define them in a comprehensive and flexible way as, for example, Kelly Askin has suggested,[583] appears to this author to offer a reasonable solution to the current problem of fragmentary and incoherent standards. Another advantage of a holistic approach would be that such a document may cover all the relevant branches of law as well as put reproductive crimes in the broader context of gender equality. The later interrelationship is not discernible in contemporary international humanitarian law norms.

It is my belief, furthermore, that the significance of the *ad hoc* Tribunals' proceedings will extend beyond the immediate time in which they are taking place, and that they shall have an positive effect on expanding the meaning and the legal status of the norms prohibiting rape and other forms of sexual assaults in general. There is today a challenging opportunity to advance international law in regard to the content of its norms and enforcement capacity.

The terrible sexual atrocities committed in the former Yugoslavia have much facilitated the acceptance of an expansive interpretation of the crime rape and sexual assault, and it constitutes today a solid basis for international prosecution. Gender concerns have been, moreover, integrated to certain extend into the operation of the Tribunal. This assertion can be supported by several examples where the Prosecutor has issued indictments, which charged rape as both a war crime and a crime against humanity.[584] In the indictment of, for example, the defendant M. Radić, who on several occasions has repeatedly subjected "A" to forcible sexual intercourse, the *ad hoc* Tribunal has submitted a comment to the effect that when causing great suffering the incidents constitute a grave breach in accordance with Article 2(c) of the Statute and, alternatively, when considered as cruel treatment they constitute a violation of the laws or customs of war in accordance with Article 3 of the Statute. Lastly, the third incident when the victim was raped has been con-

---

[582] The Inter-American Court, on the other hand, raised but did not deal with questions in the examination of rape as a human rights violation in the *María Elena Loayza Tamayo v. Peru* case. See Inter-American Commission on Human Rights, Report 38/96, Case No. 10.506 and IACHR, Sentencia de 17 de septiembre de 1997, OEA/Ser.L/V/II.98, Doc. 7 rev., April 13, 1998, p. 1002. See UN Doc. E/CN.6/1998/5, § 53.

[583] *K.D. Askin*, pp. 380–403. See also UN Doc. E/CN.4/Sub.2/1998/13, § 24. On the need for a new instrument see *J. Fitzpatrick*, pp. 556–557 and *J. Gardam*, pp. 77–80.

[584] Some of the indictments have defined sexual violence as torture, inhuman punishment and great suffering or serious injury. In the context of the proceedings before the Rwanda Tribunal see *The Prosecutor v. Jean Paul Akayesu*, Case No. ICTR-96-4-T, Judgment of 2 September 1998. Counts 13 and 15 are based on the understanding that rape is punishable by Article 3 of the Statute and as a crime against humanity as well as violation of Article 3 common to the Geneva Conventions and Article 4(2)(e) of Additional Protocol 2, as incorporated by Article 4(e) of the Tribunal's Statute.

sidered a crime against humanity recognised by Article 5(g) of the Statute.[585] This is undoubtedly a positive break-through in the normative development of contemporary international humanitarian law. In consequence, rape has been criminalised explicitly as a war crime and a crime against humanity in the Statute of the ICC. More importantly, forced pregnancy and enforced sterilisation outspoken have been classified as such crimes.[586] Nevertheless, the discriminatory nature of these crimes has still to be recognised *verbatim*.

Moreover, the *ad hoc* Tribunals have not yet delivered any judgments on the issue of homosexual rape.[587] This is an important issue since there seems to exist

---

[585] The International Criminal Tribunal for the Former Yugoslavia, *The Prosecutor of the Tribunal against Z. Meakić et al.*, §§ 22.2 – 22.16. Accusations on the same basis as regards victim "F", a prisoner in early June 1992 in the Omarska camp, have been brought up for Gruban (§§ 25.2–25.4), P. Kostić (§§ 26.2–26.4), M. Babić (§§ 30.1–30.4) and D. Tadić (*The International Criminal Tribunal for the Former Yugoslavia, the Prosecutor of the Tribunal against D. Tadić and G. Borovnica*, §§ 4.2–4.4). There were approximately 40 women who were held captive in the above mentioned camp at that time.

The Office of the Prosecutor has at the time of writing brought rape charges in six of the public indictments of the ICTY and in two of the public indictments of the ICTR. This fact has been used by the Special Rapporteur on violence against women to criticise the ICTR as not being pro-active on the question of sexual violence. UN Doc. E/CN.4/1998/54/Add.1, pp. 12–13. For a recent and comprehensive review of the decisions and the indictments issued by both *ad hoc* Tribunals on the issue of gender-based violence see *K.D. Askin*, Sexual Violence, pp. 97–124.

[586] The ICC Statute sets, in addition, a standard for domestic as well as international proceedings. The structural and procedural provisions of the Statute have been considered fundamental to ensuring that the future court addresses violations of reproductive rights. *K.H. Martinez*, p. 21; *I.L. Sajor*, p. 15.

[587] The 1994 Final Report of the UN Commission of Experts establishes that "violent crimes of a homosexual nature are not explicitly mentioned in international humanitarian law. That international humanitarian law, insofar as it provides protection against rape and other sexual assaults, is applicable to men as well as women is beyond any doubt as the international human right not to be discriminated against does not allow derogation". See Rape and Sexual Assault, A/1994/674/Add.2, Vol. I, annex II, note 4, quoted in UN Doc. E/CN.4/Sub.2/1998/13, § 24.

As already mentioned earlier, in the context of the genocide in Rwanda several women are being charged with war crimes. Some of them have perpetrated sexual violence against other women. UN Doc. E/CN.4/1998/54, § 11. Of relevance is, therefore, to mention the extensive definition of rape which has been adopted by the Trial Chamber I in the *Akayesu* case. It reads as follows: "The Chamber defines rape as a physical invasion of a sexual nature, committed on a person under circumstances which are coercive. Sexual violence, including rape, is not limited to physical invasion of the human body and may include acts which do not involve penetration or even physical contact". See Press Release AFR/94/L/2895, 2 September 1998.

However, there are still numerous different formulations of rape in municipal legal systems. This author can give the Swedish criminal legislation, which has been revised and adapted to modern developments, as an example. The term rape according to the Swedish Criminal Code (BrB 6:1) has, on the basis of Law 1992:147, been changed and given gender neutral content, *i.e.,* it is presumed that rape can be committed both by men and women against a person of the same or the opposite sex. Moreover, according to the Penal Code, rape covers not only sexual intercourse, but intercourse comparable thereto. From the 1 of July 1998 the law has been changed to include also acts of sexual violence not necessarily comparable to intercourse. See prop. 1997/98:55, Kvinnofrid, Stockholm 1998. In cases of grave rape the perpetrators will be sentenced to between 4 and 10 years in prison. See generally on the Swedish debate on the subject matter of rape SOU 1982:61, Våldtäkt och andra sexuella övergrepp, Stockholm 1982. In other jurisdictions, as for example in England, according to the Sexual Offences Act the offence "rape" covers solely vaginal penetration by the penis. Forced acts of oral sex and penetration by objects or other parts of the body do not amount to rape but are covered under the heading of indecent assault.

evidence that men have been subjected to rape and other forms of sexual assaults.[588] In several societies there is an understanding that males cannot be victims of this offence and in Nigerian law perpetration of the crime by females is even not recognised. In some jurisdictions the term "rape" has been replaced among others for that purpose with either an offence of "sexual conduct" as, *e.g.*, in Michigan or "sexual assault" as in Canada and New South Wales.[589] At the same time as Professor Bassiouni has observed, the expectations of legal standards of specificity in international criminal law cannot be the same as in domestic legislation.[590] Thus, it develops gradually on the basis of, among other things, states' practices and judicial decisions by international organs. However, although the type of sexual violence referred to above has not occurred on the same scale as rape of women by men, it is of great importance that these victims are not ignored but that they also obtain redress. The EC mission earlier referred to emphasised in its report that sexual abuse of men in detention camps has occurred, and that these victims as well must be the concern of the international community.[591] There are some indications that the *ad hoc* Tribunal might interpret the term extensively, *i.e.*, to comprise, as, *e.g.*, the Swedish legislation does, acts of rape committed against both sexes. In the background material to the indictment of the 21 individuals charged for crimes committed in the Omarska camp it is, *e.g.*, stated that both female and male prisoners were raped and sexually assaulted and humiliated. There is in my view not only practical but also symbolic value in applying an extensive concept of rape in order to convey fully the horror of the event so that the public will continue to consider such a conduct with an appropriate degree of revulsion and that it be punished.

Despite the progressive developments referred to above in international humanitarian law, there are still areas of concern, *e.g.*, the continuing gender imbalance in the composition of the Tribunals. Only two of the fourteen elected judges to serve on the *ad hoc* Tribunal for Yugoslavia and one of the six judges of the Rwanda Tribunal are women with experience of gender-related discrimination.[592] Apparently this situation is unsatisfactory in view of the fact that a great part of the work of the Tribunals will centre around sexual violence. The appointment of a woman Prosecutor in 1996 who is experienced in the prosecution of sex crimes, as well as of gender equality, and the election of women to act as the ICTY's President and

---

588 *R. Copelon*, Gendered War Crimes, p. 209, note 5.

589 *A.S. Pepple*, p. 53.

590 *M.C. Bassiouni*, Crimes Against Humanity: The Need for a Specialized Convention, p. 470.

591 UN Doc. S/25240, p. 4.

592 On the basis of the S.C. Res. 1166, adopted on 13 May 1998, the number of the ICTY's judges was expanded from eleven to fourteen. The three additional judges who were elected on 16 October 1998 are all men. Nevertheless, the fact that women serve in high-level capacities in both Tribunals has been considered to be "a monumental advance over women's traditionally minimized role and status in international law bodies or organizations, including in prior international war crimes tribunals". *K.D. Askin*, Sexual Violence, p. 98.

Articles 36(8)(a)(iii) & 44(2) of the ICC Statute requires that "fair representation of female and male judges" be taken into account in the judicial process.

Vice-President, is a welcome step in what this author hopes will be a progressive process of change of the status quo.

Another area of law, which still needs improvement, is the issue of reparation for violations. The Special Rapporteur on the Right to Restitution, Compensation and Rehabilitation of Victims of Flagrant Violations of Human Rights, Professor Theo van Boven, has defined the term "reparation" as follows: "Reparations shall be proportionate to the gravity of the violations and the resulting damage and shall include restitution, compensation, rehabilitation, satisfaction and guarantees of non-repetition".[593]

The Statutes of the *ad hoc* Tribunals do not provide any mechanism for, *e.g.*, compensation for personal as opposed to property damage. In my view it is equally important to the implementation of the principle of individual responsibility for the commitment of international crimes to grant compensation to the victims of violations of international humanitarian law. Nevertheless, Rule 106 (B) of the ICTY Rules of Procedure and Evidence is in this respect of significance for the victims. On their basis a victim or person claiming through him/her may bring an action in a national court or other competent body to obtain compensation.[594]

The recent developments in international law referred to above as regards the condemnation and prosecution of international crimes committed on women, including the recent adoption of the Statute of a permanent International Criminal Court with jurisdiction over crimes under general international law, are an important step in the struggle for justice and a welcome effort aimed at ensuring the respect of the rule of law among nations and more specifically women's rights (including reproductive freedom). The international community has taken some, albeit still very few, concrete measures to ensure that perpetrators are made accountable for the violations of human rights and international humanitarian law that they have committed. Seen in this context the establishment of the *ad hoc* Tribunal for the former Yugoslavia is undoubtedly to be regarded as an important precedent both for other similar *ad hoc* tribunals, *e.g.*, Rwanda, as well as for the establishment of the ICC.

It should also be remembered that only a couple of years ago ideas about the creation of an international criminal tribunal were deemed practically impossible to realise in the near future and even considered undesirable by some international lawyers.[595] The recent advancement of public international law is consequently

---

[593] UN Doc. E/CN.4/Sub.2/1996/17, p. 3. The Commission on Human Rights decided at its 54th session in 1998 (resolution 1998/43) to appoint an expert to prepare a revised version of the draft basic principles and guidelines elaborated by Mr. van Boven with view to its adoption by the GA. The Statute of the ICC enables the future court to award reparations to, or in respect of, victims, including restitution, compensation, and rehabilitation, upon request or on its own notion (Article 75).

A few writers, among them Ms. Aafjes, has proposed that remedies for victims of rape should include the right to medical services, including abortion, and counselling. *A. Aafjes*, p. 110.

[594] See UN Doc. E/CN.4/Sub.2/1990/10, § 33; UN Doc. E/CN.4/Sub.2/1996/17; UN Doc. E/CN.4/Sub.2/1998/13, §§ 88–90 and *N. Roth-Arriaza*, p. 53.

[595] *S.E. Nahlik*, p. 176. For further references on that matter of dispute see *J. Crawford*, p. 415.

favourable for securing effective measures against impunity,[596] which is indeed a very serious threat to the rule of law.[597]

In this respect I feel that it is important to stress once more that *all* sides involved in the conflicts in the former Yugoslavia have committed, although to varying degrees, atrocities and therefore none of them should go unpunished. Croatian women have been targets for rape at the same time as it has been pointed out that the Croatian Government has sought to "cleanse" Croatia of Serbs.[598] In addition, there are reports that rape has been committed by Muslims.[599] The American Bar Association has stressed that for the prosecution of war crimes in the former Yugoslavia to be successful, "it is imperative that the Tribunal not be used as a political tool, but solely as a means to try those suspected of violating international law".[600]

Finally, I would like to mention another legal area of concern, international refugee law, which has some relevance to the previous discussion. It is a well-established fact that actual or feared breaches of international humanitarian law lead to refugee outflows. Victims of war and armed conflicts, therefore, deserve international protection, which may take the shape of asylum. In other words, gender-based violence is an issue that can and should be addressed in the context of

---

596 The issue has been given prominent attention within the UN and some regions of the world. The Latin American and Caribbean Regional Programme of Action, (1995–2001) underlines, for example, that obstacles still remain in this region of the world permitting impunity for those who commit crimes against women and that appropriate measures are needed in order to counteract impunity. UN Doc. E/CN.6/1995/5/Add. 3, § 175(i). See also Inter-American Commission on Human Rights, Report No. 34/96, 15 October 1996, IHRR 1999, Vol. 6, pp. 89–113.

The UN Commission on Human rights, in addition, insisted during its 54th session in 1998, on the importance of the struggle against impunity and stressed how important it was to take all the necessary steps possible so that those responsible for violations of international law, especially human rights and humanitarian law, would be accountable for their acts. See resolution 1998/53.

597 The concept "The Rule of Law", which is based on the German term *Rechtsstaat*, refers to a social order, in which law is the guiding factor for all activities of the public authorities. Impunity for violations of international human rights and humanitarian law comprises moral, political and legal dimensions. It means also additional violations of the victim's rights. It is also believed that some of those who survived the genocide and other atrocities especially in Rwanda will predictably resort to summary revenge and further killing unless they can see justice done lawfully. Human Rights Watch World Report 1995, p. xx. Amnesty International takes a similar view by emphasising that: "letting killers and torturers off the hook undermines long-term solutions to the human rights crises because it sends a message that they can continue their abuses". Amnesty International, Report 1995, p. 38. Also during the Vancouver meeting of experts in 1993 it was emphasised that only through the determination to bring to justice those individuals who commit or order atrocities can the world community "hope to break the cycles of war, death and misery in which one generation's atrocities become the genesis of those of the future". Report by the International Centre for Criminal Law Reform and Criminal Justice Policy, 1993, p. 23.

598 See the reference to the findings of an international team of medical experts based on its on-site investigations in the former Yugoslavia carried out in 1993. Serb women have on several occasions reported that many women have been raped by Croat and Muslim men in positions of authority. See UN Doc. E/CN.4/1993/50, pp. 19 and 71.

599 *R. Copelon*, Gendered War Crimes, p. 209.

600 Report by the International Centre for Criminal Law Reform, ibid., p. 8.

refugee law as well. In the Beijing Platform for Action states agree to "consider recognising as refugees those women whose claim to refugee status is based upon a well-founded fear of persecution...(i)ncluding persecution through sexual violence or other gender-related persecution".[601]

The key concept in the 1951 Geneva Convention Relating to the Status of Refugees, which differs from its predecessors by defining a refugee in general terms rather in categories, is the notion "persecution".[602] Yet its designers left the expression undefined, since at the time of the treaty's drafting there was a consensus that it is impossible to enumerate "in advance all of the forms of maltreatment, which might legitimately entitle persons to benefit from the protection of a foreign state".[603] Against this background it can, therefore, be argued that there is no obstacle to the notion "fear of persecution" being interpreted and applied in the context of modern developments and changed realities. Circumstances differ today considerably from the ones existing when the 1951 Geneva Convention came into being. Persecution is generally viewed today as encompassing serious violations of basic human rights as well as severe discrimination leading to consequences of a substantially prejudicial nature for the person concerned.[604] One might not without reason argue that violations of a woman's physical security and bodily integrity should be protected under refugee law as well.[605]

It is, however, clear that the discussed concept then and now presupposes a risk of serious harm. On this basis and with reference to the UNHCR's official

---

[601] Beijing Declaration and Platform for Action, § 147 (h,i).

[602] According to Article 1(A)(2) of the Convention a refugee is anyone who: "owing to a well-founded fear of being persecuted for reasons of race, religion, nationality, membership of a particular social group or political opinion, is outside the country of his nationality and is unable or, owing to such fear, is unwilling to avail himself of the protection of that country of his former habitual residence is unable or, owing to such fear, is unwilling to return to it".

[603] *J.C. Hathaway*, Reconceiving Refugee Law as Human Rights Protection, in Problems and Prospects of Refugee Law, V. Gowlland & K. Samson (eds.), Geneva 1992, p. 19.

[604] During its 41st session in 1990, the UNCHR Executive Committee stated that severe discrimination experienced by women and prohibited by the Women's Convention can form the basis for the granting of refugee status. See Note on Refugee Women and International Protection, EC/SCP/59, 28 August 1990, § 18. However, the line between "mere" discrimination and persecution is not a clear one but requires case by case determination. In evaluating a claim based on discriminatory treatment, the adjudicator must evaluate all of the circumstances, including the type of right denied, the manner in which it is denied, the seriousness of the harm to the applicant, and the non-persecutory justification for the discriminatory treatment. UNCHR, Handbook on Procedures and Criteria for Determining Refugee Status, Geneva 1992, §§ 54 and 55. In the view of this author the Declaration on Violence against Women can also be used as a point of reference. Recently, a UN Expert Group Meeting, held in November 1997, noted that although the term "gender-based prosecution" does not appear within any of the relevant international legal instruments, it encompasses "the forms of harm that are regularly suffered by women and girls everywhere and which are directed at them because of their sex". *Human Rights Watch*, Justice in The Balance, p. 42.

[605] *P. Goldberg*, Where in the World is There Safety for Me?, in Women's rights, human rights, J. Peters & A. Wolper (eds.), p. 347; *A. Macklin*, Refugee Women and the Imperative of Categories, HRQ 1995, Vol. 17, p. 227.

standpoint on that question,[606] I may therefore establish that rape and other types of grave sexual violence, such as forced impregnation, forcible abortion or sterilisation, committed for reasons of race, religion, nationality, political opinion or membership of a particular social group should be considered to be a kind of harmful behaviour, *i.e.*, they amount to persecution under the definition of the term "refugee" in the 1951 Geneva Convention and its 1967 Additional Protocol and should constitute a basis for establishing eligibility for refugee status.[607] Also in my opinion the well-founded fear of *threat* of rape and other forms of sexual assault, when linked to women's social, political or religious status, should justify the granting of a conventional refugee status.[608]

Such a decision should be made independent of considerations of whether the asylum-seeker is fleeing from a territory where an armed conflict is going on or not. In traditional refugee law, persons compelled to leave their country of origin, as a result of international or internal armed conflicts,[609] have as a rule not been considered refugees in the sense of Article 1A, paragraph 2 of the 1951 Geneva Convention and the 1967 Protocol. Unfortunately since the outbreak of war in 1992 the arrival of 540,000 asylum-seekers from Bosnia-Herzegovina to Western European countries has resulted in the introduction of a new form of European refugee status, the so called TPS (temporary protected status) in the national legislation of most countries members of the EU.[610] It is obvious that governments of these states are anxious to keep refugees away from their frontiers and to limit their opportunities to be granted protection.

---

606 See UNCHR, Refugee, Asylum Seekers and Displaced Women in the ECE Region, ECE High-Level Regional Preparatory Meeting for the Fourth World Conference on Women, Vienna October 1994, p. 7. See also UN Doc. E/CN.6/1994/4, p. 12 ; The Executive Committee "Note on Certain Aspects of Sexual Violence against Refugee Women", A/AC.96/822 and Corr. 1 and The Executive Committee, Conclusion No. 81, "General Conclusions on International Protection", Geneva 1997.

607 See CAT, Communication No. 41/1996, *Pauline Muzonzo Paku Kisoki v. Sweden*, IHHR 1997, Vol. 1, p. 78 ff. See also UN Doc. E/CN.6/1998/5, § 71.

608 That the threat of rape is degrading act and that it constitutes an attack on the moral integrity of the person, and thereby is to be considered as "persecution of the most vile sort", was stressed already in the *M.V.R.S. Araya* case in 1977 by the Canadian Immigration Appeal Board. *J.C. Hathaway*, The Law of Refugee Status, Vancouver 1991, p. 112, note 109. Canadian tribunals have continued thereafter to view threats of rape and rape itself as "degrading and constitute quite clearly an attack on the moral integrity of the person and, hence, persecution of the most vile sort". See *A. Macklin*, p. 227. For more recent case law in the Canadian, English and American jurisdictions see <http://www.unchr.ch/refworld/legal/refcas.htm.>.

Gender-based persecution as a legitimate basis for granting refugee status can reasonably be expanded to incorporate other forms of violations of women's reproductive freedom and the non-discrimination principle, *i.e.*, coercive abortion, coercive sterilisation etc. For a similar opinion see *A. Macklin*, p. 231.

609 *O. Kimminich*, Asylrecht, Berlin 1968, pp. 7–53 and Der Aufenthalt von Ausländern in der Bundesrepublik Deutschland, Baden-Baden 1980, pp. 135–173; *J.C. Hathaway*, The Law of Refugee Status, pp. 185–187; *G. Melander*, The Two Refugee Definitions, Raoul Wallenberg Institute, Report No. 4, Lund 1987, pp. 9–20; *M.K. Eriksson*, Swedish Refugee Law and Practice in the Light of International Law, TfR 1995, No. 4, pp. 626–627.

610 SOU 1994:135, The Key to Europe – a comparative analysis of entry and asylum policies in Western countries, Stockholm 1994, p. 77; *J.C. Hathaway & J.A. Dent*, Refugee Rights, Report on a Comparative Survey, Toronto 1995, p. 8.

Although it is theoretically possible to interpret the refugee definition to include the experiences of women, this is in practice rarely done. Only few of the refugee receiving countries in the Western hemisphere accept women victims of gender-specific abuses such as sexual violence, as refugees. So far none of these countries have adopted policies to the effect that when rape or other forms of gender-based violence has been committed, such acts should under certain circumstances provide a judicial basis for a claim to refugee status in accordance with the 1951 Geneva Convention and its Protocol. Nor have they demonstrated an acceptance of the UNHCR conclusions. On the contrary, most of the domestic legislations do not explicitly acknowledge gender-related persecution.[611] On the other hand, during the regional ECE meeting, which took place in October 1994, the UNHCR representatives expressed their belief in gradually achieving a more positive attitude towards the recognition of women asylum- seekers as refugees on the basis of the earlier mentioned grounds. This is also my hope. The UN Secretary- General indicated in his report on the second review of the implementation of the Nairobi Strategies that systematic sexual violence against women and girls is "one of the major causes of internal displacement and the decision to seek asylum abroad".[612] Moreover, § 136 of the Beijing Declaration and Platform of Action clearly states that women may be forced to flee as a result of a well-founded fear of persecution, including persecution through "sexual violence or other gender-related persecution". An expanded interpretation of the refugee definition seems to be a reasonable method to extend the ambit of the 1951 Refugee Convention, which like many other international law instruments is modelled on a male reality, in order to provide protection to women fleeing gender-based persecution (including sexual violence). Governments should, in addition, seek to remove legal and administrative barriers to women seeking asylum on the basis of gender-based persecution.[613]

It is thus essential that the international community deals with and fights effectively and decisively the roots of refugee flows, *i.e.*, ignorance and disregard for basic human rights and the rules of international humanitarian law of relevance for among other things reproductive freedom.

---

[611] *J. Greatbatch*, The Gender Difference: Feminist Critiques of Refugee Discourse, IJRL 1989, Vol. 1, p. 518; *N. Kelly*, Gender-Related Persecution: Assessing Asylum Claims of Women, Cornell ILJ 1993, Vol. 26, p. 625 ff.; *N. Mahmud*; Crimes Against Honour: Women in International Refugee Law, Journal of Refugee Studies 1996, Vol. 9, p. 367 ff.

[612] UN Doc. E/CN.6/1995/3, § 9.

[613] UN Doc. E/CN.4/1998/54, p. 41 and *A. Aafjes*, p. 117.

*Part IV*

# Conclusions and Recommendations

*Chapter 9*

# Summary and Concluding Remarks – *De lege lata* and *de lege ferenda*

## 9.1. Challenging the Content of Prevailing Concepts

The present study has clarified that there can be little doubt that enjoyment of reproductive freedom is a *sine qua non* condition for the attainment of substantial equality between women and men. And yet very few human rights and humanitarian law issues have for such a long time received as little attention, at the global, regional and national level, as reproductive freedom has.

A general conclusion, which emerges from the previous analysis, is that the essence of the concept has not been grasped satisfactorily and in a broad manner by the international organs, which have the authority to interpret the contours of human rights and humanitarian law norms. On the contrary, the definition of several key terms, which form part of it, has remained rigid and narrow. There continues, in addition, to exist "a widespread failure to consider gender as a factor in defining the substantive content"[1] of human rights such as, for example, the right to life, the right to health and the prohibition of torture. From the very recent case law of international organs as well as UN reports (produced, *e.g.*, by the Special Rapporteur on Violence against Women, the Special Rapporteur on Systematic Rape during Periods of Armed Conflict and the Special Rapporteur on Traditional Practices affecting the Health of Women and Children), which I have discussed earlier, it would appear nevertheless that various human rights organs (mainly at the regional level) and special investigatory mechanisms have began to consider, *e.g.*, rape within the legal construction of torture.[2] Some of the UN Rapporteurs on country situations have, moreover, paid attention, albeit limited, to different forms of reproductive crimes, as, for example, in the country reports on Rwanda, the former Yugoslavia, Myanmar and Sudan.

---

[1] *A. Gallagher*, p. 290.

[2] The previous UN Special Rapporteur on Torture, Professor Kooijmans, has, *e.g.*, contributed to rape being considered under certain circumstances as a serious violation of the prohibition of torture and inhuman treatment under international law. See UN Doc. E/CN.4/1992/84. It should, in addition, be noted that the Office of the Prosecutor for the ICTY has brought, as earlier mentioned, charges under common Article 3 of the Geneva Conventions by interpreting the term torture to include rape.

Violence against women is one of the major issues that women's human rights advocates have used to demonstrate how human rights law has excluded women. The present study has illustrated that women's experiences have increasingly begun to be included in the definitions of several international human rights and humanitarian law norms. The jurisprudence of the regional human rights courts as well as of the *ad hoc* Tribunals supports this proposition. Rape and other forms of sexual violence are being considered as crimes against humanity, grave breaches of the 1949 Geneva Conventions, genocide, war crimes and as violations of common Article 3 of the 1949 Geneva Conventions and the 1977 Additional Protocols.[3] The *Akayesu* judgment of the *ad hoc* Tribunal for Rwanda is groundbreaking in the context of international condemnation and persecution of gender crimes.[4] The Prosecutor for the *ad hoc* Tribunals has, in addition, issued indictments, which regarded rape as both a war crime and crime against humanity.[5] Another example of a recent date and which is crucial for the advancement of reproductive freedom, is the unprecedented inclusion of rape, forced pregnancy and enforced sterilisation within the notion of war crimes as well as of crimes against humanity in the ICC Statute. In addition, violence against women (including sexual violence) has been recognised as a form of discrimination and as comprised within the ambit of the Women's Convention as well as of the Inter-American Convention on the Prevention, Punishment and Eradication of Violence against Women.

Despite the above and other encouraging trends within international law identified in the present enquiry, this author feels that the purposeful work for a more open, flexible and creative interpretation and application of human rights and humanitarian law norms has to continue.[6]

---

[3] These reformative and gender-sensitive precedents are, *e.g.*, the *Tadić*, *Celibići*, *Furundžija* and *Akayesu* cases.

[4] Nevertheless, the UN Special Rapporteur on Violence against Women, Mrs. Coomaraswamy has taken a critical position, and rightly so, in her report to the Human Rights Commission in 1998 in regard to the circumstances that after hearing of a very large number of women victims of sexual abuse, the first indictment on the grounds of sexual violence at the *ad hoc* Tribunal for Rwanda was issued only in August 1997, and only after heavy international pressure from women's groups and by Judge Pillay, the sole woman on the panel. In her view the inability of the system to prosecute and punish those who have committed sexual crimes is a serious failure of the humanitarian law system at large and of the ICTR in particular. UN Doc. E/CN.4/1998/54. See also *K.D. Askin*, Sexual Violence, p. 106 and *D.M. Amann*, p. 196.

[5] The Office of the Prosecutor has so far brought charges of gender-based (including reproductive) crimes in twelve of the indictments of the *ad hoc* Tribunal for the Former Yugoslavia and in two of the indictments of the Rwanda Tribunal.

[6] It remains to be seen whether international judicial bodies will consider certain forms of sexual violence, affecting reproductive freedom, as comprised within the definition of genocide. Helen Fein's definition of genocide as "purposeful action by a perpetrator to physically destroy a collectivity directly or indirectly, through interdiction of the biological and social reproduction of group members, sustained regardless of the surrender or lack of threat offered by the victim", clarifies this possible interrelationship. *H. Fein*, Genocide, A Sociological Perspective, London 1993, p. 23. See also from the same author: Genocide, Terror, Life Integrity, and War Crimes: The Case for Discrimination, in The Conceptual and Historical Dimensions of Genocide, G. Andreopoulos (ed.), Philadelphia 1994, pp. 95–108.

At the time of writing sexual violence has been considered as a fundamental and integral part of genocide, committed in Rwanda in general, only in one case (*Akayesu v. Prosecutor*, Judgment, §§ 416–460)

The present author has been able to show that the prevailing understanding of some of the core elements of reproductive freedom, *i.e.*, the right to family planning and the right to found a family in international treaty law, does not correspond to, and does not reflect, the latest developments in science (especially in biomedicine[7]) and in social realities. Profound social changes demand matching changes in law and practice in order to uphold its legitimacy and to keep it viable. The risk is otherwise overwhelming that a static and from social realities abstracted law becomes a dead letter. International monitoring bodies continue, however, to refrain from taking a clear standpoint on some aspects of the phenomenon under consideration such as the abortion issue, access to new techniques for assisted reproduction as well as certain issues of gender-based violence. One of the reasons probably is that these subject matters are ethically and morally difficult to decide upon, but also that human rights of special interest for women and substantial gender equality until recently have not been a high priority within the international community. Since infertility rates are increasing, especially in the industrialised world, access to alternative reproductive technologies has become more important and individuals increasingly consider it as legitimate legal claim. The intensified mobility of the modern citizen over nation borders makes domestic legal solutions to the above mentioned, and several other questions of relevance to our subject matter, insufficient. International human rights law has not yet met this new challenge in a satisfactory manner. The present author has argued that placing family planning in a broader reproductive health framework and in the context of gender equality, as well as the use of among others the teleological method of interpretation of the relevant treaty provisions, may forward its expansive reading. In my view a dynamic interpretation of the provisions in question might require, if that can improve the position of the individual concerned, (*i.e.*, that the interpretation makes the provisions more effective and useful from the point of view of the individual[8]), that other

---

decided by the ICTR. Nevertheless, the Trial Chamber of the ICTY presumed in the *Karadžić and Mladić Rule 61* decision, that forced impregnation may constitute evidence of genocidal intent. Cases Nos. IT-95-5-R61 and IT-95-18-R61.

In the view of the present author refugee law is, in addition, an area of law that urgently needs reformation and reconceptualisation from a gender perspective. Many women are victims of particular forms of sexual violence due to their gender. Whenever that violence deprives them of their fundamental human rights (including reproductive freedom) and there is no effective protection available, women are victims of persecution within the meaning of the 1951 Refugee Convention and its additional Protocol of 1967. The concept of refugee can and should be, therefore, interpreted in a more gender sensitive manner as already is the case in some national jurisdictions. See *C. Bunch & R. Carrillo*, p. 10.

[7] General principles of relevance for this enquiry are, however, contained in the 1997 European Convention on Human Rights and Biomedicine.

[8] There are, of course, opposite opinions on that issue. In the view of Heribert Golsong supervisory organs should be cautious when interpreting international human rights treaties since too excessive and broad interpretation of, for example, the European Convention may "not always be in line with the noble purpose of the Convention". An expansive reading of the Convention's provisions may, according to the same author, resemble an act "of usurpation of overreaching power or at least an act of *détournement de pouvoir*". *H. Golsong*, Interpreting the European Convention on Human Rights Beyond the Confines of the Vienna Convention on the Law of Treaties?, in The European System for the Protection of Human Rights, R. St. J. Macdonald, F. Matcher & H. Petzold (eds.), p. 162.

treaties[9] and the most recent declaratory documents adopted by the international community be consulted and relied upon.[10] In that way a greater coherence in the human rights system can be secured. In other words, the recent endorsement of the concept "reproductive health" in international law necessitates a holistic, comprehensive and visionary approach to existing law. One method in the determination of the content of a specific norm under scrutiny would be to take more frequently into account the interplay of several provisions within and among various human rights instruments. In addition to that, the result-oriented models of gender equality can be used as a justification and support for inventive interpretation of law, *e.g.*, the recognition of an emerging right to legal and safe abortion in international law.

At the same time this author is aware of the fact that the case law of the universal, as well as of regional supervisory human rights bodies, is based on individual complaints. Thus, these organs cannot tackle problems of their own motion, which they consider raise issues under the relevant conventions. Education has much to contribute in this regard. International procedures have remained beyond the reach of many women because of the deficient information about human rights obligations of the state as well as non-recognition of the jurisdiction of the treaty bodies mainly by states with poor human rights record. That girls and women should know about their human rights is, therefore, an essential prerequisite for them to be able to demand their recognition and respect. A further recommendation made by Andrew Byrnes is to build better linkages between national institutions (including NGOs) and organizations working at the international level in order to improve the dissemination of information about international procedures.[11] The UN's Plan of Action for the UN Decade for Human Rights Education (1995–2004)[12] supports these proposals.

Of critical importance for the reformation, reconceptualisation and extension of international law norms so that they better respond to and incorporate the specific needs and concerns of women is having an equality of representation of women in all international law-making forums and implementing bodies. On the basis of the facts presented in this study, it can be safely established that women continue

---

[9] See, *e.g.*, *S. Davidson*, The Inter-American Human Rights System, Aldershot 1997, p. 74 and *S.D. Murphy*, Progress and Jurisprudence of the International Criminal Tribunal for the Former Yugoslavia, AJIL 1999, Vol. 93, p. 96.

[10] The inventive use of "soft law" instruments is indeed another challenge to the normative structure and the traditional sources of international law. *C.M. Chinkin*, The Challenge of Soft Law: Development and Change in International Law, ICLQ 1989, Vol. 38, p. 866. See also *W.M. Reisman*, The Concept and Functions of Soft Law in International Politics, in Essays in honour of Judge Taslim Olawale Elias, Vol. I, E.G. Bello & B.A. Ajibola, San (eds.), Dordrecht 1992, pp. 135–145; *J. Klabbers*, The Redundancy of Soft Law, NJIL 1996, Vol. 65, pp. 167–182; *H. Combrinck*, Positive State Duties to Protect Women from Violence: Recent South African Developments, HRQ 1998, Vol. 20, p. 675.

[11] *A. Byrnes*, Toward More Effective Enforcement of Women's Human Rights Through the Use of International Human Rights Law and Procedures, in Human Rights of Women, R.J. Cook (ed.), p. 221.

[12] The United Nations General Assembly proclaimed by resolution 49/184 of 23 December 1994 the UN Decade for Human Rights Education. See *T.S. Orlin*, The UN and Human Rights Education, ASIL, Human Rights Interest Group, Newsletter November/December 1998, pp. 27–36.

largely to be underrepresented in the process of the formation of international law as well as in its application.[13] Few women, with only one exception (CEDAW), have been appointed to strategically important positions which would allow them to influence the interpretation of, and the elaboration upon, the meaning of international law norms in a gender-sensitive manner. For obvious reasons this situation cannot be tolerated any longer and it is logical to recommend that the proportion of women sitting on treaty bodies, tribunals, investigating mechanisms and in official human rights and humanitarian agencies be increased whenever there are vacancies on them. The presence of a greater number of women on the international supervisory bodies can make an important difference and can have positive effects on the outcome of the efforts to advance women's issues globally, regionally and nationally and to contribute to the elimination of gender discrimination.[14] Seen against this background the appointment of Mary Robinson in 1997 as the UN High Commissioner for Human Rights, and in 1998 of Louise Fréchette as the very first vice Secretary-General of the UN, and of Gro Harlem as the Director of WHO, is an encouraging trend.

Several authors, among them Professor Charlesworth, have pointed to the variety of techniques that can be used for the purpose of enhancing *de iure* as well as *de facto* equality. Expert committees can, *e.g.*, issue general comments "to broaden the traditionally androcentric scope of rights"[15] and this is more likely to be done with a better gender balanced composition of the international bodies. More importantly, according to the same scholar "redefining the traditional scope of international human rights law so as to acknowledge the interests of women may lead international actors to pursue change that will allow for the reimagination of gender difference"[16] and in my view hopefully to strengthening the conceptional as well as the institutional framework of international law so that substantial gender equality more easily can be achieved. We should also bear in mind that rigid and limited understanding of rights and freedoms leads to limited compliance and understanding of international obligations.

Finally, this author recognises the significance of the integrating of women's concerns in all human rights issues. Taking into account the reality we live in I am

---

[13] See also *K. Knop*, Why Rethinking the Sovereign State is Important for Women's International Human Rights Law, in Human Rights of Women, R.J. Cook (ed.), p. 160; *A. Byrnes*, p. 200; *C. Medina*, Toward a More Effective Guarantee of the Enjoyment of Human Rights by Women in the Inter-American System, p. 258; *A. Gallagher*, p. 331. At the time of writing only 5 out of 30 UN Special Rapporteurs appointed by the Commission on Human Rights were women. UN Doc. E/CN.4/1998/1/Add.1, pp. 43–44.

[14] Ensuring more gender-sensitive interpretation and application of domestic laws is equally important. Africa and the Caribbean have higher numbers of female judges and magistrates than do other regions of the world. States with legal systems based on Islamic law have clearly fewer female judges and magistrates. UN Doc. E/CN.6/1996/3/Add.7, §§ 24–25. It should be noted here that also in Western countries, such as the United States of America and Great Britain, women are fewer than 10 per cent of the judiciary. *G. Binion*, p. 513, note 17.

[15] *H. Charlesworth*, Human Rights as Men's Rights, p. 111.

[16] *Op. cit.*, p. 111.

supportive of the idea of building upon and using the existing human rights and humanitarian law framework while at the same time revising both branches of law from a woman's perspective and keeping in mind the limitations of the rights discourse.[17] Other solutions should not be excluded of course, *e.g.*, filling normative gaps with the elaboration of new substantive instruments such as, for example, the proposed additional protocol on equality between the sexes to the European Convention[18] as well as something I have already suggested, a universal convention on the prevention, punishment and eradication of violence against women including a comprehensive catalogue with definitions of among other things reproductive crimes.

## 9.2. Identification of Human Rights and Humanitarian Law Obligations

The next step, after establishing the substantial scope and the legally binding character of a specific rule in public international law, is to determine the obligations it creates. Otherwise, rights and freedoms would be "worth very little to women where there are no corresponding duties on the part of governments, organizations, and individuals to respect those rights".[19] Nevertheless, many states have remained reluctant to abandon limitations on their sovereignty by accepting *precise* international obligations.[20] Some states, albeit few, have consistently refused to become parties to human rights treaties for such reasons.[21] The number of governments who have not yet taken the step of submitting themselves to international control, *i.e.*, by accepting the jurisdiction of supervisory bodies under various human rights conventions remains substantial. The same is partly valid for judicial organs with the mandate to implement humanitarian law. The Government in Belgrade refuses so far to recognise the ICTY jurisdiction. It refused recently (November 1998) to issue an entry visa to the Tribunal's Prosecutor Judge Arbour who intended to investigate claims of crimes committed in the Kosovo province.

Encouraging states to accept the competence of international judicial and quasi-judicial treaty bodies should be a primary goal for the international community. A valuable development is discernible in this regard within the Council of Europe

---

[17] *R.J. Cook*, Women's International Human Rights Law: The Way Forward, pp. 4–5; *C.Bunch*, Organizing for Women's Human Rights Globally, in Ours by Right, J. Kerr (ed.), London 1993, p. 141; *H. Charlesworth*, What are "Women's International Human Rights?", in Human Rights of Women, R.J. Cook (ed.), pp. 60–62.

[18] Resolution 1018(1994), ERS 1018.WP.1403-24/1/94-21-E. See *G.H. Thune*, Kvinner og menneskerettigheter-refleksjoner i en europeisk ramme, Mennesker og rettigheter 1994, No. 2, p. 110.

[19] *R.J. Cook*, International Human Rights and Women's Reproductive Health, p. 270.

[20] By the submission of reservations upon signature or ratification of a human rights treaty a government may limit the scope of the instrument's applicability to that state.

[21] Recent global and regional high level conferences have repeatedly encouraged those states to become parties to human rights treaties, inclusive the Women's Convention. The UN's goal is to achieve universal ratification of the Women's Convention and the Convention on the Rights of the Child by all member states by the year 2000.

and it can be used as an inspiration for reforming other organizations as well. Since the 1990s not only do the prerequisites of a democratic society have to be fulfilled in order for a state to become a member of the organization but it has become accepted that membership involves a duty on the part of states to accept the jurisdiction of the European Court of Human Rights and to recognise the right of individuals to lodge complaints against member states.[22]

The nature of a state's international obligations varies considerably and depends on the scope of each human right. Implementation bodies and courts have the task to determine the duties which correlate to rights/freedoms that are embodied in human rights treaties. In regard to reproductive freedom this study has demonstrated that it is a composite right,[23] *i.e.*, it involves and interrelates civil and political rights with economic, social and cultural rights. It is thus a concept manifesting the natural unity of human rights and their intimate interlinkeage. Reproductive freedom is, in other words, a clear expression of the principle of the indivisibility, interrelatedness and interdependence of all categories of human rights, which is a fundamental UN doctrine on human rights.[24] This author has, therefore, tried to treat reproductive freedom as a coherent concept and in the context of gender equality. It must be, however, acknowledged that a composite right/freedom such as reproductive freedom can be problematic for implementation because of its legal construction. Some of its elements are founded on soft law documents, others constitute part of customary law and a few norms; especially certain forms of sexual violence in the context of armed conflicts, have acquired the status of *ius cogens* notions. The inadequacy of the traditional international law theory on, *e.g.*, sources and the hierarchy among them, which is value-based and predominantly male oriented, becomes thus apparent when dealing with contemporary legal phenomenon such as the one under consideration here.

By adherence to international treaties, but also on the grounds of general principles of international human rights law and *ius cogens* norms,[25] states are obliged to

---

[22] *M.K. Eriksson*, Demokrati i ljuset av det expanderande Europarådet, in Högskolan i Örebro Skriftserie 66, Örebro 1998, p. 13. Mention can be also made here of another remarkable dramatic change that has recently taken place within the European system for the protection of human rights. On the basis of the 11th additional protocol to the European Convention the position of the individual has been strengthened since the victim of a human rights violation has been granted full procedural capacity before the European Court. In November 1998 the European Court streamlined its procedures and absorbed the European Commission on Human Rights.

[23] *R.J. Cook*, International Protection of Women's Reproductive Rights, p. 653.

[24] The principle of interrelation and inderdependence between all human rights is central for the UDHR, the Women's Convention and the Convention on the Rights of the Child. See also § 5 (Part I) of the 1993 Vienna Declaration and Programme of Action. In addition, one of the more recent consensual documents, *i.e.*, the 1995 Beijing Declaration and Platform for Action underlines the same idea.

[25] The normative structure of international law needs to be further developed and modernised in the direction of the contemporary overall objectives of the international community. Being such an example, the principle of non-discrimination on the basis of sex is in the view of this author a strong candidate for becoming part of *ius cogens*. I have also argued in Part I of this study that it creates an *erga omnes* obligation for all the states comprising the international community.

respect, to protect and to ensure the realisation of human rights/freedoms of individuals under their jurisdiction.[26]

The various kinds of obligations imposed on states by international human rights law can be generally classified as follows. To begin with, a state's duty "to respect", which is a minimal undertaking,[27] implies that it has to abstain from interference with the exercise by the individual living on its territory of her/his human rights and fundamental freedoms. In other words, states are required to refrain from intruding into specifically outlined areas. To respect means also that the government in question must equally respect the dignity and worth of each single individual. In the context of the Women's Convention, for example, this confers outright obligations on states parties to refrain from engaging in any act or practice of discrimination against women (*e.g.*, Articles 2(d) and 16(2)). A state would be in breach of its international obligations if it enacts/tolerates laws and/or practises that "on their face or in the application, expressly discriminate".[28] In more concrete terms this can be the case if prosecutors ignore, as a matter of policy, certain reproductive crimes. In some instances, the duty incumbent upon states is to establish a specific, protective machinery. Thus, a systematic failure to provide an effective remedy for violations of human rights may be regarded as the responsibility of the state concerned.[29]

Generally speaking, observance of international human rights obligations would mean that governments have to take, or refrain from taking, certain actions, depending on the situation, in order to prevent violations of human rights, if the circumstances so require. Often obligations to "respect", to "protect" and to "prevent" can arise interchangeably. A state would commit a violation, among other things, if it permits groups or individuals whose acts it is aware of, and it is in position to prevent, to commit with impunity, either in the name of the state or in their own name, acts punishable by law against individuals or groups in the society in question.[30] Various governmental measures might be necessary in order to effectively protect individuals against violence, including violence committed by non-state actors, *e.g.*, to establish and "administer an adequate system of police, law enforcement, and civil and criminal justice".[31] As has been mentioned earlier in this monograph, many of the abuses against women have not been acknowledged as human rights violations because they were committed by private persons rather than by

---

[26] See *A. Eide & T. Opsahl*, General Report on "Equality and non-discrimination", Council of Europe, Strasbourg 1990, p. 5; *G.J.H. van Hoof*, The Legal Nature of Economic, Social and Cultural Rights, in the Right to Food, P. Alston & K. Tomaševski (eds.), Oxford 1984 p. 279; *R. Künnemann*, A Coherent Approach to Human Rights, HRQ 1995, Vol. 17, p. 328; *H.J. Steiner & P. Alston*, p. 907.

[27] *R.J. Cook*, Accountability in International Law for Violations of Women's Rights by Non-state Actors, in Reconceiving Reality: Women and International Law, D.G. Dallmeyer (ed.), p. 103.

[28] *R.J. Cook & J.M. Haws*, The United Nations Convention on the Rights of Women: Opportunities for Family Planning Providers, International Family Planning Perspectives 1983, Vol. 12, No. 2, p. 49.

[29] *C.W. Howland*, The Challenge of Religious Fundamentalism to the Liberty and Equality Rights of Women: An Analysis under the United Nations Charter, Columbia Journal of Transnational Law 1997, Vol. 35, p. 368.

[30] UN Doc. A/CONF.157/PC/60/Add.2, p. 14.

[31] *H.J. Steiner & P. Alston*, p. 907.

agents of the state.[32] The nature of such a division between public and private in international law is apparently gender biased. It has justified female subordination. Nevertheless, the demarcation of public and private life has been challenged by a number international law scholars,[33] and some international treaty bodies have began to expand the application of international law norms to include the private sphere of life and to hold states responsible for acts performed by private persons.[34]

---

[32] See also *D. Sullivan*, The Public/Private Distinction in International Human Rights Law, in Women's rights, human rights, J. Peters & A. Wolper (eds.), p. 126; UN Doc. E/CN.4/1995/42, § 100; *K. Tomaševski*, A Primer on CEDAW for International Development Co-operation Personnel, SIDA, Stockholm 1998, p. 8.

[33] See, for example, *L. Henkin*, Human Rights, in Encyclopedia of Public International Law, R. Bernhardt (ed.), Amsterdam 1985, Vol. 8, p. 272; *D. Shelton*, Private Violence, Public Wrongs, and the Responsibility of States, Fordham ILJ 1990, Vol. 13, p. 1 *et seq.*; *D. Shelton*, State Responsibility for Covert and Indirect Forms of Violence, in Human Rights in the Twenty-first Century, K.E. Mahoney & P. Mahoney (eds.), p. 265 *et seq.*; *J. Kokott*, No Impunity for Human Rights Violations in the Americas, HRLJ 1993, Vol. 14, Nos. 5–6, pp. 154–155; *R.J. Cook*, Women's International Human Rights Law: The Way Forward, p. 250; *D.Q. Thomas & M.E. Beasley*, Domestic Violence as a Human Rights Issue, HRQ 1993, Vol. 15, p. 41; *C. Romany*, State Responsibility Goes Private: A Feminist Critique of the Public/Private Distinction in International Human Rights Law, in Human Rights of Women, R.J.Cook (ed.), p. 101; *R. Künnemann*, pp. 328–329; *R.J. Cook*, State Responsibility for Violations of Women's Human Rights, Harvard Human Rights Law Journal 1994, Vol. 7, p. 126 ff.; *T. Buergenthal*, The Normative and Institutional Evolution of International Human Rights, p. 719.

Professor Trindade has argued, furthermore, that fundamental human rights having *erga omnes* validity require protection against "any encroachment, by public or private bodies or any individual". *A.A. Cançado Trindade*, Environmental Protection and the Absence of Restrictions, in Human Rights in the Twenty-first Century, K.E. Mahoney & P. Mahoney (eds.), p. 587.

[34] This modern approach as regards states' international obligations has been accepted within the various conventional regimes. As early as in 1977 the then member of the HRC, Mr. Tarnopolski expressed the view during the Committee's consideration of the periodic report of Finland that "Article 26 might require protection against discrimination by private individuals against private individuals". UN Doc. CCPR/C/SR.30, § 36. See also HRC's General Comment No. 6/16, UN Doc. CCPR/C/21/Rev.1.1989, § 3.

CERD has adopted this approach too. See for example *Yilmaz-Dogan v. The Netherlands*, Communication No. 1/1984, UN Doc. A/43/18, 1988, p. 59.

Traditionally, as I already have pointed out, the doctrine on state responsibility is coupled with the exercise of state power. One of the important elements of the concept is an internationally wrongful act performed by representatives of state authorities. In the "classic" sense the concept has been related to the responsibility of states for injuries to aliens and the reparation of loss or injuries caused to them. In the modern international law doctrine distinction is made between inter-state accountability, involving a "duty to provide an explanation for an act, which is apparently contrary to international law" and inter-state responsibility, involving "a duty to provide reparation for an internationally wrongful act". *T. van Boven*, Book Review, HRQ 1992, Vol. 14, p. 562. In other words, responsibility denotes in international law the consequences arising from the violation of an international obligation. In the context of international law yet another word is often used, "liability", when indicating the obligation to make compensation for damage suffered as a result of an act, which is not prohibited by international law. In 1973 the UN GA proposed the extending of the ILC study on states' responsibility to include general liability. *A. Miatello*, International Responsibility for the Use of Nuclear Energy, in United Nations Codification of State Responsibility, M. Spinedi & B. Simma (eds.), New York 1987, p. 305. See generally *A. Rosas*, State Responsibility and Liability under Civil Liability Regimes, in Current International Law Issues, Essays in Honour of Jerzy Sztucki, O. Bring & S. Mahmoudi (eds.), Stockholm 1994, p. 161; *R. Higgins*, International Law and How We Use It, pp. 39–46. The most recent report on state responsibility was presented by Professor James Crawford at the ILC's 50th session in 1998. UN Doc. A/CN.4/490, Adds. 1–6.

Geraldine Van Bueren has argued in the following manner: "The fact that women... have not been adequately protected by international human rights law strengthens the case for a reassessment of the boundaries of the private. This factor alone serves to undermine assumptions that the historical origins of international human rights law should predetermine its ambit".[35] It would not be wrong to assume that gender equality issues have benefited from the dramatic changes, which international law is undergoing and to which the *Drittwirkung* doctrine has contributed significantly. The *Drittwirkung* doctrine is simply about the extent to which international conventions are applicable to the behaviour of non-state actors.[36] The idea is that fundamental human rights should be respected both by public bodies and individuals. According to this new perception, the provisions of human rights conventions shall have an impact in two directions: in the *vertical* application of human rights, *i.e.*, the regulation of the relationship between individuals and the state, and in the *horizontal* application, *i.e.*, relations between individuals are affected.

However, not all rights and freedoms[37] can have *Drittwirkung* though we might find general statements on third-party applicability such as the preambles of the ICCPR and the ICESCR. Both documents proclaim, for example, in identical wording that: "the individual, having duties to other individuals and to the community to which he belongs, is under a responsibility to strive for the promotion and observance of the rights recognised in the present Covenant". I may also refer to provisions on the regional level such as Article 17 of the European Convention, which stipulates that: "Nothing in this Convention may be interpreted as implying

---

For further useful deliberations on the conceptual difference between the terms "responsibility" and "accountability" for violations of human rights see also *R.J. Cook*, Accountability in International Law for Violations of Women's Rights by Non-state Actors, p. 94; UN Doc. E/CN.4/1997/47, § 14 and *M. Singer*, The Future of International Human Rights, International Rule of Law Center Occasional Papers, Second Series, Number 2, Washington D.C. 1997. For a very stimulating discussion of accountability in the context of Shakespeare's plays see *T. Meron*, Crimes and Accountability in Shakespeare, AJIL 1998, Vol. 92, pp. 1–41.

[35] *G. Van Bueren*, Conference paper presented at Cardiff in 1994, p. 17.

[36] What is meant by *Drittwirkung* was developed mainly in Germany in the context of the impact of constitutionally safeguarded human rights on relations between private individuals. See generally *A. Clapham*, The "Drittwirkung" of the Convention, in The European System for The Protection of Human Rights, R. St. J. Macdonald, F. Matscher & H. Petzold (eds.), p. 163. Generally a distinction can be made between "mittelbare Drittwirkung", the theory of indirect impact on third parties (*i.e.*, principles relevant to constitutional fundamental rights are to be considered by the courts in decisions of private-law character) and "unmittellbare Drittwirkung" /direkte Drittwirkung, the theory of direct impact on third parties, (*i.e.*, rights can be applied in a direct manner against private bodies by the courts). See *M. Stathopoulos*, Equality in the Law of Contract, Law in Motion, Conference paper, Part I, Brussels 1996, p. 290; *S. Davidson*, The Inter-American Court of Human Rights, p. 150; *C. Jochnick*, Confronting the Impunity of Non-State Actors: New Fields for the Promotion of Human Rights, HRQ 1999, Vol. 21, pp. 62–64.

[37] In regard to the application of the European Convention, the Commission reached the conclusion in the *X and Y v. The Netherlands* case that in order for a right to be applicable amongst third parties "it is necessary that its contents are unequivocal and not subject to a divergence opinion of the different Member States". See § 56 of the Commission's Report.

for any State, group or person any right to engage in any activity or perform any act aimed at the destruction of the rights and freedoms set forth herein or at their limitation to a greater extent than is provided for in the Convention".[38] At the same time only states parties can be held responsible at the international level for failing to protect individuals against violations by other individuals due to "the fault of domestic legislation, of the courts, or the administrative authorities".[39]

The *Drittwirkung doctrine* has found expression in the Inter-American Court's case law and it has been spelled out explicitly as a matter of principle, for example, in the *Velásquez* case.[40] The Court found the Government of Honduras responsible for a breach of the right to life in circumstances where enforced disappearances of political opponents have been carried out between 1981 and 1984 with impunity by members of the Honduras military, acting as private individuals or unidentified groups.[41]

The same principle has been espoused also by the European Court of Human Rights. The *X and Y v the Netherlands* case[42] evidences the Court's willingness to expand the traditional scope of international commitment. The case dealt with the consequences of lack of criminal evidence provisions in the Netherlands. The circumstances in the case under consideration revealed that the existing domestic remedies did not provide the necessary basis for the national authorities to prosecute an alleged rapist of an mentally handicapped girl, Miss Y. The European Court found for these reasons Miss Y to be the victim of a violation of Article 8 of the European Convention. In the view of the Court, obligations under Article 8 of the Convention "may involve the adoption of measures designed to secure respect for private life even in the sphere of relations of individuals between themselves".[43] This and other decisions of international judicial and quasi-judicial bodies can, and should be, used as an important precedental basis for the further extension of the

---

[38] Several domestic courts in Europe have often applied some of the provisions of the European Convention to private relations. See *A. Drzemczewski*, The European Convention on Human Rights and Relations Between Private Parties, NILR 1979, Vol. 26, p. 163; *E.A. Alkema*, The third-party applicability or "Drittwirkung" of the European Convention on Human Rights, in Protecting Human Rights: The European Dimension, F. Matscher & H. Petzold (eds.), Köln 1988, p. 38.

[39] *E.A. Alkema*, p. 38.

[40] *Velásquez Rodríguez v. Honduras* case, Inter-American Court of Human Rights, Ser. C, No. 4, Judgment of 29 July 1988, 28 ILM 291, §§ 172 and 174–175. On the other hand the Court has indicated in the *Caballero Delgado & Santana* case that there is no individual right within the Inter-American system to require a state to prosecute a human rights violator. See IACHR, Ser. C, No. 17, 1994 cited in *M. Singer*, p. 5, note 3.

[41] The Court ruled in this case that states parties to the American Convention on Human Rights are obliged to prevent and prosecute violations of the guaranteed rights/freedoms by both state agents and non-state actors. The Court explained that: "An illegal act, which violates human rights and which is initially not directly imputable to a State (for example, because it is the act of a private person or because the person responsible has not been identified) can lead to international responsibility of the State, not because of the act itself, but because of the lack of due diligence to prevent the violation or to respond to it as required by the Convention". Ibid., § 172.

[42] *X and Y v the Netherlands*, ECHR Judgment of 26 March 1985, Ser. A, No. 91. See also *Young, James and Webster v. the UK*, ECHR Judgment of 26 June 1981, Ser. A., No. 44, § 49.

[43] *Supra*, case *X and Y v. The Netherlands*, § 23.

theory of accountability for violations of human rights as well as the idea of states' international obligation to include the enforcement of criminal laws against private acts of violence against women.[44]

A more modern and refined approach to the doctrine of state responsibility is necessary because it can also disclose patterns of discriminatory non-prosecution of violations of the human rights of women. It has been suggested that such a doctrinal shift would have appropriate consequences for certain national cultures, where violence against women is culturally systematic.[45]

One of the unique and important features of the Women's Convention, which expands the traditional theories of human rights, is that it requires states' parties to tackle discrimination in the private lives of women under their jurisdiction as well as the activities of the governmental authorities, in particular within families, and that it is, moreover, the obligation of states to eliminate it.[46] CEDAW's General Recommendation No. 19 makes it furthermore clear that the Women's Convention obliges states parties to eliminate violence perpetrated by public authorities *and* by private persons, organizations or enterprises.[47] In consequence, a state will be in breach of its human rights obligations if it fails to prosecute crimes against women perpetrated by family members.

The Convention on the Rights of the Child imposes also explicit duties on the states' parties to prevent violations by private persons.[48]

---

[44] The European Commission has, on the other hand, expressed the view in a case dealing with a complaint from a woman who was dismissed from her employment after her complaint against the employer of sexual harassment failed, that "the applicant's complaints, as submitted by her did not disclose any elements, which indicated that the United Kingdom Government was subject to a duty imposed by Article 1 of the European Convention in respect to the alleged matters". See Application No.12597/86 (unpublished), referred to in Equality between the sexes and the European Convention on Human Rights, *M. Buquicchio-de Boer*, p. 22. It should be born in mind, however, that this is not the first time that the European Commission and the European Court disagree on the application of international principles in practice. Even though the Commission's role in adopting a report on the merits of an application is judicial, the Court and the Committee of Ministers had the final saying at that time. A progressive development towards greater acceptance of *Drittwirkung* of human rights norms might be expected also on the basis of Article 5 of the seventh Additional Protocol to the European Convention. For a recent discussion on this issue within the UN see UN Doc. E/CN.4/Sub.2/1997/28, § 16 and UN Doc. E/CN.4/1998/87, § 65.

[45] *M. Singer*, p. 5.

[46] An important step has been taken in contemporary international law as regards prosecution of acts of rape as has been explained earlier. *P.F. Marshall,* Violence Against Women in Canada by Non-State Actors, Human Rights in the Twenty-first Century, in K.E. Mahoney & P. Mahoney (eds.), p. 319. See also *R.J. Cook*, Reservations to the Convention on the Elimination of All Forms of Discrimination against Women, Virginia Journal of International Law 1990, Vol. 30, No. 3, p. 706.

[47] As already mentioned earlier, the UN Declaration on Violence against Women and the Inter-American Convention on Prevention, Punishment and Eradication of Violence against Women contain among other things obligations for governments that target abuses of physical power.

[48] It can be mentioned here that one of the then members of the CRC, Mr. Hammarberg, submitted at the 6th meeting of the Committee that the CRC was concerned with the situation of children and ways to protect them, and according to him "it should also be able to examine cases of violations committed by individuals even if that was not strictly in accordance with its mandate". None of the other members of the Committee objected to this proposition. See UN Doc. CRC/C/1991/SR.6, p. 5; *P. Goldberg*, p. 347.

This relatively new approach in international law to state responsibility, which brings into focus states responsibility for non-state and private individuals, has very important consequences. The UN Special Rapporteur on Violence against Women has considered it as "one of the most important contributions of the women's movement to the issue of human rights".[49] As yet, however, there is no clear tendency discernible of a coherent and consistent practice in this regard by the international human rights bodies.[50]

This study has, furthermore, discussed the existence of an international law obligation for states to investigate and prosecute individuals who have violated the rules of international humanitarian law. While rules for the imposition of individual responsibility for international crimes have been for a long time in existence, it is only recently that the Statute for a permanent International Criminal Court (ICC) with the jurisdiction to implement them, and by that to ensure effective enforcement of humanitarian law, was adopted. As already mentioned, currently both *ad hoc* Tribunals make efforts to prosecute gender-specific war crimes of violence against women. It should be noted once again that the theory that both war crimes and crimes against humanity enjoy universal jurisdiction gains with each day that passes increased international support. This means that any government has the right to try any perpetrator of, *e.g.*, reproductive crimes, no matter where the crime was committed or by whom. The recent arrest of General Pinochet is a significant attempt to enforce international criminal responsibility. The British Law Lords ruled that the former dictator Augusto Pinochet, who is facing charges of torture, kidnapping and murder of Spanish citizens in Chile during the 1980s,[51] as well as crimes against nationals of other countries, was not immune from prosecution as a former head of state.[52] Extradition requests for Pinochet from France, Switzerland and Belgium, following the one from Spain, suggest that several countries take a similar view.

---

[49] UN Doc. E/CN.4/1995/42, § 107.

[50] Mention can be made of the on-going work within the UN Commission on Human Rights on a Declaration on the Right and Responsibility of Individuals, Groups and Organs of Society to Promote and Protect Universally Recognised Human Rights and Fundamental Freedoms, a work which began in 1987. Moreover, the Commission adopted without a vote on 6 March 1991 resolution 1991/72 on Responsibility for the Violations of Human Rights and Fundamental Freedoms. The Commission stressed in it that, notwithstanding existing separate norms and principles which establish responsibility for violations of obligations concerning human rights, further efforts should be undertaken with a view to elaborate legal regimes with clear rules regulating responsibility. It is, furthermore, hoped that such rules would serve as a deterrent and as preventive guarantees aimed at averting any infringements of human rights and fundamental freedoms. The Commission decided to consider the question again at its 48th session. However, there has been no follow-up either at the 48th, 49th and 50th sessions of the Commission.

[51] Pinochet can only be extradited as regards charges of crimes committed after 1988, the point in time when the acts in question were international crimes also under British Law. 1988 is the year when the UK ratified the UN Convention against Torture.

[52] See Judgments – *Regina v. Bartle and the Commissioner of Police for the Metropolis and others Ex Parte Pinochet* (on appeal from a Divisional Court of the Queen's Bench Division; *Regina v. Evans and another and the Commissioner of the Police for the Metropolis and others Ex Parte Pinochet* (on appeal from a Divisional Court of the Queen's Bench Division), 25 November 1998, House of Lords Sessions, Publications on the Internet. The Spanish warrant is based on the European Convention on Extradition.

Lastly, the category of state obligations under international law still to be mentioned is the duty "to ensure" and the duty "to promote" realisation of the rights/freedoms in question which may comprise among other things educational measures in order to reduce violation of rights and that individuals "gain recognition of their own right".[53] This type of obligations requires, furthermore, states to take appropriate legislative, administrative, budgetary, judicial and other measures towards the full realisation of such rights.[54] The realisation of a certain guaranteed right/freedom means that the individual is able to actually enjoy it. For that purpose governments may need to provide opportunities for those who lack them and also direct provisions of services and benefits for the fulfilment of the right/s in question.

On the basis of the previous discussion it seems that international human rights obligations might consist of both a negative element (*passive* obligation), *i.e.*, an obligation for the states' authorities to abstain from intervention[55] as well as a positive element (*active* obligation),[56] *i.e.*, a duty to act. Governments are expected to create conditions for, and to provide the means for, the enjoyment of the human rights/freedoms in a convention. Some of the obligations require immediate action and/or the adoption of measures to be implemented progressively, that is, within a reasonable time.[57] While negative obligations entail few costs for the state, positive obligations require expenditures. The fulfilment of this type of obligation may, in other words, depend upon the availability of adequate financial and material resources. This does not mean that a state may legitimately discharge its international obligations by simply claiming that it lacks adequate resources. The Limburg Principles (25–28)[58] refute, for example, arguments based on financial constraints

---

[53] *H.J. Steiner & P. Alston*, p. 907.

[54] The Limburg Principles, § 6 and CESCR, General Comment No. 3, § 7. The Limburg Principles on the Implementation of the International Covenant on Economic, Social and Cultural Rights, UN Doc. E/CN.4/1987/17, Appendix. The text has been reprinted in HRQ 1987, Vol. 9, pp. 73–87. The principles are not legally binding but they have been given considerable weight in the doctrine and by supervisory human rights bodies. The Limburg Principles were formulated by a group of researchers, international lawyers and human rights activists who attempted to clarify the scope of states obligations under the ICESCR. In January 1997, on the occasion of the tenth anniversary of the Limburg Principles on the Implementation of the ICESCR, a meeting was convened in Maastricht with the objective to elaborate on principles regarding the nature and scope of violations of economic, social and cultural rights. See The Maastricht Guidelines on Violations of Economic, Social and Cultural Rights, HRQ 1998, Vol. 20, p. 691 *et seq.*

[55] See for example Article 2(1) of the ICCPR according to which each state party to the Covenant "undertakes to respect and to ensure to all individuals within its territory and subject to its jurisdiction the rights recognized in the present Covenant".

[56] According to CEDAW's General Recommendation No. 8 of 1988 the Women's Convention imposes, *e.g.*, duties on states parties to "take further *direct* measures in accordance with Article 4 of the Convention" in order to achieve equality between men and women.

[57] While Article 2 of the ICCPR provides that the protected rights be respected and guaranteed immediately, Article 2 of the ICESCR provides that states should "recognize" the rights contained in the Covenant and should implement them progressively, *i.e.*, continuously improve their implementation of these rights.

[58] See also *C. Apodaca*, Measuring Women's Economic and Social Rights Achievements, HRQ 1998, Vol. 20, p. 145. Lastly, I would also like to mention the 1997 project on the identification of the minimum core content of the protected rights by the ICESCR, which was carried out by the American Association for the Advancement of Science as a valuable source.

as a hinder for a government to give effect to protected human rights. The starting point must be that regardless of the level of economic development of a society, states parties to the ICESCR are under a duty to ensure minimum subsistence rights for all and to move "as expeditiously as possible towards the realization of the rights".[59] Also the Committee on Economic, Social and Cultural Rights has emphasised in its third GC of 1990 on the nature of states parties obligations (Article 2(1)), that even in times of severe resource constraints, the vulnerable members of society "can and indeed must be protected by the adoption of relatively low-cost targeted programs".[60] Thus, lack of infrastructure, economic resources due to drought, armed conflict or external debt payment obligations, may not be accepted as justifications for non-compliance with the international obligations in regard to reproductive freedom. Undoubtedly, such an approach reflects a broadened sense of governmental responsibility for the welfare of individuals within its jurisdiction as well as a more inclusive understanding of human rights. In fact, a dichotomous division of positive/negative obligations cannot be upheld strictly. Neither does such a distinction correspond to the distinction between civil and political and economic and social rights, which rested on political controversy during the cold war. The rigid traditional distinction between the two categories of rights, *i.e.*, civil and political on the one hand and economic, social and cultural rights on the other hand, cannot be upheld today. The dividing line between the two sets of rights is simply not watertight.[61] Elements of one and the same right/freedom or composite right/freedom, such as reproductive freedom, require both a hands-off duty and considerable activity from the state for its full enjoyment. In other words, most human rights have dual nature and they are not by their terms restricted to either of the above mentioned obligations. The variation of state obligations in regard to human rights is nothing other than a difference in degree of specification and application and not of substance or approach.[62] A consideration of the Women's Convention indicates, for example, that the obligations imposed upon, and accepted by, states parties to the Convention are variable. It includes obligations for governments to undertake certain activities, *e.g.*, Article 2 "to pursue by all appropriate means[63] and without delay a policy of eliminating discrimination against women". The Women's Convention is, on the other hand, partly promotional, since it requires in Article 3 only that states parties "take in all fields, in particular in the political, social, economic and cultural fields, all appropriate measures, including legislation, to ensure the full development

---

[59] The Limburg Principles, § 21.

[60] UN Doc. HRI/GEN/1/Rev.1, 29 July 1994, p. 103, § 12.

[61] For further discussion on this subject see *M. Pellonpää*, Economic, Social and Cultural Rights, in The European System for the Protection of Human Rights, R. St. J. Macdonald, F. Matcher & H. Petzold (eds.), p. 858; *D. Türk*, Final Report on the Realization of Economic, Social and Cultural Rights, UN Doc. E/CN.4/Sub.2/1992/16; *A. Eide, C. Krause & A. Rosas* (eds.), Economic, Social and Cultural Rights: A Textbook, Dordrecht 1995.

[62] *R. Künnemann*, p. 327.

[63] For deliberations on the content of this phrase see *R.J. Cook*, State Responsibility for Violations of Women's Human Rights, p. 161. An in-depth analysis of Article 2 of the Convention is contained in UN Doc. CEDAW/C/1995/4.

and advancement of women, for the purpose of guaranteeing them the exercise and enjoyment of human rights and fundamental freedoms on a basis of equality with men". Against this background Katarina Tomaševski has identified three levels of governmental obligations embodied in the Women's Convention. They are "1. Formal recognition that all human rights and fundamental freedoms apply to women as they do to men; 2. Prohibition of discrimination in the enjoyment of those formally guaranteed rights and creation of equal opportunities for women to exercise all rights and freedoms; and 3. Identification and elimination of gender-specific obstacles to the equal enjoyment of rights and freedoms".[64]

It is, however, generally left to the discretion of states parties to treaties to relatively freely choose the means to ensure the commitments they have undertaken, *i.e.*, to fulfil their international obligations. While there is no requirement in the conventions[65] under consideration that they be incorporated into domestic legal systems, this is undoubtedly the best method to implement and to forward the realisation of the protected rights since incorporation would oblige in a strict manner national courts and administrative agencies to have regard to the conventions in question. Incorporation may ensure that national law will be brought into conformity with corresponding international law rules. Nevertheless, very few states have so far done so. The most important argument in favour of incorporating the Women's Convention into Norwegian law was, moreover, the symbolic effect this would have internationally and nationally.[66]

It remains finally to summarise the above discussion on international obligations in the context of reproductive freedom and to evaluate what kind of implications they can have for states.[67] The tentative recommendations in this regard are as follows:

**1. The right to marry and to found a family**

*A. Obligations of abstention*

- Governments should not restrict the right to marry on racial, religious and other discriminatory grounds. Certain absolute and permanent marriage impediments could be considered as a violation of the right.
- Governments (legislature, executive branch or any judicial officer) must not interfere with a person's choice to have a child as well as the choice not to have any child at all. Governments must not prescribe the compulsory use of

---

[64] *K. Tomaševski*, A Primer on CEDAW, p. 10.

[65] Strictly speaking there is no universal uniform practice stipulating how states should transform international law into their domestic legal systems. Some of the international supervisory organs have, however, on several occasions explicitly encouraged states parties to incorporate a specific convention as, for example, the CRC did in connection with the review of the first report presented by Sweden under the Convention on the Rights of the Child. See also the *Swedish Engine Drivers' Union* case, ECHR Judgment of 6 February 1976, Ser. A, No. 20, § 18.

[66] Regrettably, Norway decided to postpone the incorporation of the Convention into the municipal legal system. *K.A. Grannes*, Lovgivning om likstelling – bør FNs kvinnekonvensjon inkorporeres i norsk rett?, Mennesker og rettigheter 1994, Vol. 12, p. 123.

[67] Useful tables containing references to the elements which comprise reproductive freedom and the corresponding articles in different conventional texts can be found in *R.J. Cook*, Human Rights and Reproductive Self-determination, pp. 980–981 and in *C.A.A. Packer*, pp. 36–41.

contraceptives, neither ban nor severely restrict the availability and accessibility of contraception.

- Forced pregnancy, forced sterilisation and/or forced abortion for individuals belonging to certain groups of people (*e.g.*, mentally disabled, people with AIDS, criminals, or people of certain ethnicity) would also deny their reproductive freedom.

B. *Obligations to take action to secure and safeguard the freedom in question*

- Governments should enact and strictly enforce laws that prohibit child marriages. Girls who marry early do not only become pregnant early but they also tend to have more children and at shorter intervals (which may impair their health and the right to education) than the ones who marry later. Through the enforcement of a minimum age of marriage (not less than 15 and preferably 18 years of age) adolescent pregnancies can be prevented. Equalising the legal minimum age requirement for marriage of women and men and with the legal majority age can promote gender equality.
- States should legally prohibit and take necessary measures to eradicate polygamy which is counterproductive to gender equality and which can impair women's' reproductive freedom. Registration of marriages should be enforced.[68]
- States should eradicate practices reflecting preference for sons. This can be done by for instance: 1. Enactment of legislation which enables women to maintain their maiden name and to pass it to their children so that the desire, where it exists, to continue the family name is fulfilled. 2. Enactment of legislation which guarantees social security for elderly people in order to free them from dependence upon economic support from their sons.
- The use of technology which makes it possible for individuals and couples to determine the sex of the foetus, and which is likely to result in selective abortion of female foetuses, should be prohibited by domestic law.
- Sterilisation should be legally regulated. Legal norms should guarantee free and informed consent of the person concerned.
- Victims of forced sterilisation should be granted compensation.
- In the light of new developments in biomedicine governments can be obliged to make treatment of infertility available under certain circumstances.
- Governments should ensure access to remedy for women affected by discriminatory laws, practices or policies.

**2. The right to decide freely and responsibly on the number and spacing of children**

- Governments must not interfere in a person's decisions with regard to the number of desired children, neither their spacing. It must not prescribe a determined number of children per family.

---

[68] CEDAW identified, for example, during its review of the initial report of Namibia in 1997 polygamous marriages and non-registration of customary marriages as issues of concern. It recommended, furthermore, during the same session that the Government of Bangladesh takes measures to enforce laws prohibiting child marriages and polygamy.

- A government would be in breach of its obligations if, for example, care facilities, health subsidies, maternity leave and access to land in rural areas are conditioned by compliance with state-imposed restrictions on the number of children.

  However, governments may enjoy a certain margin of discretion as to establishing some requirements for responsible parenthood.
- Availability of contraceptives should be guaranteed to the whole population in order to make it possible for individuals to exercise the right to responsible parenthood consciously.

**3. The right to life, to bodily integrity and to health**

- The right to life and to health should entitle women to have access to reproductive health services. A state must not, in other words, prohibit or in practical ways obstruct individuals from accessing family planning services. Following my assertion that abortion should be considered as an emerging right in international law, the corresponding duty on the state would then imply an obligation to liberalise abortion laws and to provide safe and free abortions at the early stages of pregnancy. Actions should be taken for the decriminalisation of women who have undergone illegal abortion.
- States should guarantee women freedom from sexual violence by, *e.g.*, the criminalisation in domestic law of marital rape. Every state should ensure that forced pregnancy is a criminal offence, whether committed during war or peace, and whether the perpetration is a private person or a state agent.
- Governments should prosecute perpetrators of war crimes and crimes against humanity (including reproductive crimes) and individuals who are engaged in practices of sexual slavery and equivalent institutions.
- The 1951 Refugee Convention and the 1967 Protocol thereto, should be extended to include gender-based violence as a ground for granting refugee status. States parties to these documents should, in other words, grant refugee status to those girls and women who have suffered, or have a well-founded fear of suffering, sexual violence and/or other forms of gender-based discrimination because of their race, religion, nationality, political opinion or membership in a particular social group, when the government of their country of origin is unwilling or unable to protect them from reproductive crimes.

**4. The right to access to family planning information and education**

- A government must not impede an individual from seeking and receiving the desired information concerning family planning methods and services, including information about abortion.

Increasingly the right to information has been understood as an obligation for governments to *provide* information and quality counselling for women and adolescents, including the risks of unwanted pregnancy. Such information must be accessible.

Since reproductive behaviour can be influenced through education, states should enforce compulsory sex education in school curricula.

Finally, the point can be made that a state's international obligations in relation to reproductive freedom may require both negative and positive action on its part.

A state must not, for instance, obstruct access to information on family planning methods and services but should undertake public education programmes. From what has been said it is easy to see clearly the manifold interrelationships between a wide range of human rights, their interconnectedness and that the notion of reproductive freedom crosses traditional dichotomies. Dispensing with such a dichotomization of human rights/freedoms largely reflects social reality.

Apart from the above very brief review of concrete state obligations which are required in regard to reproductive freedom, the creation of conditions for its full realisation may necessitate much more demanding, comprehensive, complicated and long-term actions on the part of governments. The transformation of patriarchal social structures, which are likely to obstruct its *de facto* enjoyment, is one such example. This author hopes to have been able to demonstrate that the asymmetrical approach to equality has great potential in challenging the gender hierarchy, which forms the base for women's inequality.

A further challenge is to move beyond the mere exposition of gender aspects of human rights and humanitarian law to actual accountability for their violation.

## 9.3. Monitoring the Implementation of Human Rights and Humanitarian Law Obligations

### *9.3.1. Generally*

For more than 50 years the international community has witnessed impressive and consistent norm-setting activity and legal changes in the area of human rights and humanitarian law. Hardly any other branch of international law is able to display more norms and institutions. Yet the UN spends less than 2 per cent of its budget (except for the expenses on relief for refugees)[69] on human rights and the legal situation generally remains unimpressive, principally because the international standards have not been translated into practice and they have not been implemented in a satisfactory manner so that their credibility is fully endorsed. Thus, the implementation and enforcement of human rights and humanitarian law still depends greatly on voluntary compliance[70] and political pressure. The true effectiveness of an international norm lies consequently in the extent to which states apply it at the national level.[71]

---

69 *D. Manasian*, The conscience of mankind, p. 5.

70 René Cassin, one of the drafters of the UDHR, has remarked that "the key to the effectiveness of the Universal Declaration of Human Rights is to be found in a loyal collaboration between States and the United Nations and its specialised agencies". *A. Jacques*, Human Rights at the expense of realism, Human Rights Monitor 1998, No. 41, p. 1.

71 In the words of Professor Theo van Boven: "International procedures can never be considered as substitutes for national mechanisms and national measures with the aim to give effect to human rights standards. Human rights have to be implemented first and foremost at national local levels. The primary responsibility of States to realize human rights *vis-à-vis* the people who live under the jurisdiction of these States". *T. van Boven*, The International System of Human Rights: An Overview, in UN Manual on Human Rights Reporting, New York 1991, p. 10.

Their successful implementation at the international level depends on, as the late Professor Richard Lillich has explained, in addition to the normative quality of the rules, "their accompanying procedural or enforcement methodologies".[72] Most of the human rights monitoring bodies at the universal as well as at the regional level have developed general criteria for human rights compliance[73] as well as various mechanisms for monitoring, *i.e.*, periodic public debates, examinations of periodic state reports, complaint procedures, *ex officio* investigations by expert committees or special rapporteurs.

### *9.3.2. Institutions and Procedures*

The following comments and recommendations concern the United Nations' activities with regard to monitoring the implementation of human rights and humanitarian law. Some of the critical standpoints were, however, of relevance to the regional systems for the protection of human rights and which have been reviewed in more detail in the previous parts of this study.

#### *9.3.2.1. Charter-based Organs*

All the principal organs of the UN perform functions in the field of human rights. The charter-based organs have a broad mandate and every member state of the organization is an "actual or potential respondent or client"[74] regardless of its specific treaty obligations.

The Security Council, which is entrusted with the primary responsibility for the maintenance of international peace and security, has increasingly begun to take decisions with implications for human rights and humanitarian law. It may take and has done so, as this study has shown, enforcement measures under Chapter VII and Article 2.7. In fact, however, the situations in which the Security Council could act to safeguard human rights and humanitarian law were very few. Having failed to take action to halt the atrocities (including systematic and repeated rape of thousands of women and young girls) on the territory of the former Yugoslavia and in Rwanda, the Security Council took steps to hold the violators accountable. But despite its condemnation of violations of international humanitarian law (including rape) committed during the Gulf War, a Tribunal was not set up to bring the responsible to justice. For reasons of such selectivity, among others, this author is not supportive of the idea of the "mutation" of this highly political and to power relations sensitive organ into the main human rights deterrence organ.

---

[72] ILA, First Report of the Committee on International Human Rights Law and Practice, London 1996, p. 338.

[73] The framework for monitoring compliance with the human rights obligations under the Women's Convention, *e.g.*, comprises according to *Tomaševski* the following four levels: "adherence to international human rights standards, their transformation into domestic law, their implementation in governmental policy and practice, and identification and adjudication of discrepancies between international human rights law and domestic practice". *K. Tomaševski*, A Primer on CEDAW, p. 10.

[74] *O.W. Thiis*, The International Human Rights Machinery, in Manual on Human Rights Monitoring, Norwegian Institute of Human Rights, Oslo 1997, Chapter 2, p. 10.

The supreme governing body of the organization, the General Assembly, has paid increasing attention to the human rights of women during the general debate and has passed resolutions on several aspects of the human rights of women. Although human rights are presently of concern for the whole UN, most of the organizations' discussion and action have taken place in the Commission on Human Rights. For monitoring states' compliance with human rights obligations for states that are not parties to human rights treaties of relevance to this survey, the activities of the UN Commission on the Status of Women[75] and the UN Commission on Human Rights are, in other words, of special significance. Worthy to be quoted once again is resolution 1993/8, which was adopted without dissent by the Human Rights Commission, and which stated for the first time in the history of humanitarian law that rape is an international crime. However, both commissions are political organs. They are thus composed of representatives of governments, which requires that the role of NGOs in the monitoring process as representatives for civil society be strengthened. NGOs in a consultative status should, *e.g.*, be allowed to participate also during that part of the Commission on Human Rights closed sessions when human rights violations are revised. NGOs may ensure a better integration of women's perspective on human rights protection and their knowledge of reality makes a concrete contribution to the process of implementing international human rights and humanitarian law standards.

The special procedures mechanisms of the Commission, *i.e.*, special rapporteurs and working groups, should pay greater attention to the gender dimension especially in identifying gender-specific violations and formulating appropriate responses.[76] A gender perspective must in other words become an integral part of the on-going reporting.[77] Although the issue of women is increasingly being incorporated in the activities of the special rapporteurs, very few[78] of the special rapporteurs on country situations have as yet included specific human rights and humanitarian law violations affecting girls and women in their reports. Most of the information in the country specific reports focus, moreover, on violence against women, and important aspects of reproductive freedom were as a rule excluded.

---

[75] In addition to the Commission's procedure for the purposes of identifying specific situations in which women need redress, responsibility for monitoring progress on the Beijing Platform for Action is vested, furthermore, with the Commission. In March 1996 the CSW discussed its schedule for consideration of the implementation of the strategies and objectives in critical areas of concern. Women's human rights, the girl child and violence against women were discussed in 1998 and family planning in the context of reproductive health will be considered in 1999.

[76] UN Doc. E/CN.4/1998/122, p. 21.

[77] See Res.1993/46 of 8 March 1993 adopted by the UN Commission on Human Rights. It urges the special rapporteurs and working groups on various human rights to supply information on women's issues in their investigations. It has been suggested, furthermore, that gender-specific reporting and analysis should entail an examination of the effects of gender on "the form which a human rights violation takes, the circumstances in which a violation occurs; the consequences of that violation for the victim and the availability and accessibility of remedies". *D. Sullivan & S. Abeyesekera*, Integration of Women's Human Rights into the Work of the Special Rapporteurs, UNIFEM 1996, p. 4.

[78] See, for example, the Report on the Human Rights Situation in the Islamic Republic of Iran and the reports on Afghanistan and Equatorial Guinea.

The special rapporteurs should more frequently asses the compatibility of domestic law and practice under review affecting women's human rights with international law, including humanitarian law.

Violations of women's human rights by non-state actors and the scope of state responsibility for those abuses should regularly be addressed.

Each succeeding report should include information on governmental response to prior recommendations concerning women's human rights.[79]

There is still a need for an improved response mechanism on an urgent basis with regard to allegations regarding women's human rights. The establishment of the High Commissioner for Human Rights, who is the UN official with principal responsibility for the human rights activities of the organization, constitutes one important first step towards "quicker response and a more preventive system".[80] The Commissioner is thus vested with the power to remedy violations of human rights norms as well as to play an active role in their prevention. The High Commissioner has established a Human Rights Hot Line with the purpose of assisting the Centre for Human Rights to monitor and react rapidly to human rights emergencies. The Line will be available to victims of human rights violations, their relatives and NGOs. Despite some of the above mentioned progressive developments increased attention from the Commissioner to gender issues is still very much needed. Although Mary Robinson, the present High Commissioner for Human Rights, has raised issues relating to the promotion of the rights of women, her first report to the Commission on Human Rights[81] is disappointing. Section E of the report, which has been entirely devoted to gender and the human rights of women, mentions reproductive health only on one occasion and in a very limited context, *i.e.*, the future cooperation between the High Commissioner's Office and the UNPF.

### *9.3.2.2. Treaty Bodies*

#### 9.3.2.2.1. Reporting Procedures

A number of specialised bodies have been created with the purpose to oversee implementation of the human rights conventions by governments, which have ratified them. The primary supervisory mechanism within the UN human rights treaty system is the process of periodic reporting on compliance. States are required to supply information at regular intervals to the six treaty bodies (committees) on the steps and specific measures they have taken to implement their treaty obliga-

---

[79] Amnesty International recommended recently that the special procedures provide more information on the implementation of their recommendations in their reports and draw appropriate conclusions. AI 1999 UN Commission on Human Rights, Making Human Rights Work: Time to Strengthen the Special Procedures. AI Index: IOR/41/01/99, p. 7. See also UN Doc. E/CN.4/1999/3, § 61.

[80] *M. Tardu*, The International Protection of Human Rights after Vienna: The Future of the United Nations Supervisory System, Acta Juridica Hungarica 1993, No. 1, p. 176. For a comment on the mandate of the High Commissioner for Human Rights see *T. Buergenthal*, International Human Rights, St. Paul 1995, pp. 95–97.

[81] UN Doc. E/CN.4/1998/122.

tions and to specify the difficulties they have experienced so far in the implementation of the provisions. One of the common problems that all these committees encounter is the failure of many states to comply with their reporting obligations.

Today participation in the treaty system is extensive. As of March 1999, 161 governments had ratified the Women's Convention and 191 were party to the Convention on the Rights of the Child. The ICCPR had received 140 ratifications and the ICESCR 137. Yet, no one can claim that the success of the monitoring system has been great. One reason is that the number of countries, whose reports are overdue, is constantly increasing. Others with poor human rights records have not submitted any report at all. Professor Alston pointed out in the earlier referred to study on the effective operation of the treaty monitoring bodies that non-reporting has reached chronic proportions.[82] Periodicity seems, furthermore, to be too burdensome for developing countries, especially for those, which do not have the necessary technical, administrative or financial resources. In the light of the current situation it is obvious that the existing reporting system is unsustainable and this author is, therefore, in favour of the idea of consolidated reports based on guidelines tailored to each state's situation and that the number of treaty bodies be reduced (by consolidation).[83] Opponents of the proposal tend to focus mainly on the risk that such a body would adopt a lowest common denominator for judging compliance with human rights obligations.[84] One could also argue, on the contrary, that depending on the mandate of this "super body" there is an equal chance of raising the standard of states' compliance with existing treaty obligations. The creation of a Permanent International Court on Human Rights is an old idea[85] whose time has thus come. The Court should be given power to undertake certain functions relating to the UN Charter and other instruments affecting human rights. It should deal with individual petitions arising from all the six core human rights treaties.[86] Such a body would counteract the disturbing tendency of increased politicisation of human rights issues within, for example, the activities of the extra conventional bodies, such as the Commission on Human Rights. Thus, efforts must be made to advance the objectivity in the way situations are dealt with.

---

[82] See also ILA, Committee on International Human Rights Law and Practice, p. 347. The suggestion made during the meeting of the chairpersons of human rights treaty bodies in 1998 that there is sufficient basis, in both law and policy, to support the consideration of a situation in a country even in the absence of a report, once a repeated request had failed to persuade the government in question to fulfil its treaty obligation, seems therefore reasonable.

[83] The UN Secretary-General presented an analytical report of the comments and observations received from governments, specialised agencies and NGOs on the above proposal made by Professor Alston to the 54th session of the Human Rights Commission in 1998. Several governments, as well as some of the committees, were negative to the prospect of a possible merger between the supervisory bodies.

[84] See for example the comment on that issue expressed by Mr. Kamminga during the ILA's 67th Conference. The statement is reproduced in ILA, Report of the 67th Conference Helsinki, London 1996, p. 364.

[85] *R.S. Clark*, A United Nations High Commissioner for Human Rights, The Hague 1972, p. 40; *R. Müllerson*, The efficiency of individual complaint procedures: the experience of CCPR, CERD, CAT and ECHR, in Monitoring Human Rights in Europe, A. Bloed *et al.* (eds.), p. 43.

[86] ILA, First Report of the Committee on International Human Rights Law and Practice, p. 357.

Moreover, since states reports contain to a great extent self-evaluation and are "self-serving" the role of NGOs can and should be greatly enhanced in regard to their active participation in the monitoring process of the treaty bodies.[87] Very often the information contained in the country reports is limited to existing domestic legal provisions. Securing reproductive freedom and achieving gender equality entails obligations for the public authorities, which reach far beyond a legal prohibition of discrimination. Therefore, independent non-governmental sources of complementary information, especially on the actual conditions of women and girls in a country, are crucial in monitoring state compliance with their obligations and should be encouraged by the international community.

Today only CRC, CAT[88] and CESCR are strictly speaking entitled to receive information from NGOs. These Committee's rules of procedure provide for formal involvement by NGOs in their work. According to Article 22 of the Women's Convention, there is a possibility mainly for the specialised agencies[89] to influence the activities of CEDAW. Bearing in mind that the majority of women who are working for the full realisation of human rights standards are still involved on a grass-root level, *i.e.*, they are involved in the activities of national NGOs, there should be no formal legal obstacle for NGOs to provide reports on state compliance directly to CEDAW.[90]

In addition to the above, NGO presence is important at the sessions of the human rights supervisory bodies, since its members, for example, the members of CEDAW, are often closely connected with their respective governmental authorities and the impartiality of these persons can be therefore questioned.[91]

---

[87] The need for corrective information was emphasised already in 1980 at the session of the Third Committee of the United Nations GA dealing with social, humanitarian and cultural questions. See *L. Reanda*, Human Rights and Women's Rights: The United Nations Approach, HRQ 1981, Vol. 3, p. 16.

The important role of the NGOs was once more recognised by the Vienna World Conference on Human Rights in 1993. See § 38 of the Vienna Declaration, UN Doc. A/CONF.157/23, p. 12.

[88] CAT, Rules of Procedure, UN Doc. CAT/C/3/Rev.1, Rule 62. See furthermore *A. Byrnes*, The Committee against Torture, in The United Nations and Human Rights, A Critical Appraisal, P. Alston (ed.), Oxford 1992, p. 524; *V. Dimitrijevic*, The monitoring of human rights and the prevention of human rights violations through reporting procedures, in Monitoring Human Rights in Europe, A. Bloed *et al.* (eds.), p. 19.

[89] NGOs are, however, allowed to be present at the sessions of CEDAW, but they have no mandate to participate in the discussions. See on this issue *R. Jacobson,* The Committee on the Elimination of Discrimination against Women, in The United Nations and Human Rights, A Critical Appraisal, P. Alston (ed.), p. 466; *M.K. Eriksson*, Non-Governmental Organizations, in Manual on Human Rights Monitoring, Chapter 4, Oslo 1997, pp. 3–5.

[90] In can be noted here that CEDAW requested the Secretariat in 1992 to include in its publication *Women 2000* an invitation to NGOs to provide members of the Committee with information for their use. UN General Assembly, 46th session, UN Doc. A/46/38, Chapter V, Section 8.

[91] In 1986 twelve of the nominees were members of the respective governments' ministries or are in their countries diplomatic service. See *R. Jacobson,* p. 472. The Swedish member of CEDAW, Mr. Johan Nordenfeldt, was, *e.g.*, at the time of his membership on the Committee (1982–1984), employed at the Swedish Ministry for Foreign Affairs. Citizens of the former communist countries in Eastern Europe and who were members of CEDAW were mainly government employees, and because of their dependence on their respective country's government they have for a very long time opposed the competence of CEDAW to adopt general recommendations. The first General Recommendation was

Finally, it should be noted that the concluding observations on the country reports made by the various human rights committees and which identify difficult areas for the state in question to meet its substantive treaty obligations have become, as this study has illustrated, increasingly but not yet sufficiently gender sensitive.

The treaty bodies should ensure therefore that a gender perspective be incorporated into the new general comments on the interpretation of the particular treaty provisions, recommendations and guidelines as well as into the revised comments. The preparation of a joint general comment on gender equality by CEDAW should be also encouraged.

Many states have entered reservations upon ratification of the core human rights treaties, which undoubtedly places an inhibition upon the extent of the examination of the periodic reports. It is, therefore, important that the procedures for dealing with the profusion of reservations by the committees are improved. States should be questioned on their reservations and they should be encouraged to withdraw reservations that are incompatible with the object and purpose of the treaty, *e.g.*, certain reservations to the non-discrimination provisions and more specifically to Article 16 of the Women's Convention which undermine respect for reproductive freedom. It is encouraging that the six chairpersons of the monitoring treaty bodies at their 9th session in February 1998 expressed support for the approach followed by the HRC in its GC No. 24. The chairpersons affirmed that the capacity of a monitoring body to perform its function of determining the scope of the provisions of the relevant convention cannot be performed effectively if it is precluded from exercising a similar function in relation to reservations.[92]

9.3.2.2.2. Complaint Procedures

Complaint procedures are an additional method of monitoring compliance with international human rights standards. At the time of writing such procedures are available under three of the six core human rights treaties and all of them are optional. Many states that ratify the treaties still refuse to permit individual complaints.[93] Another serious shortcoming of the system is that the potential to lodge petitions is under-utilised. The existing procedures still attract very few claims. An average of not more than 40–50 cases per year has been registered by the HRC since the beginning of the 1990s. The Committee has expressed about 25 views per

---

adopted as late as in 1986 at the fifth session of CEDAW. During CEDAW meetings members' representatives of the above mentioned countries have regularly consulted diplomats from their respective countries.

[92] It should be noted here that a resolution (1998/13) on this issue was adopted by the Sub-Commission at its 50th session in 1998. The Sub-Commission decided to ask Ms. Hampson to prepare a working paper on "the question of reservations to human rights treaties, including examination of the number and scope of such reservations, their impact on the scope of the obligation accepted by States, reservations to the procedural provisions of human rights treaties, including opting out clauses, and the role and responsibility of monitoring bodies in relation to reservations to human rights treaties".

[93] As of June 1998, 93 states have accepted, *e.g.*, the HRC competence to review individual complaints

year. More disturbing is the fact that very few of the reviewed cases relate to gender issues and more specifically reproductive freedom. Clearly women and lawyers are not familiar with the existing procedures or ignore to use them in such matters. From that it follows that supervisory bodies should make it a priority to encourage more petitions, especially from women. The committees should hold for that purpose regional meetings with lawyers and local human rights defenders in order to explain the petition process.[94]

In addition to the above recommended measures, strengthening the implementation procedure under the Women's Convention and the ICESCR through the adoption of additional protocols extending the right of individual petition and inter-state complaint procedure under these conventions must be considered a matter of urgency.

#### 9.3.2.2.3. Monitoring Humanitarian Law

The present study has shown that human rights and humanitarian law are complementary and that the traditional view of a clear distinction between those branches of international law cannot be upheld unchallenged any longer. But while respect for human rights and their implementation has improved considerably during the 1980s and 1990s, international supervision of the implementation of international humanitarian law has remained rather sluggish and it would be no overstatement to suggest that despite the prospects of the imminent establishment of the ICC, it is still very weak and underdeveloped. There is simply no centralised and effective system for implementing sanctions. Humanitarian law places emphasis on cooperation between the parties to an armed conflict and a neutral intermediary with a view to prevent violations. Apart from the International Humanitarian Fact-Finding Commission[95] and some regional arrangements, a key role for the monitoring of respect for humanitarian law has been vested in the ICRC, which is designed to give assistance and protection in armed conflicts. The principles of neutrality and impartiality, which have to be regarded by the organization are, however, an obstacle for its effective monitoring.[96] It is apparent that there is currently a need for an improvement of the monitoring system. This author agrees with the opinion that the creation of a new, single monitoring and enforcement institution for situations of armed conflict and/or tensions and disturbances is not a realistic goal.[97] Instead,

---

[94] ILA, First Report of the Committee on International Human Rights Law and Practice, p. 355.

[95] It can be noted here that at the invitation of Switzerland, the state depository of the 1949 Geneva Conventions and their Additional Protocols, a conference was held in Bern in 1996 to elect the 15 members of the International Fact-Finding Commission, which according to Article 90 of the First Additional Protocol is competent to enquire into any facts alleged to be a grave breach of the Geneva Conventions or the first Protocol, and to use its good offices to restore "an attitude of respect for the Conventions and this Protocol". In addition, the Commission may institute an enquiry at the request of all parties to the conflict.

[96] In the view of Mr. Ramcharan a periodic reporting system is not necessarily incompatible with the functions of the ICRC. *B.G. Ramcharan*, A Reporting System for International Humanitarian Law?, in Essays in Honour of Judge Taslim Olawale Elias, E.G. Bello & Bola A. Ajibola, SAN (eds.), p. 131.

[97] *A. Rosas*, International monitoring mechanisms in situations of armed conflict, in Monitoring Human Rights in Europe, A. Bloed *et al.* (eds.), p. 244.

the existing human rights mechanisms should be used more frequently and in close cooperation with each other in monitoring the compliance with humanitarian law as well.

The UN Commission on Human Rights has, as this study has shown, on several occasions condemned violations of humanitarian law principles. It took, for example, at its 54th session in 1998 a particular stand against all violations of fundamental rights of women in situations of armed conflict, notably rape, sexual slavery and forced pregnancy. This gives us some hope.

I will conclude the present book as I began, with reference to the Universal Declaration of Human Rights, which celebrated its golden anniversary of 50 in 1998. The UN High Commissioner for Human Rights, Ms. Mary Robinson, has described it as "embodying the hopes and even the dreams of people still scared from two world wars, newly fearful of the Cold War and just beginning the great liberation of peoples, which came about with the dismantling of the European empires".[98] The present study has demonstrated that some of these dreams and hopes have become reality. The UN and the world have greatly changed, since the adoption of the Universal Declaration. There still remains, however, much scope for the positive evolution and adjustment of international human rights and humanitarian law to the needs of the female half of humanity.

---

[98] Turning 50, in Focus, Newsletter of HURIGHTS, Osaka, March 1998, p. 1.

# Abbreviations

| | |
|---|---|
| AI | artificial insemination |
| AJIL | American Journal of International Law |
| ASIL | American Society of International Law |
| | |
| BVerfG | Bundesverfassungsgericht |
| BYIL | British Yearbook of International Law |
| | |
| CAT | Committee Against Torture |
| CEDAW | Committee on the Elimination of Discrimination Against Women |
| CERD | Committee on the Elimination of Racial Discrimination |
| Cornell ILJ | Cornell International Law Journal |
| CSCE | Conference on Security and Cooperation in Europe |
| CESCR | Committee on Economic, Social and Cultural Rights |
| CRC | UN Committee on the Rights of the Child |
| | |
| DR | Decisions and Reports |
| | |
| EC | European Community |
| ECHR | European Court of Human Rights |
| ECJ | Court of Justice of the European Communities (European Court of Justice) |
| ECOSOC | UN Economic and Social Council |
| ECHR | European Court of Human Rights |
| *e.g.* | *exempli gratia* (for example) |
| EJIL | European Journal of International Law |
| ELR | European Law Review |
| ET | embryo transfer |
| *et al* | *et alia* (and others) |
| EU | European Union |
| | |
| FGM | Female genital mutilation |
| Fordham ILJ | Fordham International Law Journal |
| | |
| GA | UN General Assembly |
| GAOR | General Assembly Official Records |
| GYIL | German Yearbook of International Law |
| | |
| Harv.L.Rev. | Harvard Law Review |
| HRLJ | Human Rights Law Journal |
| HRQ | Human Rights Quarterly |

| | |
|---|---|
| *ibid.* | *ibidem* (the same as the previous citation) |
| ICESCR | International Covenant on Economic, Social and Cultural Rights |
| ICC | International Criminal Court |
| ICCPR | International Covenant on Civil and Political Rights |
| ICJ | International Court of Justice |
| ICLQ | International and Comparative Law Quarterly |
| ICPD | International Conference on Population and Development |
| ICRC | International Committee of the Red Cross |
| ICTY | International Criminal Tribunal for the Former Yugoslavia |
| ICTR | International Criminal Tribunal for Rwanda |
| *i.e.* | *id est* (that is to say) |
| IFOR | Peace Implementation Force (in former Yugoslavia) |
| IHRR | International Human Rights Reports |
| ILA | International Law Association |
| ILC | UN International Law Commission |
| ILM | International Legal Materials |
| *inter alia* | amongst others |
| IPPF | International Planned Parenthood Federation |
| IRRC | International Review of the Red Cross |
| Israel LR | Israel Law Review |
| IVF | *in vitro* fertilisation |
| IWRAW | International Women's Rights Action Watch |
| JO | Justitieombudsman |
| NATO | North Atlantic Treaty Organization |
| NGO | Non-governmental organization |
| NILR | Netherlands International Law Review |
| NJIL | Nordic Journal of International Law |
| NQHR | Netherlands Quarterly of Human Rights |
| NYUJILP | New York University Journal of International Law and Politics |
| OAS | Organization of American States |
| OAU | Organization of African Unity |
| *Op. cit.* | *opere citato* (in the work already cited) |
| OSCE | Organisation for Security and Cooperation in Europe |
| OXFAM | Oxford Committee for Famine Relief |
| PCIJ | Permanent Court of International Justice |
| Prop. | proposition (Swedish legislative bill) |
| RdC | Recueil des Cours de l'Académie de Droit International |

| | |
|---|---|
| SIDA | Swedish International Development Authority |
| SOU | Sveriges offentliga utredningar |
| SC | Security Council |
| SFOR | Stabilization Force |
| SvJT | Svensk Juristtidning |
| | |
| TfR | Tidskrift for Rettsvitenskap |
| TIAS | Treaties and Other International Acts Series |
| | |
| UNDP | United Nations Development Programme |
| UNFPA | United Nations Fund for Population Activities |
| UNHCR | United Nations High Commissioner for Refugees |
| UNIFEM | United Nations Fund for Women |
| UNICEF | United Nations International Children's Emergency Fund |
| UNPROFOR | United Nations Protection Force |
| UNTS | United Nations Treaty Series |
| | |
| Vand.JTL | Vanderbilt Journal of Transnational Law |
| VCLT | Vienna Convention on the Law of Treaties |
| Virginia JIL | Virginia Journal of International Law |
| | |
| WHO | World Health Organization |
| | |
| YJIL | Yale Journal of International Law |
| | |
| ZaöRV | Zeitschrift für ausländisches und öffentliches Recht und Völkerrecht |

# Bibliography

## *1. Official Documents*


*UN Security Council*

UN Security Council, Report to European Community Foreign Ministers, European Community investigative mission into the treatment of Muslim women in former Yugoslavia, S/25240, 3 February 1993.

UN Security Council, Letter dated 18 February from the permanent representative of Sweden to the United Nations addressed to the Secretary-General, S/25307, 18 February 1993.

UN Security Council, Report of the Secretary-General on the Establishment of the Commission of Experts on Rwanda Pursuant to Resolution 935 (1994), S/1994/879, 26 July 1994.

UN Security Council, Letter dated 1 October 1994 from the Secretary-General to the President of the Security Council transmitting the interim report of the Commission of Experts on the evidence of grave violations of international humanitarian law in Rwanda, including possible acts of genocide, S/1994/1125, 4 October 1994.

UN Security Council, Letter dated 9 December 1994 from the Secretary-General addressed to the President of the Security Council, S/1994/1405, 9 December 1994; Annex: Final Report of the Commission of Experts established pursuant to Security Council Resolution 935 (1994) (Rwanda).

UN Security Council, Report of the Secretary-General Pursuant to Paragraph 5 of Security Council Resolution 955 (1994), S/1995/134, 13 February 1995.

UN Security Council, Further Report of the Secretary-General Pursuant to Paragraph 5 of Security Council Resolution 955 (1994), S/1995/533, 30 June 1995.

UN Security Council, Third report of the Secretary-General reviewing progress made regarding arrangements for establishing the seat of the International Tribunal for Rwanda at Arusha, S/1995/741, 25 August 1995.

*UN General Assembly*

UN GA, Secretary-General, An Agenda for Peace: Peacemaking and Peace-Keeping, Report pursuant to the statement adopted by the Summit Meeting of the Security Council, January 31, New York, 1992.

UN GA, Secretary-General, Report pursuant to paragraph 2 of Security Council Resolution 808, Doc. S/2504, Add.1 of 3 May 1993.

UN GA, Report of the Secretary-General, Rape and abuse of women in the areas of armed conflict in former Yugoslavia, A/48/858, 29 January 1994.

UN GA, Report of the Secretary-General, Advancement of Women, A/49/349, 30 August 1994.

UN GA, Report of the Secretary-General, Sustainable Development and International Economic Cooperation, A/49/378, 12 September 1994.

UN GA, Supplement to an Agenda for Peace: Position Paper of the Secretary-General on the Occasion of the Fiftieth Anniversary of the United Nations, A/50/60, 3 January 1995.

UN GA, Report of the Secretary-General, Financing of the International Criminal Tribunal for the Prosecution of Persons Responsible for Genocide and Other Serious Violations of International Humanitarian Law Committed in the Territory of Rwanda and Rwandese Citizens Responsible for Genocide and other Such Violations Committed in the Territory of Neighbouring States Between 1 January and 31 December 1994, A/C.5/49/68, 29 June 1995.

UN GA, Secretary-General, Confronting New Changes, Report on the Work of the Organization from the 49th to the 50th Sessions of the General Assembly, A/50/1, 22 August 1995.

UN GA, Report of the Secretary-General, Implementation of the Outcome of the Fourth World Conference on Women: Action for Equality, Development and Peace, A/50/744, 10 November 1995.

UN GA, Report of the Secretary-General, financing of the International Criminal Tribunal for the Prosecution of Persons Responsible for Genocide and Other Serious Violations of International Humanitarian Law committed in the Territory of Rwanda, A/C.5/50/54, 11 March 1996.

UN GA, The 50th Anniversary, Annual Report on the Work of the Organization, from the 50th to the 51st Session of the General Assembly, A/51/1, 20 August 1996.

UN GA, Report of the Secretary-General, Advancement of Women, Traffic in women and girls, A/51/309, 27 August 1996.

UN GA, Report of the Secretary-General, Rape and abuse of women in the areas of armed conflict in the former Yugoslavia, A/51/557, 25 October 1996.

UN GA, Report of the Secretary-General, International Year of the Family, A/52/57, E/1997/4, 6 January 1997.

UN GA, UN Secretary-General, Kofi Annan, Renewing the United Nations: A Programme for Reform, A/51/950, 14 July 1997.

UN GA, Report of the International Tribunal for the Prosecution of Persons Responsible for Serious Violations of International Humanitarian Law Committed in the Territory of the Former Yugoslavia since 1991, A/52/375, S/1997/729, 18 September 1997.

UN GA, Report of the United Nations High Commissioner for Human Rights, Follow-up to the World Conference on Human Rights, A/53/372, 11 September 1998.

### *UN Commission on the Status of Women*

UN Commission on the Status of Women, Report of the Secretary-General, Review and Appraisal of the Implementation of the Nairobi Forward-Looking Strategies for the Advancement of Women, E/CN.6/1990/5, 22 November 1989.

UN Commission on the Status of Women, Report by the Secretary-General, Peace: Measures to eradicate violence against women in the family and society, E/CN.6/1994/4, 21 January 1994.

UN Commission on Status of Women, Report by the Secretary-General, Preparations for the fourth world conference on women: action for equality, development and peace, E/CN.6/1994/9, 7 February 1994.

UN Commission on the Status of Women, Report by the Secretary-General, Preparations for the fourth World Conference on Women: Action for Equality, Development and Peace, E/CN.6/1994/10, 2 March 1994.

UN Commission on the Status of Women, Report by the Secretary-General, Monitoring the implementation of the Nairobi Forward-Looking strategies for the advancement of women, 3 March 1994.

UN Commission on the Status of Women, African Platform for Action, E/CN.6/1995/5/Add.2, 29 December 1994.

UN Commission on the Status of Women, Jakarta Declaration and Plan of Action for the Advancement of Women in Asia and the Pacific, E/CN.6/1995/5/Add.1, 4 January 1995.

UN Commission on the Status of Women, Regional Programme of Action for the Women of Latin America and the Caribbean, 1995–2001, E/CN.6/1995/5/Add.3, 4 January 1995.

UN Commission on the Status of Women, Arab Plan of Action for the Advancement of Women to the Year 2000, E/CN.6/1995/5/Add.5, 23 February 1995.

UN, Commission on the Status of Women, Report of the Secretary-General, Second Review and Appraisal of the Implementation of the Nairobi Forward-Looking Strategies for the Advancement of Women, E/CN.6/1995/3, 10 January 1995; E/CN.6/1995/3/Add.3, 27 February 1995; E/CN.6/1995/9, 15 February 1995; E/CN.6/1995/3/Add.7, 14 March 1995.

UN, Commission on the Status of Women, Report of the Secretary-General, Peace: Women in International Decision-making, E/CN.6/1995/12, 21 February 1995.

UN, Commission on the Status of Women, Report of the 39th Session, E/CN.6/1995/14, 15 March–7 April 1995.

UN, Commission on the Status of Women, Report of the Secretary-General, Follow up to the Fourth World Conference on Women, Proposed System-wide Medium-term Plan for the Advancement of Women 1996–2001, E/CN.6/1996/CRP.2, 1996.

UN, Commission on the Status of Women, Report of the Secretary-General, Elaboration of a draft optional protocol to the Convention on the Elimination of All Forms of Discrimination against Women, E/CN.6/1996/10, 10 January 1996.

UN, Commission on the Status of Women, Report of the Secretary-General, Synthesized report on national action plans and strategies for implementation of the Beijing Platform for Action, 22 December 1997.

UN, Commission on the Status of Women, Report of the Secretary-General, Follow-up to the Fourth World Conference on Women: Implementation of Strategic Objectives and Action in the Critical Areas of Concern, E/CN.6/1998/5, 23 January 1998.

UN, Commission on the Status of Women, Report of the Secretary-General, Follow-up to the Fourth World Conference on Women, Thematic issues before the Commission on the Status of Women, E/CN.6/1999/4.

*UN Commission on Population and Development*

UN, Commission on Population and Development, Report of the Secretary-General, Concise report on world population monitoring, 1996: reproductive rights and reproductive health, E/CN.9/1996/2, 15 January 1996.

UN, Commission on Population and Development, Report of the Secretary-General, Activities of intergovernmental and non-governmental organizations in the area of reproductive rights and reproductive health, E/CN.9/1996/5, 19 January 1996.

*UN Economic and Social Council*

ECOSOC, Report of the Secretary-General, Protection of women and children in emergency and armed conflict in the struggle for peace, self-determination, national liberation and independence, E/CN.6/ 586, 1973.

ECOSOC, Commission on Human Rights, Report on the situation of human rights in the territory of the former Yugoslavia submitted by Mr. T. Mazowiecki, Special Rapporteur of the Commission on Human Rights, pursuant to Commission res. 1992/S–1/1 of August 1992, E/CN.4/1993/50.

ECOSOC, Commission on Human Rights, Fifth periodic report on the situation of human rights in the territory of the former Yugoslavia submitted by Mr. T. Mazowiecki, Special

Rapporteur of the Commission on Human Rights, pursuant to § 32 of the Commissions res. 1993/7 of 23 February 1993, E/CN.4/1994/47, 17 November 1993.

ECOSOC, Commission on Human Rights, Sixth periodic report on the situation of human rights in the territory of the former Yugoslavia submitted by Mr. T. Mazowiecki, Special Rapporteur of the Commission on Human Rights, pursuant to § 32 of the Commissions res. 1993/7 of 23 February 1993, E/CN.4/1994/110, 21 February 1994.

ECOSOC, Commission on Human Rights, Rape and abuse of women in the territory of the former Yugoslavia, Report of the Secretary-General, E/CN.4/1994/5, 30 June 1993.

ECOSOC, Commission on Human Rights, Drafting of a declaration on the right and responsibility of individuals, groups and organs of society to promote and protect universally recognized human rights and fundamental freedoms, E/CN.4/1994/81, 4 March 1994.

ECOSOC, Commission on Human Rights, Question of human rights of persons subjected to any form of detention or imprisonment, Preliminary report on opposition to the impunity of perpetrators of human rights violations (economic, social and cultural rights), prepared by Mr. Guissé and Mr. Joinet, pursuant to Sub-Commission res. 1993/37, E/CN.4/Sub.2/1994/11, 22 June 1994.

ECOSOC, Commission on Human Rights, Report on the situation of human rights in Rwanda submitted by Mr. René Degni-Ségui, Special Rapporteur of the Commission on Human Rights, E/CN.4/1995/7, 28 June 1994.

ECOSOC, Commission on Human Rights, The human rights dimensions of population transfer, including the implantation of settlers, Progress report prepared by Mr. A. Al-Khasawneh, Special Rapporteur, E/CN.4/Sub.2/1994/18, 30 June 1994.

ECOSOC, Commission on Human Rights, Report of the Second United Nations Regional Seminar on Traditional Practices Affecting the Health of Women and Children, E/CN.4/Sub.2/1994/10, 28 July 1994.

ECOSOC, Commission on Human Rights, Report on the sessional working group on the administration of justice and the question of compensation, E/CN.4/Sub.2/1994/22, 15 August 1994.

ECOSOC, Commission on Human Rights, Report on the situation of human rights in Rwanda submitted by Mr. René Degni-Ségui, Special Rapporteur of the Commission on Human Rights, E/CN.4/1995/12, 12 August 1994.

ECOSOC, Commission on Human Rights, Report of the Secretary-General, Human rights and bioethics, E/CN.4/1995/74, 15 November 1994.

ECOSOC, Commission on Human Rights, Report of the Special Rapporteur, Mr. Nigel S. Rodley, submitted pursuant to Commission on Human Rights resolution 1992/32, E/CN.4/1995/34, 12 January 1995.

ECOSOC, Commission on Human Rights, Report on the situation of human rights in Rwanda submitted by Mr. René Degni-Séqui, Special Rapporteur of the Commission on Human Rights, E/CN.4/1995/70, 11 November 1994 and E/CN.4/1995/71, 17 January 1995.

ECOSOC, Commission on Human Rights, Preliminary report submitted by the Special Rapporteur on violence against women, its causes and consequences, Ms. R. Coomaraswamy, in accordance with Commission on Human Rights res. 1994/45; E/CN.4/1995/42, 22 November 1994.

ECOSOC, Commission on Human Rights, Report of the United Nations High Commissioner for Human Rights, Mr. José Ayala Lasso, E/CN.4/1995/98, 15 February 1995.

ECOSOC, Commission on Human Rights, Final periodic report on the situation of human rights in the territory of the former Yugoslavia submitted by Mr. T. Mazowiecki, E/CN.4/1996/9, 22 August 1995.

ECOSOC, Commission on Human Rights, Report of the Special Rapporteur on the situation of human rights in Rwanda, E/CN.4/1996/68, 29 January 1996.

ECOSOC, Commission on Human Rights, Report of the Special Rapporteur on Violence against Women, its causes and consequences, Ms. R. Coomaraswamy, Report on the mission of the Special Rapporteur to Poland on the issue of trafficking and forced prostitution of women, E/CN.4/1997/47/Add.1, 10 December 1996.

ECOSOC, Commission on Human Rights, Report on the mission of the Special Rapporteur to Brazil on the issue of domestic violence, Ms. R.Coomaraswamy, E/CN.4/1997/47/Add.2, 21 January 1997.

ECOSOC, Commission on Human Rights, Report of the Special Rapporteur on Violence against Women, Ms. R. Coomaraswamy, E/CN.4/1997/47/Add.4, 30 January 1997.

ECOSOC, Commission on Human Rights, Report on the mission of the Special Rapporteur to South Africa on the issue of rape in the community, E/CN.4/1997/47/Add.3, 24 February 1997.

ECOSOC, Commission on Human Rights, Report of the Special Rapporteur on Violence against Women, its causes and consequences, Ms. R.Coomaraswamy, E/CN.4/1997/47, 12 February 1997.

ECOSOC, Commission on Human Rights, Report of the Secretary-General on Minimum humanitarian standards, E/CN.4/1998/87, 5 January 1998.

ECOSOC, Commission on Human Rights, Report of the Special Rapporteur on Violence against Women, its causes and consequences, E/CN.4/1998/54, 26 January 1998.

ECOSOC, Commission on Human Rights, Report of the Special Rapporteur on violence against women on the mission in Rwanda on the issues of Violence against Women in situations of armed conflict, E/CN.4/1998/54/Add.1, 4 February 1998.

### *UN Sub-Commission on Prevention of Discrimination and Protection of Minorities*

Sub-Commission on Prevention of Discrimination and Protection of Minorities, Final report of the Special Rapporteur on traditional practices affecting the health of women and children, E/CN.4/Sub.2/1996/6, 14 June 1996.

Sub-Commission on Prevention of Discrimination and Protection of Minorities, Contemporary Forms of Slavery, Preliminary report presented by Ms. L.Chavez, E/CN.4/Sub.2/1996/26, 16 July 1996.

Sub-Commission on Prevention of Discrimination and Protection of Minorities, Revised Set of Basic Principles and Guidelines on the Right to Reparation for Victims of Gross Violations of Human Rights and Humanitarian Law, prepared by Mr. Theo van Boven, E/CN.4/Sub.2/1996/17, 24 May 1996.

Sub-Commission on the Prevention of Discrimination and Protection of Minorities, Report on systematic rape, sexual slavery and slavery-like practices during armed conflict, E/CN.4/Sub.2/1998/13, 22 June 1998.

### *International Law Commission*

UN GA, International Law Commission, Eleventh report on the draft code of crimes against peace and security of mankind by Mr. D. Thiam, Special Rapporteur, "Draft Statute of an International Criminal Court", A/CN.4/449, 25 March 1993.

UN GA, International Law Commission, Twelfth report on the draft code of crimes against the peace and security of mankind by Mr. D. Thiam, Special Rapporteur, A/CN.4/460, 15 April 1994.

UN GA, International Law Commission, Report of the ILC on the Work of its Forty-sixth Session, A/49/10, 2 May–22 July 1994.

UN GA, Report of the International Law Commission on the work of its forty-eight session, A/51/10, 1996.
UN GA, Report of the International Law Commission on the work of its forty-ninth session, A/52/10, 1997.
UN GA, Report of the International Law Commission on the work of its fiftieth session, A/53/10 and Corr.1, 1998.
UN GA, International Law Commission, First Report on State Responsibility, A/CN.4/490 and Adds. 1–6, 1998.
UN GA, International Law Commission, Third Report of the Special Rapporteur on the Definition of Reservations, A/CN.4/491 and Adds. 1–6, 1998.

## *2. Table of Cases*

### *2.1. International*

### 2.1.1. PCIJ and ICJ

#### A. The Permanent Court of International Justice

Advisory Opinion on *Settlers of German Origin in the Territory Ceded by Germany to Poland*, PCIJ (1923), Ser. B, No. 6.
Advisory Opinion on *Minority Schools in Albania*, PCIJ (1935), Ser. A/B, No. 64.

#### B. The International Court of Justice

*Reservations to the Genocide Convention,* ICJ Rep. 1951.
*Anglo-Iranian Oil Co.,* Judgment of 22 July 1952, ICJ Rep. 1952.
*South West Africa (Second Phase),* Judgment of 18 July 1966, ICJ Rep. 1966.
*Barcelona Traction, Light and Power Co. Ltd. Case* (Belgium v. Spain), Judgment of 5 February 1970, ICJ Rep. 1970.
*US Diplomatic and Consular Staff in Tehran*, ICJ Rep. 1980.
*Military and Paramilitary Activities in and Against Nicaragua* (Nicaragua v. United States), ICJ Rep. 1986.
*East Timor (Portugal v. Australia)*, Judgment of 30 June 1995, ICJ Rep. 1995.
Case concerning application of the Convention on the prevention and punishment of the crime of genocide, (*Bosnia-Herzegovina v. Yugoslavia*), Preliminary Objections, 11 July 1996, General List No. 91. <http://www.law.cornell.edu/icj/icj4/judgment.htm>
Advisory Opinion on Namibia, ICJ Rep. 1971.
*Order on Request for the Indication of Provisional Measures in Case Concerning Application of the Convention on the Prevention and Punishment of the Crime of Genocide (Bosnia-Herzegovina v. Yugoslavia (Serbia and Montenegro),* ICJ Reports of Judgments, Advisory Opinions and Orders, Order of April 8, 1993.

### 2.1.2. International Tribunal for the Prosecution of Persons Responsible for Serious Violations of International Humanitarian Law Committed in the Territory of Former Yugoslavia since 1991

Case No. IT-94-1-D, *In the Matter of A Proposal for a Formal Request for Deferral to the Competence of the International Tribunal in the Matter of Duško Tadić (Pursuant to Rules 9 and 10 of the Rules of Procedure and Evidence*), 8 November 1994; Case No. IT-94-1-I, indictment of 13 February 1995 against D. Tadić and G. Borovnica/Responsibility for the killings within and outside the Omarska camp between May and August 1992; amended No. IT-94-1-T, 1 September 1995 and No. IT-94-1-T, 14 December 1995.

Case No. IT-95-4-I, indictment of 13 February 1995 against 19 members of the Serb forces (*Z. Meakić et al.*) who were commanders, guards or others responsible for the conditions and mistreatment of prisoners in the Omarska camp between May and August 1992.
Case No. IT-95-4-D, *Prosecutor's application for deferral of criminal proceedings against 27 accused (i.e., military and political Bosnian Croat leaders) to investigate on crimes against the Muslim population in the Lašva River valley area allegedly committed between September 1992 and June 1993*, 21 April 1995.
Case No. IT-95-5-D, *In the Matter of a Proposal for a Formal Request for Deferral to the Competence of the Tribunal Addressed to the Republic of Bosnia-Herzegovina in respect to Radovan Karadžić, Ratko Mladić and Mico Stanisić*, 16 May 1995.
Case No. IT-95-6-D, *In the Matter of a Proposal for a Formal Request for Deferral to the Competence of the Tribunal Addressed to the Republic of Bosnia-Herzegovina in respect to Crimes Against the Population of the Lašva River Valley*, 11 May 1995.
Case No. IT-95-9-I, *Miljković and Others, Bosanski Šamac*, indictment of 21 July 1995.
Case No. IT-95-10, *Jelisić and Cesić*, "*Brčko*", indictment of 21 July 1995, amended No. IT-95-10-PT, 3 March 1998.
Case No. IT-95-8, *Sikirica and Others, "Keraterm",* indictment of 21 July 1995.
Case No. IT-95-5, *Karadžić and Mladić*, indictment of 25 July 1995, *Review of the Indictment Pursuant to Rule 61*, Nos. IT-95-5-R61 and IT-95-18-R61, 11 July 1996.
Case No. IT-94-1-AR72 , *Prosecutor v. Duško Tadić*, Appeal on Jurisdiction, Decision of 2 October 1995.
Case No. IT-94-2-R61, *Nikolić, Review of the Indictment Pursuant to Rule 61*, Decision of 20 October 1995.
Case No. IT-95-17/1-PT, *Furundžija, Lašva River Valley*, indictment of 10 November 1995, amended 2 June 1998.
Case No. IT-95-13-R61, *Mile Msksić, Miroslav Radić, and Veselin Sljivančanin, Review of the Indictment Pursuant to Rule 61 of the Rules of Procedure and Evidence*, Trial Chamber, Judgment 13 April 1996.
Case No. IT-96-21, *Delalić and Others, Celebići Camp*, indictment of 21 March 1996.
Case No. IT-96-23, *Gagović and Others, Foča*, indictment of 26 June 1996; amended No. IT-96-23-I, 13 July 1998.
*International Arrest Warrants and Orders for Surrender for Radovan Karadžić and Ratko Mladić*, 11 July, 1996.
Case No. IT-97-24, *Kovačević and Drljaca*, indictment of 13 March 1997.
Case IT-94-1-T , *Prosecutor v. Tadić*, Opinion and Judgment of 7 May 1997.
Case No. IT-96-23A, *Prosecutor v. Erdemović*, Appeals Chamber Judgment of 7 October 1997.
Case No. IT-95-13-AR108 bis, *Prosecutor v. Blaškic*, Appeals Chamber Judgment of 29 October 1997.
Case No. IT-96-21-T, *Prosecutor v. Delalić and Others*, Judgment of 16 November 1998.
Case No. IT-95-17/1-T, *Prosecutor v. Furundžija*, Judgment of 10 December 1998.

### 2.1.3. The International Criminal Tribunal for Rwanda

Case No. ICTR-96-15-T, *Prosecutor v. Kanyabashi*, Decision on Jurisdiction of 18 June 1997.
Case No. ICTR-97-21-I, *Nyiramasuhuko and Ntahobali*, indictment of 26 May 1997.
Case No. ICTR-96-4-T, *Prosecutor v. Akayesu*, indictment of 13 February 1996, amended No. ICTR-96-4-I, 17 June 1997; Judgment 2 September 1998.
Case No. ICTR-97-23-S, *Prosecutor v. Kambanda*, Judgment of 4 September 1998.

### 2.1.4. The UN Human Rights Committee

*Aumeeruddy S.-Cziffra et al. v. Mauritius*, Communication No. 35/1987, Decision 9 April 1981, Selected Decisions under the Optional Protocol, Vol. I, New York 1985, pp. 67–72.

*Ato Avellanal v. Peru*, Communication No. 202/1986, Decision of 28 October 1988, UN Doc. A/44/40, p. 196 *et seq*.

*Broeks S.W.M. v. The Netherlands*, Communication No.172/1984, Decision of 9 April 1987, UN Doc. A/42740, p. 139 *et seq*.

*Danning L.G. v. The Netherlands*, Communication No. 180/1984, Decision of 16 April 1987, CCPR/C/29/D/180/1984.

*Gueye and Others v. France*, UN Doc. A/44/40, p. 189 *et seq*.

*Hertzberg L. R. v. Finland*, Communication No. 61/1979, Decision of 2 April 1982, HRC Selected Decisions under the Optional Protocol, Vol. I, pp. 124–127.

*Lovelace S. v. Canada*, Communication No. 24/1977, Decision of 18 April 1979, UN Doc. A/36/40, p. 166 *et seq*.

*Pauger v. Austria*, Communication No. 415/1990, Decision of 26 March 1992, UN Doc. A/47/40.

*Toonen vs. Australia*, Communication No. 488/1992, UN Doc. CCPR/C/50/D/488/1992, Decision of 31 March 1994.

*Vos v. The Netherlands*, Communication No. 218/1986, Decision of 1989, UN Doc. A/44/40, p. 232*et seq*.

*Zwaan F.H. de Vriez v. The Netherlands*, Communication No.182/1984; Decision of 9 April 1987, Selected Decisions of the HRC under the Optional Protocol, Vol. 2, p. 209.

### 2.1.5. CERD

*Yilmaz-Dogan v. The Netherlands*, Communication No. 1/1984, A/43/1988, p. 59 *et seq*.

### 2.1.6. UN Committee against Torture

Communication No. 41/1996, *Pauline Muzonzo Paku Kisoki v. Sweden*, (CAT/C/16/D/1995), IHRR 1997, Vol. 4, p. 78 ff.

### 2.1.7. The European Court of Human Rights

*A.v. The United Kingdom,* (199/1997/884/1096), ECHR Judgment of 23 September 1998.

*Abdulaziz, Cabales and Balkandali v. United Kingdom*, ECHR Judgment of 28 June 1985, Ser. A, No. 94.

*Aydin v. Turkey*, ECHR Judgment of 25 September 1997, <http://www.dhcour.coe.fr/eng/AYDIN.E.html.>

*Belgian Linguistic Case*, (Case relating to certain aspects of the laws on the use of languages in education in Belgium), ECHR Judgment of 23 July 1968, Ser. A, No. 6.

*Bowman v. the United Kingdom*, ECHR Judgment of 19 February 1998, HRLJ 1998, Vol. 19, pp. 84–92.

*Burghartz v. Switzerland*, ECHR Judgment of 22 February 1994, Ser. A 280–B.

*Chahal v. United Kingdom*, (79/1995/576/662), ECHR Judgment of 15 November 1996.

*Cossey v. the United Kingdom*, ECHR Judgment of 27 September 1990, Ser. A, No. 184.

*Costello-Roberts v. The United Kingdom*, ECHR Judgment of 25 March 1993, Ser. A, No. 247.

*C.R. v. the United Kingdom*, ECHR Judgment of 22 November 1995, Ser. A, No. 335-C.

*Darby v. Sweden*, ECHR Judgment of 23 October 1990, Ser. A, No. 187.

*Handyside v. the United Kingdom*, ECHR Judgment of 7 December 1976, Ser. A, No. 24.

*Dudgeon v. the UK*, ECHR Judgment of 22 October 1981, Ser. A, No. 45.
*Gaskin v. the UK*, ECHR Judgment of 7 July 1989, Ser. A, No. 146.
*Inze v. Austria*, ECHR Judgment of 28 October 1987, Ser. A, No. 126.
*Johnston and others v. Republic of Ireland*, ECHR Judgment of 18 December 1986, Ser. A, No.112.
*Keegan v. Ireland*, ECHR Judgment of 26 Maj 1994, Ser. A, No. 290.
*Kroon v the Netherlands*, ECHR Judgment of 27 October 1994, Ser. A, No. 197-C.
*Lithgow and others v. the UK*, ECHR Judgment of 8 July 1986, Ser. A, No. 102.
*Marckx P. v. Belgium*, ECHR Judgment of 18 December 1979, Ser. A, No. 31.
*Modinos v. Cyprus*, ECHR Judgment of 22 April 1993, Ser. A, No. 259.
*Open Door Counselling Ltd. And Dublin Well Women Centre Ltd. v. Ireland*, ECHR Judgment of 29 October 1992, Ser. A, No. 246.
*Rasmussen v. Denmark*, ECHR Judgment of 28 November 1984, Ser. A, No.87.
*Rees v. the UK*, ECHR Judgment of 17 October 1986, Ser. A, No. 106.
*Schuler-Zgraggen v. Switzerland*, ECHR Judgment of 24 June 1993, Ser. A, No. 263.
*Silver and Others*, ECHR Judgment of 25 March 1983, Ser. A, No. 61.
*Sunday Times v. United Kingdom*, ECHR Judgment of 26 April 1979, Ser. A, No. 30.
*S.W. v. the United Kingdom*, ECHR Judgment of 22 November 1995, Ser. A, No. 335-B.
*Schmidt v. Germany*, ECHR Judgment of 18 July 1994, Ser. A, No. 291-B.
*Tyrer v. the UK*, ECHR Judgment of 18 January 1978, Ser. A, No. 25.
*Van der Mussele v. Belgium*, ECHR Judgment of 23 November 1983, Ser. A, No. 70.
*Van Raalte v. Netherlands*, ECHR Judgment of 21 February 1997, Reports of Judgments and Decisions 1997–I 173.
*Wemhof v. Germany*, ECHR Judgment of 27 June 1968, Ser. A, No. 7.
*X and Y v. the Netherlands*, ECHR Judgment of 26 March 1985, Ser. A, No. 91.
*F. v Switzerland*, ECHR Judgment of 18 December 1987, Ser. A, No. 128.

### 2.1.8. The European Commission of Human Rights

*Brüggemann and Scheuten v. the FRG*, Report of 12 March 1977.
*Hendriks, W. v. The Netherlands*, Report of 8 March 1982.
*Knudsen v. Norway*, D&R 42, p. 247 *et seq.*
*Open Door Counselling Ltd and Dublin Well Woman Centre Ltd and others against Ireland*, Report of 7 March 1991.
*Paton v. The United Kingdom*, Report of 13 March 1980.
*E. Sutherland v. the U.K.*, Report adopted by the Commission on 1 July 1997.
*X. v. Austria*, D&R 7, p. 87 *et seq.*
*X. v. Norway*, YB 4, p. 270 *et seq.*

### 2.1.9. The Court of Justice of the European Communities

Case C-4/73, *Nold v. Commission*, ECJ Judgment of 14 May 1974, ECR 491.
Case C-159/90, *The Society for the Protection of Unborn Children Ireland Ltd v. S. Grogan and Others, 3 CMLR 849, 1991.*
Case C-13/94, *P v S and Cornwall County Council,* Judgment of 30 April 1996, ECR, 2143.
Case C-450/93, *Eckhard Kalanke v. Freie Hansestadt Bremen*, Judgment of 17 Oktober 1995, 35 I.L.M. 265, (1996).
Case C-158/97, *Badeck and Those, HessSTGH*, Decision of 14 April 1997.
Case C-409/95, *Helmut Marschall v. Land Nordrhein-Westfalen*, Judgment of 11 November 1997, HRLJ 1998, Vol. 19, p. 114 ff.
Case C-249/96, *Grant v. South-West, Ltd.,* Judgment of 17 February 1998.
Case T-264/97, *D.v.Council*, Judgment of 28 January 1999.

### 2.1.10. The Inter-American Court of Human Rights

Case No. G 101/81, *In the Matter of Viviana Gallardo et al. v. Costa Rica*, Decision of November 13, 1981, Ser. A & B.

*Velásquez Rodríguez v. Honduras*, IACHR Judgment of July 29, 1988, Ser. C, No. 4.

*Neira Alegría et al. v. Perú* – Preliminary Objections, Judgment of 11 December 1991.

*María Elena Loayaza Tamayo v. Peru*, Case No. 10.506, Sentencia de 17 de septiembre de 1997.

### Advisory opinions

OC-4/84, Proposed Amendments to the Naturalization Provisions of the Constitution of Costa Rica, 19 January 1984, Requested by Costa Rica.

OC-10/89, Interpretation of the American Declaration of the Rights and Duties of Man Within the Framework of Article 64 of the American Convention on Human Rights, 14 July 1989, Requested by Colombia.

OC-14/94, State and individual responsibility regarding laws, which manifestly violate the American Convention/Re-introduction of the death penalty in the Peruvian Constitution, 9 December 1994, Requested by the Inter-American Commission on Human Rights.

### 2.1.11. Inter-American Commission on Human Rights

Case 10.970, *Fernando and Raquel Mejía v. Peru*, Report No. 5/96, Decision 1 March 1996.

Cases 11.228, 11.229, 11.231 and 11.182, *Inan Meneses et al. v. Chile*, Report No. 34/96, Decision of 15 October 1996.

## *2.2. Domestic case law*

**Canada**

*R.v. Hess*, 1991, 59 CCC(3d) 161 (SCC)

*Layland v. Ontario*, 1993, 14 O.R.(3d) 658 (Gen. Div.)

*The Secretary of State for the Home Department v. Fatemah Firouz Ranjabar*, Immigration Appeal Tribunal, HX/70912/94 (11105), 28 June 1994.

*Egan v. Canada*, 1995, 12 R.F.L. (4th) 201, 124 D.L.R. (4th) 609 (S.C.C.)

*M. v. H.*, 1996, 17 R.F.L. (4th) 365 (Ont.Gen.Div.) affd. (1996), 25 R.F.L. (4th) 116 (Ont. C.A.)

*Korn v. Potter*, 1996, B.C.J. 692 (B.C.S.C.)

**Denmark**

*Prosecution v. Refic Sarić*, Supreme Court of Denmark, 15 August 1995.

**Germany**

*Prosecution v. Novislav Djajić*, Bayerisches Oberstes Landesgericht, 23 May 1997.

*Prosecution v. Nikola Jorgić*, Oberlandesgericht Düsseldorf, 26 September 1997.

**Ireland**

*The Attorney General v X and Others*, Judgment of the Supreme Court of Ireland, 5 March 1992.

**Israel**

*Attorney-General v. Adolf Eichmann,* Supreme Court of Israel, 29 May 1962, 36 ILR 5.

*Daniel Nachmani v. Ruti Nachmani*, Supreme Court of Israel, Judgment of 12 September 1996, C.A.H. 2401/95.

**The United States of America**

*Griswold v. Connecticut,* 381 U.S. 479 (1965)

*Roe v Wade*, 410 U.S. 113(1973)

*Michael M. v. Superior Court of Sonoma County*, 450 U.S. 464 (1981)
*City of Akron v Akron Center for Reproductive Health Inc.*, 462 U.S. 416 (1983)
*Webster v Reproductive Health Services*, 106 L Ed 2d 410 (1989)
*Planned Parenthood v Casey*, No. 91–744 (1992)
*Davis v. Davis*, 842 S.W.2d 588 (Tennessee 1992)
*Jane Doe et al v. Radovan Karadžić*, Civil Action No. 93 Civ. 0878 (PKL), Southern District of New York; 866 F. Supp. 734 (S.D.N.Y. 1994)
*S.Kadić v. Radovan Karadžić,* Civil Action No. 93 Civ. 1163 (PKL), Southern District of New York.
*Kass v. Kass*, 1995 WL 110368 (N.Y. Sup.)
*Baehr v. Lewin*, 852 P.2d 44 (Haw.1993); *Baehr v. Miike*, Hawaii Cir Ct 1st Cir, No. 91-1394, December 3, 1996, <http://www.hawaii.gov/lrb/cpt6.html.>

## Literature

### *General works and articles*

Abi-Saab, G.: *The implementation of humanitarian law*, in The New Humanitarian Law of Armed Conflict, A. Cassese (ed.), Napoli 1979, 310–346.
—— *The Concept of "International Crimes" and its Place in Contemporary International Law*, in J.H.H. Weiler *et al.* (eds.), 141–151.
—— *The 1977 Additional Protocols and general international law: some preliminary reflections,* in Humanitarian Law of Armed Conflicts, Challenges Ahead, Essays in Honour of Fritz Kalshoven, A.J.M. Delissen & G.J. Tanja (eds.), Dordrecht 1991, 115–127.
Abu-Hamad, A.: *A Breakthrough: Canada grants political asylum to a Saudi feminist*, Human Rights Watch 1993, Vol. 11, 7 *et seq.*
Agell, A.: *Familjestöd, familjebegrepp, underhållsskyldighet mot barn*, Uppsala 1996.
—— *Äktenskap, samboende, partnerskap*, Uppsala 1998.
Akehurst, M.: *The hierarchy of the sources of international law*, BYIL 1974–1975, Vol. 47, 273 *et seq.*
Akhavan, P.: *Punishing War Crimes in the Former Yugoslavia: A Critical Juncture for the New World Order*, HRQ 1993, Vol. 15, 246–289.
—— *Justice in The Hague, Peace in the Former Yugoslavia? A Commentary on the United Nations War Crimes Tribunal,* HRQ 1998, Vol. 20, 737–816.
van den Akker, P.A.M.: *Unmarried Young Girls and Motherhood, An International Comparison*, in Unwanted Pregnancies and Public Policy, H. Correa (ed.), 79–92.
Alfredsson, G. & Tomaševski, K. (eds.): *A Thematic Guide to Documents on the Human Rights of Women*, The Hague 1995.
Alfredsson, G. & Macalister–Smith, P. (eds.): *The Living Law of Nations*, Kehl 1996.
Alkema, E.A.: *The third-party applicability or "Drittwirkung" of the European Convention on Human Rights*, in Protecting Human Rights: The European Dimension, F. Matscher & H. Petzold (eds.), Köln 1988, 33–45.
de Alonso, A.R.: *Unwanted vs. Unplanned Pregnancies: Conceptual Differences and Emotional Implications on the Experience of Abortion*, in Unwanted Pregnancies and Public Policy, H. Correa (ed.), 17–26.
Alpern, K.D.: *The Ethics of Reproductive Technology*, Oxford 1992.

Alston, P.: *Conjuring Up New Human Rights: a Proposal for Quality Control*, AJIL 1984, Vol. 78, 607 *et seq.*

—— *The United Nations and Human Rights, A Critical Appraisal,* Oxford 1992.

Amann, D.M: *Prosecutor v. Akayesu, Judgment by the International Criminal Tribunal for Rwanda on charges of genocide and international crimes of sexual violence*, AJIL 1999, Vol. 93, 195–199.

Amaro, H.: *Women's Reproductive Rights in the Age of AIDS: New Threats to Informed Consent*, in From Abortion to Reproductive Freedom, M.G. Fried (ed.), 245–254.

Amnesty International: *1999 UN Commission on Human Rights, Making human rights work: time to strengthen the special procedures*, AI Index: IOR/41/01/1999.

An-Na'im Ahmed, A.: *Toward a Cross-Cultural Approach to Defining International Standards of Human Rights*, in Human Right in Cross-Cultural Perspectives, A Quest for Consensus, A. Ahmed An-Na'im (ed.), Philadelphia 1991.

Ansbach, T.: *Die Unterkommission zur Verhinderung der Diskriminierung und zum Schutze von Minderheiten – Perspektiven ihrer weiteren Arbeit*, Archiv des Völkerrechts 1993, Band 31, 230–257.

Aréchaga de Jiménez, E.: *International Law in the Past Third of a Century*, RdC 1978, Vol. I, 64 *et seq.*

Aréchaga de Jiménez E. & Tanzi A.: *International State Responsibility*, in International Law: Achievements and Prospects, M. Bedjaoui (ed.), 348–376.

Armstrong, A. *et al.*: *Uncovering Reality: Excavating Women's Rights in African Family Law*, International Journal of Law and the Family, December 1993, 314 *et seq.*

Arsanjani, H.M.: *The Rome Statute of the International Criminal Court*, AJIL 1999, Vol. 93, 22–43.

Askin, K.D.: *War Crimes Against Women*, Prosecution in International War Crimes Tribunals, The Hague 1997.

—— *Sexual Violence in Decisions and Indictments of the Yugoslav and Rwandan Tribunals: Current Status*, AJIL 1999, Vol. 93, 97–124. (cit. Sexual Violence)

Aswad, E.M.: *Torture by Means of Rape,* Georgetown Law Journal 1996, Vol. 84, No. 5, 1943 *et seq.*

Atkins, S. & Hogget, B.: *Women and the Law*, Oxford 1984.

Austin, R.H.F.: *The Law of International Armed Conflicts*, in International Law: Achievements and Prospects, M. Bedjaoui (ed.), 765–787.

Aydelot, D.: *Mass rape during war: prosecuting Bosnian rapist under international law*, Emory International Law Review 1993, Vol. 7, 631 ff.

Axelrod, R.H.: *Whose womb is it anyway, are paternal rights alive and well despite Danforth*?, Cardozo Law Review 1990, Vol. 3, 705 *et seq.*

Bacchi, C.: *Pregnancy, the Law and the Meaning of Equality*, in Equality Politics and Gender, E. Meehan & S. Sevenhuijsen (eds.), 71–88.

Baehr, P.R.: *The Security Council and Human Rights*, in The Dynamics of the Protection of Human Rights in Europe, Essays in Honour of Henry G. Schermers, R. Lawson & M. de Blois (eds.), Dordrecht 1994, 15–33.

Balakrishnan, R.: *The Social Context of Sex Selection and the Politics of Abortion in India*, in Population Policies Reconsidered, G. Sen & R.C. Snow (eds.), 267–287.

Barry, K.: *Female Sexual Slavery: Understanding the International Dimensions of Women's Oppression*, HRQ 1981, Vol. 3, 49 *et seq.*

Bartholet, E.: *Adoption Rights and Reproductive Wrongs*, in Population Policies Reconsidered, G. Sen & R.C. Snow (eds.), 177–205.

Bartlett, K.B. & Kennedy, R. (eds.): *Feminist Legal Theory, Readings in Law and Gender*, Oxford 1991.

Bassiouni, M.Cherif (ed.): *International Criminal Law*, Vol. I, Crimes, New York 1986.
—— *International Criminal Law*, (ed.), Vol. III, Enforcement, New York 1987.
—— *Crimes Against Humanity*, in International Criminal Law, Vol. III, 51–72.
—— *Introduction to the History of Establishing an International Criminal Court*, in International Criminal Law, Vol. III, 181–185.
—— *Crimes Against Humanity in International Criminal Law*, Dordrecht 1992.
—— *Investigating Violations of International Humanitarian Law in the Former Yugoslavia*, Occasional Paper No. 2, International Human Rights Law Institute, DePaul University College of Law, 1996.
Bassiouni, M.C. & Wise, E.M.: *Aut Dedere Aut Judicare: The Duty to Extradite or Prosecute in International Law*, Dordrecht 1995.
Bassiouni, M.C. & McCormick, M.: *Sexual Violence, An Invisible Weapon of War in the Former Yugoslavia*, Occasional Paper No.1, International Human Rights Law Institute, DePaul University College of Law, 1996.
Bassioni, M.C. with the Collaboration of P. Manikas: *The Law of the International Criminal Tribunal for the Former Yugoslavia*, New York 1996.
Baxter, Q.: *Human rights and humanitarian law*, The Australian Yearbook of International Law 1985, Vol. 9, 94–105.
Baxter, R.R.: *The law of war*, in The Present State of International law and Other Essays, M. Bos (ed.), Deventer 1973, 107–124.
Bayefsky, A.F.: *The Principle of Equality or Non-discrimination in International Law*, HRLJ 1990, Vol. 11, 1–34.
Beddard, R.: *Human Rights and Europe*, Cambridge 1993.
Bedjaoui, M. (ed.): *International Law: Achievements and Prospects*, UNESCO Paris 1991.
Bell, N.W. & Vogel, E.F. (eds.): *A Modern Introduction to The Family*, Toronto 1968.
Bello, E.G. & San, B.A.A.: *Essays in honour of Judge Taslim Olawale Elias*, Vol. I, Contemporary International Law and Human Rights, Dordrecht 1991.
Benedek, W.: *The Judiciary and Human Rights in Africa*, HRLJ 1990, 251 *et seq.*
Berger, V.: *Case Law of the European Court of Human Rights*, Vol. I: 1960–1987, Dublin 1989.
Bergsmo, M.: *The Establishment of the International Tribunal on War Crimes*, HRLJ 1993, Vol. 14, 371–373.
—— *International Criminal Tribunal for the Former Yugoslavia, Recent Developments*, HRLJ 1994, Vol. 15, 405–410.
Bergström, S., Molin, A. & Povey, G.W.: *International maternal health care* 1993, Uppsala 1994.
Bertrand, M: *The Historical Development of Efforts to Reform the UN*, in United Nations, Divided World, The UN's Roles in International Relations, A. Roberts & B. Kingsbury, Oxford 1993 (2nd ed.), 420–437.
Bernat, E.R.: *Rechtsfragen medizinisch assistierter Zeugung*, Frankfurt am Main 1989.
Bernhardt, R.: *Interpretation of International Law*, in Encyclopedia of Public International Law, Amsterdam 1984, Vol. 7, 322 *et seq.*
—— *Völkerrechtliche Verbote der Diskriminierung von Individuen*, in Des Menschen Recht zwischen Freiheit und Verantwortung, Festschrift für Karl Josef Partsch zum 75. Geburtstag, J. Jekewitz *et al.* (eds.), Berlin 1989, 97–102.
Best, G.: *Humanity in Warfare; The Modern History of the International Law of Armed Conflicts*, London 1980.
Bierzanek, R.: *War Crimes: History and Definition*, in International Criminal Law, Vol. III Enforcement, M.C. Bassiouni (ed.), New York 1987, 29–50.

Binion, G.: *Feminist Theory Confronts US Supreme Court Rhetoric: The Case of Abortion Rights*, International Journal of Law, Policy and the Family 1997, Vol. 11, 63–86.

Blank, R.H.: *Reproductive Technologies and Public Policy: The Gap Widens*, in Unwanted Pregnancies and Public Policy, H. Correa (ed.), 27–51.

Blatt, D.: *Recognizing Rape as a Method of Torture*, NYU Review of Law and Social Change 1992, Vol. 19, 821 *et seq.*

Blishchenko, I.P.: *Responsibility in breaches of international humanitarian law*, in International Dimensions of Humanitarian Law, UNESCO, Dordrecht 1988, 283–297.

Bloed, A., Leicht, L., Nowak, M. & Rosas, A. (eds.): *Monitoring Human Rights in Europe, Comparing International Procedures and Mechanisms*, Dordrecht 1993.

Blomquist, C.: *Medicinsk etik*, Stockholm 1971.

Blyth, E.: *Donor assisted conception and donor offspring rights to genetic origins information*, The International Journal of Children's Rights 1998, Vol. 6, 237–253.

Boch, C.: *During Pregnancy, Females are Pregnant*, European Law Review 1998, No. 5, 488–494.

Bogdan, M.: *Registrerat partnerskap och svensk internationell privaträtt*, SvJT 1994, No. 9, 773–784.

Bondeson, W.B. *et al.* (eds.): *Abortion and the Status of the Fetus*, Dordrecht 1984.

Borkowski, A.: *Textbook on Roman Law*, London 1994.

Bothe, M.; Partsch, K.J. & Solf, W.: *New Rules for Victims of Armed Conflicts: Commentary on the two 1977 Protocols additional to the Geneva Conventions of 1949*, The Hague 1982.

Boucaud, P.: *The Council of Europe's standard-setting activities relating to equality of the sexes*, Strasbourg 1989.

van Boven, T.C.: *Survey of the Positive International Law of Human Rights,* in The International Dimensions of Human Rights, K. Vasak (ed.), UNESCO 1982, Vol. 1, 87–111.

—— *Reliance on norms of humanitarian law by United Nation's organs*, in Humanitarian Law of Armed Conflict, A.J.M. Delissen & G.J. Tanja (eds.), 495–515.

—— *The International System of Human Rights: An Overview*, in Manual on Human Rights Reporting, UN New York 1991, 3–13.

Brackman, A.C.: *The Other Nuremberg – The Untold Story of the Tokyo War Crimes Trials*, New York 1989.

Brandt, M.: *Doe v. Karadžić*: Redressing Non-State Acts of Gender – Specific Abuse Under the Alien Tort Statute, Minnesota Law Review 1995, Vol. 79, 1413–1446.

Brownlie, I.: *Basic Documents on Human Rights*, Oxford 1981.

—— *International law at the fiftieth anniversary of the United Nations*, 255 Recueil' des Cours de l' Academie de Droit International de la Haye 1995, 9–228.

Brownmiller, S.: *Making Female Bodies the Batterfield*, in Mass Rape, A. Stiglmayer (ed.), 180–183.

Brett, R.: *The contribution of NGOs to the monitoring and protection of human rights in Europe: an analysis of the role and access of NGOs to the intergovernmental organisations*, in Monitoring Human Rights in Europe, A. Bloed *et al.* (eds.), Dordrecht 1993, 121–145.

Bring, O.: *FN-stadgans folkrätt,* Stockholm 1992.

—— *Folkrätt för totalförsvaret*, Stockholm 1994.

Brodie, J.: *Health versus Rights: Comparative Perspectives on Abortion Policy in Canada and the United States*, in Power and Decision, G. Sen & R.C. Snow (eds.), 123–147.

Broms, B.: *The Definition of Aggression*, Recueil des Cours 1977, Vol. I, 299–400.

—— *Security Council Resolution 808 (1993),* in Current International Law Issues, Nordic Perspectives, Essays in Honour of Jerzy Sztucki, O. Bring & S. Mahmoudi (eds.), Stockholm 1994, 51–65.

Brownlie, I.: *Principles of Public International Law*, Oxford 1990.

—— *The History of State Responsibility*, in New Directions in International Law, Essays in Honour of Wolfgang Abendroth – Festschrift zu seinem 75. Geburtstag, R.G. Girardot *et al.* (eds.), 19–27.

—— *Discussion Theme I*, in Universality of Human Rights In A Pluralistic World, Council of Europe, Strasbourg 1990, 92–93.

—— *Basic Documents, International Law*, Oxford 1995.

Bruce, N.: *The Child's Right to Know*, International Children's Rights Monitor 1986, Vol. 3, 14 *et seq.*

Bryde, B.O.; *Verpflichtungen Erga Omnes als Menschenrechten*, in Aktuelle Probleme des Menschenrechtsschutzes, Berichte der Deutschen Gesellschaft für Völkerrecht, Heidelberg 1994, 165–189.

Buergenthal, T.: *The Effect of the European Convention on Human Rights on the Internal Law of Member States,* ICLQ, Supplementary Publication 1965, No. 11, 76–106.

—— *The Revised OAS Charter and the Protection of Human Rights,* AJIL 1975, Vol. 69, 828–836.

—— *The American and European Conventions on Human Rights, Similarities and Differences,* The American University Law Review 1980, Vol. 30, 155–166.

—— *Menschenrechtsschutz im inter-amerikanischen System*, EuGRZ 1984, Vol. 11, 169–189.

—— *The Inter-American Court, Human Rights and the OAS*, HRLJ 1986, Vol. 7, 157–165.

—— *Human Rights in the Americas: View from the Inter-American Court*, Connecticut Journal of International Law 1987, Vol. 2, 303–310.

—— *The Inter-American System for the Protection of Human Rights*, in Human Rights in International Law: Legal and Political Issues, T. Meron (ed.), Oxford 1988, 439–493.

—— *The OAS and the Protection of Rights*, Emory Journal of International Dispute Resolution 1988, Vol. 3, 1–24.

—— *The OAS Charter After Forty Years*, American Society of International Law Proceedings 1988, Vol. 82, 114–118 .

—— *International Human Rights*, St.Paul 1995.

—— *The Normative and Institutional Evolution of International Human Rights,* HRQ 1997, Vol. 19, 703–723.

Buergenthal, T. & Norris, R.E.: *Human Rights: The Inter-American System*, Vols. 1 and 2, New York 1982, Vol. 3, New York 1983.

Buergenthal, T., Norris, R.E., & Shelton, D.: *Protecting Human Rights in the Americas, Selected Problems*, Kehl 1986.

Buergenthal, T. & Shelton, D.: *Protecting Human Rights in the Americas*, Strasbourg 1995.

Van Bueren, G.: *The International Law on the Rights of the Child,* Dordrecht 1995.

Bumiller, E.: *May You Be the Mother of a Hundred Sons*, New York 1990.

Bunch, C. & Carillo, R.: *Gender Violence, A Development and Human Rights Issue*, New Jersey 1991.

Bunch, C.: *Transforming Human Rights from a Feminist Perspective*, in Women's rights, human rights, J. Peters & A. Wolper (eds.), 11–18.

Burckhardt, W.: *Die Völkerrechtliche Haftung der Staaten*, Bern 1924.

Bussemaker, J.: *Equality, Autonomy and Feminist Politics*, in Equality Politics and Gender, E. Meehan & S. Sevenhuijsen (eds.), 52–71.

Buquicchio-de Boer, M.: *Sexual equality in the European Convention of Human Rights, a survey of case-law*, Strasbourg 1989.

Byrnes, A.: *CEDAW's 10th Session*, NQHR 1991, Vol. 3, 345 *et seq.*

—— *Women, Feminism and International Human Rights Law Methodological Myopia, Fundamental Flaws or Meaningful Marginalization?,* Australian Yearbook of International Law 1992, Vol. 12, 1 *et seq.*

—— *Toward More Effective Enforcement of Women's Human Rights Through the Use of International Human Rights Law and Procedures*, in Human Rights of Women, R.J. Cook (ed.), 189–228.

Byrnes, A., Connors, J. & Bik, L. (eds.): *Advancing the Human Rights of Women: Using International Human Rights Standards in Domestic Litigation*, London 1997.

Cabranes, J.A.: *The Protection of Human Rights by the Organization of American States*, AJIL 1968, Vol. 62, 889–908.

Camargo, P.P.: *The American Convention on Human Rights*, HRLJ 1970, Vol. 3, 333–356.

Cameron, I. & Eriksson, M.K.: *An Introduction to the European Convention on Human Rights*, Uppsala 1995.

Cançado Trindade, A.A.: *The Domestic Jurisdiction of States in the Practice of the UN and Regional Organizations*, ICLQ 1976, Vol. 25, 715–765.

—— *Co-Existence and Co-ordination of International Protection of Human Rights – At Global and Regional Level*, Recueil des Cours de l'Académie de Droit International 1987, Vol. 202, 190–209.

Cass, D.Z.: *Navigating the Newstream: Recent Critical Scholarship in International Law*, NJIL 1996, Vol. 65, 341–383.

Cassese, A.: *The International Fight Against Torture*, Baden–Baden 1991.

—— *Individuals*, in International Law: Achievements and Prospects, M. Bedjaoui (ed.), 113–120.

—— *Prohibition of Torture and Inhumane or Degrading Treatment or Punishment*, in The European System for the Protection of Human Rights, R. St. J. Macdonald *et al.* (eds.), Dordrecht 1993, 225–261.

—— *On the Current Trends towards Criminal Prosecution and Punishment of Breaches of International Humanitarian Law*, European Journal of International Law 1998, Vol. 9, No. 1, 2–17.

Cassese, A. & Spinedi, M. (eds.): *International Crimes of State, A Critical Analysis of the ILC's Draft Article 19 on State Responsibility*, Berlin 1989, 215–216.

Cerna, C. & Young W.: *The Inter-American Commission on Human Rights and the Death Penalty*, Federal Bar News & Journal 1987, Vol. 34, 398–402.

Cerna, C.M.: *Universality of Human Rights and Cultural Diversity: Implementation of Human Rights in Different Socio-Cultural Contexts*, HRQ 1994, Vol. 16, 740–752.

Chahar, S.: *Offence of Rape: The Marital Exception*, Indian Socio-Legal Journal 1996, Vol. XXII, 35–43.

Chapman, A.R.: *A New Approach to Monitoring the International Covenant on Economic, Social and Cultural Rights*, in The Review (ICJ) December 1995, No. 55, 23–38.

Charlesworth, H.: *What are "Women's International Human Rights"?,* in Human Rights of Women, R.J. Cook (ed.), 58–85.

—— *Alienating Oscar? Feminist Analysis of International Law*, in Reconceiving Reality: Women and International Law, D.G. Dallmeyer (ed.), 1–19.

—— *Human Rights as Men's Rights*, in Women's rights, human rights, J. Peters & A. Wolper (eds.), 103–114.

—— *Cries and Whispers: Responses to Feminist Scholarship in International Law*, NJIL 1996, Vol. 65, 557–568.

Charlesworth, H. & Chinkin, C.: *The Gender of Jus Cogens*, HRQ 1993, Vol. 15, 63–76

Charlesworth, H., Chinkin, C. & Wright, S.: *Feminist Approaches to International Law*, AJIL 1991, Vol. 85, 625–645.

Charpentier, L.: *The European Court of Justice and the Rhetoric of Affirmative Action*, ELJ 1998, Vol. 4, 167–195.

Chen, Lung-Chu: *An Introduction to Contemporary International Law, A Policy-Oriented Perspective*, London 1989.

Cheng, B.: *Introduction to Subjects of International Law*, in International Law: Achievements and Prospects, M. Bedjaoui (ed.), 23–40.

Chinkin, C.M.: *The Challenge of Soft Law: Development and Change in International Law*, International and Comparative Law Quarterly 1989, Vol. 38, 850–866.

—— *Peace and Force in International Law*, in Reconceiving Reality: Women and International Law, D.G. Dallmeyer (ed.), 203–231.

—— *Due Process and Witness Anonymity*, AJIL 1997, Vol. 91, 75–79.

Clapham, A.: *The "Drittwirkung" of the Convention*, in The European System for the Protection of Human Rights, R. St. J. Mcdonald *et al.* (eds.), 163–207.

Clark, B.: *The Vienna Convention Reservations Regime and the Convention on Discrimination against Women*, AJIL 1991, Vol. 85, 281 *et seq.*

Clark, R.S.: A *United Nations High Commissioner for Human Rights*, The Hague 1972.

Coleman, M.N.: *Embryo Transplant, Parental Conflict and Reproductive Freedom: a Prospective Analysis of Issues and Arguments Created by Forthcoming Technology*, Hofstra Law Review 1987, Vol. 15, 611 *et seq.*

Coliver, S.: *The Right to Information Necessary for Reproductive Health and Choice under International Law*, The American University Law Review 1995, Vol. 44, 1279–1303.

Connery, J.S.J.: *Abortion: The Development of the Roman Catholic Perspective*, Chicago 1977.

Connors, J.F.: *Violence Against Women in the Family*, UN New York 1989.

Cook, B.W.: *Eleanor Roosevelt and Human Rights: The Battle for Peace and Planetary Decency*, in Women and American Foreign Policy: Lobbyists, Critics, and Insiders, E.P. Crapol (ed.), New York 1987.

Cook, R.J.: *Reservations to the Convention on the Elimination of All Forms of Discrimination Against Women*, Virginia JIL 1990, Vol. 30, 643–716.

—— *International Protection of Women's Reproductive Rights*, New York University Journal of International Law and Politics 1992, Vol. 24, 646 *et seq.*

—— *Women's International Human Rights Law: The Way Forward*, HRQ 1993, Vol. 15, 241 *et seq.*

—— *Human Rights in Relation to Women's Health*, WHO publication, June 1993.

—— *Accountability in International Law for Violations of Women's Rights by Non-state Actors*, in Reconceiving Reality: Women and International Law, D.G. Dallmeyer (ed.), 93–117.

—— *Women's International Human Rights Law: The Way Forward*, in Human Rights of Women, National and International Perspectives, R.J. Cook (ed.), Philadelphia 1994, 3–37.

—— *State Accountability Under the Convention on the Elimination of All Forms of Discrimination Against Women*, in Human Rights of Women, R.J. Cook (ed.), 228–257.

—— *State Responsibility for Violations of Women's Human Rights*, Harvard Human Rights Journal 1994, Vol. 7, 125–175.

—— *International Human Rights and Women's Reproductive Health*, in Women's rights, human rights, J. Peters & A. Wolper (eds.), 256–279.

—— *Human Rights and Self-determination*, The American University Law Review 1995, Vol. 44, 976–1475.

—— *Women*, in The United Nations and International Law, C.C. Joyner (ed.), 181–208.

Cook, R.J. & Haws, J.M.: *The United Nations Convention on the Rights of Women: Opportunities for Family Planning Providers*, International Family Planning Perspectives 1983, Vol. 12, p. 45 *et seq.*

Cook, R.J. & Plata, M.I.: *Women's Reproductive Self-Determination: evolutionary models*, Development 1994: 3, 29–34.

Copelon, R.: *Surfacing Gender: Reconceptualizing Crimes against Women in Time of War*, in Mass Rape, A. Stiglmayer (ed.), 197–219.

—— *Intimate Terror: Understanding Domestic Violence as Torture*, in Human Rights of Women, R.J. Cook (ed.), 116–152.

—— *Recognizing the Egregious in the Everyday: Domestic Violence as Torture*, Columbia Human Rights Law Review 1994, Vol. 25, 291–367.

—— *Gendered War Crimes: Reconceptualizing Rape in Time of War*, in Women's rights, human rights, J. Peters & A. Wolper (eds.), 197–215.

—— *From Privacy to Autonomy: The Conditions for Sexual and Reproductive Freedom*, in From Abortion to Reproductive Freedom, M.G. Fried (ed.), 27–45.

Correa, H. (ed.): *Unwanted Pregnancies and Public Policy: An International Perspective*, New York 1993.

—— *The Impact of Abortion Legislation*, ibid., 155–162.

Craven, M.: *The International Covenant on Economic, Social and Cultural Rights: A Perspective on Its Development*, Oxford 1995.

Crawford, J. (ed.): *The Rights of Peoples*, Oxford 1988.

—— *The ILC's Draft Statute for an International Criminal Tribunal*, AJIL 1994, Vol. 88, 140 ff.

—— *The ILC Adopts A Statute For An International Criminal Court*, AJIL 1995, Vol. 89, 404–416.

D'Amato, A.: *Peace vs. Accountability in Bosnia*, AJIL 1994, Vol. 88, 500–506.

Daes, E.: *New Types of War Crimes and Crimes against Humanity: Violations of International Humanitarian and Human Rights Law*, in International Geneva Yearbook 1993, Vol. 7, 55–78.

Dallmeyer, D.G.: *Reconceiving Reality: Women and International Law,* Studies in Transnational Legal Policy, No. 25, ASIL, Washington D.C. 1993.

Danelius, H.: *Mänskliga rättigheter*, Stockholm, 1993.

—— *The International Protection against Torture and Inhumane or Degrading Treatment or Punishment,* in Collected Courses of the Academy of European Law, Dordrecht 1993, Vol. II, 151–198.

—— *Protection Against Torture in Europe and the World*, in The European System for the Protection of Human Rights, R. St. J. Macdonald *et al.* (eds.), 263–277.

—— *Mänskliga rättigheter i europeisk praxis*, Stockholm 1997.

Danelius & Burger: *The United Nations Convention against Torture. A Handbook on the Convention against Torture and Other Cruel, Inhumane or Degrading Treatment or Punishment,* Dordrecht 1988.

Daniels, C.: *Gender Difference, Fetal Rights, and the Politics of Protectionism: Workplace Issues*, in From Abortion to Reproductive Freedom, M.G. Fried (ed.), 271–281.

Dankwa, E.V.: *Conference on Regional Systems of Human Rights Protection in Africa, the Americas and Europe,* HRLJ 1992, Vol.13, 316 *et seq.*

David, H.P. and A. Titkow: *Abortion and Women's Rights in Poland, 1994*, Studies in Family Planning 1994, Vol. 25, 239–243.

Davidson, S.: *The Inter American Court of Human Rights,* Dartmouth 1992.

—— *Human Rights*, Philadelphia 1993.

Davis, A.: *Racism, Birth Control, and Reproductive Rights*, in From Abortion to Reproductive Freedom, M.G. Fried (ed.), 15–27.

Delissen, A.J.M. & Tanja, G.J. (eds.): *Humanitarian Law of Armed Conflict, Challenges Ahead,* Essays in Honour of Fritz Karlshoven, Dordrecht 1991.

Delmas, M. Marty: *The European Convention for the Protection of Human Rights. International Protection versus National Restrictions,* Dordrecht 1992.

Deodhar, N.S.: *First Contentious Cases Before the Inter-American Court of Human Rights*, The American University Journal of International Law and Policy 1988, Vol. 3, 283–286.

Detrick, S.: *The United Nations Convention on the Rights of the Child, A Guide to the "Travaux Préparatoires",* Dordrecht 1992.

—— *The Irish case*, International Children's Rights Monitor 1992, Vol. 9, 6 *et seq.*

Detter De Lupis, I.: *The Concept of International Law*, Stockholm 1987.

—— *The Law of War*, Cambridge 1987.

—— *International Law*, Stockholm 1991.

Dewar, J.: *Fathers in Law? The Case of AID*, in Birthrights, Law and Ethics at the Beginning of Life, R. Lee & D. Morgan (eds.), London 1989.

van Dijk, P.: *Judicial Review of Governmental Action and the Requirement of an Interest to Sue*, Dordrecht 1980.

—— *Common Standard of Achievement*, NQHR 1995, Vol. 2, 119 *et seq.*

van Dijk, P. & van Hoof, G.: *Theory and Practice of the European Convention on Human Rights,* Deventer, 1990.

Dimitrijevic, V.: *The Human Dimension of Post-totalitarianism*, in The Future of Human Rights Protection in a Changing World, A. Eide & J. Helgesen (eds.), Oslo 1991.

Dinstein, Y.: *The Defence of "Obedience to Superior Orders" in International Law*, Leyden 1965.

—— *The Law of Armed Conflict and Human Rights: Convergence and Integration*, International Institute of Human Rights, sixth course, Strasbourg 1974.

—— *Collective Human Rights of Peoples and Minorities*, ICLQ 1976, Vol. 25, 102–120.

—— *The Right to Life, Physical Integrity and Liberty*, in The International Bill of Rights, L. Henkin (ed.), New York 1981.

—— *Discrimination and International Human Rights*, Israel Yearbook of Human Rights 1985, Vol. 15, 11–27.

—— *International Criminal Law*, Israel Law Review 1985, Vol. 20, 206–242.

—— *Human Rights in Armed Conflict: International Humanitarian Law*, in Human Rights in International Law, T. Meron (ed.), Oxford 1988, 345–368.

—— *The erga omnes applicability of Human Rights*, Archiv des Völkerrechts 1992, 16–21.

Dinstein, Y. & Tabory, M. (eds.): *International Law at a Time of Perplexity*, Essays in Honour of Shabtai Rosenne, Dordrecht 1989.

—— *War Crimes in International Law*, The Hague 1996.

Dixon-Mueller, R.: *Population Policy & Women's Rights, Transforming Reproductive Choice*, London 1993.

Dolfe, I.: *Internationell tribunal för brott mot humanitär rätt i f.d. Jugoslavien*, SvJT 1995, 609–616.

Donnelly, J.: *Human Rights and Human Dignity: an analytical critique of non-Western conceptions of human rights*, American Political Science Review 1982, Vol. 76, 312 *et seq.*

—— *Universal Human Rights in Theory and Practice*, Ithaca, NY 1989.

—— *International Human Rights*, Oxford 1993.

Donner, L.A.: *Gender Bias in Drafting International Discrimination Conventions: The 1979 Women's Convention Compared with the 1965 Racial Convention*, California Western International Law Journal 1994, Vol. 24, 241–254.

Donoho, D.: *Relativism versus Universalism in Human Rights: The Search for Meaningful Standard*, Stanford Journal of International Law 1991, Vol. 27, 354–391.

Dorf, J.& Pérez, G.C.: *Discrimination and the Tolerance of Difference: International Lesbian Human Rights*, in Women's rights, human rights, J. Peters & A. Wolper (eds.), 324–335.

Doswald-Beck, L.: *The Civilian in the Crossfire*, Journal of Peace Research 1987, Vol. 24, No. 3, 251–262.

Draper, G.I.A.D.: *The development of international humanitarian law*, in International Dimensions of Humanitarian Law, 67–93.

Drost, P.N.: *The Crime of State*, Vol. II Genocide, Leyden 1959.

Drzemczewski, A.: *European Human Rights Convention in Domestic Law, A Comparative Study*, Oxford, 1985.

—— *The Role of NGOs in Human Rights Matters in the Council of Europe*, HRLJ 1987, Vol. 8, 273–281.

Drzewicki, K.: *Reporting mechanism for supervision of national legislation implementing international humanitarian law*, in Humanitarian Law of Armed Conflict, A.J.M. Delissen & G.J. Tanja (eds.), 545–567.

Dunshee de Abranches, C.A.: *The Inter-American Court of Human Rights*, American University Law Review 1981, Vol. 30, 79 *et seq.*

Dworkin, R.M.: *Taking Rights Seriously*, London 1977.

—— *The Philosophy of Law*, Oxford University Press 1977.

—— *Life's Dominion, An Argument about Abortion and Euthanasia*, London 1993.

Dwyer, A.S.: *The Inter-American Court of Human Rights: Toward Establishing an Effective Regional Contentious Jurisdiction*, Boston College International & Comparative Law Review 1990, Vol. 13, 127–166.

Eagleton, C.: *The Responsibility of States in International Law*, New York 1928.

Eduards *et al.* (eds.): *Kön, Makt, Medborgarskap. Kvinnan i politiskt tänkande från Platon till Engels*, Stockholm 1983.

Eide, A.: *The laws of war and human rights – Differences and convergences*, in Studies and essays on international humanitarian law and Red Cross principles in honour of Jean Pictet, ICRC 1984, 675–697.

Eide, A. & Opsahl, T.: *General Report on Equality and Non-discrimination*, Council of Europe, Strasbourg 1990.

Eide, A., Rosas, A. & Meron, T: *Combating Lawlessness in Gray Zone Conflicts through Minimum Humanitarian Standards*, AJIL 1995, Vol. 89, 215 *et seq.*

Eiriksson, G.: *The Work of the International Law Commission at its 47th Session*, NJIL 1995, 169–186.

Ek, L.: *Barnkonventionens skydd för ofödda barn*, SvJT 1993, 914–923.

Eklund, R.: *Gender-based affirmative action*, in Lex Ferenda, J. Rosén (ed.), Stockholm 1996, 29–50.

—— *The Swedish Case – The Promised Land of Sex Equality?*, in Sex Equality Law in the European Union, Hervey & O´Keeffee (eds.), Wiley 1996, 337–356.

Elder, B.G.: *Human Rights and the United Nations*, Crime and Social Justice 1986, Vol. 25, 21 *et seq.*

Elkind, J.B.: *Interim Protection, A Functional Approach*, The Hague 1981.

Engle, K.: *After the Collapse of the Public/Private Distinction: Strategizing Women's Rights*, in Reconceiving Reality: Women and International Law, D.G. Dallmeyer (ed.), 143–157.

Epiney, A.: *Die völkerrechtliche Verantwortlichkeit von Staaten für rechtswidriges Verhalten im Zusammenhang mit Aktionen Privater*, Baden–Baden 1992.

Eriksson, A. & Saldeen, Å.: *Parenthood and Science – Establishing and Contesting Parentage*, in Parenthood in Modern Society, J. Eekelaar & P. Sarcevic (eds.), 67–75.

Eriksson, M.K.: *Barnets folkrättsliga skydd*, SvJT 1988, 437–480.
—— *The Right to Marry and to Found a Family, A World-Wide Human Right*, Uppsala 1990.
—— *Article 16*, in A. Eide *et al.* (eds.), The Universal Declaration of Human Rights. A Commentary, Oxford 1992, 243–255.
—— *Family Planning as a Human Rights Issue*, in Parenthood in Modern Society, J. Eekelaar & P. Sarcević (eds.), Dordrecht 1993, 191–207.
—— *The Legal Position of the Unborn Child in International Law*, GYIL 1993, Vol. 36, 86–130.
—— *Swedish Refugee Law and Practice in the Light of International Law*, TfR 1995, No. 4, 623–686.
Ermacora, F., Nowak, M. & Tretter, H.: *International Human Rights*, Vienna 1993.
Evans, D. (ed.): *Creating the Child*, The Hague 1996.
Fahrenhorst, I.: *Fortpflanzungstechnologien und Europäische Menschenrechtskonvention*, EuGRZ 1988, 129 *et seq.*
Farer, T.J. & Gaer, F.: *The UN and Human Rights: At the End of the Beginning*, in United Nations, Divided World, A. Roberts & B. Kingsbury (eds.), Oxford 1993, 240–297.
Fawcett, J.E.S.: *The Application of the European Convention on Human Rights*, Oxford 1987.
Ferencz, B.B.: *Crimes Against Humanity*, in Encyclopedia of Public International Law, R.Bernhardt (ed.), Vol. 8, 107–109.
Fitzpatrick, J.: *The Use of International Human Rights Norms to Combat Violence Against Women*, in Human Rights of Women, R.J. Cook (ed.), 532–573.
Flanz, G.H.: *Gender-based discrimination in spite of equal treatment laws? Legal and linguistic aspects*, in Festschrift für Felix Ermacora, M. Nowak *et al.* (eds.), Strasbourg 1988, 439 *et seq.*
Fleen, R.H.: *Abortion and Exposure in Ancient Greece: Assessing the Status of the Fetus and "Newborn" from Classical Sources*, in Abortion and the Status of the Fetus, W.B. Bondeson *et al.* (eds.), Dordrecht 1984.
Forbes, I.: *Equal Opportunity: Radical, Liberal and Conservative Critiques,* in Equality Politics and Gender, E. Meehan & S. Sevenhuijsen (eds.), 17–36.
Forbes Martin, S.: *Refugee Women*, London 1991.
Forsythe, D.P.: *Human Rights After the Cold War*, NQHR 1993, Vol. 11, 393–412.
Francioni, F.: *International 'soft law': a contemporary assessment*, in Fifty Years of International Court of Justice – Essays in honour of Sir Robert Jennings, Lowe & Fitzmaurice (eds.), Cambridge 1996, 167–178.
Frankowski, J. & Cole, G.: *Abortion and Protection of the Human Foetus*, Dordrecht 1987.
Fraser, A.S.: *The U.N. Decade for Women*, Documents and Dialogue, Colorado 1987.
Freeman, M.A.: *Measuring equality: a comparative perspective on women's legal capacity and constitutional rights in five Commonwealth countries*, Commonwealth Law Bulletin, October 1990, 1423 *et seq.*
—— *The Human Rights of Women in the Family: Issues and Recommendations for Implementation of the Women's Convention*, in Women's rights, human rights, J. Peters & A. Wolper (eds.), 149–167.
Freeman, M. and Veerman, P. (eds.): *The Ideologies of Children's Rights*, Dordrecht 1992.
Fried, M.G. (ed.): *From Abortion to Reproductive Freedom: Transforming a Movement*, Boston 1990.
Friedman, E.: *Women's Human Rights: The Emergence of a Movement*, in Women's rights, human rights, J. Peters & A. Wolper (eds.), 18–36.
Frost, L.E.: *The Evolution of the Inter-American Court of Human Rights: Reflections of Present and Former Judges*, HRQ 1992, Vol. 14, 171–205.

Frowein, J.A.: *The European and American Conventions on Human Rights – A Comparison*, HRLJ 1980, Vol. 1, 44–65.
Frowein, J.A. & Peukert, W.: *Europäische Menschenrechtskonvention, EMRK – Kommentar*, Kehl 1996.
Fürst-Mellström, G. & Sterner, M.: *Kvinnors värde i männens värld*, Angered 1983.
Fyzee, Asaf, A.A.: *Outlines of Muhammadan Law*, Oxford 1993.
Gallagher, A.: *Ending the Marginalization: Strategies for Incorporating Women into the United Nations Human Rights System*, HRQ 1997, Vol. 19, 283–333.
Gallagher, J.: *Embryos and Foetuses: Anxiety and the Law*, in Reproductive Technologies, M. Stanworth (ed.), Oxford 1987, 148 *et seq*.
Gardam, J.G.: *The Law of Armed Conflict: A Gendered Regime?*, in Reconceiving Reality: Women and International Law, D.G. Dallmeyer (ed.), 171–203.
Gasser, H.-P.: *Der Internationale Strafgerichtshof für das frühere Jugoslavien und das "Kriegsrecht und die Kriegsgebräuche" – Eine Glosse zu Artikel 3 des Statuts*, in Humanitäres Völkerrecht, Deutsches Rotes Kreuz 1993, Nr. 2, 60–63.
Giegerich, T.: *Vorbehalte zu Menschenrechtsabkommen: Zulässigkeit, Gültigkeit und Prüfungskompetenzen von Vertragsgremien, Ein konstitutioneller Ansatz*, ZaöRV 1995, 55/3, 713–782.
Gingsburgs, G. & Kudrjavcev, N.V., (eds.): *The Nuremberg Trial and International Law*, Dordrecht 1990.
Glendon, M.A.: *Abortion and Divorce in Western Law*, Cambridge 1987.
Glueck, S.: *War Criminals – Their Prosecution and Punishment*, New York 1944.
Goldberg, P.: *Where in the World is There Safety for Me?: Women Fleeing Gender-Based Persecution*, in Women's rights, human rights, J. Peters & A. Wolper (eds.), 345–356.
Goldsmith, M.: *Women at War*, London 1943.
Gomien, D., Harris, D. & Zwaak, L.: *Law and Practice of the European Convention on Human Rights and the European Social Charter*, Strasbourg 1996.
Gornig, G.H.: *Das Refoulement Verbot im Völkerrecht*, Wien 1987.
Graber, M.A.: *Rethinking Abortion*, Princeton 1996.
Grahl-Madsen, A.: *The Status of Refugees in International Law*, Vol. II, Leyden 1972.
Grayson, J.W.: *The Defence of Superior Orders in the International Criminal Court*, NJIL 1995, 243–260.
Greig, D.W.: *Reservations: Equity as a Balancing Factor?*, Australian Year Book of International Law 1995, 21–173.
Grotzky, J.: *Balkankrieg. Der Zerfall Jugoslawiens und die Folgen für Europa*, München 1993.
Gruskin, S.: *Negotiating the Relationship of HIV/AIDS to Reproductive Health and Reproductive Rights*, The American University Law Review 1995, Vol. 44, 1191–1206.
Guest, I.: *On Trial: The United Nations, War Crimes, and the Former Yugoslavia*, Refugee Policy Group, Washington D.C. 1995.
Gutman, R.: *Augenzeuge des Völkermords*, Göttingen 1994.
Hadley, J.: *Abortion, Between Freedom and Necessity*, London 1996.
Halberstam, M. & Defeis, E.F.: *Women's Legal Rights. International Covenants an Alternative to ERA?*, New York 1989.
Hamand, J.: *Working for Change in the Arab World*, IPPF 1996/1, 5–8.
Hamand, J. & Yang, L.: *"Backers of the people" in China*, IPPF 1996/1, 25–28.
Hampson, F.J.: *The International Criminal Tribunal for Yugoslavia and the Reluctant Witness*, ICLQ 1998, Vol. 47, 50–74.
Hanigan, J.P.: *Unwanted Pregnancies and the Common Good*, in Unwanted Pregnancies and Public Policy, H. Correa (ed.), 1–16.

Hannikainen, L.: *Peremptory Norms (jus cogens) in International Law, Historical Development, Criteria, Present Status,* Helsinki 1988.

Hannum, H. (ed.): *Guide to International Human Rights Practice*, Philadelphia 1986.

Hardon, A. & Hayes, E.: *Reproductive Rights in Practice*, London 1997.

Hardy, E. *et al.*: *Illegal Induced Abortion Among Female Employees of a Brazilian University*, in Unwanted Pregnancies and Public Policies, H. Correa (ed.), 109–122.

Harris, D.J. & Warbrick, C.: *The Law of the European Convention on Human Rights*, London 1995.

Harrison, B.W.: *Our Right to Choose, Towards a New Ethic of Abortion*, Boston 1983.

Hartman, J.F.: *Derogation from Human Rights Treaties in Public Emergencies: a Critique of Implementation by the European Commission and Court of Human Rights and the Human Rights Committee of the United Nations*, Harvard International Law Journal 1981, Vol. 22, 1–52.

Hathaway, J.C.: *The Law of Refugee Status*, Vancouver 1991.

—— *Reconceiving Refugee Law as Human Rights Protection*, in Problems and Prospects of Refugee Law, V. Gowlland & K. Samson (eds.), Geneva 1992, 9–31.

Hathaway, J.C. & Dent J.A.: *Refugee Rights*, Report on a Comparative Survey, Toronto 1995.

Healey, S.A.: *Prosecuting Rape Under the Statute of the War Crimes Tribunal for the Former Yugoslavia*, Brooklyn Journal of International Law 1995, Vol. 21, No. 2, 369 *et seq.*

Hebel von, H.: *An International Tribunal for the Former Yugoslavia; An Act of Powerlessness or a new Challenge for the International Community?*, NQHR 1993, Vol. 11, 437–456.

Heise, L.L.: *Freedom Close to Home: The Impact of Violence Against Women on Reproductive Rights*, in Women's rights, human rights, J. Peters & A. Wolper (eds.), 238–256.

Henkin, A.H.(ed.): *Human Dignity, The Internalization of Human Rights*, New York 1979.

Henkin, L., Pugh, R.C., Schachter, O. & Smith, H.: *International Law, Cases and Materials*, Minnesota 1987.

Henkin, L.: *The Ghost of Senator Bricker*, AJIL 1995, Vol. 89, 341–350.

—— *International Law: Politics and Values*, Dordrecht 1995.

Higgins, R.: *Internal war and international law*, in the Future of the International Legal Order, R. Higgins (ed.), Princeton 1971, 81–121.

—— *The United Nations Human Rights Committee*, in Human Rights for the 1990s Legal, Political and Ethical Issues, R. Blackbum & J.M. Taylor (eds.), London 1991.

—— *Problems and Process – International Law and How to Use It,* Oxford 1994.

Hill, H.H.: *Central American Court of Justice*, in Encyclopedia of Public International Law 1981, Vol. 1, 41–45.

Hong, Z.: *The Testimony of Women Writers: The Situation of Women in China*, in Women's rights, human rights, J. Peters & A. Wolper (eds.), 96–103.

Horn, F.: *Reservations and Interpretative Declarations to Multilateral Treaties*, Uppsala 1988.

Hosken, P.F.: *Toward a Definition of Women's Human Rights*, HRQ 1981, Vol. 3, 1 *et seq.*

Hosoyal, C., Ando, N., Onuma Y. & Minear, R.: *The Tokyo War Crimes Trial – An International Symposium*, Tokyo 1988.

Howen, N.: *From Nuremberg to the Balkans: The international war crimes tribunal for the former Yugoslavia*, in Monitoring Human Rights in Europe, A. Bloed *et al.* (eds.), 261–285.

Howard, M., Andreopoulos, G.J. & Schulman, M.R. (eds.): *The Laws of War: Constraints on Warfare in the Western World,* Yale University Press New Haven 1994.

Howard, R.: *Cultural Absolutism and the Nostalgia for Community*, HRQ 1993, Vol. 15, 315–338.

Howland, C.W.: *The Challenge of Religious Fundamentalism to the Liberty and Equality Rights of Women: An Analysis under the United Nations Charter,* Columbia Journal of Transnational Law 1997, Vol. 35, 271–377.

Hubbard, R.: *The Politics of Fetal/Maternal Conflict,* in Power and Decision, G. Sen & R.C. Snow (eds.), 311–325.

Hudson, M.O.: *The Central American Court of Justice*, AJIL 1932, Vol. 26, 759–786.

Human Rights Watch: *Justice in The Balance*, New York 1998.

Humphry, J.B.: *No distant millennium: the international law of human rights*, UNESCO Paris 1989.

Ilic, Z.: *The Convention on the Elimination of All Forms of Discrimination against Women*, in Manual on Human Rights Reporting, UN New York 1991, 153–177.

Imbert, P.H.: *Rights of the Poor, Poor Rights?,* in The Review (ICJ), December 1995, No. 55, 85–97.

Ingelse, C: "*Soft Law"?,* Polish Yearbook of International Law 1993, Vol. 20, 75–90.

Jacobson, R.: *The Committee on the Elimination of Discrimination against Women,* in The United Nations and Human Rights, P. Alston (ed.), 444–473.

Jacobs, F.G. & White, R.C.A.: *The European Convention on Human Rights*, Oxford 1996.

Jaising, I.: *Violence Against Women: The Indian Perspective*, in Women's rights, human rights, J. Peters & A. Wolper (eds.), 51–57.

Jareborg, N.: *Essays in Criminal Law*, Uppsala 1988.

Jenkins, S.: *Abortion Rights, Poor Women, and Religious Diversity*, in From Abortion to Reproductive Freedom, M.G. Fried (ed.), 151–157.

Jennings, R. & Watts, A.: *Oppenheim's International Law*, Vol. I, PEACE, London 1992.

Jeschek, H.-H.: *Genocide*, in Encyclopedia of Public International Law, Vol. 8, 255–258.

Johnson, S.P.: *World Population – Turning the Tide*, Three decades of progress, London 1994.

Jónasdottir, A.G.: *Love Power and Political Interests*, Örebro Studies No. 7, Kumla 1991.

Jung, S.: *Die Rechtsprobleme der Nürnberger Prozesse*, Tübingen 1992.

Kaganas, F.: *Rape in Marriage – Law Reform in Scotland and South Africa*, International Journal of Law and the Family 1990, Vol. 4, 320 *et seq.*

Kalshoven, F.: *Constraints on the Waging of War*, ICRC, Geneva 1991.

Kalshoven, F. & Sandoz, Y.: *Implementation of International Humanitarian Law*, Dordrecht 1989.

Kaufman, N.H. & Lindquist, A.S.: *Critiquing Gender-Neutral Treaty Language: The Convention on the Elimination of All Forms of Discrimination Against Women*, in Women's rights, human rights, J. Peters & A. Wolper (eds.), 114–126.

Kee, H.P.: *Abortion in Singapore: a Legal Perspective*, ICLQ 1993, Vol. 42, 392 *et seq.*

Kelsen, H.: *Pure Theory of Law*, Berkeley 1967.

Kennedy, D.: *International Legal Structures,* Baden–Baden 1987.

Khushalani, Y.: *Dignity and Honour of Women as Basic and Fundamental Human Rights*, The Hague 1982.

Kirsch, P. & Holmes, J.T.: *The Rome Conference on an International Criminal Court*, AJIL 1999, Vol. 93, 2–12.

Klabbers, J.: *The redundancy of soft law*, NJIL 1996, Vol. 65, 167–182.

Kodjo, E.: *The African Charter on Human and Peoples' Rights*, HRLJ 1990, Vol. 11, 271–283.

Kohen, M.G.: *The Universal Declaration of Human Rights and Latin America*, ICJ The Review 1988, 44–47

Kokott, J.: *Das interamerikanische System zum Schutz der Menschenrechte*, Berlin 1986.
Kolbert, K.: *Developing a Reproductive Rights Agenda for the 1990s*, in M.G. Fried (ed.), 297–306.
Koskenniemi, M.: *From Apology to Utopia, The Structure of International Legal Argument,* Helsinki 1989.
Knoppers, B.M.: *Modern Birth Technology and Human Rights*, AJIL 1985, Vol. 33, p. 22 *et seq.*
Kréca, M: *Some General Reflections on Main Features of Ius Cogens as Notion of International Public Law*, in New Directions in International Law, Essays in Honour of Wolfgang Abendroth – Festschrift zu seinem 75. Geburtstag, R.G. Girardot *et al.* (eds.), 27–41.
Krill, F.: *The Protection of Women in International Humanitarian Law*, International Review of the Red Cross, No. 249, Geneva 1985.
Kritchevsky, B.: *The Unmarried Woman's Right to Artificial Insemination: a Call for an Expanded Definition of Family*, Harvard Women's Law Journal 1981, Vol. 4, 1 *et seq.*
Kuhn, A.K.: *The Genocide Convention and State Rights*, AJIL 1949, Vol. 43, 498–501.
Kurczewski, J. & Maclean, M. (eds.): *Family Law and Family Policy in the New Europe,* Aldershot 1997.
Kuzmanovic, J.: *Legacies of Invisibility: Past Silence, Present Violence Against Women in the Former Yugoslavia*, in Women's rights, human rights, J. Peters & A. Wolper (eds.), 57–62.
Kwakwa, E.K.: *The International Law of Armed Conflict: Personal and Material Fields of Application*, Dordrecht 1992.
Kälin, W., Riedel E., Karl, W., Bryde, B.-O., von Bar, C. & Geimer, R.: *Aktuelle Probleme des Menschenrechtsschutzes*, Heidelberg 1994.
Lacey, N.: *Unspeakable Subjects – Feminist Essays in Legal and Social Theory*, Oxford 1998.
Lackland, T.H.: *Towards Creating a Philosophy of Fundamental Human Rights*, Columbia Human Rights Law Review 1975, Vol. 6, 489 *et seq.*
Lal, A.: *Abortion under the Indian Penal Code and the Medical Termination of Pregnancy Act – A Comparative View*, Indian Socio-Legal Journal 1996, Vol. XXII, 93–103.
Lauterpacht, H.: *An International Bill of the Rights of Man*, New York 1945.
Lawson, R. & deBlois, M.: *The Dynamics of the Protection of Human Rights in Europe*, Dordrecht 1994.
Leary, V.A.: *The Right to Reproductive Health in International Human Rights Law*, Health and Human Rights 1994, Vol. 1, 25–56.
—— *Justiciability and Beyond; Complaint Procedures and the Right to Health*, The Review, December 1995, No. 55, 105–122.
Lemkin, R.: *Axis Rule in Occupied Europe*, Washington 1944.
—— *Genocide as a Crime Under International Law*, AJIL 1947, Vol. 41, 145–151.
Lerner, N.: *Group Rights and Discrimination in International Law*, Dordrecht 1991.
Lescure, K. & Trintignac, F.: *International Justice for Former Yugoslavia*, The Hague 1996.
Lillich, R.: *Civil Rights*, in Human Rights in International Law: Legal and Policy Issues, T. Meron (ed.), Oxford 1988, 115–170.
Lindholm, T.: *Article 1*, in The Universal Declaration of Human Rights, A Commentary, A. Eide *et al.* (eds.), Oslo 1992, 31–57.
Lippman, M.: *Nuremberg: Forty Five Years Later*, Connecticut Journal of International Law 1991, Vol. 7, 1–65.
Little, H.: *Non-Consensual Sterilization of the Intellectually Disabled in the Australian Context: Potential for Human Rights Abuse and the Need for Reform*, The Australian Yearbook of International Law 1993, Vol. 14, 203–226.

Littleton, C.A.: *Reconstructing Sexual Equality*, in Feminist Legal Theory, K.T.Bartlett & R.Kennedy (eds.), 35–56.

Loenen, T.: *Rethinking Sex Equality as a Human Rights*, NQHR 1994, Vol. 12, 253–270.

Lundström, K.: *Jämlikhet mellan kvinnor och män i EG-rätten*, Uppsala 1999.

Lysén, G.: *State Responsibility and International Liability of States for Lawful Acts*, Uppsala 1997.

Macdonald, R.St.J.: *The Use of Force by States in International Law*, in International Law: Achievements and Prospects, M. Bedjaoui (ed.), 717–740.

Macdonald, R.St.J., Matscher, F. & Petzold, H. (eds.): *The European System for the Protection of Human Rights*, Dordrecht 1993.

Macfarline, L.J.: *The Theory and Practice of Human Rights*, London 1985.

MacKinnon, C.A.: *Feminism Unmodified*, Cambridge 1987.

—— *Reflections on Sex Equality Under Law*, The Yale Law Journal 1991, Vol. 100, 1281–1297.

—— *Comment: "Theory is not a Luxury"*, in Reconceiving Reality: Women and International Law, D.G. Dallmeyer (ed.), 83–93.

—— *Turning Rape into Pornography: Postmodern Genocide*, in Mass Rape, A. Stiglmayer (ed.), 73–82.

—— *Rape, Genocide, and Women's Human Rights*, in A. Stiglmayer (ed.), 183–197.

Macphee, D. & Forest, K.: *Surrogacy: Programme Comparison and Policy Implications*, International Journal of Law and the Family 1990, 309 *et seq*.

Mahoney, P.: *Judicial Activism and Judicial Self-Restraint in the European Court of Human Rights: Two Sides of the Same Coin*; HRLJ 1990, Vol. 11, 57 *et seq*.

Mahoney, K.E.: *Canadian Approaches to Equality Rights and Gender Equality in the Courts*, in Human Rights of Women, R.J. Cook (ed.), 438–461.

Mahoney, K.E. & Mahoney, P.: *Human Rights in the Twenty-First Century*, A Global Challenge, Dordrecht 1992.

Malanczuk, P.: *Akehurst's Modern Introduction to International Law*, London 1997.

Malekian, F.: *International Criminal Law, The Legal and Critical Analysis of International Crimes*, Vol. I, Uppsala 1991.

Mansfield, L.: *Crimes against Humanity: Reflections on the Fiftieth Anniversary of Nuremberg and a Forgotten Legacy*, NJIL 1995, 293–341.

Marcelino, A.B.: *Combating Opposition in the Philippines*, IPPF 1996/1, 28–30.

Marks, S.P.: *Principles and norms of human rights applicable in emergency situations: Underdevelopment, catastrophes and armed conflicts*, in The International Dimensions of Human Rights, Vol. 1, K. Vasak (ed.), Paris 1982, 175–212.

Marwick, A.: *Women at War-1914–1918*, Glasgow 1977.

Matscher, F. & Petzold, H. (eds.): *Protecting Human Rights: the European Dimension*: Studies in Honour of Gérard J. Wiarda, Köln 1988.

Mayer, E.A.: *Cultural Particularism as a Bar to Women's Rights: Reflections on the Middle Eastern Experience*, in Women's rights, human rights, J. Peters & A. Wolper (eds.), 176–189.

Mbaya, E.: *Menschenrechtskodifikation in Afrika*, Vereinte Nationen 1984, Nr. 4, 132–136.

McCann, T.: *The American Convention on Human Rights toward Uniform Interpretation of Human Rights Law*, Fordham International Law Journal, 1983, Vol. 6, 610–635.

McConell, M.: *Feminist Theory as the Embodiment of Marginalization*, in Reconceiving Reality: Women and International Law, D.G. Dallmeyer (ed.), 61–83.

McCormack, T.L.H. & Simpson, G.J.: *A New International Criminal Law Regime?,* NILR 1995, 177–206.

McCormack, T.L.H. & Simpson, G.J. (eds.): *The Law of War Crimes: National and International Approaches*, The Hague 1997.

McCoubrey, H.: *International Humanitarian Law, The Regulation of Armed Conflicts*, Dartmouth 1990.

McDougal, M.S. & Feliciano, F.P.: *Law and Minimum World Public Order: The Legal Regulation of International Coercion*, New Haven 1961.

McDougal, M.S. & Reisman, W.M.: *International Law in Contemporary Perspective, The Public Order of the World Community*, Mineola 1981.

McDougal, Lasswell & Chen: *Human Rights for Women and World Public Order: The Outlawing of Sex-Based Discrimination*, AJIL 1975, Vol. 69, 497 *et seq.*

McGoldrick, D.: *The Human Rights Committee: It's Role in the Development of the International Covenant on Civil and Political Rights*, Oxford 1991.

McKean, W.: *Equality and Discrimination under International Law*, Oxford 1983.

McLean, S.(ed.): *Legal Issues in Human Reproduction*, Brookfield 1990.

McNeil, M., Varcoe & Jearley, S. (eds.): *The New Reproductive Technologies,* London 1990.

Medina, C.: *The Inter-American Commission on Human Rights and the Inter-American Court of Human Rights: Reflections on a Joint Venture*, HRQ 1990, Vol. 12, 439–464.

Meehan, E. & Sevenhuijsen, S.: *Equality Politics and Gender*, London 1991.

Meindersma, C.: *Applicability of Humanitarian Law in International and Internal Armed Conflict*, Hague Yearbook of International Law 1994, Vol. 7, 113–140.

Melander, G.: *The Two Refugee Definitions*, Raoul Wallenberg Institute, Report No. 4, Lund 1987.

Mercado, E.: *Consequences of Unwanted Pregnancies in Bolivia: An Overview*, in Unwanted Pregnancies and Public Policy, H. Correa (ed.), 179–193.

Merrills, G.: *The Development of International Law by the European Court of Human Rights*, Manchester 1983.

Meron, T.: *Human Rights Law-Making in the United Nations*, Oxford 1986.

—— *The Geneva Conventions as customary law*, AJIL 1987, Vol. 81, 348–370.

—— *Human Rights in International Law: Legal and Policy Issues*, Oxford 1988.

—— *Human Rights and Humanitarian Norms as Customary Law,* Oxford 1989.

—— *Enhancing the Effectiveness of the Prohibition of Discrimination against Women*, AJIL 1990, 216 *et seq.*

—— *The protection of the human person under human rights law and humanitarian law*, Bulletin of Human Rights 1991, 33–46.

—— *Rape as a Crime under International Humanitarian Law*, AJIL 1993, Vol. 87, 424 *et seq.*

—— *War Crimes in Yugoslavia and the Development of International Law*, AJIL 1994, Vol. 88, 78–88.

—— *International Criminalization of Internal Atrocities*, AJIL 1995, Vol. 89, 554–577.

—— *Is International Law Moving towards Criminalization?,* European Journal of International Law 1998, Vol. 9, No. 1, 18–31.

Meron, T. & Rosas, A.: *A Declaration of Minimum Humanitarian Standards*, AJIL 1991, Vol. 85, 375–381.

Mertus, J.: *State Discriminatory Family Law and Customary Abuses*, in Women's rights, human rights, J. Peters & A. Wolper (eds.), 135–149.

Meulders-Klein, M.: *The Position of the Father in European Legislation*, International Journal of Law and the Family 1990, Vol. 4, 136 *et seq.*

Miller, B.D.: *Unwanted Daughters in Northwest India*, in H. Correa (ed.), 193–203.

Mirhosseini, A.: *After the Revolution: Violations of Women's Human Rights in Iran*, in Women's rights, human rights, J. Peters & A. Wolper (eds.), 72–78.

Monroy Cabra, M.G.: *Rights and Duties Established by the American Convention on Human Rights*, The American University Law Review 1980, Vol. 30, 21–63.

Morgan, M.: *Founding Mothers: Women's Voices and Stories*, Boston University Law Review 1990, Vol. 70, 45 *et seq.*

Morgan, W.: *Sexuality and Human Rights: The First communication by an Australian to the Human Rights Committee under the Optional Protocol to the International Covenant on Civil and Political Rights*, The Australian Year Book of International Law 1993, Vol. 14, 277–292.

Morosin, M.N.: *Double Jeopardy and International Law: Obstacles to Formulating a General Principle*, NJIL 1995, 261–274.

Morris, A.E. & Nott, S.M.: *Working Women and the Law: Equality and Discrimination in Theory and Practice*, London 1991.

Morris, M.: *By Force of Arms: Rape, War, And Military Culture*, Duke Law Journal 1996, Vol. 45, 651–781.

Morris, V. & Scharf, M.P.: *An Insider's Guide to The International Criminal Tribunal for The Former Yugoslavia*, New York 1995.

Mumtaz, K.: *The Woman not the Womb: Population Policy in Pakistan*, Development 1994: 1, 26–30.

Murphy, S.D.: *Progress and Jurisprudence of the International Criminal Tribunal for the Former Yugoslavia*, AJIL 1999, Vol. 93, 57–97.

Nahlik, E.S.: *From reprisals to individual penal responsibility*, in Humanitarian Law of Armed Conflict Challenges Ahead, A.J.M. Delissen & G.J. Tanja (eds.), 165–177.

Nelson, A.: *Swedish and Foreign Crimes in the Swedish Criminal Justice System,* in Double Criminality, Studies in International Criminal Law, N. Jareborg (ed.), Uppsala 1989, 11–39.

—— *Kring födelse och död-några juridiska reflexioner*, Annales Societatis Litterarum Humaniorum Regiae Upsaliensis 1997, 109–138.

Nguema, I.: *Human Rights Perspectives in Africa, The Roots of a Constant Challenge,* HRLJ 1990, Vol. 11, 261–271.

Nielsen, L.: *Family Rights and the 'Registered Partnership' in Denmark,* International Journal of Law and the Family 1990, Vol. 4, 297 *et seq.*

—— *The Right to a Child versus the Right of a Child*, in Parenthood in Modern Society, J. Ekelaar & P. Sarcevic (eds.), 213–223.

—— *Legal consensus and divergence in Europe in the area of assisted conception-room for harmonization?,* in Creating the Child, D. Evans (ed.), pp. 305–325.

Nino, C.S.: *The Ethics of Human Rights*, Oxford 1991.

Noonan, J.T.: *Contraception*, Cambridge MA, 1965.

Nordborg, G.(ed.): *13 kvinnoperspektiv på rätten*, Uppsala 1995.

Norrie, K.Mck.: *Reproductive Technology, Transsexualism and Homosexuality: New Problems for International Private Law*, ICLQ 1994, Vol. 43, 757–775.

Norris, R.E.: *Bringing Human Rights Petitions Before the Inter-American Commission*, Santa Clara Law Review 1980, Vol. 20, 733–757.

Nowak, M.: *U. N. Covenant on Civil and Political Rights, CCPR Commentary*, Strasbourg 1993.

—— *World Conference on Human Rights*, Vienna 1993, The Contributions of NGOs, Reports and Documents, Wien 1994.

—— *The Need for an Optional Protocol to the International Covenant on Economic, Social and Cultural Rights*, The Review, December 1995, No. 55, 153–165.

Nowak, M. & Suntinger W.: *International mechanisms for the prevention of torture*, in Monitoring Human Rights in Europe, A. Bloed *et al.* (eds.), 145–169.

Nyong´O, D. & Oodit, G.: *Tackling unsafe abortions in Mauritius*, IPPF 1996/1, 35–38.

Obermeyer, C.M.: *Religious Doctrine, State Ideology, and Reproductive Options in Islam*, in Power and Decision, G. Sen & R.C. Snow (eds.), 59–77.

O'Brien, J.C.: *The International Tribunal For Violations of International Humanitarian Law in former Yugoslavia*, AJIL 1993, Vol. 87, 639–659.

O' Donovan, K.: *What shall we tell the children? Reflections on children's perspectives and the reproduction revolution*, in R. Lee & D. Morgan (eds.), 96 *et seq.*

O'Donovan, K. & Szyszczak, E.: *Equality and Sex Discrimination Law*, Oxford 1988.

O'Flaherty, M.: *Human Rights and the UN,* Practice before the treaty bodies, London 1996.

Okere, O.: *The Protection of Human Rights in Africa and the African Charter on Human and Peoples' Rights: a Comparative Analysis with the European and American Systems*, HRQ 1984, Vol. 6, 141–159.

Olsen, F.E.: *International Law: Feminist Critiques of the Public/Private Distinction*, in Reconceiving Reality: Women in International Law, D.G. Dallmeyer (ed.), 157–171.

—— *Feminist Legal Theory I: Foundations and Outlooks,* Dartmouth 1995.

—— *Feminist Legal Theory II: Positioning Feminist Theory Within the Law*, Dartmouth 1995.

Opsahl, T.: *The Convention and the Right to Respect for Family Life*, in Privacy and Human Rights, A.A. Robertson (ed.), Manchester 1970, 192–247.

—— *Ni års sameksistens mellom Europa- og FN-systemene*, Mennesker & rettigheter, 1986, No. 2, 47–55.

—— *Instruments of Implementation of Human Rights*, HRLJ 1989, Vol. 10, 13–34.

—— *The Human Rights Committee*, in The United Nations and Human Rights, P. Alston (ed.), 369–444.

Oraá, J.: *Human Rights in States of Emergency in International Law*, Oxford 1992.

Orentlicher, D.F.: *Setting Accounts: The Duty to Prosecute Human Rights Violations of a Prior Regime*, Yale Law Journal 1991, Vol. 100, 2537–2614.

Outshoorn, J.: *Is This What We Wanted? Positive Action as Issue Perversion*, in Equality Politics and Gender, E. Meehan & S. Sevenhuijsen (eds.), 104–122.

Packer, C.A.A.: *The Right to Reproductive Choice, A Study in International Law*, Åbo 1996.

Palm-Risse, M.: *Der völkerrechtliche Schutz von Ehe und Familie*, Berlin 1990.

Partsch, K.J.: *Fundamental Principles of Human Rights: Self-Determination, Equality and Non-discrimination*, in The International Dimensions of Human Rights, K. Vasak (ed.), Vol. 1, UNESCO 1982, 61–87.

—— *Discrimination,* in The European System for the Protection of Human Rights, R.St. J. Macdonald, F. Matscher & H. Petzold, The European System for the Protection of Human Rights, 571–593.

Paust, J.J.: *Superior Orders and Command Responsibility*, in International Criminal Law, Vol. III Enforcement, M.C. Bassiouni (ed), 73–88.

—— *Peace-Making and Security Council Powers: Bosnia-Herzegovina Raises International and Constitutional Questions*, Southern Illinois University Law Journal 1994, Vol. 19, 131–143.

—— *The Politics of Establishing an International Criminal Court*, Duke Journal of Comparative and International Law 1995, Vol. 6, 167–173.

Pellonpää, M.: *Economic, Social and Cultural Rights*, in The European System for the Protection of Human Rights, R.St.J. Macdonald *et al.* (eds.), Dordrecht 1993, 855–875.

Peng, X.: *Demographic Transition in China: Fertility Trends since the 1950s,* Beijing 1991.

Pepple, A.S.: *Socio-legal and Contemporary Problems of Rape in Nigeria*, Indian Socio-Legal Journal 1996, Vol. XXII, 43–57.

Petchesky, R.P.: *Reproductive Freedom: Beyond "A Woman's Right to Choose",* SIGNS, Journal of Women in Culture and Society 1980, Vol. 5, 661–685.

Petchesky, R.P. & Judd, K.: *Negotiating Reproductive Rights*, London 1998.

Peters, J. & Wolper, A. (eds.): *Women's Rights, Human Rights*, International Feminist Perspectives, New York 1995.

—— Introduction, *ibid.*, 1–11.

Pictet, J.: *Development and Principles of International Humanitarian Law*, Dordrecht 1985.

—— *Humanitarian Law and the Protection of War Victims*, Henry Dunant Institute, Geneva 1986.

—— *Humanitarian ideas shared by different schools of thought and cultural traditions*, in International Dimensions of Humanitarian Law, UNESCO, Dordrecht 1988, 3–5.

Pitanguy, J.: *Feminist Politics and Reproductive Rights: The Case of Brazil*, in Power and Decision, G. Sen & R.C. Snow (eds.), 101–123.

Pojman, P.L. & Westmoreland, R.: *Equality, Selected Readings*, New York 1997.

Pocar, F.: *The International Covenant on Civil and Political Rights*, in Manual on Human Rights Reporting, UN New York 1991, 79–127.

Preux de, J.: *Special protection of women and children*, International Review of the Red Cross, Geneva 1985, No. 248, 292–302.

Prunier, G.: *The Rwanda Crisis, History of a Genocide*, New York 1995.

Puls, K.E.: *Report on The International Tribunal to Adjudicate War Crimes Committed in the Former Yugoslavia*, Boston University International Law Journal 1994, Vol. 12: 139, 139–152.

Pyne, H.H.: *Reproductive Experiences and Needs of Thai Women: Where Has Development Taken Us?*, in Power and Decision, G. Sen & R.C. Snow (eds.), 19–43.

Rabledo, Gómez, A.: *El Ius Cogens Internacional*, UNAM, Mexico City 1982.

Ragazzi, M.: *The Concept of International Obligations Erga Omnes*, Oxford 1997.

Rademakers, J.: *Teenage Pregnancy and Contraceptive Behavior in the Netherlands*, in Unwanted Pregnancies and Public Policy, H. Correa (ed.), 59–68.

—— *Abortion Laws and Practice: An International Comparison*, ibid., 163–171.

Ramcharan, B.G.: *Equality and Non-discrimination*, in The International Bill of Rights: The Covenant on Civil and Political Rights, L. Henkin (ed.), New York 1981.

—— *The Right to Life in International Law*, Boston 1985.

Rao, A.: *The Politics of Gender and Culture in International Human Rights Discourse*, in Women's rights, human rights, J. Peters & A. Wolper (eds.), 167–176.

Rasmussen, M.A.: *Rules of Evidence for the International Criminal Court*, NJIL 1995, 275–291.

Rathfelder, E.: *Krieg auf dem Balkan-die europäische Verantwortung*, Reinbek 1992.

Reanda, L.: *Human Rights and Women's Rights: The United Nations Approach*, HRQ 1981, Vol. 3, 15 *et seq.*

—— *The Commission on the Status of Women*, in The United Nations and Human Rights, P. Alston (ed.), 265–304.

Reardon, B.: *Discrimination*, World in Focus 1977, Vol. 2, 10 *et seq.*

Rehof, L.A.: *Guide to the Travaux Préparatoires of the United Nations Convention on the Elimination of All Forms of Discrimination against Women*, Dordrecht 1993.

Reisman, W.M.: *The Concept and Functions of Soft Law in International Politics,* in E.G. Bello & B.A.A. San (eds.), 135–145.

Reissmüller, J.G.: *Die bosnische Tragödie*, Stuttgart 1993.

Reoch, R. (ed.): *Human Rights: the new consensus*, London 1994.

Roberts, A. & Kingsbury B. (eds.): *United Nations, Divided World*, The UN's Roles in International Relations, Oxford 1993.

Robertson, A.H.: *The American Convention on Human Rights and the European Convention: a Comparative Study*, Annuaire European 1981, Vol. XXIX, 50–76.

Robertson, A.H. & Merrills, J.G.: *Human Rights in the World*, Oxford 1993.
Robinson, D.: *Defining "Crimes against Humanity" at the Rome Conference*, AJIL 1999, Vol. 93, 43–57.
Rodley, N: *The Treatment of Prisoners under International Law*, Oxford 1987.
Roggemann, H.: *Krieg und Frieden auf dem Balkan. Historische Kriegsursachen, wirtschaftliche und soziale Kriegsfolgen, politische und rechtliche Friedensvoraussetzungen*, Berlin 1993.
—— *Der Internationale Strafgerichtshof der Vereinten Nationen von 1993 und der Krieg auf dem Balkan*, Berlin 1994.
Romans-Clarkson, S.E.: *What Role for Induced Abortion in the Management of Unwanted Pregnancies?,* in Unwanted Pregnancies and Public Policy, H. Correa (ed.), 123–144.
Rosas, A.: *De nordiska ländernas politik i fråga om mänskliga rättigheter*, Mennesker og Rettigheter 1986, No. 2, 38–44.
—— *Democracy and Human Rights,* in Human Rights in a Changing East-West Perspective, Rosas, A. & Helgesen, J. (eds.), London 1990.
—— *State Responsibility and Liability under Civil Liability Regimes*, in Current International Law Issues, O. Bring & S. Mahmoudi (eds.), 161–183.
—— *International monitoring mechanisms in situations of armed conflict*, in Monitoring Human Rights in Europe, A. Bloed *et al.* (eds.), 221–247.
Rosenstock, R.: *The Forty-Sixth Session of the International Law Commission*, AJIL 1995, Vol. 89, 390–395.
Roth, K.: *Domestic Violence as an International Human Rights Issue*, in Human Rights of Women, R.J. Cook (ed.), 326–340.
Roht-Arriaza, N. (ed.): *Impunity and Human Rights in International Law and Practice*, New York 1995.
Rozakis, C.L.: *The Concept of Jus Cogens in the Law of Treaties*, Amsterdam 1976.
Rumage, S.A.: *Resisting the West: The Clinton Administration's Promotion of Abortion at the 1994 Cairo Conference and the Strength of the Islamic Response*, California Western International Law Journal 1996, Vol. 27, 1–100.
Rüpke, G.: *Das Verbot Willkürlicher Gleichbehandlung in Seiner Bedeutung für Soziale Grundrechte*, in Festschrift für F. Ermacora, 484 *et seq.*
Rwomire, A.: *Adolescent Fertility in African Countries: Causes, Consequences, and Policies*, in Unwanted Pregnancies and Public Policy, H. Correa (ed.), 99–108.
Sadik, N.: *Panel Statement*, in Development Cooperation for Human Rights and Democracy, Ministry for Foreign Affairs, Stockholm 1993, 35–42.
Sahovic, M.: *Medunarodno Pravo i Jugoslovenska Kriza*, Beograd 1996.
Saito, Y.: *Judge Tanaka, natural law and the principle of equality*, in The Living Law of Nations, G. Alfredsson & P. Macalister-Smith (eds.), 399–409.
Saldeen, Å.: *Sweden: Family Counselling, the Tortuous Liability of Parents and Homosexual Partnership*, University of Louisville Journal of Family Law 1994–95, Vol. 33, 513–523,
—— *The Rights of Children to Speak for Themselves and Obtain Access to Information Concerning Their Biological Origins Etc..*, in The International Survey of Family Law 1994, A. Bainham (ed.), The Hague 1996, 441–449,
—— *Barnets rätt till sitt ursprung*, in De lege, Uppsala 1996, 249–275,
—— *Rights of the unborn child and questions of custody, access and residence*, in The International Survey of Family Law 1995, A. Bainham (ed.), The Hague 1997, 477–487.
—— *Barn och föräldrar*, Uppsala 1997.
Sandoz, Y.: *Implementing international humanitarian law*, in International Dimensions of Humanitarian Law, 259–283.

Sajor, L.: *Common Grounds, Violence Against Women in War and Armed Conflict Situations*, Asian Center for Women's Human Rights 1998.
Scott, C.: *The Interdependence and Permeability of Human Rights Norms: Towards a Partial Fusion of the International Covenants on Human Rights*, Osgoode Hall Law Journal 1989, Vol. 27, p. 770 *et seq.*
Schachter, O.: *General Course in International Law*, RdC 1982, Vol. 178, 182 *et seq.*
—— *Human Dignity as a Normative Concept*, AJIL 1983, Vol. 77, 848–854.
—— *International Law in Theory and Practice*, Dordrecht 1991.
Schaefer, K.: *In-vitro Fertilisation, Frozen Embryos, and The Right to Privacy – Are Mandatory Donation Laws Constitutional ?*, Pacific Law Journal 1990, Vol. 22, 87 *et seq.*
Schick, P.I.: *Law and Moral Dilemmas Affecting Life and Death*, Council of Europe, Strasbourg 1990.
Schindler, D. & Toman, J. (eds.): *The Laws of Armed Conflicts: a Collection of Conventions, Resolutions and Other Documents*, Dordrecht 1988.
Schmale, W.: *Human Rights and Cultural Diversity*, Goldbach 1993.
Schmidt, M.G.: *Individual Human Rights Complaints Procedures Based on United Nations Treaties and the Need for Reform*, ICLQ 1992, Vol. 41, 645 *et seq.*
Schutter de, O.: *L'interprétation de la Convention Européenne des Droits de l'Homme – Un Essai de Démolition*, Revue de Droit International de Sciences Diplomatiques 1992, 93 *et eq.*
Schutte, J.J.E.: *The system of repression of breaches of Additional Protocol I,* in Humanitarian Law of Armed Conflict, A.J.M. Delissen & G.J. Tanja (eds.), 177-197.
Schutz, R.: *The Right to Parenthood: Surrogacy and Frozen Embryos*, in The International Survey of Family Law 1996, The Hague 1998, 237-257.
Schwarzeberger, G.: *A Manual of International Law*, London 1960.
—— *International Law as Applied by International Courts and Tribunals*, Vol. II, The Law of Armed Conflict, London 1968.
Schwelb, E.: *Some Aspects of International Jus Cogens as Formulated by the International Law Commission*, AJIL 1967, Vol. 61, 948 *et seq.*
—— *The Abuse of the Right to Petition*, Revue des Droits de l'Homme 1970, 313 *et seq.*
Scott, E.S.: *Rational Decisionmaking About Marriage and Divorce*, Virginia Law Review 1990, Vol. 76, 9-94.
Scharf, M.P.: *Balkan Justice, The Story Behind the First International War Crimes Trial Since Nuremberg*, Durham 1997.
Seifert, R.: *War and Rape: A Preliminary Analysis*, in Mass Rape, A. Stiglmayer (ed.), 54–73.
Sen, G. & Snow, R.C. (eds.): *Power and Decision, The Social Control of Reproduction*, Harvard University Press, Boston 1994.
Sen, G.; Germain, A. & Chen, L.C.: *Population Policies Reconsidered, Health, Empowerment, and Rights*, (eds.), Harvard University Press 1994.
Shalev, C.: *Women in Israel: Fighting Tradition*, in Women's rights, human rights, J. Peters & A. Wolper (eds.), 89-96.
Shaw, M.N.: *Genocide and International Law*, in International Law at a Time of Perplexity, Y. Dinstein & M. Tabory (ed.), 797-820.
Shelton, D.: *Abortion and the Right to Life in the Inter-American System: The Case of "Baby Boy"*, HRLJ 1981, Vol. 2, 309 *et seq.*
—— *Improving the Status of Women Through International Law*, Whittier Law Review 1987, Vol. 9, 414 *et seq.*
—— *Improving Human Rights Protections: Recommendations for Enhancing the Effectiveness of the Inter-American Commission and the Inter-American Court of Human*

*Rights*, The American University Journal of International Law and Policy 1988, Vol. 3, 323–329.

—— *Private Violence, Public Wrongs, and the Responsibility of States*, Fordham ILJ 1990, Vol. 13, 1 *et seq.*

Shifman, P.: *Involuntary Parenthood: Misrepresentation as to the Use of Contraceptives*, International Journal of Law and the Family 1990, Vol. 4, 284 *et seq.*

Shiota, K.: *Induced Abortion and Unwanted Pregnancies in Japan*, in Unwanted Pregnancies and Public Policy, H. Correa (ed.), 145–154.

Sieghart, P.: *The International Law of Human Rights*, Oxford 1983.

—— *AIDS and Human Rights, A UK Perspective*, London 1989.

Sima, B. & Alston, P.: *The Sources of Human Rights Law: Custom, Jus Cogens & General Principles*, Australian YIL 1992, Vol. 12, 82–108.

Sokolovic, D.: *Organiseret forbrydelse*, Mennesker og rettigheter 1995, No. 3, 278–282.

Sommaruga, C.: *Human rights and international humanitarian law*, Bulletin of Human Rights 1991, 55–63.

Soupart, P.: *Present and Possible Future Research in the USA of Human Embryos*, in The Contraceptive Ethos, S.S. Spicker, B. Bondeson & H.T. Engelhardt (eds.), Dordrecht 1987, 68 *et seq.*

Spinedi, M. & Simma, B.: *United Nations Codification of State Responsibility*, New York 1987.

Stamatopoulou, E.: *Women's Rights and the United Nations*, in Women's rights, human rights, J. Peters & A. Wolper (eds.), 36–51.

Stark, B.: *The "Other" Half of the International Bill of Rights as a Postmodern Feminist Text*, in Reconceiving Reality: Women and International Law, D.G. Dallmeyer (ed.), 19–61.

Steiner, J.H. & Alston, P. (eds.): *International Human Rights in Context*, Law, Politics, Morals, *Text and Materials*, Oxford 1996.

Stiglmayer, A. (ed.): *Mass Rape. The War Against Women in Bosnia-Herzegovina*, University of Nebraska Press 1994.

—— *The War in the Former Yugoslavia*, ibid., 1–35.

—— *The Rapes in Bosnia-Herzegovina*, ibid., 82–170.

Strömholm, S.: *Rätt, rättskällor och rättstillämpning,* Stockholm 1991.

Suikkari, S.: *Debate in the United Nations on the International Law Commission's Draft Statute for an International Criminal Court*, NJIL 1995, 205–221.

Sullivan, D.J.: *Women's Human Rights and the 1993 World Conference on Human Rights*, AJIL 1994, Vol. 88, 152–167.

—— *The Private/Public Distinction in International Human Rights Law*, in Women's rights, human rights, J. Peters & A. Wolper (eds.), 126–135.

Sundberg, J.W.F.: *Om positivering av mänskliga rättigheter* (1982), Sundberg & Sundberg, Lagen och Europakonventionen, Institutet för offentlig och internationell rätt, nr. 95, Stockholm 1992.

—— *Laws, Rights and the European Convention on Human Rights*, Colorado 1986.

Sundberg, F.G.E.: *The European Experience of Human Rights Proceedings: The Precedent Value of the European Court's Decisions,* Akron Law Review 1987, Vol. 20, 629–647.

Sundberg-Weitman, B.: *Legal Test for Applying the European Convention on Human Rights and Freedoms in Adjudicating on Alleged Discrimination*, NTIR 1980, Vol. 49, 31–58.

Sundman, P.: *Human Rights, Justifications, and Christian Ethics,* Uppsala 1996.

Sundström, K.: *Abortion – A Reproductive Health Issue*, Stockholm 1993.

Sunga, L.S.: *Individual Responsibility in International Law for Serious Human Rights Violations*, Dordrecht 1992.

—— *The Commission of Experts on Rwanda and the Creation of the International Criminal Tribunal for Rwanda*/A note, HRLJ 1995, Vol. 16, 121–124.

Suy, E. *et al.*: *The Concept Jus Cogens in Public International Law*, in Langonissi Conference on International Law, Geneva 1967.

Szasz, P.C.: *The Proposed War Crimes Tribunal for Ex-Yugoslavia*, New York University Journal of International Law and Politics 1993, Vol. 25, 405–488.

Sztucki, J.: *Jus Cogens and the Vienna Convention on the Law of Treaties: A Critical Appraisal*, Vienna 1974.

—— *Interim Measures in The Hague Court, An Attempt at a Scrutiny*, Deventer 1983.

—— *The European Convention on Human Rights and National Law*, NTIR 1986, 219–231.

—— *Reflections on International "Soft Law"*, in Festskrift till Lars Hjerner, Studies in International Law, Stockholm 1990, 132–148.

Tabory, M.: *The Status of Women in Humanitarian Law*, in International Law at a Time of Perplexity, Y. Dinstein & M. Tabory (eds.), 941–951.

Tardu, M.E.: *The Protocol to the United Nations Covenant on Civil and Political Rights and the Inter-American System: a Study of Co-Existing Petition Procedures*, AJIL 1976, Vol. 70, 778–800.

—— *Human Rights, The International Petition System*, (section III B), New York, 1985.

—— *The Right of Individual Complaint to the United Nations for Violations of Human Rights*, in International Human Rights Law, Theory and Practice, I. Cotler & F.P. Eliadis (eds.), The Canadian Human Rights Foundation 1992, 405–434.

Taub, N.: *International Conference on Population and Development*, ASIL, Issue Papers on World Conferences, No. 1, Washington, D.C. 1994.

Teske, L.R.: *Power: An Interdisciplinary Approach*, in Reconceiving Reality: Women and International Law, D.G. Dallmeyer (ed.), 231–267.

Thomas, D.Q. & Beasley, M.E.: *Domestic Violence as a Human Rights Issue*, HRQ 1993, Vol. 15, 37 *et seq.*

Thornberry, P.: *International Law and the Rights of Minorities*, Oxford 1992.

Tickner, J.A.: *Feminist Approaches to Issues of War and Peace*, in Reconceiving Reality: Women and International Law, D.G. Dallmeyer (ed.), 267–275.

Tomaševski, K.: *Women and Human Rights*, London 1993.

—— *Human Rights in Population Policies, A Study for SIDA*, Lund 1994.

—— *Justiciability of Economic, Social and Cultural Rights*, The Review, December 1995, No. 55, 203–218.

—— *European Approaches to Enhancing Reproductive Freedom*, The American University Law Review 1995, Vol. 44, 1037–1051.

Tomuschat, C.: *Der Ausschuss für Menschenrechte – Recht und Praxis*, Vereinte Nationen 1981, Nr. 5, 141–148.

—— *Is Universality of Human Rights Standards an Outdated and Utopian Concept?*, in Das Europa der zweiten Generation, Strasbourg 1981.

—— *A System of International Criminal Prosecution is Taking Shape*, The Review 1993, No. 50, 56–71.

—— *Ein Internationaler Strafgerichtshof als Element einer Weltfriedensordnung*, Europa-Archiv 1994, 61 *et seq.*

di Torella, E.C.: *Maternity and Equal Treatment*, European Law Review 1998, No. 2, 165–170.

Toro, M.S.: *Popularizing Women's Human Rights at the Local Level: A Grassroots Methodology for Setting the International Agenda*, in Women's rights, human rights, J. Peters & A. Wolper (eds.), 189–197.

Tribe, L.H.: *Abortion, The Clash of Absolutes*, New York 1990.

Triffterer, O.: *Dogmatische Untersuchungen zur Entwicklung des materiellen Völkerstrafrechts seit Nürnberg*, Freiburg 1966.

Törnudd, K.: *Finland and the International Norms of Human Rights*, Dordrecht 1986.

Umozurike, O.: *Protection of victims of armed conflicts: III. civilian population*, in International Dimensions of Humanitarian Law, 187–203.

Vargas, M.D.: *Individual Access to the Inter-American Court of Human Rights*, New York University Journal of International Law and Politics, 1984, Vol. 16, 601–617.

Vasak, K.: *The International Dimensions of Human Rights*, 2 volumes, UNESCO, Paris 1982.

Vasilijević, V.A.: *Zločin i Odgovornost*, Beograd 1995.

—— *Medunarodni Krivični Tribunal*, Beograd 1996.

de Verannes, F.: *Asia-Pacific Human Rights Documents*, The Hague 1998.

Verdross, A.: *Jus Dispositivum and Jus Cogens in International Law*, AJIL 1966, Vol. 60, 217 *et seq.*

Verno, G.: *Gjennombrudd, etappeseier eller slag i luften? Kvinnene og Verdenskonferansen om menneskerettigheter*, Mennesker og rettigheter 1993, Vol. 11, 307 *et seq.*

Verschraegen, B.: *Gleichgeschlechtliche "Ehen"*, Wien 1994.

—— *Die Kinderrechtekonvention*, Wien 1996.

Verzijl, J.H.W.: *International Law in Historical Perspective*, Part IX – A: The Laws of War, The Netherlands 1978.

Vierdag, E.W.: *Non-discrimination and Justice*, Archiv für Rechts – und Sozialphilosophie 1971, Vol. LVII, 187 *et seq.*

—— *The Concept of Discrimination in International Law*, The Hague 1973.

Wajcman, J.: *Delivered into Men's Hands? The Social Construction of Reproductive Technology*, in Power and Decision, G. Sen & R.C. Snow (eds.), 153–177.

Wali, S.: *Human Rights for Refugee and Displaced Women*, in Women's rights, human rights, J. Peters & A. Wolper (eds.), 335–345.

Warbrick, C.: *Co-operation with the International Criminal Tribunal for Yugoslavia*, ICLQ 1996, Vol. 45, 947–954.

Wash, L.J., Suagee, D.B. & Schlanger, P.: *Conference Report, Inter-American Human Rights System: into the 1990s and Beyond*, The American University Journal of International Law and Policy 1988, Vol. 3, 517–565.

Webb, J.: *Genocide Treaty: ethnic cleansing, substantive and procedural hurdles in the application of the Genocide Convention to alleged crimes in the former Yugoslavia*, Georgia Journal of International and Comparative Law 1993, 391 *et seq.*

Weeramantry, C.G.: *Islamic Jurisprudence, An International Perspective*, London 1988.

Weil, P.: *Towards Relative Normativity in International Law*, AJIL 1983, Vol. 77, 413–432.

Welch, C.E.: *Human Rights and African Women: a Comparison of Protection Under Two Major Treaties*, HRQ 1993, Vol. 15, 565 *et seq.*

West, R.: *Jurisprudence and Gender*, The University of Chicago Law Review 1988, Vol. 55, 1–72.

Westman, P.: *Protection of the Unborn Child and the Rights of Parents, Recent Developments in Swedish and English Law*, SvJT 1993, 479–498.

Westen, P.: *The Empty Idea of Equality*, Harvard Law Review 1982, Vol. 95, 537–596.

Weston, H.B., Lukes, A.R. & Hnatt, K.M.: *Regional Human Rights*, Vanderbilt Journal of Transnational Law 1987, Vol. 20, 585–637.

Whitman, J. & Pocock, D.: *After Rwanda*, The Coordination of United Nations Humanitarian Assistance, London 1996.

Wieruszewski, R.: *Case study on the former Yugoslavia: The international mechanisms, their efficiency and failures*, in Monitoring Human Rights in Europe, A. Bloed *et al.* (eds.), 285–319.

Wilenski, P.: *The Structure of the UN in the Post-Cold War Period*, in United Nations: Divided World, A.Roberts & B.Kingsbury (eds.), 437–468.

Wright, S.: *Human Rights and Women's Rights*, in Human Rights in the Twenty-First Century: A Global Challenge, K.E. Mahoney & P. Mahoney (eds.), 80 *et seq.*

—— *Economic Rights, Social Justice and the State: A Feminist Reappraisal*, in Reconceiving Reality, Women in International Law, D.G. Dallmeyer (ed.), 117–143.

Wyngaert, Chr. van den: *The suppression of war crimes under Additional Protocol I*, in Humanitarian Law of Armed Conflict, A.J.M. Delissen & G.J. Tanja (eds.), 197–209.

Zayas, A. de, Möller, J. Opsahl, T.: *Application of the International Covenant on Civil And Political Rights Under the Optional Protocol by the Human Rights Committee*, GYIL 1989, Vol. 28, 9–64.

Zayas, A. de: *Human Rights and Humanitarian Law*, NJIL 1994, Vols. 61/62, 243–253.

—— *An International Criminal Court*, NJIL 1994, Vols. 61/62, 271–279.

Zearfoss, S.C.: *The Convention for the Elimination of All Forms of Discrimination Against Women: Radical, Reasonable, or Reactionary?,* Michigan Yearbook of International Legal Studies 1991, Vol. 12, 903–942.

Zemanek, K.: *Responsibility of States: General Principles*, in Encyclopedia of Public International Law, Vol. 10, Amsterdam 1987, 362–372.

Zipper, J. & Sevenhuijsen, S.: *Surrogacy: Feminist Notions of Motherhood, Reconsidered*, in Reproductive Technologies, M.Stanworth (ed.) Oxford 1987, 119 *et seq.*

Zülch, T. (ed.): *"Ethnische Säuberungen" – Völkermord für Grosserbien*, Hamburg 1992.

Österdahl, I.: *Räddaren i nöden? Den afrikanska stadgan för människans och folkens rättigheter*, SvJT 1993, 134–169.

—— *Threat to the Peace*, Uppsala 1998.

# Index

# International Studies in Human Rights

1. B.G. Ramcharan (ed.): *International Law and Fact-finding in the Field of Human Rights*. 1982 ISBN 90-247-3042-2
2. B.G. Ramcharan: *Humanitarian Good Offices in International Law*. The Good Offices of the United Nations Secretary-General in the Field of Human Rights. 1983 ISBN 90-247-2805-3
3. B.G. Ramcharan (ed.): *The Right to Life in International Law*. 1985 ISBN 90-247-3074-0
4. P. Alston and K. Tomaševski (eds.): *The Right to Food*. 1984 ISBN 90-247-3087-2
5. A Bloed and P. van Dijk (eds.): *Essays on Human Rights in the Helsinki Process*. 1985 ISBN 90-247-3211-5
6. K. Trnudd: *Finland and the International Norms of Human Rights*. 1986 ISBN 90-247-3257-3
7. H. Thoolen and B. Verstappen: *Human Rights Missions*. A Study of the Fact-finding Practice of Non-governmental Organizations. 1986 ISBN 90-247-3364-2
8. H. Hannum: *The Right to Leave and Return in International Law and Practice*. 1987 ISBN 90-247-3445-2
9. J.H. Burgers and H. Danelius: *The United Nations Convention against Torture*. A Handbook on the Convention against Torture and Other Cruel, Inhuman or Degrading Treatment or Punishment. 1988 ISBN 90-247-3609-9
10. D.A. Martin (ed.): *The New Asylum Seekers: Refugee Law in the 1980s*. The Ninth Sokol Colloquium on International Law. 1988 ISBN 90-247-3730-3
11. C.M. Quiroga: *The Battle of Human Rights*. Gross, Systematic Violations and the Inter-American System. 1988 ISBN 90-247-3687-0
12. L.A. Rehof and C. Gulmann (eds.): *Human Rights in Domestic Law and Development Assistance Policies of the Nordic Countries*. 1989 ISBN 90-247-3743-5
13. B.G. Ramcharan: *The Concept and Present Status of International Protection of Human Rights*. Forty Years After the Universal Declaration. 1989 ISBN 90-247-3759-1
14. A.D. Byre and B.Y. Byfield (eds.): *International Human Rights Law in the Commonwealth Caribbean*. 1991 ISBN 90-247-3785-0
15. N. Lerner: *Groups Rights and Discrimination in International Law*. 1991 ISBN 0-7923-0853-0
16. S. Shetreet (ed.): *Free Speech and National Security*. 1991 ISBN 0-7923-1030-6
17. G. Gilbert: *Aspects of Extradition Law*. 1991 ISBN 0-7923-1162-0
18. P.E. Veerman: *The Rights of the Child and the Changing Image of Childhood*. 1991 ISBN 0-7923-1250-3
19. M. Delmas-Marty (ed.): *The European Convention for the Protection of Human Rights*. International Protection versus National Restrictions. 1991 ISBN 0-7923-1283-X

# International Studies in Human Rights

20. A. Bloed and P. van Dijk (eds.): *The Human Dimension of the Helsinki Process*. The Vienna Follow-up Meeting and its Aftermath. 1991 ISBN 0-7923-1337-2
21. L.S. Sunga: *Individual Responsibility in International Law for Serious Human Rights Violations*. 1992 ISBN 0-7923-1453-0
22. S. Frankowski and D. Shelton (eds.): *Preventive Detention*. A Comparative and International Law Perspective. 1992 ISBN 0-7923-1465-4
23. M. Freeman and P. Veerman (eds.): *The Ideologies of Children's Rights*. 1992 ISBN 0-7923-1800-5
24. S. Stavros: *The Guarantees for Accused Persons Under Article 6 of the European Convention on Human Rights*. An Analysis of the Application of the Convention and a Comparison with Other Instruments. 1993 ISBN 0-7923-1897-8
25. A. Rosas and J. Helgesen (eds.): *The Strength of Diversity*. Human Rights and Pluralist Democracy. 1992 ISBN 0-7923-1987-7
26. K. Waaldijk and A. Clapham (eds.): *Homosexuality: A European Community Issue*. Essays on Lesbian and Gay Rights in European Law and Policy. 1993 ISBN 0-7923-2038-7; Pb: 0-7923-2240-1
27. Y.K. Tyagi: *The Law and Practice of the UN Human Rights Committee*. 1993 ISBN 0-7923-2040-9
28. H.Ch. Yourow: *The Margin of Appreciation Doctrine in the Dynamics of European Human Rights Jurisprudence*. 1996 ISBN 0-7923-3338-1
29. L.A. Rehof: *Guide to the* Travaux PrÇparatoires *of the United Nations Convention on the Elimination of All Forms of Discrimination against Women*. 1993 ISBN 0-7923-2222-3
30. A. Bloed, L. Leicht, M. Novak and A. Rosas (eds.): *Monitoring Human Rights in Europe*. Comparing International Procedures and Mechanisms. 1993 ISBN 0-7923-2383-1
31. A. Harding and J. Hatchard (eds.): *Preventive Detention and Security Law*. A Comparative Survey. 1993 ISBN 0-7923-2432-3
32. Y. Beigbeder: *International Monitoring of Plebiscites, Referenda and National Elections*. Self-determination and Transition to Democracy. 1994 ISBN 0-7923-2563-X
33, T.D. Jones: *Human Rights: Group Defamation, Freedom of Expression and the Law of Nations*. 1997 ISBN 90-411-0265-5
34. D.M. Beatty (ed.): *Human Rights and Judicial Review*. A Comparative Perspective. 1994 ISBN 0-7923-2968-6
35. G. Van Bueren, *The International Law on the Rights of the Child*. 1995 ISBN 0-7923-2687-3
36. T. Zwart: *The Admissibility of Human Rights Petitions*. The Case Law of the European Commission of Human Rights and the Human Rights Committee. 1994 ISBN 0-7923-3146-X; Pb: 0-7923-3147-8
37. H. Lambert: *Seeking Asylum*. Comparative Law and Practice in Selected European Countries. 1995 ISBN 0-7923-3152-4

# International Studies in Human Rights

38. E. Lijnzaad: *Reservations to UN-Human Rights Treaties*. Ratify and Ruin? 1994 ISBN 0-7923-3256-3
39. L.G. Loucaides: *Essays on the Developing Law of Human Rights*. 1995 ISBN 0-7923-3276-8
40. T. Degener and Y. Koster-Dreese (eds.): *Human Rights and Disabled Persons*. Essays and Relevant Human Rights Instruments. 1995 ISBN 0-7923-3298-9
41. J.-M. Henckaerts: *Mass Expulsion in Modern International Law and Practice*. 1995 ISBN 90-411-0072-5
42. N.A. Neuwahl and A. Rosas (eds.): *The European Union and Human Rights*. 1995 ISBN 90-411-0124-1
43. H. Hey: *Gross Human Rights Violations: A Search for Causes*. A Study of Guatemala and Costa Rica. 1995 ISBN 90-411-0146-2
44. B.G. Tahzib: *Freedom of Religion or Belief*. Ensuring Effective International Legal Protection. 1996 ISBN 90-411-0159-4
45. F. de Varennes: *Language, Minorities and Human Rights*. 1996 ISBN 90-411-0206-X
46. J. Räikkä (ed.): *Do We Need Minority Rights?* Conceptual Issues. 1996 ISBN 90-411-0309-0
47. J. Bröhmer: *State Immunity and the Violation of Human Rights*. 1997 ISBN 90-411-0322-8
48. C.A. Gearty (ed.): *European Civil Liberties and the European Convention on Human Rights*. A Comparative Study. 1997 ISBN 90-411-0253-1
49. B. Conforti and F. Francioni (eds.): *Enforcing International Human Rights in Domestic Courts*. 1997 ISBN 90-411-0393-7
50. A. Spiliopoulou Åkermark: *Justifications of Minority Protection in International Law*. 1997 ISBN 90-411-0424-0
51. A. Boulesbaa: *The U.N. Convention on Torture and the Prospects for Enforcement*. 1997 ISBN 90-411-0457-7
52. S. Bowen (ed.): *Human Rights, Self-Determination and Political Change in the Occupied Palestinian Territories*. 1997 ISBN 90-411-0502-6
53. M. O'Flaherty and G. Gisvold (eds.): *Post-War Protection of Human Rights in Bosnia and Herzegovina*. 1998 ISBN 90-411-1020-8
54. A.-L. Svensson-McCarthy: *The International Law of Human Rights and States of Exception*. With Special Reference to the *Travaux Préparatoires* and Case-Law of the International Monitoring Organs. 1998 ISBN 90-411-1021-6
55. G. Gilbert: *Transnational Fugitive Offenders in International Law*. Extradition and Other Mechanisms. 1998 ISBN 90-411-1040-2

# International Studies in Human Rights

56. M. Jones and L.A. Basser Marks (eds.): *Disability, Divers-ability and Legal Change*. 1998 ISBN 90-411-1086-0
57. T. Barkhuysen, M.L. van Emmerik and P.H.P.H.M.C. van Kempen (eds.): *The Execution of Strasbourg and Geneva Human Rights Decisions in the National Legal Order*. 1999 ISBN 90-411-1152-2
58. S. Coliver, P. Hoffman, J. Fitzpatrick and S. Bowen (eds.): *Secrecy and Liberty: National Security, Freedom of Expression and Access to Information*. 1999 ISBN 90-411-1191-3
59. W.S. Heinz and H. Frühling: *Determinants of Gross Human Rights Violations by State and State-Sponsored Actors in Brazil, Uruguay, Chile and Argentina*. 1960–1990. 1999 ISBN 90-411-1202-2
60 M. Kirilova Eriksson: *Reproductive Freedom*. In the Context of International Human Rights and Humanitarian Law. 1999 ISBN 90-411-1249-9
61. M. Bedri Eryilmaz: *Arrest and Detention Powers in English and Turkish Law and Practice in the Light of the European Convention on Human Rights*. 1999 ISBN 90-411-1269-3

This series is designed to shed light on current legal and political aspects of process and organization in the field of human rights.

MARTINUS NIJHOFF PUBLISHERS – THE HAGUE/BOSTON/LONDON